KEY TO WORLD MAP PAGES

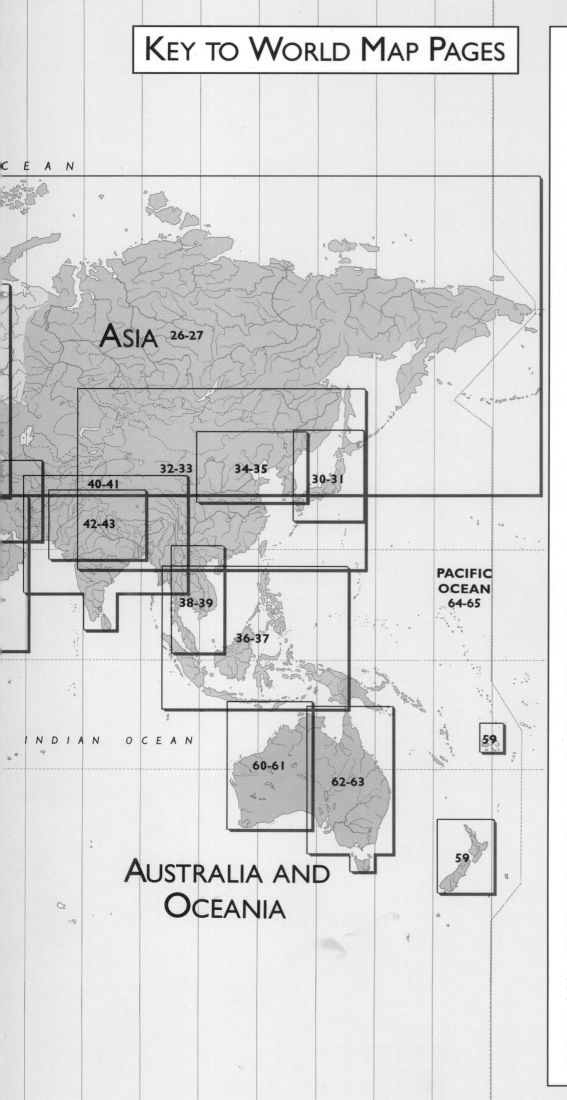

OCEAN

ASIA 26-27

PACIFIC OCEAN 64-65

INDIAN OCEAN

AUSTRALIA AND OCEANIA

32-33

34-35

30-31

40-41

42-43

38-39

36-37

60-61

62-63

59

59

COUNTRY INDEX

PHILIP'S

WORLD ATLAS
& GAZETTEER

Introduction to World Geography
Cartography by Philip's

Picture Acknowledgements
Page 14
Science Photo Library/NOAA

Illustrations
Stefan Chabluk

CONSULTANTS
Philip's are grateful to the following people for acting as specialist geography consultants on the '*Introduction to World Geography*' front section:

Professor D. Brunsden, Kings College, University of London, UK
Dr C. Clarke, Oxford University, UK
Dr. I. S. Evans, Durham University, UK
Professor P. Haggett, University of Bristol, UK
Professor K. McLachlan, University of London, UK
Professor M. Monmonier, Syracuse University, New York, USA
Professor M-L. Hsu, University of Minnesota, Minnesota, USA
Professor M. J. Tooley, University of St Andrews, UK
Dr T. Unwin, Royal Holloway, University of London, UK

Published in Great Britain in 1997
by George Philip Limited,
an imprint of Reed Books,
Michelin House, 81 Fulham Road, London SW3 6RB,
and Auckland and Melbourne

Cartography by Philip's

ISBN 0–540–07256–7

A CIP catalogue record for this book is available
from the British Library

Printed in Hong Kong

PHILIP'S

WORLD ATLAS & GAZETTEER

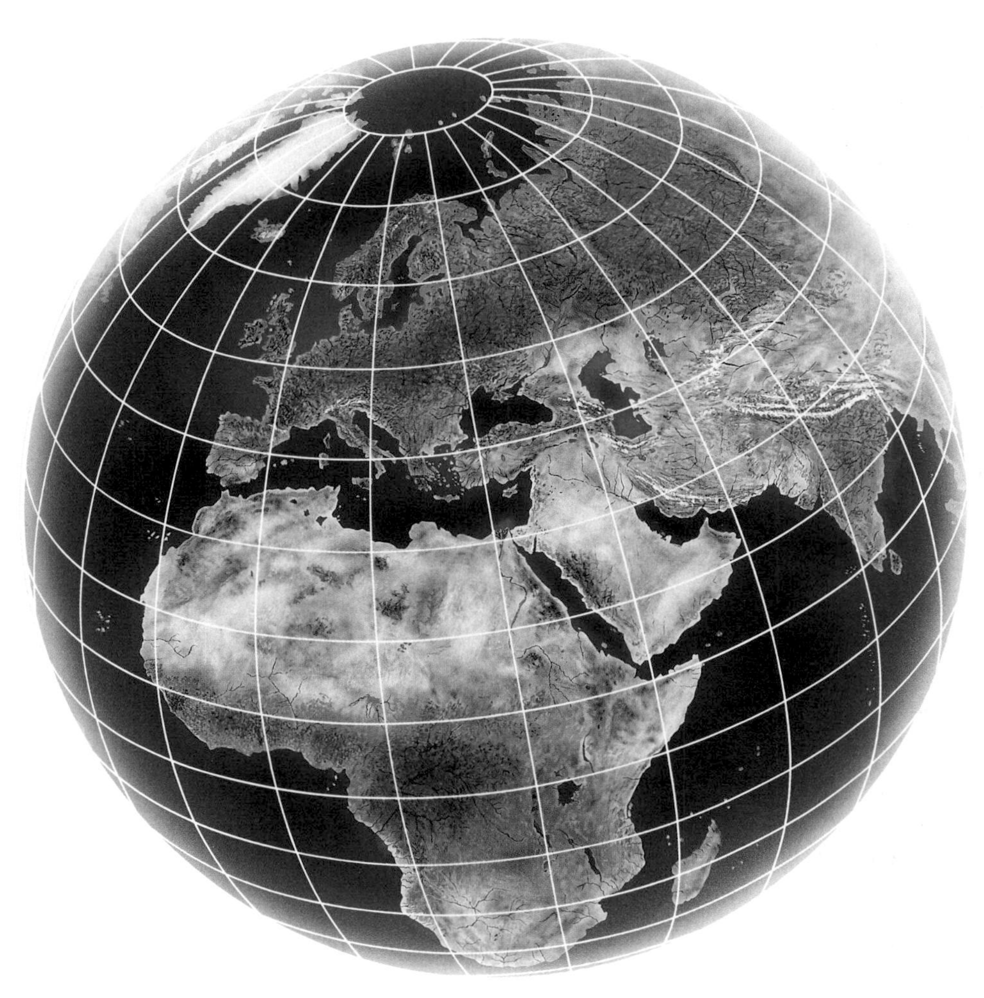

Fifth Edition

CONTENTS

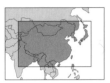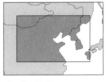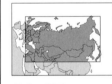

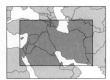

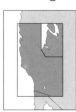

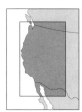

v

World Statistics: Countries

This alphabetical list includes all the countries and territories of the world. If a territory is not completely independent, then the country it is associated with is named. The area figures give the total area of land, inland water and ice. The population figures are the latest available estimates. The annual income is the Gross National Product per capita in US dollars for 1995.

Country/Territory	Area km² *Thousands*	Area miles² *Thousands*	Population *Thousands*	Capital	Annual Income US $
Adélie Land (Fr.)	432	167	0.03	–	–
Afghanistan	652	252	19,509	Kabul	220
Albania	28.8	11.1	3,458	Tirana	340
Algeria	2,382	920	27,936	Algiers	1,650
American Samoa (US)	0.20	0.08	58	Pago Pago	2,600
Andorra	0.45	0.17	65	Andorra La Vella	14,000
Angola	1,247	481	10,844	Luanda	600
Anguilla (UK)	0.1	0.04	8	The Valley	6,800
Antigua & Barbuda	0.44	0.17	67	St John's	6,390
Argentina	2,767	1,068	34,663	Buenos Aires	7,290
Armenia	29.8	11.5	3,603	Yerevan	660
Aruba (Neths)	0.19	0.07	71	Oranjestad	17,500
Ascension Is. (UK)	0.09	0.03	1.5	Georgetown	–
Australia	7,687	2,968	18,107	Canberra	17,510
Austria	83.9	32.4	8,004	Vienna	23,120
Azerbaijan	86.6	33.4	7,559	Baku	730
Azores (Port.)	2.2	0.87	240	Ponta Delgada	4,500
Bahamas	13.9	5.4	277	Nassau	11,500
Bahrain	0.68	0.26	558	Manama	7,870
Bangladesh	144	56	118,342	Dhaka	220
Barbados	0.43	0.17	263	Bridgetown	6,240
Belarus	207.6	80.1	10,500	Minsk	2,930
Belgium	30.5	11.8	10,140	Brussels	21,210
Belize	23	8.9	216	Belmopan	2,440
Benin	113	43	5,381	Porto-Novo	420
Bermuda (UK)	0.05	0.02	64	Hamilton	27,000
Bhutan	47	18.1	1,639	Thimphu	170
Bolivia	1,099	424	7,900	La Paz/Sucre	770
Bosnia-Herzegovina	51	20	4,400	Sarajevo	2,500
Botswana	582	225	1,481	Gaborone	2,590
Brazil	8,512	3,286	161,416	Brasilia	3,020
British Indian Ocean Terr. (UK)	0.08	0.03	0	–	–
Brunei	5.8	2.2	284	Bandar Seri Begawan	9,000
Bulgaria	111	43	8,771	Sofia	1,160
Burkina Faso	274	106	10,326	Ouagadougou	300
Burma (Myanmar)	677	261	46,580	Rangoon	950
Burundi	27.8	10.7	6,412	Bujumbura	180
Cambodia	181	70	10,452	Phnom Penh	600
Cameroon	475	184	13,232	Yaoundé	770
Canada	9,976	3,852	29,972	Ottawa	20,670
Canary Is. (Spain)	7.3	2.8	1,700	Las Palmas/Santa Cruz	7,900
Cape Verde Is.	4	1.6	386	Praia	870
Cayman Is. (UK)	0.26	0.10	31	George Town	20,000
Central African Republic	623	241	3,294	Bangui	390
Chad	1,284	496	6,314	Ndjaména	200
Chatham Is. (NZ)	0.96	0.37	0.05	Waitangi	–
Chile	757	292	14,271	Santiago	3,070
China	9,597	3,705	1,226,944	Beijing	490
Christmas Is. (Aus.)	0.14	0.05	2	The Settlement	–
Cocos (Keeling) Is. (Aus.)	0.01	0.005	0.6	West Island	–
Colombia	1,139	440	34,948	Bogotá	1,400
Comoros	2.2	0.86	654	Moroni	520
Congo	342	132	2,593	Brazzaville	920
Cook Is. (NZ)	0.24	0.09	19	Avarua	900
Costa Rica	51.1	19.7	3,436	San José	2,160
Croatia	56.5	21.8	4,900	Zagreb	4,500
Cuba	111	43	11,050	Havana	1,250
Cyprus	9.3	3.6	742	Nicosia	10,380
Czech Republic	78.9	30.4	10,500	Prague	2,730
Denmark	43.1	16.6	5,229	Copenhagen	26,510
Djibouti	23.2	9	603	Djibouti	780
Dominica	0.75	0.29	89	Roseau	2,680
Dominican Republic	48.7	18.8	7,818	Santo Domingo	1,080
Ecuador	284	109	11,384	Quito	1,170
Egypt	1,001	387	64,100	Cairo	660
El Salvador	21	8.1	5,743	San Salvador	1,320
Equatorial Guinea	28.1	10.8	400	Malabo	360
Eritrea	94	36	3,850	Asmara	500
Estonia	44.7	17.3	1,531	Tallinn	3,040
Ethiopia	1,128	436	51,600	Addis Ababa	100
Falkland Is. (UK)	12.2	4.7	2	Stanley	–
Faroe Is. (Den.)	1.4	0.54	47	Tórshavn	23,660
Fiji	18.3	7.1	773	Suva	2,140
Finland	338	131	5,125	Helsinki	18,970
France	552	213	58,286	Paris	22,360
French Guiana (Fr.)	90	34.7	154	Cayenne	5,000
French Polynesia (Fr.)	4	1.5	217	Papeete	7,000
Gabon	268	103	1,316	Libreville	4,050
Gambia, The	11.3	4.4	1,144	Banjul	360
Georgia	69.7	26.9	5,448	Tbilisi	560
Germany	357	138	82,000	Berlin/Bonn	23,560
Ghana	239	92	17,462	Accra	430
Gibraltar (UK)	0.007	0.003	28	Gibraltar Town	5,000
Greece	132	51	10,510	Athens	7,390
Greenland (Den.)	2,176	840	59	Godthåb (Nuuk)	9,000
Grenada	0.34	0.13	96	St George's	2,410
Guadeloupe (Fr.)	1.7	0.66	443	Basse-Terre	9,000
Guam (US)	0.55	0.21	155	Agana	6,000
Guatemala	109	42	10,624	Guatemala City	1,110
Guinea	246	95	6,702	Conakry	510
Guinea-Bissau	36.1	13.9	1,073	Bissau	220
Guyana	215	83	832	Georgetown	350
Haiti	27.8	10.7	7,180	Port-au-Prince	800
Honduras	112	43	5,940	Tegucigalpa	580
Hong Kong (China)	1.1	0.40	6,000	–	17,860
Hungary	93	35.9	10,500	Budapest	3,330
Iceland	103	40	269	Reykjavik	23,620
India	3,288	1,269	942,989	New Delhi	290
Indonesia	1,905	735	198,644	Jakarta	730
Iran	1,648	636	68,885	Tehran	4,750
Iraq	438	169	20,184	Baghdad	2,000
Ireland	70.3	27.1	3,589	Dublin	12,580
Israel	27	10.3	5,696	Jerusalem	13,760
Italy	301	116	57,181	Rome	19,620
Ivory Coast	322	125	14,271	Yamoussoukro	630
Jamaica	11	4.2	2,700	Kingston	1,390
Jan Mayen Is. (Nor.)	0.38	0.15	0.06	–	–
Japan	378	146	125,156	Tokyo	31,450
Johnston Is. (US)	0.002	0.0009	1	–	–
Jordan	89.2	34.4	5,547	Amman	1,190
Kazakstan	2,717	1,049	17,099	Alma-Ata	1,540
Kenya	580	224	28,240	Nairobi	270
Kerguelen Is. (Fr.)	7.2	2.8	0.7	–	–
Kermadec Is. (NZ)	0.03	0.01	0.1	–	–
Kiribati	0.72	0.28	80	Tarawa	710
Korea, North	121	47	23,931	Pyŏngyang	1,100
Korea, South	99	38.2	45,088	Seoul	7,670
Kuwait	17.8	6.9	1,668	Kuwait City	23,350
Kyrgyzstan	198.5	76.6	4,738	Bishkek	830
Laos	237	91	4,906	Vientiane	290
Latvia	65	25	2,558	Riga	2,030
Lebanon	10.4	4	2,971	Beirut	1,750
Lesotho	30.4	11.7	2,064	Maseru	660

Country/Territory	Area km² *Thousands*	Area miles² *Thousands*	Population *Thousands*	Capital	Annual Income US $
Liberia	111	43	3,092	Monrovia	800
Libya	1,760	679	5,410	Tripoli	6,500
Liechtenstein	0.16	0.06	31	Vaduz	33,510
Lithuania	65.2	25.2	3,735	Vilnius	1,310
Luxembourg	2.6	1	408	Luxembourg	35,850
Macau (Port.)	0.02	0.006	490	Macau	7,500
Macedonia	25.7	9.9	2,173	Skopje	730
Madagascar	587	227	15,206	Antananarivo	240
Madeira (Port.)	0.81	0.31	300	Funchal	4,500
Malawi	118	46	9,800	Lilongwe	220
Malaysia	330	127	20,174	Kuala Lumpur	3,160
Maldives	0.30	0.12	254	Malé	820
Mali	1,240	479	10,700	Bamako	300
Malta	0.32	0.12	370	Valletta	6,800
Marshall Is.	0.18	0.07	55	Dalap-Uliga-Darrit	1,500
Martinique (Fr.)	1.1	0.42	384	Fort-de-France	3,500
Mauritania	1,030	412	2,268	Nouakchott	510
Mauritius	2.0	0.72	1,112	Port Louis	2,980
Mayotte (Fr.)	0.37	0.14	101	Mamoundzou	1,430
Mexico	1,958	756	93,342	Mexico City	3,750
Micronesia, Fed. States of	0.70	0.27	125	Palikir	1,560
Midway Is. (US)	0.005	0.002	2	–	–
Moldova	33.7	13	4,434	Chişinău	1,180
Monaco	0.002	0.0001	32	Monaco	16,000
Mongolia	1,567	605	2,408	Ulan Bator	400
Montserrat (UK)	0.10	0.04	11	Plymouth	4,500
Morocco	447	172	26,857	Rabat	1,030
Mozambique	802	309	17,800	Maputo	80
Namibia	825	318	1,610	Windhoek	1,660
Nauru	0.02	0.008	12	Yaren District	10,000
Nepal	141	54	21,953	Katmandu	160
Netherlands	41.5	16	15,495	Amsterdam/The Hague	20,710
Neths Antilles (Neths)	0.99	0.38	202	Willemstad	9,700
New Caledonia (Fr.)	19	7.2	181	Nouméa	6,000
New Zealand	269	104	3,567	Wellington	12,900
Nicaragua	130	50	4,544	Managua	360
Niger	1,267	489	9,149	Niamey	270
Nigeria	924	357	88,515	Abuja	310
Niue (NZ)	0.26	0.10	2	Alofi	–
Norfolk Is. (Aus.)	0.03	0.01	2	Kingston	–
Northern Mariana Is. (US)	0.48	0.18	50	Saipan	11,500
Norway	324	125	4,361	Oslo	26,340
Oman	212	82	2,252	Muscat	5,600
Pakistan	796	307	143,595	Islamabad	430
Palau	0.46	0.18	18	Koror	2,260
Panama	77.1	29.8	2,629	Panama City	2,580
Papua New Guinea	463	179	4,292	Port Moresby	1,120
Paraguay	407	157	4,979	Asunción	1,500
Peru	1,285	496	23,588	Lima	1,490
Philippines	300	116	67,167	Manila	830
Pitcairn Is. (UK)	0.03	0.01	0.05	Adamstown	–
Poland	313	121	38,587	Warsaw	2,270
Portugal	92.4	35.7	10,600	Lisbon	7,890
Puerto Rico (US)	9	3.5	3,689	San Juan	7,020
Qatar	11	4.2	594	Doha	15,140
Queen Maud Land (Nor.)	2,800	1,081	0	–	–
Réunion (Fr.)	2.5	0.97	655	Saint-Denis	3,900
Romania	238	92	22,863	Bucharest	1,120
Russia	17,075	6,592	148,385	Moscow	2,350
Rwanda	26.3	10.2	7,899	Kigali	200
St Helena (UK)	0.12	0.05	6	Jamestown	–
St Kitts & Nevis	0.36	0.14	45	Basseterre	4,470
St Lucia	0.62	0.24	147	Castries	3,040
St Pierre & Miquelon (Fr.)	0.24	0.09	6	Saint Pierre	–
St Vincent & Grenadines	0.39	0.15	111	Kingstown	1,730
San Marino	0.06	0.02	26	San Marino	20,000
São Tomé & Príncipe	0.96	0.37	133	São Tomé	330
Saudi Arabia	2,150	830	18,395	Riyadh	8,000
Senegal	197	76	8,308	Dakar	730
Seychelles	0.46	0.18	75	Victoria	6,370
Sierra Leone	71.7	27.7	4,467	Freetown	140
Singapore	0.62	0.24	2,990	Singapore	19,310
Slovak Republic	49	18.9	5,400	Bratislava	1,900
Slovenia	20.3	7.8	2,000	Ljubljana	6,310
Solomon Is.	28.9	11.2	378	Honiara	750
Somalia	638	246	9,180	Mogadishu	500
South Africa	1,220	471	44,000	C. Town/Pretoria/Bloem.	2,900
South Georgia (UK)	3.8	1.4	0.05	–	–
Spain	505	195	39,664	Madrid	13,650
Sri Lanka	65.6	25.3	18,359	Colombo	600
Sudan	2,506	967	29,980	Khartoum	750
Surinam	163	63	421	Paramaribo	1,210
Svalbard (Nor.)	62.9	24.3	4	Longyearbyen	–
Swaziland	17.4	6.7	849	Mbabane	1,050
Sweden	450	174	8,893	Stockholm	24,830
Switzerland	41.3	15.9	7,268	Bern	36,410
Syria	185	71	14,614	Damascus	5,700
Taiwan	36	13.9	21,100	Taipei	11,000
Tajikistan	143.1	55.2	6,102	Dushanbe	470
Tanzania	945	365	29,710	Dodoma	100
Thailand	513	198	58,432	Bangkok	2,040
Togo	56.8	21.9	4,140	Lomé	330
Tokelau (NZ)	0.01	0.005	2	Nukunonu	–
Tonga	0.75	0.29	107	Nuku'alofa	1,610
Trinidad & Tobago	5.1	2	1,295	Port of Spain	3,730
Tristan da Cunha (UK)	0.11	0.04	0.33	Edinburgh	–
Tunisia	164	63	8,906	Tunis	1,780
Turkey	779	301	61,303	Ankara	2,120
Turkmenistan	488.1	188.5	4,100	Ashkhabad	1,400
Turks & Caicos Is. (UK)	0.43	0.17	15	Cockburn Town	5,000
Tuvalu	0.03	0.01	10	Fongafale	600
Uganda	236	91	21,466	Kampala	190
Ukraine	603.7	233.1	52,027	Kiev	1,910
United Arab Emirates	83.6	32.3	2,800	Abu Dhabi	22,470
United Kingdom	243.3	94	58,306	London	17,970
United States of America	9,373	3,619	263,563	Washington, DC	24,750
Uruguay	177	68	3,186	Montevideo	3,910
Uzbekistan	447.4	172.7	22,833	Tashkent	960
Vanuatu	12.2	4.7	167	Port-Vila	1,230
Vatican City	0.0004	0.0002	1	–	–
Venezuela	912	352	21,810	Caracas	2,840
Vietnam	332	127	74,580	Hanoi	170
Virgin Is. (UK)	0.15	0.06	20	Road Town	–
Virgin Is. (US)	0.34	0.13	102	Charlotte Amalie	12,000
Wake Is.	0.008	0.003	0.30	–	–
Wallis & Futuna Is. (Fr.)	0.20	0.08	13	Mata-Utu	–
Western Sahara	266	103	220	El Aaiún	300
Western Samoa	2.8	1.1	169	Apia	980
Yemen	528	204	14,609	Sana	800
Yugoslavia	102.3	39.5	10,881	Belgrade	1,000
Zaïre	2,345	905	44,504	Kinshasa	500
Zambia	753	291	9,500	Lusaka	370
Zimbabwe	391	151	11,453	Harare	540

World Statistics: Physical dimensions

Each topic list is divided into continents and within a continent the items are listed in order of size. The bottom part of many of the lists is selective in order to give examples from as many different countries as possible. The order of the continents is the same as in the atlas, beginning with Europe and ending with South America. The figures are rounded as appropriate.

World, Continents, Oceans

	km²	miles²	%
The World	509,450,000	196,672,000	–
Land	149,450,000	57,688,000	29.3
Water	360,000,000	138,984,000	70.7
Asia	44,500,000	17,177,000	29.8
Africa	30,302,000	11,697,000	20.3
North America	24,241,000	9,357,000	16.2
South America	17,793,000	6,868,000	11.9
Antarctica	14,100,000	5,443,000	9.4
Europe	9,957,000	3,843,000	6.7
Australia & Oceania	8,557,000	3,303,000	5.7
Pacific Ocean	179,679,000	69,356,000	49.9
Atlantic Ocean	92,373,000	35,657,000	25.7
Indian Ocean	73,917,000	28,532,000	20.5
Arctic Ocean	14,090,000	5,439,000	3.9

Ocean Depths

Atlantic Ocean	m	ft
Puerto Rico (Milwaukee) Deep	9,220	30,249
Cayman Trench	7,680	25,197
Gulf of Mexico	5,203	17,070
Mediterranean Sea	5,121	16,801
Black Sea	2,211	7,254
North Sea	660	2,165

Indian Ocean	m	ft
Java Trench	7,450	24,442
Red Sea	2,635	8,454

Pacific Ocean	m	ft
Mariana Trench	11,022	36,161
Tonga Trench	10,882	35,702
Japan Trench	10,554	34,626
Kuril Trench	10,542	34,587

Arctic Ocean	m	ft
Molloy Deep	5,608	18,399

Mountains

Europe		m	ft
Mont Blanc	*France/Italy*	4,807	15,771
Monte Rosa	*Italy/Switzerland*	4,634	15,203
Dom	*Switzerland*	4,545	14,911
Liskamm	*Switzerland*	4,527	14,852
Weisshorn	*Switzerland*	4,505	14,780
Taschorn	*Switzerland*	4,490	14,730
Matterhorn/Cervino	*Italy/Switzerland*	4,478	14,691
Mont Maudit	*France/Italy*	4,465	14,649
Dent Blanche	*Switzerland*	4,356	14,291
Nadelhorn	*Switzerland*	4,327	14,196
Grandes Jorasses	*France/Italy*	4,208	13,806
Jungfrau	*Switzerland*	4,158	13,642
Grossglockner	*Austria*	3,797	12,457
Mulhacén	*Spain*	3,478	11,411
Zugspitze	*Germany*	2,962	9,718
Olympus	*Greece*	2,917	9,570
Triglav	*Slovenia*	2,863	9,393
Gerlachovka	*Slovak Republic*	2,655	8,711
Galdhöpiggen	*Norway*	2,468	8,100
Kebnekaise	*Sweden*	2,117	6,946
Ben Nevis	*UK*	1,343	4,406

Asia		m	ft
Everest	*China/Nepal*	8,848	29,029
K2 (Godwin Austen)	*China/Kashmir*	8,611	28,251
Kanchenjunga	*India/Nepal*	8,598	28,208
Lhotse	*China/Nepal*	8,516	27,939
Makalu	*China/Nepal*	8,481	27,824
Cho Oyu	*China/Nepal*	8,201	26,906
Dhaulagiri	*Nepal*	8,172	26,811
Manaslu	*Nepal*	8,156	26,758
Nanga Parbat	*Kashmir*	8,126	26,660
Annapurna	*Nepal*	8,078	26,502
Gasherbrum	*China/Kashmir*	8,068	26,469
Broad Peak	*China/Kashmir*	8,051	26,414
Xixabangma	*China*	8,012	26,286
Kangbachen	*India/Nepal*	7,902	25,925
Trivor	*Pakistan*	7,720	25,328
Pik Kommunizma	*Tajikistan*	7,495	24,590
Elbrus	*Russia*	5,642	18,510
Demavend	*Iran*	5,604	18,386
Ararat	*Turkey*	5,165	16,945
Gunong Kinabalu	*Malaysia (Borneo)*	4,101	13,455
Fuji-San	*Japan*	3,776	12,388

Africa		m	ft
Kilimanjaro	*Tanzania*	5,895	19,340
Mt Kenya	*Kenya*	5,199	17,057
Ruwenzori (Margherita)	*Uganda/Zaire*	5,109	16,762
Ras Dashan	*Ethiopia*	4,620	15,157
Meru	*Tanzania*	4,565	14,977
Karisimbi	*Rwanda/Zaïre*	4,507	14,787
Mt Elgon	*Kenya/Uganda*	4,321	14,176
Batu	*Ethiopia*	4,307	14,130
Toubkal	*Morocco*	4,165	13,665
Mt Cameroon	*Cameroon*	4,070	13,353

Oceania		m	ft
Puncak Jaya	*Indonesia*	5,029	16,499
Puncak Trikora	*Indonesia*	4,750	15,584
Puncak Mandala	*Indonesia*	4,702	15,427
Mt Wilhelm	*Papua New Guinea*	4,508	14,790
Mauna Kea	*USA (Hawaii)*	4,205	13,796
Mauna Loa	*USA (Hawaii)*	4,170	13,681
Mt Cook	*New Zealand*	3,753	12,313
Mt Kosciusko	*Australia*	2,237	7,339

North America		m	ft
Mt McKinley (Denali)	*USA (Alaska)*	6,194	20,321
Mt Logan	*Canada*	5,959	19,551
Citlaltepetl	*Mexico*	5,700	18,701
Mt St Elias	*USA/Canada*	5,489	18,008
Popocatepetl	*Mexico*	5,452	17,887
Mt Foraker	*USA (Alaska)*	5,304	17,401
Ixtaccihuatl	*Mexico*	5,286	17,342
Lucania	*Canada*	5,227	17,149
Mt Steele	*Canada*	5,073	16,644
Mt Bona	*USA (Alaska)*	5,005	16,420
Mt Whitney	*USA*	4,418	14,495
Tajumulco	*Guatemala*	4,220	13,845
Chirripó Grande	*Costa Rica*	3,837	12,589
Pico Duarte	*Dominican Rep.*	3,175	10,417

South America		m	ft
Aconcagua	*Argentina*	6,960	22,834
Bonete	*Argentina*	6,872	22,546
Ojos del Salado	*Argentina/Chile*	6,863	22,516
Pissis	*Argentina*	6,779	22,241
Mercedario	*Argentina/Chile*	6,770	22,211
Huascaran	*Peru*	6,768	22,204
Llullaillaco	*Argentina/Chile*	6,723	22,057
Nudo de Cachi	*Argentina*	6,720	22,047
Yerupaja	*Peru*	6,632	21,758
Sajama	*Bolivia*	6,542	21,463
Chimborazo	*Ecuador*	6,267	20,561
Pico Colon	*Colombia*	5,800	19,029
Pico Bolivar	*Venezuela*	5,007	16,427

Antarctica		m	ft
Vinson Massif		4,897	16,066
Mt Kirkpatrick		4,528	14,855

Rivers

Europe		km	miles
Volga	*Caspian Sea*	3,700	2,300
Danube	*Black Sea*	2,850	1,770
Ural	*Caspian Sea*	2,535	1,575
Dnepr (Dnipro)	*Volga*	2,285	1,420
Kama	*Volga*	2,030	1,260
Don	*Volga*	1,990	1,240
Petchora	*Arctic Ocean*	1,790	1,110
Oka	*Volga*	1,480	920
Dnister (Dniester)	*Black Sea*	1,400	870
Vyatka	*Kama*	1,370	850
Rhine	*North Sea*	1,320	820
N. Dvina	*Arctic Ocean*	1,290	800
Elbe	*North Sea*	1,145	710

Asia		km	miles
Yangtze	*Pacific Ocean*	6,380	3,960
Yenisey–Angara	*Arctic Ocean*	5,550	3,445
Huang He	*Pacific Ocean*	5,464	3,395
Ob–Irtysh	*Arctic Ocean*	5,410	3,360
Mekong	*Pacific Ocean*	4,500	2,795
Amur	*Pacific Ocean*	4,400	2,730
Lena	*Arctic Ocean*	4,400	2,730
Irtysh	*Ob*	4,250	2,640
Yenisey	*Arctic Ocean*	4,090	2,540
Ob	*Arctic Ocean*	3,680	2,285
Indus	*Indian Ocean*	3,100	1,925
Brahmaputra	*Indian Ocean*	2,900	1,800
Syrdarya	*Aral Sea*	2,860	1,775
Salween	*Indian Ocean*	2,800	1,740
Euphrates	*Indian Ocean*	2,700	1,675
Amudarya	*Aral Sea*	2,540	1,575

Africa		km	miles
Nile	*Mediterranean*	6,670	4,140
Zaïre/Congo	*Atlantic Ocean*	4,670	2,900
Niger	*Atlantic Ocean*	4,180	2,595
Zambezi	*Indian Ocean*	3,540	2,200
Oubangi/Uele	*Zaïre*	2,250	1,400
Kasai	*Zaïre*	1,950	1,210
Shaballe	*Indian Ocean*	1,930	1,200
Orange	*Atlantic Ocean*	1,860	1,155
Cubango	*Okavango Swamps*	1,800	1,120
Limpopo	*Indian Ocean*	1,600	995
Senegal	*Atlantic Ocean*	1,600	995

Australia		km	miles
Murray–Darling	*Indian Ocean*	3,750	2,330
Darling	*Murray*	3,070	1,905
Murray	*Indian Ocean*	2,575	1,600
Murrumbidgee	*Murray*	1,690	1,050

North America		km	miles
Mississippi–Missouri	*Gulf of Mexico*	6,020	3,740
Mackenzie	*Arctic Ocean*	4,240	2,630
Mississippi	*Gulf of Mexico*	3,780	2,350
Missouri	*Mississippi*	3,780	2,350
Yukon	*Pacific Ocean*	3,185	1,980
Rio Grande	*Gulf of Mexico*	3,030	1,880
Arkansas	*Mississippi*	2,340	1,450
Colorado	*Pacific Ocean*	2,330	1,445
Red	*Mississippi*	2,040	1,270
Columbia	*Pacific Ocean*	1,950	1,210
Saskatchewan	*Lake Winnipeg*	1,940	1,205

South America		km	miles
Amazon	*Atlantic Ocean*	6,450	4,010
Paraná–Plate	*Atlantic Ocean*	4,500	2,800
Purus	*Amazon*	3,350	2,080
Madeira	*Amazon*	3,200	1,990
São Francisco	*Atlantic Ocean*	2,900	1,800
Paraná	*Plate*	2,800	1,740
Tocantins	*Atlantic Ocean*	2,750	1,710
Paraguay	*Paraná*	2,550	1,580
Orinoco	*Atlantic Ocean*	2,500	1,550
Pilcomayo	*Paraná*	2,500	1,550
Araguaia	*Tocantins*	2,250	1,400

Lakes

Europe		km²	miles²
Lake Ladoga	*Russia*	17,700	6,800
Lake Onega	*Russia*	9,700	3,700
Saimaa system	*Finland*	8,000	3,100
Vänern	*Sweden*	5,500	2,100

Asia		km²	miles²
Caspian Sea	*Asia*	371,800	143,550
Aral Sea	*Kazakstan/Uzbekistan*	33,640	13,000
Lake Baykal	*Russia*	30,500	11,780
Tonlé Sap	*Cambodia*	20,000	7,700
Lake Balqash	*Kazakstan*	18,500	7,100

Africa		km²	miles²
Lake Victoria	*East Africa*	68,000	26,000
Lake Tanganyika	*Central Africa*	33,000	13,000
Lake Malawi/Nyasa	*East Africa*	29,600	11,430
Lake Chad	*Central Africa*	25,000	9,700
Lake Turkana	*Ethiopia/Kenya*	8,500	3,300
Lake Volta	*Ghana*	8,500	3,300

Australia		km²	miles²
Lake Eyre	*Australia*	8,900	3,400
Lake Torrens	*Australia*	5,800	2,200
Lake Gairdner	*Australia*	4,800	1,900

North America		km²	miles²
Lake Superior	*Canada/USA*	82,350	31,800
Lake Huron	*Canada/USA*	59,600	23,010
Lake Michigan	*USA*	58,000	22,400
Great Bear Lake	*Canada*	31,800	12,280
Great Slave Lake	*Canada*	28,500	11,000
Lake Erie	*Canada/USA*	25,700	9,900
Lake Winnipeg	*Canada*	24,400	9,400
Lake Ontario	*Canada/USA*	19,500	7,500
Lake Nicaragua	*Nicaragua*	8,200	3,200

South America		km²	miles²
Lake Titicaca	*Bolivia/Peru*	8,300	3,200
Lake Poopo	*Peru*	2,800	1,100

Islands

Europe		km²	miles²
Great Britain	*UK*	229,880	88,700
Iceland	*Atlantic Ocean*	103,000	39,800
Ireland	*Ireland/UK*	84,400	32,600
Novaya Zemlya (N.)	*Russia*	48,200	18,600
Sicily	*Italy*	25,500	9,800
Corsica	*France*	8,700	3,400

Asia		km²	miles²
Borneo	*South-east Asia*	744,360	287,400
Sumatra	*Indonesia*	473,600	182,860
Honshu	*Japan*	230,500	88,980
Celebes	*Indonesia*	189,000	73,000
Java	*Indonesia*	126,700	48,900
Luzon	*Philippines*	104,700	40,400
Hokkaido	*Japan*	78,400	30,300

Africa		km²	miles²
Madagascar	*Indian Ocean*	587,040	226,660
Socotra	*Indian Ocean*	3,600	1,400
Réunion	*Indian Ocean*	2,500	965

Oceania		km²	miles²
New Guinea	*Indonesia/Papua NG*	821,030	317,000
New Zealand (S.)	*Pacific Ocean*	150,500	58,100
New Zealand (N.)	*Pacific Ocean*	114,700	44,300
Tasmania	*Australia*	67,800	26,200
Hawaii	*Pacific Ocean*	10,450	4,000

North America		km²	miles²
Greenland	*Atlantic Ocean*	2,175,600	839,800
Baffin Is.	*Canada*	508,000	196,100
Victoria Is.	*Canada*	212,200	81,900
Ellesmere Is.	*Canada*	212,000	81,800
Cuba	*Caribbean Sea*	110,860	42,800
Hispaniola	*Dominican Rep./Haiti*	76,200	29,400
Jamaica	*Caribbean Sea*	11,400	4,400
Puerto Rico	*Atlantic Ocean*	8,900	3,400

South America		km²	miles²
Tierra del Fuego	*Argentina/Chile*	47,000	18,100
Falkland Is. (E.)	*Atlantic Ocean*	6,800	2,600

PHILIP'S WORLD MAPS

The reference maps which form the main body of this atlas have been prepared in accordance with the highest standards of international cartography to provide an accurate and detailed representation of the Earth. The scales and projections used have been carefully chosen to give balanced coverage of the world, while emphasizing the most densely populated and economically significant regions. A hallmark of Philip's mapping is the use of hill shading and relief colouring to create a graphic impression of landforms: this makes the maps exceptionally easy to read. However, knowledge of the key features employed in the construction and presentation of the maps will enable the reader to derive the fullest benefit from the atlas.

Map sequence

The atlas covers the Earth continent by continent: first Europe; then its land neighbour Asia (mapped north before south, in a clockwise sequence), then Africa, Australia and Oceania, North America and South America. This is the classic arrangement adopted by most cartographers since the 16th century. For each continent, there are maps at a variety of scales. First, physical relief and political maps of the whole continent; then a series of larger-scale maps of the regions within the continent, each followed, where required, by still larger-scale maps of the most important or densely populated areas. The governing principle is that by turning the pages of the atlas, the reader moves steadily from north to south through each continent, with each map overlapping its neighbours. A key map showing this sequence, and the area covered by each map, can be found on the endpapers of the atlas.

Map presentation

With very few exceptions (e.g. for the Arctic and Antarctic), the maps are drawn with north at the top, regardless of whether they are presented upright or sideways on the page. In the borders will be found the map title; a locator diagram showing the area covered and the page numbers for maps of adjacent areas; the scale; the projection used; the degrees of latitude and longitude; and the letters and figures used in the index for locating place names and geographical features. Physical relief maps also have a height reference panel identifying the colours used for each layer of contouring.

Map symbols

Each map contains a vast amount of detail which can only be conveyed clearly and accurately by the use of symbols. Points and circles of varying sizes locate and identify the relative importance of towns and cities; different styles of type are employed for administrative, geographical and regional place names. A variety of pictorial symbols denote features such as

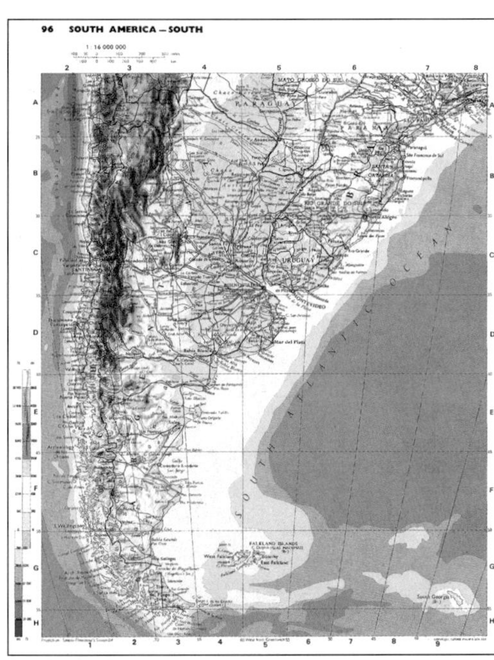

glaciers and marshes, as well as man-made structures including roads, railways, airports, canals and dams. International borders are shown by red lines. Where neighbouring countries are in dispute, for example in the Middle East, the maps show the *de facto* boundary between nations, regardless of the legal or historical situation. The symbols are explained on the first page of the World Maps section of the atlas.

Map scales

The scale of each map is given in the numerical form known as the 'representative fraction'. The first figure is always one, signifying one unit of distance on the map; the second figure, usually in millions, is the number by which the map unit must be multiplied to give the equivalent distance on the Earth's surface. Calculations can easily be made in centimetres and kilometres, by dividing the Earth units figure by 100 000 (i.e. deleting the last five 0s). Thus 1:1 000 000 means 1 cm = 10 km. The calculation for inches and miles is more laborious, but 1 000 000 divided by 63 360 (the number of inches in a mile) shows that the ratio 1:1 000 000 means approximately 1 inch = 16 miles. The table below provides distance equivalents for scales down to 1:50 000 000.

LARGE SCALE		
1:1 000 000	1 cm = 10 km	1 inch = 16 miles
1:2 500 000	1 cm = 25 km	1 inch = 39.5 miles
1:5 000 000	1 cm = 50 km	1 inch = 79 miles
1:6 000 000	1 cm = 60 km	1 inch = 95 miles
1:8 000 000	1 cm = 80 km	1 inch = 126 miles
1:10 000 000	1 cm = 100km	1 inch = 158 miles
1:15 000 000	1 cm = 150 km	1 inch = 237 miles
1:20 000 000	1 cm = 200 km	1 inch = 316 miles
1:50 000 000	1 cm = 500 km	1 inch = 790 miles
SMALL SCALE		

Measuring distances

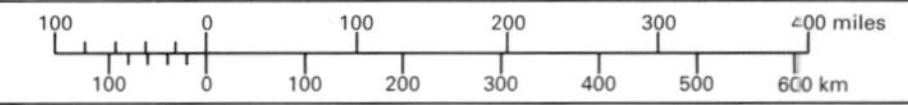

Although each map is accompanied by a scale bar, distances cannot always be measured with confidence because of the distortions involved in portraying the curved surface of the Earth on a flat page. As a general rule, the larger the map scale (i.e. the lower the number of Earth units in the representative fraction), the more accurate and reliable will be the distance measured. On small-scale maps such as those of the world and of entire continents, measurement may only be accurate along the 'standard parallels', or central axes, and should not be attempted without considering the map projection.

Latitude and longitude

Accurate positioning of individual points on the Earth's surface is made possible by reference to the geometrical system of latitude and longitude. Latitude *parallels* are drawn west–east around the Earth and numbered by degrees north and south of the Equator, which is designated 0° of latitude. Longitude *meridians* are drawn north–south and numbered by degrees east and west of the *prime meridian*, 0° of longitude, which passes through Greenwich in England. By referring to these co-ordinates and their subdivisions of minutes ($^1/60$th of a degree) and seconds ($^1/60$th of a minute), any place on Earth can be located to within a few hundred metres. Latitude and longitude are indicated by blue lines on the maps; they are straight or ·curved according to the projection employed. Reference to these lines is the easiest way of determining the relative positions of places on different maps, and for plotting compass directions.

Name forms

For ease of reference, both English and local name forms appear in the ' atlas. Oceans, seas and countries are shown in English throughout the atlas; country names may be abbreviated to their commonly accepted form (e.g. Germany, not The Federal Republic of Germany). Conventional English forms are also used for place names on the smaller-scale maps of the continents. However, local name forms are used on all large-scale and regional maps, with the English form given in brackets only for important cities – the large-scale map of Russia and Central Asia thus shows Moskva (Moscow). For countries which do not use a Roman script, place names have been transcribed according to the systems adopted by the British and US Geographic Names Authorities. For China, the Pin Yin system has been used, with some more widely known forms appearing in brackets, as with Beijing (Peking). Both English and local names appear in the index, the English form being cross-referenced to the local form.

THE WORLD OF NATIONS

An A – Z Gazetteer of Countries 1– 47
Index and Notes 48

AFGHANISTAN

After many changes since the late 1970s, a new flag was introduced in December 1992 based on the colours used by the Mujaheddin during the civil war. The flag bears the new national arms which show wheatsheaves and the shahada, *the Muslim statement of faith, above a mosque.*

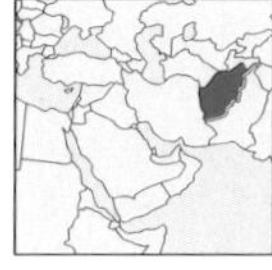

GEOGRAPHY Nearly 75% of Afghanistan is mountainous, comprising most of the Hindu Kush and its foothills. The remainder of the country is desert or semi-desert.

HISTORY AND POLITICS Afghanistan has always been in a critical position in Asia: the Khyber Pass being the gateway to India and the back door to Russia. Numerous historical invasions cul-

minated in the 1979 Soviet invasion, resulting in civil war. The Soviet troops withdrew in 1988–9, but the civil war continued. Mujaheddin forces set up an Islamic government in 1992, but a militant Islamic faction, Taliban, had gained control by late 1996.

ECONOMY Up to 70% of the workforce are peasant farmers. Natural gas is the country's biggest export.

AREA 652,090 sq km [251,772 sq mls]
POPULATION 19,509,000
CAPITAL (POPULATION) Kabul (1,424,000)
GOVERNMENT Islamic republic
ETHNIC GROUPS Pashtun ('Pathan') 52%, Tajik 20%, Uzbek 9%, Hazara 9%
LANGUAGES Pashto 50%, Dari (Persian)
RELIGIONS Sunni Muslim 84%, Shiite Muslim 15%
CURRENCY Afghani = 100 puls
MAIN EXPORTS Natural gas 42%, dried fruit 26%, fresh fruit 9%, carpets and rugs 7%

ALBANIA

The name of the country means 'land of the eagle'. Following the formation of a non-Communist government in March 1992, the star that had been placed above the eagle's head in 1946 was removed and the flag has reverted to its original form.

GEOGRAPHY Bordering the Adriatic Sea, Albania has a mountainous interior, with ranges rising to almost 2,000 m [6,500 ft]. The coastal lowlands have a Mediterranean-type climate with hot, dry summers and temperatures that rarely drop below freezing.

HISTORY AND POLITICS As Europe's poorest country, Albania has always been one of the most isolated and backward. Under Enver Hoxha it was run as a rigid Communist state virtually cut

off from the outside world. Changes in Eastern Europe in the early 1990s spread to Albania and reforms were started. However, in early 1997 civil unrest spread throughout the country.

ECONOMY Two-thirds of the population live in villages and most people live by farming, with maize, wheat, barley and fruits being the predominant crops. There are large reserves of petroleum, brown coal and iron, but there is still limited industrialization and a poor transport system.

AREA 28,750 sq km [11,100 sq mls]
POPULATION 3,458,000
CAPITAL (POPULATION) Tirana (251,000)
GOVERNMENT Multiparty republic with a unicameral legislature
ETHNIC GROUPS Albanian 96%, Greek 2%, Romanian, Macedonian, Montenegrin, Gypsy
LANGUAGES Albanian (official)
RELIGIONS Sunni Muslim 65%, Christian 33%
CURRENCY Lek = 100 qindars
MAIN EXPORTS Chrome, crude oil, nickel, iron ore, coal

ALGERIA

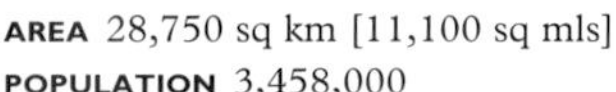

Algeria's flag features traditional Islamic symbols and colours, and the design dates back to the early 19th century. Used by the liberation movement that fought against French rule after 1954, it was adopted on independence in 1962.

GEOGRAPHY Algeria is the world's 11th largest nation, with 85% (2 million sq km [772,200 sq mls]) of its land area covered by the Sahara Desert. Over 90% of the population live in the Mediterranean coastlands, where the climate is milder.

HISTORY AND POLITICS Algeria was the first Maghreb country to be conquered by France and the last to gain independence

after a bitter war between nationalist guerillas and the French.

ECONOMY Revenues from oil (discovered in 1956 in the desert) and natural gas provide 65% of all revenue and account for over 90% of exports. This has enabled rapid industrialization and economic development with industries such as food processing, car manufacturing and oil refining.

AREA 2,381,740 sq km [919,590 sq mls]
POPULATION 27,936,000
CAPITAL (POPULATION) Algiers (1,722,000)
GOVERNMENT Socialist multiparty republic with a unicameral legislature
ETHNIC GROUPS Arab 83%, Berber 16%
LANGUAGES Arabic (official), Berber, French
RELIGIONS Sunni Muslim 99%
CURRENCY Algerian dinar = 100 centimes
MAIN EXPORTS Crude oil, petroleum products, natural gas
URBAN POPULATION 53% of population

AMERICAN SAMOA

A flag was introduced in 1960 for this American dependency. It shows the American eagle holding two typically Samoan objects: a war-club and a fly-whisk, both symbols of a chief's authority. The colours used on the flag are those of the American flag.

AREA 200 sq km [77 sq mls]
POPULATION 58,000
CAPITAL (POPULATION) Pago Pago (3,519)
GOVERNMENT Self-governing 'unincorporated territory of the USA'
ETHNIC GROUPS Samoan 90%, Caucasian 2%, Tongan 2%
LANGUAGES Samoan, English
RELIGIONS Christian

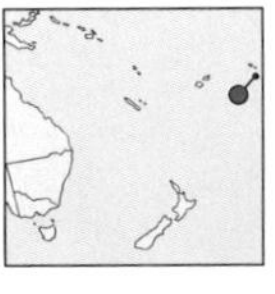

American Samoa is a group of five volcanic islands and two atolls in the South Pacific, with Tutuila the largest. The Samoan Islands were divided between Germany and the USA in 1899, and although the US naval base closed in 1951, there remains a strong American influence, with substantial grants from the USA and with 90% of Samoan exports going to the USA.

ANDORRA

Andorra is traditionally said to have been granted independence by Charlemagne in the 9th century, after the Moorish Wars. The flag, adopted in 1866, sometimes features the state coat of arms on the obverse in the central yellow band.

AREA 453 sq km [175 sq mls]
POPULATION 65,000
CAPITAL (POPULATION) Andorra La Vella (23,000)
GOVERNMENT Co-principality of Spain and France
ETHNIC GROUPS Spanish 46%, Andorran 28%, Portuguese 11%, French 8%
LANGUAGES Catalan (official), French
RELIGIONS Roman Catholic

Andorra consists mainly of six valleys (the Valls) that drain to the River Valira at the eastern end of the high central Pyrenees. There are deep glaciated valleys lying at altitudes of around 1,000 to 2,900 m [3,280 to 9,500 ft]. The climate is severe in winter and cool in summer. Andorra's economy is very dependent on tourism (skiing) and duty-free sales (every year over 10 million visitors come to shop); other sources of income include stock-rearing and agriculture, especially tobacco.

ANGOLA

The flag is based on that of the Popular Movement for the Liberation of Angola during the struggle for independence from Portugal (1975). The emblem, incorporating a half gearwheel and a machete, symbolizes Angola's socialist ideology.

AREA 1,246,700 sq km [481,351 sq mls]
POPULATION 10,844,000
CAPITAL (POPULATION) Luanda (2,250,000)
GOVERNMENT Multiparty republic
ETHNIC GROUPS Ovimbundu 37%, Mbundu 23%, Kongo, Luimbe, Humbe
LANGUAGES Portuguese (official), Umbundu 38%, Kimbundu 27%
RELIGIONS Roman Catholic 69%, Protestant 20%, traditional beliefs 10%
CURRENCY New kwanza = 100 lwei

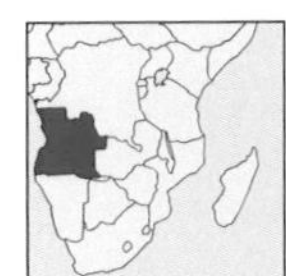

GEOGRAPHY Angola extends through 13° of latitude, with climate and vegetation varying from desert on the south coast to equatorial and montane conditions in the centre and north.
HISTORY AND POLITICS As a Portuguese colony, Angola was a centre of the slave trade (with some 3 million captives going to the Americas). Development has been slow, hampered by a civil war between the MPLA government and UNITA rebels, which finally ended when a peace accord was signed in 1994.
ECONOMY Potentially, Angola could be very rich, since there are oil reserves, diamonds, copper, manganese and phosphates.

ANGUILLA

This flag came into use in 1993 and, since Anguilla is a British dependency, the British Blue Ensign is flown. The three dolphins depicted on the shield represent strength, unity and endurance, while the white stands for peace and the blue for the sea.

AREA 96 sq km [37 sq mls]
POPULATION 8,000
CAPITAL (POPULATION) The Valley (2,000)
GOVERNMENT British Dependent Territory
ETHNIC GROUPS Mainly of African descent
LANGUAGES English and Creole
RELIGIONS Christian
CURRENCY East Caribbean $ = 100 cents

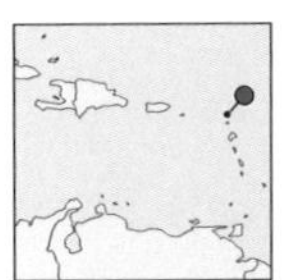

Discovered by Columbus in 1493, Anguilla is a long and thin coral atoll (*anguil* is Spanish for eel) covered by poor soil and scrub. It has been a British colony since 1650 and its main source of revenue is now tourism.

ANTIGUA AND BARBUDA

The design of the flag was decided in a competition in 1967. The V depicted in the design denotes victory and the golden sun symbolizes the dawning of a new era. The black represents African heritage and the soil, blue is for hope and red for the dynamism of the people.

AREA 440 sq km [170 sq mls]
POPULATION 67,000
CAPITAL (POPULATION) St John's (38,000)
GOVERNMENT Multiparty constitutional monarchy with a bicameral legislature
ETHNIC GROUPS Of African descent
LANGUAGES English and local dialects
RELIGIONS Christian
CURRENCY East Caribbean $ = 100 cents

Antigua and Barbuda are part of the Leeward Islands; Barbuda is a wooded low coral atoll, while Antigua is higher with no rivers or forests, but over 365 sandy beaches. Independence from Britain was gained in 1981 and the economy relies heavily on tourism. There is also the production of Sea Island cotton, sugar cane crops and lobster fishing.

ARGENTINA

The 'celeste' and white stripes, symbol of independence since 1810 around Buenos Aires, became the national flag in 1816 and influenced other Latin American countries. A yellow May Sun, only used on the state flag, was added two years later.

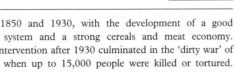

AREA 2,766,890 sq km [1,068,296 sq mls]
POPULATION 34,663,000
CAPITAL (POPULATION) Buenos Aires (10,990,000)
GOVERNMENT Republic
ETHNIC GROUPS European 85%, Mestizo, Amerindian
LANGUAGES Spanish (official) 95%, Italian, Guarani
RELIGIONS Roman Catholic 93%, Protestant 2%
CURRENCY Peso = 10,000 australs
MAIN EXPORTS Vegetable products 43%, textiles and manufactures 4%
MAIN IMPORTS Machinery 23%

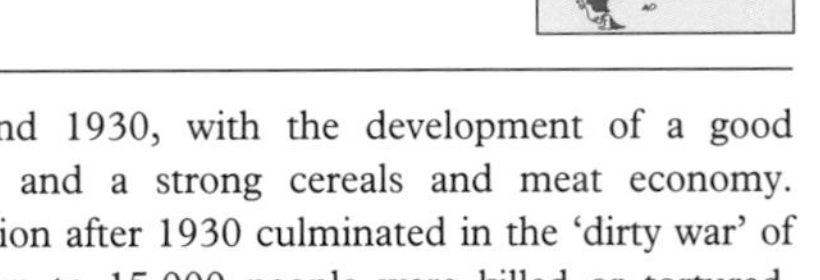

GEOGRAPHY Argentina is the world's eighth largest country and stretches from the Tropic of Capricorn almost into Antarctica. The Andes mountains are to the west, with Mt Aconcagua, at 6,960 m [22,834 ft], the tallest mountain in the western hemisphere. The pampas grasslands cover much of central Argentina and most of the population lives on this fertile land; in the far south are the plateaux of Patagonia.
HISTORY AND POLITICS The 'land of silver' emerged as a national entity in 1816 and there was great economic prosperity between 1850 and 1930, with the development of a good transport system and a strong cereals and meat economy. Military intervention after 1930 culminated in the 'dirty war' of 1976–82, when up to 15,000 people were killed or tortured. After an unsuccessful invasion of the Falkland Islands in 1982, there was a return to constitutional rule.
ECONOMY Economic problems have included a large foreign debt and inflation rates of 3,084%. There are rich natural resources, with agriculture making up 70% of export earnings.

ARMENIA

The flag used in the period 1918–22 was readopted on 24 August 1990. The colours represent the blood shed in the past (red), the land of Armenia (blue), and the unity and courage of the people (orange).

Armenia is a mountainous country, landlocked between hostile neighbours. The economy is weak, with few natural resources and limited industry; agricultural products include wine and tobacco. Historically its peoples have been subject to war and occupation and the western regions are still recovering from an earthquake in 1988, which killed 55,000.

AREA 29,800 sq km [11,506 sq mls]
POPULATION 3,603,000
CAPITAL (POPULATION) Yerevan (1,226,000)
GOVERNMENT Multiparty republic
ETHNIC GROUPS Armenian 93%, Azerbaijani 3%, Russian 2%, Kurd 2%
LANGUAGES Armenian 89%, Azerbaijani, Russian
CURRENCY Dram = 100 couma

ARUBA

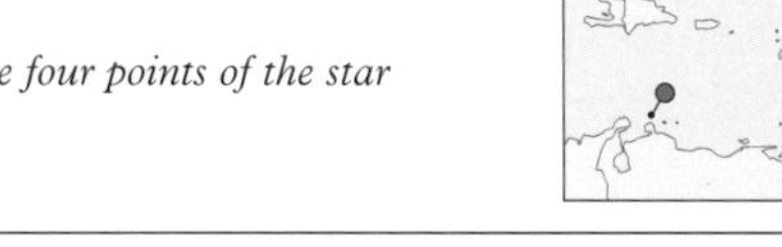

The flag of this Dutch overseas territory was introduced in 1976. The four points of the star represent the four main language groups of the area.

Aruba is the most western of the Lesser Antilles and is a dry, flat limestone island. A Dutch territory, it was part of the Netherlands Antilles until 1986. About half of export earnings come from beverages and tobacco; tourism is also important.

AREA 193 sq km [75 sq mls]
POPULATION 71,000
CAPITAL (POPULATION) Oranjestad (21,000)
GOVERNMENT Self-governing Dutch Territory
ETHNIC GROUPS Mixed European/Caribbean Indian 80%
LANGUAGES Dutch, Papiamento, English

ASCENSION

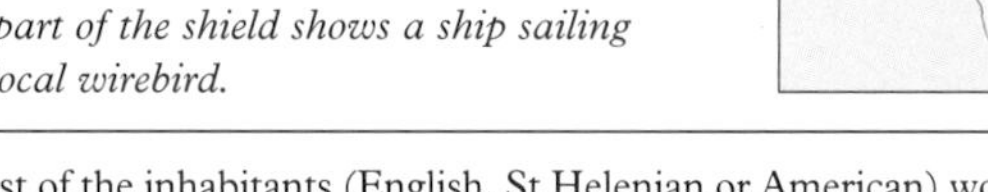

As a dependency of St Helena, Ascension uses her flag, which shows the shield from her coat of arms in the fly of the British Blue Ensign. The main part of the shield shows a ship sailing towards the island, and the chief is yellow and shows a local wirebird.

Ascension is a triangular volcanic island standing on the Mid-Atlantic Ridge, with a single high peak and a cool, damp climate. Most of the inhabitants (English, St Helenian or American) work in telecommunications or on the mid-ocean airstrip.

AREA 88 sq km [34 sq mls]
POPULATION 1,500
CAPITAL (POPULATION) Georgetown (1,500)
GOVERNMENT British Dependent Territory
ETHNIC GROUPS No native ones
LANGUAGES English
POPULATION DENSITY 17 people per sq km [44 per sq ml]

AUSTRALIA

Showing its historical link with Britain, Australia's flag, adopted in 1901, features the British Blue Ensign. The five stars represent the Southern Cross constellation and, together with the larger star, symbolize the six states. Since 1995, the Aboriginal flag has had equal status.

GEOGRAPHY The landscape is largely made up of low to medium plateaus of desert and semi-desert stretching for hundreds of kilometres. At the edges of these plateaus, there are more diverse landscapes: for example, the gorges in the Hamersley Range and Kimberley area of the north and the forests of eucalyptus hardwoods in the extreme south-west of Western Australia. The Great Artesian Basin in the central lowlands is the world's largest underground natural reservoir, discharging some 1,500 million litres [330 million gallons] of water a day. Along the east coast of Queensland lies the Great Barrier Reef, a coral reef stretching about 2,000 km [1,250 mls] with the 2,500 reefs exposed only at low tide.

HISTORY AND POLITICS Aborigines arrived in Australia from Asia over 40,000 years ago, while European settlement did not begin until 1788 when the British established a penal colony first in New South Wales and then in Queensland and Tasmania. During the 19th century the continent was divided into colonies and in 1901 these came together to create the Commonwealth of Australia. Immigration since 1960 has changed the ethnic character of Australia, with Greek, Italian, Turkish and Lebanese communities now living alongside the longer-established Aboriginal, British, Dutch and Chinese communities. Some 60% of the total Australian population live in Sydney, Melbourne, Adelaide, Brisbane, Perth and Hobart. A good transport system and good communications, particularly radio, help the many remote and isolated settlements. Since 1991, with a worsening economic situation and Britain's closer links with the European Union, Australia has increasingly turned to the Pacific countries, especially Japan, for trade. The former prime minister, Paul Keating, was a keen republican but the new prime minister, John Howard, is keen to maintain Australia's ties with the UK.

ECONOMY Much of Australia's early development was based on its mineral resources, such as copper, lead, zinc and silver. In 1993, it produced over a third of the world's diamonds and bauxite, 11% of iron ore, 7% of uranium and over 5% of zinc and lead. On the agricultural side, there is extensive sheep and cattle production, with 140 million sheep producing 25% of the world's wool. Metals, minerals and farm products account for the bulk of Australia's exports. Wine production around Perth, Adelaide and in Victoria has expanded in recent years.

AREA 7,686,850 sq km [2,967,893 sq mls]
POPULATION 18,107,000
CAPITAL (POPULATION) Canberra (328,000)
GOVERNMENT Federal constitutional monarchy with a bicameral legislature
ETHNIC GROUPS White 94%, Aboriginal 1.5%, Asian 1.3%
LANGUAGES English (official)
RELIGIONS Roman Catholic 26%, Anglican 24%, other Christian 22%
CURRENCY Australian dollar = 100 cents
MAIN EXPORTS Food and live animals 22%, coal, oil and gas 19%, metallic ores 14%

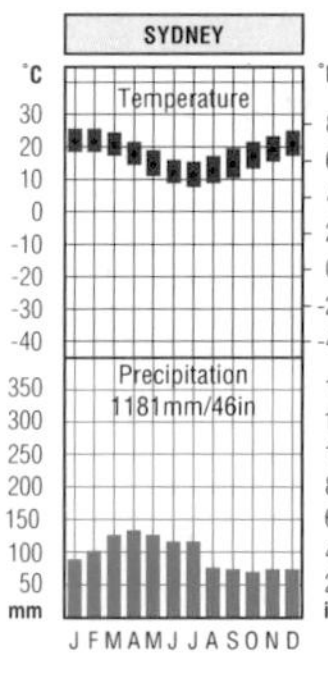

In the south-east, the annual rainfall total is fairly high, with maxima between April and June. Rain falls on 12–13 days each month. The valleys inland of the Great Divide, in the lee of rain-bearing winds, are drier. Temperatures are moderate, with winter night frosts in the south and interior, but the lowest temperatures in Sydney are 2–4°C [36–39°F].

AUSTRIA

According to legend, the colours of the Austrian flag date from the battle of Ptolemais in 1191, when the only part of the Duke of Bebenberg's tunic not bloodstained was under his swordbelt. The design was officially adopted in 1918.

GEOGRAPHY Austria is a mountainous country, with two-thirds of its territory and slightly less than a third of its population within the eastern Alps. Forests cover 37% of the country.

HISTORY AND POLITICS Austria's boundaries derive from the Versailles Treaty of 1919, which dissolved the Austro-Hungarian Empire. It regained its full independence in 1955 after occupation by the Germans in 1938 and the Allies in 1945. A member of EFTA since 1960, in 1994 two-thirds of the population voted in favour of joining the European Union, and on 1 January 1995 Austria became a member (at the same time as Finland and Sweden).

ECONOMY There are important heavy industries based mainly on indigenous resources; oil and gas are found in the Vienna Basin and the mountains are a source of hydroelectric power.

AREA 83,850 sq km [32,374 sq mls]
POPULATION 8,004,000
CAPITAL (POPULATION) Vienna (1,560,000)
GOVERNMENT Federal multiparty republic
ETHNIC GROUPS Austrian 94%, Slovene 2%, Turkish, German
LANGUAGES German 94% (official), Slovene, Croat, Turkish, Slovak, Magyar
RELIGIONS Roman Catholic 78%, Protestant 6%, Muslim 2%
CURRENCY Schilling = 100 Groschen
MAIN EXPORTS Machinery and transport equipment 34%, iron and steel 7%

AZERBAIJAN

This flag was instituted on 5 February 1991. The blue stands for the sky, the red for freedom and the green for land and the Islamic religion; the crescent and star symbolize Islam, and the points of the star represent the eight races of Azerbaijan.

AREA 86,600 sq km [33,436 sq mls]
POPULATION 7,559,000
CAPITAL (POPULATION) Baku (1,081,000)
GOVERNMENT Transitional government
ETHNIC GROUPS Azerbaijani 83%, Russian 6%, Armenian 6%, Daghestani 3%
LANGUAGES Azerbaijani 82%, Russian, Armenian
RELIGIONS Muslim 87%, Christian
CURRENCY Manat = 100 gopik
URBAN POPULATION 55% of population

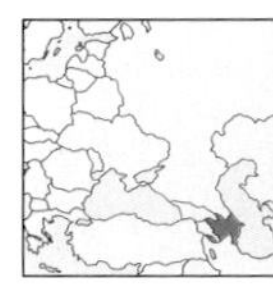

GEOGRAPHY Azerbaijan is mostly semi-arid, with the Caspian Sea to the east and the Caucasus Mountains to the north.
HISTORY AND POLITICS Independence was declared in 1991 but fighting broke out with Armenia over the predominantly Armenian enclave of Nagorno-Karabakh in the south-west. A cease-fire was agreed in 1994, however, with about 20% of Azerbaijan territory under Armenian control. Azerbaijan has its own enclave, Nakhichevan, between Armenia and Turkey.
ECONOMY The country became an oil exporter for the first time in early 1997 when a new pipeline agreement came into effect.

AZORES

The flag dates from 1979 and shows the hawk (or açor) after which the islands are named, below an arc of nine stars (one for each island). The colours recall the fact that the old Portuguese flag was first adopted in the Azores.

AREA 2,247 sq km [868 sq mls]
POPULATION 240,000
CAPITAL (POPULATION) Ponta Delgada (21,000)
GOVERNMENT Portuguese Autonomous Region
ETHNIC GROUPS Portuguese
CURRENCY Portuguese escudo

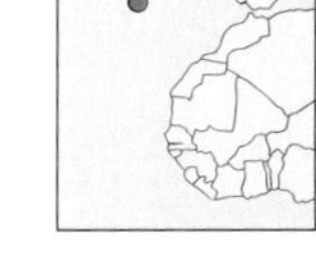

Part of the Mid-Atlantic Ridge, the Azores comprise nine large and several smaller islands; of recent volcanic origin, they have high cliffs and narrow beaches. Occupations include small-scale farming and fishing, with the export of fruit and canned fish.

BAHAMAS

The black hoist triangle symbolizes the unity of the Bahamian people and their resolve to develop the island's natural resources. The golden sand and blue sea of the islands are depicted by the yellow and aquamarine stripes.

AREA 13,880 sq km [5,359 sq mls]
POPULATION 277,000
CAPITAL (POPULATION) Nassau (190,000)
GOVERNMENT Constitutional monarchy with a bicameral legislature
ETHNIC GROUPS Black 80%, Mixed 10%, White 10%
LANGUAGES English, English Creole 80%
RELIGIONS Christian 95%

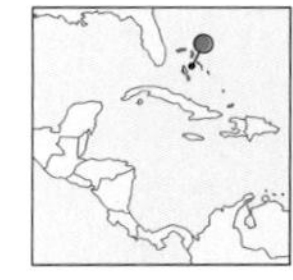

The Bahamas are made up of a coral-limestone archipelago of 29 inhabited low-lying islands and over 3,000 uninhabited cays, reefs and rocks; tourism now accounts for more than half the country's revenue (over 90% of its visitors are American) and involves 40% of the workforce. Other activities include offshore banking and some traditional fishing and agriculture.

BAHRAIN

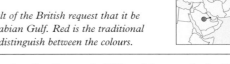

The flag dates from about 1932, with the white section a result of the British request that it be included in the flags of all friendly Arab states around the Arabian Gulf. Red is the traditional colour of Kharijite Muslims. The serrated edge was added to distinguish between the colours.

AREA 678 sq km [262 sq mls]
POPULATION 558,000
CAPITAL (POPULATION) Manama (143,000)
GOVERNMENT Monarchy (emirate) with a cabinet appointed by the Emir
ETHNIC GROUPS Bahraini Arab 68%, Persian, Indian and Pakistani 25%, other Arab 4%, European 3%
LANGUAGES Arabic (official), English
RELIGIONS Muslim 85%, Christian 7%

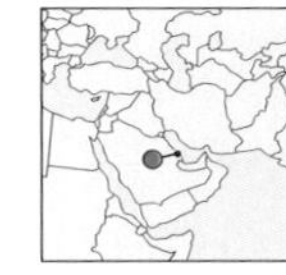

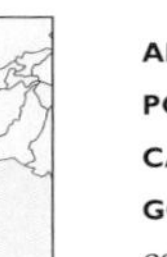

GEOGRAPHY Bahrain comprises 35 small islands in the southern Gulf, the largest of which is called Bahrain. Most of the land is barren, but soil imports have created fertile areas.
HISTORY, POLITICS AND ECONOMY Bahrain led the region into oil production after discovery in 1932, and there are also banking and aluminium-smelting activities. Tensions between the Sunni and majority Shiite population (the latter favouring an Islamic republic) have always been a problem.

BANGLADESH

Bangladesh adopted this flag in 1971 following the break from Pakistan. The green is said to represent the fertility of the land, while the red disc, as the sun of independence, commemorates the blood shed in the struggle for freedom.

AREA 144,000 sq km [55,598 sq mls]
POPULATION 118,342,000
CAPITAL (POPULATION) Dhaka (7,832,000)
GOVERNMENT Multiparty republic
ETHNIC GROUPS Bengali 98%, Bihari, tribal groups
LANGUAGES Bengali (official), English, nearly 100 tribal dialects
RELIGIONS Sunni Muslim 87%, Hindu 12%, Buddhist, Christian
CURRENCY Taka = 100 paisas
MAIN EXPORTS Jute goods and raw jute 33%, fish and fish preparations 12%

GEOGRAPHY Apart from hills covered in bamboo forest in the south-east, Bangladesh consists of lowlands made up mostly from the (greater) eastern part of the huge delta formed jointly by the Ganges and Brahmaputra. Known as the 'active delta', it frequently floods, making it hazardous to life, health and property, but also creating fertile alluvial silts.
HISTORY AND POLITICS Once known as Golden Bengal, Bangladesh was East Pakistan until 1971 when the state of 'Free Bengal' was set up. It is now one of Asia's poorest countries, with the world's ninth biggest population. In 1991 Bangladesh held its first free elections since independence.
ECONOMY Up to three rice crops a year and the world's best jute are grown on the fertile delta areas, but political problems, flooding and sheer population numbers hinder development.

BARBADOS

The flag was adopted on independence in 1960. The trident had been part of the colonial badge of Barbados and was retained as the centre to its flag, maintaining the link between old and new. The gold stripe represents the beaches and the two blue stripes the sea and the sky.

AREA 430 sq km [166 sq mls]
POPULATION 263,000
CAPITAL (POPULATION) Bridgetown (8,000)
GOVERNMENT Constitutional monarchy with a bicameral legislature
ETHNIC GROUPS Black 80%, Mixed 16%, White 4%
LANGUAGES English (official), Creole 90%
RELIGIONS Protestant 65%, Roman Catholic 4%
CURRENCY Barbados dollar = 100 cents

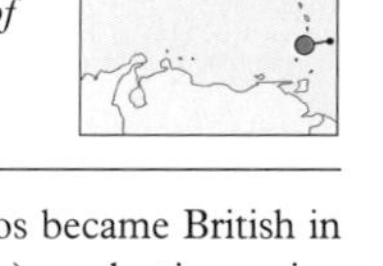

GEOGRAPHY Barbados is the easternmost of the West Indies, and its landscape is underlain with limestone and capped with coral. The coral structure acts as a natural filter and makes the water very pure. Soils are fertile and deep. It has a mild climate, but its location makes it susceptible to hurricanes.
HISTORY, POLITICS AND ECONOMY Barbados became British in 1627 and sugar (one of the principal exports) production, using African slave labour, began then. Tourism is now the leading industry; the island itself is densely populated and emigration is high, particularly to the USA and the UK.

BELARUS

In September 1991, Belarus adopted a red and white flag to replace the one used in the Soviet era. But, in June 1995, after a referendum in which Belarussians voted to improve relations with Russia, this was replaced with a design similar to that of 1958 minus the hammer and sickle.

AREA 207,600 sq km [80,154 sq mls]
POPULATION 10,500,000
CAPITAL (POPULATION) Minsk (1,658,000)
ETHNIC GROUPS Belarussian 78%, Russian 14%, Polish 4%, Ukrainian 3%, Jewish 1%
LANGUAGES Belarussian 70%, Russian 25%
RELIGIONS Belarussian Orthodox, Roman Catholic, Evangelical

GEOGRAPHY The Republic of Belarus ('White Russia') is a landlocked country in Eastern Europe, formerly part of the Soviet Union. The land is low-lying and mostly flat. In the south, much of the land is marshy. This area contains Europe's largest marsh and peat bog, the Pripet Marshes. A hilly region extends from north-east to south-west through the centre of the country. Forests cover about a third of the country, but farmland and pasture have replaced most of the original forest.

HISTORY AND POLITICS In 1918, Belarus became an independent republic, but Russia invaded the country and, in 1919, a Communist state was set up. In 1922, Belarus became a founder republic of the Soviet Union. Most observers were surprised when this most conservative and Communist-dominated of parliaments declared independence on 25 August 1991, forcing the Party president to stand down. The quiet state of the European Soviet Union, it played a big supporting role in its deconstruction and the creation of the CIS; the latter's first meeting was in Minsk – subsequently chosen as its capital. Like the Ukraine, Belarus has been a separate UN member since 1945, the end of World War II, during which it bore much of the force of the German invasion; one in four of its population died.

ECONOMY The World Bank classifies Belarus as an 'upper-middle-income' economy. It faces many problems in working to turn a government-run economy into a free-market one. Though mainly agricultural – 46% of the land is used efficiently for flax, potatoes, cereals, dairying, pigs and peat digging – it also has the largest petrochemical complex in Europe and the giant Belaz heavy-truck plants; these, however, like its many light industries, are heavily reliant on Russia for electricity and raw materials, including steel.

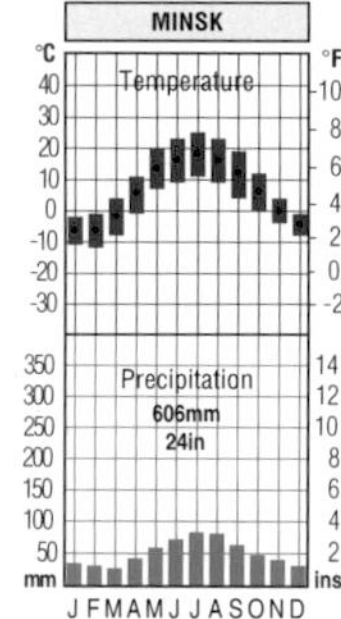

The climate of Belarus is affected by both the moderating influence of the Baltic Sea to the extreme north of the country and the continental conditions to the east. The winter months are cold and the summers warm. The average annual rainfall is between about 550 mm and 700 mm [22 in to 28 in], falling mainly in the summer months.

BELGIUM

The colours of Belgium's flag derive from the arms of the province of Brabant which rebelled against Austrian rule in 1787. It was adopted as the national flag in 1830 when Belgium gained independence from the Netherlands.

AREA 30,510 sq km [11,780 sq mls]
POPULATION 10,140,000
CAPITAL (POPULATION) Brussels (952,000)
GOVERNMENT Constitutional monarchy with a bicameral legislature
ETHNIC GROUPS Fleming 55%, Walloon 34%, Italian 3%, German, French, Dutch, Turkish, Moroccan
LANGUAGES Flemish (Dutch) 57%, Walloon (French) 32%, German 1% – all official languages; 10% of population is officially bilingual
RELIGIONS Roman Catholic 72%, Protestant, Muslim
CURRENCY Belgian franc = 100 centimes
MAIN EXPORTS Vehicles 15%, chemicals 13%, foodstuffs 9%, iron and steel 7%

GEOGRAPHY Physically Belgium may be divided into the uplands of the Ardennes in the south-east and the lowland plains which are drained by the rivers Meuse and Schelde. The Ardennes, rising in Belgium to about 700 m [2,296 ft] at the highest point, is largely moorland, peat bogs and woodland. There is a cool temperate maritime climate and temperatures may reach 30°C [86°F] between May and September.

HISTORY AND POLITICS After the Napoleonic Wars, from 1815, Belgium and the Netherlands were united as the 'Low Countries', but Belgium regained independence in 1830, although it was occupied by Germany in both world wars. Since the end of World War II economic progress has been fast, since its geographical position gives it a significant position in Europe, especially in the European Union (it was a founder member of the European Community). There are tensions between its peoples, however – with the Flemings of Flanders in the north and the Walloons of Wallonia in the south.

ECONOMY Belgium has a very high urban population (97%), and most of its people work in industry. Coal is the only significant mineral resource and the other raw materials that are needed are imported. The textile industry, in existence since medieval times, is important, based around Ghent.

BELIZE

The badge shows loggers bearing axes and oars, tools employed in the industry responsible for developing Belize. The motto underneath reads 'Sub Umbra Floreo' ('Flourish in the Shade') and the tree is a mahogany, the national tree.

AREA 22,960 sq km [8,865 sq mls]
POPULATION 216,000
CAPITAL (POPULATION) Belmopan (4,000)
GOVERNMENT Constitutional monarchy with a bicameral National Assembly
ETHNIC GROUPS Mestizo (Spanish Maya) 44%, Creole 30%, Mayan Indian 11%, Garifuna (Black Carib Indian) 7%, White 4%, East Indian 3%
LANGUAGES English and Spanish (official), Creole, Indian, Carib
RELIGIONS Roman Catholic 58%

GEOGRAPHY Belize is a sparsely populated enclave on the Caribbean coast of Central America. The northern half is low-lying swamp, the south a high plateau, while offshore is the world's second biggest coral reef. The climate is hot and wet.

HISTORY AND POLITICS Formerly known as British Honduras, Belize became independent in 1981. There has been a long border dispute with Guatemala, but British troops, stationed here since the 1970s, were finally withdrawn at the end of 1993.

ECONOMY After independence there was an economic boom, with the processing of citrus fruits and tourism helping to allay the dependency on timber, bananas and sugar. Sugar still accounts for 30% of export earnings.

BENIN

This flag, showing the red, yellow and green Pan-African colours, was first used after independence from France in 1960 and has now been readopted. While Benin was a Communist state after 1975, another flag, showing a red Communist star, was used.

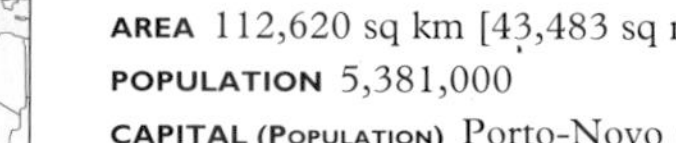

AREA 112,620 sq km [43,483 sq mls]
POPULATION 5,381,000
CAPITAL (POPULATION) Porto-Novo (179,000)
GOVERNMENT Multiparty republic with a unicameral legislature
ETHNIC GROUPS Fon 66%, Bariba 10%, Yoruba 9%, Somba 5%
LANGUAGES French (official), Fon 47%
RELIGIONS Traditional beliefs 61%, Christian 23%, Sunni Muslim 15%
CURRENCY CFA franc = 100 centimes
MAIN EXPORTS Fuels, raw cotton, palm products
MAIN IMPORTS Manufactured goods, textiles
URBAN POPULATION 30% of population

GEOGRAPHY Benin is one of Africa's smallest countries, with a coastline that is only 100 km [62 mls] long. The equatorial and more fertile south is the most populated area and has a hot and humid climate. There is a central rainforest belt and savanna in the far north.

HISTORY AND POLITICS Known as Dahomey until 1975, Benin was inhabited by the Portuguese in the 16th century. They were expelled by the Dutch in 1642 and Dahomey became the base of a flourishing slave trade, mainly going to Brazil. Until 1850, when the French began to establish control, many rival tribal kingdoms flourished. In 1904 Dahomey became part of French West Africa. After independence in 1960 a series of coups and power struggles followed, until multiparty elections in 1991. There was an unexpected victory for the former military dictator General Kérékou, in the presidential elections of 1996.

ECONOMY During the 18th and 19th centuries Benin was a major trading point for pepper and ivory. Now Benin exports only palm-oil produce, cotton and groundnuts. There is some offshore oil production, but this has been hampered by low prices. There are hopes for increased tourism in the future.

BERMUDA

BERMUDA

Instead of the customary British Blue Ensign, the Red Ensign with the shield from Bermuda's badge is on the fly. The shield depicts a red lion holding another shield in which the shipwreck of the Sea Venture *in 1609 is shown.*

AREA 53 sq km [20 sq mls]
POPULATION 64,000
CAPITAL (POPULATION) Hamilton (6,000)
GOVERNMENT British Dependent Territory
ETHNIC GROUPS Black 61%, White 37%
LANGUAGES English
RELIGIONS Anglican 37%, Roman Catholic 14%, other Christian 25%
CURRENCY Bermuda dollar = 100 cents
MAIN EXPORTS Drugs (legal), medicines

Comprising about 150 small islands, the coral caps of ancient submarine volcanoes rising over 4,000 m [13,000 ft] from the ocean floor, Bermuda has a mild climate. Twenty of the islands are inhabited, particularly the biggest island of Great Bermuda.

It is Britain's oldest dependency, but has strong ties with the USA. Tourism is vital to the economy, with over 500,000 visitors a year, and the islands are also a tax haven for companies and individuals; foodstuffs and energy dominate imports.

BHUTAN

The striking image on Bhutan's flag is explained by the name of this Himalayan kingdom in the local language, Druk Yil, *which means 'land of the dragon'. The saffron colour stands for royal power and the orange-red for Buddhist spiritual power.*

AREA 47,000 sq km [18,147 sq mls]
POPULATION 1,639,000
CAPITAL (POPULATION) Thimphu (31,000)
GOVERNMENT Constitutional monarchy
ETHNIC GROUPS Bhote 60%, Nepalese 33%
LANGUAGES Dzongkha (official, a Tibetan dialect), Sharchop, Bumthap, Nepali and English
RELIGIONS Buddhist 75%, Hindu 25%
CURRENCY Ngultrum = 100 chetrum
MAIN EXPORTS Cement, talcum, timber
URBAN POPULATION 6% of the population

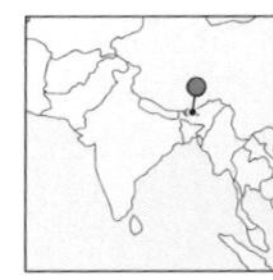

GEOGRAPHY Bhutan is a remote mountain kingdom that lies in the eastern Himalayas and is the world's most 'rural' country, with less than 6% of the population living in towns. Rainfall is high and temperatures are very varied.

HISTORY AND POLITICS Although Bhutan is ruled by a king, its foreign affairs are under Indian guidance following a treaty of

1949. There were small-scale pro-democracy demonstrations in 1990, but there has been little political progress since then.

ECONOMY Over 90% of the population are dependent on agriculture, producing mainly rice and maize as staple crops and fruit and cardamom as cash crops. Cement and talcum exports earn much-needed foreign exchange.

BOLIVIA

Dating from liberation in 1825, the tricolour has been used as both national and merchant flag since 1888. The red stands for Bolivia's animals and the army's courage, the yellow for mineral resources and the green for its agricultural wealth.

AREA 1,098,580 sq km [424,162 sq mls]
POPULATION 7,900,000
CAPITAL (POPULATION) La Paz (1,126,000)/ Sucre (131,000)
GOVERNMENT Unitary multiparty republic with a bicameral legislature
ETHNIC GROUPS Mestizo 31%, Quechua 25%, Aymara 17%, White 15%
LANGUAGES Spanish, Aymara, Quechua
RELIGIONS Roman Catholic 94%
CURRENCY Boliviano = 100 centavos
MAIN EXPORTS Tin, zinc, natural gas
POPULATION DENSITY 7 per sq km [19 per sq ml]

GEOGRAPHY Bolivia is landlocked and made up of a wide stretch of the Andes and a long, broad Oriente – part of the south-western fringe of the Amazon Basin. To the east lies the Altiplano, a high grassland plateau, which in prehistoric times was a great lake; Lake Titicaca, the highest navigable body of water in the world, lies at its northern end.

HISTORY AND POLITICS In pre-Conquest days Bolivia was the homeland of the Tiahuanaco culture (7th to 11th centuries AD) and was later absorbed into the Inca empire. The silver mines of

the high Andean plain area were exploited by Spanish *conquistadores*. The local population seized independence in 1824. Today Bolivia is one of the poorest South American republics and is renowned for its political volatility.

ECONOMY Bolivia has abundant natural resources, especially petroleum and natural gas but there is a lack of investment. The collapse of a dam at the El Porco zinc mine near Potosí in 1996 released 400,000 tonnes of heavy-metal sludge and was one of the worst environmental disasters ever in Latin America.

BOSNIA-HERZEGOVINA

The flag was adopted when independence was declared in April 1992 and has a shield recalling the ancient Bosnian monarchy of pre-Turkish times. The fleur-de-lis is thought to be derived from the lily specific to Bosnia, Lilium bosniacum.

AREA 51,129 sq km [19,745 sq mls]
POPULATION 4,400,000
CAPITAL (POPULATION) Sarajevo (526,000)
ETHNIC GROUPS Muslim, Serb, Croat
LANGUAGES Serbo-Croat 99%
RELIGIONS Muslim 40%, Orthodox 31%, Roman Catholic 15%
CURRENCY Dinar = 100 paras
POPULATION DENSITY 86 per sq km [223 per sq ml]
LAND USE Arable 16%, grass 31%, forest 48%

Bosnia-Herzegovina has been in a state of chaos since declaring independence in April 1992. The latest figures put its population at 49% Muslim, 31% Serb and 17% Croat – a mixture that has proved unworkable. At first the Muslim-dominated government allied itself uneasily with the Croat minority, but was at once under attack from the local Serbs, supported by their co-nationals

from beyond Bosnia's borders. By early 1993, the Muslims controlled less than a third of the former federal republic and the capital, Sarajevo, became disputed territory. In 1995, the warring parties agreed to a solution. This involved dividing the country into two self-governing provinces: a Bosnian-Serb one and a Muslim-Croat one, under a central, multi-ethnic government.

BOTSWANA

Botswana's flag dates from independence from Britain in 1966. The white-black-white zebra stripe represents the racial harmony of the people and the coat of the zebra, the national animal. The blue symbolizes the country's most vital need – rainwater.

AREA 581,730 sq km [224,606 sq mls]
POPULATION 1,481,000
CAPITAL (POPULATION) Gaborone (135,000)
GOVERNMENT Multiparty republic
ETHNIC GROUPS Tswana 76%, Shona 12%, San (Bushmen) 3%
LANGUAGES English (official), Setswana (Siswana, Tswana – national language)
RELIGIONS Traditional beliefs 50%, Christian (mainly Anglican) 30%
CURRENCY Pula = 100 thebe
MAIN EXPORTS Diamonds, copper-nickel matte, meat and meat products
MAIN IMPORTS Food, beverages, tobacco, machinery, electrical goods

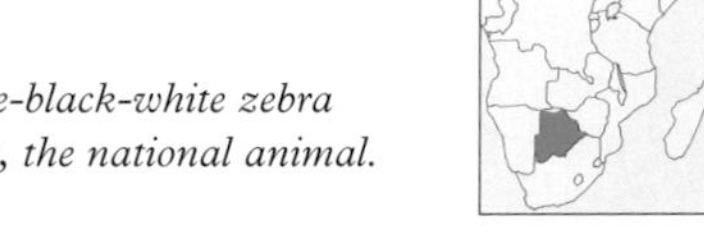

GEOGRAPHY More than half of Botswana's land area is covered by the Kalahari Desert, which stretches into Namibia and South Africa in the south-west. The desert is not uniform; occasional rainfall allows the growth of grasses and thorny scrub, on which cattle can graze. Much of the rest of the country is taken up by salt pans and the Okavango Swamp in the north-west.

HISTORY AND POLITICS Botswana was the British protectorate of Bechuanaland from 1885 to 1966, when it became independent after a peaceful six-year transition period. Political

stability has been achieved since then, first under Seretse Khama and then under Quett Masire.

ECONOMY Large numbers of cattle are kept by the Bantu-speaking herdsmen, and provide the main export. Diamonds (Botswana is the world's third largest producer) and copper are mined in the east. Recently, tourism has become important: 17% of the land (Africa's highest figure) is set aside for wildlife conservation and game reserves and attracts some half a million visitors a year, particularly from South Africa.

BRAZIL

The sphere bears the motto 'Order and Progress' and its 27 stars, arranged in the pattern of the night sky over Rio de Janeiro, represent the states and federal district. Green symbolizes the nation's rainforests, and the yellow diamond represents its mineral wealth.

GEOGRAPHY Brazil covers nearly 48% of South America and is the world's fifth largest country. In the north, the huge Amazon Basin covers the landscape, once an inland sea and now drained by a river system that carries one-fifth of the Earth's running water. The rainforest here is the world's largest, although it is being destroyed at an alarming rate, and the rest of the area is covered by an upland plateau of thorny scrub forest. In the centre and south of Brazil lies the Brazilian Highlands, a huge extent of hard crystalline rock deeply dissected into rolling uplands. Here the vegetation of wooded savanna (*campo cerrado*) covers 2 million sq km [770,000 sq mls]. The narrow coastal plain is fertile and swampy in places, with high rainfall all year. Over 60% of the population live in four southern and south-eastern states that make up only 17% of the total land area.

HISTORY AND POLITICS Brazil was 'discovered' by Pedro Alvarez Cabral in 1500 and gradually penetrated by Portuguese settlers and explorers during the 17th and 18th centuries. In 1822 Brazil declared itself independent from Portugal and established an empire, first under Pedro I and then ruled by his son, Pedro II, whose liberal policies included the abolition of slavery in 1888. In 1889 Brazil became a republic. Since then there have been dictatorships and military rule: between 1964 and 1985 there were five military presidents. A new constitution came into force in 1988, with a return to democracy in 1990.

ECONOMY Brazil is one of the world's largest farming countries, with agriculture employing a quarter of the population and providing 40% of exports. The main agricultural exports are coffee, sugar, soya beans, orange juice concentrates, beef, cocoa, poultry, sisal, tobacco, maize and cotton. There are also huge mineral resources, particularly in Minas Gerais and the Amazon area, including bauxite, tin, iron ore, chrome, nickel, uranium, industrial diamonds, platinum and manganese.

AREA 8,511,970 sq km [3,286,472 sq mls]
POPULATION 161,416,000
CAPITAL (POPULATION) Brasília (1,596,000)
GOVERNMENT Federal republic with a bicameral legislature
ETHNIC GROUPS White 53%, Mulatto 22%, Mestizo 12%, Black 11%, Amerindian
LANGUAGES Portuguese, Spanish, English, French, native dialects

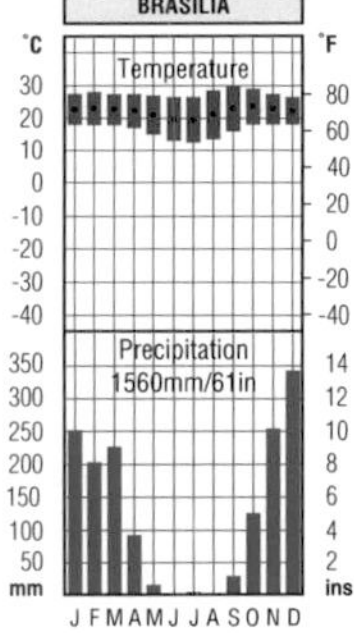

Brazil lies almost entirely within the tropics. The monthly temperatures are high – over 25°C [77°F] – and there is little annual variation. Brasília has only a 4°C [7°F] difference between July and October; Rio has twice this range. The hottest part of the country is in the north-east. Frosts do occur in the eastern highlands and in the far south.

BRUNEI

The yellow background represents the flag of the Sultan, with the black and white stripes standing for his two main advisers (wazirs). The arms contain the inscription in Arabic 'Brunei, Gate of Peace' and a crescent, the symbol of Islam.

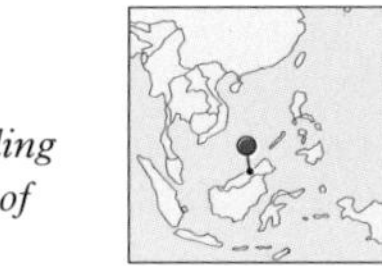

GEOGRAPHY Brunei comprises two enclaves on the north-east coast of Borneo. The landscape rises from humid plains to forested mountains over 1,800 m [6,000 ft] high along the Malaysian border. The climate is tropical with high rainfall and temperatures varying between 24°C [75°F] and 30°C [86°F].

HISTORY AND POLITICS Brunei was a British protectorate from 1888 to 1971 and still retains very close ties with the UK. The Sultan and his family now rule Brunei by ancient hereditary rights and the Sultan himself, through the oil and gas revenues, is thought to be one of the world's richest men.

ECONOMY The oil and gas fields lie offshore and account for 70% of GDP and even more of exports earnings (oil 41%, gas 53%). Machinery, manufactures and foodstuffs are imported. There is no income tax, and free health services and education.

AREA 5,770 sq km [2,228 sq mls]
POPULATION 284,000
CAPITAL (POPULATION) Bandar Seri Begawan (55,000)
GOVERNMENT Constitutional monarchy with an advisory council
ETHNIC GROUPS Malay 69%, Chinese 18%, Indian
LANGUAGES Malay (official), English, Chinese
RELIGIONS Muslim 63%, Buddhist 14%, Christian 10%
CURRENCY Brunei dollar = 100 cents

BULGARIA

The Slav colours of white, green and red were used in the Bulgarian flag from 1878. The national emblem, incorporating a lion (a symbol of Bulgaria since the 14th century), was first added to the flag in 1947, but the crest is now only added for official government occasions.

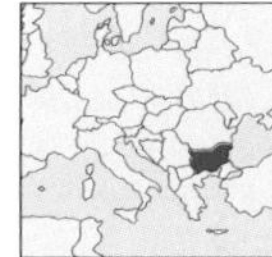

GEOGRAPHY Bulgaria lies in south-eastern Europe, with a coastline on the Black Sea. The Balkan Mountains (Stara Planina), in central Bulgaria, rise to heights of over 2,000 m [6,500 ft]. These are separated from the Rhodopi Mountains in the south by the central valley of the River Maritsa, which is the main farming region. The climate is varied, with the south generally warmer and drier than the north.

HISTORY AND POLITICS From 1396 Bulgaria was ruled by Islamic Turks as part of the Ottoman Empire; in 1878 Russian forces helped liberate the country and it became an independent country. After World War II, Bulgaria was heavily dependent on the USSR and was one of the last Communist governments to fall in the early 1990s. The first free elections in 44 years were held in 1991 and free-market reforms have since been initiated.

ECONOMY Fertile soils means that agriculture is important, with the most productive land found on the lowland plains. Crops include maize, wheat and fruits. Attar of roses is exported worldwide to the cosmetics industry. However, Bulgaria's economy suffers many problems such as inflation, rising unemployment, strikes and a large foreign debt.

AREA 110,910 sq km [42,822 sq mls]
POPULATION 8,771,000
CAPITAL (POPULATION) Sofia (1,114,000)
GOVERNMENT Multiparty republic
ETHNIC GROUPS Bulgarian 85%, Turkish 9%, Gypsy 3%, Macedonian 3%, Armenian, Romanian, Greek
LANGUAGES Bulgarian (official), Turkish, Romany
RELIGIONS Eastern Orthodox 80%, Sunni Muslim
CURRENCY Lev = 100 stotinki
MAIN EXPORTS Machinery and equipment 57%, foodstuffs, wine and tobacco 14%
MAIN IMPORTS Machinery and equipment 43%, fuels, mineral raw materials

BURKINA FASO

Formerly Upper Volta, this country adopted a new name and flag in 1984, replacing those used since independence from France in 1960. The colours are the Pan-African shades of Burkina Faso's neighbours, representing the desire for unity.

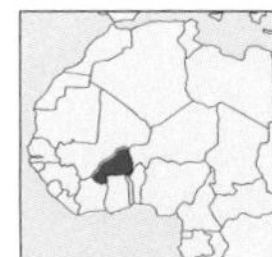

GEOGRAPHY Landlocked Burkina Faso ('land of upright people') is a West African country made up mostly of low plateaux. The valleys, drained by the Black, Red and White Volta rivers, have the most fertile and best watered lands. Among these is the 'W' national park, shared with Niger and Benin.

HISTORY AND POLITICS Burkina Faso is the successor to Mossi, an early West African state dating from 1100. In 1919 Upper Volta was created as a French colony; it became independent in 1960 before changing its name to Burkina Faso in 1984. Since then there has been a long period of military rule, broken in 1991, when the first elections for a decade were held and a new constitution was drawn up.

ECONOMY With low and erratic rainfall, thin, eroded soils and a lack of natural resources, the country remains very poor and heavily reliant on aid. Cotton, millet, guinea corn and groundnuts are grown for food; migrants working in other countries send money back and provide most of the foreign income. Manganese and gold mining could be developed.

AREA 274,200 sq km [105,869 sq mls]
POPULATION 10,326,000
CAPITAL (POPULATION) Ouagadougou (634,000)
GOVERNMENT Multiparty republic
ETHNIC GROUPS Mossi 48%, Mande 8%, Fulani 8%
LANGUAGES French (official)
RELIGIONS Traditional beliefs 45%, Sunni Muslim 43%, Christian 12%
CURRENCY CFA franc = 100 centimes
MAIN EXPORTS Ginned cotton, livestock
MAIN IMPORTS Transport equipment, non-electrical machinery, petroleum products and cereals

BURMA (MYANMAR)

The colours were adopted following independence from Britain in 1948. The Socialist symbol, added in 1974, includes a ring of 14 stars for the country's states. The gearwheel represents industry and the rice plant symbolizes agriculture.

GEOGRAPHY Burma's core area is a great structural depression, largely drained by the Chindwin and Irrawaddy rivers. Within this, the region between Prome and Mandalay is a 'dry zone', sheltered from the monsoon and receiving less than 1,000 mm [40 in] of rain a year. To the west are the fold mountains of the Arakan Yoma, and to the east rises the Shan Plateau. In the south-east, along the isthmus that leads on to the Malay Peninsula, are the Tenasserim uplands, with hundreds of islands along the coast. More than 60% of the country is forested, with teak as the indigenous species.

HISTORY AND POLITICS Burma was annexed by Britain in 1895 and separated from India as a crown colony in 1937. In 1948 it became an independent republic and left the Commonwealth. A military dictatorship was replaced by a one-party state in 1974 and 'The Burmese Way to Socialism' has seen rigid state control, Buddhism and international isolation. Prosperity has turned to poverty. The results of a multiparty election in 1990 were disallowed by the ruling junta and much of the country remains closed to foreigners.

ECONOMY More than 60% of the working population are farmers and the largest crop is rice (until 1964 Burma was the world's leading exporter). There are also reserves of oil and natural gas. However, more than 35% of the budget is spent on the suppression of political opposition and of human rights.

AREA 676,577 sq km [261,228 sq mls]
POPULATION 46,580,000
CAPITAL (POPULATION) Rangoon (2,513,000)
GOVERNMENT Transitional government
ETHNIC GROUPS Burman 69%, Shan 9%, Karen 6%, Rakhine 5%, Mon 2%, Chin 2%, Kachin 1%
LANGUAGES Burmese (official), English
RELIGIONS Buddhist 85%, Christian 5%, Muslim 4%, Hindu, animist
CURRENCY Kyat = 100 pyas
MAIN EXPORTS Rice 41%, teak 24%, metals and ores 9%
MAIN IMPORTS Machinery 18%, base metals 10%, transport equipment 8%
POPULATION DENSITY 69 per sq km [178 per sq ml]
URBAN POPULATION 25% of population

BURUNDI

Burundi adopted this unusual design when it became a republic in 1966. The three stars symbolize the nation's motto 'Unity, Work, Progress'. Green represents hope for the future, red the struggle for independence, and white the desire for peace.

GEOGRAPHY From the captial of Bujumbura on Lake Tanganyika a great escarpment rises in the west to the rift highlands (reaching 2,670 m [8,769 ft]) and makes up most of Burundi. In the east there are plateaux with steep slopes and swamps. The climate is cool, with two wet seasons. This small country must support a dense population and employment is often sought in neighbouring countries.

HISTORY AND POLITICS In 1897 the region became part of the German East African colony and from 1919 it formed part of Ruanda-Urundi, a Belgian trust territory. After independence in 1962 a monarchy existed until 1966 when a republic was established. Ancient rivalries exist between the Hutu and Tutsi tribes and have led to periodic outbreaks of fighting. An estimated 150,000 people have been killed in ethnic violence since 1993. A military coup in July 1996 installed Major Buyoya as President.

ECONOMY Coffee is widely grown for export throughout the highlands (80% of total earnings). Cotton and tea are also exported, and goats make up the largest numbers of livestock.

AREA 27,830 sq km [10,745 sq mls]
POPULATION 6,412,000
CAPITAL (POPULATION) Bujumbura (235,000)
GOVERNMENT Transitional government
ETHNIC GROUPS Hutu 85%, Tutsi 14%, Twa 1%
LANGUAGES French and Kirundi (both official)
RELIGIONS Roman Catholic 62%, traditional beliefs 30%, Protestant 5%
CURRENCY Burundi franc = 100 centimes
MAIN EXPORTS Coffee, tea, cotton
POPULATION DENSITY 230 per sq km [597 per sq ml]
URBAN POPULATION 7% of population

CAMBODIA

As well as being associated with Communism and revolution, red is the traditional colour of Cambodia. The silhouette is the historic temple of Angkor Wat. The blue symbolizes the water resources which are so vital to the people of Cambodia.

GEOGRAPHY At the heart of Cambodia is a wide basin drained by the Mekong River, at the centre of which lies the Tonlé Sap ('Great Lake'), a former arm of the sea surrounded by a broad plain. During the rainy season and period of high river water between June and October the lake more than doubles its size to become the largest freshwater lake in Asia. Up to 90% of the population live on these fertile plains, while in the north the Phanom Dangrek uplands bound the country with a prominent sandstone escarpment. Three-quarters of Cambodia is forested and there is a tropical monsoon climate.

HISTORY AND POLITICS The Tonlé Sap lowlands were the cradle of the Khmer Empire, which lasted from 802 to 1432, during which time the great temple of Angkor Wat was built (together with Angkor Thom, these 600 Hindu temples form the world's largest group of religious buildings). Cambodia was under French rule from 1863 to 1954, when it became independent. The ruthless dictatorship of the Khmer Rouge and several civil wars in the 1970s and 1980s left Cambodia devastated and up to 2.5 million people dead. Following UN-supervised elections in 1993 a government of national unity was formed with Prince Sihanouk becoming monarch.

ECONOMY The economy is based largely on agriculture (rice and maize) and rubber plantations, but these have been widely destroyed in the civil wars. There are few mineral resources.

AREA 181,040 sq km [69,900 sq mls]
POPULATION 10,452,000
CAPITAL (POPULATION) Phnom Penh (920,000)
GOVERNMENT Constitutional monarchy with a unicameral legislature
ETHNIC GROUPS Khmer 93%, Vietnamese, Chinese, Cham, Thai, Lao, Kola
LANGUAGES Khmer (official), French
RELIGIONS Buddhist 88%, Muslim 2%
CURRENCY Riel = 100 sen
MAIN EXPORTS Iron and steel, rubber manufactures
MAIN IMPORTS Machinery and transport equipment
POPULATION DENSITY 58 per sq km [150 per sq ml]
URBAN POPULATION 12% of population

CAMEROON

Cameroon's flag employs the Pan-African colours, as used by many former African colonies. The design, with the yellow liberty star, dates from 1975 and is based on the tricolour adopted in 1957 before independence from France in 1960.

GEOGRAPHY Located in west-central Africa on the Gulf of Guinea, Cameroon has a mixture of vegetation, with desert to the north, dense tropical rainforest in the south and dry savanna in the middle. The mountains on the border with Nigeria are mostly volcanic in origin, including Mt Cameroon (4,070 m [13,353 ft]), which is sometimes active.

HISTORY AND POLITICS The word Cameroon comes from the Portuguese *camarões* – prawns fished by Portuguese explorers in the coastal estuaries in the 1400s. It was ruled as a German protectorate from 1884, but divided between France (mainly) and Britain. French Cameroon became independent in 1960 and southern British Cameroon in 1961; a republic was created in 1984. Since 1987 President Paul Biya has led a repressive regime, but elections were held in 1992. Cameroon joined the Commonwealth in November 1995.

ECONOMY Cameroon is one of tropical Africa's richer nations, with self-sufficiency in food. There is diverse agriculture; coffee, cocoa and aluminium products are the chief exports.

AREA 475,440 sq km [183,567 sq mls]
POPULATION 13,232,000
CAPITAL (POPULATION) Yaoundé (750,000)
GOVERNMENT Multiparty republic with a unicameral legislature
ETHNIC GROUPS Fang 20%, Bamileke and Mamum 19%, Duala, Luanda and Basa 15%, Fulani 10%
LANGUAGES French and English (both official), Sudanic, Bantu
RELIGIONS Animist 25%, Sunni Muslim 22%, Roman Catholic 21%, Protestant 18%
CURRENCY CFA franc = 100 centimes
URBAN POPULATION 42% of population

CANADA

The British Red Ensign was used from 1892 but became unpopular with Canada's French community. After many attempts to find a more acceptable design, the present flag – featuring the simple maple leaf emblem – was finally adopted in 1965.

GEOGRAPHY Canada is the world's second largest country (after Russia) and has an even longer coastline (250,00 km [155,000 mls]). Some 80% of the land is uninhabited and there are huge areas of virtually unoccupied mountains, forests, tundra and polar desert in the north and west. To the east lie the Maritime provinces of Newfoundland, Nova Scotia, New Brunswick, Prince Edward Islands and Québec; they are clustered about the Gulf of St Lawrence and based on ancient worn-down mountains – the northern extension of the Appalachians – and the eastern uptilted edge of the even older Canadian Shield. The central province of Ontario borders the Great Lakes and further to the west are the prairie provinces of Manitoba, Saskatchewan and Alberta. Most of the population is to be found on the fertile farmland in the south of these provinces and in Québec and Ontario. A large part of the Rocky Mountains are found in south-west Alberta, with peaks rising to over 4,000 m [13,120 ft]. In the huge northern area tundra replaces boreal forest; here, glaciation has scoured the rocks and although the surface of the soil thaws in summer, the subsoil remains frozen.

HISTORY AND POLITICS John Cabot's discovery of North America in 1497 began the annex of lands and wealth, with France and Britain the main contenders. The French established themselves first by discovering the St Lawrence River in 1534 and then the Great Lakes. British settlers based themselves on the Atlantic coast and in the 1780s moved north from the USA into Nova Scotia, New Brunswick and Lower Canada.

Eventually, the bulk of Canada east and west became predominantly British, while the fertile lowlands of the St Lawrence Basin and on the Shield remained French. The union of British Upper Canada and French Lower Canada was sealed by the Confederation of 1867 and Canada became largely self-governing, although it remained technically subject to the British Imperial parliament until 1931. The creation of the British Commonwealth made the country a sovereign nation under the crown. The proximity of the USA and its economic dominance has caused problems, as has the persistence of French culture in Québec province. In 1995, Québeckers voted against a move to make Québec a sovereign state, but the majority was less than 1% and this issue seems unlikely to disappear.

ECONOMY Agriculture plays an important role with 50% of produce being exported. Industry has transformed some of the more remote areas: cheap hydroelectric power in Québec and Ontario, coupled with improved transmission technology, has encouraged the further development of wood pulp and paper industries, even in distant parts of the northern forests, and stimulated industry and commerce in the south. Over 90% of the country's oil output comes from Alberta. Trade with the USA represents the world's largest single bilateral trade route. There is still potential for development in the north, with abundant mineral resources under the frozen subsoil, and although the cost of their extraction and transportation is very high construction began in late 1996 on the country's first diamond mine.

AREA 9,976,140 sq km [3,851,788 sq mls]
POPULATION 29,972,000
CAPITAL (POPULATION) Ottawa (921,000)
GOVERNMENT Federal multiparty republic with a bicameral legislature
ETHNIC GROUPS British 40%, French 27%, other European 20%, Asiatic 2%, Amerindian/Inuit (Eskimo) 2%
LANGUAGES English 63% and French 25% (both official)
RELIGIONS Roman Catholic 47%, Protestant 41%, Eastern Orthodox, Jewish, Muslim, Hindu
CURRENCY Canadian dollar = 100 cents
MAIN EXPORTS Passenger vehicles, trucks and parts 26%, food, feed, beverages and tobaco 6%, timber 5%, newspaper print 5%, wood pulp 4%, petroleum 4%, natural gas 3%, industrial machinery 3%

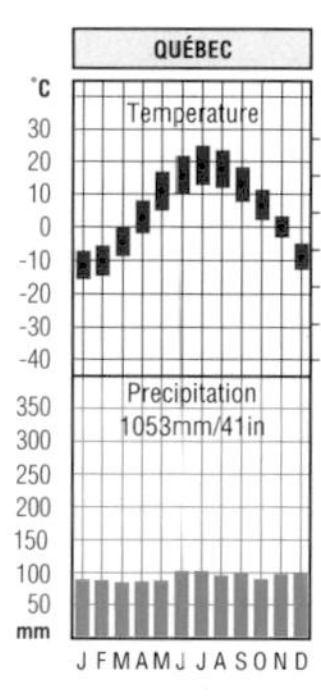

The effect of the Great Lakes is felt in the Ontario Peninsula with slightly warmer winters than in Québec. The temperatures in northern Canada are violent; along the Arctic Circle the mean monthly temperatures for over seven months are below freezing. In Québec rainfall is moderate throughout the year, with some snow.

CANARY ISLANDS

As a Spanish Autonomous Region, the Canary Islands have their own arms and flag. This flag was adopted in 1982 on the basis of colours used by the dominant political movement. The arms can be added in the centre.

Ceded to Spain from Portugal in 1479, the Canary Islands comprise seven large islands and numerous small volcanic islands situated off southern Morocco, the nearest within 100 km [60 mls] of the mainland. The islands have a subtropical climate, dry at sea level but damp on higher ground. Soils are fertile and there is large-scale irrigation. Industries include food and fish processing, boat-building and crafts; the islands are also a year-round major tourist destination.

AREA 7,273 sq km [2,807 sq mls]
POPULATION 1,700,000
CAPITAL (POPULATION) Las Palmas (342,000)/Santa Cruz (223,000)
GOVERNMENT Spanish Autonomous Region
LANGUAGES Spanish
RELIGIONS Roman Catholic
POPULATION DENSITY 234 per sq km [606 per sq ml]

CAPE VERDE

This new flag was adopted in September 1992 to replace the red-yellow-green one adopted in 1975. The flag was adopted to symbolize the end of the rule of the 'Partido Africano da Independencia de Cabo Verde' and the election of the Movement for Democracy.

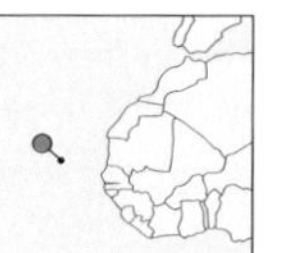

GEOGRAPHY Cape Verde is an archipelago of ten large and five small islands off the coast of Senegal. They are volcanic and mainly mountainous, with steep cliffs and rocky headlands; the highest, Fogo, rises to 2,829 m [9,281 ft] and is active. The islands are tropical, hot for most of the year and mainly dry at sea level. Endemic droughts have killed 75,000 since 1900.

HISTORY, POLITICS AND ECONOMY Portuguese since the 15th century, the colony became an overseas territory in 1951 and independent in 1975. In the first multiparty elections in 1991, the ruling socialist PAICV was beaten by a newly legalized opposition. Poor soils and the lack of surface water have hindered development and much food is imported. Exports comprise mainly bananas (36%) and tuna (30%); there is a dependency on foreign aid and much emigration.

AREA 4,030 sq km [1,556 sq mls]
POPULATION 386,000
CAPITAL (POPULATION) Praia (69,000)
GOVERNMENT Multiparty republic
ETHNIC GROUPS Mixed 71%, Black 28%, White 1%
LANGUAGES Portuguese (official), Crioulo
RELIGIONS Roman Catholic 97%, Protestant 2%
CURRENCY Cape Verde escudo = 100 centavos
POPULATION DENSITY 96 per sq km [248 per sq ml]

CAYMAN ISLANDS

As a British Dependency, the Cayman Islands fly the Blue Ensign with a white roundel, depicting the islands' coat of arms in the fly. The coat of arms shows an English heraldic lion, with the blue and white wavy lines representing the sea.

The Cayman Islands comprise three low-lying islands south of Cuba, with the capital George Town on the biggest, Grand Cayman. A dependent territory of Britain (Crown Colony since 1959), they were occupied mainly with farming and fishing until the 1960s, when an economic revolution turned them into the world's biggest offshore financial centre, offering a tax haven to 18,000 companies and 450 banks. The luxury tourist industry accounts for more than 70% of the official GDP and foreign earnings. An immigrant labour force, chiefly Jamaican, makes up about a fifth of the population.

AREA 259 sq km [100 sq mls]
POPULATION 31,000
CAPITAL (POPULATION) George Town (14,000)
ETHNIC GROUPS Mixed 40%, White 20%, Black 20%
LANGUAGES English (official)
RELIGIONS Christian
CURRENCY Caymanian dollar = 100 cents
POPULATION DENSITY 120 per sq km [310 per sq ml]

CENTRAL AFRICAN REPUBLIC

The national flag of the Central African Republic, adopted in 1958, combines the green, yellow and red of Pan-African unity with the blue, white and red of the flag of the country's former colonial ruler, France.

GEOGRAPHY Central African Republic is landlocked, lying on an undulating plateau between the Chad and Zaïre (Congo) basins. The vegetation is mostly savanna and the climate is tropical, with day temperatures rarely falling below 30°C [86°F].

HISTORY AND POLITICS The country became an independent republic in 1960, having been part of the colony of French Equatorial Africa since 1910. The repressive regime of Jean-Bedel Bokassa lasted from 1976 to 1979, when the army took over. Multiparty elections took place in 1993.

ECONOMY Only 5% of the land is cultivated, yet 90% of the population are involved in agriculture, mainly for subsistence. Coffee, cotton, groundnuts and diamonds are exported.

AREA 622,980 sq km [240,533 sq mls]
POPULATION 3,294,000
CAPITAL (POPULATION) Bangui (706,000)
GOVERNMENT Multiparty republic
ETHNIC GROUPS Banda 29%, Baya 25%, Ngbandi 11%, Azande 10%, Sara, Mbaka
LANGUAGES French (official), Sango (linguafranca)
RELIGIONS Traditional beliefs 57%, Christian 35%, Sunni Muslim 8%
CURRENCY CFA franc = 100 centimes
URBAN POPULATION 38% of population

CHAD

Adopted in 1959, Chad's colours are a compromise between the French and Pan-African flags. Blue represents the sky, the streams of the south and hope, yellow represents the sun and the Sahara Desert in the north, and red represents national sacrifice.

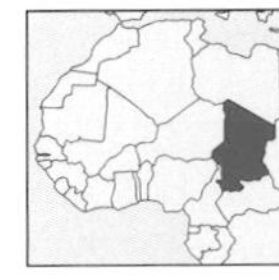

GEOGRAPHY Chad is Africa's largest landlocked country, with part of the Sahara Desert in the north (containing the volcanic Tibesti Mountains). In the south there is wooded savanna, while Lake Chad, in the west, is the focal point of much of Chad's drainage, affecting two-thirds of the country.

HISTORY AND POLITICS After independence from France in 1960 Chad has been plagued by almost continuous civil wars, primarily between the Muslim Arab north and the Christian and animist black south. In 1973 Libya, supporters of the Arabs, occupied the mineral-rich Aozou Strip in the north and tried further incursions in 1983 and 1987. In 1994 the International Court of Justice ruled in favour of Chad, but Libyan troops remained within the strip.

ECONOMY Over 90% of the population work in crop cultivation or herding and there is little industry. A large foreign debt and frequent droughts have caused much poverty.

AREA 1,284,000 sq km [495,752 sq mls]
POPULATION 6,314,000
CAPITAL (POPULATION) Ndjaména (530,000)
GOVERNMENT Transitional government
ETHNIC GROUPS Bagirmi, Sara and Kreish 31%, Sudanic Arab 26%, Teda, Mbum
LANGUAGES French and Arabic (official), but more than 100 languages and dialects are spoken
RELIGIONS Sunni Muslim 44%, animist 38%, various Christian 17%
CURRENCY CFA franc = 100 centimes
MAIN EXPORTS Cotton, live cattle, animal products

CHILE

Inspired by the US Stars and Stripes, the flag was designed by an American serving with the Chilean Army in 1817 and adopted that year. White represents the snow-capped Andes, blue the sky and red the blood of the nation's patriots.

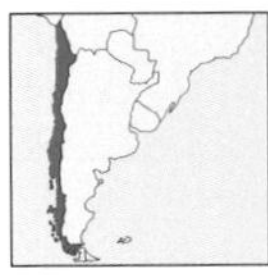

GEOGRAPHY Chile runs down the west coast of South America, extending from latitude 17°30'S (inside the Tropics) to 55°50'S at Cape Horn, and is the world's thinnest country. There are three parallel zones: from the Bolivian border runs an extension of the high plateau of Bolivia, with several volcanic peaks of more than 6,000 m [19,680 ft]; there is then a sheltered and fertile central valley, with 60% of the population living in an 800 km [500 ml] stretch of land south of Santiago. Finally, the parallel coastal ranges create a rolling, hilly belt, rising no more than 3,000 m [10,000 ft].

HISTORY AND POLITICS A Spanish colony from the 16th century, Chile developed as a mining enterprise in the north and a series of vast ranches, or haciendas, in the fertile central region. Chile became independent in 1818. In 1970 Chile had the world's first democratically elected Marxist government under President Allende; this was overthrown in a CIA-backed military coup in 1973 and General Pinochet took control, establishing a repressive regime. Free elections finally took place in 1989 and there has been a gradual return to democracy.

ECONOMY Chile's economy continues to depend on agriculture (crops include wheat, barley and rice), fishing (anchovetas, mackerel and sardines) and, particularly, mining: the country is the world's leading producer of copper ore (22% of the world total) and it accounts for nearly half of all export earnings.

AREA 756,950 sq km [292,258 sq mls]
POPULATION 14,271,000
CAPITAL (POPULATION) Santiago (4,628,000)
GOVERNMENT Multiparty republic with a bicameral legislature
ETHNIC GROUPS Mestizo 92%, Amerindian 7%
LANGUAGES Spanish (official)
RELIGIONS Roman Catholic 80%, Protestant 6%
CURRENCY Peso = 100 centavos
MAIN EXPORTS Copper, iron, molybdenum, nitrate, pulp and paper, fishmeal, fruit
POPULATION DENSITY 19 per sq km [49 per sq ml]
URBAN POPULATION 86% of population
ADULT LITERACY 93%

CHINA

Red, the traditional colour of both China and Communism, was chosen for the People's Republic flag in 1949. The large star represents the Communist Party programme; the small stars represent the four principal social classes.

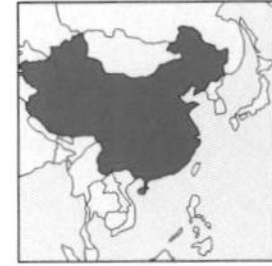

GEOGRAPHY China is the world's most populous country, with its population making up 20% of the world's total, and its land area is the world's third largest. It also has the greatest number of international frontiers in the world (15), but its huge size and complex landscape have meant that one of the main determining influences on the evolution of Chinese civilization has been its geographical isolation from the rest of the world. Landscapes include two intersecting mountain chains, one stretching from the north-east to the south-west, the other from east to west; in the south the Yangtze delta is made up of large lakes; and in the south-west, the Red Basin of Sichuan (Szechwan) is protected by high mountains and, with its mild climate and fertile soils, is one of the most densely populated and productive regions of China.

HISTORY AND POLITICS The earliest Chinese civilization began on the North China Plain over 4,000 years ago, but it was not until the 3rd century BC that China was unified into a centrally administered empire. The Great Wall of China, the world's longest fortification at 6,400 km [4,000 mls] long, was completed under the Ch'in dynasty (221–206 BC). Over the centuries the population has gradually moved from the north to the warmer and more productive south, often accelerated by northern invasions. China became a republic in 1912, from when followed a long period of anarchy until the Communists declared a People's Republic of China in October 1949. Under the centrally planned economy and despite many problems, order was brought to China and living standards raised.

ECONOMY Although only 10% of the land is suitable for agriculture, farmers and their families make up 73% of the population and China is the world's leading producer of rice. Since 1976 industrialization has become important, with sufficient resources in oil, coal and iron ore to support an independent economy.

AREA 9,596,960 sq km [3,705,386 sq mls]
POPULATION 1,226,944,000
CAPITAL (POPULATION) Beijing (12,362,000)
GOVERNMENT Single-party Communist State
ETHNIC GROUPS Han (Chinese) 93%, 55 others
LANGUAGES Mandarin Chinese; local dialects spoken in the south and west

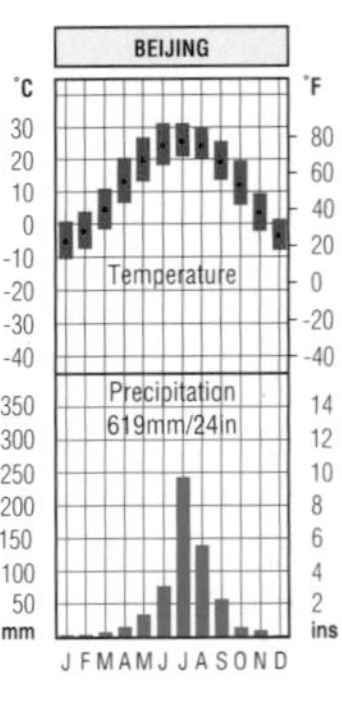

China's climate is controlled by the air masses of Asia and the Pacific, and the mountains in the west. In winter the cold, dry Siberian air blows southwards. In summer the tropical Pacific air dominates, bringing rain and high temperatures. Annual rain decreases from over 2,000 mm [80 in] in the south to the desert conditions of the north-west.

COLOMBIA

Colombia's colours – showing the (yellow) land of the nation separated by the (blue) sea from the tyranny of Spain, whose rule the people fought with their (red) blood – are shared by Ecuador and Venezuela. It was first used in 1806.

GEOGRAPHY The Andes cross Colombia from south to north, fanning out into three ranges with two intervening fertile valleys, in which some three-quarters of the population live. North-west of the mountains lies the broad Atlantic plain crossed by many rivers. The Andean foothills to the east, falling away into the Orinoco and Amazon basins and densely covered with rainforest, occupy about two-thirds of the total land area. The tropical climate is affected by the altitude of the Andes, causing lower temperatures and increased rainfall.

HISTORY AND POLITICS Christopher Columbus sighted what was to become Colombia in 1499, and the Spanish conquest of the territory began ten years later. Independence was gained in 1819, and since the 19th century the two political parties (Conservatives and Liberals) have alternated in power. There have been two civil wars (1899–1902 and 1949–57), in which some 400,000 people have been killed. A coalition in 1957 was unsuccessful and led to the election of a Liberal president in 1986, but there is still political instability.

ECONOMY The variety of climates and conditions result in many crops, including coffee, bananas and cotton. There are huge coal reserves, as well as gold, silver and emeralds. Drugs, however, may be the country's biggest industry.

AREA 1,138,910 sq km [439,733 sq mls]
POPULATION 34,948,000
CAPITAL (POPULATION) Bogotá (5,026,000)
GOVERNMENT Multiparty republic
ETHNIC GROUPS Mestizo 68%, White 20%, Amerindian 7%, Black 5%
LANGUAGES Spanish (official), over 100 Indian languages and dialects
RELIGIONS Roman Catholic 95%
CURRENCY Peso = 100 centavos
MAIN EXPORTS Coffee 43%, crude petroleum 8%, bananas 6%, cotton 3%
MAIN IMPORTS Machinery 28%, chemicals 18%, vehicles 13%
POPULATION DENSITY 31 per sq km [79 per sq ml]
URBAN POPULATION 71% of population

COMOROS

Since independence in 1975 a flag depicting a crescent and four stars has been flown. This design, first adopted in 1978 and slighty altered in 1996, shows the crescent representing the Muslim faith, and the stars representing the four islands, on a plain green background representing Islam.

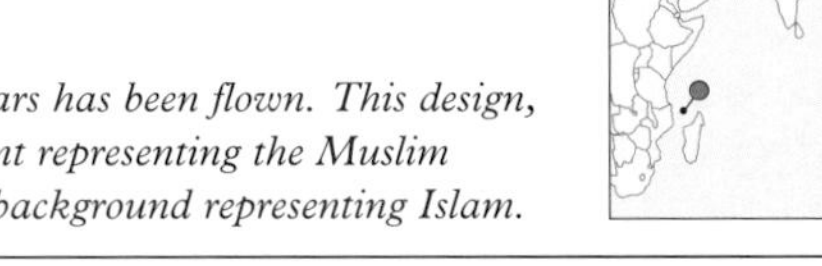

The Comoros are three large mountainous islands and several smaller coral islands lying between Madagascar and the East African coast. Formerly a French overseas territory, the Comoros became independent following a referendum in 1974.

Fertile soils, originally forested, are now mostly under subsistence agriculture and produce coconuts, coffee, cocoa and spices, with vanilla accounting for 78% of exports. The islands remain one of the world's poorest countries.

AREA 2,230 sq km [861 sq mls]
POPULATION 654,000
CAPITAL (POPULATION) Moroni (23,000)
GOVERNMENT Islamic republic
ETHNIC GROUPS Mainly mixture of Arab, Bantu and Malagasy peoples
LANGUAGES Shaafi (Swahili dialect), Malagasy, French
RELIGIONS Sunni Muslim 86%, Roman Catholic 14%

CONGO

The People's Republic of the Congo was created in 1970, ten years after it achieved independence from France, becoming Africa's first Communist state. Marxism was officially abandoned in 1990 and this new flag was adopted.

GEOGRAPHY Congo lies across the Equator, but only the near-coastal Mayombe ridges and the east-central and northern parts of the Congo basin have a truly equatorial climate and vegetation, with swamps and rainforests. The climate is hot all year round and there is heavy rainfall.

HISTORY AND POLITICS Part of French Equatorial Africa until 1960 when it gained independence, Congo became Africa's first declared Communist state in 1970. Marxism was officially abandoned in 1990 and elections were held in 1992 to create a multiparty republic, with further elections in 1993.

ECONOMY The vast deposits of offshore oil have become the main source of revenue; there are also reserves of diamonds, lead and copper. About a third of the workforce work in subsistence agriculture, mainly for cassava, but also bananas and maize. The timber industry is potentially important, but is hampered by a lack of transport.

AREA 342,000 sq km [132,046 sq mls]
POPULATION 2,593,000
CAPITAL (POPULATION) Brazzaville (938,000)
GOVERNMENT Multiparty republic
ETHNIC GROUPS Kongo 52%, Teke 17%, Mboshi 12%, Mbete 5%
LANGUAGES French (official), Kongo, Teke, Ubangi
RELIGIONS Roman Catholic 54%, Protestant 24%
CURRENCY CFA franc = 100 centimes
MAIN EXPORTS Petroleum, timber, diamonds
MAIN IMPORTS Machinery, iron, steel

COSTA RICA

Dating from 1848, Costa Rica's ('rich coast') national flag is based on the blue/white/blue sequence of the flag of the Central American Federation (see Guatemala), which is itself based on the Argentinian flag, but with an additional red stripe in the centre.

GEOGRAPHY Three mountain ranges running the length of the country make up the skeleton landscape and provide fertile uplands for growing crops. There are coastlines with both the Pacific Ocean and Caribbean Sea, where the climate is hot and humid and there are thick forests.

HISTORY, POLITICS AND ECONOMY With the first free elections in Central America in 1890, Costa Rica established a record of democratic and stable government and is exceptional among the other Central American republics. Coffee is the most important crop; together with bananas, they supply about half of the country's overseas earnings. Cattle are raised in the far north-west and there are reserves of gold and silver.

AREA 51,100 sq km [19,730 sq mls]
POPULATION 3,436,000
CAPITAL (POPULATION) San José (1,186,000)
GOVERNMENT Multiparty republic
ETHNIC GROUPS White 87%, Mestizo 7%
LANGUAGES Spanish (official), Creole, Indian
RELIGIONS Roman Catholic 92%
CURRENCY Colón = 100 céntimos
POPULATION DENSITY 67 per sq km [174 per sq ml]
URBAN POPULATION 50% of population

CROATIA

The red, white and blue flag was originally adopted in 1848. During the Communist period a red star appeared in the centre, but this was replaced by the present arms, which symbolize the various parts of the country.

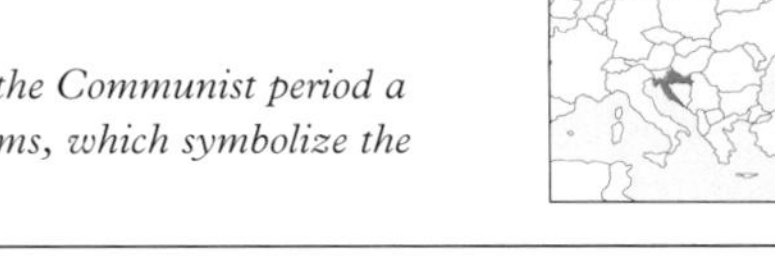

Croatia has a narrow strip of land running along the Adriatic Sea and then curves inland in the north. The coast is fairly mountainous and barren, with a climate of warm winters and hot, dry summers. Formerly Yugoslavia's second largest and second most populous republic, Croatia suffered some of the worst damage in the war following the break-up of Yugoslavia. The tourist industry has been devastated, especially the medieval city of Dubrovnik on the Dalmatian coast and a massive reconstruction programme is needed. In 1995 Croatia helped to draw up the Dayton Peace Accord in Bosnia-Herzegovina.

AREA 56,538 sq km [21,824 sq mls]
POPULATION 4,900,000
CAPITAL (POPULATION) Zagreb (931,000)
GOVERNMENT Multiparty republic
ETHNIC GROUPS Croat 78%, Serb 12%, Muslim 1%
LANGUAGES Serbo-Croat 96%
RELIGIONS Roman Catholic 77%, Orthodox 11%
POPULATION DENSITY 87 per sq km [225 per sq ml]

CUBA

CUBA

First designed in 1849, Cuba's flag, the 'Lone Star' banner, was not officially adopted until the island finally gained its independence from Spain in 1901. The red triangle represents the Cuban people's bloody struggle for independence.

AREA 110,860 sq km [42,803 sq mls]
POPULATION 11,050,000
CAPITAL (POPULATION) Havana (2,143,000)
GOVERNMENT Socialist republic
ETHNIC GROUPS White 66%, Mulatto 22%, Black 12%
LANGUAGES Spanish (official)
RELIGIONS Roman Catholic 40%, Protestant 3%
CURRENCY Cuban peso = 100 centavos
MAIN EXPORTS Sugar, tobacco
POPULATION DENSITY 97 per sq km [258 sq ml]

GEOGRAPHY Cuba is only 193 km [120 mls] across at its widest, but stretches for over 1,200 km [750 mls] from the Gulf of Mexico to the Windward Passage. There is a varied landscape, including mountains and fertile plains. The climate is tropical, with high temperatures and some hurricanes.

HISTORY AND POLITICS A colony until 1898, Cuba took on many Spanish immigrants in the early years of independence.

The revolution in 1959 deposed the right-wing dictator Fulgencio Batista and brought Fidel Castro to power – 600,000 people fled the island. A close ally of the former USSR, the rapid changes in Eastern Europe and the USSR have left Cuba isolated as a hardline Marxist state.

ECONOMY Sugar cane is the most important cash crop, taking up a third of the cultivated land and making up 75% of exports.

CYPRUS

The design, featuring a map of the island with two olive branches, has been the official state flag since independence from Britain in 1960. However, Cyprus is now divided and the separate communities fly the Greek and Turkish flags.

AREA 9,250 sq km [3,571 sq mls]
POPULATION 742,000
CAPITAL (POPULATION) Nicosia (178,000)
GOVERNMENT Multiparty republic
ETHNIC GROUPS Greek Cypriot 81%, Turkish Cypriot 19%
LANGUAGES Greek, Turkish
RELIGIONS Greek Orthodox, Muslim
CURRENCY Cyprus pound = 100 cents
MAIN EXPORTS Wine, vegetables, fruit, clothing, shoes

Cyprus is a small but strategically situated Mediterranean island, comprising a detached fragment of the mainland mountains to the east. The northern coast is backed by the long limestone range of Kyrenia and in the south is the broad massif of Troodos. The fertile central plain grows fruits, flowers and early vegetables. In 1968 the Turkish Cypriots set up an 'autonomous administration' in the north, but in 1974 Turkey invaded the mainland and took control of the northern 40% of the country, displacing 200,000 Greek Cypriots. The UN has since supervised an uneasy partition of the country.

CZECH REPUBLIC

On independence in January 1993, the Czech Republic adopted the flag of the former Czechoslovakia. It features the red and white of Bohemia with the blue of Moravia and Slovakia, the colours of Pan-Slavic liberation.

AREA 78,864 sq km [30,449 sq mls]
POPULATION 10,500,000
CAPITAL (POPULATION) Prague (1,217,000)
GOVERNMENT Multiparty republic with a bicameral legislature
ETHNIC GROUPS Czech 81%, Moravian 13%, Slovak 3%
LANGUAGES Czech
RELIGIONS Roman Catholic, Protestant
CURRENCY Koruna = 100 haler
MAIN EXPORTS Machinery, vehicles
URBAN POPULATION 65% of population

The Czech Republic has 61% of the land area of the former Czechoslovakia; it is split into two units, Bohemia in the west, with Prague at its centre, and Moravia, divided from Bohemia by a plateau known as the Moravian Heights. There are rich mineral resources in the mountains and reserves of hard coal and lignite. Agriculture is also well developed. The 'velvet revolution' of 1989 was one of the easiest transitions in Eastern Europe, replacing Communism with a multiparty system. The move to democracy was not as easy and resurgent Slovak nationalism in 1992 ended the old federation and split the country into two. Czechs and Slovaks have maintained some economic ties and the break-up has been amicable.

DENMARK

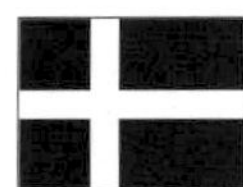

The Dannebrog ('the spirit of Denmark') flag is said to represent King Waldemar II's vision of a white cross against a red sky before the Battle of Lyndanisse in 1219, and is possibly the oldest national flag in continuous use.

AREA 43,070 sq km [16,629 sq mls]
POPULATION 5,229,000
CAPITAL (POPULATION) Copenhagen (1,353,000)
GOVERNMENT Constitutional monarchy with a unicameral legislature
ETHNIC GROUPS Danish 97%
LANGUAGES Danish (official)
RELIGIONS Lutheran 91%, Roman Catholic 1%
CURRENCY Krone = 100 øre
MAIN EXPORTS Meat, dairy produce, fish 27%, machinery and electronic equipment 24%, chemicals
MAIN IMPORTS Machinery and transport equipment 31%, chemicals 10%
URBAN POPULATION 86% of population

GEOGRAPHY Denmark consists of the Jutland (Jylland) peninsula, which is an extension of the North German Plain, and an archipelago of 406 islands, of which 89 are inhabited. The largest and most densely populated of the islands is Zealand (Sjaelland), which lies close to the coast of Sweden. The climate reflects Denmark's position at the meeting of the Arctic, continental and maritime influences, giving it warm summers and average rainfall. Structurally the land is made up of low-lying sedimentary rocks, nowhere higher than 171 m [561 ft].

HISTORY AND POLITICS Control of the entrances to the Baltic Sea contributed to the power of Denmark in the Middle Ages, when the kingdom dominated its neighbours and expanded its territories to include Norway, Iceland, Greenland and the Faroe Islands. Greenland and the Faroes still retain connections. Denmark has good relations with its neighbours and partners, as a member of the EU and as part of the Nordic Council (with the other Scandinavian countries).

ECONOMY There are few mineral resources and no coal, but there is some oil and natural gas from the North Sea. Denmark is, however, one of Europe's wealthiest industrial nations, with a strong agricultural base and advanced methods of processing and distributing farm produce.

DJIBOUTI

Djibouti's flag was adopted on independence from France in 1977, though its use by the independence movement had begun five years earlier. The colours represent the two principal peoples in the country: the Issas (blue) and the Afars (green).

AREA 23,200 sq km [8,958 sq mls]
POPULATION 603,000
CAPITAL (POPULATION) Djibouti (383,000)
GOVERNMENT Multiparty republic
ETHNIC GROUPS Issa 47%, Afar 38%, Arab 6%
LANGUAGES Arabic and French (official), Cushitic
RELIGIONS Sunni Muslim 94%, Roman Catholic 4%
CURRENCY Djibouti franc = 100 centimes

Djibouti was previously the French territory of the Afars and the Issas and lies in the Afro-Asian rift valley system at the mouth of the Red Sea. Part of the country lies below sea level; much of this is hot, arid and unproductive basalt plain. Mt Goudah, the principal mountain, rises to 1,783 m [5,850 ft], and is covered with juniper and box forest. Djibouti is important because of the railway link with Addis Ababa and is Ethiopia's main artery for overseas trade. The capital city grew from 1862 around a French naval base and the French still maintain a garrison there and offer support to the government.

DOMINICA

The Caribbean island of Dominica adopted its flag on independence from Britain in 1978 and slightly amended it in 1981. The parrot, from the coat of arms, is the national bird, the sisserou, and the stars represent the ten island parishes.

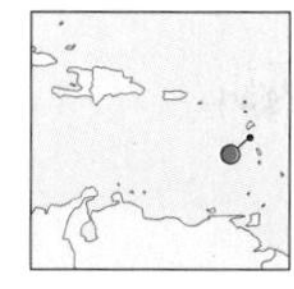

AREA 751 sq km [290 sq mls]
POPULATION 89,000
CAPITAL (POPULATION) Roseau (21,000)
GOVERNMENT Multiparty republic with a unicameral legislature
ETHNIC GROUPS Of African descent
LANGUAGES English (official), French patois
RELIGIONS Roman Catholic 75%, Protestant 15%

Dominica has been an independent republic since 1978, after 11 years as a self-governing UK colony. A mountainous ridge forms the island's spine, and it is from this central region that the main rivers flow to the indented coast. Rich soils support dense vegetation, but less than 10% is cultivated. Bananas account for 48% of exports, coconut-based soaps for 25%. Much food is imported and future prospects depend greatly on the development of luxury tourism.

DOMINICAN REPUBLIC

The Dominican Republic's flag dates from 1844, when the country finally gained its independence from both Spain and Haiti. The design developed from Haiti's flag, adding a white cross and rearranging the position of the colours.

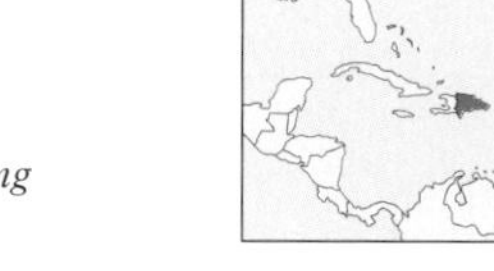

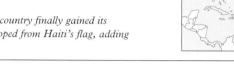

AREA 48,730 sq km [18,815 sq mls]
POPULATION 7,818,000
CAPITAL (POPULATION) Santo Domingo (2,100,000)
GOVERNMENT Multiparty republic
ETHNIC GROUPS Mulatto 73%, White 16%, Black 11%
LANGUAGES Spanish (official)
RELIGIONS Roman Catholic 93%
CURRENCY Peso = 100 centavos
URBAN POPULATION 62% of population

Second largest of the Caribbean nations in both area and population, the Dominican Republic shares the island of Hispaniola with Haiti, occupying the eastern two-thirds. Steep-sided mountains are dominant, although to the east lie fertile valleys and lowlands, including the coastal plains where most of the sugar plantations are found. Hispaniola was a Spanish colony before it won independence in 1821. Haiti then held the territory until 1844, when sovereignty was restored. Recently a fragile democracy has been established. Industry, mining and tourism help the traditional agricultural economy.

ECUADOR

Shared in different proportions by Colombia and Venezuela, Ecuador's colours were used in the flag created by the patriot Francisco de Miranda in 1806 and flown by Simón Bolívar, whose armies also liberated Peru and Bolivia.

AREA 283,560 sq km [109,483 sq mls]
POPULATION 11,384,000
CAPITAL (POPULATION) Quito (1,101,000)
GOVERNMENT Unitary multiparty republic with a unicameral legislature
ETHNIC GROUPS Mestizo 40%, Amerindian 40%, White 5%, Black 5%
LANGUAGES Spanish 93% (official), Quechua
RELIGIONS Roman Catholic 93%, Protestant 6%
CURRENCY Sucre = 100 centavos
MAIN EXPORTS Petroleum and derivatives, seafood, bananas, coffee
POPULATION DENSITY 40 per sq km [104 per sq ml]

GEOGRAPHY Ecuador's name comes from the Equator, which divides the country unequally. There are three distinct regions – the coastal plain (Costa), the Andes, and the eastern alluvial plains of the Oriente. The coastal plain, averaging 100 km [60 mls] wide, is a hot, fertile area of variable rainfall that has now been cleared to create good farmland. The Galápagos Islands lie 970 km [610 mls] west of Ecuador and consist of six main islands and over 50 smaller ones: they contain many unique species of flora and fauna.

HISTORY AND POLITICS The Incas of Peru conquered Ecuador in the 15th century, but in 1532 a colony was founded by the Spaniards in the territory, then called Quito. Independence from Spain was achieved in 1822, when it became part of Gran Colombia, and full independence was gained in 1830. Since then it has remained a democratic republic.

ECONOMY Originally the economy was based on the export of bananas (and they are still the biggest export), but in 1972 oil was first exploited and petroleum and derivatives now account for about 40% of export earnings. There have been recent problems with foreign debt repayment.

EGYPT

Egypt has flown a flag of red, white and black (the Pan-Arab colours) since 1958 but with various emblems in the centre. The present design, with the gold eagle emblem symbolizing the Arab hero Saladin, was introduced in 1984.

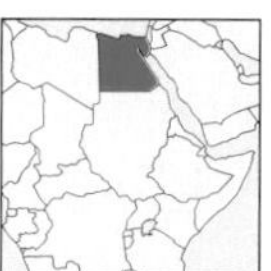

AREA 1,001,450 sq km [386,660 sq mls]
POPULATION 64,100,000
CAPITAL (POPULATION) Cairo (9,656,000)
GOVERNMENT Multiparty republic with a bicameral legislature
ETHNIC GROUPS Egyptian 99%
LANGUAGES Arabic (official), French, English
RELIGIONS Sunni Muslim 90%
CURRENCY Egyptian pound = 100 piastres or 1,000 millièmes
MAIN EXPORTS Mineral products including crude petroleum 65%, textiles
POPULATION DENSITY 64 per sq km [166 per sq ml]

GEOGRAPHY The vast majority of Egypt is made up of desert and semi-desert, both with varied landscapes. For example, the Western Desert includes almost three-quarters of Egypt and consists of low vales and scarps, while the Sinai peninsula in the south is mountainous and rugged. The Nile Valley and its delta supports 96% of the population and was one of the cradles of civilization; now the control and storage of the water is essential.

HISTORY AND POLITICS Egypt was part of the Ottoman Empire from 1517, though British influence was important after 1882 and the country was a British protectorate from 1914 to 1922, when it acquired limited independence. In 1952 the corrupt regime of King Farouk, the last ruler of a dynasty dating back to 1841, was toppled by the army. Arab nationalism was then prominent until 1970.

ECONOMY Industrial development has become important since World War II, with textiles forming the largest industry. Other manufactures derive from local agricultural and mineral raw materials (for example, sugar refining and milling).

EL SALVADOR

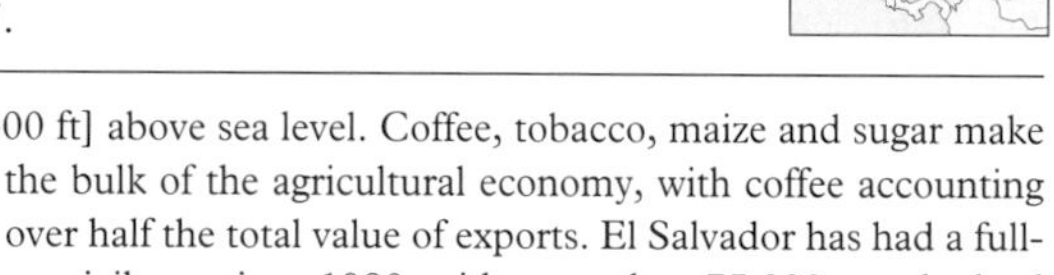

The original flag, the 'Stars and Stripes', was replaced in 1912 by the current one. The blue and white stripes are a common feature of the flags of Central American countries that gained their independence from Spain at the same time in 1821.

AREA 21,040 sq km [8,124 sq mls]
POPULATION 5,743,000
CAPITAL (POPULATION) San Salvador (1,522,000)
GOVERNMENT Republic with a unicameral legislature
ETHNIC GROUPS Mestizo 90%, Indian 5%, White 5%
LANGUAGES Spanish (official)
RELIGIONS Roman Catholic 75%
CURRENCY Colón = 100 céntavos
URBAN POPULATION 44% of population

El Salvador is the only Central American country without a Caribbean coastline, and is also the smallest and most densely populated. The Pacific coastal plain is narrow and backed by a volcanic range averaging about 1,200 m [4,000 ft] in altitude. The country has over 20 volcanoes, some still active, and crater lakes occupying a central fertile plain 400 to 800 m [1,300 to 2,600 ft] above sea level. Coffee, tobacco, maize and sugar make up the bulk of the agricultural economy, with coffee accounting for over half the total value of exports. El Salvador has had a full-blown civil war since 1980, with more than 75,000 people dead and many homeless. A cease-fire took effect in February 1992 but the country remains in chaos.

EQUATORIAL GUINEA

Equatorial Guinea's flag dates from independence from Spain in 1968. Green represents the country's natural resources, blue the sea, red the nation's struggle for independence and the white stands for peace.

AREA 28,050 sq km [10,830 sq mls]
POPULATION 400,000
CAPITAL (POPULATION) Malabo (35,000)
GOVERNMENT Multiparty republic (transitional)
ETHNIC GROUPS Fang 83%, Bubi 10%, Ndowe 4%
LANGUAGES Spanish (official), Fang, Bubi
RELIGIONS Christian (mainly Roman Catholic) 89%
CURRENCY CFA franc = 100 centimes
POPULATION DENSITY 14 per sq km [36 per sq ml]

GEOGRAPHY Equatorial Guinea comprises the low-lying mainland area of Mbini in West Africa and five volcanic and mountainous offshore islands, the largest of which is Fernando Poó (now known as Bioko) which lies in the Gulf of Guinea and contains the capital city.
HISTORY AND POLITICS Guinea, a name which derives from an ancient African kingdom, was once used to describe the whole coastal region of West Africa. Equatorial Guinea was granted partial autonomy from Spain in 1963, and gained full independence in 1968. The ensuing 11-year dictatorship of President Macias Nguema left the economy in ruins and some 100,000 Equatorial Guineans now live outside the country.
ECONOMY Cocoa and coffee plantations are found on the islands, with cocoa beans as the chief cash crop. There is also some oil.

ERITREA

The new flag was hoisted on 24 May 1993 to celebrate independence from Ethiopia. It is a variation on the flag of the Eritrean People's Liberation Front, and shows an olive wreath which featured on the flag of the region between 1952 and 1959.

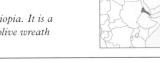

AREA 94,000 sq km [36,293 sq mls]
POPULATION 3,850,000
CAPITAL (POPULATION) Asmara (367,500)
GOVERNMENT Transitional government
ETHNIC GROUPS Tigre, Afar, Beja, Saho, Agau
LANGUAGES Arabic, English, Tigrinya, Tigre, Saho, Agail, Afar
RELIGIONS Coptic Christian 50%, Muslim 50%

Until May 1993 Eritrea was the far northern and third largest province of Ethiopia. It was an Italian colony until 1941, when it passed to British military administration. In 1952 it became an autonomous region within the Federation of Ethiopia and Eritrea; in 1962 the region was annexed by Emperor Haile Selassie. The Eritrean People's Liberation Front (EPLF) then pushed for independence, with a guerilla campaign, until it was granted after the fall of the Mengistu regime in 1991.

ESTONIA

Used for the independent republic of 1918–40, the Estonian flag was readopted in June 1988. The colours are said to symbolize the country's blue skies, its black earth and the snows of its long winter.

AREA 44,700 sq km [17,300 sq mls]
POPULATION 1,531,000
CAPITAL (POPULATION) Tallinn (490,000)
ETHNIC GROUPS Estonian 62%, Russian 30%, Ukrainian 3%, Belarussian 2%
LANGUAGES Estonian 64% (official), Russian 31%
RELIGIONS Christian (Lutheran and Orthodox)
CURRENCY Kroon = 100 sents
POPULATION DENSITY 34 per sq km [88 per sq ml]

GEOGRAPHY Estonia is the smallest of the three Baltic States, bounded on the north by the Gulf of Finland and on the west by the Baltic Sea. The country mainly comprises flat, rock-strewn, glaciated lowlands and has over 1,500 lakes.
HISTORY, POLITICS AND ECONOMY Estonia and the other Baltic States became part of the Russian Empire in the 18th century, and after a period of independence in the early 20th century, became part of the USSR in 1940. All three states became independent in 1990. The timber industry is one of the country's most important industries, together with metal-working, ship-building and food processing. Oats, barley and potatoes are grown and fishing is a major occupation.

ETHIOPIA

Ethiopia's tricolour was first flown as three separate pennants, one above the other. The colours date from the late 19th century but the present sequence was not adopted until 1941. The national emblem, which represents the common will of the 68 ethnic groups, was added in 1996.

AREA 1,128,000 sq km [435,521 sq mls]
POPULATION 51,600,000
CAPITAL (POPULATION) Addis Ababa (2,316,000)
GOVERNMENT Federal republic with a unicameral legislature
ETHNIC GROUPS Amharic 38%, Galla 35%, Tigre 9%, Gurage 3%, Ometo 3%
LANGUAGES Amharic, Galla, Tigre
RELIGIONS Ethiopian Orthodox 53%, Muslim 31%, traditional beliefs 11%
CURRENCY Ethiopian Birr = 100 cents
MAIN EXPORTS Coffee 56%, hides and skins 11%
MAIN IMPORTS Machinery and transport equipment 39%, petroleum 17%
POPULATION DENSITY 46 per sq km [118 per sq ml]

GEOGRAPHY The main geographical feature is a massive block of volcanic mountains, rising to 4,620 m [15,150 ft] and divided into the Western and Eastern Highlands by the Great Rift Valley. The Western Highlands, generally higher and far more extensive and deeply trenched, are the sources of the Blue Nile and its tributaries. Off their north-eastern flank lies the Danakil Depression, an extensive desert that falls to 116 m [380 ft] below sea level. Ethiopia suffers periodically from severe droughts, which cause widespread famine.
HISTORY AND POLITICS Ethiopia (then known as Abyssinia) was a colonial power between 1897 and 1908, taking Somali and other peoples into its feudal empire. Invaded by Italy in 1935, Ethiopia became independent again in 1941 when British troops forced the Italians out. Emperor Haile Selassie ('the lion of Judah') was deposed after his 44-year rule by a revolutionary military government in 1974. Ethiopia became a socialist state and President Mengistu took control in 1977, with his period of 'Red Terror' causing the deaths of many thousands of people. In 1991 the military regime collapsed and in 1995 Ethiopia was divided into nine provinces, each with its own regional assembly.
ECONOMY Most people make a living from agriculture, with such crops as maize, barley, sugar cane and coffee. Coffee is the main cash crop and the main industry is textiles. The droughts and civil wars have caused serious economic problems, however.

FALKLAND ISLANDS

The white roundel in the flag contains the islands' badge which shows the ship Desire, *which discovered the islands in 1592, and a sheep, representing the main farming activity.*

AREA 12,170 sq km [4,699 sq mls]
POPULATION 2,000
CAPITAL (POPULATION) Stanley (2,120)
GOVERNMENT British Dependent Territory
ETHNIC GROUPS British
LANGUAGES English
RELIGIONS Christian
CURRENCY Falkland pound = 100 pence
POPULATION DENSITY 0.2 per sq km [0.5 per sq ml]
LAND USE Grass 98%

Comprising two main islands and over 200 small islands, the Falkland Islands lie 480 km [300 mls] from South America. The landscape is covered with peat moorland and tussock grass. Sheep farming is the main activity. Discovered in 1592, the Falklands were first occupied by the French and the British. Argentina, on independence in 1806, assumed the French interest and the British, who had withdrawn in 1774, returned to dispossess the Argentinians in 1832 and create a Crown Colony. Argentina invaded in 1982 only to be thrown out by the British, who refuse to discuss the issue of sovereignty.

FRANCE

FAROE ISLANDS

In 1948 the Faroe Islands, which are part of Denmark, adopted a flag combining the local arms with the Danish arms. The cross, like that on other Scandinavian flags, is slightly off-centre. Red and blue are ancient Faroese colours and the white represents the foam of the sea.

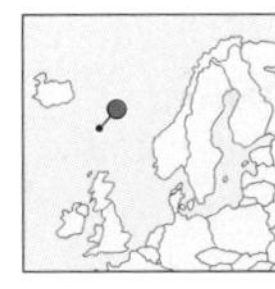

The Faroes are a group of rocky islands situated in the North Atlantic 450 km [280 mls] south-east of Iceland. They are mostly composed of volcanic material, which has been dramatically moulded by glacial action. Sheep farming is the main occupation, but salted, dried, processed and frozen fish, fishmeal and oil comprise the chief exports. The islands have been part of the Danish kingdom since 1386, although they secured a large degree of self-government in 1948.

AREA 1,400 sq km [541 sq mls]
POPULATION 47,000
CAPITAL (POPULATION) Tórshavn (14,601)
GOVERNMENT Danish self-governing region
ETHNIC GROUPS Of Scandinavian descent
LANGUAGES Faroese (official), Danish
CURRENCY Faroese króna
MAIN EXPORTS Fish products
POPULATION DENSITY 34 per sq km [13 per sq ml]

FIJI

The Fijian flag, based on the British Blue Ensign, was adopted in 1970 after independence from Britain. The state coat of arms shows a British lion, sugar cane (the most important crop), a coconut palm, bananas and a dove of peace.

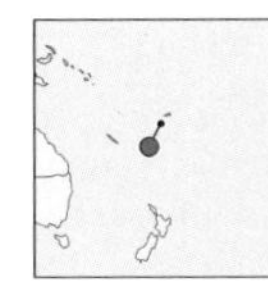

GEOGRAPHY Fiji comprises more than 800 Melanesian islands, the larger one volcanic, mountainous and surrounded by coral reefs, the rest being low coral atolls. The biggest are Viti and Vanua Levu. The south-east trade winds blow all year round and rain usually falls on 200 days per year.

HISTORY AND POLITICS Fiji became a British Crown Colony in 1874 and the British brought in Indians to work on the sugar plantations, which has caused many racial problems as the Indians now outnumber the native Fijians. Two military coups in 1987 overthrew the first Indian-majority government and suspended the constitution. Full civilian rule returned in 1990.

ECONOMY The economy is largely agricultural, with sugar cane making up 45% of exports. Ginger, copra, fish and timber are also important, as well as the sale of gold abroad.

AREA 18,270 sq km [7,054 sq mls]
POPULATION 773,000
CAPITAL (POPULATION) Suva (75,000)
GOVERNMENT Republic with a non-elected senate
ETHNIC GROUPS Fijian 48%, Indian 46%
LANGUAGES English, Bauan, Hindustani
RELIGIONS Christian 53%, Hindu 38%, Muslim 8%
CURRENCY Fiji dollar = 100 cents
MAIN EXPORTS Sugar, gold, food products
POPULATION DENSITY 42 per sq km [110 per sq ml]

FINLAND

Finland became an independent republic only in 1917 after separation from Russia, then in the throes of the Revolution, and the present flag was adopted soon after. The colours symbolize Finland's blue lakes and white snow.

GEOGRAPHY Located almost entirely between latitudes 60°N and 70°N, Finland is the most northerly state on the mainland of Europe; a third of its total area lies within the Arctic Circle. Geologically, Finland is made up of a central plateau of ancient crystalline rocks surrounded by lowlands composed of recent glacial deposits. More than two-thirds of the country is covered by lakes (which are long, narrow and shallow) and forests (mainly of pine, spruce and birch). Winters are long and cold and in severe cases the sea freezes over for several miles offshore. Summers are short but can be warm: July temperatures at Helsinki have an average of 17°C [63°F].

HISTORY AND POLITICS Between 1150 and 1809 Finland was under Swedish rule and, as a legacy of this period, there is a Swedish-speaking minority in the country. In 1809 Finland was annexed by Russia and did not become independent until 1917. Formerly a member of EFTA, Finland joined the EU on 1 January 1995, following a referendum in 1994.

ECONOMY With forests occupying 60% of the land surface, forest-based products form the majority of Finland's exports. Since World War II engineering, shipbuilding and metallurgical industries have greatly expanded. Acid rain and pollution from wood processing and fertilizers are continuing problems.

AREA 338,130 sq km [130,552 sq mls]
POPULATION 5,125,000
CAPITAL (POPULATION) Helsinki (525,000)
GOVERNMENT Multiparty republic
ETHNIC GROUPS Finnish 93%, Swedish 6%
LANGUAGES Finnish and Swedish (both official)
RELIGIONS Lutheran 87%, Greek Orthodox 1%
CURRENCY Markka = 100 penniä
MAIN EXPORTS Machinery 27%, paper and paperboard 26%, wood, lumber, cork and wastepaper 10%
MAIN IMPORTS Machinery and transport equipment 44%, basic manufactures, textiles and metals 16%, petroleum and petroleum products 10%, chemicals 10%

FRANCE

The colours of the French flag originated during the Revolution of 1789. The red and blue are said to represent Paris and the white the monarchy. The present design, adopted in 1794, is meant to symbolize republican principles.

GEOGRAPHY France is Europe's third largest country after Russia and the Ukraine. Some 60% of the country lies less than 250 m [800 ft] above sea level. Rivers, including the Rhône, Garonne, Loire and Seine, along with their many tributaries, drain large lowland basins. There are also several distinctive upland areas, particularly the Alps and the Pyrenees, and also the ancient massifs of Brittany and the Central Plateau. The Alps are formed of complex folded rocks of intricate structure, with relief made even more complicated by the successive glaciations of the Ice Age. Areas of permanent snow exist on Mont Blanc and many other high peaks. Almost half of France's frontiers (which total 5,500 km [3,440 mls]) consist of sea coast and another 1,000 km [620 mls] winds through the Pyrenees and the Alps. The Paris basin is a vast area of sedimentary rocks, while Paris lies on the Île de la Cité, where the River Seine was easily crossed.

HISTORY AND POLITICS France has a long history dating back to the 50s BC when it was conquered by the Romans; in the south there are famous Roman remains – for example, at Arle and Carcassonne. It became an independent kingdom in AD 486, although the monarchy was overthrown by the Revolution in 1789. Local government was reorganized, with the country divided into *départements* – areas in which everyone could reach the central town within one day. There followed many changes, with the country becoming first a republic, then an empire, a monarchy, a republic, and another empire before finally being established as a republic in 1875. France was invaded by Germany in both world wars, but Germany has since become one of France's closest allies, while France itself was one of the founder members of the European Community. François Mitterrand, president of France from 1981–95 died in January 1996 and was succeeded by Jacques Chirac of the centre-right.

ECONOMY Agriculture is a very important part of the economy, making up 17% of export earnings, with about 5% of the world's barley and wheat produced in France. Other crops include maize, a wide range of vegetables, olives and grapes. In terms of minerals, France is a declining but still significant producer of iron ore (mostly from Lorraine), and also bauxite, potash, salt and sulphur. New sources of energy are used, including experiments with solar power in the Pyrenees and the world's first major tidal power station on the Rance estuary in Brittany.

AREA 551,500 sq km [212,934 sq mls]
POPULATION 58,286,000
CAPITAL (POPULATION) Paris (9,469,000)
GOVERNMENT Multiparty republic with a bicameral legislature
ETHNIC GROUPS French 93%, Arab 3%, German 2%, Breton 1%, Catalan 1%
LANGUAGES French (official), Arabic, Breton, Catalan, Basque
RELIGIONS Roman Catholic 76%, other Christian 4%, Muslim 3%
CURRENCY Franc = 100 centimes
URBAN POPULATION 73% of population

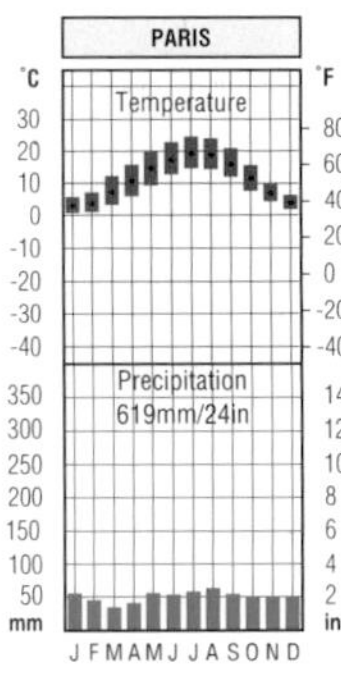

The climate of France is formed from three influences: the Atlantic, the Mediterranean and the continent. With no mountain barriers to affect it the Atlantic regime extends far inland, giving mild weather with wind and rain, but little snow. To the east the climate gets warmer, but with colder winters. At Paris low rainfall is evenly distributed all year.

FRENCH GUIANA

FRENCH GUIANA

The official flag flown over 'Guyane' is the French tricolour. A French possession since 1676 (apart from 1809–17), the territory is treated as part of mainland France and its citizens send representatives to the Paris parliament.

AREA 90,000 sq km [34,749 sq mls]
POPULATION 154,000
CAPITAL (POPULATION) Cayenne (42,000)
GOVERNMENT Overseas Department of France
ETHNIC GROUPS Creole 42%, Chinese 14%, French 10%, Haitian 7%
LANGUAGES French (official), Creole patois
RELIGIONS Roman Catholic 80%, Protestant 4%

French Guiana is the smallest country in South America and has a narrow coastal plain covered with mangrove swamps and marshes, and a drier, forested interior. A French settlement was established in 1604 by a group of merchant adventurers, but it did not become permanently French until 1817. From 1852 to 1939 it was used as a French penal colony, (the notorious Devil's Island was located here, but this was closed in 1945). The economy is very dependent on France for food and manufactured goods. Timber is the most important natural resource; fishing (for shrimps) and tourism are also important.

FRENCH POLYNESIA

The flag was adopted in 1984 and is in the traditional colours of Tahiti, but can only be flown in conjunction with the French tricolour since it is still a French territory. The emblem in the centre is a native canoe (pirogue) against the background of a rising sun over the sea.

AREA 3,941 sq km [1,520 sq mls]
POPULATION 217,000
CAPITAL (POPULATION) Papeete (78,000)
GOVERNMENT Overseas Territory of France
ETHNIC GROUPS Polynesian 78%, Chinese 12%, French
LANGUAGES French (official), Tahitian
RELIGIONS Protestant 54%, Roman Catholic 30%
CURRENCY CFP franc = 100 centimes
URBAN POPULATION 67% of population

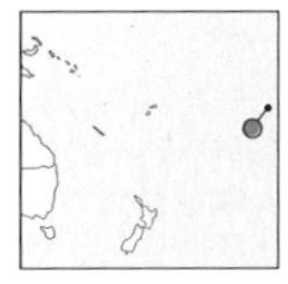

French Polynesia consists of 130 islands, scattered over 4 million sq km [1.5 million sq mls] of ocean halfway between Australia and South America. Tahiti is the largest island and the climate is warm and humid. The tribal chiefs eventually agreed to a French protectorate in 1843, and by the end of the century France controlled all the present islands. They formed an overseas territory from 1958 and in 1984 gained increased autonomy with a territorial assembly; there are calls for independence, but the high standard of living comes largely from the links with France, including a military presence. The main earners are petroleum re-exports, cultured pearls, vanilla and citrus fruits. Tourism is vital to the economy – there were 150,000 tourists in 1994.

GABON

Gabon's tricolour was adopted on independence from France in 1960. The yellow, now representing the sun, used to be thinner to symbolize the Equator on which the country lies. The green stands for Gabon's forests and blue for the sea.

AREA 267,670 sq km [103,347 sq mls]
POPULATION 1,316,000
CAPITAL (POPULATION) Libreville (418,000)
GOVERNMENT Multiparty republic
ETHNIC GROUPS Fang 36%, Mpongwe 15%, Mbete 14%, Punu 12%
LANGUAGES French (official), Bantu languages
RELIGIONS Christian 96% (Roman Catholic 65%)
CURRENCY CFA franc = 100 centimes
URBAN POPULATION 48% of population

Gabon lies in south-west Africa and derives its name from that given by a 16th-century Portuguese explorer. Most of the country is densely forested (covering 75% of the land) and the climate is mainly equatorial with uniform heat and humidity throughout the year and very high rainfall. The capital city of Libreville was founded in 1849 by the French as a home for slaves rescued from illegal slaving ships. Timber was the main export until 1962, when minerals began to be developed, but largely by foreign companies whose profits leave the country. Oil now provides 65% of export earnings and Gabon has about a quarter of the world's known reserves of manganese; there are also reserves of natural gas and uranium.

GAMBIA, THE

The blue stripe in the Republic of The Gambia's flag represents the Gambia River that flows through the country, while the red stands for the sun overhead and the green for the land. The design was adopted on independence from Britain in 1965.

AREA 11,300 sq km [4,363 sq mls]
POPULATION 1,144,000
CAPITAL (POPULATION) Banjul (150,000)
GOVERNMENT Military government
ETHNIC GROUPS Madinka 40%, Fulani 19%, Wolof 15%, Jola 10%, Soninke 8%
LANGUAGES English (official), Madinka, Fula, Wolof
RELIGIONS Sunni Muslim 95%, Christian 4%
CURRENCY Dalasi = 100 butut
POPULATION DENSITY 101 per sq km [262 per sq ml]

GEOGRAPHY The smallest and most westerly country in mainland Africa, The Gambia is low-lying and forms a narrow strip on either side of the River Gambia, making it almost an enclave of Senegal. The capital, Banjul, is the main port and is by far the largest town. All the large settlements are on the river, which provides the main source of communication.
HISTORY AND POLITICS The Gambia was a British colony (the first one) from 1888 and became independent in 1965 (the last to gain independence). A republic was created in 1970. A coup in 1994 brought the military to power. There are close links with Senegal but The Gambia rejects any suggestions of unification.
ECONOMY Rice is grown in swamps and on the floodplains of the river, with millet, sorghum and cassava on the higher ground. Groundnuts provide nine-tenths of export earnings but tourism is by far the country's biggest foreign exchange earner; in 1990–91, 101,500 tourists visited the country.

GEORGIA

The flag was first adopted in 1917 and lasted until 1921. The colours represent the good times of the past and the future (wine-red), the period of Russian rule (black) and the hope for peace (white). It was readopted on independence in 1990.

AREA 69,700 sq km [26,910 sq mls]
POPULATION 5,448,000
CAPITAL (POPULATION) Tbilisi (1,279,000)
GOVERNMENT Multiparty republic
ETHNIC GROUPS Georgian 70%, Armenian 8%, Russian 6%
LANGUAGES Georgian 69%, Armenian 8%, Russian 6%, Azerbaijani 5%, Ossetian 3%
RELIGIONS Orthodox (Georgian 65%, Russian 10%, Armenian 8%), Muslim 11%
CURRENCY Lari
POPULATION DENSITY 78 per sq km [202 per sq ml]
URBAN POPULATION 57% of population
LAND USE Arable 3%, grass 30%

GEOGRAPHY Positioned between Russia and Turkey, Georgia comprises four main areas: the Caucasus Mountains in the north; the Black Sea coastal plain in the west; the eastern end of the mountains of Asia Minor to the south; and a low plateau in the east, protruding into Azerbaijan. Separating the two mountain sections is the crucial Kura Valley.
HISTORY AND POLITICS Georgia has a strong national culture. Land of the legendary Golden Fleece of Greek mythology, the area was conquered by the Romans, Persians and Arabs before establishing autonomy in the 10th century. It came under Russian rule in 1800 and was the first Soviet republic to declare independence after the Baltic states and the only one not to join the CIS at its inception (it later joined in 1994). The former Soviet foreign minister, Eduard Shevardnadze, became head of state in 1992, but there have been recent political problems.
ECONOMY Important crops include citrus fruits, wine, tea, tobacco, wheat, barley and vegetables. Perfume is made from flowers and herbs and there is a silk industry in Imeretiya.

GERMANY

The red, black and gold, dating back to the Holy Roman Empire, are associated with the struggle for a united Germany from the 1830s. The horizontal design was officially adopted for the FRG in 1949, and accepted by 'East Germany' on reunification.

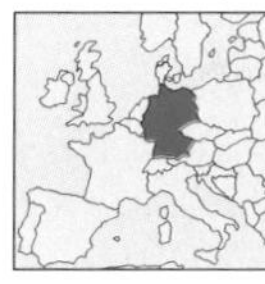

GEOGRAPHY Germany extends from the North Sea and Baltic coasts in the north to the flanks of the central Alps in the south and has the most international borders of any European country. Although there is only a narrow fringe of Alpine mountains, there is a wide section of the associated Alpine foreland bordering Switzerland and Austria that is largely covered by moraines and outwash plains as relics of the last Ice Age. Much of the rest of the country is covered by the central uplands of Europe, including block mountains, which are remnants of pre-Alpine fold mountains and down-faulted basins filled with softer deposits of more recent age (for example, the Upper Rhine plain between Basle and Mainz). The northern lowlands and coast owe much of their topography to glaciation and the retreat of the ice-sheets, with the leached older moraines leaving poor soils.

HISTORY AND POLITICS The German Empire was created under Prussian dominance in 1871 and comprised four kingdoms, six grand duchies, five duchies and seven principalities, and centred on the great imperial capital of Berlin. Following the fall of Hitler in 1945, a defeated Germany was obliged to transfer to Poland and the Soviet Union nearly a quarter of the country's pre-war area. The German-speaking inhabitants were expelled and the remainder of Germany was occupied by the four victorious Allied powers. The dividing line between the zones occupied by the three Western Allies (USA, UK and France) and that occupied by the USSR rapidly became a political boundary dividing the country. In 1948 West Germany was proclaimed as the independent Federal Republic of Germany and East Germany became the German Democratic Republic. In 1990 West and East Germany reunited and the former East Germany was absorbed into the European Union. Problems have arisen from the huge cost of reconstruction and the length of time it was taking to achieve.

ECONOMY Germany has impressive agriculture and industry. In agricultural production it is the world's third largest producer of rye (11% of the total), sugar beet and cheese, and fourth in barley, butter and milk. There are important coal reserves; oil and gas are extracted from beneath the northern lowland; and potash is mined south of the Harz.

AREA 356,910 sq km [137,803 sq mls]
POPULATION 82,000,000
CAPITAL (POPULATION) Berlin (3,475,000)/ Bonn (297,000)
GOVERNMENT Federal multiparty republic with a bicameral legislature
ETHNIC GROUPS German 93%, Turkish, Yugoslav, Italian, Greek, Polish, Spanish
LANGUAGES German (official)
RELIGIONS Protestant 45%, Roman Catholic 37%, Muslim 2%
CURRENCY Deutschmark = 100 Pfennig

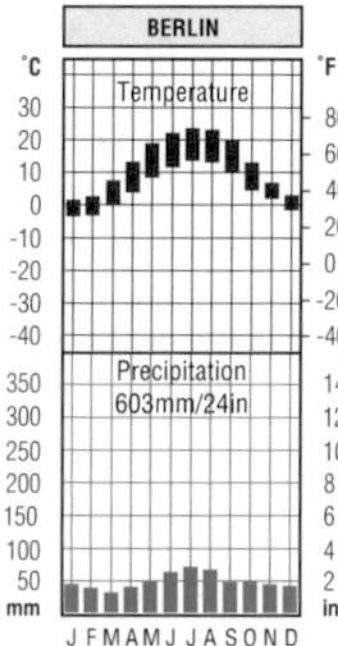

The climate of northern Germany is due mainly to the weather coming in from the the Atlantic. January and February are the only months with mean temperatures just below 0°C [32°F], and the summers are warm. Humidity is always high, with fog in the autumn. In the south the climate is a little warmer in summer and a little colder in winter. It is also wetter.

GHANA

Adopted on independence from Britain in 1957, Ghana's flag features the colours first used by Ethiopia, Africa's oldest independent nation. Following Ghana's lead, other ex-colonies adopted them as a symbol of black Pan-African unity.

GEOGRAPHY Ghana is located in West Africa, with a southern coast on the Atlantic Ocean. It is mostly low-lying and has a climate with uniformly high temperatures and humidity. Lake Volta, one of the world's largest artificial lakes, is located here.

HISTORY AND POLITICS Ghana was known as the Gold Coast from the 8th to the 13th centuries. In 1957 it became the first tropical African country to become independent of colonial rule, and was led by Dr Kwame Nkrumah, a prominent Third World spokesman and pioneer of Pan-African socialism. He was overthrown in 1966 and replaced in 1981 by a hardline regime led by Flight Lieutenant Jerry Rawlings. In 1992, a democratic constitution was adopted and multiparty elections were won by Rawlings.

ECONOMY Cocoa has been the leading export since 1924 with a recent expansion of fishing, tourism and agriculture.

AREA 238,540 sq km [92,100 sq mls]
POPULATION 17,462,000
CAPITAL (POPULATION) Accra (1,390,000)
GOVERNMENT Multiparty republic with a unicameral legislature
ETHNIC GROUPS Akan, Mossi, Ewe, Ga-Adangme, Gurma
LANGUAGES English (official), Akan 54%, Mossi 16%, Ewe 12%, Ga-Adangme 8%, Gurma 3%, Yoruba 1%, Hausa
RELIGIONS Protestant 28%, traditional beliefs 21%, Roman Catholic 19%, Muslim
CURRENCY Cedi = 100 pesewas

GIBRALTAR

The official flag is the Union Jack but this flag has been in use unofficially (on land only) since about 1966. It is a banner of the city arms granted to Gibraltar in 1502 by Spain; the key symbolizes Gibraltar's strategic importance as the gateway to the Mediterranean.

The Rock, as it is popularly known, stands at the north-eastern end of the Strait of Gibraltar, largely consisting of a narrow ridge thrusting south along the eastern side of Algeciras Bay. The topography prohibits cultivation, so the Gibraltarians rely on the port, the ship-repairing yards, the military and air bases, and on tourism for their livelihood. It was formally recognized as a British possession at the Treaty of Utrecht in 1713 and has remained so ever since.

AREA 6.5 sq km [2.5 sq mls]
POPULATION 28,000
CAPITAL Gibraltar Town
GOVERNMENT British Dependent Territory
ETHNIC GROUPS British, Spanish, Maltese, Portuguese
LANGUAGES English, Spanish
RELIGIONS Roman Catholic 74%, Protestant 11%, Muslim 8%
CURRENCY Gibraltar pound = 100 pence

GREECE

Blue and white became Greece's national colours during the war of independence. Finally adopted in 1970, the stripes represent the battle cry 'Eleutheria i thanatos' ('Freedom or Death') used during the struggle against Ottoman (Turkish) domination in the war of 1821–9.

GEOGRAPHY Mainland Greece consists of a mountainous peninsula which projects 500 km [312 mls] into the Mediterranean and an 80 km [50 ml] coastal belt along the northern shore of the Aegean Sea. Nearly a fifth of the total land area of Greece is made up of its 2,000 or so islands, mainly in the Aegean Sea, of which only 154 are inhabited. The Pindos Mountains are the main structural feature, extending southeastwards from the Albanian border to cover most of the peninsula. Nowhere in Greece is more than 80 km [50 mls] from the sea, and most of the towns are on the coast.

HISTORY AND POLITICS In the days of classical Greece, during the thousand years before Christ, Greek colonies were established all round the shores of the Mediterranean, and for a short period in the 4th century BC Alexander the Great built a huge empire extending from the Danube to northern India. Greece was ruled by the Romans in 146 BC and then by Turkey from AD 365; in 1830 it became independent as a monarchy. Greece joined the European Union in 1981, but a vast economic difference has always existed between it and the other members.

ECONOMY Only a third of the land area is suitable for cultivation, yet 40% of the population depend on agriculture for their living, the major crops being wheat, olives, vines and citrus fruits. The tourist industry is vital to the economy. There are few industrial raw materials and most energy is imported.

AREA 131,990 sq km [50,961 sq mls]
POPULATION 10,510,000
CAPITAL (POPULATION) Athens (3,097,000)
GOVERNMENT Multiparty republic
ETHNIC GROUPS Greek 96%, Macedonian 2%, Turkish 1%, Albanian, Slav
LANGUAGES Greek (official)
RELIGIONS Greek Orthodox 97%, Muslim 2%
CURRENCY Drachma = 100 lepta
MAIN EXPORTS Foodstuffs, olive oil and tobacco 28%, textiles 23%, petroleum products 8%
MAIN IMPORTS Machinery and transport equipment 23%, foodstuffs 17%
POPULATION DENSITY 80 per sq km [206 per sq ml]
URBAN POPULATION 64% of population

GREENLAND

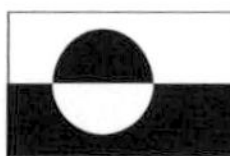

The flag was introduced in 1985 after a competition to decide a design and can be used on land and at sea. The design is in the Danish colours, with the red depicting the midsummer sun rising over the (white) polar ice.

AREA 2,175,600 sq km [839,999 sq mls]
POPULATION 59,000
CAPITAL (Population) Godthåb (12,550)
GOVERNMENT Self-governing overseas region of Denmark
ETHNIC GROUPS Greenlander 86%, Danish 14%
LANGUAGES Inuit (official), Danish
RELIGIONS Lutheran
CURRENCY Danish krone
MAIN EXPORTS Shrimps, prawns and molluscs, fish, lead, zinc

Recognized by geographers as the world's largest island, Greenland is almost three times the size of the second largest, New Guinea. More than 85% of the land is covered in continuous permafrost, an ice-cap with an average depth of about 1,500 m [5,000 ft], and though there are a few sandy and clay plains in the ice-free areas, settlement is confined to the rocky coasts. Greenland became a Danish possession in 1380 and part of the Danish kingdom in 1953; full internal self-government was granted in 1981. The economy still depends greatly on Danish subsidies and Denmark remains its chief trading partner. The main rural occupations are sheep rearing and fishing and the main manufacturing is fish canning.

GRENADA

Each star represents one of Grenada's seven parishes. The country's traditional cash crop, nutmeg, is depicted in the hoist triangle. The people are represented by the colours red (for unity) and yellow (for friendliness and the sunshine), the island by the colour green.

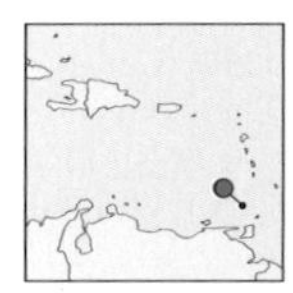

AREA 344 sq km [133 sq mls]
POPULATION 96,000
CAPITAL (Population) St George's (7,000)
GOVERNMENT Constitutional monarchy with a bicameral legislature
ETHNIC GROUPS Black 85%, Mixed 11%, East Indian 3%, White 1%
LANGUAGES English, French patois
RELIGIONS Roman Catholic 64%, Protestant 34%
CURRENCY East Caribbean $ = 100 cents
MAIN EXPORTS Nutmeg, bananas
POPULATION DENSITY 273 per sq km [707 per sq ml]

GEOGRAPHY Grenada is the most southern of the Windward Islands and the territory also includes the Southern Grenadines, principally Carriacou. The landscape is mountainous, consisting of the remains of extinct volcanoes; the only flat land is along the rivers' lower courses and part of the coastline. A hurricane in 1955 virtually destroyed the capital of St George's.
HISTORY AND POLITICS British since 1783, Grenada became a self-governing colony in 1967 and independent in 1974. It went Communist after a coup in 1979 when links with Cuba were established by Maurice Bishop. Bishop was executed in 1983 and the USA sent in troops to restore democracy; since then there has been a heavy reliance on American aid.
ECONOMY Grenada is known as 'the spice island of the Caribbean' and is the world's leading producer of nutmeg, its main crop. Cocoa, bananas and mace are also produced. The tourist industry has gradually recovered since the 1983 invasion.

GUADELOUPE

As an overseas department of France, Guadeloupe uses the French tricolour for its flag.

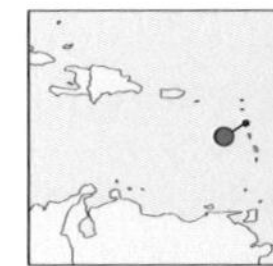

AREA 1,710 sq km [660 sq mls]
POPULATION 443,000
CAPITAL (Population) Basse-Terre (15,000)
GOVERNMENT Overseas Department of France
ETHNIC GROUPS Mixed (Black and White) 90%
LANGUAGES French
RELIGIONS Roman Catholic 88%
CURRENCY French franc

Slightly the larger of France's two Caribbean overseas departments, Guadeloupe comprises seven islands including Saint-Martin and Saint-Barthélemy to the north-west. Over 90% of the area, however, is taken up by Basse-Terre, which is volcanic, and the smaller Grande-Terre, made of low limestone. Food is the main import (mostly from France) and bananas are the biggest export. French aid has helped create a reasonable standard of living, although unemployment is high.

GUAM

The flag was adopted in 1917. The badge in the centre is based on the island seal and depicts the mouth of the Agana River and a prao *sailing off Point Ritidian. Guam has been a dependency of the USA since 1898 and flies its flag only with the American 'Stars and Stripes'.*

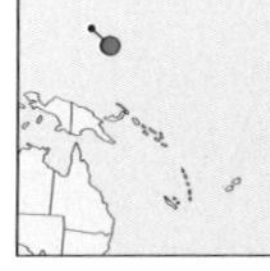

AREA 541 sq km [209 sq mls]
POPULATION 155,000
CAPITAL (Population) Agana (4,000)
GOVERNMENT US Territory
ETHNIC GROUPS Chamorro 47%, Filipino 25%, American
LANGUAGES English, Chamorro, Japanese
RELIGIONS Roman Catholic 98%
MAIN EXPORTS Textiles, beverages, tobacco, copra

Largest of the Mariana Islands, Guam is composed mainly of a coralline limestone plateau, with mountains in the south, hills in the centre and narrow coastal lowlands in the north. Populated for over 3,000 years, colonized by Spain from 1668, but ceded to the USA after the 1896–8 war and occupied by the Japanese 1941–4, it is today of huge strategic importance to the USA and a third of its usable land is taken up by American naval and airforce establishments.

GUATEMALA

The simple design of Guatemala's flag was adopted in 1871, but its origins date back to the Central American Federation (1823–39) formed with Honduras, El Salvador, Nicaragua and Costa Rica after the break from Spanish rule in 1821.

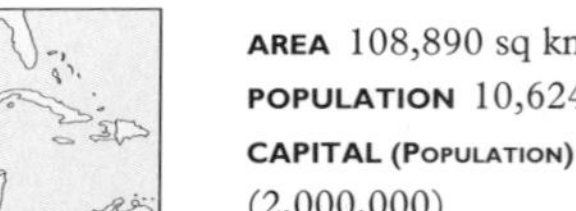

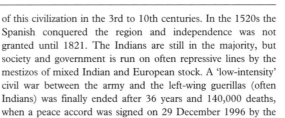

AREA 108,890 sq km [42,042 sq mls]
POPULATION 10,624,000
CAPITAL (Population) Guatemala City (2,000,000)
GOVERNMENT Republic with a unicameral legislature
ETHNIC GROUPS Mayaquiche Indian 55%, Ladino (Mestizo) 42%
LANGUAGES Spanish (official) 40%, 20 Indian dialects
RELIGIONS Roman Catholic 75%, Protestant 23%
CURRENCY Guatemalan quetzal = 100 centavos
MAIN EXPORTS Coffee, bananas, sugar, cardamom
POPULATION DENSITY 98 per sq km [253 per sq ml]

GEOGRAPHY Most populous of the Central American countries, Guatemala's Pacific coastline, two and a half times longer than its Caribbean coast, is backed by broad alluvial plains, formed from material washed down from the 27 volcanoes that front the ocean. These include extinct Tajumulco (4,217 m [13,830 ft]), the highest peak in central America. Its position between the seas and its mountainous interior gives Guatemala a variety of climates. On the Caribbean coast, with the trade winds always blowing onshore, rainfall is high in all months, whereas inland there is a dry, almost arid, season in January and February.
HISTORY AND POLITICS The remains of the largest of the pre-Colombian Maya Indian cities at Tikal indicates the importance of this civilization in the 3rd to 10th centuries. In the 1520s the Spanish conquered the region and independence was not granted until 1821. The Indians are still in the majority, but society and government is run on often repressive lines by the mestizos of mixed Indian and European stock. A 'low-intensity' civil war between the army and the left-wing guerillas (often Indians) was finally ended after 36 years and 140,000 deaths, when a peace accord was signed on 29 December 1996 by the commanders of the guerillas and President Alvaro Irigoyen.
ECONOMY Coffee production dominates the economy, with the lower mountain slopes providing ideal conditions for growth. Bananas, cotton and cattle are also important.

GUINEA

Guinea's Pan-African colours, adopted on independence from France in 1958, represent the three words of the national motto 'Travail, Justice, Solidarité': Work (red), Justice (yellow) and Solidarity (green). The design is based on the French tricolour.

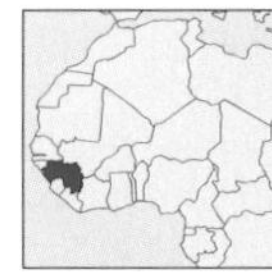

GEOGRAPHY Guinea is a country of varied landscapes, ranging from the grasslands and scattered woodland of the interior highlands and Upper Niger plains, to the swampy mangrove-fringed plains of the Atlantic coast. Dense forests occupy the western foothills of the Fouta Djalon plateau.

HISTORY AND POLITICS In the 1400s the Portuguese developed a slave trade from Guinea, before the French took over after 1849. Independence was granted in 1958 after a referendum (it became the first independent state of French-speaking Africa) and until 1984 Guinea was ruled by the repressive regime of President Ahmed Sékou Touré, who isolated Guinea from the West. It was not until after his death that economic reforms began to work and relations with France were restored.

ECONOMY Two-thirds of the population are involved in agriculture and there are also considerable natural resources: huge reserves of bauxite account for 80% of export earnings.

AREA 245,860 sq km [94,927 sq mls]
POPULATION 6,702,000
CAPITAL (POPULATION) Conakry (1,508,000)
GOVERNMENT Multiparty republic
ETHNIC GROUPS Fulani 40%, Malinké 26%, Susu 11%
LANGUAGES French (official), Susu, Malinké
RELIGIONS Muslim 85%, traditional beliefs 5%
CURRENCY Guinean franc = 100 cauris
POPULATION DENSITY 27 per sq km [71 per sq ml]
URBAN POPULATION 28% of population

GUINEA-BISSAU

This flag, using the Pan-African colours, was adopted on gaining independence from Portugal in 1973. It is based on the one used by the PAIGC political party that led the struggle from 1962, who in turn based it on the flag of Ghana, the first of the African colonies to gain independence.

GEOGRAPHY Guinea-Bissau lies between Guinea and Senegal in West Africa. Thick forest and mangrove swamps cover the area nearest to the Atlantic Ocean, with savanna covering the inland area. The climate is tropical.

HISTORY AND POLITICS Formerly known as Portuguese Guinea, Portugal ruled for 500 years before independence was granted in 1973 after a guerilla war. In 1991 the Supreme Court ended 17 years of Socialist one-party rule by legalizing the opposition Democratic Front; multiparty elections were held in 1994.

ECONOMY About 85% of the active population are subsistence farmers. A fishing industry and cash crops such as tropical fruits, cotton and tobacco are being developed.

AREA 36,120 sq km [13,946 sq mls]
POPULATION 1,073,000
CAPITAL (POPULATION) Bissau (125,000)
GOVERNMENT Multiparty republic
ETHNIC GROUPS Balante 27%, Fulani 23%, Malinké 12%, Mandyako 11%, Pepel 10%
LANGUAGES Portuguese (official), Crioulo
RELIGIONS Traditional beliefs 54%, Muslim 38%
CURRENCY Peso = 100 centavos
POPULATION DENSITY 30 per sq km [77 per sq ml]

GUYANA

This striking design, adopted by Guyana on independence from Britain in 1966, has colours representing the people's energy building a new nation (red), their perseverance (black), minerals (yellow), rivers (white), and agriculture and forests (green).

GEOGRAPHY With its name meaning 'land of many waters', Guyana has a vast interior with low forest-covered plateaux, the wooded Rapunumi savannas, river valleys and the Roraima Massif on the Venezuela-Brazil border. The coastal plain is mainly artificial, reclaimed from the marshes and swamps.

HISTORY, POLITICS AND ECONOMY Guyana was settled by the Dutch between 1616 and 1621. The territory was ceded to Britain in 1814 and became British Guiana. Independent since 1966, Guyana became a republic in 1970. It is largely uninhabited, with 95% of the population living within a few kilometres of the coast. Sugar production, bauxite mining and alumina production provide 80% of the overseas earnings.

AREA 214,970 sq km [83,000 sq mls]
POPULATION 832,000
CAPITAL (POPULATION) Georgetown (200,000)
GOVERNMENT Multiparty republic with a unicameral legislature
ETHNIC GROUPS Asian Indian 49%, Black 36%, Amerindian 7%, Mixed 7%
LANGUAGES English (official), Hindi, Urdu, Amerindian dialects
RELIGIONS Hindu 34%, Protestant 34%, Roman Catholic 18%, Sunni Muslim 9%

HAITI

Although the colours, first used in 1803, are said to represent the country's two communities (the blacks [blue] and the mulattos [red]), the design of Haiti's flag derives from that of France, to which it once belonged. The present version was first used in 1843 and restored in 1986.

GEOGRAPHY Occupying the western third of Hispaniola, the Caribbean's second largest island, Haiti is mainly mountainous with a long, indented coast. Most of the country is centred around the Massif du Nord, with the narrow Massif de la Hotte forming the southern peninsula.

HISTORY AND POLITICS Ceded to France in 1697, Haiti developed as a sugar-producing colony. Once the richest part of the Caribbean, it is now one of the world's poorest nations. Since a slave revolt in 1804, it has been plagued by continuous instability and violence, particularly during the regimes of François Duvalier ('Papa Doc') and his son Jean-Claude ('Baby Doc') from 1957. The first multiparty elections were held in 1990, but the military took over in 1991. In 1994, the USA sent in troops to restore democracy and in 1996 René Préval was elected president.

ECONOMY With few natural resources, coffee is the main cash crop; 60% of the population live at or below the poverty line.

AREA 27,750 sq km [10,714 sq mls]
POPULATION 7,180,000
CAPITAL (POPULATION) Port-au-Prince (1,402,000)
GOVERNMENT Multiparty republic
ETHNIC GROUPS Black 95%, Mulatto 5%
LANGUAGES French (official) 10%, Haitian Creole 88%
RELIGIONS Christian (Roman Catholic 80%), Voodoo
CURRENCY Gourde = 100 centimes
POPULATION DENSITY 259 per sq km [670 per sq ml]

HONDURAS

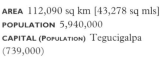

Officially adopted in 1949, the flag of Honduras is based on that of the Central American Federation (see Guatemala). Honduras left the organization in 1838, but in 1866 added the five stars to the flag to express a hope for a future federation.

GEOGRAPHY Some 80% of Honduras is mountainous, with peaks of more than 2,500 m [8,000 ft] in the west. The mountain ranges are metalliferous: gold and silver deposits were, and still are, very important to the economy.

HISTORY AND POLITICS The first Spanish *conquistadores* came to Honduras to search for gold and founded the capital city in 1524. It became an independent republic in 1838, and after a civil war in the 1920s a series of military regimes ruled until 1980, when civilians took over. Since then there have been democratic governments but the military retains an interest.

ECONOMY Bananas and coffee are the chief cash crops and there is little industrialization. Lead, silver and zinc are mined.

AREA 112,090 sq km [43,278 sq mls]
POPULATION 5,940,000
CAPITAL (POPULATION) Tegucigalpa (739,000)
GOVERNMENT Multiparty republic with a unicameral legislature
ETHNIC GROUPS Mestizo 90%, Amerindian 7%, Black (including Black Carib) 2%, White 1%
LANGUAGES Spanish (official), Black Carib (Garifuna), English Creole, Miskito
RELIGIONS Roman Catholic 85%

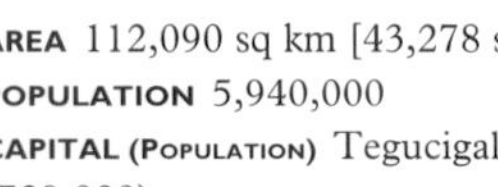

HONG KONG

HONG KONG

Hong Kong flew the Blue Ensign from 1841 when it became a British dependent territory until July 1997 when it reverted to Chinese control and this new flag was adopted. The five stars and the red background come from the Chinese flag and the white flower is a symbol of Hong Kong.

AREA 1,071 sq km [413 sq mls]
POPULATION 6,000,000
CAPITAL –
GOVERNMENT Special Administrative Region of China
ETHNIC GROUPS Chinese 97%, others 2% (including European)
LANGUAGES English and Chinese (official)
RELIGIONS Buddhist majority, Confucian, Taoist, Christian, Muslim, Hindu, Sikh, Jewish
CURRENCY Hong Kong dollar = 100 cents
MAIN EXPORTS Textiles, clothing, plastic and light metal products
POPULATION DENSITY 5,602 per sq km [14,527 per sq ml]

GEOGRAPHY The Special Administrative Region of Hong Kong is made up of Hong Kong Island (which is 13 km [8 mls] long), about 235 smaller islands, the Kowloon peninsula in the Chinese province of Guangdong and the 'New Territories' adjoining it. Summers are hot and humid with heavy rain, while winters are mild and dry. Hong Kong is very densely populated, but has few natural resources of its own and most of its water, food and raw materials comes from China.

HISTORY AND POLITICS Hong Kong was acquired by Britain in three stages between 1842 and 1898. In 1898 Britain signed a 99-year lease with the Chinese government, and in 1997 the country reverted to Chinese rule. Under a 1984 accord, China agreed to allow Hong Kong full economic autonomy and the ability to pursue its capitalist path for at least another 50 years, by operating it as a Special Administrative Region.

ECONOMY Hong Kong's successful economy is based on manufacturing (including textiles and plastics), banking and commerce. It has the world's biggest container port, is the biggest exporter of clothes and the tenth biggest trader. China increased its export earnings by over 25% on changeover.

HUNGARY

The tricolour became popular in the European revolutions of 1848, though the colours had been in the Hungarian arms since the 15th century. Adopted in 1919, the design was amended in 1957 to remove the state emblem, which had been added in 1949.

AREA 93,030 sq km [35,919 sq mls]
POPULATION 10,500,000
CAPITAL (POPULATION) Budapest (2,009,000)
GOVERNMENT Multiparty republic
ETHNIC GROUPS Magyar 97%, Gypsy, German, Slovak
LANGUAGES Hungarian (official), German, Slovak
RELIGIONS Roman Catholic 68%, Protestant 25%
CURRENCY Forint = 100 fillér
MAIN EXPORTS Machinery, vehicles, iron and steel
POPULATION DENSITY 113 per sq km [292 per sq ml]

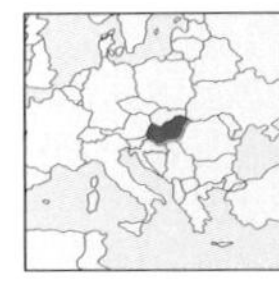

GEOGRAPHY Hungary has two large lowland areas – the Great Plain (Nagyalföld) in the south-east, which is dissected by the country's two main rivers, the Danube and the Tisza, and the Little Plain (Kisalföld) in the north-west. These plains make extremely fertile agricultural land. Europe's second longest river, the Danube, flows through Hungary on its way to the Black Sea.

HISTORY AND POLITICS As a large part of the Austro-Hungarian Empire, Hungary enjoyed an autonomous position within the Dual Monarchy from 1867, but defeat in World War I saw nearly 70% of its territory apportioned to Czechoslovakia, Yugoslavia and Romania. A Communist state was established in 1949 after occupation by the Soviet Red Army. The Uprising of 1956 was put down by Soviet troops, but successive governments have been fairly progressive. In 1989 a new constitution was adopted, making Hungary a multiparty state.

ECONOMY There are reserves of gas and bauxite, but other natural resources are scarce. Many raw materials are imported and the main industrial centres are in the north.

ICELAND

Dating from 1915, the flag became official on independence from Denmark in 1944. It uses the traditional Icelandic colours of blue and white and is in fact the same as the Norwegian flag, but with the blue and red colours reversed.

AREA 103,000 sq km [39,768 sq mls]
POPULATION 269,000
CAPITAL (POPULATION) Reykjavik (103,000)
GOVERNMENT Multiparty republic with a unicameral parliament
ETHNIC GROUPS Icelandic 97%
LANGUAGES Icelandic (official)
RELIGIONS Lutheran 92%, Roman Catholic 1%
CURRENCY Króna = 100 aurar
MAIN EXPORTS Fish products, unwrought aluminium
POPULATION DENSITY 3 per sq km [8 per sq ml]

GEOGRAPHY Iceland is situated far out in the North Atlantic Ocean and arises geologically from the boundary between Europe and America – the Mid-Atlantic Ridge. A central zone of recently active volcanoes and fissures crosses Iceland from north to south: in the thousand years of settlement, between 150 and 200 eruptions have occurred in the active zones. Four large ice-caps cover 11% of the land surface.

HISTORY AND POLITICS Colonized by Viking farmers in the 9th century, Iceland became a dependency of first Norway, and then Denmark, although it was mainly self-governing after what is thought to be one of the world's earliest parliaments was set up in AD 930. In 1944 it became a republic after sharing a sovereign with Denmark after 1918.

ECONOMY The economy is based on deep-sea fishing; fish and fish products make up 70% of exports. About a fifth of the land is used for agriculture, mostly to graze cattle and sheep.

INDIA

India's flag evolved during the struggle for freedom from British rule. The orange represents the Hindu majority, green the country's many Muslims and white peace. The Buddhist wheel symbol, the blue charka, was added on independence in 1947.

AREA 3,287,590 sq km [1,269,338 sq mls]
POPULATION 942,989,000
CAPITAL (POPULATION) New Delhi (301,000)
GOVERNMENT Multiparty federal republic with a bicameral legislature
ETHNIC GROUPS Indo-Aryan (Caucasoid) 72%, Dravidian (Aboriginal) 25%, other (mainly Mongoloid) 3%

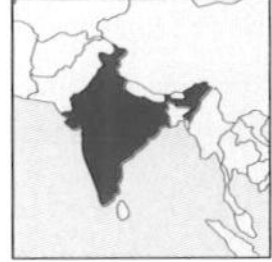

GEOGRAPHY India is the world's seventh largest country and extends from high in the Himalayas through the Tropic of Cancer to the warm waters of the Indian Ocean at 8°N. There are a wide variety of landscapes. These include: the Himalayan foothills in the north, where there are harsh, dry highlands and fertile valleys with rice-terraces; the lowlands of Uttar Pradesh, criss-crossed by the Ganges and Jumna rivers and their many tributaries and densely populated; the Thar or Great Indian Desert which lies mostly in Rajasthan; and the coastline of peninsular India lined with coconut groves, rising to the mountain chain of the Western Ghats.

HISTORY AND POLITICS India's earliest settlers were widely scattered across the subcontinent in Stone Age times. The first of its civilizations developed in the Indus Valley about 2600 BC and by the 3rd and 4th centuries BC Pataliputra (modern Patna) formed the centre of a loosely held empire that extended across the peninsula and beyond into Afghanistan. By 1805 the British East India Company was virtually in control after many battles fought by Britain in both Europe and India to gain superiority over local factions and other European rivals (such as Denmark and France). In 1947 the Indian subcontinent became independent from Britain, but divided into India (Hindu) and Pakistan (Muslim). The sheer size and population of India has caused many problems of organization and development, leaving a complex society.

ECONOMY Some 70% of the population works in agriculture, mostly on small farms and growing crops such as rice, wheat, tea, barley, jute, sorghum and millet. India is the world's third largest coal producer and industrialization has progressed rapidly since independence, with a series of five-year plans.

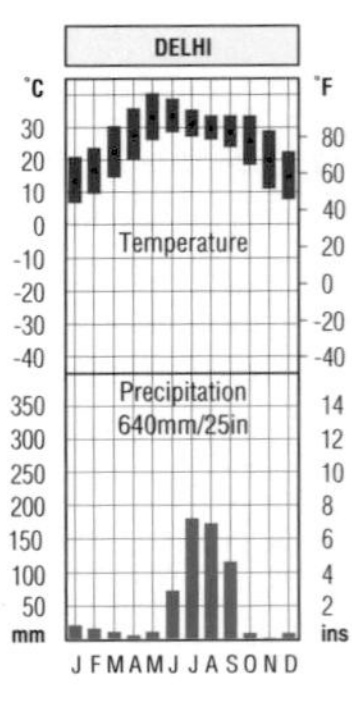

The summer rains, typical of the Indian monsoon, arrive later and are less intense at Delhi than in the lower parts of the Ganges Valley. Between November and May, the dry season, there is abundant sunshine and temperatures increase rapidly until the arrival of the rains in June. During the rainy season the temperature is uniformly hot.

INDONESIA

While the colours date back to the Middle Ages, they were adopted by political groups in the struggle against the Netherlands in the 1920s and became the national flag in 1945, when Indonesia finally proclaimed its independence.

GEOGRAPHY Indonesia is the world's largest island chain with about 13,000 islands, of which less than half are inhabited. There are over 100 active volcanoes – the eruption of Krakatoa in 1883 killed 30,000 people. All the islands are mountainous. The natural vegetation of the tropical lowlands is rainforest, much of which has now been cleared for cultivation. Rainfall is heaviest in summer, most of it falling in thunderstorms. Temperatures are high throughout the year.

HISTORY AND POLITICS From the 16th century onwards the influences of European powers grew, dominated by the Dutch

East India Company. Freedom movements in the early 20th century found expression under Japanese occupation in World War II, and Indonesia declared independence in 1945. After four years of fighting, the Dutch finally recognized the country as a sovereign state in 1949. There has been recent social unrest.

ECONOMY Indonesia is a mainly agricultural nation with about a tenth of the land area under permanent cultivation, mostly producing rice, maize, cassava and sweet potato. There are also large plantations of rubber (second in the world), sugar cane, coffee and tea. The tourist industry is growing rapidly.

AREA 1,904,570 sq km [735,354 sq mls]
POPULATION 198,644,000
CAPITAL (POPULATION) Jakarta (11,500,000)
GOVERNMENT Multiparty republic
ETHNIC GROUPS Javanese 39%, Sundanese 16%, Bahasa Indonesian 12%, Madurese 5%, over 300 others
LANGUAGES Bahasa Indonesia (official), Javanese, Sundanese, Dutch, over 20 others
RELIGIONS Sunni Muslim 87%, Christian 10% (Roman Catholic 4%), Hindu 2%, Buddhist 1%
CURRENCY Rupiah = 100 sen
POPULATION DENSITY 104 per sq km [270 per sq ml]

IRAN

Iran's flag has been in use since July 1980 after the fall of the Shah and the rise of the Islamic Republic. Along the edges of the stripes is the legend 'Allah Akbar' (God is Great) repeated 22 times; in the centre is the new national emblem, symbolizing Allah (God).

GEOGRAPHY The deserts of Kavir and Lut lie in the middle of Iran, surrounded by mountain ranges, which broaden in the west into the high plateaux of the Zagros. Fertile land is found near the Caspian Sea in the north, an area which is subject to earthquakes. The cities of the interior depend on complex arrangements of tunnels and channels for tapping underground water, and these have been supplemented by high dams, notably at Dezful. Most of the population live in the mountainous north and west of the country.

HISTORY AND POLITICS Before 1935 Iran was called Persia and retained its Shah until 1979 when a revolution toppled the

regime and replaced it with a radical fundamentalist Islamic republic, led by the exiled Ayatollah Khomeini. The Iran-Iraq war of 1980–8 saw Iranian casualties of between 150,000 and 630,000 and left its vital oil production at less than half the 1979 level (although still seventh in the world); consequently, Iran began to look to Western powers and recent years have seen closer links with many of them.

ECONOMY Oil and natural gas deposits are Iran's most important sources of wealth (oil was first discovered in 1908). About 20% of the population work on the land, while Iran is also known for its caviar and its carpets and rugs.

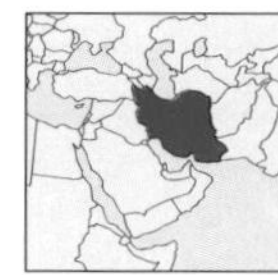

AREA 1,648,000 sq km [636,293 sq mls]
POPULATION 68,885,000
CAPITAL (POPULATION) Tehran (6,476,000)
GOVERNMENT Unitary Islamic republic, religious leader (elected by Council of Experts) exercises supreme authority
ETHNIC GROUPS Persian 46%, Azerbaijani 17%, Kurdish 9%, Gilaki 5%, Luri, Mazandarani, Baluchi, Arab
LANGUAGES Farsi (Persian) 48% (official), Kurdish, Baluchi, Turkic, Arabic, French
RELIGIONS Shiite Muslim 91%, Sunni Muslim 8%
CURRENCY Rial = 100 dinars
POPULATION DENSITY 42 per sq km [108 per sq ml]
URBAN POPULATION 57% of population

IRAQ

Using the four Pan-Arab colours, Iraq's flag was adopted in 1963 at the time of the proposed federation with Egypt and Syria. Iraq retained the three green stars, symbolizing the three countries, even though the union failed to materialize.

GEOGRAPHY Iraq essentially comprises the lower valleys and combined deltas of the Tigris and Euphrates rivers, which provide fertile land when supplied with water. In the north-east there is a hilly region, including part of the Zagros Mountains, and in the west is a large part of the Hamad or Syrian Desert. The country is landlocked except for its outlet to the Gulf at Shatt Al Arab Waterway, which is shared with Iran.

HISTORY AND POLITICS Absorbed into the Ottoman Empire in the 16th century, Iraq was captured by British forces in 1916 and run as a virtual colony. The Hashemite dynasty ruled an independent kingdom from 1932, but in 1958 a republic was set up after a military coup. In 1968 the Pan-Arab Baathists seized

control and Saddam Hussein became president in 1979. The Iran-Iraq war of 1980–8 left over a million Iraqi men killed or wounded and nearly crippled the economy; this was worsened by the Second Gulf War when Iraq invaded Kuwait in August 1990 and annexed it as an Iraqi province. The international community first imposed sanctions and then sent in a multi-national force to drive back the Iraqis, leaving Iraq with a crumbling infrastructure and a severe shortage of food.

ECONOMY The chief mineral resource is oil, with some sulphur and gypsum deposits and some crops (such as dates) and livestock. However, sanctions and war damage have caused economic chaos and much personal hardship.

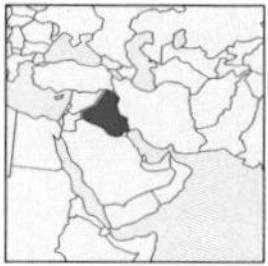

AREA 438,320 sq km [169,235 sq mls]
POPULATION 20,184,000
CAPITAL (POPULATION) Baghdad (3,841,000)
GOVERNMENT Unitary republic
ETHNIC GROUPS Arab 77%, Kurd 19%, Turkmen 2%, Persian 2%, Assyrian
LANGUAGES Arabic (official), Kurdish, Turkish
RELIGIONS Shiite Muslim 62%, Sunni Muslim 34%
CURRENCY Dinar = 20 dirhams = 1,000 fils
MAIN EXPORTS Fuels and other energy 98%
MAIN IMPORTS Machinery and transport equipment, manufactured goods
POPULATION DENSITY 46 per sq km [119 per sq ml]
URBAN POPULATION 73% of population

IRELAND

The Irish flag was first used by nationalists in 1848 in the struggle for freedom from Britain and adopted in 1922 after independence. Green represents the Roman Catholics and orange the Protestants, with white in the middle representing the desire for peace between the two.

GEOGRAPHY The word 'Ireland' is today used as shorthand for the Republic of Ireland, which occupies some 80% of the whole island of Ireland, with the rest as Northern Ireland, which remains part of the United Kingdom. The landscape is made up of a central lowland and a series of different mountain chains, including the Wicklow Mountains in the south-east. The climate is mild and damp with high humidity and frequent fog.

HISTORY AND POLITICS The Anglo-Irish Treaty of 1921 established southern Ireland – Eire – as an independent state,

after it had been part of the United Kingdom since 1801. It became a republic in 1949 and joined the EU in 1973.

ECONOMY Agriculture is the traditional occupation of the Irish, together with fishing, home crafts and local labouring as extra sources of income. The eastern and south-eastern areas tend to be richer than the western areas, with large farms supporting cattle, sheep and racehorses. European Union grants have helped greatly and increased prosperity. Tourism and high-tech industries are important in the north-east.

AREA 70,280 sq km [27,135 sq mls]
POPULATION 3,589,000
CAPITAL (POPULATION) Dublin (1,024,000)
GOVERNMENT Unitary multiparty republic with a bicameral legislature
ETHNIC GROUPS Irish 94%
LANGUAGES Irish and English (both official)
RELIGIONS Roman Catholic 93%, Protestant 3%
CURRENCY Punt = 100 pence
MAIN EXPORTS Machinery and transport equipment 32%
POPULATION DENSITY 51 per sq km [132 per sq ml]

ISRAEL

ISRAEL

The blue and white stripes on Israel's flag are based on the tallit, *a Hebrew prayer shawl. In the centre is the ancient six-pointed Star of David. The flag was designed in America in 1891 and officially adopted by the new Jewish state in 1948.*

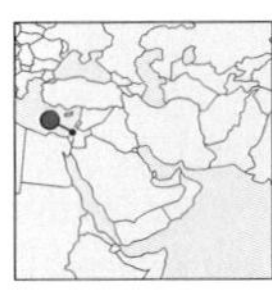

GEOGRAPHY About half of the total territory of Israel is covered by the desert plateau of the Negev in the south of the country. Its bedrock is covered with blown sand and loess, which, if irrigated, will grow grapes and tomatoes. The Dead Sea to the east is the world's lowest point (396 m [1,279 ft] below sea level), while in the north the Sea of Galilee is Israel's main reservoir of fresh water. The north has the most fertile land; the excellent farmland in the Upper Jordan Valley is reclaimed from Lake Huleh.

HISTORY AND POLITICS The state of Israel was created in 1948 and the return of the Jewish people to their homeland marked the end of 18 centuries of exile. After the Six Day War in 1967 Israel took over the administration of the 'West Bank' (from Jordan), the Gaza Strip (from Egypt) and the Golan Heights (from Syria). There have been five wars since 1948 in which Arab nations and Palestinians have fought against Israel. A peace accord was signed in September 1993 between Israel and the Palestinian Liberation Organization (PLO) and Palestinian self-rule has been established in the Gaza Strip and part of the West Bank. On 4 November 1995, the prime minister Yitzhak Rabin was assassinated. His successor Simon Peres was narrowly defeated by right-wing Benjamin Netanyahu in elections in 1996.

ECONOMY Israel is the world's top recipient of aid, mainly from the USA, and has become the most industrialized country in the Near East. Important industries include textiles and ceramics, plus iron smelting and chemical manufacturing at Haifa. Agriculture is important, especially oranges and olives.

AREA 26,650 sq km [10,290 sq mls]
POPULATION 5,696,000
CAPITAL (POPULATION) Jerusalem (550,000)
GOVERNMENT Multiparty republic
ETHNIC GROUPS Jewish 82%, Arab 18%
LANGUAGES Hebrew and Arabic (official)
RELIGIONS Jewish 82%, Muslim 14%, Christian 2%
CURRENCY New Israeli shekel = 100 agorat
MAIN EXPORTS Machinery 29%, diamonds 29%, chemicals 22%, textiles 8%, foodstuffs 5%
MAIN IMPORTS Diamonds 20%, capital goods 15%, consumer goods 11%, fuels and lubricants 8%
POPULATION DENSITY 214 per sq km [554 per sq ml]
URBAN POPULATION 91% of population
LAND USE Arable 21%, grass 7%

ITALY

When Napoleon invaded Italy in 1796, the French Republican National Guard carried a military standard of vertical green, white and red stripes. After many changes, it was finally adopted as the national flag after the unification of Italy in 1861.

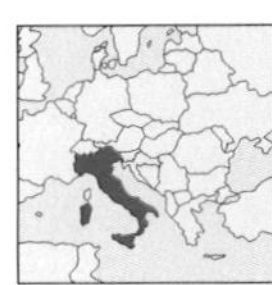

GEOGRAPHY The Alpine period of mountain building, when the main ranges of the Alps and the Apennines were uplifted together, determined much of Italy's topographical structure. The Apennines, in central Italy, reach their highest peaks – almost 3,000 m [9,800 ft] – in the Gran Sasso range overlooking the central Adriatic Sea near Pescara. Between the mountains are long, narrow basins, some of which contain lakes. In the north lies the large Lombardy plain, drained by the River Po, and the most productive industrial and agricultural area in Italy. The islands of Sicily and Sardinia are also Italian; Sardinia lies 480 km [300 mls] from the Italian coast and has a rugged, windswept terrain.

HISTORY AND POLITICS In 1800 present-day Italy was made up of several political units, including the Papal States, and a substantial part of the north-east was occupied by Austria. Unification – the *Risorgimento* – began early in the 19th century, but little progress was made until an alliance between France and Piedmont drove Austria from Lombardy in 1859. The other states were soon brought into the alliance and by 1861 King Victor Emmanuel was proclaimed ruler of a united Italy, with Venetia acquired from Austria in 1866 and Rome annexed in 1871. A republic was set up in 1946 and Italy was a founder member of the EC. Northern and southern Italy still have very different characteristics, due to their very disparate social and historical backgrounds and the distance between them.

ECONOMY With few natural resources, Italy has managed to make great economic progress. Textiles, metal-working, engineering and food processing industries all flourish in the north and crops include grapes, olives, tomatoes and wheat. The black economy may boost official GNP by as much as 10%.

AREA 301,270 sq km [116,320 sq mls]
POPULATION 57,181,000
CAPITAL (POPULATION) Rome (2,723,000)
GOVERNMENT Multiparty republic with a bicameral legislature
ETHNIC GROUPS Italian 94%, German
LANGUAGES Italian 94%, Sardinian 3%
RELIGIONS Roman Catholic 83%

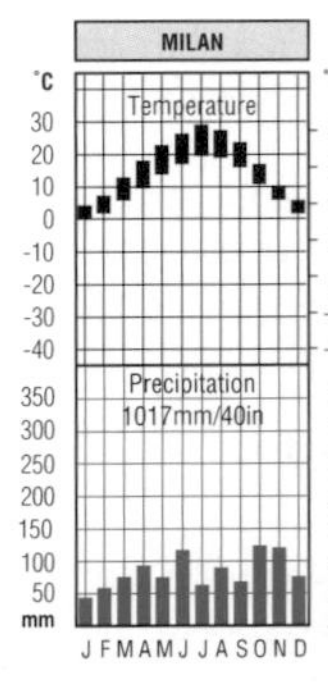

Although the plains of Lombardy lie within the Mediterranean basin they have a climate more like that of central Europe, though with hotter summers and warmer winters. Sunshine averages under 5 hours a day, whereas in southern Italy it can average 8 to 10 hours between May and September. Winter is relatively dry and cold with some snow.

IVORY COAST (CÔTE D'IVOIRE)

On independence from France in 1960 this former colony adopted a compromise between the French tricolour and the colours of the Pan-African movement. Orange represents the northern savannas, white is for peace and unity, and green for the forests and agriculture.

GEOGRAPHY Known as the Côte d'Ivoire since 1986, it is located in West Africa with a coastline on the Gulf of Guinea. There are substantial rainforests in the south, although their rate of depletion is rapid. The climate has uniformly high temperatures and humidity.

HISTORY AND POLITICS France came to the region in the 1500s, when traders started buying slaves and ivory. It became a colony in 1893 and part of French West Africa in 1904. In 1960 independence was gained and in 1990 the first multiparty elections were held, returning to power (until his death in 1993) Felix Houphouët-Boigny, Africa's longest-ruling head of state.

ECONOMY The Ivory Coast is the world's largest producer and exporter of cocoa and Africa's biggest producer of coffee. Its free-market economy has attracted many foreign investors.

AREA 322,460 sq km [124,502 sq mls]
POPULATION 14,271,000
CAPITAL (POPULATION) Yamoussoukro (126,000)
GOVERNMENT Multiparty republic
ETHNIC GROUPS Akan 41%, Kru 18%, Voltaic 16%, Malinké 15%, Southern Mande 10%
LANGUAGES French (official), African languages
RELIGIONS Muslim 38%, Christian 38%, traditional beliefs 17%
CURRENCY CFA franc = 100 centimes

JAMAICA

Jamaica's distinctive flag dates from independence from Britain in 1962. The gold stands for the country's natural resources and sunshine, the green for its agriculture and hope for the future, and black for the nation's hardships.

GEOGRAPHY Third largest of the Caribbean islands, Jamaica has a central range culminating in Blue Mountain Peak (2,256 m [7,402 ft]). Called Xaymaca ('land of wood and water') by the Arawak Indians, half the country lies above 300 m [1,000 ft] and moist south-east trade winds bring rain to the mountains. There is a rich variety of tropical and subtropical vegetation.

HISTORY AND POLITICS Britain took Jamaica from the Spaniards in the 17th century and it became a centre of slavery before emancipation in 1838. After independence Michael Manley led a democratic socialist government, which led to some economic growth in the 1980s, but migration, unemployment and underemployment levels remain high.

ECONOMY Tourism and bauxite production are the most important industries, having replaced the traditional sugar trade.

AREA 10,990 sq km [4,243 sq mls]
POPULATION 2,700,000
CAPITAL (POPULATION) Kingston (644,000)
GOVERNMENT Constitutional monarchy
ETHNIC GROUPS Black 76%, Afro-European 15%, East Indian and Afro-East Indian 3%, White 3%
LANGUAGES English (official), English Creole, Hindi, Chinese, Spanish
RELIGIONS Protestant 70%, Roman Catholic 8%
POPULATION DENSITY 246 per sq km [636 per sq ml]

JAPAN

The geographical position of Japan in the East is expressed in the name of the country, Nihon-Koku *(Land of the Rising Sun), and in the flag. Officially adopted in 1870, the simple design had been used by Japanese emperors for many centuries.*

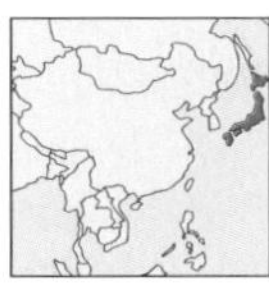

AREA 377,800 sq km [145,869 sq mls]
POPULATION 125,156,000
CAPITAL (POPULATION) Tokyo (11,927,000)
GOVERNMENT Constitutional monarchy with a bicameral legislature

GEOGRAPHY The Japanese archipelago lies off the Asian mainland and 98% of the territory is on four large and closely grouped islands (Hokkaido, Honshu, Shikoku and Kyushu), the remainder being made up of some 4,000 smaller islands. Japan is predominantly mountainous and only 16% of the land is cultivable; this small area of land must support the eighth largest population in the world. The islands are located in one of the Earth's zones of geological instability, meaning volcanic eruptions and earthquakes are frequent. The folding and faulting has produced a wide variety of landforms.

HISTORY AND POLITICS Early Japanese development saw the arrival of many immigrants from Korea and elsewhere in Asia, so that by the 5th century BC the country was divided into numerous clans. The Japanese imperial dynasty emerged from about AD 200 and government was conducted in the name of the emperor by warrior leaders (*shoguns*). Modern Japan has seen the power of the emperor reduced, with rapid industrialization and the growth of overseas colonies in the early 20th century; after World War II there was a period of US administration, during which many reforms were enacted, until 1952.

ECONOMY The Japanese boom of the late 20th century gave Japan the world's second most powerful economy, leading world markets in high-technology and electronic equipment. Its huge trade surpluses have caused some resentment worldwide.

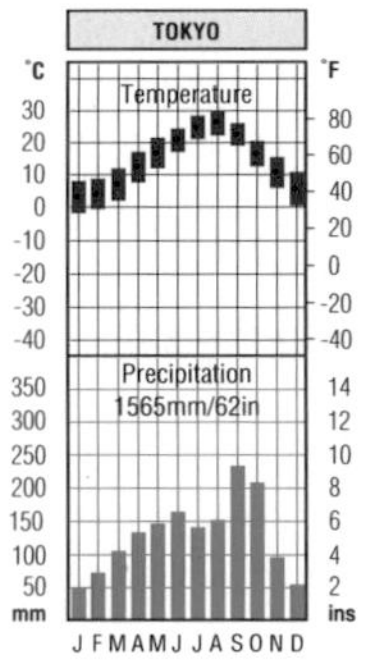

Despite its maritime location, Tokyo has a large annual range of temperature (23°C [41°F]) due to the seasonal reversal of wind, blowing from the cold heart of Asia in winter and from the warm Pacific in the summer. Winter weather is usually fine and sunny with some frost, while summer in Tokyo is hot and humid with abundant rainfall.

JORDAN

Green, white and black are the colours of the three tribes that led the Arab Revolt against the Turks in 1917, while red is the colour of the Hussein dynasty. The star was added in 1928 with its seven points representing the first seven verses of the Koran.

AREA 89,210 sq km [34,444 sq mls]
POPULATION 5,547,000
CAPITAL (POPULATION) Amman (1,300,000)
GOVERNMENT Constitutional monarchy with a bicameral legislature
ETHNIC GROUPS Arab 99%, (Palestinian 60%)
LANGUAGES Arabic (official)
RELIGIONS Sunni Muslim 93%, Christian 5%
CURRENCY Jordan dinar = 1,000 fils
MAIN EXPORTS Potash, phosphates, citrus fruits, vegetables
POPULATION DENSITY 62 per sq km [161 per sq ml]
URBAN POPULATION 70% of population

GEOGRAPHY Jordan lies to the east of Israel and some 87% of the land is desert. There is a small stretch of Red Sea coast centred on the important port of Aqaba, and fertile uplands are found above the rift valley that contains the River Jordan and the Dead Sea along the border with Israel.

HISTORY AND POLITICS After World War I the Arab territories of the Ottoman Empire were divided up and Jordan (known as Transjordan until 1949) passed from Turkish to British control. In 1946 it became independent and in 1948 acquired the crucial Palestinian West Bank area, but lost it to Israel in the 1967 Arab-Israeli war. In 1988 King Hussein renounced all responsibility for the West Bank, but ten UN refugee camps for Palestinians are located within Jordan and 60% of the population is Palestinian. There have been signs of political progress with martial law lifted in 1991 after 21 years.

ECONOMY Only 5% of the land is cultivable and the 1967 war deprived Jordan of 80% of its fruit-growing area (the West Bank). The limited agricultural base (including tomatoes, olives, barley and wheat) and few natural resources are supported by the mining of phosphates and potash, the main exports.

KAZAKSTAN

The flag of Kazakstan was adopted on 4 June 1992. The soaring eagle and the golden sun represent the love of freedom and the blue represents the cloudless skies. There is also a hoist-based vertical strip of golden ornamentation.

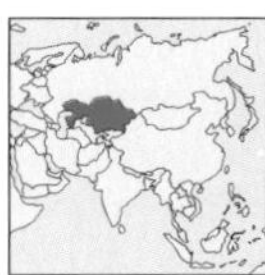

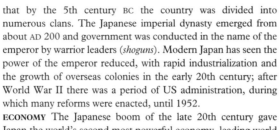

AREA 2,717,300 sq km [1,049,150 sq mls]
POPULATION 17,099,000
CAPITAL (POPULATION) Alma-Ata (1,198,000)
GOVERNMENT Multiparty republic
ETHNIC GROUPS Kazak 41%, Russian 37%, German 5%, Ukrainian 5%, Uzbek, Tatar
LANGUAGES Kazak, Russian
RELIGIONS Sunni Muslim, Christian
CURRENCY Tenge = 500 rubles
MAIN INDUSTRIES Oil refining (notably for aviation fuel), metallurgy, engineering, chemicals, footwear
POPULATION DENSITY 6 per sq km [16 per sq ml]
URBAN POPULATION 58% of population

GEOGRAPHY Kazakstan is a huge country, ninth largest in the world, and comprises mainly vast plains with a (mineral-rich) central plateau. North to south the steppe gradually gives way to desert. The climate is continental with hot summers and very cold winters.

HISTORY AND POLITICS Successive Soviet regimes have used Kazakstan as a dumping-ground and test-bed (for nuclear weapons) and the Aral Sea has shrunk by 70% after Soviet irrigation projects dried up its two feeder rivers. However, in 1991 it led the Central Asian states into the new Commonwealth of States (CIS) as an independent republic and has now emerged as a powerful country, wealthier and more diversified than the other Asian republics.

ECONOMY There are rich deposits of oil and gas, as well as coal, iron ore, bauxite and gold, and rapid industrialization (for example, chemical and footwear industries) has taken place in recent years. Agriculture is mostly concentrated on livestock rearing, although there is quite substantial grain production.

KENYA

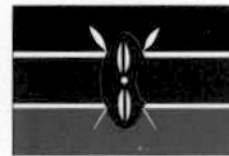

The Kenyan flag, which dates from independence from Britain in 1963, is based on the flag of the Kenya African National Union, which led the colonial struggle. The Masai warrior's shield and crossed spears represent the defence of freedom.

AREA 580,370 sq km [224,081 sq mls]
POPULATION 28,240,000
CAPITAL (POPULATION) Nairobi (2,000,000)
GOVERNMENT Multiparty republic with a unicameral legislature
ETHNIC GROUPS Kikuyu 18%, Luhya 12%, Luo 11%, Kamba 10%, Kalenjin 10%
LANGUAGES Swahili and English (both official), Kikuyu, over 200 tribal languages
RELIGIONS Christian 73% (Roman Catholic 27%, Protestant 19%, others 27%), African indigenous 19%, Muslim 6%
CURRENCY Kenyan shilling = 100 cents
POPULATION DENSITY 49 per sq km [126 per sq ml]
URBAN POPULATION 25% of population
LAND USE Arable 4%, grass 67%

GEOGRAPHY Lying on the Equator, most of Kenya comprises plains cut across old crystalline rocks. The Kenya Highlands were formed by volcanoes and lava flows, with Mt Kenya at 5,199 m [17,000 ft], and are bisected by the Great Rift Valley. Some 80% of the population live on about 15% of the plains in the south-west, where average rainfalls of over 750 mm [30 in] a year support the dense farming populations. The climate is tropical, but greatly affected by altitude; for example, in summer, Nairobi is 10°C [18°F] cooler than Mombasa on the coast.

HISTORY AND POLITICS Kenya has been known as the 'cradle of mankind' since the discovery of the earliest human bones on the shores of Lake Turkana. It had one of the world's highest birth rates (47 per 1,000) but has made substantial efforts to reduce this in recent years. The first multiparty elections for 26 years were held in 1992, although Daniel arap Moi was re-elected amid allegations of vote-rigging.

ECONOMY By some African standards and even being such a large aid recipient, Kenya has a fairly stable economy. About 80% of the population work in agriculture, producing crops such as maize, coffee, tea (Kenya is the world's fourth largest producer) and sisal. Tourism is now a very important source of foreign exchange, with many game parks and beach resorts.

KIRIBATI

The flag is a banner of the arms granted to the Gilbert and Ellice Islands in 1937 and was adopted on independence in 1979. Kiribati is the sole Commonwealth country to use an armorial banner, that is, a flag whose design corresponds exactly to the shield of its arms.

AREA 728 sq km [281 sq mls]
POPULATION 80,000
CAPITAL (POPULATION) Tarawa (20,000)
GOVERNMENT Multiparty republic
ETHNIC GROUPS Micronesian
LANGUAGES English (official), Gilbertese
RELIGIONS Roman Catholic 53%, Protestant 51%
CURRENCY Australian dollar
URBAN POPULATION 39% of population

Known as the Gilbert Islands until independence from Britain in 1979, Kiribati comprises three groups of coral atolls scattered over 5 million sq km [2 million sq mls] of the Pacific Ocean. Very little of the islands rises over 4 m [13 ft] and temperatures are always high. The main crops are coconuts, bananas, papayas and taro (*babai* – the staple vegetable), and the main export is copra. There is a heavy dependency on foreign aid and a real problem of overcrowding.

KOREA, NORTH

The Korean Democratic People's Republic has flown this flag since the country was split into two separate states in 1948. The colours are those of the traditional Korean standard, but in a new Communist design with a red star.

AREA 120,540 sq km [46,540 sq mls]
POPULATION 23,931,000
CAPITAL (POPULATION) Pyongyang (2,639,000)
GOVERNMENT Single-party socialist republic
ETHNIC GROUPS Korean 99%
LANGUAGES Korean (official), Chinese
RELIGIONS Traditional beliefs 16%, Chondogyo 14%, Buddhist 2%, Christian 1%
CURRENCY North Korean won = 100 chon
POPULATION DENSITY 199 per sq km [514 per sq ml]

GEOGRAPHY North Korea covers the northern half of the Korean peninsula (with 55% of the land area) and has a largely mountainous landscape. Only 20% of the surface area is suitable for cultivation and the climate can be harsh, with long and severe winters. Coniferous and broadleaf forests cover some two-thirds of the country.

HISTORY AND POLITICS After World War II Korea split into North and South and the Soviet Union installed a Stalinist regime in the North. In the Korean War of 1950–3 North Korea was supported by China and a demilitarized zone was established between North and South. Despite the death of the dictator Kim Il Sung in July 1994, the country remains isolated.

ECONOMY 90% of cultivated land is under the control of co-operative farms and four out of every ten North Koreans work on the land. There are rich deposits of minerals, including coal, which supplies 70% of energy needs.

KOREA, SOUTH

Adopted in 1950, South Korea's flag is the traditional white of peace. The central emblem signifies nature's opposing forces: the black symbols stand for the four seasons, the points of the compass, and the Sun, Moon, Earth and Heaven.

AREA 99,020 sq km [38,232 sq mls]
POPULATION 45,088,000
CAPITAL (POPULATION) Seoul (11,641,000)
GOVERNMENT Unitary multiparty republic
ETHNIC GROUPS Korean 99%
LANGUAGES Korean (official)
RELIGIONS Buddhist 28%, Protestant 19%, Roman Catholic 6%, Confucian 1%
CURRENCY South Korean won = 100 chon
MAIN EXPORTS Transport equipment 11%, electrical machinery 9%, footwear 6%, textile fabrics 5%
MAIN IMPORTS Petroleum and petroleum products 11%, electronic components 6%
POPULATION DENSITY 455 per sq km [1,179 per sq ml]

GEOGRAPHY South Korea has a smaller land area than North Korea but about twice as many people. The landscape is mostly made up of highlands (the Taebaek Mountains), with an eastern coastline that is steep and largely uninhabited and a western coastline that is indented, with many islands and natural harbours. Summers are hot and wet, and winters are cold and dry with strong north-westerly winds blowing from central Asia.

HISTORY AND POLITICS Before partition Korea was known as the 'Land of the Morning Calm' and was very much a united kingdom. After the civil war at the beginning of the 1950s, South Korea had a very different development to North Korea. An economic miracle based on slender natural resources and cheap and plentiful labour transformed the economy and made South Korea into one of the strongest countries in Asia (the economy grew at nearly 9% a year between 1960 and 1990).

ECONOMY South Korea is now a world leader in the manufacture of footwear and consumer electronics and in shipbuilding. The manufacturing base of textiles remains important, as does agriculture; rice is the main crop and South Korea's fishing fleet is ninth in the world, with, for example, catches of oysters.

KUWAIT

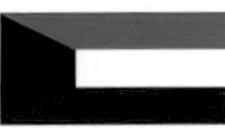

Kuwait's national flag dates from 1961, when the country ceased to be a British protectorate and gained its independence. The flag features the four Pan-Arab colours, the black portion having an unusual trapezium shape.

AREA 17,820 sq km [6,880 sq mls]
POPULATION 1,668,000
CAPITAL (POPULATION) Kuwait City (189,000)
GOVERNMENT Constitutional monarchy
ETHNIC GROUPS Kuwaiti Arab 44%, non-Kuwaiti Arab 36%, various Asian 20%
LANGUAGES Arabic 78%, Kurdish 10%, Farsi 4%
RELIGIONS Muslim 90% (Sunni 63%), Christian 8%, Hindu 2%
CURRENCY Kuwaiti dinar = 1,000 fils

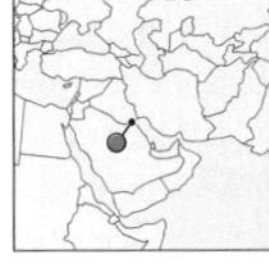

GEOGRAPHY Kuwait lies at the northern end of the Arabian Gulf, and is largely made up of desert, with a climate of high summer temperatures and little rainfall.

HISTORY, POLITICS AND ECONOMY A former British protectorate, Kuwait became fully independent in 1961. Its oil reserves are the third largest in the world and have made it very prosperous. However, in 1990 Iraq invaded Kuwait and claimed it as its own. A multinational force liberated Kuwait in January 1991, but not before almost all industrial and commercial installations had been destroyed and the Iraqis had set fire to more than 500 oil-wells. In spite of the devastation, oil and gas production remains the mainstay of the Kuwaiti economy.

KYRGYZSTAN

The flag was adopted in March 1992 and depicts a bird's-eye view of a yurt *within a radiant sun. The* yurt *stands for the ancient nomadic way of life and the rays of the sun for the 40 traditional tribes.*

AREA 198,500 sq km [76,640 sq mls]
POPULATION 4,738,000
CAPITAL (POPULATION) Bishkek (597,000)
GOVERNMENT Multiparty republic
ETHNIC GROUPS Kyrgyz 53%, Russian 22%, Uzbek 13%, Ukrainian 3%, Tatar 2%, German 2%
LANGUAGES Kyrgyz and Russian (both official)
RELIGIONS Sunni Muslim, Christian
CURRENCY Som = 100 tyiyn
URBAN POPULATION 39% of population

GEOGRAPHY Kyrgyzstan is geographically isolated and mainly mountainous, dominated by the western end of the Tian Shan, with peaks rising to the 7,439 m [24,405 ft] of Pik Pobedy.

HISTORY AND POLITICS 'European'-style policies towards a capitalist democracy have been pursued since independence in 1991. The president, Askar Akayev (re-elected in 1996), has encouraged rapid privatization and foreign trade and has established important links with China.

ECONOMY Kyrgyzstan has a strong agricultural economy producing such crops as cotton, tobacco, mulberry trees and sugar beet. The main manufacturing industry is textiles and there are large reserves of uranium, mercury and gold.

LAOS

Since 1975 Laos has flown the flag of the Pathet Lao, the Communist movement which won the long struggle for control of the country. The blue stands for the Mekong River, the white disc for the moon, the red for the unity and purpose of the people.

GEOGRAPHY Laos is a narrow, landlocked, largely mountainous country in South-east Asia, with no railways – the Mekong River is the main artery. The hilly terrain broadens in the north to a wide plateau, 2,000 m [6,500 ft] above sea level. The climate is affected by the seasonal reversal of winds associated with the monsoon, with a wet season between April and October.

HISTORY AND POLITICS Laos became a French protectorate in 1893 and was ruled as part of Indochina. Independence was granted in 1954, after which followed two decades of civil war. The Communists took power in 1975 and some reforms began in 1986, but Laos remains one of Asia's poorest countries and there is little chance of a multiparty democracy very soon.

ECONOMY Some 85% of the sparse population work on collective farms at subsistence level, growing mainly rice.

AREA 236,800 sq km [91,428 sq mls]
POPULATION 4,906,000
CAPITAL (POPULATION) Vientiane (449,000)
GOVERNMENT Single-party socialist republic with a unicameral legislature
ETHNIC GROUPS Lao 67%, Palaung-Wa 12%, Thai 8%, Man 5%
LANGUAGES Laotian (official), French
RELIGIONS Buddhist 58%, tribal religionist 34%, Christian 2%, Muslim 1%
CURRENCY Kip = 100 at
POPULATION DENSITY 21 per sq km [54 per sq ml]

LATVIA

The burgundy and white Latvian flag, revived after independence from the USSR in 1991, dates back to at least 1280. According to one legend, it was first made from a white sheet stained with the blood of a Latvian hero who was wrapped in it.

GEOGRAPHY Its Baltic coast heavily indented by the Gulf of Riga, Latvia is a small country of flat glaciated lowland. The land is covered by coniferous forests and lakes. The climate has long, cold winters and short summers, the warmest months being June to August, when temperatures may rise over 15°C [59°F].

HISTORY AND POLITICS The native Latvians (Letts) have a long history and highly developed culture, with nationalist move-ments dating to the late 19th century. Over 100 years later, Latvia became independent from the Soviet Union in 1991 and had joined the UN by the end of the year, together with the two other Baltic states (Estonia and Lithuania). Strong ties with Russia and the Ukraine remain, especially for energy supplies.

ECONOMY Latvia contains many of the less traditional former Soviet industries, such as electronics and consumer goods.

AREA 64,589 sq km [24,938 sq mls]
POPULATION 2,558,000
CAPITAL (POPULATION) Riga (840,000)
GOVERNMENT Multiparty republic
ETHNIC GROUPS Latvian 54%, Russian 33%, Belarussian 4%, Ukrainian 3%, Polish 2%
LANGUAGES Latvian (official) 54%, Russian 40%
RELIGIONS Christian (Lutheran, Catholic, Orthodox)
POPULATION DENSITY 40 per sq km [103 per sq ml]

LEBANON

Adopted on independence in 1943, Lebanon's colours are those of the Lebanese Legion in World War I. The cedar tree, many of which grow in the country's mountains, has been a Lebanese symbol since biblical times. The colours of the cedar tree were slightly altered in 1996.

GEOGRAPHY Lebanon is located on the eastern shores of the Mediterranean, with the Lebanon Mountains rising behind a narrow coastal plain, and the fertile land of the Beqaa Valley covering much of central Lebanon.

HISTORY AND POLITICS Lebanon was originally part of the Ottoman Empire, before coming under French rule in 1918. Independence was granted in 1944 and there followed three decades of relative peace and prosperity. Beirut, the capital, was a centre of international commerce and a playground for the wealthy. However, in 1975 civil war broke out between the Christians, Muslims and Druses and plunged Lebanon into chaos, with frequent bombings, assassinations and kidnappings, made more complicated by the involvement of Israeli troops, Palestinians, the Syrian army and the UN. Israel still occupies the south of the country from where it launched a military offensive, with heavy civilian casualties, against Hezbollah in April 1996 in retaliation for rocket attacks by this group on northern Israel.

ECONOMY The economy has been severely damaged by the war.

AREA 10,400 sq km [4,015 sq mls]
POPULATION 2,971,000
CAPITAL (POPULATION) Beirut (1,500,000)
GOVERNMENT Multiparty republic
ETHNIC GROUPS Arab 93% (Lebanese 83%, Palestinian 10%), Armenian 5%
LANGUAGES Arabic and French (official), English, Armenian
RELIGIONS Muslim 57%, Christian 40%, Druse 3%
CURRENCY Lebanese pound = 100 piastres
POPULATION DENSITY 286 per sq km [740 per sq ml]
MAIN EXPORTS Clothing, jewellery, aluminium and pharmaceutical products

LESOTHO

In 1987 this succeeded the flag adopted on independence from Britain in 1966. The white, blue and green represent peace, rain and prosperity – the words of the national motto. The emblem comprises a shield, knobkerrie and ostrich feather sceptre.

Consisting mainly of a high mountainous plateau deeply fretted by the headwaters of the Orange (Oranje) River, Lesotho declines altitudinally from east to west. The higher ridges are treeless and the steep valleys suffer from an excess of water, making the land boggy in summer and frozen in winter. This physical environment and the presence on all sides of South Africa causes major political and economic problems for Lesotho. Most of the population survive on subsistence farming and there is migration to the small towns or to the mines in South Africa to look for work. Tourism is developing.

AREA 30,350 sq km [11,718 sq mls]
POPULATION 2,064,000
CAPITAL (POPULATION) Maseru (367,000)
GOVERNMENT Constitutional monarchy
ETHNIC GROUPS Sotho 85%, Zulu 15%
LANGUAGES Sesotho and English (both official)
RELIGIONS Christian 93% (Roman Catholic 44%)
POPULATION DENSITY 68 per sq km [176 per sq ml]

LIBERIA

Liberia was founded in the early 19th century as an American colony for freed black slaves. The flag, based on the American flag, was adopted on independence in 1847, with its 11 red and white stripes representing the 11 men who signed the Liberian declaration of independence.

GEOGRAPHY Liberia is West Africa's oldest independent state. Sparsely populated, it has large tracts of inaccessible tropical rainforest, with a coastal plain made up of swamps and savanna.

HISTORY, POLITICS AND ECONOMY Liberia became an inde-pendent republic in 1847, thus lacking a legacy of colonial administration. In 1989 civil war broke out when a force invaded from the Ivory Coast. The president was assassinated and conflicts broke out between the rebel forces, with peacekeeping forces from five West African countries unable to stop the fight-ing. In 1995 a cease-fire was finally agreed and a council of state was set up, but the fighting flared up again in early 1996. The largely agricultural economy has been devastated by the civil war.

AREA 111,370 sq km [43,000 sq mls]
POPULATION 3,092,000
CAPITAL (POPULATION) Monrovia (490,000)
GOVERNMENT Multiparty republic
ETHNIC GROUPS Kpelle 19%, Bassa 14%, Grebo 9%, Gio 8%, Kru 7%, Mano 7%
LANGUAGES English (official), Mande, West Atlantic, Kwa
RELIGIONS Christian 68%, traditional beliefs 18%, Muslim 14%
POPULATION DENSITY 28 per sq km [72 per sq ml]

LIBYA

The simplest of all world flags, Libya's flag represents the nation's quest for a green revolution in agriculture. Libya flew the flag of the Federation of Arab Republics until 1977, when it left the organization.

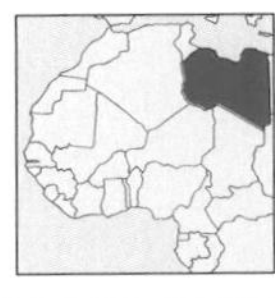

GEOGRAPHY Located in North Africa with a coastline on the Mediterranean, Libya has a mainly desert environment with a largely nomadic population. The climate on the coast has less extreme temperatures and higher rainfall than inland.

HISTORY AND POLITICS Italy controlled Libya from 1912 until it was defeated in World War II and lost the colony. In 1951 it became an independent monarchy under King Idris. In 1969 a group of 12 army officers overthrew the king in a coup and control passed to the Revolutionary Command Council under Colonel Gaddafi, with pro-Palestinian and anti-Western policies and continual disputes with Libya's neighbours.

ECONOMY Until 1959, when vast reserves of oil and natural gas were discovered, Libya was very poor. Since then standards of living have risen dramatically.

AREA 1,759,540 sq km [679,358 sq mls]
POPULATION 5,410,000
CAPITAL (POPULATION) Tripoli (960,000)
GOVERNMENT Single-party socialist state
ETHNIC GROUPS Arab-Berber 89%
LANGUAGES Arabic, Berber
RELIGIONS Sunni Muslim 97%
CURRENCY Libyan dinar = 1,000 dirhams
POPULATION DENSITY 3 per sq km [8 per sq ml]
MAIN EXPORTS Oil, natural gas
URBAN POPULATION 84% of population
LAND USE Arable 1%, grass 8%

LIECHTENSTEIN

The colours of Liechtenstein's flag originated in the early part of the 19th century. The gold crown, often rotated 90° so that the flag can be hung vertically, was added in 1937 to avoid confusion with the flag then used by Haiti.

Standing at the end of the eastern Alps between Austria and Switzerland, the tiny state of Liechtenstein became an independent principality within the Holy Roman Empire in 1719. Since 1923 Liechtenstein has been in customs and currency union with Switzerland, which also provides overseas representation, but it does retain full sovereignty in other spheres. It is particularly known abroad for its postage stamps and as a haven for international companies, with low taxation and strict, secretive banking codes. Tourism has been increasing over recent years as has a growth in specialized manufacturing.

AREA 157 sq km [61 sq mls]
POPULATION 31,000
CAPITAL (POPULATION) Vaduz (5,067)
GOVERNMENT Principality
ETHNIC GROUPS Alemannic 95%
LANGUAGES German, Alemannic dialects
RELIGIONS Roman Catholic 81%, Protestant 7%
CURRENCY Swiss franc
POPULATION DENSITY 197 per sq km [508 per sq ml]

LITHUANIA

The flag was created in 1918, at the birth of the independent republic; it was suppressed after the Soviet annexation in 1940, and restored in November 1988. The colours are reputed to represent Lithuania's rich forests and agricultural wealth.

Lithuania is the largest and most populous of the Baltic States, with a landscape consisting mostly of a low, glaciated but fairly fertile central plain. In the east of the country is an area of forested sandy ridges, dotted with lakes. Lithuania was the first of the former Soviet republics to declare itself an independent, non-Communist country in March 1990. This resulted in the occupation of much of Vilnius by Soviet troops and a crippling economic blockade. The situation improved under the presidency of Vytautas Landsbergis, who was later defeated by Algirdas Brazauskas in elections in 1992. There are a range of industries, many of them the most advanced in the former Soviet Union, including timber, fertilizers and plastics.

AREA 65,200 sq km [25,200 sq mls]
POPULATION 3,735,000
CAPITAL (POPULATION) Vilnius (576,000)
GOVERNMENT Multiparty republic
ETHNIC GROUPS Lithuanian 81%, Russian 9%, Polish 7%, Belarussian 2%
LANGUAGES Lithuanian 70%, Russian 30%
RELIGIONS Christian
CURRENCY Litas = 100 centai
POPULATION DENSITY 57 per sq km [148 per sq ml]
URBAN POPULATION 57% population

LUXEMBOURG

Luxembourg's colours are taken from the Grand Duke's 14th-century coat of arms. The Grand Duchy's flag is almost identical to that of the Netherlands, but the blue stripe is a lighter shade and the flag itself is longer.

GEOGRAPHY Located in central Europe and bordered by France, Germany and Belgium, Luxembourg consists partly of the picturesque Ardennes region in the north, well wooded and famed for its deer and wild boar. Further south the land is flatter and more fertile. The climate is fairly mild with some rain, making it ideal for farming.

HISTORY AND POLITICS Declaring itself a Grand Duchy in 1354, Luxembourg was ruled by Spain and then Austria until 1795. It was then annexed by France before becoming part of the Netherlands in 1815. Part of the Grand Duchy was taken by Belgium in 1831 and the rest became independent in 1839. It is now the only one out of hundreds of independent duchies, which once comprised much of continental Europe, still surviving. In 1922 Luxembourg formed an economic union with Belgium, which was extended in 1944 to include the Netherlands under the composite name of Benelux. Luxembourg was a founder member of NATO in 1949 and of the EEC in 1957 and therefore plays an important part in Western European affairs.

ECONOMY Stock-rearing, especially of dairy cattle, is important, and crops include grains, potatoes, roots and fruit, and vines in the Moselle Valley. There is also a prosperous iron and steel industry based on rich iron-ore deposits.

AREA 2,590 sq km [1,000 sq mls]
POPULATION 408,000
CAPITAL (POPULATION) Luxembourg (76,500)
GOVERNMENT Constitutional monarchy with a bicameral legislature
ETHNIC GROUPS Luxembourger 70%, Portuguese 11%, Italian 5%, French 4%, German 2%, Belgian 1%
LANGUAGES Letzeburgish (Luxembourgian – official), French, German
RELIGIONS Roman Catholic 94%
CURRENCY Luxembourg franc = 100 centimes
POPULATION DENSITY 158 per sq km [408 per sq ml]
MAIN EXPORTS Base metals, plastic and rubber manufactures

MACAU

Portugal declared Macau independent from China in 1849, and a century later proclaimed it an Overseas Province. This new flag for Macau replaces that of Portugal in the run-up to retrocession to China, on 20 December 1999.

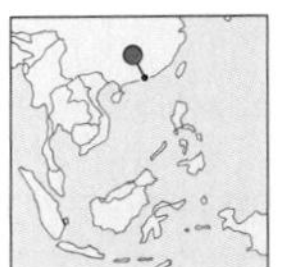

Macau is a peninsula at the head of the Zhu Jiang (Pearl) River, 64 km [40 mls] west of Hong Kong and connected to China by a narrow isthmus. As a Portuguese colony from 1557, Macau was for 200 years one of the great trading centres for silk, gold, spices and opium. In 1979 the status of Macau was redefined as a 'Chinese territory under Portuguese administration' and in 1987 it was agreed that the territory will return to China in 1999 as a Special Administrative Region. Its main industries are textiles and tourism but Macau is heavily reliant on China for water, food and raw materials. A new $1 billion airport opened in 1995.

AREA 16 sq km [6 sq mls]
POPULATION 490,000
GOVERNMENT Overseas Territory of Portugal
ETHNIC GROUPS Chinese 95%, Portuguese 3%
LANGUAGES Cantonese, Portuguese
RELIGIONS Buddhist 45%, Roman Catholic 7%
POPULATION DENSITY 30,625 per sq km [81,667 per sq ml]

MACEDONIA

Macedonia's flag was first introduced in August 1992 but was altered by parliamentary decree on 5 October 1995. The effect was to replace the 'Star of Vergina' on the previous flag with a modified form of sunburst. This follows a treaty with Greece, who had objected to the star.

With a northern frontier dangerously contiguous with Serbia's troubled Kosovo region, Macedonia has so far avoided the long-running and devastating civil war that has marked the disintegration of the former Yugoslavia. It is a landlocked and mountainous country surrounded by Greece, Bulgaria and Albania. International recognition proved difficult to obtain at first, since Greece vetoed any acknowledgement of an independent Macedonia. Diplomatic relations with Greece were assumed in 1995 when Greece recognized the Former Yugoslav Republic of Macedonia (FYROM) as an independent country.

AREA 25,710 sq km [9,927 sq mls]
POPULATION 2,173,000
CAPITAL (POPULATION) Skopje (563,000)
ETHNIC GROUPS Macedonian 65%, Albanian 21%
LANGUAGES Macedonian 70%, Albanian 21%, Turkish, Serbo-Croat
RELIGIONS Eastern Orthodox, Muslim
CURRENCY Dinar = 100 paras
POPULATION DENSITY 87 per sq km [226 per sq ml]

MADAGASCAR

Madagascar's colours are those of historical flags of South-east Asia, from where the island's first inhabitants came before AD 1000. The present flag was adopted in 1958 when the country first became a republic after French rule.

GEOGRAPHY The world's fourth largest island, Madagascar has a huge variety of physical, ecological and cultural features. Most geological eras are represented and made more vivid by steep faulting and deeply-trenched valleys. The coasts are hostile, with little natural shelter, and the climate is varied, from hot and wet in the north and east to arid in the south and south-west.

HISTORY AND POLITICS Separated from the African mainland for more than 50 million years, Madagascar contains a distinct flora and fauna and mixture of peoples. A monarchy existed before French occupation in 1895, and after independence in 1958 the government continued the links with France until 1975 when Didier Ratsiraka seized power and established a dictatorial socialist one-party state, plunging Madagascar into poverty. He was defeated in elections in 1993 but was re-elected in 1997.

ECONOMY Two-thirds of the world's vanilla is produced here, along with other crops of coffee, sugar, spices and essential oils. With 90% of its forest gone (it once covered most of the island), Madagascar is today one of the most eroded places in the world.

AREA 587,040 sq km [226,656 sq mls]
POPULATION 15,206,000
CAPITAL (POPULATION) Antananarivo (1,053,000)
GOVERNMENT Unitary republic with a bicameral legislature
ETHNIC GROUPS Merina 26%, Betsimisaraka 15%, Betsileo 12%
LANGUAGES Malagasy, French, English
RELIGIONS Christian 51% (Roman Catholic 28%), traditional beliefs 47%, Muslim 2%
CURRENCY Malagasy franc = 100 centimes
POPULATION DENSITY 26 per sq km [67 per sq ml]

MADEIRA

The emblem in the flag is the cross of the Order of Christ, which inspired the colonization of the islands in the 15th century. The flag was adopted in 1978.

Madeira is the largest of the group of picturesque volcanic islands of that name lying 550 km [350 mls] from the Moroccan coast in the Atlantic Ocean and 900 km [560 mls] south-west of the national Portuguese capital, Lisbon. Porto Santo and the uninhabited Ilhas Selvagens and Sesertas complete the group. With a warm temperate climate and good soils, Madeira was originally forested, but early settlers cleared the uplands for plantations. Tourism is now very important to the economy.

AREA 813 sq km [314 sq mls]
POPULATION 300,000
CAPITAL (POPULATION) Funchal (45,000)
GOVERNMENT Portuguese Autonomous Region
LANGUAGES Portuguese
RELIGIONS Roman Catholic
CURRENCY Portuguese escudo
POPULATION DENSITY 369 per sq km [955 per sq ml]

MALAWI

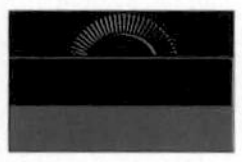

The colours in Malawi's flag come from the flag adopted by the Malawi Congress Party in 1953. The rising sun symbol, representing the beginning of a new era for Malawi and Africa, was added when the country gained independence from Britain in 1964.

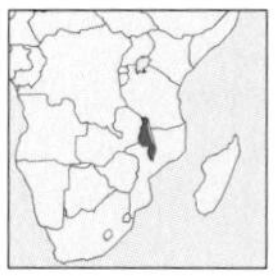

GEOGRAPHY A small and hilly country, Malawi is nowhere more than 160 km [100 mls] wide and was derived from a 19th-century missionaries' and traders' route up the Zambezi, Shire and Lake Nyasa (Malawi). The climate around the lake is very hot and humid, with cooler conditions in the south.

HISTORY AND POLITICS Malawi's recent history has been dominated by one man, Dr Hastings Kamuzu Banda, who led the country to independence in 1964 and then declared a one-party republic, with himself as president for life, in 1971. At first successful in helping the economy, his austere regime saw a return to poverty and a high incidence of AIDS in the late 1980s. In 1993 there was a return to a multiparty system, and in the 1994 presidential elections Banda was defeated by Bakili Muluzi.

ECONOMY Agriculture is the mainstay of the economy.

AREA 118,480 sq km [45,745 sq mls]
POPULATION 9,800,000
CAPITAL (POPULATION) Lilongwe (268,000)
GOVERNMENT Multiparty republic
ETHNIC GROUPS Maravi 58%, Lomwe 18%, Yao 13%, Ngoni 7%
LANGUAGES Chichewa, English
RELIGIONS Christian 64%, Muslim 16%, Animist
CURRENCY Kwacha = 100 tambala
POPULATION DENSITY 83 per sq km [214 per sq ml]
MAIN EXPORTS Tobacco, tea and sugar

MALAYSIA

The red and white bands date back to a revolt in the 13th century. The star and crescent are symbols of Islam; the blue represents Malaysia's role in the Commonwealth. This version of the flag was first flown after federation in 1963.

GEOGRAPHY The present federation of Malaysia comprises 11 states and a federal territory (Kuala Lumpur) on the Malay Peninsula, and two states and a federal territory (Labuan) in northern Borneo. The Peninsula is dominated by fold mountains with a north-south axis. There are seven or eight ranges, with frequently exposed granite cores. The natural vegetation of most of Malaysia is lowland rainforest and its montane variants.

HISTORY AND POLITICS In the 15th century Malay political power was at its peak with the rise of the kingdom of Malacca, which controlled the important sea routes and trade of the region. In 1414 the ruler of Malacca accepted the Islamic faith, which remains the official religion today. There is, however, a great diversity of ethnic and religious groups, and tensions have arisen between the politically dominant Muslim Malays and the economically dominant Buddhists, mostly Chinese.

ECONOMY Economic growth has been rapid with rice, plus exports of rubber, palm oil and tin, as the traditional mainstays of the economy, together with a growing tourist industry.

AREA 329,750 sq km [127,316 sq mls]
POPULATION 20,174,000
CAPITAL (POPULATION) Kuala Lumpur (1,145,000)
GOVERNMENT Federal constitutional monarchy with a bicameral legislature
ETHNIC GROUPS Malay 62%, Chinese 30%, Indian 8%
LANGUAGES Malay, Chinese, Tamil, Iban, Dusan, English
RELIGIONS Sunni Muslim 53%, Buddhist 17%, Chinese folk religionist 12%, Hindu 7%, Christian 6%
POPULATION DENSITY 61 per sq km [158 per sq ml]

MALDIVES

The Maldives used to fly a plain red flag until the Islamic green panel with white crescent was added early this century. The present design was officially adopted in 1965, after the British left the islands.

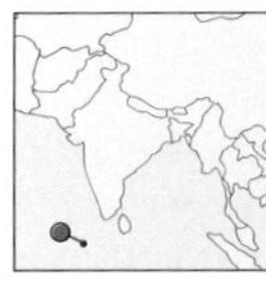

The archipelago of the Maldives comprises over 1,190 small low-lying islands and atolls (202 of them inhabited), scattered along a broad north-south line in the Indian Ocean. The islands were settled from Sri Lanka about 500 BC. They became a British protectorate in 1887, administered from Ceylon (now Sri Lanka) but retaining local sultanates. Independence was achieved in 1965 and the last sultan deposed in 1968. Fishing (for bonito and tuna) and tourism are the main activities.

AREA 298 sq km [115 sq mls]
POPULATION 254,000
CAPITAL (Population) Malé (56,000)
GOVERNMENT Republic with a unicameral legislature
ETHNIC GROUPS Mixture of Sinhalese, Indian and Arab
LANGUAGES Divehi (Sinhala dialect)
RELIGIONS Sunni Muslim
CURRENCY Rufiyaa = 100 laaris

MALI

Adopted on independence from France in 1960, Mali's flag uses the Pan-African colours, employed by the African Democratic Rally, and symbolizing the desire for African unity. Its design is based on the French tricolour.

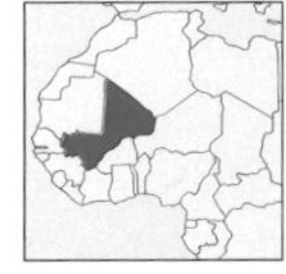

In the 14th century the centre of a huge West African Malinka empire based on the legendary city of Timbuktu, Mali is today a poor, landlocked country consisting mainly of empty Saharan desert plains. Lack of water is a real problem and most of the country's population lives along the Senegal and Niger rivers, which provide water for stock and irrigation and act as communication routes. Millet, cotton and groundnuts are grown on unirrigated land, while rice is grown intensively with irrigation. Industry is very limited. The 23-year repressive regime of Moussa Traoré ended in 1991 after student-led protests.

AREA 1,240,190 sq km [478,837 sq mls]
POPULATION 10,700,000
CAPITAL (Population) Bamako (746,000)
GOVERNMENT Multiparty republic with a unicameral legislature
ETHNIC GROUPS Bambara 32%, Fulani 14%, Senufo 12%, Soninké 9%
LANGUAGES French, languages of the Mande group 60%
RELIGIONS Muslim 90%, traditional Animist beliefs 9%, Christian 1%

MALTA

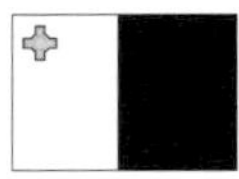

The colours of Malta's flag, adopted on independence in 1964, are those of the Knights of Malta, who ruled the islands from 1530 to 1798. The George Cross was added in 1943 to commemorate the heroism of the Maltese people during World War II.

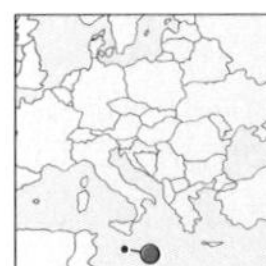

Malta lies in the centre of the Mediterranean, roughly halfway between Gibraltar and Suez and 290 km [180 mls] from North Africa. The three islands of Malta, Comino and Gozo have few natural resources (apart from building stone) and with no rivers and little rainfall, agricultural possibilities are limited. Its strategic importance arises from its position and good natural harbours. The port, wharf and storage facilities at the Kalafrana freeport are important to the economy, as is year-round tourism.

AREA 316 sq km [122 sq mls]
POPULATION 370,000
CAPITAL (Population) Valletta (102,500)
GOVERNMENT Multiparty republic
ETHNIC GROUPS Maltese 96%, English 2%
LANGUAGES Maltese, Arabic, English
RELIGIONS Roman Catholic 96%
CURRENCY Maltese lira = 100 cents
POPULATION DENSITY 1,171 per sq km [3,033 per sq ml]

MARSHALL ISLANDS

The flag dates from 1 May 1979 and has two rays which represent the two chains of islands: Ratik (Sunrise) is in orange and Ralik (Sunset) is in white. The 24 points on the star represent the municipalities of the area, all set against the blue of the Pacific Ocean.

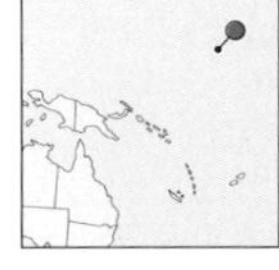

The Marshall Islands comprise over 1,250 islands and atolls – including the former US nuclear testing sites of Bikini and Enewetak – located in the Pacific Ocean. The islands became a republic 'in free association with the USA' in 1986, moving from Trust Territory status to a sovereign state responsible for its own foreign policy but not (until 2001) for its defence and security. The economy, based on agriculture and tourism, is very heavily supported by aid from the USA.

AREA 181 sq km [70 sq mls]
POPULATION 55,000
CAPITAL (Population) Dalap-Uliga-Darrit (20,000)
GOVERNMENT Republic with a unicameral legislature
ETHNIC GROUPS Micronesian
LANGUAGES English, Marshallese dialects, Japanese
RELIGIONS Christian (mainly Protestant)

MARTINIQUE

The appearance of the French tricolour here is a reminder that there are three overseas departments of France in this region: Martinique, Guadeloupe and French Guiana.

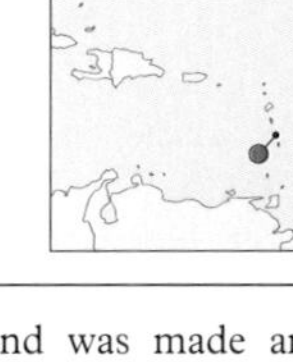

Martinique comprises three groups of volcanic hills and the intervening lowlands in the Caribbean Sea. It was 'discovered' by Columbus in 1493, colonized by France from 1635 and, apart from brief British interludes, has been French ever since. It became an overseas department in 1946 and was made an administrative region in 1974. Bananas (40%), rum and pineapples are the main agricultural exports, but tourism is the biggest earner. Oil products account for another 14% of exports.

AREA 1,100 sq km [425 sq mls]
POPULATION 384,000
CAPITAL (Population) Fort-de-France (102,000)
GOVERNMENT Overseas Department of France
ETHNIC GROUPS Of African descent, Mixed, White
LANGUAGES French, Creole patois
RELIGIONS Roman Catholic 85%

MAURITANIA

The Mauritanian Islamic Republic's flag features the star and the crescent, traditional symbols of the Islamic religion, as is the colour green. It was adopted in 1959, the year before the country gained its independence from France.

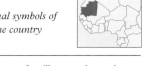

Over two-thirds of Mauritania consists of desert wastes, much of it in the Sahara. Apart from the main north-south highway and routes associated with mineral developments, land communications consist of rough tracks. The only permanent arable agriculture is in the south, concentrated in a narrow strip along the Senegal River. Crops of millet, sorghum, beans, peanuts and rice are grown. The fishing industry, based off the Atlantic coast, is still growing and a new port and capital city have been constructed at Nouakchott. Democratization did not reach Mauritania until the early 1990s when elections were held.

AREA 1,030,700 sq km [412,280 sq mls]
POPULATION 2,268,000
CAPITAL (Population) Nouakchott (600,000)
GOVERNMENT Multiparty Islamic republic
ETHNIC GROUPS Moor (Arab-Berber) 70%, Wolof 7%, Tukulor 5%, Soninké, Fulani
LANGUAGES Arabic, Soninké, Wolof, French
RELIGIONS Sunni Muslim 99%
CURRENCY Ouguiya = 5 khoums

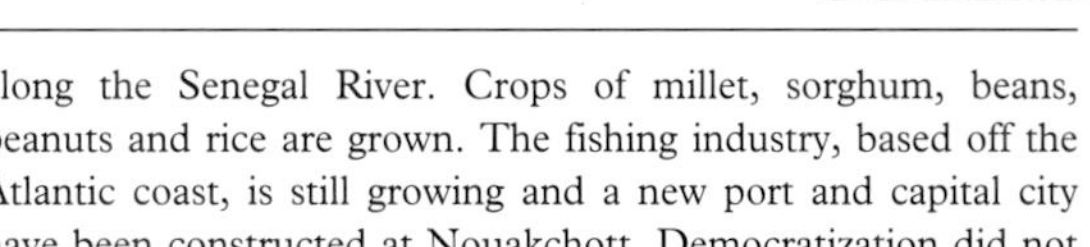

MAURITIUS

The flag of this small island state was adopted on independence from Britain in 1968. Red stands for the struggle for independence, blue for the Indian Ocean, yellow for the bright future, and green for the lush vegetation.

AREA 1,860 sq km [718 sq mls]
POPULATION 1,112,000
CAPITAL (POPULATION) Port Louis (144,000)
GOVERNMENT Multiparty republic with a unicameral legislature
ETHNIC GROUPS Indian 68%, Creole 27%, Chinese 3%, White 2%
LANGUAGES English, Creole, French
RELIGIONS Hindu 51%, Roman Catholic

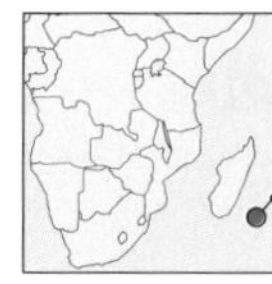

Mauritius consists of the main island, which is fringed with coral reefs, Rodrigues, 20 nearby islets and the dependencies of the Agalega Islands and the tiny Cargados Carajas shoals (St Brandon). French from 1715 and British from 1810, the colony gained independence in 1968. Sugar cane accounts for over 40% of exports and tourism and textiles have become very important.

MEXICO

The stripes on the Mexican flag were inspired by the French tricolour and date from 1821. The emblem of the eagle, snake and cactus is based on an ancient Aztec legend about the founding of Mexico City. The design was adopted for the Olympic year, 1968.

AREA 1,958,200 sq km [756,061 sq mls]
POPULATION 93,342,000
CAPITAL (POPULATION) Mexico City (15,643,000)
GOVERNMENT Federal multiparty republic
ETHNIC GROUPS Mestizo 60%, Amerindian 30%, European 9%
LANGUAGES Spanish 92%, 59 native dialects
RELIGIONS Roman Catholic 90%, Protestant 5%
POPULATION DENSITY 48 per sq km [123 per sq ml]

GEOGRAPHY Mexico is the world's largest and most populous Spanish-speaking nation and is a land of great physical variety. The northern, emptier, half is open basin-and-range country of the Mesa Central; mountains dominate southern Mexico, broken only by the low, narrow isthmus of Tehuantepec. In the south-east is the flat, low-lying Yucatán peninsula.
HISTORY AND POLITICS After independence in 1821 there was a century of political chaos, climaxing in the violent revolution of 1920–21. The PRI was then in power for more than six decades after 1929 and instituted crucial land reforms in the 1930s. There has been a recent resurgence in guerrilla attacks.
ECONOMY Mexico is the world's fifth biggest producer of oil, much of it exported to the USA, but the economy is very diverse with important silver production and also textiles and tourism.

MICRONESIA, FEDERATED STATES OF

The flag was adopted in 1978 when the country broke away from the United States Trust Territory of Micronesia and became the Federated States of Micronesia. The four stars stand for the four states (Kosrai, Pohnpei, Truk and Yap) that remained in the federation.

AREA 705 sq km [272 sq mls]
POPULATION 125,000
CAPITAL Palikir
GOVERNMENT Federal multiparty republic with a unicameral legislature
ETHNIC GROUPS Micronesian, Polynesian
LANGUAGES English, local languages
RELIGIONS Christian
CURRENCY US currency

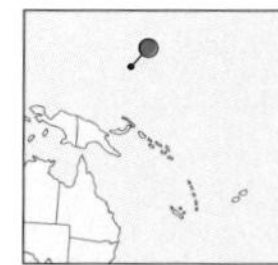

Comprising the bulk of the Caroline Islands, the Federation stretches across more than 2,300 km [2,000 mls] of the Pacific Ocean, with the Equator as the southern boundary. The 607 islands divide into four groups and range from mountains to low atolls. Traditional subsistence farming and fishing are still important, with copra as the main crop and tuna the main export.

MOLDOVA

The flag and eagle are based on those of pre-Communist Romania, and the bull's head is the distinctive emblem of Moldova. The flag was adopted in November 1990. According to the official description, the tricolour represents 'the past, present and future' of Moldova.

AREA 33,700 sq km [13,010 sq mls]
POPULATION 4,434,000
CAPITAL (POPULATION) Chişinău (667,000)
GOVERNMENT Multiparty republic
ETHNIC GROUPS Moldovan 65%, Ukrainian 14%, Russian 13%, Gagauz 4%, Jewish 2%, Bulgarian
LANGUAGES Moldovan 61%, Russian
RELIGIONS Russian Orthodox, Evangelical
CURRENCY Leu = 100 bani

Moldova is the most densely populated of the former Soviet republics and has an ethnically complex society. The majority 'Moldovan' population is Romanian, while there are Gagauz (the Christian Orthodox Turks) in the south and Russians and Ukrainians. Independence from Moscow was declared in August 1991 and multiparty elections were held in February 1994. The economy is fairly prosperous; fertile lands and a tolerant climate provide vines, tobacco and honey. Light industry is expanding.

MONACO

An independent state since AD 980, Monaco has been ruled by the Grimaldi family since 1297. The colours of the flag, which was officially adopted in 1881, come from the Prince of Monaco's coat of arms, which dates to medieval times.

AREA 1.5 sq km [0.6 sq mls]
POPULATION 32,000
CAPITAL Monaco
GOVERNMENT Constitutional monarchy with a unicameral legislature
ETHNIC GROUPS French 47%, Monégasque 16%, Italian 16%
LANGUAGES French, Monégasque
RELIGIONS Roman Catholic 95%
CURRENCY French franc

The tiny principality of Monaco comprises a rocky peninsula and a narrow stretch of coast, but has increased in size by 20% since its land reclamation programme began in 1958. The greater part of it was annexed by France in 1848 and the remainder came under its protection in 1861 – a situation that essentially survives today within a customs union. Its considerable income is mostly derived from services: banking, finance and, especially, tourism; this is based not only on its climate but also on its famous casino.

MONGOLIA

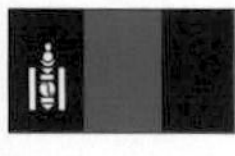

On Mongolia's flag the blue represents the country's national colour. In the hoist is the Golden Soyonbo, a Buddhist symbol, representing freedom. Within this, the flame is seen as a promise of prosperity and progress.

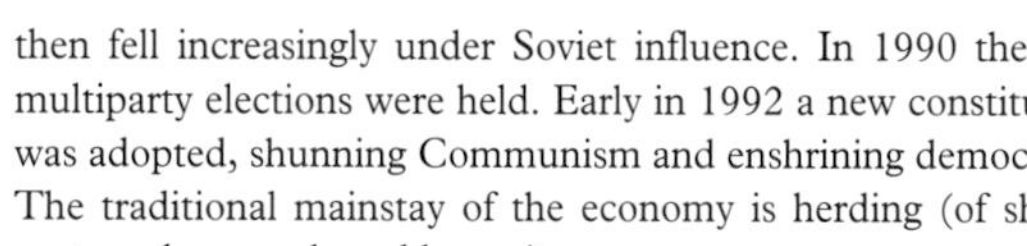

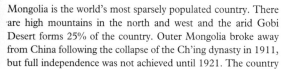

AREA 1,566,500 sq km [604,826 sq mls]
POPULATION 2,408,000
CAPITAL (POPULATION) Ulan Bator (601,000)
GOVERNMENT Multiparty republic
ETHNIC GROUPS Khalkha Mongol 79%, Kazak 6%
LANGUAGES Khalkha Mongolian, Chinese, Russian
RELIGIONS Buddhist, Shamanist, Muslim
CURRENCY Tugrik = 100 möngös
URBAN POPULATION 59% of population

Mongolia is the world's most sparsely populated country. There are high mountains in the north and west and the arid Gobi Desert forms 25% of the country. Outer Mongolia broke away from China following the collapse of the Ch'ing dynasty in 1911, but full independence was not achieved until 1921. The country then fell increasingly under Soviet influence. In 1990 the first multiparty elections were held. Early in 1992 a new constitution was adopted, shunning Communism and enshrining democracy. The traditional mainstay of the economy is herding (of sheep, goats, yaks, camels and horses).

MONTSERRAT

The flag is the British Blue Ensign with the arms in a white roundel in the fly. The shield dates from 1909 and shows a black Passion cross rising from the (brown) ground, grasped in the right arm of a female figure in a green robe, representing the Irish origin of the island's immigrants.

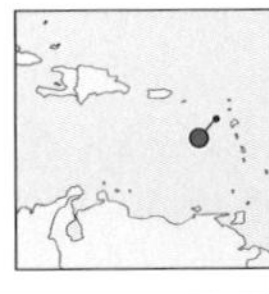

Located in the middle of the Caribbean Sea with a warm, tropical climate, Montserrat was colonized by Britain from 1632, which brought in Irish settlers. Although it is still a dependent territory of the UK, it became self-governing in 1960. Cotton was once the main industry, but with generous tax concessions new ones moved in. Tourism is now the mainstay of the economy (30% of GDP in 1994), supported by exports of electronic equipment, Sea Island cotton, fruit and vegetables.

AREA 102 sq km [39 sq mls]
POPULATION 11,000
CAPITAL (POPULATION) Plymouth (3,500)
GOVERNMENT British Dependent Territory
ETHNIC GROUPS Black, European
LANGUAGES English
RELIGIONS Christian
POPULATION DENSITY 108 per sq km [282 per sq ml]
CURRENCY East Caribbean $ = 100 cents

MOROCCO

A red flag had been flown in Morocco since the 16th century and the star-shaped green pentagram, the Seal of Solomon, was added in 1915. This design was retained when Morocco gained independence from French and Spanish rule in 1956.

GEOGRAPHY The name Morocco is derived from the Arabic *Maghreb-el-Aksa* ('the Farthest West'), due to its position in the far north-western corner of Africa. More than a third of the country is mountainous, with the main uplands being 'arms' of the Atlas Mountains in the west and north.

HISTORY AND POLITICS Morocco was the last North African country to succumb to European colonialism; not until 1912 did the Sultan of Morocco accept the French protectorate, with Spain controlling certain areas. In 1956 Morocco became independent (with Tangier incorporated into a unified Morocco in 1958). Since 1961 it has been ruled by the authoritarian regime of King Hassan II. The state of Western Sahara lies between Mauritania and the Atlantic coast and is occupied by Morocco in a long-running dispute. Morocco claims that the northern two-thirds are historically part of 'Greater Morocco'.

ECONOMY Peasant cultivation and nomadic pastoralism exist in the mountains, while modern economic development is found in the Atlantic plains and plateaux. Tourism is now very important.

AREA 446,550 sq km [172,413 sq mls]
POPULATION 26,857,000
CAPITAL (POPULATION) Rabat (1,220,000)
GOVERNMENT Constitutional monarchy
ETHNIC GROUPS Arab 70%, Berber 30%
LANGUAGES Arabic, Berber
RELIGIONS Muslim 99%, Christian 1%
POPULATION DENSITY 60 per sq km [156 per sq ml]
MAIN EXPORTS Food and beverages 27%, phosphoric acid 15%, phosphates 13%, clothing 10%
MAIN IMPORTS Capital goods 21%, crude oil 15%, consumer goods 12%
CURRENCY Dirham = 100 centimes

MOZAMBIQUE

The green stripe represents the fertile land, the black stripe Africa and the yellow stripe mineral wealth. The badge on the red triangle contains a rifle, hoe, cogwheel and book, which are all Marxist symbols of the struggle against colonialism.

GEOGRAPHY With the warm Mozambique (Agulhas) Current running offshore in the Indian Ocean, all the country is tropical. Coral reefs lie just offshore, and the only real natural harbour is Maputo (Lourenço Marques). The coastal plain is wide and the only high area is found around the inner borderlands.

HISTORY AND POLITICS Mozambique developed (like many other ex-Portuguese colonies) from the search for a route round Africa to the riches of Asia. Independence from Portugal was granted in 1975, with civil wars both before and after, and a series of droughts and floods, leaving it as one of the world's poorest countries. The civil war officially ended in 1992 and multiparty elections were held in 1994.

ECONOMY Coconut, sisal and sugar are grown on the plains, and maize, groundnuts and cotton are produced on the higher ground. Large deposits of coal, copper and bauxite have yet to be exploited.

AREA 801,590 sq km [309,494 sq mls]
POPULATION 17,800,000
CAPITAL (POPULATION) Maputo (2,000,000)
GOVERNMENT Multiparty republic
ETHNIC GROUPS Makua/Lomwe 47%, Tsonga 23%, Malawi 12%, Shona 11%, Yao 4%, Swahili 1%, Makonde 1%
LANGUAGES Portuguese, Bantu
RELIGIONS Traditional beliefs 48%, Roman Catholic 31%, Muslim 13%
POPULATION DENSITY 22 per sq km [56 per sq ml]
CURRENCY Metical = 100 centavos
URBAN POPULATION 30% of population

NAMIBIA

Namibia adopted its flag after independence from South Africa in 1990. The red and white colours symbolize the country's human resources, while the green, blue and the gold sun represent the natural resources, mostly minerals.

GEOGRAPHY Namibia has a diverse physical landscape, with the arid Namib Desert fringing the southern Atlantic coastline. A major escarpment separates this from a north-south spine of mountains which culminate in the Khomas Highlands near Windhoek. To the east the country occupies the fringes of the Kalahari Desert. The climate is very dry, with much sunshine.

HISTORY AND POLITICS Apart from the British enclave of Walvis Bay, Namibia was (as South West Africa) a German protectorate from 1884 before being occupied by the Union of South Africa at the request of the Allied powers in 1915. South Africa began a long period of exploitation of Namibia and in 1971 the International Court of Justice ruled that its occupation was illegal; but it was not until 1990 that independence was gained.

ECONOMY Some 90% of Namibia's income comes from exports of minerals, particularly uranium and diamonds. There are rich fishing grounds offshore and good prospects for oil and gas.

AREA 825,414 sq km [318,434 sq mls]
POPULATION 1,610,000
CAPITAL (POPULATION) Windhoek (126,000)
GOVERNMENT Multiparty republic
ETHNIC GROUPS Ovambo 47%, Kavango 9%, Herero 7%, Damara 7%, White 6%, Nama 5%
LANGUAGES English, Afrikaans
RELIGIONS Christian 90% (Lutheran 51%), animist
POPULATION DENSITY 2 per sq km [5 per sq ml]
CURRENCY Namibian dollar = 100 cents
URBAN POPULATION 34% of population

NAURU

The flag represents the geographical location of Nauru, south of the Equator in the middle of the Pacific Ocean. The 12 points of the star stand for the traditional tribes, and the flag was adopted on independence in 1968.

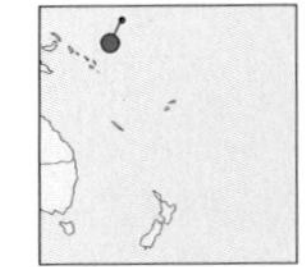

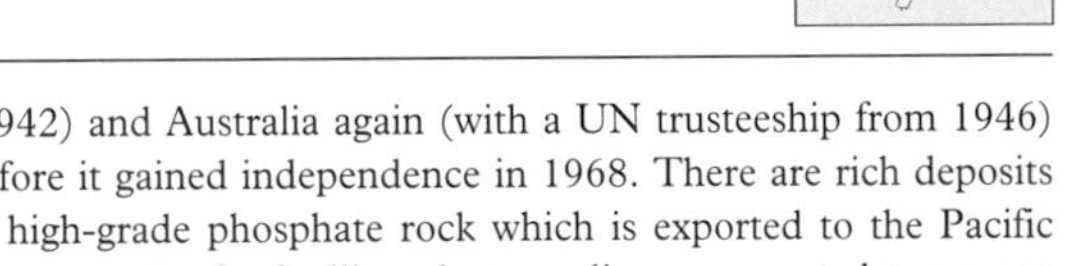

A low-lying coral atoll located halfway between Australia and Hawaii, 40 km [25 mls] south of the Equator, Nauru is the world's smallest republic. The climate is hot and wet, though the rains can fail. Discovered by Britain in 1798, the island was under the control of Germany (1888), Australia (1914), Japan (1942) and Australia again (with a UN trusteeship from 1946) before it gained independence in 1968. There are rich deposits of high-grade phosphate rock which is exported to the Pacific Rim countries for fertilizers but supplies are expected to run out by the end of 1997, leaving a legacy of environmental damage.

AREA 21 sq km [8 sq mls]
POPULATION 12,000
CAPITAL Yaren District
GOVERNMENT Democratic republic
ETHNIC GROUPS Nauruan 58%, other Pacific groups 26%
LANGUAGES Nauruan, English
RELIGIONS Christian
POPULATION DENSITY 571 per sq km [1,500 per sq ml]
CURRENCY Australian dollar

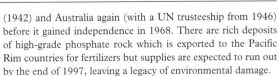

NEPAL

This Himalayan kingdom's uniquely shaped flag was adopted in 1962. It came from the joining together in the 19th century of two triangular pennants – the royal family's crescent moon emblem and the powerful Rana family's sun symbol.

GEOGRAPHY Over three-quarters of Nepal lies in a mountain heartland located between the Himalayas, the subject of an inconclusive boundary negotiation with China in 1961, and the far lower Siwalik Range overlooking the Ganges plain. The high altitude gives sub-zero temperatures in some parts.

HISTORY AND POLITICS Before 1951 (when it was first opened up to foreigners) Nepal had been a patchwork of feudal valley kingdoms until they were conquered by the Gurkhas in the 18th century to form the present country. Local leaders remained loyal to their clans and reduced the power of the central king, although in 1951 the monarchy was re-established. A new constitution incorporating basic human rights was drawn up and the first democratic elections for 32 years were held in 1991.

ECONOMY Nepal remains an under-developed rural country.

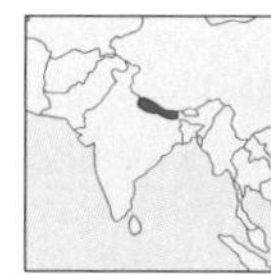

AREA 140,800 sq km [54,363 sq mls]
POPULATION 21,953,000
CAPITAL (POPULATION) Katmandu (535,000)
GOVERNMENT Constitutional monarchy
ETHNIC GROUPS Nepalese 53%, Bihari 18%, Tharu 5%, Tamang 5%, Newar 3%
LANGUAGES Nepali 58%
RELIGIONS Hindu 86%, Buddhist 8%, Muslim 4%
POPULATION DENSITY 156 per sq km [404 per sq ml]
CURRENCY Nepalese rupee = 100 paisa

NETHERLANDS

The Dutch national flag dates from 1630, during the long war of independence from Spain that began in 1568. The tricolour became a symbol of liberty and inspired many other revolutionary flags around the world.

GEOGRAPHY The Netherlands (the 'Low Countries') is a low-lying country of which more than two-fifths would be flooded without the protection of dykes and sand dunes along the coast. Reclamation since 1900 has added almost 3,000 sq km [1,160 sq mls] to the land area, but the danger of flooding remains. The countryside is mostly made up of richly cultivated fields, mainly rectangular, with water-filled ditches between them. It is a very crowded country, with the greatest concentration of population in the towns and cities of Randstad Holland.

HISTORY AND POLITICS The Dutch gained independence after 1648, following periods of rule under the dukes of Burgundy, the German empire and then Spain. In 1948 the Netherlands formed a customs union with Belgium and Luxembourg called Benelux and in 1957 it became a member of the EEC.

ECONOMY Industry and commerce are important, with good mineral resources including china clay, natural gas and oil. There is widespread production of flowers and vegetables and a very successful port and industrial complex at Europoort.

AREA 41,526 sq km [16,033 sq mls]
POPULATION 15,495,000
CAPITAL (POPULATION) Amsterdam (1,100,000); Seat of government: The Hague (695,000)
GOVERNMENT Constitutional monarchy with a bicameral legislature
ETHNIC GROUPS Dutch 95%, Indonesian, Turkish, Moroccan, Surinamese, German
LANGUAGES Dutch
RELIGIONS Roman Catholic 33%, Dutch Reformed Church 15%, Reformed Churches 8%, Muslim 3%
CURRENCY Guilder (florin) = 100 cents
URBAN POPULATION 89% of population

NETHERLANDS ANTILLES

The flag was originally introduced in 1959 with six white stars in the centre, but these were reduced to five in 1986 when Aruba became a separate territory. Each star represents one of the five islands that make up the territory.

The Netherlands Antilles consists of two very different island groups – Curaçao and Bonaire, off the coast of Venezuela, and Saba, St Eustatius and the southern part of St Maarten, at the northern end of the Leeward Islands, some 800 km [500 mls] away. With Aruba, they formed part of the Dutch West Indies before attaining internal self-government in 1954. Curaçao is dominant, with 45% of the land area and 80% of the population. Tourism, offshore banking and oil refining buoy the economy.

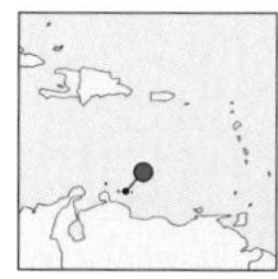

AREA 993 sq km [383 sq mls]
POPULATION 202,000
CAPITAL (POPULATION) Willemstad (125,000)
GOVERNMENT Self-governing Dutch Territory
ETHNIC GROUPS African descent 85%, European
LANGUAGES Dutch, Papiamento (Span., Port., Dutch and Eng. dialect), English
RELIGIONS Christian

NEW CALEDONIA

New Caledonia has been a French possession since 1853. It became a French Overseas Territory in 1958 and therefore uses the French tricolour as its flag.

Most southerly of the Melanesian countries in the Pacific Ocean, New Caledonia comprises the main island of Grande Terre and the dependencies of the Loyalty Islands. The remaining islands are all small and uninhabited. A French possession since 1853 and Overseas Territory since 1958, there is today a fundamental split over the question of independence between the indigenous Melanesians and the French settlers. The country is rich in minerals resources, most notably nickel.

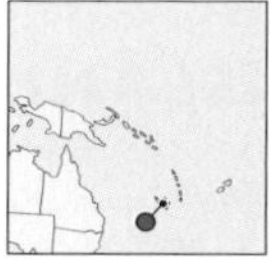

AREA 18,580 sq km [7,174 sq mls]
POPULATION 181,000
CAPITAL (POPULATION) Nouméa (98,000)
GOVERNMENT French Overseas Territory
ETHNIC GROUPS Melanesian 43%, European 37%
LANGUAGES French, Melanesian and Polynesian dialects
RELIGIONS Roman Catholic 60%, Protestant 30%

NEW ZEALAND

Like Australia, New Zealand flies a flag based on the design of the British Blue Ensign. Designed in 1869 and adopted in 1907 on acquiring Dominion status, it displays four of the five stars of the Southern Cross constellation.

GEOGRAPHY Geologically part of the Circum-Pacific Mobile belt of tectonic activity, New Zealand is mountainous and partly volcanic with about 75% of the total land area rising above the 200 m [650 ft] contour. Much of the North Island was formed by volcanic action, mainly in the last 1 to 4 million years. Minor earthquakes are common and there are several areas of volcanic and geothermal activity. The location of New Zealand in the huge Pacific Ocean moderates temperatures and there is a well-distributed rainfall throughout the year.

HISTORY AND POLITICS New Zealand was discovered by Abel Tasman in 1642 and then charted by James Cook in 1769–70. Already settled there were Maoris-Polynesians, who were joined by about 2,000 Europeans by the early 1830s. In 1840 Britain took possession and thousands of new settlers began to arrive, leading to problems of land ownership with the Maoris (these still exist). Recently, New Zealand has begun to look towards Asia for new markets, as its links with Britain begin to decline.

ECONOMY The economy is prosperous and agricultural products are the main exports. New Zealand is the world's third largest producer of lamb, with wheat and other cereals also grown.

AREA 268,680 sq km [103,737 sq mls]
POPULATION 3,567,000
CAPITAL (POPULATION) Wellington (329,000)
GOVERNMENT Constitutional monarchy with a unicameral legislature
ETHNIC GROUPS White 74%, Maori 10%, Polynesian 4%
LANGUAGES English, Maori
RELIGIONS Anglican 21%, Presbyterian 16%, Roman Catholic 15%, Methodist 4%
POPULATION DENSITY 13 per sq km [34 per sq ml]
MAIN EXPORTS Meat and meat preparations 20%, wool 14%, fruit and vegetables 7%, forestry products 7%

NICARAGUA

Nicaragua's flag, adopted in 1908, is identical to that of the Central American Federation (see Guatemala) to which it once belonged. Except for a difference in the shading of the blue and the motif, it is also the same as the flag of El Salvador.

GEOGRAPHY The largest and least densely populated country in South America, Nicaragua has an almost empty eastern half. The Caribbean plain is extensive, and the coast contains lagoons and sandy beaches. Inland mountain ranges are broken by fertile valleys and contain some 40 volcanoes, many still active.
HISTORY AND POLITICS Independence was granted in 1821 from Spain. Between 1832 and 1838 the country was part of the Central American Federation, and between 1937 and 1979 it was ruled by the corrupt Samoza family. Civil war was virtually continuous from the 1960s until a cease-fire in 1989. An uprising by the Sandinistas saw the end of the Samozas' rule. Elections in 1996 brought the Liberal Alliance party to power.
ECONOMY Cotton and coffee provide the main exports, but the economy is in a chaotic state as a result of the fighting.

AREA 130,000 sq km [50,193 sq mls]
POPULATION 4,544,000
CAPITAL (POPULATION) Managua (974,000)
GOVERNMENT Multiparty republic
ETHNIC GROUPS Mestizo 69%, White 17%, Black 9%
LANGUAGES Spanish, Indian, Creole
RELIGIONS Christian (Roman Catholic 89%)
POPULATION DENSITY 35 per sq km [91 per sq ml]
CURRENCY Córdoba = 100 centavos
URBAN POPULATION 62% of population

NIGER

Niger's flag was adopted shortly before independence from France in 1960. The circle represents the sun, the orange stripe the Sahara Desert in the north, the green stripe the grasslands of the south, divided by the (white) River Niger.

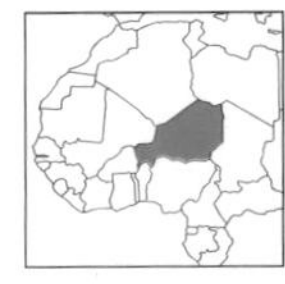

GEOGRAPHY Although Niger's name comes from the Tuareg word meaning 'flowing water', the country (apart from its fertile southern area where the River Niger flows) is arid and hot, with sandy and stony basins. The Aïr Mountains rise to 1,900 m [6,230 ft] above the desert in the north. Droughts are common.
HISTORY AND POLITICS Niger came under French colonial rule between 1922 and 1960. The post-independence government was overthrown in 1974 by the military. Civilian control was reinstated in 1989 and in 1992 a multiparty constitution was adopted. In January 1996 the military once again took control.
ECONOMY Drought and desertification have caused widespread poverty and migration to the already crowded cities.

AREA 1,267,000 sq km [489,189 sq mls]
POPULATION 9,149,000
CAPITAL (POPULATION) Niamey (398,000)
GOVERNMENT Multiparty republic suspended by a military regime
ETHNIC GROUPS Hausa 53%, Djerma-Songhai 21%, Tuareg 11%, Fulani 10%
LANGUAGES French, Hausa
RELIGIONS Sunni Muslim 99%
POPULATION DENSITY 7 per sq km [19 per sq ml]
CURRENCY CFA franc = 100 centimes

NIGERIA

The design of Nigeria's flag was selected after a competition to find a new national flag in time for independence from Britain in 1960. The green represents the country's forests and the white is for peace.

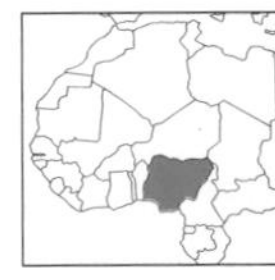

GEOGRAPHY Nigeria is Africa's most populous country. The landscape is varied: savanna in the north gives way to mountains and tropical rainforests and then to mangrove swamps and sandy beaches on the Gulf of Guinea. Much of the coast is formed by the Niger delta and its many creeks.
HISTORY AND POLITICS Nigeria was a British colony between 1914 and 1960 and became a full republic in 1963. A tripartite federal structure first introduced in 1954 was unable to contain rivalries between the 250 ethnic and linguistic groups that make up Nigeria. A military coup in 1966 saw the start of a vicious civil war, in which the Eastern Region (Biafra) attempted to split from the rest of the country; this ended in 1971. Between 1960 and 1997, Nigeria has enjoyed only nine years of civilian rule.
ECONOMY Oil accounts for over 90% of exports, although 50% of the population rely on farming. Serious economic problems have been exacerbated by falling oil prices.

AREA 923,770 sq km [356,668 sq mls]
POPULATION 88,515,000
CAPITAL Abuja (306,000)
GOVERNMENT Transitional government
ETHNIC GROUPS Hausa 21%, Yoruba 21%, Ibo 18%, Fulani 11%, Ibibio 6%
LANGUAGES English, Hausa, Yoruba, Ibo
RELIGIONS Sunni Muslim 45%, Protestant 26%, Roman Catholic 12%, African indigenous 11%
POPULATION DENSITY 96 per sq km [248 per sq ml]
CURRENCY Naira = 100 kobo
URBAN POPULATION 37% of population

NORTHERN MARIANA ISLANDS

The sea-blue flag of this island group shows a grey latte stone, a Polynesian taga, surrounded by a wreath of flowers and shells. The flag was originally adopted in 1972 and the wreath was added in 1989. The latte stone represents the old traditions of the Chamorro people.

The Northern Marianas in the Pacific Ocean comprise all 17 Mariana Islands except Guam. Part of the US Trust Territory of the Pacific from 1947, its people voted in a 1975 plebiscite for Commonwealth status in union with the USA. US citizenship was granted in 1976 and internal self-government followed in 1978. The tourist industry is growing rapidly.

AREA 477 sq km [184 sq mls]
POPULATION 50,000
CAPITAL (POPULATION) Saipan (39,000)
GOVERNMENT Commonwealth in union with USA
ETHNIC GROUPS Chamorro, Micronesian, Spanish
LANGUAGES English, Chamorro
RELIGIONS Christian

NORWAY

Norway's flag has been used since 1898, though its use as a merchant flag dates back to 1821. The design is based on the Dannebrog flag of Denmark, which ruled Norway from the 14th century to the early 19th century.

GEOGRAPHY A distinctly shaped country, Norway occupies the western part of the Scandinavian peninsula. The relatively small population lives mainly in the southern half of the country. The landscape is mountainous, dominated by rolling plateaux, the *vidda*, generally 300 to 900 m [1,000 to 3,000 ft] high; these are broken by deep river valleys. The highest areas retain permanent ice fields. The coastline is the longest in Europe, with long, narrow, steep-sided fjords. Hundreds of islands offshore protect the inner coast from the Atlantic waves.
HISTORY AND POLITICS The sea has been very important throughout Norway's history. A thousand years ago Viking sailors from Norway travelled around the northern seas, founding colonies around the coasts of Britain, Iceland and North America. Today fishing, shipbuilding and the merchant fleets are of vital importance to the economy. Norway is a member of NATO and EFTA (but not the EU), and co-operates closely with its Scandinavian neighbours on many issues.
ECONOMY Rapid industrial development since World War II has given Norway a prosperous economy. There are many mineral resources, particularly oil and natural gas from the North Sea.

AREA 323,900 sq km [125,050 sq mls]
POPULATION 4,361,000
CAPITAL (POPULATION) Oslo (714,000)

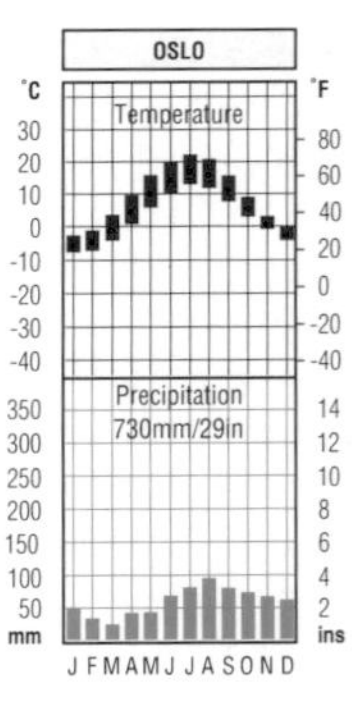

The warm waters and cyclones of the North Atlantic Ocean give the western coastlands of Norway a warm maritime climate of mild winters and cool summers, although wet. The rainfall is heavy on the coast but less inland and northwards. Inland the winters are more severe and the summers warmer. At Oslo the snows may last from November to March.

OMAN

Formerly Muscat and Oman, the state's flag was plain red – the traditional colour of the people who lived in the area. When Oman was established in 1970, the state arms of sword and dagger were added with stripes of white and green. The proportions of the stripes were changed in 1995.

AREA 212,460 sq km [82,031 sq mls]
POPULATION 2,252,000
CAPITAL (POPULATION) Muscat (350,000)
GOVERNMENT Monarchy with a unicameral consultative council
ETHNIC GROUPS Omani Arab 74%, other Asian 25%
LANGUAGES Arabic, Baluchi, English
RELIGIONS Muslim 86%, Hindu 13%
POPULATION DENSITY 11 per sq km [27 per sq ml]

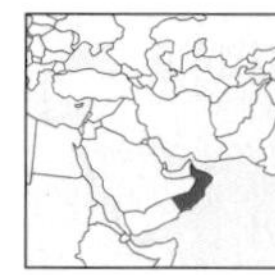

GEOGRAPHY Located on the south-eastern coast of the Persian Gulf, Oman has an arid and inhospitable landscape, where temperatures are high all year round.

HISTORY AND POLITICS Oman was backward compared to the other Gulf countries before 1970, with Sultan Said in power, and a civil war against Yemen-backed separatist guerillas in the southern province of Dhofar (Zufar). Sultan Said was deposed by his son Qaboos in 1970 and growth has since been rapid.

ECONOMY Petroleum accounts for 90% of government revenues and huge reserves of natural gas were discovered in 1991.

PAKISTAN

Pakistan's flag was adopted when the country gained independence from Britain in 1947. The green, the crescent moon and five-pointed star are traditionally associated with Islam. The white stripe represents Pakistan's other religions.

AREA 796,100 sq km [307,374 sq mls]
POPULATION 143,595,000
CAPITAL (POPULATION) Islamabad (204,000)
GOVERNMENT Federal republic
ETHNIC GROUPS Punjabi 60%, Pushtun 13%, Sindhi 12%, Baluchi, Muhajir
LANGUAGES Punjabi 60%, Pashto 13%, Sindhi 12%, Urdu 8%, Baluchi, Brahvi, English
RELIGIONS Muslim 96%, Hindu, Christian, Buddhist
POPULATION DENSITY 180 per sq km [467 per sq ml]
CURRENCY Rupee = 100 paisa

GEOGRAPHY The Indus delta and its tributaries on the coast of Pakistan have been vital for development, supplying irrigation for farming. West of the delta the arid coastal plain of Makran rises first to the Coast Range, then in successive ridges to the north. In the North-West Frontier province is the world's second highest mountain, K2, on the border with China.

HISTORY AND POLITICS Pakistan was part of the British Indian Empire until 1947, when Pakistan was granted independence as a separate Muslim state. East Pakistan (Bangladesh) broke away from the west in 1971, following a bitter civil war and Indian military intervention. Pakistan has been subject to military rule and martial law for most of its life, interspersed with periods of fragile democracy resting on army consent. Benazir Bhutto, the Muslim world's first female prime minister, was arrested in 1996 and democratic elections were held in February 1997.

ECONOMY Reserves of some minerals have yet to be exploited (such as copper and bauxite). However, the economy faces many problems, including a chronic trade deficit and debt burden.

PALAU

The flag dates from 1980 when Palau became a republic and depicts a full moon over the blue Pacific Ocean. The moon stands for national unity and destiny and the blue sea for the achievement of independence.

AREA 458 sq km [177 sq mls]
POPULATION 18,000
CAPITAL (POPULATION) Koror (10,000)
GOVERNMENT Republic
ETHNIC GROUPS Palauan (mixture of Polynesian, Melanesian and Malay)
LANGUAGES Palauan (official), English
RELIGIONS Christian (mainly Roman Catholic)
POPULATION DENSITY 39 per sq km [102 per sq ml]
CURRENCY US dollar
MAIN EXPORTS Copra

The Republic of Palau comprises an archipelago of six Caroline groups, totalling 26 islands and over 300 islets varying in terrain from mountain to reef. Eight of the islands are permanently inhabited. Agriculture is still largely at subsistence level, with copra the main export crop, but luxury tourism is growing, based strongly on scuba-diving and sea fishing. The country relies heavily on US aid. The last remaining member of the four states that comprised the US Trust Territory of the Pacific, established under UN mandate in 1947, Palau voted to break away from the Federated States of Micronesia in 1978. The territory then entered into 'free association with the USA', but in 1983 the people voted to reject the association, since the USA refused to accede to a 1979 referendum that declared the nation a nuclear-free zone. The result was stalemate until 1 October 1994 when the republic became independent. Palau joined the UN, as the 185th member, in December of the same year.

PANAMA

The Panamanian flag dates from the break with Colombia in 1903. Blue stands for the Conservative Party, red for the Liberal Party and white for the hope of peace. The red star represents law and order and the blue star represents 'public honesty'.

AREA 77,080 sq km [29,761 sq mls]
POPULATION 2,629,000
CAPITAL (POPULATION) Panama City (500,000)
GOVERNMENT Multiparty republic
ETHNIC GROUPS Mestizo 64%, Black and Mulatto 14%, White 10%, Amerindian 8%
LANGUAGES Spanish
RELIGIONS Roman Catholic 80%, Protestant 10%, Muslim 5%
CURRENCY Balboa = 100 centésimos

GEOGRAPHY Less than 60 km [37 mls] wide at its narrowest point, the Isthmus of Panama not only links Central and South America but also, via its canal, the Atlantic and Pacific Oceans. Most of the country, including some 750 offshore islands, lies below 700 m [2,300 ft], with a hot and humid climate.

HISTORY, POLITICS AND ECONOMY A French company began cutting the canal in 1880, but various problems stopped work after ten years. In 1903 the province of Panama declared independence from Colombia and granted the USA rights in perpetuity over a 16 km [10 ml] wide Canal Zone (this reverted to Panama in 1979). The canal opened for shipping in 1914. In 1994, 12,337 commercial vessels passed through the canal.

PAPUA NEW GUINEA

When Papua New Guinea became independent from Australia in 1975, it adopted a flag which had been used for the country since 1971. The design includes a local bird of paradise, the kumul, in flight and the stars of the Southern Cross constellation.

AREA 462,840 sq km [178,703 sq mls]
POPULATION 4,292,000
CAPITAL (POPULATION) Port Moresby (193,000)
GOVERNMENT Constitutional monarchy with a unicameral legislature
ETHNIC GROUPS Papuan 84%, Melanesian 15%
LANGUAGES Motu, English
RELIGIONS Christian, traditional beliefs
POPULATION DENSITY 9 per sq km [24 per sq ml]

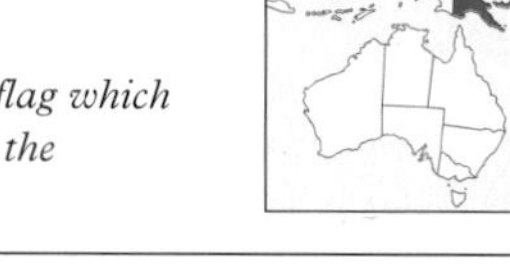

GEOGRAPHY Forming part of Melanesia, Papua New Guinea is the eastern section of the island of New Guinea, plus the Bismarck Archipelago and the island of Bougainville. The main island has a high cordillera of rugged fold mountains covered with montane 'cloud' forest. With few roads, communication is dependent on the country's 400 airports and strips.

HISTORY, POLITICS AND ECONOMY The first European contact was in 1526, but it was not until the late 19th century that permanent British and German settlements were established. After World War II it was governed by Australia, until independence in 1975. Some 80% of the population live by agriculture, but minerals have become increasingly important.

PARAGUAY

PARAGUAY

Paraguay's tricolour is a national flag with different sides. On the obverse the state emblem, illustrated here, displays the May Star to commemorate liberation from Spain (1811); the reverse shows the treasury seal – a lion and staff, with the words 'Peace and Justice'.

GEOGRAPHY A landlocked nation in the heart of South America, Paraguay is bounded mainly by rivers; for example, the Paraná (South America's second longest) in the south and east. The eastern area is an extension of the Brazilian plateau and is densely forested. In the west is the Northern Chaco, a flat, alluvial plain that rises gently from the Paraguay river valley.

HISTORY AND POLITICS Paraguay was settled in 1537 by the Spanish, and from 1766 formed part of the Rio de la Plata Viceroyalty. It broke free in 1811 and achieved independence in 1813. A long period of internal conflict then followed, including the dictatorship of General Stroessner which lasted from 1954 to 1989. General Rodríguez took over and a new constitution was drawn up but he was replaced in 1993 by Juan Carlos Wasmosy, Paraguay's first civilian president since 1954.

ECONOMY There was considerable economic growth in the 1970s, but debt and inflation problems have now arisen.

AREA 406,750 sq km [157,046 sq mls]
POPULATION 4,979,000
CAPITAL (POPULATION) Asunción (945,000)
GOVERNMENT Multiparty republic
ETHNIC GROUPS Mestizo 90%, Amerindian 3%
LANGUAGES Spanish 60%, Guarani 40%
RELIGIONS Roman Catholic 93%
POPULATION DENSITY 12 per sq km [32 per sq ml]
CURRENCY Guaraní = 100 céntimos
URBAN POPULATION 51% of population
MAIN EXPORTS Cotton, soya, oil seeds, timber

PERU

Flown since 1825, the flag's colours are said to have come about when the Argentine patriot General José de San Martin, arriving to liberate Peru from Spain in 1820, saw a flock of red and white flamingos flying over his marching army.

GEOGRAPHY Peru is spread over coastal plain, mountains and forested Amazon lowlands in the interior, with a coastline on the Pacific Ocean. The Amazon lowlands themselves are hot and wet with dense tropical rainforest.

HISTORY AND POLITICS Peru was the homeland of Inca and other ancient civilizations, and has a history of human settlement stretching back over 10,500 years. The last Inca empire ended in the 16th century with the arrival of the Spaniards, who made Peru the most important of their viceroyalties in South America. Independence was gained in 1824, but development has been hampered by problems of communication, political strife, an unbalanced economy and periodic earthquakes.

ECONOMY Agricultural production has failed to keep up with population, so many foods are imported. Peru is the leading producer of coca, used in the production of cocaine. Fishing is also important, and copper, silver and zinc are exported.

AREA 1,285,220 sq km [496,223 sq mls]
POPULATION 23,588,000
CAPITAL (POPULATION) Lima (6,601,000)
GOVERNMENT Unitary republic
ETHNIC GROUPS Quechua 47%, Mestizo 32%, White 12%
LANGUAGES Spanish, Quechua, Aymara
RELIGIONS Roman Catholic 93%
CURRENCY New sol = 100 centavos
MAIN EXPORTS Copper 19%, petroleum and derivatives 10%, lead 9%, zinc 8%, fishmeal 8%, coffee 5%
MAIN IMPORTS Fuels, machinery, chemicals, food

PHILIPPINES

The eight rays of the large sun represent the eight provinces that led the revolt against Spanish rule in 1898 and the three smaller stars stand for the three main island groups. The flag was adopted on independence from the USA in 1946.

GEOGRAPHY The Republic of the Philippines consists of 7,107 islands stretching for 1,800 km [1,120 mls]. About 1,000 of the islands are inhabited. There are over 20 active volcanoes in the islands, including Mt Apo and Mt Pinatubo, which erupted violently in 1991.

HISTORY AND POLITICS After 300 years of Spanish rule, the islands were ceded to the USA in 1898. Ties with the USA have remained strong even through the corrupt regime of President Ferdinand Marcos from 1965–86. Marcos was overthrown by the 'people power' revolution that brought to office Corazon Aquino, but the political situation has remained extremely volatile. Fidel Ramos became president in the 1992 elections.

ECONOMY There are few natural resources. Although there is high unemployment there are signs of economic growth.

AREA 300,000 sq km [115,300 sq mls]
POPULATION 67,167,000
CAPITAL (POPULATION) Manila (9,280,000)
GOVERNMENT Unitary republic with a bicameral legislature
ETHNIC GROUPS Tagalog 30%, Cebuano 24%, Ilocano 10%, Hiligayon Ilongo 9%, Bicol 6%, Samar-Leyte 4%
LANGUAGES Pilipino (Tagalog) and English (both official), Spanish, Cebuano, Ilocano, over 80 others
RELIGIONS Roman Catholic 84%, Agilpayan
CURRENCY Peso = 100 centavos

PITCAIRN ISLANDS

A flag for local use was granted to Pitcairn in 1984. The flag is the British Blue Ensign with the whole arms in the fly. The arms were first used in 1969.

Pitcairn is a British dependent territory of four islands situated halfway between New Zealand and Panama. Uninhabited until 1790, Pitcairn was occupied by nine mutineers from HMS *Bounty* and some people from Tahiti. The islands were annexed by Britain in 1902. The present population all live in the capital, administered by the British High Commission in New Zealand.

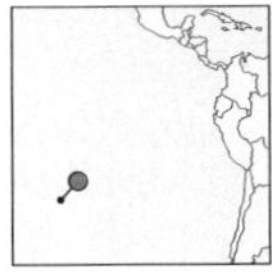

AREA 48 sq km [19 sq mls]
POPULATION 54
CAPITAL (POPULATION) Adamstown (54)
GOVERNMENT British Dependent Territory
ETHNIC GROUPS English, Tahitian
POPULATION DENSITY 1.1 per sq km [2.8 per sq ml]
CURRENCY New Zealand dollar

POLAND

The colours of Poland's flag were derived from the 13th-century coat of arms of a white eagle on a red field, which still appears on the Polish merchant flag. The flag's simple design was adopted when Poland became a republic in 1919.

GEOGRAPHY Poland's geographical location has had a strong influence on the country's complex history. Invasions by neighbouring countries have changed the frontiers on several occasions, most recently after the end of World War II, when 17% of the population was lost and territory was given up to the USSR in return for land from Germany. Part of these gains was a length of Baltic coastline, giving Poland a chance to develop its maritime interests; as a result, it is now a leading fishing nation.

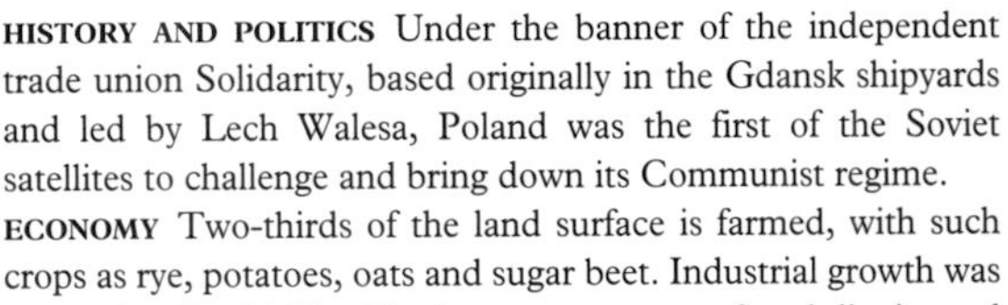

HISTORY AND POLITICS Under the banner of the independent trade union Solidarity, based originally in the Gdansk shipyards and led by Lech Walesa, Poland was the first of the Soviet satellites to challenge and bring down its Communist regime.

ECONOMY Two-thirds of the land surface is farmed, with such crops as rye, potatoes, oats and sugar beet. Industrial growth was rapid after World War II – there are reserves of coal, lignite and lead – but restructuring and diversification is now needed.

AREA 312,680 sq km [120,726 sq mls]
POPULATION 38,587,000
CAPITAL (POPULATION) Warsaw (1,643,000)
GOVERNMENT Multiparty republic
ETHNIC GROUPS Polish 99%, Ukrainian
LANGUAGES Polish (official)
RELIGIONS Roman Catholic 91%, Orthodox 2%
POPULATION DENSITY 123 per sq km [320 per sq ml]
CURRENCY Zloty = 100 groszy
MAIN EXPORTS Machinery and transport equipment 39%, chemicals 11%, fuel and power 10%, metals 10%, textiles 7%

PORTUGAL

Portugal's colours, adopted in 1910 when it became a republic, represent the soldiers who died in the war (red) and hope (green). The armillary sphere – an early navigational instrument – reflects Portugal's leading role in world exploration.

GEOGRAPHY Portugal occupies an oblong coastland in the south-west of the Iberian peninsula, facing the Atlantic Ocean. Here the Meseta edge has splintered and in part foundered to leave upstanding mountain ranges, particularly in the Serra da Estrêla. Over a quarter of the country is forested, with tree growth helped by the mild, moist airflow from the Atlantic. Pines are the most common species, especially on the sandy 'littorals' near the coast. The climate is drier and warmer in the south.

HISTORY AND POLITICS Portugal had an important historical role in maritime exploration and established colonies in Africa and Asia. The country became a republic in 1910 and joined the European Union in 1986, but is one of its poorest members.

ECONOMY The Portuguese economy relies heavily on agriculture and fishing, which together employ over a quarter of the national workforce. These industries are still fairly primitive, but produce a wide range of crops including maize, rye, olives and grapes. Fish include oysters, sardines and cod. The manufacture of textiles and ceramics is also important, as is the tourist industry.

AREA 92,390 sq km [35,670 sq mls]
POPULATION 10,600,000
CAPITAL (POPULATION) Lisbon (2,561,000)
GOVERNMENT Multiparty republic with a unicameral legislature
ETHNIC GROUPS Portuguese 99%, Cape Verdean, Brazilian, Spanish, British
LANGUAGES Portuguese
RELIGIONS Roman Catholic 95%
POPULATION DENSITY 115 per sq km [297 per sq ml]
CURRENCY Escudo = 100 centavos
MAIN EXPORTS Clothing 26%, machinery and transport equipment 20%, paper and paper products 8%, footwear 8%

PUERTO RICO

Puerto Rico fought with Cuba for independence from Spain and their flags are almost identical (the red and blue colours are transposed). The island is a dependent territory of the United States and the flag, adopted in 1952, is flown only with the American 'Stars and Stripes'.

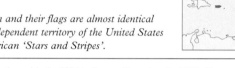

GEOGRAPHY Puerto Rico is the easternmost of the major Greater Antilles and is mainly mountainous, with a narrow coastal plain. Cerro de Punta (1,338 m [4,389 ft]) is the highest peak. The climate is hot and wet, but there are no great extremes of temperature; the winds from the north-east or east, blowing over a warm sea, cause rain which falls on over 200 days a year.

HISTORY AND POLITICS Ceded by Spain to the USA in 1898, Puerto Rico became a 'self-governing Commonwealth in free association with the USA' after a referendum in 1952. Even with this degree of autonomy, there is a strong US influence; as full US citizens Puerto Ricans pay no federal taxes, but neither do they vote in US elections. Migration to the USA is common.

ECONOMY The island is the most industrialized in the Caribbean with chemicals constituting 36% of exports and metal products (based on copper deposits) a further 17%. Manufacturing and tourism are growing and crops include sugar, coffee and spices.

AREA 8,900 sq km [3,436 sq mls]
POPULATION 3,689,000
CAPITAL (POPULATION) San Juan (1,816,000)
GOVERNMENT Self-governing Commonwealth in association with the USA
ETHNIC GROUPS Spanish 99%, African American, Indian
LANGUAGES Spanish, English
RELIGIONS Christian (mainly Roman Catholic)
POPULATION DENSITY 414 per sq km [1,074 per sq ml]
CURRENCY US dollar
URBAN POPULATION 77% of population

QATAR

The flag was adopted in 1971. The maroon colour is said to result from the natural effect of the sun on the traditional red banner, while the white was added after a British request in 1820 that white should be included in the flags of friendly states in the Arabian Gulf.

Qatar occupies a low, barren peninsula that extends northwards into the Arabian Gulf. The climate is hot and dry all year round and much of the landscape is made up of desert. A British protectorate between 1916 and 1971, there is a high standard of living for its inhabitants, which is mainly derived from oil and gas. These two account for over 80% of exports. There has been some recent diversification into cement, steel and fertilizers. Much of the workforce is made up of immigrant labour.

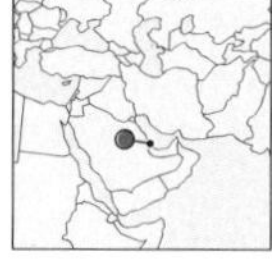

AREA 11,000 sq km [4,247 sq mls]
POPULATION 594,000
CAPITAL (POPULATION) Doha (243,000)
GOVERNMENT Constitutional absolute monarchy
ETHNIC GROUPS Southern Asian 34%, Qatari 20%
LANGUAGES Arabic
RELIGIONS Sunni Muslim 92%, Christian, Hindu

RÉUNION

As a French Overseas Department, Réunion uses the French tricolour as its flag.

Réunion is the largest of the Mascarene Islands, lying in the Indian Ocean east of Madagascar and south-west of Mauritius. The island is made up of a rugged, mountainous forested centre surrounded by a fertile coastal plain. The volcanic mountains rise to the peak of Piton des Neiges (3,070 m [10,076 ft]). It became an overseas department of France in 1946 and the French still subsidize Réunion heavily in return for the use of the island as its main military base in the area. Intensive cultivation takes place on the lowlands, with sugar cane providing 75% of exports. Vanilla, perfume and tea are also produced.

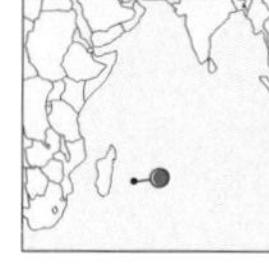

AREA 2,510 sq km [969 sq mls]
POPULATION 655,000
CAPITAL (POPULATION) St-Denis (207,000)
GOVERNMENT Overseas Department of France
ETHNIC GROUPS Mixed 64%, East Indian 28%, Chinese 2%, White 2%
LANGUAGES French, Creole
RELIGIONS Roman Catholic 90%, Muslim 1%
CURRENCY French franc

ROMANIA

Romania's colours come from the arms of the provinces that united to form the country in 1861, and the design was adopted in 1948. The central state coat of arms, added in 1965, was deleted in 1990 after the fall of the Communist Ceausescu regime.

GEOGRAPHY Romania has clearly defined natural borders on three sides: the Danube in the south, the Black Sea coast in the east and the River Prut in the north-east. The landscape is dominated by an arc of high fold mountains, the Carpathians; south and east of these lie the plains of the lower Danube.

HISTORY AND POLITICS Romania was formed in 1861 when the provinces of Moldavia and Wallachia united. It became a Communist republic in 1946 and the dictator Nicolae Ceausescu took control in 1965. His corrupt regime lasted for 24 years, until he and his wife were executed following an army-backed revolt in 1989. In the 1970s his programmes of industrialization and urbanization caused severe food shortages. In 1990, Romania held its first free elections since the end of the World War II. Presidential elections in 1996 were won by Emil Constantinescu.

ECONOMY Despite the industrialization programmes, Romania is an agricultural nation, with crops of cereals, timber and fruit.

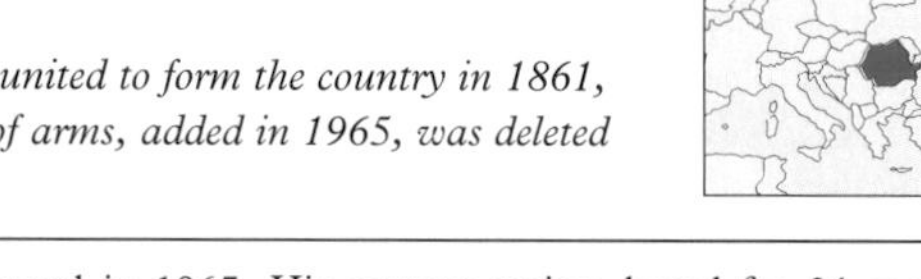

AREA 237,500 sq km [91,699 sq mls]
POPULATION 22,863,000
CAPITAL (POPULATION) Bucharest (2,061,000)
GOVERNMENT Multiparty republic
ETHNIC GROUPS Romanian 89%, Hungarian 8%
LANGUAGES Romanian, Hungarian, German
RELIGIONS Romanian Orthodox 87%, Roman Catholic 5%, Greek Orthodox 4%
POPULATION DENSITY 96 per sq km [249 per sq ml]
CURRENCY Leu = 100 bani

RUSSIA

RUSSIA

Distinctive Russian flags were first instituted by Peter the Great, based on those of the Netherlands. This flag became the official national flag in 1799 but was suppressed in the Bolshevik Revolution. It was restored on 22 August 1991.

GEOGRAPHY Even with the break-up of the Soviet Union in 1991, the Russian Federation remains the largest country in the world. The landscape and climates are very diverse, ranging from tundra in the north, to the coniferous forests of the taiga, to the steppe regions of the south, once grassland but now largely under cultivation. There are several mountain ranges, including the Ural Mountains, and many long rivers, including the Volga, which flows for 3,700 km [2,300 mls] to the Caspian Sea.

HISTORY AND POLITICS The present size of Russia is the product of a long period of evolution dating to early medieval times. It has always been a centralized state. The 1917 Revolution, when the Tsarist Order was overthrown and a Communist government established under Lenin, was a landmark in Russian history. The next fundamental changes began when Gorbachev took charge after 1985. Russia's huge size and numbers of different peoples have always posed problems and continue to do so.

ECONOMY The Soviet economy was transformed after 1917 into one of the most industrialized in the world, based initially on the iron and steel industry. Although strong, the Russian economy is now in chaos, with food shortages and unemployment.

AREA 17,075,000 sq km [6,592,800 sq mls]
POPULATION 148,385,000
CAPITAL (POPULATION) Moscow (9,233,000)
GOVERNMENT Federal republic
ETHNIC GROUPS Russian 82%, Tatar 4%, Ukrainian 3%, Chuvash 2%
LANGUAGES Russian
RELIGIONS Christian, Muslim, Buddhist
POPULATION DENSITY 9 per sq km [22 per sq ml]
CURRENCY Rouble = 100 kopeks
URBAN POPULATION 75% of population
LAND USE Arable 8%, grass 6%, forest 45%
ANNUAL INCOME $2,350 per person

RWANDA

Adopted in 1961, Rwanda's tricolour in the Pan-African colours features the letter 'R' to distinguish it from Guinea's flag. Red represents the blood shed in the 1959 revolution, yellow for victory over tyranny, and green for hope.

GEOGRAPHY Rwanda is a small, landlocked and poor rural country and Africa's most densely populated. Geological uplift of the western arm of the Great Rift Valley has raised most of the country to well over 2,000 m [6,000 ft].

HISTORY, POLITICS AND ECONOMY Rwanda was merged with Burundi by Germany in 1899, making Ruanda-Urundi part of German East Africa. Belgium occupied it during World War I and then administered it afterwards. It was divided into two in 1959, with Rwanda achieving full independence in 1962. Civil war erupted in 1994, with appalling loss of life.

AREA 26,340 sq km [10,170 sq mls]
POPULATION 7,899,000
CAPITAL (POPULATION) Kigali (235,000)
GOVERNMENT Transitional government
ETHNIC GROUPS Hutu 90%, Tutsi 9%, Twa 1%
LANGUAGES English, French, Kinyarwanda
RELIGIONS Roman Catholic 65%, Protestant 12%, traditional beliefs 17%, Muslim 9%
CURRENCY Rwandan franc = 100 centimes

ST HELENA

Since 1984 the British dependent territory of St Helena, with its dependencies of Ascension Island and the Tristan da Cunha group, has used the shield from its new coat of arms in the fly of the British Blue Ensign. The main part of the shield shows a ship sailing towards the island.

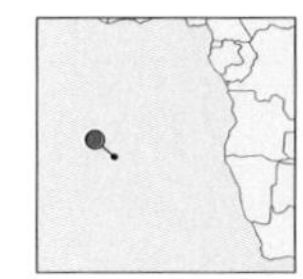

St Helena is an isolated rectangular island of old volcanic rocks in the southern Atlantic Ocean. It has been a British colony since 1834 and the administrative centre for six of the UK's South Atlantic islands and is very dependent on subsidies.

AREA 122 sq km [47 sq mls]
POPULATION 6,000
CAPITAL (POPULATION) Jamestown (1,500)
GOVERNMENT British Dependent Territory
ETHNIC GROUPS Mixed European (British), Asian and African
LANGUAGES English
CURRENCY St Helena pound = 100 pence

ST KITTS AND NEVIS

The colours represent fertility (green), sunshine (yellow), the independence struggle (red) and the African heritage (black); the two stars stand for hope and liberty. The flag was adopted on independence from Britain in 1983.

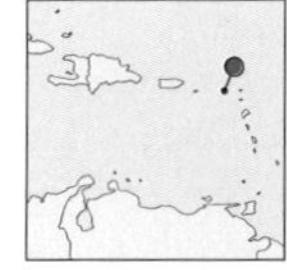

St Kitts (formerly St Christopher) and Nevis are two well-watered volcanic islands, about 20% forested. They were the first West Indian islands to be colonized by Britain – in 1623 and 1628. Tourism has now replaced sugar as the main earner.

AREA 360 sq km [139 sq mls]
POPULATION 45,000
CAPITAL (POPULATION) Basseterre (15,000)
GOVERNMENT Constitutional monarchy
ETHNIC GROUPS Of African descent
LANGUAGES English
RELIGIONS Christian
CURRENCY East Caribbean $ = 100 cents

ST LUCIA

This Caribbean island became an Associated State of Great Britain in 1967 and adopted this modern-looking flag. It is a symbolic representation of St Lucia itself: the black volcanic hills of the island rising from the blue ocean.

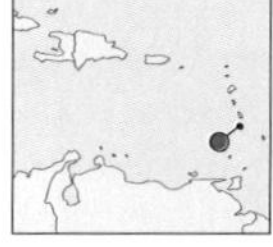

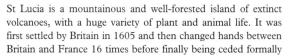

St Lucia is a mountainous and well-forested island of extinct volcanoes, with a huge variety of plant and animal life. It was first settled by Britain in 1605 and then changed hands between Britain and France 16 times before finally being ceded formally in 1814. It gained full independence in 1979. St Lucia is still overdependent on bananas, which provide 71% of exports but are easily destroyed by hurricane and disease. Other crops include cocoa and coconuts. Clothing is the second main export.

AREA 610 sq km [236 sq mls]
POPULATION 147,000
CAPITAL (POPULATION) Castries (54,000)
GOVERNMENT Constitutional monarchy
ETHNIC GROUPS African descent 90%, Mixed 6%, East Indian 3%
LANGUAGES English, French patois
RELIGIONS Roman Catholic 79%, Protestant 16%, Anglican
CURRENCY East Caribbean $ = 100 cents

ST VINCENT AND THE GRENADINES

On independence from Britain in 1979, St Vincent adopted this tricolour, but with the islands' coat of arms in the centre. In 1985 this was replaced by the present three green diamonds representing the islands as the 'gems of the Antilles'.

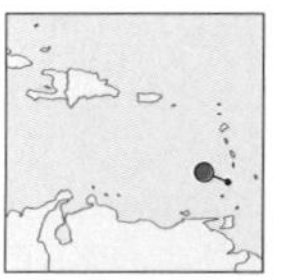

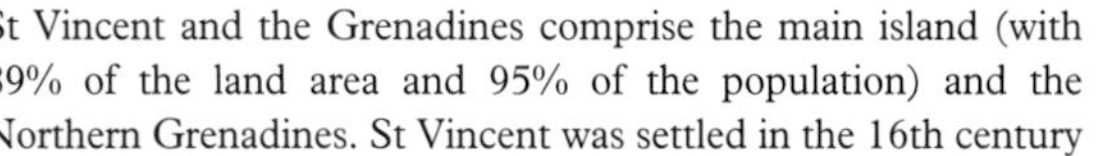

St Vincent and the Grenadines comprise the main island (with 89% of the land area and 95% of the population) and the Northern Grenadines. St Vincent was settled in the 16th century and became a British colony in 1783. The colony became self-governing in 1969 and independent in 1979. Less prosperous than some of its neighbours, the tourist industry is growing.

AREA 388 sq km [150 sq mls]
POPULATION 111,000
CAPITAL (POPULATION) Kingstown (27,000)
GOVERNMENT Constitutional monarchy
ETHNIC GROUPS Of African descent
LANGUAGES English, French patois
RELIGIONS Christian
POPULATION DENSITY 286 per sq km [740 per sq ml]

SAN MARINO

The tiny republic of San Marino, enclosed completely within the territory of Italy, has been an independent state since AD 885. The flag's colours – white for the snowy mountains and blue for the sky – derive from the state coat of arms.

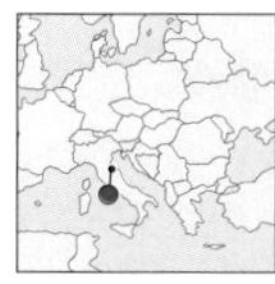

San Marino is the world's smallest republic and lies 20 km [12 mls] south-west of Rimini. The territory consists mainly of the limestone mass of Monte Titano. Most of the population live in the medieval fortified city of San Marino. There is a friendship and co-operation treaty with Italy dating back to 1862 and tourism and limestone quarrying are the chief occupations.

AREA 61 sq km [24 sq mls]
POPULATION 26,000
CAPITAL (POPULATION) San Marino (4,335)
GOVERNMENT Multiparty republic with an elected council
ETHNIC GROUPS San Marinese, Italian
LANGUAGES Italian
RELIGIONS Roman Catholic
CURRENCY Italian lira and San Marino lira

SÃO TOMÉ AND PRÍNCIPE

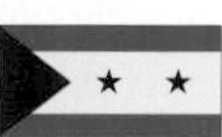

Adopted on independence from Portugal in 1975, this variation of the familiar Pan-African colours had previously been the emblem of the national liberation movement. The two black stars represent the two islands that comprise the country.

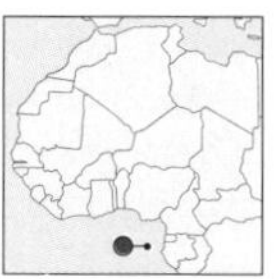

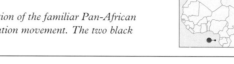

São Tomé and Príncipe are two mountainous, volcanic and heavily forested Atlantic islands some 145 km [90 mls] apart. A Portuguese colony since 1522, the islands were suddenly granted independence in 1975 and a one-party Socialist state was set up. Marxism was abandoned in 1990 and São Tomé held multiparty elections in 1991 and 1996. Cocoa is the most important crop.

AREA 964 sq km [372 sq mls]
POPULATION 133,000
CAPITAL (POPULATION) São Tomé (43,000)
GOVERNMENT Multiparty republic
ETHNIC GROUPS Mainly descendants of slaves
LANGUAGES Portuguese
RELIGIONS Christian (mainly Roman Catholic)

SAUDI ARABIA

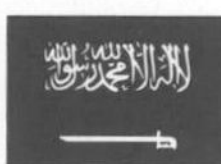

The inscription on the Saudi flag above the sword means 'There is no God but Allah, and Muhammad is the Prophet of Allah'. The only national flag with an inscription as its main feature, the design was adopted in 1938.

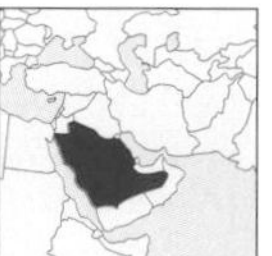

GEOGRAPHY Saudi Arabia is the largest state in the Middle East but is more than 95% desert. At its heart is the province of Najd, containing three main groups of oases. To the south lies the Rub 'al Khali ('empty quarter'), the world's largest expanse of sand.
HISTORY, POLITICS AND ECONOMY During and shortly after World War I, the Saudis of Najd (central Arabia) extended their territory and took control over the greater part of the Arabian peninsula, including the holy city of Mecca. Its vast reserves of oil (the world's largest) were discovered after World War II and the strictly Muslim society soon had some of the world's most advanced facilities. Saudi Arabia has always been an ally of the West, but this has conflicted with its Islamic role.

AREA 2,149,690 sq km [829,995 sq mls]
POPULATION 18,395,000
CAPITAL (POPULATION) Riyadh (2,000,000)
GOVERNMENT Absolute monarchy with a consultative assembly
ETHNIC GROUPS Arab 92% (Saudi 82%, Yemeni 10%)
LANGUAGES Arabic
RELIGIONS Muslim 99%, Christian 1%
CURRENCY Saudi riyal = 100 halalas
POPULATION DENSITY 9 per sq km [22 per sq ml]

SENEGAL

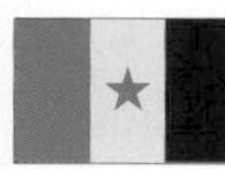

Apart from the green five-pointed star, which symbolizes the Muslim faith of the majority of the population, Senegal's flag is identical to that of Mali. It was adopted in 1960 when the country gained its independence from France.

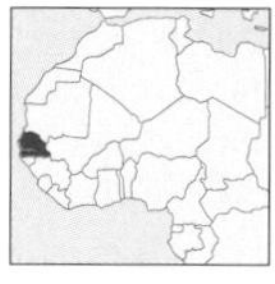

GEOGRAPHY One-fifth of Senegal's population lives in Dakar and the area around volcanic Cape Verde, the most westerly point on mainland Africa. In the north-east there is scrub and semi-desert, while the south is wetter and more fertile.
HISTORY, POLITICS AND ECONOMY Senegal's name derives from the Zenega Berbers, who invaded from Mauritania in the 14th century. The country became the administrative centre for French West Africa, benefitting from this with a good road network and a well-planned capital. Groundnuts dominate the economy and exports, with phosphates as the other main export.

AREA 196,720 sq km [75,954 sq mls]
POPULATION 8,308,000
CAPITAL (POPULATION) Dakar (1,729,000)
GOVERNMENT Multiparty republic with a unicameral legislature
ETHNIC GROUPS Wolof 44%, Fulani 23%, Serer 14%, Tukulor 8%, Dyola 8%
LANGUAGES French, African languages
RELIGIONS Sunni Muslim 94%, Christian 5%, animist
CURRENCY CFA franc = 100 centimes

SEYCHELLES

This new flag was introduced on 5 June 1996 following the abolition of one-party rule and the introduction of a new constitution. Red, white and green are the colours of the ruling party and the blue and gold are the colours of the main opposition party.

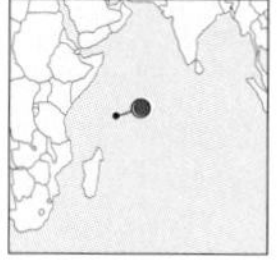

The Seychelles are a compact group of four large and 36 small granitic islands, plus a wide scattering of coralline islands lying mainly to the south and west. Some 98% of the population live on the four main islands, particularly on the biggest, Mahé. French from 1756 and British from 1814, the islands gained independence in 1976. A one-party Socialist state was set up in 1977; multiparty democracy was restored after elections in 1992. Fishing and luxury tourism are the two main industries.

AREA 455 sq km [176 sq mls]
POPULATION 75,000
CAPITAL (POPULATION) Victoria (30,000)
GOVERNMENT Multiparty republic
ETHNIC GROUPS Mixture of African, Asian and European
LANGUAGES English, French, Creole
RELIGIONS Roman Catholic 89%, Anglican 9%
CURRENCY Seychelles rupee = 100 cents

SIERRA LEONE

The colours of Sierra Leone's flag, adopted on independence from Britain in 1961, come from the coat of arms. Green represents the country's agriculture, white stands for peace and blue for the Atlantic Ocean.

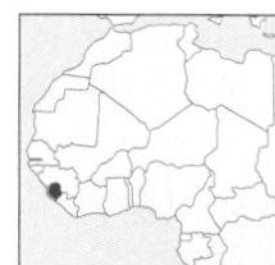

GEOGRAPHY Sierra Leone ('lion mountain') is located in West Africa and has a coastline on the Atlantic Ocean. The interior of the country is made up of plateaux and mountains, while the coastal plain is more swampy. The climate is tropical.
HISTORY, POLITICS AND ECONOMY The capital was established as a settlement for freed slaves in the 18th century and the country became a British colony in 1808. Independence was gained in 1961. Multiparty elections were held in 1996, ending 19 years of one-party or military rule. Diamonds and iron-ore mining provide revenue.

AREA 71,740 sq km [27,699 sq mls]
POPULATION 4,467,000
CAPITAL (POPULATION) Freetown (505,000)
GOVERNMENT Transitional government
ETHNIC GROUPS Mende 34%, Temne 31%, Limba 8%, Kono 5%
LANGUAGES English, Creole, Mende, Limba, Temne
RELIGIONS Traditional beliefs 51%, Sunni Muslim 39%, Christian 9%
CURRENCY Leone = 100 cents

SINGAPORE

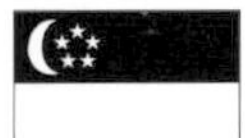

Adopted in 1959, this flag was retained when Singapore broke away from the Federation of Malaysia in 1963. The crescent stands for the nation's ascent and the stars for its aims of democracy, peace, progress, justice and equality.

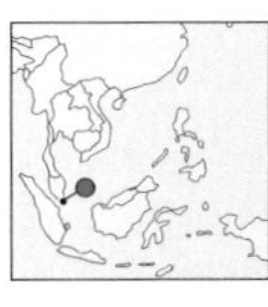

GEOGRAPHY Singapore comprises the main island itself and an additional 54 much smaller islands lying within its territorial waters. The highest point on the main island is Bukit Tiamah (177 m [581 ft]). The uplands were originally forested, while the lowlands were swampy with mangrove forests along the inlets. Much of the forest has been cleared for farming and building, creating problems of soil erosion. Temperatures are uniformly high throughout the year, with high humidity and heavy rain.

HISTORY AND POLITICS Its position at the southernmost point of the Malay Peninsula has been of great strategic importance to Singapore. A British colony from 1867, it became self-governing in 1959. Part of the Federation of Malaysia from 1963, it became fully independent in 1965. Singapore's success owes much to Lee Kuan Yew, prime minister from 1959 to 1990, who brought in an ambitious, but rigid, policy of industrialization. His successor, Goh Chok Tong, has continued his work.

ECONOMY The successful economy is based on its vast port, and its manufacturing, commercial and financial services.

AREA 618 sq km [239 sq mls]
POPULATION 2,990,000
CAPITAL (POPULATION) Singapore (2,874,000)
GOVERNMENT Unitary multiparty republic with a unicameral legislature
ETHNIC GROUPS Chinese 76%, Malay 14%, Indian 7%
LANGUAGES Chinese, Malay, Tamil, English
RELIGIONS Buddhist 28%, Muslim 15%, Christian 13%, Taoist 13%, Hindu 4%
CURRENCY Singapore dollar = 100 cents
POPULATION DENSITY 4,838 per sq km [12,510 per sq ml]

SLOVAK REPUBLIC

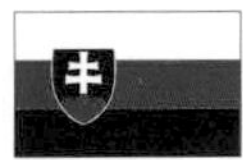

The horizontal tricolour which the Slovak Republic adopted in September 1992 dates from 1848. The red, white and blue colours are typical of Slavonic flags. The three blue mounds in the shield represent the traditional mountains of Slovakia: Tatra, Matra and Fatra.

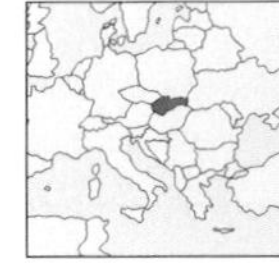

GEOGRAPHY One part of the former Czechoslovakia, the Slovak Republic consists of a mountainous region in the north, part of the Carpathian system that divides Slovakia from Poland, and a southern lowland area drained by the River Danube.

HISTORY AND POLITICS As part of the Austro-Hungarian Empire the Slovaks were subject to enforced 'Magyarization' and their development was stifled. They gained independence from it in 1918 and joined the Czechs to form Czechoslovakia. This was formally broken up in January 1993, but the split was amicable and the two new states maintain close links with each other.

ECONOMY There are reserves of coal, copper, lead and zinc. Agriculture is important, with crops of potatoes and sugar beet.

AREA 49,035 sq km [18,932 sq mls]
POPULATION 5,400,000
CAPITAL (POPULATION) Bratislava (448,000)
GOVERNMENT Multiparty republic with a unicameral legislature
ETHNIC GROUPS Slovak, Hungarian, Czech
LANGUAGES Slovak (official)
RELIGIONS Roman Catholic 60%, Protestant 8%, Orthodox 3%
CURRENCY Slovak koruna = 100 halierov
POPULATION DENSITY 110 per sq km [285 per sq ml]

SLOVENIA

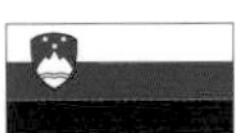

The Slovene flag, based on the flag of Russia, was originally adopted in 1848. During the Communist period a red star appeared in the centre. This was replaced in June 1991 after independence, with the new emblem showing an outline of Mount Triglav.

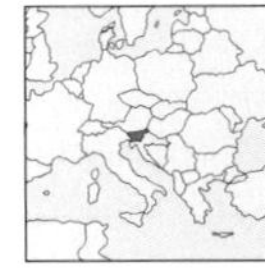

GEOGRAPHY Slovenia is a mountainous state at the northern end of the former Yugoslavia. It has access to the Adriatic Sea through the port of Koper, near the Italian border, giving it a flourishing trade from landlocked central Europe.

HISTORY AND POLITICS Part of the Austro-Hungarian Empire until 1918, Slovenia's Roman Catholic population found support from neighbours Italy and Austria as well as Germany during its fight for independence in 1991. The most ethnically homogeneous of Yugoslavia's component republics, it made the transition to independence fairly peacefully.

ECONOMY There are strong agricultural sectors (wheat, maize) and industry (textiles, timber) and some mineral resources.

AREA 20,251 sq km [7,817 sq mls]
POPULATION 2,000,000
CAPITAL (POPULATION) Ljubljana (323,000)
GOVERNMENT Multiparty republic
ETHNIC GROUPS Slovene 88%, Croat 3%, Serb 2%, Muslim 1%
LANGUAGES Slovene 90%, Serbo-Croat 7%
RELIGIONS Roman Catholic 98%, Orthodox 2%, Muslim 1%
POPULATION DENSITY 99 per sq km [256 per sq ml]

SOLOMON ISLANDS

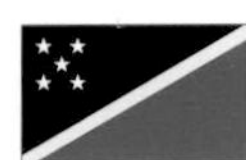

In 1978 the Solomon Islands became independent from Britain and adopted a new flag. The five white-pointed stars represent the five main islands, whilst the colours stand for the forests (green) and waters (blue) lighted by the sun (yellow).

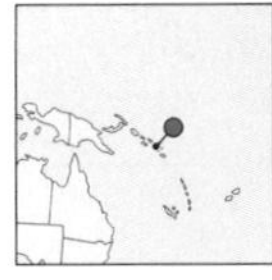

The double chain of islands forming the Solomons and Vanuatu extends for some 2,250 km [1,400 mls] in the Pacific Ocean. It represents the drowned outermost crustal fold on the borders of the ancient Australian continent. Occupied by the Japanese during World War II, the islands were the scene of fierce fighting, notably the battle for the island of Guadalcanal, on which the capital stands. Known as the British Solomons, the islands won full independence in 1978. Subsistence farming occupies about 90% of the population. Coconuts and cocoa are the most important exports, while tuna fish is the main earner.

AREA 28,900 sq km [11,158 sq mls]
POPULATION 378,000
CAPITAL (POPULATION) Honiara (37,000)
GOVERNMENT Constitutional monarchy with a unicameral legislature
ETHNIC GROUPS Melanesian 94%, Polynesian 4%
LANGUAGES Many Melanesian languages, English
RELIGIONS Christian
CURRENCY Solomon Is. $ = 100 cents

SOMALIA

In 1960 British Somaliland united with Italian Somaliland to form present-day Somalia and the flag of the southern region was adopted. It is based on the colours of the UN flag with the points of the star representing the five regions of East Africa where Somalis live.

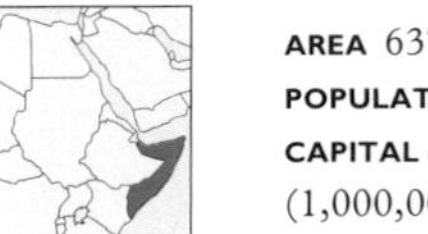

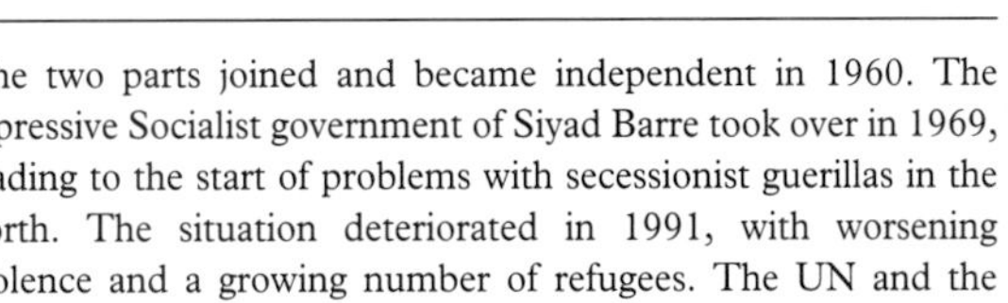

With a coastline on the Gulf of Aden in the north and one on the Indian Ocean in the east, Somalia occupies the literal 'Horn of Africa'. The northern area is the highest and most arid, with mountains rising to 2,408 m [7,900 ft] and wooded with box and cedar. In the south there is low plain or plateau, covered in grass and thorn bush; bananas are a major export from this area. Northern Somalia was ruled as British Somaliland from the 1880s and the south was ruled as Italian Somaliland after 1905. The two parts joined and became independent in 1960. The repressive Socialist government of Siyad Barre took over in 1969, leading to the start of problems with secessionist guerillas in the north. The situation deteriorated in 1991, with worsening violence and a growing number of refugees. The UN and the USA sent in troops in 1993 but they had to withdraw in 1994. In 1997 representatives of 26 factions formed a National Salvation Council in an attempt to restore law and order to the country.

AREA 637,660 sq km [246,201 sq mls]
POPULATION 9,180,000
CAPITAL (POPULATION) Mogadishu (1,000,000)
GOVERNMENT Single-party republic, suspended due to civil war
ETHNIC GROUPS Somali 98%, Arab 1%
LANGUAGES Somali, Arabic, English, Italian
RELIGIONS Sunni Muslim 99%
CURRENCY Shilling = 100 cents
POPULATION DENSITY 14 per sq km [37 per sq ml]
URBAN POPULATION 25% of population

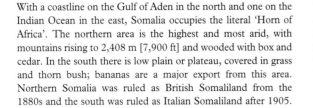

SOUTH AFRICA

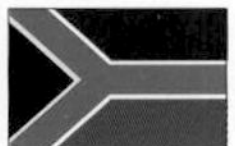

This new flag was adopted in May 1994, after the country's first multiracial elections were held in April and a new constitution was drawn up. The colours are a combination of the ANC colours (black, yellow and green) and the traditional Afrikaner ones (red, white and blue).

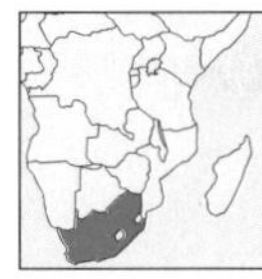

AREA 1,219,916 sq km [470,566 sq mls]
POPULATION 44,000,000
CAPITAL (POPULATION) Pretoria (1,080,000)/
Cape Town (1,912,000)/
Bloemfontein (300,000)
GOVERNMENT Multiparty republic

GEOGRAPHY South Africa is divisible into two major natural zones – the interior and the coastal fringe, with the interior itself divisible into two major parts. Most of Northern Cape Province and Free State are drained by the Orange River and its tributaries. The Northern Transvaal is occupied by the Bushveld, an area of granites and igneous intrusions. The coastal fringe is divided from the interior by the Fringing Escarpment; in the east this is shown by the huge rock wall of the Drakensberg, which rises to over 3,000 m [over 10,000 ft].

HISTORY AND POLITICS The country was first peopled by negroids from the north, who moved southwards into land occupied by Bushmanoid peoples and reached the south-east by the 18th century. At the same time Europeans were establishing a site for the Dutch East India Company on what is now Cape Town; they then spread out throughout the south of the country. Eventually black and white met near the Kei River and the black-dominated and white-dominated areas first arose. The policy of apartheid was instituted by the ruling National Party in 1948, with racial segregation and discrimination against the blacks rigidly enforced. It was not until President F.W. de Klerk was elected in 1989 that reforms slowly began. The first multiracial elections were held in April 1994, with Nelson Mandela elected president, after which all the internal boundaries were changed.

ECONOMY Despite apartheid, South Africa's economy has been very successful (for the white population). There are valuable mineral resources, such as gold, chrome, uranium and nickel.

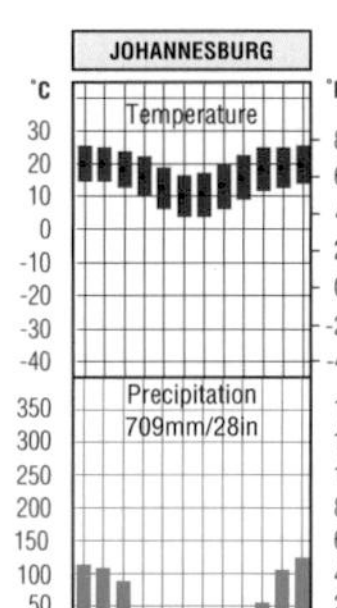

In winter the air is very dry and the sky almost cloudless on the High Veld. The large diurnal range of temperature resembles that of other places on the high plateaux of southern Africa; it often exceeds 15°C [27°F]. Summer is the rainy season, when north-easterly winds bring moist air from the Indian Ocean. In winter it rains on 1–3 days per month.

SPAIN

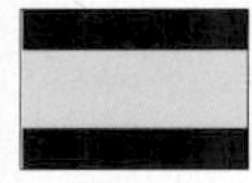

The colours of the Spanish flag date back to the old kingdom of Aragon in the 12th century. The present design, in which the central yellow stripe is twice as wide as each of the red stripes, was adopted during the Civil War in 1938.

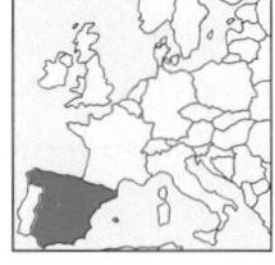

AREA 504,780 sq km [194,896 sq mls]
POPULATION 39,664,000
CAPITAL (POPULATION) Madrid (3,041,000)
GOVERNMENT Constitutional monarchy
CURRENCY Peseta = 100 céntimos

GEOGRAPHY Spain occupies an important geographical position between Europe and Africa, with the narrow Strait of Gibraltar encouraging African contact. The chief physical feature of Spain is the vast central plateau, the Meseta, which tilts gently towards Portugal. This is crossed by the mountain range of the Central Sierras. In the north-east and south of the country are lowlands, while in Andalusia (in the south) a mountain chain rises to the peak of the Sierra Nevada (3,478 m [11,400 ft]). Spain has three main categories of vegetation: forests (about 10% of the land surface) in the north and north-west, *matorral* (which is scrub and covers a fifth of the land), and steppe.

HISTORY AND POLITICS Spain became united in 1479 when the different independent kingdoms that existed joined together after the marriage of Isabella of Castille and Ferdinand of Aragon. The country remained neutral in both world wars, but suffered a civil war between 1936 and 1939, which was won by the Nationalists under Franco. He then ruled as a dictator until 1975 when democracy was restored under King Juan Carlos.

ECONOMY Agriculture occupies nearly one-third of the work-force, even though the soils are poor and there is little rain. Crops include wheat, maize, barley, olives and vines, with vegetables and fruit grown where there is irrigation. Spain is one of the world's largest producers of olive oil. Manufacturing industries include textiles and food processing. Tourism is very important.

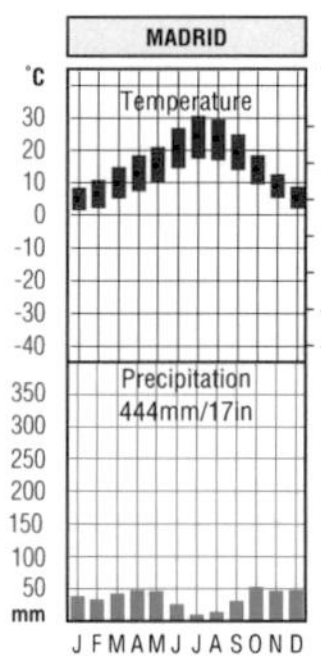

The interior of Spain is a high plateau, isolated from the seas which surround the Iberian Peninsula. Summer days are very hot despite the altitude, above 25°C [77°F] June to September during the day, but at night temperatures fall sharply. Madrid has an average of eight hours of sunshine a day over the year. Winters are colder than in coastal districts.

SRI LANKA

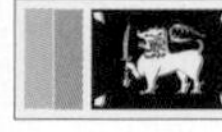

This unusual flag was adopted in 1951, three years after 'Ceylon' gained independence from Britain. The lion banner represents the ancient Buddhist kingdom and the stripes the island's minorities – Muslims (green) and Hindus (orange).

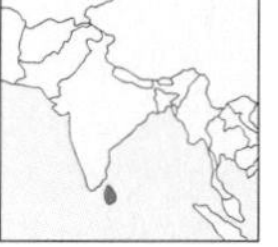

AREA 65,610 sq km [25,332 sq mls]
POPULATION 18,359,000
CAPITAL (POPULATION) Colombo (1,863,000)
GOVERNMENT Unitary multiparty republic with a unicameral legislature
ETHNIC GROUPS Sinhalese 74%, Tamil 18%, Sri Lankan Moor 7%
LANGUAGES Sinhala, Tamil, English
RELIGIONS Buddhist 69%, Hindu 16%, Muslim 8%, Christian 7%
CURRENCY Rupee = 100 cents
POPULATION DENSITY 280 per sq km [725 per sq ml]
URBAN POPULATION 22% of population

GEOGRAPHY The island of Sri Lanka (known as Ceylon until 1972) lies in the Indian Ocean and has a mountainous core. The 'wet zone' of the south-west supports rainforests and tea gardens near Kandy and evergreen forests and palm-fringed beaches in between Colombo and Galle. The north and east are drier.

HISTORY AND POLITICS The island was first inhabited by forest-dwelling Veddas and then by Aryans from India. Portuguese, Dutch and then British (who ruled from 1796 to 1948) traders and colonists came to Sri Lanka, as well as immigrant Tamils. Civil war and violence have been common since independence, with the main conflict between the Sinhalese Buddhist majority and the Tamil Hindu minority. The conflict has been almost continuous since 1983 as the Tamils fight for independence in the north, despite Indian attempts to manage a cease-fire.

ECONOMY Tea, rubber and coconuts are the main products, with some light industry, but the violence has slowed progress.

SUDAN

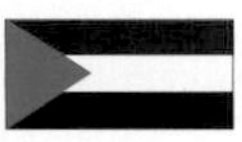

The design of Sudan's flag is based on the flag of the Arab revolt used in Syria, Iraq and Jordan after 1918. Adopted in 1969, it features the Pan-Arab colours and an Islamic green triangle symbolizing material prosperity and spiritual wealth.

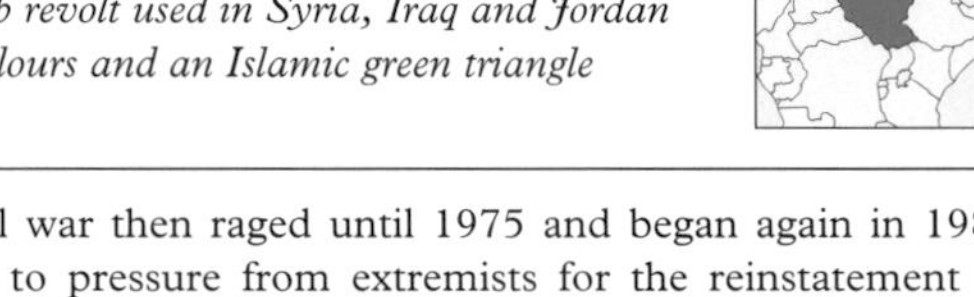

AREA 2,505,810 sq km [967,493 sq mls]
POPULATION 29,980,000
CAPITAL (POPULATION) Khartoum (561,000)
GOVERNMENT Multiparty republic
ETHNIC GROUPS Sudanese Arab 49%, Dinka 12%, Nuba 8%, Beja 6%, Nuer 5%, Azande 3%
LANGUAGES Arabic, Nubian, local languages, English
RELIGIONS Sunni Muslim 75%, traditional beliefs 17%, Roman Catholic 4%, Protestant 2%
CURRENCY Dinar = 10 Sudanese pounds
POPULATION DENSITY 12 per sq km [31 per sq ml]

GEOGRAPHY The Sudan is the largest African state and consists mainly of huge clay plains and sandy areas, part of the Nile basin and the Sahara Desert. The extreme north is virtually uninhabited and most of the population is concentrated in a belt across the centre of the country, especially near the Blue and White Niles. The climate changes from desert to equatorial as the influence of the inter-tropical rainbelt increases southwards.

HISTORY AND POLITICS Sudan was ruled as an Anglo-Egyptian Condominium from 1889 and gained independence in 1956. Civil war then raged until 1975 and began again in 1983 due to pressure from extremists for the reinstatement of fundamental Sharic law. The rivalries of the Arab north and the non-Muslim south have led to many hundreds of thousands of deaths. The first democratic elections since a coup in 1989 were won by Omar Hassan al-Bashir in 1996.

ECONOMY Cotton and oilseed are grown for export, but civil war, repression, a huge foreign debt, prolonged drought and food shortages have caused economic chaos.

SURINAM

SURINAM

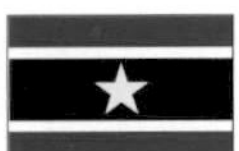

Adopted on independence from the Dutch in 1975, Surinam's flag features the colours of the main political parties, the yellow star symbolizing unity and a golden future. The red is twice the width of the green, and four times that of the white.

AREA 163,270 sq km [63,039 sq mls]
POPULATION 421,000
CAPITAL (POPULATION) Paramaribo (201,000)
GOVERNMENT Multiparty republic with a unicameral legislature
ETHNIC GROUPS Creole 35%, Asian Indian 33%, Indonesian 16%, Black 10%, Amerindian 3%
LANGUAGES Dutch, English
RELIGIONS Hindu, Roman Catholic

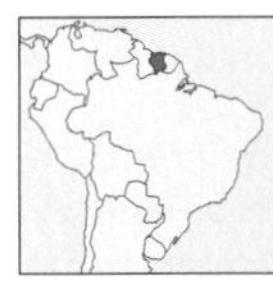

Surinam has a coastline of 350 km [218 mls] of Amazonian mud and silt, fringed by extensive mangrove swamps. Behind lies an old coastal plain of sands and clays, bordering a stretch of savanna. Forest covers 92% of the land surface. The country was first settled by British colonists in 1651. It was ceded to Holland in 1667 and became Dutch Guiana in 1816. Independence was won in 1975. Since 1992 there has been some instability. Bauxite and its derivatives, bananas and shrimps are the main exports.

SWAZILAND

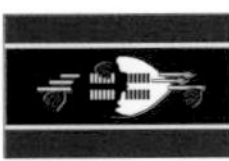

The kingdom has flown this distinctive flag, whose background is based on that of the Swazi Pioneer Corps of World War II, since independence from Britain in 1968. The emblem has the weapons of a warrior – ox-hide shield, two assegai *(spears) and a fighting stick.*

AREA 17,360 sq km [6,703 sq mls]
POPULATION 849,000
CAPITAL (POPULATION) Mbabane (42,000)
GOVERNMENT Monarchy with a bicameral legislature
ETHNIC GROUPS African 97%, European 3%
LANGUAGES English, Swazi
RELIGIONS Christian 77%, traditional beliefs 21%
CURRENCY Lilangeni = 100 cents

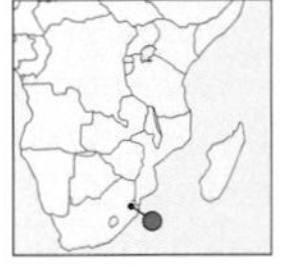

Swaziland is the smallest state in sub-Saharan Africa, but has a wide variety of landscapes. From west to east the land descends in three altitudinal steps: the High Veld (1,200 m [4,000 ft]), the Middle Veld and the Low Veld (270 m [900 ft]). In the east are the Lebombo Mountains. Europeans settled Swaziland in the late 19th century. Independence was won from Britain in 1968 and Swaziland is part of a customs union which includes South Africa. Swaziland has some mineral reserves (such as iron ore, coal, gold and diamonds) and tourism is increasing in importance. Sugar, citrus fruits and wood pulp are exported.

SWEDEN

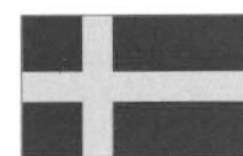

While Sweden's national flag has been flown since the reign of King Gustavus Vasa in the early 16th century, it was not officially adopted until 1906. The colours were derived from the ancient state coat of arms dating from 1364.

AREA 449,960 sq km [173,730 sq mls]
POPULATION 8,893,000
CAPITAL (POPULATION) Stockholm (1,539,000)
GOVERNMENT Constitutional monarchy and a parliamentary state with a unicameral legislature
ETHNIC GROUPS Swedish 90%, Finnish 2%
LANGUAGES Swedish, Finnish
RELIGIONS Lutheran 88%, Roman Catholic 2%
CURRENCY Swedish krona = 100 öre
POPULATION DENSITY 20 per sq km [51 per sq ml]

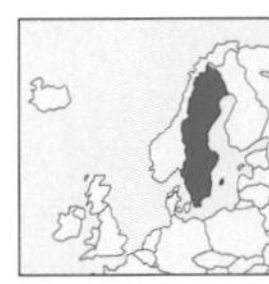

GEOGRAPHY Sweden occupies the eastern half of the Scandinavian peninsula, with a much smaller Arctic area than Finland or Norway. The northern part of the country forms part of the Baltic or Fenno-Scandian Shield, and is an area of low plateaux. In the south there is a belt of lowlands, which contain several large lakes (including Vänern). The topography has been greatly affected by the Ice Age, which has shaped the lakes and left fertile soils. Half of Sweden's land area is covered by forests.
HISTORY AND POLITICS Between 1397 and 1523 Sweden was united with Norway and Denmark, and after it broke away it was for a period the leading Baltic nation. More recent history has seen the end of the Social Democrat government in 1991, which had been in power for all but six years since 1932. Sweden applied for entry to the EU in 1991 and finally joined on 1 January 1995, following a referendum.
ECONOMY Sweden is famous for high-quality engineering products such as ball-bearings, agricultural machines, cars and ships. It is also the world's largest exporter of wood pulp.

SWITZERLAND

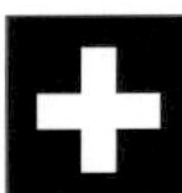

Switzerland's square flag was officially adopted in 1848, though the white cross on a red shield has been the Swiss emblem since the 14th century. The flag of the International Red Cross, based in Geneva, derives from this Swiss flag.

AREA 41,290 sq km [15,942 sq mls]
POPULATION 7,268,000
CAPITAL (POPULATION) Bern (299,000)
GOVERNMENT Federal state with a bicameral legislature
ETHNIC GROUPS Swiss German 65%, Swiss French 18%, Swiss Italian 10%, Spanish 2%, Yugoslav 2%, Romansch 1%
LANGUAGES French, German, Italian, Romansch
RELIGIONS Roman Catholic 46%, Protestant 40%, Muslim 2%
CURRENCY Swiss franc = 100 centimes
POPULATION DENSITY 176 per sq km [456 per sq ml]
URBAN POPULATION 60% of population

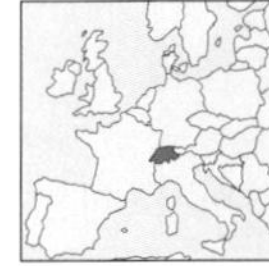

GEOGRAPHY Nearly 60% of Swiss territory is in the Alps, with two notable peaks on the Italian border: the Matterhorn (4,478 m [14,700 ft]) and the Monte Rosa (4,634 m [15,200 ft]). The Alps are drained by the upper Rhine tributaries and by the Rhône Valley via Lac Léman (Lake Geneva). Within the mountains are many lakes and much permanent snow.
HISTORY AND POLITICS Switzerland is made up of 26 multilingual cantons, each of which has control over housing and economic policy. Six of the cantons are French-speaking, one Italian-speaking, one with a significant Romansch-speaking community and the rest German-speaking. It is a strongly united country and is politically stable. It remained neutral in both world wars and has a high standard of living, helped by its central European location and good organizational ability. It is now the location of many headquarters of international bodies, including the Red Cross and 10 UN agencies in Geneva.
ECONOMY Agriculture is efficient, with a wide range of produce including maize and other cereals, fruits and vegetables. Industry is progressive, particularly engineering. There are strong banking and insurance industries and the Alps attract many tourists.

SYRIA

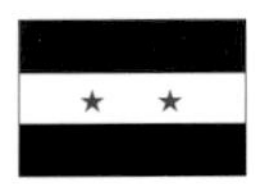

The flag of Syria is the one adopted in 1958 by the former United Arab Republic and is in the colours of the Pan-Arab movement. At various times in their history Egypt and Syria have shared the same flag, but since 1980 Syria has used this design.

AREA 185,180 sq km [71,498 sq mls]
POPULATION 14,614,000
CAPITAL (POPULATION) Damascus (2,230,000)
GOVERNMENT Unitary multiparty republic with a unicameral legislature
ETHNIC GROUPS Arab 89%, Kurdish 6%
LANGUAGES Arabic, Kurdish, Armenian
RELIGIONS Muslim 90%, Christian 9%
CURRENCY Syrian pound = 100 piastres
POPULATION DENSITY 79 per sq km [204 per sq ml]

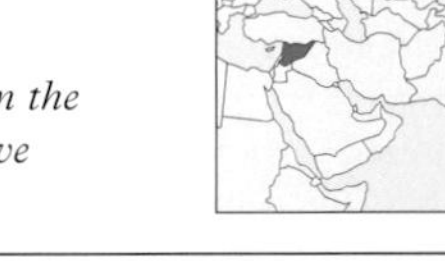

GEOGRAPHY Syria stretches from the Mediterranean to the Tigris and has most of the Hamad or stony desert in the south. There is one large harbour, at Latakia, and the Lebanon and Anti-Lebanon Mountains are found in the west and south-west.
HISTORY AND POLITICS Syria now occupies what was the northern part of the Ottoman province of Syria. It became an independent country in 1946 but was then part of the United Arab Republic, with Egypt and Yemen, between 1958 and 1961. Syria has always played a key role in Middle East affairs, usually with a pro-Arab stance (except during the 1991 Gulf War).
ECONOMY Crops include cotton and cereals and there are good irrigation schemes. Oil has been struck in the far north-east.

TAIWAN

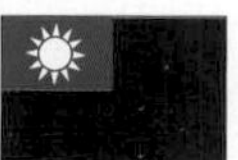

In 1928 the Nationalists adopted this design as China's national flag and used it in the long struggle against Mao Tse-tung's Communist army. When they were forced to retreat to Taiwan (then Formosa) in 1949, the flag went with them.

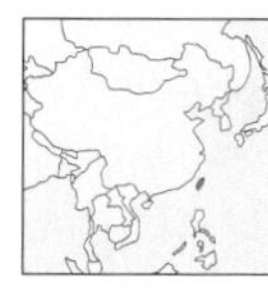

GEOGRAPHY Taiwan was formerly known by the Portuguese as Isla Formosa, meaning 'beautiful island'. High mountain ranges, extending the length of the island, occupy the central and eastern areas and carry dense forests. The climate is warm and moist, thereby producing a good environment for agriculture.
HISTORY AND POLITICS Chinese settlers occupied Taiwan from the 7th century onwards, before the Portuguese discovered it in 1590. In 1895 the province was seized by Japan and developed as a colony. Returned to China after World War II, Taiwan became the final refuge of the Nationalists that had been driven from China by Mao Tse-tung's forces in 1949. With US help, Taiwan set about ambitious land reforms and industrial expansion. The first full general election was held in 1991.
ECONOMY A wide range of manufactured goods are produced, including colour television sets, electronic calculators, footwear and clothing, and Taiwan is the world's leading shipbreaker.

AREA 36,000 sq km [13,900 sq mls]
POPULATION 21,100,000
CAPITAL (POPULATION) Taipei (2,653,000)
GOVERNMENT Unitary multiparty republic with a unicameral legislature
ETHNIC GROUPS Taiwanese (Han Chinese) 84%, mainland Chinese 14%
LANGUAGES Mandarin Chinese
RELIGIONS Buddhist 43%, Taoist & Confucian 49%, Christian 7%
CURRENCY New Taiwan dollar = 100 cents
POPULATION DENSITY 586 per sq km [1,518 per sq ml]
URBAN POPULATION 75% of population

TAJIKISTAN

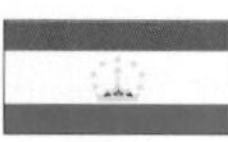

The new flag was adopted early in 1993 and denotes a gold crown of unusual design under an arc of seven stars. The proportions of the flag are 1:2.

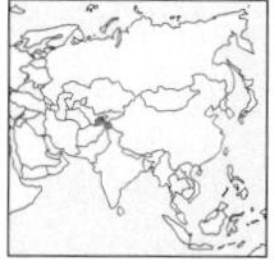

Tajikistan lies on the borders of Afghanistan and China and only 7% of the land area lies below 1,000 m [3,280 ft]. The eastern half is almost all above 3,000 m [9,840 ft]. The country is the poorest of the former Soviet republics and independence (in 1991) brought huge economic problems. As a Persian people the Tajiks are more likely to follow Islamic influences rather than Western ones. In 1992, civil war broke out between the government and an alliance of democrats and Islamic forces.

AREA 143,100 sq km [55,250 sq mls]
POPULATION 6,102,000
CAPITAL (POPULATION) Dushanbe (602,000)
GOVERNMENT Transitional democracy
ETHNIC GROUPS Tajik 64%, Uzbek 24%, Russian 7%
LANGUAGES Tajik
RELIGIONS Sunni Muslim, some Christian
CURRENCY Tajik rouble = 100 kopeks
URBAN POPULATION 32% of population

TANZANIA

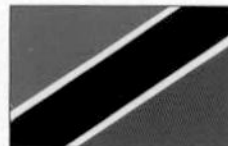

In 1964 Tanganyika united with the island of Zanzibar to form the United Republic of Tanzania and a new flag was adopted. The colours represent agriculture (green), minerals (yellow), the people (black), water and Zanzibar (blue).

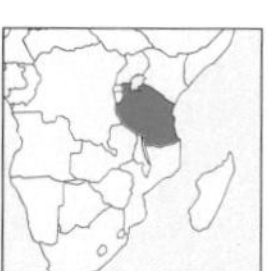

GEOGRAPHY Tanzania extends across the high plateau of eastern Africa, mostly above 1,000 m [3,000 ft], to the rift valleys filled by Lakes Tanganyika and Nyasa (Malawi). The Northern Highlands are part of the eastern rift valley and are dominated by the ice-capped extinct volcano of Kilimanjaro, the highest mountain in Africa. Temperatures are uniformly high all year.
HISTORY AND POLITICS Tanzania was formed in 1964 when mainland Tanganyika (which had become independent from Britain in 1961) was joined by the island state of Zanzibar. For 20 years President Julius Nyerere ruled with policies of self-help (*ujamaa*) and egalitarian socialism. Progress was slowed and Nyerere's successor is now attempting to liberalize the economy.
ECONOMY Export crops include coffee, tea, cotton, sisal and tobacco. A nickel mine, the country's first, was opened in 1996.

AREA 945,090 sq km [364,899 sq mls]
POPULATION 29,710,000
CAPITAL (POPULATION) Dodoma (204,000)
GOVERNMENT Multiparty republic
ETHNIC GROUPS Nyamwezi and Sukuma 21%, Swahili 9%, Hehet and Bena 7%, Makonde 6%, Haya 6%
LANGUAGES English and Swahili (both official)
RELIGIONS Christian 34%, Sunni Muslim 33%, traditional beliefs
CURRENCY Shilling = 100 cents
URBAN POPULATION 22% of population

THAILAND

The two red and white stripes are all that remains of Thailand's traditional red-on-white elephant emblem, removed from the flag in 1916. The blue stripe was added in 1917 to show solidarity with the Allies in World War I.

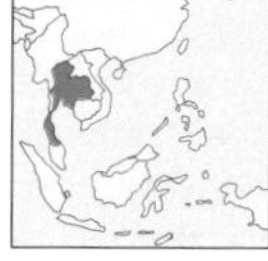

GEOGRAPHY Thailand is centred on the valley of the Chao Phraya River that flows across the central plain extending from the Gulf of Siam to the foothills of the northern fold mountains. In the east, separated from the central plain by low hills, is the Khorat Plateau, which is covered by savanna woodlands. The long southern part of Thailand, linked to the Malay Peninsula by the Isthmus of Kra, is a forested region. The climate is tropical, with fairly high rainfall and temperatures all year round.
HISTORY AND POLITICS Known as Siam until 1939, Thailand is the only South-east Asian country that has not been colonized, or occupied by foreign powers, except in war. It was an absolute monarchy until 1932, when the king surrendered. Military rulers dominated the next 40 years; after being forced into alliance with Japan in World War II, the Thais then aligned themselves to the USA after 1945. The country now has a system of constitutional rule that has helped it to prosper.
ECONOMY Rice is the most important crop, with others such as rubber and sugar. Manufacturing is increasing rapidly.

AREA 513,120 sq km [198,116 sq mls]
POPULATION 58,432,000
CAPITAL (POPULATION) Bangkok (5,876,000)
GOVERNMENT Constitutional monarchy with a multiparty bicameral legislature
ETHNIC GROUPS Thai 80%, Chinese 12%, Malay 4%, Khmer 3%
LANGUAGES Thai, Chinese, Malay
RELIGIONS Buddhist 95%, Muslim 4%, Christian 1%
CURRENCY Baht = 100 satang
POPULATION DENSITY 114 per sq km [295 per sq ml]
URBAN POPULATION 19% of population
LAND USE Arable 33%, forest 26%

TOGO

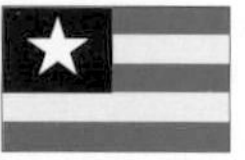

Togo's Pan-African colours stand for agriculture and the future (green), mineral wealth and the value of hard work (yellow), and the blood shed in the struggle for independence from France in 1960 (red), with the white star for national purity.

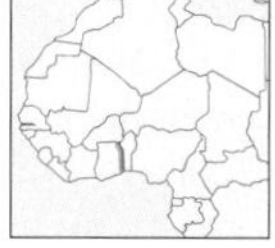

GEOGRAPHY A small country in West Africa nowhere more than 120 km [75 mls] wide, Togo stretches inland from the Gulf of Guinea. The Togo-Atacora Mountains cross the country from south-west to north-east and there are forests in the south-west.
HISTORY, POLITICS AND ECONOMY As Togoland, the country was colonized by Germany in 1884 and then occupied by Franco-British troops during World War I. It was partitioned between the two powers in 1922, with British Togoland later becoming part of Ghana and the larger eastern French section gaining independence as Togo in 1960. In 1991 multiparty elections ended the military regime, but there has since been fighting. Phosphates, coffee and cocoa are the main exports.

AREA 56,790 sq km [21,927 sq mls]
POPULATION 4,140,000
CAPITAL (POPULATION) Lomé (590,000)
GOVERNMENT Multiparty republic
ETHNIC GROUPS Ewe-Adja 43%, Tem-Kabre 26%, Gurma 16%
LANGUAGES French, Ewe, Kabre
RELIGIONS Traditional beliefs 59%, Christian 28%, Sunni Muslim 12%
CURRENCY CFA franc = 100 centimes
POPULATION DENSITY 73 per sq km [189 per sq ml]

TONGA

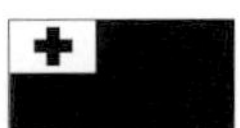

The flag was introduced in 1862 by Taufa'ahau Tupou, the first king of all Tonga, and represents the Christian faith of the islanders. The red cross, similar to the methodist badge and the Red Cross flag, illustrates the Tongans' adherence to the Christian religion.

The Tongan archipelago comprises more than 170 islands in the southern Pacific Ocean, 36 of which are inhabited. The landscape is a mixture of low coralline and higher volcanic outcrops covered with dense vegetation. Nearly two-thirds of the population live on the largest island of Tongatapu. Tonga has been ruled by Taufa'ahau Tupou IV since 1965, who presided over the transition of the islands to an independent state in 1970. Coconut oil products and bananas are the main exports.

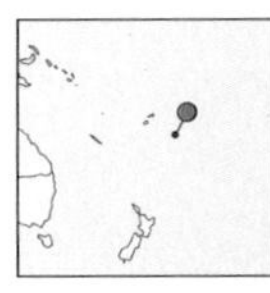

AREA 750 sq km [290 sq mls]
POPULATION 107,000
CAPITAL (POPULATION) Nuku'alofa (30,000)
GOVERNMENT Constitutional monarchy
ETHNIC GROUPS Tongan 96%
LANGUAGES Tongan, English
RELIGIONS Christian
CURRENCY Pa'anga = 100 seniti
POPULATION DENSITY 143 per sq km [369 per sq ml]

TRINIDAD AND TOBAGO

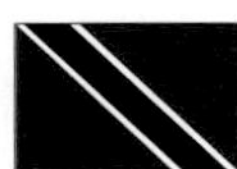

The islands of Trinidad and Tobago have flown this flag since independence from Britain in 1962. Red stands for the people's warmth and vitality, black for their strength, and white for their hopes and the surf of the sea.

GEOGRAPHY Furthest south of the West Indies, Trinidad is an island situated just 16 km [10 mls] off Venezuela. Tobago is a detached extension of its Northern Range of hills, lying 34 km [21 mls] to the north-east. The landscape is forested and hilly.
HISTORY, POLITICS AND ECONOMY Trinidad was 'discovered' by Columbus in 1498 and then settled by Spanish and French. It became British in 1797. Tobago came under British control in 1814, with the two islands joining to form a united colony in 1899. Independence came in 1962 and a republic was formed in 1976, although Tobago is keen for internal self-government. Oil was very important in economic development, but falling prices have caused problems. There are also reserves of asphalt and gas.

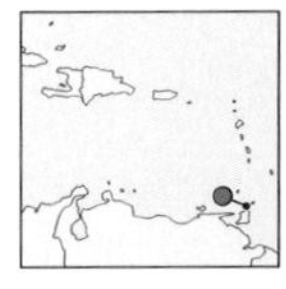

AREA 5,130 sq km [1,981 sq mls]
POPULATION 1,295,000
CAPITAL (POPULATION) Port of Spain (60,000)
GOVERNMENT Republic with a bicameral legislature
ETHNIC GROUPS Black 40%, East Indian 40%, Mixed 18%, White 1%, Chinese 1%
LANGUAGES English
RELIGIONS Christian 40%, Hindu 24%, Muslim 6%

TRISTAN DA CUNHA

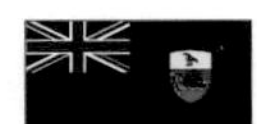

The flag is the British Blue Ensign with the shield from the arms in the fly. A new coat of arms was introduced in 1984.

Tristan da Cunha is located towards the southern end of the Mid-Atlantic Ridge and has a volcanic cone ringed by a lava plain that drops steeply to the sea. The small population live on a flat coastal strip. It is administered as a dependency of St Helena.

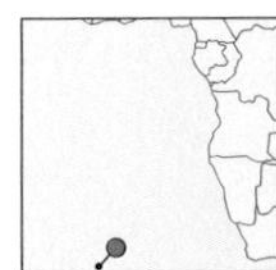

AREA 104 sq km [40 sq mls]
POPULATION 330
CAPITAL Edinburgh
GOVERNMENT Dependent Territory of the UK
LANGUAGES English
POPULATION DENSITY 3.2 per sq km [8 per sq ml]

TUNISIA

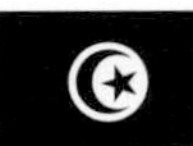

The Tunisian flag features the crescent moon and five-pointed star, traditional symbols of Islam. It originated in about 1835 when the country was still officially under Turkish rule and was adopted after independence from France in 1956.

GEOGRAPHY Tunisia is the smallest of the three Maghreb countries that comprise north-west Africa. The country is made up of the eastern end of the Atlas Mountains together with the central steppelands to the south, which are separated from the country's Saharan sector by the huge low-lying saltpans of the Chott Djerid. In the north the lower Medjerda Valley and the low-lying plains of Bizerte and Tunis were densely colonized.
HISTORY AND POLITICS Tunisia has a long and varied history. It was the first part of the region to be conquered by the Phoenicians, Romans (Carthage is now a suburb of Tunis) and later the Arabs and Turks (as part of the Ottoman Empire after 1537). Each successive civilization has left a marked impression on the country, giving Tunisia a distinct national identity. France established a protectorate in 1881 and Tunisia became independent in 1956. Today it is effectively ruled by one party, the RCD, with some elements of democracy slowly introduced.
ECONOMY Major irrigation schemes in the northern lowlands have turned it into an important agricultural area, producing cereals, vines, citrus fruits, olives and vegetables. New industries and some tourism have been important along the coast.

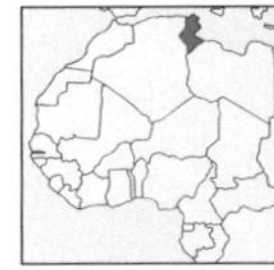

AREA 163,610 sq km [63,170 sq mls]
POPULATION 8,906,000
CAPITAL (POPULATION) Tunis (1,827,000)

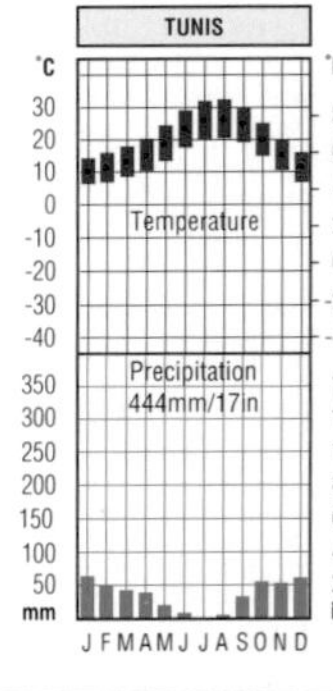

Although most of the rain in Tunisia falls in winter when the region is affected by low pressure, prevailing north-easterly winds from the sea in summer result in a shorter dry season than is found in other parts of the Mediterranean. Rain falls on only a few days throughout the summer. The influence of the sea moderates extremes of temperatures.

TURKEY

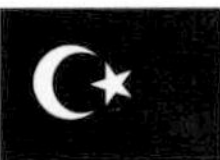

Although the crescent moon and the five-pointed star are symbols of Islam, their presence on Turkey's flag dates from long before the country became a Muslim state. The flag was officially adopted when the republic was founded in 1923.

GEOGRAPHY The most populous country in south-west Asia, Turkey comprises the broad peninsula of Asia Minor and in Europe that part of Thrace (Thraki) which lies to the east of the lower Maritsa River. The Straits separating the European (5%) and Asiatic parts of Turkey have been of strategic importance for thousands of years. The heart of the country is the high karst plateau of Anatolia with semi-desert around the central salt lake. The northern Pontic ranges are wooded, with fertile plains. Istanbul controls the straits between the Black Sea and the Mediterranean and is Turkey's chief port and commercial city.
HISTORY AND POLITICS The huge Ottoman Empire of Constantinople (modern Istanbul) extended through the Balkans to south-west Asia and north Africa for many hundreds of years. After alliance with Germany in World War I, all non-Turkish areas were lost. Nationalists led by Mustafa Kemal rejected peace proposals favouring Greece and after a civil war set up a republic. Turkey's present frontiers were established in 1923, when Atatürk became president, and until 1938 he ruled as a virtual dictator, secularizing and modernizing the traditional Islamic state. Democracy has been relatively stable since 1983 with the return of civilian rule, but there is a poor human rights record and a low standard of living.
ECONOMY Manufacturing is important, particularly textiles and clothing. Export crops include tobacco, figs and cotton.

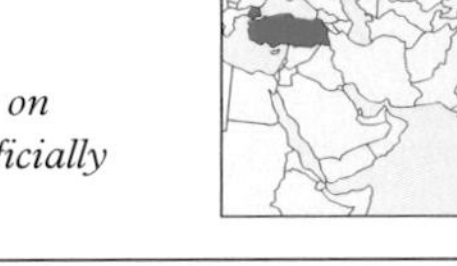

AREA 779,450 sq km [300,946 sq mls]
POPULATION 61,303,000
CAPITAL (POPULATION) Ankara (3,028,000)
GOVERNMENT Multiparty republic with a unicameral legislature

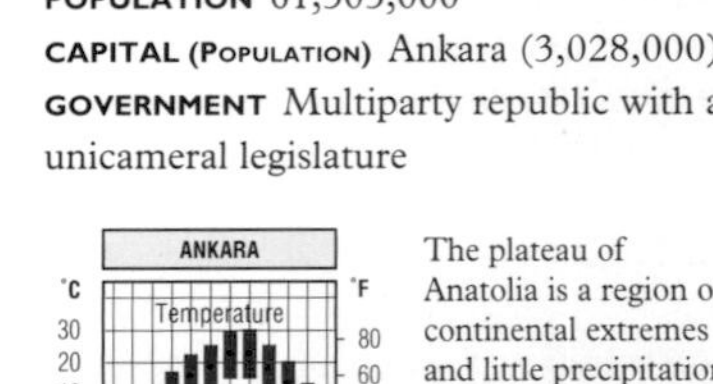

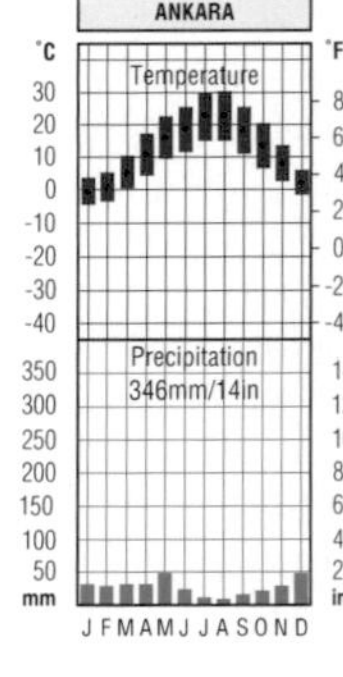

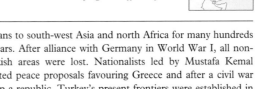

The plateau of Anatolia is a region of continental extremes and little precipitation. Ankara lies just to the north of the driest part of the plateau which is situated around the large saltwater Lake Tuz. Summer days are hot and sunny and nights pleasantly cool; over 11 hours of sunshine and 15–30°C [59–86°F]. Annual rainfall is low.

TURKMENISTAN

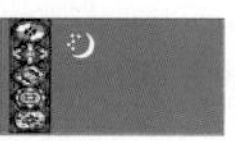

The flag dates from February 1992 and depicts a typical Turkmen carpet design and a crescent and five stars. The stars and the five elements of the carpet represent the traditional tribes of Turkmenistan.

AREA 488,100 sq km [188,450 sq mls]
POPULATION 4,100,000
CAPITAL (POPULATION) Ashkhabad (411,000)
GOVERNMENT Single-party republic
ETHNIC GROUPS Turkmen 73%, Russian 10%, Uzbek 9%, Kazak 2%
LANGUAGES Turkmen 72%, Russian 12%
RELIGIONS Sunni Muslim 85%, Christian
CURRENCY Manat
POPULATION DENSITY 8 per sq km [22 per sq ml]

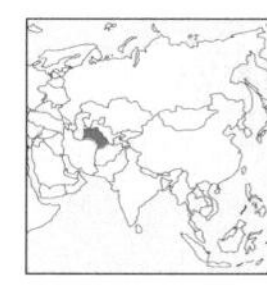

More than 90% of Turkmenistan is arid, with over half the country covered by the Karakum, Asia's largest sand desert. It declared independence from the former Soviet Union in October 1991 and has since looked south to the Muslim countries more than the CIS for support. Like its Turkic associates, Azerbaijan and Uzbekistan, it has joined the Economic Co-operation Organization formed by Turkey, Iran and Pakistan in 1985. Crops include cereals, cotton and fruit. Apart from astrakhan rugs and food processing, industry is confined to mining sulphur and salt and the production of natural gas, its biggest export.

TURKS AND CAICOS ISLANDS

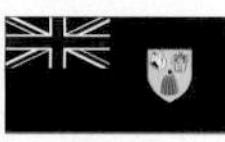

Since this group of islands is a British dependent territory, the flag has the same basic design of the British Blue Ensign. The gold roundel in the fly contains the islands' badge which shows a conch shell, a spiny lobster and a turk's head cactus, all of which are found on the islands.

AREA 430 sq km [166 sq mls]
POPULATION 15,000
CAPITAL (POPULATION) Cockburn Town (4,000)
GOVERNMENT British Dependent Territory
ETHNIC GROUPS Of African descent
LANGUAGES English
RELIGIONS Christian
CURRENCY US dollar
URBAN POPULATION 55% of population

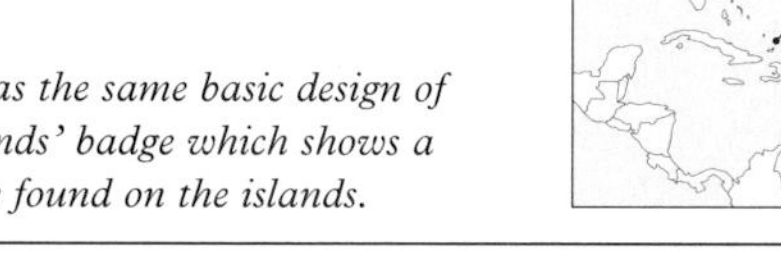

A group of 30 islands (eight of them inhabited), lying at the eastern end of the Grand Bahama Bank, north of Haiti, the Turks and Caicos are composed of low, flat limestone terrain with scrub, marsh and swamp providing little agriculture. They have been British since 1766, administered with Jamaica from 1873 to 1959 and a separate British dependency since 1973. Tourism (71,000 visitors in 1994) has replaced fishing as the main industry. Offshore banking facilities are also expanding.

TUVALU

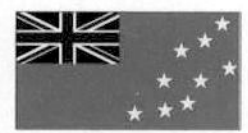

A new flag was adopted on Independence Day on 1 October 1995 but the flag shown left, based on the British Blue Ensign, was reinstated in February 1997. It features nine yellow stars representing the geographical position of the nine main islands and was first adopted in 1978.

AREA 24 sq km [9 sq mls]
POPULATION 10,000
CAPITAL (POPULATION) Fongafale (2,810)
GOVERNMENT Constitutional monarchy
ETHNIC GROUPS Polynesian
LANGUAGES Tuvaluan, English
RELIGIONS Christian
CURRENCY Tuvaluan dollar = 100 cents
POPULATION DENSITY 417 per sq km [1,111 per sq ml]

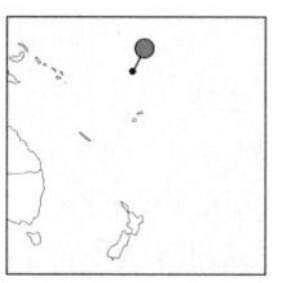

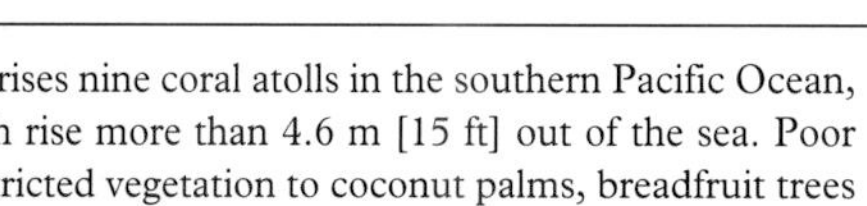

Tuvalu comprises nine coral atolls in the southern Pacific Ocean, none of which rise more than 4.6 m [15 ft] out of the sea. Poor soils have restricted vegetation to coconut palms, breadfruit trees and bush. The islands became an independent constitutional monarchy within the Commonwealth in 1978, three years after separation from the Gilbert Islands. The population survive by subsistence farming and by fishing. Copra and the sale of elaborate postage stamps are the main foreign exchange earners.

UGANDA

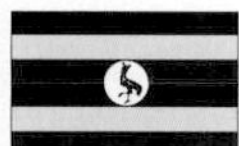

Adopted on independence from Britain in 1962, Uganda's flag is that of the party which won the first national election. The colours represent the people (black), the sun (yellow), and brotherhood (red); the country's emblem is a crested crane.

AREA 235,880 sq km [91,073 sq mls]
POPULATION 21,466,000
CAPITAL (POPULATION) Kampala (773,000)
GOVERNMENT Transitional republic
ETHNIC GROUPS Baganda 18%, Banyoro 14%, Teso 9%, Banyan 8%, Basoga 8%, Bagisu 7%, Bachiga 7%, Lango 6%, Acholi 5%
LANGUAGES English, Swahili
RELIGIONS Roman Catholic 40%, Protestant 29%, animist 18%, Sunni Muslim 7%
CURRENCY Shilling = 100 cents
POPULATION DENSITY 91 per sq km [236 per sq ml]
URBAN POPULATION 12% of population

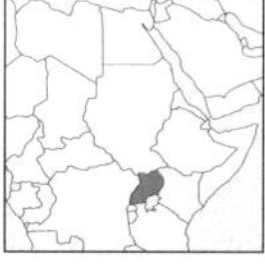

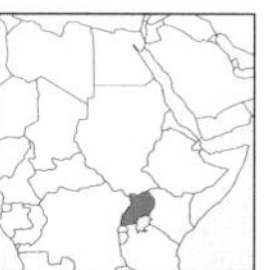

GEOGRAPHY Extending from Lake Victoria to the western arm of the Great Rift Valley, landlocked Uganda has many lakes originating from the tilting and faulting associated with the rift valley system. On the western side of the country the Ruwenzori block has been uplifted to 5,109 m [16,762 ft], while the eastern frontier bisects the large extinct volcano of Mt Elgon. In the south rainfall is abundant in two seasons, and patches of the original rainforest (25% of the land area) remain. To the north, one rainy season supports a savanna of trees and grassland.
HISTORY AND POLITICS Uganda was a British protectorate from 1894 to 1962. After independence the country suffered a succession of linked civil wars, violent coups, armed invasions and tribal massacres. The worst period was during the regime of Idi Amin, who in 1971 replaced the first prime minister Milton Obote. His eight-year reign saw up to 300,000 deaths and the suspension of all political and human rights. Obote returned to power briefly after Amin was removed, but he was ousted again in 1985. Museveni took over in 1986 and began some reforms.
ECONOMY Uganda is the world's seventh largest coffee producer. Other crops include tea and sugar.

UKRAINE

The colours of the Ukrainian flag were first adopted in 1848 and were heraldic in origin, first used on the coat of arms of one of the medieval Ukrainian kingdoms. The flag was first used in the period 1918–20 and was readopted on 4 September 1991.

AREA 603,700 sq km [233,100 sq mls]
POPULATION 52,027,000
CAPITAL (POPULATION) Kiev (2,643,000)
GOVERNMENT Multiparty republic

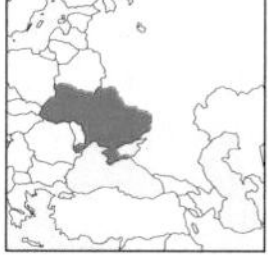

GEOGRAPHY The Ukraine became the largest nation wholly within Europe following its declaration of independence on 24 August 1991 and the subsequent disintegration of the Soviet Union. The western Ukraine comprises the fertile uplands of Volhynia, with the Carpathians in the far western corner of the country. The north is mainly lowlands, with the Dnepr River at its heart; this was the area that suffered most from the Chernobyl nuclear disaster of 1986, with huge areas of land contaminated by radioactivity. In the south are dry lowlands bordering the Black Sea and the Sea of Azov, with Odesa the main port.
HISTORY AND POLITICS The Ukraine was invaded in 1941 by the Germans who stayed until 1944 and were responsible for the deportation and deaths of more than 5 million Ukrainians and Ukrainian Jews. After Soviet control was reinstated in 1945, the Ukraine was given a seat on the UN as some sort of compensation. The Ukraine's declaration of independence was ratified by referendum in December 1991 and Leonid Kravchuk was voted president. In 1996 a new constitution was adopted granting new powers to the president and a right to private ownership.
ECONOMY The main industries are coalmining, iron and steel, agricultural machinery, petrochemicals and plastics. Chronic food shortages and hyperinflation have caused problems.

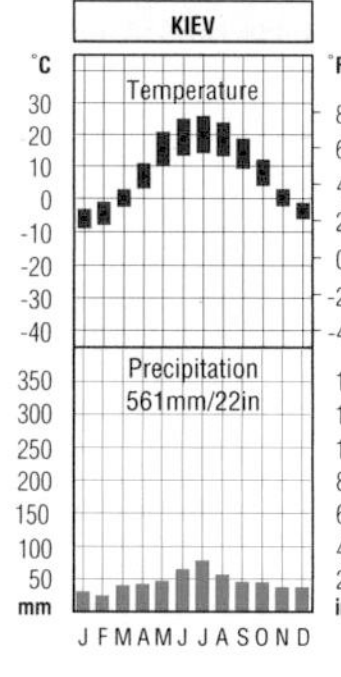

Although on the same latitude as many European cities, Kiev is distant from maritime effects. Rainfall is low and evenly distributed throughout the year with a slight summer peak. Snow may lie for over 80 days, and there is precipitation on over 160 days in the year. Winter temperatures are not too severe and only four months of the year are sub-zero.

UNITED ARAB EMIRATES

UNITED ARAB EMIRATES

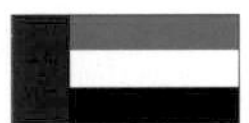

When seven small states around the Gulf combined to form the United Arab Emirates in 1971, this flag was agreed for the new nation. It features the Pan-Arab colours, first used in the Arab revolt against the Turks from 1916.

AREA 83,600 sq km [32,278 sq mls]
POPULATION 2,800,000
CAPITAL (POPULATION) Abu Dhabi (243,000)
GOVERNMENT Federation of seven emirates, each with its own government
ETHNIC GROUPS Arab 87%, Indo-Pakistani 9%, Iranian 2%
LANGUAGES Arabic, English
RELIGIONS Muslim 95%, Christian 4%
CURRENCY Dirham = 100 fils
POPULATION DENSITY 33 per sq km [87 per sq ml]

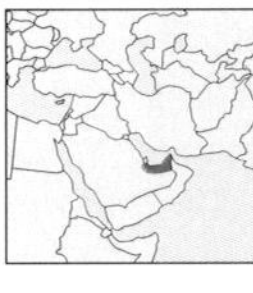

The United Arab Emirates (UAE) were formed in 1971, when six of the British-run Trucial States of the Gulf – Abu Dhabi, Ajman, Dubai, Fujairah, Sharjah and Umm al-Qaiwain – opted to join together and form their own independent country. The state of Ras-al-Khaimah joined in 1972. The country has a coastline on the Gulf and comprises mainly low-lying desert, with little fertile land. The climate is very hot and arid. The oil and gas reserves have provided the highest GNP per capita figure in Asia after Japan. However, only 20% of the population are citizens; the rest are expatriate workers. There is some agriculture, but only where there are oases or the land is irrigated. Crops grown include dates, fruits and vegetables.

UNITED KINGDOM

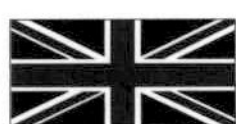

The first Union flag, combining England's cross of St George and Scotland's cross of St Andrew, dates from 1603 when James VI became James I of England. The Irish emblem, the cross of St Patrick, was added in 1801 to form the present flag.

AREA 243,368 sq km [94,202 sq mls]
POPULATION 58,306,000
CAPITAL (POPULATION) London (6,967,000)
GOVERNMENT Constitutional monarchy with a bicameral legislature
ETHNIC GROUPS White 94%, Asian Indian 1%, West Indian 1%, Pakistani 1%
LANGUAGES English, Welsh, Scots-Gaelic
RELIGIONS Anglican 57%, Roman Catholic 13%, Presbyterian 7%, Methodist 4%, other Christian 6%, Muslim 2%, Jewish 1%, Hindu 1%, Sikh 1%
CURRENCY Pound sterling = 100 pence
POPULATION DENSITY 240 per sq km [619 per sq ml]

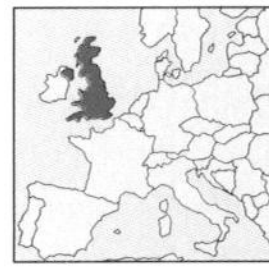

GEOGRAPHY The British Isles stand on the westernmost edge of the continental shelf – two large and several hundred small islands. The United Kingdom of Great Britain and Northern Ireland is made up of England, Scotland and Wales (Great Britain), Northern Ireland and the many off-lying islands from the Scillies to the Shetlands. The Isle of Man and the Channel Islands are separate dependencies of the Crown, with a degree of political autonomy and their own taxation systems. There are a variety of physical landscapes. The present English landscape has been marked by events in the past, including complex folding, laval outpourings, volcanic upheavals and eruptions, glacial planing, and changes of sea level. Upland areas include the Pennines, the Lake District and Exmoor, while lowland areas largely consist of chalk downlands – examples are the North Downs and the Hampshire Downs. Wales is predominantly hilly and mountainous, although two-thirds of the rural area is farmland and one-third is moorland. Scotland is also hilly, with a landscape of many deep, glaciated valleys dominated by mountains. Despite its subarctic position Britain is favoured climatically; this is due to the North Atlantic Drift, a current of warm surface water from the southern Atlantic Ocean.

HISTORY AND POLITICS While Britain is physically close to the rest of Europe (32 km [20 mls] at the nearest point), it has a long history of political independence from its neighbours. Its peoples are of mixed stock, after invasions by several groups and immigrants arriving from all over the world. The most important invasions were those of the Romans in AD 43, the Anglo-Saxons after AD 500 and the Normans in 1066. The United Kingdom itself was formed by the unions of the different kingdoms. England became the most powerful kingdom in the Middle Ages and annexed Wales in 1535. The Union of 1707 joined Scotland, with Ireland joining in 1800. Southern Ireland broke away in 1921 to form what is now the Republic of Ireland.

ECONOMY Historically the growth of the British economy was due to an agricultural revolution and the Industrial Revolution in the 18th and 19th centuries. Today only 2% of the working population is employed in agriculture, but there is a wide range of produce, particularly wheat, dairy products, vegetables and wool. The Industrial Revolution was based on coal and iron ore reserves, found largely in northern areas, and there was a huge growth in towns and communications at this time. The discovery of North Sea oil and gas in the 1960s gave a vital boost to the economy as mineral reserves diminished. Important industries today include textiles and high-skilled engineering.

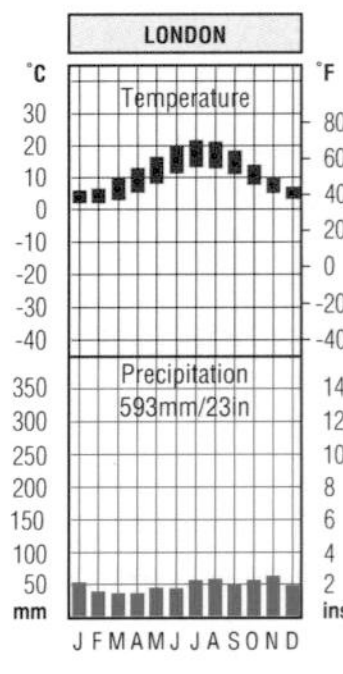

South-eastern England, sheltered from the ocean to the west, is one of the driest parts of the British Isles. Although rainfall varies little throughout the year, greater evaporation creates a deficit between May and August. Like other parts of north-west Europe, London has a small temperature range. The metropolis creates its own local climate.

UNITED STATES OF AMERICA

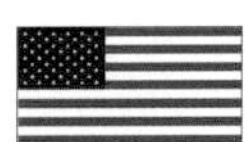

The 'Stars and Stripes' has had the same basic design since 1777, during the War of Independence. The 13 stripes represent the original colonies that rebelled against British rule, and the 50 stars are for the present states of the Union.

AREA 9,372,610 sq km [3,618,765 sq mls]
POPULATION 263,563,000
CAPITAL (POPULATION) Washington, DC (4,360,000)
GOVERNMENT Federal republic with a bicameral legislature
ETHNIC GROUPS White 85%, African American 12%, other races 8%
LANGUAGES English, Spanish
RELIGIONS Protestant 53%, Roman Catholic 26%, Jewish 2%, Eastern Orthodox 2%, Muslim 2%
CURRENCY United States $ = 100 cents
POPULATION DENSITY 28 per sq km [73 per sq ml]

GEOGRAPHY The United States of America is the world's fourth largest country and the third most populous. It fills the North American continent between Canada and Mexico and also includes Alaska and Hawaii. Geographically, the bulk of the USA falls into three main sections: eastern, central and western. Eastern North America is crossed by a band of low, folded mountains which nowhere rise more than 2,000 m [6,500 ft] and include the Appalachians. The coastal plain includes the six New England states with their fertile, wooded landscape. The central section is very different in character. Within the 1,400 km [875 mls] from the Mississippi River to the foothills of the Rockies, the land rises 3,000 m [9,580 ft] almost imperceptibly. The plains are crossed by a series of rivers that drain off the Rockies. This area suffers great seasonal contrasts of climate with hot, moist air from the Gulf of Mexico in the summer and cold, dry Arctic air in winter. The western USA is a complex mountain and plateau system bordered by a rugged coast that starts in the semi-desert of the south and ends in the coniferous forests of the north. The Rocky Mountains are the highest in the area, rising in Colorado to over 3,000 m [10,000 ft].

HISTORY AND POLITICS The USA was established in 1776 after 13 colonies declared their independence from Britain and set up a federal republic. This spread westwards and southwards, especially after the Civil War (1861–5) when slaves were freed from the southern states. The eastern USA is the heartland of many of America's rural and urban traditions. In the 19th century many European immigrants arrived in Boston, New York, Philadelphia and Baltimore, with some then moving into the interior. As resources were discovered here new cities began to develop, such as Chicago. The patterns established then still exist, with the highest concentrations of industry and population in the north-east. The central and western states were first inhabited by over 30 major tribes of Native Americans. Their ways of life were transformed (and often ruined) by the arrival of the Europeans. Americans began to arrive in the west in the 1840s and the south-west became part of the USA. Today the USA has one of the most diverse populations in the world.

ECONOMY The USA became the world's leading industrial society after the Civil War and still maintains very high standards of living and levels of production. Agriculture is now a highly mechanized industry and the USA is a leading producer of many crops, including corn and cotton, as well as meat and dairy foods. It is also one of the leading oil producers. Other industries include iron and steel, uranium and many manufacturing industries.

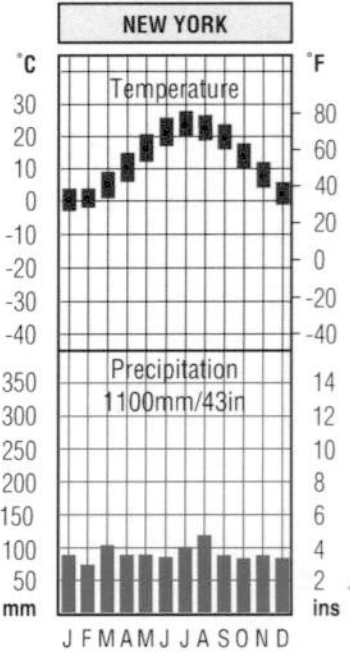

New York is 40°N, but its average temperature December to February is only just above freezing. Temperatures below −20°C [−4°F] have been recorded between December and February, while daily high from May to August is above 20°C [68°F]. Rain and snow are evenly distributed throughout the year, with rainfall on about a third of the days.

URUGUAY

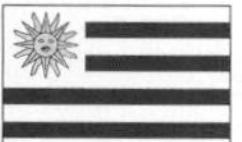

Displayed since 1830, the stripes represent the nine provinces of Uruguay on independence from Spain two years earlier. The blue and white and the May Sun derive from the flag originally employed by Argentina in the colonial struggle.

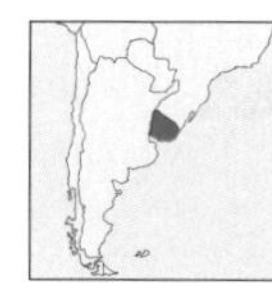

GEOGRAPHY After Surinam, Uruguay is the smallest South American state. It is a low-lying country of tall prairie grasses and woodlands with the highest land less than 600 m [2,000 ft] above sea level. The Atlantic coast and River Plate estuary are fringed with lagoons and sand dunes; the centre of the country is a low plateau, rising in the north towards the Brazilian border. The Uruguay River forms the western border with Argentina.

HISTORY AND POLITICS Uruguay was once simply a hinterland to the Spanish base at Montevideo, forming a buffer area between northern Portuguese and western Spanish territories.

Spain gained control of Uruguay in 1777 but the country became independent in 1828. Since this time Uruguay has been dominated by two political parties – Colorados (Liberals) and Blancos (Conservatives). From 1973 to 1985, there was a strict military regime, with an appalling human rights record. A civilian (Blanco) government is now back in office.

ECONOMY Historically, the economy was based on a meat-and-hide export industry and today it still depends largely on exports of animal products (especially meat, wool and dairy products) for revenue. The country is moderately prosperous.

AREA 177,410 sq km [68,498 sq mls]
POPULATION 3,186,000
CAPITAL (POPULATION) Montevideo (1,384,000)
GOVERNMENT Unitary multiparty republic with a bicameral legislature
ETHNIC GROUPS White 86%, Mestizo 8%, Black 6%
LANGUAGES Spanish
RELIGIONS Roman Catholic 66%, Protestant 2%, Jewish 1%
CURRENCY Peso = 100 centésimos
POPULATION DENSITY 18 per sq km [47 per sq ml]
URBAN POPULATION 90% of population
LAND USE Grass 77%, arable 7%

UZBEKISTAN

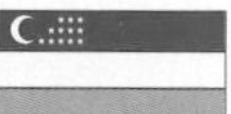

This flag replaced the Soviet-style flag on 18 November 1991. The blue recalls the blue flag of Timur (a former ruler), the white peace, the green nature and the red vitality. The crescent moon is for Islam and the 12 stars represent the months of the Islamic calendar.

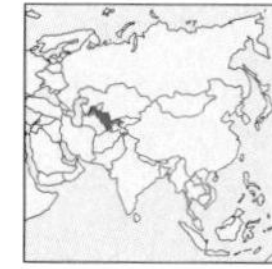

Uzbekistan stretches from the shores of the Aral Sea in the north, through desert and increasingly fertile semi-arid lands, to the peaks of the Western Pamirs and the mountainous border with Afghanistan, with a populous eastern spur jutting into Kyrgyzstan. There is little rainfall and very high summer temperatures.

The Uzbeks were the ruling race in southern central Asia before the Russians took over in the 19th century. The country declared its independence from the former Soviet Union in 1990 and joined the CIS in 1991. Cotton production is important to the economy, and there are also oil, gas, coal and copper reserves.

AREA 447,400 sq km [172,740 sq mls]
POPULATION 22,833,000
CAPITAL (POPULATION) Tashkent (2,113,000)
GOVERNMENT Socialist republic
ETHNIC GROUPS Uzbek 73%, Russian 8%, Tajik 5%, Kazak 4%, Tatar 2%, Kara-Kalpak 2%
LANGUAGES Uzbek 85%, Russian 5%
RELIGIONS Sunni Muslim 75%
CURRENCY Som = 100 tiyin
URBAN POPULATION 41% of population

VANUATU

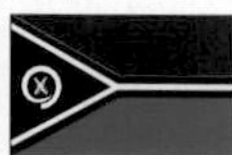

The device in the triangle is a boar's tusk surrounding two crossed fern leaves, the emblems of war and peace. The flag is in the colours of the Vanuaaku Pati, the dominant political party at the time of independence in 1980.

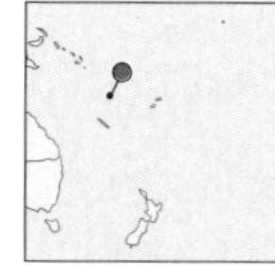

Vanuatu is an archipelago of 13 large islands and 70 islets in the southern Pacific Ocean. The majority of them are mountainous and volcanic in origin, with coral beaches, reefs and forest.

Formerly the New Hebrides and governed jointly by France and Britain from 1906, the islands became independent in 1980. Copra (45% of total), beef and veal are the main exports.

AREA 12,190 sq km [4,707 sq mls]
POPULATION 167,000
CAPITAL (POPULATION) Port-Vila (20,000)
GOVERNMENT Multiparty republic
ETHNIC GROUPS Melanesian 98%, French 1%
LANGUAGES English, French, Pidgin
RELIGIONS Christian
CURRENCY Vatu = 100 centimes

VATICAN CITY

Since the 13th century the emblem on the flag has represented the Vatican's role as the headquarters of the Roman Catholic Church. Consisting of the triple tiara of the Popes above the keys of heaven given to St Peter, it was adopted in 1929.

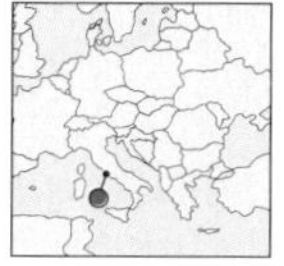

The Vatican City State is a walled enclave on the west bank of the River Tiber in Rome and is the world's smallest nation. It exists to provide an independent base for the Holy See, governing body of the Roman Catholic Church. It is all that

remains of the Papal States, which until 1870, occupied most of central Italy. The Popes have lived here since the 5th century. The Vatican City has its own newspaper and radio station, police and railway station, and issues its own stamps and coins.

AREA 0.44 sq km [0.17 sq mls]
POPULATION 1,000
CAPITAL –
GOVERNMENT Papal Commission
ETHNIC GROUPS Italian, Swiss
LANGUAGES Latin, Italian
RELIGIONS Roman Catholic
CURRENCY Vatican lira = 100 centesimi
POPULATION DENSITY 2,273 per sq km [5,882 per sq ml]

VENEZUELA

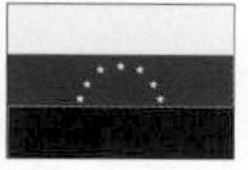

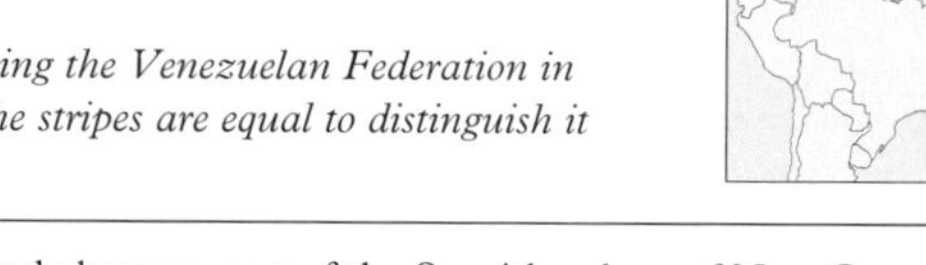

The seven stars on the tricolour represent the provinces forming the Venezuelan Federation in 1811 (see Colombia and Ecuador). The proportions of the stripes are equal to distinguish it from the flags of Colombia and Ecuador.

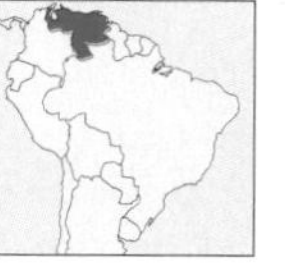

GEOGRAPHY Venezuela ('Little Venice') lies in northern South America with a coastline on the Atlantic Ocean. In the north and north-west of the country, where 90% of the population lives, the Andes split to form two ranges separated from each other by the Maracaibo basin. Above 3,000 m [10,000 ft] are the *paramos* – regions of grassland vegetation, with fertile land and mild temperatures. By contrast the rest of the country has a humid tropical climate. The mountains running west to east behind the coast from Valencia to Trinidad have a gentler topography, with fertile alluvial basins between the ranges. South of the mountains are the *llanos* of Orinoco – a vast savanna of trees and grassland.

HISTORY AND POLITICS First sighted by Columbus in 1498,

Venezuela became part of the Spanish colony of New Granada. In 1821 it became independent, first in federation with Colombia and Ecuador and then, from 1830, as a separate independent republic under Simón Bolívar. Between 1830 and 1945 the country was governed mainly by dictators; after frequent changes of president a new constitution came into force in 1961. Since then a fragile democracy has existed but it has rested on a system of widespread repression and corruption.

ECONOMY Oil has made Venezuela prosperous, but the wealth is unevenly distributed. It provides 86% of export earnings and there are signs of overdependence on this single commodity. Principal crops include coffee, sugar cane and bananas.

AREA 912,050 sq km [352,143 sq mls]
POPULATION 21,810,000
CAPITAL (POPULATION) Caracas (2,784,000)
GOVERNMENT Federal republic with a bicameral legislature

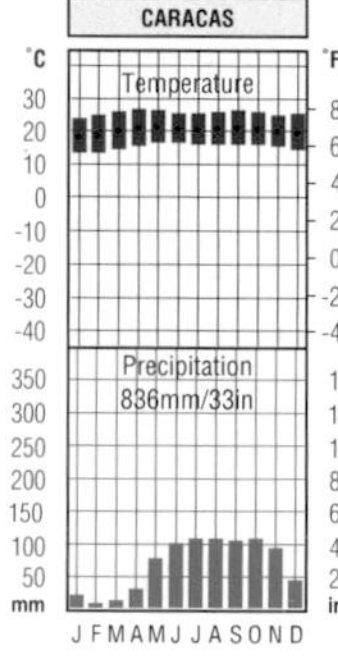

The country has a tropical climate. There is little variation in the temperature from month to month, but there are marked wet and dry seasons, the rain falling from May to November. The north-east trade winds leave little rain in the coastal lowlands, but the total increases when they hit the mountains. Some of the Andean peaks have permanent snow.

VIETNAM

VIETNAM

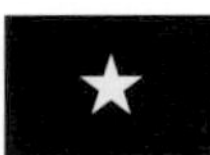

First used by the forces of Ho Chi Minh in the liberation struggle against Japan in World War II, the design was adopted as the national flag of North Vietnam in 1945. It was retained when the two parts of the country were reunited in 1975.

AREA 331,689 sq km [128,065 sq mls]
POPULATION 74,580,000
CAPITAL (POPULATION) Hanoi (3,056,000)
GOVERNMENT Unitary single-party socialist republic
ETHNIC GROUPS Vietnamese 87%, Tho (Tay) 2%, Chinese (Hoa) 2%, Meo 2%, Thai 2%, Khmer, Muong, Nung
LANGUAGES Vietnamese, Chinese, Tho, Khmer, Muong, Thai, Nung, Miao, Jarai, Rhadé, Hre, Bahnar
RELIGIONS Buddhist 67%, Roman Catholic 8%
CURRENCY Dong = 10 hao or 100 xu

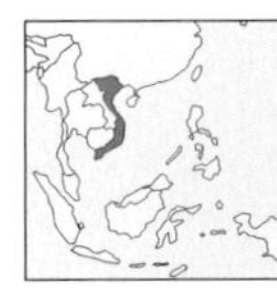

GEOGRAPHY Vietnam is one of Asia's most strangely shaped countries. In the north coastal lands widen into the valley and delta of the Hongha (Red) River and the valley of the Da. These lowlands are backed in the west by mountains of the Anamite chain. To the north are the plateaux of Laos and Tongking.
HISTORY, POLITICS AND ECONOMY Vietnam became a French protectorate in 1883 and was later joined by Laos and Cambodia in the French Indo-Chinese Union. Communist-led guerillas under Ho Chi Minh declared Vietnam free after Japanese occupation in World War II, before embarking on a war with the French between 1946 and 1954. This produced a Communist North Vietnam and a non-Communist South Vietnam and saw the start of the war against the USA between 1964 and 1976, when Vietnam was reunited as a Communist state. The war left economic chaos, from which it is only now beginning to emerge. Much of the population subsists on agriculture.

VIRGIN ISLANDS, BRITISH

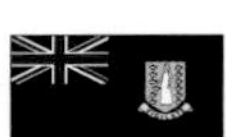

In the British Blue Ensign is the green badge of the islands, which shows a vestal virgin dressed in white and carrying a lamp. On either side of her are rows of lamps, five on the left and six on the right. Below the shield is a gold scroll bearing the motto Vigilate *('Be Alert').*

AREA 153 sq km [59 sq mls]
POPULATION 20,000
CAPITAL (POPULATION) Road Town (6,500)
GOVERNMENT British Dependent Territory
ETHNIC GROUPS African American 90%
LANGUAGES English
RELIGIONS Protestant 86%
CURRENCY US dollar
POPULATION DENSITY 131 per sq km [339 per sq ml]

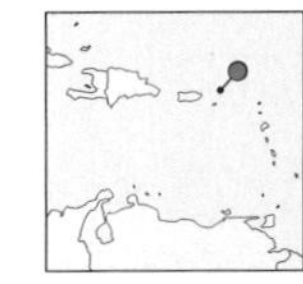

Most northerly of the Lesser Antilles, the British Virgin Islands comprise four low-lying islands and 36 islets and cays. Three-quarters of the population live on the largest island, Tortola. Dutch from 1648 but British since 1666, they are now a British dependency enjoying (since 1977) a strong measure of self-government. The main source of income is tourism. Offshore banking has been important since 1985 and the facilities are increasingly a rival to the Caymans and the Turks and Caicos.

VIRGIN ISLANDS, US

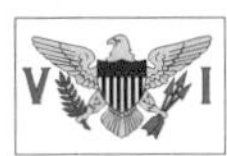

The flag was adopted in 1921 and is based on the seal of the USA. The three arrows grasped by the eagle stand for the three main islands. The emblem appears between the initial letters of the islands' name, 'V' and 'I', in blue.

AREA 340 sq km [130 sq mls]
POPULATION 102,000
CAPITAL (POPULATION) Charlotte Amalie (12,330)
GOVERNMENT Self-governing US Territory
ETHNIC GROUPS Black 80%, White 15%
LANGUAGES English, Spanish, Creole
RELIGIONS Baptist 42%, Roman Catholic 34%

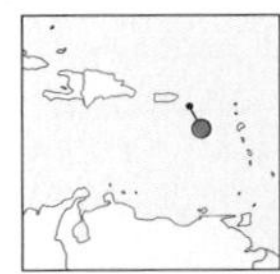

St Thomas, St Croix and St John are the largest of the 68 islands of the US Virgin Islands. The islands were Spanish from 1553, Danish from 1672 and, for a sum of US$25 million, American in 1917 – so they could protect the approaches to the newly-built Panama Canal. From 1973 they have had an elected delegate in the House of Representatives. Tourism is the main industry.

WALLIS AND FUTUNA ISLANDS

As a French Overseas Territory, the Wallis and Futuna Islands use the French tricolour as their flag.

AREA 200 sq km [77 sq mls]
POPULATION 13,000
CAPITAL (POPULATION) Mata-Utu (850)
GOVERNMENT French Overseas Territory
ETHNIC GROUPS Polynesian
LANGUAGES French, Wallisian
RELIGIONS Roman Catholic
POPULATION DENSITY 65 per sq km [169 per sq ml]

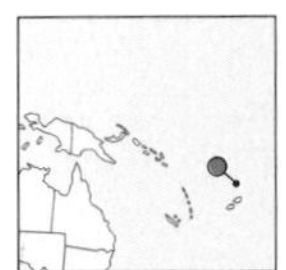

The smallest, least populous and poorest of France's three Pacific Overseas Territories, the Wallis and Futuna Islands comprise three main islands and numerous islets. Futuna and uninhabited Alofi are mountainous; the much larger Uvea is hilly with coral reefs and contains 60% of the population. The economy is based mainly on tropical subsistence agriculture.

WESTERN SAMOA

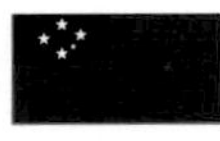

The red and white are traditional colours used in Samoan flags of the 19th century. The design of the flag, in use since 1948 (14 years before independence), links Samoa with other nations of the southern hemisphere by its inclusion of the Southern Cross constellation.

AREA 2,840 sq km [1,097 sq mls]
POPULATION 169,000
CAPITAL (POPULATION) Apia (37,000)
GOVERNMENT Constitutional monarchy
ETHNIC GROUPS Samoan, mixed European and Polynesian
LANGUAGES Samoan, English
RELIGIONS Christian
CURRENCY Tala = 100 sene

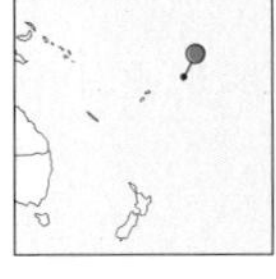

Western Samoa comprises two large islands, seven small islands and a number of islets, all lying in the Pacific Ocean. The cradle of Polynesian civilization, the islands were first independent in 1889, but became a German protectorate in 1899. They were administered by New Zealand from 1920 until independence in 1962. Coconut oil, taro and cocoa are the main exports.

YEMEN

The new straightforward design of Yemen's flag, incorporating the Pan-Arab colours, dates from 1990 when the Yemen Arab Republic (in the north and west) united with the People's Democratic Republic of Yemen (in the south and east).

AREA 527,970 sq km [203,849 sq mls]
POPULATION 14,609,000
CAPITAL (POPULATION) Sana (972,000)
GOVERNMENT Multiparty republic
ETHNIC GROUPS Arab 96%, Somali 1%
LANGUAGES Arabic
RELIGIONS Sunni Muslim, Shiite Muslim
CURRENCY N. Yemeni riyal = 100 fils, S. Yemeni dinar = 1,000 fils
POPULATION DENSITY 28 per sq km [72 per sq ml]

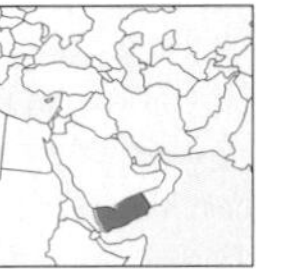

Located at the southern end of the Arabian peninsula, Yemen has a coastline on the Gulf of Aden. There is a narrow coastal plain behind which rise mountains and plateaus. There is little annual rainfall. Aden in South Yemen was a British colony from 1839 to 1967 and an important British staging post on the journey to India. The two states of North Yemen (an independent kingdom since 1918) and South Yemen (under Marxist control) united in 1990 to form the Yemeni Republic. Clashes between the north and south in 1994 escalated into a full civil war until June when government troops captured Aden.

YUGOSLAVIA (SERBIA AND MONTENEGRO)

Only the republics of Serbia and Montenegro now remain in Yugoslavia. The same flag is still used with its colours identifying it as a Slavic state which was once part of the Austro-Hungarian Empire. It used to have a red star in the centre, but this was dropped in 1992.

AREA 102,170 sq km [39,449 sq mls]
POPULATION 10,881,000
CAPITAL (POPULATION) Belgrade (1,137,000)
GOVERNMENT Federal republic
ETHNIC GROUPS Serb 62%, Albanian 17%, Montenegrin 5%, Hungarian 4%
LANGUAGES Serbo-Croatian
RELIGIONS Orthodox 65%, Muslim 19%
CURRENCY New Yugoslav dinar = 100 paras
POPULATION DENSITY 106 per sq km [276 per sq ml]
URBAN POPULATION 52% of population
LAND USE Arable 36%, grass 21%, forest 30%

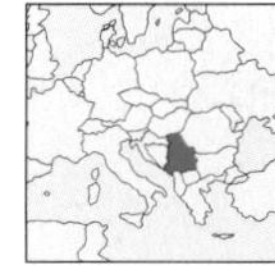

'Yugoslavia' today only contains the federal republics of Serbia and Montenegro and further changes are likely. Known from 1918 as the Kingdom of the Serbs, Croats and Slovenes, and from 1929 as Yugoslavia ('land of the South Slavs'), the unity of the country has always been fragile, with a long history of nationalist and ethnic tensions. In the interwar period the country was virtually a 'Greater Serbia', and after Hitler invaded in 1941 Yugoslavs fought both the Germans and each other. The Communist-led partisans of 'Tito' (a Croat) were the victors in 1945 and reformed Yugoslavia as a republic based on the Soviet model. The region was fairly peaceful until Tito died in 1990. In the first free elections since the war there were nationalist victories in four out of the six federal republics. Slovenia and Croatia became independent in 1991 with Bosnia-Herzegovina following in 1992. Bosnia was at once the centre of a vicious civil war until a fragile peace was negotiated at the end of 1995. The Yugoslavia that now exists is therefore much reduced, with many problems of its own, including severe trade sanctions.

ZAÏRE

The Pan-African colours of red, yellow and green were adopted for Zaïre's flag in 1971. The central emblem symbolizes the revolutionary spirit of the nation and was used by the Popular Movement of the Revolution, formed in 1967.

AREA 2,344,885 sq km [905,365 sq mls]
POPULATION 44,504,000
CAPITAL (POPULATION) Kinshasa (3,804,000)
GOVERNMENT Transitional government
URBAN POPULATION 29% of population

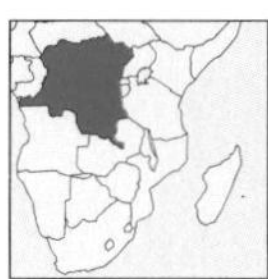

GEOGRAPHY Zaïre is Africa's third biggest country and the world's 12th biggest, and is 77 times the size of its former colonial ruler, Belgium. Much of the northern part of the country lies in the equatorial Congo Basin, the world's second largest river drainage system, where the landscape is mostly tropical rainforest. The Congo (Zaïre) River was developed as a major artery, its rapids and falls bypassed by railways. In the south and east is part of the Great Rift Valley and there are highlands and plateaus. Despite its huge size, it has a coastline on the Atlantic Ocean of only 27 km [17 mls].

HISTORY AND POLITICS Zaïre was made up of several African kingdoms before becoming the Congo Free State between 1884 and 1908, owned by Belgium's King Léopold II. The country then became the Belgian Congo colony until independence in 1960. Soon after independence a violent civil war began which lasted until General Mobutu seized power in 1965, declaring a one-party state in 1967 and renaming the country Zaïre as part of a wide-ranging Africanization policy. His long dictatorship was characterized by repression and inefficiency and by 1990 increasing protests forced him to agree to multiparty elections. A civil war erupted in October 1996.

ECONOMY Minerals provide much of Zaïre's export income. Copper accounts for more than half, with cobalt, manganese, tin and diamonds also important. Coffee is also exported.

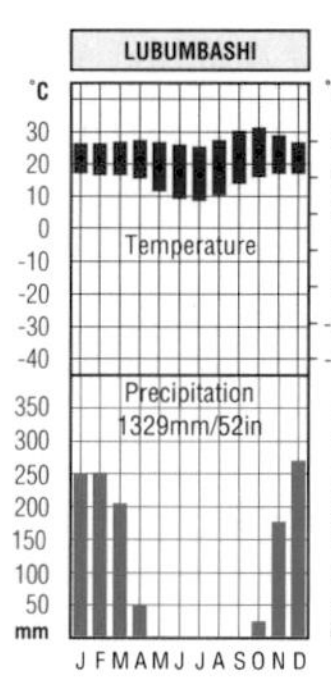

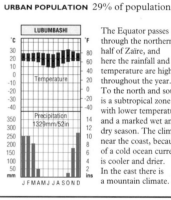

The Equator passes through the northern half of Zaïre, and here the rainfall and temperature are high throughout the year. To the north and south is a subtropical zone with lower temperatures and a marked wet and dry season. The climate near the coast, because of a cold ocean current, is cooler and drier. In the east there is a mountain climate.

ZAMBIA

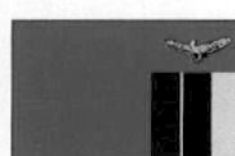

The colours of Zambia's distinctive national flag are those of the United Nationalist Independence Party, which led the struggle against Britain. The flying eagle represents freedom. The design was adopted on independence in 1964.

AREA 752,614 sq km [290,586 sq mls]
POPULATION 9,500,000
CAPITAL (POPULATION) Lusaka (982,000)
GOVERNMENT Multiparty republic with a unicameral legislature
ETHNIC GROUPS Bemba 36%, Nyanja 18%, Malawi 14%, Lozi 9%, Tonga 5%
LANGUAGES English, Bemba, Tonga, Nyanja, Lozi, Lunda, Luvale, Kaonde
RELIGIONS Christian 72%, animist
CURRENCY Kwacha = 100 ngwee
POPULATION DENSITY 13 per sq km [33 per sq ml]
URBAN POPULATION 42% of population
LAND USE Arable 7%, grass 40%, forest 39%

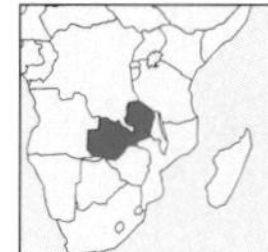

GEOGRAPHY A vast expanse of high plateaus (about 1,200 m [3,900 ft] above sea level) in the interior of south-central Africa, most of Zambia is drained by the Zambezi and two of its major tributaries, the Kafue and the Luangwa. In the south the latter and the central section of the Zambezi occupy a low-lying rift valley bounded by rugged escarpments. The Victoria Falls lie on the border with Zimbabwe. In the north are the swamps of the Bangweulu Depression and the Muchinga Mountains.

HISTORY AND POLITICS In the 1890s Britain took control over Zambia and named it Northern Rhodesia. Between 1953 and 1963 it was part of a federation with Southern Rhodesia (now Zimbabwe) and Nyasaland. It became independent in 1964 and Kenneth Kaunda became president. His 27-year, single-party rule (he declared his party, the UNIP, the only legal party in 1972) ended in 1991 when he conceded to multiparty elections and union leader Frederick Chiluba became president.

ECONOMY Zambia is the world's fifth biggest producer of copper ore and the economy is heavily dependent on the income gained from this, despite attempts to diversify. There are high levels of rural-urban migration, mostly in search of scarce employment.

ZIMBABWE

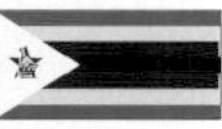

Adopted when legal independence was secured in 1980, Zimbabwe's flag is based on the colours of the ruling Patriotic Front. Within the white triangle is the soapstone bird national emblem and a red star, symbolizing the party's socialist policy.

AREA 390,579 sq km [150,873 sq mls]
POPULATION 11,453,000
CAPITAL (POPULATION) Harare (1,189,000)
GOVERNMENT Multiparty republic

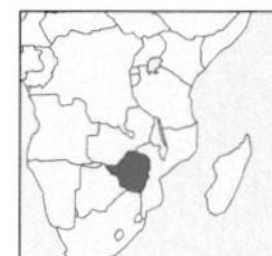

GEOGRAPHY Zimbabwe is a landlocked country lying astride the high plateaus between the Zambezi (in the north) and Limpopo (in the south) rivers. Almost all the country is over 300 m [1,000 ft] above sea level. In the north-west it shares Lake Kariba, Africa's second largest artificial lake, with Zambia. The vegetation on the plateaus is that of the High Veld, which is mostly grassland.

HISTORY AND POLITICS Britain controlled Zimbabwe from 1894, naming it Southern Rhodesia after the politician Cecil Rhodes and nurturing it as a 'white man's country'. From 1923 it became a self-governing colony and in 1965 Ian Smith's white government declared itself independent as Rhodesia. The ensuing guerrilla action against Smith led to a full-scale civil war and eventually forced a move to black majority rule in 1980. The rift that followed independence, between Robert Mugabe's ruling ZANU and Joshua Nkomo's ZAPU, was resolved in 1989 when they merged and Mugabe renounced his Marxist ideology. In 1990 Mugabe was elected president and the state of emergency that had lasted since 1965 was ended.

ECONOMY The economy is relatively strong, founded on gold and tobacco but now more diverse. There are varied mineral resources, including copper, nickel and iron ore.

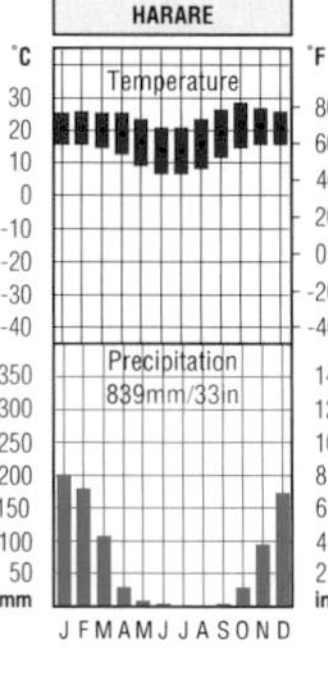

Like other places on the high interior plateau of southern Africa, Harare has a large diurnal range of temperature, particularly in the dry, sunny winter, and is much cooler than lowlands at the same latitude. Frosts have been recorded between June and August. The main rains of summer are brought by south-easterly winds from the Indian Ocean.

WORLD OF NATIONS: INDEX TO COUNTRIES

NOTES

The countries are arranged alphabetically, with Afghanistan as the first entry and Zimbabwe as the last. Information is given for all countries and territories, except for some of the smallest and near uninhabited islands.

The form of names for the many new countries that now exist follows the conventions used in all Philip's world atlases. The region that is generally called Serbia is listed under Yugoslavia (Serbia and Montenegro) and for two countries the traditional English conventional name has been used: Burma (Myanmar) and Ivory Coast (Côte d'Ivoire).

The statistical data is the latest available, usually for 1995. In the statistics' boxes:
Country area includes inland water and land areas covered in ice, as in Greenland and Canada, for example.
City populations are usually those of the 'urban agglomerations' rather than within the legal city boundaries.

INTRODUCTION TO
WORLD GEOGRAPHY

PLANET EARTH

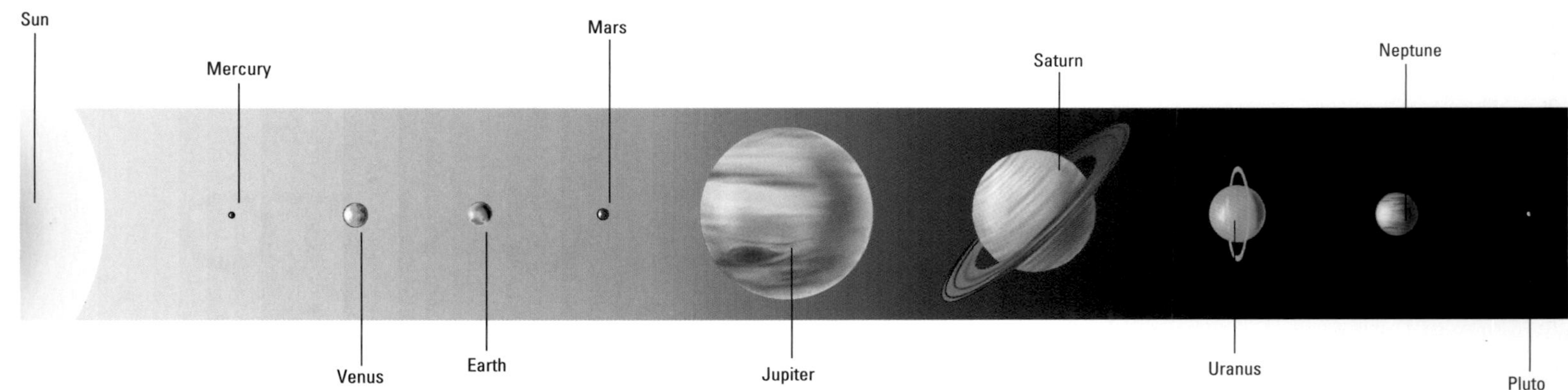

Sun · Mercury · Venus · Earth · Mars · Jupiter · Saturn · Uranus · Neptune · Pluto

THE SOLAR SYSTEM

A minute part of one of the billions of galaxies (collections of stars) that comprises the Universe, the Solar System lies some 27,000 light-years from the centre of our own galaxy, the 'Milky Way'. Thought to be over 4,700 million years old, it consists of a central sun with nine planets and their moons revolving around it, attracted by its gravitational pull. The planets orbit the Sun in the same direction – anti-clockwise when viewed from the Northern Heavens – and almost in the same plane. Their orbital paths, however, vary enormously.

The Sun's diameter is 109 times that of Earth, and the temperature at its core – caused by continuous thermonuclear fusions of hydrogen into helium – is estimated to be 15 million degrees Celsius. It is the Solar System's only source of light and heat.

PROFILE OF THE PLANETS

	Mean distance from Sun (million km)	Mass (Earth = 1)	Period of orbit (Earth years)	Period of rotation (Earth days)	Equatorial diameter (km)	Number of known satellites
Mercury	57.9	0.055	0.24 years	58.67	4,878	0
Venus	108.2	0.815	0.62 years	243.00	12,104	0
Earth	149.6	1.0	1.00 years	1.00	12,756	1
Mars	227.9	0.107	1.88 years	1.03	6,787	2
Jupiter	778.3	317.8	11.86 years	0.41	142,800	16
Saturn	1,427	95.2	29.46 years	0.43	120,000	20
Uranus	2,871	14.5	84.01 years	0.75	51,118	15
Neptune	4,497	17.1	164.80 years	0.80	49,528	8
Pluto	5,914	0.002	248.50 years	6.39	2,320	1

All planetary orbits are elliptical in form, but only Pluto and Mercury follow paths that deviate noticeably from a circular one. Near perihelion – its closest approach to the Sun – Pluto actually passes inside the orbit of Neptune, an event that last occurred in 1983. Pluto will not regain its station as outermost planet until February 1999.

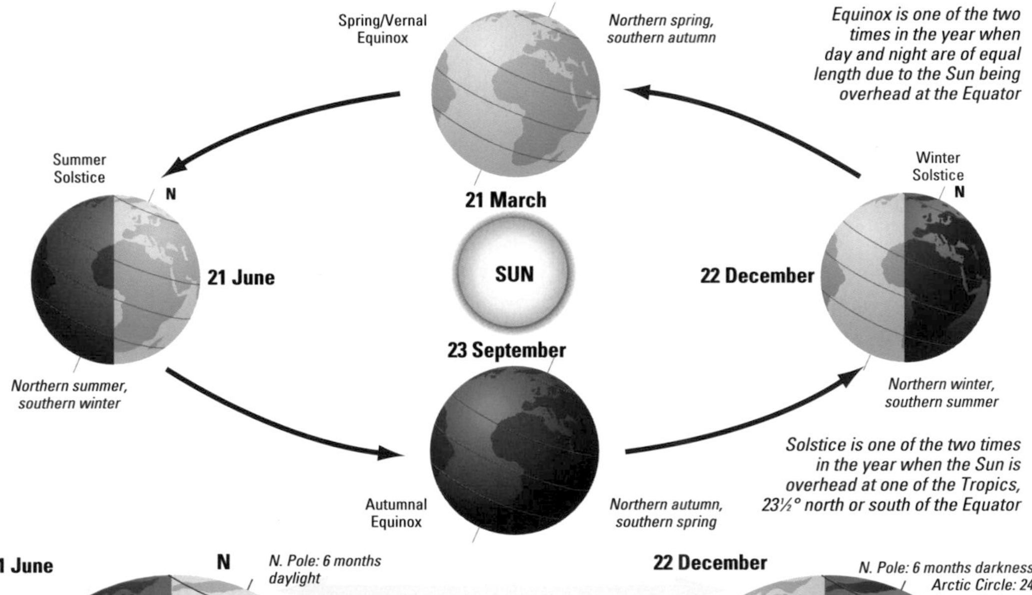

Spring/Vernal Equinox

Northern spring, southern autumn

Equinox is one of the two times in the year when day and night are of equal length due to the Sun being overhead at the Equator

Summer Solstice

21 March

Winter Solstice

21 June · SUN · 22 December

23 September

Northern summer, southern winter

Autumnal Equinox

Northern autumn, southern spring

Northern winter, southern summer

Solstice is one of the two times in the year when the Sun is overhead at one of the Tropics, 23½° north or south of the Equator

21 June
N. Pole: 6 months daylight
66½°
SHORT NIGHT
12 hours daylight
LONG DAY
13½ hours daylight
Equator
23½°
Sun's rays
0°
12 hours daylight
SHORT DAY
23½°
10½ hours daylight
Antarctic Circle: 24 hours darkness
S. Pole: 6 months darkness

22 December
N. Pole: 6 months darkness
Arctic Circle: 24 hours darkness
10½ hours daylight
23½°
SHORT DAY
66½°
12 hours daylight
0°
Equator
23½°
LONG DAY
12 hours daylight
Antarctic Circle: 24 hours daylight
S. Pole: 6 months daylight

THE SEASONS

The Earth revolves around the Sun once a year in an 'anti-clockwise' direction, tilted at a constant angle of 23½°. In June, the northern hemisphere is tilted towards the Sun: as a result it receives more hours of sunshine in a day and therefore has its warmest season, summer. By December, the Earth has rotated halfway round the Sun so that the southern hemisphere is tilted towards the Sun and has its summer; the hemisphere that is tilted away from the Sun has winter. On 21 June the Sun is directly overhead at the Tropic of Cancer (23½° N), and this is midsummer in the northern hemisphere. Midsummer in the southern hemisphere occurs on 21 December, when the Sun is overhead at the Tropic of Capricorn (23½° S).

DAY AND NIGHT

The Sun appears to rise in the east, reach its highest point at noon, and then set in the west, to be followed by night. In reality it is not the Sun that is moving but the Earth revolving from west to east. Due to the tilting of the Earth the length of day and night varies from place to place and month to month, as shown on the diagram on the left.

At the summer solstice in the northern hemisphere (21 June), the Arctic has total daylight and the Antarctic total darkness. The opposite occurs at the winter solstice (21 December). At the Equator, the length of day and night are almost equal all year, at latitude 30° the length of day varies from about 14 hours to 10 hours, and at latitude 50° from about 16 hours to about 8 hours.

TIME

Year: The time taken by the Earth to revolve around the Sun, or 365.24 days.
Leap Year: A calendar year of 366 days, 29 February being the additional day. It offsets the difference between the calendar and the solar year.
Month: The approximate time taken by the Moon to revolve around the Earth. The 12 months of the year in fact vary from 28 (29 in a Leap Year) to 31 days.
Week: An artificial period of 7 days, not based on astronomical time.
Day: The time taken by the Earth to complete one rotation on its axis.
Hour: 24 hours make one day. Usually the day is divided into hours AM (ante meridiem or before noon) and PM (post meridiem or after noon), although most timetables now use the 24-hour system, from midnight to midnight.

SUNRISE

SUNSET

THE MOON

Distance from Earth: 356,410 km – 406,685 km; Mean diameter: 3,475.1 km; Mass: approx. 1/81 that of Earth; Surface gravity: one-sixth of Earth's; Daily range of temperature at lunar equator: 200°C; Average orbital speed: 3,683 km/h

PHASES OF THE MOON

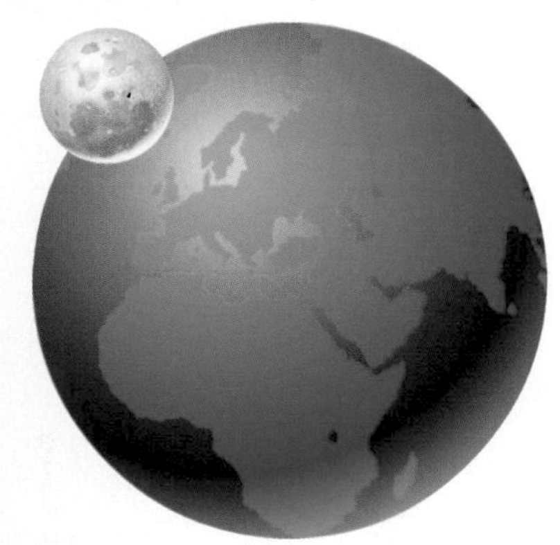

New Moon | Crescent | First quarter | Gibbous | Full Moon | Gibbous | Last quarter | Crescent | New Moon

The Moon rotates more slowly than the Earth, making one complete turn on its axis in just over 27 days. Since this corresponds to its period of revolution around the Earth, the Moon always presents the same hemisphere or face to us, and we never see 'the dark side'. The interval between one full Moon and the next (and between new Moons) is about 29½ days – a lunar month. The apparent changes in the shape of the Moon are caused by its changing position in relation to the Earth; like the planets, it produces no light of its own and shines only by reflecting the rays of the Sun.

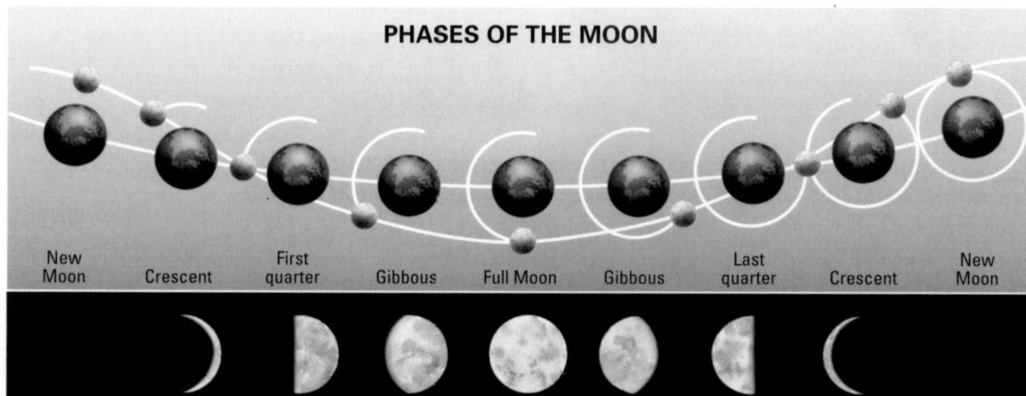

Partial eclipse (1)

P P P

Solar eclipse

Total eclipse (2)

Lunar eclipse

ECLIPSES

When the Moon passes between the Sun and the Earth it causes a partial eclipse of the Sun (1) if the Earth passes through the Moon's outer shadow (P), or a total eclipse (2) if the inner cone shadow crosses the Earth's surface. In a lunar eclipse, the Earth's shadow crosses the Moon and, again, provides either a partial or total eclipse. Eclipses of the Sun and the Moon do not occur every month because of the 5° difference between the plane of the Moon's orbit and the plane in which the Earth moves. In the 1990s only 14 lunar eclipses are possible, for example, seven partial and seven total; each is visible only from certain, and variable, parts of the world. The same period witnesses 13 solar eclipses – six partial (or annular) and seven total.

TIDES

The daily rise and fall of the ocean's tides are the result of the gravitational pull of the Moon and that of the Sun, though the effect of the latter is only 46.6% as strong as that of the Moon. This effect is greatest on the hemisphere facing the Moon and causes a tidal 'bulge'. When the Sun, Earth and Moon are in line, tide-raising forces are at a maximum and Spring tides occur: high tide reaches the highest values, and low tide falls to low levels. When lunar and solar forces are least coincidental with the Sun and Moon at an angle (near the Moon's first and third quarters), Neap tides occur, which have a small tidal range.

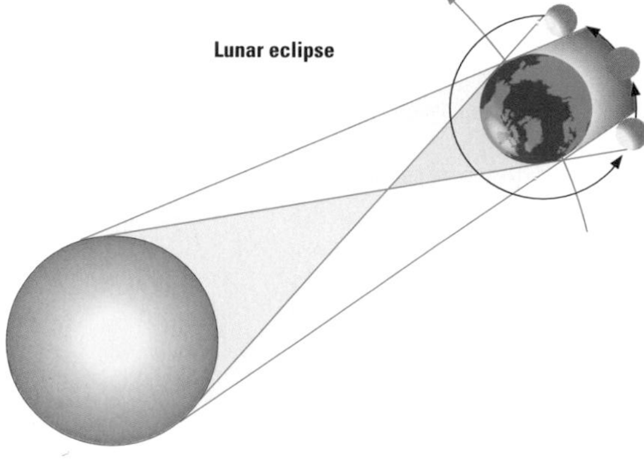

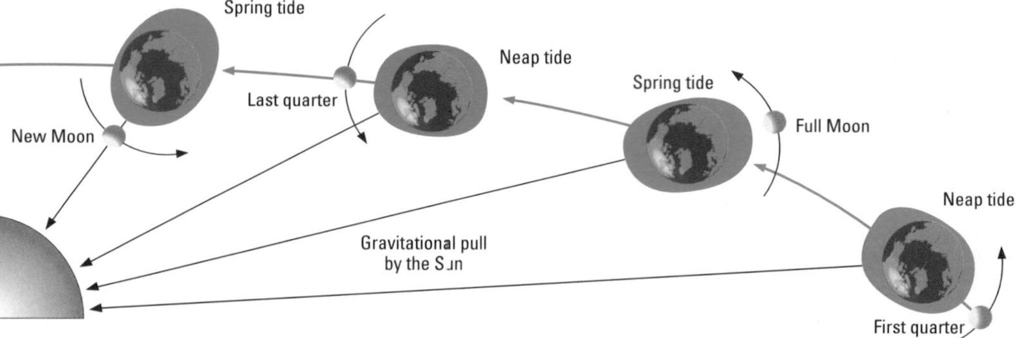

Spring tide

Neap tide

Last quarter

Spring tide

New Moon

Full Moon

Neap tide

Gravitational pull by the Sun

First quarter

RESTLESS EARTH

THE EARTH'S STRUCTURE

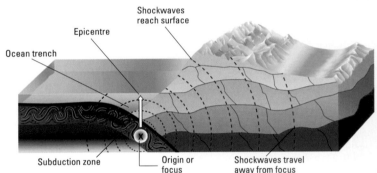

Upper mantle (c. 370 km)
Crust (average 5–50 km)
Transitional zone (600 km)
Outer core (2,100 km)
Lower mantle (1,700 km)
Inner core (1,350 km)

CONTINENTAL DRIFT

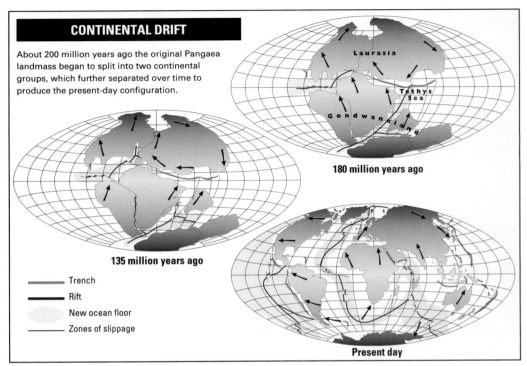

About 200 million years ago the original Pangaea landmass began to split into two continental groups, which further separated over time to produce the present-day configuration.

Laurasia

Tethys Sea

Gondwanaland

180 million years ago

135 million years ago

	Trench
	Rift
	New ocean floor
	Zones of slippage

Present day

EARTHQUAKES

Earthquake magnitude is usually rated according to either the Richter or the Modified Mercalli scale, both devised by seismologists in the 1930s. The Richter scale measures absolute earthquake power with mathematical precision: each step upwards represents a tenfold increase in shockwave amplitude. Theoretically, there is no upper limit, but the largest earthquakes measured have been rated at between 8.8 and 8.9. The 12–point Mercalli scale, based on observed effects, is often more meaningful, ranging from I (earthquakes noticed only by seismographs) to XII (total destruction); intermediate points include V (people awakened at night; unstable objects overturned), VII (collapse of ordinary buildings; chimneys and monuments fall) and IX (conspicuous cracks in ground; serious damage to reservoirs).

Shockwaves reach surface
Epicentre
Ocean trench
Subduction zone
Origin or focus
Shockwaves travel away from focus

NOTABLE EARTHQUAKES SINCE 1900

Year	Location	Richter Scale	Deaths
1906	San Francisco, USA	8.3	503
1906	Valparaiso, Chile	8.6	22,000
1908	Messina, Italy	7.5	83,000
1915	Avezzano, Italy	7.5	30,000
1920	Gansu (Kansu), China	8.6	180,000
1923	Yokohama, Japan	8.3	143,000
1927	Nan Shan, China	8.3	200,000
1932	Gansu (Kansu), China	7.6	70,000
1934	Bihar, India/Nepal	8.4	10,700
1935	Quetta, India (now Pakistan)	7.5	60,000
1939	Chillan, Chile	8.3	28,000
1939	Erzincan, Turkey	7.9	30,000
1960	Agadir, Morocco	5.8	12,000
1962	Khorasan, Iran	7.1	12,230
1968	N.E. Iran	7.4	12,000
1970	N. Peru	7.7	66,794
1972	Managua, Nicaragua	6.2	5,000
1974	N. Pakistan	6.3	5,200
1976	Guatemala	7.5	22,778
1976	Tangshan, China	8.2	255,000
1978	Tabas, Iran	7.7	25,000
1980	El Asnam, Algeria	7.3	20,000
1980	S. Italy	7.2	4,800
1985	Mexico City, Mexico	8.1	4,200
1988	N.W. Armenia	6.8	55,000
1990	N. Iran	7.7	36,000
1993	Maharashtra, India	6.4	30,000
1994	Los Angeles, USA	6.6	61
1995	Kobe, Japan	7.2	5,000
1995	Sakhalin Is., Russia	7.5	2,000
1997	N.W. Iran	6.1	965

The highest magnitude recorded on the Richter scale is 8.9 in Japan on 2 March 1933 which killed 2,990 people. The most devastating earthquake ever was at Shaanxi (Shenshi) province, central China, on 3 January 1556, when an estimated 830,000 people were killed.

STRUCTURE AND EARTHQUAKES

	Mobile land areas
	Submarine zones of mobile land areas
	Stable land platforms
	Submarine extensions of stable land platforms
	Mid-oceanic volcanic ridges
	Oceanic platforms
1976 ○	Principal earthquakes and dates

Earthquakes are a series of rapid vibrations originating from the slipping or faulting of parts of the Earth's crust when stresses within build up to breaking point. They usually happen at depths varying from 8 km to 30 km. Severe earthquakes cause extensive damage when they take place in populated areas, destroying structures and severing communications. Most initial loss of life occurs due to secondary causes such as falling masonry, fires and flooding.

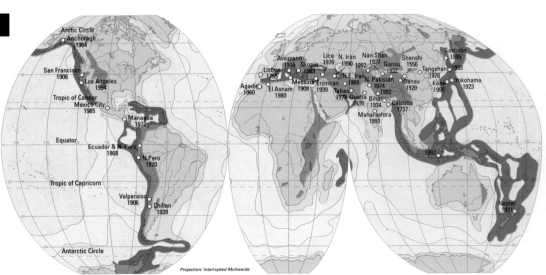

Projection: Interrupted Mollweide

PLATE TECTONICS

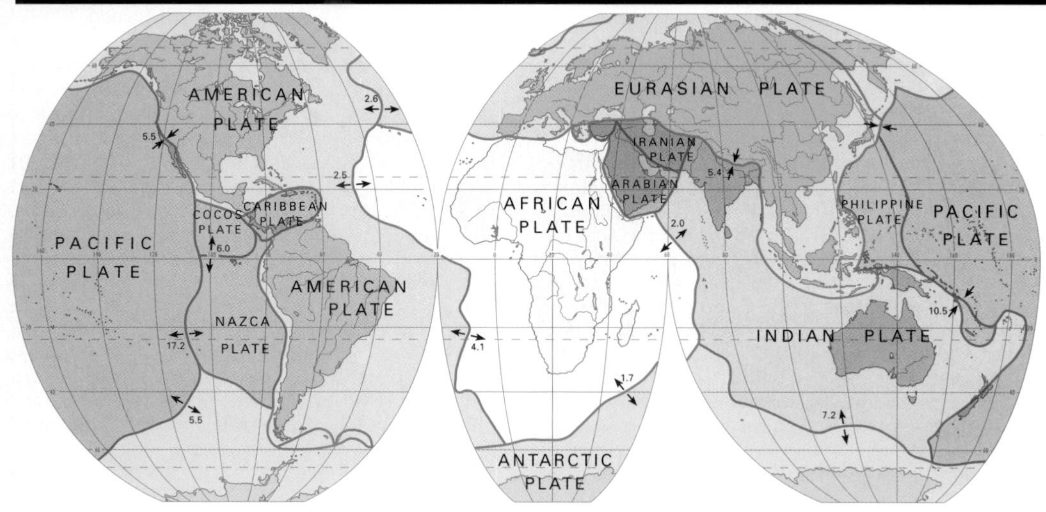

— Plate boundaries

PACIFIC Major plates

→ Direction of plate movements and rate of movement (cm/year)

The drifting of the continents is a feature that is unique to Planet Earth. The complementary, almost jigsaw-puzzle fit of the coastlines on each side of the Atlantic Ocean inspired Alfred Wegener's theory of continental drift in 1915. The theory suggested that the ancient super-continent, which Wegener named Pangaea, incorporated all of the Earth's landmasses and gradually split up to form today's continents.

The original debate about continental drift was a prelude to a more radical idea: plate tectonics. The basic theory is that the Earth's crust is made up of a series of rigid plates which float on a soft layer of the mantle and are moved about by continental convection currents within the Earth's interior. These plates diverge and converge along margins marked by seismic activity. Plates diverge from mid-ocean ridges where molten lava pushes upwards and forces the plates apart at rates of up to 40 mm [1.6 in] a year.

The three diagrams, right, give some examples of plate boundaries from around the world. Diagram a) shows sea-floor spreading at the Mid-Atlantic Ridge as the American and African plates slowly diverge. The same thing is happening in b) where sea-floor spreading at the Mid-Indian Ocean Ridge is forcing the Indian plate to collide into the Eurasian plate. In c) oceanic crust (sima) is being subducted beneath lighter continental crust (sial).

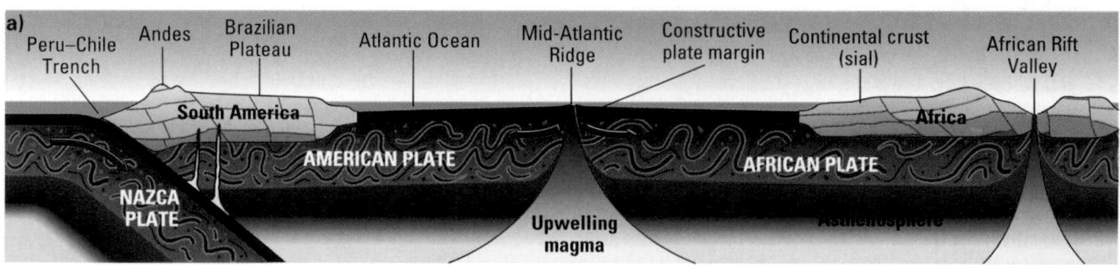

VOLCANOES

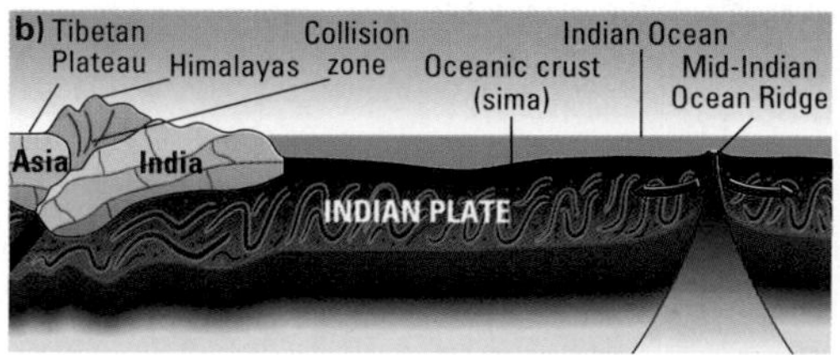

Volcanoes occur when hot liquefied rock beneath the Earth's crust is pushed up by pressure to the surface as molten lava. Some volcanoes erupt in an explosive way, throwing out rocks and ash, whilst others are effusive and lava flows out of the vent. There are volcanoes which are both, such as Mount Fuji. An accumulation of lava and cinders creates cones of variable size and shape. As a result of many eruptions over centuries Mount Etna in Sicily has a circumference of more than 120 km [75 miles].

Climatologists believe that volcanic ash, if ejected high into the atmosphere, can influence temperature and weather for several years afterwards. The eruption of Mount Pinatubo in the Philippines ejected more than 20 million tonnes of dust and ash 32 km [20 miles] into the atmosphere and is believed to have accelerated ozone depletion over a large part of the globe.

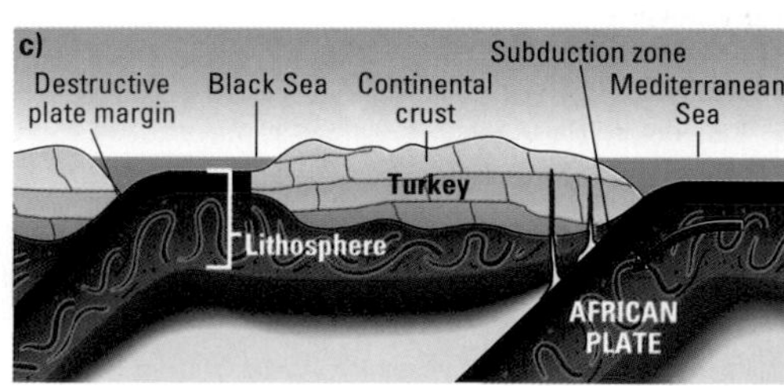

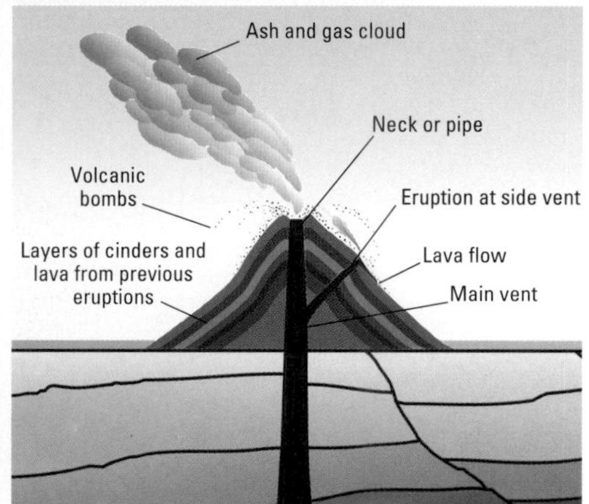

[Diagrams not to scale]

DISTRIBUTION OF VOLCANOES

Today volcanoes may be the subject of considerable scientific study but they remain both dramatic and unpredictable, if not exactly supernatural: in 1991 Mount Pinatubo, 100 km [62 miles] north of the Philippines capital Manila, suddenly burst into life after lying dormant for more than six centuries. Most of the world's active volcanoes occur in a belt around the Pacific Ocean, on the edge of the Pacific plate, called the 'ring of fire'. Indonesia has the greatest concentration with 90 volcanoes, 12 of which are active. The most famous, Krakatoa, erupted in 1883 with such force that the resulting tidal wave killed 36,000 people and tremors were felt as far away as Australia.

○ Submarine volcanoes

▲ Land volcanoes active since 1700

— Boundaries of tectonic plates

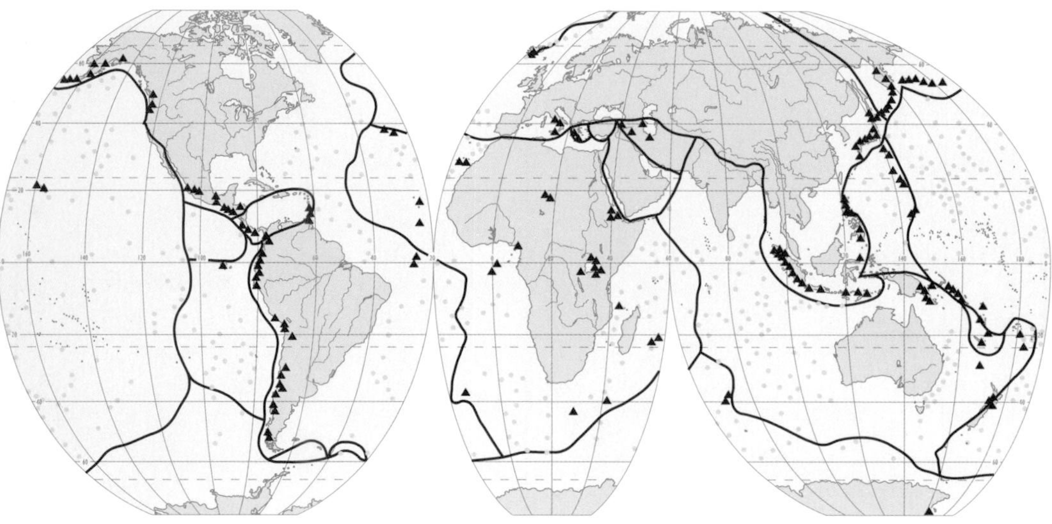

LANDFORMS

THE ROCK CYCLE

James Hutton first proposed the rock cycle in the late 1700s after he observed the slow but steady effects of erosion.

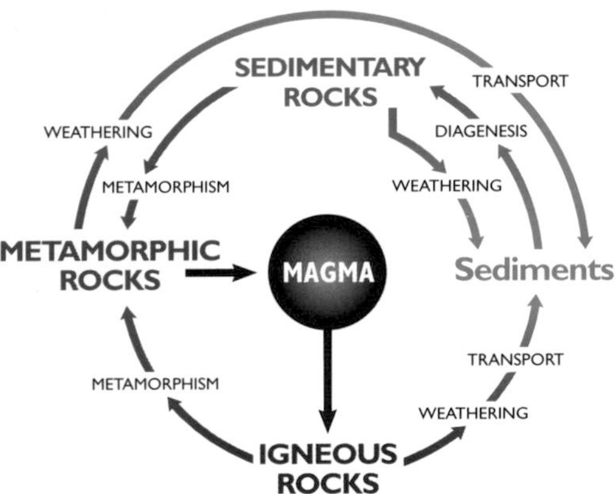

Above and below the surface of the oceans, the features of the Earth's crust are constantly changing. The phenomenal forces generated by convection currents in the molten core of our planet carry the vast segments or 'plates' of the crust across the globe in an endless cycle of creation and destruction. A continent may travel little more than 25 mm [1 in] per year, yet in the vast span of geological time this process throws up giant mountain ranges and creates new land.

Destruction of the landscape, however, begins as soon as it is formed. Wind, water, ice and sea, the main agents of erosion, mount a constant assault that even the most resistant rocks cannot withstand. Mountain peaks may dwindle by as little as a few millimetres each year, but if they are not uplifted by further movements of the crust they will eventually be reduced to rubble and transported away. Water is the most powerful agent of erosion – it has been estimated that 100 billion tonnes of sediment are washed into the oceans every year. Three Asian rivers account for 20% of this total, the Huang He, in China, and the Brahmaputra and Ganges in Bangladesh.

Rivers and glaciers, like the sea itself, generate much of their effect through abrasion – pounding the land with the debris they carry with them. But as well as destroying they also create new landforms, many of them spectacular: vast deltas like those of the Mississippi and the Nile, or the deep fjords cut by glaciers in British Columbia, Norway and New Zealand.

Geologists once considered that landscapes evolved from 'young', newly uplifted mountainous areas, through a 'mature' hilly stage, to an 'old age' stage when the land was reduced to an almost flat plain, or peneplain. This theory, called the 'cycle of erosion', fell into disuse when it became evident that so many factors, including the effects of plate tectonics and climatic change, constantly interrupt the cycle, which takes no account of the highly complex interactions that shape the surface of our planet.

MOUNTAIN BUILDING

Mountains are formed when pressures on the Earth's crust caused by continental drift become so intense that the surface buckles or cracks. This happens where oceanic crust is subducted by continental crust or, more dramatically, where two tectonic plates collide: the Rockies, Andes, Alps, Urals and Himalayas resulted from such impacts. These are all known as fold mountains because they were formed by the compression of the rocks, forcing the surface to bend and fold like a crumpled rug. The Himalayas are formed from the folded former sediments of the Tethys Sea which was trapped in the collision zone between the Indian and Eurasian plates.

The other main mountain-building process occurs when the crust fractures to create faults, allowing rock to be forced upwards in large blocks; or when the pressure of magma within the crust forces the surface to bulge into a dome, or erupts to form a volcano. Large mountain ranges may reveal a combination of those features; the Alps, for example, have been compressed so violently that the folds are fragmented by numerous faults and intrusions of molten igneous rock.

Over millions of years, even the greatest mountain ranges can be reduced by the agents of erosion (most notably rivers) to a low rugged landscape known as a peneplain.

Types of faults: Faults occur where the crust is being stretched or compressed so violently that the rock strata break in a horizontal or vertical movement. They are classified by the direction in which the blocks of rock have moved. A normal fault results when a vertical movement causes the surface to break apart; compression causes a reverse fault. Horizontal movement causes shearing, known as a strike-slip fault. When the rock breaks in two places, the central block may be pushed up in a horst fault, or sink (creating a rift valley) in a graben fault.

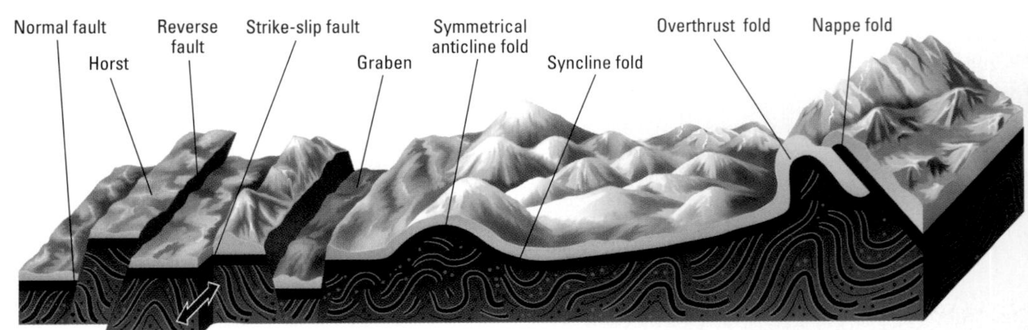

Normal fault   Reverse fault   Strike-slip fault   Symmetrical anticline fold   Overthrust fold   Nappe fold

Horst   Graben   Syncline fold

Types of fold: Folds occur when rock strata are squeezed and compressed. They are common therefore at destructive plate margins and where plates have collided, forcing the rocks to buckle into mountain ranges. Geographers give different names to the degrees of fold that result from continuing pressure on the rock. A simple fold may be symmetric, with even slopes on either side, but as the pressure builds up, one slope becomes steeper and the fold becomes asymmetric. Later, the ridge or 'anticline' at the top of the fold may slide over the lower ground or 'syncline' to form a recumbent fold. Eventually, the rock strata may break under the pressure to form an overthrust and finally a nappe fold.

CONTINENTAL GLACIATION

Ice sheets were at their greatest extent about 200,000 years ago. The maximum advance of the last Ice Age was about 18,000 years ago, when ice covered virtually all of Canada and reached as far south as the Bristol Channel in Britain.

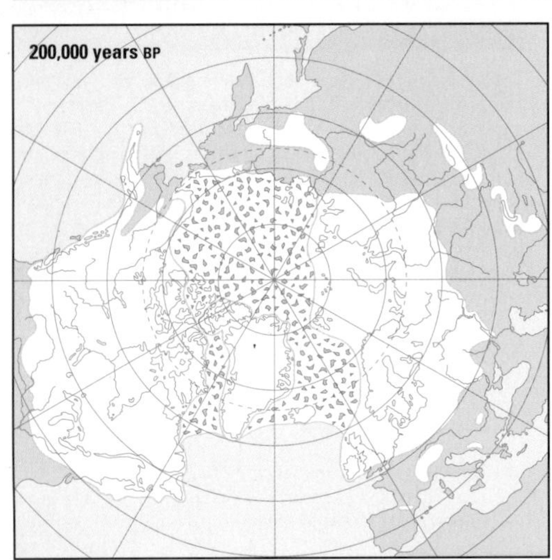

200,000 years BP

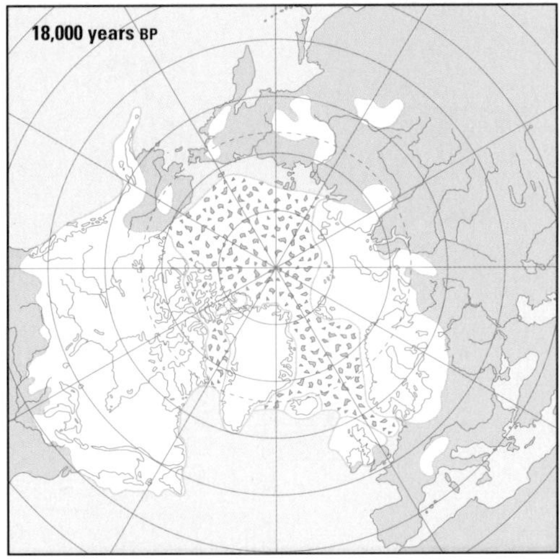

18,000 years BP

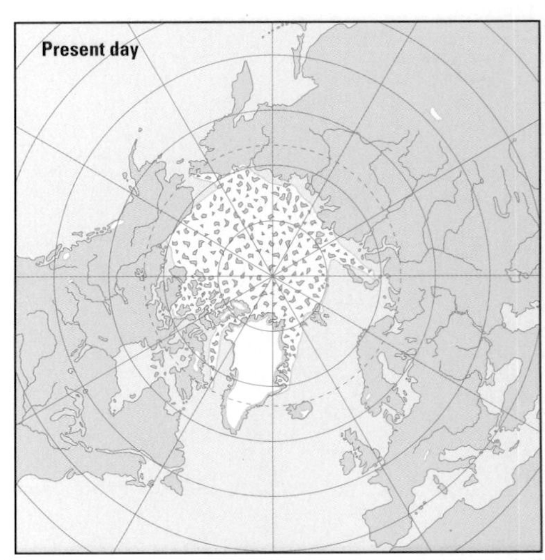

Present day

A stylized diagram to show a selection of landforms found in the mid-latitudes.

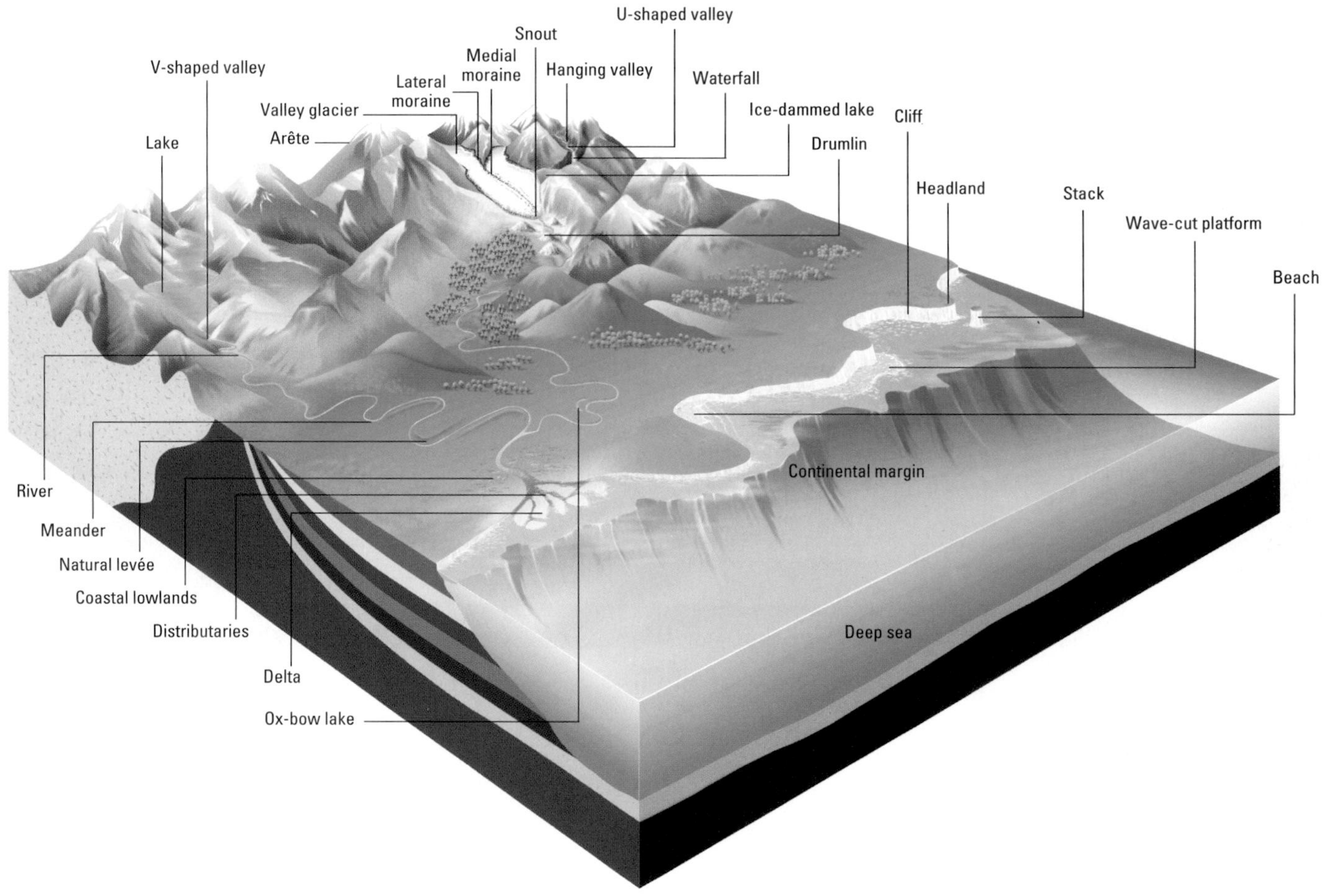

Labels on diagram: V-shaped valley · Snout · U-shaped valley · Medial moraine · Hanging valley · Waterfall · Lateral moraine · Valley glacier · Ice-dammed lake · Cliff · Lake · Arête · Drumlin · Headland · Stack · Wave-cut platform · Beach · Continental margin · River · Meander · Natural levée · Coastal lowlands · Distributaries · Delta · Ox-bow lake · Deep sea

DESERT LANDSCAPES

The popular image that deserts are all huge expanses of sand is wrong. Despite harsh conditions, deserts contain some of the most varied and interesting landscapes in the world. They are also one of the most extensive environments – the hot and cold deserts together cover almost 40% of the Earth's surface.

The three types of hot desert are known by their Arabic names: sand desert, called *erg*, covers only about one-fifth of the world's desert; the rest is divided between *hammada* (areas of bare rock) and *reg* (broad plains covered by loose gravel or pebbles).

In areas of *erg*, such as the Namib Desert, the shape of the dunes reflects the character of local winds. Where winds are constant in direction, crescent-shaped *barchan* dunes form. In areas of bare rock, wind-blown sand is a major agent of erosion. The erosion is mainly confined to within two metres of the surface, producing characteristic, mushroom-shaped rocks.

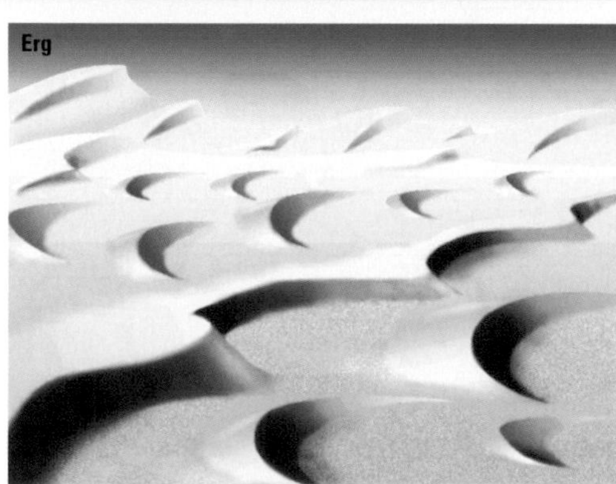

Erg

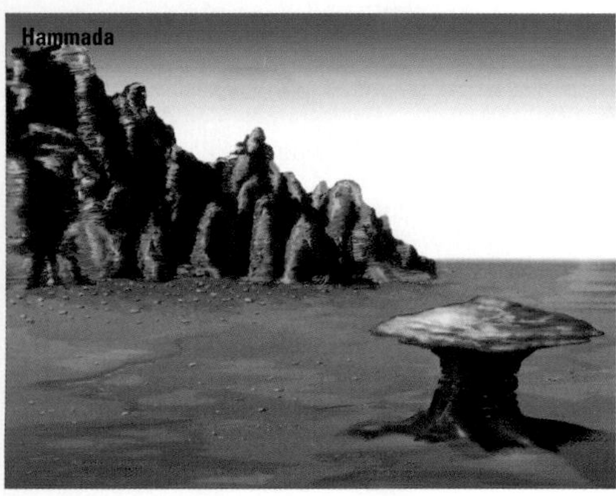

Hammada

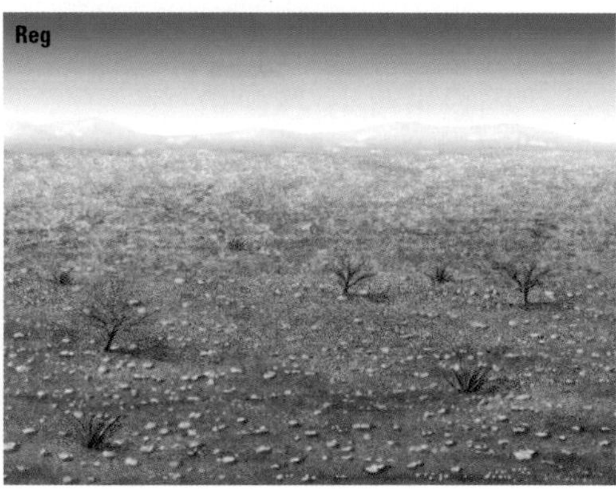

Reg

SURFACE PROCESSES

Catastrophic changes to natural landforms are periodically caused by such phenomena as avalanches, landslides and volcanic eruptions, but most of the processes that shape the Earth's surface operate extremely slowly in human terms. One estimate, based on a study in the United States, suggested that one metre of land was removed from the entire surface of the country, on average, every 29,500 years. However, the time-scale varies from 1,300 years to 154,200 years depending on the terrain and climate.

In hot, dry climates, mechanical weathering, a result of rapid temperature changes, causes the outer layers of rock to peel away, while in cold mountainous regions, boulders are prised apart when water freezes in cracks in rocks. Chemical weathering, at its greatest in warm, humid regions, is responsible for hollowing out limestone caves and decomposing granites.

The erosion of soil and rock is greatest on sloping land and the steeper the slope, the greater the tendency for mass wasting – the movement of soil and rock downhill under the influence of gravity. The mechanisms of mass wasting (ranging from very slow to very rapid) vary with the type of material but the presence of water as a lubricant is usually an important factor.

Running water is the world's leading agent of erosion and transportation. The energy of a river depends on several factors, including its velocity and volume, and its erosive power is at its peak when it is in full flood. Sea waves also exert tremendous erosive power during storms when they hurl pebbles against the shore, undercutting cliffs and hollowing out caves.

Glacier ice forms in mountain hollows and spills out to form valley glaciers, which transport rocks shattered by frost action. As glaciers move, rocks embedded into the ice erode steep-sided, U-shaped valleys. Evidence of glaciation in mountain regions includes cirques, knife-edged ridges, or arêtes, and pyramidal peaks.

OCEANS

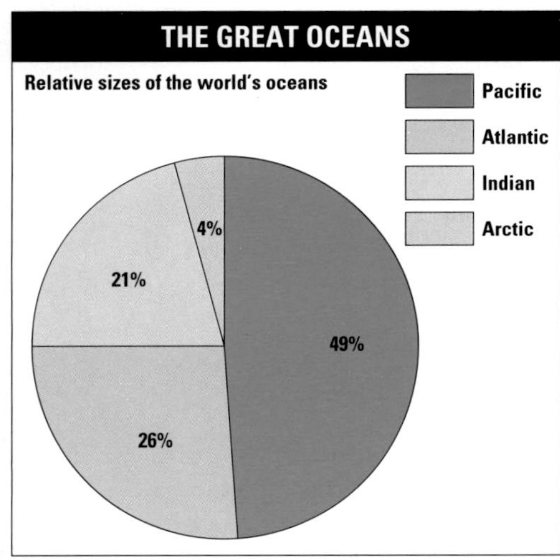
The Earth is a watery planet: more than 70% of its surface – over 360,000,000 square kilometres – is covered by the oceans and seas. The mighty Pacific alone accounts for nearly 36% of the total, and 49% of the sea area. Gravity holds in around 1,400 million cubic kilometres of water, of which over 97% is saline.

The vast underwater world starts in the shallows of the seaside and plunges to depths of more than 11,000 metres. The continental shelf, part of the landmass, drops gently to around 200 metres; here the seabed falls away suddenly at an angle of 3° to 6° – the continental slope. The third stage, called the continental rise, is more gradual with gradients varying from 1 in 100 to 1 in 700. At an average depth of 5,000 metres there begins the aptly-named abyssal plain – massive submarine depths where sunlight fails to penetrate and few creatures can survive.

From these plains rise volcanoes which, taken from base to top, rival and even surpass the biggest continental mountains in height. Mount Kea, on Hawaii, reaches a total of 10,203 metres, some 1,355 metres more than Mount Everest, though scarcely 40% is visible above sea level.

In addition there are underwater mountain chains up to 1,000 kilometres across, whose peaks sometimes appear above sea level as islands such as Iceland and Tristan da Cunha.

THE OCEAN DEPTHS

Average and maximum depths of the world's great oceans, in metres

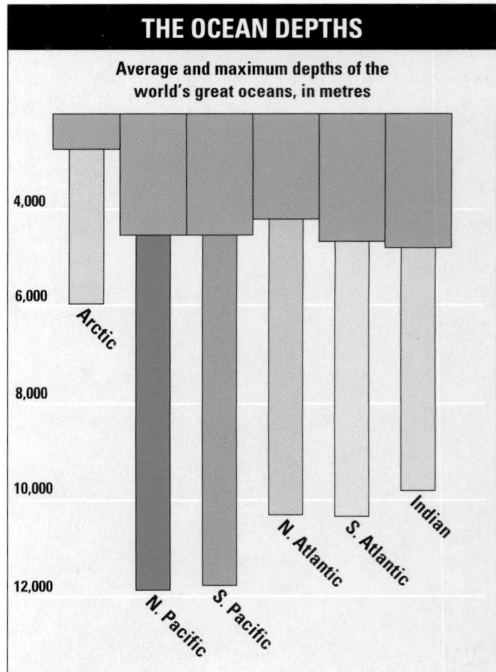

OCEAN CURRENTS

January temperatures and ocean currents

ACTUAL SURFACE TEMPERATURE

°C
30
20
10
0
−10
−20
−30
−40

OCEAN CURRENTS

Cold	Warm	Speed (knots)
◄- -	◄—	Less than 0.5
◄—	◄—	0.5 – 1.0
◄—	◄—	Over 1.0

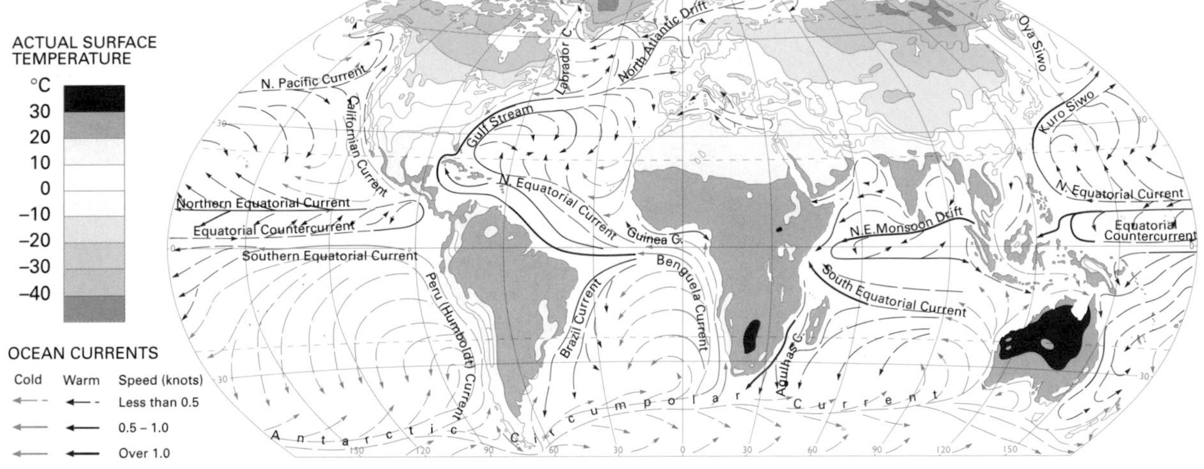

July temperatures and ocean currents

ACTUAL SURFACE TEMPERATURE

°C
30
20
10
0
−10

OCEAN CURRENTS

Cold	Warm	Speed (knots)
◄- -	◄—	Less than 0.5
◄—	◄—	0.5 – 1.0
◄—	◄—	Over 1.0

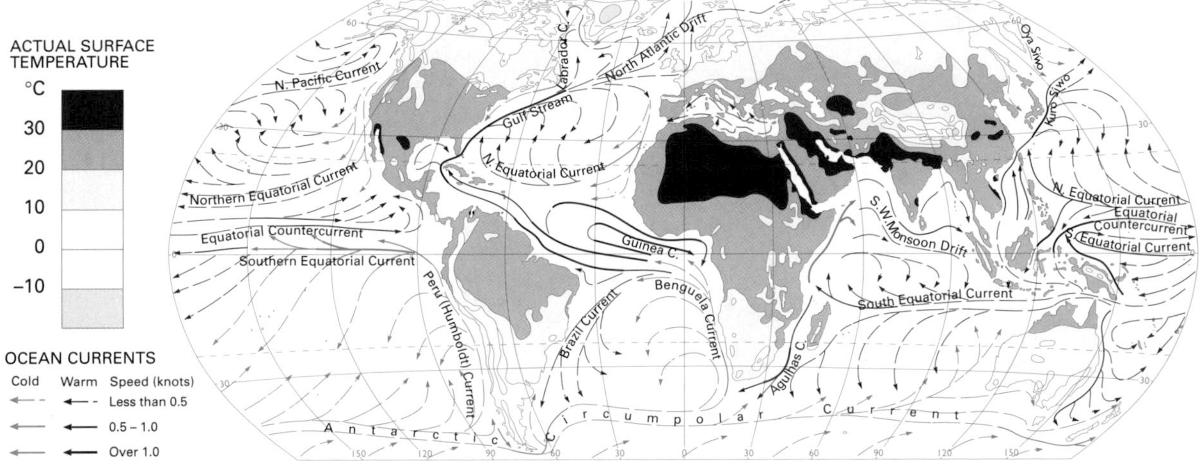

Moving immense quantities of energy as well as billions of tonnes of water every hour, the ocean currents are a vital part of the great heat engine that drives the Earth's climate. They themselves are produced by a twofold mechanism. At the surface, winds push huge masses of water before them; in the deep ocean, below an abrupt temperature gradient that separates the churning surface waters from the still depths, density variations cause slow vertical movements.

The pattern of circulation of the great surface currents is determined by the displacement known as the Coriolis effect. As the Earth turns beneath a moving object – whether it is a tennis ball or a vast mass of water – it appears to be deflected to one side. The deflection is most obvious near the Equator, where the Earth's surface is spinning eastwards at 1,700 km/h; currents moving polewards are curved clockwise in the northern hemisphere and anti-clockwise in the southern.

The result is a system of spinning circles known as gyres. The Coriolis effect piles up water on the left of each gyre, creating a narrow, fast-moving stream that is matched by a slower, broader returning current on the right. North and south of the Equator, the fastest currents are located in the west and in the east respectively. In each case, warm water moves from the Equator and cold water returns to it. Cold currents often bring an upwelling of nutrients with them, supporting the world's most economically important fisheries.

Depending on the prevailing winds, some currents on or near the Equator may reverse their direction in the course of the year – a seasonal variation on which Asian monsoon rains depend, and whose occasional failure can bring disaster to millions.

WORLD FISHING AREAS

Main commercial fishing areas (numbered FAO regions)

Catch by top marine fishing areas, thousand tonnes (1992)

1.	Pacific, NW	[61]	24,199	29.3%
2.	Pacific, SE	[87]	13,899	16.8%
3.	Atlantic, NE	[27]	11,073	13.4%
4.	Pacific, WC	[71]	7,710	9.3%
5.	Indian, W	[51]	3,747	4.5%
6.	Indian, E	[57]	3,262	4.0%
7.	Atlantic, EC	[34]	3,259	3.9%
8.	Pacific, NE	[67]	3,149	3.8%

Principal fishing areas

Leading fishing nations

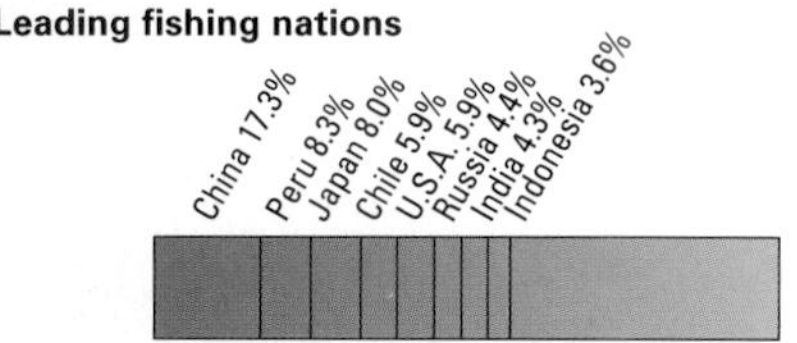

China 17.3% Peru 8.3% Japan 8.0% Chile 5.9% U.S.A. 5.9% Russia 4.4% India 4.3% Indonesia 3.6%

World total (1993): 101,417,500 tonnes
(Marine catch 83.1% Inland catch 16.9%)

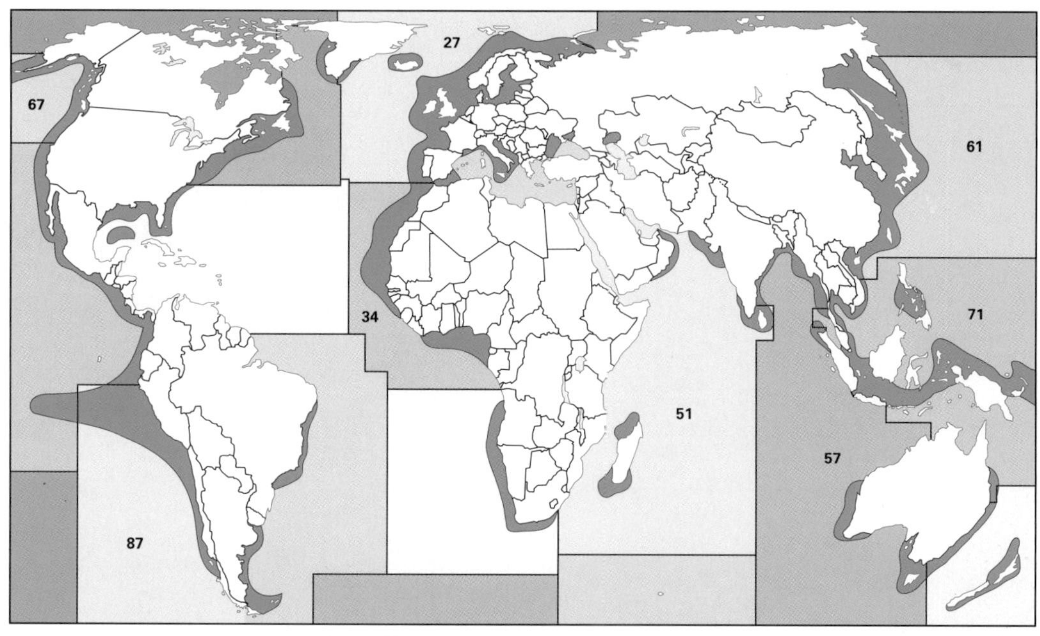

MARINE POLLUTION

Sources of marine oil pollution (latest available year)

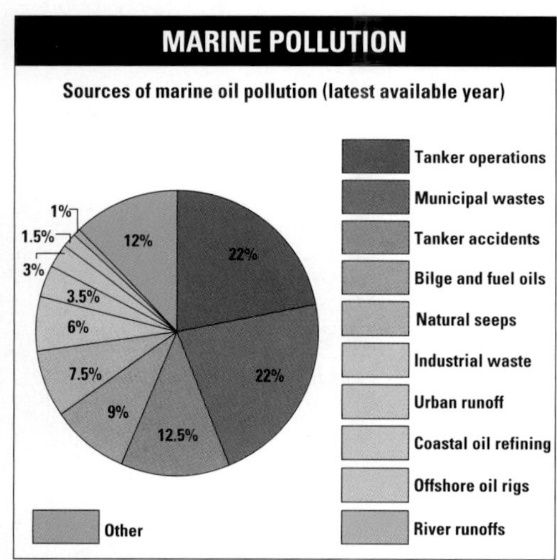

- Tanker operations
- Municipal wastes
- Tanker accidents
- Bilge and fuel oils
- Natural seeps
- Industrial waste
- Urban runoff
- Coastal oil refining
- Offshore oil rigs
- River runoffs
- Other

OIL SPILLS

Major oil spills from tankers and combined carriers

Year	Vessel	Location	Spill (barrels)**	Cause
1979	Atlantic Empress	West Indies	1,890,000	collision
1983	Castillo De Bellver	South Africa	1,760,000	fire
1978	Amoco Cadiz	France	1,628,000	grounding
1991	Haven	Italy	1,029,000	explosion
1988	Odyssey	Canada	1,000,000	fire
1967	Torrey Canyon	UK	909,000	grounding
1972	Sea Star	Gulf of Oman	902,250	collision
1977	Hawaiian Patriot	Hawaiian Is.	742,500	fire
1979	Independenta	Turkey	696,350	collision
1993	Braer	UK	625,000	grounding
1996	Sea Empress	UK	515,000	grounding

Other sources of major oil spills

Year				
1983	Nowruz oilfield	The Gulf	4,250,000[†]	war
1979	Ixtoc 1 oilwell	Gulf of Mexico	4,200,000	blow-out
1991	Kuwait	The Gulf	2,500,000[†]	war

** 1 barrel = 0.136 tonnes/159 lit./35 Imperial gal./42 US gal. [†] estimated

RIVER POLLUTION

Sources of river pollution, USA (latest available year)

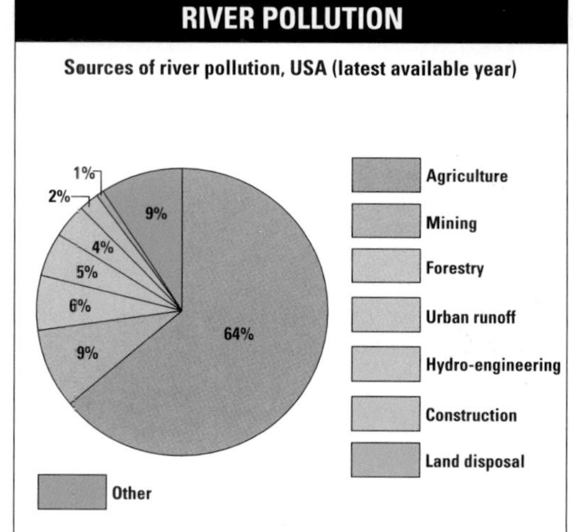

- Agriculture
- Mining
- Forestry
- Urban runoff
- Hydro-engineering
- Construction
- Land disposal
- Other

WATER POLLUTION

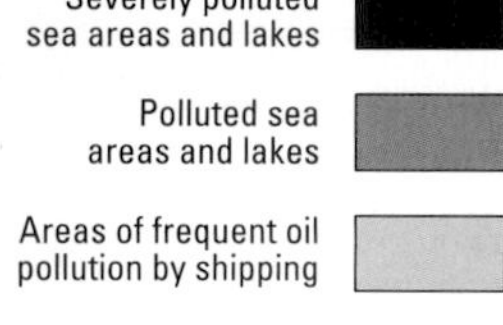

Severely polluted sea areas and lakes

Polluted sea areas and lakes

Areas of frequent oil pollution by shipping

▶ Major oil tanker spills

▲ Major oil rig blow-outs

▼ Offshore dumpsites for industrial and municipal waste

— Severely polluted rivers and estuaries

The most notorious tanker spillage of the 1980s occurred when the *Exxon Valdez* ran aground in Prince William Sound, Alaska, in 1989, spilling 267,000 barrels of crude oil close to shore in a sensitive ecological area. This rates as the world's 28th worst spill in terms of volume.

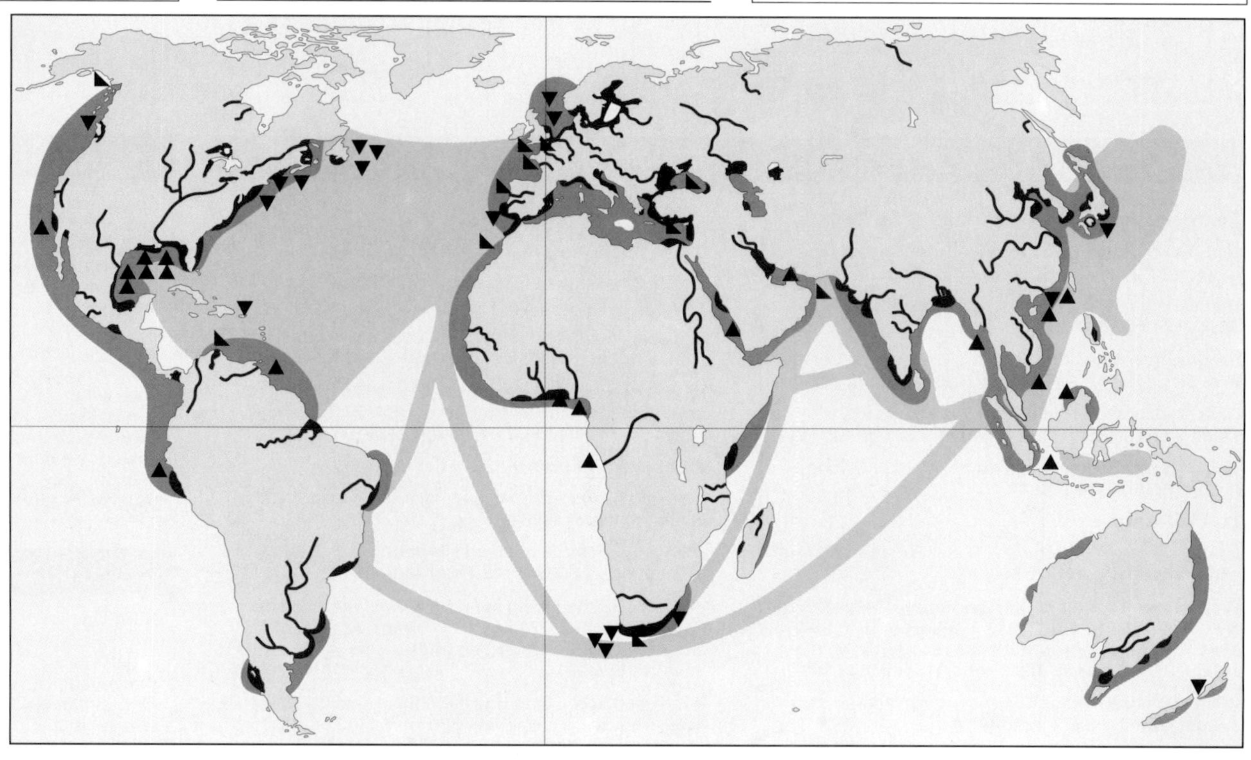

CLIMATE

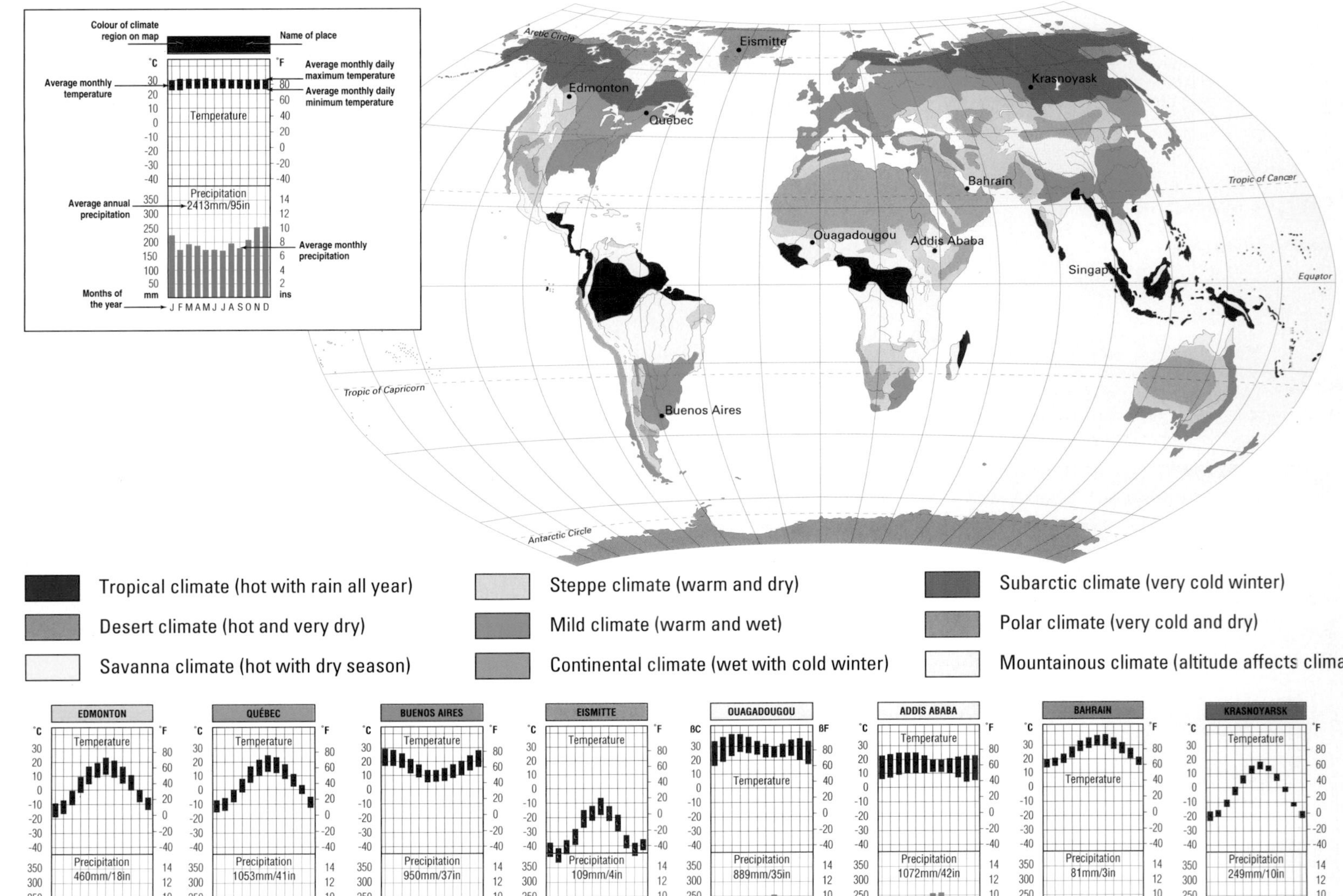

Tropical climate (hot with rain all year)

Desert climate (hot and very dry)

Savanna climate (hot with dry season)

Steppe climate (warm and dry)

Mild climate (warm and wet)

Continental climate (wet with cold winter)

Subarctic climate (very cold winter)

Polar climate (very cold and dry)

Mountainous climate (altitude affects climate)

CLIMATE RECORDS

Temperature

Highest recorded shade temperature: Al Aziziyah, Libya, 58°C [136.4°F], 13 September 1922.

Highest mean annual temperature: Dallol, Ethiopia, 34.4°C [94°F], 1960–66.

Longest heatwave: Marble Bar, W. Australia, 162 days over 38°C [100°F], 23 October 1923 to 7 April 1924.

Lowest recorded temperature (outside poles): Verkhoyansk, Siberia, –68°C [–90°F], 6 February 1933.

Lowest mean annual temperature: Plateau Station, Antarctica, –56.6°C [–72.0°F]

Precipitation

Longest drought: Calama, N. Chile, no recorded rainfall in 400 years to 1971.

Wettest place (12 months): Cherrapunji, Meghalaya, N. E. India, 26,470 mm [1,040 in], August 1860 to August 1861. Cherrapunji also holds the record for the most rainfall in one month: 2,930 mm [115 in], July 1861.

Wettest place (average): Mawsynram, India, mean annual rainfall 11,873 mm [467.4 in].

Wettest place (24 hours): Cilaos, Réunion, Indian Ocean, 1,870 mm [73.6 in], 15–16 March 1952.

Heaviest hailstones: Gopalganj, Bangladesh, up to 1.02 kg [2.25 lb], 14 April 1986 (killed 92 people).

Heaviest snowfall (continuous): Bessans, Savoie, France, 1,730 mm [68 in] in 19 hours, 5–6 April 1969.

Heaviest snowfall (season/year): Paradise Ranger Station, Mt Rainier, Washington, USA, 31,102 mm [1,224.5 in], 19 February 1971 to 18 February 1972.

Pressure and winds

Highest barometric pressure: Agata, Siberia (at 262 m [862 ft] altitude), 1,083.8 mb, 31 December 1968.

Lowest barometric pressure: Typhoon Tip, Guam, Pacific Ocean, 870 mb, 12 October 1979.

Highest recorded wind speed: Mt Washington, New Hampshire, USA, 371 km/h [231 mph], 12 April 1934. This is three times as strong as hurricane force on the Beaufort Scale.

Windiest place: Commonwealth Bay, Antarctica, where gales frequently reach over 320 km/h [200 mph].

CLIMATE

Climate is weather in the long term: the seasonal pattern of hot and cold, wet and dry, averaged over time (usually 30 years). At the simplest level, it is caused by the uneven heating of the Earth. Surplus heat at the Equator passes towards the poles, levelling out the energy differential. Its passage is marked by a ceaseless churning of the atmosphere and the oceans, further agitated by the Earth's diurnal spin and the motion it imparts to moving air and water. The heat's means of transport – by winds and ocean currents, by the continual evaporation and recondensation of water molecules – is the weather itself. There are four basic types of climate, each of which can be further subdivided: tropical, desert (dry), temperate and polar.

COMPOSITION OF DRY AIR

Nitrogen	78.09%	Sulphur dioxide	trace
Oxygen	20.95%	Nitrogen oxide	trace
Argon	0.93%	Methane	trace
Water vapour	0.2–4.0%	Dust	trace
Carbon dioxide	0.03%	Helium	trace
Ozone	0.00006%	Neon	trace

EL NIÑO

In a normal year, south-easterly trade winds drive surface waters westward off the coast of South America, drawing cold, nutrient-rich water up from below. In an El Niño year (which occurs every 2 to 7 years), warm water from the west Pacific suppresses upwelling in the east depriving the region of nutrients. The water is warmed by as much as 7°C, disturbing the tropical atmospheric circulation. During an intense El Niño, the south-east trade winds change direction and become equatorial westerlies resulting in climatic extremes in many regions of the world, such as drought in parts of Australia and India, and heavy rainfall in south-eastern USA. The UK experiences exceptionally mild and wet winters.

Normal year

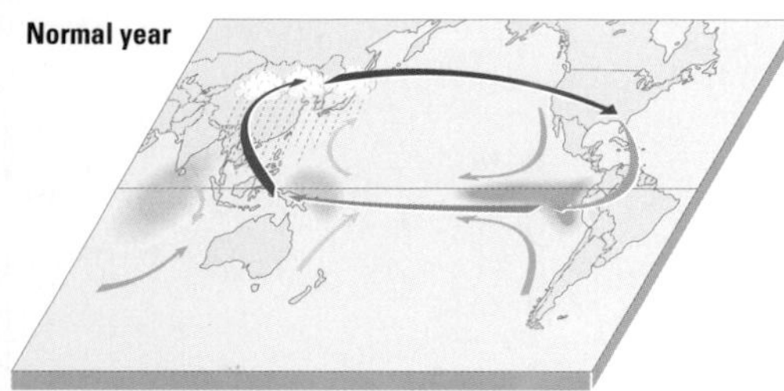

El Niño event

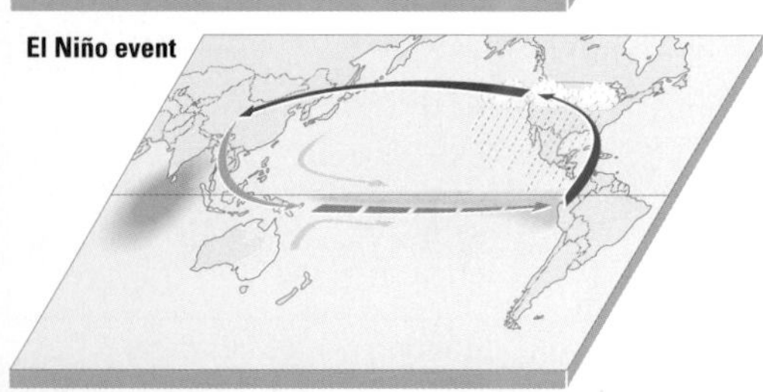

BEAUFORT WIND SCALE

Named after the 19th-century British naval officer who devised it, the Beaufort Scale assesses wind speed according to its effects. It was originally designed as an aid for sailors, but has since been adapted for use on the land.

Scale	Wind speed km/h	mph	Effect
0	0–1	0–1	**Calm** Smoke rises vertically
1	1–5	1–3	**Light air** Wind direction shown only by smoke drift
2	6–11	4–7	**Light breeze** Wind felt on face; leaves rustle; vanes moved by wind
3	12–19	8–12	**Gentle breeze** Leaves and small twigs in constant motion; wind extends small flag
4	20–28	13–18	**Moderate** Raises dust and loose paper; small branches move
5	29–38	19–24	**Fresh** Small trees in leaf sway; wavelets on inland waters
6	39–49	25–31	**Strong** Large branches move; difficult to use umbrellas
7	50–61	32–38	**Near gale** Whole trees in motion; difficult to walk against wind
8	62–74	39–46	**Gale** Twigs break from trees; walking very difficult
9	75–88	47–54	**Strong gale** Slight structural damage
10	89–102	55–63	**Storm** Trees uprooted; serious structural damage
11	103–117	64–72	**Violent storm** Widespread damage
12	118+	73+	**Hurricane**

Conversions
°C = (°F −32) x 5/9; °F = (°C x 9/5) + 32; 0°C = 32°F
1 in = 25.4 mm; 1 mm = 0.0394 in; 100 mm = 3.94 in

TEMPERATURE

Average temperature in January

Temperature
30°C
20°C
10°C
0°C
−10°C
−20°C
−30°C
−40°C

Average temperature in July

Temperature
30°C
20°C
10°C
0°C
−10°C

PRECIPITATION

Average annual precipitation
3,000 mm
2,000 mm
1,000 mm
500 mm
250 mm

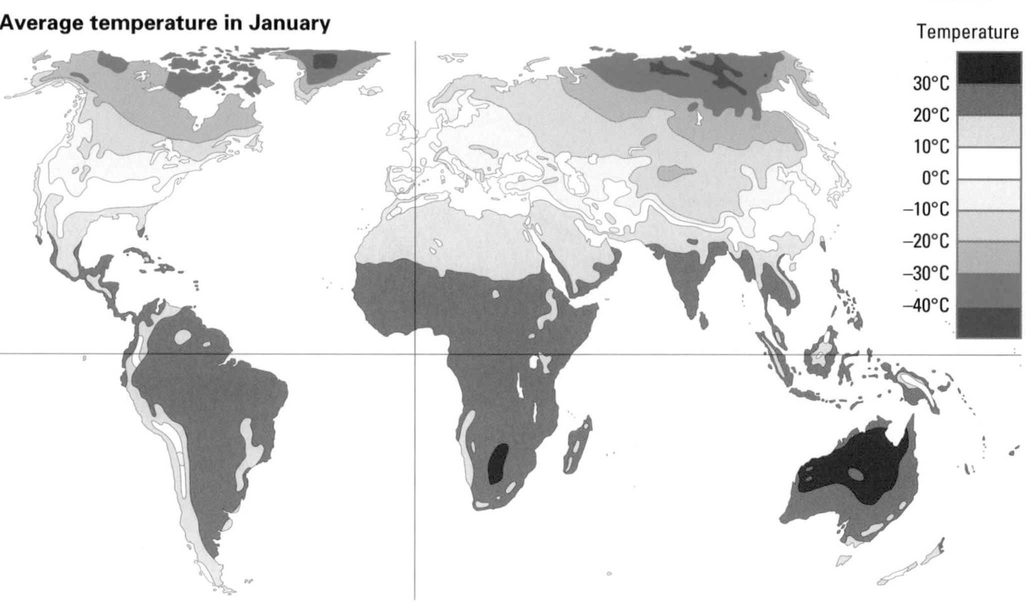

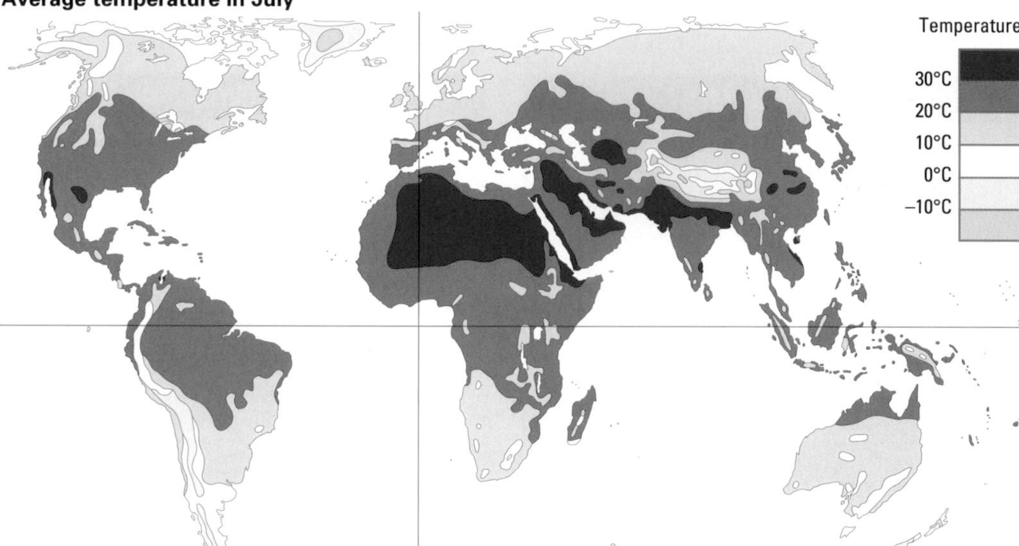

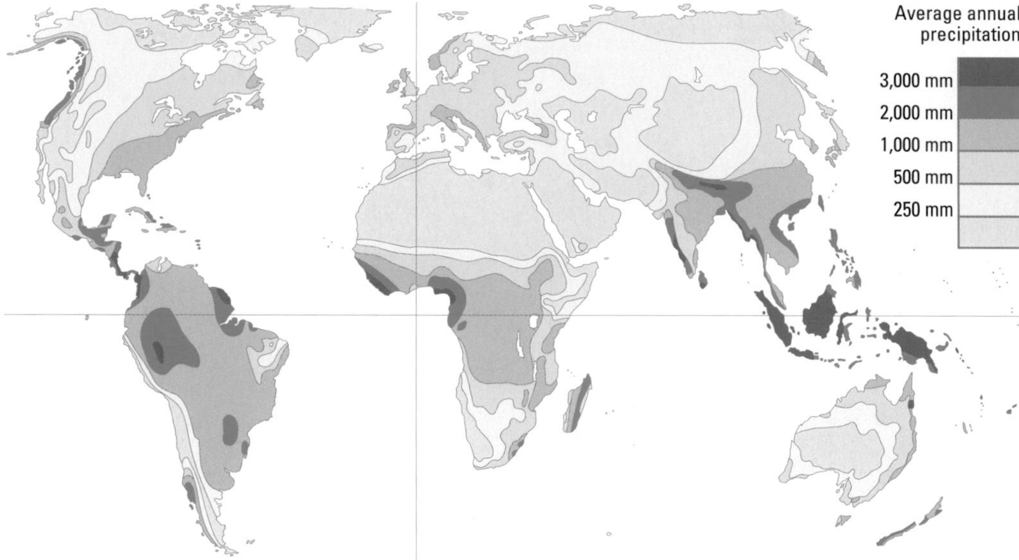

WATER AND VEGETATION

THE HYDROLOGICAL CYCLE

The world's water balance is regulated by the constant recycling of water between the oceans, atmosphere and land. The movement of water between these three reservoirs is known as the hydrological cycle. The oceans play a vital role in the hydrological cycle: 74% of the total precipitation falls over the oceans and 84% of the total evaporation comes from the oceans.

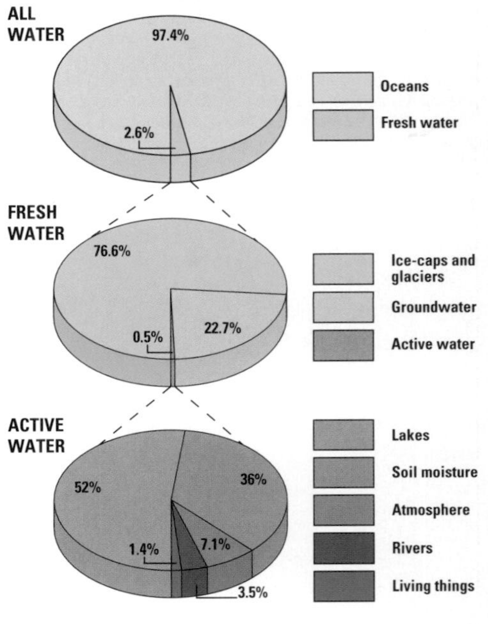

WATER DISTRIBUTION

The distribution of planetary water, by percentage. Oceans and ice-caps together account for more than 99% of the total; the breakdown of the remainder is estimated.

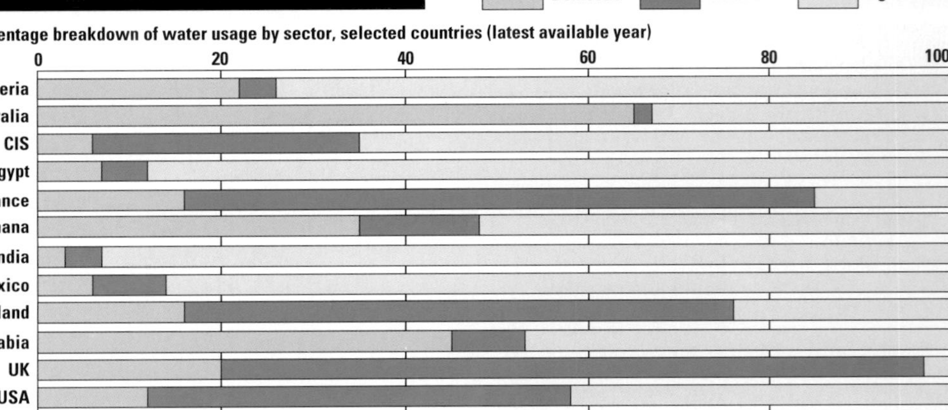

ALL WATER
- 97.4% Oceans
- 2.6% Fresh water

FRESH WATER
- 76.6% Ice-caps and glaciers
- 0.5% Groundwater
- 22.7% Active water

ACTIVE WATER
- 52% Lakes
- 1.4% Soil moisture
- 7.1% Atmosphere
- 36% Rivers
- 3.5% Living things

WATER USAGE

Almost all the world's water is 3,000 million years old, and all of it cycles endlessly through the hydrosphere, though at different rates. Water vapour circulates over days, even hours, deep ocean water circulates over millennia, and ice-cap water remains solid for millions of years.

Fresh water is essential to all terrestrial life. Humans cannot survive more than a few days without it, and even the hardiest desert plants and animals could not exist without some water. Agriculture requires huge quantities of fresh water: without large-scale irrigation most of the world's people would starve. In the USA, agriculture uses 43% and industry 38% of all water withdrawals.

The United States is one of the heaviest users of water in the world. According to the latest figures the average American uses 380 litres a day and the average household uses 415,000 litres a year. This is two to four times more than in Western Europe.

WATER UTILIZATION

□ Domestic ■ Industrial □ Agriculture

The percentage breakdown of water usage by sector, selected countries (latest available year)

Algeria, Australia, CIS, Egypt, France, Ghana, India, Mexico, Poland, Saudi Arabia, UK, USA

WATER SUPPLY

Percentage of total population with access to safe drinking water (1992)

- Over 90% with safe water
- 75 – 90% with safe water
- 60 – 75% with safe water
- 45 – 60% with safe water
- 30 – 45% with safe water
- Under 30% with safe water

◊ Under 80 litres per person per day domestic water consumption

♦ Over 320 litres per person per day

Least well-provided countries

Country	%	Country	%
Central African Rep.	12%	Madagascar	23%
Uganda	15%	Guinea-Bissau	25%
Ethiopia	18%	Laos	28%
Mozambique	22%	Swaziland	30%
Afghanistan	23%	Tajikistan	30%

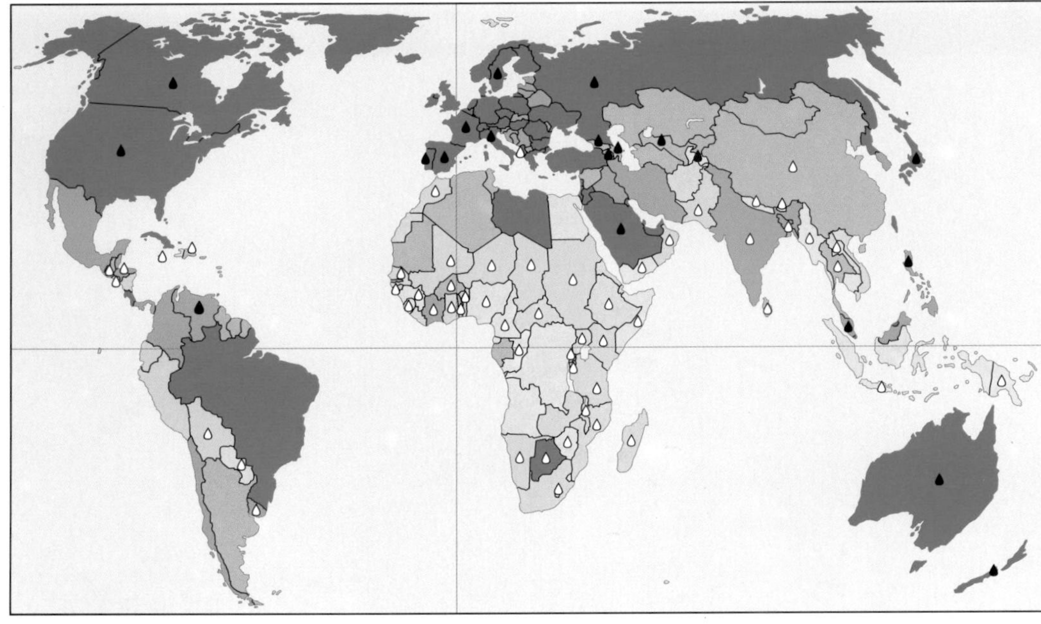

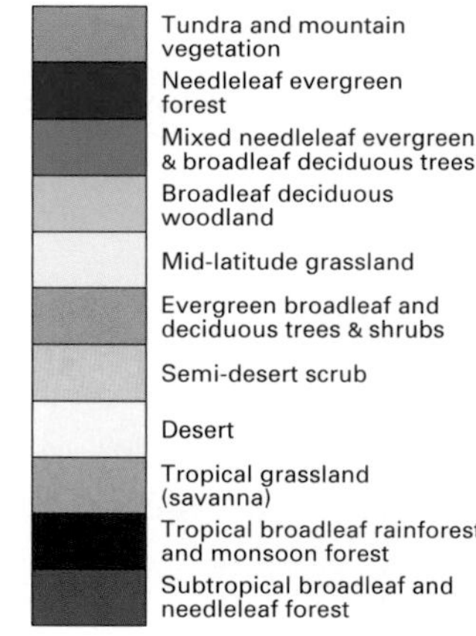

NATURAL VEGETATION

Regional variation in vegetation

- Tundra and mountain vegetation
- Needleleaf evergreen forest
- Mixed needleleaf evergreen & broadleaf deciduous trees
- Broadleaf deciduous woodland
- Mid-latitude grassland
- Evergreen broadleaf and deciduous trees & shrubs
- Semi-desert scrub
- Desert
- Tropical grassland (savanna)
- Tropical broadleaf rainforest and monsoon forest
- Subtropical broadleaf and needleleaf forest

The map shows the natural 'climax vegetation' of regions, as dictated by climate and topography. In most cases, however, agricultural activity has drastically altered the vegetation pattern. Western Europe, for example, lost most of its broadleaf forest many centuries ago, while irrigation has turned some natural semi-desert into productive land.

LAND USE BY CONTINENT

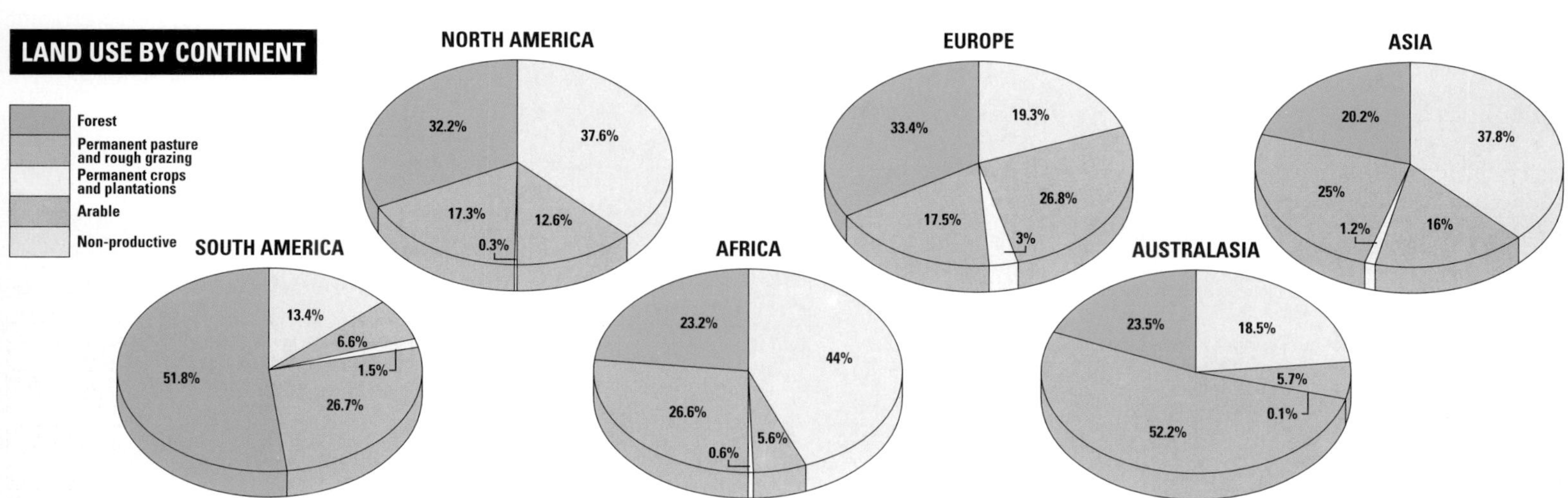

- Forest
- Permanent pasture and rough grazing
- Permanent crops and plantations
- Arable
- Non-productive

NORTH AMERICA: 37.6%, 12.6%, 0.3%, 17.3%, 32.2%

EUROPE: 19.3%, 26.8%, 3%, 17.5%, 33.4%

ASIA: 37.8%, 16%, 1.2%, 25%, 20.2%

SOUTH AMERICA: 13.4%, 6.6%, 1.5%, 26.7%, 51.8%

AFRICA: 44%, 5.6%, 0.6%, 26.6%, 23.2%

AUSTRALASIA: 18.5%, 5.7%, 0.1%, 52.2%, 23.5%

FORESTRY: PRODUCTION

	Forest & woodland (million hectares)	Annual production (1993, million cubic metres)	
		Fuelwood & charcoal	Industrial roundwood*
World	*3,987.9*	*1,875.8*	*1,528.5*
CIS	827.8	51.5	172.9
S. America	829.3	247.8	122.0
N. & C. America	709.8	156.7	586.7
Africa	684.6	493.6	59.5
Asia	490.2	866.4	278.1
Europe	157.3	50.9	272.2
Australasia	157.2	8.7	36.9

PAPER AND BOARD

Top producers (1993)**		Top exporters (1993)**	
USA	77,250	Canada	12,896
Japan	27,764	Finland	8,526
China	23,816	USA	7,146
Canada	17,557	Sweden	7,008
Germany	13,034	Germany	4,763

* roundwood is timber as it is felled

** in thousand tonnes

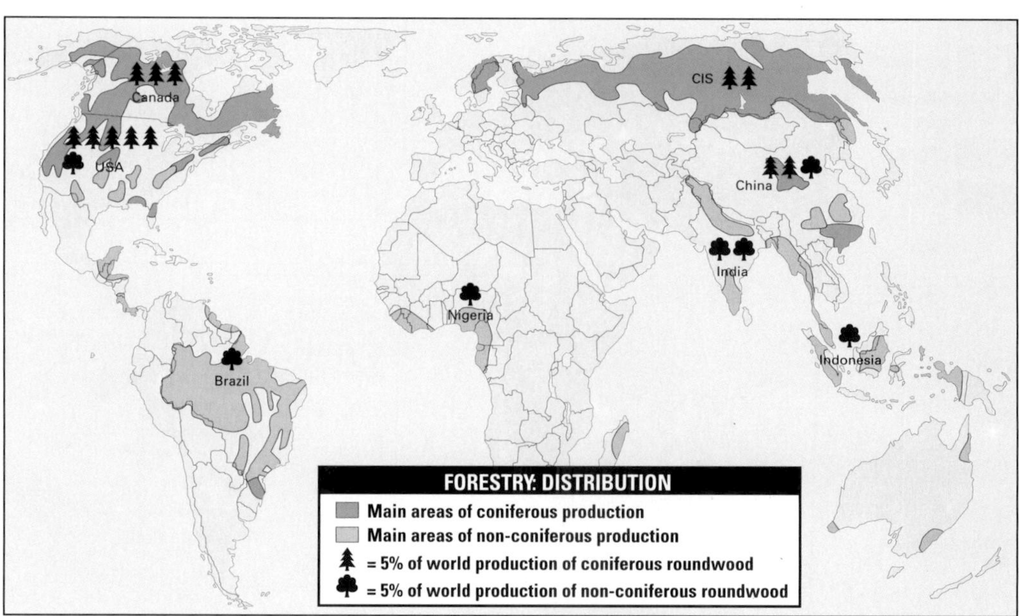

FORESTRY: DISTRIBUTION

- Main areas of coniferous production
- Main areas of non-coniferous production
- 🌲 = 5% of world production of coniferous roundwood
- ♣ = 5% of world production of non-coniferous roundwood

ENVIRONMENT

Humans have always had a dramatic effect on their environment, at least since the development of agriculture almost 10,000 years ago. Generally, the Earth has accepted human interference without obvious ill effects: the complex systems that regulate the global environment have been able to absorb substantial damage while maintaining a stable and comfortable home for the planet's trillions of lifeforms. But advancing human technology and the rapidly-expanding populations it supports are now threatening to overwhelm the Earth's ability to compensate.

Industrial wastes, acid rainfall, desertification and large-scale deforestation all combine to create environmental change at a rate far faster than the great slow cycles of planetary evolution can accommodate. As a result of overcultivation, overgrazing and overcutting of groundcover for firewood, desertification is affecting as much as 60% of the world's croplands. In addition, with fire and chain-saws, humans are destroying more forest in a day than their ancestors could have done in a century, upsetting the balance between plant and animal, carbon dioxide and oxygen, on which all life ultimately depends.

The fossil fuels that power industrial civilization have pumped enough carbon dioxide and other so-called greenhouse gases into the atmosphere to make climatic change a near-certainty. As a result of the combination of these factors, the Earth's average temperature has risen by approximately 0.5°C since the beginning of the 20th century, and it is still rising.

GLOBAL WARMING

Carbon dioxide emissions in tonnes per person per year (1991)

⬛	Over 10 tonnes of CO_2
⬛	5 – 10 tonnes of CO_2
⬜	1 – 5 tonnes of CO_2
⬜	Under 1 tonne of CO_2

Changes in CO_2 emissions 1980–90

▲ Over 100% increase in emissions

▲ 50–100% increase in emissions

▽ Reduction in emissions

── Coastal areas in danger of flooding from rising sea levels caused by global warming

High atmospheric concentrations of heat-absorbing gases, especially carbon dioxide, appear to be causing a steady rise in average temperatures worldwide – up to 1.5°C by the year 2020, according to some estimates. Global warming is likely to bring with it a rise in sea levels that may flood some of the Earth's most densely populated coastal areas.

GREENHOUSE POWER

Relative contributions to the Greenhouse Effect by the major heat-absorbing gases in the atmosphere.

The chart combines greenhouse potency and volume. Carbon dioxide has a greenhouse potential of only 1, but its concentration of 350 parts per million makes it predominant. CFC 12, with 25,000 times the absorption capacity of CO_2, is present only as 0.00044 ppm.

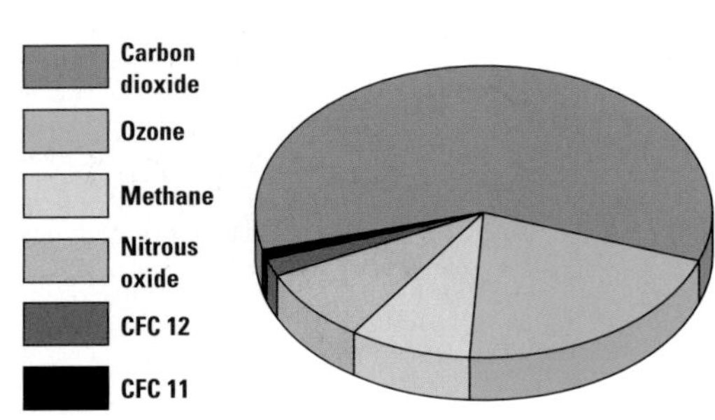

- Carbon dioxide
- Ozone
- Methane
- Nitrous oxide
- CFC 12
- CFC 11

CARBON DIOXIDE

Carbon dioxide released in millions of tonnes (1992)

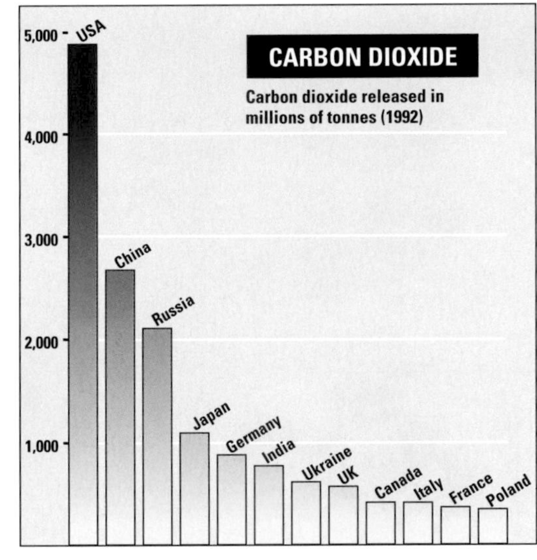

USA, China, Russia, Japan, Germany, India, Ukraine, UK, Canada, Italy, France, Poland

OZONE LAYER

The ozone 'hole' over the northern hemisphere on 12 March 1995.

The colours represent Dobson Units (DU). The ozone 'hole' is seen as the dark blue and purple patch in the centre, where ozone values are around 120 DU or lower. Normal levels are around 280 DU. The ozone 'hole' over Antarctica is much larger.

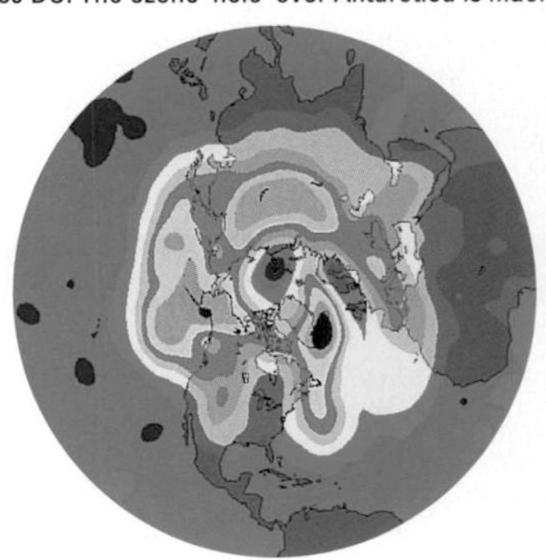

THE GREENHOUSE EFFECT

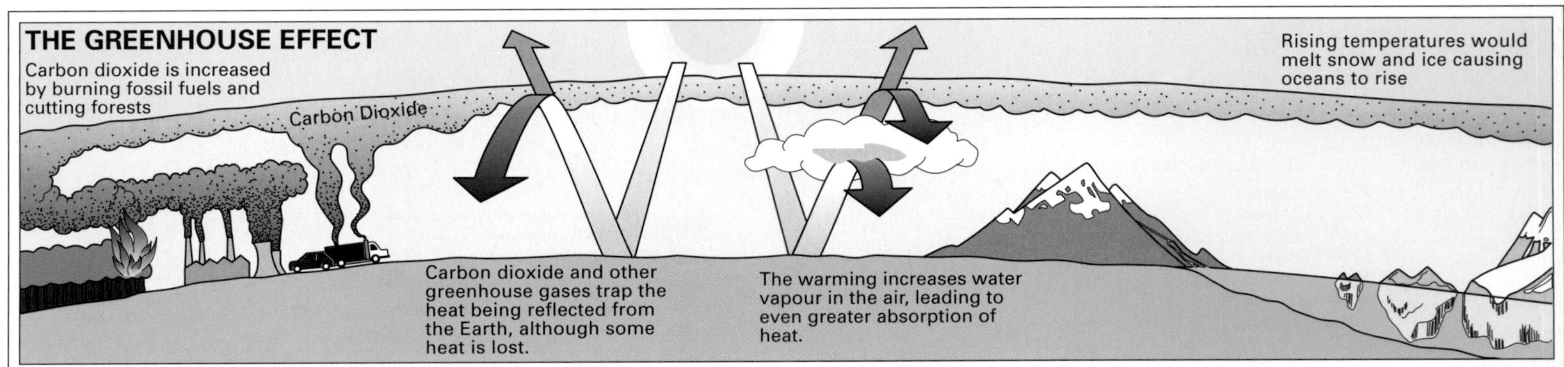

Carbon dioxide is increased by burning fossil fuels and cutting forests

Carbon Dioxide

Rising temperatures would melt snow and ice causing oceans to rise

Carbon dioxide and other greenhouse gases trap the heat being reflected from the Earth, although some heat is lost.

The warming increases water vapour in the air, leading to even greater absorption of heat.

DESERTIFICATION

- Existing deserts
- Areas with a high risk of desertification
- Areas with a moderate risk of desertification
- Former areas of rainforest
- Existing rainforest

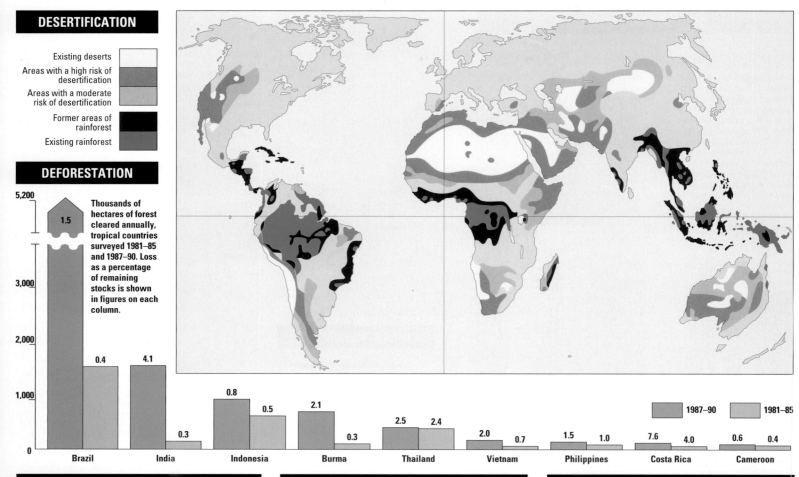

DEFORESTATION

Thousands of hectares of forest cleared annually, tropical countries surveyed 1981–85 and 1987–90. Loss as a percentage of remaining stocks is shown in figures on each column.

■ 1987–90   ■ 1981–85

Country	1987–90	1981–85
Brazil	1.5	0.4
India	4.1	0.3
Indonesia	0.8	0.5
Burma	2.1	0.3
Thailand	2.5	2.4
Vietnam	2.0	0.7
Philippines	1.5	1.0
Costa Rica	7.6	4.0
Cameroon	0.6	0.4

OZONE DEPLETION

The ozone layer (25–30 km above sea level) acts as a barrier to most of the Sun's harmful ultra-violet radiation, protecting us from the ionizing radiation that can cause skin cancer and cataracts. In recent years, however, two holes in the ozone layer have been observed during winter; one over the Arctic and the other, the size of the USA, over Antarctica. By 1996, ozone had been reduced to around a half of its 1970 amount. The ozone (O_3) is broken down by chlorine released into the atmosphere as CFCs (chlorofluorocarbons) – chemicals used in refrigerators, packaging and aerosols.

DEFORESTATION

The Earth's remaining forests are under attack from three directions: expanding agriculture, logging, and growing consumption of fuelwood, often in combination. Sometimes deforestation is the direct result of government policy, as in the efforts made to resettle the urban poor in some parts of Brazil; just as often, it comes about despite state attempts at conservation. Loggers, licensed or unlicensed, blaze a trail into virgin forest, often destroying twice as many trees as they harvest. Landless farmers follow, burning away most of what remains to plant their crops, completing the destruction.

ACID RAIN

Killing trees, poisoning lakes and rivers and eating away buildings, acid rain is mostly produced by sulphur dioxide emissions from industry and volcanic eruptions. By the mid 1990s, acid rain had sterilized 4,000 or more of Sweden's lakes and left 45% of Switzerland's alpine conifers dead or dying, while the monuments of Greece were dissolving in Athens' smog. Prevailing wind patterns mean that the acids often fall many hundred kilometres from where the original pollutants were discharged. In parts of Europe acid deposition has slightly decreased, following reductions in emissions, but not by enough.

WORLD POLLUTION

Acid rain and sources of acidic emissions (latest available year)

Acid rain is caused by high levels of sulphur and nitrogen in the atmosphere. They combine with water vapour and oxygen to form acids (H_2SO_4 and HNO_3) which fall as precipitation.

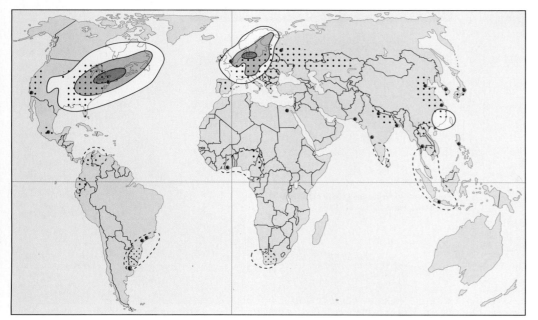

▨ Regions where sulphur and nitrogen oxides are released in high concentrations, mainly from fossil fuel combustion

• Major cities with high levels of air pollution (including nitrogen and sulphur emissions)

Areas of heavy acid deposition

pH numbers indicate acidity, decreasing from a neutral 7. Normal rain, slightly acid from dissolved carbon dioxide, never exceeds a pH of 5.6.

- pH less than 4.0 (most acidic)
- pH 4.0 to 4.5
- pH 4.5 to 5.0
- Areas where acid rain is a potential problem

POPULATION

DEMOGRAPHIC PROFILES

Developed nations such as the UK have populations evenly spread across the age groups and, usually, a growing proportion of elderly people. The great majority of the people in developing nations, however, are in the younger age groups, about to enter their most fertile years. In time, these population profiles should resemble the world profile (even Kenya has made recent progress with reducing its birth rate), but the transition will come about only after a few more generations of rapid population growth.

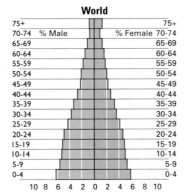

World

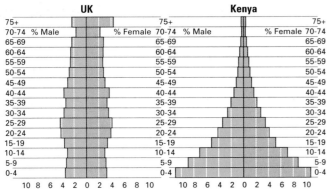

UK   Kenya

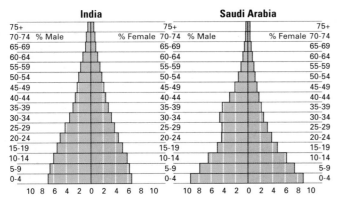

India   Saudi Arabia

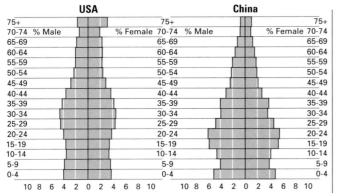

USA   China

MOST POPULOUS NATIONS [in millions (1995)]

1. China	1,227	9. Bangladesh	118	17. Turkey	61
2. India	943	10. Mexico	93	18. Thailand	58
3. USA	264	11. Nigeria	89	19. UK	58
4. Indonesia	199	12. Germany	82	20. France	58
5. Brazil	161	13. Vietnam	75	21. Italy	57
6. Russia	148	14. Iran	69	22. Ukraine	52
7. Pakistan	144	15. Philippines	67	23. Ethiopia	52
8. Japan	125	16. Egypt	64	24. Burma	47

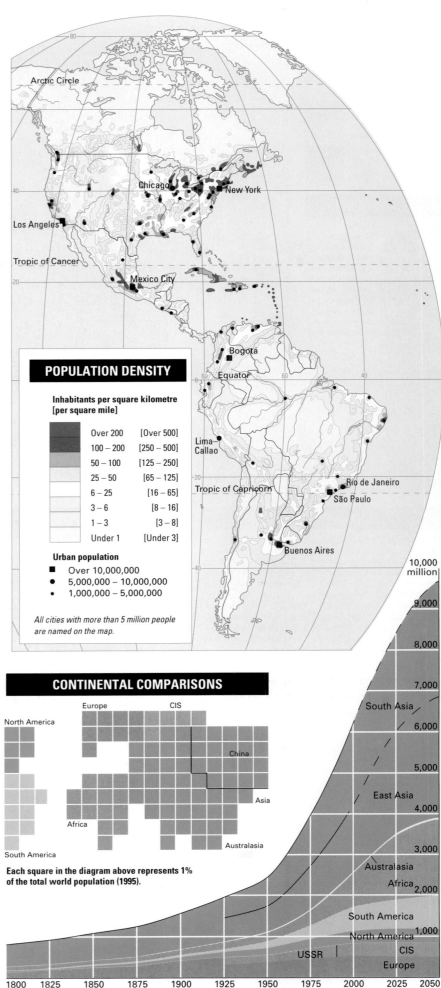

POPULATION DENSITY

Inhabitants per square kilometre [per square mile]

Over 200	[Over 500]
100 – 200	[250 – 500]
50 – 100	[125 – 250]
25 – 50	[65 – 125]
6 – 25	[16 – 65]
3 – 6	[8 – 16]
1 – 3	[3 – 8]
Under 1	[Under 3]

Urban population

■ Over 10,000,000
● 5,000,000 – 10,000,000
· 1,000,000 – 5,000,000

All cities with more than 5 million people are named on the map.

CONTINENTAL COMPARISONS

Each square in the diagram above represents 1% of the total world population (1995).

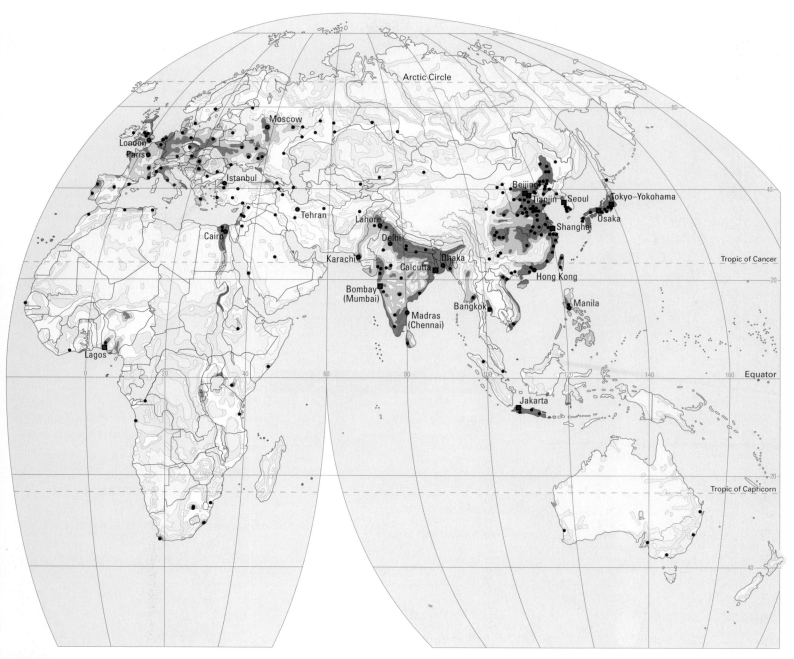

URBAN POPULATION

Percentage of total population living in towns and cities (1993)

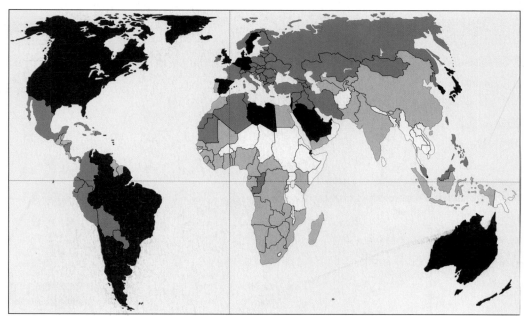

Over 75%
50 – 75%
25 – 50%
10 – 25%
Under 10%

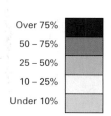

Most urbanized		Least urbanized	
Singapore	100%	Bhutan	6%
Belgium	97%	Rwanda	6%
Kuwait	96%	Burundi	7%
Venezuela	92%	Nepal	12%
Israel	91%	Uganda	12%
	[UK 89%]		

THE HUMAN FAMILY

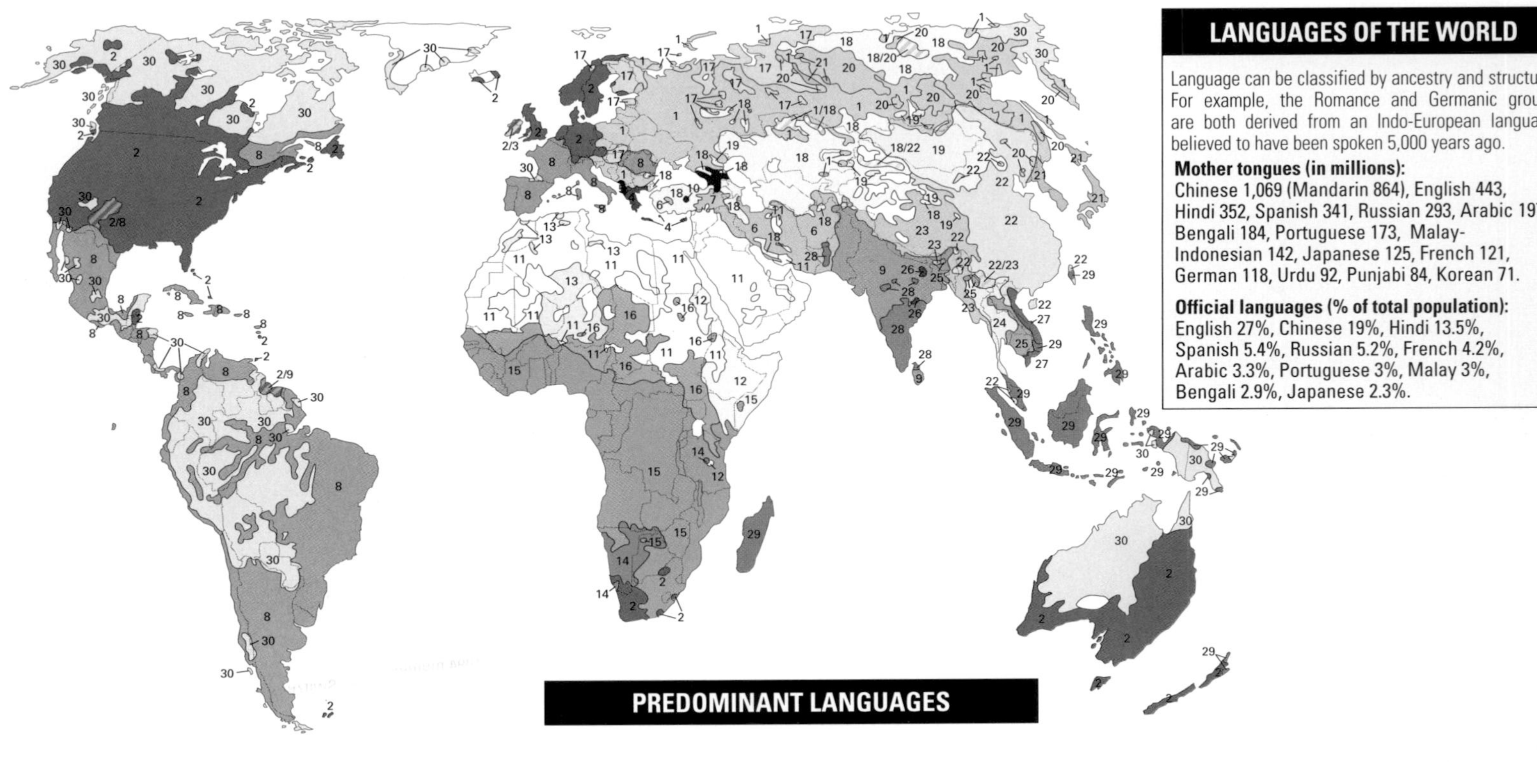

LANGUAGES OF THE WORLD

Language can be classified by ancestry and structure. For example, the Romance and Germanic groups are both derived from an Indo-European language believed to have been spoken 5,000 years ago.

Mother tongues (in millions):
Chinese 1,069 (Mandarin 864), English 443, Hindi 352, Spanish 341, Russian 293, Arabic 197, Bengali 184, Portuguese 173, Malay-Indonesian 142, Japanese 125, French 121, German 118, Urdu 92, Punjabi 84, Korean 71.

Official languages (% of total population):
English 27%, Chinese 19%, Hindi 13.5%, Spanish 5.4%, Russian 5.2%, French 4.2%, Arabic 3.3%, Portuguese 3%, Malay 3%, Bengali 2.9%, Japanese 2.3%.

PREDOMINANT LANGUAGES

INDO-EUROPEAN FAMILY

1	Balto-Slavic group (incl. Russian, Ukrainian)
2	Germanic group (incl. English, German)
3	Celtic group
4	Greek
	Albanian
6	Iranian group
	Armenian
8	Romance group (incl. Spanish, Portuguese, French, Italian)
9	Indo-Aryan group (incl. Hindi, Bengali, Urdu, Punjabi, Marathi)

CAUCASIAN FAMILY

AFRO-ASIATIC FAMILY

11	Semitic group (incl. Arabic)
12	Kushitic group
13	Berber group

14 **KHOISAN FAMILY**

15 **NIGER-CONGO FAMILY**

16 **NILO-SAHARAN FAMILY**

17 **URALIC FAMILY**

ALTAIC FAMILY

18	Turkic group
19	Mongolian group
20	Tungus-Manchu group
21	Japanese and Korean

SINO-TIBETAN FAMILY

22	Sinitic (Chinese) languages
23	Tibetic-Burmic languages

24 **TAI FAMILY**

AUSTRO-ASIATIC FAMILY

25	Mon-Khmer group
26	Munda group
27	Vietnamese

28 **DRAVIDIAN FAMILY** (incl. Telugu, Tamil)

29 **AUSTRONESIAN FAMILY** (incl. Malay-Indonesian)

30 **OTHER LANGUAGES**

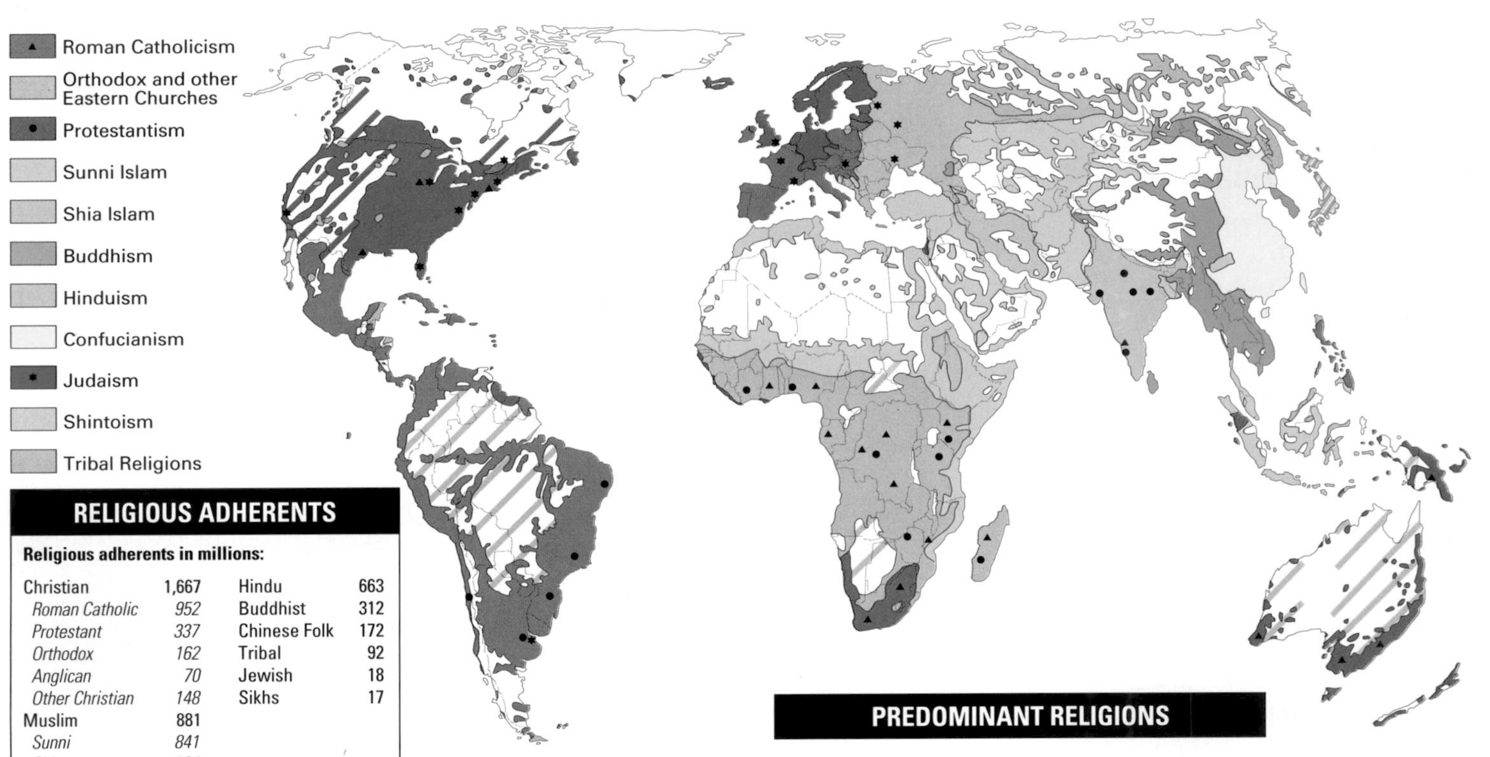

- Roman Catholicism
- Orthodox and other Eastern Churches
- Protestantism
- Sunni Islam
- Shia Islam
- Buddhism
- Hinduism
- Confucianism
- Judaism
- Shintoism
- Tribal Religions

RELIGIOUS ADHERENTS

Religious adherents in millions:

Christian	1,667	Hindu	663
Roman Catholic	*952*	Buddhist	312
Protestant	*337*	Chinese Folk	172
Orthodox	*162*	Tribal	92
Anglican	*70*	Jewish	18
Other Christian	*148*	Sikhs	17
Muslim	881		
Sunni	*841*		
Shia	*104*		

PREDOMINANT RELIGIONS

UNITED NATIONS

Created in 1945 to promote peace and co-operation and based in New York, the United Nations is the world's largest international organization, with 185 members and an annual budget of US $2.6 billion (1996–97). Each member of the General Assembly has one vote, while the permanent members of the 15-nation Security Council – USA, Russia, China, UK and France – hold a veto. The Secretariat is the UN's principal administrative arm. The 54 members of the Economic and Social Council are responsible for economic, social, cultural, educational, health and related matters. The UN has 16 specialized agencies – based in Canada, France, Switzerland and Italy, as well as the USA – which help members in fields such as education (UNESCO), agriculture (FAO), medicine (WHO) and finance (IFC). By the end of 1994, all the original 11 trust territories of The Trusteeship Council had become independent.

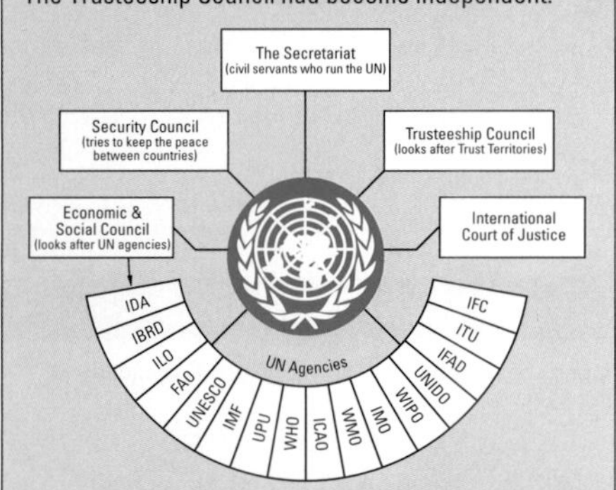

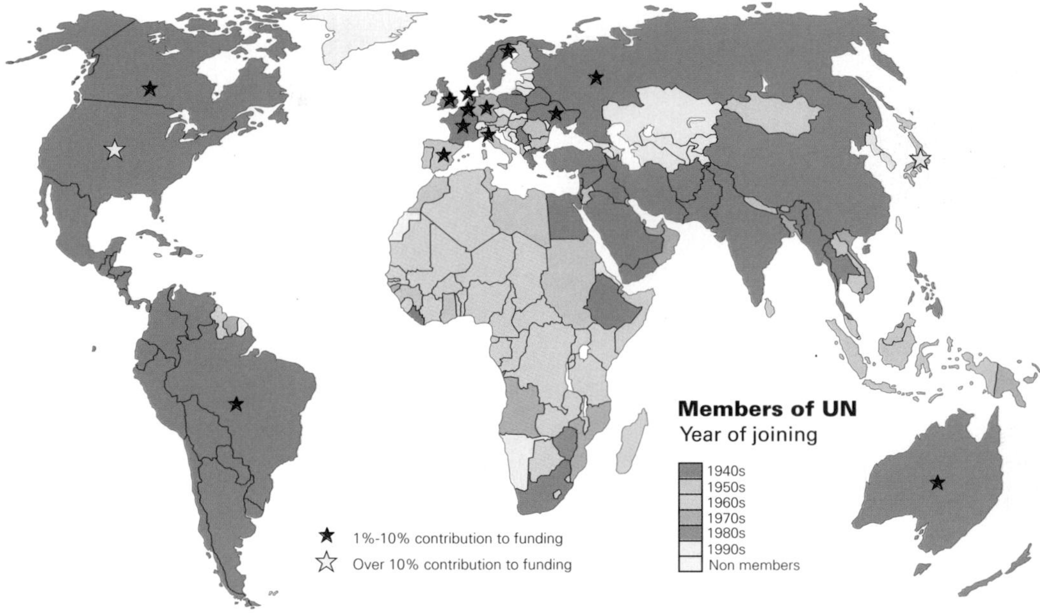

Members of UN
Year of joining

- 1940s
- 1950s
- 1960s
- 1970s
- 1980s
- 1990s
- Non members

★ 1%–10% contribution to funding

☆ Over 10% contribution to funding

MEMBERSHIP OF THE UN In 1945 there were 51 members; by December 1994 membership had increased to 185 following the admission of Palau. There are 7 independent states which are not members of the UN – Kiribati, Nauru, Switzerland, Taiwan, Tonga, Tuvalu and the Vatican City. All the successor states of the former USSR had joined by the end of 1992. The official languages of the UN are Chinese, English, French, Russian, Spanish and Arabic.

FUNDING The UN budget for 1996–97 was US $2.6 billion. Contributions are assessed by the members' ability to pay, with the maximum 25% of the total, the minimum 0.01%. Contributions for 1996 were: USA 25.0%, Japan 15.4%, Germany 9.0%, France 6.4%, UK 5.3%, Italy 5.2%, Russia 4.5%, Canada 3.1%, Spain 2.4%, Brazil 1.6%, Netherlands 1.6%, Australia 1.5%, Sweden 1.2%, Ukraine 1.1%, Belgium 1.0%.

INTERNATIONAL ORGANIZATIONS

EU European Union (evolved from the European Community in 1993). The 15 members – Austria, Belgium, Denmark, Finland, France, Germany, Greece, Ireland, Italy, Luxembourg, Netherlands, Portugal, Spain, Sweden and the UK – aim to integrate economies, co-ordinate social developments and bring about political union. These members of what is now the world's biggest market share agricultural and industrial policies and tariffs on trade. The original body, the European Coal and Steel Community (ECSC), was created in 1951 following the signing of the Treaty of Paris.

EFTA European Free Trade Association (formed in 1960). Portugal left the original 'Seven' in 1989 to join what was then the EC, followed by Austria, Finland and Sweden in 1995. Only 4 members remain: Norway, Iceland, Switzerland and Liechtenstein.

ACP African-Caribbean-Pacific (formed in 1963). Members have economic ties with the EU.

NATO North Atlantic Treaty Organization (formed in 1949). It continues after 1991 despite the winding up of the Warsaw Pact. There are 16 member nations.

OAS Organization of American States (formed in 1948). It aims to promote social and economic co-operation between developed countries of North America and developing nations of Latin America.

ASEAN Association of South-east Asian Nations (formed in 1967). Vietnam joined in July 1995.

OAU Organization of African Unity (formed in 1963). Its 53 members represent over 94% of Africa's population. Arabic, French, Portuguese and English are recognized as working languages.

LAIA Latin American Integration Association (1980). Its aim is to promote freer regional trade.

OECD Organization for Economic Co-operation and Development (formed in 1961). It comprises the 29 major Western free-market economies. Poland, Hungary and South Korea joined in 1996. 'G7' is its 'inner group' comprising the USA, Canada, Japan, UK, Germany, Italy and France.

COMMONWEALTH The Commonwealth of Nations evolved from the British Empire; it comprises 16 Queen's realms, 32 republics and 5 indigenous monarchies, giving a total of 53.

OPEC Organization of Petroleum Exporting Countries (formed in 1960). It controls about three-quarters of the world's oil supply. Gabon left the organization in 1996.

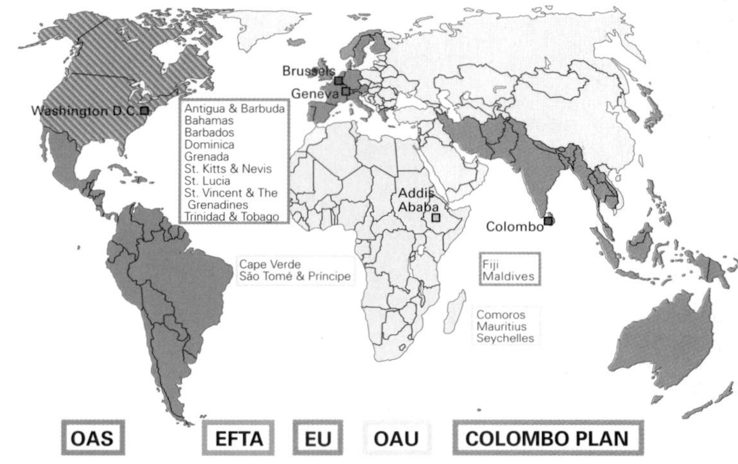

OAS   EFTA   EU   OAU   COLOMBO PLAN

ARAB LEAGUE (formed in 1945). The League's aim is to promote economic, social, political and military co-operation. There are 21 member nations.

COLOMBO PLAN (formed in 1951). Its 26 members aim to promote economic and social development in Asia and the Pacific.

★ G7   OECD   ACP   OPEC   CIS

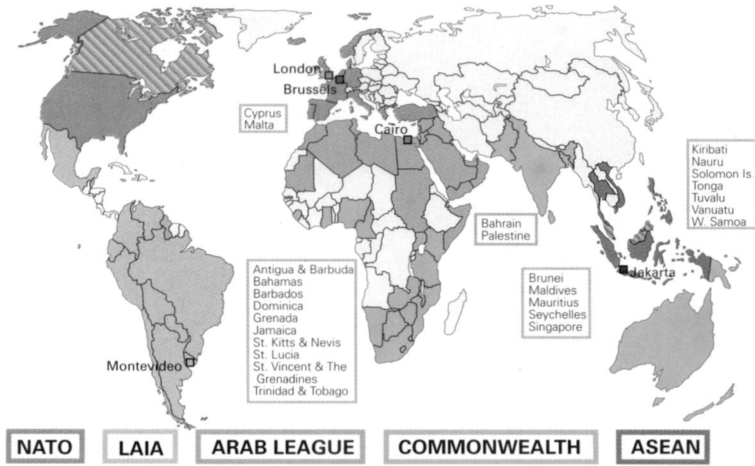

NATO   LAIA   ARAB LEAGUE   COMMONWEALTH   ASEAN

WEALTH

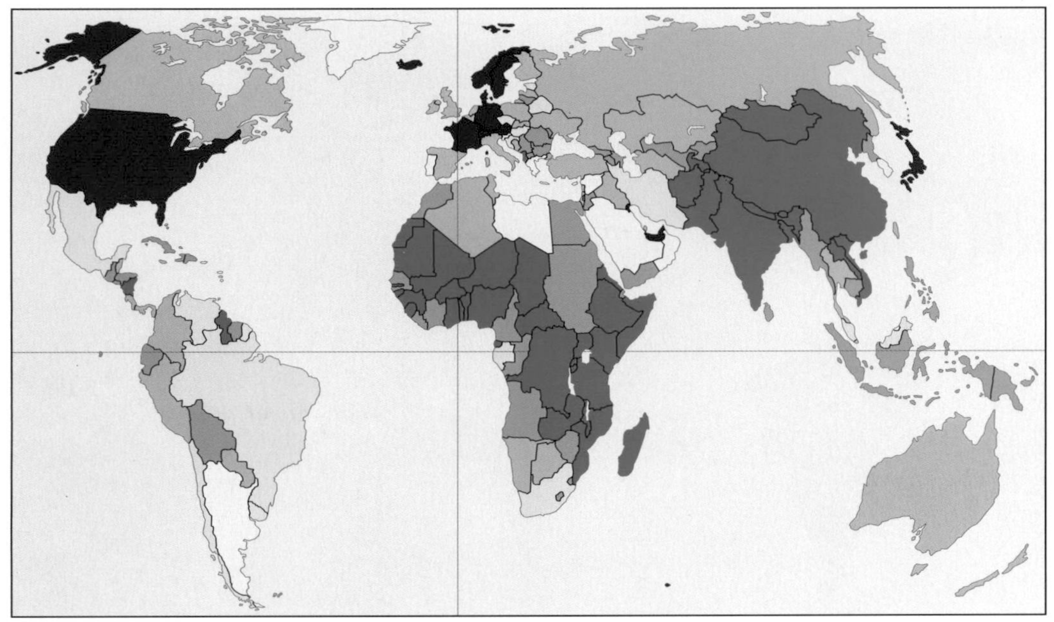

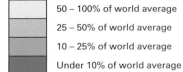

WEALTH CREATION

The Gross National Product (GNP) of the world's largest economies, US $ million (1994)

1.	USA	6,737,367	23.	Indonesia	167,632
2.	Japan	4,321,136	24.	Turkey	149,002
3.	Germany	2,075,452	25.	Denmark	145,384
4.	France	1,355,039	26.	Thailand	129,864
5.	Italy	1,101,258	27.	Saudi Arabia	126,597
6.	UK	1,069,457	28.	South Africa	125,225
7.	China	630,202	29.	Norway	114,328
8.	Canada	569,949	30.	Finland	95,817
9.	Brazil	536,309	31.	Poland	94,613
10.	Spain	525,334	32.	Portugal	92,124
11.	Russia	392,496	33.	Ukraine	80,921
12.	Mexico	368,679	34.	Greece	80,194
13.	South Korea	366,484	35.	Syria	80,120
14.	Netherlands	338,144	36.	Israel	78,113
15.	Australia	320,705	37.	Malaysia	68,674
16.	India	278,739	38.	Singapore	65,842
17.	Argentina	275,657	39.	Philippines	63,311
18.	Switzerland	264,974	40.	Venezuela	59,025
19.	Belgium	231,051	41.	Colombia	58,935
20.	Taiwan	228,000	42.	Pakistan	55,565
21.	Sweden	206,419	43.	Chile	50,051
22.	Austria	197,475	44.	Ireland	48,275

THE WEALTH GAP

The world's richest and poorest countries, by Gross National Product per capita in US $ (1994)

1.	Luxembourg	39,850	1.	Rwanda	80
2.	Switzerland	37,180	2.	Mozambique	80
3.	Japan	34,630	3.	Ethiopia	130
4.	Liechtenstein	33,510	4.	Tanzania	140
5.	Denmark	28,110	5.	Malawi	140
6.	Norway	26,480	6.	Sierra Leone	150
7.	USA	25,860	7.	Burundi	150
8.	Germany	25,580	8.	Chad	190
9.	Austria	24,950	9.	Vietnam	190
10.	Iceland	24,590	10.	Nepal	200
11.	Sweden	23,630	11.	Uganda	200
12.	France	23,470	12.	Haiti	220
13.	Singapore	23,360	13.	Afghanistan	220
14.	UAE	23,000	14.	Madagascar	230
15.	Belgium	22,920	15.	Bangladesh	230
16.	Netherlands	21,970	16.	Guinea-Bissau	240
17.	Hong Kong	21,650	17.	Mali	250
18.	Canada	19,570	18.	São Tomé & P.	250
19.	Italy	19,270	19.	Kenya	260
20.	Kuwait	19,040	20.	Yemen	280

GNP per capita is calculated by dividing a country's Gross National Product by its total population. GNP per capita in the UK is $18,410.

CONTINENTAL SHARES

Shares of population and of wealth (GNP) by continent

POPULATION

- 12%
- 6.7%
- 7.1%
- 15.5%
- 0.4%
- 58.3%

GNP

- 32.6%
- 3.7%
- 2.2%
- 24.7%
- 1.4%
- 35.3%

Europe	Asia	South America
Australia	Africa	North America

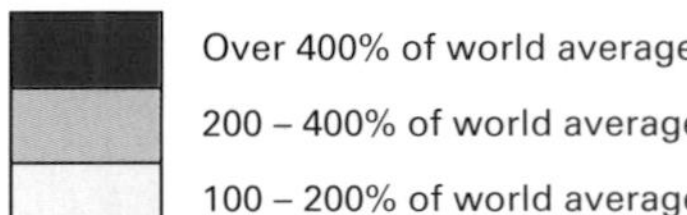

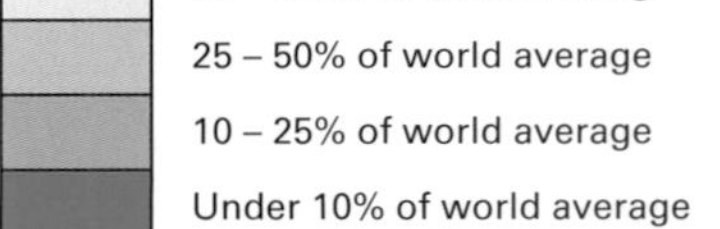

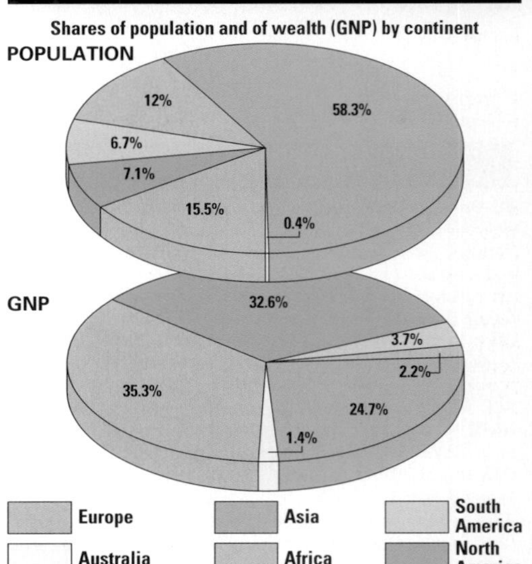

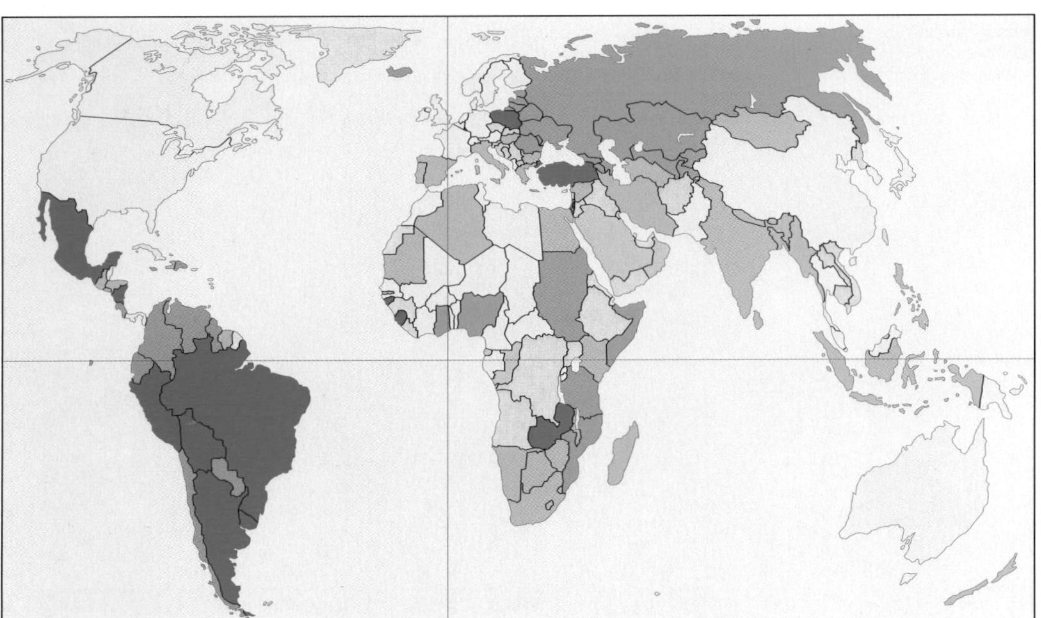

INFLATION

Average annual rate of inflation (1980–93)

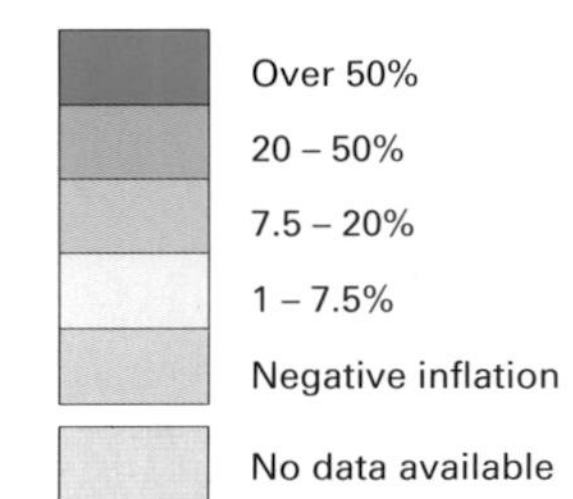

- Over 50%
- 20 – 50%
- 7.5 – 20%
- 1 – 7.5%
- Negative inflation
- No data available

Highest average inflation		Lowest average inflation	
Nicaragua	665%	Brunei	–5.1%
Brazil	423%	Oman	–2.3%
Argentina	374%	Saudi Arabia	–2.1%
Peru	316%	Equatorial Guinea	–0.6%
Bolivia	187%	Congo	–0.6%
Israel	70%	Bahrain	–0.3%
Poland	69%	Libya	0.2%

INTERNATIONAL AID

Aid provided or received, divided by the total population, in US $ (1994)

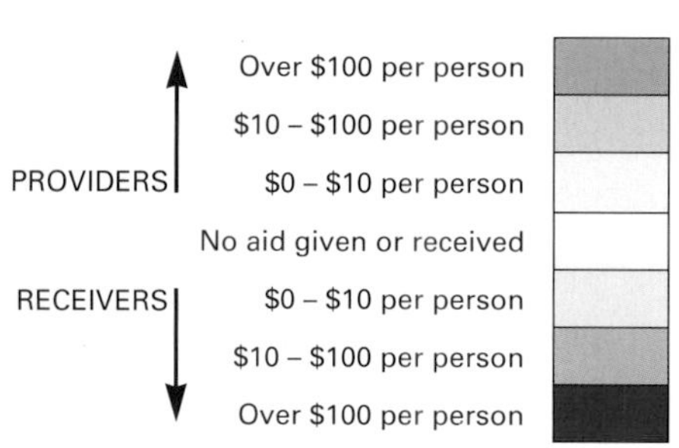

PROVIDERS
- Over $100 per person
- $10 – $100 per person
- $0 – $10 per person
- No aid given or received

RECEIVERS
- $0 – $10 per person
- $10 – $100 per person
- Over $100 per person

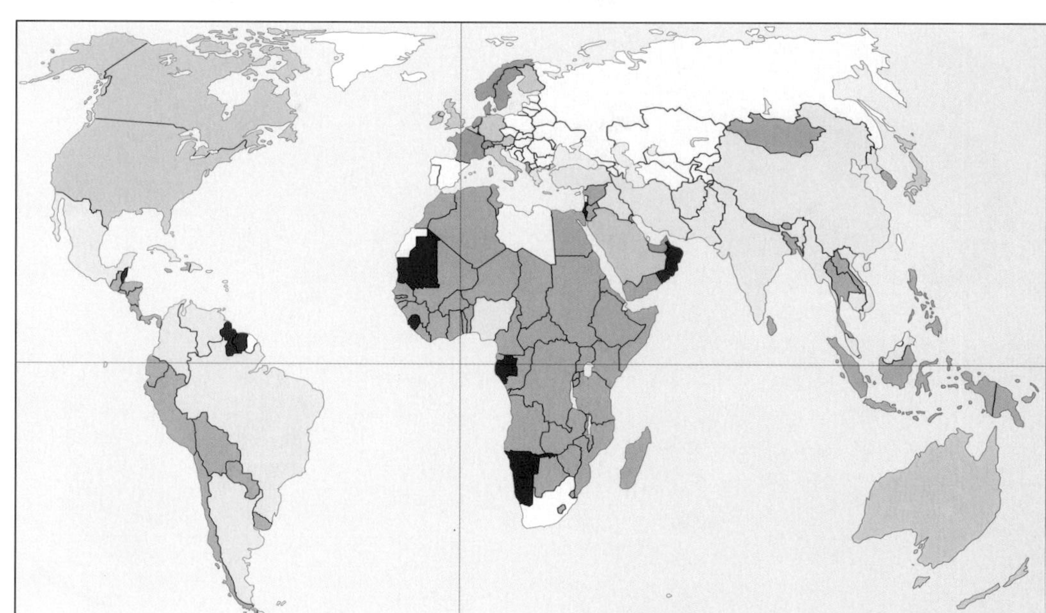

Top 5 providers per capita

France	$279
Denmark	$260
Norway	$247
Sweden	$201
Germany	$166

Top 5 receivers per capita

São Tomé & P.	$378
Cape Verde	$314
Djibouti	$235
Surinam	$198
Mauritania	$153

DEBT AND AID

International debtors and the aid they receive (1993)

Although aid grants make a vital contribution to many of the world's poorer countries, they are usually dwarfed by the burden of debt that the developing economies are expected to repay. In 1992, they had to pay US $160,000 million in debt service charges alone – more than two and a half times the amount of Official Development Assistance (ODA) the developing countries were receiving, and US $60,000 million more than total private flows of aid in the same year. In 1990, the debts of Mozambique, one of the world's poorest countries, were estimated to be 75 times its entire earnings from exports.

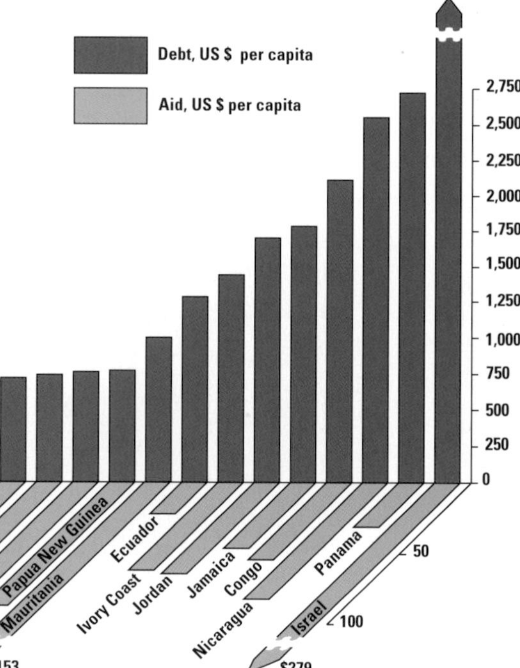

- Debt, US $ per capita
- Aid, US $ per capita

DISTRIBUTION OF SPENDING

Percentage share of household spending, selected countries

- Food
- Medicine & Education
- Clothing
- Transport
- Energy & Housing
- Other

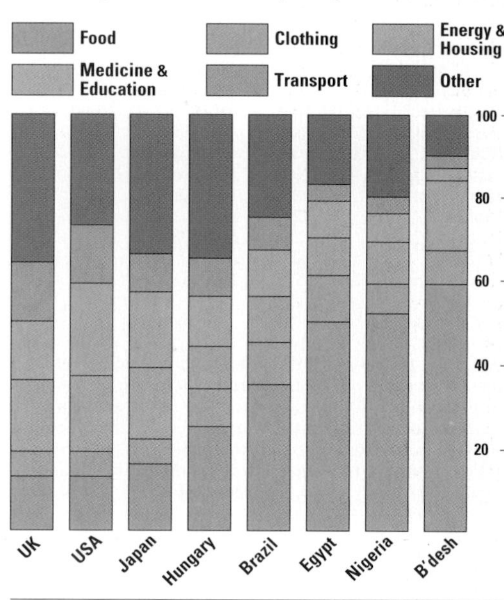

UK, USA, Japan, Hungary, Brazil, Egypt, Nigeria, B'desh

HIGH INCOME

Number of cars, televisions and telephones for each 10,000 people, selected high income countries (1993)

- Cars
- Televisions
- Telephones

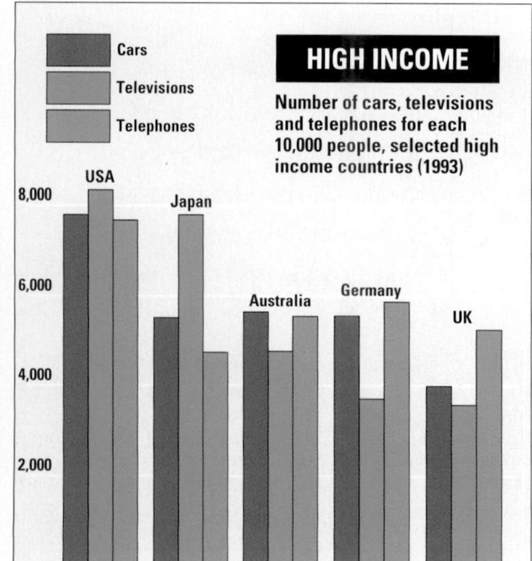

MIDDLE INCOME

Number of cars, televisions and telephones for each 10,000 people, selected middle income countries (1993)

- Cars
- Televisions
- Telephones

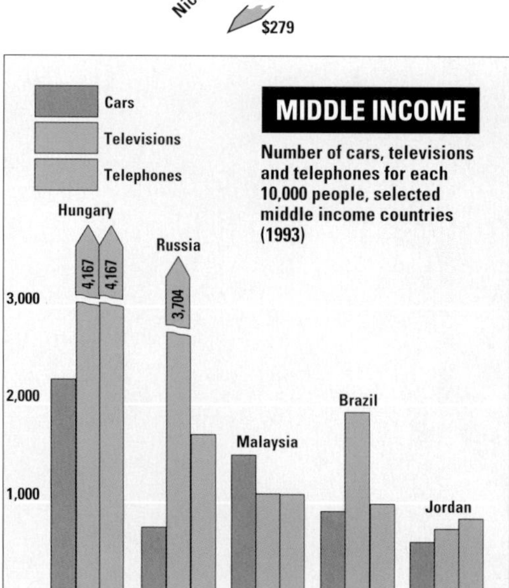

LOW INCOME

Number of cars, televisions and telephones for each 10,000 people, selected low income countries (1993)

- Cars
- Televisions
- Telephones

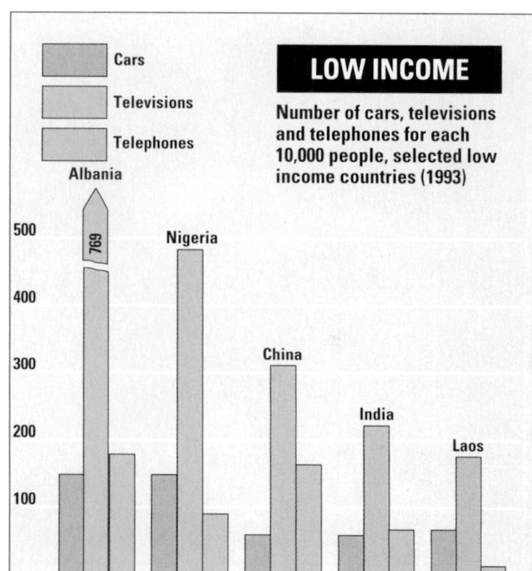

QUALITY OF LIFE

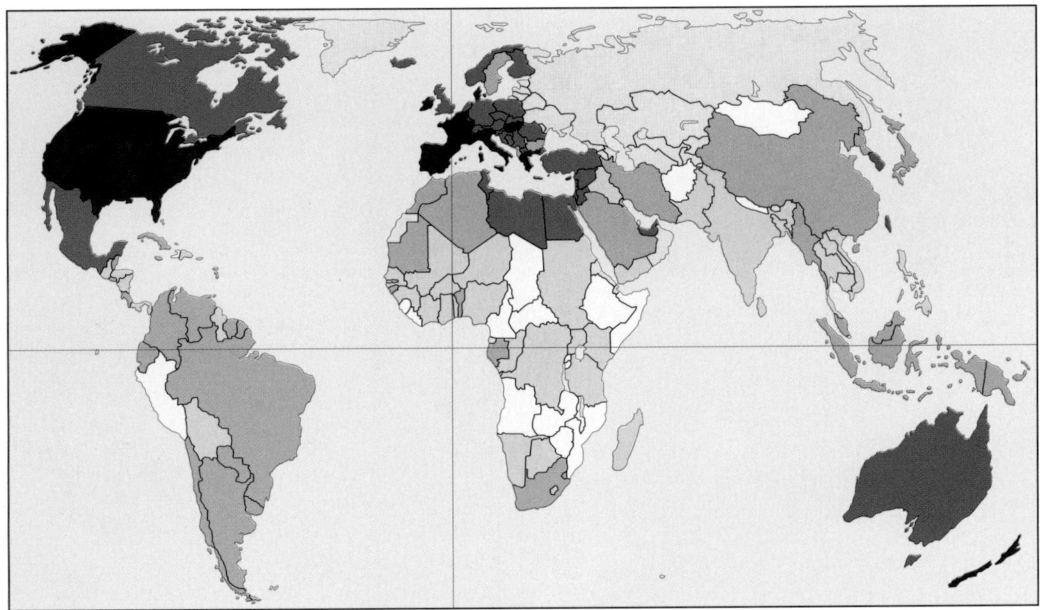

DAILY FOOD CONSUMPTION

Average daily food intake in calories per person (latest available year)

- Over 3,500 calories per person
- 3,000 – 3,500 calories per person
- 2,500 – 3,000 calories per person
- 2,000 – 2,500 calories per person
- Under 2,000 calories per person
- No available data

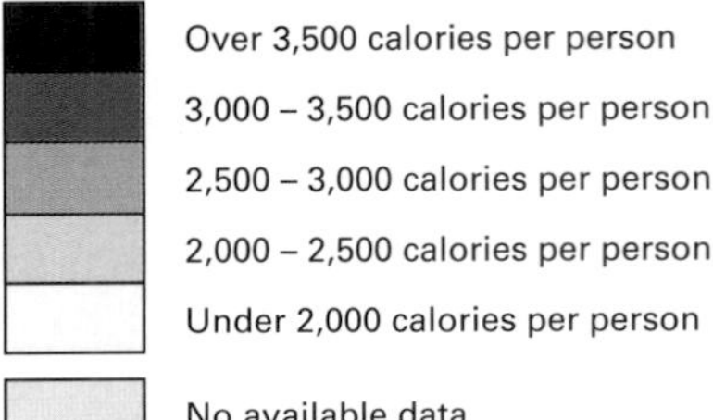

Top 5 countries		Bottom 5 countries	
Ireland	3,847 cal.	Mozambique	1,680 cal.
Greece	3,815 cal.	Liberia	1,640 cal.
Cyprus	3,779 cal.	Ethiopia	1,610 cal.
USA	3,732 cal.	Afghanistan	1,523 cal.
Spain	3,708 cal.	Somalia	1,499 cal.

[UK 3,317 calories]

HOSPITAL CAPACITY

Hospital beds available for each 1,000 people (1993)

Highest capacity		Lowest capacity	
Japan	13.6	Bangladesh	0.2
Kazakstan	13.5	Ethiopia	0.2
Ukraine	13.5	Nepal	0.3
Russia	13.5	Burkina Faso	0.4
Latvia	13.5	Afghanistan	0.5
North Korea	13.5	Pakistan	0.6
Moldova	12.8	Niger	0.6
Belarus	12.7	Mali	0.6
Finland	12.3	Indonesia	0.6
France	12.2	Guinea	0.6

[UK 6.4] [USA 4.6]

Although the ratio of people to hospital beds gives a good approximation of a country's health provision, it is not an absolute indicator. Raw numbers may mask inefficiency and other weaknesses: the high availability of beds in Kazakstan, for example, has not prevented infant mortality rates over three times as high as in the United Kingdom and the United States.

LIFE EXPECTANCY

Years of life expectancy at birth, selected countries (1990–95)

The chart shows combined data for both sexes. On average, women live longer than men worldwide, even in developing countries with high maternal mortality rates. Overall, life expectancy is steadily rising, though the difference between rich and poor nations remains dramatic.

Sierra Leone	39
Nigeria	50
India	60
Brazil	66
Hungary	69
UK	76
Japan	79

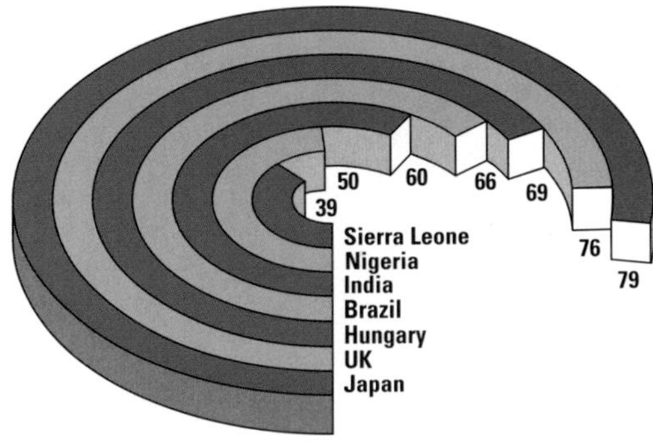

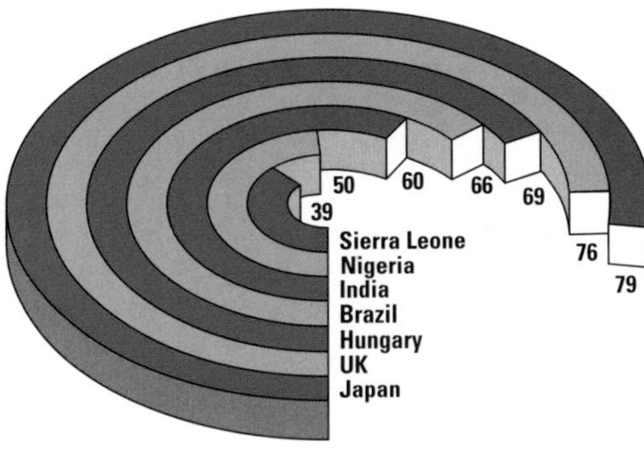

CAUSES OF DEATH

Causes of death for selected countries by % (1992–94)

China Japan Mexico Morocco Russia UK USA

- Infectious & parasitic diseases
- Cancers
- Metabolic disorders
- Nervous & circulatory diseases
- Respiratory & digestive diseases
- Accidents, poisoning & violence

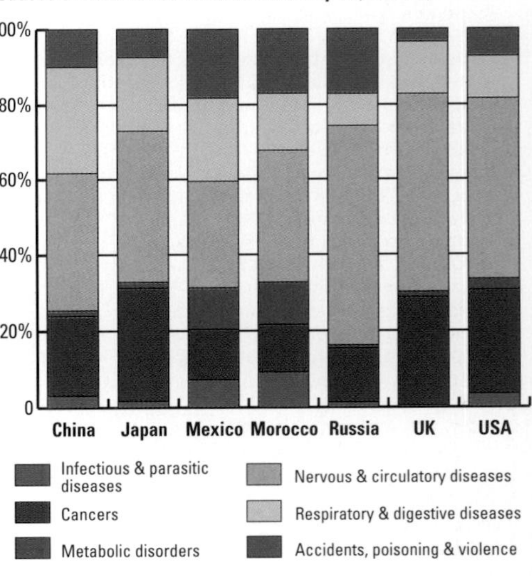

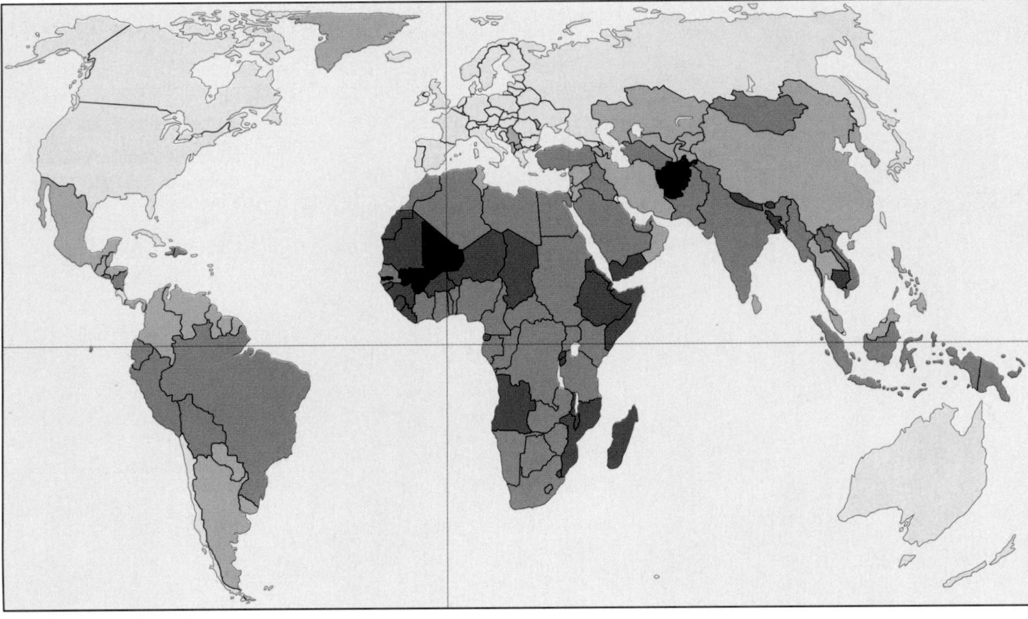

CHILD MORTALITY

Number of babies who will die under the age of one, per 1,000 births (average 1990–95)

- Over 150 deaths per 1,000 births
- 100 – 150 deaths per 1,000 births
- 50 – 100 deaths per 1,000 births
- 20 – 50 deaths per 1,000 births
- 10 – 20 deaths per 1,000 births
- Under 10 deaths per 1,000 births

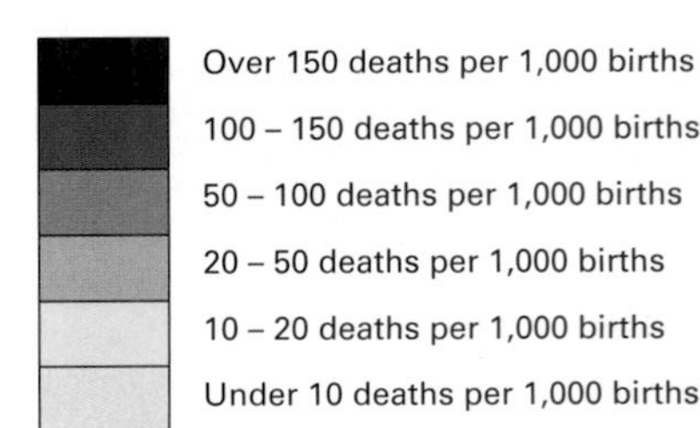

Highest child mortality		Lowest child mortality	
Afghanistan	162	Hong Kong	6
Mali	159	Denmark	6
Sierra Leone	143	Japan	5
Guinea-Bissau	140	Iceland	5
Malawi	138	Finland	5

[UK 8 deaths]

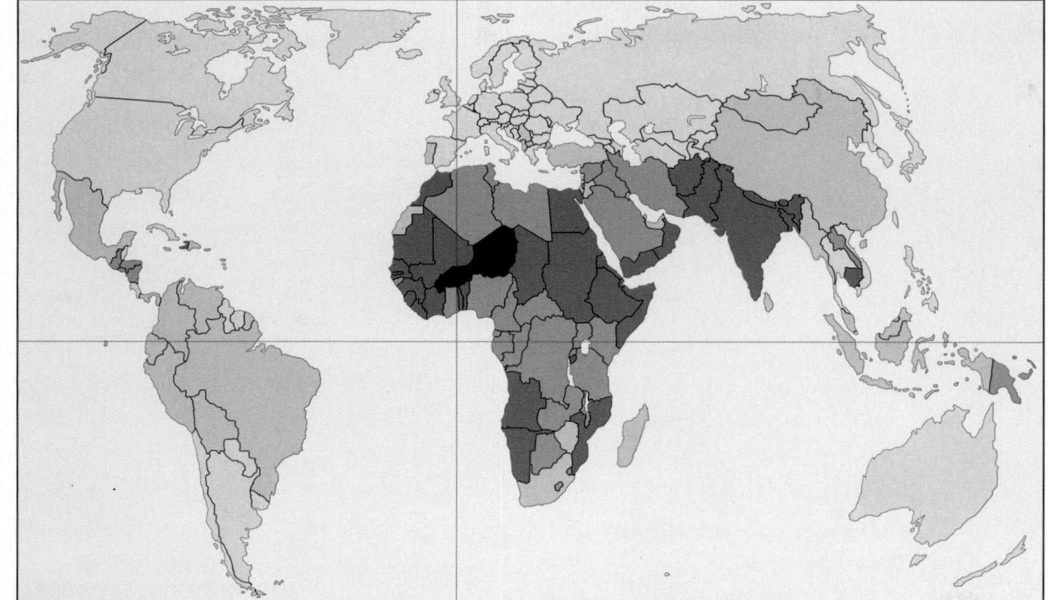

Percentage of the total population unable to read or write (latest available year)

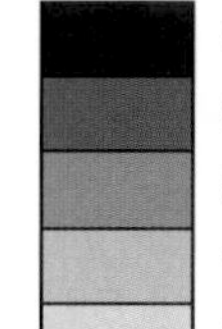

- Over 75% of population illiterate
- 50 – 75% of population illiterate
- 25 – 50% of population illiterate
- 10 – 15% of population illiterate
- Under 10% of population illiterate

Educational expenditure per person (latest available year)

Top 5 countries		Bottom 5 countries	
Sweden	$997	Chad	$2
Qatar	$989	Bangladesh	$3
Canada	$983	Ethiopia	$3
Norway	$971	Nepal	$4
Switzerland	$796	Somalia	$4

[UK $447]

LIVING STANDARDS

At first sight, most international contrasts in living standards are swamped by differences in wealth. The rich not only have more money, they have more of everything, including years of life. Those with only a little money are obliged to spend most of it on food and clothing, the basic maintenance costs of their existence; air travel and tourism are unlikely to feature on their expenditure lists. However, poverty and wealth are both relative: slum dwellers living on social security payments in an affluent industrial country have far more resources at their disposal than an average African peasant, but feel their own poverty nonetheless. A middle-class Indian lawyer cannot command a fraction of the earnings of a counterpart living in New York, London or Rome; nevertheless, he rightly sees himself as prosperous.

The rich not only live longer, on average, than the poor, they also die from different causes. Infectious and parasitic diseases, all but eliminated in the developed world, remain a scourge in the developing nations. On the other hand, more than two-thirds of the populations of OECD nations eventually succumb to cancer or circulatory disease.

FERTILITY AND EDUCATION

Fertility rates compared with female education, selected countries (1992–95)

- Fertility rate: average number of children borne per woman
- Percentage of females aged 12–17 in secondary education

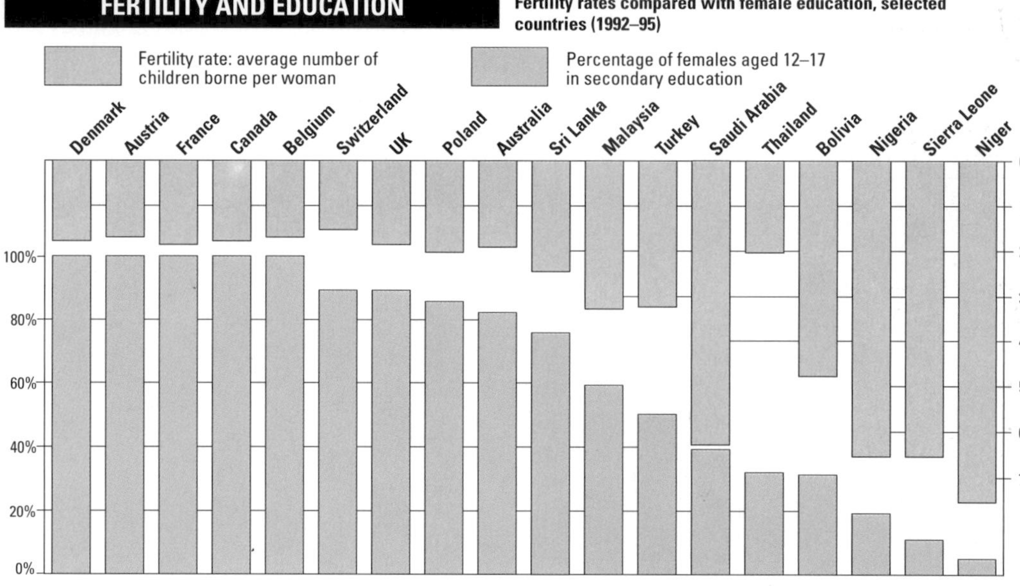

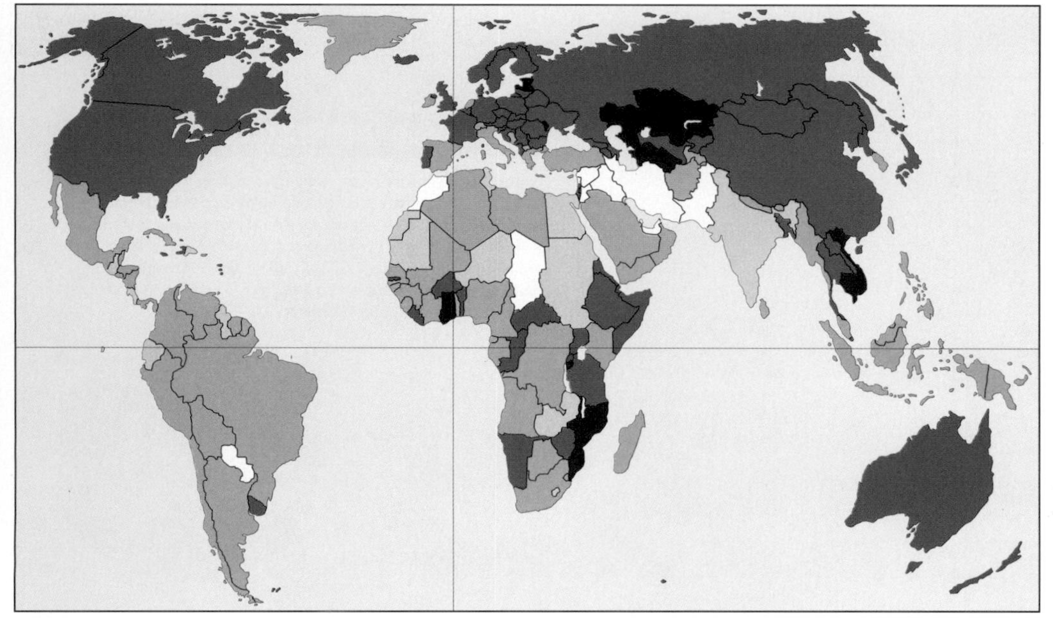

WOMEN IN THE WORKFORCE

Women in paid employment as a percentage of the total workforce (latest available year)

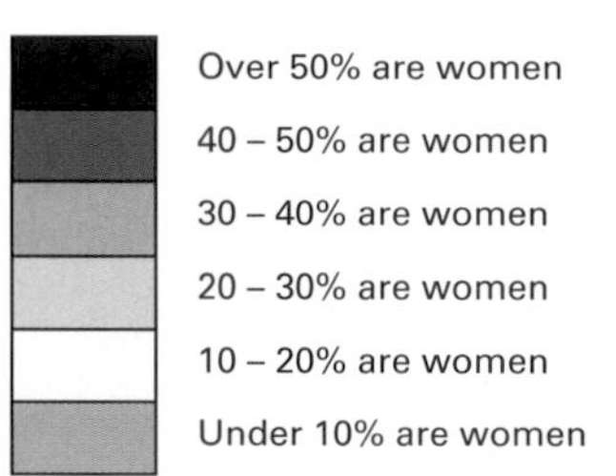

- Over 50% are women
- 40 – 50% are women
- 30 – 40% are women
- 20 – 30% are women
- 10 – 20% are women
- Under 10% are women

Most women in the workforce		Fewest women in the workforce	
Cambodia	56%	Saudi Arabia	4%
Kazakstan	54%	Oman	6%
Burundi	53%	Afghanistan	8%
Mozambique	53%	Algeria	9%
Turkmenistan	52%	Libya	9%

[USA 45] [UK 44]

ENERGY

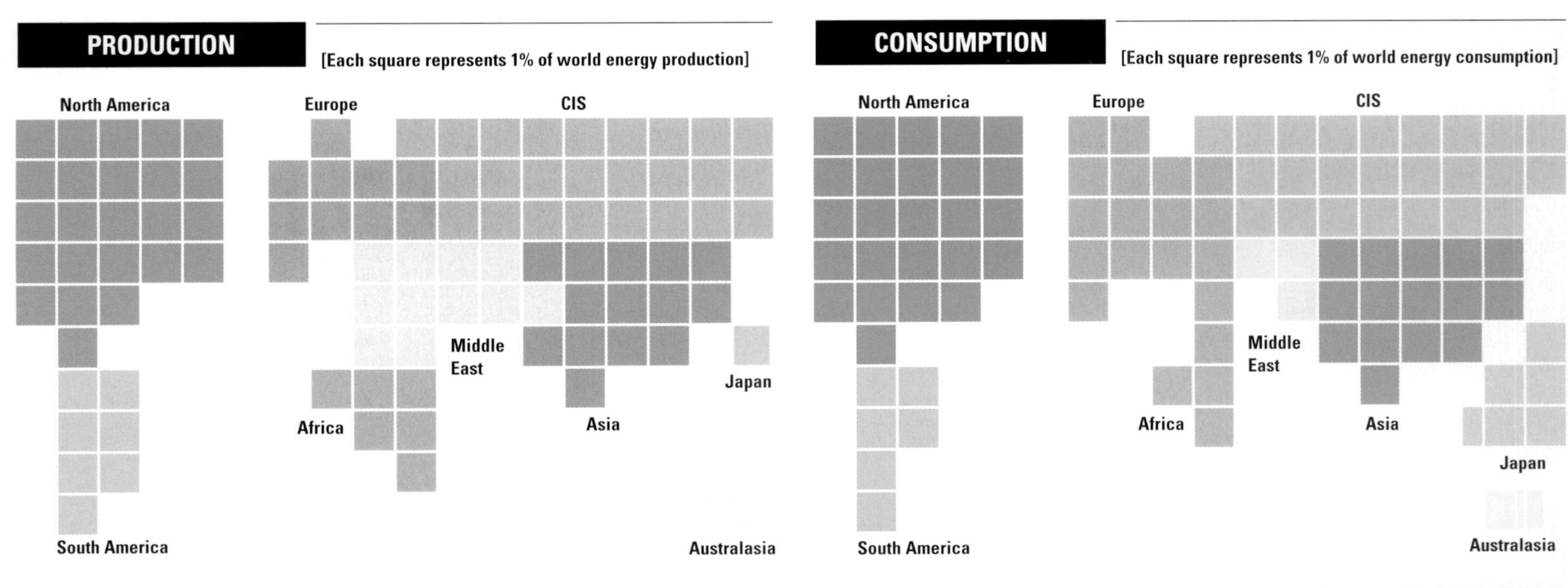

PRODUCTION
[Each square represents 1% of world energy production]

North America
Europe
CIS
Middle East
Africa
Asia
Japan
South America
Australasia

CONSUMPTION
[Each square represents 1% of world energy consumption]

North America
Europe
CIS
Middle East
Africa
Asia
Japan
South America
Australasia

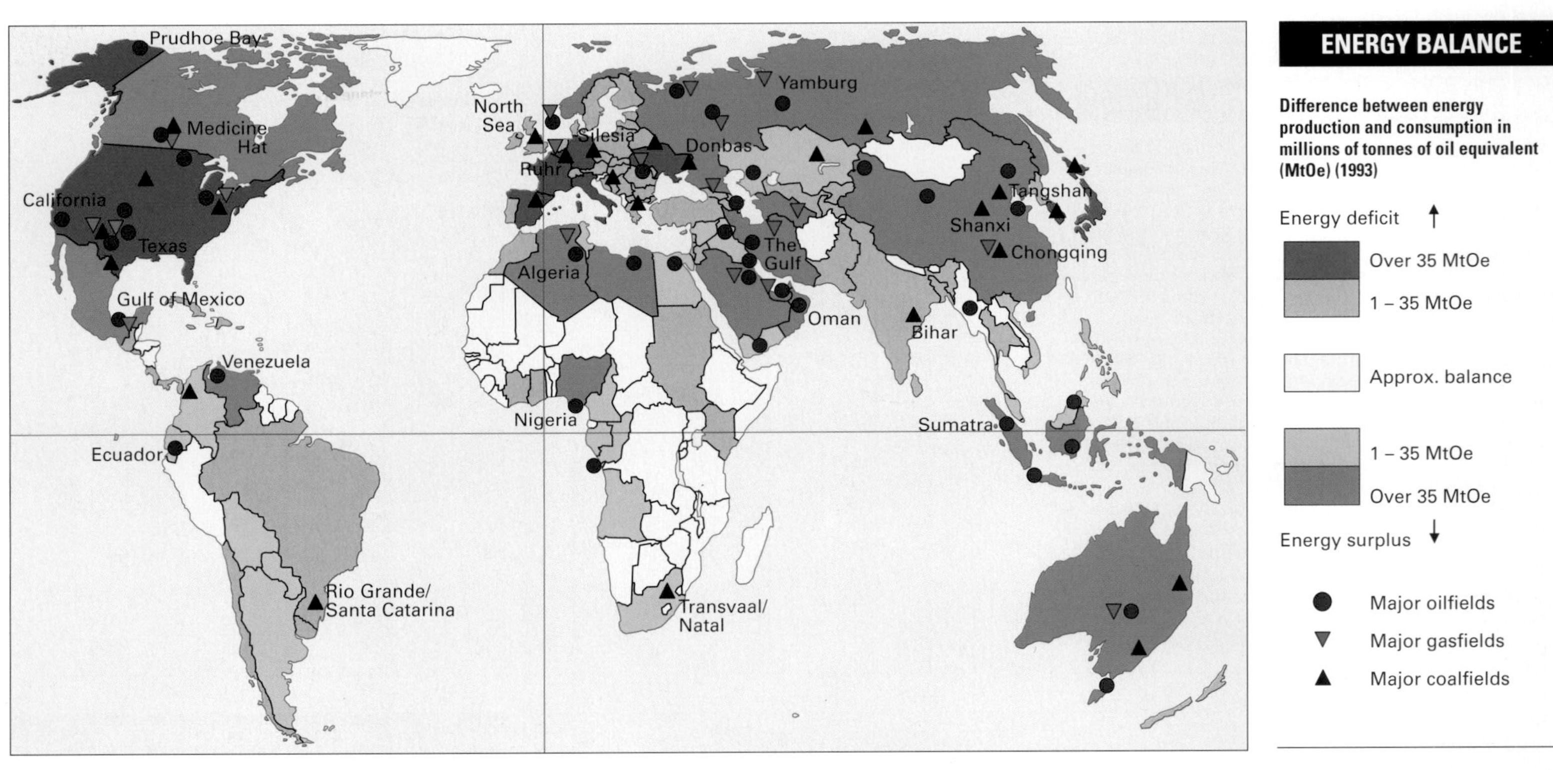

Prudhoe Bay
Medicine Hat
California
Texas
Gulf of Mexico
Venezuela
Ecuador
Rio Grande/Santa Catarina
North Sea
Silesia
Ruhr
Algeria
Nigeria
Donbas
Yamburg
The Gulf
Oman
Bihar
Shanxi
Chongqing
Tangshan
Sumatra
Transvaal/Natal

ENERGY BALANCE

Difference between energy production and consumption in millions of tonnes of oil equivalent (MtOe) (1993)

Energy deficit ↑
- Over 35 MtOe
- 1 – 35 MtOe

Approx. balance

- 1 – 35 MtOe
- Over 35 MtOe
Energy surplus ↓

● Major oilfields
▽ Major gasfields
▲ Major coalfields

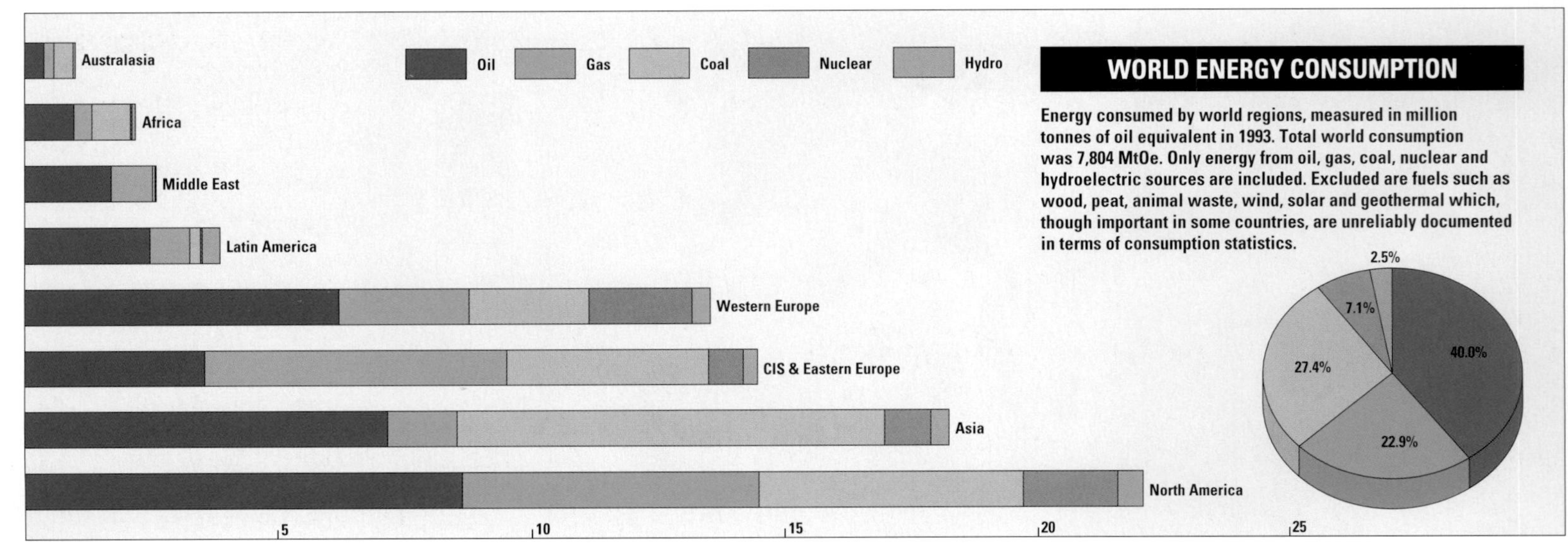

Australasia
Africa
Middle East
Latin America
Western Europe
CIS & Eastern Europe
Asia
North America

Oil | Gas | Coal | Nuclear | Hydro

WORLD ENERGY CONSUMPTION

Energy consumed by world regions, measured in million tonnes of oil equivalent in 1993. Total world consumption was 7,804 MtOe. Only energy from oil, gas, coal, nuclear and hydroelectric sources are included. Excluded are fuels such as wood, peat, animal waste, wind, solar and geothermal which, though important in some countries, are unreliably documented in terms of consumption statistics.

2.5%
7.1%
27.4%
40.0%
22.9%

ENERGY

Energy is used to keep us warm or cool, fuel our industries and our transport systems, and even feed us; high-intensity agriculture, with its use of fertilizers, pesticides and machinery, is heavily energy-dependent. Although we live in a high-energy society, there are vast discrepancies between rich and poor; for example, a North American consumes 13 times as much energy as a Chinese person. But even developing nations have more power at their disposal than was imaginable a century ago.

The distribution of energy supplies, most importantly fossil fuels (coal, oil and natural gas), is very uneven. In addition, the diagrams and map opposite show that the largest producers of energy are not necessarily the largest consumers. The movement of energy supplies around the world is therefore an important component of international trade. In 1995, total world movements in oil amounted to 1,815 million tonnes.

As the finite reserves of fossil fuels are depleted, renewable energy sources, such as solar, hydro-thermal, wind, tidal and biomass, will become increasingly important around the world.

NUCLEAR POWER

Percentage of electricity generated by nuclear power stations, leading nations (1994)

1. Lithuania	76%	11. Spain	35%
2. France	75%	12. Taiwan	32%
3. Belgium	56%	13. Finland	30%
4. Sweden	51%	14. Germany	29%
5. Slovak Rep.	49%	15. Ukraine	29%
6. Bulgaria	46%	16. Czech Rep.	28%
7. Hungary	44%	17. Japan	27%
8. Slovenia	38%	18. UK	26%
9. Switzerland	37%	19. USA	22%
10. South Korea	36%	20. Canada	19%

Although the 1980s were a bad time for the nuclear power industry (major projects ran over budget, and fears of long-term environmental damage were heavily reinforced by the 1986 disaster at Chernobyl), the industry picked up in the early 1990s. However, whilst the number of reactors is still increasing, orders for new plants have shrunk. This is partly due to the increasingly difficult task of disposing of nuclear waste.

HYDROELECTRICITY

Percentage of electricity generated by hydroelectric power stations, leading nations (1993)

1. Paraguay	99.9%	11. Zaïre	97.3%
2. Norway	99.6%	12. Cameroon	97.1%
3. Bhutan	99.6%	13. Tajikistan	96.5%
4. Zambia	99.5%	14. Albania	96.5%
5. Ghana	99.4%	15. Sri Lanka	95.4%
6. Congo	99.3%	16. Laos	95.2%
7. Uganda	99.1%	17. Iceland	94.4%
8. Rwanda	98.3%	18. Nepal	93.5%
9. Buruni	98.3%	19. Brazil	93.3%
10. Malawi	98.0%	20. Honduras	91.9%

Countries heavily reliant on hydroelectricity are usually small and non-industrial: a high proportion of hydroelectric power more often reflects a modest energy budget than vast hydroelectric resources. The USA, for instance, produces only 9% of power requirements from hydroelectricity; yet that 9% amounts to more than three times the hydro power generated by all of Africa.

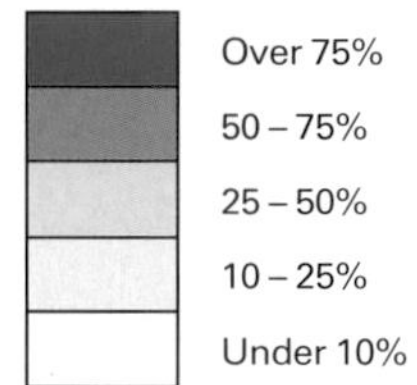

FUEL EXPORTS

Fuels as a percentage of total value of exports (1990–94)

- Over 75%
- 50 – 75%
- 25 – 50%
- 10 – 25%
- Under 10%

CONVERSION RATES

1 barrel = 0.136 tonnes or 159 litres or 35 Imperial gallons or 42 US gallons

1 tonne = 7.33 barrels or 1,185 litres or 256 Imperial gallons or 261 US gallons

1 tonne oil = 1.5 tonnes hard coal or 3.0 tonnes lignite or 12,000 kWh

1 Imperial gallon = 1.201 US gallons or 4.546 litres or 277.4 cubic inches.

MEASUREMENTS
For historical reasons, oil is traded in 'barrels'. The weight and volume equivalents (shown right) are all based on average-density 'Arabian light' crude oil.

The energy equivalents given for a tonne of oil are also somewhat imprecise: oil and coal of different qualities will have varying energy contents, a fact usually reflected in their price on world markets.

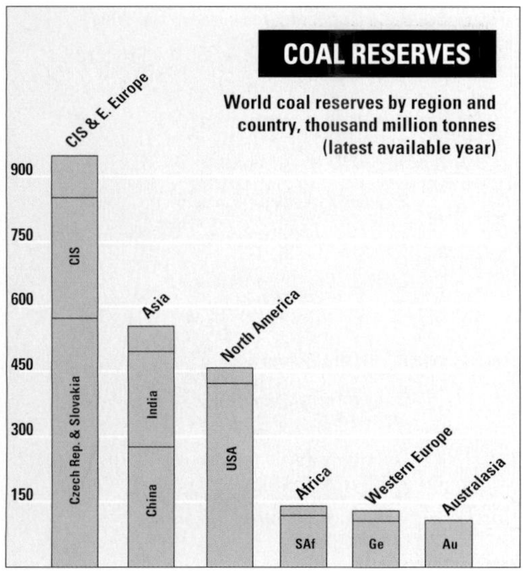

COAL RESERVES
World coal reserves by region and country, thousand million tonnes (latest available year)

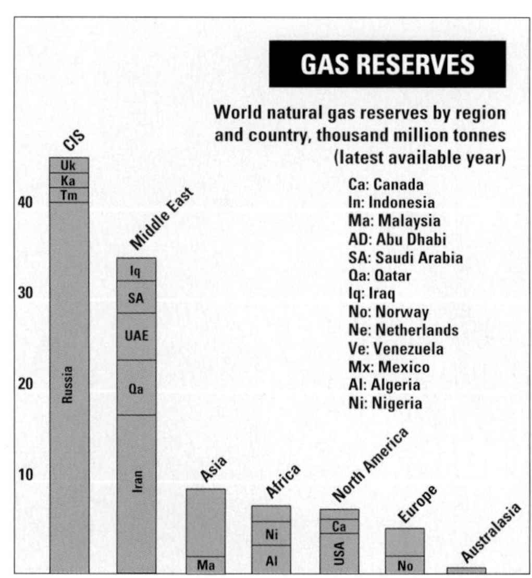

GAS RESERVES
World natural gas reserves by region and country, thousand million tonnes (latest available year)

Ca: Canada
In: Indonesia
Ma: Malaysia
AD: Abu Dhabi
SA: Saudi Arabia
Qa: Qatar
Iq: Iraq
No: Norway
Ne: Netherlands
Ve: Venezuela
Mx: Mexico
Al: Algeria
Ni: Nigeria

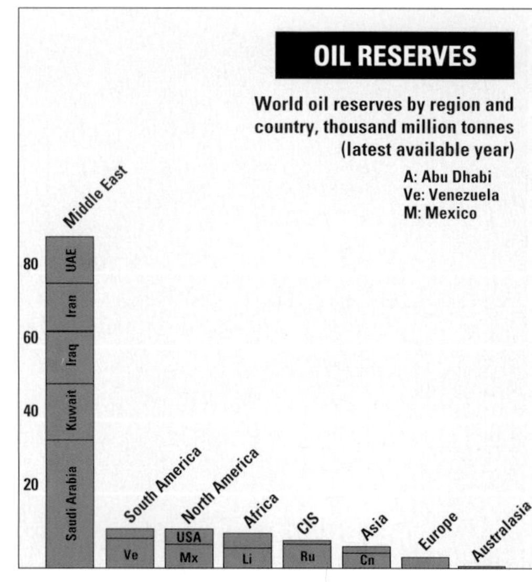

OIL RESERVES
World oil reserves by region and country, thousand million tonnes (latest available year)

A: Abu Dhabi
Ve: Venezuela
M: Mexico

PRODUCTION

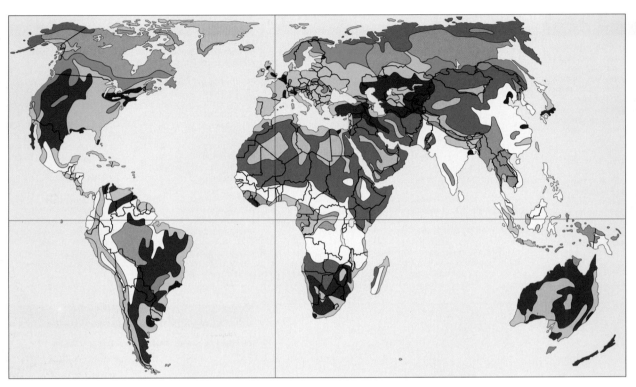

AGRICULTURE

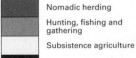

Predominant type of farming or land use.

- Nomadic herding
- Hunting, fishing and gathering
- Subsistence agriculture
- Commercial ranching
- Commercial livestock and grain farming
- Urban areas
- Forestry
- Unproductive land

The development of agriculture transformed human existence more than any other. The whole business of farming is constantly developing: due mainly to new varieties of rice and wheat, world grain production has increased by over 70% since 1965. New machinery and modern agricultural techniques enable relatively few farmers to produce enough food for the world's 5,800 million people.

STAFF CROPS

STAPLE CROPS

Wheat

China 18.6% USA 11.6% India 10.1% Russia 7.5% France 5.2% Canada 4.9%

World total (1993): 564,457,000 tonnes

Rice
China 35.4% India 21.0% Indonesia 9.1% Bangladesh 5.3% Vietnam 4.2% Thailand 3.6%

World total (1993): 527,413,000 tonnes

Maize
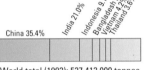
USA 35.8% China 22.9% Brazil 6.7% Mexico 4.1% France 3.3%

World total (1993): 450,570,000 tonnes

Potatoes
Russia 13.2% Poland 12.6% China 12.2% Ukraine 7.3% USA 6.6% India 5.5%

World total (1993): 288,183,000 tonnes

Millet
India 37.8% China 15.0% Nigeria 14.4% Niger 5.4% Russia 4.2%

World total (1993): 26,442,000 tonnes

Rye
Russia 34.9% Poland 19.0% Germany 11.2% Belarus 10.7% Ukraine 4.5%

World total (1993): 26,200,000 tonnes

Soya

USA 44.3% Brazil 20.5% China 11.7% Argentina 9.6% India 4.1%

World total (1993): 111,011,000 tonnes

Cassava
Brazil 14.1% Nigeria 13.7% Zaire 13.6% Thailand 12.8% Indonesia 10.6% Tanzania 4.4%

World total (1993): 153,628,000 tonnes

SUGARS

Sugar cane
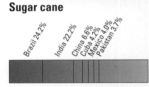
Brazil 24.2% India 22.2% China 6.6% Cuba 4.2% Mexico 4.0% Pakistan 3.7%

World total (1993): 1,040,600,000 tonnes

Sugar beet
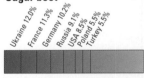
Ukraine 12.0% France 11.3% Germany 10.2% Russia 9.1% USA 8.5% Poland 5.5% Turkey 5.5%

World total (1993): 281,682,000 tonnes

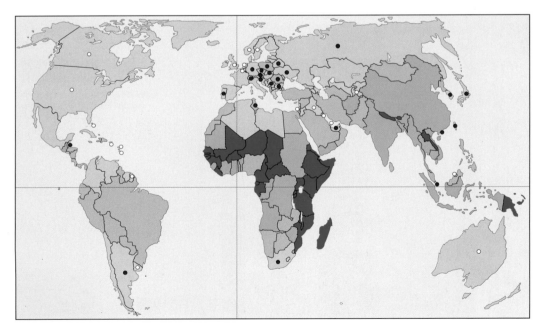

BALANCE OF EMPLOYMENT

Percentage of total workforce employed in agriculture, including forestry and fishing (1990–92)

- Over 75% in agriculture
- 50 – 75% in agriculture
- 25 – 50% in agriculture
- 10 – 25% in agriculture
- Under 10% in agriculture

Employment in industry and services

- ● Over a third of total workforce employed in manufacturing
- ○ Over two-thirds of total workforce employed in service industries (work in offices, shops, tourism, transport, construction and government)

MINERAL PRODUCTION

*Figures for aluminium are for refined metal; all other figures refer to ore production.

Copper
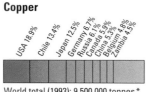
USA 18.9% · Chile 13.4% · Japan 12.5% · Germany 6.7% · Russia 6.1% · Canada 5.9% · China 5.3% · Belgium 4.8% · Zambia 4.5%

World total (1993): 9,500,000 tonnes *

Iron
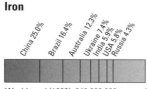
China 25.0% · Brazil 16.4% · Australia 12.3% · Ukraine 7.4% · India 5.9% · USA 5.8% · Russia 4.3%

World total (1993): 940,000,000 tonnes *

Chromium
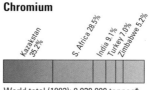
Kazakstan 35.2% · S. Africa 28.5% · India 9.1% · Turkey 7.0% · Zimbabwe 5.2%

World total (1993): 9,930,000 tonnes *

Gold
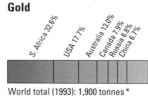
S. Africa 32.6% · USA 17.7% · Australia 13.0% · Canada 7.9% · Russia 6.6% · China 6.7%

World total (1993): 1,900 tonnes *

Uranium
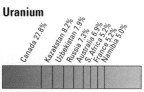
Canada 27.8% · Kazakstan 8.2% · Uzbekistan 7.9% · Russia 7.3% · Australia 6.9% · S. Africa 5.2% · France 5.2% · Namibia 5.0%

World total (1993): 33,000 tonnes *

Lead
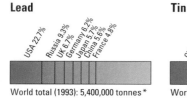
USA 22.7% · Russia 9.3% · UK 6.7% · Germany 6.2% · Japan 5.7% · China 5.6% · France 4.8%

World total (1993): 5,400,000 tonnes *

Tin
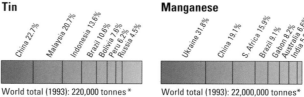
China 22.7% · Malaysia 20.7% · Indonesia 13.6% · Brazil 10.6% · Bolivia 7.6% · Peru 6.2% · Russia 4.5%

World total (1993): 220,000 tonnes *

Manganese
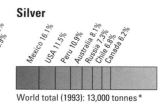
Ukraine 31.8% · China 19.1% · S. Africa 15.9% · Brazil 8.9% · Gabon 8.2% · Australia 6.6% · India 5.9%

World total (1993): 22,000,000 tonnes *

Silver
Mexico 16.1% · USA 11.5% · Peru 10.9% · Australia 8.1% · Russia 7.3% · Chile 6.8% · Canada 6.2%

World total (1993): 13,000 tonnes *

Aluminium
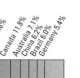
USA 33.8% · Russia 15.8% · Canada 11.8% · Australia 7.1% · China 6.2% · Brazil 6.0% · Germany 5.4%

World total (1993): 19,609,000 tonnes *

Mercury
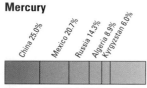
China 25.0% · Mexico 20.7% · Russia 14.3% · Algeria 8.9% · Kyrgyzstan 6.0%

World total (1993): 4,200 tonnes *

Zinc

China 11.8% · Japan 10.3% · Canada 9.3% · Germany 7.7% · Belgium 5.6% · USA 5.6% · Russia 4.9%

World total (1993): 7,127,000 tonnes *

Nickel
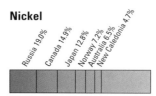
Russia 19.0% · Canada 14.9% · Japan 12.8% · Norway 7.2% · Australia 6.5% · New Caledonia 4.7%

World total (1993): 790,000 tonnes *

Diamonds
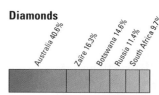
Australia 40.6% · Zaire 16.3% · Botswana 14.6% · Russia 11.4% · South Africa 9.7%

World total (1993): 100,850,000 carats

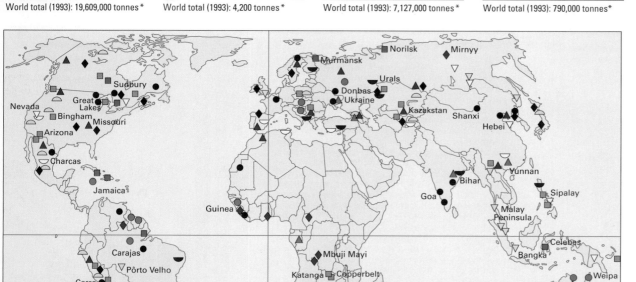

MINERAL DISTRIBUTION

The map shows the richest sources of the most important minerals. Major mineral locations are named.

Light metals
● Bauxite

Base metals
■ Copper
▲ Lead
▽ Mercury
▽ Tin
◆ Zinc

Iron and ferro-alloys
● Iron
◗ Chrome
▲ Manganese
■ Nickel

Precious metals
▽ Gold
◡ Silver

Precious stones
◆ Diamonds

The map does not show undersea deposits, most of which are considered inaccessible.

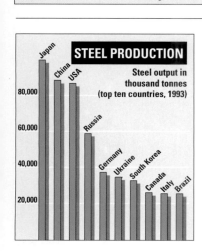

STEEL PRODUCTION
Steel output in thousand tonnes (top ten countries, 1993)

SHIPBUILDING
Merchant vessels launched, in thousand gross registered tonnes (top ten countries, 1993)

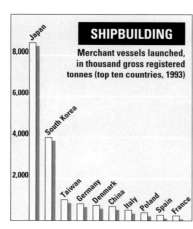

AUTOMOBILES
Production of passenger cars in thousands (top ten countries, 1993)

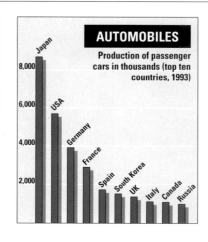

COMMERCIAL VEHICLES
Trucks, buses and coaches produced by the top ten manufacturing countries, in thousands (1993)

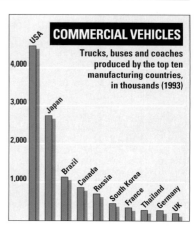

TRADE

Percentage share of total world exports by value (1993)

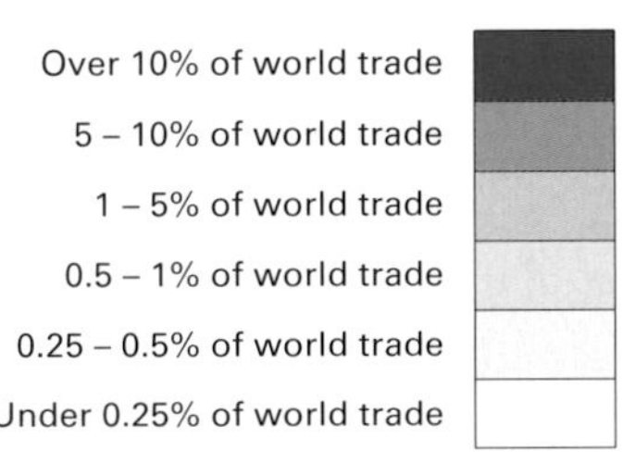

Over 10% of world trade
5 – 10% of world trade
1 – 5% of world trade
0.5 – 1% of world trade
0.25 – 0.5% of world trade
Under 0.25% of world trade

International trade is dominated by a handful of powerful maritime nations. The members of 'G7', the inner circle of OECD (see page 19), and the top seven countries listed in the diagram below, account for more than half the total. The majority of nations – including all but four in Africa – contribute less than one quarter of 1% to the worldwide total of exports; the EU countries account for 40%, the Pacific Rim nations over 35%.

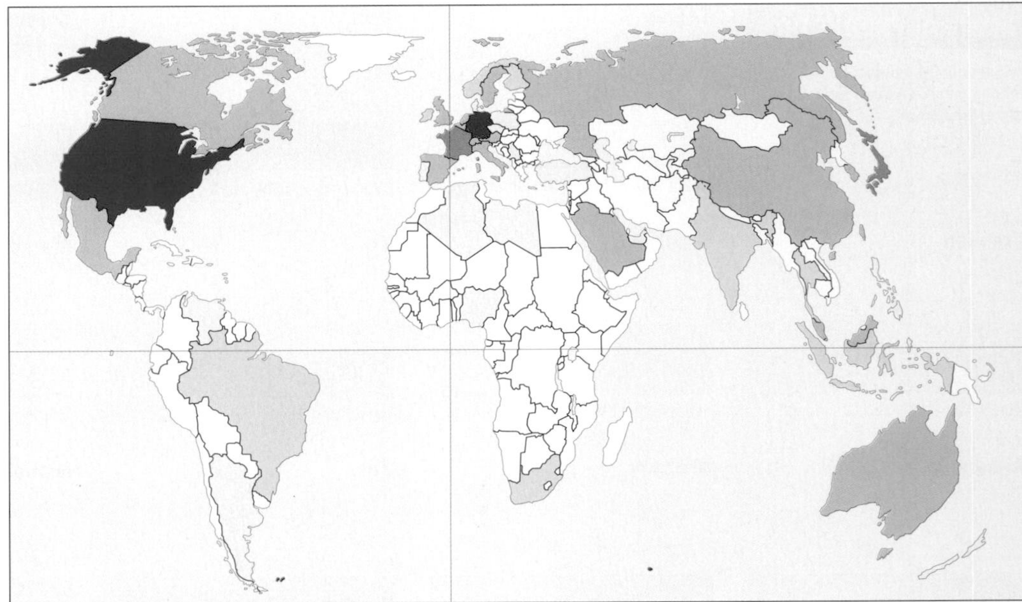

THE MAIN TRADING NATIONS

The imports and exports of the top ten trading nations as a percentage of world trade (1994). Each country's trade in manufactured goods is shown in dark blue.

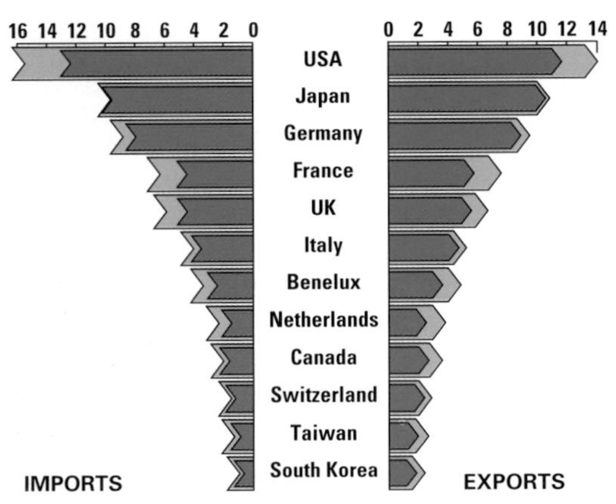

16 14 12 10 8 6 4 2 0   0 2 4 6 8 10 12 14

USA
Japan
Germany
France
UK
Italy
Benelux
Netherlands
Canada
Switzerland
Taiwan
South Korea

IMPORTS   EXPORTS

PATTERNS OF TRADE

Thriving international trade is the outward sign of a healthy world economy, the obvious indicator that some countries have goods to sell and others the means to buy them. Global exports expanded to an estimated US $3.92 trillion in 1994, an increase due partly to economic recovery in industrial nations but also to export-led growth strategies in many developing nations and lowered regional trade barriers. International trade remains dominated, however, by the rich, industrialized countries of the Organization for Economic Development: between them, OECD members account for almost 75% of world imports and exports in most years. However, continued rapid economic growth in some developing countries is altering global trade patterns. The 'tiger economies' of South-east Asia are particularly vibrant, averaging more than 8% growth between 1992 and 1994. The size of the largest trading economies means that imports and exports usually represent only a small percentage of their total wealth. In export-concious Japan, for example, trade in goods and services amounts to less than 18% of GDP. In poorer countries, trade – often in a single commodity – may amount to 50% of GDP.

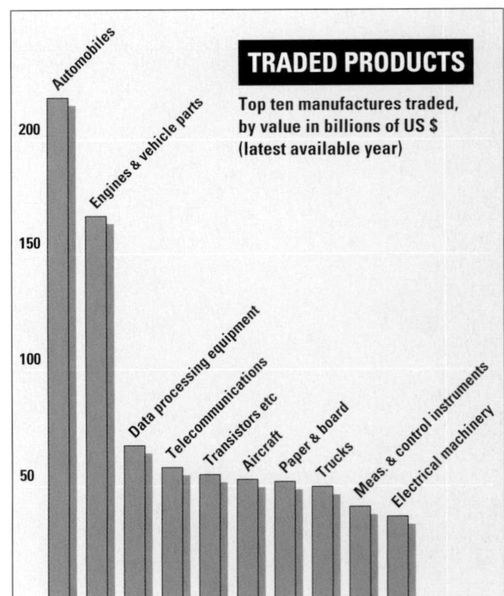

TRADED PRODUCTS

Top ten manufactures traded, by value in billions of US $ (latest available year)

Automobiles
Engines & vehicle parts
Data processing equipment
Telecommunications
Transistors etc
Aircraft
Paper & board
Trucks
Meas. & control instruments
Electrical machinery

200
150
100
50

BALANCE OF TRADE

Value of exports in proportion to the value of imports (1993)

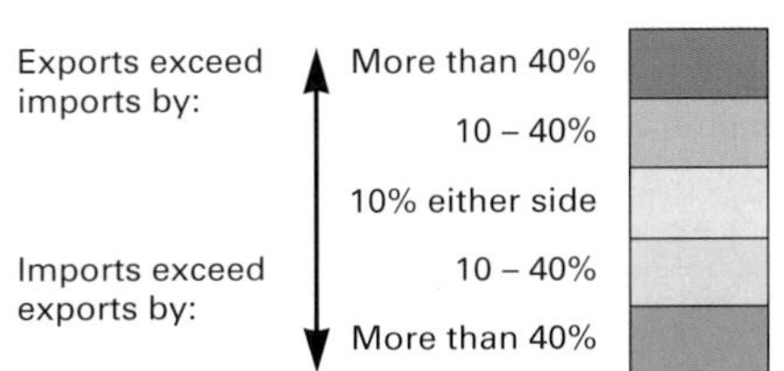

Exports exceed imports by:
More than 40%
10 – 40%
10% either side
Imports exceed exports by:
10 – 40%
More than 40%

The total world trade balance should amount to zero, since exports must equal imports on a global scale. In practice, at least $100 billion in exports go unrecorded, leaving the world with an apparent deficit and many countries in a better position than public accounting reveals. However, a favourable trade balance is not necessarily a sign of prosperity: many poorer countries must maintain a high surplus in order to service debts, and do so by restricting imports below the levels needed to sustain successful economies.

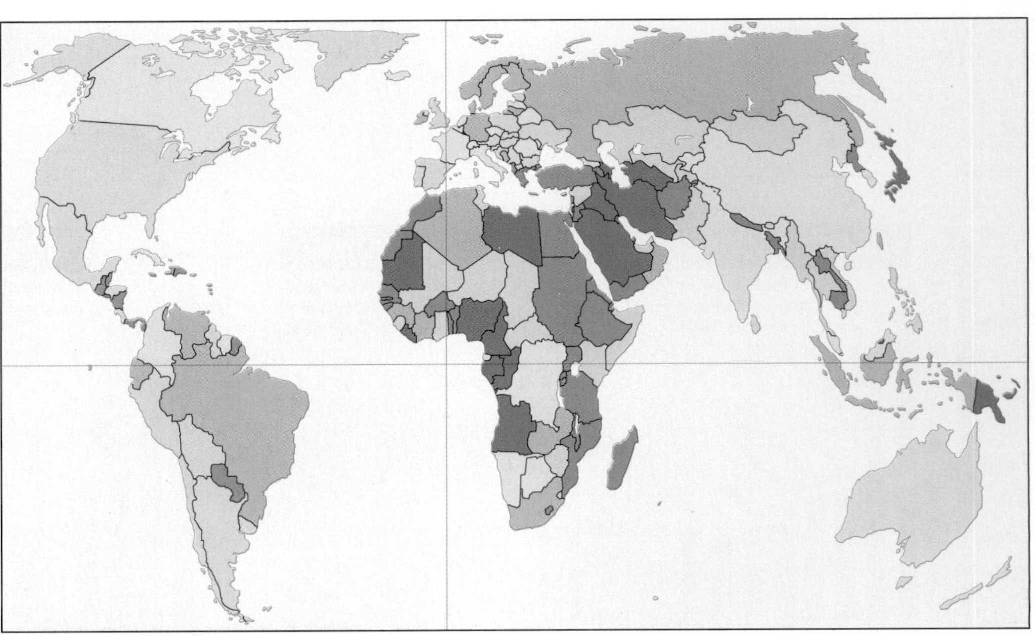

SEABORNE FREIGHT

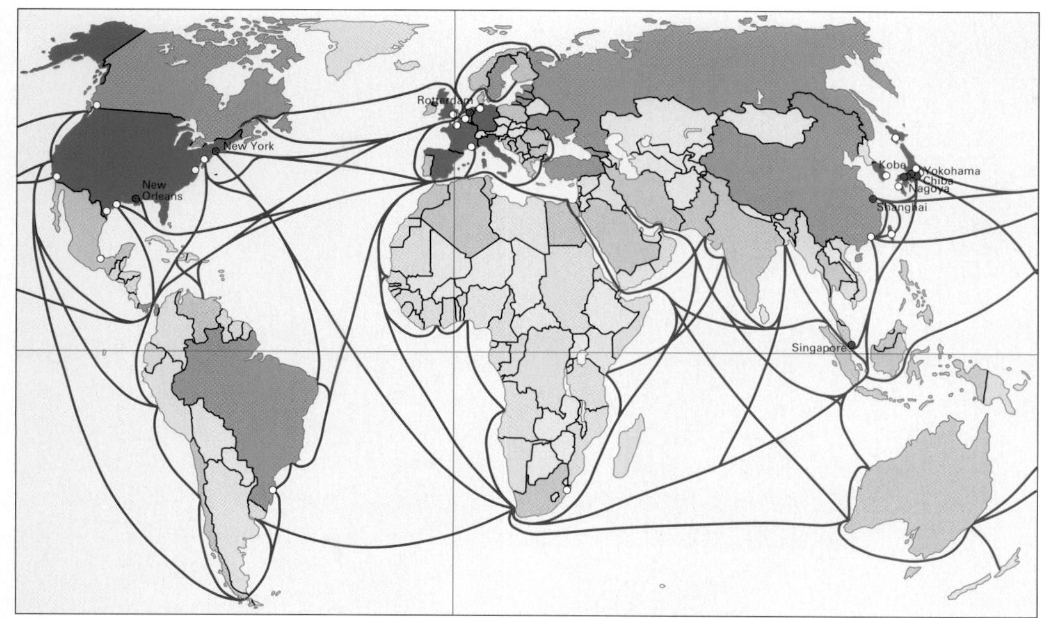

Freight unloaded in millions of tonnes (latest available year)

- Over 100
- 50 – 100
- 10 – 50
- 5 – 10
- Under 5
- Landlocked countries

Major seaports

- ● Over 100 million tonnes per year
- ○ 50–100 million tonnes per year
- ━ Major shipping routes

CARGOES

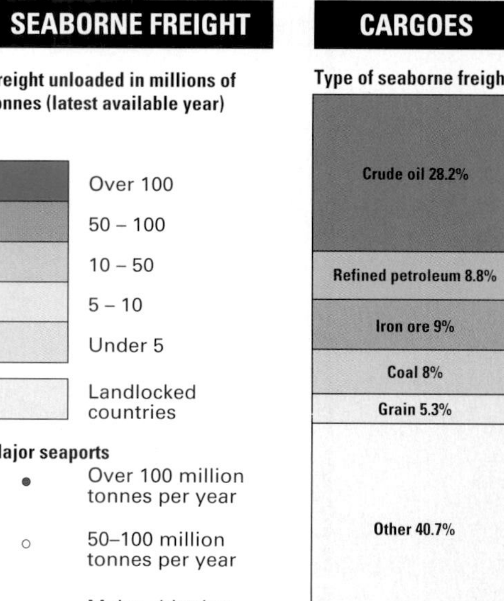

Type of seaborne freight

- Crude oil 28.2%
- Refined petroleum 8.8%
- Iron ore 9%
- Coal 8%
- Grain 5.3%
- Other 40.7%

MERCHANT FLEETS

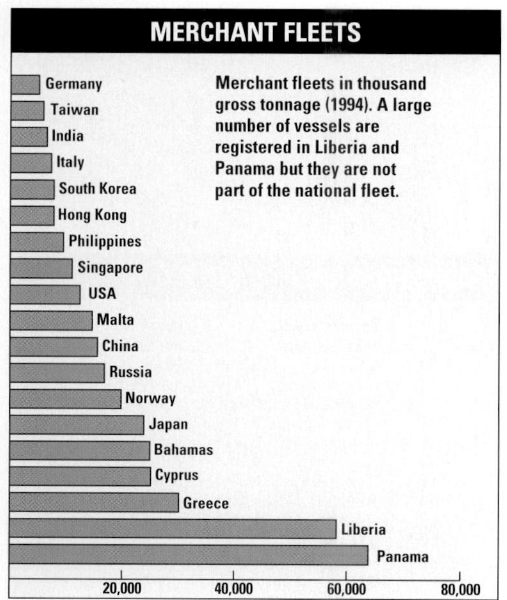

Merchant fleets in thousand gross tonnage (1994). A large number of vessels are registered in Liberia and Panama but they are not part of the national fleet.

Germany, Taiwan, India, Italy, South Korea, Hong Kong, Philippines, Singapore, USA, Malta, China, Russia, Norway, Japan, Bahamas, Cyprus, Greece, Liberia, Panama

20,000 40,000 60,000 80,000

WORLD SHIPPING

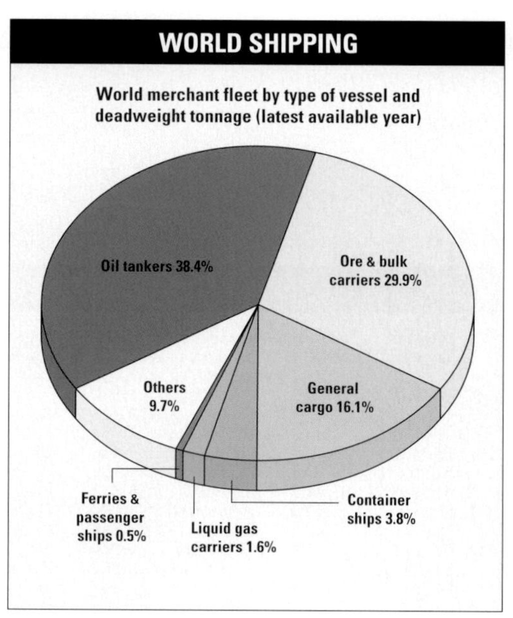

World merchant fleet by type of vessel and deadweight tonnage (latest available year)

- Oil tankers 38.4%
- Ore & bulk carriers 29.9%
- General cargo 16.1%
- Others 9.7%
- Container ships 3.8%
- Liquid gas carriers 1.6%
- Ferries & passenger ships 0.5%

THE GREAT PORTS

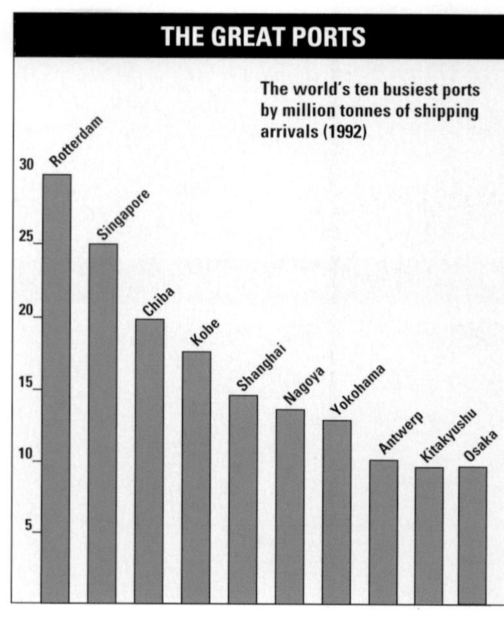

The world's ten busiest ports by million tonnes of shipping arrivals (1992)

Rotterdam, Singapore, Chiba, Kobe, Shanghai, Nagoya, Yokohama, Antwerp, Kitakyushu, Osaka

DEPENDENCE ON TRADE

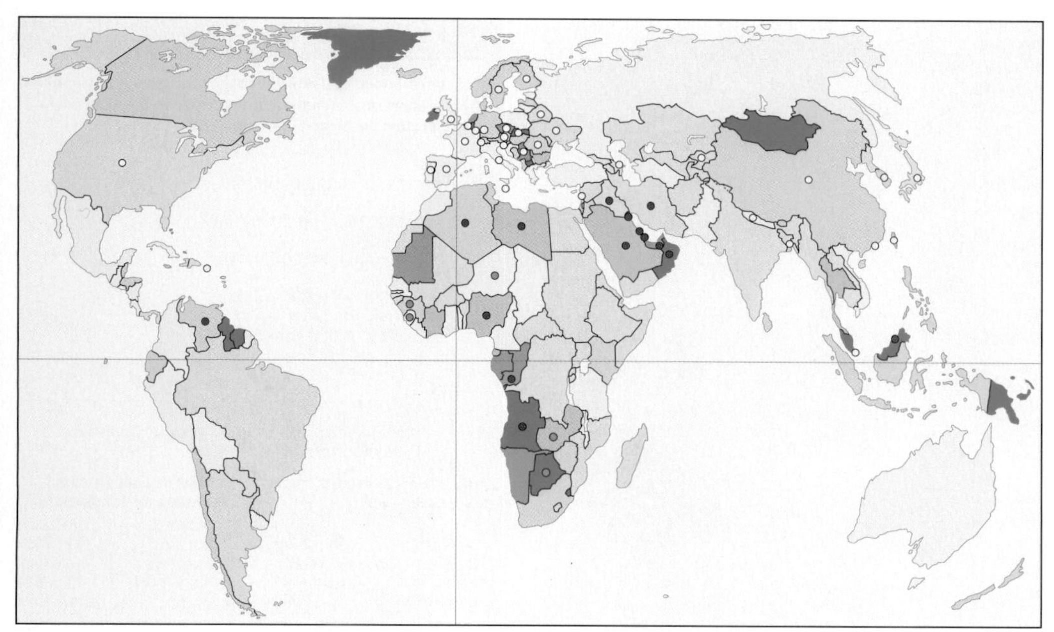

Value of exports as a percentage of Gross Domestic Product (1993)

- Over 50% GDP
- 40 – 50% GDP
- 30 – 40% GDP
- 20 – 30% GDP
- 10 – 20% GDP
- Under 10% GDP

- ○ Most dependent on industrial exports (over 75% of total exports)
- ● Most dependent on fuel exports (over 75% of total exports)
- 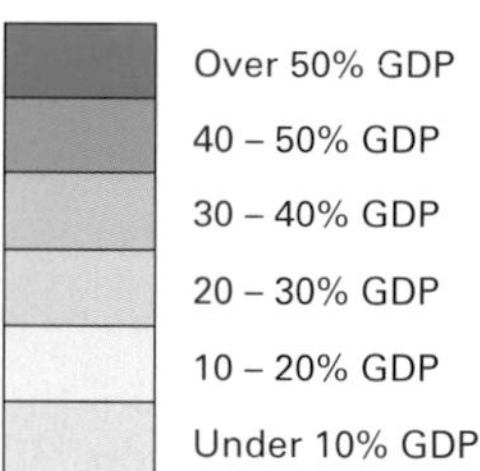 Most dependent on mineral and metal exports (over 75% of total exports)

TRAVEL AND TOURISM

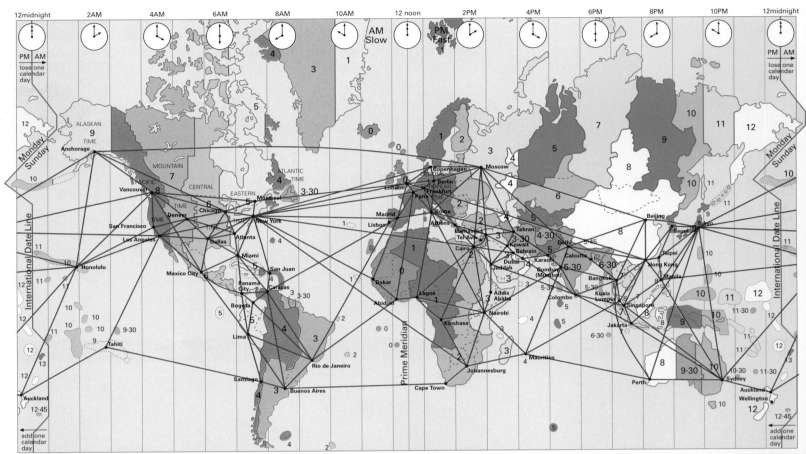

12midnight | 2AM | 4AM | 6AM | 8AM | 10AM | 12 noon | 2PM | 4PM | 6PM | 8PM | 10PM | 12midnight

AM Slow / PM Fast

PM | AM — lose one calendar day

Monday / Sunday

add one calendar day

TIME ZONES

▓ Zones using GMT	▓ Zones fast of GMT
▓ Zones slow of GMT	▓ Half-hour zones
– – – International boundaries	—— Time zone boundaries
10 Hours slow or fast of GMT	—— International Date Line
	Selected air routes

The world is divided into 24 time zones, each centred on meridians at 15° intervals, which is the longitudinal distance the sun travels every hour. The meridian running through Greenwich, London, passes through the middle of the first zone.

Certain time zones are affected by the incidence of 'summer time' in countries where it is adopted.

Actual Solar Time, when it is noon at Greenwich, is shown along the top of the map.

RAIL AND ROAD: THE LEADING NATIONS

Total rail network ('000 km)	Passenger km per head per year	Total road network ('000 km)	Vehicle km per head per year	Number of vehicles per km of roads
1. USA 239.7	Japan 2,017	USA...........6,277.9	USA.............12,505	Hong Kong ...284
2. Russia 87.5	Belarus 1,880	India 2,962.5	Luxembourg.7,989	Taiwan 211
3. India 62.5	Russia...........1,826	Brazil 1,824.4	Kuwait...........7,251	Singapore.....152
4. China 54.0	Switzerland..1,769	Japan 1,130.9	France 7,142	Kuwait...........140
5. Germany 40.4	Ukraine.........1,456	China 1,041.1	Sweden.........6,991	Brunei 96
6. Australia 35.8	Austria 1,168	Russia 884.0	Germany 6,806	Italy 91
7. Argentina 34.2	France 1,011	Canada.........849.4	Denmark 6,764	Israel 87
8. France............32.6	Netherlands 994	France 811.6	Austria 6,518	Thailand..........73
9. Mexico............26.5	Latvia..............918	Australia 810.3	Netherlands...5,984	Ukraine 73
10. Poland 24.9	Denmark 884	Germany 636.3	UK 5,738	UK 67
11. South Africa ...23.6	Slovak Rep. 862	Romania 461.9	Canada..........5,493	Netherlands....66
12. Ukraine...........22.6	Romania.........851	Turkey 388.1	Italy 4,852	Germany.........62

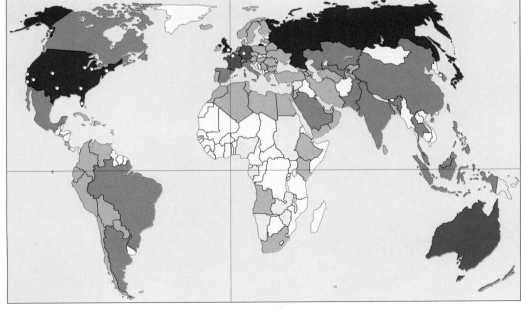

AIR TRAVEL

Passenger kilometres (the number of passengers – international and and domestic – multiplied by the distance flown by each passenger from the airport of origin) (1994)

▓	Over 100,000 million
▓	50,000 – 100,000 million
▓	10,000 – 50,000 million
▓	1,000 – 10,000 million
▓	500 – 1,000 million
▓	Under 500 million
○	Major airports (handling over 25 million passengers in 1994)

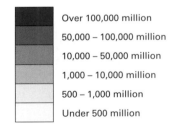

World's busiest airports (total passengers)		World's busiest airports (international passengers)	
1. Chicago	(O'Hare)	1. London	(Heathrow)
2. Atlanta	(Hatsfield)	2. London	(Gatwick)
3. Dallas	(Dallas/Ft Worth)	3. Frankfurt	(International)
4. London	(Heathrow)	4. New York	(Kennedy)
5. Los Angeles	(Intern'l)	5. Paris	(De Gaulle)

DESTINATIONS

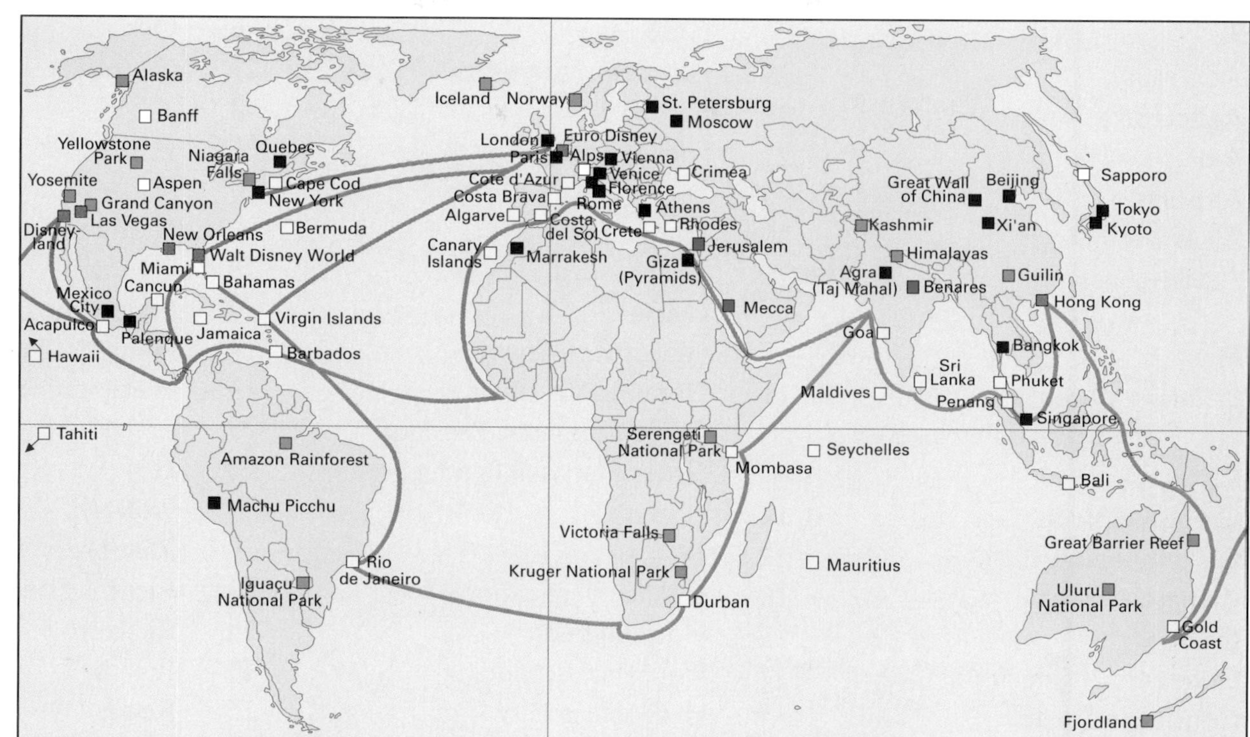

- ■ Cultural & historical centres
- ☐ Coastal resorts
- ☐ Ski resorts
- ▨ Centres of entertainment
- ▨ Places of pilgrimage
- ▨ Places of great natural beauty
- — Popular holiday cruise routes

Map labels: Alaska, Banff, Yellowstone Park, Niagara Falls, Quebec, Yosemite, Aspen, Cape Cod, New York, Grand Canyon, Las Vegas, Disneyland, New Orleans, Walt Disney World, Miami, Cancun, Bahamas, Bermuda, Mexico City, Acapulco, Palenque, Jamaica, Virgin Islands, Barbados, Hawaii, Tahiti, Amazon Rainforest, Machu Picchu, Iguaçu National Park, Rio de Janeiro, Iceland, Norway, London, Euro Disney, Paris, St. Petersburg, Moscow, Alps, Vienna, Cote d'Azur, Venice, Florence, Crimea, Costa Brava, Rome, Athens, Algarve, Costa del Sol, Crete, Rhodes, Canary Islands, Marrakesh, Jerusalem, Giza (Pyramids), Mecca, Serengeti National Park, Mombasa, Seychelles, Victoria Falls, Kruger National Park, Mauritius, Durban, Great Wall of China, Beijing, Sapporo, Tokyo, Kyoto, Xi'an, Kashmir, Himalayas, Guilin, Agra (Taj Mahal), Benares, Hong Kong, Goa, Bangkok, Sri Lanka, Phuket, Maldives, Penang, Singapore, Bali, Great Barrier Reef, Uluru National Park, Gold Coast, Fjordland

VISITORS TO THE USA

Overseas travellers to the USA, thousands (1997 projections)

1. Canada 13,900
2. Mexico 12,370
3. Japan 4,640
4. UK 3,350
5. Germany 1,990
6. France 1,030
7. Taiwan 885
8. Venezuela 860
9. South Korea 800
10. Brazil 785

In 1996, the USA earned the most from tourism, with receipts of more than US $64 billion.

TOURIST SPENDING

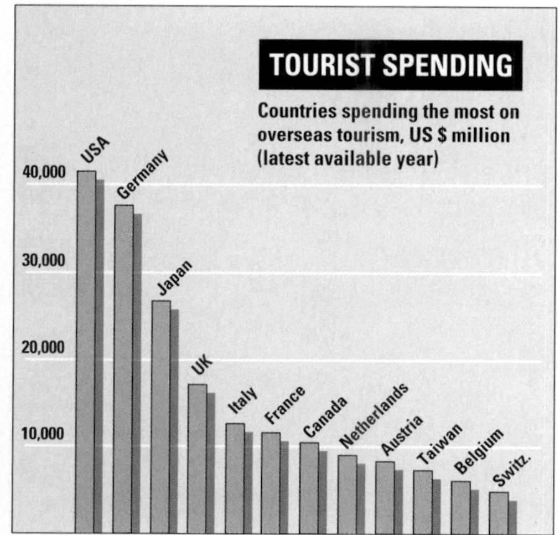

Countries spending the most on overseas tourism, US $ million (latest available year)

Bars: USA, Germany, Japan, UK, Italy, France, Canada, Netherlands, Austria, Taiwan, Belgium, Switz.

IMPORTANCE OF TOURISM

	Arrivals from abroad (1995)	% of world total (1995)
1. France	60,584,000	10.68%
2. Spain	45,125,000	7.96%
3. USA	44,730,000	7.89%
4. Italy	29,184,000	5.15%
5. China	23,368,000	4.12%
6. UK	22,700,000	4.00%
7. Hungary	22,087,000	3.90%
8. Mexico	19,870,000	3.50%
9. Poland	19,225,000	3.39%
10. Austria	17,750,000	3.13%
11. Canada	16,854,000	2.97%
12. Czech Republic	16,600,000	2.93%

The latest figures reveal a 4.6% rise in the total number of people travelling abroad in 1996, to 593 million. Small economies in attractive areas are often completely dominated by tourism: in some West Indian islands, for example, tourist spending provides over 90% of total income.

TOURIST EARNING

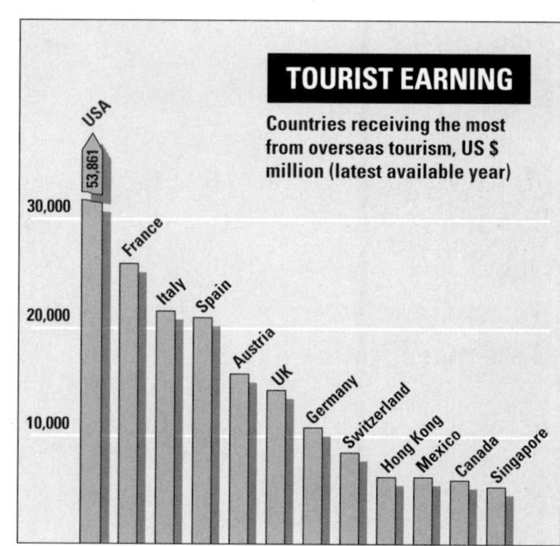

Countries receiving the most from overseas tourism, US $ million (latest available year)

Bars: USA (53,861), France, Italy, Spain, Austria, UK, Germany, Switzerland, Hong Kong, Mexico, Canada, Singapore

TOURISM

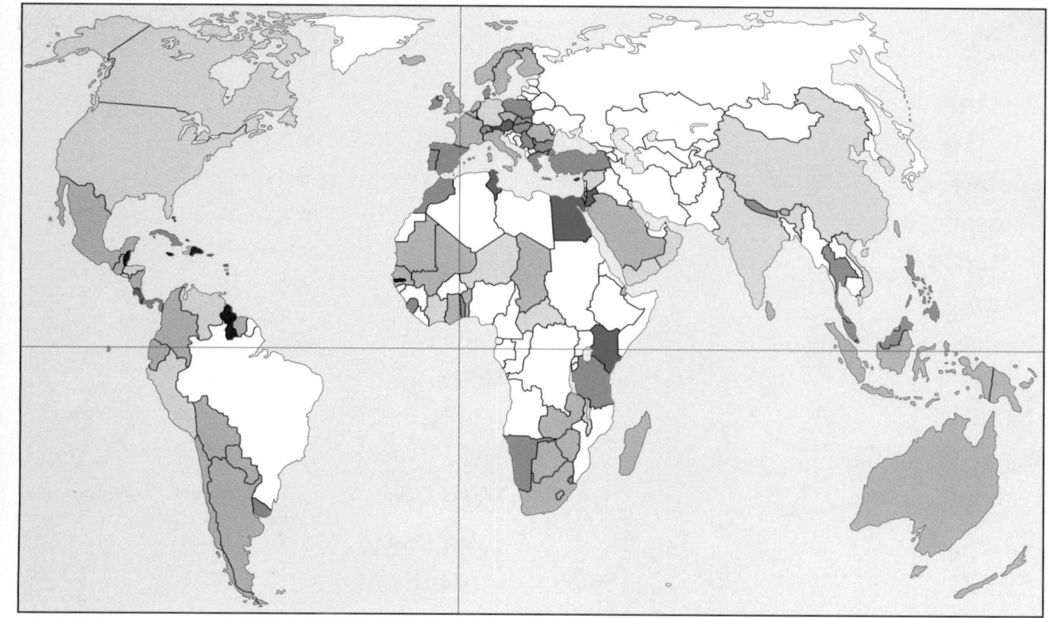

Tourism receipts as a percentage of Gross National Product (1994)

- ■ Over 10% of GNP from tourism
- ▨ 5 – 10% of GNP from tourism
- ▨ 2.5 – 5% of GNP from tourism
- ▨ 1 – 2.5% of GNP from tourism
- ▨ 0.5 – 1% of GNP from tourism
- ☐ Under 0.5% of GNP from tourism

Countries spending the most on promoting tourism, millions of US $ (1996)

Australia 88
Spain 79
UK 79
France 73
Singapore 54

Fastest growing tourist destinations, % change in receipts (1994–5)

South Korea 49%
Czech Republic 27%
India 21%
Russia 19%
Philippines 18%

INTRODUCTION TO WORLD GEOGRAPHY: INDEX

WORLD MAPS

SETTLEMENTS

◻ **PARIS**   ◼ **Berne**   ◉ **Livorno**   ● Brugge   ◉ Algeciras   ○ Fréjus   ○ Oberammergau   ○ Thira

Settlement symbols and type styles vary according to the scale of each map and indicate the importance
of towns on the map rather than specific population figures

∴   Ruins or Archæological Sites   ⌣   Wells in Desert

ADMINISTRATION

——— International Boundaries

– – – International Boundaries
(Undefined or Disputed)

⋯⋯ Internal Boundaries

National Parks

Country Names

NICARAGUA

Administrative
Area Names

KENT

CALABRIA

International boundaries show the *de facto* situation where there are rival claims to territory

COMMUNICATIONS

——— Principal Roads

⌣ Other Roads

-·-·- Trails and Seasonal Roads

� Passes

⚬ Airfields

⌣ Principal Railroads

-·-·- Railroads
Under Construction

⌣ Other Railroads

⌐--⌐ Railroad Tunnels

⋯⋯ Principal Canals

PHYSICAL FEATURES

⌣ Perennial Streams

-·-· Intermittent Streams

◯ Perennial Lakes

⬭ Intermittent Lakes

Swamps and Marshes

Permanent Ice
and Glaciers

▲ 8848 Elevations (m)

▾ 8050 Sea Depths (m)

1134 Height of Lake Surface
Above Sea Level (m)

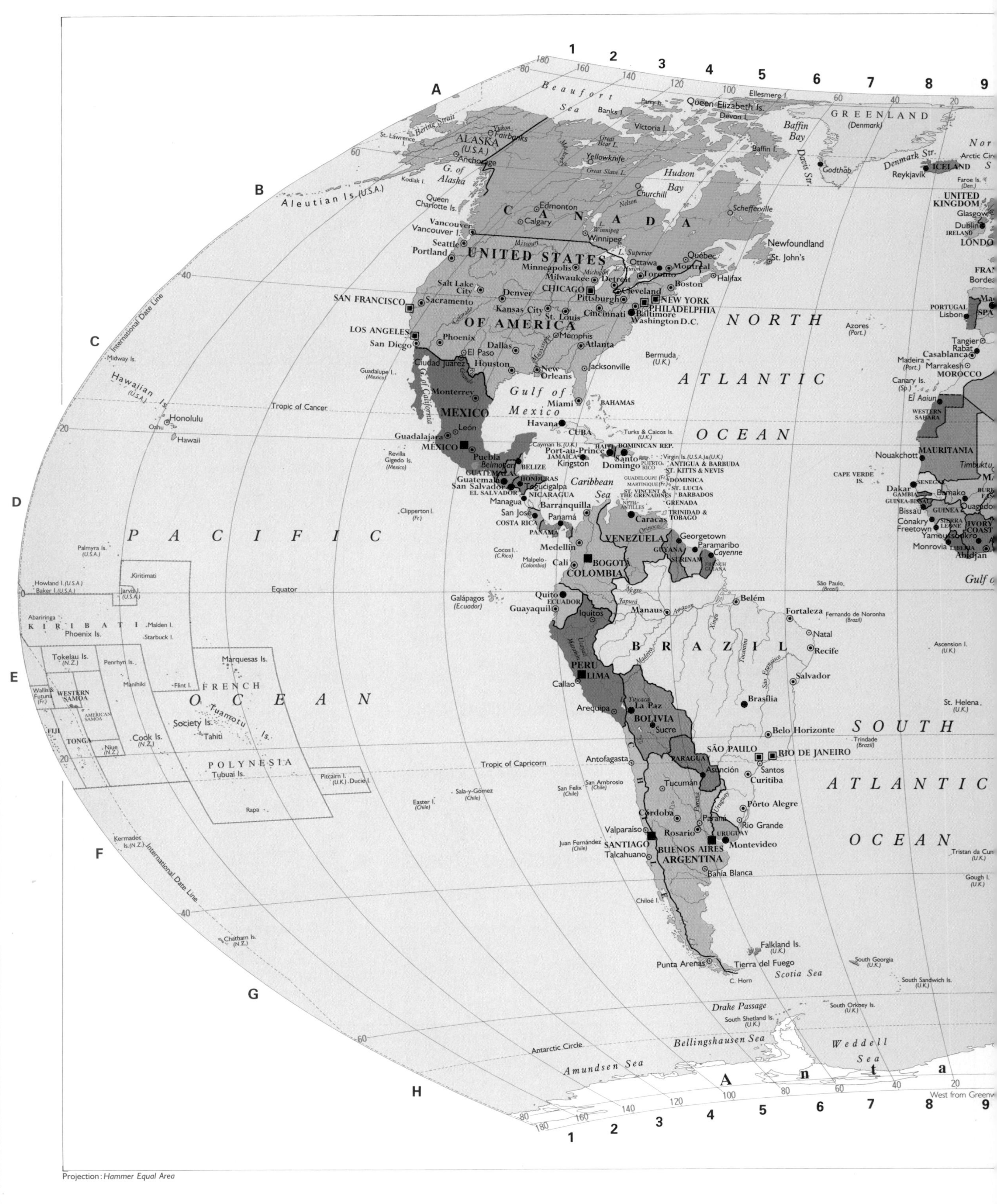

Projection: *Hammer Equal Area*

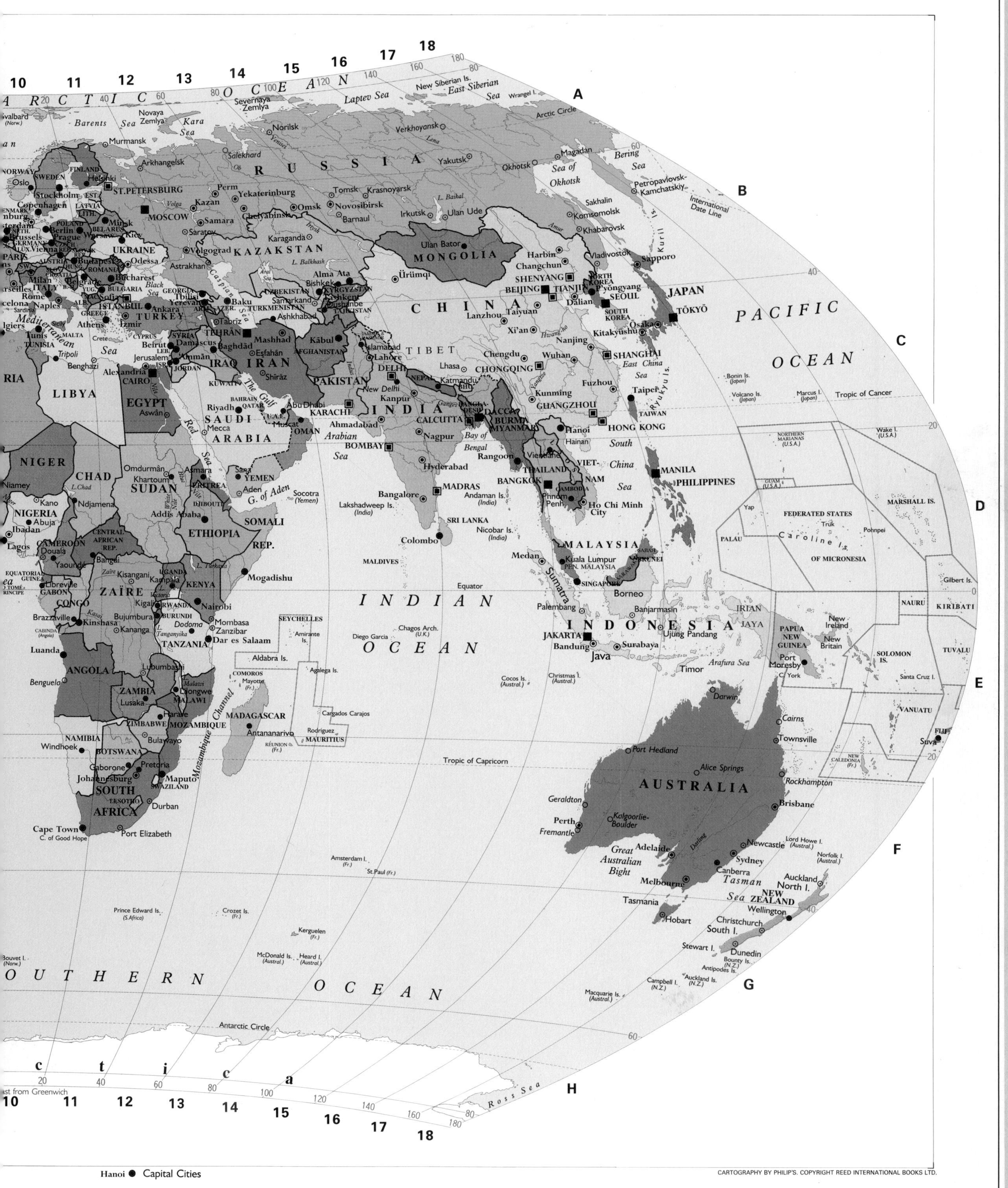

CARTOGRAPHY BY PHILIP'S. COPYRIGHT REED INTERNATIONAL BOOKS LTD.

Hanoi ● Capital Cities

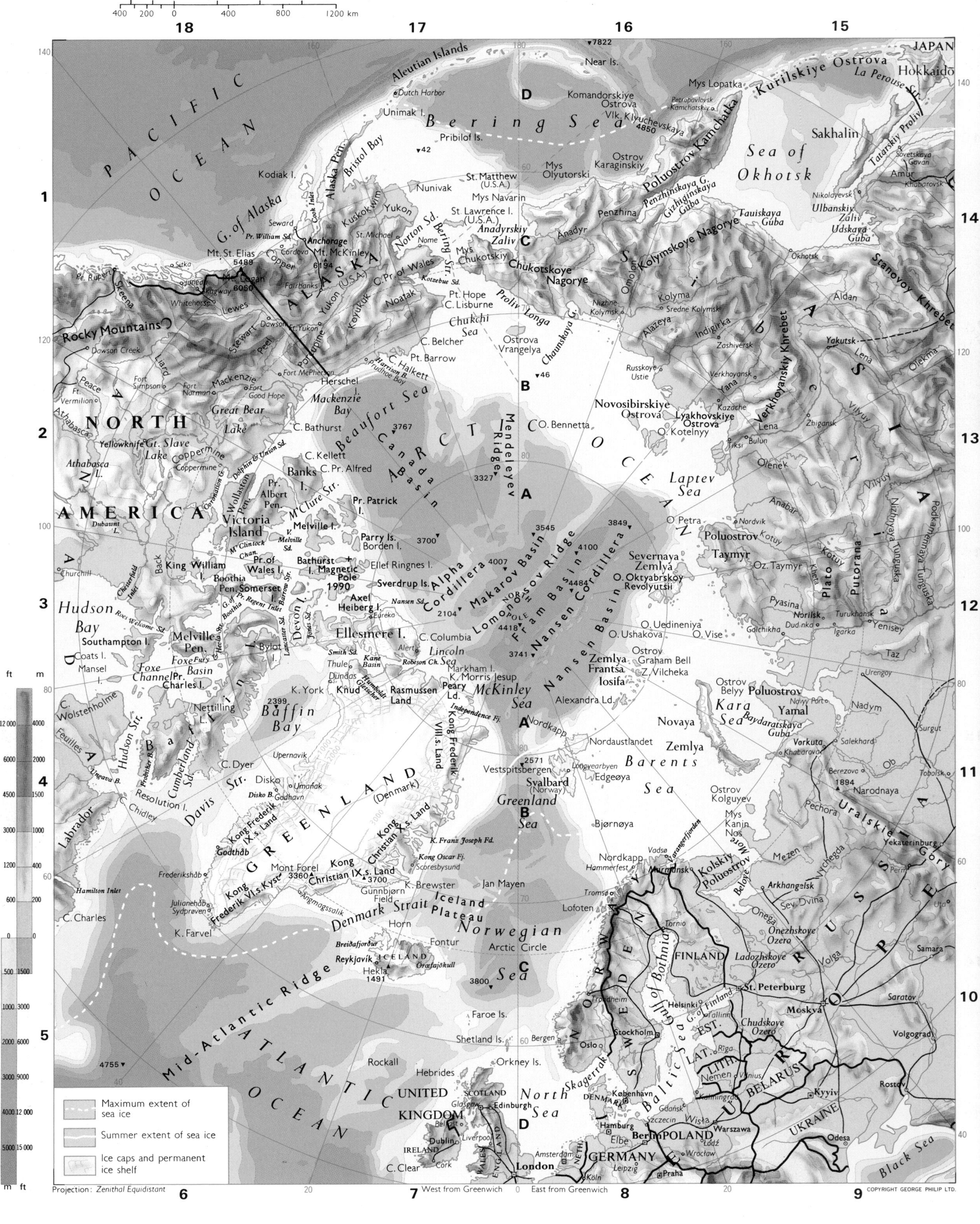

1:35 000 000

| 200 | 100 | | 400 | | 600 miles |
| 400 | 200 | 0 | 400 | 800 | 1200 km |

18　　　　**17**　　　　**16**　　　　**15**

PACIFIC OCEAN

Aleutian Islands
Near Is.
▼7822
Dutch Harbor
Bering Sea
Komandorskiye Ostrova
Petropavlovsk-Kamchatskiy
Vlk. Klyuchevskaya 4850
Kurilskiye Ostrova
La Perouse Str.
JAPAN
Hokkaido
Unimak I.
Mys Lopatka
Poluostrov Kamchatka
Sakhalin
Sovetskaya
Govan
▼42
Pribilof Is.
Ostrov Karaginskiy
Sea of Okhotsk
Tatarskiy Proliv
Kodiak I.
Mys Olyutorski
Nikolayevsk
Ulbanskiy Zaliv
Amur
Khabarovsk
G. of Alaska
St. Matthew (U.S.A.)
60
Mys Navarin
Penzhina
Penzhinskaya G.
Gizhiginskaya Guba
Tauiskaya Guba
Udskaya Guba
Bristol Bay
Seward
Nunivak
St Lawrence I. (U.S.A.)
Anadyrskiy Zaliv
Anadyr
S
Okhotsk
Stanovoy Khrebet
Kuskokwim
Yukon
Nome
Bering Str.
Chukotskoye Nagorye
Kolymskoye Nagorye
ALASKA (U.S.A.)
C. Pr. of Wales
Mys Chukotskiy
Kolyma
Aldan
Anchorage
St Michael
Norton Sd.
Kotzebue Sd.
Nizhne Kolymsk
Sredne Kolymsk
Yakutsk
Cordova
Mt. McKinley 6194
Koyukuk
Pt. Hope
Proliv Longa
Alazeya
Indigirka
Verkhoyansk
Lena
Olekma
Mt. St. Elias 5488
Copper
Fairbanks
Noatak
C. Lisburne
Zashiversk
Olenek
 Mt. Logan 6050
Pr. William Sd.
Chukchi Sea
Ostrova Vrangelya
Russkoye Ustie
Yana
Verkhoyanskiy Khrebet
Zhigansk
 120
Sitka
C. Halkett
Chaunskaya G.
Tiksi
Bulun
Vilyuy
120
Rocky Mountains
Whitehorse
Lewes
Pt. Barrow
▼46
Novosibirskiye Ostrova
Lyakhovskiye Ostrova
Kazache
Verkhoyanskiy Khrebet
Yenisey
Dawson
Fort Yukon
Harrison B.
Prudhoe Bay
Kazache
S
Peel
Herschel
B
Mendeleyev Ridge
C. O. Bennetta
A
Laptev Sea
NORTH
Great Bear Lake
Mackenzie Bay
Beaufort Sea
R
C
T
O. Kotelnyy
Lena
Olenek
2
Yellowknife
Gt. Slave Lake
C. Bathurst
▼3767
Canada Basin
80
Anabar
Nordvik
Kotuy
13
Athabasca L.
Coppermine
C. Kellett
I
O. Petra
Poluostrov Taymyr
Putorana
AMERICA
Banks I.
C. Pr. Alfred
3327
▼3545
E
O. Oktyabrskoy Revolyutsii
Oz. Taymyr
Pyasina
Dubawnt
Pr. Albert Pen.
Mt. Clure Str.
▼3849
Severnaya Zemlya
4100
A
N
Plato
Kheta
Churchill
Victoria Island
Melville I.
Pr. Patrick
Alpha Cordillera 4007
Makarov Basin
Norilsk
Turukhansk
Igarka
3
Hudson Bay
King William I.
M'Clintock Chan.
Bathurst I.
Parry Is.
Borden I.
3700▼
Lomonosov Ridge
44484
Z
O. Uedineniya
Golchikha
Dud.nka
12
Southampton I.
Back
Boothia Pen.
Somerset I.
Prince of Wales I.
Magnetic Pole 1990
Ellef Ringnes I.
Sverdrup Is.
2104
POLE
Fram Basin
4418
Nansen Basin
O. Vise
Coats I.
Mansel
Foxe Channel
Fury & Hecla Str.
Axel Heiberg I.
Devon I.
Nansen Cordillera
3741
Zemlya Frantsa Iosifa
Kara Sea
Ostrov Belyy
Poluostrov
80
Charles I.
Eureka
Ellesmere I.
C. Columbia
Markham I.
K. Morris Jesup
McKinley Sea
Zemlya Graham Bell
Z. Vilcheka
Baydaratskaya Guba
Novyy Port
Nadym
ft m
C. Wolstenholme
Nettilling
Baffin Bay
Thule
Kane Basin
Robeson Ch.
Lincoln Sea
Alert
Peary Ld.
A
Novaya
O. Ushakova
Alexandra Ld.
Vorkuta
Ob
Surgut
K. York
Knud
Smith Sd.
Dundas
Rasmussen Land
Kong Frederik VIII's Land
Nordkapp
Zemlya
Ostrov Kolguyev
URALSKIE
Narodnaya
12 000 4000
Feuilles
Cumberland Sd.
C. Dyer
Upernavik
Kong Christian IX's Land
K. Franz Joseph Fd.
Barents Sea
Novaya Zemlya
1894
GORY
6000 2000
Resolution I.
Disko
Disko B.
Godhavn
Nordaustlandet
Edgeøya
Mys Kanin Nos
Pechora
Berezovo
Nadym
Salekhard
4500 1500
Chidley
Ungava B.
Davis Str.
Umanak
Vestspitsbergen
Svalbard (Norway)
Bjørnøya
More
Mezen
Vorkuta
Tobolsk
Khabarovo
3000 1000
Labrador
Godthåb
GREENLAND (Denmark)
Kong Frederik IX's Land
Longyearbyen
Greenland Sea
Kolskiy Poluostrov
Arkhangelsk
60
1200 400
Hamilton Inlet
Frederikshåb
Mont Forel
Kong Christian IX's Land
2571
Vadsø
Nordkapp
Hammerfest
Murmansk
Beloye
Onega
Sev. Dvina
R
600 200
C. Charles
Julianehåb
Sydprøven
3360
3700
K. Franz Joseph Fd.
Kong Oscar Fj.
Scoresbysund
Tromsø
Lofoten
Finland
Ladozhskoye Ozero
Nychegda
Vychegda
Perm
0
K. Farvel
Gunnbjørn Field
K. Brewster
Jan Mayen
Iceland
Onezhskoye Ozero
St. Peterburg
Moskva
Samara
Angmagssalik
Horn
Plateau
Arctic Circle
Norwegian
Trondheim
Gulf of Bothnia
Helsinki
Chudskoye Ozero
E
500 1500
Breiðafjörður
Fontur
Denmark Strait
Sea
Oslo
Stockholm
Tallinn
EST.
Saratov
1000 3000
Reykjavík
ICELAND
Hekla 1491
Oræfajökull
3800▼
C
Bergen
60
SWEDEN
Riga
LAT.
Volga
Volgograd
2000 6000
5
Mid-Atlantic Ridge
Faroe Is.
Gulf of Finland
LITH.
Vilnius
R
3000 9000
4755▼
Shetland Is.
Bergen
North Sea
København
Baltic Sea
Nemen
BELARUS
Rostov
4000 12 000
ATLANTIC OCEAN
Rockall
Hebrides
Orkney Is.
Skagerrak
DENMARK
Gdańsk
Kaliningrad
Kyyiv
UKRAINE
Black Sea
Odesa
5000 15 000
UNITED KINGDOM
SCOTLAND
Glasgow
Edinburgh
Hamburg
Szczecin
Wisła
Warszawa
Łódź
Wrocław
40
m ft
Belfast
ENGLAND
Amsterdam
NETH.
Berlin
POLAND
Elbe
Leipzig
Praha
Dublin
IRELAND
Liverpool
WALES
London
GERMANY
Köln
Cork
C. Clear

Maximum extent of sea ice

Summer extent of sea ice

Ice caps and permanent ice shelf

Projection: Zenithal Equidistant

6　　20　　**7** West from Greenwich 0 East from Greenwich **8**　　20　　**9** COPYRIGHT GEORGE PHILIP LTD.

1:35 000 000

200 100 0 200 400 600 miles
400 200 0 400 800 1200 km

West from Greenwich   East from Greenwich

ATLANTIC OCEAN

INDIAN OCEAN

SOUTHERN

Atlantic - Indian Basin

Atlantic - Indian Basin

▼8265
Zavodovski I.
Visokoi I.
Leskov I.   Candlemas I.
Saunders I.   S. Sandwich Is. (U.K.)
Montagu I.   Bristol I.

South Georgia
Bird I. (U.K.)

Bases on
King George Island:
Jubany (Argentina)
Com. Ferraz (Brazil)
Ten. Rodolfo Marsh (Chile)
Great Wall (China)
King Sejong (Korea)
Arctowski (Poland)
Artigas (Uruguay)

Antarctic Circle

6739 ▼

Georg Forster (Germany)
Dakshin Gangotri (India)
Sanae (S. Afr.)
Georg von Neumayer (Germany)

Prinsesse Astrid Kyst   Prinsesse Ragnhild Kyst
Kronprinsesse Martha Kyst   2717   Sør-Rondane   3630
Mühlig-Hofmann Kyst
Prins Harald Kyst
Lützow-Holmbukta   Syowa (Japan)
Kronprins Olav Kyst
Mizuho (Japan)

Riiser-Larsen-halvøya

Enderby Ld.   2260
Kemp Land   Stefansson B.

C. Borley

Mawson (Austr.)

▼5552
Orcadas (Arg.)
Signy I. (U.K.)   South Orkney Is.
Coronation I.   (U.K.)

Stanley (U.K.)
Falkland Is. (U.K.)

Clarence I.
Elephant I.
South   Kg.George
Shetland Is.
Deception I.
Gen. Bernardo O'Higgins (Chile)
Joinville I.
Esperanza (Arg.)
Marambio (Arg.)
Capitan Arturo Prat (Chile)
James Ross I.
Robertson I.

ARGENTINA
Tierra del Fuego
C. de Hornos
I. Hoste
CHILE

Queen Maud Land   3212   3039
3318   2990
2311   1431
Coats Land
Caird Coast
Luitpold Coast

3556   2600

3355   2600
Prince Charles Mts.
Lambert Glacier
Amery Ice Shelf
American Highland   1800   1040
Zhongshan (China)
Davis (Austr.)
Prydz Bay

Mac-Robertson Land   2645
C. Darnley

Graham Land
Palmer (U.S.A.)
Anvers I.
Vernadsky (Ukr.)
Biscoe Is.
Adelaide I.
Rothera (U.K.)
Alexander I.   2987
Charcot I.   C. Byrd
Peter I. Øy (Nor.)

Larsen Ice Shelf
Antarctic Peninsula
Palmer Land
Dyer Plateau   4191
George VI Sound   3658
Ronne Ice Shelf
975   Berkner I.   158   1312
Filchner Ice Shelf
2896

Halley Bay (U.K.)
Vahsel Bay
Pensacola Mountains   3657

4030   1040
East Antarctica
4000

SOUTH POLE   2773   Amundsen-Scott (U.S.A.)   2407

Wilhelm II Coast
West Ice Shelf

Davis Sea
Drygalski I.
Masson I.
Shackleton Ice Shelf

Queen Mary Land   3030   2570
3488   3700

Weddell Sea

Siple (U.S.A.)
Ellsworth Mts.   Vinson Massif   4897
Ellsworth Land
1797   4335   3022
Thiel Mts.
Horlick Mts.   3810
Transantarctica

West Antarctica

Thurston I.   1036
Hudson Mts.
C. Flying Fish
Bellingshausen Sea

2407   3087
Shackleton Inlet
2801   3491
Beardmore Glacier
4176   4528
Queen Maud Mts.
Queen Alexandra Ra.
Mt. Markham   4349

Bowman I.
Mill I.
Scott Gl.
Knox Coast
Budd Coast   Casey (Austr.)
Sabrina Coast   Totten Glacier
Banzare Coast
Dalton Iceberg Tongue

Amundsen Sea
Marie Byrd Land
Kohler Ra.   Mt. Sidley   4181
3109   Getz Ice Shelf
C. Dart   3496   Hobbs Coast
Walgreen Coast
Bakutis Coast
Rockefeller Plateau   666   2080
Edward VII Land
Sulzberger Ice Shelf   Roosevelt I.
Bay of Whales

Ross Ice Shelf   Roosevelt

Mt. Erebus   3743   Mt. Lister   4023
McMurdo (U.S.A.)
Scott (N.Z.)
Ross I.   McMurdo
C. Colbeck
Franklin I.
Victoria Land
Pr. Albert Mts.
Mt. Murchison   3502
Ross Sea
Coulman I.
Possession I.
C. Adare   3719

2216   2798
Clarie Coast
Terre Adélie
Dumont d'Urville (Fr.)
Porpoise Bay
Blodgett Iceberg Tongue
2435   4776
George V Land

SOUTHEAST PACIFIC OCEAN
Southeast Pacific Basin
Pacific Basin
Pacific Ocean
Antarctic Ridge
PACIFIC OCEAN

Antarctic Circle

Scott I.   Balleny Is.

Wilkes Land

Oates Land
C. Freshfield
Commonwealth B.
+ Magnetic Pole 1990

Southeast Indian Rise

▼6240

Macquarie Is. (Austr.)

Southwestern Pacific Basin
Campbell I. (N.Z.)
Auckland Is. (N.Z.)
Antipodes Is.
Campbell Plateau
Bounty Is.   Stewart I.
Dunedin   NEW ZEALAND

Tasman Plat.
Tasman Sea
Tasmania   Bass Strait
Hobart
Melbourne
AUSTRALIA

Legend

Ice cap

Permanent ice shelf

Maximum extent of sea ice

March (Summer) extent of sea ice

▲3488   3700   Surface elevation and depth of ice (in metres)

• Stanley (U.K.)   Permanent bases

Projection: *Zenithal Equidistant*

COPYRIGHT GEORGE PHILIP LTD.

The Antarctic Treaty was signed in Washington in 1959 so that scientific and technical research could continue unhampered by international politics.

All territorial claims covering land areas south of latitude 60°S have been suspended. Those claims were:

Norwegian claim   45°E – 20°W
Australian claims   { 45°E – 136°E
                    { 142°E – 160°E
French claim   136°E – 142°E
New Zealand claim   160°E – 150°W
Chilean claim   90°W – 53°W
British claim   80°W – 20°W
Argentine claim   74°W – 53°W

ft   m
12 000   4000
6000   2000
4500   1500
3000   1000
1200   400
600   200
0   0
500   1500
1000   3000
2000   6000
3000   9000
4000   12 000
5000   15 000
m   ft

EUROPE : Physical

1:20 000 000

100 0 100 200 300 400 miles

100 0 100 200 300 400 500 600 km

m: 5000, 4000, 2000, 1000, 400, 200, 0, 200, 1000, 2000, 4000

ft: 15 000, 12 000, 6000, 3000, 1200, 600, 0, 600, 3000, 6000, 12 000

Projection: Bonne

West from Greenwich 0 East from Greenwich

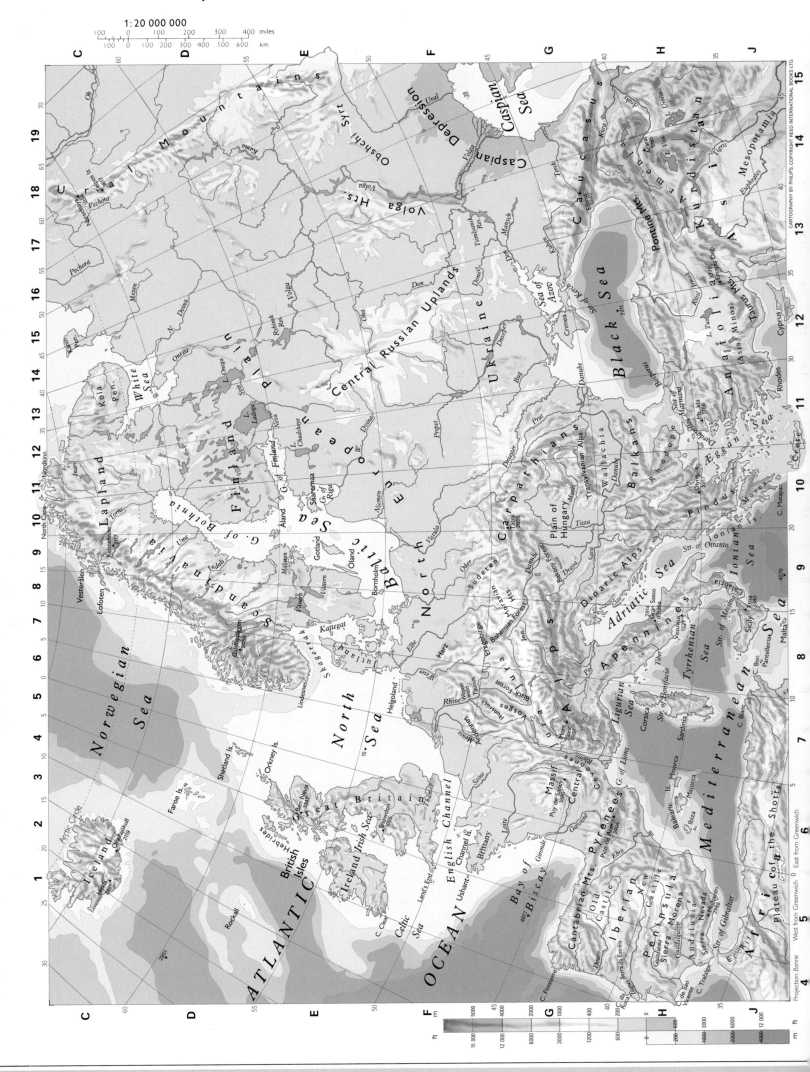

1 : 20 000 000

100   0   100   200   300   400 miles

100   0   100   200 300 400 500 600 km

ATLANTIC OCEAN

Norwegian Sea

ICELAND
Reykjavik

Arctic Circle

UNITED KINGDOM

IRELAND
Dublin
Cork

SCOTLAND
Glasgow
Edinburgh
Aberdeen
Dundee
Newcastle-upon-Tyne
WALES
Cardiff
ENGLAND
Birmingham
Bristol
Manchester
Leeds
Sheffield
Liverpool
Southampton
Plymouth
LONDON

Shetland Is.
Orkney Is.
Hebrides
Faroe Is. (Den.)

North Sea

NORWAY
Oslo
Bergen
Stavanger
Trondheim
Narvik
Tromsø

SWEDEN
Stockholm
Göteborg
Malmö
Uppsala
Gävle
Örebro
Gotland

FINLAND
Helsinki
Turku
Tampere
Vaasa

G. of Bothnia

Baltic Sea

DENMARK
Copenhagen
Århus
Odense

ESTONIA
Tallinn

LATVIA
Riga

LITHUANIA
Vilnius
Kaunas
Kaliningrad

BELARUS
Minsk

RUSSIA
MOSCOW
ST. PETERSBURG
Murmansk
Arkhangelsk

White Sea
L. Onega
L. Ladoga

NETHER-LANDS
Amsterdam
The Hague
Rotterdam

BELGIUM
Brussels

GERMANY
Berlin
Hamburg
Hannover
Bremen
Cologne
Bonn
Dortmund
Essen
Frankfurt am Main
Munich
Nuremberg
Stuttgart
Leipzig
Dresden
Magdeburg
Halle

POLAND
Warsaw
Kraków
Łódź
Poznań
Wrocław
Gdansk
Szczecin
Katowice
Lublin
Białystok
Bydgoszcz

CZECH REP.
Prague

SLOVAK REP.
Bratislava

AUSTRIA
Vienna
Graz
Linz
Innsbruck
Salzburg

SWITZERLAND
Zurich
Geneva
Bern

FRANCE
PARIS
Lyon
Marseille
Bordeaux
Toulouse
Nantes
Lille
Strasbourg
Dijon
Nice
Le Havre
Rouen
Brest
St-Etienne
Limoges

SPAIN
Madrid
Barcelona
Valencia
Seville
Zaragoza
Bilbao
Málaga
Murcia
Córdoba
Granada
Alicante
Valladolid
La Coruña
Vigo

PORTUGAL
Lisbon
Porto

ANDORRA

ITALY
Rome
Milan
Naples
Turin
Genoa
Florence
Venice
Bologna
Palermo
Catania
Bari
Sicily
Sardinia

HUNGARY
Budapest
Miskolc
Debrecen

SLOVENIA
Ljubljana

CROATIA
Zagreb

BOSNIA-HERZ.
Sarajevo

YUGOSLAVIA
Belgrade
SERBIA

ROMANIA
Bucharest
Cluj-Napoca
Timişoara
Braşov
Galaţi
Ploieşti

BULGARIA
Sofia
Plovdiv
Varna

MACEDONIA
Skopje

ALBANIA
Tirana

GREECE
Athens
Thessaloniki
Patras

MOLDOVA
Kishinev

UKRAINE
Kiev
Kharkov
Dnepropetrovsk
Odessa
Lvov
Donetsk
Zaporozhye

Black Sea

Crimea
Sevastopol

TURKEY
Ankara
Istanbul
Izmir
Konya
Adana
Antalya
Kayseri

CYPRUS
Nicosia

SYRIA
Aleppo

IRAQ
Baghdad

IRAN
Tabriz

GEORGIA
Tbilisi

ARMENIA

AZERBAIJAN
Baku

KAZAKSTAN

Caspian Sea

Mediterranean Sea

Adriatic Sea

Ionian Sea

Tyrrhenian Sea

Aegean Sea

Crete

MALTA
Valletta

MONACO

SAN MARINO

LIECHT.

LUXEMBOURG

MOROCCO
ALGERIA
TUNISIA
Algiers
Tunis

Africa

English Channel

Bay of Biscay

North Sea

Kattegat

Balearic Is.
Majorca
Minorca
Ibiza

Corsica

Volga

■ LONDON Capital Cities

West from Greenwich   0   East from Greenwich

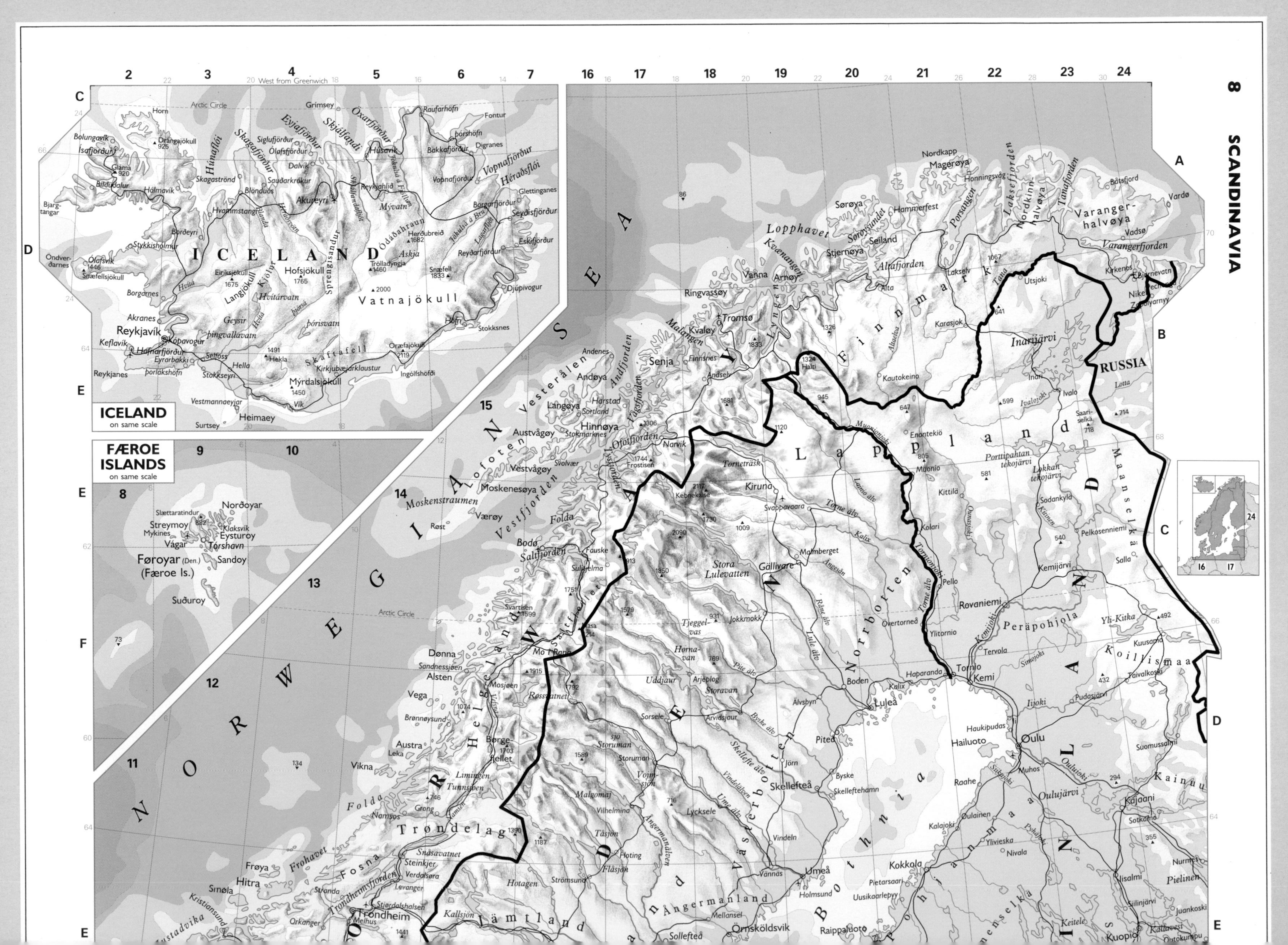
ICELAND
on same scale
FÆROE ISLANDS
on same scale
ICELAND
Vatnajökull
Hofsjökull
Langjökull
Mýrdalsjökull
Reykjavík
Keflavík
Hafnarfjörður
Akureyri
Húsavík
Heimaey
Vestmannaeyjar
Surtsey
Hekla
Askja
Grímsey
Arctic Circle
West from Greenwich
Føroyar (Den.)
(Færoe Is.)
Tórshavn
Streymoy
Eysturoy
Vágar
Sandoy
Suðuroy
Norðoyar
Mykines
NORWEGIAN SEA
RUSSIA
FINLAND
Lappland
Finnmark
Maanselkä
Norrbotten
Västerbotten
Ångermanland
Jämtland
Trøndelag
Lofoten
Vesterålen
Vestfjorden
Moskenesøya
Moskenstraumen
Værøy
Røst
Vestvågøy
Austvågøy
Hinnøya
Andøya
Langøya
Senja
Kvaløya
Ringvassøy
Vanna
Arnøy
Sørøya
Seiland
Stjernøya
Magerøya
Nordkapp
Hammerfest
Alta
Tromsø
Narvik
Bodø
Mo i Rana
Mosjøen
Trondheim
Kristiansund
Smøla
Hitra
Frøya
Kiruna
Gällivare
Luleå
Boden
Piteå
Skellefteå
Umeå
Örnsköldsvik
Kemi
Tornio
Haparanda
Oulu
Kajaani
Kokkola
Rovaniemi
Inarijärvi
Ivalo
Kirkenes
Vadsø
Vardø
Varangerfjorden
Varangerhalvøya
Tanafjorden
Porsangen
Laksefjorden
Lyngen
Malangen
Ofotfjorden
Tysfjorden
Saltfjorden
Trondheimsfjorden
Kebnekaise
Torneträsk
Stora Lulevatten
Hornavan
Storuman
Lule älv
Torne älv
Skellefte älv
Ume älv
Ångermanälven
Pello
Kittilä
Sodankylä
Kemijärvi
Karasjok
Kautokeino
Utsjoki

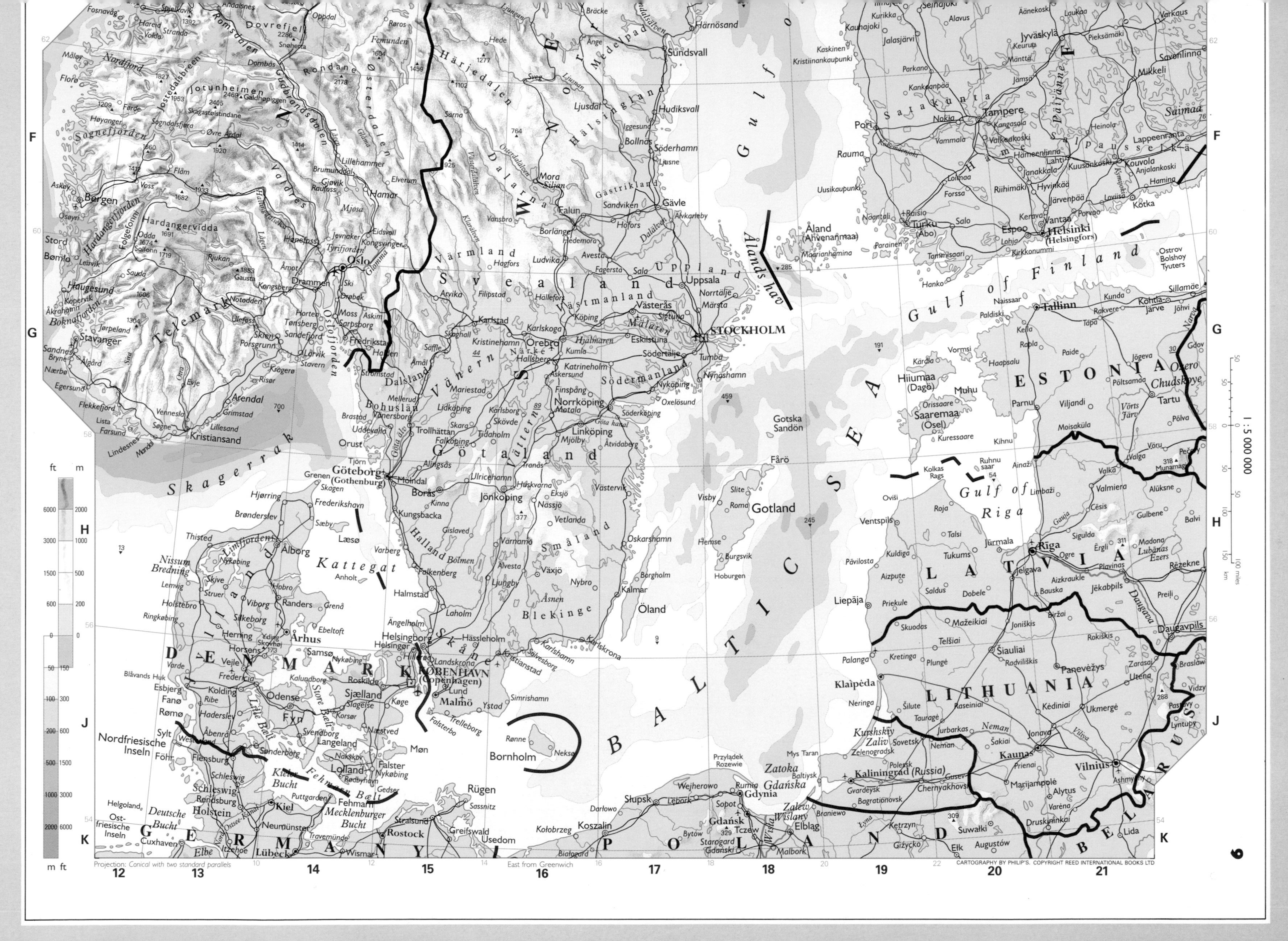

1 : 5 000 000
50 0 50 100 miles
50 0 50 100 150 km
9
NORWAY
SWEDEN
FINLAND
ESTONIA
LATVIA
LITHUANIA
BELARUS
POLAND
GERMANY
DENMARK
BALTIC SEA
Gulf of Bothnia
Gulf of Finland
Gulf of Riga
Ålands hav
Skagerrak
Kattegat
Zatoka Gdańska
Kurshskiy Zaliv
Zalew Wiślany
Fehmarn Bælt
Store Bælt
Lille Bælt
Kieler Bucht
Mecklenburger Bucht
Deutsche Bucht
Chudskoye Ozero
Oslofjorden
Sognefjorden
Hardangerfjorden
Nordfjord
Hardangervidda
Jotunheimen
Dovrefjell
Rondane
Telemark
Valdres
Gudbrandsdalen
Østerdalen
Härjedalen
Dalarna
Värmland
Svealand
Götaland
Uppland
Västmanland
Södermanland
Småland
Blekinge
Skåne
Halland
Bohuslän
Dalsland
Gästrikland
Hälsingland
Medelpad
Satakunta
Häme
Salpausselkä
Saimaa
Päijänne
Vänern
Vättern
Mälaren
Hjälmaren
Jylland
Sjælland
Fyn
Lolland
Falster
Møn
Bornholm
Gotland
Öland
Gotska Sandön
Fårö
Åland (Ahvenanmaa)
Hiiumaa (Dagö)
Saaremaa (Ösel)
Muhu
Rügen
Usedom
Nordfriesische Inseln
Ostfriesische Inseln
STOCKHOLM
Oslo
København (Copenhagen)
Helsinki (Helsingfors)
Tallinn
Riga
Vilnius
Göteborg (Gothenburg)
Malmö
Bergen
Stavanger
Kristiansand
Turku (Åbo)
Tampere
Tartu
Kaunas
Klaipėda
Liepāja
Daugavpils
Kaliningrad (Russia)
Gdańsk
Gdynia
Kiel
Lübeck
Rostock
Århus
Ålborg
Odense
Uppsala
Västerås
Örebro
Norrköping
Linköping
Jönköping
Gävle
Sundsvall
Projection: Conical with two standard parallels
East from Greenwich
CARTOGRAPHY BY PHILIP'S. COPYRIGHT REED INTERNATIONAL BOOKS LTD
ft m
6000 2000
3000 1000
1500 500
600 200
0 0
150 50
300 100
600 200
1500 500
3000 1000
6000 2000
m ft

English Unitary Authorities
(from April 1996)

12. Hartlepool
13. Stockton-on-Tees
14. Middlesbrough
15. Redcar and Cleveland
16. Darlington
17. City of York
18. Kingston upon Hull
19. Stoke-on-Trent
20. Derby City
21. Leicester City
22. Rutland
23. Milton Keynes
24. Luton
25. Thamesdown
26. South Gloucester
27. City and County of Bristol
28. North Somerset
29. Bath and N.E. Somerset
30. Southampton
31. Portsmouth
32. Brighton and Hove
33. Bournemouth
34. Poole

Welsh Unitary Authorities
(from April 1996)

1. Neath Port Talbot
2. Rhondda Cynon Taff
3. Bridgend
4. Merthyr Tydfil
5. Caerphilly
6. Vale of Glamorgan
7. Cardiff
8. Blaenau Gwent
9. Torfaen
10. Newport
11. Monmouthshire

NORTH SEA

IRISH SEA

North Channel

SCOTLAND

NORTHUMBERLAND

DURHAM

N. YORKSHIRE

EAST RIDING OF YORKSHIRE

LANCASHIRE

MERSEYSIDE

CHESHIRE

DERBY

NOTT

LINCOLN

GWYNEDD

ANGLESEY

ISLE OF MAN

Edinburgh · Glasgow · Paisley · Dumfries · Carlisle · Newcastle · Sunderland · Middlesbrough · Hartlepool · Scarborough · Whitby · Kingston upon Hull · Lincoln · Leeds · Bradford · Sheffield · Manchester · Liverpool · Blackpool · Preston · Lancaster · Barrow · Workington · Belfast · Douglas

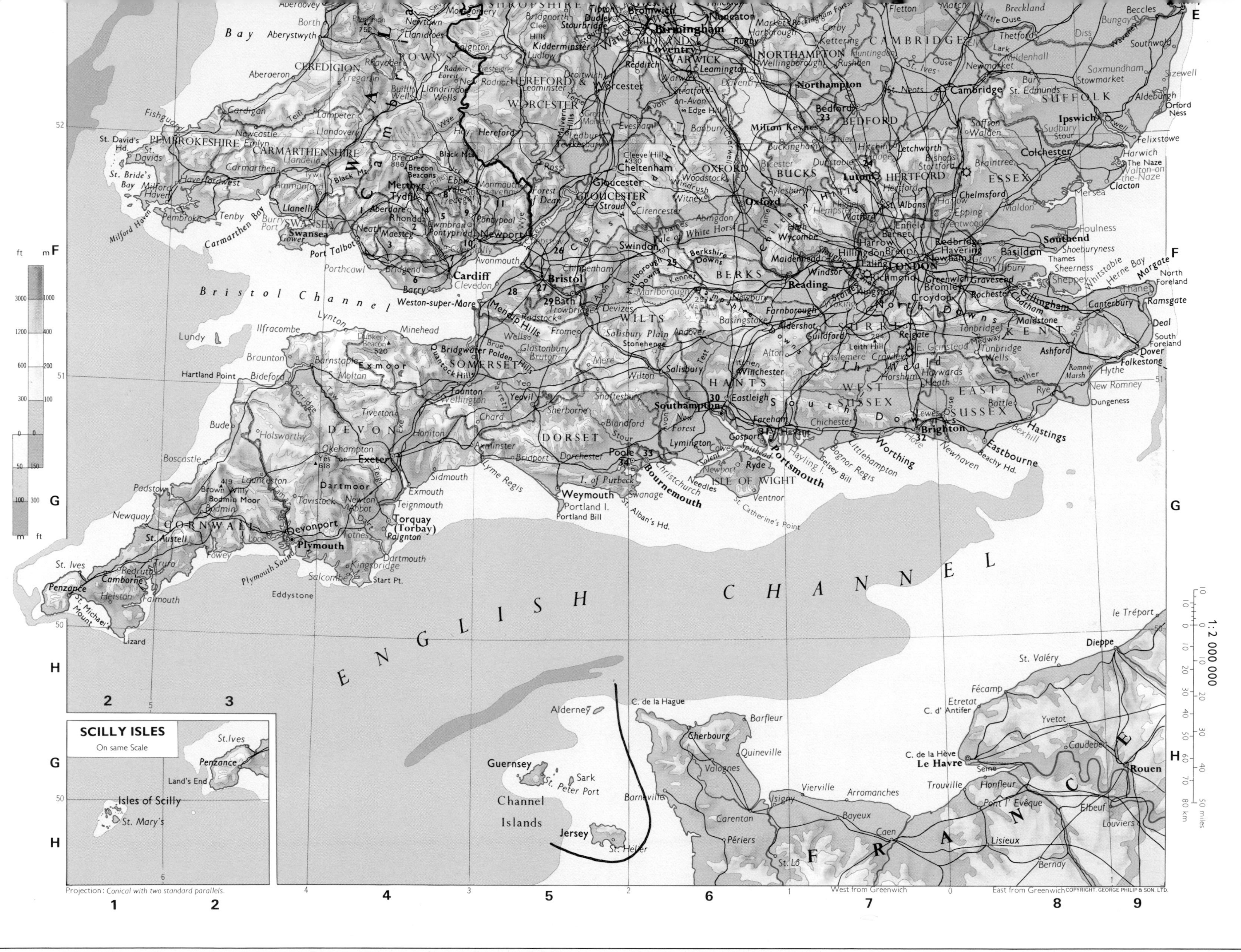

1 : 2 000 000

10   0   10   20   30   40   50 miles
10   0   10   20   30   40   50   60   70   80 km

East from Greenwich. COPYRIGHT GEORGE PHILIP & SON LTD.

E N G L I S H   C H A N N E L

F R A N C E

Rouen
Dieppe
le Tréport
St. Valéry
Fécamp
Yvetot
Caudebec
Étretat
C. d'Antifer
C. de la Hève
Le Havre
Honfleur
Trouville
Port l'Évêque
Lisieux
Louviers
Brionne
Bernay
Pont-Audemer
Seine

Alderney
C. de la Hague
Cherbourg
Valognes
Quineville
Carentan
Barfleur
St. Vaast
Périers
St. Lô
Coutances
Isigny
Bayeux
Caen
Arromanches
Vierville
Barneville

Guernsey
St. Peter Port
Sark
Jersey
St. Helier
Channel Islands

SUFFOLK
Beccles
Southwold
Bungay
Diss
Stowmarket
Saxmundham
Aldeburgh
Sizewell
Orford Ness
Harwich
The Naze
Walton-on-the-Naze
Felixstowe
Ipswich
Woodbridge
Clacton
Mersea I.
Foulness
Colchester
ESSEX
Braintree
Chelmsford
Maldon
Southend
Shoeburyness
Basildon
Havering
Margate
North Foreland
Ramsgate
Deal
Dover
Folkestone
Hythe
New Romney
Dungeness
Rye
Hastings
Bexhill
Battle
Eastbourne
Beachy Hd.

CAMBRIDGE
Cambridge
St. Edmunds
Newmarket
BEDFORD
Bedford
Luton
HERTFORD
St. Albans
LONDON
Windsor
Reading
BERKS
Berkshire Downs
WILTS
Swindon
Marlborough
Devizes
Salisbury Plain
Salisbury
Stonehenge
DORSET
Dorchester
Weymouth
Portland I.
Portland Bill
Poole
Bournemouth
Christchurch
ISLE OF WIGHT
Newport
Ryde
Ventnor
Portsmouth
Gosport
Fareham
HANTS
Southampton
Winchester
Eastleigh
Worthing
Brighton
WEST SUSSEX
Chichester
Bognor Regis
Littlehampton
Selsey Bill
Hayling I.
EAST SUSSEX

SCILLY ISLES
On same Scale

SCILLY ISLES
On same Scale

Isles of Scilly
St. Mary's

St. Ives
Penzance
Land's End

DEVON
Exeter
Dartmoor
Plymouth
Devonport
Torquay (Torbay)
Paignton
Exmouth
Sidmouth
CORNWALL
Bodmin Moor
Newquay
St. Austell
Truro
Redruth
Camborne
Helston
St. Michael's Mount
Lizard
Penzance
St. Ives

SOMERSET
Taunton
Bridgwater
Weston-super-Mare
Clevedon
Cardiff
Newport
Mendip Hills
Bristol
Bath
GLOUCESTER
Cheltenham
Stroud
Cirencester
Gloucester

WALES
Swansea
Llanelli
CARMARTHENSHIRE
PEMBROKESHIRE
Milford Haven
Tenby
CEREDIGION
Aberystwyth
Cardigan Bay

Projection: Conical with two standard parallels.
West from Greenwich

G   H

1:2 000 000

10 0 10 20 30 40 50 miles
10 0 10 20 30 40 50 60 70 80 km

Scottish Local Authorities
(From April 1996)
1. City of Aberdeen
2. Dundee City
3. West Dunbartonshire
4. East Dunbartonshire
5. City of Glasgow
6. Inverclyde
7. Renfrewshire
8. East Renfrewshire
9. North Lanarkshire
10. Falkirk
11. Clackmannan
12. West Lothian
13. City of Edinburgh
14. Midlothian

ORKNEY IS.
On same scale

Westray
Rousay
Eday
Sanday
Stronsay
Shapinsay
Mainland
ORKNEY
Stromness
Kirkwall
Scapa Flow
Hoy
South Ronaldsay
Pentland Firth
Dunnet Hd.
J. o' Groats
North Ronaldsay

SHETLAND IS.
On same scale
Unst
Yell Sound
Yell
Fetlar
Whalsay
SHETLAND
Mainland
Bressay
Scalloway
Lerwick
Foula
Sumburgh Hd.

ATLANTIC OCEAN

WESTERN ISLES
Flannan Is.
Butt of Lewis
L. Roag
Stornoway
Broad Bay
Lewis
Eye Pen.
Tarbert
L. Seaforth
Harris
Sound of Harris
North Uist
Lochmaddy
Monach Is.
Benbecula
South Uist
Ben More 620
Lochboisdale
Sound of Barra
Barra
Barra Hd.

Inner Hebrides
Outer Hebrides
North Minch
Little Minch
The Minch

C. Wrath
Durness
Cape Wrath
Faraid Hd.
Kyle of Durness
Strathy Pt.
Tongue
Halladale
Dunnet Hd.
Dounreay
Thurso
Wick
Noss Hd.
Pentland Firth
John o' Groats

Ben Hope 927
Reay Forest
Ben Loyal
Naver
L. Laxford
Eddrachillis Bay
Lochinver
Enard Bay
L. Assynt
B. More Assynt
Loch Shin
Lairg
Helmsdale
Ord of Caithness
Helmsdale
Lybster

Ullapool
L. Broom
Oykel
Brora
Golspie
Dornoch
Dornoch Firth
Tain
Tarbat Ness
Moray Firth
Lossiemouth
Cullen
Portsoy
Banff
Macduff
Kinnaird's Head
Fraserburgh
Rattray Head
Peterhead
Buchan Ness

Fannich
B. Dearg 1081
Conon
Dingwall
Beauly
Inverness
Culloden Moor
Nairn
Forres
Elgin
Keith
Turriff
Deveron
Ythan
Elon
BUCHAN
Rubha Hunish
Trotternish
L. Gairloch
L. Maree
Strathpeffer
Fortrose
Cromarty
Ben Wyvis 1045
Invergordon

Rona
Raasay
Portree
Sound of Raasay
Scalpay
Kyle of Lochalsh
Stromeferry
Dornie
L. Torridon
L. Bracadale
Cuillin Hills
Cuillin Sound
Canna
Rhum
Eigg
Muck
Coll
Tiree
Staffa
Iona
Mull
Ben More 966
Tobermory
Sound of Mull
Morvern

HIGHLAND
WEST HIGHLANDS
Loch Ness
Glen Affric
Glen Moriston
Fort Augustus
L. Garry
Glen Garry
Glen Spean
L. Oich
L. Lochy
Spean
Loch Linnhe
Ben Nevis 1343
Fort William
Ardgour
Pt. of Ardnamurchan
Arisaig
Mallaig
Morar
L. Morar
L. Eil
L. Shiel
Glenfinnan
L. Moidart
L. Sunart

Farrar
Monadhliath Mts.
Aviemore
Grantown-on-Spey
Kingussie
Newtonmore
Cairn Gorm
Cairngorm Mts. 1245
Cairn Toul 1293
Ben Macdhui 1311
Braemar
Balmoral
Lochnagar
Forest of Atholl
Blair Atholl
Pass of Killiecrankie
Pitlochry
L. Rannoch
L. Tummel
Rannoch Moor
Glen Coe
Ballachulish

MORAY
Dufftown
Huntly
Tomintoul
Alford
Don
Inverurie
ABERDEENSHIRE
Aboyne
Ballater
Banchory
Stonehaven
Inverbervie
Laurencekirk
Aberdeen
Girdle Ness
GRAMPIAN HIGHLANDS
Badenoch
Braes of Angus
ANGUS
Brechin
Montrose
N. Esk
S. Esk
Kirriemuir
Forfar
Arbroath
Broughty Ferry

ARGYLL & BUTE
Oban
Firth of Lorn
Colonsay
Crinan
Lochgilphead
L. Awe
Inveraray
Ben Cruachan 1124
Ben More 1174
Ben Vorlich 983
L. Katrine
Trossachs
Callander
Crieff
PERTH
Aberfeldy
Ben Lawers 1214
L. Tay
Breadalbane
Killin
KINROSS
Dunkeld
Blairgowrie
Alyth
Sidlaw Hills
Scone
Perth
Dundee
Tay
Firth of Tay
Tayport
Newport
St. Andrews
Fife Ness
Anstruther
Crail
Cupar
FIFE
Leven
Glenrothes
Buckhaven
Kirkcaldy
Markinch
Loch Leven
Kinross

STIRLING
Dunblane
Bridge of Allan
Bannockburn
Stirling
Alloa
Dunfermline
Rosyth
Forth
North Berwick
Bass Rock
Dunbar
St. Abbs Hd.
Eyemouth
Berwick-upon-Tweed

L. Lomond
Ben Lomond 974
Helensburgh
Dumbarton
Clydebank
Cumbernauld
Kilsyth
Grangemouth
Falkirk
Linlithgow
Bathgate
Livingston
Edinburgh
Leith
Musselburgh
Haddington
EAST LOTHIAN
Pentland Hills
Penicuik
WEST LOTHIAN
Dunoon
Greenock
Port Glasgow
Paisley
Johnstone
Glasgow
Rutherglen
Airdrie
Coatbridge
Motherwell
Wishaw
Hamilton
E. Kilbride
Carstairs
SOUTH LANARKSHIRE
Lanark
Biggar
Peebles
Moorfoot Hills
Lammermuir Hills
Duns
Galashiels
Melrose
Kelso
Coldstream
Selkirk
Jedburgh
Hawick
The Cheviot 816
BORDERS
Broad Law 840
Tweed

NORTH AYRSHIRE
Dumoon
Rothesay
Bute
Largs
Ardrossan
Saltcoats
Irvine
Kilmarnock
EAST AYRSHIRE
Troon
Prestwick
Ayr
SOUTH AYRSHIRE
Cumnock
Goat Fell 874
Arran
Brodick
Kilbride

Kintyre
Tarbert
Gigha
Jura
Sound of Jura
Islay
Bowmore
Port Ellen
Rubh a' Mhail
Rathlin
Fair Hd.
Ballycastle
Campbeltown
Mull of Kintyre
Ailsa Craig
Girvan
Ballymena
Larne
Portrush
Trostan 554
NORTHERN IRELAND
Belfast
Belfast Lough
Bangor
Newtownards
North Channel
Firth of Clyde

Dalmellington
Sanquhar
Leadhills
Moffat
Langholm
Lockerbie
Gretna
Merrick 843
DUMFRIES AND GALLOWAY
Dumfries
Annan
SOUTHERN UPLANDS
South of Galloway
Stranraer
Portpatrick
Newton Stewart
Castle Douglas
Dalbeattie
Kirkcudbright
Wigtown
Whithorn
Luce Bay
Mull of Galloway
Wigtown Bay
Solway Firth
Workington
Carlisle
HADRIAN'S WALL
Hexham
ENGLAND
Penrith
Skiddaw 931
Ullswater
Cross Fell 893
Cumbrian Mts.
Alston
N. Tyne
S. Tyne
Wear
Tees
Barnard Castle
Derwent
Flodden

NORTH SEA

West from Greenwich

Projection: Conical with two standard parallels.

ft m
3000 1000
1200 400
600 200
300
0
50 150
100 300
m ft

1:2 000 000

10   0   10   20   30   40   50 miles
10   0   10   20   30   40   50   60   70   80 km

1   2   3   4   5   6

A

B

C

D

E

ATLANTIC OCEAN

IRISH SEA

St. Georges Channel

North Channel

Kintyre   Arran
Campbeltown
Rathlin I.   Ailsa Craig
Mull of Kintyre
Fair Hd.
Stranraer
Portpatrick
I. Magee

Malin Hd.
Lough Swilly
Tory I.   Horn Hd.
Sheep Haven
Carndonagh
Inishowen Pen.
Moville
Buncrana
Bloody Foreland
Giant's Causeway
Portrush
Coleraine   Ballymoney   Ballycastle
Limavady   △554 Trostan
Gweedore Mts.
△752 Errigal
Derryveagh Mts.
Aran I.
Letterkenny
Londonderry   Sperrin Mts.
Sawel 683
Ballymena
Larne
DONEGAL   Strabane
Magherafelt   Antrim
Gweebarra B.
Finn   Lifford
Glenties
Bluestack 676
Cookstown
Lough Neagh
Belfast   Belfast L.
Carrickfergus   Bangor   Donaghadee
Rossan Pt.   Killybegs   Mourne
Donegal   Derg
NORTHERN IRELAND   Lisburn   Newtownards
Downpatrick Hd.   Killala Hd.   Dungannon   Lurgan (Craigavon)   Ards Pen.
Donegal Bay   Ballyshannon   L. Omagh   Portadown
Broad Haven   Bundoran   Banbridge   7
Erris Hd.   Enniskillen   Lower L. Erne   Armagh   Downpatrick   Dundrum
Belmullet   Killala B.   1   Slieve Donard 852   Newcastle
Mullet Peninsula   Sligo B.   Sligo   Monaghan   Newry   Mourne Mts.   Dundrum Bay
Killala   Collooney   Upper L. Erne   Sl. Gullion 577   8   Warrenpoint
Ballina   Clones   Castleblayney   Carlingford L.
Achill Hd.   Moy   Ox Mts.   Allen   Leitrim   Arrow   Belturbet   Annalee   Cootehill   Greenore   Dundalk
Achill I.   L. Conn   Nephin 806   **CAVAN**   Carrickmacross   Dundalk Bay
MAYO   Castlebar   Roscommon   Carrick-on-Shannon   Cavan   Kingscourt   Louth   **LOUTH**   Ardee
Clare I.   Clew Bay   L. Gowna   Oldcastle   Ceanannas Mor (Kells)
Croagh Patrick △765   **CONNACHT**   Castlerea   L. Sheelin
Westport   Granard   Longford   An Uaimh (Navan)   Drogheda
Killary Harbour   Mweelrea △819   **ROSCOMMON**   **LONGFORD**   Athboy   Trim   Boyne   Balbriggan
Inishbofin   L. Mask   Ballinrobe   Robe   L. Ree   **MEATH**   Swords
Twelve Pins   Claremorris   Mullingar   Maynooth   Lambay I.
Clifden   Tuam   **WESTMEATH**   **DUBLIN**   Ireland's Eye
Connemara   L. Corrib   Athlone   Howth Head
Slyne Hd.   **GALWAY**   **IRELAND**   Clara   Edenderry   **Dublin** (Baile Atha Cliath)   Dublin Bay
Ballinasloe   Clara   Daingean   Droichead Nua   Celbridge   **Dun Laoghaire**
Galway   Athenry   Clare   Tullamore   Naas   Bray
Galway Bay   Loughrea   Brosna   **OFFALY**   Kildare   Kippure 754
Inishmore   Portumna   Birr   Mountmellick   Poulaphouca Res.
Aran Is.   Slieve Aughty   **L. SL BLOOM**   Portarlington   Port Laoise   **KILDARE**
Kilkieran B.   Gort   L. Derg   **LEINSTER**   Wicklow
Hags Hd.   Ennistymon   **LAOIS**   Athy   Lugnaquilla 923   Wicklow Hd.
Liscannor Bay   Rossa   Carlow   Rathdrum
Mal Bay   **CLARE**   Killaloe   Nenagh   Templemore   **CARLOW**   Mizen Hd.
Miltown Malbay   Ennis   Ballina   Keeper 694   Tullow   Shillelagh   Arklow
Kilkee   Ardnacrusha   Thurles   Muine Bheag   Gorey
Loop Hd.   Kilrush   Limerick   **TIPPERARY**   Cashel   **KILKENNY**   Mt. Leinster 796   Enniscorthy
R. Shannon   Foynes   Slievenamon   **KILKENNY**   **WEXFORD**
Kerry Hd.   Listowel   **LIMERICK**   Golden Vale   Kilkenny   Callan   Cahore Pt.
Tralee Bay   Rathkeale   Newcastle   **Tipperary**   Clonmel   Carrick-on-Suir   New Ross
Brandon Bay   Tralee   Rath Luirc (Charleville)   Galtymore 920   Galtee Mts.   Slievenamon   **Wexford**   Wexford Harbour
Brandon Mt. 953   **MUNSTER**   Newmarket   Mitchelstown   Knockmealdown Mts.   Comeragh Mts.   Rosslare   Greenore Pt.
Dingle   Slieve Mish   **KERRY**   Kanturk   Mallow   Fermoy   **WATERFORD**   **Waterford**   Tramore   Tuscar Rock
Dingle Bay   Maine   Blackwater   Lismore   Dungarvan   Carnsore Pt.
Valencia Harbour   Killarney   Boggeragh Mts.   Macroom   Youghal   Saltee Is.   St. David's Hd.
Valencia I.   Cahirciveen   Macgillycuddy's Reeks   Lakes of Killarney   Blarney   **Cork**   Youghal Harbour   Hook Hd.   Waterford Harbour
Skellig Rocks   Carrauntuohill 1040   Kenmare   **CORK**   Lee   Midleton   Cobh
Ballinskelligs B.   Caha Mts.   Glengarriff   Passage West   Cork Harbour
Castletown Bearhaven   Kenmare River   Bandon   Crosshaven   Kinsale
Crow Hd.   Bear I.   Bantry   Clonakilty   Kinsale
Dunmanus Hd.   Bantry Bay   Skull   Skibbereen   Old Head of Kinsale
Mizen Hd.   Fastnet Rock   Baltimore   Clear I.   Galley Hd.   C. Clear

Towns underlined in Northern Ireland give their names to the Districts in which they stand
The remaining Districts are:—
1 Fermanagh   5 Castlereagh
2 Moyle   6 Ards
3 Newtownabbey   7 Down
4 North Down   8 Newry & Mourne

ft   m
3000   1000
1200   400
600   200
300   100
0   0
100   300
200   600
m   ft

Projection: Conical with two standard parallels.
West from Greenwich
COPYRIGHT. GEORGE PHILIP & SON. LTD.

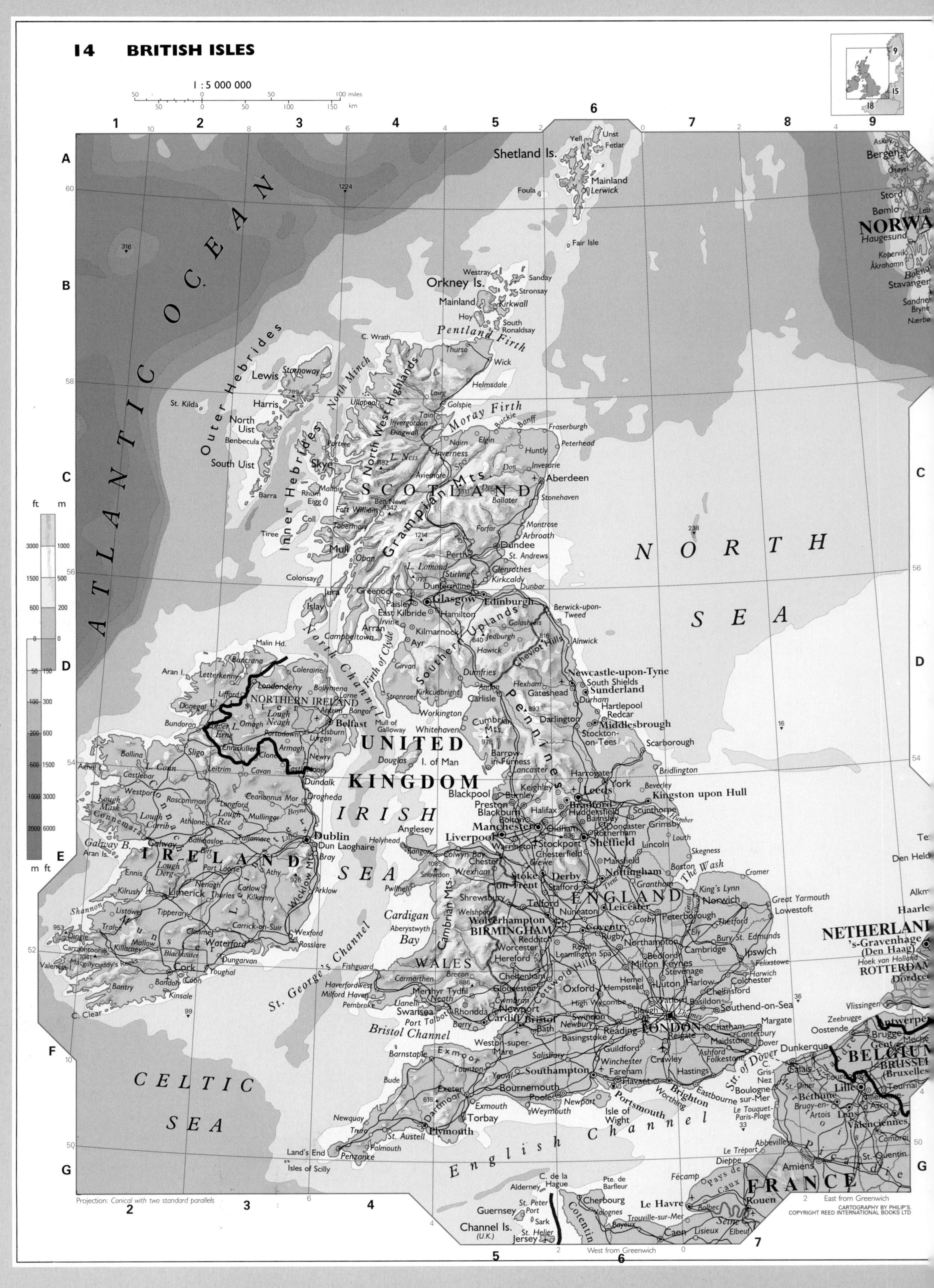

1 : 5 000 000

50   0   50   100 miles

50   0   50   100   150
km

ATLANTIC OCEAN

Shetland Is.
Yell Unst Fetlar
Foula Mainland
Lerwick
Fair Isle

Orkney Is.
Westray Sanday
Mainland Stronsay
Kirkwall
Hoy South
Ronaldsay

C. Wrath
Pentland Firth
Thurso
Wick
Helmsdale
Golspie
Lewis Stornoway
Laing
Outer Hebrides
Harris
St. Kilda
North Minch
Ullapool
Moray Firth
North West Highlands
Invergordon Nairn Buckie Fraserburgh
North Dingwall Banff
Uist Inverness Elgin Peterhead
Benbecula L. Ness Huntly
South Uist Skye Aviemore Inverurie
Barra Aberdeen
Rhum Fort William Ben Nevis 1342 SCOTLAND Ballater Stonehaven
Eigg Grampian Mts.
Coll Mull 1214 Forfar Montrose
Tiree Oban Perth St. Andrews Arbroath
Colonsay L. Lomond Stirling Dundee
Islay Jura Glenrothes
Greenock Dunfermline Kirkcaldy
Paisley Glasgow Edinburgh Dunbar
East Kilbride Hamilton Berwick-upon-Tweed
Arran Kilmarnock Southern Uplands Galashiels
Campbeltown Irvine Hawick Cheviot Hills Alnwick
Ayr Jedburgh
Malin Hd. Girvan Dumfries Newcastle-upon-Tyne
Buncrana Kirkcudbright South Shields
Londonderry North Channel Stranraer Annan Hexham Gateshead Sunderland
Coleraine Carlisle Durham
Aran I. Ballymena Larne Pennines Hartlepool
Letterkenny Antrim Workington Redcar
Lifford NORTHERN IRELAND Bangor Cumbrian Darlington Middlesbrough
Donegal Omagh Lough Belfast Whitehaven Mts. Stockton-on-Tees
Neagh Lisburn Scarborough
Bundoran Enniskillen Lurgan Barrow-in-Furness Bridlington
L. Erne Portadown Douglas
Ballina Sligo Armagh I. of Man Harrogate
Leitrim Newry UNITED York Beverley
Castlebar Cavan Dundalk Blackpool Leeds Kingston upon Hull
Lough Roscommon KINGDOM Preston Bradford
Conn Drogheda Burnley Halifax Huddersfield Doncaster Grimsby
Westport Longford Boyne IRISH Blackburn Bolton Barnsley Scunthorpe
Lough Athlone Dublin SEA Anglesey Liverpool Manchester Oldham Rotherham Lincoln Louth
Mask Ballinasloe Mullingar Dun Laoghaire Stockport Sheffield
Lough Bray Bangor Holyhead Chester Crewe Chesterfield Skegness
Galway B. Corrib Ceanannus Mor Colwyn Bay Mansfield Boston The Wash
Galway Tullamore Snowdon Wrexham Stoke- Derby Nottingham
Aran Is. Lough Birr Wicklow Mts. on-Trent Granth am King's Lynn Cromer
Ennis Ree Arklow Stafford Trent
Kilrush Nenagh Carlow Kilkenny Shrewsbury Telford ENGLAND Leicester Norwich Great Yarmouth
Limerick Thurles Cambrian Mts. Nuneaton Peterborough Lowestoft
Listowel Tipperary Clonmel Wexford Welshpool Wolverhampton Corby
Tralee Carrick-on-Suir Cardigan Aberystwyth BIRMINGHAM Coventry Rugby Northampton Thetford
Dingle Mallow Bay Redditch Bedford Cambridge Ipswich
Killarney Blackwater Worcester Royal Bury St. Edmunds
Carrauntoohill Waterford Hereford Leamington Spa Milton Keynes Felixstowe
Macgillycuddy's Reeks Dungarvan WALES Cheltenham Harwich
Kilkenny Gloucester Oxford Hemel Colchester
Cork Merthyr Tydfil Cwmbran Hempstead Luton Harlow Chelmsford
Valencia Youghal Carmarthen Neath Cotswold Hills High Wycombe Stevenage
Bandon Milford Haven Llanelli Rhondda Newport Slough Watford Southend-on-Sea
Kinsale Haverfordwest Swansea Cardiff Bristol Reading LONDON
Bantry Pembroke Port Talbot Barry Bath Newbury Basildon
C. Clear St. George's Channel Fishguard Weston-super- Swindon Basingstoke Reigate Maidstone Margate
Mare Bristol Channel Guildford Chatham Canterbury Dover
Barnstaple Exmoor Salisbury Winchester Crawley Ashford Folkestone
CELTIC Bude Taunton Yeovil Fareham Brighton Hastings Str. of Dover
Southampton Havant Worthing Eastbourne Boulogne
SEA Exeter Bournemouth Poole Portsmouth
Newquay Dartmoor Exmouth Weymouth Isle of Wight English Channel
Truro St. Austell Plymouth Torbay Newport
Land's End Falmouth
Penzance
Isles of Scilly

ENGLISH CHANNEL

NORTH
SEA

BERGEN
NORWAY
Haugesund
Kopervik
Åkrahamn
Stord
Bømlo
Stavanger
Sandnes
Bryne
Nærbø

NETHERLAND
Haarle
's-Gravenhage
(Den Haag)
Hoek van Holland
ROTTERDAM
Dordrec

BELGIUM
Brussel
Bruxelles
Antwerp
Gent
Brugge
Oostende
Zeebrugge
Vlissingen

Calais
Dunkerque
Gris Nez
St-Omer
Béthune
Lens
Lille
Tournai
Valenciennes
Cambrai
St. Quentin

FRANCE
C. de la Hague
Pte. de Barfleur
Cherbourg
St. Peter Port
Guernsey
Sark
Jersey
St. Helier
Channel Is. (U.K.)
Cotentin
Valognes
Bayeux
Caen
Lisieux
Le Havre
Trouville-sur-Mer
Bolbec
Rouen
Seine
Elbeuf
Pays de Caux
Fécamp
Le Tréport
Dieppe
Abbeville
Amiens
Picardie
Le Touquet-Paris-Plage
Bruay-en-Artois
Doullens

West from Greenwich   East from Greenwich

CARTOGRAPHY BY PHILIP'S
COPYRIGHT REED INTERNATIONAL BOOKS LTD

Projection: Conical with two standard parallels

ft   m
3000   1000
1500   500
600   200
0   0
50   150
100   300
200   600
500   1500
1000   3000
2000   6000
m   ft

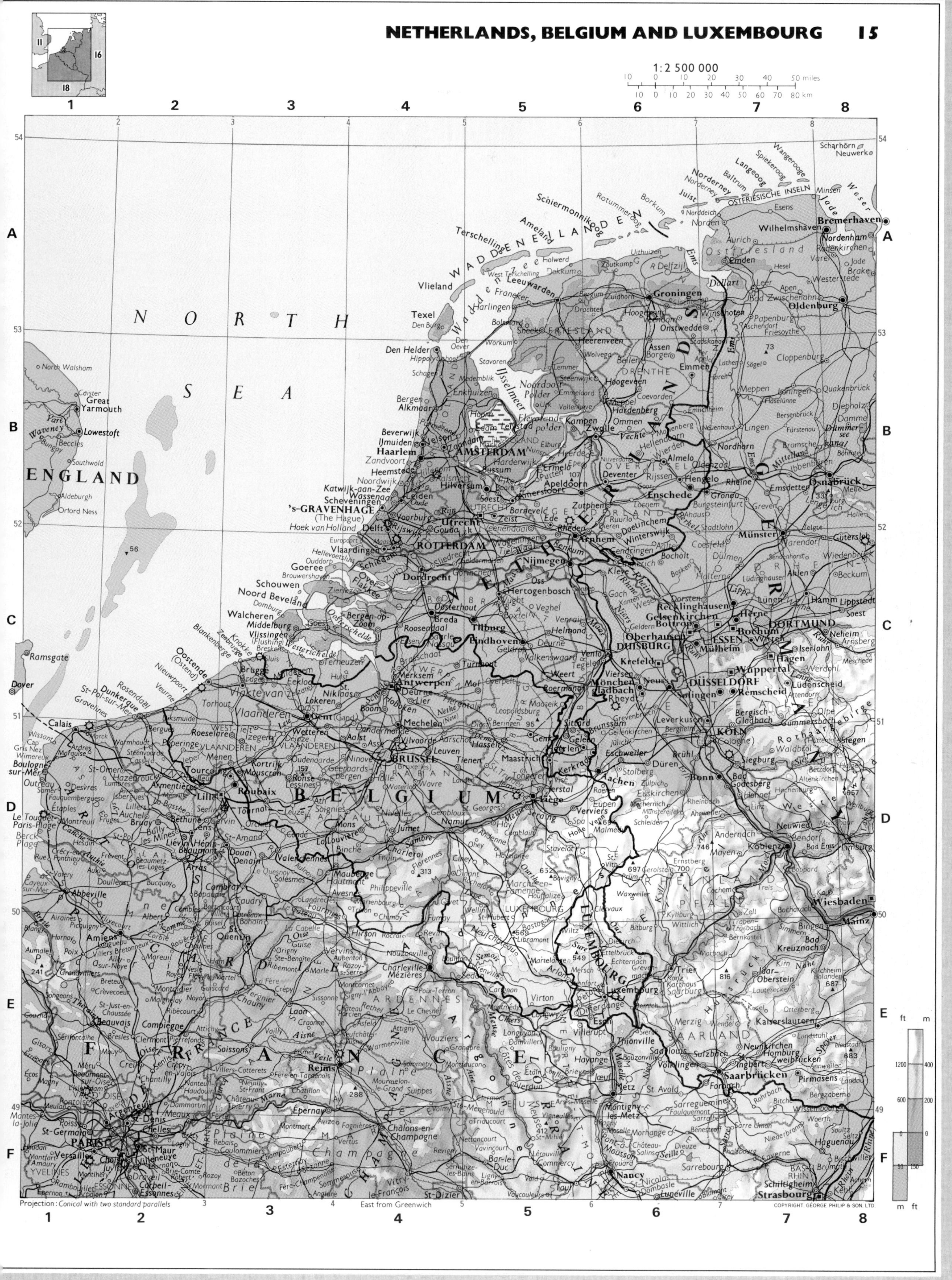
1:2 500 000
miles
km
NORTH SEA
ENGLAND
NETHERLANDS
BELGIUM
LUXEMBOURG
FRANCE
GERMANY
WADDENZEE
WADDENEILANDEN
IJsselmeer
Texel
Vlieland
Terschelling
Ameland
Schiermonnikoog
Borkum
Juist
Norderney
Baltrum
Langeoog
Spiekeroog
Wangerooge
OSTFRIESISCHE INSELN
AMSTERDAM
'S-GRAVENHAGE
(The Hague)
ROTTERDAM
Utrecht
Haarlem
Leiden
Delft
Hoek van Holland
Dordrecht
Breda
Tilburg
Eindhoven
Nijmegen
Arnhem
Apeldoorn
Zwolle
Deventer
Enschede
Hengelo
Almelo
Groningen
Leeuwarden
Den Helder
Alkmaar
Hilversum
Amersfoort
Maastricht
Middelburg
Vlissingen
(Flushing)
Oostende
(Ostend)
Brugge
Gent
Antwerpen
Mechelen
Leuven
BRUSSEL
Liège
Namur
Charleroi
Mons
Kortrijk
Luxembourg
Lille
Roubaix
Tourcoing
Calais
Dunkerque
Dover
Ramsgate
Lowestoft
Great Yarmouth
Amiens
Reims
Metz
Nancy
Strasbourg
Saarbrücken
Trier
Koblenz
Bonn
KÖLN
DÜSSELDORF
DUISBURG
ESSEN
DORTMUND
Wuppertal
Aachen
Münster
Osnabrück
Oldenburg
Emden
Bremerhaven
Wiesbaden
Mainz
PARIS
Versailles
SAARLAND
Projection: Conical with two standard parallels
East from Greenwich
COPYRIGHT. GEORGE PHILIP & SON, LTD.

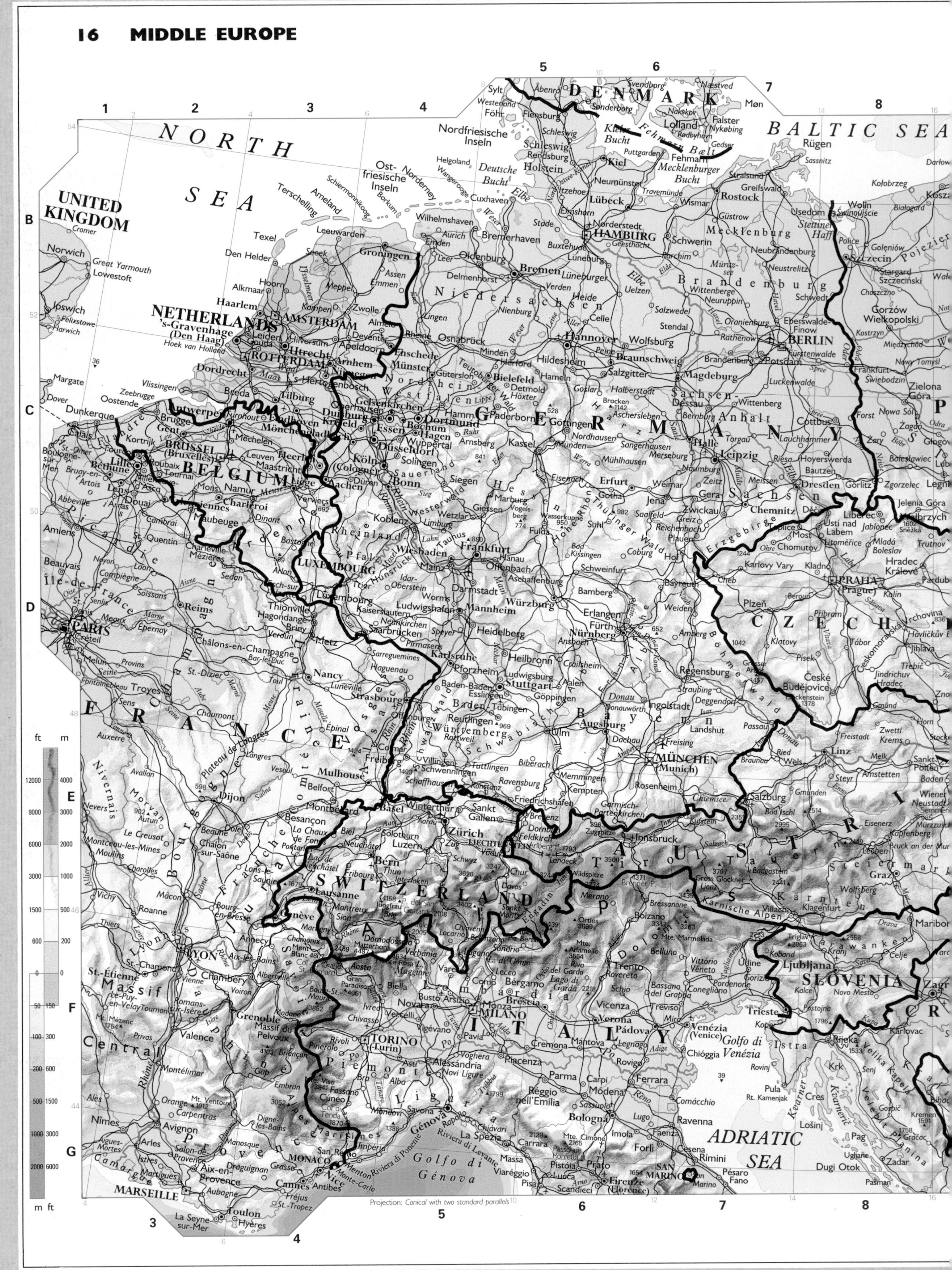
NORTH SEA
BALTIC SEA
UNITED KINGDOM
DENMARK
NETHERLANDS
BELGIUM
LUXEMBOURG
GERMANY
FRANCE
SWITZERLAND
LIECHTENSTEIN
AUSTRIA
ITALY
CZECH
SLOVENIA
MONACO
SAN MARINO
ADRIATIC SEA
Golfo di Génova
Golfo di Venézia
Deutsche Bucht
Kieler Bucht
Mecklenburger Bucht
Fehmarn Bælt
Nordfriesische Inseln
Ost-friesische Inseln
Niedersachsen
Nordrhein-Westfalen
Hessen
Rheinland-Pfalz
Baden-Württemberg
Bayern
Sachsen
Sachsen-Anhalt
Brandenburg
Mecklenburg
Thüringer Wald
Schwarzwald
Schwäbische Alb
Böhmerwald
Erzgebirge
Harz
Ardennes
Picardie
Île-de-France
Champagne
Lorraine
Alsace
Bourgogne
Franche-Comté
Jura
Plateau de Langres
Massif Central
Morvan
Nivernais
Lyonnais
Dauphiné
Savoie
Provence
Alpes Maritimes
Piemonte
Liguria
Lombardia
Dolomiti
Tirol
Tauern
Steiermark
Kärnten
Karawanken
Karnische Alpen
Istra
Velika Kapela
Velebit planina
Riviera di Ponente
Riviera di Levante
AMSTERDAM
's-Gravenhage (Den Haag)
ROTTERDAM
BRUSSEL (Bruxelles)
PARIS
BERLIN
HAMBURG
MÜNCHEN (Munich)
PRAHA (Prague)
LYON
MILANO
TORINO (Turin)
MARSEILLE
Frankfurt
Köln (Cologne)
Düsseldorf
Stuttgart
Zürich
Bern
Genève
Innsbruck
Salzburg
Linz
Graz
Ljubljana
Venézia (Venice)
Génova
Bologna
Firenze (Florence)
Nice
Strasbourg
Dijon
Leipzig
Dresden
Hannover
Bremen
Nürnberg
Projection: Conical with two standard parallels
ft m
12000 4000
9000 3000
6000 2000
3000 1000
1500 500
600 200
0 0
50 150
100 300
200 600
500 1500
1000 3000
2000 6000
m ft

1:5 000 000

50 0 50 100 miles
50 0 50 100 150 km

9 10 11 12 13 14 15 16

LITHUANIA
BELARUS

Zatoka Gdańska
Wejherowo Rumia Baltiysk
Sopot Gdynia
Lębork Gdańsk Tczew Elblag Zalew Wiślany
Bytów 329 Braniewo Żyna Ketrzyn Giżycko Suwałki
Chojnice Starogard Gdański Malbork Kwidzyn Iława Ostróda 309 Ełk Augustów
Świecie Grudziądz Brodnica Działdowo Narew Łomża Białystok Sokółka
Bydgoszcz Chełmno Pojezierze Mazurskie Szczytno Ostrołęka Ostrów Mazowiecka Hajnówka
Toruń Rypin Mława Ciechanów Pułtusk Bug Biała Podlaska Brest
Inowrocław Włocławek Płock Legionowo Mińsk Mazowiecki Siedlce Międzyrzec Podlaski Malaryta
Gniezno Września WARSZAWA (Warsaw) Otwock Łuków Wlodawa
Poznań Konin Koło Kutno Łowicz Pruszków Żyrardów Skierniewice Grójec Garwolin
Srem Turek Łódź Pabianice Tomaszów Mazowiecki Radom Puławy Lublin Chełm
Kościan Kalisz Zduńska Wola Sieradz Piotrków Trybunalski Kańskie Radomsko Starachowice Świdnik
Krotoszyn Ostrów Wielkopolski Wieluń Radomsko Kielce Ostrowiec-Świętokrzyski Sandomierz Kraśnik Zamość
Oleśnica Wrocław Opole Częstochowa Myszków Jędrzejów Pińczów Tarnobrzeg Stalowa Wola Novovolynsk
Brzeg Olawa Kluczbork Tarnowskie Góry Zawiercie Mielec Rzeszów Nowy Sącz

POLAND
UKRAINE

Zabrze Bytom Sosnowiec Katowice Tarnów Dębica Jarosław Przemyśl Lviv (Lvov)
Gliwice Chorzów Tychy Kraków Bochnia Jasło Krosno Sanok Ternopil Khmelnytskyy
Ostrava Frýdek-Místek Bielsko-Biała Żywiec Nowy Targ Zakopane Bardejov Prešov Humenné Ivano-Frankivsk Vinnytsya
Přerov Zlín Žilina Ružomberok Poprad Košice Uzhhorod Chernivtsi

SLOVAK REP.

Martin Nízke Tatry Banská Bystrica Zvolen Michalovce Mukacheve Chernivtsi
Trenčín Prievidza Topol'čany Levice Lučenec Chop Berehove Khust
Bratislava Nitra Nové Zámky Komárno Salgótarján Ózd Miskolc Satu Mare Baia Mare

HUNGARY
MOLDOVA

Győr Tatabánya Esztergom Vác Gyöngyös Eger Mezőkövesd Nyíregyháza Chișinău Tiraspol
Sopron BUDAPEST Jászberény Hajdúböszörmény Debrecen Iași Tighina
Székesfehérvár Cegléd Szolnok Karcág Oradea Cluj-Napoca Piatra Neamț
Veszprém Dunaújváros Kecskemét Nagykőrös Mezőtúr Dej Turda Tîrgu Mureș Bacău
Nagykanizsa Kiskunfélegyháza Csongrád Békéscsaba Salonta Zalău Alba-Iulia Bîrlad Cahul
Kaposvár Szekszárd Kiskőrös Kiskunhalas Szentes Gyula Orosháza Arad Sighișoara Vaslui Galați
Pécs Baja Hódmezővásárhely Makó Timișoara Deva Sibiu Brașov Focșani

ROMANIA

Szeged Subotica Kikinda Lugoj Hunedoara Caransebeș Petroșani Cîmpulung Buzău Brăila Tulcea
Novi Sad Zrenjanin Vršac Reșița Rîmnicu Vîlcea Tîrgoviște Ploiești Slobozia Constanța
Osijek Vukovar Vinkovci Vrbas Bela Crkva Turnu Severin Drăgășani Pitești BUCUREȘTI (Bucharest) Călărași
Slavonski Brod Sremska Mitrovica Pančevo Orșova Dobreta-Turnu-Severin Craiova Slatina Mangalia

YUGOSLAVIA
BULGARIA

BEOGRAD (Belgrade) Smederevo Požarevac Negotin Roșiori-de-Vede Alexandria Turnu Măgurele Giurgiu Ruse Dobrich
Šabac Valjevo Kragujevac Svetozarevo Bor Vidin Corabia Băilești Caracal Zimnicea Razgrad Varna

BOSNIA-HERZEGOVINA

Sarajevo Višegrad Tuzla Zenica

East from Greenwich

CARTOGRAPHY BY PHILIP'S. COPYRIGHT REED INTERNATIONAL BOOKS LTD

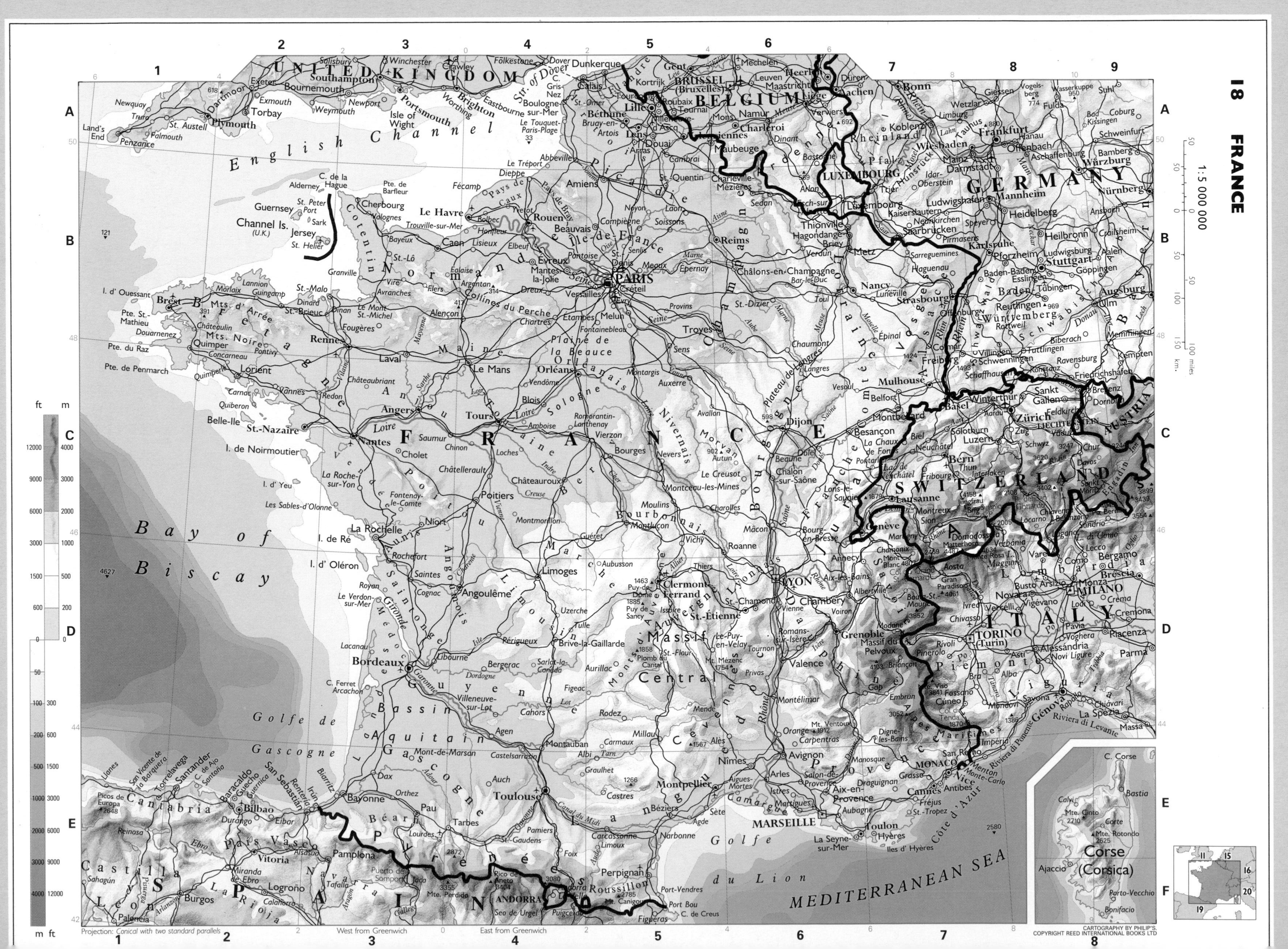

1:5 000 000

MEDITERRANEAN SEA

Corse (Corsica)

GERMANY

SWITZERLAND

ITALY

BELGIUM

LUXEMBOURG

UNITED KINGDOM

English Channel

Bay of Biscay

PARIS

MARSEILLE

SPAIN

Projection: Conical with two standard parallels

CARTOGRAPHY BY PHILIP'S
COPYRIGHT REED INTERNATIONAL BOOKS LTD

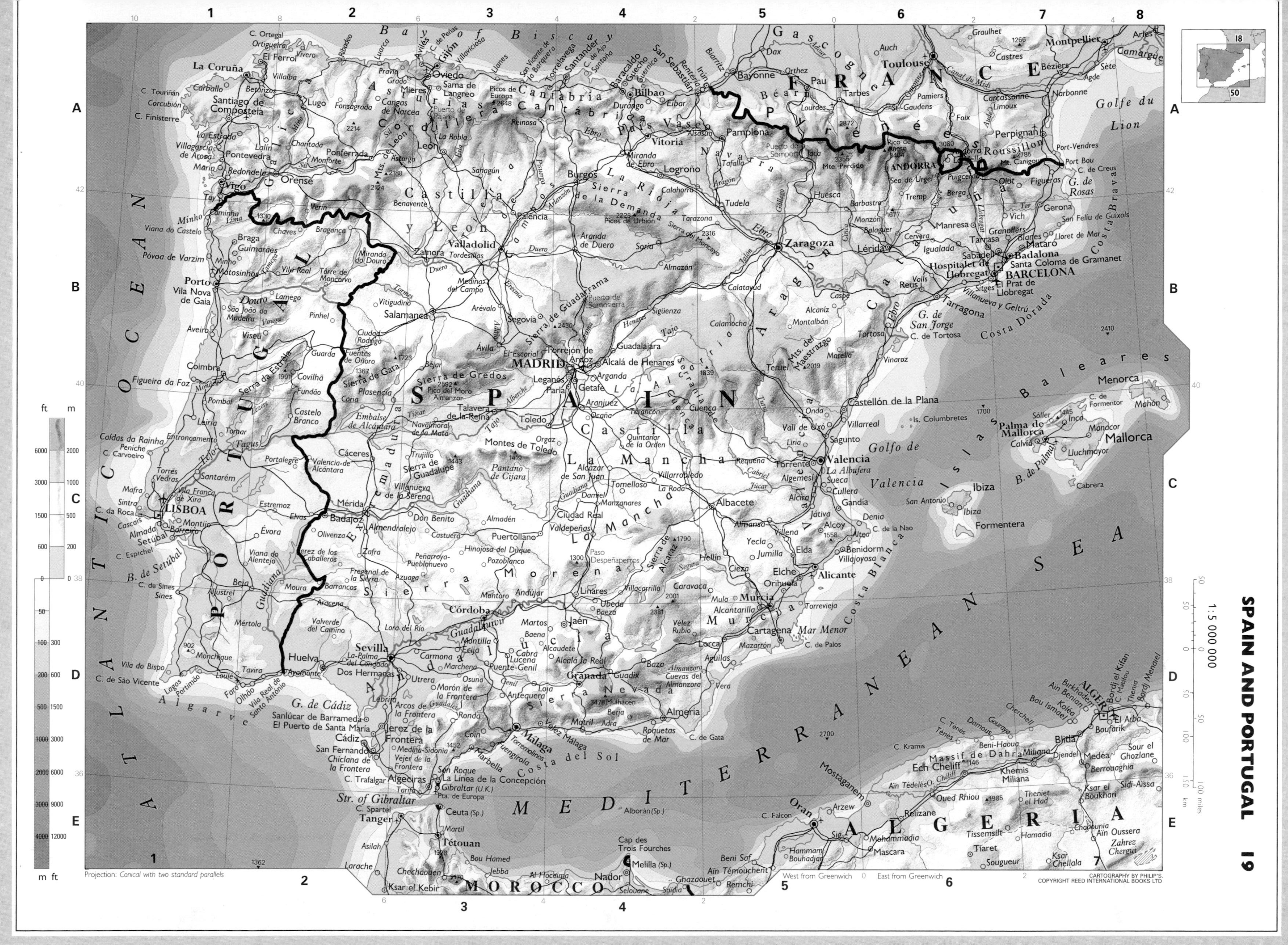
1:5 000 000
50 0 50 100 miles
50 0 50 100 150 km
SPAIN
PORTUGAL
FRANCE
ANDORRA
ALGERIA
MOROCCO
MADRID
LISBOA
BARCELONA
Valencia
Zaragoza
Sevilla
Málaga
Bilbao
Porto
Córdoba
Granada
Alicante
Murcia
Valladolid
Salamanca
Toledo
Cádiz
Gibraltar (U.K.)
Str. of Gibraltar
Ceuta (Sp.)
Melilla (Sp.)
Tanger
Tétouan
Oran
ALGER
Mallorca
Menorca
Ibiza
Formentera
Palma de Mallorca
Islas Baleares
Bay of Biscay
Golfe du Lion
Golfo de Valencia
G. de Cádiz
ATLANTIC OCEAN
MEDITERRANEAN SEA
Pyrénées
Sierra Nevada
Sierra Morena
Sierra de Gredos
Costa del Sol
Costa Brava
Costa Blanca
Costa Dorada
Algarve
Tajo
Duero
Ebro
Guadiana
Guadalquivir
Projection: Conical with two standard parallels
West from Greenwich
East from Greenwich
ft m
6000 2000
3000 1000
1500 500
600 200
0
m ft
4000 12000
3000 9000
2000 6000
1000 3000
500 1500
200 600
100 300
50
CARTOGRAPHY BY PHILIP'S.
COPYRIGHT REED INTERNATIONAL BOOKS LTD

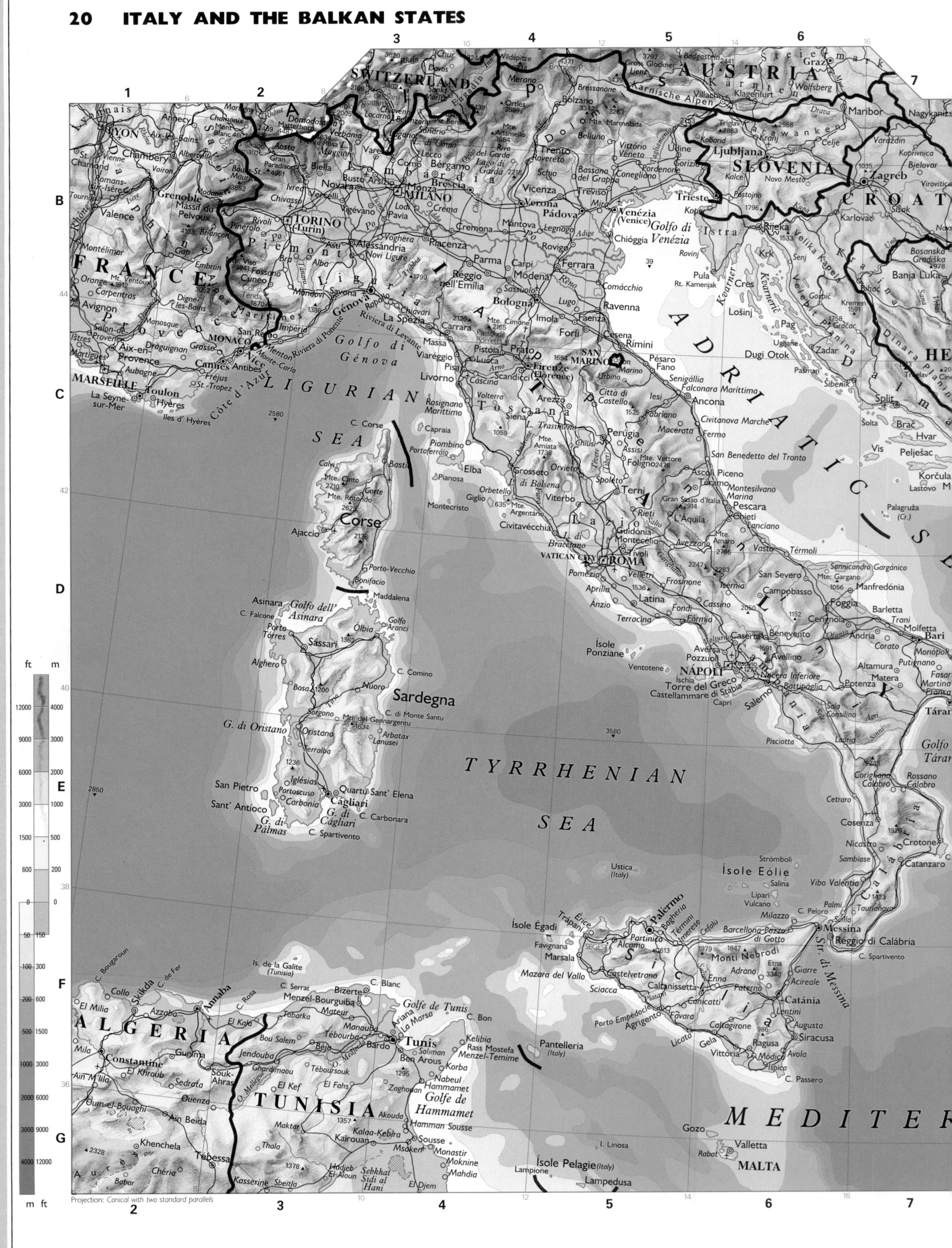

Projection: Conical with two standard parallels

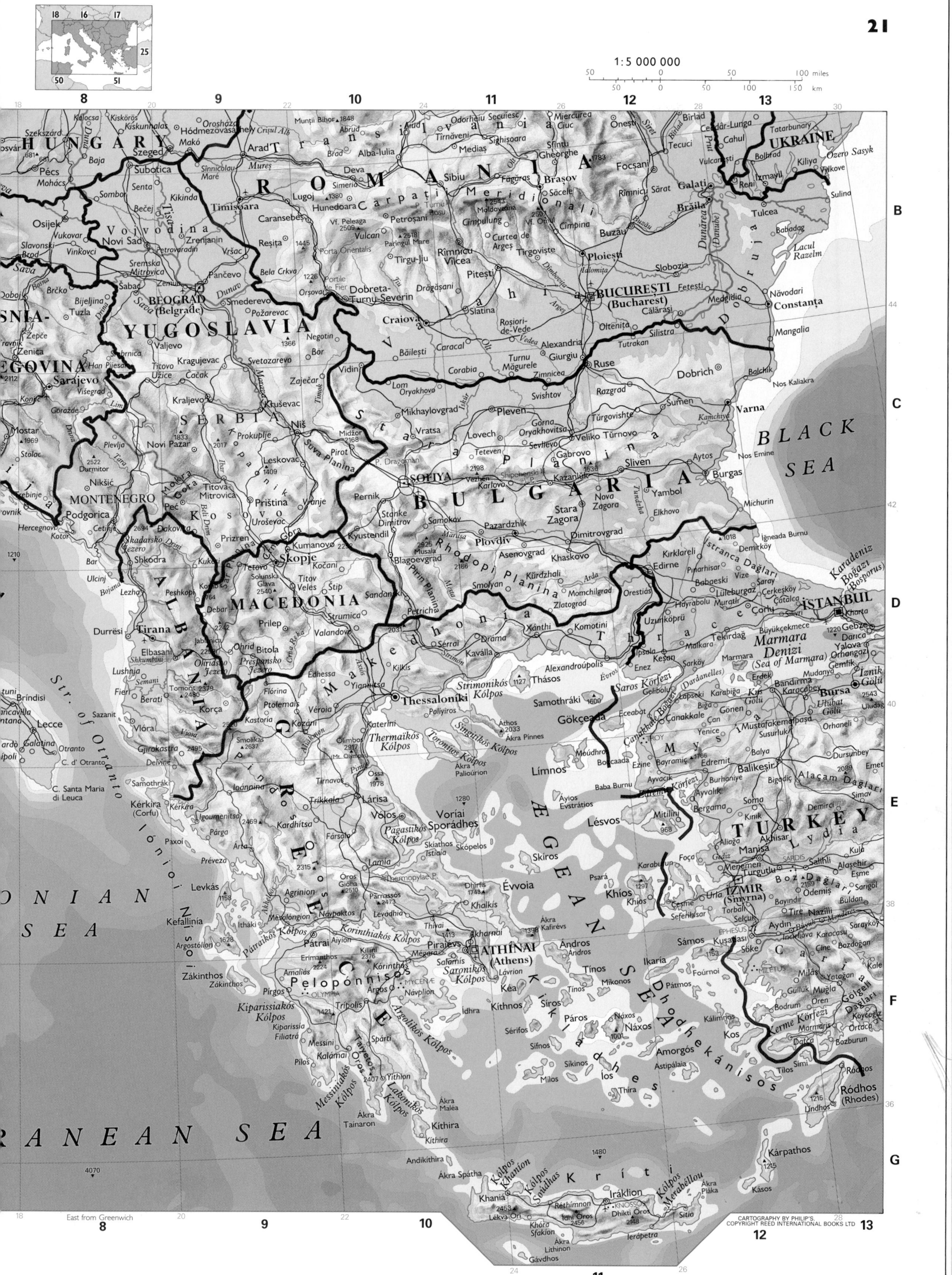
1:5 000 000
50 0 50 100 miles
50 0 50 100 150 km
HUNGARY
ROMANIA
UKRAINE
YUGOSLAVIA
SERBIA
Vojvodina
Kosovo
MONTENEGRO
ALBANIA
MACEDONIA
BULGARIA
GREECE
TURKEY
BLACK SEA
ÆGEAN SEA
IONIAN SEA
MEDITERRANEAN SEA
Transilvania
Carpaţii Meridionali
Vlahia
Dobruja
Stara Planina
Rhodopi Planina
Makedhonía
Thrace
Pelopónnisos
Kikládhes
Dhodhekánisos
Kríti
BUCUREŞTI (Bucharest)
BEOGRAD (Belgrade)
SOFIYA
Skopje
Tirana
ATHÍNAI (Athens)
ISTANBUL
IZMIR (Smyrna)
Thessaloníki
Szeged
Timişoara
Craiova
Constanţa
Varna
Burgas
Plovdiv
Ruse
Pleven
Niš
Sarajevo
Podgorica
Edirne
Bursa
Marmara Denizi (Sea of Marmara)
Kárpathos
Ródhos (Rhodes)
Iráklion
Khania
Lésvos
Khíos
Sámos
Límnos
Évvoia
Kérkira (Corfu)
Kefallinía
Zákinthos
Kithira
East from Greenwich
CARTOGRAPHY BY PHILIP'S. COPYRIGHT REED INTERNATIONAL BOOKS LTD

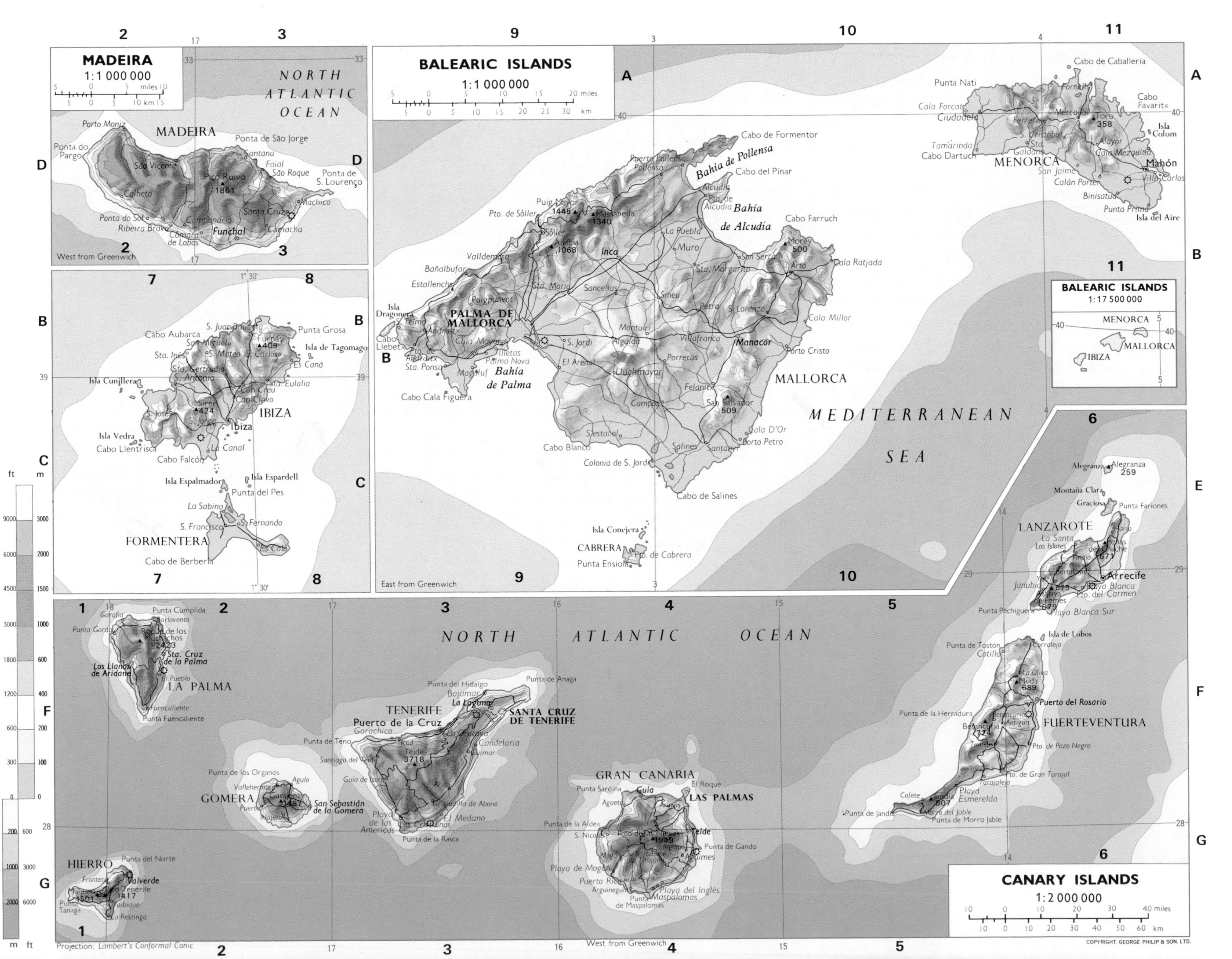
MADEIRA
1:1 000 000
NORTH ATLANTIC OCEAN
Porto Moniz
Ponta de São Jorge
Pico Ruivo 1861
Santa Cruz
Funchal
West from Greenwich
BALEARIC ISLANDS
1:1 000 000
Cabo de Formentor
Bahía de Pollensa
Bahía de Alcudia
Cabo Farruch
Puig Mayor 1445
Inca
PALMA DE MALLORCA
Bahía de Palma
Manacor
MALLORCA
MEDITERRANEAN SEA
Cabo de Salines
CABRERA
East from Greenwich
Cabo de Caballería
Ciudadela
MENORCA
Mahón
Isla del Aire
BALEARIC ISLANDS
1:17 500 000
MENORCA
MALLORCA
IBIZA
Punta Grosa
Isla de Tagomago
IBIZA
Ibiza
FORMENTERA
Cabo de Berbería
NORTH ATLANTIC OCEAN
LA PALMA
Sta. Cruz de la Palma
Los Llanos de Aridane
HIERRO
Valverde
GOMERA
San Sebastián de la Gomera
TENERIFE
Puerto de la Cruz
SANTA CRUZ DE TENERIFE
Teide 3718
GRAN CANARIA
LAS PALMAS
Telde
Playa del Inglés
LANZAROTE
Arrecife
Alegranza 259
Isla de Lobos
FUERTEVENTURA
Puerto del Rosario
Punta de Jandía
CANARY ISLANDS
1:2 000 000
Projection: Lambert's Conformal Conic
West from Greenwich
COPYRIGHT, GEORGE PHILIP & SON, LTD.

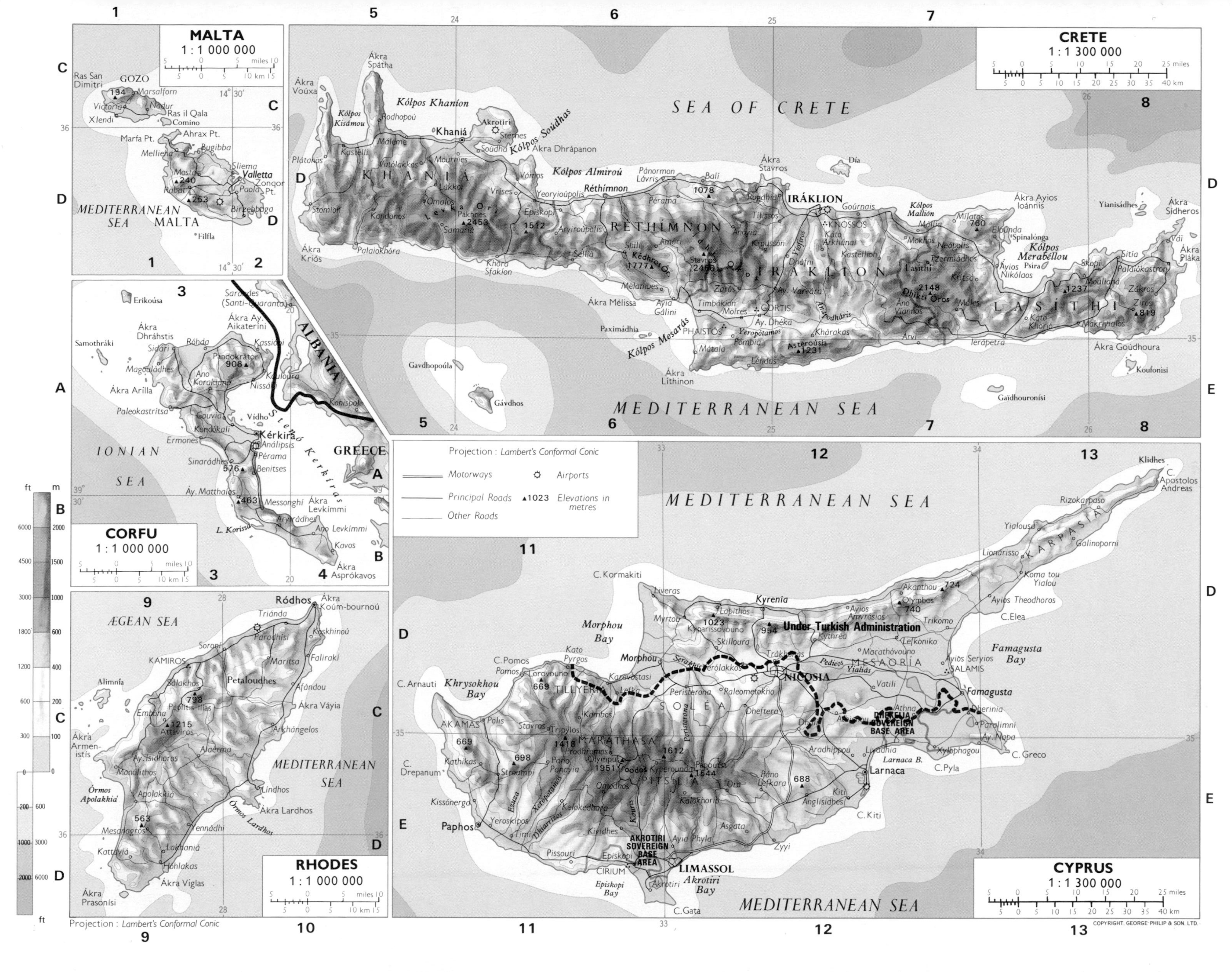

CRETE
1 : 1 300 000

SEA OF CRETE

Akra Sidheros
Akra Plâka
Yianísadhes
Koufonísi
Zâkros
2349
Skópi
Akra Goúdhoura
Kólpos Merabéllou
Ayios Nikólaos
Ieràpetra
Gaidhouronisi

KHANIÁ

RETHÍMNON

IRÁKLION

LASÍTHI

MEDITERRANEAN SEA

Kôlpos Khaniôn
Khaniá
Rethímnon
Kólpos Almiroú
Kôlpos Mesará
PHAISTÓS

MALTA
1 : 1 000 000

GOZO
Ras San Dimitri
Xlendi
Valletta
MALTA
MEDITERRANEAN SEA

CORFU
1 : 1 000 000

ALBANIA
GREECE
Kérkira
Kérkiras
IONIAN SEA

Projection : Lambert's Conformal Conic

Motorways
Airports
Principal Roads ▲1023 Elevations in metres
Other Roads

CYPRUS
1 : 1 300 000

COPYRIGHT, GEORGE PHILIP & SON, LTD.

Klídhes
C. Apóstolos Andréas
KARPASÍA
Rizokárpaso
Koma tou Yialoú
Famagusta Bay
MESAORIA
NICOSIA
Under Turkish Administration
Famagusta
SALAMIS
Kyrenia
Larnaca
MEDITERRANEAN SEA
Morphou Bay
Morphou
Paphos
Limassol
AKROTIRI SOVEREIGN BASE AREA
Akrotiri Bay
MEDITERRANEAN SEA

RHODES
1 : 1 000 000

Ródhos
AEGEAN SEA
KAMIROS
MEDITERRANEAN SEA

Projection : Lambert's Conformal Conic

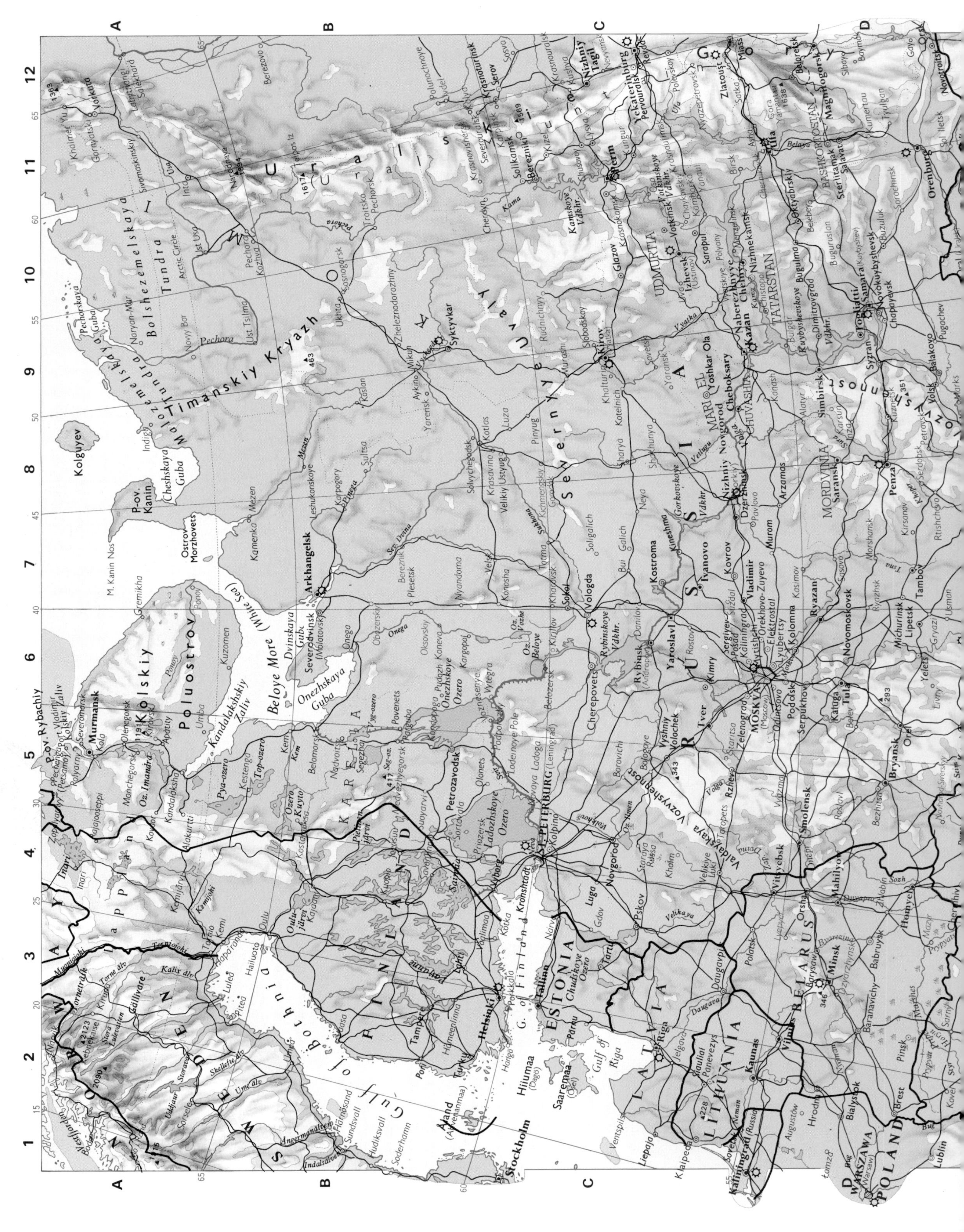

FINLAND
ESTONIA
LATVIA
LITHUANIA
BELARUS
POLAND
KARELIA
UDMURTIA
TATARSTAN
MORDVINIA
MOSKVA
(Moscow)
ST PETERSBURG
(Leningrad)
Helsinki
Tallinn
Riga
Vilnius
Minsk
Stockholm
Arkhangelsk
Murmansk
Beloye More
(White Sea)
Gulf of Bothnia
G. of Finland
Gulf of Riga
Kolskiy Poluostrov
Timanskiy Kryazh
Bolshezemelskaya Tundra
Severnyye Uvaly
Kolguyev
Ladozhskoye Ozero
Onezhskoye Ozero

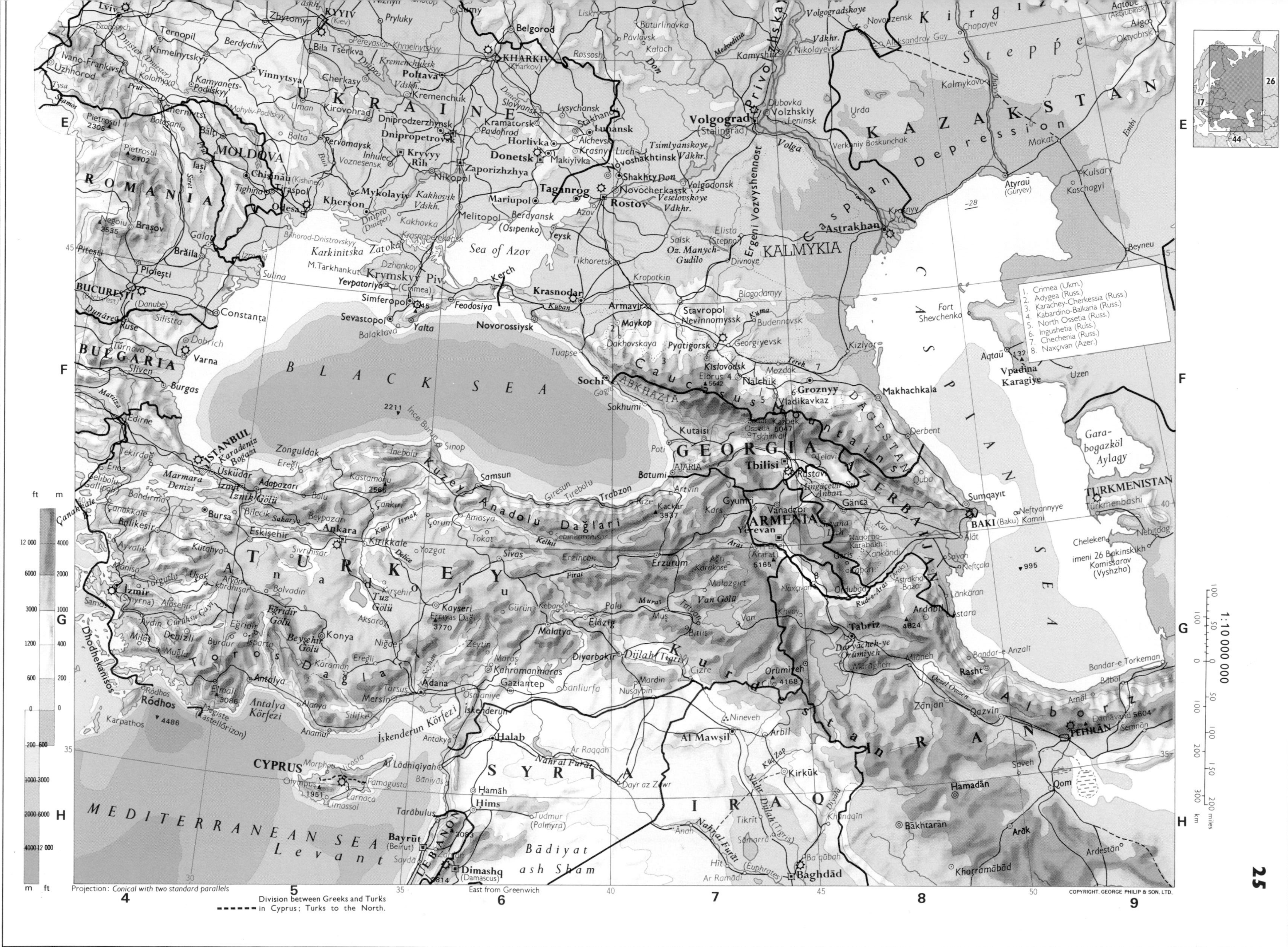
1:10 000 000
100 50 0 50 100 150 200 miles
100 0 100 200 300 km
1. Crimea (Ukr.)
2. Adygea (Russ.)
3. Karachey-Cherkessia (Russ.)
4. Kabardino-Balkaria (Russ.)
5. North Ossetia (Russ.)
6. Ingushetia (Russ.)
7. Chechenia (Russ.)
8. Naxçıvan (Azer.)
UKRAINE
MOLDOVA
ROMANIA
BULGARIA
TURKEY
GEORGIA
ARMENIA
AZERBAIJAN
KAZAKSTAN
TURKMENISTAN
KALMYKIA
ABKHAZIA
AJARIA
DAGESTAN
CYPRUS
LEBANON
SYRIA
IRAQ
IRAN
BLACK SEA
CASPIAN SEA
Sea of Azov
MEDITERRANEAN SEA
Levant
Caucasus Mountains
Anadolu Dağlari
Toros Dağlari
Kurdistan
Alborz
Caspian Depression
Kirgiz Steppe
Bādiyat ash Sham
Gara-bogazköl Aylagy
KYYIV (Kiev)
KHARKIV (Kharkov)
Volgograd (Stalingrad)
Astrakhan
Rostov
Donetsk
Odesa
Chişinău
BUCUREŞTI (Bucharest)
İSTANBUL
Ankara
İzmir (Smyrna)
Tbilisi
Yerevan
BAKI (Baku)
TEHRĀN
Baghdād
Dimashq (Damascus)
Bayrūt (Beirut)
Krasnodar
Groznyy
Makhachkala
Tabrīz
Sochi
Trabzon
Sevastopol
Simferopol
Atyraū (Guryev)
Aqtaū
Elbrus 5642
Kazbek 5047
Ağrı Dağı (Ararat) 5165
Damāvand 5604
Projection: Conical with two standard parallels
Division between Greeks and Turks in Cyprus; Turks to the North.
East from Greenwich
ft m
12 000 4000
6000 2000
3000 1000
1200 400
600 200
0 0
200 600
1000 3000
2000 6000
4000 12 000
m ft

1:20 000 000

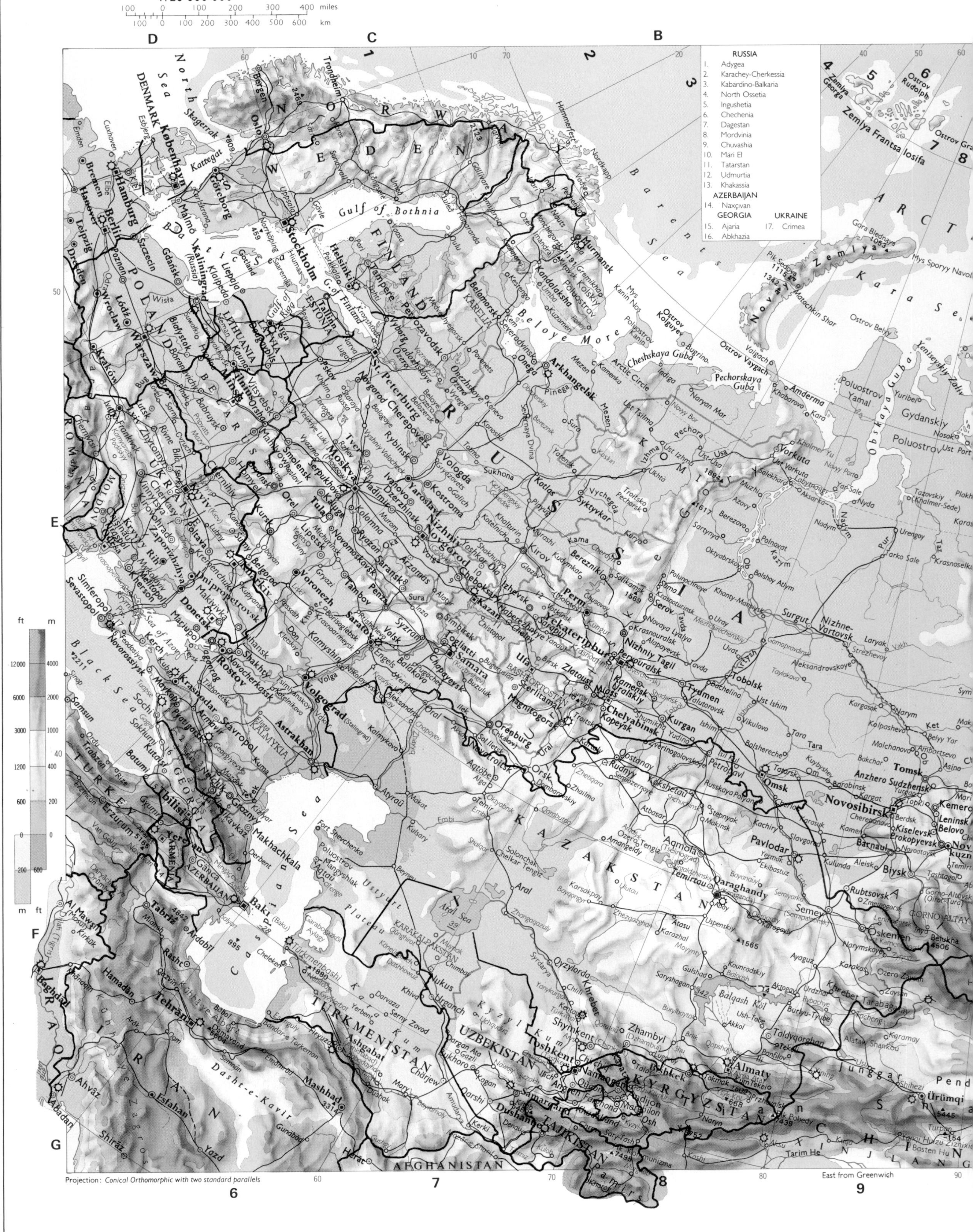

	RUSSIA
1.	Adygea
2.	Karachey-Cherkessia
3.	Kabardino-Balkaria
4.	North Ossetia
5.	Ingushetia
6.	Chechenia
7.	Dagestan
8.	Mordvinia
9.	Chuvashia
10.	Mari El
11.	Tatarstan
12.	Udmurtia
13.	Khakassia
	AZERBAIJAN
14.	Naxçivan
	GEORGIA UKRAINE
15.	Ajaria 17. Crimea
16.	Abkhazia

Projection: Conical Orthomorphic with two standard parallels

East from Greenwich

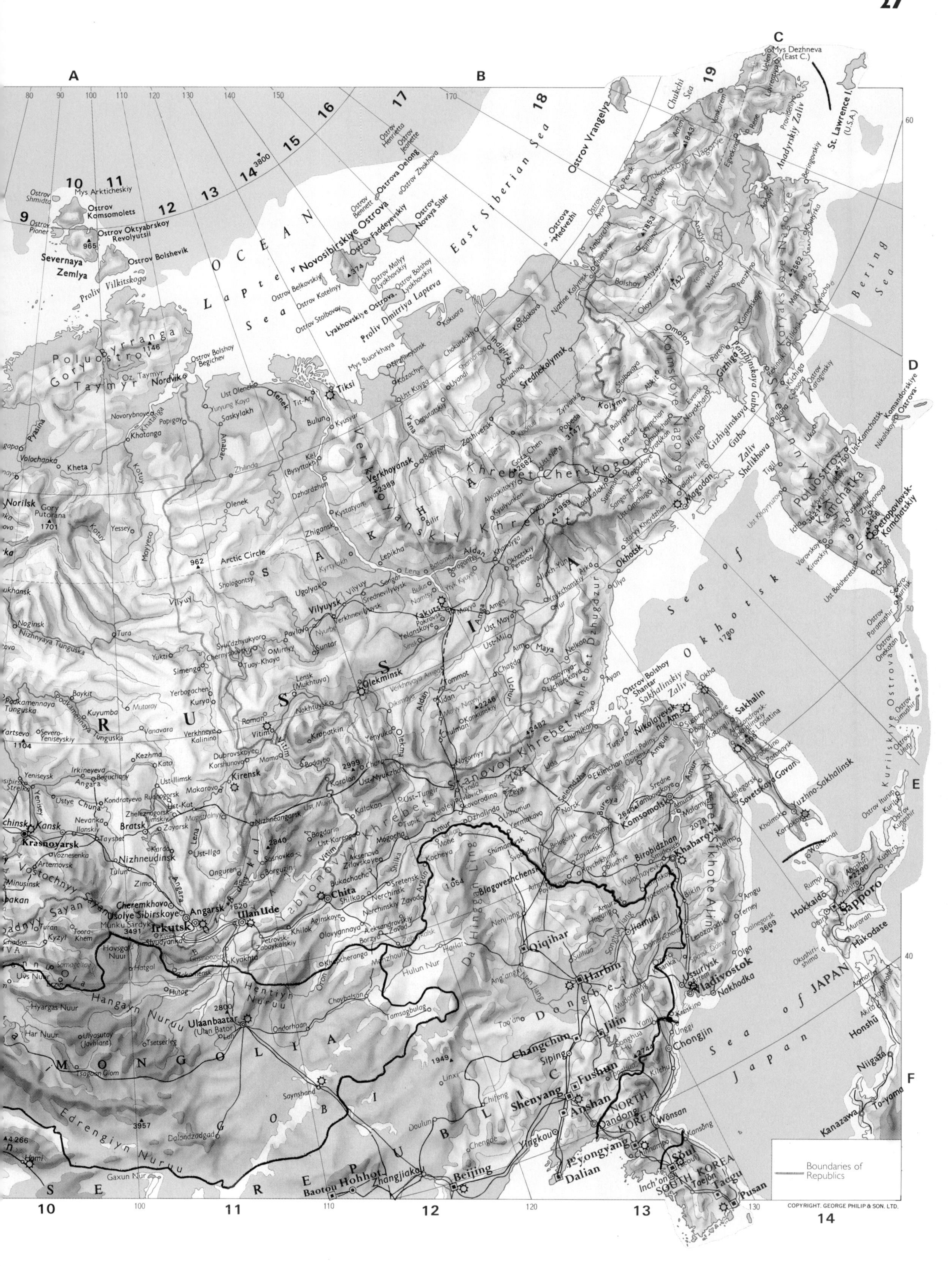

A   B   C

D

E

F

9 10 11 12 13 14 15 16 17 18 19

10 11 12 13 14

ARCTIC OCEAN

Laptev Sea

East Siberian Sea

Chukchi Sea

Bering Sea

R U S S I A

Sea of Okhotsk

Sea of JAPAN

M O N G O L I A

C H I N A

NORTH KOREA

SOUTH KOREA

Mys Dezhneva (East C.)

St. Lawrence I. (U.S.A.)

Severnaya Zemlya

Ostrov Shmidta

Mys Arkticheskiy

Ostrov Komsomolets

Ostrov Pioner

Ostrov Oktyabrskoy Revolyutsii

965

Ostrov Bolshevik

Proliv Vilkitskogo

Poluostrov Taymyr

Gory Byrranga

Nordvik

Novosibirskiye Ostrova

Ostrova Delong

Ostrov Henrietta

Ostrov Zhokhova

Ostrov Bennett

Ostrov Vrangelya

Ostrova Medvezhi

Ostrov Bolshoy Lyakhovskiy

Ostrov Faddeyevskiy

Ostrov Novaya Sibir

Ostrov Kotelny

Ostrov Belkovskiy

Ostrov Stolbovoy

3800

Proliv Dmitriya Lapteva

Lyakhovskiye Ostrova

Mys Suorkhaya

Tiksi

Nordvik

Khatanga

Olenek

Norilsk

Gory Putorana

1701

Arctic Circle

962

Verkhoyansk

2389

Khrebet Cherskogo

Srednekolymsk

Kolyma

2595

Zyryanka

Oymyakon

Magadan

Poluostrov Kamchatka

Petropavlovsk-Kamchatskiy

Zaliv Shelikhova

Penzhinskaya Guba

Gizhiginskaya Guba

Gizhiga

Kolymskoye Nagorye

Omolon

Anadyrskiy Zaliv

Sredinnyy Khrebet

1883

1762

3621

Yakutsk

Vilyuysk

Olekminsk

Lensk (Mukhtuya)

Vitim

Kirensk

2999

Bratsk

Nizhneudinsk

Krasnoyarsk

Kansk

Irkutsk

Angarsk

Ulan Ude

Usolye Sibirskoye

Cheremkhovo

Munku Sardyk 3491

Chita

Stanovoy Khrebet

Khrebet Dzhugdzhur

Okhotsk

Ayan

Ostrov Bolshoy Shantar

Sakhalinskiy Zaliv

Nikolayevsk-na-Amur

Sakhalin

Yuzhno-Sakhalinsk

Sovetskaya Gavan

Kurilskiye Ostrova

Komsomolsk

Birobidzhan

Khabarovsk

Khrebet Sikhote Alin

2078

Amur

Blagoveshchensk

Jiamusi

Qiqihar

Harbin

Changchun

Jilin

Vladivostok

Nakhodka

Ussuriysk

Chongjin

Hokkaido

Sapporo

Hakodate

Honshu

Niigata

Kanazawa

Toyama

Sea of Japan

Pyongyang

Wonsan

Seoul

Inch'on

Taejon

Taegu

Pusan

Dalian

Dandong

Anshan

Fushun

Shenyang

Yingkou

Chengde

Beijing

Zhangjiakou

Hohhot

Baotou

Ulaanbaatar (Ulan Bator)

Hangayn Nuruu

Hentiyn Nuruu

Hövsgöl Nuur

Uvs Nuur

Har Nuur

Hyargas Nuur

GOBI DESERT

Edrengiyn Nuruu

4266

Da Hinggan Ling

Dong

3957

Boundaries of Republics

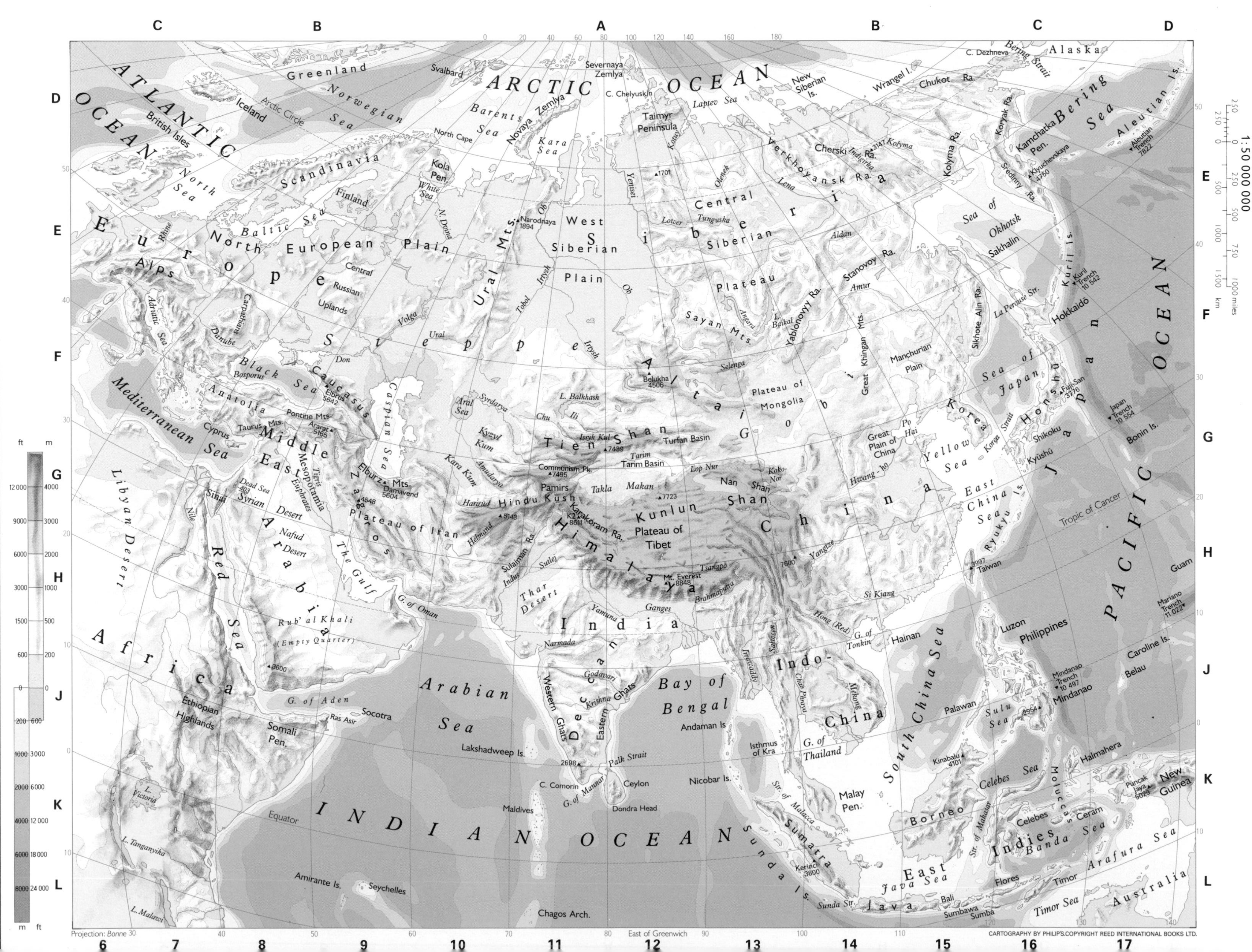

1 : 50 000 000

250   0   250   500   750   1000 miles
250   0   500   1000   1500   km

CARTOGRAPHY BY PHILIPS.COPYRIGHT REED INTERNATIONAL BOOKS LTD.

Projection: Bonne 30

1:50 000 000

250   0   250   500   750   1000 miles

250   0   500   1000   1500 km

CARTOGRAPHY BY PHILIP'S. COPYRIGHT REED INTERNATIONAL BOOKS LTD.

Projection: Bonne 30

East from Greenwich

Hanoi ● Capital Cities

Oceans and Seas

ARCTIC OCEAN
ATLANTIC OCEAN
PACIFIC OCEAN
INDIAN OCEAN
Bering Sea
Sea of Okhotsk
Sea of Japan
Yellow Sea
East China Sea
South China Sea
Philippine Sea
Celebes Sea
Sulu Sea
Banda Sea
Arafura Sea
Timor Sea
Java Sea
Bay of Bengal
Arabian Sea
Caspian Sea
Aral Sea
Black Sea
Mediterranean Sea
Red Sea
G. of Aden
The Gulf
G. of Oman
Barents Sea
Kara Sea
Laptev Sea
North Sea
White Sea

Countries

RUSSIA
KAZAKSTAN
MONGOLIA
CHINA
TIBET
SINKIANG
UIGHUR
INDIA
PAKISTAN
AFGHANISTAN
IRAN
IRAQ
SAUDI ARABIA
TURKEY
SYRIA
JORDAN
ISRAEL
LEBANON
CYPRUS
YEMEN
OMAN
UNITED ARAB EMIRATES
QATAR
BAHRAIN
KUWAIT
UZBEKISTAN
TURKMENISTAN
TAJIKISTAN
KYRGYZSTAN
AZERBAIJAN
ARMENIA
GEORGIA
UKRAINE
FINLAND
SWEDEN
NORWAY
GERMANY
FRANCE
UNITED KINGDOM
ITALY
ICELAND
GREENLAND
JAPAN
NORTH KOREA
SOUTH KOREA
TAIWAN
VIETNAM
LAOS
THAILAND
CAMBODIA
BURMA (MYANMAR)
MALAYSIA
BRUNEI
SINGAPORE
INDONESIA
PHILIPPINES
NEPAL
BHUTAN
BANGLADESH
SRI LANKA
MALDIVES
SOMALI REP.
ETHIOPIA
ERITREA
DJIBOUTI
SUDAN
EGYPT
LIBYA
KENYA
TANZANIA
UGANDA
ZAIRE
ZAMBIA
MALAWI
AUSTRALIA
SEYCHELLES

Capital and major cities

TOKYO, Yokohama, Osaka, Sapporo, Sendai
SEOUL, PYONGYANG
BEIJING, SHANGHAI, TIANJIN, SHENYANG, GUANGZHOU, HANGZHOU, CHONGQING, Harbin, Changchun, Jinan, Nanjing, Wuhan, Xian, Chengdu, Kunming, Lanzhou, Baotou, Taiyuan, Nanchang, Fuzhou, Hong Kong, Macau (Port.), Hainan
Ulan Bator
TAIPEI
MANILA, Davao, Mindanao, Luzon
JAKARTA, Bandung, Surabaya, Semarang, Palembang, Medan
Kuala Lumpur, SINGAPORE
BANGKOK
Phnom Penh, Ho Chi Minh City
HANOI, Haiphong
RANGOON, Mandalay
DACCA, Chittagong
CALCUTTA, MADRAS, BOMBAY, New Delhi, DELHI, Hyderabad, Bangalore, Ahmadabad, Kanpur, Lucknow, Nagpur, Jaipur, Indore, Bhopal, Surat, Vadodara, Pune, Madurai, Patna, Varanasi
Colombo
KARACHI, Lahore, Islamabad, Faisalabad
Kabul, Qandahar, Herat
TEHRAN, Esfahan, Shiraz, Mashhad, Tabriz, Zahedan
BAGHDAD, Basra, Mosul
Riyadh, Mecca, Medina, Jedda
Kuwait
Abu Dhabi, Doha, Manama, Muscat
ISTANBUL, Ankara, Izmir, Bursa, Adana, Konya
Damascus, Aleppo
Amman
Beirut
Jerusalem
Nicosia
Sana, Aden
ALMA ATA, Karaganda, Semey, Pavlodar, Omsk
MOSCOW, ST. PETERSBURG, Nizhniy Novgorod, Kazan, Samara, Ufa, Perm, Yekaterinburg, Chelyabinsk, Volgograd, Rostov, Saratov, Novosibirsk, Novokuznetsk, Omsk, Tomsk, Krasnoyarsk, Irkutsk, Yakutsk, Vladivostok, Khabarovsk, Magadan, Petropavlovsk, Murmansk, Arkhangelsk, Norilsk, Yakutsk
Tashkent, Samarkand
Ashkhabad
Dushanbe
Bishkek
Baku
Yerevan
Tbilisi
Odessa, Kharkov
LONDON, PARIS, Berlin, Vienna, Warsaw, Budapest, Belgrade, Rome, Athens
CAIRO, Alexandria, Aswan, Suez, Port Sudan, Khartoum, Addis Ababa, Mogadishu, Nairobi, Mombasa, Dar es Salaam
Victoria

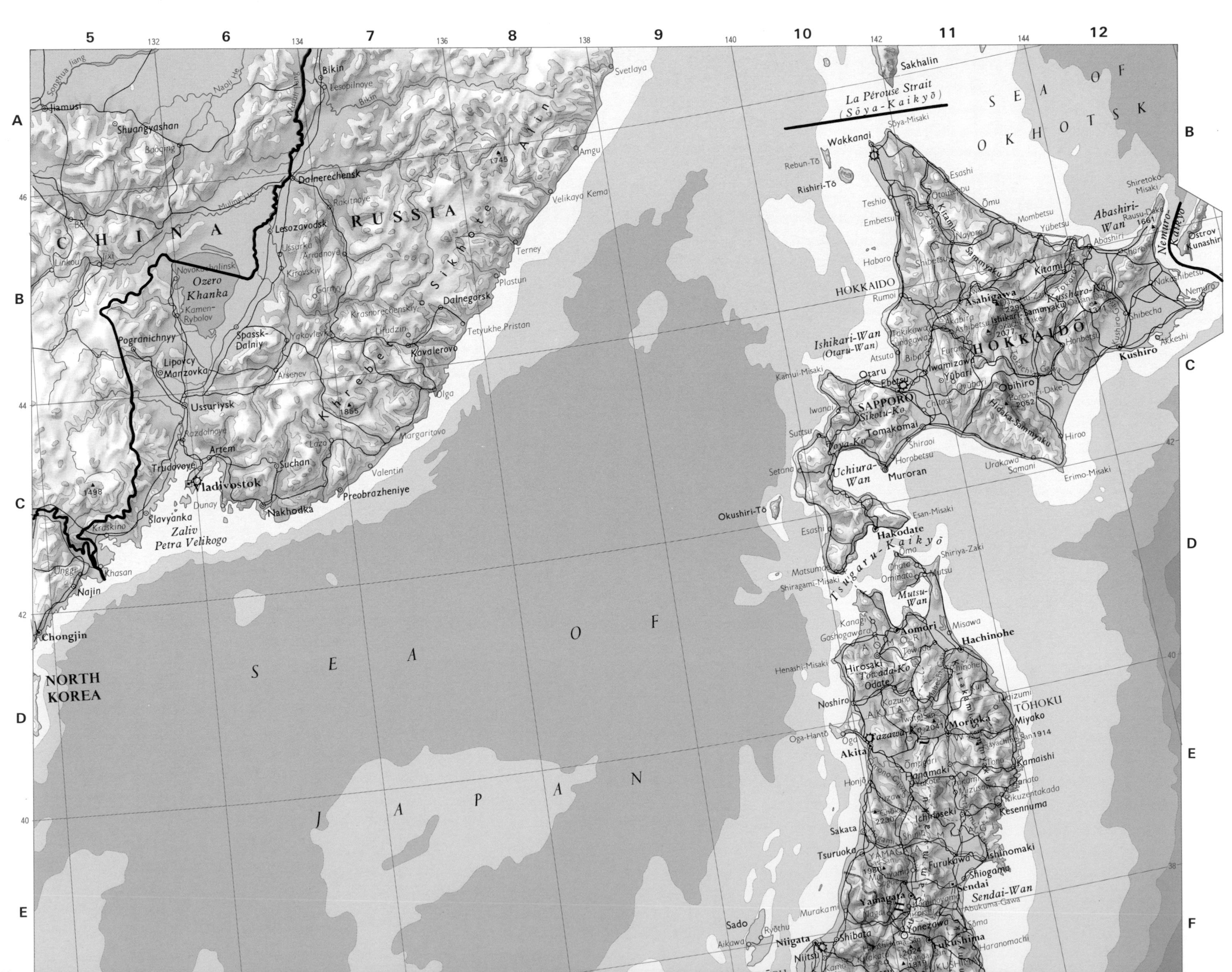

SEA OF OKHOTSK

HOKKAIDO

La Pérouse Strait
(Sōya-Kaikyō)

Wakkanai

SAPPORO

Hakodate

Tsugaru-Kaikyō

TŌHOKU

Hachinohe

Aomori

Akita

HONSHU

SEA OF JAPAN

RUSSIA

SIKHOTE ALIN

Vladivostok

Zaliv Petra Velikogo

CHINA

NORTH KOREA

Chŏngjin

Najin

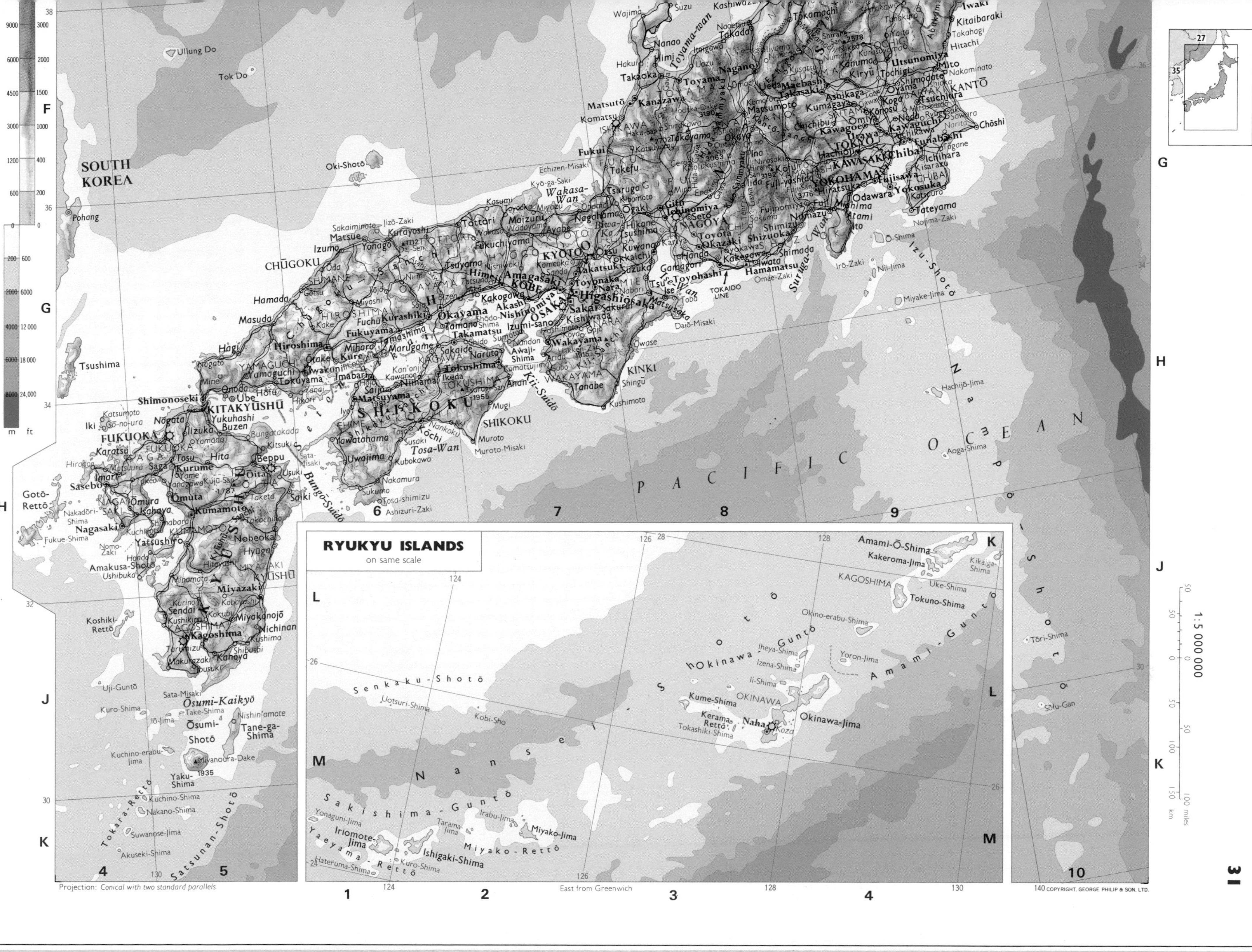
SOUTH KOREA
Pohang
Ullung Do
Tok Do
Oki-Shotō
Tsushima
Iki
Gotō-Rettō
Koshiki-Rettō
CHŪGOKU
SHIKOKU
KYŪSHŪ
KINKI
KANTŌ
KITAKYŪSHŪ
Shimonoseki
FUKUOKA
Nagasaki
Sasebo
Kumamoto
Kagoshima
Miyazaki
Nobeoka
Ōita
Beppu
Hiroshima
Okayama
Matsuyama
Takamatsu
Tokushima
Kōchi
KŌBE
ŌSAKA
KYŌTO
NAGOYA
Hamamatsu
Shizuoka
YOKOHAMA
KAWASAKI
TŌKYŌ
Chiba
Yokosuka
Kanazawa
Toyama
Nagano
Fukui
Tottori
Hamada
Masuda
Hagi
Wakasa-Wan
Tosa-Wan
Kii-Suidō
Bungo-Suidō
Ōsumi-Kaikyō
Tane-ga-Shima
Yaku-Shima
Tokara-Rettō
Satsunan-Shotō
Izu-Shotō
Hachijō-Jima
Miyake-Jima
Tōri-Shima
Sōfu-Gan
PACIFIC OCEAN
Nampō-Shotō
TOKAIDO LINE
RYUKYU ISLANDS
on same scale
Amami-Ō-Shima
Kakeroma-Jima
Tokuno-Shima
KAGOSHIMA
Okino-erabu-Shima
Yoron-Jima
Amami-Guntō
Okinawa-Guntō
OKINAWA
Okinawa-Jima
Naha
Kume-Shima
Kerama-Rettō
Senkaku-Shotō
Nansei-Shotō
Sakishima-Guntō
Miyako-Jima
Miyako-Rettō
Ishigaki-Shima
Iriomote-Jima
Yonaguni-Jima
Yaeyama-Rettō
1:5 000 000
Projection: Conical with two standard parallels
East from Greenwich
COPYRIGHT. GEORGE PHILIP & SON, LTD.

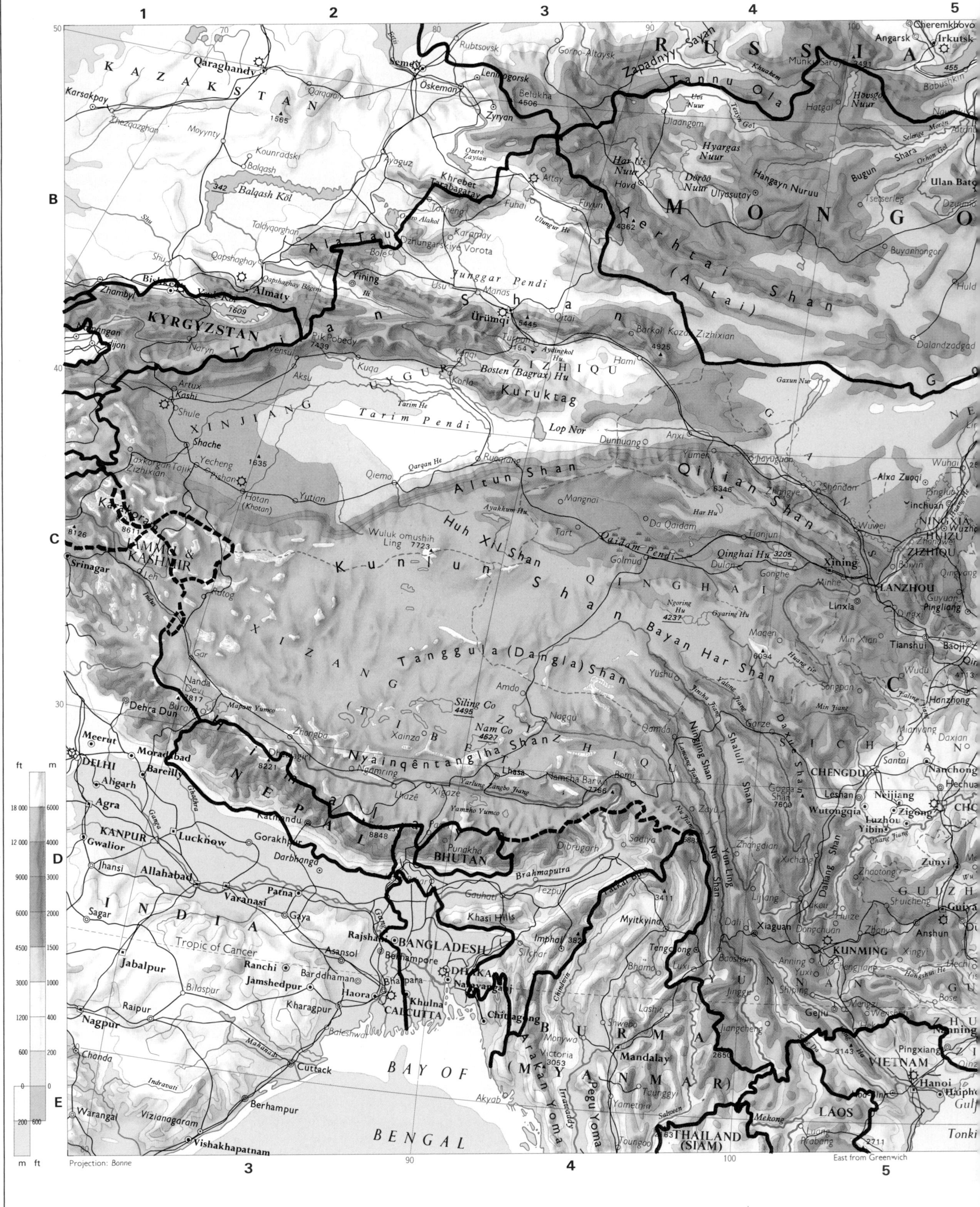
KAZAKSTAN
RUSSIA
MONGOLIA
KYRGYZSTAN
XINJIANG UYGUR ZIZHIQU
XIZANG ZIZHIQU (TIBET)
QINGHAI
SICHUAN
NEPAL
BHUTAN
BANGLADESH
INDIA
BURMA (MYANMAR)
THAILAND (SIAM)
LAOS
VIETNAM
JAMMU & KASHMIR
Tarim Pendi
Kunlun Shan
Tanggula (Dangla) Shan
Altun Shan
Qilian Shan
Bayan Har Shan
Tian Shan
Aerhtai (Altai) Shan
Junggar Pendi
Himalaya
Balqash Köl
Lop Nor
Qinghai Hu
Ürümqi
Lhasa
Kathmandu
DELHI
CALCUTTA
DHAKA
CHENGDU
KUNMING
LANZHOU
Xining
Hanoi
Mandalay
BAY OF BENGAL
Tropic of Cancer
Projection: Bonne
East from Greenwich

27
40 37
38
6

1 : 15 000 000

100 0 100 200 300 400 miles
100 0 100 200 300 400 500 600 km

7 8 9

z. Baykal
Ulan Ude • Chita Sretensk Nerchinsk
Ilan Ude Bukachacha
Borzya Svobodny
Olovyannaya Blagoveshchensk
Nerchinsk Aihui Bureya
Manzhouli Oroqen Zizhiqi
Komsomolsk
C. Terpeniya
Poronaysk
Aleksandrovsk
Sakhalin
Dolinsk
Khabarovsk Yuzhno-Sakhalinsk
Kholmsk

B

Hailar Qiqihar Nenjiang Yichun Hegang
Butha Qi Jiamusi
Suihua Shuangyashan
HARBIN Hulin Mishan
Jixi
Horqin Youyi Qianqi Ulan Hot Baicheng
Shuangcheng Mudanjiang oz. Khanka
Tao'an Asahigawa
Changchun Jilin HOKKAIDO
Shuangliao Dunhua SAPPORO
Linxi Siping Liaoyuan Yanji Muroran Kushiro
Vladivostok C. Erimo
Hohhot Chifeng Fuxin Chongjin Hakodate
Erenhot FUSHUN Aomori Hachinohe
Zhangjiakou Chengde SHENYANG NORTH Akita Morioka
BEIJING Tangshan ANSHAN Dandong Ishinomaki
TAIYUAN TIANJIN P'YONGYANG Hungnam Sendai
Baoding Shijiazhuang Wonsan Niigata Sado
DALIAN Kaesong TOKYO
Yantai Weihai SOUL NAGOYA YOKOHAMA
QINGDAO SEOUL Kanazawa
JINAN Inch'on SOUTH KOBE KYOTO OSAKA
YELLOW Taejon TAEGU Yokosuka
SEA PUSAN Hiroshima Shizuoka
Kwangju Masan Okayama SHIKOKU
Cheju Do KITAKYUSHU Kochi Wakayama
FUKUOKA Matsuyama
Sasebo Kumamoto KYUSHU
Nagasaki
Kagoshima

C

HENAN ZHENGZHOU Kaifeng Xuzhou
XI'AN Luoyang Qingjiang
Nanyang Shangqiu Huaibei
Shangshui Fuyang Bengbu Yangzhou
WUHAN Hefei NANJING SHANGHAI
Huangshi Tongling Wuxi Suzhou
Changde HUNAN Hangzhou
Nanchang Shaoxing Ningbo
Changsha JIANGXI Jinhua
Xiangtan Pingxiang Qu Xian Wenzhou

D

EAST CHINA SEA
Ryūkyū-rettō
Amami-ō-Shima
Okinawa Naha
Tropic of Cancer

PACIFIC

Guilin Ganzhou FUJIAN Fuzhou
Hengyang Shaoguan Quanzhou
GUANGDONG Xiamen Chilung TAIPEI
GUANGZHOU Shantou Changhua
HONG KONG TAIWAN (FORMOSA)
Macau T'ainan T'aitung
Zhanjiang Kaohsiung Pingtung

O C E A N

E

Hainan Dao
HAINAN Pratas Batan Is.
Yacheng SOUTH CHINA Babuyan Is.
Haikou SEA

6 120 7 130 8

COPYRIGHT GEORGE PHILIP & SON LTD

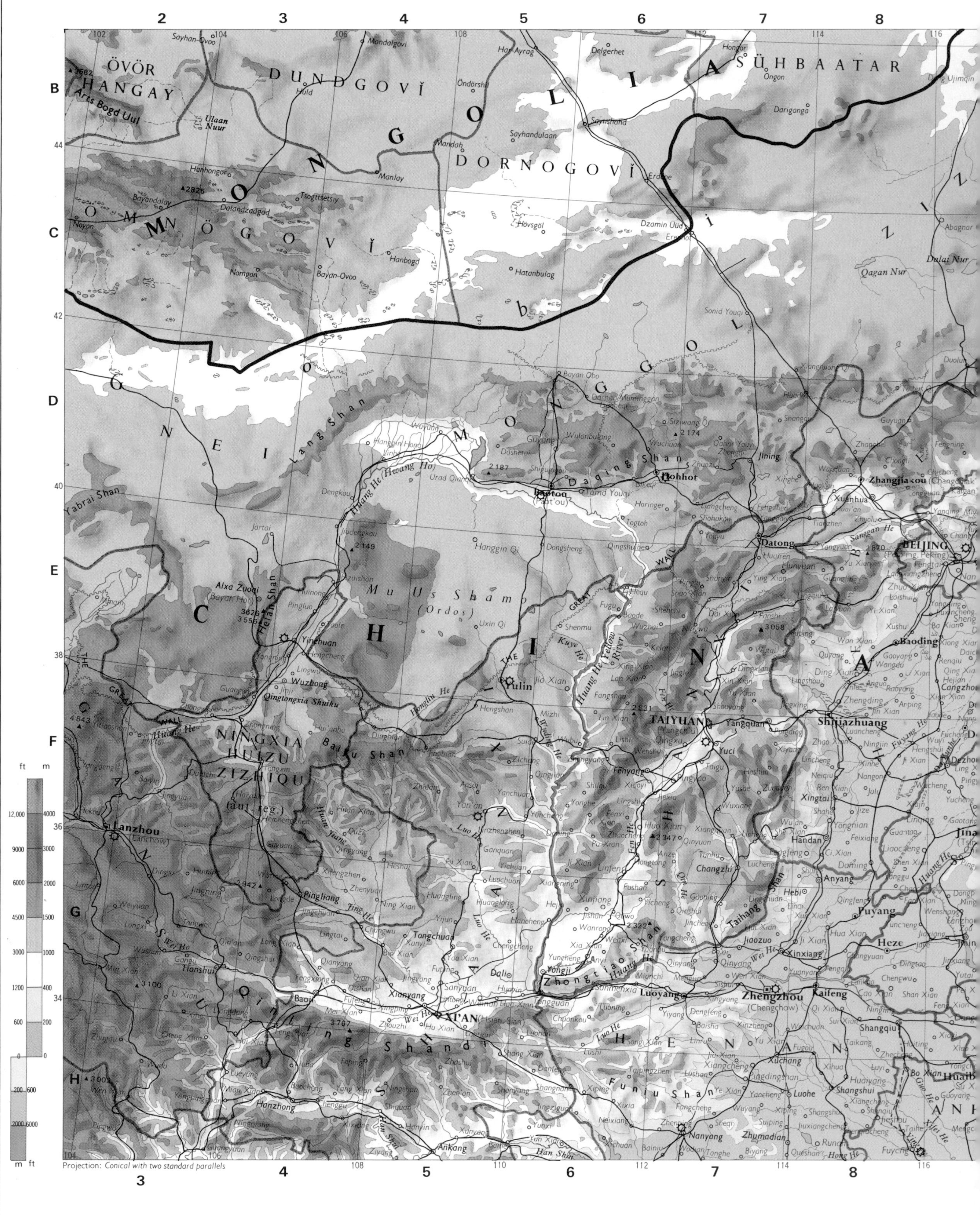
MONGOLIA
DUNDGOVĬ
DORNOGOVĬ
ÖMNÖGOVĬ
ÖVÖR HANGAY
SÜHBAATAR
NEI MONGOL ZIZHIQU
NINGXIA HUIZU ZIZHIQU (aut. reg.)
SHAANXI
SHANXI
HEBEI
HENAN
GANSU
Mu Us Shamo (Ordos)
Lang Shan
Daqing Shan
Helan Shan
Qinling Shandi
Taihang Shan
Zhongtiao Shan
Funiu Shan
Huang He (Hwang Ho)
BEIJING
TAIYUAN
Lanzhou
Xi'an
Zhengzhou
Luoyang
Baotou
Hohhot
Datong
Yinchuan
Shijiazhuang
Zhangjiakou
Projection: Conical with two standard parallels

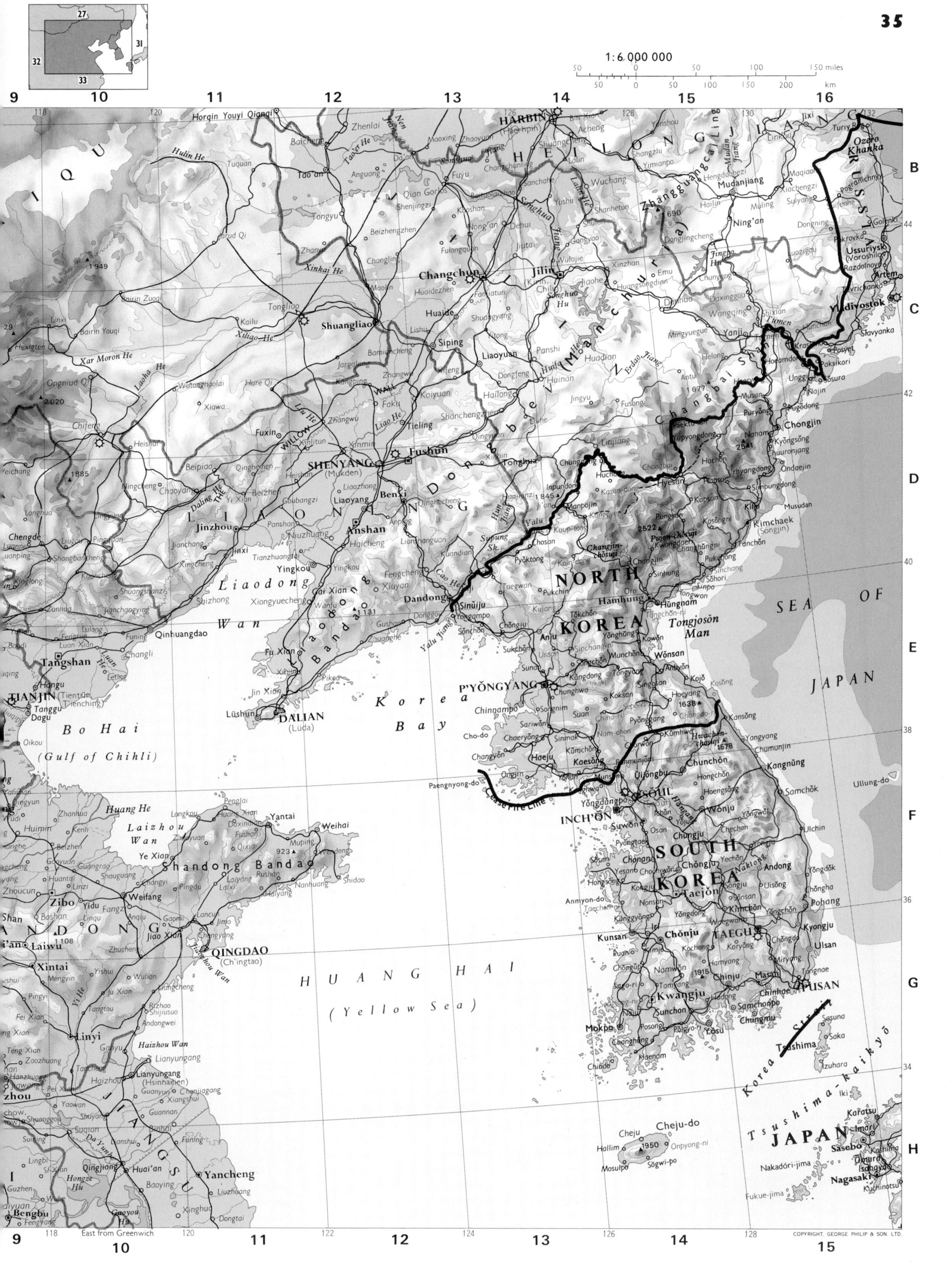
1: 6 000 000
50 0 50 100 150 miles
50 0 50 100 150 200 km
27
31
32
33
9
10
11
12
13
14
15
16
B
C
D
E
F
G
H
HARBIN
(Haerhpin)
HEILONGJIANG
RUSSIA
Ozero Khanka
Mudanjiang
Ning'an
Jixi
Ussuriysk (Voroshilov)
Artem
Vladivostok
Changchun
Jilin
(Kirin)
Shuangliao
Siping
Liaoyuan
JILIN
Tongliao
Xiliao He
Xar Moron He
Laoha He
Chifeng
Fuxin
Tieling
Fushun
SHENYANG
(Mukden)
Benxi
Liaoyang
Anshan
Jinzhou
Chengde
LIAONING
Yingkou
Dandong
Liaodong Wan
Liaodong Bandao
Qinhuangdao
Tangshan
TIANJIN
(Tientsin)
Tianjin
Tanggu
Dagu
Bo Hai
(Gulf of Chihli)
Lüshun
DALIAN
(Lüda)
Korea Bay
Yalu Jiang
Changbai Shan
Paektu-san
Hyesan
Chongjin
Kimchaek
(Songjin)
Hamhung
Hungnam
NORTH KOREA
Sinŭiju
P'YŎNGYANG
Chinnampo
Haeju
Kaesŏng
Wŏnsan
Tongjosŏn Man
Cease Fire Line
Paengnyong-do
SŎUL
INCH'ŎN
Suwŏn
Ch'unch'ŏn
Kangnŭng
SOUTH KOREA
Taejŏn
Chŏnju
Kunsan
TAEGU
Kwangju
Mokpo
Yŏsu
PUSAN
Ulsan
Pohang
Ullung-do
SEA OF JAPAN
Korea Strait
Tsushima
Tsushima-kaikyō
Cheju
Cheju-do
1950
JAPAN
Sasebo
Nagasaki
Iki
Shandong Bandao
SHANDONG
Yantai
Weihai
Weifang
Zibo
Laizhou Wan
Huang He
QINGDAO
(Ch'ingtao)
Jiaozhou Wan
HUANG HAI
(Yellow Sea)
Lianyungang
(Hsinhaihsien)
Haizhou Wan
Linyi
Xintai
Laiwu
JIANGSU
Yancheng
Huai'an
Qingjiang
Bengbu
East from Greenwich
COPYRIGHT. GEORGE PHILIP & SON. LTD.

32 33
58
60 62

1   2   3   4   5

A

B

C

D

E

F

15

10

5

0

5

BURMA (MYANMAR)
THAILAND
LAOS
VIETNAM
CAMBODIA
MALAYSIA
PENINSULAR MALAYSIA
SINGAPORE
SUMATERA
BORNEO
KALIMANTAN
SARAWAK
SABAH
BRUNEI
INDONESIA

ANDAMAN SEA
Gulf of Thailand
SOUTH CHINA SEA
Strait of Malacca
INDIAN OCEAN
JAVA SEA
Java Sea (Jawa)
Greater Sunda Islands
NUSA TENGGARA

RANGOON
G. of Martaban
Moulmein
Thaton
Maubin
Pyapon
Bassein
Tavoy
Moscos Is.
Mergui
Myeik
Kyunzu
BANGKOK
Nakhon Ratchasima (Khorat)
Phra Nakhon Si Ayutthaya
Kho Khot Kra
Surat Thani
Ko Samui
Nakhon Si Thammarat
Thung Song
Phuket
Trang
Songkhla (Singora)
Pattani
Yala
Kota Baharu
George Town
Pinang
Butterworth
Taiping
Ipoh
Kuala Lumpur
Melaka
Johor Baharu
SINGAPORE
Vientiane
Udon Thani
Thakhek
Savannakhet
Hue
Da Nang
Quang Ngai
Qui Nhon
An Nhon (Binh Dinh)
Nha Trang
Phan Rang
PHANH BHO HO CHI MINH (Saigon)
Bien Hoa
Vung Tau
Phnom Penh
Battambang
Siem Reap
Kompong Cham
Kompong Som
Kampot
Takeo
Phu Quoc
Ca Mau
Rach Gia
Can Tho
My Tho

Paracel I.
Spratly Is.
Itu Aba
Spratly I.
Amboyna Cay
Con Son

Kota Kinabalu
Kota Belud
Victoria
Bandar Seri Begawan
BRUNEI
Miri
Bintulu
SARAWAK
Sibu
Kuching
Pontianak
Singkawang
Kepulauan Natuna Besar
Kepulauan Anambas
Kepulauan Riau
Tanjungpinang
Bintan
Pekanbaru
Medan
Belawan
Sibolga
Padang
JAMBI
Palembang
Muaraenim
Bengkulu
LAMPUNG
Tanjungkarang Telukbetung
JAKARTA
Serang
Bogor
Bandung
Cirebon
Pekalongan
Semarang
Surakarta
Yogyakarta
Surabaya
Madiun
Madura
BALI
Denpasar
Lombok
Banjarmasin
Balikpapan
Pontianak
Ketapang
Pangkalpinang
Bangka
Belitung (Billiton)

Projection: Mercator
East from Greenwich

ft   m
12 000   4000
9000   3000
6000   2000
4500   1500
3000   1000
1200   400
600   200
0   0
200   600
2000   6000
4000   12 000
6000   18 000
8000   24 000
m   ft

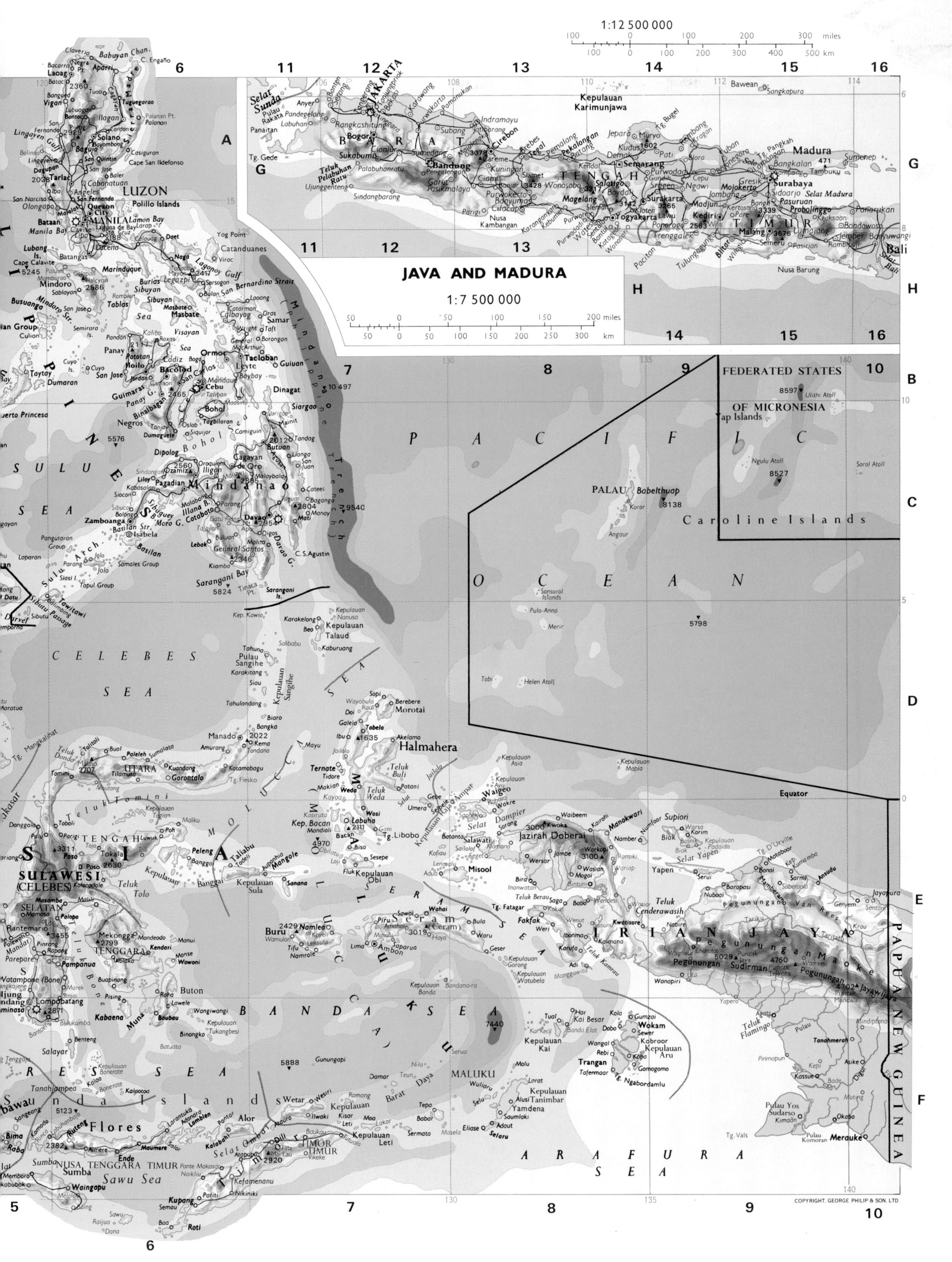

1:12 500 000

100 0 100 200 300 miles

100 0 100 200 300 400 500 km

JAVA AND MADURA

1:7 500 000

50 0 50 100 150 200 miles

50 0 50 100 150 200 250 300 km

PACIFIC

OCEAN

FEDERATED STATES

OF MICRONESIA

Caroline Islands

Equator

SULU SEA

CELEBES SEA

CELEBES SEA

MOLUCCA SEA

Halmahera

SULAWESI (CELEBES)

Mindanao

LUZON

PHILIPPINE

Madura

Bali

Buru

SERAM SEA

BANDA SEA

MALUKU

FLORES

TIMUR

ARAFURA SEA

IRIAN JAYA

PAPUA NEW GUINEA

Sawu Sea

NUSA TENGGARA TIMUR

Merauke

COPYRIGHT. GEORGE PHILIP & SON. LTD.

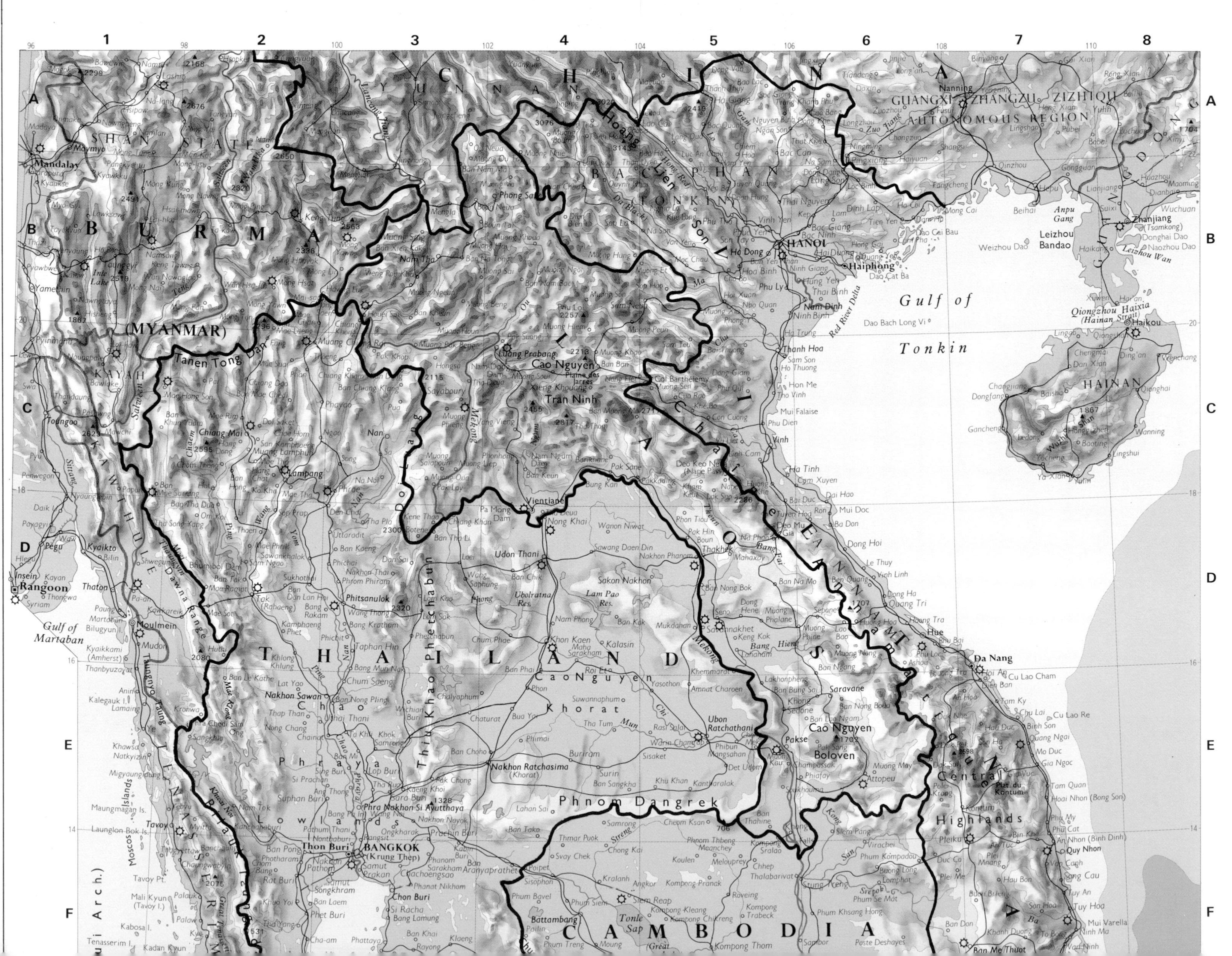
Gulf of Tonkin
HAINAN
Qiongzhou Haixia (Hainan Strait)
Haikou
Leizhou Bandao
Zhanjiang
Nanning
GUANGXI ZHANGZU ZIZHIQU AUTONOMOUS REGION
YUNNAN
HANOI
Haiphong
Red River Delta
Thanh Hoa
Vinh
Hue
Da Nang
Central Highlands
Quy Nhon
Vientiane
Luang Prabang
Udon Thani
Khon Kaen
Nakhon Ratchasima (Khorat)
Ubon Ratchathani
Pakse
Mekong
Phnom Dangrek
CAMBODIA
Battambang
Tonle Sap
BANGKOK (Krung Thep)
Thon Buri
Chiang Mai
Lampang
Phitsanulok
Nakhon Sawan
Moulmein
Dawna Range
Tavoy
Thaton
Pegu
Rangoon
Gulf of Martaban
Mandalay
SHAN STATE
BURMA
(MYANMAR)
KAYAH
THAILAND
LAOS
Salween
Sittang

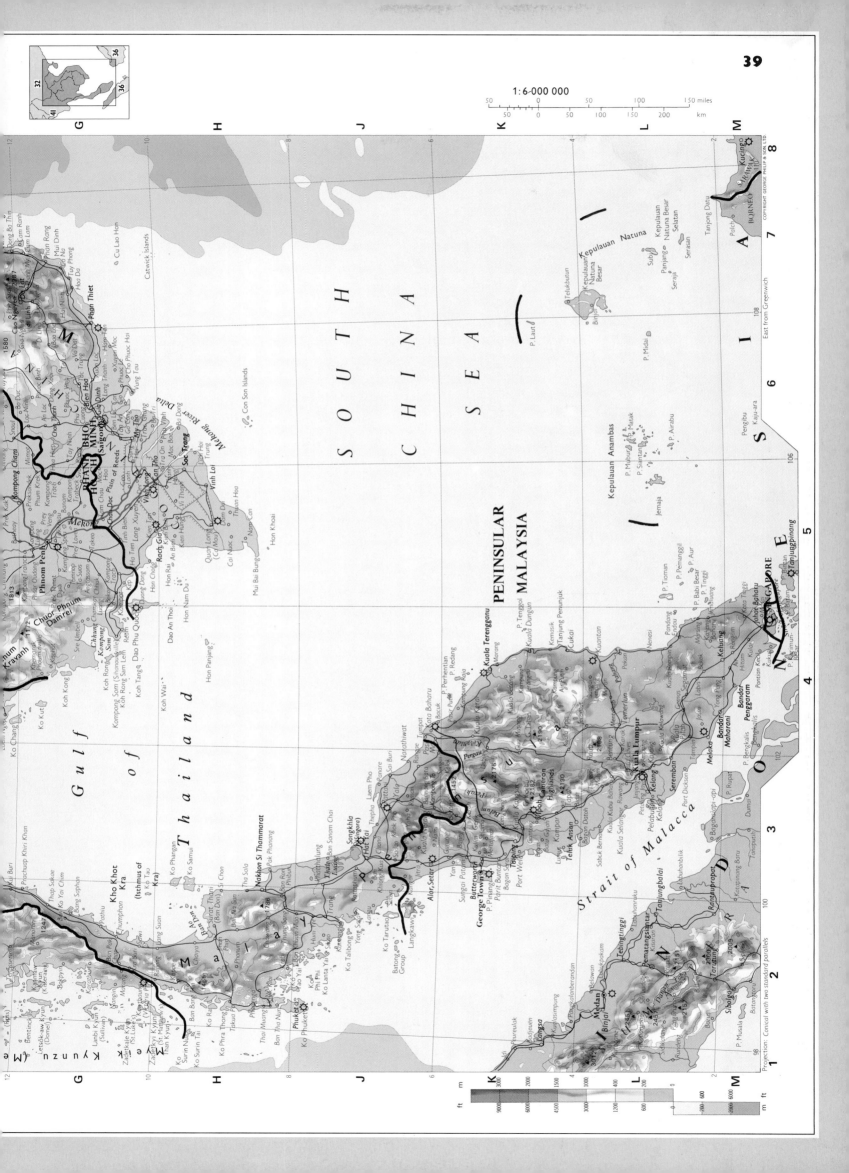

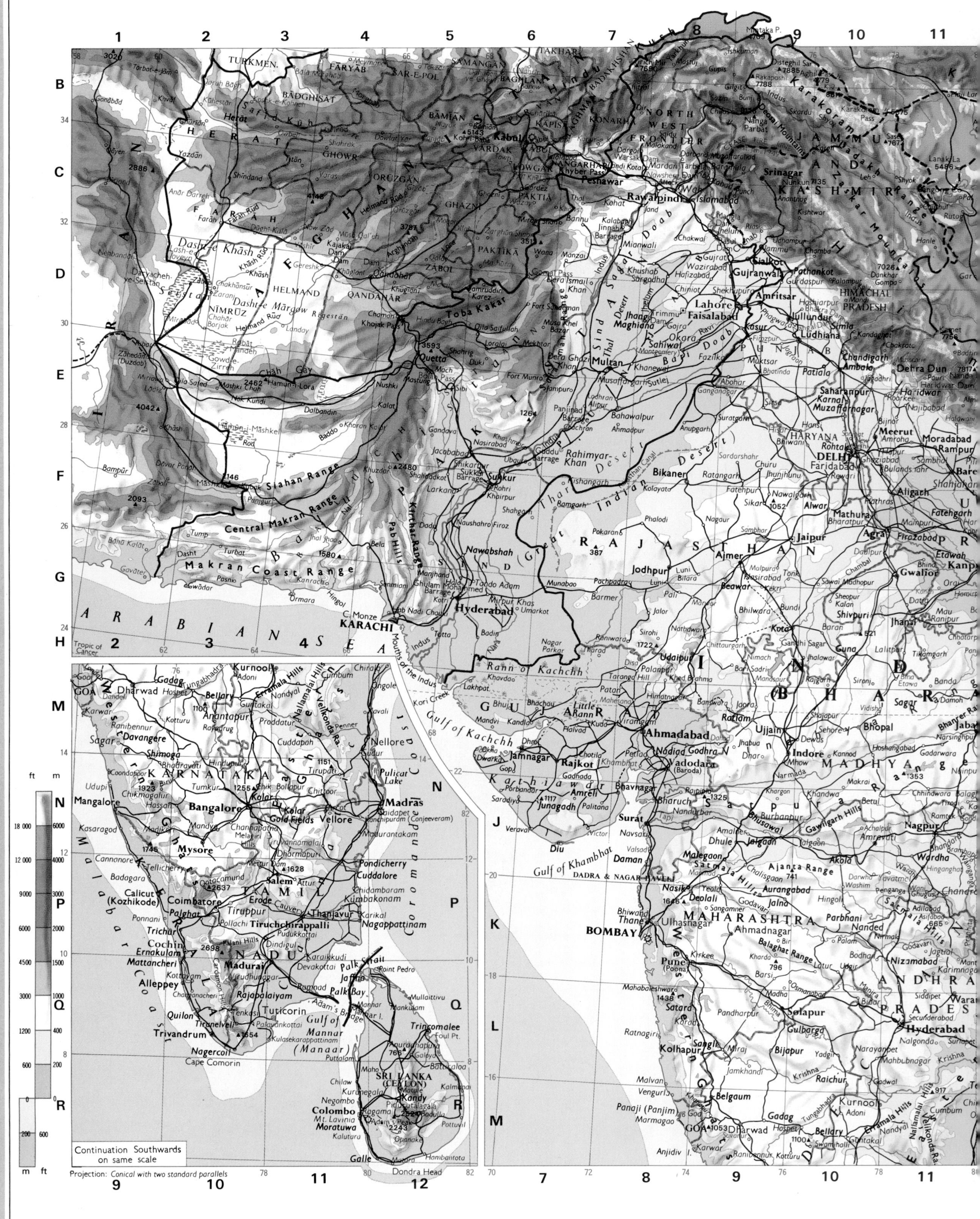
ARABIAN SEA
Tropic of Cancer
AFGHANISTAN
PAKISTAN
INDIA
IRAN
SRI LANKA (CEYLON)
HERAT
FARAH
HELMAND
NĪMRŪZ
QANDAHĀR
ORŪZGĀN
GHAZNI
PAKTIA
PAKTIKĀ
ZĀBOL
BĀMIĀN
GHOWR
BĀDGHĪSĀT
FĀRYĀB
SAR-E-POL
SAMANGĀN
BAGHLĀN
KĀPĪSĀ
KONARH
LOWGAR
VARDAK
NANGARHĀR
BADAKHSHĀN
NORTH WEST FRONTIER
JAMMU AND KASHMIR
HIMACHAL PRADESH
PUNJAB
HARYANA
DELHI
RAJASTHAN
SIND
GUJARAT
MADHYA PRADESH
MAHARASHTRA
ANDHRA PRADESH
KARNATAKA
KERALA
TAMIL NADU
GOA
DADRA & NAGAR HAVELI
Kabul
Herāt
Qandahār
Peshawar
Rawalpindi
Islamabad
Lahore
Faisalabad
Multan
Quetta
Hyderabad
KARACHI
Srinagar
Amritsar
Ludhiana
Jullundur
Chandigarh
Meerut
Jaipur
Ajmer
Jodhpur
Bikaner
Ahmadabad
Vadodara (Baroda)
Surat
Rajkot
Jamnagar
Indore
Bhopal
Nagpur
BOMBAY
Pune (Poona)
Solapur
Hyderabad
Bangalore
Madras
Mysore
Coimbatore
Madurai
Tiruchchirappalli
Calicut (Kozhikode)
Cochin
Trivandrum
Mangalore
Colombo
Kandy
Jaffna
Trincomalee
Galle
Dashte Khāsh
Dasht-e Mārgow
Rīgestān
Hindu Kush
Karakoram
Toba Kakar
Siahan Range
Central Makran Range
Makran Coast Range
Kirthar Range
Thar or Great Indian Desert
Rann of Kachchh
Gulf of Kachchh
Gulf of Khambhat
Satpura Range
Ajanta Range
Western Ghats
Malabar Coast
Coromandel Coast
Palk Strait
Palk Bay
Gulf of Mannar
Cape Comorin
Dondra Head
Indus
Mouths of the Indus
Tropic of Cancer
ft m
18 000 6000
12 000 4000
9000 3000
6000 2000
4500 1500
3000 1000
1200 400
600 200
0 0
200 600
m ft
Continuation Southwards on same scale
Projection: Conical with two standard parallels

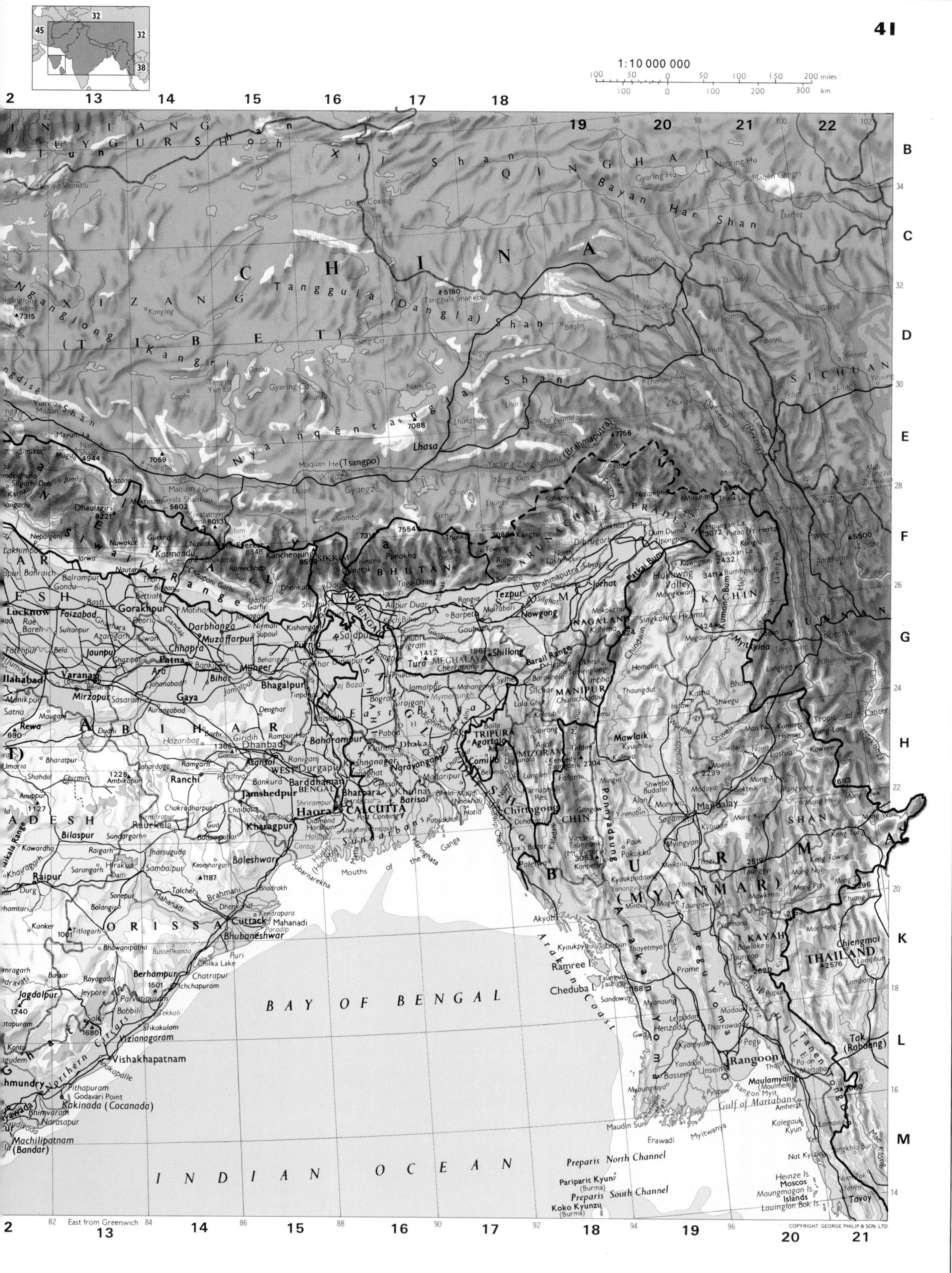
1:10 000 000
BAY OF BENGAL
INDIAN OCEAN
CHINA
XIZANG (TIBET)
QINGHAI
SICHUAN
YUNNAN
BHUTAN
SIKKIM
BANGLADESH
BURMA (MYANMAR)
THAILAND
BIHAR
ORISSA
WEST BENGAL
MEGHALAYA
MANIPUR
MIZORAM
TRIPURA
NAGALAND
ARUNACHAL PRADESH
Lhasa
CALCUTTA
Dhaka
Rangoon
Mandalay
Chittagong
Patna
Varanasi
Kanchenjunga 8598
Everest 8848
Gulf of Martaban
Mouths of the Ganga
Northern Circars
East from Greenwich

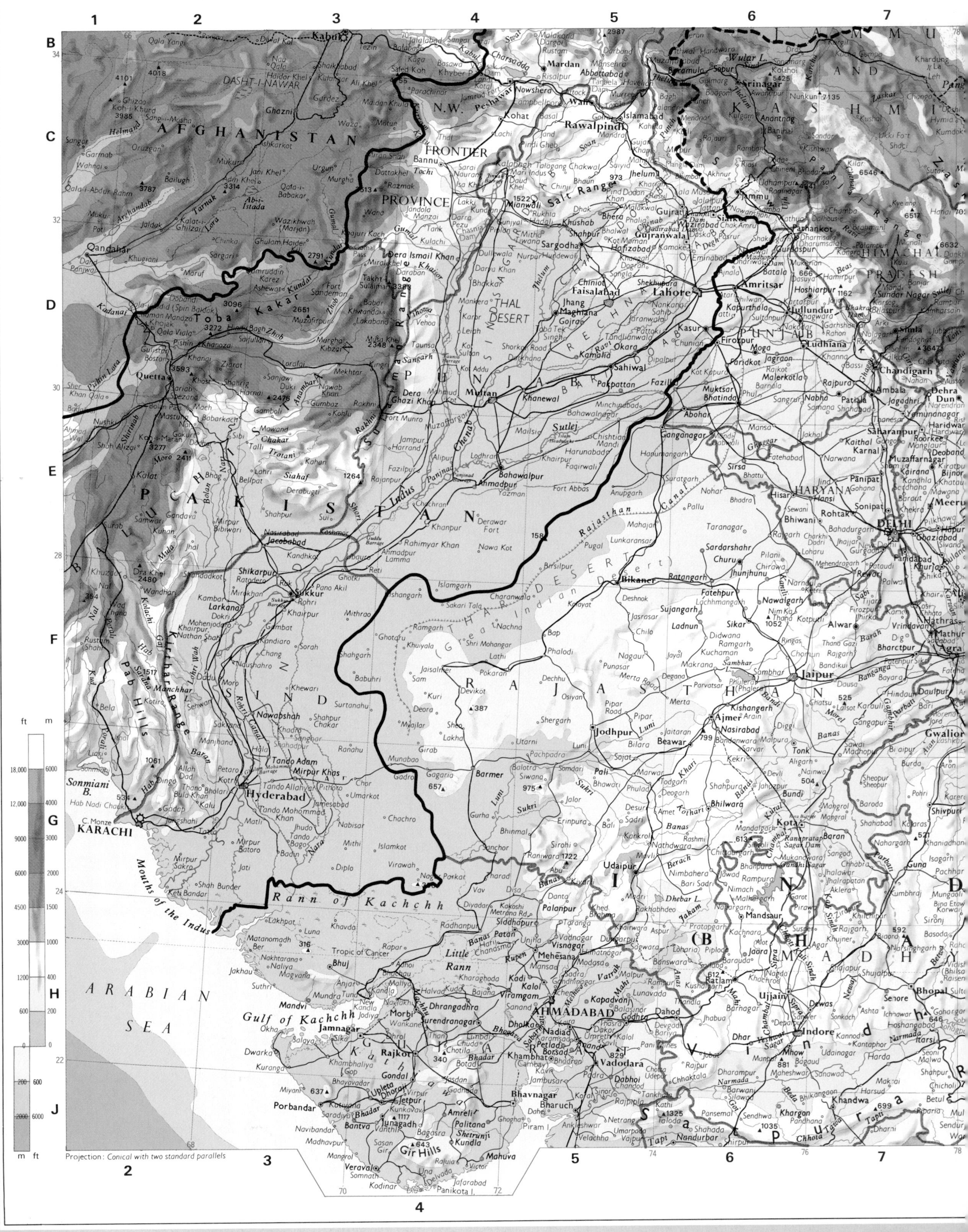
AFGHANISTAN
DASHT-I-NAWAR
N.W. FRONTIER PROVINCE
PAKISTAN
BALUCHISTAN
PUNJAB
SIND
RAJASTHAN
HARYANA
HIMACHAL PRADESH
JAMMU AND KASHMIR
GUJARAT
MADHYA PRADESH
THAL DESERT
THAR DESERT (Great Indian Desert)
Rann of Kachchh
Little Rann
Gulf of Kachchh
ARABIAN SEA
Mouths of the Indus
Salt Range
Toba Kakar Range
Sulaiman Range
Kirthar Range
Pab Hills
Gir Hills
Tropic of Cancer
Kabul
Peshawar
Rawalpindi
Islamabad
Srinagar
Jammu
Lahore
Amritsar
Faisalabad
Multan
Quetta
Hyderabad
KARACHI
Sukkur
Bahawalpur
Chandigarh
DELHI
Jaipur
Agra
Jodhpur
Ajmer
Bikaner
Udaipur
AHMADABAD
Vadodara
Rajkot
Bhavnagar
Indore
Ujjain
Bhopal
Gwalior
Qandahar
Ghazni
Projection: Conical with two standard parallels

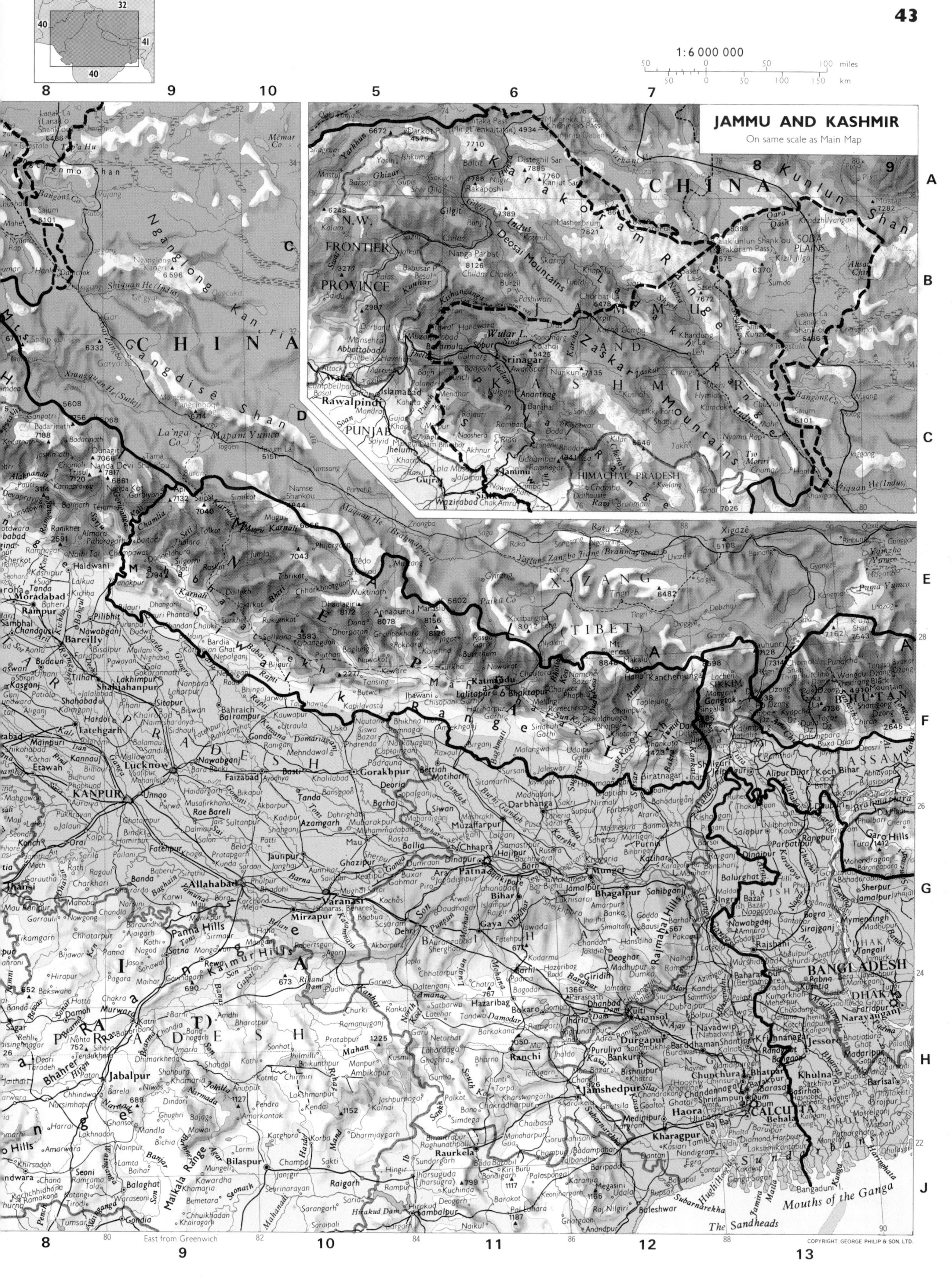

JAMMU AND KASHMIR
On same scale as Main Map

1:6 000 000

50   0   100 miles
50   0   50   100   150 km

CHINA

N.W. FRONTIER PROVINCE

Karakoram Range

Kunlun Shan

SODA PLAINS

Aksai Chin

Rawalpindi
Islamabad
Srinagar
Wular L.
Anantnag
Baramula
Gilgit
Nanga Parbat
Deosai Mountains
Zaskar Range
Pir Panjal Range
KASHMIR
Leh
Ladakh Range
Zaskar Mountains

PUNJAB
Jhelum
Jammu
Udhampur
HIMACHAL PRADESH
Tso Morari

Ngangong Co
Zangdise Shan
CHINA

Mapam Yumco
Nanda Devi
Alaknanda

XIZANG (TIBET)

Maquan He (Brahmaputra)
Xigazê

Mt. Everest
8848
Makalu
Kanchenjunga
SIKKIM
Gangtok
Darjiling
BHUTAN

Moradabad
Rampur
Bareilly
Shahjahanpur
Lucknow
KANPUR
Faizabad
Gorakhpur
U T T A R   P R A D E S H

Katmandu
Bhaktapur
Lalitpur
N E P A L
Mahabharat Range
Biratnagar

ASSAM
Koch Bihar
Brahmaputra

Allahabad
VARANASI
Mirzapur
B I H A R
Patna
Muzaffarpur
Darbhanga
Bhagalpur
Munger
Purnia

Gaya
Hazaribag
Ranchi
Dhanbad
Asansol
Durgapur
Jamshedpur
Raurkela

BANGLADESH
DHAKA
Narayanganj
Faridpur
Jessore
Khulna
Barisal

M A D H Y A   P R A D E S H
Jabalpur
Satna
Rewa
Panna Hills
Kaimur Hills
Malkala Range
Bilaspur
Raigarh
Sambalpur
Hirakud Dam

W E S T   B E N G A L
CALCUTTA
Haora
Kharagpur
Medinipur
Sundarbans

O R I S S A

Mouths of the Ganga
The Sandheads

East from Greenwich
COPYRIGHT. GEORGE PHILIP & SON. LTD.

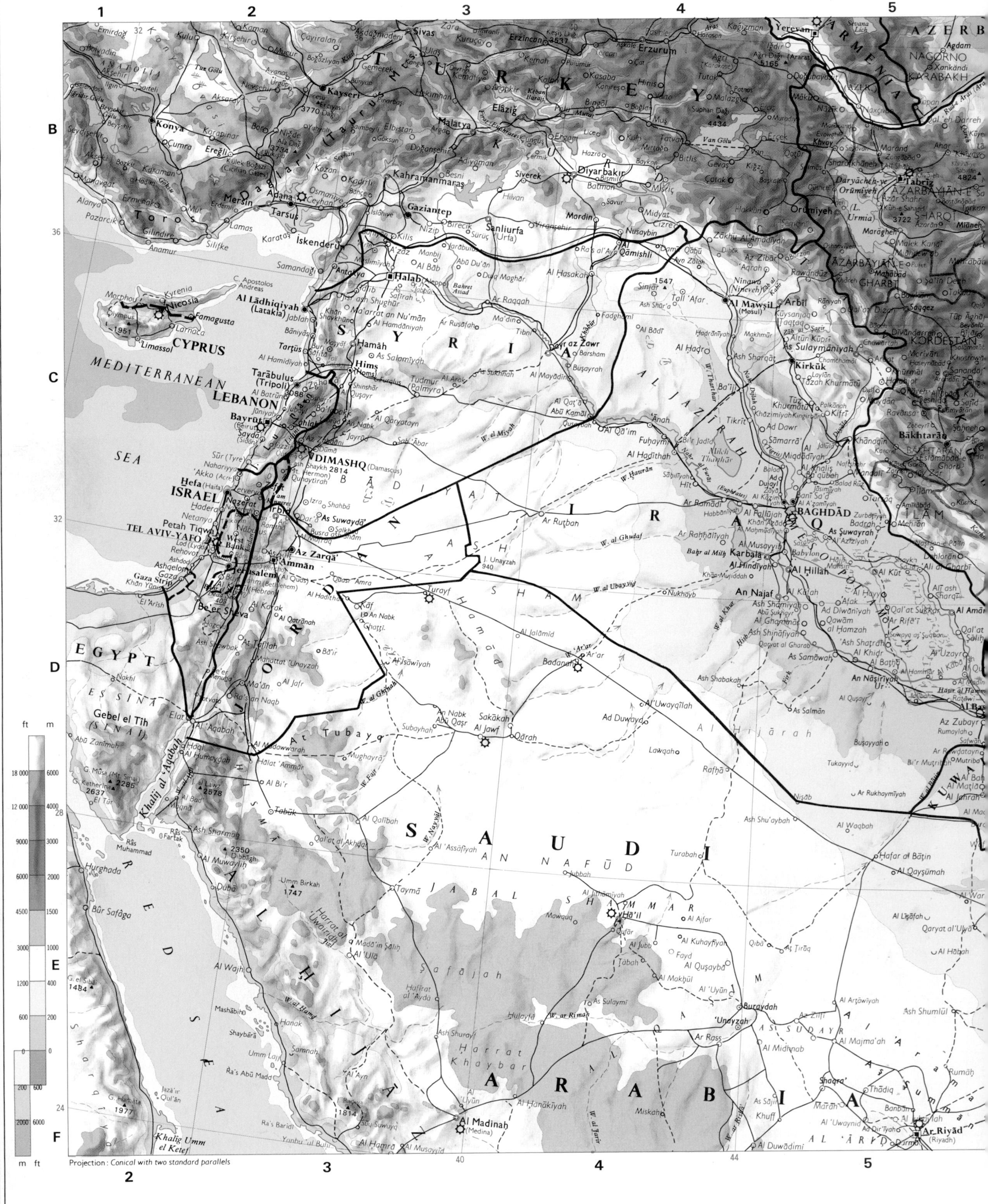

Projection: Conical with two standard parallels

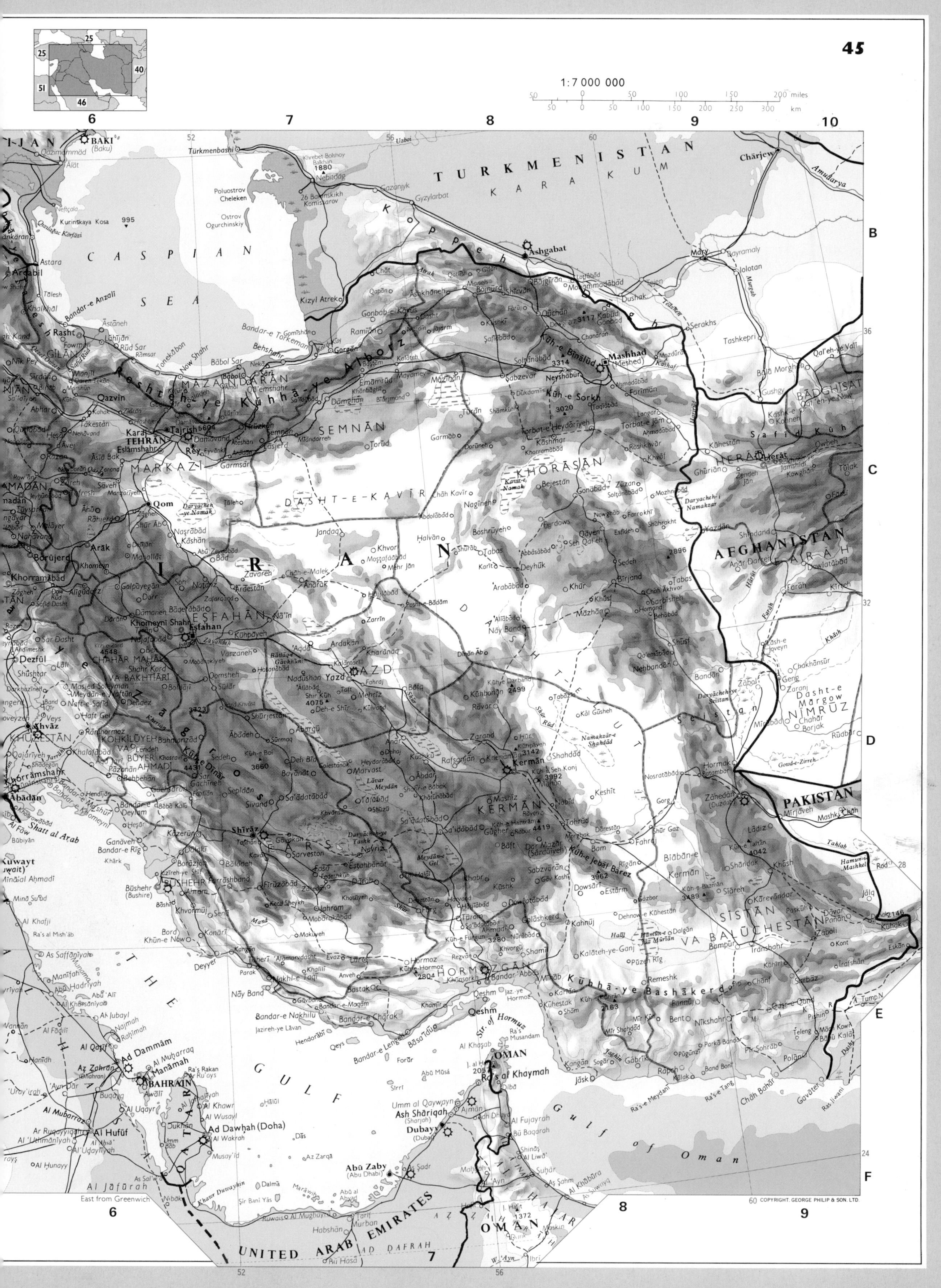
1:7 000 000
50 0 50 100 150 200 miles
50 0 50 100 150 200 250 300 km
6
7
8
9
10
B
C
D
E
F
TURKMENISTAN
KARAKUM
Kopeh Dagh
CASPIAN SEA
IRAN
DASHT-E-KAVĪR
DASHT-E LUT
AFGHANISTAN
PAKISTAN
OMAN
UNITED ARAB EMIRATES
THE GULF
Gulf of Oman
Str. of Hormuz
QATAR
BAHRAIN
Reshteh-ye Kūhhā-ye Alborz
Kūhhā-ye Zāgros
Kūhhā-ye Bashākerd
Kūh-e Jebāl Bārez
Kūh-e Bīnālūd
Kūh-e Sorkh
Kūh-e Dīnār
Safīd Kūh
Dasht-e Mārgow
Shatt al Arab
BAKI (Baku)
TEHRĀN
Tajrīsh 5604
Qom
Esfahan
Yazd
Shīrāz
Kermān
Mashhad (Meshed)
Ashgabat
Mary
Chärjew
Herāt
Zāhedān (Duzdab)
Ahvāz
Ābādān
Khorramshahr
Bandar-e 'Abbās
Būshehr (Bushire)
Ad Dammām
Al Manāmah
Ad Dawhah (Doha)
Dubayy (Dubai)
Abū Zaby (Abu Dhabi)
Ash Shāriqah (Sharjah)
Ra's al Khaymah
Al Hufūf
Kuwayt (Kuwait)
Türkmenbashi
Rasht
Qazvin
Arāk
Hamadān
Dezfūl
Semnān
Sabzevār
Neyshābūr
Bīrjand
Tabas
Kāshān
MĀZANDARĀN
GĪLĀN
MARKAZĪ
SEMNĀN
KHORĀSĀN
ESFAHĀN
YAZD
KERMĀN
FĀRS
HORMOZGĀN
BŪSHEHR
KHŪZESTĀN
SĪSTĀN VA BALŪCHESTĀN
CHAHĀR MAHĀL VA BAKHTĪĀRĪ
KOHKĪLŪYEH VA BŪYER AHMADĪ
BĀDGHĪSĀT
FARĀH
NĪMRŪZ
Al Jāfūrah
East from Greenwich
COPYRIGHT, GEORGE PHILIP & SON, LTD.

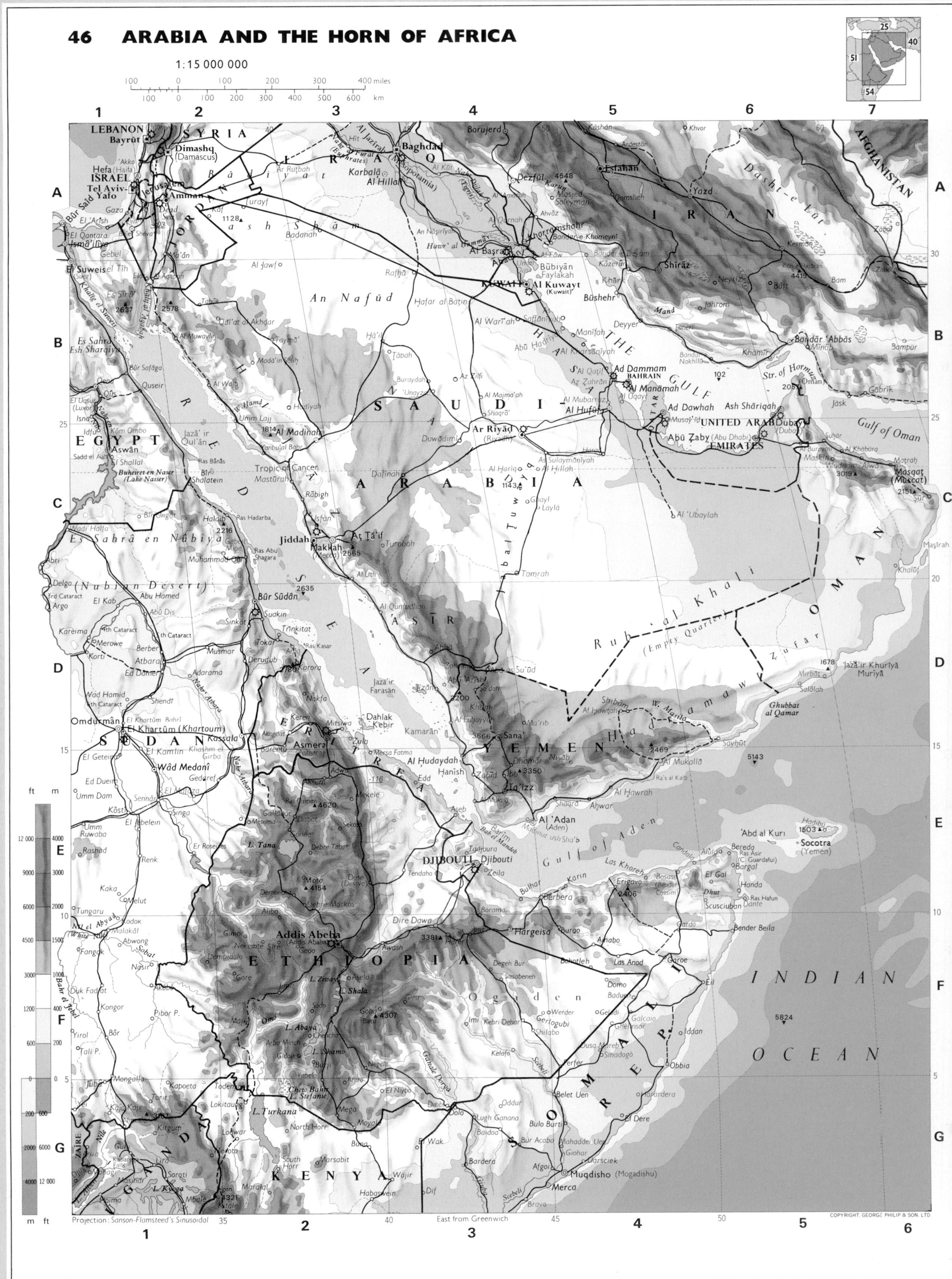

46 ARABIA AND THE HORN OF AFRICA

1:15 000 000

Projection: Sanson-Flamsteed's Sinusoidal   East from Greenwich

COPYRIGHT. GEORGE PHILIP & SON LTD.

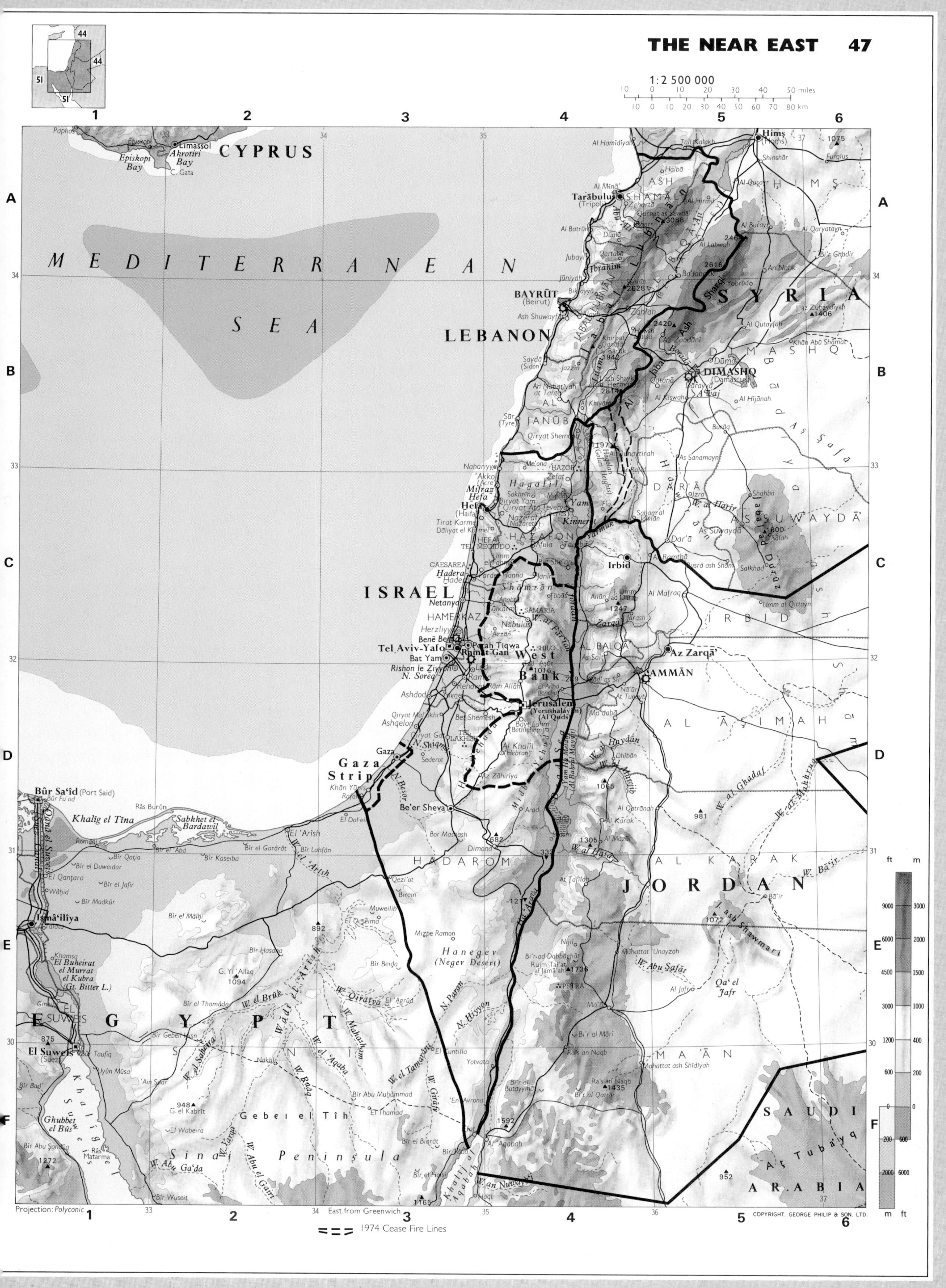

1 : 2 500 000

10   0   10   20   30   40   50 miles
10   0   10   20   30   40   50   60   70   80 km

CYPRUS
Paphos
Episkopi Bay
Akrotiri Bay
Limassol
C. Gata

M E D I T E R R A N E A N

S E A

Hims
(Homs)
Al Hamidiyah
Tall Kalakh
Fuqlus
Halbā
ASH
Al Qusayr
Al Qaryatayn
Al Mīnā'
SHAMĀL
Bi'r Ghadīr
Tarābulus
(Tripoli)
HIMS
Al Batrūn
Dūma
An Nabk
Jubayl
2616
Yabrūd
Ibrahim
2628
SYRIA
BAYRŪT
(Beirut)
Ash Shuwayfāt
'az Zubaydīyah
1406
Zahlah
Al Qutayfah
LEBANON
Saydā
(Sidon)
DIMASHQ
DIMASHQ
(Damascus)
Jazzīn
1944
Al Kiswah
A'laj
AL
Sūr
(Tyre)
JANŪB
Al Hijānah
Qiryat Shemo
DARʿĀ
AS SUWAYDĀ'
Nahariyya
HAZOR
1800
'Akko
(Acre)
Hagalil
Zefat
Kinner
Shahba
Mifrag
Hefa
Qiryat Yam
Yam
As Suwayda
Hefa
(Haifa)
Nazerat
(Nazareth)
Teverya
Dar'ā
Tirat Karme
HEFA
TEL MEGIDDO
HADAROM
CAESAREA
Hadera
ISRAEL
Shomron
SAMARIA
Irbid
Netanya
Herzliyya
Nābulus
IRBID
HAMERKAZ
Benē Beraq
Zarqā
Tel Aviv-Yafo
Ramat Gan
West
Az Zarqā'
Bat Yam
Bank
AMMĀN
Rishon le Ziyyon
N. Soreq
Ashdod
Jerusalem
(Yerushalayim)
(Al Quds)
AL 'ĀSIMAH
Qiryat Malakhi
Bet Shemesh
Ashqelon
Qiryat Gat
Al Khalīl
(Hebron)
Gaza
N. Shiq
Gaza
Strip
Sederot
Az Zāhiriya
Be'er Sheva
Bûr Sa'id (Port Said)
Bûr Fu'âd
AL KARAK
Râs Burûn
Khalîg el Tîna
Sabkhet el Bardawil
Dimona
El 'Arîsh
JORDAN
Ismâ'îliya
HADAROM
El Buheirat el Murrat el Kubra
(Gt. Bitter L.)
Mizpe Ramon
PETRA
EGYPT
Hanegev
(Negev Desert)
MAʿĀN
El Suweis
El Suweis (Suez)
Gebel el Tîh
Sinai Peninsula
SAUDI
Al 'Aqabah
ARABIA
Ghubbet el Bûs

Projection: Polyconic   East from Greenwich   COPYRIGHT. GEORGE PHILIP & SON. LTD.

= = = 1974 Cease Fire Lines

ft   m
9000   3000
6000   2000
4500   1500
3000   1000
1200   400
600
0
0
200   600
2000 6000
m   ft

1 : 42 000 000

200   0   200   400   600   800   1000   1200 miles
200   0   200   400   600   800   1000   1200   1400   1600   1800 km

1   2   3   4   5   6   7   8   9   10

NORTH
ATLANTIC
OCEAN

British Isles

E u r o p e

Carpathians

B. of Biscay

Mont Blanc
4807

Alps

Dinaric Alps

Black Sea

Caucasus

Elbrus
5633

Caspian Sea

Aral Sea

Azores

Pyrénées

Apennines

Adriatic Sea

Anatolia

A s i a

6578

Iberian
Peninsula

Corsica

Sardinia

Sicily

Crete

Cyprus

Levant

Mesopotamia

Tigris

Madeira

Str. of Gibraltar

C. Bon

Malta

5121

Syrian Desert

Euphrates

The Gulf

M e d i t e r r a n e a n   S e a

Canary Is.

4165 Middle Atlas
High Atlas
Toubkal

High Plateaux
Saharan Atlas

G. of Gabès

Chott Djerid

G. of Sidra

Tripolitania

Cyrenaica

Siwa Oasis

Libyan Desert

Egypt

Arabian Desert

Mt. Sinai
2285

H e j a z

A r a b i a

Red Sea

Tenerife

Anti Atlas

Tropic of Cancer

Tasili Plateau

Hoggar

Al Kufrah

El Khārga

Nubian Desert

Nubia

Ras Nouâdhibou

El Djouf

Adrar

Aïr

Tibesti

S   a   h   a   r   a

Bilma

Ras Dashen
4620

116

Cape Verde Is.

C. Vert

Senegal

Niger

Volta

Niger

L. Chad

Bahr el Ghazal

Wadai

Darfur

Kordofân

White Nile

Blue Nile

Atbara

L. Tana

Barim
Bab el Mandeb

G. of Aden

Ras Asir

Soco

Senegambia
Gambia

Fouta
Djalon

S   u   d   a   n

Chari

Ethiopian
Highlands

Somali
Peninsula

G u i n e a

Benue

Dar Banda

Bahr el
Ghazâl

Bahr el Jebel

Shabelle

Grain Coast

Gold Coast

Ivory Coast

Slave Coast

Bight of Benin

Mt. Cameroon
4070

Adamawa
Highlands

Uele

Ubangi

L. Turkana

Juba

C. Palmas

Bioko

Bight of Bonny

I. de Principe

São Tomé

Congo

Zaïre

Chutes
Boyoma

L. Albert
Ruwenzori
5109

4321

Mt. Elgon

5199

Mt. Kenya

Tana

Gulf of Guinea

Equator

C. Lopez

Ogooué

Annobón

B a s i n

L. Edward

L. Victoria

5895

Kilimanjaro

Pemba I.

INDIAN

Seychelle

Zaïre

Kasai

Sankuru

L. Lualaba

L. Kivu

OCEAN

Ascension I.

Cuango

Kasai

Lukuga

L. Tanganyika

Rungwe
2961

Aldabra
Is.

SOUTH

Cuanza

L. Mweru

Shaba

Bangweulu
Swamp

L. Nyasa
(L. Malawi)

C. Delgado

Comoros

ATLANTIC

Biê
Plateau

Luapula

Zambezi

St. Helena

Cubango

Cuando

Zambezi

Shire

Madagascar

OCEAN

Cunene

C. Fria

Victoria
Falls

2643

Mauri

Namib Desert

Okavango Swamps

Limpopo

Réunion

Mozambique Channel

Tropic of Capricorn

Walvis Bay

K a l a h a r i

Vaal

High Veld

Drakensberg

Delagoa B.

3482

Orange

Compass Mt.
2505

Nieuveldberge
Great Karoo
Swartberge

Algoa B.

C. of Good Hope

C. Agulhas

Tristan da Cunha

West from Greenwich   East from Greenwich

1   2   3   4   5   6   7   8   9

Projection: Azimuthal Equidistant

ft   m
12000 4000
9000   3000
6000   2000
3000   1000
1500   500
600   200
0   0
600   200
3000   1000
6000   2000
12000 4000
m ft

1 : 42 000 000

200   0   200   400   600   800   1000   1200 miles
200   0   200   400   600   800   1000 1200 1400 1600 1800 km

1   2   3   4   5   6   7   8   9   10

20   0   20   40   50   60

B

NORTH

ATLANTIC

OCEAN

UNITED
KINGDOM
LONDON

NETH.   GERMANY   POLAND   Warsaw
BELG.   Kiev   RUSSIA
PARIS   PRAGUE   Volgograd   KAZAKHSTAN
FRANCE   CZECH REP.   UKRAINE
SWITZ.   Vienna   SLOVAK REP.
B. of Biscay   AUSTRIA   HUNGARY
CROATIA   ROMANIA   Odessa
BOS.-HERZ.   YUG.   GEORGIA   AZER.
Corsica   Rome   ITALY   BULGARIA   Black Sea   ARM.   Baku   TURKMEN.
Madrid   Sardinia   MAC.   Ankara   Caspian Sea
SPAIN   GREECE   TURKEY   Mosul   Eşfahān
Lisbon   PORTUGAL   Athens   IRAN
            Sicily   Crete   CYPRUS   Aleppo   TEHRĀN
Mediterranean Sea   SYRIA   Damascus   Baghdād
Algiers   Annaba   Tunis   MALTA   Tel Aviv-Jaffa   Basra
Constantine   TUNISIA   Jerusalem   ISRAEL   JORDAN   KUWAIT
Sfax   Tripoli   Misrātah   Alexandria   Port Said   Suez
Benghazi   CAIRO   El Faiyûm   Riyadh
Casablanca   Fès   Syrian Desert
Rabat   Tétouan   Medina   BAHRAIN   QATAR
Marrakesh   SAUDI   The Gulf
Canary Is.   ALGERIA   LIBYA   EGYPT   ARABIA
El Aaiún   In Salah   Marzûq   Aswân   Jedda   Mecca
Dakhla   Tropic of Cancer   Al Jawf   Wādī Halfa
Fdérik   Sahara   Port Sudan   YEMEN
Ras Nouâdhibou   MAURITANIA   Atbara
VERDE IS.   Nouakchott   NIGER   CHAD   Om durmân   Khartoum   ERITREA   Asmera
St-Louis   Tombouctou   Agades   L. Chad   Abéché   El Fâsher   SUDAN   Wād Medani   DJIBOUTI   G. of Aden
C. Vert   Senegal   Niamey   Kano   Maiduguri   Ndjamena   El Obeid   Addis Ababa   Djibouti   Socotra (Yemen)   Ras Asir
Dakar   SENEGAL   MALI   BURKINA FASO   NIGERIA   CENTRAL   L. Tana   Harer   Berbera
GAMBIA   Banjul   Bamako   Ouagadougou   Abuja   AFRICAN REP.   Bangui   ETHIOPIA
GUINEA-BISSAU   Bissau   Bobo Dioulasso   BENIN   Ibadan   Enugu   Benue   Douala   Yaoundé   CAMEROON   Wau   L. Turkana   SOMALI REP.
Conakry   GUINEA   IVORY COAST   GHANA   TOGO   Lagos   Malakal   L. Albert   Shabelle
Freetown   SIERRA LEONE   Bouaké   Kumasi   Porto Novo   EQUATORIAL GUINEA   UGANDA   KENYA   Mogadishu
Monrovia   LIBERIA   Yamoussoukro   Accra   Bight of Benin   Port Harcourt   Malabo   Libreville   CONGO   ZAÏRE   Kisangani   Kampala   Kisumu   Nairobi   Juba
Abidjan   Sekondi-Takoradi   SÃO TOMÉ & PRINCIPE   GABON   Brazzaville   Mbandaka   L. Edward   RWANDA   Kigali   L. Victoria   Mombasa   Kismayu
Gulf of Guinea   C. Lopez   Annobón   Pointe Noire   Kinshasa   Kasai   L. Kivu   BURUNDI   Bujumbura   INDIAN
Equator   Matadi   CABINDA (Angola)   Kananga   TANZANIA   Dodoma   Zanzibar   OCEAN   SEYCHELLES
Ascension I. (U.K.)   Luanda   Lobito   L. Tanganyika   Dar es Salaam
SOUTH   ANGOLA   Huambo   Likasi   Lubumbashi   L. Malawi   C. Delgado   COMOROS   Antsiranana
ATLANTIC   Namibe   Ndola   Lilongwe   MALAWI   Mayotte (Fr.)   Mahajanga
St. Helena (U.K.)   C. Fria   ZAMBIA   Lusaka   Blantyre   MOZAMBIQUE   Toamasina   Antananarivo
OCEAN   NAMIBIA   Livingstone   Harare   Beira   MADAGASCAR   MAURITIUS
            Windhoek   BOTSWANA   Bulawayo   ZIMBABWE   Limpopo   Fianarantsoa   Réunion (Fr.)
Tropic of Capricorn   Gaborone   Pretoria   Mbabane   SWAZ.   Maputo
            Johannesburg   Vaal   Mozambique Channel
            Kimberley   Orange   Maseru   LESOTHO   Durban
SOUTH AFRICA   East London
Cape Town   C. of Good Hope   C. Agulhas   Port Elizabeth

Tristan da Cunha (U.K.)

Projection: Azimuthal Equidistant   West from Greenwich   East from Greenwich   ● Dakar   Capital Cities   CARTOGRAPHY BY PHILIP'S COPYRIGHT REED INTERNATIONAL BOOKS LTD

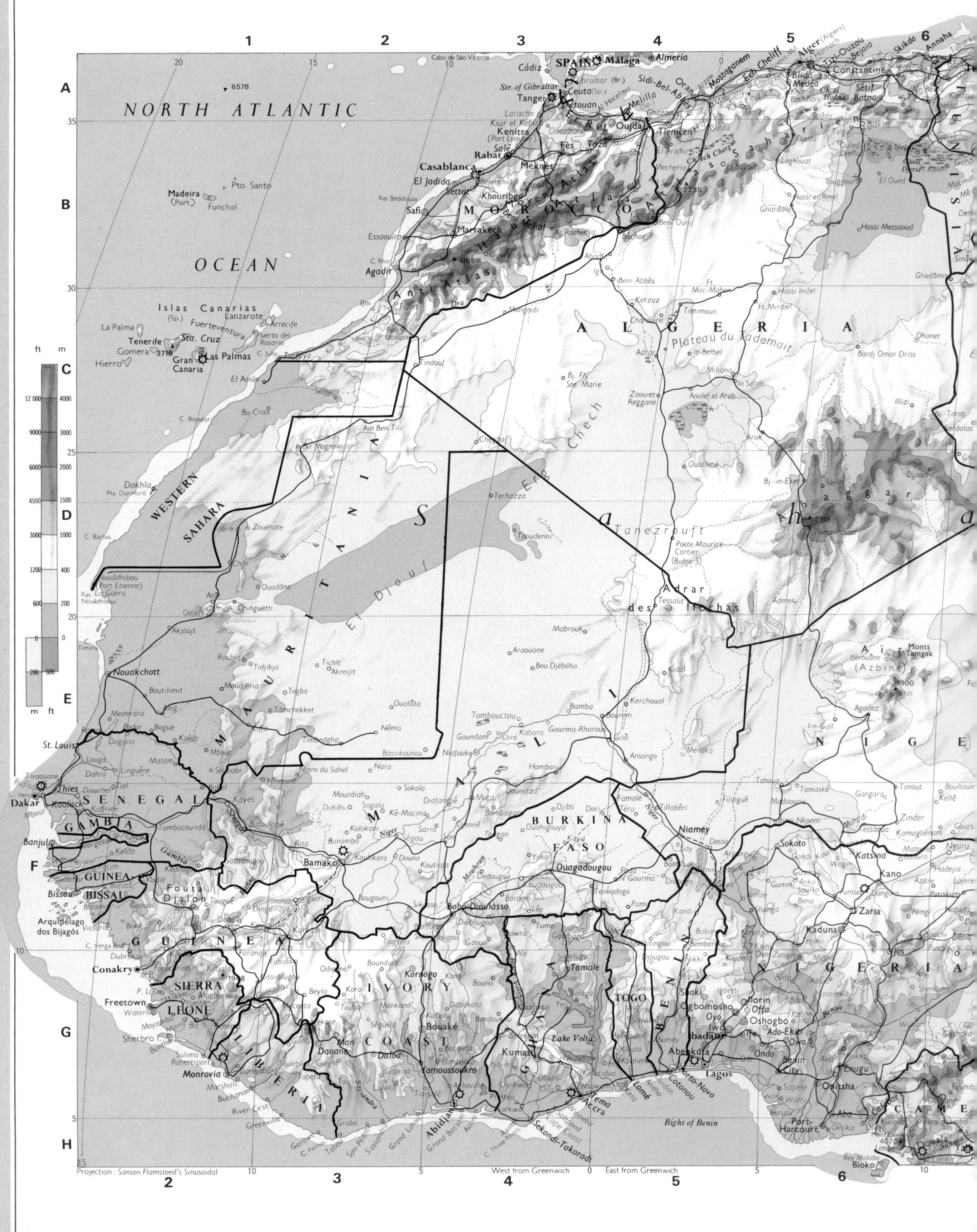
NORTH ATLANTIC
OCEAN
Madeira (Port.)
Pto. Santo
Funchal
Islas Canarias (Sp.)
Lanzarote
Fuerteventura
La Palma
Tenerife
Sta. Cruz
Gomera
Hierro
Gran Canaria
Las Palmas
SPAIN
Málaga
Almería
Cádiz
Str. of Gibraltar
Gibraltar (Br.)
Tanger
Ceuta (Sp.)
Tetouan
Melilla (Sp.)
Oran
Mostaganem
Alger (Algiers)
Blida
Medea
Constantine
Annaba
Skikda
Bejaia
Tizi-Ouzou
Sétif
Batna
Biskra
Laghouat
Ghardaïa
Touggourt
Ouargla
Hassi Messaoud
El Oued
Sidi-Bel-Abbès
Tlemcen
Oujda
Fès
Taza
Meknès
Rabat
Salé
Kenitra (Port Lyautey)
Larache
Ksar el Kebir
Casablanca
El Jadida
Settat
Khouribga
Safi
Beni Mellal
Marrakech
Essaouira
Agadir
MOROCCO
Haut Atlas
Moyen Atlas
Anti Atlas
Er Rif
Ar Rachidiya
Béchar
Beni Abbès
Tindouf
ALGERIA
Plateau du Tademait
Timimoun
Adrar
In Salah
Reggane
Ahaggar
Tamanrasset
Djanet
Illizi
Tanezrouft
Adrar des Iforhas
Tessalit
Poste Maurice Cortier (Bidon 5)
WESTERN SAHARA
El Aaiún
Semara
Bu Craa
Dakhla
C. Bojador
Tarfaya
C. Barbas
Nouâdhibou (Port Etienne)
La Guera
Ras Nouâdhibou
C. Timiris
MAURITANIA
Zouérate
Atar
Chinguetti
Akjoujt
Nouakchott
Tidjikja
Tichit
Kiffa
Néma
Rosso
Boghé
Kaédi
Sélibabi
El Djouf
Erg Chech
Taoudenni
MALI
Tombouctou
Gao
Kidal
Mopti
Ségou
Bamako
Kayes
Nioro du Sahel
Sikasso
SENEGAL
Dakar
Thiès
Kaolack
St. Louis
Tambacounda
Ziguinchor
C. Vert
GAMBIA
Banjul
GUINEA-BISSAU
Bissau
Arquipélago dos Bijagós
GUINEA
Conakry
Fouta Djalon
Kankan
SIERRA LEONE
Freetown
LIBERIA
Monrovia
IVORY COAST
Abidjan
Yamoussoukro
Bouaké
BURKINA FASO
Ouagadougou
Bobo-Dioulasso
GHANA
Kumasi
Accra
Tema
Lake Volta
Tamale
Sekondi-Takoradi
TOGO
Lomé
BENIN
Cotonou
Porto-Novo
Bight of Benin
NIGER
Niamey
Agadez
Zinder
Aïr (Azbine)
NIGERIA
Lagos
Ibadan
Kano
Kaduna
Zaria
Sokoto
Port Harcourt
Enugu
Onitsha
Benin City
Oshogbo
Ogbomosho
Abeokuta
CAMEROON
Douala
Bioko
Projection: Sanson Flamsteed's Sinusoidal
West from Greenwich
East from Greenwich
ft m
12 000 4000
9000 3000
6000 2000
4500 1500
3000 1000
1200 400
600 200
0 0
200 600
m ft

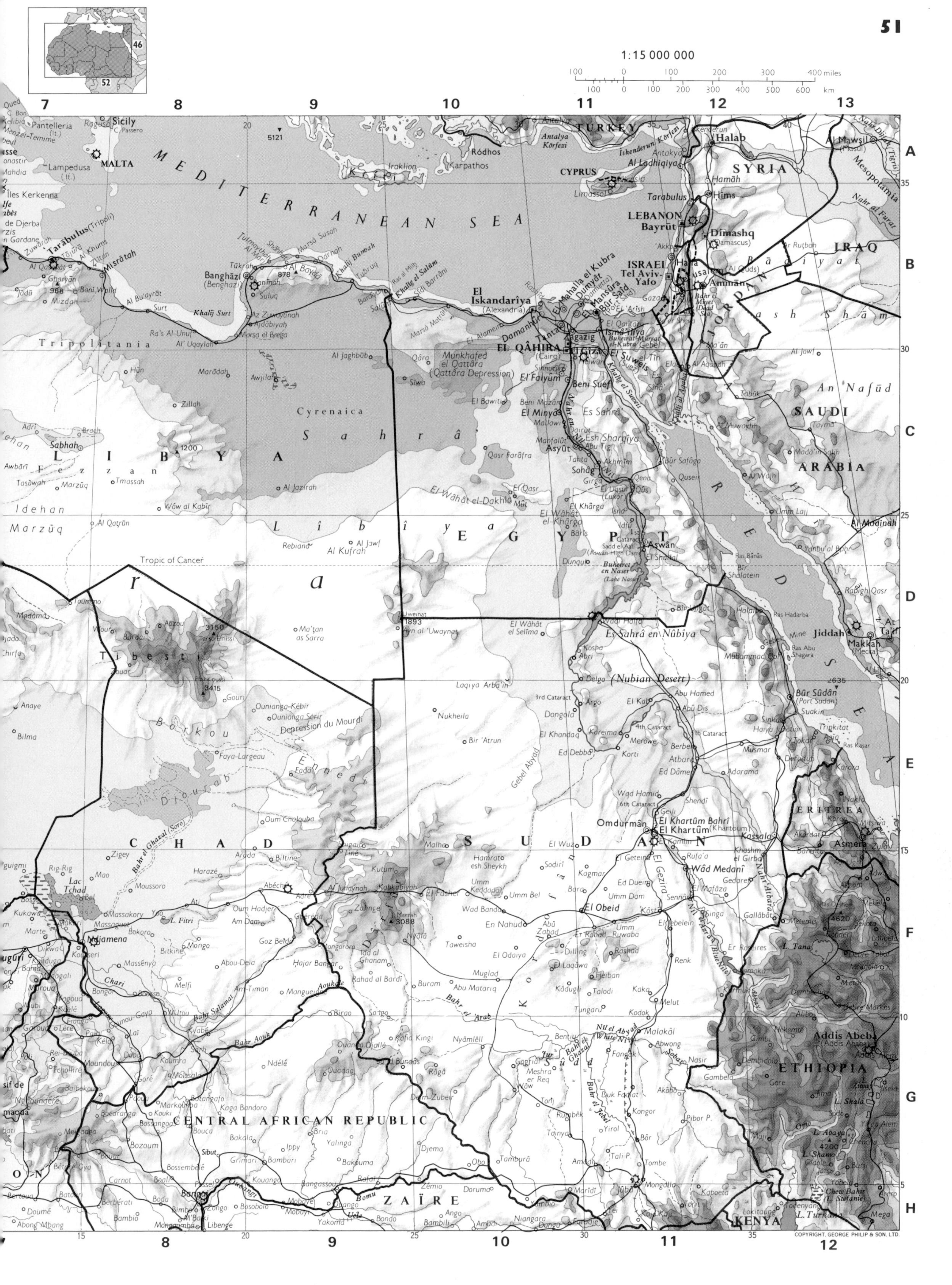

46
52
1:15 000 000
100 0 100 200 300 400 miles
100 0 100 200 300 400 500 600 km
7 8 9 10 11 12 13
A B C D E F G H
MEDITERRANEAN SEA
TURKEY
SYRIA
LEBANON
ISRAEL
JORDAN
IRAQ
CYPRUS
MALTA
Sicily
Pantelleria
Lampedusa
Kriti
Rodhos
Karpathos
Halab
Hamāh
Hims
Tarabulus
Bayrūt
Dimashq
(Damascus)
Tel Aviv-Yafo
Ammān
Al Mawsil
(Mosul)
Mesopotamia
Nahr al Furat
Bādiyat ash Shām
An Nafūd
SAUDI ARABIA
Al Madinah
Jiddah
Makkah
(Mecca)
At Tā'if
Yanbu' al Bahr
Rābigh
Tabūk
Al Wajh
Umm Lajj
Ras Banâs
Ras Hadarba
RED SEA
Tarābulus (Tripoli)
Misrātah
Banghāzī
(Benghazi)
Surt
Khalīj Surt
Tripolitania
Cyrenaica
Fezzan
Sabhah
Marzūq
Idehan Marzūq
Al Jaghbūb
Al Kufrah
Al Jawf
Tropic of Cancer
LIBYA
Sahra' Libiya
Sahara
EGYPT
El Iskandarîya
(Alexandria)
EL QÂHIRA
(Cairo)
El Gîza
Bûr Sa'îd
(Port Said)
El Suweis
(Suez)
Dumyât
Mansûra
Tanta
Zagazig
Ismâ'ilîya
Damanhûr
El Faiyûm
Beni Suef
El Minya
Asyût
Sohâg
Qena
Luxor
Aswân
Buheiret en Naser
(Lake Nasser)
Munkhafed el Qattâra
(Qattâra Depression)
Siwa
El Wâhât el Dakhla
El Khârga
Qasr Farâfra
Es Sahrâ esh Sharqîya
Es Sahrâ en Nûbîya
(Nubian Desert)
Wadi Halfa
Bûr Sûdân
(Port Sudan)
Suakin
Atbara
Omdurman
El Khartûm
(Khartoum)
El Khartûm Bahrî
Kassala
Wâd Medanî
El Obeid
Kordofan
Dârfûr
El Fasher
Nyala
Malakâl
Juba
Wau
Bahr el Ghazal
Bahr el Jebel
Nil el Abyad
(White Nile)
Bahr el Azraq
(Blue Nile)
Nahr Atbara
SUDAN
Tibesti
Borkou
Ennedi
Djourab
Faya-Largeau
Abéché
Lac Tchad
Ndjamena
CHAD
Chari
Sarh
Moundou
Bangui
Berbérati
Bambari
CENTRAL AFRICAN REPUBLIC
ZAÏRE
Ubangi
Bomu
Uele
ERITREA
Asmera
Mitsiwa
ETHIOPIA
Addis Abeba
(Addis Ababa)
L. Tana
Gonder
KENYA
L. Turkana
COPYRIGHT, GEORGE PHILIP & SON, LTD.

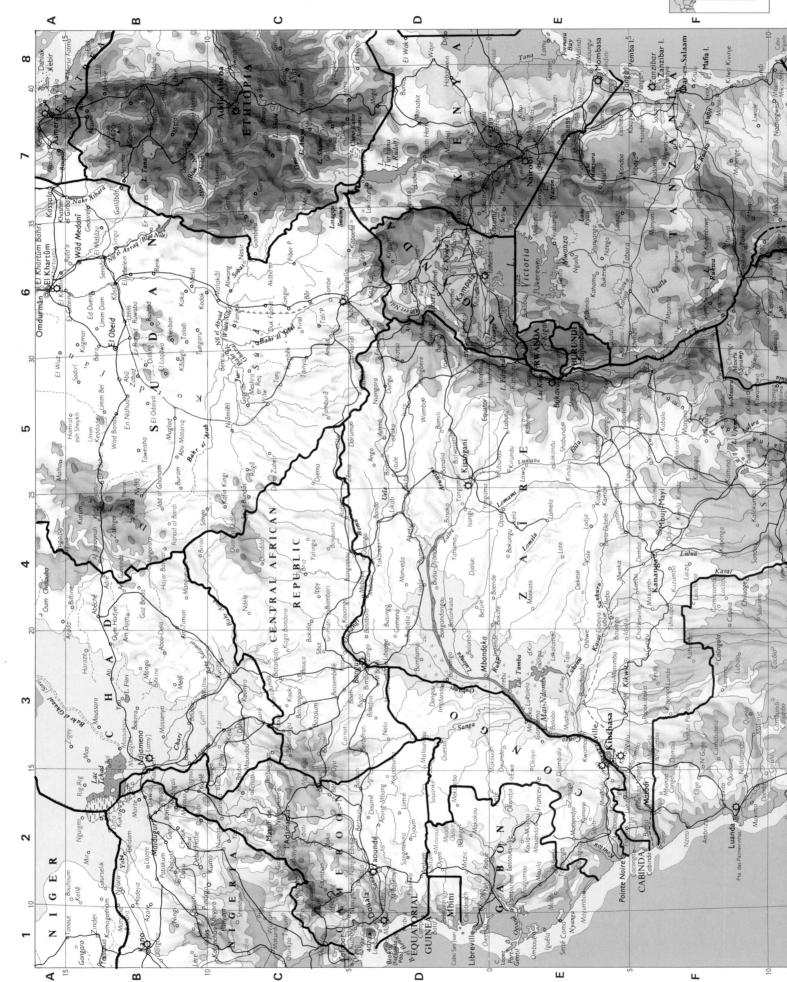

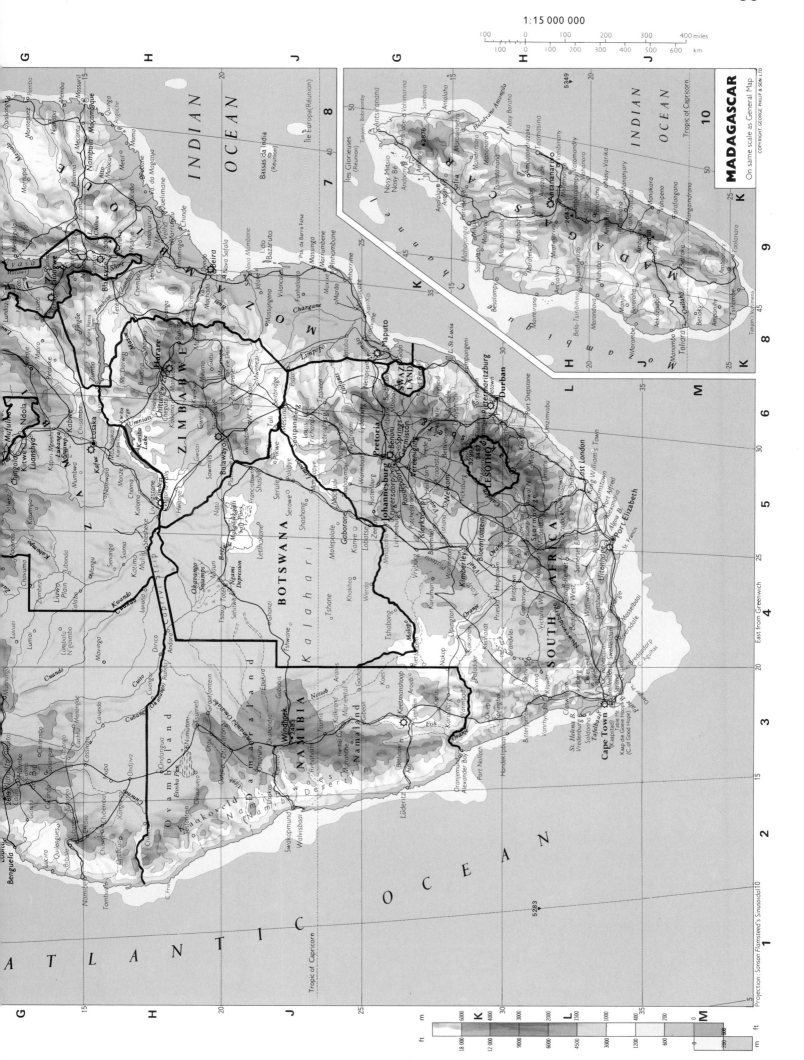

1:15 000 000

MADAGASCAR
On same scale as General Map
COPYRIGHT. GEORGE PHILIP & SON. LTD.

INDIAN OCEAN

ATLANTIC OCEAN

Projection: Sanson Flamsteed's Sinusoidal

SOUTH AFRICA

NAMIBIA

BOTSWANA

ZIMBABWE

Kalahari

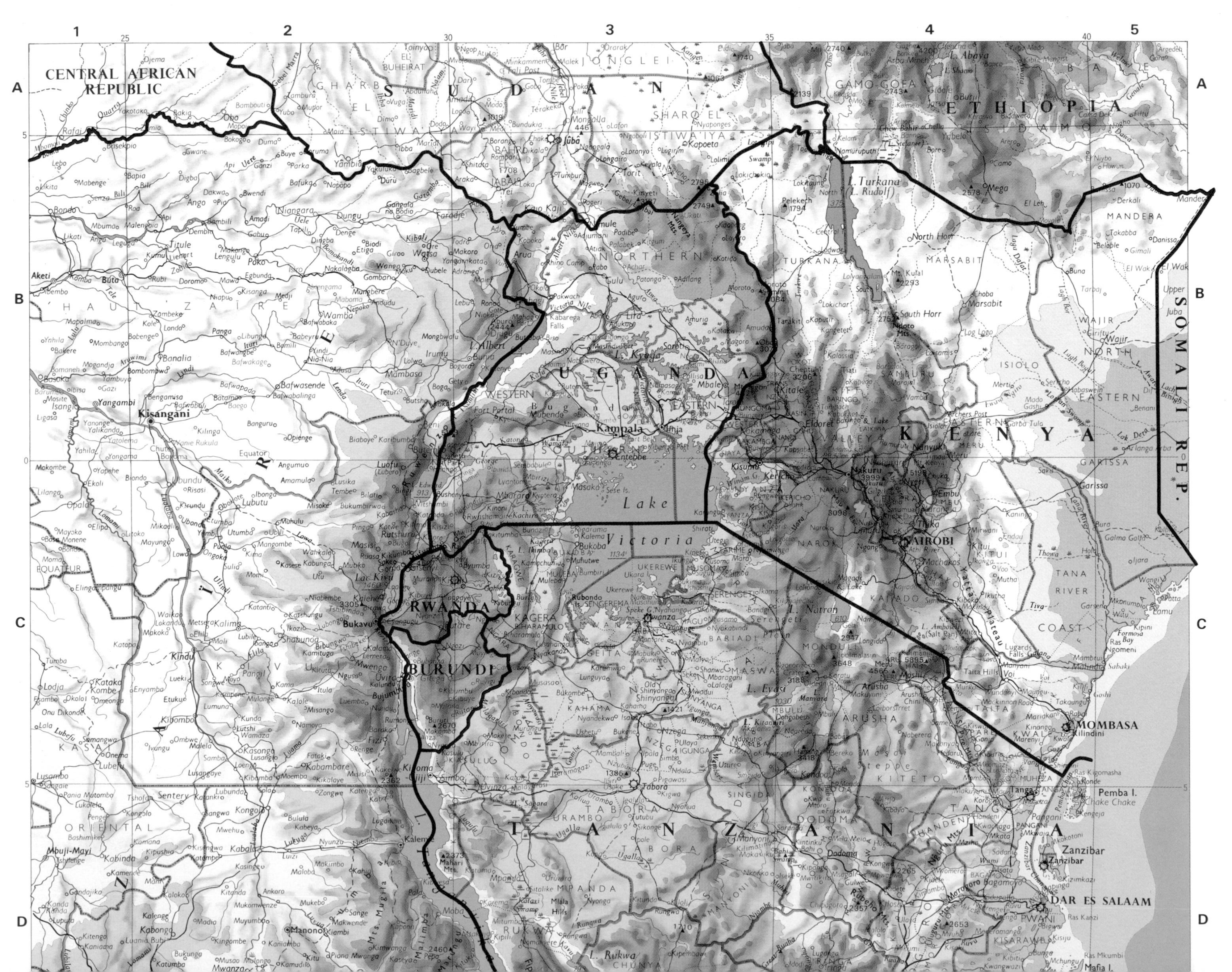
CENTRAL AFRICAN REPUBLIC
SUDAN
ETHIOPIA
SOMALI REP.
KENYA
UGANDA
TANZANIA
RWANDA
BURUNDI
ZAIRE
NAIROBI
MOMBASA
DAR ES SALAAM
Zanzibar
Pemba I.
Lake Victoria
Kampala
Entebbe
Kisangani
Juba
Tabora
Mwanza
Bukavu
Dodoma
Tanga
Kisumu
Nakuru
L. Turkana (L. Rudolf)
L. Albert
L. Natron
L. Eyasi
L. Kivu
Garissa
Marsabit
Mega
Aketi
Yangambi
Kindu
Mbuji-Mayi
Manono
Ujiji
Kigoma

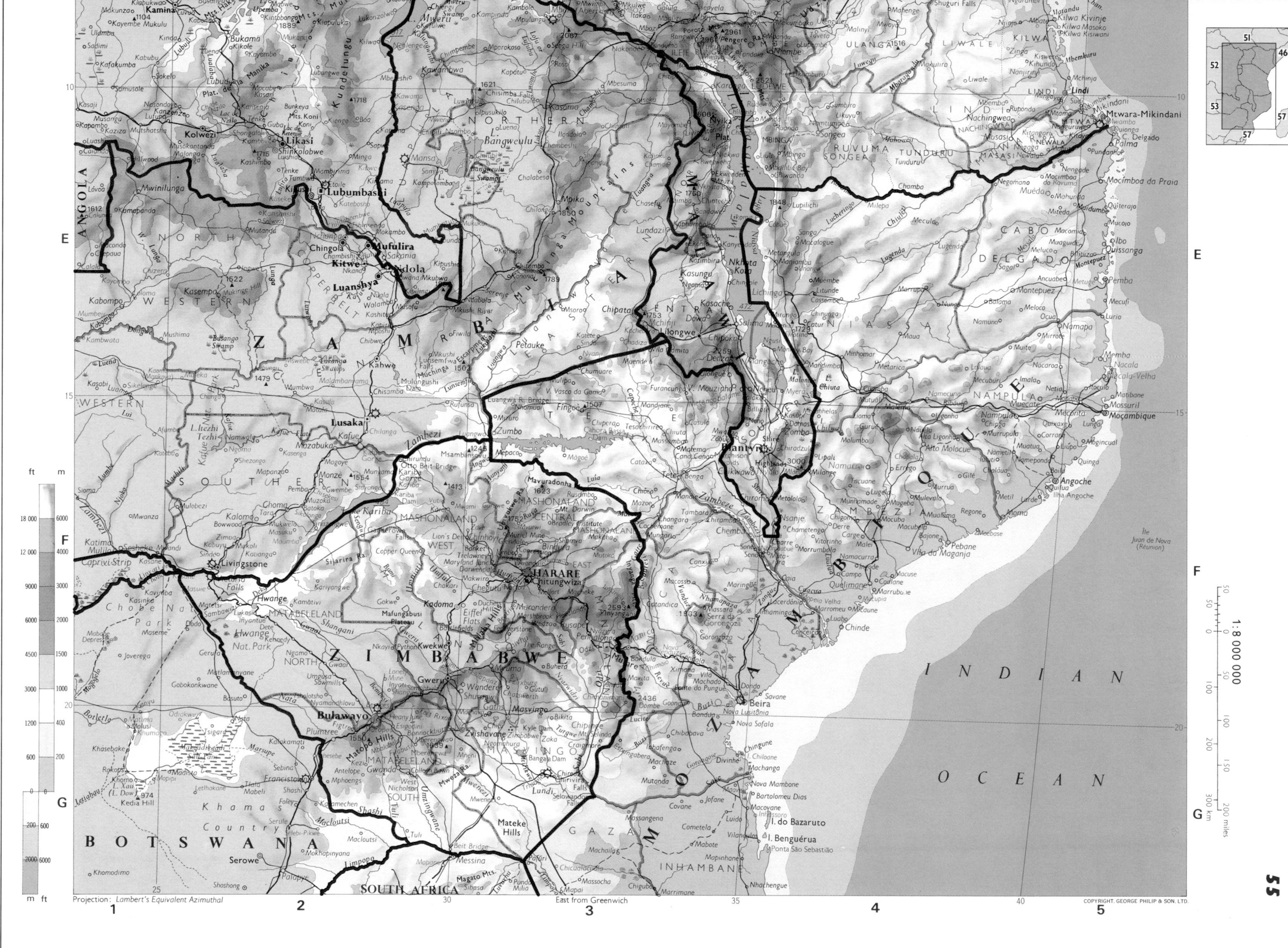

1 : 8 000 000

Projection: Lambert's Equivalent Azimuthal

East from Greenwich

53 | 55

ANGOLA

NAMIBE

ZAMBIA

CUANDO CUBANGO

WESTERN

SOUTH

Livingstone
Victoria Falls

Caprivi Strip

Chobe Nat. Park
Hwange Nat. Park

Okavango Swamps

Ngami Depression

Mababe Depression

NAMIBIA

Ovamboland

Etosha Pan

Tsumeb
Grootfontein
Otavi 2148
Uchab

Outjo
Okakuejo
Otjiwarongo

Kaukauveld

Sandveld

BOTSWANA

Ghanzi

Serowe
Palapye
Mahalapye
Shoshong

Kalahari

Khamas Country

NAMIBIA

Brandberg 2606
Omaruru
Hochfeld
Erongo 2350
Okahandja
Swakopmund
Walvisbaai (Walvis Bay)
Windhoek 2483
Khomas Hochland
Rehoboth 2351
Gobabis

Tropic of Capricorn

Conception B.

Sandwich B.

Spencer B.

Meob B.

Sossus Vlei

Namaland

Mariental
Maltahöhe

Lüderitzbaai
Lüderitz

Keetmanshoop

Kalahari Gemsbok National Park

Molepolole
Gaborone
Kanye
Ramotswa
Lobatse

NORTH-WEST
Mafikeng
Zeerust

Kuruman

Kroonstad
Welkom
Virginia

FREE STATE

Kimberley
Bloemfontein

Oranjemund
Alexander Bay

Port Nolloth

Springbok
Namaqualand

SOUTH AFRICA

NORTHERN CAPE

ATLANTIC

OCEAN

De Aar

Queenstown
Cradock 2369

EASTERN CAPE

Graaff-Reinet
Beaufort West

Great Karoo

Uitenhage
PORT ELIZABETH
Algoa Bay

Vredenburg
Saldanha
Moorreesburg

WESTERN CAPE

Worcester
Oudtshoorn
George
Knysna
Mosselbaai

CAPE TOWN (Kaapstad)
Table Mt. 1086
Stellenbosch
Paarl
Strand

Simonstown
Kaap die Goeie Hoop (Cape of Good Hope)
C. Agulhas

ft | m
9000 | 3000
6000 | 2000
4500 | 1500
3000 | 1000
1200 | 400
600 | 200
200 | 600
2000 | 6000
4000 | 12,000
m | ft

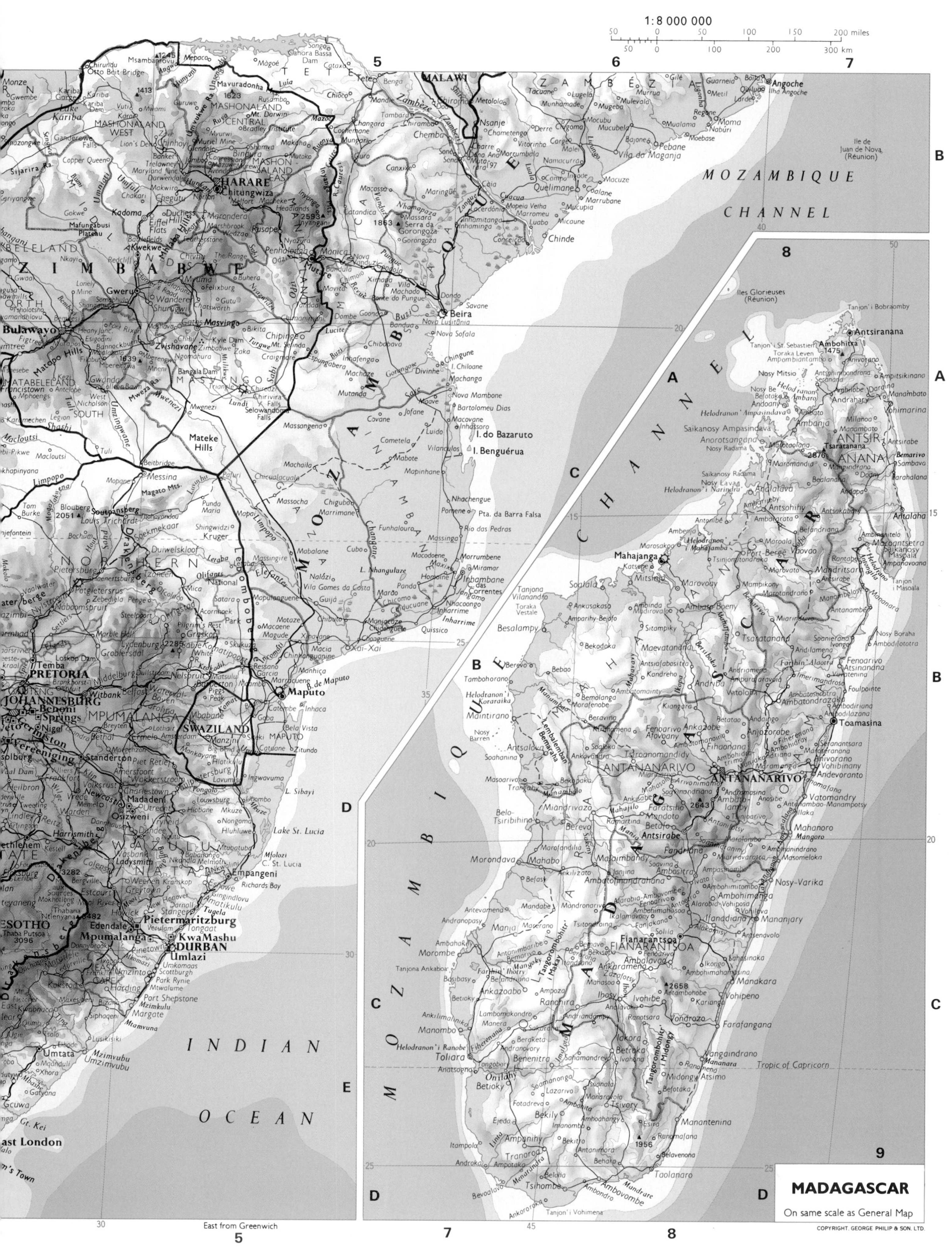

1:8 000 000

50   0   50   100   150   200 miles
50   0   100   200   300 km

M O Z A M B I Q U E

C H A N N E L

*Ile de
Juan de Nova
(Réunion)*

ZIMBABWE

HARARE
Chitungwiza

Gweru

Bulawayo

MASHONALAND

MASHONALAND
WEST

MASHONALAND
CENTRAL

MASHONALAND
EAST

Beira

Nova Sofala

MATABELELAND
SOUTH

MASVINGO

Messina

Quelimane

Chinde

*Iles Glorieuses
(Réunion)*

Antsiranana

Nosy Be

Mahajanga

M A D A G A S C A R

ANTANANARIVO

Antsirabe

Fianarantsoa

Toamasina

Toliara

Tropic of Capricorn

PRETORIA

JOHANNESBURG

SWAZILAND

MAPUTO

Maputo

PIETERMARITZBURG

DURBAN

Umlazi

LESOTHO

I N D I A N

O C E A N

East London

East from Greenwich

M O Z A M B I Q U E

MADAGASCAR

On same scale as General Map

COPYRIGHT. GEORGE PHILIP & SON. LTD.

1 : 50 000 000

Physical map (top):

ft / m elevation scale
12000 4000
9000 3000
6000 2000
3000 1000
1500 500
600 200
0 0

m ft

Malay Peninsula
Sumatra
Str. of Malacca
Borneo
Celebes Sea
Halmahera
Celebes
Sula Is.
Buru
Ceram
Ambon
G. of Sarera
Maoke Mts.
Puncak Jaya 5029
New Guinea
Admiralty Is.
New Ireland
Bismarck Arch.
Nauru
Gilbert Is.
PACIFIC
Java Sea
Java
Sumbawa
Sumba
Flores Sea
Flores
Timor
Aru Is.
Tanimbar Is.
Arafura Sea
Fly
G. of Papua
Owen Stanley Ra. 9103
New Britain
Bougainville
Solomon Is.
Malaita
San Cristobal
Santa Cruz Is.
Espíritu Santo
Rotuma
Samoan Is.
Torres Strait
Thursday I.
C. York
Great Barrier Reef
Coral Sea
D'Entrecasteaux Is.
Louisiade Arch.
Guadalcanal
New Hebrides
Fiji Is.
Vanua Levu
Viti Levu
Savai'i
Upolu
Banda Sea
Timor Sea
Melville I.
C. Arnhem
Arnhem Land
Gulf of Carpentaria
Cape York Pen.
Chesterfield Is.
Ellice Is.
INDIAN
King Sd.
Victoria
Barkly Tableland
Tanami Desert
Fitzroy
Flinders
New Caledonia
Loyalty Is.
Tonga Is.
Tongatapu
OCEAN
North West C.
Mt. Bruce 1227
L. Disappointment
Macdonnell Ras.
Sandy C.
Hervey B.
C. Byron
New England Ra.
Norfolk I.
Kermadec Is.
Ashburton
6658
L. Mackay
L. Amadeus
Australia
Darling Downs
Darling
Shark Bay
Gascoyne
Musgrave Ra.
L. Eyre
Cooper
Warrego
Lord Howe I.
Tropic of Capricorn
L. Burley
L. Torrens
Frome
Lachlan
Murray
Botany Bay
Tasman Sea
Geographe Bay
Darling Ra.
Nullarbor Plain
Gaudner
Flinders Ras.
Eyre Pen.
Spencer Gulf
North C.
C. Naturaliste
C. Leeuwin
Great Australian Bight
Kangaroo I.
Encounter B.
Australian Alps
C. Howe
10047
Bay of Plenty
East C.
North I.
Ruapehu 2797
L. Taupo
Hawke B.
P. Phillip B.
Bass Str.
Flinders I.
King I.
South C.
Tasmania
Mt. Cook 3753
Southern Alps
South I.
New Zealand
Stewart I.

Political map (bottom):

m ft

MALAYSIA
BRUNEI
PALAU
FEDERATED STATES OF MICRONESIA
MARSHALL IS.
Kuala Lumpur
SINGAPORE
Borneo
Sula Is.
Ceram
IRIAN JAYA
PAPUA NEW GUINEA
New Ireland
NAURU
KIRIBATI
PACIFIC
Sumatra
Celebes
Buru
Aru Is.
New Guinea
Madang
Rabaul
New Britain
Bougainville I.
Ujung Pandang
INDONESIA
Banda Sea
Tanimbar Is.
Lae
Choiseul
Santa Isabel
SOLOMON IS.
TUVALU
Java Sea
Arafura Sea
Fly
Port Moresby
Honiara
Malaita
San Cristóbal
JAKARTA
Java
Sumbawa
Flores
Timor
Kupang
Torres Strait
Guadalcanal
Santa Cruz Is.
Funafuti
Sumba
Timor Sea
Darwin
Katherine
Gulf of Carpentaria
Cooktown
CORAL SEA ISLANDS TERRITORY
Espíritu Santo
VANUATU
Rotuma
Is. Wallis & Futuna
WESTERN SAMOA
Wyndham
Cairns
NORTHERN TERRITORY
QUEENSLAND
Townsville
Chesterfield Is.
Port Vila
Viti Levu
Vanua Levu
Broome
Mount Isa
Charters Towers
NEW CALEDONIA (Fr.)
Suva
INDIAN
Dampier
WESTERN AUSTRALIA
Rockhampton
Nouméa
Loyalty Is.
FIJI
Onslow
Alice Springs
Longreach
AUSTRALIA
Quilpie
Charleville
Toowoomba
Brisbane
Norfolk I. (Aust.)
TONGA
Tropic of Capricorn
Oodnadatta
Wiluna
SOUTH
Cunnamulla
Warwick
Nuku'alofa
Geraldton
Bourke
OCEAN
Port Pirie
AUSTRALIA
NEW SOUTH WALES
Newcastle
Lord Howe I. (Aust.)
Kermadec Is. (N.Z.)
OCEAN
Perth
Kalgoorlie-Boulder
Broken Hill
Mildura
A.C.T.
Sydney
Tasman Sea
Fremantle
Esperance
Great Australian Bight
Port Pirie
Adelaide
Canberra
North I.
NEW ZEALAND
Albany
VICTORIA
Auckland
Ballarat
Geelong
Melbourne
New Plymouth
Hamilton
King I.
Bass Str.
Napier
Launceston
South I.
Greymouth
Nelson
Wellington
TASMANIA
Hobart
Chatham Is. (N.Z.)
Invercargill
Dunedin
Christchurch
International Date Line

Projection: Bonne
90 East from Greenwich 100

● Canberra Capital Cities

CARTOGRAPHY BY PHILIP'S. COPYRIGHT REED INTERNATIONAL BOOKS LTD

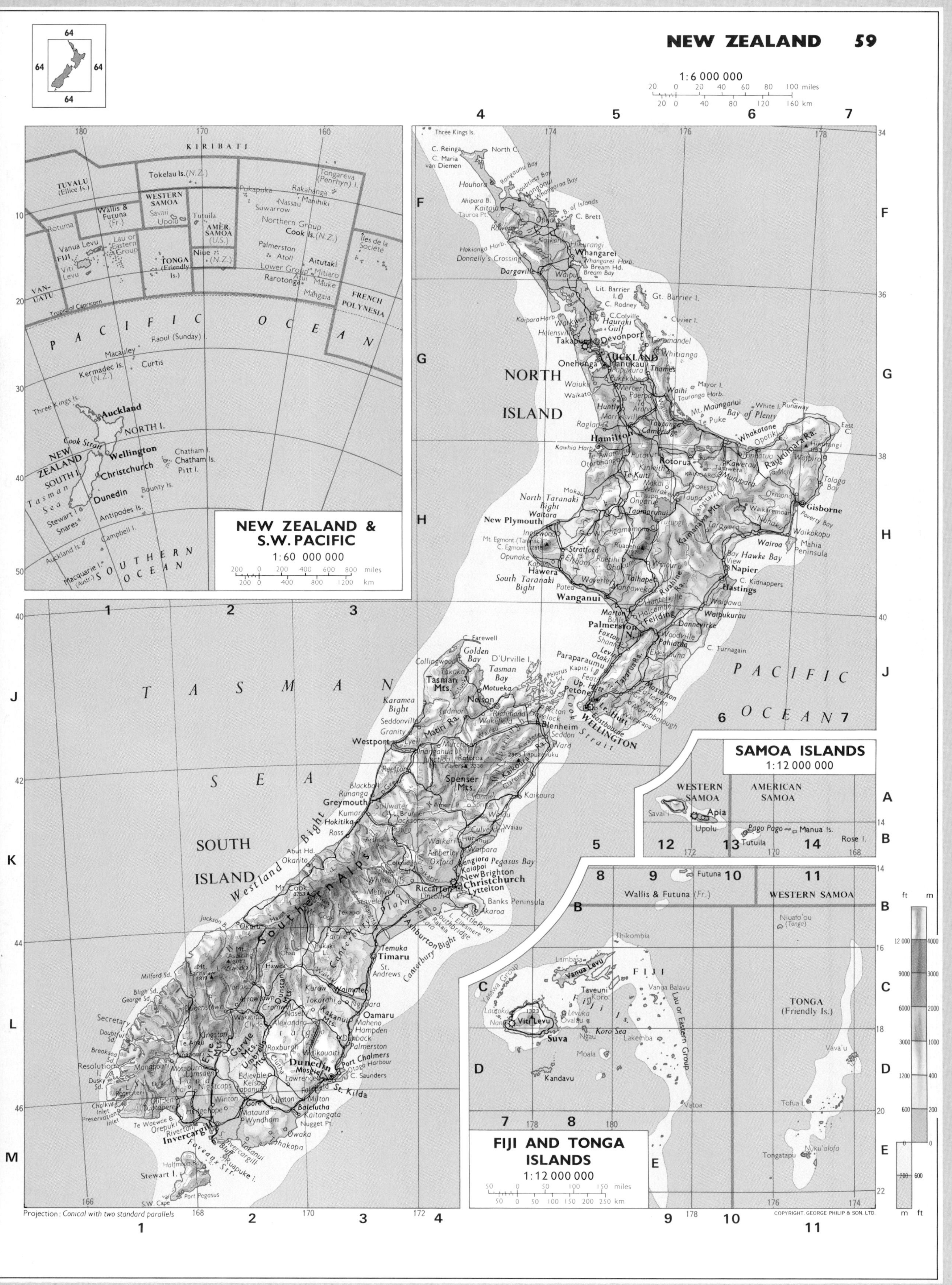
1:6 000 000
NEW ZEALAND & S.W. PACIFIC
1:60 000 000
SAMOA ISLANDS
1:12 000 000
FIJI AND TONGA ISLANDS
1:12 000 000
NORTH ISLAND
SOUTH ISLAND
TASMAN SEA
PACIFIC OCEAN
Auckland
Wellington
Christchurch
Dunedin
Projection: Conical with two standard parallels
COPYRIGHT, GEORGE PHILIP & SON, LTD.

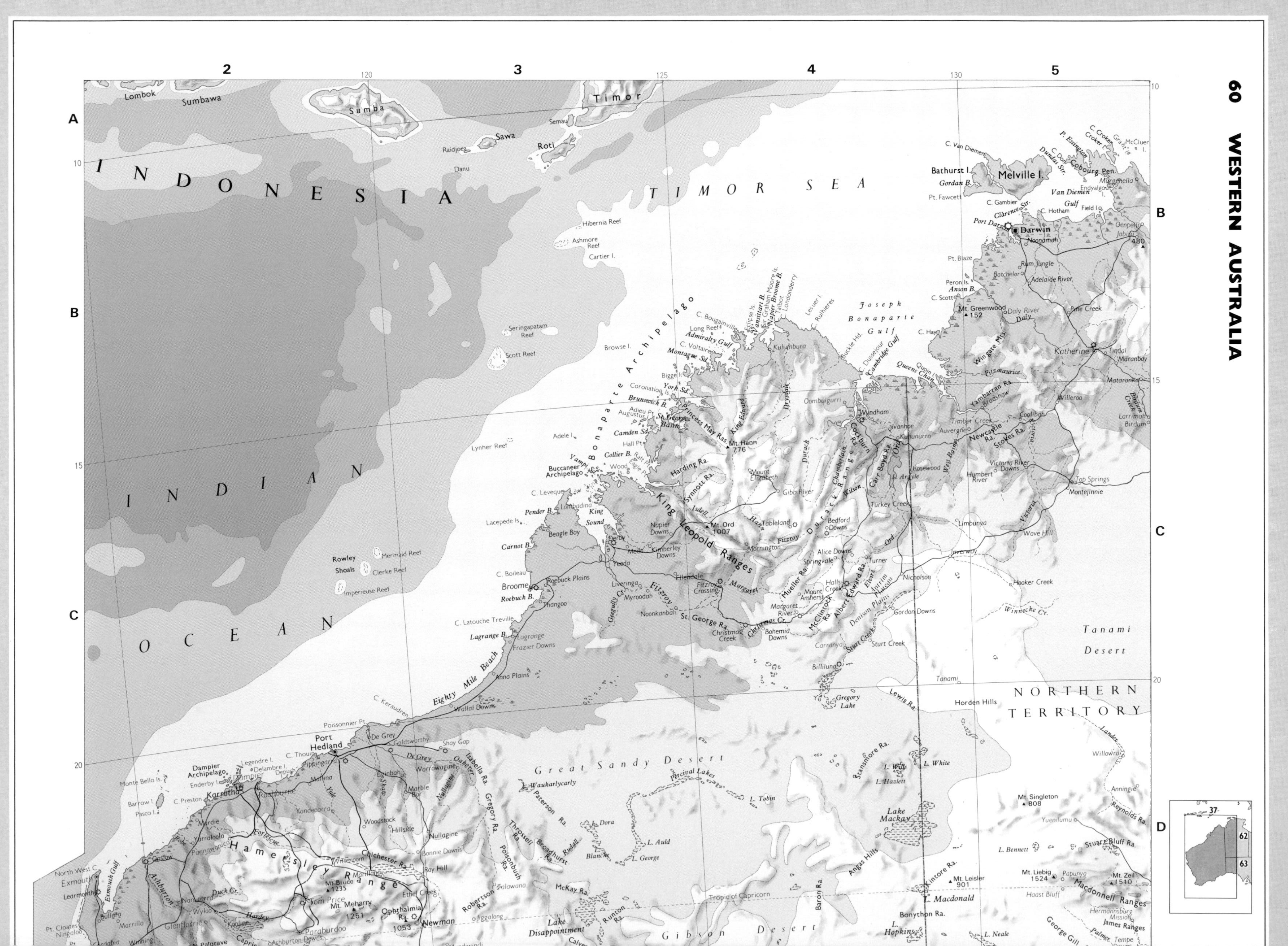
INDONESIA
TIMOR SEA
INDIAN OCEAN
NORTHERN TERRITORY
Tanami Desert
Great Sandy Desert
Gibson Desert
Timor
Sumba
Sumbawa
Lombok
Roti
Sawa
Melville I.
Bathurst I.
Darwin
Katherine
Joseph Bonaparte Gulf
Bonaparte Archipelago
King Leopold Ranges
Kimberley Downs
Wyndham
Broome
Eighty Mile Beach
Port Hedland
Dampier Archipelago
Karratha
Hamersley Range
Newman
Exmouth Gulf
Rowley Shoals
Scott Reef
Lake Mackay
Lake Disappointment
Macdonnell Ranges
Tropic of Capricorn

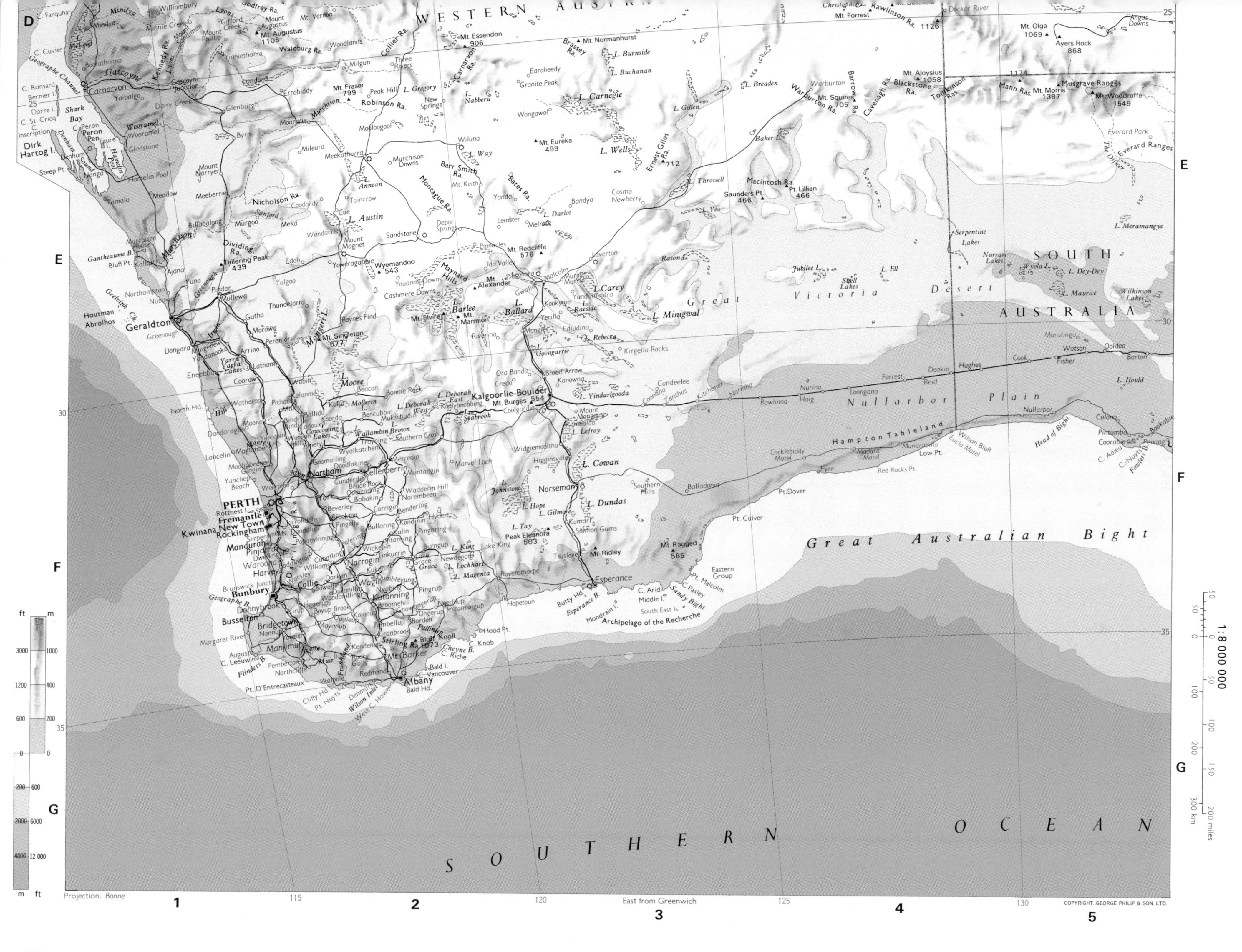

61

1 : 8 000 000

50 0 50 100 150 200 miles
50 0 100 200 300 km

Projection. Bonne

COPYRIGHT. GEORGE PHILIP & SON LTD.

W E S T E R N   A U S T R A L I A

S O U T H   A U S T R A L I A

Great Victoria Desert

Nullarbor Plain

Hampton Tableland

Great Australian Bight

S O U T H E R N   O C E A N

Ayers Rock
868

Mt. Olga
1069

Musgrave Ranges

Mt. Woodroffe
1549

Mann Ra. Mt. Morris
1387

PERTH
Fremantle
New Town
Rockingham
Kwinana

Geraldton

Bunbury
Busselton

Albany

Kalgoorlie-Boulder
554

Norseman

Esperance

ft   m
3000 1000
1200 400
600   200
0
-200 -600
2000 6000
4000 12 000

m   ft
1000
400
200
0

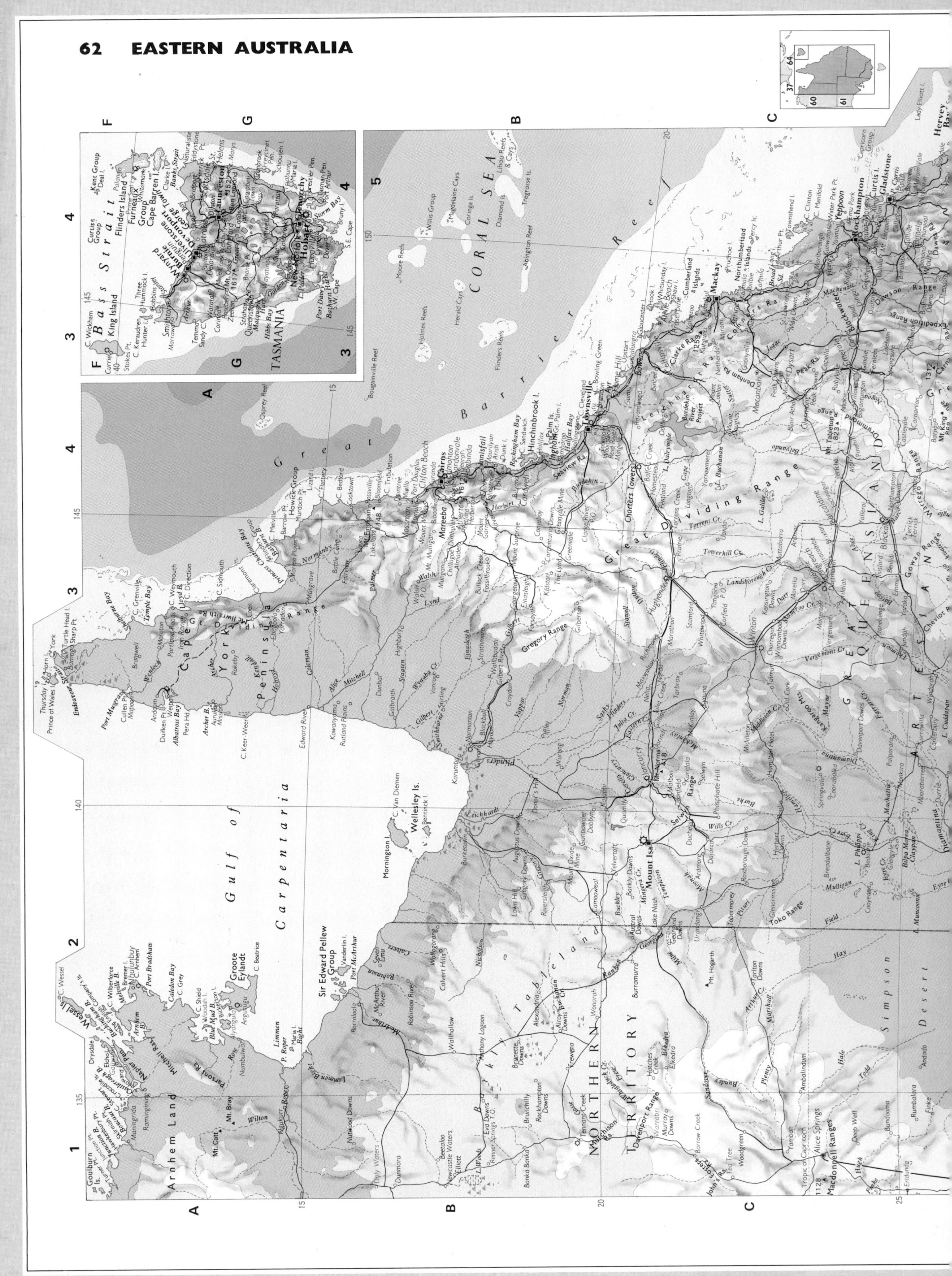
Gulf of Carpentaria
Great Barrier Reef
CORAL SEA
Cape York Peninsula
Arnhem Land
Groote Eylandt
Sir Edward Pellew Group
Wellesley Is.
Mornington I.
NORTHERN TERRITORY
QUEENSLAND
Barkly Tableland
Great Dividing Range
Gregory Range
Simpson Desert
Macdonnell Ranges
Alice Springs
Mount Isa
Cloncurry
Townsville
Cairns
Mackay
Rockhampton
Gladstone
Charters Towers
Hughenden
Winton
Longreach
Mareeba
Bowen
Cooktown
Burketown
Normanton
Karumba
Camooweal
Tennant Creek
Borroloola
Cumberland Islands
Northumberland Islands
Hinchinbrook I.
Whitsunday I.
TASMANIA
Bass Strait
King Island
Flinders Island
Furneaux Group
Cape Barren I.
Launceston
Hobart
Devonport
Burnie
Storm Bay
Kent Group
Tropic of Capricorn
Hervey Bay

1:8 000 000

50   0   50   100   150   200 miles
50   0   50   100   150   200   300 km

COPYRIGHT. GEORGE PHILIP & SON. LTD.

T A S M A N   S E A

S O U T H   A U S T R A L I A

N E W   S O U T H   W A L E S

V I C T O R I A

G R E A T   D I V I D I N G   R A N G E

BRISBANE

SYDNEY

CANBERRA
FEDERAL COMMONWEALTH TERR.

MELBOURNE

ADELAIDE

Newcastle

Wollongong

Geelong

Broken Hill

Bass Strait

King Island

Flinders Island

Furneaux Group

Kangaroo I.

Spencer Gulf

Gulf St. Vincent

Lake Eyre

Lake Torrens

Lake Frome

Lake Gairdner

Fraser Island

Maryborough

Gympie

Toowoomba

Ipswich

Coffs Harbour

Port Macquarie

Tamworth

Dubbo

Orange

Bathurst

Goulburn

Wagga Wagga

Albury

Bendigo

Ballarat

Port Augusta

Port Pirie

Whyalla

Port Lincoln

Mount Gambier

Murray Bridge

Eyre Peninsula

Yorke Peninsula

Darling R.

Murray R.

Murrumbidgee R.

Lachlan R.

Projection: Bonne

East from Greenwich

135   140   145   150

ft   m
15000   4500
12000   3000
6000   2000
2000   1200
600   600
0   200
0
—200 —600

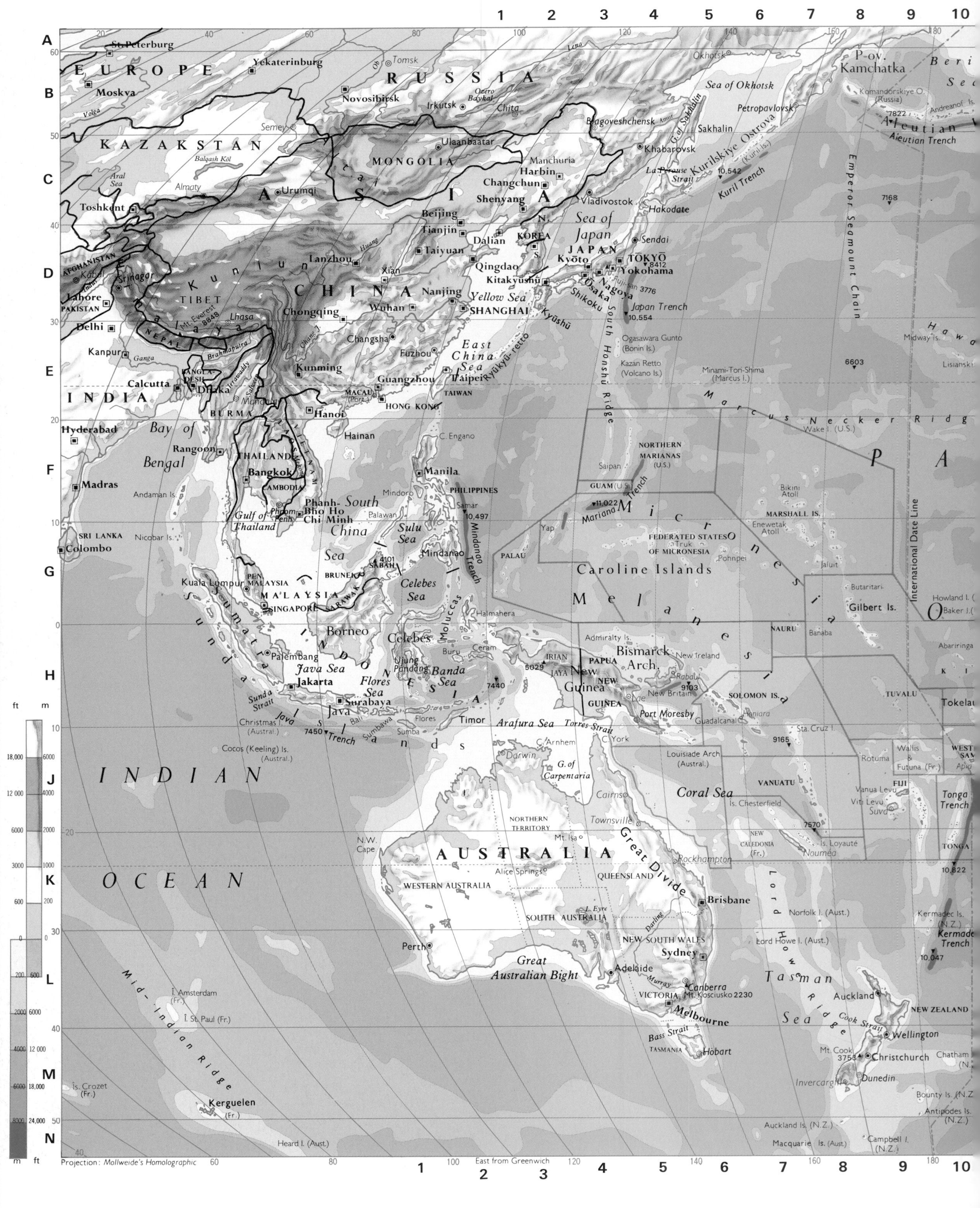
EUROPE
RUSSIA
St. Peterburg
Moskva
Yekaterinburg
Novosibirsk
Irkutsk
Chita
Ozero Baykal
Tomsk
Semey
KAZAKSTAN
Balqash Köl
Aral Sea
Almaty
Toshkent
Urumqi
MONGOLIA
Ulaanbaatar
Sea of Okhotsk
Okhotsk
P-ov. Kamchatka
Petropavlovsk
Sakhalin
Blagoveshchensk
Khabarovsk
Manchuria
Harbin
Changchun
Shenyang
Vladivostok
Hakodate
La Perouse Strait
Kurilskiye Ostrova
Kuril Trench
10,542
Komandorskiye O. (Russia)
Aleutian Trench
Emperor Seamount Chain
7168
ASIA
Beijing
Tianjin
Taiyuan
Dalian
KOREA
Sea of Japan
JAPAN
Sendai
TŌKYŌ
Yokohama
8412
Kyōto
Nagoya
Ōsaka
Shikoku
Kyūshū
Kitakyūshū
Qingdao
Lanzhou
Xian
Kunlun
AFGHANISTAN
Kabul
Srinagar
Lahore
PAKISTAN
Delhi
TIBET
Mt. Everest 8848
Lhasa
NEPAL
CHINA
Nanjing
Yellow Sea
SHANGHAI
Wuhan
Chongqing
Changsha
Fuzhou
East China Sea
Ryūkyū-retto
Japan Trench
10,554
3776
South Honshu Ridge
Ogasawara Gunto (Bonin Is.)
Kazan Retto (Volcano Is.)
Minami-Tori-Shima (Marcus I.)
Midway Is.
6603
Lisianski
Kanpur
Ganga
Brahmaputra
BANGLADESH
Dhaka
Calcutta
INDIA
Kunming
Guangzhou
Taipei
TAIWAN
MACAU (Port.)
HONG KONG
Hanoi
BURMA
Mandalay
Hainan
Marcus Necker Ridge
Wake I. (U.S.)
Hyderabad
Bay of Bengal
Rangoon
THAILAND
Bangkok
CAMBODIA
Phnom Penh
Phanh-Bho Ho Chi Minh
South China Sea
Gulf of Thailand
C. Engano
Manila
PHILIPPINES
Mindoro
Palawan
Samar
10,497
Mindanao
Mindanao Trench
Sulu Sea
NORTHERN MARIANAS (U.S.)
Saipan
GUAM (U.S.)
11,022
Mariana Trench
Micronesia
Bikini Atoll
MARSHALL IS.
Enewetak Atoll
Madras
Andaman Is.
SRI LANKA
Colombo
Nicobar Is.
Yap
PALAU
FEDERATED STATES OF MICRONESIA
Truk
Pohnpei
Jaluit
Caroline Islands
Butaritari
Gilbert Is.
International Date Line
Howland I.
Baker I.
Kuala Lumpur
PEN. MALAYSIA
MALAYSIA
SINGAPORE
BRUNEI
SABAH
SARAWAK
4101
Celebes Sea
Halmahera
Melanesia
Sumatra
Borneo
Celebes
Moluccas
Ceram
Buru
Palembang
Java Sea
Jakarta
Sunda Strait
Surabaya
Java
INDONESIA
Ujung Pandang
Flores Sea
Banda Sea
7440
IRIAN JAYA
5029
New Guinea
PAPUA NEW GUINEA
Admiralty Is.
Bismarck Arch.
New Ireland
Rabaul
New Britain
9103
Lae
NAURU
Banaba
SOLOMON IS.
Honiara
Guadalcanal
TUVALU
Abariringa
Tokelau
Christmas I. (Austral.)
Java Trench
7450
Sunda Islands
Bali
Sumbawa
Sumba
Flores
Timor
Arafura Sea
Torres Strait
Port Moresby
C. York
Sta. Cruz I.
9165
Cocos (Keeling) Is. (Austral.)
C. Arnhem
Darwin
G. of Carpentaria
Louisiade Arch. (Austral.)
Rotuma
Wallis & Futuna (Fr.)
WESTERN SAMOA
Apia
INDIAN OCEAN
Cairns
Coral Sea
VANUATU
Is. Chesterfield
FIJI
Vanua Levu
Viti Levu
Suva
Tonga Trench
NORTHERN TERRITORY
Townsville
Mt. Isa
N.W. Cape
AUSTRALIA
Great Dividing Range
7570
NEW CALEDONIA (Fr.)
Is. Loyauté
Nouméa
TONGA
10,822
Alice Springs
Rockhampton
WESTERN AUSTRALIA
QUEENSLAND
Lord Howe Ridge
Brisbane
L. Eyre
SOUTH AUSTRALIA
Norfolk I. (Aust.)
Kermadec Is. (N.Z.)
Kermadec Trench
10,047
Darling
NEW SOUTH WALES
Lord Howe I. (Aust.)
Perth
Sydney
Great Australian Bight
Adelaide
Murray
Tasman Sea
Canberra
Mt. Kosciusko 2230
VICTORIA
Melbourne
Auckland
NEW ZEALAND
I. Amsterdam (Fr.)
I. St. Paul (Fr.)
Mid-Indian Ridge
Bass Strait
TASMANIA
Hobart
Cook Strait
Wellington
Mt. Cook 3753
Christchurch
Chatham
Invercargill
Dunedin
Is. Crozet (Fr.)
Kerguelen (Fr.)
Bounty Is.
Antipodes Is. (N.Z.)
Auckland Is. (N.Z.)
Heard I. (Aust.)
Macquarie Is. (Aust.)
Campbell I. (N.Z.)
Projection: Mollweide's Homolographic
East from Greenwich
ft
m
18,000
6000
12 000
4000
6000
2000
3000
1000
600
200
0
600
2000
6000
4000
12 000
6000
18,000
8000
24,000

1:54 000 000

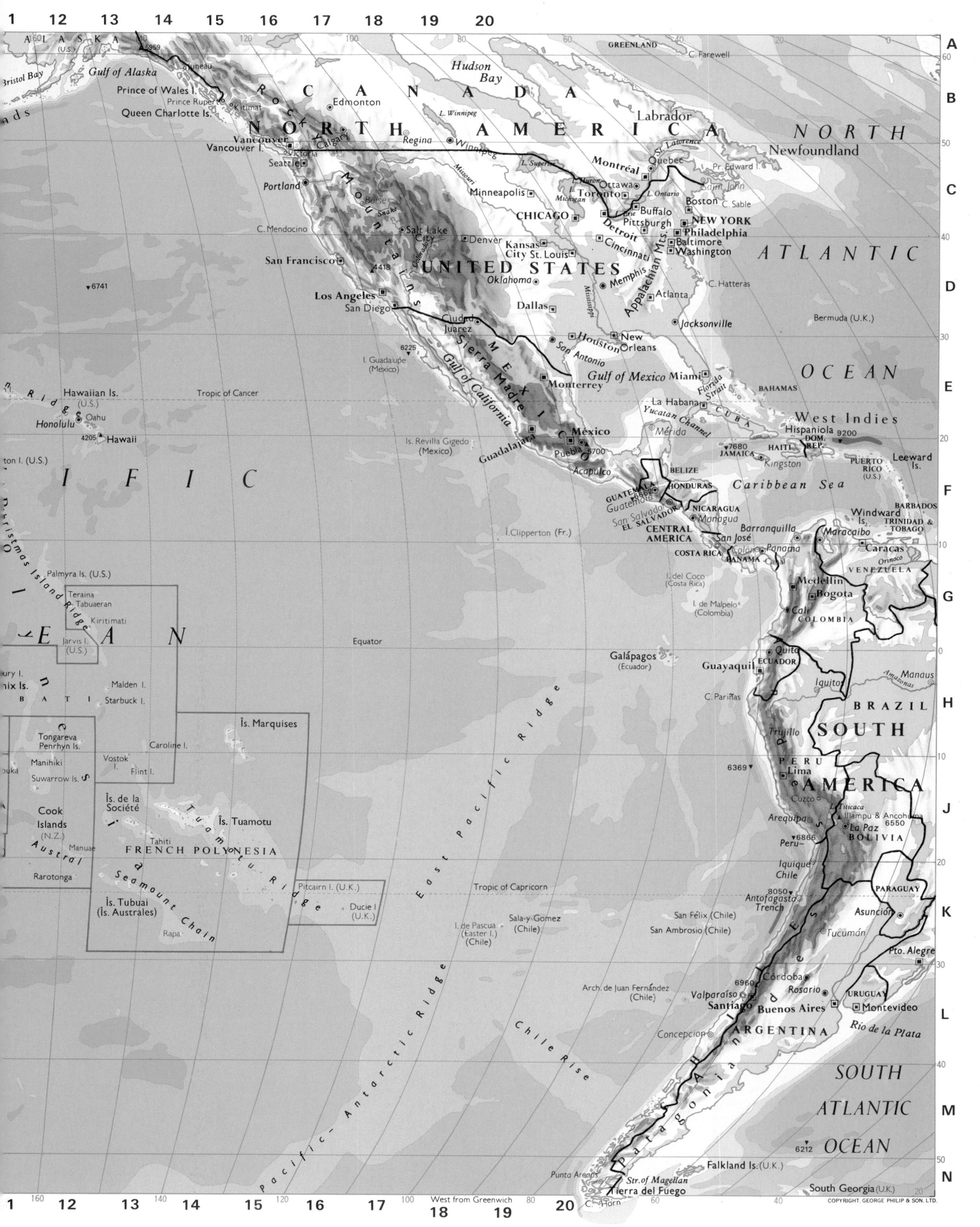

NORTH AMERICA
CANADA
UNITED STATES
MEXICO
Hudson Bay
Labrador
Newfoundland
Rocky Mountains
Gulf of Alaska
Prince of Wales I.
Queen Charlotte Is.
Vancouver
Vancouver I.
Seattle
Portland
Edmonton
Calgary
Regina
Winnipeg
L. Winnipeg
Montréal
Quebec
Ottawa
Toronto
Minneapolis
CHICAGO
Detroit
Buffalo
Pittsburgh
Boston
NEW YORK
Philadelphia
Baltimore
Washington
Salt Lake City
Denver
Kansas City
St. Louis
San Francisco
Los Angeles
San Diego
Oklahoma
Dallas
Memphis
Atlanta
Jacksonville
Houston
New Orleans
San Antonio
Monterrey
Gulf of Mexico
Miami
Ciudad Juarez
Sierra Madre
Gulf of California
Guadalajara
México
Puebla
Acapulco
ATLANTIC OCEAN
West Indies
BAHAMAS
CUBA
La Habana
Hispaniola
HAITI
DOM. REP.
JAMAICA
Kingston
PUERTO RICO (U.S.)
Leeward Is.
Caribbean Sea
BELIZE
GUATEMALA
HONDURAS
NICARAGUA
EL SALVADOR
COSTA RICA
PANAMA
CENTRAL AMERICA
Windward Is.
BARBADOS
TRINIDAD & TOBAGO
Caracas
VENEZUELA
Bogota
Medellin
Cali
COLOMBIA
Quito
ECUADOR
Guayaquil
Galápagos (Ecuador)
SOUTH AMERICA
BRAZIL
PERU
Lima
Manaus
Iquitos
Trujillo
Arequipa
Cuzco
La Paz
BOLIVIA
PARAGUAY
Asunción
Iquique
Antofagasta
Tucumán
Córdoba
Rosario
Valparaíso
Santiago
Buenos Aires
Montevideo
URUGUAY
ARGENTINA
Rio de la Plata
Concepcion
Patagonia
Andes
Punta Arenas
Str. of Magellan
Tierra del Fuego
C. Horn
Falkland Is. (U.K.)
South Georgia (U.K.)
SOUTH ATLANTIC OCEAN
PACIFIC OCEAN
Hawaiian Is. (U.S.)
Honolulu
Oahu
Hawaii
Tropic of Cancer
Equator
Tropic of Capricorn
Palmyra Is. (U.S.)
Kiritimati
Jarvis I. (U.S.)
Malden I.
Starbuck I.
Îs. Marquises
Caroline I.
Vostok I.
Flint I.
Cook Islands (N.Z.)
Îs. de la Société
Tahiti
Îs. Tuamotu
FRENCH POLYNESIA
Îs. Tubuai (Îs. Australes)
Rarotonga
Pitcairn I. (U.K.)
Ducie I (U.K.)
I. de Pascua (Easter I.) (Chile)
Sala-y-Gomez (Chile)
San Félix (Chile)
San Ambrosio (Chile)
Arch. de Juan Fernández (Chile)
I. Clipperton (Fr.)
I. del Coco (Costa Rica)
I. de Malpelo (Colombia)
I. Guadalupe (Mexico)
Is. Revilla Gigedo (Mexico)
East Pacific Ridge
Pacific-Antarctic Ridge
Chile Rise
Tuamotu Ridge
Seamount Chain
Bermuda (U.K.)
C. Hatteras
C. Mendocino
C. Farewell
GREENLAND
West from Greenwich
COPYRIGHT, GEORGE PHILIP & SON, LTD.

1 : 35 000 000

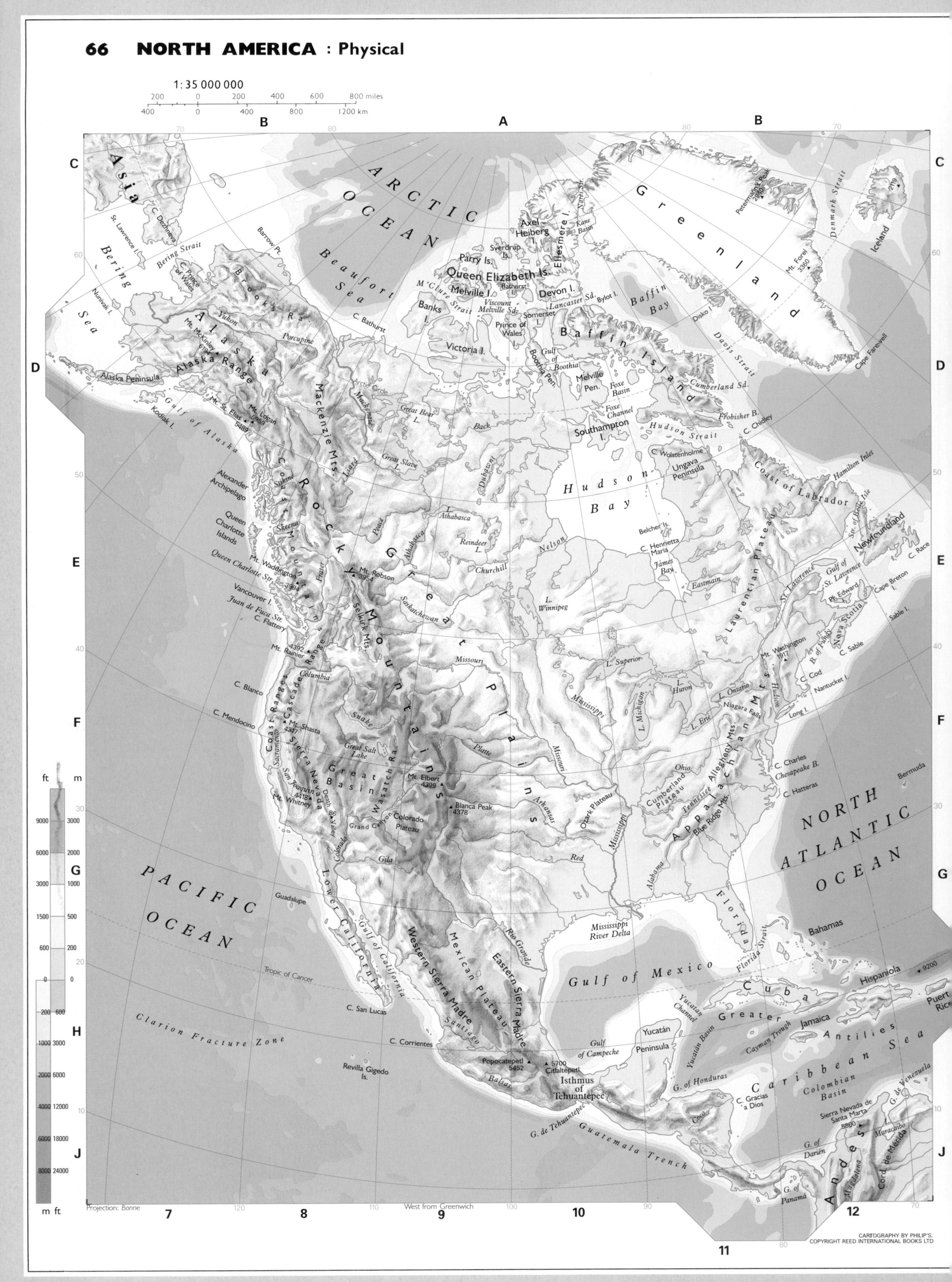

Projection: Bonne

West from Greenwich

CARTOGRAPHY BY PHILIP'S.
COPYRIGHT REED INTERNATIONAL BOOKS LTD

1 : 35 000 000

200 0 200 400 600 800 miles
400 0 400 800 1200 km

C **RUSSIA** A s i a

St. Lawrence
Bering Strait
Bering Sea

International Date Line

A R C T I C O C E A N

Beaufort Sea

Queen Elizabeth Is.

Ellesmere I.

GREENLAND

(Denmark)

Denmark Strait

ICELAND

Reykjavik

Godthåb

Baffin Bay

Davis Strait

Cape Farewell

ALASKA (U.S.A.)
Yukon
Porcupine
Fairbanks
Anchorage
Kodiak I.
Gulf of Alaska
Whitehorse
Juneau

YUKON TERRITORY
Arctic Circle
Mackenzie
Great Bear L.
Yellowknife

NORTHWEST TERRITORIES

Victoria I.

Baffin Island

Hudson Strait

NEWFOUNDLAND

C A N A D A

BRITISH COLUMBIA
Skeena
Fraser
Peace
Liard

ALBERTA
Athabasca
Edmonton
Calgary
Saskatchewan

Great Slave L.
Athabasca
Churchill

SASKATCHEWAN
Regina

MANITOBA
Nelson
Winnipeg

Back
Dubawnt

H u d s o n B a y

Eastmain

Q U É B E C

St. Lawrence

Labrador

St. John's

St-Pierre Et Miquelon (Fr.)

Victoria
Vancouver
Olympia
Seattle
WASHINGTON
Portland
Salem
OREGON
Columbia
Snake
IDAHO
Boise

MONTANA
Missouri
Helena

WYOMING
Cheyenne

Winnipeg
L. Superior

ONTARIO
Ottawa
Toronto
Buffalo

Montréal

NEW BRUNSWICK
Fredericton
PRINCE EDWARD I.
Charlottetown
NOVA SCOTIA
Halifax
C. Sable
MAINE
Augusta
VER.
N.H.
Concord
MASS.
Boston
Providence
Hartford
NEW YORK CITY

NORTH DAKOTA
Bismarck
SOUTH DAKOTA
MINNESOTA
Minneapolis
WISCONSIN
Madison
Milwaukee
L. Michigan
MICHIGAN
Lansing
L. Huron
Detroit
Cleveland
PA.
Pittsburgh
PHILADELPHIA
NEW YORK

Sacramento
Carson City
NEVADA
Salt Lake City
UTAH
SAN FRANCISCO
San Jose
CALIFORNIA
Las Vegas
LOS ANGELES
San Diego

Denver
COLORADO

NEBRASKA
Lincoln

IOWA
Des Moines

CHICAGO
ILLINOIS
Springfield
INDIANA
Indianapolis
OHIO
Columbus
Cincinnati
Washington D.C.
W.V.
MD.
Baltimore
DEL.
Richmond
VIRGINIA

Kansas City
KANSAS
Topeka

Santa Fe
Albuquerque
NEW MEXICO
ARIZONA
Phoenix
Tucson
El Paso

U N I T E D   S T A T E S

MISSOURI
St. Louis
KENTUCKY
TENNESSEE
Nashville
Memphis

Oklahoma City
OKLAHOMA
Little Rock
ARKANSAS

NORTH CAROLINA
Raleigh
Charlotte
SOUTH CAROLINA
Columbia
Charleston

Dallas
TEXAS
Austin
Houston
San Antonio

MISSISSIPPI
Jackson
ALABAMA
Montgomery
Birmingham
GEORGIA
Atlanta
LOUISIANA
Baton Rouge
New Orleans
Tallahassee
Jacksonville
FLORIDA
Tampa
Miami

N O R T H   A T L A N T I C   O C E A N

Bermuda (U.K.)

P A C I F I C   O C E A N

Guadalupe (Mex.)
Hermosillo
Culiacán
M E X I C O
Monterrey
Tropic of Cancer

Revilla Gigedo Is. (Mex.)

Guadalajara
MÉXICO
Puebla
Acapulco
Mérida

G u l f   o f   M e x i c o

Florida Str.
Havana
C U B A
Cayman Is. (U.K.)
JAMAICA
Kingston

Nassau
BAHAMAS
Turks & Caicos Is. (U.K.)

HAITI
Port-au-Prince
DOMINICAN REP.
Santo Domingo
San Juan
PUERTO RICO (U.S.A.)

C a r i b b e a n   S e a

Belmopan
BELIZE
GUATEMALA
Guatemala
San Salvador
EL SALVADOR
HONDURAS
Tegucigalpa
Managua
NICARAGUA
L. Nicaragua
COSTA RICA
San José
PANAMA
Panamá
COLOMBIA
Medellín

Maracaibo
Barranquilla
VENEZUELA

S o u t h
A m e r i c a

Projection: Bonne

7 ■ MÉXICO Capital Cities 8

120 110

West from Greenwich

9 10 90 11 12 70 80

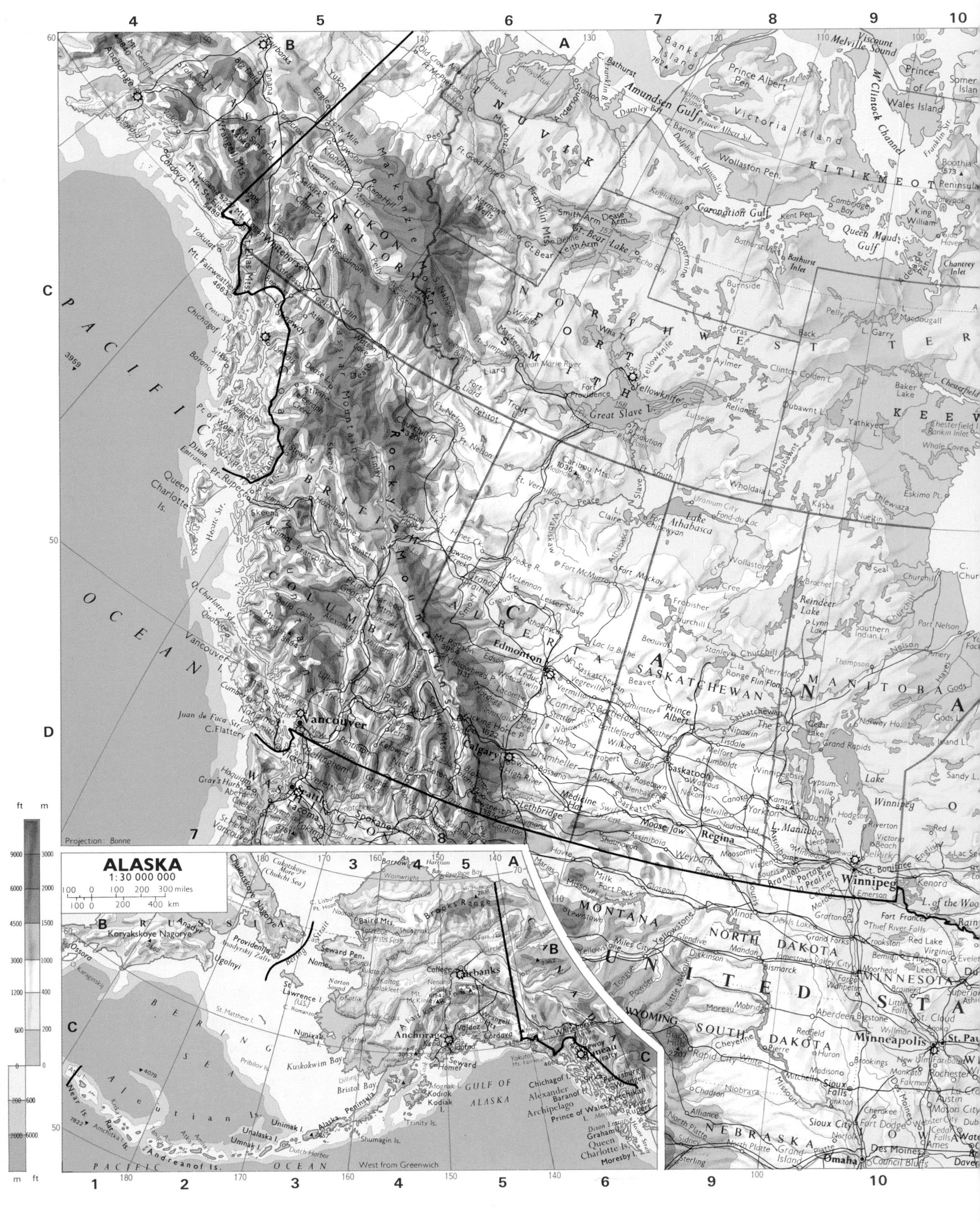
ALASKA
1:30 000 000
Projection: Bonne
West from Greenwich
PACIFIC OCEAN
BRITISH COLUMBIA
ALBERTA
SASKATCHEWAN
MANITOBA
YUKON TERRITORY
NORTHWEST TERRITORIES
UNITED STATES
Vancouver
Edmonton
Calgary
Winnipeg
Regina
Saskatoon
Anchorage
Fairbanks
Juneau

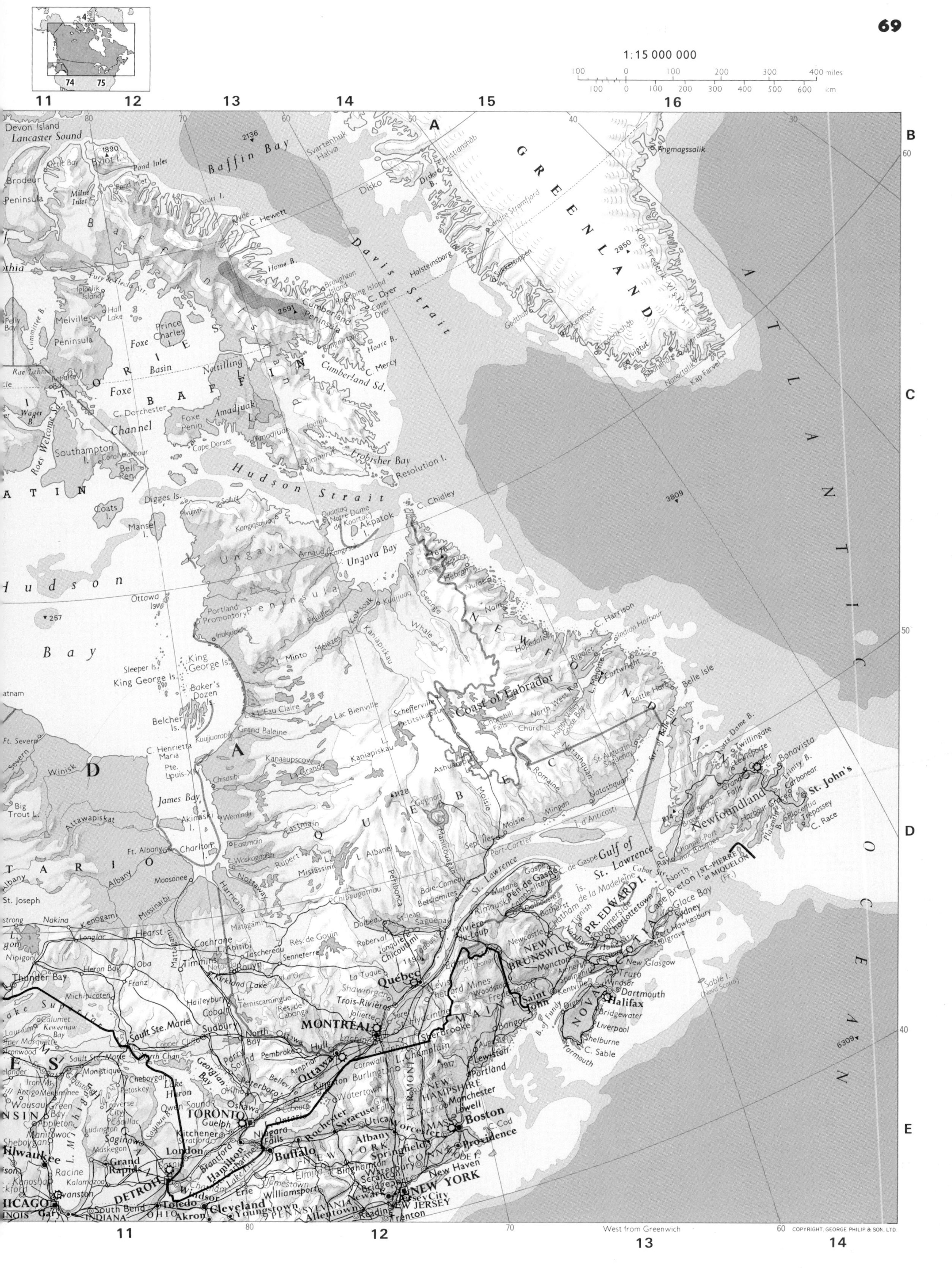
1:15 000 000
miles
km
GREENLAND
ATLANTIC OCEAN
Baffin Bay
Davis Strait
Hudson Strait
Ungava Bay
Ungava Peninsula
Hudson Bay
James Bay
Foxe Basin
Foxe Channel
BAFFIN I.
Cumberland Sd.
Frobisher Bay
Labrador Sea
Coast of Labrador
NEWFOUNDLAND
Newfoundland
St. John's
Gulf of St. Lawrence
QUEBEC
ONTARIO
NEW BRUNSWICK
NOVA SCOTIA
PR. EDWARD I.
Halifax
Québec
MONTREAL
Ottawa
TORONTO
Boston
NEW YORK
Buffalo
Cleveland
DETROIT
CHICAGO
Thunder Bay
Sault Ste. Marie
Lake Superior
Lake Huron
Lake Ontario
Lake Erie
VERMONT
NEW HAMPSHIRE
MAINE
West from Greenwich
COPYRIGHT, GEORGE PHILIP & SON, LTD.

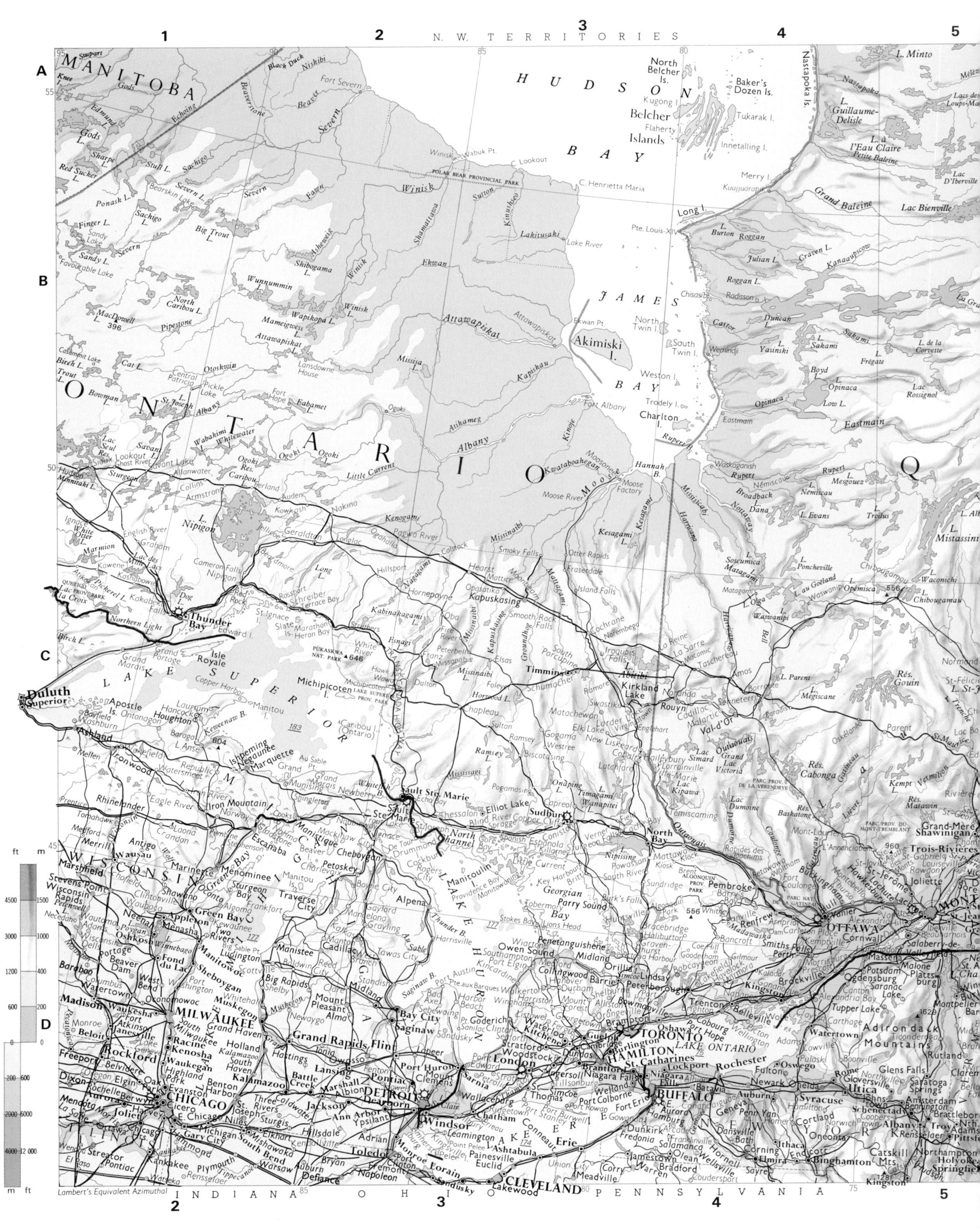
1
2
3
4
5
A
B
C
D
N. W. TERRITORIES
MANITOBA
HUDSON BAY
JAMES BAY
ONTARIO
Q
North Belcher Is.
Baker's Dozen Is.
Kugong I.
Belcher Islands
Flaherty I.
Tukarak I.
Innetalling I.
Nastapoka Is.
Nastapoka
L. Minto
Mélèzes
Lacs des Loups-Marins
L. Guillaume-Delisle
L. à l'Eau Claire
Petite Baleine
Lac D'Iberville
Grand Baleine
Lac Bienville
Merry I.
Kuujjuarapik
C. Henrietta Maria
C. Lookout
Winisk
Wabuk Pt.
POLAR BEAR PROVINCIAL PARK
Long I.
Pte. Louis-XIV
L. Burton
Roggan
Julian L.
Craven L.
Kanaaupscow
Roggan L.
Chisasibi
Radisson
North Twin I.
South Twin I.
Ekwan Pt.
Akimiski I.
Weston I.
Trodely I.
Charlton I.
Fort Albany
Duncan L.
Castor
Wemindji
Yasinski
L. Sakami
Sakami
L. de la Corvette
Frégate
Boyd
Opinaca
Lac Rossignol
Low L.
Eastmain
Rupert B.
Hannah B.
Moosonee
Moose Factory
Moose River
Waskaganish
Rupert
Némiscau
Broadback
Nottaway
L. Mesgouez
L. Nemiscau
L. Dana
L. Evans
L. Troilus
L. Mistassini
Fort Severn
Beaver
Beaverstone
Severn
Niskibi
Black Duck
Stupart
Knee L.
Gods
Echoing
Edmund L.
Gods L.
Sharpe L.
Red Sucker L.
Stull L.
Sachigo
Severn L.
Bearskin Lake
Ponask L.
Sachigo L.
Big Trout L.
Finger L.
Sandy Lake
Sandy L.
Favourable Lake
Fawn
Sutton
Kinushseo
Lakitusaki
Lake River
Shamattawa
Ekwan
Asheweig
Shibogama L.
Wunnummin L.
North Caribou L.
Winisk L.
Wapikopa L.
Mameigwess L.
Attawapiskat L.
Attawapiskat
Pipestone
MacDowell L.
396
Cat L.
Otoskwin
Central Patricia
Pickle Lake
Lansdowne House
Missisa L.
Kapiskau
St. Joseph
Albany
Fort Hope
Eabamet L.
Ogoki
Attikameg
Kinoje
Kwataboahegan
Wabakimi L.
Whitewater
Lac Seul
Sioux Lookout
Savant L.
Sturgeon
Allanwater
Ogoki Res.
Caribou
Little Current
Nakina
Armstrong
L. Nipigon
Kenogami
Pagwa River
Missinaibi
Kesagami L.
Harricana
Missisicabi
Hudson
English River
Graham
Geraldton
Longlac
Calstock
Hearst
Smoky Falls
Otter Rapids
Fraserdale
Marmion
Lac des Mille Lacs
Kashabowie
Cameron Falls
Nipigon
Long L.
Hillsport
Hornepayne
Mattice
Kapuskasing
Opasatika
Island Falls
Kabinakagami L.
Smooth Rock Falls
Cochrane
Soscumica
Matagami
Poncheville
L. au Goéland
Waswanipi
L. Olga
L. Waswanipi
Chibougamau
Opémisca
Waconichi
Bell
Thunder Bay
Dog L.
Rossport
Schreiber
Terrace Bay
Marathon
Heron Bay
Red Rock
St. Ignace
Slate Is.
Northern Light L.
Edward I.
Birch L.
Isle Royale
Grand Marais
LAKE SUPERIOR
PUKASKWA NAT. PARK
646
White River
Franz
Missanabie
Peterbell
Esnagi L.
Elsas
Groundhog
Timmins
South Porcupine
Iroquois Falls
La Reine
La Sarre
Macamic
Taschereau
Amos
L. Abitibi
Michipicoten I.
Dulton
Foleyet
Horwood L.
Chapleau
Schumacher
Kirkland Lake
Rouyn
Noranda
Senneterre
L. Parent
Mégiscane
Rés. Gouin
Duluth
Superior
Apostle Is.
Bayfield
Washburn
Ashland
Ontonagon
Houghton
Hancock
Keweenaw B.
Copper Harbor
Manitou I.
Caribou I. (Ontario)
183
Sultan
Ramsey
Gogama
Westree
Matachewan
Elk Lake
New Liskeard
Swastika
Cadillac
Malartic
Val-d'Or
Parent
Mont-Laurier
Ishpeming
Negaunee
Marquette
Au Sable Pt.
Grand Marais
Munising
Newberry
Whitefish B.
Mississagi
Biscotasing
Ramsey L.
Cobalt
Haileybury
Lorrainville
Ville-Marie
Latchford
Lac Simard
Grand Lac Victoria
Lac Kipawa
Rés. Cabonga
PARC PROV. DE LA VERENDRYE
Lac Dumoine
Témiscaming
Onaping
L. Timagami
L. Wanapitei
Capreol
Sault Ste. Marie
Echo Bay
Elliot Lake
Sudbury
Copper Cliff
Blind River
Spragge
Espanola
North Bay
Mattawa
Rapides des Joachims
Baskatong
Grand-Mère
Shawinigan
Trois-Rivières
Joliette
PARC PROV. DU MONT-TREMBLANT
960
Mont-Laurier
L'Annonciation
St-Jérôme
Lachute
Hawkesbury
Buckingham
Ironwood
Rhinelander
Eagle River
Iron Mountain
Norway
Crandon
Laona
Tomahawk
Medford
Merrill
Antigo
Wausau
Marinette
Menominee
Escanaba
Manistique
Mackinaw City
St. Ignace
Cheboygan
Petoskey
Charlevoix
Drummond I.
De Tour
Cockburn I.
Manitoulin I.
Little Current
Gore Bay
Killarney
Key Harbour
Britt
Nipissing
Powassan
South River
Kiosk
ALGONQUIN PROV. PARK
Pembroke
Barry's Bay
Renfrew
Ottawa
Hull
Vanier
Montréal
Cornwall
Salaberry-de-Valleyfield
Smiths Falls
Perth
Brockville
Kingston
WISCONSIN
MICHIGAN
Marshfield
Stevens Point
Wisconsin Rapids
Shawano
Oconto
Green Bay
Sturgeon Bay
Algoma
Kewaunee
Two Rivers
Manitowoc
Appleton
Menasha
Neenah
Oshkosh
Fond du Lac
Sheboygan
Port Washington
Beaver Dam
Portage
Baraboo
Madison
Watertown
Oconomowoc
Waukesha
MILWAUKEE
Racine
Kenosha
Waukegan
Highland Park
Evanston
CHICAGO
Cicero
Joliet
Gary
Hammond
Rockford
Belvidere
Freeport
Beloit
Janesville
Fort Atkinson
Monroe
Elgin
Aurora
Dixon
Rochelle
Streator
Pontiac
Kankakee
Watseka
Traverse City
Frankfort
Manistee
Ludington
Cadillac
Grayling
Gaylord
Alpena
Harrisville
Tawas City
Big Rapids
Midland
Bay City
Saginaw
Flint
Mount Pleasant
Alma
Muskegon
Grand Haven
Holland
Grand Rapids
Kalamazoo
Battle Creek
Marshall
Albion
Jackson
Lansing
Owosso
Ann Arbor
Ypsilanti
DETROIT
Dearborn
Pontiac
Port Huron
Mount Clemens
Sarnia
Windsor
Leamington
Chatham
St. Thomas
London
Woodstock
Stratford
Kitchener
Guelph
Brantford
HAMILTON
TORONTO
St. Catharines
Niagara Falls
BUFFALO
Lockport
Rochester
Oswego
Syracuse
Utica
Rome
Schenectady
Albany
Troy
Binghamton
Elmira
Ithaca
Cortland
Oneonta
Geneva
Auburn
Batavia
Fulton
Watertown
Ogdensburg
Potsdam
Malone
Tupper Lake
Saranac Lake
Plattsburg
Glens Falls
Saratoga Springs
Amsterdam
Gloversville
Adirondack Mountains
Rutland
Catskill Mts.
Kingston
Northampton
Holyoke
Springfield
Brattleboro
Pittsfield
Owen Sound
Southampton
Port Elgin
Kincardine
Goderich
Wingham
Collingwood
Midland
Penetanguishene
Orillia
Barrie
Lindsay
Peterborough
Cobourg
Port Hope
Oshawa
Bowmanville
Belleville
Trenton
Huntsville
Bracebridge
Parry Sound
Georgian Bay
Tobermory
Lions Head
Stokes Bay
LAKE HURON
LAKE ONTARIO
LAKE ERIE
Simcoe
Port Dover
Welland
Port Colborne
Fort Erie
Dunkirk
Fredonia
Jamestown
Erie
Conneaut
Ashtabula
Painesville
Euclid
CLEVELAND
Lakewood
Lorain
Sandusky
Toledo
Monroe
Adrian
Hillsdale
Napoleon
Defiance
Fremont
Bryan
Auburn
Elkhart
South Bend
Mishawaka
Niles
St. Joseph
Benton Harbor
South Haven
Three Rivers
Sturgis
Plymouth
Warsaw
Michigan City
Meadville
Corry
Warren
Bradford
Olean
Salamanca
Hornell
Wellsville
Coudersport
Corning
Sayre
Dansville
Bath
Penn Yan
Hamburg
Aurora
Canandaigua
INDIANA
OHIO
PENNSYLVANIA
NEW YORK
ILLINOIS
Lambert's Equivalent Azimuthal
95
90
85
80
75
55
50
45
ft
m
4500
1500
3000
1000
1200
400
600
200
0
0
200
600
2000
6000
4000
12 000
m
ft

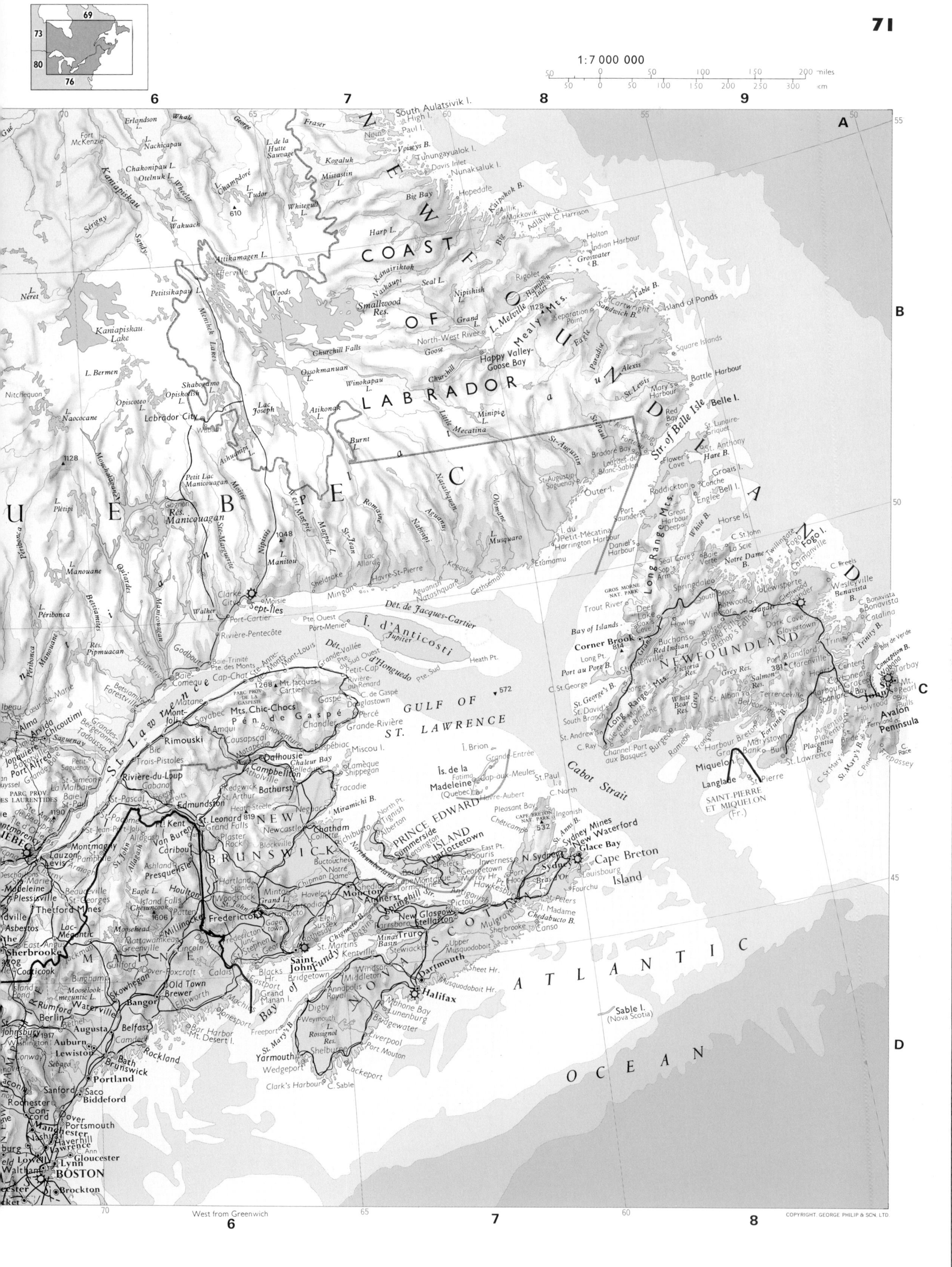
69
73
80
76
1:7 000 000
50 0 50 100 150 200 miles
50 0 50 100 150 200 250 300 km
6
7
8
9
A
B
C
D
COAST OF LABRADOR
NEWFOUNDLAND
QUEBEC
LABRADOR
Labrador
South Aulatsivik I.
Nain
Hopedale
Makkovik
Kaipokok B.
Big Bay
Harp L.
Kogaluk
Mistastin L.
Fraser
George
Whale
Erlandson L.
Fort McKenzie
Nachicapau
Chakonipau L.
Otelnuk L.
L. Champdoré
L. Tudor
Whitegull L.
Kaniapiskau
Sérigny
Wakuach
Attikamagen L.
Schefferville
Petitsikapau L.
Woods L.
Smallwood Res.
Kanairiktok
Naskaupi
Seal L.
Nipishish L.
Grand L.
L. Melville
Hamilton Inlet
Rigolet
Mealy Mts.
1128
Happy Valley-Goose Bay
North-West River
Goose
Churchill Falls
Churchill
Winokapau L.
Ossokmanuan L.
Atikonak L.
Cartwright
Sandwich B.
Table B.
Island of Ponds
Separation Point
Square Islands
Eagle
Paradise
Alexis
Battle Harbour
Mary's Harbour
St. Lewis
Holton
Indian Harbour
Groswater B.
C. Harrison
Kaniapiskau Lake
L. Bermen
Nitchequon
Opiscoteo L.
Shabogamo L.
Lac Joseph
Labrador City
Wabush
Ashuanipi L.
Minipi L.
Little Mecatina
Burnt L.
St-Augustin
Belle I.
Str. of Belle Isle
Red Bay
Blanc-Sablon
Bradore Bay
St. Lunaire-Griquet
St. Anthony
Hare B.
Groais I.
Bell I.
Horse Is.
Roddickton
Englee
Outer I.
Port Saunders
Great Harbour Deep
White B.
Long Range Mts.
Daniel's Harbour
Harrington Harbour
Petit-Mécatina
Musquaro
Olomane
Natashquan
Aguanus
Nabisipi
Romaine
St-Jean
Magpie L.
West Magpie
Moisie
Manitou
1048
Havre-St-Pierre
Mingan
Sheldrake
Aguanish
Kegaska
Natashquan
Gethsémani
Etamamu
Petit Lac Manicouagan
Gagnon
Rés. Manicouagan
Ste-Marguerite
Plétipi
L. Manouane
Péribonca
Sept-Îles
Clarke City
Port-Cartier
Walker L.
Rivière-Pentecôte
Godbout
Baie-Trinité
Pte. des Monts
Baie-Comeau
Forestville
Rés. Pipmuacan
Dét. de Jacques-Cartier
Î. d'Anticosti
Port-Menier
Pte. Ouest
Heath Pt.
Dét. d'Honguedo
Gaspé
Mts. Chic-Chocs
Pén. de Gaspé
1268 Mt. Jacques-Cartier
Matane
Mont-Joli
Rimouski
Amqui
Causapscal
Chandler
Percé
Grande-Rivière
Douglastown
C. de Gaspé
Petit-Cap
Paspébiac
Miscou I.
Lamèque
Shippegan
GULF OF ST. LAWRENCE
St. Lawrence
Chicoutimi
Jonquière
Arvida
Alma
Saguenay
Tadoussac
Port Alfred
Rivière-du-Loup
Trois-Pistoles
Bic
Dalhousie
Chaleur Bay
Campbellton
Bathurst
Tracadie
Miramichi B.
Edmundston
St. Leonard
Grand Falls
NEW BRUNSWICK
Newcastle
Chatham
Fredericton
Moncton
Saint John
Bay of Fundy
PRINCE EDWARD ISLAND
Summerside
Charlottetown
Îs. de la Madeleine
Madeleine (Quebec)
Cap-aux-Meules
Î. Brion
St. Paul I.
C. North
Cabot Strait
Pleasant Bay
Chéticamp
Ingonish
532
Sydney Mines
New Waterford
Glace Bay
N. Sydney
Sydney
Cape Breton Island
Louisbourg
Bras d'Or
St. Peters
I. Madame
Chedabucto B.
Canso
Sherbrooke
Mulgrave
Antigonish
Pictou
New Glasgow
Stellarton
Truro
Amherst
Springhill
Minas Basin
Kentville
Windsor
Dartmouth
Halifax
NOVA SCOTIA
Bridgetown
Middleton
Annapolis Royal
Digby
Weymouth
Lunenburg
Mahone Bay
Bridgewater
Liverpool
Port Mouton
Shelburne
Yarmouth
Wedgeport
Clark's Harbour
C. Sable
Lockeport
Sheet Hr.
Musquodoboit Hr.
Sable I. (Nova Scotia)
ATLANTIC OCEAN
Corner Brook
814
Bay of Islands
Trout River
Deer Lake
Humber
Long Pt.
Port au Port B.
St. George's B.
Stephenville
C. St. George
St. David's
South Branch
St. Andrew's
C. Ray
Channel-Port aux Basques
Burgeo
Ramea
Red Indian L.
Buchans
Victoria L.
Grand Falls
Bishop's Falls
Botwood
Windsor
Howley
NEWFOUNDLAND
Grey Res.
Salmon Res.
White Bear Res.
St. Alban's
Terrenceville
Harbour Breton
Fortune B.
Grand Bank
Marystown
Burin
St. Lawrence
Placentia B.
St. Mary's B.
C. Pine
Trepassey
C. Race
Avalon Peninsula
St. John's
Holyrood
Ferryland
Conception B.
Torbay
Bay de Verde
Trinity B.
Catalina
Bonavista
C. Bonavista
Wesleyville
Clarenville
Glovertown
Gander
Gambo
Lewisporte
Springdale
Notre Dame B.
Fogo I.
Twillingate
Carmanville
C. Freels
C. St. John
La Scie
Baie Verte
Sop's Arm
Seal Cove
GROS MORNE NAT. PARK
Miquelon
Langlade
St. Pierre
SAINT-PIERRE ET MIQUELON (Fr.)
Thetford Mines
Plessisville
Lévis
Montmagny
Asbestos
Sherbrooke
Coaticook
Lac-Mégantic
MAINE
Houlton
Presque Isle
Caribou
Van Buren
Ft. Kent
Millinocket
Moosehead L.
Greenville
Lincoln
Calais
Eastport
Grand Manan I.
Machias
Old Town
Brewer
Bangor
Ellsworth
Bar Harbor
Mt. Desert I.
Belfast
Camden
Rockland
Skowhegan
Waterville
Augusta
Bath
Brunswick
Lewiston
Auburn
Portland
Saco
Biddeford
Sanford
Rumford
Berlin
Rochester
Concord
Dover
Portsmouth
Manchester
Nashua
Haverhill
Lawrence
Lowell
Lynn
Gloucester
C. Ann
Waltham
BOSTON
Brockton
70
65
60
55
50
45
West from Greenwich
6
7
8

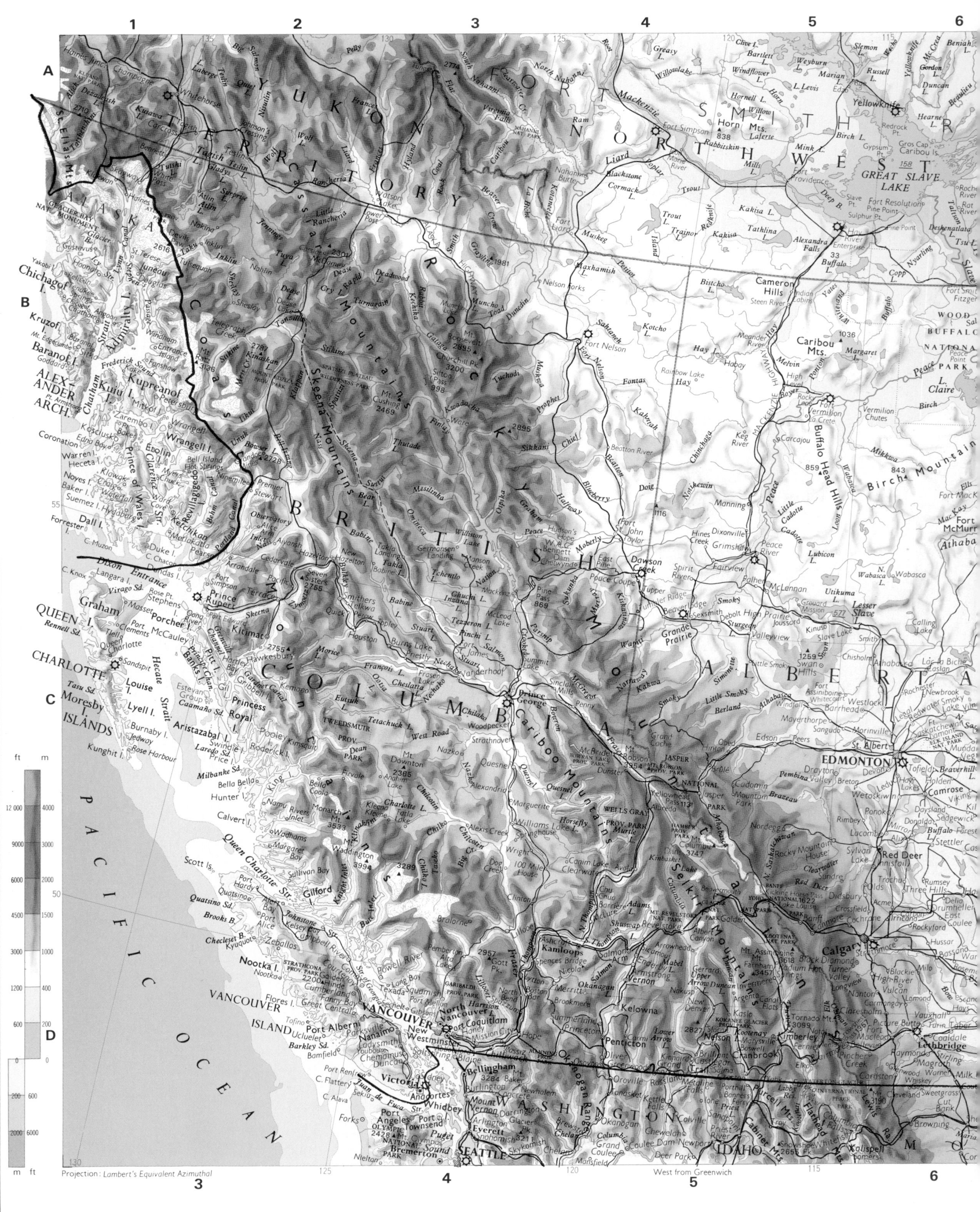
YUKON TERRITORY
NORTHWEST TERRITORIES
FORT SMITH
BRITISH COLUMBIA
ALBERTA
ALASKA
WASHINGTON
IDAHO
PACIFIC OCEAN
QUEEN CHARLOTTE ISLANDS
VANCOUVER ISLAND
GREAT SLAVE LAKE
Skeena Mountains
Cassiar Mountains
Cariboo Mountains
Selkirk Mountains
Rocky Mountains
Coast Mountains
Caribou Mts.
Buffalo Head Hills
Birch Mountains
Cameron Hills
Whitehorse
Yellowknife
Fort Simpson
Fort Nelson
Fort St. John
Dawson Creek
Grande Prairie
Peace River
Prince Rupert
Prince George
Kamloops
Kelowna
Penticton
Vancouver
Victoria
Nanaimo
Port Alberni
Bellingham
Seattle
Edmonton
Red Deer
Calgary
Lethbridge
Jasper
Banff
Juneau
Ketchikan
Hay River
Fort Resolution
Fort Vermilion
Camrose
Medicine Hat
Projection: Lambert's Equivalent Azimuthal
West from Greenwich
1
2
3
4
5
6
A
B
C
D
ft
m
12 000
4000
9000
3000
6000
2000
4500
1500
3000
1000
1200
400
600
200
0
0
200
600
2000
6000

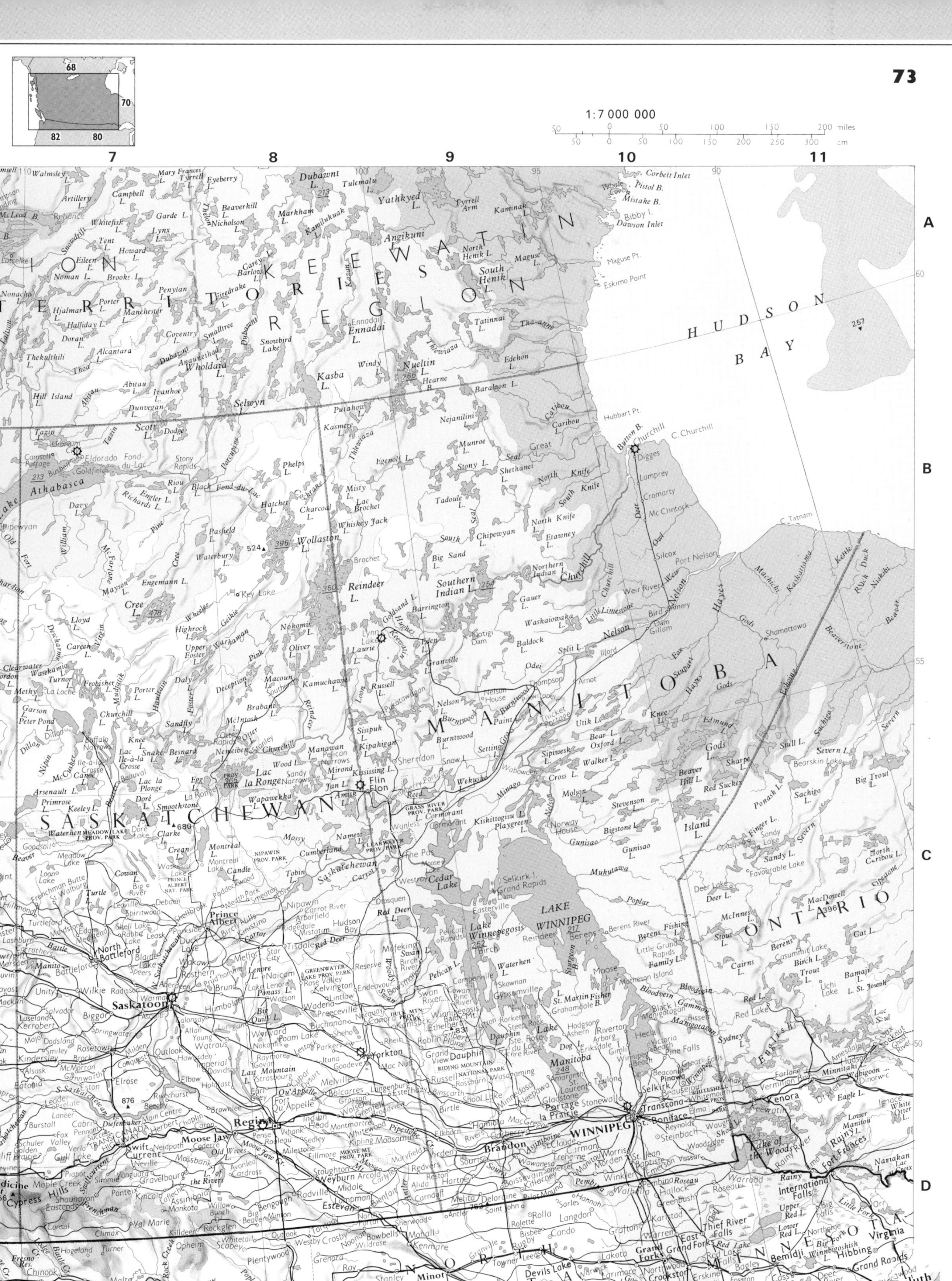
1:7 000 000
miles
km
A
B
C
D
7
8
9
10
11
KEEWATIN
REGION
TERRITORIES
HUDSON BAY
MANITOBA
SASKATCHEWAN
ONTARIO
NORTH DAKOTA
MONTANA
MINNESOTA
Lake Athabasca
Wollaston L.
Reindeer L.
Southern Indian L.
Nueltin L.
Kasba L.
Dubawnt L.
Yathkyed L.
Lac la Ronge
Cedar Lake
Lake Winnipegosis
LAKE WINNIPEG
Lake Manitoba
Lake of the Woods
Churchill
C. Churchill
Port Nelson
Flin Flon
The Pas
Thompson
Prince Albert
North Battleford
Saskatoon
Yorkton
Regina
Moose Jaw
Swift Current
Medicine Hat
Brandon
WINNIPEG
St. Boniface
Dauphin
Portage la Prairie
Kenora
International Falls
Fort Frances
Minot
Grand Forks
Devils Lake
Bemidji
Duluth
Williston
Havre
Cypress Hills
Nelson
Hayes
Saskatchewan
COPYRIGHT. GEORGE PHILIP & SON. LTD.

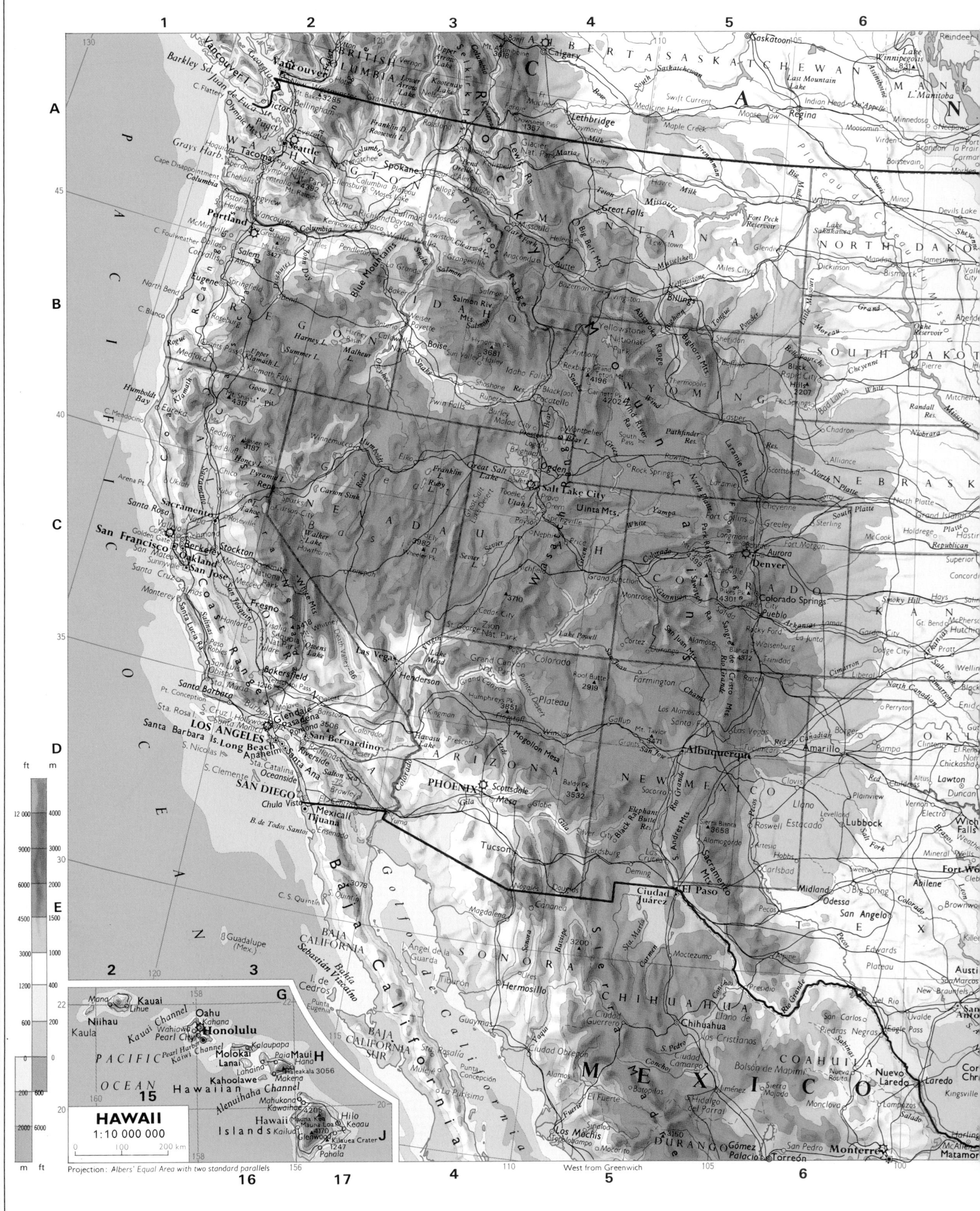

HAWAII
1:10 000 000

0   100   200 km

Projection: Albers' Equal Area with two standard parallels

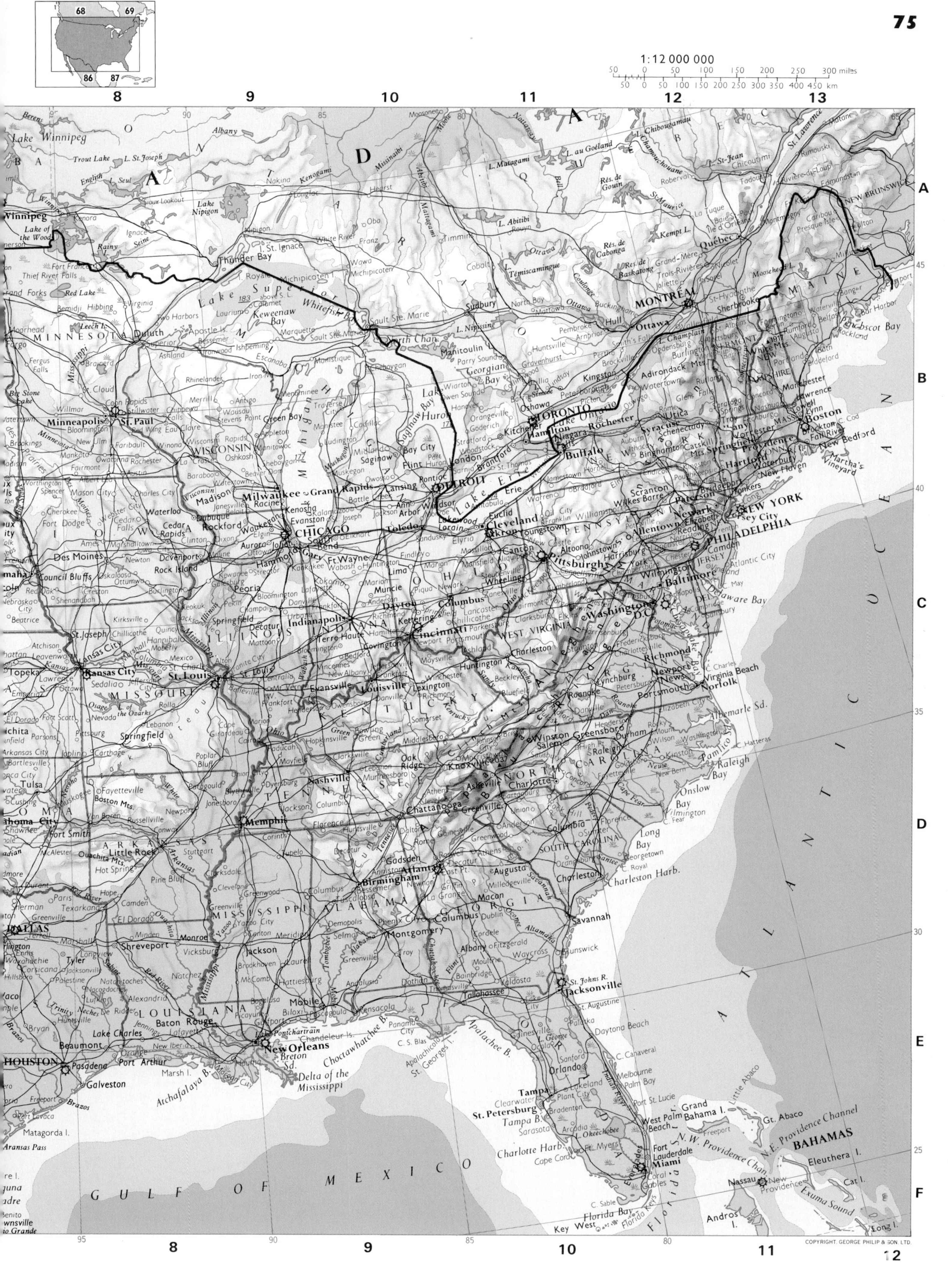
68
69
86
87
1:12 000 000
50 0 50 100 150 200 250 300 miles
50 0 50 100 150 200 250 300 350 400 450 km
8
9
10
11
12
13
A
B
C
D
E
F
Lake Winnipeg
Winnipeg
Lake of the Woods
Thunder Bay
Lake Superior
MINNESOTA
Duluth
Minneapolis
St. Paul
WISCONSIN
Green Bay
Milwaukee
Madison
Lake Michigan
Lake Huron
Georgian Bay
Sault Ste. Marie
Sudbury
Ottawa
MONTRÉAL
Québec
TORONTO
Hamilton
Lake Ontario
Rochester
Buffalo
Lake Erie
DETROIT
Windsor
Cleveland
Toledo
CHICAGO
Grand Rapids
Lansing
Flint
Saginaw
IOWA
Des Moines
Cedar Rapids
Waterloo
ILLINOIS
Peoria
Springfield
INDIANA
Indianapolis
Ft. Wayne
OHIO
Columbus
Dayton
Cincinnati
Akron
Youngstown
Pittsburgh
PENNSYLVANIA
Harrisburg
Allentown
Scranton
Wilkes Barre
PHILADELPHIA
NEW YORK
Syracuse
Utica
Albany
Hartford
Providence
Boston
Worcester
Springfield
New Haven
Bridgeport
MAINE
VERMONT
NEW HAMPSHIRE
NEW BRUNSWICK
Cape Cod
Martha's Vineyard
New Bedford
Newark
Camden
Trenton
Atlantic City
Wilmington
Baltimore
Washington D.C.
Delaware Bay
Chesapeake Bay
WEST VIRGINIA
Charleston
Richmond
Norfolk
Newport News
Portsmouth
Virginia Beach
Roanoke
Lynchburg
Kansas City
Topeka
St. Joseph
St. Louis
MISSOURI
Springfield
Evansville
Louisville
Lexington
KENTUCKY
Nashville
Knoxville
Chattanooga
TENNESSEE
Memphis
Winston Salem
Greensboro
Durham
Raleigh
NORTH CAROLINA
Charlotte
Asheville
Greenville
Columbia
SOUTH CAROLINA
Charleston
Savannah
Augusta
Atlanta
GEORGIA
Macon
Columbus
Birmingham
ALABAMA
Montgomery
Mobile
MISSISSIPPI
Jackson
LOUISIANA
Baton Rouge
New Orleans
Shreveport
Little Rock
ARKANSAS
Fort Smith
Tulsa
Oklahoma City
DALLAS
HOUSTON
Galveston
Beaumont
Port Arthur
Pasadena
Lake Charles
Tallahassee
Jacksonville
St. Augustine
Daytona Beach
Orlando
Tampa
St. Petersburg
Sarasota
C. Canaveral
West Palm Beach
Fort Lauderdale
Miami
Key West
Florida Bay
Florida Keys
Grand Bahama I.
Gt. Abaco
BAHAMAS
Nassau
Andros I.
Eleuthera I.
Cat I.
Exuma Sound
Long I.
N.W. Providence Chan.
N.E. Providence Channel
GULF OF MEXICO
ATLANTIC OCEAN
Delta of the Mississippi
Apalachee B.
Charlotte Harb.
Tampa B.
Onslow Bay
Raleigh Bay
Long Bay
Albemarle Sd.
Pamlico Sd.
C. Hatteras
95
90
85
80
75
45
40
35
30
25
COPYRIGHT. GEORGE PHILIP & SON. LTD.

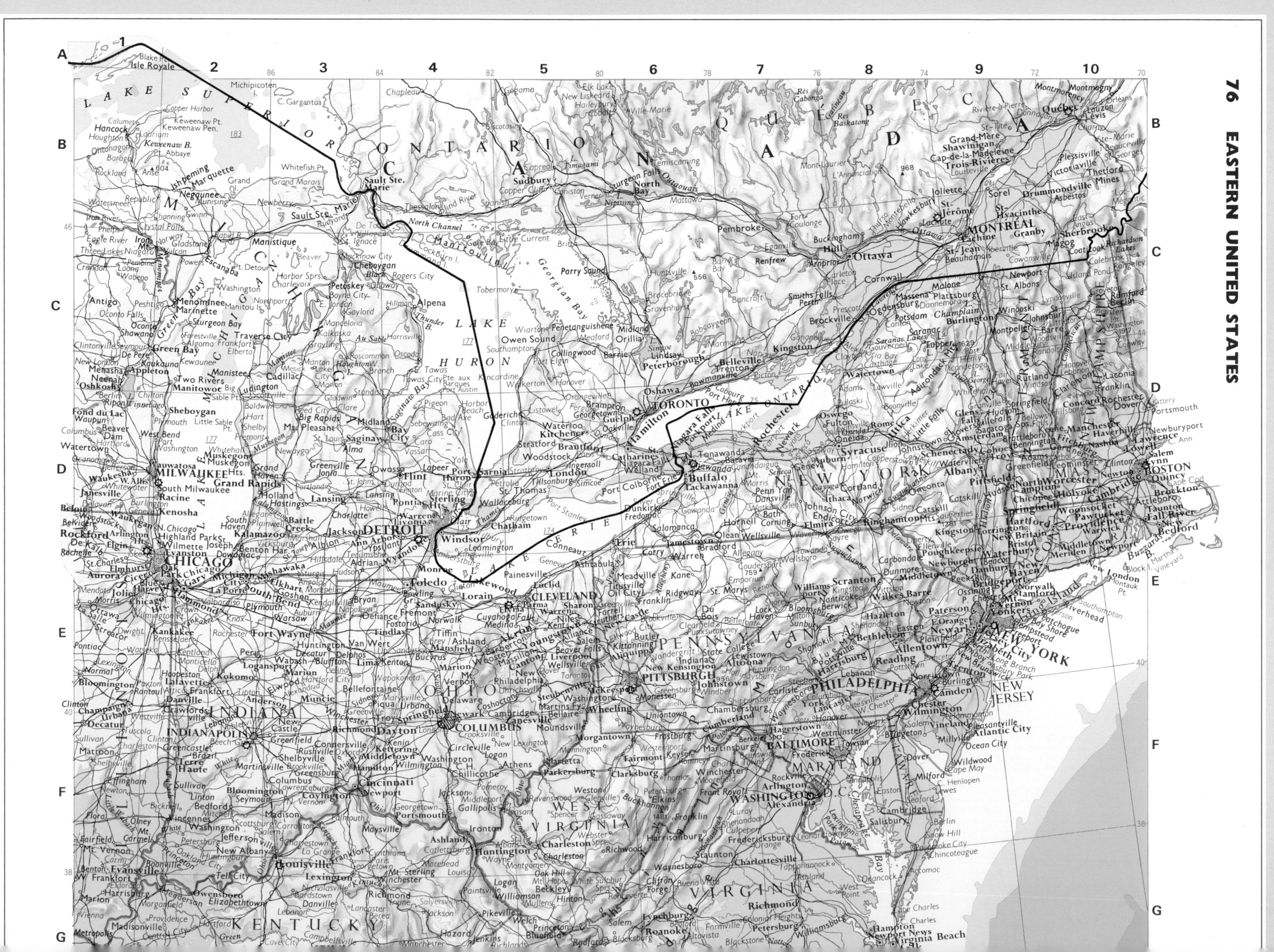
LAKE SUPERIOR
LAKE HURON
Georgian Bay
LAKE ONTARIO
LAKE ERIE
ONTARIO
QUÉBEC
CANADA
MICHIGAN
NEW YORK
PENNSYLVANIA
OHIO
INDIANA
ILLINOIS
WEST VIRGINIA
VIRGINIA
KENTUCKY
MARYLAND
NEW JERSEY
VERMONT
NEW HAMPSHIRE
MASSACHUSETTS
CHICAGO
MILWAUKEE
DETROIT
TORONTO
MONTRÉAL
Ottawa
Québec
CLEVELAND
PITTSBURGH
COLUMBUS
INDIANAPOLIS
PHILADELPHIA
BALTIMORE
WASHINGTON D.C.
NEW YORK
BOSTON
Buffalo
Rochester
Syracuse
Albany
Louisville
Cincinnati
Dayton
Toledo
Hamilton
Windsor
London
Kingston
Sudbury
Sault Ste. Marie

1 : 6 000 000

50 0 50 100 150 miles
50 0 50 100 150 200 km

Continuation Eastwards On same scale.

NEW HAMPSHIRE

MAINE

ATLANTIC OCEAN

BAHAMAS

Little Abaco I.
Gt. Guana Cay
Hope Town
Great Abaco I.
Grand Bahama I.
Freeport
Settlement Pt.
Grand Cays

VIRGINIA

NORTH CAROLINA

SOUTH CAROLINA

GEORGIA

FLORIDA

ALABAMA

MISSISSIPPI

TENNESSEE

KENTUCKY

GULF OF MEXICO

Wilmington
Raleigh
Charlotte
Columbia
Charleston
Savannah
Jacksonville
Atlanta
Birmingham
Montgomery
Mobile
Pensacola
Tallahassee
Panama City
Tampa
St. Petersburg
Orlando
Miami
Ft. Lauderdale
West Palm Beach
Key West
Nashville
Chattanooga
Knoxville
Asheville

West from Greenwich

Projection: Alber's Equal Area with two standard parallels

COPYRIGHT GEORGE PHILIP & SON, LTD.

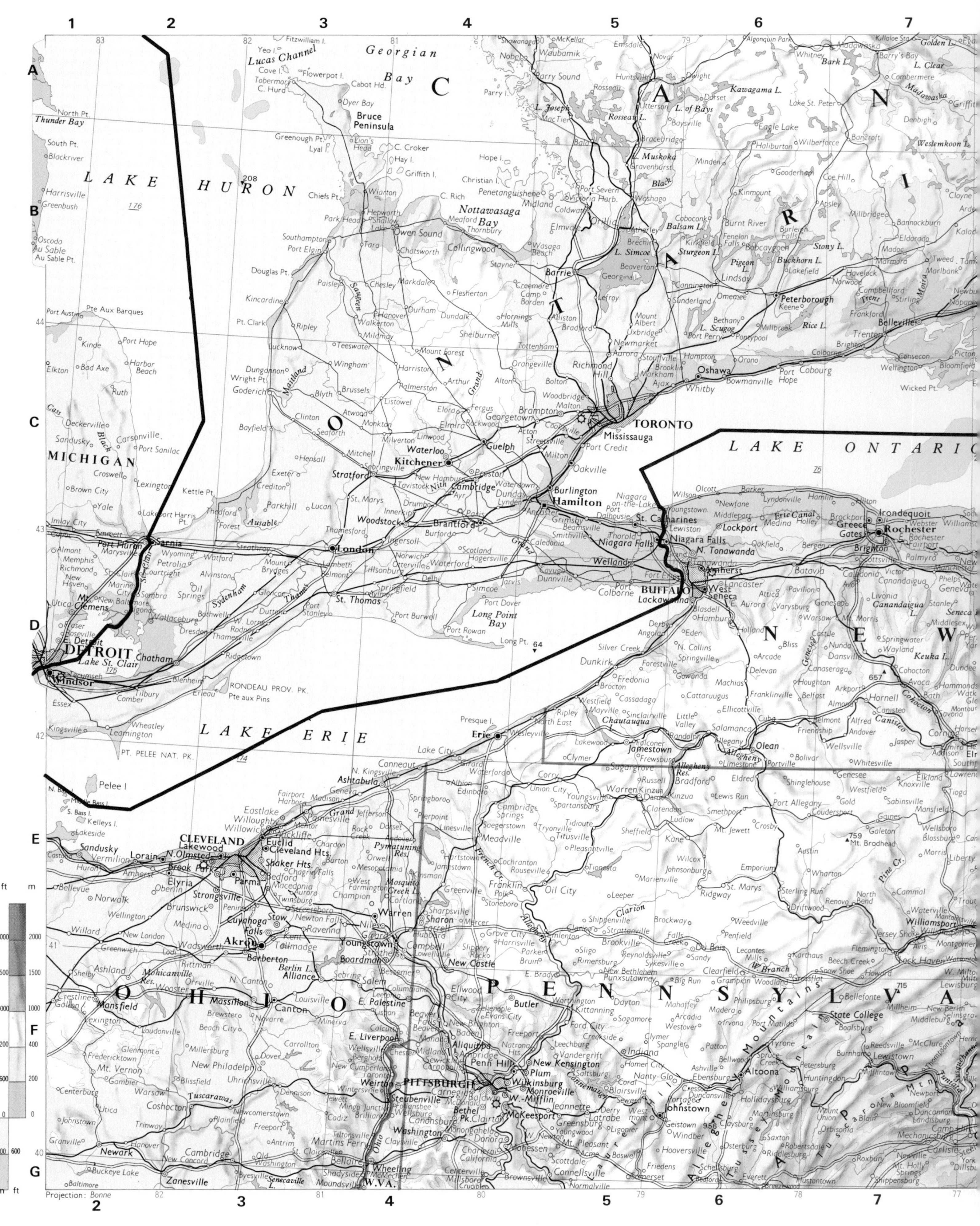
LAKE HURON
LAKE ERIE
LAKE ONTARIO
Georgian Bay
MICHIGAN
OHIO
PENNSYLVANIA
ONTARIO
CANADA
TORONTO
DETROIT
CLEVELAND
BUFFALO
PITTSBURGH
Projection: Bonne

1:2 500 000

10   0   10   20   30   40   50 miles
10 0 10 20 30 40 50 60 70 80 km

CANADA

QUÉBEC

MONTREAL

MAINE

VERMONT

NEW HAMPSHIRE

NEW YORK

MASSACHUSETTS

RHODE ISLAND

CONNECTICUT

NEW JERSEY

NEW YORK

PENNSYLVANIA

Lake Champlain

Long Island

Long Island Sound

Block Island Sound

ATLANTIC OCEAN

Ottawa
Hull
Cornwall
Ogdensburg
Potsdam
Watertown
Syracuse
Utica
Rome
Oneida L.
Gloversville
Amsterdam
Schenectady
Troy
Albany
Saratoga Springs
Glens Falls
Lake George
Ticonderoga
Burlington
Montpelier
Mt. Washington 1917
Mt. Marcy 1629
Lake Placid
Saranac Lakes
Concord
Manchester
Nashua
Lowell
Lawrence
Haverhill
Portsmouth
Pittsfield
Northampton
Springfield
Holyoke
Chicopee
Worcester
Framingham
BOSTON
Cambridge
Newton
Waltham
Quincy
Brockton
Fall River
New Bedford
Providence
Pawtucket
Cranston
Warwick
Newport
Hartford
New Britain
Waterbury
Meriden
New Haven
Bridgeport
Stamford
Norwalk
Danbury
New London
Norwich
Poughkeepsie
Kingston
Newburgh
Middletown
Binghamton
Ithaca
Cortland
Scranton
Wilkes-Barre
Allentown
Bethlehem
Easton
Reading
Pottstown
Norristown
Lancaster
PHILADELPHIA
Camden
Trenton
New Brunswick
Perth Amboy
Newark
Elizabeth
Bayonne
Jersey City
Paterson
Passaic
Yonkers
White Plains
New Rochelle
Mt. Vernon
Hackensack
Montclair
Long Branch
Asbury Park
Montauk Pt.

COPYRIGHT GEORGE PHILIP & SON LTD

West from Greenwich

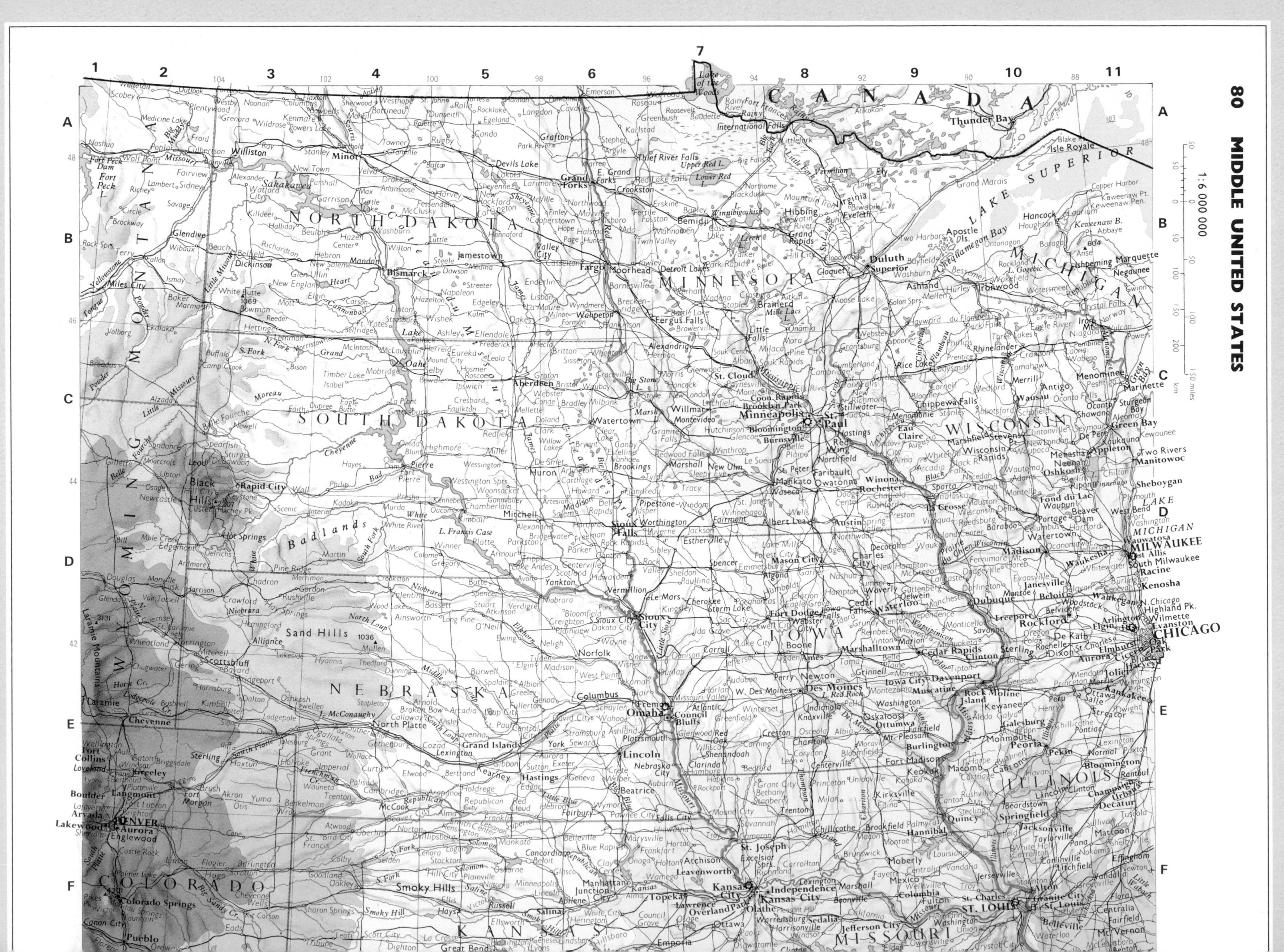
1:6 000 000
50 0 50 100 150 miles
50 0 50 100 150 200 km
CANADA
LAKE SUPERIOR
LAKE MICHIGAN
MICHIGAN
WISCONSIN
MINNESOTA
NORTH DAKOTA
SOUTH DAKOTA
IOWA
ILLINOIS
NEBRASKA
KANSAS
MISSOURI
MONTANA
WYOMING
COLORADO
MILWAUKEE
CHICAGO
ST. LOUIS
DENVER
Minneapolis
St. Paul
Des Moines
Omaha
Kansas City
Sand Hills
Badlands
Black Hills
Laramie Mountains

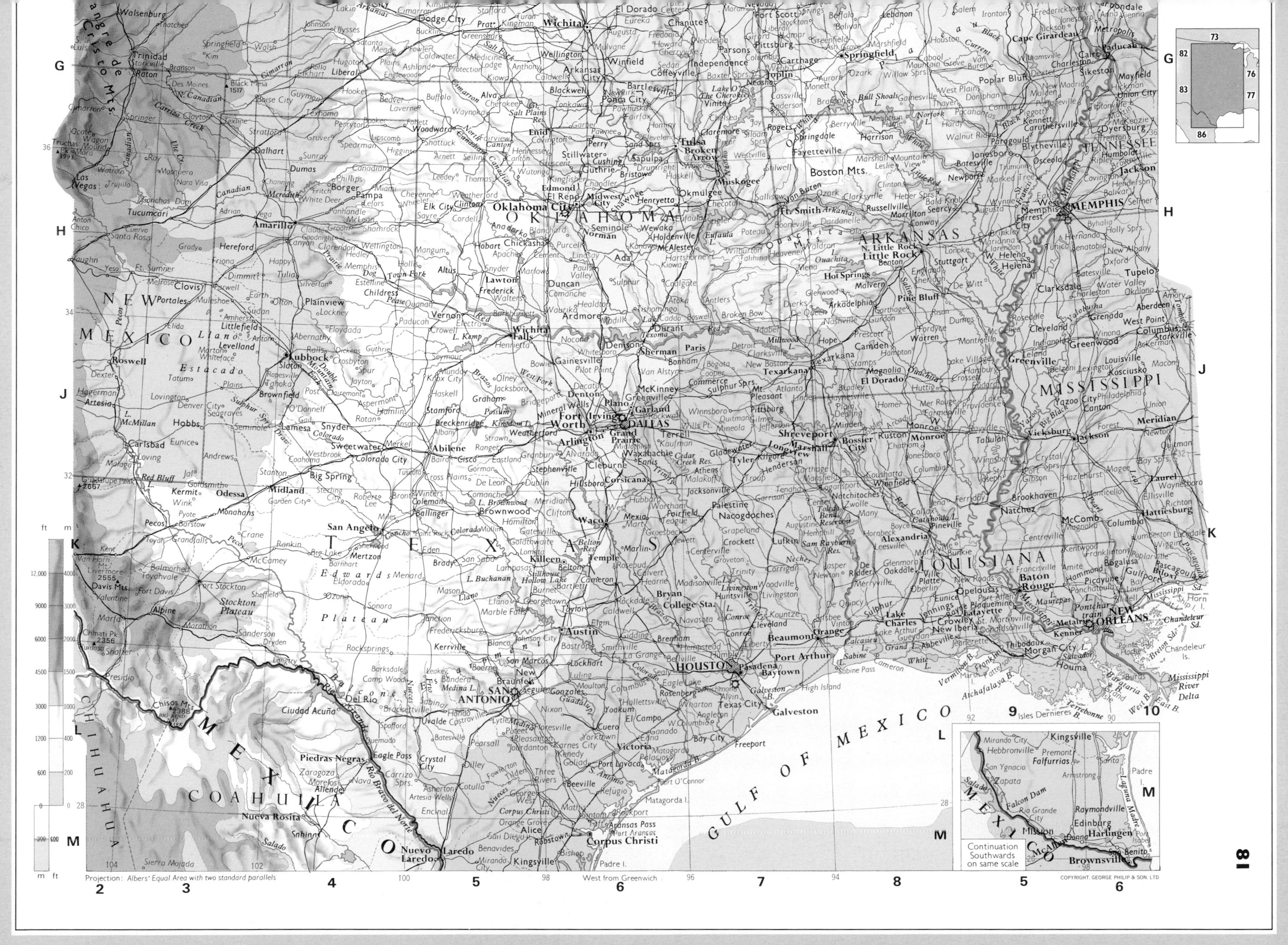
OKLAHOMA
ARKANSAS
MISSISSIPPI
LOUISIANA
TEXAS
NEW MEXICO
TENNESSEE
MEXICO
COAHUILA
CHIHUAHUA
GULF OF MEXICO
DALLAS
HOUSTON
SAN ANTONIO
Oklahoma City
MEMPHIS
NEW ORLEANS
Little Rock
Shreveport
Fort Worth
Austin
Amarillo
Lubbock
Wichita
Tulsa
Baton Rouge
Jackson
Corpus Christi
Galveston
Sangre de Cristo Mts.
Boston Mts.
Edwards Plateau
Llano Estacado
Continuation Southwards on same scale
Projection: Albers' Equal Area with two standard parallels
West from Greenwich
COPYRIGHT GEORGE PHILIP & SON, LTD

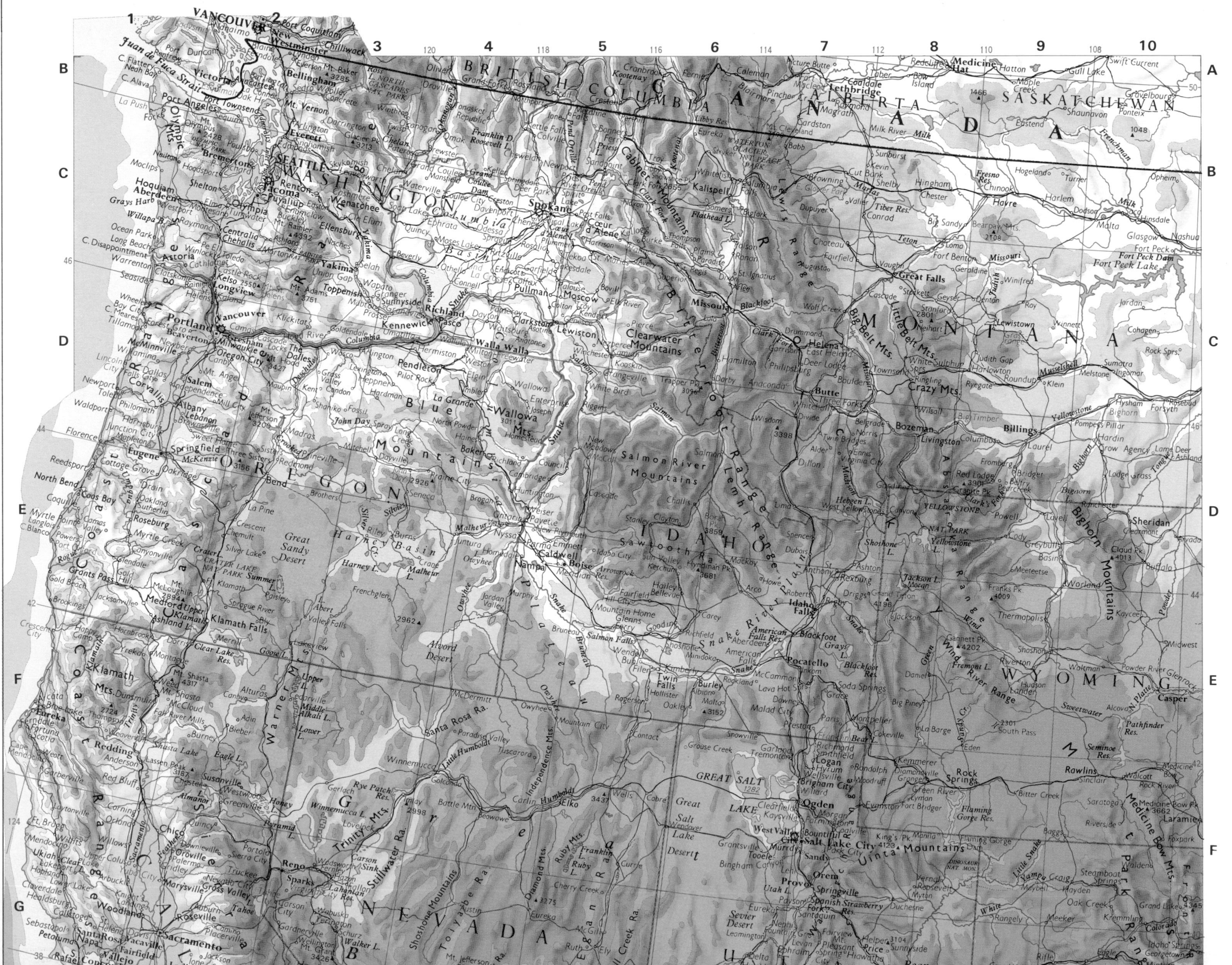
BRITISH COLUMBIA
ALBERTA
SASKATCHEWAN
CANADA
WASHINGTON
OREGON
IDAHO
MONTANA
WYOMING
NEVADA
Olympic Mts.
Blue Mountains
Salmon River Mountains
Clearwater Mountains
Bitterroot Range
Lemhi Range
Sawtooth Range
Bighorn Mountains
Wind River Range
Uinta Mountains
Medicine Bow Mts.
Cabinet Mountains
Great Salt Lake Desert
Great Sandy Desert
Harney Basin
Snake River Plain
Seattle
Portland
Spokane
Boise
Salt Lake City
Ogden
Helena
Butte
Great Falls
Billings
Sacramento
Reno
Vancouver
Victoria
Lethbridge
Medicine Hat

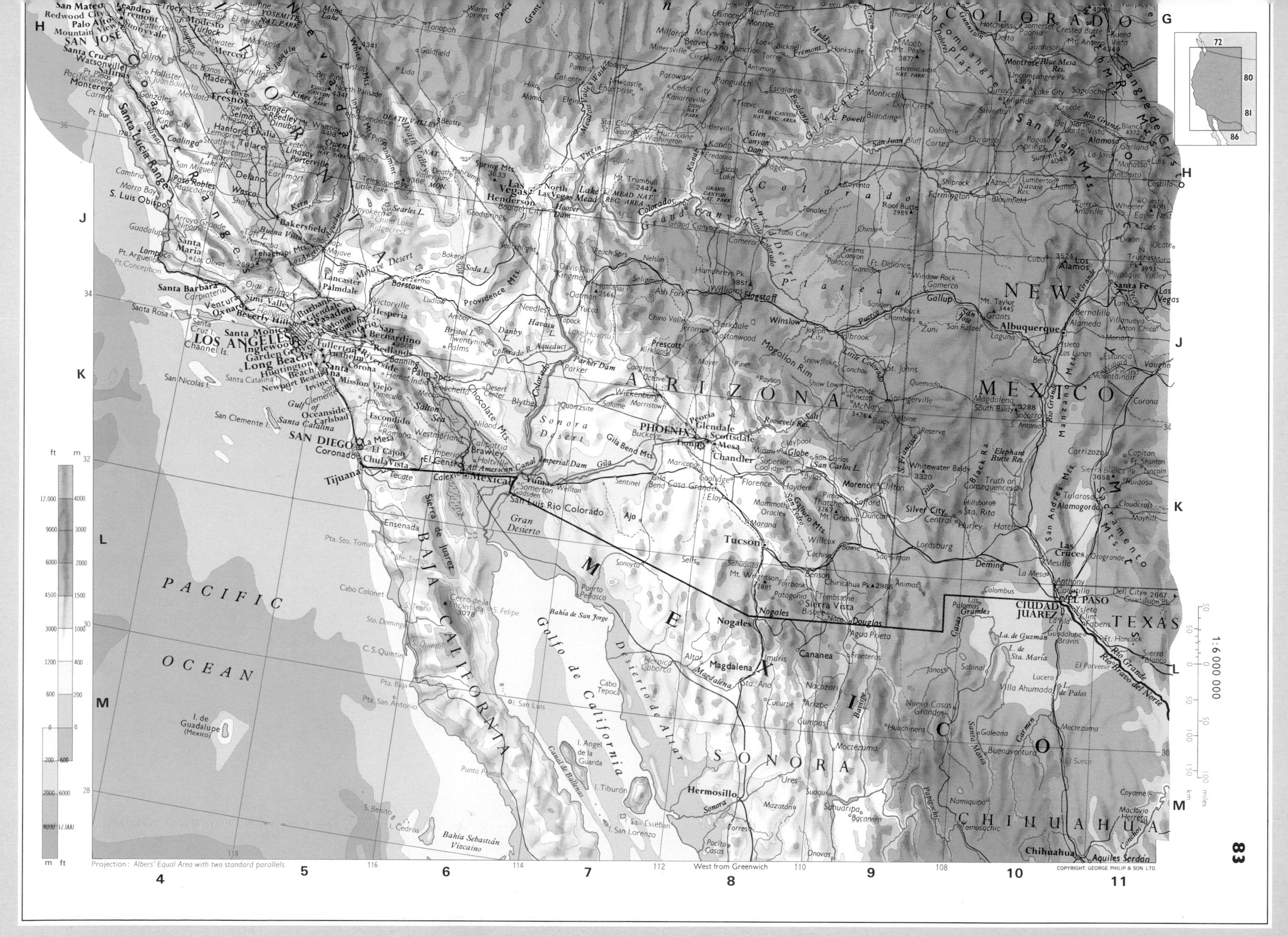

1:6 000 000
50 0 50 100 miles
50 0 50 100 150 km
CALIFORNIA
NEVADA
ARIZONA
NEW MEXICO
COLORADO
TEXAS
MEXICO
SONORA
CHIHUAHUA
BAJA CALIFORNIA
PACIFIC OCEAN
Golfo de California
Desierto de Altar
Sonora Desert
Gran Desierto
Colorado Plateau
Painted Desert
Grand Canyon
Mojave Desert
Death Valley
Coast Ranges
Santa Lucia Range
San Juan Mts.
Sangre de Cristo Mts.
Sacramento Mts.
Mogollon Rim
LOS ANGELES
SAN DIEGO
SAN JOSE
PHOENIX
Tucson
Albuquerque
Santa Fe
EL PASO
CIUDAD JUAREZ
Las Vegas
Tijuana
Mexicali
Hermosillo
Chihuahua
Fresno
Bakersfield
Santa Barbara
Flagstaff
Yuma
Nogales
Channel Is.
I. Tiburón
I. Angel de la Guarda
I. de Guadalupe (Mexico)
Rio Grande
Colorado
Gila
West from Greenwich
Projection: Albers' Equal Area with two standard parallels
ft m
m ft

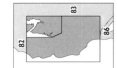

SEATTLE-PORTLAND
REGION
On same scale

1:2 500 000

10 0 10 20 30 40 50 miles
10 0 10 20 30 40 50 60 70 80 km

NEVADA

ARIZONA

CALIFORNIA

MEXICO

PACIFIC OCEAN

Lake Mead
LAKE HEAD NATIONAL RECREATION AREA

Las Vegas
North Las Vegas
Henderson
Paradise
Sunrise Manor

LOS ANGELES
SAN BERNARDINO
Pasadena
Glendale
Long Beach
Santa Ana
Anaheim
Riverside
Santa Monica
Inglewood
Torrance
Redondo Beach
Huntington Beach
Newport Beach
Costa Mesa
Orange
Corona
Ontario
Pomona
Fullerton
Whittier
Norwalk
Lancaster
Palmdale
Santa Clarita
Oxnard
Ventura
Santa Barbara
Santa Maria
Bakersfield
Hillcrest Center
Victorville
Hesperia
Apple Valley
Barstow
Needles

SAN DIEGO
Chula Vista
Tijuana
Mexicali
El Centro
Escondido
Oceanside
Carlsbad
Encinitas
El Cajon
National City
Coronado
Imperial Beach

Death Valley
Amargosa Range
Panamint Range
Providence Mts.
Sonora Desert
Colorado Desert
Chocolate Mts.
San Bernardino Mts.
San Gabriel Mts.
Tehachapi Mts.
San Rafael Mts.
Santa Ynez Mts.

Santa Barbara Channel
San Pedro Channel
Channel Islands
Santa Catalina
Santa Cruz I.
Santa Rosa I.
San Miguel I.
San Nicolas I.
San Clemente I.
Santa Barbara I.

Salton Sea
Imperial Valley
Coachella Canal
All American Canal
Colorado R. Aqueduct

COPYRIGHT GEORGE PHILIP & SON LTD.

West from Greenwich

Projection: Bonne

m ft
12 000
9000
6000
4500
3000
1200
600
0
ft 4000 3000 2000 1500 1000 400 200 0 m

H J K L M
13
114
12
115
11
116
10
117
9
118
8
119
N P

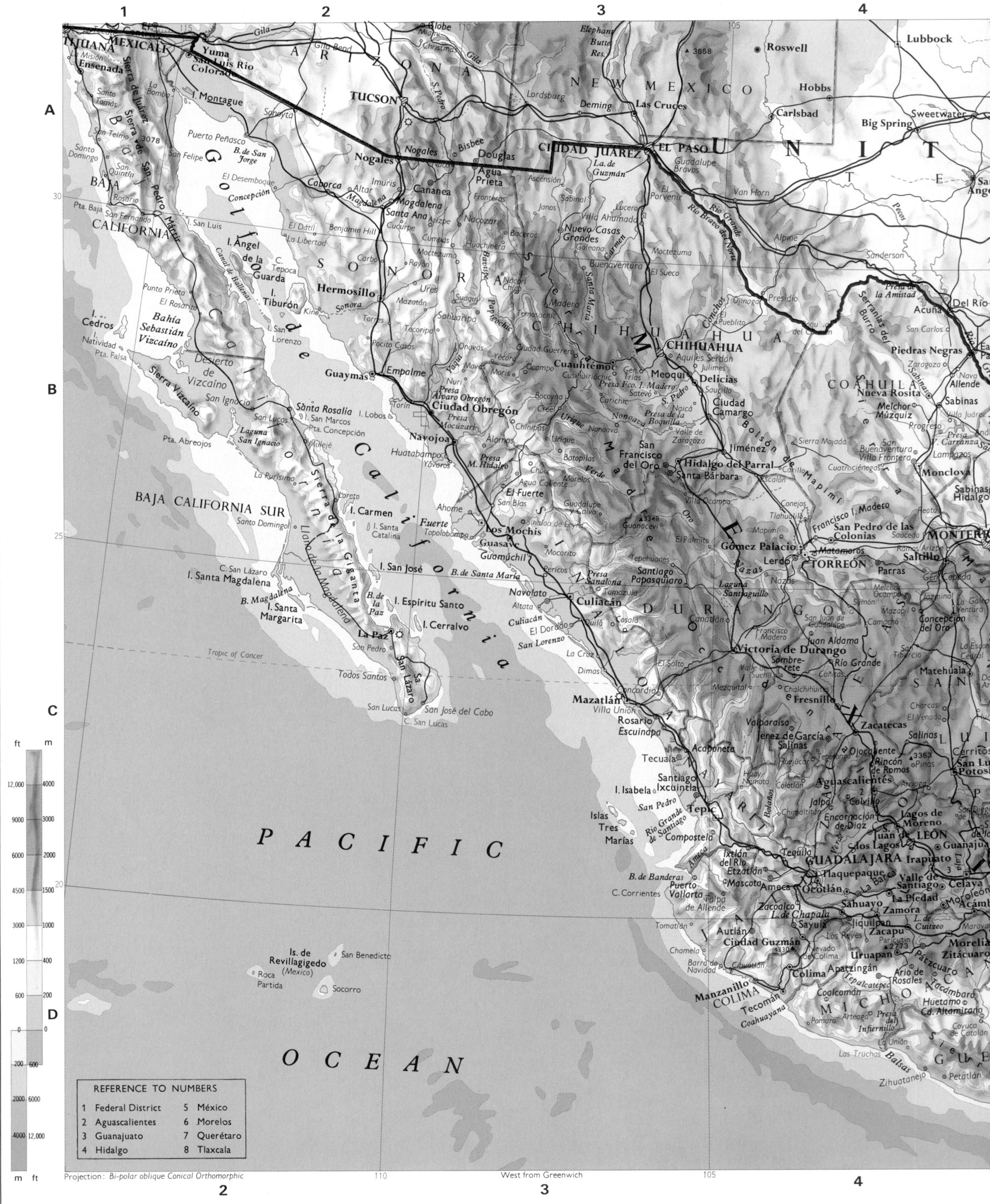

REFERENCE TO NUMBERS

1	Federal District	5	México
2	Aguascalientes	6	Morelos
3	Guanajuato	7	Querétaro
4	Hidalgo	8	Tlaxcala

Projection: Bi-polar oblique Conical Orthomorphic

West from Greenwich

74 75
88
5

1 : 8 000 000
50 0 50 100 150 200 miles
50 0 100 200 300 km

5 6 7 8

Wichita Falls
Denison
Sherman
Paris
Texarkana
Camden
Greenville
Tuscaloosa
Opelika
Columbus
McRae

Denton
Greenville
Texarkana
El Dorado
MISSISSIPPI
ALABAMA
Phenix City
Americus
Cordele
Tifton
GEORGIA

FORT WORTH
DALLAS
Marshall
Longview
Monroe
Vicksburg
Meridian
Montgomery
Troy
Albany
Waycross

Ranger
Cleburne
Tyler
Shreveport
Tallulah
Jackson
Selma
Dothan
Valdosta

Hillsboro
Corsicana
Palestine
Nacogdoches
Natchez
Laurel
Hattiesburg
Flomaton
Tallahassee
Lake City

Brownwood
Waco
Jewett
Lufkin
Sam Rayburn Res.
Alexandria
McComb
Bogalusa
Biloxi
MOBILE
Panama City
FLORIDA

Temple
Huntsville
Bryan
Toledo Bend Res.
Baton Rouge
Hammond
Gulfport
Pensacola
C. San Blas
Apalachee Bay
Suwannee

Austin
Navasota
Beaumont
Lafayette
NEW ORLEANS
Mobile Bay

HOUSTON
Port Arthur
Atchafalaya Bay
Breton Sound
Mississippi Delta

SAN ANTONIO
Rosenberg
Galveston
Terrebonne B.
Clearwater

Dilley
Victoria
Nueces

Alice
Corpus Christi

Laredo
Kingsville

Nuevo Laredo
Zapata
Brownsville
Harlingen
Laguna Madre

GULF OF MEXICO

Camargo
Mc Allen
Reynosa
Matamoros
Valle Hermoso
Santa Teresa

Laguna Madre
Méndez
San Fernando
Linares
Villagrán
Soto la Marina
La Pesca

Tropic of Cancer

CUBA
Guane
La Fé
Corrientes

Ciudad Victoria
Sierra de Tamaulipas
Pta. Jerez

Ciudad Mante
Altamira
Ciudad Madero
Tampico
Pánuco
Isla Desterrada
Isla Pérez
Canal de Yucatán
C. San Antonio

Ciudad de Valles
Laguna de Tamiahua
C. Rojo
Pta. Yalkubul
Rio Lagartos
Pta. Catoche

Tuxpan
Ozuluama
Progreso
Dzilam de Bravo
El Cuyo
Cancún
Pto. Juárez

Tantoyuca
Tamazunchale
Poza Rica
Papantla
Nautla
Mérida
Motul
Temax
Izamal
Tizimín
Espita
Puerto Morelos

Huauchinango
Tulancingo
Tezlutlán
Misantla
YUCATAN
Maxcanú
Sotuta
Valladolid
Cozumel
Isla Cozumel

Pachuca
Jalapa Enríquez
Zempoala
Ticul
Uman
Tekax
Peto

MEXICO
Tlaxcala
Coatepec
Veracruz
Llave
Tenabo
Vigía Chico

PUEBLA
Orizaba
Córdoba
Alvarado
Campeche
Champotón
Chenkán
Hopelchén
Felipe Carrillo Puerto
B. de la Ascensión
B. del Espíritu Santo

Cuernavaca
Tehuacán
Cosamaloapan
San Andrés Tuxtla
Ciudad del Carmen
Laguna de Términos
QUINTANA ROO
Bacalar
Banco Chinchorro

Iguala
Coatzacoalcos
Frontera
CAMPECHE
Chetumal

Chilapa
Chilpancingo
TABASCO
Villahermosa
Paraíso
Palizada
Concepción
Matamoros
Orange Walk

OAXACA
Oaxaca
Minatitlán
Cárdenas
Acayucan
Ambergris Cay

Istmo de Tehuantepec
La Venta
Turneffe Is.

San Cristóbal de las Casas
Palenque
Uaxactún
BELIZE City
Belmopan
BELIZE

CHIAPA
Tuxtla Gutiérrez
Comitán
Tikal
L. Petén Itzá
La Libertad
Flores
Benque Viejo
Dangriga

Acapulco
Pinotepa
Ometepec
Ejutla
Tehuantepec
Matías Romero
Ixtepec
Juchitán
San Luis
San Antonio
Maya Mts.
Golfo de Honduras
Roatán
Islas de la Bahía

Salina Cruz
Golfo de Tehuantepec
Tonalá
Arriaga
Puerto Gordo
Livingston
Puerto Barrios
Tela
La Ceiba
San Pedro Sula

Puerto Ángel
Huixtla
GUATEMALA
Cobán
Zacapa
Santa Rosa de Copán
HONDURAS

Tapachula
GUATEMALA
Quezaltenango
Antigua
Teguicigalpa

COPYRIGHT. GEORGE PHILIP & SON. LTD.

Projection: Bi-polar oblique Conical Orthomorphic

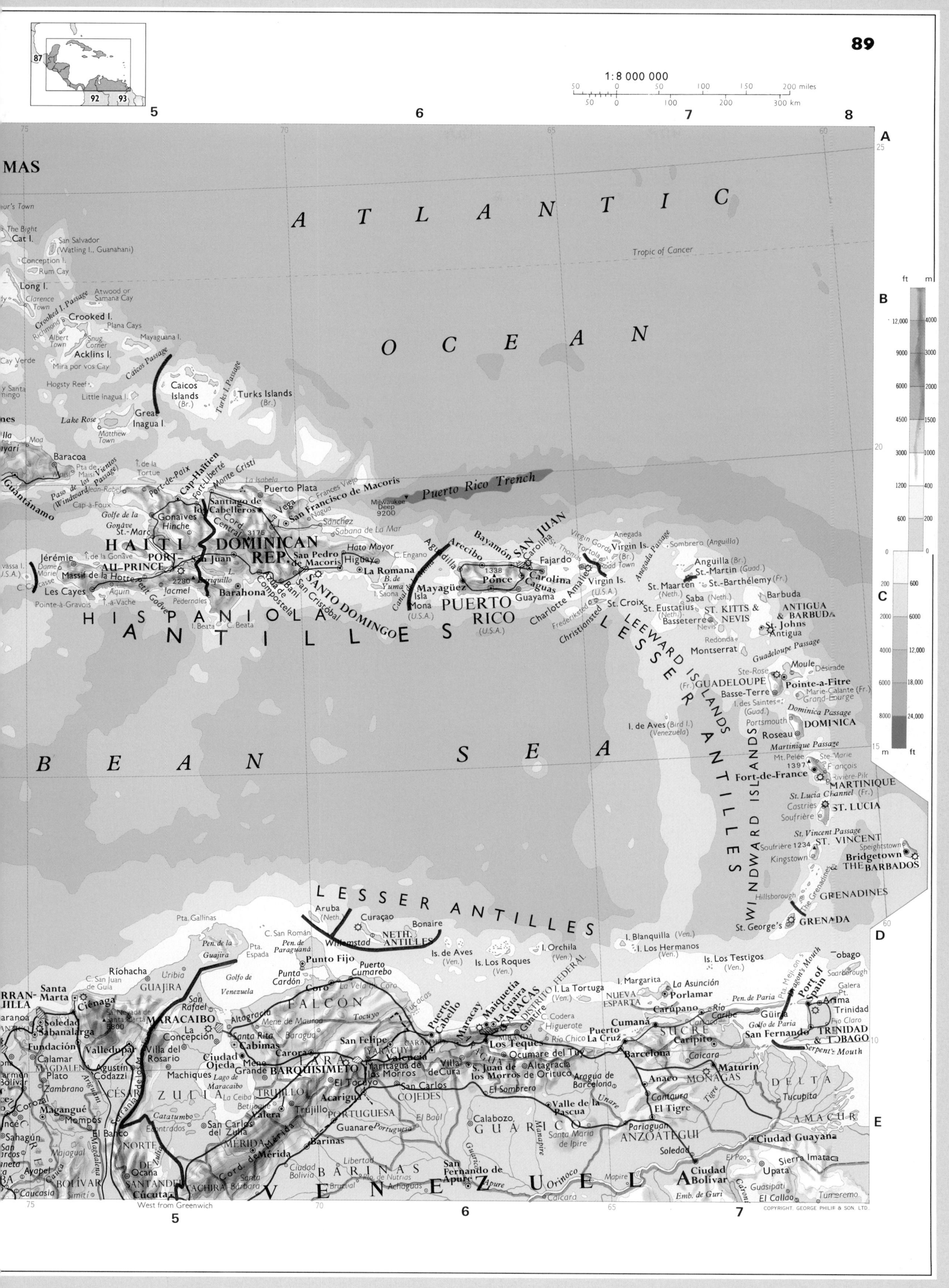

1:8 000 000

50   0   50   100   150   200 miles
50 0   100   200   300 km

ATLANTIC

OCEAN

Tropic of Cancer

MAS

Cat I.
The Bight
San Salvador
(Watling I., Guanahani)
Conception I.
Rum Cay
Long I.
Clarence Town
Atwood or Samana Cay
Richmond
Albert Town
Crooked I.
Snug Corner
Acklins I.
Mira por vos Cay
Plana Cays
Mayaguana I.
Hogsty Reef
Little Inagua I.
Lake Rose
Matthew Town
Great Inagua I.

Caicos Islands (Br.)
Turks Islands (Br.)

Puerto Rico Trench

Milwaukee Deep 9200

Baracoa
Guantánamo
Paso de los Vientos (Windward Passage)
Cap-à-Foux
Cap-Haïtien
Port-de-Paix
Î. de la Tortue
Fort-Liberté
Monte Cristi
La Isabela
Puerto Plata
C. Francés Viejo
San Francisco de Macorís
Santiago de los Caballeros
Gonaïves
Hinche
Cord. Central
3175
Vega
San Juan
Sabana de la Mar
Sánchez
Bayamón
SAN JUAN
Carolina
Arecibo
Virgin Is.
Anegada
Sombrero (Anguilla)

HAITI
DOMINICAN REP.
PORT-AU-PRINCE
San Juan
Hato Mayor
C. Engaño
Aguadilla
1338
Ponce
Fajardo
Carolina
Virgin Is. (U.S.A.)
Anguilla (Br.)
St-Martin (Guad.)
St-Barthélemy (Fr.)

Jérémie
Massif de la Hotte
2280
Jacmel
Barriquillo
La Romana
B. de Yuma
Higüey
Mayagüez
Isla Mona
Guayama
Charlotte Amalie
St. Croix
Frederiksted
Christiansted
St. Maarten (Neth.)
Saba (Neth.)
St. Eustatius (Neth.)
Basseterre
Barbuda
Antigua

Les Cayes
Aquin
I.-à-Vache
Barahona
San Cristóbal
PUERTO RICO (U.S.A.)
ST. KITTS & NEVIS
Nevis
ANTIGUA & BARBUDA
St. Johns
Antigua

Pointe-à-Gravois
Pedernales
I. Beata
C. Beata
Redonda
Montserrat
Guadeloupe Passage

HISPANIOLA
ANTILLES
Ste-Rose
Moule
Désirade

I. de Aves (Bird I.) (Venezuela)
GUADELOUPE
Basse-Terre
Marie-Galante (Fr.)
Grand-Bourge
Pointe-à-Pitre

Dominica Passage
Portsmouth
DOMINICA
Roseau

BEAN   SEA

Mt. Pelée
1397
Ste-Marie
St-François
Rivière-Pilote
Fort-de-France
MARTINIQUE

Martinique Channel (Fr.)
St. Lucia Channel (Fr.)
Castries
ST. LUCIA
Soufrière

St Vincent Passage
Soufrière 1234
ST. VINCENT
Speightstown
Kingstown
Bridgetown
THE BARBADOS

Hillsborough
The Grenadines
GRENADINES

St. George's
GRENADA

LESSER ANTILLES

LEEWARD ISLANDS
WINDWARD ISLANDS

Pta. Gallinas
Aruba (Neth.)
Curaçao
Bonaire
NETH. ANTILLES
Is. de Aves (Ven.)
I. Orchila (Ven.)
I. Blanquilla (Ven.)
I. Los Hermanos (Ven.)
Tobago

C. San Román
Willemstad
Is. Los Roques (Ven.)
Is. Los Testigos (Ven.)
Port of Spain
Saarbourg

Pen. de la Guajira
Pta. Espada
Pen. de Paraguaná
Punto Fijo
Puerto Cumarebo
I. Margarita
La Asunción
NUEVA ESPARTA
Porlamar
Pen. de Paria
Galera Pt.
Arima
Trinidad

Ríohacha
Uribia
GUAJIRA
Punta Cardón
Puerto La Vela de Coro
Coro
Tucacas
I. La Tortuga
Carúpano
Güiria
TRINIDAD & TOBAGO

Santa Marta
C. San Juan de Guía
Golfo de Venezuela
FALCÓN
Mene de Mauroa
Puerto Cabello
Maracay
Maiquetía
La Guaira
CARACAS
DISTRITO FEDERAL
Cumaná
SUCRE
Caripito
San Fernando

BARRAN-QUILLA
Soledad
Sabanalarga
Ciénaga
Sierra Nevada de Santa Marta 5800
MARACAIBO
La Concepción
Santa Rita
Baragua
San Felipe
Valencia
YARACUY
CARABOBO
Los Teques
Río Chico
La Cruz
Barcelona
Caicara
Maturín
MONAGAS
TRINIDAD

Fundación
Calamar
Plato
Zambrano
Magangué
Mompós
CÉSAR
ZULIA
Machiques
Lago de Maracaibo
Cabimas
Ciudad Ojeda
Mene Grande
LARA
BARQUISIMETO
El Tocuyo
Carora
Villa de Cura
Cagua
S. Juan de los Morros
Chaguaramas
Ocumare del Tuy
Altagracia de Orituco
Valle de la Pascua
El Tigre
Anaco
Cantaura
El Pao
Sierra Imataca
DELTA AMACUR
Tucupita

NORTE
Agustín Codazzi
TRUJILLO
Acarigua
Betijoque
Trujillo
PORTUGUESA
COJEDES
San Carlos
El Baúl
El Sombrero
GUÁRICO
Calabozo
Santa María de Ipire
El Tigre
ANZOÁTEGUI
Soledad
Ciudad Guayana

El Banco
Ocaña
SANTANDER
San Carlos del Zulia
MÉRIDA
Cord. de Mérida
Valera
Ciudad Bolivia
BARINAS
Libertad
Barinas
San Fernando de Apure
Pariaguán
Ciudad Bolívar
Upata
El Callao

Cúcuta
TÁCHIRA
Santa Bárbara
San Cristóbal
Pen. de Nutrias
APURE
Achaguas
Orinoco
Mapire
Emb. de Guri
Guasipati
El Callao
Turemero

VENEZUELA

West from Greenwich

ft   m
12,000 4000
9000   3000
6000   2000
4500   1500
3000   1000
1200   400
600   200
0   0
200   600
2000   6000
4000   12,000
6000   18,000
8000   24,000
m   ft

I : 35 000 000

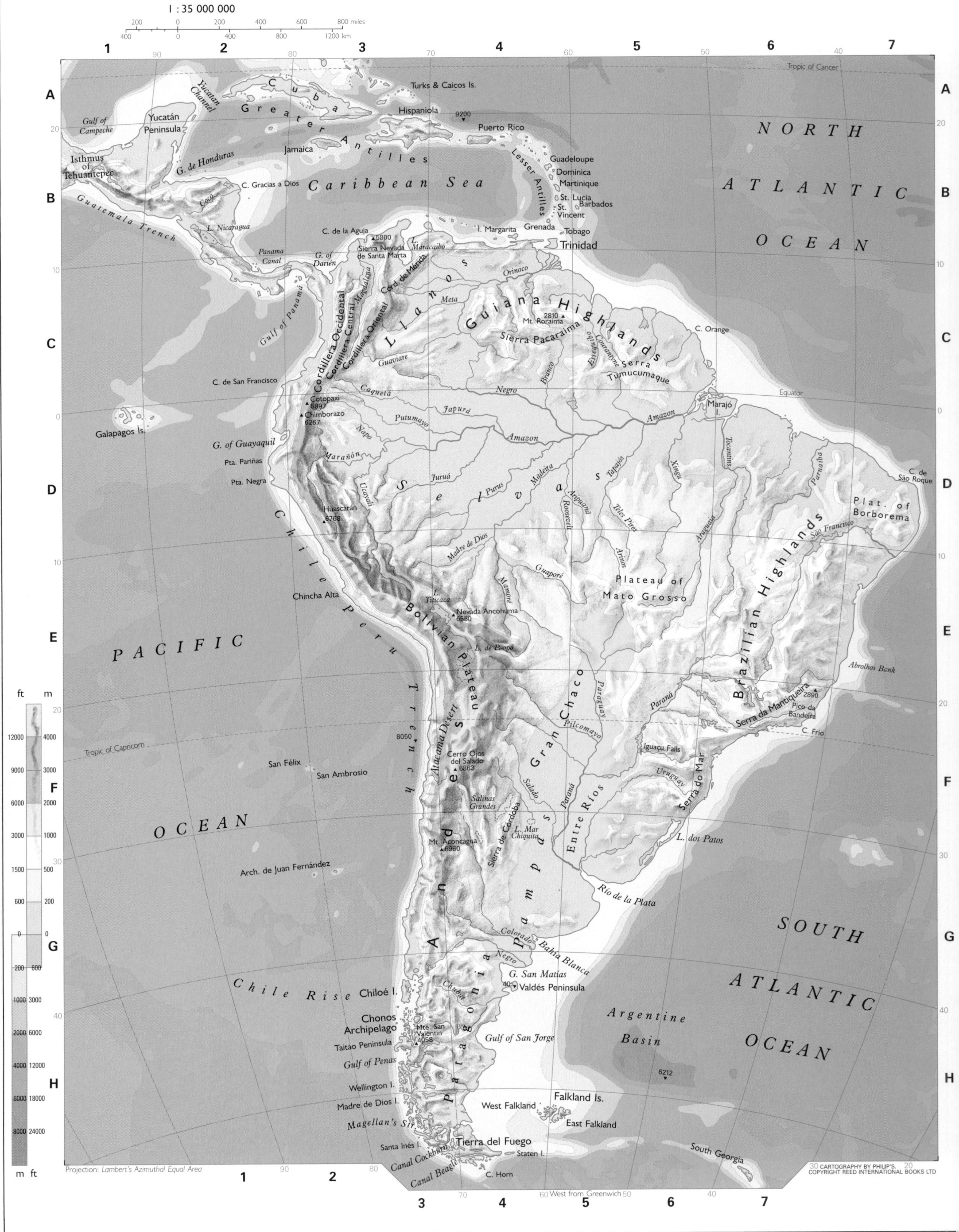

200 0 200 400 600 800 miles
400 0 400 800 1200 km

1 90 **2** 80 **3** 70 **4** 60 **5** 50 **6** 40 **7**

Tropic of Cancer

A

Gulf of Campeche
Yucatán Peninsula
Yucatán Channel
Cuba
Greater Antilles
Turks & Caicos Is.
Hispaniola
9200
Puerto Rico
Isthmus of Tehuantepec
G. de Honduras
Jamaica
Lesser Antilles
Guadeloupe
Dominica
Martinique
St. Lucia
St. Vincent
Barbados
Grenada
Tobago
Trinidad

NORTH
ATLANTIC
OCEAN

B

Guatemala Trench
C. Gracias a Dios
Coco
L. Nicaragua
Caribbean Sea
Panama Canal
G. of Darién
Gulf of Panamá
C. de la Aguja
Sierra Nevada de Santa Marta
5800
L. Maracaibo
Córd. de Mérida
I. Margarita

C

Cordillera Occidental
Cordillera Central
Cordillera Oriental
Llanos
Meta
Orinoco
Guiana Highlands
Mt. Roraima 2810
Sierra Pacaraima
C. Orange
Guaviare
Serra Tumucumaque
Caquetá
Branco
Negro
Equator
Marajó I.

C. de San Francisco
Cotopaxi 5897
Chimborazo 6267
Putumayo
Japurá
Amazon
Tocantins
C. de São Roque

D

Galapagos Is.
G. of Guayaquil
Pta. Pariñas
Pta. Negra
Napo
Marañón
Ucayali
Juruá
Purus
Madeira
Tapajós
Xingu
Araguaia
Parnaíba
São Francisco
Plat. of Borborema

Huascarán 6768
Madre de Dios
Roosevelt
Arinos

E

PACIFIC
Chincha Alta
Bolivian Plateau
L. Titicaca
Nevada Ancohuma 6550
L. de Poopó
Guaporé
Mamoré
Plateau of Mato Grosso
Brazilian Highlands
Abrolhos Bank

ft m
12000 4000
9000 3000
6000 2000
3000 1000
1500 500
600 200
0 0
200 600
1000 3000
2000 6000
4000 12000
6000 18000
8000 24000
m ft

F

Tropic of Capricorn
San Félix
San Ambrosio
Atacama Desert
8050
Cerro Ojos del Salado 6863
Salinas Grandes
Gran Chaco
Paraguay
Pilcomayo
Paraná
Iguaçu Falls
Serra da Mantiqueira 2890
Pico da Bandeira
Serra do Mar
C. Frio

OCEAN
Andes
Peru Trench
Chile

G

Arch. de Juan Fernández
Salado
Sierra de Córdoba
L. Mar Chiquita
Entre Ríos
Paraná
Uruguay
L. dos Patos
Pampa
Mt. Aconcagua 6960
Río de la Plata

Colorado
Bahía Blanca

SOUTH
ATLANTIC

H

Chile Rise
Chiloé I.
Chonos Archipelago
Mte. San Valentín 4058
Taitao Peninsula
Gulf of Penas
Wellington I.
Madre de Dios I.
Magellan's Str.
Santa Inés I.
Canal Cockburn
Canal Beagle
C. Horn
Tierra del Fuego
Staten I.

Patagonia
Chubut
Negro
G. San Matías
Valdés Peninsula
Gulf of San Jorge

Argentine
Basin

6212

West Falkland
Falkland Is.
East Falkland

South Georgia

OCEAN

Projection: Lambert's Azimuthal Equal Area

3 90 **4** 70 **5** 60 West from Greenwich 50 **6** 40 **7**

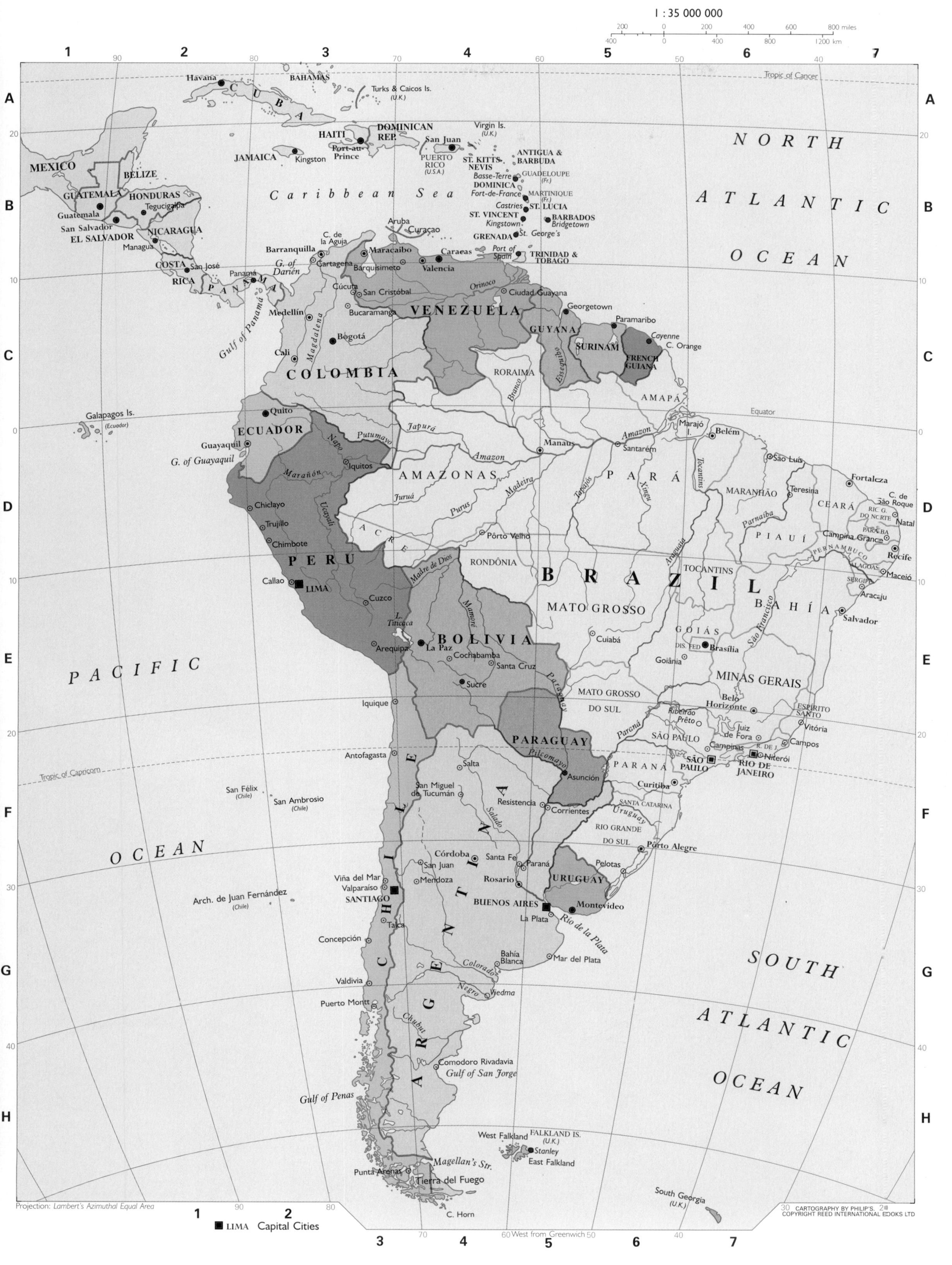

1 : 35 000 000

200   0   200   400   600   800 miles
400   0   400   1200 km

A

Tropic of Cancer

Havana CUBA   BAHAMAS
Turks & Caicos Is.
(U.K.)

NORTH

MEXICO
HAITI   DOMINICAN REP.   Virgin Is. (U.K.)   San Juan   ANTIGUA & BARBUDA
JAMAICA Kingston   Port-au-Prince   PUERTO RICO (U.S.A.)   ST. KITTS-NEVIS   GUADELOUPE (Fr.)
BELIZE   Basse-Terre   DOMINICA
GUATEMALA   HONDURAS   *Caribbean Sea*   Fort-de-France   MARTINIQUE (Fr.)
Guatemala   Tegucigalpa   Castries ST. LUCIA
San Salvador   NICARAGUA   ST. VINCENT   BARBADOS
EL SALVADOR   Managua   Kingstown   Bridgetown
COSTA   San José   GRENADA   St. George's
RICA   Panama   Aruba   Curaçao   Port of Spain   TRINIDAD & TOBAGO
Barranquilla C. de la Aguja   Maracaibo   Caracas

ATLANTIC

OCEAN

G. of Darién   Cartagena   Barquisimeto   Valencia
Medellín   Cúcuta   San Cristóbal   Orinoco   Ciudad Guayana   Georgetown
Bucaramanga   VENEZUELA   GUYANA   Paramaribo   Cayenne
Gulf of Panama   Bogotá   SURINAM   C. Orange
Cali   FRENCH GUIANA
COLOMBIA   RORAIMA
Galapagos Is.   AMAPÁ
(Ecuador)   Quito   Branco   Equator
ECUADOR   Napo   Putumayo   Marajó I.   Belém
Guayaquil   Japurá   Amazon   Santarém   São Luís
G. of Guayaquil   Marañón   Iquitos   Amazon   PARÁ   Fortaleza
AMAZONAS   Madeira   MARANHÃO   Teresina   C. de Roque
Chiclayo   Juruá   Purus   Xingu   Tocantins   RIO G. DO NORTE   Natal
Trujillo   ACRE   Pôrto Velho   PIAUÍ   PARAÍBA   Campina Grande
Chimbote   RONDÔNIA   B R A Z I L   PERNAMBUCO   Recife
PERU   Madre de Dios   TOCANTINS   ALAGOAS   Maceió
Callao LIMA   MATO GROSSO   SERGIPE   Aracaju
Cuzco   BAHÍA   Salvador
L. Titicaca   Mamoré   GOIÁS   Brasília   São Francisco
BOLIVIA   Cuiabá   DIS. FED.
Arequipa   La Paz   Cochabamba   Goiânia   MINAS GERAIS
Santa Cruz   Belo Horizonte   ESPÍRITO SANTO
Iquique   Sucre   MATO GROSSO DO SUL   Ribeirão Prêto   Juiz de Fora   Vitória
PARAGUAY   Paraná   SÃO PAULO   Campinas   Campos
Antofagasta   Salta   SÃO PAULO   RIO DE JANEIRO
San Félix   Pilcomayo   Asunción   PARANÁ   Niterói
(Chile)   San Ambrosio   Resistencia   Curitiba   SANTA CATARINA
(Chile)   San Miguel de Tucumán   Corrientes   Uruguay   RIO GRANDE DO SUL
ARGENTINA   Salado   Pôrto Alegre
Córdoba   Santa Fe   Paraná   Pelotas
Arch. de Juan Fernández   San Juan   Rosario   URUGUAY
(Chile)   Viña del Mar   Mendoza   Santa Fe   Montevideo
Valparaíso   SANTIAGO   BUENOS AIRES
Talca   La Plata   Río de la Plata
Concepción   Bahía Blanca   Mar del Plata
Valdivia   Colorado
Puerto Montt   Negro   Viedma

PACIFIC

OCEAN

SOUTH

ATLANTIC

OCEAN

Tropic of Capricorn

Comodoro Rivadavia
Gulf of San Jorge
Gulf of Penas
Chubut

West Falkland   FALKLAND IS. (U.K.)
Stanley
Magellan's Str.   East Falkland
Punta Arenas   Tierra del Fuego   South Georgia (U.K.)
C. Horn

Projection: Lambert's Azimuthal Equal Area

West from Greenwich

CARTOGRAPHY BY PHILIP'S
COPYRIGHT REED INTERNATIONAL BOOKS LTD

■ LIMA Capital Cities

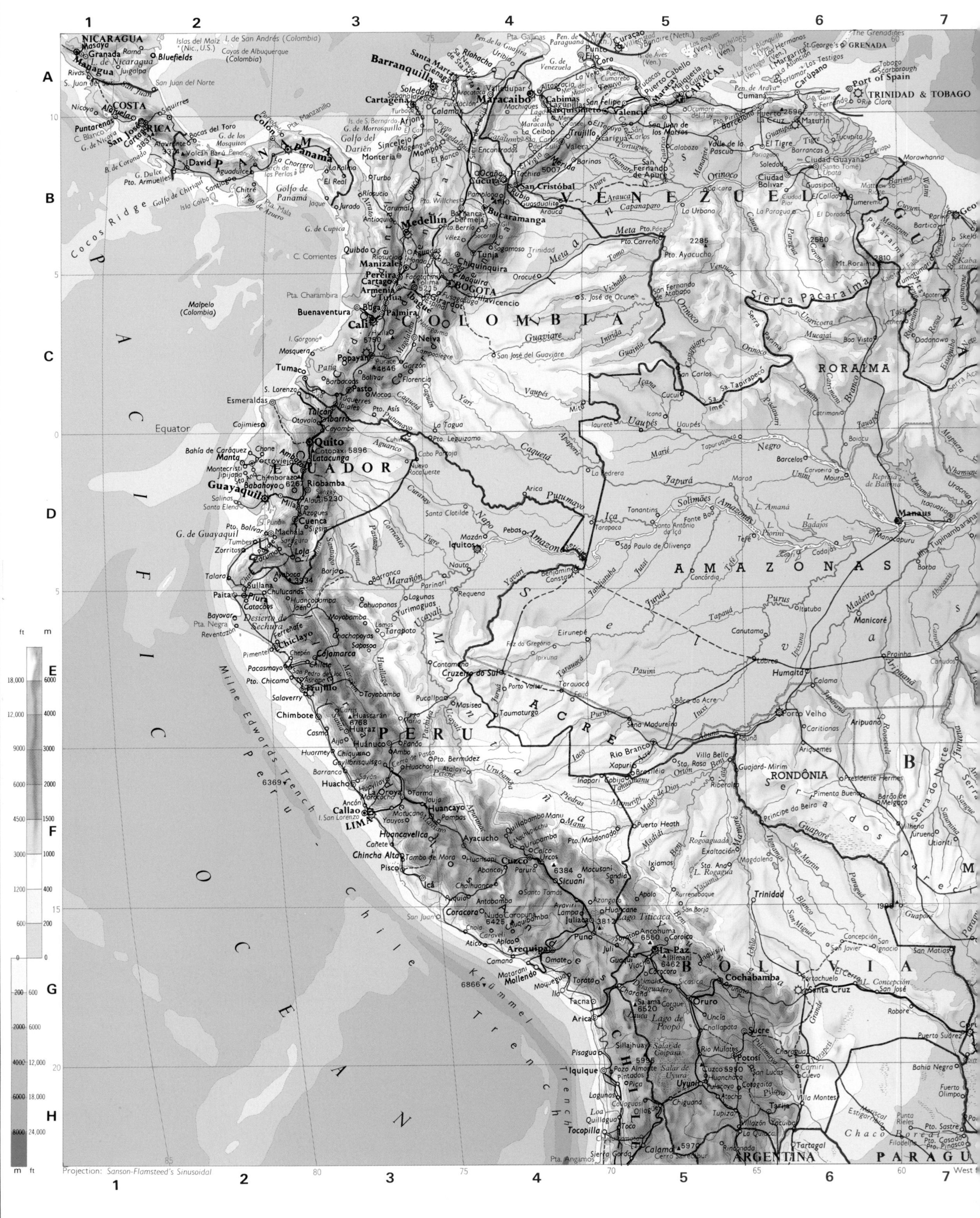

NICARAGUA
COSTA RICA
PANAMA
COLOMBIA
VENEZUELA
ECUADOR
PERU
BOLIVIA
AMAZONAS
RORAIMA
RONDÔNIA
ACRE
ARGENTINA
PARAGU
TRINIDAD & TOBAGO
GRENADA
PACIFIC OCEAN
Cocos Ridge
Milne Edwards Trench
Peru - Chile Trench
Krümmel Trench
Equator
Sierra Pacaraima
Barranquilla
Cartagena
Maracaibo
Caracas
Valencia
Medellín
Bogotá
Cali
Quito
Guayaquil
Cuenca
Chiclayo
Trujillo
Chimbote
Callao
LIMA
Arequipa
Cuzco
La Paz
Cochabamba
Oruro
Sucre
Potosí
Santa Cruz
Manaus
Porto Velho
Iquitos
Arica
Iquique
Lago Titicaca
Amazonas
Orinoco
Ucayali
Marañón
Putumayo
Madeira
Purus
Juruá
Japurá
Negro
Projection: Sanson-Flamsteed's Sinusoidal

88 89
94 95

1:16 000 000

100 50 0 100 200 300 miles
100 0 100 200 300 400 km

A T L A N T I C   O C E A N

Paramaribo
Nieuw Amsterdam
St. Laurent
Cayenne
FR. GUIANA
C. Orange
Oiapoque
AMAPÁ
C. do Norte
Macapá
Ilha de Maracá
Estuario do Rio Amazonas
Ilha Caviana
Ilha de Marajó
Equator
Belém
PARÁ
Santarém
Altamira
Amazonas (Amazon)
São Luís
Rosário
MARANHÃO
Teresina
Bacabal
Caxias
Imperatriz
Carolina
PIAUÍ
Floriano
Fortaleza
CEARÁ
Sobral
Crateús
Quixadá
Mossoró
Natal
RIO GRANDE DO NORTE
PARAÍBA
João Pessoa
Campina Grande
Caruaru
Olinda
RECIFE
PERNAMBUCO
Petrolina
Juazeiro
Paulo Afonso
Maceió
ALAGOAS
SERGIPE
Aracaju
São Cristóvão
BAHIA
Feira de Santana
Alagoinhas
Santo Amaro
Salvador
TOCANTINS
Palmas
Pôrto Nacional
Barreiras
Xique-Xique
Jacobina
Barra
Vitória da Conquista
Itabuna
Ilhéus
Fernando de Noronha (Braz.)
Rocas
C. de São Roque
BRAZIL
GOIÁS
Goiânia
Anápolis
DIST. FED.
Brasília
Montes Claros
Diamantina
MINAS GERAIS
Belo Horizonte
Uberlândia
Uberaba
Teófilo Otoni
Gov. Valadares
Nanuque
Pôrto Seguro
Belmonte
ESPÍRITO SANTO
Vitória
Vila Velha
Linhares
Cachoeiro de Itapemirim
Campos
Juiz de Fora
Petrópolis
Niterói
RIO DE JANEIRO
Cabo Frio
Campinas
Ribeirão Preto
SÃO PAULO
Bauru
Marília
Piracicaba
Botucatu
MATO GROSSO DO SUL
Campo Grande
Três Lagoas
Dourados
Planalto do Mato Grosso
Trindade (Braz.)

6059

COPYRIGHT. GEORGE PHILIP & SON, LTD.

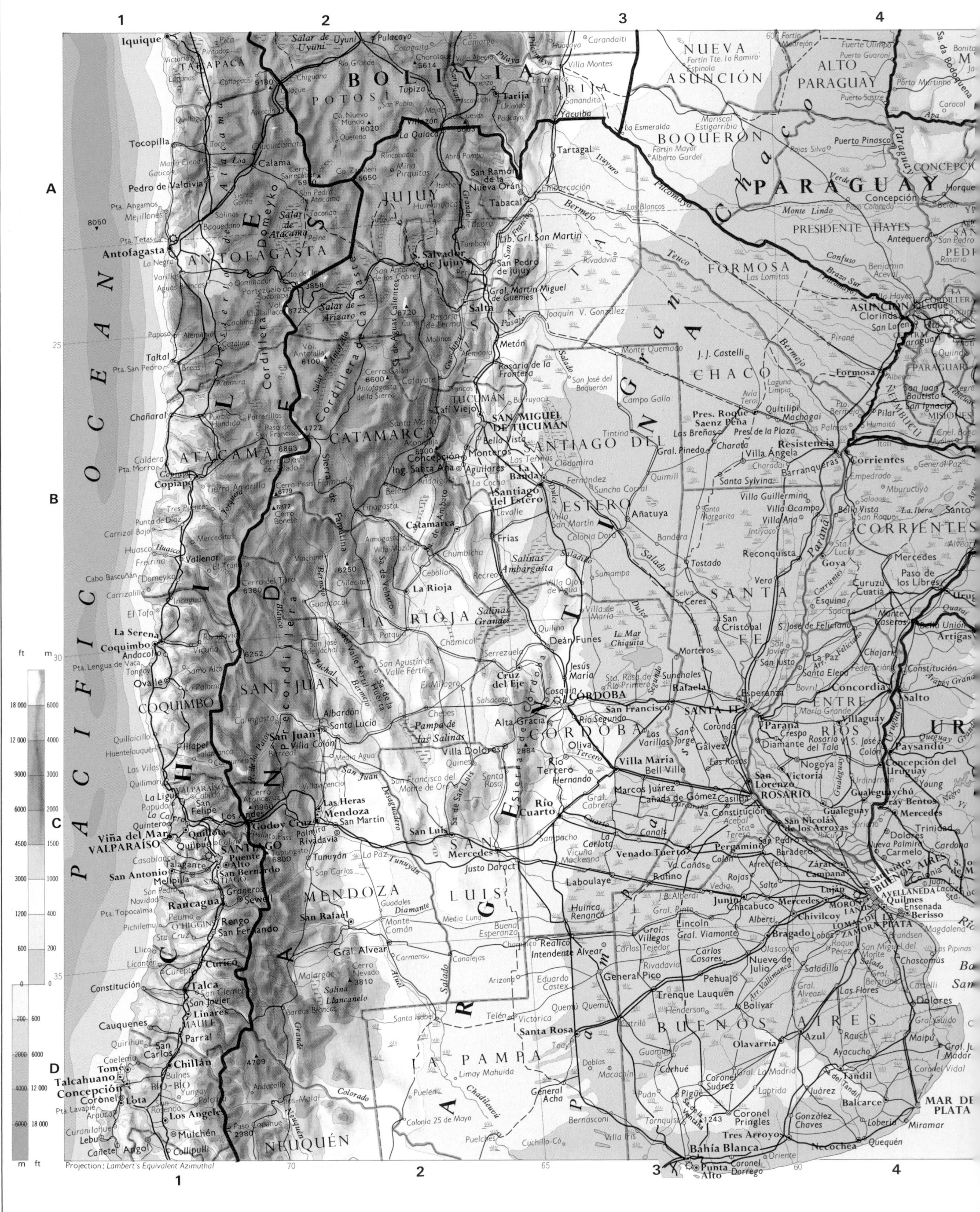

BOLIVIA
PARAGUAY
PACIFIC OCEAN
ANTOFAGASTA
ATACAMA
COQUIMBO
JUJUY
SALTA
CATAMARCA
TUCUMÁN
SANTIAGO DEL ESTERO
LA RIOJA
SAN JUAN
MENDOZA
SAN LUIS
CÓRDOBA
SANTA FE
ENTRE RIOS
CORRIENTES
CHACO
FORMOSA
BUENOS AIRES
LA PAMPA
NEUQUÉN
Iquique
Antofagasta
Calama
Tocopilla
Copiapó
La Serena
Coquimbo
VALPARAÍSO
Viña del Mar
SANTIAGO
San Antonio
Rancagua
Talca
Chillán
Concepción
Talcahuano
Los Angeles
Salta
Tucumán
Córdoba
Mendoza
San Juan
San Luis
Rosario
Santa Fe
Paraná
Corrientes
Resistencia
Formosa
ASUNCIÓN
Concepción
BUENOS AIRES
La Plata
Mar del Plata
Bahía Blanca
Santa Rosa
Tarija
Potosí
Tupiza
Villazón
Projection: Lambert's Equivalent Azimuthal

92 93
96

1 : 8 000 000

50 0 50 100 150 200 miles
50 0 50 100 200 300 km

5 6 7

MATO GROSSO DO SUL

Três Lagoas · Andradina · Mirassol · S. José do Rio Prêto · Olímpia · Passos · BELO HORIZONTE · Vitória · Itaquari
Xavantina · Mirandópolis · Araçatuba · Catanduva · Bebedouro · Ribeirão Prêto · São Seb. do Paraíso · Oliveira · Campo Belo · Cons. Lafaiete · N. Lima · Itabirito · Vila Velha
Panorama · Birigui · Taquaritinga · Jaboticabal · Mococa · Guaxupé · Três Pontas · São João del Rei · Ponte Nova · Ouro Prêto · Congonhas · Castelo · Guarapari
Pardo · Adamantina · Penápolis · Tupã · Lins · Pirajuí · Casa Branca · Alfenas · Varginha · Lavras · Barbacena · Cataguases · Cachoeiro de Itapemirim
Santo Anastácio · Presidente Prudente · Martinópolis · Marília · Paraguaçu Paulista · Garça · Bariri · Jaú · São Carlos · São João da Boa Vista · Poços de Caldas · Três Corações · Santos Dumont · Juiz de Fora · Leopoldina · Itaperuna
Rancharia · Assis · Cambará · Santa Cruz do Rio Pardo · Bauru · Rio Claro · Araras · Limeira · Pouso Alegre · Ijuhá · Três Rios · Além Paraíba · Cambuí · Alegre
Presidente Epitácio · Porto São José · Paranapanema · Porecatu · Sertanópolis · Ibaiti · Piracicaba · Americana · Cruzeiro · Volta Redonda · Barra do Piraí · Paraíba do Sul · CAMPOS · Cabo de São Tomé
Paranavaí · Londrina · Rolândia · Apucarana · Tatuí · Sorocaba · SÃO PAULO · Guaratinguetá · Mansa Mar · Nova Iguaçu · RIO DE JANEIRO · Nova Friburgo · Macaé
Umuarama · Cianorte · Maringá · Arapongas · Itapetininga · São Bernardo del Campo · SANTO ANDRÉ · Jacareí · Taubaté · S. J. dos Campos · DUQUE DE CAXIAS · SÃO GONÇALO · Cabo Frio
Cruzeiro do Oeste · Mandaguari · PARANÁ · Itapeva · São Vicente · SANTOS · Guarujá · Angra dos Reis · Ilha Grande · NITERÓI · RIO DE JANEIRO · Tropic of Capricorn
Guaíra · Goioerê · BRAZIL · Jaguariaíva · Paranaguá · Ilha de São Sebastião · Pta. de Juatinga
Pto. Mendes · Cascavel · Guarapuava · Castro · Ponta Grossa · Itapokanga · Itanhaém · Iguape · Ilha de São Sebastião · Pta. do Boi
Foz do Iguaçu · Represa de Itaipu · Pitanga · Prudentópolis · Palmeira · CURITIBA · Antonina · Ilha Comprida
Ciudad del Este · Irati · Lapa · Guaratuba · Ilha do Cardoso
Bernardo de Irigoyen · União da Vitória · Rio Negro · Mafra · São Francisco do Sul
MISIONES · Clevelândia · Palmas · Pto. União · Joinvile · 1340 · Caçador · Blumenau · Itajaí
Oberá · Chapecó · Joaçaba · SANTA CATARINA · Santa Cecília · Brusque
Santa Rosa · Erechim · Campos Novos · Rio do Sul · Ilha de Santa Catarina
Santo Ângelo · Carazinho · Passo Fundo · Lajes · 1808 · Florianópolis
São Luís Gonzaga · Cruz Alta · Vacaria · Tubarão · Laguna · Cabo Santa Marta Grande
Santiago · RIO GRANDE · Guaporé · Bento Gonçalves · Criciúma · Araranguá
Santa Maria · Santa Cruz do Sul · Caxias do Sul · Montenegro · Nôvo Hamburgo · Taquara
Alegrete · DO SUL · Canoas · São Leopoldo · Osorio · Viamão · PÔRTO ALEGRE
Santana do Livramento · São Gabriel · Dom Pedrito · Camaquã · Mostardas
Bagé · Canguçu · Pelotas · Lagoa dos Patos
URUGUAY · Melo · Jaguarão · Rio Grande
Treinta y Tres · Santa Vitória do Palmar · Lagoa Mirim · Lagoa Mangueira
José Batlle y Ordóñez · Lascano · Aigua · Castillos
Minas · Rocha · San Carlos · Maldonado
MONTEVIDEO

ATLANTIC OCEAN

5304

1 : 16 000 000

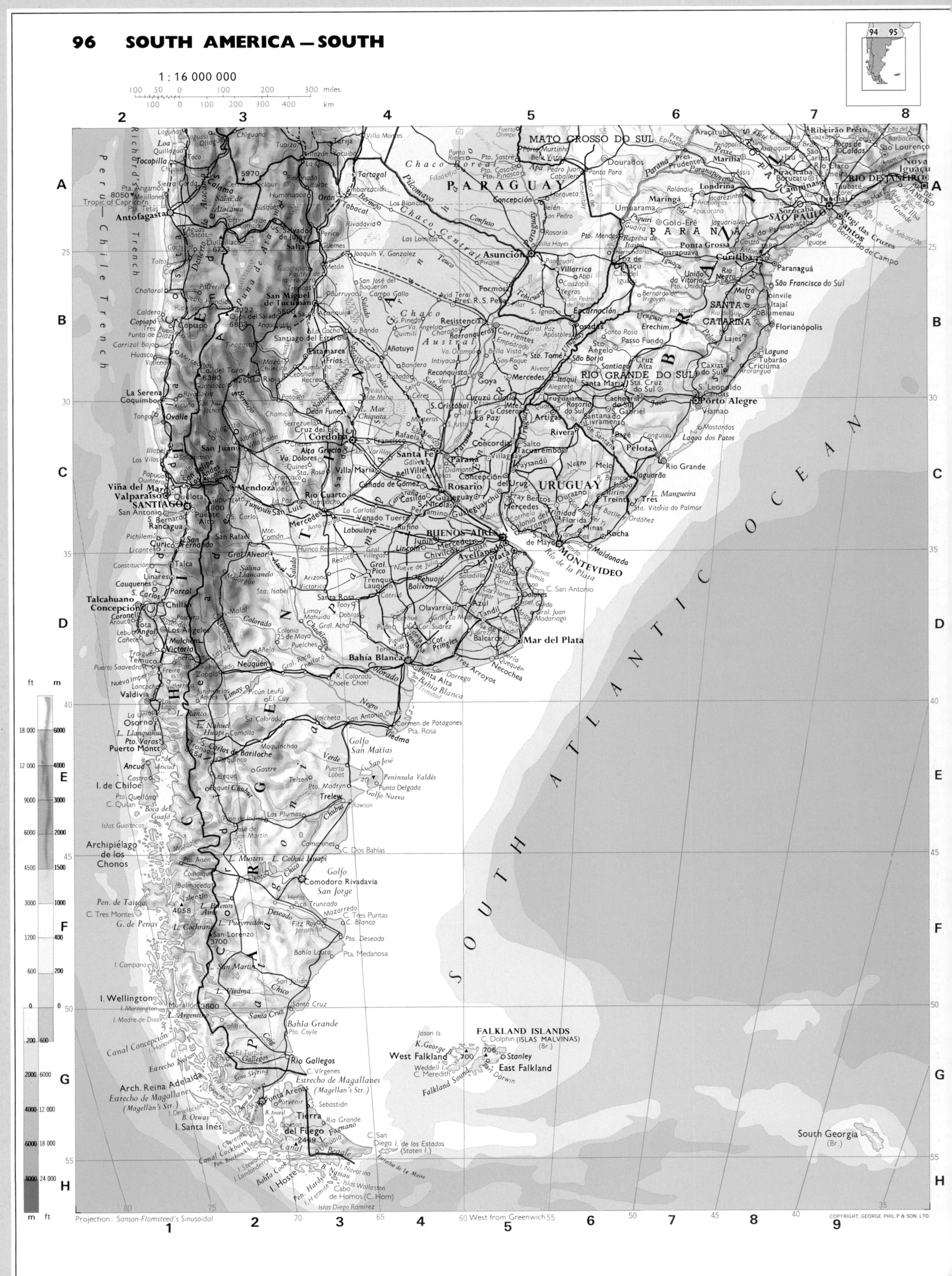

Projection: Sanson-Flamsteed's Sinusoidal

COPYRIGHT. GEORGE PHIL. P & SON. LTD.

INDEX

The index contains the names of all the principal places and features shown on the World Maps. Each name is followed by an additional entry in italics giving the country or region within which it is located. The alphabetical order of names composed of two or more words is governed primarily by the first word and then by the second. This is an example of the rule:

Mīr Kūh, *Iran*	**45 E8**	26	22 N	58	55 E
Mīr Shahdād, *Iran*	**45 E8**	26	15 N	58	29 E
Miraj, *India*	**40 L9**	16	50 N	74	45 E
Miram Shah, *Pakistan*	**42 C4**	33	0 N	70	2 E
Miramar, *Mozam.*	**57 C6**	23	50 S	35	35 E

Physical features composed of a proper name (Erie) and a description (Lake) are positioned alphabetically by the proper name. The description is positioned after the proper name and is usually abbreviated:

Erie, L., *N. Amer.*	**78 D3**	42	15 N	81	0 W

Where a description forms part of a settlement or administrative name, however, it is always written in full and put in its true alphabetic position:

Mount Morris, *U.S.A.*	**78 D7**	42	44 N	77	52 W

Names beginning with M' and Mc are indexed as if they were spelled Mac. Names beginning St. are alphabetized under Saint, but Sankt, Sint, Sant', Santa and San are all spelled in full and are alphabetized accordingly. If the same place name occurs two or more times in the index and all are in the same country, each is followed by the name of the administrative subdivision in which it is located. The names are placed in the alphabetical order of the subdivisions. For example:

Jackson, *Ky., U.S.A.*	**76 G4**	37	33 N	83	23 W
Jackson, *Mich., U.S.A.*	**76 D3**	42	15 N	84	24 W
Jackson, *Minn., U.S.A.*	**80 D7**	43	37 N	95	1 W

The number in bold type which follows each name in the index refers to the number of the map page where that feature or place will be found. This is usually the largest scale at which the place or feature appears.

The letter and figure which are in bold type immediately after the page number give the grid square on the map page, within which the feature is situated. The letter represents the latitude and the figure the longitude.

In some cases the feature itself may fall within the specified square, while the name is outside. This is usually the case only with features which are larger than a grid square.

For a more precise location the geographical coordinates which follow the letter/figure references give the latitude and the longitude of each place. The first set of figures represent the latitude which is the distance north or south of the Equator measured as an angle at the centre of the Earth. The Equator is latitude 0°, the North Pole is 90°N, and the South Pole 90°S.

The second set of figures represent the longitude, which is the distance East or West of the prime meridian, which runs through Greenwich, England. Longitude is also measured as an angle at the centre of the earth and is given East or West of the prime meridian, from 0° to 180° in either direction.

The unit of measurement for latitude and longitude is the degree, which is subdivided into 60 minutes. Each index entry states the position of a place in degrees and minutes, a space being left between the degrees and the minutes.

The latitude is followed by N(orth) or S(outh) and the longitude by E(ast) or W(est).

Rivers are indexed to their mouths or confluences, and carry the symbol → after their names. A solid square ■ follows the name of a country while, an open square □ refers to a first order administrative area.

Abbreviations used in the index

A.C.T. — Australian Capital Territory
Afghan. — Afghanistan
Ala. — Alabama
Alta. — Alberta
Amer. — America(n)
Arch. — Archipelago
Ariz. — Arizona
Ark. — Arkansas
Atl. Oc. — Atlantic Ocean
B. — Baie, Bahia, Bay, Bucht, Bugt
B.C. — British Columbia
Bangla. — Bangladesh
Barr. — Barrage
Bos. & H. — Bosnia and Herzegovina
C. — Cabo, Cap, Cape, Coast
C.A.R. — Central African Republic
C. Prov. — Cape Province
Calif. — California
Cent. — Central
Chan. — Channel
Colo. — Colorado
Conn. — Connecticut
Cord. — Cordillera
Cr. — Creek
Czech. — Czech Republic
D.C. — District of Columbia
Del. — Delaware
Dep. — Dependency
Des. — Desert
Dist. — District
Dj. — Djebel
Domin. — Dominica
Dom. Rep. — Dominican Republic
E. — East

El Salv. — El Salvador
Eq. Guin. — Equatorial Guinea
Fla. — Florida
Falk. Is. — Falkland Is.
G. — Golfe, Golfo, Gulf, Guba, Gebel
Ga. — Georgia
Gt. — Great, Greater
Guinea-Biss. — Guinea-Bissau
H.K. — Hong Kong
H.P. — Himachal Pradesh
Hants. — Hampshire
Harb. — Harbor, Harbour
Hd. — Head
Hts. — Heights
I.(s). — Île, Ilha, Insel, Isla, Island, Isle
Ill. — Illinois
Ind. — Indiana
Ind. Oc. — Indian Ocean
Ivory C. — Ivory Coast
J. — Jabal, Jebel, Jazira
Junc. — Junction
K. — Kap, Kapp
Kans. — Kansas
Kep. — Kepulauan
Ky. — Kentucky
L. — Lac, Lacul, Lago, Lagoa, Lake, Limni, Loch, Lough
La. — Louisiana
Liech. — Liechtenstein
Lux. — Luxembourg
Mad. P. — Madhya Pradesh
Madag. — Madagascar
Man. — Manitoba
Mass. — Massachusetts

Md. — Maryland
Me. — Maine
Medit. S. — Mediterranean Sea
Mich. — Michigan
Minn. — Minnesota
Miss. — Mississippi
Mo. — Missouri
Mont. — Montana
Mozam. — Mozambique
Mt.(e). — Mont, Monte, Monti, Montaña, Mountain
N. — Nord, Norte, North, Northern, Nouveau
N.B. — New Brunswick
N.C. — North Carolina
N. Cal. — New Caledonia
N. Dak. — North Dakota
N.H. — New Hampshire
N.I. — North Island
N.J. — New Jersey
N. Mex. — New Mexico
N.S. — Nova Scotia
N.S.W. — New South Wales
N.W.T. — North West Territory
N.Y. — New York
N.Z. — New Zealand
Nebr. — Nebraska
Neths. — Netherlands
Nev. — Nevada
Nfld. — Newfoundland
Nic. — Nicaragua
O. — Oued, Ouadi
Okla. — Oklahoma
Ont. — Ontario
Or. — Orientale

Oreg. — Oregon
Os. — Ostrov
Oz. — Ozero
P. — Pass, Passo, Pasul, Pulau
P.E.I. — Prince Edward Island
Pa. — Pennsylvania
Pac. Oc. — Pacific Ocean
Papua N.G. — Papua New Guinea
Pass. — Passage
Pen. — Peninsula, Péninsule
Phil. — Philippines
Pk. — Park, Peak
Plat. — Plateau
P-ov. — Poluostrov
Prov. — Province, Provincial
Pt. — Point
Pta. — Ponta, Punta
Pte. — Pointe
Qué. — Québec
Queens. — Queensland
R. — Rio, River
R.I. — Rhode Island
Ra.(s). — Range(s)
Raj. — Rajasthan
Reg. — Region
Rep. — Republic
Res. — Reserve, Reservoir
S. — San, South, Sea
Si. Arabia — Saudi Arabia
S.C. — South Carolina
S. Dak. — South Dakota
S.I. — South Island
S. Leone — Sierra Leone
Sa. — Serra, Sierra
Sask. — Saskatchewan
Scot. — Scotland

Sd. — Sound
Sev. — Severnaya
Sib. — Siberia
Sprs. — Springs
St. — Saint, Sankt, Sint
Sta. — Santa, Station
Ste. — Sainte
Sto. — Santo
Str. — Strait, Stretto
Switz. — Switzerland
Tas. — Tasmania
Tenn. — Tennessee
Tex. — Texas
Tg. — Tanjung
Trin. & Tob. — Trinidad & Tobago
U.A.E. — United Arab Emirates
U.K. — United Kingdom
U.S.A. — United States of America
Ut. P. — Uttar Pradesh
Va. — Virginia
Vdkhr. — Vodokhanilishche
Vf. — Vîrful
Vic. — Victoria
Vol. — Volcano
Vt. — Vermont
W. — Wadi, West
W. Va. — West Virginia
Wash. — Washington
Wis. — Wisconsin
Wlkp. — Wielkopolski
Wyo. — Wyoming
Yorks. — Yorkshire

A Coruña

A

A Coruña = La Coruña, *Spain* **19 A1** 43 20N 8 25W
Aachen, *Germany* **16 C4** 50 45N 6 6 E
Aalborg = Ålborg, *Denmark* **9 H13** 57 2N 9 54 E
Aalen, *Germany* **16 D6** 48 51N 10 6 E
Aalsmeer, *Neths.* **15 B4** 52 17N 4 43 E
Aalst, *Belgium* **15 D4** 50 56N 4 2 E
Aalten, *Neths.* **15 C6** 51 56N 6 35 E
Äänekoski, *Finland* **9 E21** 62 36N 25 44 E
Aarau, *Switz.* **16 E5** 47 23N 8 4 E
Aare →, *Switz.* **16 E5** 47 33N 8 14 E
Aarhus = Århus, *Denmark* **9 H14** 56 8N 10 11 E
Aarschot, *Belgium* **15 D4** 50 59N 4 49 E
Aba, *Nigeria* **50 G6** 5 10N 7 19 E
Aba, *Zaïre* **54 B3** 3 58N 30 17 E
Ābādān, *Iran* **45 D6** 30 22N 48 20 E
Ābādeh, *Iran* **45 D7** 31 8N 52 40 E
Abadla, *Algeria* **50 B4** 31 2N 2 45W
Abaetetuba, *Brazil* **93 D9** 1 40S 48 50W
Abagnar Qi, *China* **34 C9** 43 52N 116 2 E
Abai, *Paraguay* **95 B4** 25 58S 55 54W
Abakan, *Russia* **27 D10** 53 40N 91 10 E
Abancay, *Peru* **92 F4** 13 35S 72 55W
Abariringa, *Kiribati* **64 H10** 2 50S 171 40W
Abarqū, *Iran* **45 D7** 31 10N 53 20 E
Abashiri, *Japan* **30 B12** 44 0N 144 15 E
Abashiri-Wan, *Japan* **30 B12** 44 0N 144 30 E
Abay, *Kazakstan* **26 E8** 49 38N 72 53 E
Abaya, L., *Ethiopia* **51 G12** 6 30N 37 50 E
Abaza, *Russia* **26 D10** 52 39N 90 6 E
'Abbāsābād, *Iran* **45 C8** 33 34N 58 23 E
Abbay = Nîl el Azraq →, *Sudan* **51 E11** 15 38N 32 31 E
Abbaye, Pt., *U.S.A.* **76 B1** 46 58N 88 8W
Abbeville, *France* **18 A4** 50 6N 1 49 E
Abbeville, *La., U.S.A.* **81 K8** 29 58N 92 8W
Abbeville, *S.C., U.S.A.* **77 H4** 34 11N 82 23W
Abbieglassie, *Australia* **63 D4** 27 15S 147 28 E
Abbot Ice Shelf, *Antarctica* **5 D16** 73 0S 92 0W
Abbotsford, *Canada* **72 D4** 49 5N 122 20W
Abbotsford, *U.S.A.* **80 C9** 44 57N 90 19W
Abbottabad, *Pakistan* **42 B5** 34 10N 73 15 E
Abd al Kūrī, *Ind. Oc.* **46 E5** 12 5N 52 20 E
Ābdar, *Iran* **45 D7** 30 16N 55 19 E
'Abdolābād, *Iran* **45 C8** 34 12N 56 30 E
Abéché, *Chad* **51 F9** 13 50N 20 35 E
Åbenrå, *Denmark* **9 J13** 55 3N 9 25 E
Abeokuta, *Nigeria* **50 G5** 7 3N 3 19 E
Aber, *Uganda* **54 B3** 2 12N 32 25 E
Aberaeron, *U.K.* **11 E3** 52 15N 4 15W
Aberayron = Aberaeron, *U.K.* **11 E3** 52 15N 4 15W
Aberconwy & Colwyn □, *U.K.* **10 D4** 53 10N 3 44W
Abercorn = Mbala, *Zambia* **55 D3** 8 46S 31 24 E
Abercorn, *Australia* **63 D5** 25 12S 151 5 E
Aberdare, *U.K.* **11 F4** 51 43N 3 27W
Aberdare Ra., *Kenya* **54 C4** 0 15S 36 50 E
Aberdeen, *Australia* **63 E5** 32 9S 150 56 E
Aberdeen, *Canada* **73 C7** 52 20N 106 8W
Aberdeen, *S. Africa* **56 E3** 32 28S 24 2 E
Aberdeen, *U.K.* **12 D6** 57 9N 2 5W
Aberdeen, *Ala., U.S.A.* **77 J1** 33 49N 88 33W
Aberdeen, *Idaho, U.S.A.* **82 E7** 42 57N 112 50W
Aberdeen, *S. Dak., U.S.A.* **80 C5** 45 28N 98 29W
Aberdeen, *Wash., U.S.A.* **84 D3** 46 59N 123 50W
Aberdeenshire □, *U.K.* **12 D6** 57 17N 2 36W
Aberdovey = Aberdyfi, *U.K.* **11 E3** 52 33N 4 3W
Aberdyfi, *U.K.* **11 E3** 52 33N 4 3W
Aberfeldy, *U.K.* **12 E5** 56 37N 3 51W
Abergavenny, *U.K.* **11 F4** 51 49N 3 1W
Abernathy, *U.S.A.* **81 J4** 33 50N 101 51W
Abert, L., *U.S.A.* **82 E3** 42 38N 120 14W
Aberystwyth, *U.K.* **11 E3** 52 25N 4 5W
Abhar, *Iran* **45 B6** 36 9N 49 13 E
Abhayapuri, *India* **43 F14** 26 24N 90 38 E
Abidjan, *Ivory C.* **50 G4** 5 26N 3 58W
Abilene, *Kans., U.S.A.* **80 F6** 38 55N 97 13W
Abilene, *Tex., U.S.A.* **81 J5** 32 28N 99 43W
Abingdon, *U.K.* **11 F6** 51 40N 1 17W
Abingdon, *Ill., U.S.A.* **80 E9** 40 48N 90 24W
Abingdon, *Va., U.S.A.* **77 G5** 36 43N 81 59W
Abington Reef, *Australia* **62 B4** 18 0S 149 35 E
Abitau →, *Canada* **73 B7** 59 53N 109 3W
Abitau L., *Canada* **73 A7** 60 27N 107 15W
Abitibi L., *Canada* **70 C4** 48 40N 79 40W
Abkhaz Republic □ = Abkhazia □, *Georgia* **25 F7** 43 12N 41 5 E
Abkhazia □, *Georgia* **25 F7** 43 12N 41 5 E
Abkit, *Russia* **27 C16** 64 10N 157 10 E
Abminga, *Australia* **63 D1** 26 8S 134 51 E
Åbo = Turku, *Finland* **9 F20** 60 30N 22 19 E
Abohar, *India* **42 D6** 30 10N 74 10 E
Abomey, *Benin* **50 G5** 7 10N 2 5 E
Abong-Mbang, *Cameroon* **52 D2** 4 0N 13 8 E
Abou-Deïa, *Chad* **51 F8** 11 20N 19 20 E
Aboyne, *U.K.* **12 D6** 57 4N 2 47W
Abra Pampa, *Argentina* **94 A2** 22 43S 65 42W
Abreojos, Pta., *Mexico* **86 B2** 26 50N 113 40W
Abri, *Sudan* **51 D11** 20 50N 30 27 E
Abrolhos, Banka, *Brazil* **93 G11** 18 0S 38 0W
Abrud, *Romania* **17 E12** 46 19N 23 5 E
Absaroka Range, *U.S.A.* **82 D9** 44 45N 109 50W
Abū al Khaşīb, *Iraq* **45 D6** 30 25N 48 0 E
Abū 'Alī, *Si. Arabia* **45 E6** 27 20N 49 27 E
Abū 'Alī →, *Lebanon* **47 A4** 34 25N 35 50 E
Abū 'Arīsh, *Si. Arabia* **46 D3** 16 53N 42 48 E
Abu Dhabi = Abū Z̧āby, *U.A.E.* **45 E7** 24 28N 54 22 E
Abū Dis, *Sudan* **51 E11** 19 12N 33 38 E
Abū Du'ān, *Syria* **44 B3** 36 25N 38 15 E
Abu el Gairi, W. →, *Egypt* **47 F2** 29 35N 33 30 E
Abu Ga'da, W. →, *Egypt* **47 F1** 29 15N 32 53 E
Abū Ḩadrīyah, *Si. Arabia* **45 E6** 27 20N 48 58 E
Abu Ḩamed, *Sudan* **51 E11** 19 32N 33 13 E
Abū Kamāl, *Syria* **44 C4** 34 30N 41 0 E
Abū Madd, Ra's, *Si. Arabia* **44 E3** 24 50N 37 7 E
Abu Matariq, *Sudan* **51 F10** 10 59N 26 9 E
Abu Şafāt, W. →, *Jordan* **47 E5** 30 24N 36 7 E
Abū Şukhayr, *Iraq* **44 D5** 31 54N 44 30 E
Abu Tig, *Egypt* **51 C11** 27 4N 31 15 E
Abû Zabad, *Sudan* **51 F10** 12 25N 29 10 E
Abū Z̧āby, *U.A.E.* **45 E7** 24 28N 54 22 E
Abū Zeydābād, *Iran* **45 C6** 33 54N 51 45 E
Abuja, *Nigeria* **50 G6** 9 16N 7 2 E
Abukuma-Gawa →, *Japan* **30 E10** 38 6N 140 52 E
Abukuma-Sammyaku, *Japan* **30 F10** 37 30N 140 45 E
Abunã, *Brazil* **92 E5** 9 40S 65 20W
Abunã →, *Brazil* **92 E5** 9 41S 65 20W
Aburo, *Zaïre* **54 B3** 2 4N 30 53 E
Abut Hd., *N.Z.* **59 K3** 43 7S 170 15 E
Abwong, *Sudan* **51 G11** 9 2N 32 14 E
Acajutla, *El Salv.* **88 D2** 13 36N 89 50W
Acámbaro, *Mexico* **86 C4** 20 0N 100 40W
Acaponeta, *Mexico* **86 C3** 22 30N 105 20W
Acapulco, *Mexico* **87 D5** 16 51N 99 56W
Acarigua, *Venezuela* **92 B5** 9 33N 69 12W
Acatlán, *Mexico* **87 D5** 18 10N 98 3W
Acayucan, *Mexico* **87 D6** 17 59N 94 58W
Accomac, *U.S.A.* **76 G8** 37 43N 75 40W
Accra, *Ghana* **50 G4** 5 35N 0 6W
Accrington, *U.K.* **10 D5** 53 45N 2 22W
Acebal, *Argentina* **94 C3** 33 20S 60 50W
Aceh □, *Indonesia* **36 D1** 4 15N 97 30 E
Achalpur, *India* **40 J10** 21 22N 77 32 E
Acheng, *China* **35 B14** 45 30N 126 58 E
Acher, *India* **42 H5** 23 10N 72 32 E
Achill, *Ireland* **13 C2** 53 56N 9 55W
Achill Hd., *Ireland* **13 C1** 53 58N 10 15W
Achill I., *Ireland* **13 C1** 53 58N 10 1W
Achill Sd., *Ireland* **13 C2** 53 54N 9 56W
Achinsk, *Russia* **27 D10** 56 20N 90 20 E
Acireale, *Italy* **20 F6** 37 37N 15 10 E
Ackerman, *U.S.A.* **81 J10** 33 19N 89 11W
Acklins I., *Bahamas* **89 B5** 22 30N 74 0W
Acme, *Canada* **72 C6** 51 33N 113 30W
Aconcagua, Cerro, *Argentina* **94 C2** 32 39S 70 0W
Aconquija, Mt., *Argentina* **94 B2** 27 0S 66 0W
Açores, Is. dos = Azores, *Atl. Oc.* **48 C1** 38 44N 29 0W
Acraman, L., *Australia* **63 E2** 32 2S 135 23 E
Acre = 'Akko, *Israel* **47 C4** 32 55N 35 4 E
Acre □, *Brazil* **92 E4** 9 1S 71 0W
Acre →, *Brazil* **92 E5** 8 45S 67 22W
Acton, *Canada* **78 C4** 43 38N 80 3W
Ad Dammām, *Si. Arabia* **45 E6** 26 20N 50 5 E
Ad Dawhah, *Qatar* **45 E6** 25 15N 51 35 E
Ad Dawr, *Iraq* **44 C4** 34 27N 43 47 E
Ad Dir'īyah, *Si. Arabia* **44 E5** 24 44N 46 35 E
Ad Dīwānīyah, *Iraq* **44 D5** 32 0N 45 0 E
Ad Dujayl, *Iraq* **44 C5** 33 51N 44 14 E
Ad Durūz, J., *Jordan* **47 C5** 32 35N 36 40 E
Ada, *Minn., U.S.A.* **80 B6** 47 18N 96 31W
Ada, *Okla., U.S.A.* **81 H6** 34 46N 96 41W
Adaja →, *Spain* **19 B3** 41 32N 4 52W
Adamaoua, Massif de l', *Cameroon* **51 G7** 7 20N 12 20 E
Adamawa Highlands = Adamaoua, Massif de l', *Cameroon* **51 G7** 7 20N 12 20 E
Adamello, Mte., *Italy* **20 A4** 46 9N 10 30 E
Adaminaby, *Australia* **63 F4** 36 0S 148 45 E
Adams, *Mass., U.S.A.* **79 D11** 42 38N 73 7W
Adams, *N.Y., U.S.A.* **79 C8** 43 49N 76 1W
Adams, *Wis., U.S.A.* **80 D10** 43 57N 89 49W
Adam's Bridge, *Sri Lanka* **40 Q11** 9 15N 79 40 E
Adams L., *Canada* **72 C5** 51 10N 119 40W
Adams Mt., *U.S.A.* **84 D5** 46 12N 121 30W
Adam's Peak, *Sri Lanka* **40 R12** 6 48N 80 30 E
Adana, *Turkey* **25 G6** 37 0N 35 16 E
Adapazarı, *Turkey* **25 F5** 40 48N 30 25 E
Adarama, *Sudan* **51 E11** 17 10N 34 52 E
Adare, C., *Antarctica* **5 D11** 71 0S 171 0 E
Adaut, *Indonesia* **37 F8** 8 8S 131 7 E
Adavale, *Australia* **63 D3** 25 52S 144 32 E
Adda →, *Italy* **20 B3** 45 8N 9 53 E
Addis Ababa = Addis Abeba, *Ethiopia* **51 G12** 9 2N 38 42 E
Addis Abeba, *Ethiopia* **51 G12** 9 2N 38 42 E
Addis Alem, *Ethiopia* **51 G12** 9 0N 38 17 E
Addison, *U.S.A.* **78 D7** 42 1N 77 14W
Addo, *S. Africa* **56 E4** 33 32S 25 45 E
Ādeh, *Iran* **44 B5** 37 42N 45 11 E
Adel, *U.S.A.* **77 K4** 31 8N 83 25W
Adelaide, *Australia* **63 E2** 34 52S 138 30 E
Adelaide, *Bahamas* **88 A4** 25 4N 77 31W
Adelaide, *S. Africa* **56 E4** 32 42S 26 20 E
Adelaide I., *Antarctica* **5 C17** 67 15S 68 30W
Adelaide Pen., *Canada* **68 B10** 68 15N 97 30W
Adelaide River, *Australia* **60 B5** 13 15S 131 7 E
Adelanto, *U.S.A.* **85 L9** 34 35N 117 22W
Adele I., *Australia* **60 C3** 15 32S 123 9 E
Adélie, Terre, *Antarctica* **5 C10** 68 0S 140 0 E
Adélie Land = Adélie, Terre, *Antarctica* **5 C10** 68 0S 140 0 E
Aden = Al 'Adan, *Yemen* **46 E4** 12 45N 45 0 E
Aden, G. of, *Asia* **46 E4** 12 30N 47 30 E
Adendorp, *S. Africa* **56 E3** 32 15S 24 30 E
Adh Dhayd, *U.A.E.* **45 E7** 25 17N 55 53 E
Adhoi, *India* **42 H4** 23 26N 70 32 E
Adi, *Indonesia* **37 E8** 4 15S 133 30 E
Adi Ugri, *Eritrea* **51 F12** 14 58N 38 48 E
Adieu, C., *Australia* **61 F5** 32 0S 132 10 E
Adieu Pt., *Australia* **60 C3** 15 14S 124 35 E
Adige →, *Italy* **20 B5** 45 9N 12 20 E
Adilabad, *India* **40 K11** 19 33N 78 20 E
Adin, *U.S.A.* **82 F3** 41 12N 120 57W
Adin Khel, *Afghan.* **40 C6** 32 45N 68 5 E
Adirondack Mts., *U.S.A.* **79 C10** 44 0N 74 0W
Adjumani, *Uganda* **54 B3** 3 20N 31 50 E
Adlavik Is., *Canada* **71 B8** 55 2N 57 45W
Admer, *Algeria* **50 D6** 20 21N 5 27 E
Admiralty G., *Australia* **60 B4** 14 20S 125 55 E
Admiralty I., *U.S.A.* **68 C6** 57 30N 134 30W
Admiralty Inlet, *U.S.A.* **82 C2** 48 8N 122 58W
Admiralty Is., *Papua N. G.* **64 H6** 2 0S 147 0 E
Ado-Ekiti, *Nigeria* **50 G6** 7 38N 5 12 E
Adonara, *Indonesia* **37 F6** 8 15S 123 5 E
Adoni, *India* **40 M10** 15 33N 77 18 E
Adour →, *France* **18 E3** 43 32N 1 32W
Adra, *India* **43 H12** 23 30N 86 42 E
Adra, *Spain* **19 D4** 36 43N 3 3W
Adrano, *Italy* **20 F6** 37 40N 14 50 E
Adrar, *Algeria* **50 C4** 27 51N 0 11W
Adré, *Chad* **51 F9** 13 40N 22 20 E
Adrī, *Libya* **51 C7** 27 32N 13 2 E
Adrian, *Mich., U.S.A.* **76 E3** 41 54N 84 2W
Adrian, *Tex., U.S.A.* **81 H3** 35 16N 102 40W
Adriatic Sea, *Medit. S.* **20 C6** 43 0N 16 0 E
Adua, *Indonesia* **37 E7** 1 45S 129 50 E
Adwa, *Ethiopia* **51 F12** 14 15N 38 52 E
Adzhar Republic □ = Ajaria □, *Georgia* **25 F7** 41 30N 42 0 E
Ægean Sea, *Medit. S.* **21 E11** 38 30N 25 0 E
Aerhtai Shan, *Mongolia* **32 B4** 46 40N 92 45 E
'Afak, *Iraq* **44 C5** 32 4N 45 15 E
Afándou, *Greece* **23 C10** 36 18N 28 12 E
Afghanistan ■, *Asia* **40 C4** 33 0N 65 0 E
Afgoi, *Somali Rep.* **46 G3** 2 7N 44 59 E
Afognak I., *U.S.A.* **68 C4** 58 15N 152 30W
'Afrīn, *Syria* **44 B3** 36 32N 36 50 E
Afton, *U.S.A.* **79 D9** 42 14N 75 32W
Afuá, *Brazil* **93 D8** 0 15S 50 20W
Afula, *Israel* **47 C4** 32 37N 35 17 E
Afyonkarahisar, *Turkey* **25 G5** 38 45N 30 33 E
Agadès = Agadez, *Niger* **50 E6** 16 58N 7 59 E
Agadez, *Niger* **50 E6** 16 58N 7 59 E
Agadir, *Morocco* **50 B3** 30 28N 9 55W
Agaete, *Canary Is.* **22 F4** 28 6N 15 43W
Agapa, *Russia* **27 B9** 71 27N 89 15 E
Agar, *India* **42 H7** 23 40N 76 2 E
Agartala, *India* **41 H17** 23 50N 91 23 E
Agassiz, *Canada* **72 D4** 49 14N 121 46W
Agats, *Indonesia* **37 F9** 5 33S 138 0 E
Agboville, *Ivory C.* **50 G4** 5 55N 4 15W
Agde, *France* **18 E5** 43 19N 3 28 E
Agen, *France* **18 D4** 44 12N 0 38 E
Āgh Kand, *Iran* **45 B6** 37 15N 48 4 E
Aginskoye, *Russia* **27 D12** 51 6N 114 32 E
Agra, *India* **42 F7** 27 17N 77 58 E
Agri →, *Italy* **20 D7** 40 13N 16 44 E
Ağri Daği, *Turkey* **25 G7** 39 50N 44 15 E
Ağri Karakose, *Turkey* **25 G7** 39 44N 43 3 E
Agrigento, *Italy* **20 F5** 37 19N 13 34 E
Agrinion, *Greece* **21 E9** 38 37N 21 27 E
Agua Caliente, *Baja Calif., Mexico* **85 N10** 32 29N 116 59W
Agua Caliente, *Sinaloa, Mexico* **86 B3** 26 30N 108 20W
Agua Caliente Springs, *U.S.A.* **85 N10** 32 56N 116 19W
Água Clara, *Brazil* **93 H8** 20 25S 52 45W
Agua Hechicero, *Mexico* **85 N10** 32 26N 116 14W
Agua Prieta, *Mexico* **86 A3** 31 20N 109 32W
Aguadas, *Colombia* **92 B3** 5 40N 75 38W
Aguadilla, *Puerto Rico* **89 C6** 18 26N 67 10W
Aguadulce, *Panama* **88 E3** 8 15N 80 32W
Aguanga, *U.S.A.* **85 M10** 33 27N 116 51W
Aguanish, *Canada* **71 B7** 50 14N 62 2W
Aguanus →, *Canada* **71 B7** 50 13N 62 5W
Aguapey →, *Argentina* **94 B4** 29 7S 56 36W
Aguaray Guazú →, *Paraguay* **94 A4** 24 47S 57 19W
Aguarico →, *Ecuador* **92 D3** 0 59S 75 11W
Aguas Blancas, *Chile* **94 A2** 24 15S 69 55W
Aguas Calientes, Sierra de, *Argentina* **94 B2** 25 26S 66 40W
Aguascalientes, *Mexico* **86 C4** 21 53N 102 12W
Aguascalientes □, *Mexico* **86 C4** 22 0N 102 20W
Aguilares, *Argentina* **94 B2** 27 26S 65 35W
Aguilas, *Spain* **19 D5** 37 23N 1 35W
Agüimes, *Canary Is.* **22 G4** 27 58N 15 27W
Aguja, C. de la, *Colombia* **90 B3** 11 18N 74 12W
Agulhas, C., *S. Africa* **56 E3** 34 52S 20 0 E
Agulo, *Canary Is.* **22 F2** 28 11N 17 12W
Agung, *Indonesia* **36 F5** 8 20S 115 28 E
Agur, *Uganda* **54 B3** 2 28N 32 55 E
Agusan →, *Phil.* **37 C7** 9 0N 125 30 E
Aha Mts., *Botswana* **56 B3** 19 45S 21 0 E
Ahaggar, *Algeria* **50 D6** 23 0N 6 30 E
Ahar, *Iran* **44 B5** 38 35N 47 0 E
Ahipara B., *N.Z.* **59 F4** 35 5S 173 5 E
Ahiri, *India* **40 K12** 19 30N 80 0 E
Ahmad Wal, *Pakistan* **42 E1** 29 18N 65 58 E
Ahmadabad, *India* **42 H5** 23 0N 72 40 E
Aḩmadābād, *Khorāsān, Iran* **45 C9** 35 3N 60 50 E
Aḩmadābād, *Khorāsān, Iran* **45 C8** 35 49N 59 42 E
Aḩmadī, *Iran* **45 E8** 27 56N 56 42 E
Ahmadnagar, *India* **40 K9** 19 7N 74 46 E
Ahmadpur, *Pakistan* **42 E4** 29 12N 71 10 E
Ahmedabad = Ahmadabad, *India* **42 H5** 23 0N 72 40 E
Ahmednagar = Ahmadnagar, *India* **40 K9** 19 7N 74 46 E
Ahome, *Mexico* **86 B3** 25 55N 109 11W
Ahram, *Iran* **45 D6** 28 52N 51 16 E
Ahrax Pt., *Malta* **23 D1** 35 59N 14 22 E
Āhū, *Iran* **45 C6** 34 33N 50 2 E
Ahuachapán, *El Salv.* **88 D2** 13 54N 89 52W
Ahvāz, *Iran* **45 D6** 31 20N 48 40 E
Ahvenanmaa = Åland, *Finland* **9 F19** 60 15N 20 0 E
Aḩwar, *Yemen* **46 E4** 13 30N 46 40 E
Aichi □, *Japan* **31 G8** 35 0N 137 15 E
Aigua, *Uruguay* **95 C5** 34 13S 54 46W
Aigues-Mortes, *France* **18 E6** 43 35N 4 12 E
Aihui, *China* **33 A7** 50 10N 127 30 E
Aija, *Peru* **92 E3** 9 50S 77 45W
Aikawa, *Japan* **30 E9** 38 2N 138 15 E
Aiken, *U.S.A.* **77 J5** 33 34N 81 43W
Aillik, *Canada* **71 A8** 55 11N 59 18W
Ailsa Craig, *U.K.* **12 F3** 55 15N 5 6W
'Ailūn, *Jordan* **47 C4** 32 18N 35 47 E
Aim, *Russia* **27 D14** 59 0N 133 55 E
Aimere, *Indonesia* **37 F6** 8 45S 121 3 E
Aimogasta, *Argentina* **94 B2** 28 33S 66 50W
Aimorés, *Brazil* **93 G10** 19 30S 41 4W
Aïn Beïda, *Algeria* **50 A6** 35 50N 7 29 E
Aïn Ben Tili, *Mauritania* **50 C3** 25 59N 9 27W
Aïn-Sefra, *Algeria* **50 B4** 32 47N 0 37W
'Ain Sudr, *Egypt* **47 F2** 29 50N 33 6 E
Ainabo, *Somali Rep.* **46 F4** 9 0N 46 25 E
Ainaži, *Latvia* **9 H21** 57 50N 24 24 E
Ainsworth, *U.S.A.* **80 D5** 42 33N 99 52W
Aïr, *Niger* **50 E6** 18 30N 8 0 E
Air Hitam, *Malaysia* **39 M4** 1 55N 103 11 E
Airdrie, *U.K.* **12 F5** 55 52N 3 57W
Aire →, *U.K.* **10 D7** 53 43N 0 55W
Aire, I. del, *Spain* **22 B11** 39 48N 4 16 E
Airlie Beach, *Australia* **62 C4** 20 16S 148 43 E
Aisne →, *France* **18 B5** 49 26N 2 50 E
Aitkin, *U.S.A.* **80 B8** 46 32N 93 42W
Aiud, *Romania* **17 E12** 46 19N 23 44 E
Aix-en-Provence, *France* **18 E6** 43 32N 5 27 E
Aix-la-Chapelle = Aachen, *Germany* **16 C4** 50 45N 6 6 E
Aix-les-Bains, *France* **18 D6** 45 41N 5 53 E
Aiyansh, *Canada* **72 B3** 55 17N 129 2W
Aiyion, *Greece* **21 E10** 38 15N 22 5 E
Aizawl, *India* **41 H18** 23 40N 92 44 E
Aizkraukle, *Latvia* **9 H21** 56 36N 25 11 E
Aizpute, *Latvia* **9 H19** 56 43N 21 40 E
Aizuwakamatsu, *Japan* **30 F9** 37 30N 139 56 E
Ajaccio, *France* **18 F8** 41 55N 8 40 E
Ajalpan, *Mexico* **87 D5** 18 22N 97 15W
Ajanta Ra., *India* **40 J9** 20 28N 75 50 E
Ajari Rep. = Ajaria □, *Georgia* **25 F7** 41 30N 42 0 E
Ajaria □, *Georgia* **25 F7** 41 30N 42 0 E
Ajax, *Canada* **78 C5** 43 50N 79 1W
Ajdâbiyah, *Libya* **51 B9** 30 54N 20 4 E
Ajka, *Hungary* **17 E9** 47 4N 17 31 E
'Ajmān, *U.A.E.* **45 E7** 25 25N 55 30 E
Ajmer, *India* **42 F6** 26 28N 74 37 E
Ajo, *U.S.A.* **83 K7** 32 22N 112 52W
Ajo, C. de, *Spain* **19 A4** 43 31N 3 35W
Akabira, *Japan* **30 C11** 43 33N 142 5 E
Akamas □, *Cyprus* **23 D11** 35 3N 32 18 E
Akanthou, *Cyprus* **23 D12** 35 22N 33 45 E
Akaroa, *N.Z.* **59 K4** 43 49S 172 59 E
Akashi, *Japan* **31 G7** 34 45N 134 58 E
Akelamo, *Indonesia* **37 D7** 1 35N 129 40 E
Aketi, *Zaïre* **52 D4** 2 38N 23 47 E
Akharnai, *Greece* **21 E10** 38 5N 23 44 E
Akhelóös →, *Greece* **21 E9** 38 19N 21 7 E
Akhisar, *Turkey* **21 E12** 38 56N 27 48 E
Akhmîm, *Egypt* **51 C11** 26 31N 31 47 E
Akhnur, *India* **43 C6** 32 52N 74 45 E
Aki, *Japan* **31 H6** 33 30N 133 54 E
Akimiski I., *Canada* **70 B3** 52 50N 81 30W
Akita, *Japan* **30 E10** 39 45N 140 7 E
Akita □, *Japan* **30 E10** 39 40N 140 30 E
Akjoujt, *Mauritania* **50 E2** 19 45N 14 15W
Akkeshi, *Japan* **30 C12** 43 2N 144 51 E
'Akko, *Israel* **47 C4** 32 55N 35 4 E
Akkol, *Kazakstan* **26 E8** 45 0N 75 39 E
Aklavik, *Canada* **68 B6** 68 12N 135 0W
Akmolinsk = Aqmola, *Kazakstan* **26 D8** 51 10N 71 30 E
Akō, *Japan* **31 G7** 34 45N 134 24 E
Akobo →, *Ethiopia* **51 G11** 7 48N 33 3 E
Akola, *India* **40 J10** 20 42N 77 2 E
Akordat, *Eritrea* **51 E12** 15 30N 37 40 E
Akpatok I., *Canada* **69 B13** 60 25N 68 8W
Åkrahamn, *Norway* **9 G11** 59 15N 5 10 E
Akranes, *Iceland* **8 D2** 64 19N 22 5W
Akreïjit, *Mauritania* **50 E3** 18 19N 9 11W
Akron, *Colo., U.S.A.* **80 E3** 40 10N 103 13W
Akron, *Ohio, U.S.A.* **78 E3** 41 5N 81 31W
Akrotiri, *Cyprus* **23 E11** 34 36N 32 57 E
Akrotiri Bay, *Cyprus* **23 E12** 34 35N 33 10 E
Aksai Chin, *India* **43 B8** 35 15N 79 55 E
Aksarka, *Russia* **26 C7** 66 31N 67 50 E
Aksay, *Kazakstan* **24 D9** 51 11N 53 0 E
Aksenovo Zilovskoye, *Russia* **27 D12** 53 20N 117 40 E
Aksu, *China* **32 B3** 41 5N 80 10 E
Aksum, *Ethiopia* **51 F12** 14 5N 38 40 E
Aktogay, *Kazakstan* **26 E8** 46 57N 79 40 E
Aktsyabrski, *Belarus* **17 B15** 52 38N 28 53 E
Aktyubinsk = Aqtöbe, *Kazakstan* **25 D10** 50 17N 57 10 E
Aku, *Nigeria* **50 G6** 6 40N 7 18 E
Akure, *Nigeria* **50 G6** 7 15N 5 5 E
Akureyri, *Iceland* **8 D4** 65 40N 18 6W
Akuseki-Shima, *Japan* **31 K4** 29 27N 129 37 E
Akyab = Sittwe, *Burma* **41 J18** 20 18N 92 45 E
Al 'Adan, *Yemen* **46 E4** 12 45N 45 0 E
Al Aḩsā, *Si. Arabia* **45 E6** 25 50N 49 0 E
Al Ajfar, *Si. Arabia* **44 E4** 27 26N 43 0 E
Al Amādīyah, *Iraq* **44 B4** 37 5N 43 30 E
Al Amārah, *Iraq* **44 D5** 31 55N 47 15 E
Al 'Aqabah, *Jordan* **47 F4** 29 31N 35 0 E
Al Arak, *Syria* **44 C3** 34 38N 38 35 E
Al 'Aramah, *Si. Arabia* **44 E5** 25 30N 46 0 E
Al Arţāwīyah, *Si. Arabia* **44 E5** 26 31N 45 20 E
Al 'Āşimah □, *Jordan* **47 D5** 31 40N 36 30 E
Al' Assāfīyah, *Si. Arabia* **44 D3** 28 17N 38 59 E
Al 'Ayn, *Oman* **45 E7** 24 15N 55 45 E
Al 'Ayn, *Si. Arabia* **44 E3** 25 4N 38 6 E
Al A'z̧amīyah, *Iraq* **44 C5** 33 22N 44 22 E
Al 'Azīzīyah, *Iraq* **44 C5** 32 54N 45 4 E
Al Bāb, *Syria* **44 B3** 36 23N 37 29 E
Al Bad', *Si. Arabia* **44 D2** 28 28N 35 1 E
Al Bādī, *Iraq* **44 C4** 35 56N 41 32 E
Al Baḩrah, *Kuwait* **44 D5** 29 40N 47 52 E
Al Balqā' □, *Jordan* **47 C4** 32 5N 35 45 E
Al Bārūk, J., *Lebanon* **47 B4** 33 39N 35 40 E
Al Başrah, *Iraq* **44 D5** 30 30N 47 50 E
Al Baţḩā, *Iraq* **44 D5** 31 6N 45 53 E
Al Batrūn, *Lebanon* **47 A4** 34 15N 35 40 E
Al Bayḑā, *Libya* **51 B9** 32 50N 21 44 E
Al Biqā □, *Lebanon* **47 A5** 34 10N 36 10 E
Al Bi'r, *Si. Arabia* **44 D3** 28 51N 36 16 E
Al Bu'ayrāt al Ḩasūn, *Libya* **51 B8** 31 24N 15 44 E
Al Burayj, *Syria* **47 A5** 34 15N 36 46 E
Al Fallūjah, *Iraq* **44 C4** 33 20N 43 55 E
Al Fāw, *Iraq* **45 D6** 30 0N 48 30 E
Al Fujayrah, *U.A.E.* **45 E8** 25 7N 56 18 E
Al Ghadaf, W. →, *Jordan* **47 D5** 31 26N 36 43 E
Al Ghammās, *Iraq* **44 D5** 31 45N 44 37 E

Amadi

Al Hābah, Si. Arabia 44 E5 27 10N 47 0 E
Al Ḩadīthah, Iraq 44 C4 34 0N 41 13 E
Al Ḩadīthah, Si. Arabia 44 D3 31 28N 37 8 E
Al Ḩājānah, Syria 47 B5 33 20N 36 33 E
Al Ḩāmad, Si. Arabia 44 D3 31 30N 39 30 E
Al Hamdānīyah, Syria 44 C3 35 25N 36 50 E
Al Ḩamīdīyah, Syria 47 A4 34 42N 35 57 E
Al Ḩammār, Iraq 44 D5 30 57N 46 51 E
Al Ḩarīr, W. →, Syria 47 C4 32 44N 35 59 E
Al Ḩasā, W. →, Jordan 47 D4 31 4N 35 29 E
Al Ḩasakah, Syria 44 B4 36 35N 40 45 E
Al Ḩawrah, Yemen 46 E4 13 50N 47 35 E
Al Ḩaydān, W. →, Jordan 47 D4 31 29N 35 34 E
Al Ḩayy, Iraq 44 C5 32 5N 46 5 E
Al Ḩijāz, Si. Arabia 46 B2 26 0N 37 30 E
Al Ḩillah, Iraq 44 C5 32 30N 44 25 E
Al Ḩillah, Si. Arabia 46 C4 23 35N 46 50 E
Al Hirmil, Lebanon 47 A5 34 26N 36 24 E
Al Hoceïma, Morocco 50 A4 35 8N 3 58W
Al Ḩudaydah, Yemen 46 E3 14 50N 43 0 E
Al Hufūf, Si. Arabia 45 E6 25 25N 49 45 E
Al Ḩumaydah, Si. Arabia 44 D2 29 14N 34 56 E
Al Ḩunayy, Si. Arabia 45 E6 25 58N 48 45 E
Al Īsāwīyah, Si. Arabia 44 D3 30 43N 37 59 E
Al Ittihad = Madīnat ash Sha'b, Yemen 46 E3 12 50N 45 0 E
Al Jafr, Jordan 47 E5 30 18N 36 14 E
Al Jaghbūb, Libya 51 C9 29 42N 24 38 E
Al Jahrah, Kuwait 44 D5 29 25N 47 40 E
Al Jalāmīd, Si. Arabia 44 D3 31 20N 39 45 E
Al Jamalīyah, Qatar 45 E6 25 37N 51 5 E
Al Janūb □, Lebanon 47 B4 33 20N 35 20 E
Al Jawf, Libya 51 D9 24 10N 23 24 E
Al Jawf, Si. Arabia 44 D3 29 55N 39 40 E
Al Jazirah, Iraq 44 C5 33 30N 44 0 E
Al Jazirah, Libya 51 C9 26 10N 21 20 E
Al Jithāmīyah, Si. Arabia 44 E4 27 41N 41 43 E
Al Jubayl, Si. Arabia 45 E6 27 0N 49 50 E
Al Jubaylah, Si. Arabia 44 E5 24 55N 46 25 E
Al Jubb, Si. Arabia 44 E4 27 11N 42 17 E
Al Junaynah, Sudan 51 F9 13 27N 22 45 E
Al Kabā'ish, Iraq 44 D5 30 58N 47 0 E
Al Karak, Jordan 47 D4 31 11N 35 42 E
Al Karak □, Jordan 47 E5 31 0N 36 0 E
Al Kāzim Tyah, Iraq 44 C5 33 22N 44 12 E
Al Khalīl, West Bank 47 D4 31 32N 35 6 E
Al Khawr, Qatar 45 E6 25 41N 51 30 E
Al Khiḑr, Iraq 44 D5 31 12N 45 33 E
Al Khiyām, Lebanon 47 B4 33 20N 35 36 E
Al Kiswah, Syria 47 B5 33 23N 36 14 E
Al Kufrah, Libya 51 D9 24 17N 23 15 E
Al Kuhayfīyah, Si. Arabia 44 E4 27 12N 43 3 E
Al Kūt, Iraq 44 C5 32 30N 46 0 E
Al Kuwayt, Kuwait 44 D5 29 30N 48 0 E
Al Labwah, Lebanon 47 A5 34 11N 36 20 E
Al Lādhiqīyah, Syria 44 C2 35 30N 35 45 E
Al Liwā', Oman 45 E8 24 31N 56 36 E
Al Luḩayyah, Yemen 46 D3 15 45N 42 40 E
Al Madīnah, Iraq 44 D5 30 57N 47 16 E
Al Madīnah, Si. Arabia 46 C2 24 35N 39 52 E
Al-Mafraq, Jordan 47 C5 32 17N 36 14 E
Al Maḩmūdīyah, Iraq 44 C5 33 3N 44 21 E
Al Majma'ah, Si. Arabia 44 E5 25 57N 45 22 E
Al Makhruq, W. →, Jordan 47 D6 31 28N 37 0 E
Al Makhūl, Si. Arabia 44 E4 26 37N 42 39 E
Al Manāmah, Bahrain 45 E6 26 10N 50 30 E
Al Maqwa', Kuwait 44 D5 29 10N 47 59 E
Al Marj, Libya 51 B9 32 25N 20 30 E
Al Maţlā, Kuwait 44 D5 29 24N 47 40 E
Al Mawjib, W. →, Jordan 47 D4 31 28N 35 36 E
Al Mawşil, Iraq 44 B4 36 15N 43 5 E
Al Mayādin, Syria 44 C4 35 1N 40 27 E
Al Mazār, Jordan 47 D4 31 4N 35 41 E
Al Midhnab, Si. Arabia 44 E5 25 50N 44 18 E
Al Mīnā', Lebanon 47 A4 34 24N 35 49 E
Al Miqdādīyah, Iraq 44 C5 34 0N 45 0 E
Al Mubarraz, Si. Arabia 45 E6 25 30N 49 40 E
Al Mughayrā', U.A.E. 45 E7 24 5N 53 32 E
Al Muḩarraq, Bahrain 45 E6 26 15N 50 40 E
Al Mukallā, Yemen 46 E4 14 33N 49 2 E
Al Mukhā, Yemen 46 E3 13 18N 43 15 E
Al Musayjid, Si. Arabia 44 E3 24 5N 39 5 E
Al Musayyib, Iraq 44 C5 32 49N 44 20 E
Al Muwayliḩ, Si. Arabia 44 E2 27 40N 35 30 E
Al Qā'im, Iraq 44 C4 34 21N 41 7 E
Al Qalībah, Si. Arabia 44 D3 28 24N 37 42 E
Al Qaryatayn, Syria 47 A6 34 12N 37 13 E
Al Qaşabāt, Libya 51 B7 32 39N 14 1 E
Al Qaţ'ā, Syria 44 C4 34 40N 40 48 E
Al Qaţīf, Si. Arabia 45 E6 26 35N 50 0 E
Al Qatrānah, Jordan 47 D5 31 12N 36 6 E
Al Qaţrūn, Libya 51 D8 24 56N 15 3 E
Al Qayşūmah, Si. Arabia 44 D5 28 20N 46 7 E
Al Quds = Jerusalem, Israel 47 D4 31 47N 35 10 E
Al Qunaytirah, Syria 47 C4 32 55N 35 45 E
Al Qurnah, Iraq 44 D5 31 1N 47 25 E
Al Quşayr, Iraq 44 D5 30 39N 45 50 E
Al Quşayr, Syria 47 A5 34 31N 36 34 E
Al Quţayfah, Syria 47 B5 33 44N 36 36 E
Al' Udaylīyah, Si. Arabia 45 E6 25 8N 49 18 E
Al 'Ulā, Si. Arabia 44 E3 26 35N 38 0 E
Al Uqaylah ash Sharqīgah, Libya 51 B8 30 12N 19 10 E
Al Uqayr, Si. Arabia 45 E6 25 40N 50 15 E
Al 'Uwaynid, Si. Arabia 44 E5 24 50N 46 0 E
Al 'Uwayqīlah, Si. Arabia 44 D4 30 30N 42 10 E
Al 'Uyūn, Si. Arabia 44 E4 26 30N 43 50 E
Al 'Uyūn, Si. Arabia 44 E3 24 33N 39 35 E
Al Wajh, Si. Arabia 44 E3 26 10N 36 30 E
Al Wakrah, Qatar 45 E6 25 10N 51 40 E
Al Wannān, Si. Arabia 45 E6 26 55N 48 24 E
Al Waqbah, Si. Arabia 44 D5 28 48N 45 33 E
Al Wari'āh, Si. Arabia 44 E5 27 51N 47 25 E
Al Wusayl, Qatar 45 E6 25 29N 51 29 E
Ala Tau Shankou = Dzhungarskiye Vorota, Kazakstan 32 B3 45 0N 82 0 E
Alabama □, U.S.A. 77 J2 33 0N 87 0W
Alabama →, U.S.A. 77 K2 31 8N 87 57W
Alaçam Dağları, Turkey 21 E13 39 18N 28 49 E
Alaérma, Greece 23 C9 36 9N 27 57 E
Alagoa Grande, Brazil 93 E11 7 3S 35 35W
Alagoas □, Brazil 93 E11 9 0S 36 0W
Alagoinhas, Brazil 93 F11 12 7S 38 20W
Alajero, Canary Is. 22 F2 28 3N 17 13W
Alajuela, Costa Rica 88 D3 10 2N 84 8W
Alakamisy, Madag. 57 C8 21 19S 47 14 E
Alakurtti, Russia 24 A5 67 0N 30 30 E
Alameda, Calif., U.S.A. 84 H4 37 46N 122 15W
Alameda, N. Mex., U.S.A. 83 J10 35 11N 106 37W
Alamo, U.S.A. 85 J11 36 21N 115 10W
Alamo Crossing, U.S.A. 85 L13 34 16N 113 33W
Alamogordo, U.S.A. 83 K11 32 54N 105 57W
Alamos, Mexico 86 B3 27 0N 109 0W
Alamosa, U.S.A. 83 H11 37 28N 105 52W
Åland, Finland 9 F19 60 15N 20 0 E
Ålands hav, Sweden 9 F18 60 0N 19 30 E
Alandur, India 40 N12 13 0N 80 15 E
Alania = North Ossetia □, Russia 25 F7 43 30N 44 30 E
Alanya, Turkey 25 G5 36 38N 32 0 E
Alaotra, Farihin', Madag. 57 B8 17 30S 48 30 E
Alapayevsk, Russia 26 D7 57 52N 61 42 E
Alaşehir, Turkey 21 E13 38 23N 28 30 E
Alaska □, U.S.A. 68 B5 64 0N 154 0W
Alaska, G. of, Pac. Oc. 68 C5 58 0N 145 0W
Alaska Highway, Canada 72 B3 60 0N 130 0W
Alaska Peninsula, U.S.A. 68 C4 56 0N 159 0W
Alaska Range, U.S.A. 68 B4 62 50N 151 0W
Älät, Azerbaijan 25 G8 39 58N 49 25 E
Alatyr, Russia 24 D8 54 55N 46 35 E
Alausi, Ecuador 92 D3 2 0S 78 50W
Alava, C., U.S.A. 82 B1 48 10N 124 44W
Alavus, Finland 9 E20 62 35N 23 36 E
Alawoona, Australia 63 E3 34 45S 140 30 E
'Alayh, Lebanon 47 B4 33 46N 35 33 E
Alayor, Spain 22 B11 39 57N 4 8 E
Alba, Italy 20 B3 44 42N 8 2 E
Alba-Iulia, Romania 17 E12 46 8N 23 39 E
Albacete, Spain 19 C5 39 0N 1 50W
Albacutya, L., Australia 63 F3 35 45S 141 58 E
Albania ■, Europe 21 D9 41 0N 20 0 E
Albany, Australia 61 G2 35 1S 117 58 E
Albany, Ga., U.S.A. 77 K3 31 35N 84 10W
Albany, Minn., U.S.A. 80 C7 45 38N 94 34W
Albany, N.Y., U.S.A. 79 D11 42 39N 73 45W
Albany, Oreg., U.S.A. 82 D2 44 38N 123 6W
Albany, Tex., U.S.A. 81 J5 32 44N 99 18W
Albany →, Canada 70 B3 52 17N 81 31W
Albardón, Argentina 94 C2 31 20S 68 30W
Albatross B., Australia 62 A3 12 45S 141 30 E
Albemarle, U.S.A. 77 H5 35 21N 80 11W
Albemarle Sd., U.S.A. 77 H7 36 5N 76 0W
Alberche →, Spain 19 C3 39 58N 4 46W
Alberdi, Paraguay 94 B4 26 14S 58 20W
Albert, L., Australia 63 F2 35 30S 139 10 E
Albert Canyon, Canada 72 C5 51 8N 117 41W
Albert Edward Ra., Australia 60 C4 18 17S 127 57 E
Albert L., Africa 54 B3 1 30N 31 0 E
Albert Lea, U.S.A. 80 D8 43 39N 93 22W
Albert Nile →, Uganda 54 B3 3 36N 32 2 E
Albert Town, Bahamas 89 B5 22 37N 74 33W
Alberta □, Canada 72 C6 54 40N 115 0W
Alberti, Argentina 94 D3 35 1S 60 16W
Albertinia, S. Africa 56 E3 34 11S 21 34 E
Alberton, Canada 71 C7 46 50N 64 0W
Albertville = Kalemie, Zaïre 54 D2 5 55S 29 9 E
Albertville, France 18 D7 45 40N 6 22 E
Albi, France 18 E5 43 56N 2 9 E
Albia, U.S.A. 80 E8 41 2N 92 48W
Albina, Surinam 93 B8 5 37N 54 15W
Albina, Ponta, Angola 56 B1 15 52S 11 44 E
Albion, Idaho, U.S.A. 82 E7 42 25N 113 35W
Albion, Mich., U.S.A. 76 D3 42 15N 84 45W
Albion, Nebr., U.S.A. 80 E5 41 42N 98 0W
Albion, Pa., U.S.A. 78 E4 41 53N 80 22W
Alborán, Medit. S. 19 E4 35 57N 3 0W
Ålborg, Denmark 9 H13 57 2N 9 54 E
Alborz, Reshteh-ye Kūhhā-ye, Iran 45 C7 36 0N 52 0 E
Albreda, Canada 72 C5 52 35N 119 10W
Albuquerque, U.S.A. 83 J10 35 5N 106 39W
Albuquerque, Cayos de, Caribbean 88 D3 12 10N 81 50W
Alburg, U.S.A. 79 B11 44 59N 73 18W
Albury, Australia 63 F4 36 3S 146 56 E
Alcalá de Henares, Spain 19 B4 40 28N 3 22W
Alcalá la Real, Spain 19 D4 37 27N 3 57W
Álcamo, Italy 20 F5 37 59N 12 55 E
Alcaniz, Spain 19 B5 41 2N 0 8W
Alcântara, Brazil 93 D10 2 20S 44 30W
Alcántara, Embalse de, Spain 19 C2 39 44N 6 50W
Alcantara L., Canada 73 A7 60 57N 108 9W
Alcantarilla, Spain 19 D5 37 59N 1 12W
Alcaraz, Sierra de, Spain 19 C4 38 40N 2 20W
Alcaudete, Spain 19 D3 37 35N 4 5W
Alcázar de San Juan, Spain 19 C4 39 24N 3 12W
Alchevsk, Ukraine 25 E6 48 30N 38 45 E
Alcira, Spain 19 C5 39 9N 0 30W
Alcoa, U.S.A. 77 H4 35 48N 83 59W
Alcova, U.S.A. 82 E10 42 34N 106 43W
Alcoy, Spain 19 C5 38 43N 0 30W
Alcudia, Spain 22 B10 39 51N 3 7 E
Alcudia, B. de, Spain 22 B10 39 47N 3 15 E
Aldabra Is., Seychelles 49 G8 9 22S 46 28 E
Aldama, Mexico 87 C5 23 0N 98 4W
Aldan, Russia 27 D13 58 40N 125 30 E
Aldan →, Russia 27 C13 63 28N 129 35 E
Aldea, Pta. de la, Canary Is. 22 G4 28 0N 15 50W
Aldeburgh, U.K. 11 E9 52 10N 1 37 E
Alder, U.S.A. 82 D7 45 19N 112 6W
Alder Pk., U.S.A. 84 K5 35 53N 121 22W
Alderney, U.K. 11 H5 49 42N 2 11W
Aldershot, U.K. 11 F7 51 15N 0 44W
Aledo, U.S.A. 80 E9 41 12N 90 45W
Aleg, Mauritania 50 E2 17 3N 13 55W
Alegranza, Canary Is. 22 E6 29 23N 13 32W
Alegranza, I., Canary Is. 22 E6 29 23N 13 32W
Alegre, Brazil 95 A7 20 50S 41 30W
Alegrete, Brazil 95 B4 29 40S 56 0W
Aleisk, Russia 26 D9 52 40N 83 0 E
Aleksandriya = Oleksandriya, Ukraine 17 C14 50 37N 26 19 E
Aleksandrovsk-Sakhalinskiy, Russia 27 D15 50 50N 142 20 E
Aleksandrovskiy Zavod, Russia 27 D12 50 40N 117 50 E
Aleksandrovskoye, Russia 26 C8 60 35N 77 50 E
Além Paraíba, Brazil 95 A7 21 52S 42 41W
Alemania, Argentina 94 B2 25 40S 65 30W
Alemania, Chile 94 B2 25 10S 69 55W
Alençon, France 18 B4 48 27N 0 4 E
Alenuihaha Channel, U.S.A. 74 H17 20 30N 156 0W
Aleppo = Ḩalab, Syria 44 B3 36 10N 37 15 E
Alert Bay, Canada 72 C3 50 30N 126 55W
Alès, France 18 D6 44 9N 4 5 E
Alessándria, Italy 20 B3 44 54N 8 37 E
Ålesund, Norway 9 E12 62 28N 6 12 E
Aleutian Is., Pac. Oc. 68 C2 52 0N 175 0W
Aleutian Trench, Pac. Oc. 64 B10 48 0N 180 0 E
Alexander, U.S.A. 80 B3 47 51N 103 39W
Alexander, Mt., Australia 61 E3 28 58S 120 16 E
Alexander Arch., U.S.A. 72 B2 56 0N 136 0W
Alexander Bay, S. Africa 56 D2 28 40S 16 30 E
Alexander City, U.S.A. 77 J3 32 56N 85 58W
Alexander I., Antarctica 5 C17 69 0S 70 0W
Alexandra, Australia 63 F4 37 8S 145 40 E
Alexandra, N.Z. 59 L2 45 14S 169 25 E
Alexandra Falls, Canada 72 A5 60 29N 116 18W
Alexandria = El Iskandarîya, Egypt 51 B10 31 13N 29 58 E
Alexandria, Australia 62 B2 19 5S 136 40 E
Alexandria, B.C., Canada 72 C4 52 35N 122 27W
Alexandria, Ont., Canada 70 C5 45 19N 74 38W
Alexandria, Romania 17 G13 43 57N 25 24 E
Alexandria, S. Africa 56 E4 33 38S 26 28 E
Alexandria, Ind., U.S.A. 76 E3 40 16N 85 41W
Alexandria, La., U.S.A. 81 K8 31 18N 92 27W
Alexandria, Minn., U.S.A. 80 C7 45 53N 95 22W
Alexandria, S. Dak., U.S.A. 80 D6 43 39N 97 47W
Alexandria, Va., U.S.A. 76 F7 38 48N 77 3W
Alexandria Bay, U.S.A. 79 B9 44 20N 75 55W
Alexandrina, L., Australia 63 F2 35 25S 139 10 E
Alexandroúpolis, Greece 21 D11 40 50N 25 54 E
Alexis →, Canada 71 B8 52 33N 56 8W
Alexis Creek, Canada 72 C4 52 10N 123 20W
Alfabia, Spain 22 B9 39 44N 2 44 E
Alfenas, Brazil 95 A6 21 20S 46 10W
Alford, U.K. 12 D6 57 14N 2 41W
Alfred, Maine, U.S.A. 79 C14 43 29N 70 43W
Alfred, N.Y., U.S.A. 78 D7 42 16N 77 48W
Alfreton, U.K. 10 D6 53 6N 1 24W
Alga, Kazakstan 25 E10 49 53N 57 20 E
Algaida, Spain 22 B9 39 33N 2 53 E
Algård, Norway 9 G11 58 46N 5 53 E
Algarve, Portugal 19 D1 36 58N 8 20W
Algeciras, Spain 19 D3 36 9N 5 28W
Algemesí, Spain 19 C5 39 11N 0 27W
Alger, Algeria 50 A5 36 42N 3 8 E
Algeria ■, Africa 50 C5 28 30N 2 0 E
Alghero, Italy 20 D3 40 33N 8 19 E
Algiers = Alger, Algeria 50 A5 36 42N 3 8 E
Algoa B., S. Africa 56 E4 33 50S 25 45 E
Algoma, U.S.A. 76 C2 44 36N 87 26W
Algona, U.S.A. 80 D7 43 4N 94 14W
Algonac, U.S.A. 78 D2 42 37N 82 32W
Alhambra, U.S.A. 74 D3 34 8N 118 6W
Alhucemas = Al Hoceïma, Morocco 50 A4 35 8N 3 58W
'Alī al Gharbī, Iraq 44 C5 32 30N 46 45 E
Alī ash Sharqī, Iraq 44 C5 32 7N 46 44 E
'Alī Khēl, Afghan. 42 C3 33 57N 69 43 E
Alī Shāh, Iran 44 B5 38 9N 45 50 E
'Alīābād, Khorāsān, Iran 45 C8 32 30N 57 30 E
'Alīābād, Kordestān, Iran 44 C5 35 4N 46 58 E
'Alīābād, Yazd, Iran 45 D7 31 41N 53 49 E
Aliağa, Turkey 21 E12 38 47N 26 59 E
Aliákmon →, Greece 21 D10 40 30N 22 36 E
Alibo, Ethiopia 51 G12 9 52N 37 5 E
Alicante, Spain 19 C5 38 23N 0 30W
Alice, S. Africa 56 E4 32 48S 26 55 E
Alice, U.S.A. 81 M5 27 45N 98 5W
Alice →, Queens., Australia 62 C3 24 2S 144 50 E
Alice →, Queens., Australia 62 B3 15 35S 142 20 E
Alice Arm, Canada 72 B3 55 29N 129 31W
Alice Downs, Australia 60 C4 17 45S 127 56 E
Alice Springs, Australia 62 C1 23 40S 133 50 E
Alicedale, S. Africa 56 E4 33 15S 26 4 E
Aliceville, U.S.A. 77 J1 33 8N 88 9W
Alick Cr. →, Australia 62 C3 20 55S 142 20 E
Alida, Canada 73 D8 49 25N 101 55W
Aligarh, Raj., India 42 G7 25 55N 76 15 E
Aligarh, Ut. P., India 42 F8 27 55N 78 10 E
Alīgūdarz, Iran 45 C6 33 25N 49 45 E
Alimnia, Greece 23 C9 36 16N 27 43 E
Alingsås, Sweden 9 H15 57 56N 12 31 E
Alipur, Pakistan 42 E4 29 25N 70 55 E
Alipur Duar, India 41 F16 26 30N 89 35 E
Aliquippa, U.S.A. 78 F4 40 37N 80 15W
Alitus = Alytus, Lithuania 9 J21 54 24N 24 3 E
Aliwal North, S. Africa 56 E4 30 45S 26 45 E
Alix, Canada 72 C6 52 24N 113 11W
Aljustrel, Portugal 19 D1 37 55N 8 10W
Alkmaar, Neths. 15 B4 52 37N 4 45 E
All American Canal, U.S.A. 83 K6 32 45N 115 15W
Allah Dad, Pakistan 42 G2 25 38N 67 34 E
Allahabad, India 43 G9 25 25N 81 58 E
Allakh-Yun, Russia 27 C14 60 50N 137 5 E
Allan, Canada 73 C7 51 53N 106 4W
Allanmyo, Burma 41 K19 19 30N 95 17 E
Allanridge, S. Africa 56 D4 27 45S 26 40 E
Allanwater, Canada 70 B1 50 14N 90 10W
Allegan, U.S.A. 76 D3 42 32N 85 51W
Allegany, U.S.A. 78 D6 42 6N 78 30W
Allegheny →, U.S.A. 78 F5 40 27N 80 1W
Allegheny Mts., U.S.A. 66 F11 38 15N 80 10W
Allegheny Plateau, U.S.A. 76 G6 38 0N 80 0W
Allegheny Reservoir, U.S.A. 78 E6 41 50N 79 0W
Allen, Bog of, Ireland 13 C4 53 15N 7 0W
Allen, L., Ireland 13 B3 54 8N 8 4W
Allende, Mexico 86 B4 28 20N 100 50W
Allentown, U.S.A. 79 F9 40 37N 75 29W
Alleppey, India 40 Q10 9 30N 76 28 E
Aller →, Germany 16 B5 52 56N 9 12 E
Alliance, Nebr., U.S.A. 80 D3 42 6N 102 52W
Alliance, Ohio, U.S.A. 78 F3 40 55N 81 6W
Allier →, France 18 C5 46 57N 3 4 E
Alliston, Canada 70 D4 44 9N 79 52W
Alloa, U.K. 12 E5 56 7N 3 47W
Allora, Australia 63 D5 28 2S 152 0 E
Alluitsup Paa = Sydprøven, Greenland 4 C5 60 30N 45 35W
Alma, Canada 71 C5 48 35N 71 40W
Alma, Ga., U.S.A. 77 K4 31 33N 82 28W
Alma, Kans., U.S.A. 80 F6 39 1N 96 17W
Alma, Mich., U.S.A. 76 D3 43 23N 84 39W
Alma, Nebr., U.S.A. 80 E5 40 6N 99 22W
Alma, Wis., U.S.A. 80 C9 44 20N 91 55W
Alma Ata = Almaty, Kazakstan 26 E8 43 15N 76 57 E
Almada, Portugal 19 C1 38 40N 9 9W
Almaden, Australia 62 B3 17 22S 144 40 E
Almadén, Spain 19 C3 38 49N 4 52W
Almanor, L., U.S.A. 82 F3 40 14N 121 9W
Almansa, Spain 19 C5 38 51N 1 5W
Almanzor, Pico del Moro, Spain 19 B3 40 15N 5 18W
Almanzora →, Spain 19 D5 37 14N 1 46W
Almaty, Kazakstan 26 E8 43 15N 76 57 E
Almazán, Spain 19 B4 41 30N 2 30W
Almeirim, Brazil 93 D8 1 30S 52 34W
Almelo, Neths. 15 B6 52 22N 6 42 E
Almendralejo, Spain 19 C2 38 41N 6 26W
Almería, Spain 19 D4 36 52N 2 27W
Almirante, Panama 88 E3 9 10N 82 30W
Almiroú, Kólpos, Greece 23 D6 35 23N 24 20 E
Almont, U.S.A. 78 D1 42 55N 83 3W
Almonte, Canada 79 A8 45 14N 76 12W
Almora, India 43 E8 29 38N 79 40 E
Alnwick, U.K. 10 E6 55 24N 1 42W
Aloi, Uganda 54 B3 2 16N 33 10 E
Alon, Burma 41 H19 22 12N 95 5 E
Alor, Indonesia 37 F6 8 15S 124 30 E
Alor Setar, Malaysia 39 J3 6 7N 100 22 E
Aloysius, Mt., Australia 61 E4 26 0S 128 38 E
Alpaugh, U.S.A. 84 K7 35 53N 119 29W
Alpena, U.S.A. 76 C4 45 4N 83 27W
Alpha, Australia 62 C4 23 39S 146 37 E
Alpine, Ariz., U.S.A. 83 K9 33 51N 109 9W
Alpine, Calif., U.S.A. 85 N10 32 50N 116 46W
Alpine, Tex., U.S.A. 81 K3 30 22N 103 40W
Alps, Europe 16 E5 46 30N 9 30 E
Alroy Downs, Australia 62 B2 19 20S 136 5 E
Alsace, France 18 B7 48 15N 7 25 E
Alsask, Canada 73 C7 51 21N 109 59W
Alsásua, Spain 19 A4 42 54N 2 10W
Alsten, Norway 8 D15 65 58N 12 40 E
Alta, Norway 8 B20 69 57N 23 10 E
Alta Gracia, Argentina 94 C3 31 40S 64 30W
Alta Lake, Canada 72 C4 50 10N 123 0W
Alta Sierra, U.S.A. 85 K8 35 42N 118 33W
Altaelva →, Norway 8 B20 69 54N 23 17 E
Altafjorden, Norway 8 A20 70 5N 23 5 E
Altagracia, Venezuela 92 A4 10 45N 71 30W
Altai = Aerhtai Shan, Mongolia 32 B4 46 40N 92 45 E
Altamaha →, U.S.A. 77 K5 31 20N 81 20W
Altamira, Brazil 93 D8 3 12S 52 10W
Altamira, Chile 94 B2 25 47S 69 51W
Altamira, Mexico 87 C5 22 24N 97 55W
Altamont, U.S.A. 79 D10 42 43N 74 3W
Altamura, Italy 20 D7 40 49N 16 33 E
Altanbulag, Mongolia 32 A5 50 16N 106 30 E
Altar, Mexico 86 A2 30 40N 111 50W
Altata, Mexico 86 C3 24 30N 108 0W
Altavista, U.S.A. 76 G6 37 6N 79 17W
Altay, China 32 B3 47 48N 88 10 E
Altea, Spain 19 C5 38 38N 0 2W
Alto Araguaia, Brazil 93 G8 17 15S 53 20W
Alto Cuchumatanes = Cuchumatanes, Sierra de los, Guatemala 88 C1 15 35N 91 25W
Alto del Inca, Chile 94 A2 24 10S 68 10W
Alto Ligonha, Mozam. 55 F4 15 30S 38 11 E
Alto Molocue, Mozam. 55 F4 15 50S 37 35 E
Alto Paraguay □, Paraguay 94 A4 21 0S 58 30W
Alto Paraná □, Paraguay 95 B5 25 30S 54 50W
Alton, Canada 78 C4 43 54N 80 5W
Alton, U.S.A. 80 F9 38 53N 90 11W
Alton Downs, Australia 63 D2 26 7S 138 57 E
Altoona, U.S.A. 78 F6 40 31N 78 24W
Altūn Kūprī, Iraq 44 C5 35 45N 44 9 E
Altun Shan, China 32 C3 38 30N 88 0 E
Alturas, U.S.A. 82 F3 41 29N 120 32W
Altus, U.S.A. 81 H5 34 38N 99 20W
Alūksne, Latvia 9 H22 57 24N 27 3 E
Alùla, Somali Rep. 46 E5 11 50N 50 45 E
Alunite, U.S.A. 85 K12 35 59N 114 55W
Alusi, Indonesia 37 F8 7 35S 131 40 E
Al'Uzayr, Iraq 44 D5 31 19N 47 25 E
Alva, U.S.A. 81 G5 36 48N 98 40W
Alvarado, Mexico 87 D5 18 40N 95 50W
Alvarado, U.S.A. 81 J6 32 24N 97 13W
Alvaro Obregón, Presa, Mexico 86 B3 27 55N 109 52W
Alvear, Argentina 94 B4 29 5S 56 30W
Alvesta, Sweden 9 H16 56 54N 14 35 E
Alvie, Australia 63 F3 38 14S 143 30 E
Alvin, U.S.A. 81 L7 29 26N 95 15W
Alvinston, Canada 78 D3 42 49N 81 52W
Älvkarleby, Sweden 9 F17 60 34N 17 26 E
Älvsbyn, Sweden 8 D19 65 40N 21 0 E
Alwar, India 42 F7 27 38N 76 34 E
Alxa Zuoqi, China 34 E3 38 50N 105 40 E
Alyaskitovyy, Russia 27 C15 64 45N 141 30 E
Alyata = Älät, Azerbaijan 25 G8 39 58N 49 25 E
Alyth, U.K. 12 E5 56 38N 3 13W
Alytus, Lithuania 9 J21 54 24N 24 3 E
Alzada, U.S.A. 80 C2 45 2N 104 25W
Am Dam, Chad 51 F9 12 40N 20 35 E
Am-Timan, Chad 51 F9 11 0N 20 10 E
Amadeus, L., Australia 61 D5 24 54S 131 0 E
Amâdi, Sudan 51 G11 5 29N 30 25 E
Amadi, Zaïre 54 B2 3 40N 26 40 E

Asike

Anzhero-Sudzhensk, *Russia* 26 D9 56 10N 86 0 E
Ánzio, *Italy* 20 D5 41 27N 12 37 E
Aoga-Shima, *Japan* 31 H9 32 28N 139 46 E
Aomori, *Japan* 30 D10 40 45N 140 45 E
Aomori □, *Japan* 30 D10 40 45N 140 40 E
Aonla, *India* 43 E8 28 16N 79 11 E
Aosta, *Italy* 20 B2 45 45N 7 20 E
Aoudéras, *Niger* 50 E6 17 45N 8 20 E
Aoulef el Arab, *Algeria* 50 C5 26 55N 1 2 E
Apa →, *S. Amer.* 94 A4 22 6S 58 2W
Apache, *U.S.A.* 81 H5 34 54N 98 22W
Apalachee B., *U.S.A.* 77 L3 30 0N 84 0W
Apalachicola, *U.S.A.* 77 L3 29 43N 84 59W
Apalachicola →, *U.S.A.* 77 L3 29 43N 84 58W
Apaporis →, *Colombia* 92 D5 1 23S 69 25W
Aparri, *Phil.* 37 A6 18 22N 121 38 E
Apàtity, *Russia* 24 A5 67 34N 33 22 E
Apatzingán, *Mexico* 86 D4 19 0N 102 20W
Apeldoorn, *Neths.* 15 B5 52 13N 5 57 E
Apennines = Appennini, *Italy* 20 B4 44 0N 10 0 E
Apia, *W. Samoa* 59 A13 13 50S 171 50W
Apiacás, Serra dos, *Brazil* 92 E7 9 50S 57 0W
Apizaco, *Mexico* 87 D5 19 26N 98 9W
Aplao, *Peru* 92 G4 16 0S 72 40W
Apo, Mt., *Phil.* 37 C7 6 53N 125 14 E
Apolakkiá, *Greece* 23 C9 36 5N 27 48 E
Apolakkiá, Órmos, *Greece* 23 C9 36 5N 27 45 E
Apollonia = Marsá Susah, *Libya* 51 B9 32 52N 21 59 E
Apolo, *Bolivia* 92 F5 14 30S 68 30W
Apostle Is., *U.S.A.* 80 B9 47 0N 90 40W
Apóstoles, *Argentina* 95 B4 28 0S 56 0W
Apostolos Andreas, C., *Cyprus* 23 D13 35 42N 34 35 E
Apoteri, *Guyana* 92 C7 4 2N 58 32W
Appalachian Mts., *U.S.A.* 76 G6 38 0N 80 0W
Appennini, *Italy* 20 B4 44 0N 10 0 E
Apple Hill, *Canada* 79 A10 45 13N 74 46W
Apple Valley, *U.S.A.* 85 L9 34 32N 117 14W
Appleby-in-Westmorland, *U.K.* 10 C5 54 35N 2 29W
Appleton, *U.S.A.* 76 C1 44 16N 88 25W
Approuague, *Fr. Guiana* 93 C8 4 20N 52 0W
Aprília, *Italy* 20 D5 41 36N 12 39 E
Apucarana, *Brazil* 95 A5 23 55S 51 33W
Apure →, *Venezuela* 92 B5 7 37N 66 25W
Apurimac →, *Peru* 92 F4 12 17S 73 56W
Aqabah = Al 'Aqabah, *Jordan* 47 F4 29 31N 35 0 E
'Aqabah, Khalīj al, *Red Sea* 44 D2 28 15N 33 20 E
'Aqdā, *Iran* 45 C7 32 26N 53 37 E
Aqīq, *Sudan* 51 E12 18 14N 38 12 E
Aqmola, *Kazakstan* 26 D8 51 10N 71 30 E
Aqrah, *Iraq* 44 B4 36 46N 43 45 E
Aqtöbe, *Kazakstan* 25 D10 50 17N 57 10 E
Aquidauana, *Brazil* 93 H7 20 30S 55 50W
Aquiles Serdán, *Mexico* 86 B3 28 37N 105 54W
Aquin, *Haiti* 89 C5 18 16N 73 24W
Aquitain, Bassin, *France* 18 D3 44 0N 0 30W
Ar Rachidiya, *Morocco* 50 B4 31 58N 4 20W
Ar Rafid, *Syria* 47 C4 32 57N 35 52 E
Ar Raḩḩālīyah, *Iraq* 44 C4 32 44N 43 23 E
Ar Ramādī, *Iraq* 44 C4 33 25N 43 20 E
Ar Ramthā, *Jordan* 47 C5 32 34N 36 0 E
Ar Raqqah, *Syria* 44 C3 35 59N 39 8 E
Ar Rass, *Si. Arabia* 44 E4 25 50N 43 40 E
Ar Rifā'ī, *Iraq* 44 D5 31 50N 46 10 E
Ar Riyāḑ, *Si. Arabia* 46 C4 24 41N 46 42 E
Ar Ru'ays, *Qatar* 45 E6 26 8N 51 12 E
Ar Rukhaymīyah, *Iraq* 44 D5 29 22N 45 38 E
Ar Ruqayyidah, *Si. Arabia* 45 E6 25 21N 49 34 E
Ar Ruşāfah, *Syria* 44 C3 35 45N 38 49 E
Ar Ruţbah, *Iraq* 44 C4 33 0N 40 15 E
Ara, *India* 43 G11 25 35N 84 32 E
'Arab, Bahr el →, *Sudan* 51 G10 9 0N 29 30 E
'Arabābād, *Iran* 45 C8 33 2N 57 41 E
Arabia, *Asia* 46 C4 25 0N 45 0 E
Arabian Desert = Es Sahrâ' Esh Sharqîya, *Egypt* 51 C11 27 30N 32 30 E
Arabian Gulf = Gulf, The, *Asia* 45 E6 27 0N 50 0 E
Arabian Sea, *Ind. Oc.* 29 H10 16 0N 65 0 E
Aracaju, *Brazil* 93 F11 10 55S 37 4W
Aracataca, *Colombia* 92 A4 10 38N 74 9W
Aracati, *Brazil* 93 D11 4 30S 37 44W
Araçatuba, *Brazil* 95 A5 21 10S 50 30W
Aracena, *Spain* 19 D2 37 53N 6 38W
Araçuai, *Brazil* 93 G10 16 52S 42 4W
'Arad, *Israel* 47 D4 31 15N 35 12 E
Arad, *Romania* 17 E11 46 10N 21 20 E
Arada, *Chad* 51 F9 15 0N 20 20 E
Aradhippou, *Cyprus* 23 E12 34 57N 33 36 E
Arafura Sea, *E. Indies* 37 F8 9 0S 135 0 E
Aragón □, *Spain* 19 B5 41 25N 0 40W
Aragón →, *Spain* 19 A5 42 13N 1 44W
Araguacema, *Brazil* 93 E9 8 50S 49 20W
Araguaia →, *Brazil* 93 E9 5 21S 48 41W
Araguari, *Brazil* 93 G9 18 38S 48 11W
Araguari →, *Brazil* 93 C9 1 15N 49 55W
Arak, *Algeria* 50 C5 25 20N 3 45 E
Arāk, *Iran* 45 C6 34 0N 49 40 E
Arakan Coast, *Burma* 41 K19 19 0N 94 0 E
Arakan Yoma, *Burma* 41 K19 20 0N 94 40 E
Araks = Aras, Rūd-e →, *Azerbaijan* 44 B5 40 5N 48 29 E
Aral, *Kazakstan* 26 E7 46 41N 61 45 E
Aral Sea, *Asia* 26 E7 44 30N 60 0 E
Aral Tengizi = Aral Sea, *Asia* 26 E7 44 30N 60 0 E
Aralsk = Aral, *Kazakstan* 26 E7 46 41N 61 45 E
Aralskoye More = Aral Sea, *Asia* 26 E7 44 30N 60 0 E
Aramac, *Australia* 62 C4 22 58S 145 14 E
Arambag, *India* 43 H12 22 53N 87 48 E
Aran I., *Ireland* 13 B3 55 0N 8 30W
Aran Is., *Ireland* 13 C2 53 6N 9 38W
Aranda de Duero, *Spain* 19 B4 41 39N 3 42W
Arandān, *Iran* 44 C5 35 23N 46 55 E
Aranjuez, *Spain* 19 B4 40 1N 3 40W
Aranos, *Namibia* 56 C2 24 9S 19 7 E
Aransas Pass, *U.S.A.* 81 M6 27 55N 97 9W
Araouane, *Mali* 50 E4 18 55N 3 30W
Arapahoe, *U.S.A.* 80 E5 40 18N 99 54W
Arapey Grande →, *Uruguay* 94 C4 30 55S 57 49W
Arapiraca, *Brazil* 93 E11 9 45S 36 39W
Arapongas, *Brazil* 95 A5 23 29S 51 28W
Ar'ar, *Si. Arabia* 44 D4 30 59N 41 2 E
Araranguá, *Brazil* 95 B6 29 0S 49 30W
Araraquara, *Brazil* 93 H9 21 50S 48 0W
Ararás, Serra das, *Brazil* 95 B5 25 0S 53 10W
Ararat, *Australia* 63 F3 37 16S 143 0 E
Ararat, Mt. = Ağrı Dağı, *Turkey* 25 G7 39 50N 44 15 E
Araria, *India* 43 F12 26 9N 87 33 E
Araripe, Chapada do, *Brazil* 93 E11 7 20S 40 0W
Araruama, L. de, *Brazil* 95 A7 22 53S 42 12W
Aras, Rūd-e →, *Azerbaijan* 44 B5 40 5N 48 29 E
Arauca, *Colombia* 92 B4 7 0N 70 40W
Arauca →, *Venezuela* 92 B5 7 24N 66 35W
Arauco, *Chile* 94 D1 37 16S 73 25W
Arauco □, *Chile* 94 D1 37 40S 73 25W
Araxá, *Brazil* 93 G9 19 35S 46 55W
Araya, Pen. de, *Venezuela* 92 A6 10 40N 64 0W
Arbat, *Iraq* 44 C5 35 25N 45 35 E
Arbatax, *Italy* 20 E3 39 56N 9 42 E
Arbil, *Iraq* 44 B5 36 15N 44 5 E
Arborfield, *Canada* 73 C8 53 6N 103 39W
Arborg, *Canada* 73 C9 50 54N 97 13W
Arbroath, *U.K.* 12 E6 56 34N 2 35W
Arbuckle, *U.S.A.* 84 F4 39 1N 122 3W
Arcachon, *France* 18 D3 44 40N 1 10W
Arcade, *U.S.A.* 78 D6 42 32N 78 25W
Arcadia, *Fla., U.S.A.* 77 M5 27 13N 81 52W
Arcadia, *La., U.S.A.* 81 J8 32 33N 92 55W
Arcadia, *Nebr., U.S.A.* 80 E5 41 25N 99 8W
Arcadia, *Pa., U.S.A.* 78 F6 40 47N 78 51W
Arcadia, *Wis., U.S.A.* 80 C9 44 15N 91 30W
Arcata, *U.S.A.* 82 F1 40 52N 124 5W
Archangel = Arkhangelsk, *Russia* 24 B7 64 38N 40 36 E
Archbald, *U.S.A.* 79 E9 41 30N 75 32W
Archer →, *Australia* 62 A3 13 28S 141 41 E
Archer B., *Australia* 62 A3 13 20S 141 30 E
Archers Post, *Kenya* 54 B4 0 35N 37 35 E
Arcila = Asilah, *Morocco* 50 A3 35 29N 6 0W
Arckaringa, *Australia* 63 D1 27 56S 134 45 E
Arckaringa Cr. →, *Australia* 63 D2 28 10S 135 22 E
Arco, *U.S.A.* 82 E7 43 38N 113 18W
Arcola, *Canada* 73 D8 49 40N 102 30W
Arcos de la Frontera, *Spain* 19 D3 36 45N 5 49W
Arcot, *India* 40 N11 12 53N 79 20 E
Arcoverde, *Brazil* 93 E11 8 25S 37 4W
Arctic Bay, *Canada* 69 A11 73 1N 85 7W
Arctic Ocean, *Arctic* 4 B18 78 0N 160 0W
Arctic Red River, *Canada* 68 B6 67 15N 134 0W
Arda →, *Bulgaria* 21 D12 41 40N 26 29 E
Ardabīl, *Iran* 45 B6 38 15N 48 18 E
Ardakān = Sepīdān, *Iran* 45 D7 30 20N 52 5 E
Ardee, *Ireland* 13 C5 53 52N 6 33W
Arden, *Canada* 78 B8 44 43N 76 56W
Arden, *Calif., U.S.A.* 84 G5 38 36N 121 33W
Arden, *Nev., U.S.A.* 85 J11 36 1N 115 14W
Ardenne, *Belgium* 15 E5 49 50N 5 5 E
Ardennes = Ardenne, *Belgium* 15 E5 49 50N 5 5 E
Ardestān, *Iran* 45 C7 33 20N 52 25 E
Ardgour, *U.K.* 12 E3 56 45N 5 25W
Ardlethan, *Australia* 63 E4 34 22S 146 53 E
Ardmore, *Australia* 62 C2 21 39S 139 11 E
Ardmore, *Okla., U.S.A.* 81 H6 34 10N 97 8W
Ardmore, *Pa., U.S.A.* 79 G9 39 58N 75 18W
Ardmore, *S. Dak., U.S.A.* 80 D3 43 1N 103 40W
Ardnacrusha, *Ireland* 13 D3 52 43N 8 38W
Ardnamurchan, Pt. of, *U.K.* 12 E2 56 43N 6 14W
Ardrossan, *Australia* 63 E2 34 26S 137 53 E
Ardrossan, *U.K.* 12 F4 55 39N 4 49W
Ards □, *U.K.* 13 B6 54 35N 5 30W
Ards Pen., *U.K.* 13 B6 54 33N 5 34W
Arecibo, *Puerto Rico* 89 C6 18 29N 66 43W
Areia Branca, *Brazil* 93 D11 5 0S 37 0W
Arena, Pt., *U.S.A.* 84 G3 38 57N 123 44W
Arendal, *Norway* 9 G13 58 28N 8 46 E
Arequipa, *Peru* 92 G4 16 20S 71 30W
Arero, *Ethiopia* 51 H12 4 41N 38 50 E
Arévalo, *Spain* 19 B3 41 3N 4 43W
Arezzo, *Italy* 20 C4 43 25N 11 53 E
Argamakmur, *Indonesia* 36 E2 3 35S 102 0 E
Arganda, *Spain* 19 B4 40 19N 3 26W
Argentan, *France* 18 B3 48 45N 0 1W
Argentário, Mte., *Italy* 20 C4 42 24N 11 9 E
Argentia, *Canada* 71 C9 47 18N 53 58W
Argentina ■, *S. Amer.* 96 D3 35 0S 66 0W
Argentina Is., *Antarctica* 5 C17 66 0S 64 0W
Argentino, L., *Argentina* 96 G2 50 10S 73 0W
Argeş →, *Romania* 17 F14 44 11N 26 25 E
Arghandab →, *Afghan.* 42 D1 31 30N 64 15 E
Argo, *Sudan* 51 E11 19 28N 30 30 E
Argolikós Kólpos, *Greece* 21 F10 37 20N 22 52 E
Árgos, *Greece* 21 F10 37 40N 22 43 E
Argostólion, *Greece* 21 E9 38 12N 20 33 E
Arguello, Pt., *U.S.A.* 85 L6 34 35N 120 39W
Arguineguín, *Canary Is.* 22 G4 27 46N 15 41W
Argun →, *Russia* 27 D13 53 20N 121 28 E
Argungu, *Nigeria* 50 F5 12 40N 4 31 E
Argus Pk., *U.S.A.* 85 K9 35 52N 117 26W
Argyle, *U.S.A.* 80 A6 48 20N 96 49W
Argyle, L., *Australia* 60 C4 16 20S 128 40 E
Argyll & Bute □, *U.K.* 12 E3 56 13N 5 28W
Århus, *Denmark* 9 H14 56 8N 10 11 E
Ariadnoye, *Russia* 30 B7 45 8N 134 25 E
Ariamsvlei, *Namibia* 56 D2 28 9S 19 51 E
Arica, *Chile* 92 G4 18 32S 70 20W
Arica, *Colombia* 92 D4 2 0S 71 50W
Arico, *Canary Is.* 22 F3 28 9N 16 29W
Arid, C., *Australia* 61 F3 34 1S 123 10 E
Arida, *Japan* 31 G7 34 5N 135 8 E
Arīḩā, *Syria* 44 C3 35 49N 36 35 E
Arilla, Ákra, *Greece* 23 A3 39 43N 19 39 E
Arima, *Trin. & Tob.* 89 D7 10 38N 61 17W
Arinos →, *Brazil* 92 F7 10 25S 58 20W
Ario de Rosales, *Mexico* 86 D4 19 12N 102 0W
Aripuanã, *Brazil* 92 E6 9 25S 60 30W
Aripuanã →, *Brazil* 92 E6 5 7S 60 25W
Ariquemes, *Brazil* 92 E6 9 55S 63 6W
Arisaig, *U.K.* 12 E3 56 55N 5 51W
Aristazabal I., *Canada* 72 C3 52 40N 129 10W
Arivaca, *U.S.A.* 83 L8 31 37N 111 25W
Arivonimamo, *Madag.* 57 B8 19 1S 47 11 E
Arizaro, Salar de, *Argentina* 94 A2 24 40S 67 50W
Arizona, *Argentina* 94 D2 35 45S 65 25W
Arizona □, *U.S.A.* 83 J8 34 0N 112 0W
Arizpe, *Mexico* 86 A2 30 20N 110 11W
Arjeplog, *Sweden* 8 D18 66 3N 18 2 E
Arjona, *Colombia* 92 A3 10 14N 75 22W
Arjuno, *Indonesia* 37 G15 7 49S 112 34 E
Arka, *Russia* 27 C15 60 15N 142 0 E
Arkadelphia, *U.S.A.* 81 H8 34 7N 93 4W
Arkaig, L., *U.K.* 12 E3 56 59N 5 10W
Arkalyk = Arqalyk, *Kazakstan* 26 D7 50 13N 66 50 E
Arkansas □, *U.S.A.* 81 H8 35 0N 92 30W
Arkansas →, *U.S.A.* 81 J9 33 47N 91 4W
Arkansas City, *U.S.A.* 81 G6 37 4N 97 2W
Arkhángelos, *Greece* 23 C10 36 13N 28 7 E
Arkhangelsk, *Russia* 24 B7 64 38N 40 36 E
Arklow, *Ireland* 13 D5 52 48N 6 10W
Arkticheskiy, Mys, *Russia* 27 A10 81 10N 95 0 E
Arlanzón →, *Spain* 19 A3 42 3N 4 17W
Arlberg P., *Austria* 16 E6 47 9N 10 12 E
Arlee, *U.S.A.* 82 C6 47 10N 114 5W
Arles, *France* 18 E6 43 41N 4 40 E
Arlington, *S. Africa* 57 D4 28 1S 27 53 E
Arlington, *Oreg., U.S.A.* 82 D3 45 43N 120 12W
Arlington, *S. Dak., U.S.A.* 80 C6 44 22N 97 8W
Arlington, *Va., U.S.A.* 76 F7 38 53N 77 7W
Arlington, *Wash., U.S.A.* 84 B4 48 12N 122 8W
Arlington Heights, *U.S.A.* 76 D2 42 5N 87 59W
Arlon, *Belgium* 15 E5 49 42N 5 49 E
Armagh, *U.K.* 13 B5 54 21N 6 39W
Armagh □, *U.K.* 13 B5 54 18N 6 37W
Armavir, *Russia* 25 E7 45 2N 41 7 E
Armenia, *Colombia* 92 C3 4 35N 75 45W
Armenia ■, *Asia* 25 F7 40 20N 45 0 E
Armenistís, Ákra, *Greece* 23 C9 36 8N 27 42 E
Armidale, *Australia* 63 E5 30 30S 151 40 E
Armour, *U.S.A.* 80 D5 43 19N 98 21W
Armstrong, *B.C., Canada* 72 C5 50 25N 119 10W
Armstrong, *Ont., Canada* 70 B2 50 18N 89 4W
Armstrong, *U.S.A.* 81 M6 26 56N 97 47W
Armstrong →, *Australia* 60 C5 16 35S 131 40 E
Arnarfjörður, *Iceland* 8 D2 65 48N 23 40W
Arnaud →, *Canada* 69 B12 60 0N 70 0W
Arnauti, C., *Cyprus* 23 D11 35 6N 32 17 E
Arnett, *U.S.A.* 81 G5 36 8N 99 46W
Arnhem, *Neths.* 15 C5 51 58N 5 55 E
Arnhem, C., *Australia* 62 A2 12 20S 137 30 E
Arnhem B., *Australia* 62 A2 12 20S 136 10 E
Arnhem Land, *Australia* 62 A1 13 10S 134 30 E
Arno →, *Italy* 20 C4 43 41N 10 17 E
Arno Bay, *Australia* 63 E2 33 54S 136 34 E
Arnold, *Calif., U.S.A.* 84 G6 38 15N 120 20W
Arnold, *Nebr., U.S.A.* 80 E4 41 26N 100 12W
Arnot, *Canada* 73 B9 55 56N 96 41W
Arnøy, *Norway* 8 A19 70 9N 20 40 E
Arnprior, *Canada* 70 C4 45 26N 76 21W
Arnsberg, *Germany* 16 C5 51 24N 8 5 E
Aroab, *Namibia* 56 D2 26 41S 19 39 E
Arqalyk, *Kazakstan* 26 D7 50 13N 66 50 E
Arrabury, *Australia* 63 D3 26 45S 141 0 E
Arrah = Ara, *India* 43 G11 25 35N 84 32 E
Arran, *U.K.* 12 F3 55 34N 5 12W
Arrandale, *Canada* 72 C3 54 57N 130 0W
Arras, *France* 18 A5 50 17N 2 46 E
Arrecife, *Canary Is.* 22 F6 28 57N 13 37W
Arrecifes, *Argentina* 94 C3 34 6S 60 9W
Arrée, Mts. d', *France* 18 B2 48 26N 3 55W
Arriaga, *Chiapas, Mexico* 87 D6 16 15N 93 52W
Arriaga, *San Luis Potosí, Mexico* 86 C4 21 55N 101 23W
Arrilalah P.O., *Australia* 62 C3 23 43S 143 54 E
Arrino, *Australia* 61 E2 29 30S 115 40 E
Arrow, L., *Ireland* 13 B3 54 3N 8 19W
Arrow Rock Res., *U.S.A.* 82 E6 43 45N 115 50W
Arrowhead, *Canada* 72 C5 50 40N 117 55W
Arrowhead, L., *U.S.A.* 85 L9 34 16N 117 10W
Arrowtown, *N.Z.* 59 L2 44 57S 168 50 E
Arroyo Grande, *U.S.A.* 85 K6 35 7N 120 35W
Ars, *Iran* 44 B5 37 9N 47 46 E
Arsenault L., *Canada* 73 B7 55 6N 108 32W
Arsenev, *Russia* 30 B6 44 10N 133 15 E
Árta, *Greece* 21 E9 39 8N 21 2 E
Artà, *Spain* 22 B10 39 41N 3 21 E
Arteaga, *Mexico* 86 D4 18 50N 102 20W
Artem, *Russia* 30 C6 43 22N 132 13 E
Artemovsk, *Russia* 27 D10 54 45N 93 35 E
Artesia = Mosomane, *Botswana* 56 C4 24 2S 26 19 E
Artesia, *U.S.A.* 81 J2 32 51N 104 24W
Artesia Wells, *U.S.A.* 81 L5 28 17N 99 17W
Artesian, *U.S.A.* 80 C6 44 1N 97 55W
Arthur →, *Australia* 62 G3 41 2S 144 40 E
Arthur Cr. →, *Australia* 62 C2 22 30S 136 25 E
Arthur Pt., *Australia* 62 C5 22 7S 150 3 E
Arthur's Pass, *N.Z.* 59 K3 42 54S 171 35 E
Arthur's Town, *Bahamas* 89 B4 24 38N 75 42W
Artigas, *Uruguay* 94 C4 30 20S 56 30W
Artillery L., *Canada* 73 A7 63 9N 107 52W
Artois, *France* 18 A5 50 20N 2 30 E
Artsyz, *Ukraine* 17 E15 46 4N 29 26 E
Artvin, *Turkey* 25 F7 41 14N 41 44 E
Aru, Kepulauan, *Indonesia* 37 F8 6 0S 134 30 E
Aru Is. = Aru, Kepulauan, *Indonesia* 37 F8 6 0S 134 30 E
Aru Meru □, *Tanzania* 54 C4 3 20S 36 50 E
Arua, *Uganda* 54 B3 3 1N 30 58 E
Aruanã, *Brazil* 93 F8 14 54S 51 10W
Aruba ■, *W. Indies* 89 D6 12 30N 70 0W
Arucas, *Canary Is.* 22 F4 28 7N 15 32W
Arumpo, *Australia* 63 E3 33 48S 142 55 E
Arun →, *Nepal* 43 F12 26 55N 87 10 E
Arunachal Pradesh □, *India* 41 E19 28 0N 95 0 E
Arusha, *Tanzania* 54 C4 3 20S 36 40 E
Arusha □, *Tanzania* 54 C4 4 0S 36 30 E
Arusha Chini, *Tanzania* 54 C4 3 32S 37 20 E
Aruwimi →, *Zaïre* 54 B1 1 13N 23 36 E
Arvada, *U.S.A.* 82 D10 44 39N 106 8W
Árvi, *Greece* 23 E7 34 59N 25 28 E
Arvida, *Canada* 71 C5 48 25N 71 14W
Arvidsjaur, *Sweden* 8 D18 65 35N 19 10 E
Arvika, *Sweden* 9 G15 59 40N 12 36 E
Arvin, *U.S.A.* 85 K8 35 12N 118 50W
Arxan, *China* 33 B6 47 11N 119 57 E
Aryirádhes, *Greece* 23 B3 39 27N 19 58 E
Aryiroúpolis, *Greece* 23 D6 35 17N 24 20 E
Arys, *Kazakstan* 26 E7 42 26N 68 48 E
Arzamas, *Russia* 24 C7 55 27N 43 55 E
Arzew, *Algeria* 50 A4 35 50N 0 23W
Aş Şadr, *U.A.E.* 45 E7 24 40N 54 41 E
Aş Şafā, *Syria* 47 B6 33 10N 37 0 E
'As Saffānīyah, *Si. Arabia* 45 D6 28 5N 48 50 E
As Safīrah, *Syria* 44 B3 36 5N 37 21 E
Aş Şahm, *Oman* 45 E8 24 10N 56 53 E
As Sājir, *Si. Arabia* 44 E5 25 11N 44 36 E
As Salamīyah, *Syria* 44 C3 35 1N 37 2 E
As Salţ, *Jordan* 47 C4 32 2N 35 43 E
As Sal'w'a, *Qatar* 45 E6 24 23N 50 50 E
As Samāwah, *Iraq* 44 D5 31 15N 45 15 E
As Sanamayn, *Syria* 47 B5 33 3N 36 10 E
As Sukhnah, *Syria* 44 C3 34 52N 38 52 E
As Sulaymānīyah, *Iraq* 44 C5 35 35N 45 29 E
As Sulaymī, *Si. Arabia* 44 E4 26 17N 41 21 E
As Summān, *Si. Arabia* 44 E5 25 0N 47 0 E
As Suwaydā', *Syria* 47 C5 32 40N 36 30 E
As Suwaydā' □, *Syria* 47 C5 32 45N 36 45 E
Aş Şuwayrah, *Iraq* 44 C5 32 55N 45 0 E
Asab, *Namibia* 56 D2 25 30S 18 0 E
Asahi-Gawa →, *Japan* 31 G6 34 36N 133 58 E
Asahigawa, *Japan* 30 C11 43 46N 142 22 E
Asansol, *India* 43 H12 23 40N 87 1 E
Asbesberge, *S. Africa* 56 D3 29 0S 23 0 E
Asbestos, *Canada* 71 C5 45 47N 71 58W
Asbury Park, *U.S.A.* 79 F10 40 13N 74 1W
Ascensión, *Mexico* 86 A3 31 6N 107 59W
Ascensión, B. de la, *Mexico* 87 D7 19 50N 87 20W
Ascension I., *Atl. Oc.* 49 G2 8 0S 14 15W
Aschaffenburg, *Germany* 16 D5 49 58N 9 6 E
Aschersleben, *Germany* 16 C6 51 45N 11 29 E
Áscoli Piceno, *Italy* 20 C5 42 51N 13 34 E
Ascope, *Peru* 92 E3 7 46S 79 8W
Ascotán, *Chile* 94 A2 21 45S 68 17W
Aseb, *Eritrea* 46 E3 13 0N 42 40 E
Asela, *Ethiopia* 51 G12 8 0N 39 0 E
Asenovgrad, *Bulgaria* 21 C11 42 1N 24 51 E
Asgata, *Cyprus* 23 E12 34 46N 33 15 E
Ash Fork, *U.S.A.* 83 J7 35 13N 112 29W
Ash Grove, *U.S.A.* 81 G8 37 19N 93 35W
Ash Shām, Bādiyat, *Asia* 28 F7 32 0N 40 0 E
Ash Shamāl □, *Lebanon* 47 A5 34 25N 36 0 E
Ash Shāmīyah, *Iraq* 44 D5 31 55N 44 35 E
Ash Shāriqah, *U.A.E.* 45 E7 25 23N 55 26 E
Ash Sharmah, *Si. Arabia* 44 D2 28 1N 35 16 E
Ash Sharqāt, *Iraq* 44 C4 35 27N 43 16 E
Ash Sharqi, Al Jabal, *Lebanon* 47 B5 33 40N 36 10 E
Ash Shaţrah, *Iraq* 44 D5 31 30N 46 10 E
Ash Shawbak, *Jordan* 44 D2 30 32N 35 34 E
Ash Shawmari, J., *Jordan* 47 E5 30 35N 36 35 E
Ash Shaykh, J., *Lebanon* 47 B4 33 25N 35 50 E
Ash Shināfīyah, *Iraq* 44 D5 31 35N 44 39 E
Ash Shu'aybah, *Si. Arabia* 44 E5 27 53N 44 43 E
Ash Shumlūl, *Si. Arabia* 44 E5 26 31N 47 20 E
Ash Shūr'a, *Iraq* 44 C4 35 58N 43 13 E
Ash Shurayf, *Si. Arabia* 44 E3 25 43N 39 14 E
Ash Shuwayfāt, *Lebanon* 47 B4 33 45N 35 30 E
Asha, *Russia* 24 D10 55 0N 57 16 E
Ashau, *Vietnam* 38 D6 16 6N 107 22 E
Ashburn, *U.S.A.* 77 K4 31 43N 83 39W
Ashburton, *N.Z.* 59 K3 43 53S 171 48 E
Ashburton →, *Australia* 60 D1 21 40S 114 56 E
Ashburton Downs, *Australia* 60 D2 23 25S 117 4 E
Ashby de la Zouch, *U.K.* 10 E6 52 46N 1 29W
Ashcroft, *Canada* 72 C4 50 40N 121 20W
Ashdod, *Israel* 47 D3 31 49N 34 35 E
Asheboro, *U.S.A.* 77 H6 35 43N 79 49W
Asherton, *U.S.A.* 81 L5 28 27N 99 46W
Asheville, *U.S.A.* 77 H4 35 36N 82 33W
Asheweig →, *Canada* 70 B2 54 17N 87 12W
Ashford, *Australia* 63 D5 29 15S 151 3 E
Ashford, *U.K.* 11 F8 51 8N 0 53 E
Ashford, *U.S.A.* 82 C2 46 46N 122 2W
Ashgabat, *Turkmenistan* 26 F6 38 0N 57 50 E
Ashibetsu, *Japan* 30 C11 43 31N 142 11 E
Ashikaga, *Japan* 31 F9 36 28N 139 29 E
Ashizuri-Zaki, *Japan* 31 H6 32 44N 133 0 E
Ashkarkot, *Afghan.* 42 C2 33 3N 67 58 E
Ashkhabad = Ashgabat, *Turkmenistan* 26 F6 38 0N 57 50 E
Ashland, *Kans., U.S.A.* 81 G5 37 11N 99 46W
Ashland, *Ky., U.S.A.* 76 F4 38 28N 82 38W
Ashland, *Maine, U.S.A.* 71 C6 46 38N 68 24W
Ashland, *Mont., U.S.A.* 82 D10 45 36N 106 16W
Ashland, *Nebr., U.S.A.* 80 E6 41 3N 96 23W
Ashland, *Ohio, U.S.A.* 78 F2 40 52N 82 19W
Ashland, *Oreg., U.S.A.* 82 E2 42 12N 122 43W
Ashland, *Pa., U.S.A.* 79 F8 40 45N 76 22W
Ashland, *Va., U.S.A.* 76 G7 37 46N 77 29W
Ashland, *Wis., U.S.A.* 80 B9 46 35N 90 53W
Ashley, *N. Dak., U.S.A.* 80 B5 46 2N 99 22W
Ashley, *Pa., U.S.A.* 79 E9 41 12N 75 55W
Ashmont, *Canada* 72 C6 54 7N 111 35W
Ashmore Reef, *Australia* 60 B3 12 14S 123 5 E
Ashmyany, *Belarus* 9 J21 54 26N 25 52 E
Ashqelon, *Israel* 47 D3 31 42N 34 35 E
Ashtabula, *U.S.A.* 78 E4 41 52N 80 47W
Ashton, *S. Africa* 56 E3 33 50S 20 5 E
Ashton, *U.S.A.* 82 D8 44 4N 111 27W
Ashton under Lyne, *U.K.* 10 D5 53 29N 2 6W
Ashuanipi, L., *Canada* 71 B6 52 45N 66 15W
Asia, Kepulauan, *Indonesia* 37 D8 1 0N 131 13 E
Āsīā Bak, *Iran* 45 C6 35 19N 50 30 E
Asifabad, *India* 40 K11 19 20N 79 24 E
Asike, *Indonesia* 37 F10 6 39S 140 24 E

Asilah

Asilah, Morocco 50 A3 35 29N 6 0W
Asinara, Italy 20 D3 41 4N 8 16 E
Asinara, G. dell', Italy 20 D3 41 0N 8 30 E
Asino, Russia 26 D9 57 0N 86 0 E
Asipovichy, Belarus 17 B15 53 19N 28 33 E
'Asīr □, Si. Arabia 46 D3 18 40N 42 30 E
Asir, Ras, Somali Rep. 46 E5 11 55N 51 10 E
Askersund, Sweden 9 G16 58 53N 14 55 E
Askham, S. Africa 56 D3 26 59S 20 47 E
Askim, Norway 9 G14 59 35N 11 10 E
Askja, Iceland 8 D5 65 3N 16 48W
Askøy, Norway 9 F11 60 29N 5 10 E
Asmara = Asmera, Eritrea 51 E12 15 19N 38 55 E
Asmera, Eritrea 51 E12 15 19N 38 55 E
Åsnen, Sweden 9 H16 56 37N 14 45 E
Asotin, U.S.A. 82 C5 46 20N 117 3W
Aspen, U.S.A. 83 G10 39 11N 106 49W
Aspermont, U.S.A. 81 J4 33 8N 100 14W
Aspiring, Mt., N.Z. 59 L2 44 23S 168 46 E
Asprókavos, Ákra, Greece 23 B4 39 21N 20 6 E
Aspur, India 42 H6 23 58N 74 7 E
Asquith, Canada 73 C7 52 8N 107 13W
Assad, Bahret, Syria 44 C3 36 0N 38 15 E
Assam □, India 41 F18 26 0N 93 0 E
Asse, Belgium 15 D4 50 24N 4 10 E
Assen, Neths. 15 B6 53 0N 6 35 E
Assini, Ivory C. 50 G4 5 9N 3 17W
Assiniboia, Canada 73 D7 49 40N 105 59W
Assiniboine →, Canada 73 D9 49 53N 97 8W
Assis, Brazil 95 A5 22 40S 50 20W
Assisi, Italy 20 C5 43 4N 12 37 E
Assynt, L., U.K. 12 C3 58 10N 5 3W
Astara, Azerbaijan 25 G8 38 30N 48 50 E
Asteroúsia, Greece 23 E7 34 59N 25 3 E
Asti, Italy 20 B3 44 54N 8 12 E
Astipálaia, Greece 21 F12 36 32N 26 22 E
Astorga, Spain 19 A2 42 29N 6 8W
Astoria, U.S.A. 84 D3 46 11N 123 50W
Astrakhan, Russia 25 E8 46 25N 48 5 E
Astrakhan-Bazàr, Azerbaijan 25 G8 39 14N 48 30 E
Asturias □, Spain 19 A3 43 15N 6 0W
Asunción, Paraguay 94 B4 25 10S 57 30W
Asunción Nochixtlán, Mexico 87 D5 17 28N 97 14W
Aswa →, Uganda 54 B3 3 43N 31 55 E
Aswân, Egypt 51 D11 24 4N 32 57 E
Aswân High Dam = Sadd el Aali, Egypt 51 D11 23 54N 32 54 E
Asyût, Egypt 51 C11 27 11N 31 4 E
At Țafilah, Jordan 47 E4 30 45N 35 30 E
At Tā'if, Si. Arabia 46 C3 21 5N 40 27 E
Aț Țirāq, Si. Arabia 44 E5 27 19N 44 33 E
Atacama □, Chile 94 B2 27 30S 70 0W
Atacama, Desierto de, Chile 94 A2 24 0S 69 20W
Atacama, Salar de, Chile 94 A2 23 30S 68 20W
Atakpamé, Togo 50 G5 7 31N 1 13 E
Atalaya, Peru 92 F4 10 45S 73 50W
Atalaya de Femes, Canary Is. 22 F6 28 56N 13 47W
Atami, Japan 31 G9 35 5N 139 4 E
Atapupu, Indonesia 37 F6 9 0S 124 51 E
Atâr, Mauritania 50 D2 20 30N 13 5W
Atascadero, U.S.A. 83 J3 35 29N 120 40W
Atasu, Kazakstan 26 E8 48 30N 71 0 E
Atauro, Indonesia 37 F7 8 10S 125 30 E
Atbara, Sudan 51 E11 17 42N 33 59 E
'Atbara →, Sudan 51 E11 17 40N 33 56 E
Atbasar, Kazakstan 26 D7 51 48N 68 20 E
Atchafalaya B., U.S.A. 81 L9 29 25N 91 25W
Atchison, U.S.A. 80 F7 39 34N 95 7W
Ath, Belgium 15 D3 50 38N 3 47 E
Athabasca, Canada 72 C6 54 45N 113 20W
Athabasca →, Canada 73 B6 58 40N 110 50W
Athabasca, L., Canada 73 B7 59 15N 109 15W
Athboy, Ireland 13 C5 53 37N 6 56W
Athenry, Ireland 13 C3 53 18N 8 44W
Athens = Athínai, Greece 21 F10 37 58N 23 46 E
Athens, Ala., U.S.A. 77 H2 34 48N 86 58W
Athens, Ga., U.S.A. 77 J4 33 57N 83 23W
Athens, N.Y., U.S.A. 79 D11 42 16N 73 49W
Athens, Ohio, U.S.A. 76 F4 39 20N 82 6W
Athens, Pa., U.S.A. 79 E8 41 57N 76 31W
Athens, Tenn., U.S.A. 77 H3 35 27N 84 36W
Athens, Tex., U.S.A. 81 J7 32 12N 95 51W
Atherley, Canada 78 B5 44 37N 79 20W
Atherton, Australia 62 B4 17 17S 145 30 E
Athienou, Cyprus 23 D12 35 3N 33 32 E
Athínai, Greece 21 F10 37 58N 23 46 E
Athlone, Ireland 13 C4 53 25N 7 56W
Athna, Cyprus 23 D12 35 3N 33 47 E
Atholl, Forest of, U.K. 12 E5 56 51N 3 50W
Atholville, Canada 71 C6 47 59N 66 43W
Áthos, Greece 21 D11 40 9N 24 22 E
Athy, Ireland 13 D5 53 0N 7 0W
Ati, Chad 51 F8 13 13N 18 20 E
Atiak, Uganda 54 B3 3 12N 32 2 E
Atico, Peru 92 G4 16 14S 73 40W
Atikokan, Canada 70 C1 48 45N 91 37W
Atikonak L., Canada 71 B7 52 40N 64 32W
Atka, Russia 27 C16 60 50N 151 48 E
Atkinson, U.S.A. 80 D5 42 32N 98 59W
Atlanta, Ga., U.S.A. 77 J3 33 45N 84 23W
Atlanta, Tex., U.S.A. 81 J7 33 7N 94 10W
Atlantic, U.S.A. 80 E7 41 24N 95 1W
Atlantic City, U.S.A. 76 F8 39 21N 74 27W
Atlantic Ocean 2 E9 0 0 20 0W
Atlas Mts. = Haut Atlas, Morocco 50 B3 32 30N 5 0W
Atlin, Canada 72 B2 59 31N 133 41W
Atlin, L., Canada 72 B2 59 26N 133 45W
Atmore, U.S.A. 77 K2 31 2N 87 29W
Atoka, U.S.A. 81 H6 34 23N 96 8W
Atolia, U.S.A. 85 K9 35 19N 117 37W
Atoyac →, Mexico 87 D5 16 30N 97 31W
Atrak = Atrek →, Turkmenistan 45 B8 37 35N 53 58 E
Atrauli, India 42 E8 28 2N 78 20 E
Atrek →, Turkmenistan 45 B8 37 35N 53 58 E
Atsuta, Japan 30 C10 43 24N 141 26 E
Attalla, U.S.A. 77 H2 34 1N 86 6W
Attáviros, Greece 23 C9 36 12N 27 50 E
Attawapiskat, Canada 70 B3 52 56N 82 24W
Attawapiskat →, Canada 70 B3 52 57N 82 18W
Attawapiskat, L., Canada 70 B2 52 18N 87 54W
Attica, U.S.A. 76 E2 40 18N 87 15W
Attikamagen L., Canada 71 A6 55 0N 66 30W
Attleboro, U.S.A. 79 E13 41 57N 71 17W
Attock, Pakistan 42 C5 33 52N 72 20 E
Attopeu, Laos 38 E6 14 48N 106 50 E
Attur, India 40 P11 11 35N 78 30 E
Atuel →, Argentina 94 D2 36 17S 66 50W
Åtvidaberg, Sweden 9 G17 58 12N 16 0 E
Atwater, U.S.A. 83 H3 37 21N 120 37W
Atwood, Canada 78 C3 43 40N 81 1W
Atwood, U.S.A. 80 F4 39 48N 101 3W
Atyraū, Kazakstan 25 E9 47 5N 52 0 E
Au Sable →, U.S.A. 76 C4 44 25N 83 20W
Au Sable Pt., U.S.A. 70 C2 46 40N 86 10W
Aubagne, France 18 E6 43 17N 5 37 E
Aubarca, C., Spain 22 B7 39 4N 1 22 E
Aube →, France 18 B5 48 34N 3 43 E
Auberry, U.S.A. 84 H7 37 7N 119 29W
Auburn, Ala., U.S.A. 77 J3 32 36N 85 29W
Auburn, Calif., U.S.A. 84 G5 38 54N 121 4W
Auburn, Ind., U.S.A. 76 E3 41 22N 85 4W
Auburn, N.Y., U.S.A. 79 D8 42 56N 76 34W
Auburn, Nebr., U.S.A. 80 E7 40 23N 95 51W
Auburn, Wash., U.S.A. 84 C4 47 18N 122 14W
Auburn Ra., Australia 63 D5 25 15S 150 30 E
Auburndale, U.S.A. 77 L5 28 4N 81 48W
Aubusson, France 18 D5 45 57N 2 11 E
Auch, France 18 E4 43 39N 0 36 E
Auckland, N.Z. 59 G5 36 52S 174 46 E
Auckland Is., Pac. Oc. 64 N8 50 40S 166 5 E
Aude →, France 18 E5 43 13N 3 14 E
Auden, Canada 70 B2 50 14N 87 53W
Audubon, U.S.A. 80 E7 41 43N 94 56W
Augathella, Australia 63 D4 25 48S 146 35 E
Augrabies Falls, S. Africa 56 D3 28 35S 20 20 E
Augsburg, Germany 16 D6 48 25N 10 52 E
Augusta, Italy 20 F6 37 13N 15 13 E
Augusta, Ark., U.S.A. 81 H9 35 17N 91 22W
Augusta, Ga., U.S.A. 77 J5 33 28N 81 58W
Augusta, Kans., U.S.A. 81 G6 37 41N 96 59W
Augusta, Maine, U.S.A. 71 D6 44 19N 69 47W
Augusta, Mont., U.S.A. 82 C7 47 30N 112 24W
Augusta, Wis., U.S.A. 80 C9 44 41N 91 7W
Augustów, Poland 17 B12 53 51N 23 0 E
Augustus, Mt., Australia 60 D2 24 20S 116 50 E
Augustus Downs, Australia 62 B2 18 35S 139 55 E
Augustus I., Australia 60 C3 15 20S 124 30 E
Aukum, U.S.A. 84 G6 38 34N 120 43W
Auld, L., Australia 60 D3 22 25S 123 50 E
Ault, U.S.A. 80 E2 40 35N 104 44W
Aunis, France 18 C3 46 5N 0 50W
Auponhia, Indonesia 37 E7 1 58S 125 27 E
Aur, P., Malaysia 39 L5 2 35N 104 10 E
Auraiya, India 43 F8 26 28N 79 33 E
Aurangabad, Bihar, India 43 G11 24 45N 84 18 E
Aurangabad, Maharashtra, India 40 K9 19 50N 75 23 E
Aurich, Germany 16 B4 53 28N 7 28 E
Aurillac, France 18 D5 44 55N 2 26 E
Aurora, Canada 78 C5 44 0N 79 28W
Aurora, S. Africa 56 E2 32 40S 18 29 E
Aurora, Colo., U.S.A. 80 F2 39 44N 104 52W
Aurora, Ill., U.S.A. 76 E1 41 45N 88 19W
Aurora, Mo., U.S.A. 81 G8 36 58N 93 43W
Aurora, Nebr., U.S.A. 80 E6 40 52N 98 0W
Aurora, Ohio, U.S.A. 78 E3 41 21N 81 20W
Aurukun Mission, Australia 62 A3 13 20S 141 45 E
Aus, Namibia 56 D2 26 35S 16 12 E
Auschwitz = Oświęcim, Poland 17 C10 50 2N 19 11 E
Austin, Minn., U.S.A. 80 D8 43 40N 92 58W
Austin, Nev., U.S.A. 82 G5 39 30N 117 4W
Austin, Pa., U.S.A. 78 E6 41 38N 78 6W
Austin, Tex., U.S.A. 81 K6 30 17N 97 45W
Austin, L., Australia 61 E2 27 40S 118 0 E
Austra, Norway 8 D14 65 8N 11 55 E
Austral Downs, Australia 62 C2 20 30S 137 45 E
Austral Is. = Tubuai Is., Pac. Oc. 65 K12 25 0S 150 0W
Austral Seamount Chain, Pac. Oc. 65 K13 24 0S 150 0W
Australia ■, Oceania 64 K5 23 0S 135 0 E
Australian Alps, Australia 63 F4 36 30S 148 30 E
Australian Capital Territory □, Australia 63 F4 35 30S 149 0 E
Austria ■, Europe 16 E8 47 0N 14 0 E
Austvågøy, Norway 8 B16 68 20N 14 40 E
Autlán, Mexico 86 D4 19 40N 104 30W
Autun, France 18 C6 46 58N 4 17 E
Auvergne, Australia 60 C5 15 39S 130 1 E
Auvergne, France 18 D5 45 20N 3 15 E
Auvergne, Mts. d', France 18 D5 45 20N 2 55 E
Auxerre, France 18 C5 47 48N 3 32 E
Avallon, France 18 C5 47 30N 3 53 E
Avalon, U.S.A. 85 M8 33 21N 118 20W
Avalon Pen., Canada 71 C9 47 30N 53 20W
Avaré, Brazil 95 A6 23 4S 48 58W
Avawatz Mts., U.S.A. 85 K10 35 40N 116 30W
Aveiro, Brazil 93 D7 3 10S 55 5W
Aveiro, Portugal 19 B1 40 37N 8 38W
Āvej, Iran 45 C6 35 40N 49 15 E
Avellaneda, Argentina 94 C4 34 50S 58 10W
Avellino, Italy 20 D6 40 54N 14 47 E
Avenal, U.S.A. 84 K6 36 0N 120 8W
Aversa, Italy 20 D6 40 58N 14 12 E
Avery, U.S.A. 82 C6 47 15N 115 49W
Aves, I. de, W. Indies 89 C7 15 45N 63 55W
Aves, Is. de, Venezuela 89 D6 12 0N 67 30W
Avesta, Sweden 9 F17 60 9N 16 10 E
Avezzano, Italy 20 C5 42 2N 13 25 E
Aviá Terai, Argentina 94 B3 26 45S 60 50W
Avignon, France 18 E6 43 57N 4 50 E
Ávila, Spain 19 B3 40 39N 4 43W
Avila Beach, U.S.A. 85 K6 35 11N 120 44W
Avilés, Spain 19 A3 43 35N 5 57W
Avoca, Ireland 13 D5 52 51N 6 13W
Avoca, U.S.A. 78 D7 42 25N 77 25W
Avoca →, Australia 63 F3 35 40S 143 43 E
Avola, Canada 72 C5 51 45N 119 19W
Avola, Italy 20 F6 36 56N 15 7 E
Avon, N.Y., U.S.A. 78 D7 42 55N 77 45W
Avon, S. Dak., U.S.A. 80 D5 43 0N 98 4W
Avon →, Australia 61 F2 31 40S 116 7 E
Avon →, Bristol, U.K. 11 F5 51 29N 2 41W
Avon →, Dorset, U.K. 11 G6 50 44N 1 46W
Avon →, Warks., U.K. 11 F5 52 10N 1 51W
Avondale, Zimbabwe 55 F3 17 43S 30 58 E
Avonlea, Canada 73 D7 50 0N 105 0W
Avonmore, Canada 79 A10 45 10N 74 58W
Avonmouth, U.K. 11 F5 51 30N 2 42W
Avranches, France 18 B3 48 40N 1 20W
A'waj →, Syria 47 B5 33 23N 36 20 E
Awaji-Shima, Japan 31 G7 34 30N 134 50 E
'Awālī, Bahrain 45 E6 26 0N 50 30 E
Awantipur, India 43 C6 33 55N 75 3 E
Awash, Ethiopia 46 F3 9 1N 40 10 E
Awatere →, N.Z. 59 J5 41 37S 174 10 E
Awbārī, Libya 51 C7 26 46N 12 57 E
Awe, L., U.K. 12 E3 56 17N 5 16W
Awjilah, Libya 51 C9 29 8N 21 7 E
Axel Heiberg I., Canada 4 B3 80 0N 90 0W
Axim, Ghana 50 H4 4 51N 2 15W
Axiós →, Greece 21 D10 40 57N 22 35 E
Axminster, U.K. 11 G4 50 46N 3 0W
Ayabaca, Peru 92 D3 4 40S 79 53W
Ayabe, Japan 31 G7 35 20N 135 20 E
Ayacucho, Argentina 94 D4 37 5S 58 20W
Ayacucho, Peru 92 F4 13 0S 74 0W
Ayaguz, Kazakstan 26 E9 48 10N 80 10 E
Ayamonte, Spain 19 D2 37 12N 7 24W
Ayan, Russia 27 D14 56 30N 138 16 E
Ayaviri, Peru 92 F4 14 50S 70 35W
Aydın, Turkey 21 F12 37 51N 27 51 E
Ayer's Cliff, Canada 79 A12 45 10N 72 3W
Ayers Rock, Australia 61 E5 25 23S 131 5 E
Ayia Aikateríni, Ákra, Greece 23 A3 39 50N 19 50 E
Ayia Dhéka, Greece 23 D6 35 3N 24 58 E
Ayia Gálini, Greece 23 D6 35 6N 24 41 E
Ayia Napa, Cyprus 23 E13 34 59N 34 0 E
Ayia Phyla, Cyprus 23 E12 34 43N 33 1 E
Ayia Varvára, Greece 23 D7 35 8N 25 1 E
Áyios Amvrósios, Cyprus 23 D12 35 20N 33 35 E
Áyios Evstrátios, Greece 21 E11 39 34N 24 58 E
Áyios Ioánnis, Ákra, Greece 23 D7 35 20N 25 40 E
Áyios Isidhoros, Greece 23 C9 36 9N 27 51 E
Áyios Matthaíos, Greece 23 B3 39 30N 19 47 E
Áyios Nikólaos, Greece 23 D7 35 11N 25 41 E
Áyios Seryios, Cyprus 23 D12 35 12N 33 53 E
Ayios Theodhoros, Cyprus 23 D13 35 22N 34 1 E
Aykino, Russia 24 B8 62 15N 49 56 E
Aylesbury, U.K. 11 F7 51 49N 0 49W
Aylmer, Canada 78 D4 42 46N 80 59W
Aylmer, L., Canada 68 B8 64 0N 110 8W
Ayolas, Paraguay 94 B4 27 10S 56 59W
Ayon, Ostrov, Russia 27 C17 69 50N 169 0 E
Ayr, Australia 62 B4 19 35S 147 25 E
Ayr, U.K. 12 F4 55 28N 4 38W
Ayr →, U.K. 12 F4 55 28N 4 38W
Ayre, Pt. of, U.K. 10 C3 54 25N 4 21W
Aytos, Bulgaria 21 C12 42 42N 27 16 E
Ayu, Kepulauan, Indonesia 37 D8 0 35N 131 5 E
Ayutla, Guatemala 88 D1 14 40N 92 10W
Ayutla, Mexico 87 D5 16 58N 99 17W
Ayvacık, Turkey 21 E12 39 36N 26 24 E
Ayvalık, Turkey 21 E12 39 20N 26 46 E
Az Zabdānī, Syria 47 B5 33 43N 36 5 E
Aẓ Ẓāhirīyah, West Bank 47 D3 31 25N 34 58 E
Aẓ Ẓahrān, Si. Arabia 45 E6 26 10N 50 7 E
Az Zarqā, Jordan 47 C5 32 5N 36 4 E
Az Zībār, Iraq 44 B5 36 52N 44 4 E
Az-Zilfī, Si. Arabia 44 E5 26 12N 44 52 E
Az Zubayr, Iraq 44 D5 30 26N 47 40 E
Az Zuwaytīnah, Libya 51 B9 30 58N 20 7 E
Azamgarh, India 43 F10 26 5N 83 13 E
Āzār Shahr, Iran 44 B5 37 45N 45 59 E
Azärbayjan = Azerbaijan ■, Asia 25 F8 40 20N 48 0 E
Āzarbāyjān-e Gharbī □, Iran 44 B5 37 0N 44 30 E
Āzarbāyjān-e Sharqī □, Iran 44 B5 37 20N 47 0 E
Azare, Nigeria 50 F7 11 55N 10 10 E
A'zāz, Syria 44 B3 36 36N 37 4 E
Azbine = Aïr, Niger 50 E6 18 30N 8 0 E
Azerbaijan ■, Asia 25 F8 40 20N 48 0 E
Azerbaijchan = Azerbaijan ■, Asia 25 F8 40 20N 48 0 E
Azimganj, India 43 G13 24 14N 88 16 E
Azogues, Ecuador 92 D3 2 35S 78 0W
Azores, Atl. Oc. 48 C1 38 44N 29 0W
Azov, Russia 25 E6 47 3N 39 25 E
Azov, Sea of, Europe 25 E6 46 0N 36 30 E
Azovskoye More = Azov, Sea of, Europe 25 E6 46 0N 36 30 E
Azovy, Russia 26 C7 64 55N 65 1 E
Aztec, U.S.A. 83 H10 36 49N 107 59W
Azúa, Dom. Rep. 89 C5 18 25N 70 44W
Azuaga, Spain 19 C3 38 16N 5 39W
Azuero, Pen. de, Panama 88 E3 7 30N 80 30W
Azul, Argentina 94 D4 36 42S 59 43W
Azusa, U.S.A. 85 L9 34 8N 117 52W
'Azzūn, West Bank 47 C4 32 10N 35 2 E

B

Ba Don, Vietnam 38 D6 17 45N 106 26 E
Ba Dong, Vietnam 39 H6 9 40N 106 33 E
Ba Ngoi = Cam Lam, Vietnam 39 G7 11 54N 109 10 E
Ba Ria, Vietnam 39 G6 10 30N 107 10 E
Ba Tri, Vietnam 39 G6 10 2N 106 36 E
Ba Xian, China 34 E9 39 8N 116 22 E
Baa, Indonesia 37 F6 10 50S 123 0 E
Baarle Nassau, Belgium 15 C4 51 27N 4 56 E
Baarn, Neths. 15 B5 52 12N 5 17 E
Bab el Mandeb, Red Sea 46 E3 12 35N 43 25 E
Baba Burnu, Turkey 21 E12 39 29N 26 2 E
Bābā Kalū, Iran 45 D6 30 7N 50 49 E
Babadag, Romania 17 F15 44 53N 28 44 E
Babadayhan, Turkmenistan 26 F7 37 42N 60 23 E
Babaeski, Turkey 21 D12 41 26N 27 6 E
Babahoyo, Ecuador 92 D3 1 40S 79 30W
Babakin, Australia 61 F2 32 7S 118 1 E
Babana, Nigeria 50 F5 10 31N 3 46 E
Babar, Indonesia 37 F7 8 0S 129 30 E
Babar, Pakistan 42 D3 31 7N 69 32 E
Babarkach, Pakistan 42 E2 29 45N 68 0 E
Babb, U.S.A. 82 B7 48 51N 113 27W
Babi Besar, P., Malaysia 39 L4 2 25N 103 59 E
Babinda, Australia 62 B4 17 20S 145 56 E
Babine, Canada 72 B3 55 22N 126 37W
Babine →, Canada 72 B3 55 45N 127 44W
Babine L., Canada 72 C3 54 48N 126 0W
Babo, Indonesia 37 E8 2 30S 133 30 E
Bābol, Iran 45 B7 36 40N 52 50 E
Bābol Sar, Iran 45 B7 36 45N 52 45 E
Baboua, C.A.R. 52 C2 5 49N 14 58 E
Babruysk, Belarus 17 B15 53 10N 29 15 E
Babura, Nigeria 50 F6 12 51N 8 59 E
Babusar Pass, Pakistan 43 B5 35 12N 73 59 E
Babuyan Chan., Phil. 37 A6 18 40N 121 30 E
Babylon, Iraq 44 C5 32 34N 44 22 E
Bac Can, Vietnam 38 A5 22 8N 105 49 E
Bac Giang, Vietnam 38 B6 21 16N 106 11 E
Bac Ninh, Vietnam 38 B6 21 13N 106 4 E
Bac Phan, Vietnam 38 B5 22 0N 105 0 E
Bac Quang, Vietnam 38 A5 22 30N 104 48 E
Bacabal, Brazil 93 D10 4 15S 44 45W
Bacalar, Mexico 87 D7 18 50N 87 27W
Bacan, Kepulauan, Indonesia 37 E7 0 35S 127 30 E
Bacan, Pulau, Indonesia 37 E7 0 50S 127 30 E
Bacarra, Phil. 37 A6 18 15N 120 37 E
Bacău, Romania 17 E14 46 35N 26 55 E
Bacerac, Mexico 86 A3 30 18N 108 50W
Bach Long Vi, Dao, Vietnam 38 B6 20 10N 107 40 E
Bachelina, Russia 26 D7 57 45N 67 20 E
Back →, Canada 68 B9 65 10N 104 0W
Backstairs Passage, Australia 63 F2 35 40S 138 5 E
Bacolod, Phil. 37 B6 10 40N 122 57 E
Bacuk, Malaysia 39 J4 6 4N 102 25 E
Bād, Iran 45 C7 33 41N 52 1 E
Bad →, U.S.A. 80 C4 44 21N 100 22W
Bad Axe, U.S.A. 78 C2 43 48N 83 0W
Bad Ischl, Austria 16 E7 47 44N 13 38 E
Bad Kissingen, Germany 16 C6 50 11N 10 4 E
Bad Lands, U.S.A. 80 D3 43 40N 102 10W
Badagara, India 40 P9 11 35N 75 40 E
Badajoz, Spain 19 C2 38 50N 6 59W
Badalona, Spain 19 B7 41 26N 2 15 E
Badalzai, Afghan. 42 E1 29 50N 65 35 E
Badampahar, India 41 H15 22 10N 86 10 E
Badanah, Si. Arabia 44 D4 30 58N 41 30 E
Badarinath, India 43 D8 30 45N 79 30 E
Badas, Brunei 36 D4 4 33N 114 25 E
Badas, Kepulauan, Indonesia 36 D3 0 45N 107 5 E
Baddo →, Pakistan 40 F4 28 0N 64 20 E
Bade, Indonesia 37 F9 7 10S 139 35 E
Baden, Austria 16 D9 48 1N 16 13 E
Baden-Baden, Germany 16 D5 48 44N 8 13 E
Baden-Württemberg □, Germany 16 D5 48 20N 8 40 E
Badenoch, U.K. 12 E4 56 59N 4 15W
Badgastein, Austria 16 E7 47 7N 13 9 E
Badger, Canada 71 C8 49 0N 56 4W
Badger, U.S.A. 84 J7 36 38N 119 1W
Bādghīsāt □, Afghan. 40 B3 35 0N 63 0 E
Badgom, India 43 B6 34 1N 74 45 E
Badin, Pakistan 42 G3 24 38N 68 54 E
Baduen, Somali Rep. 46 F4 7 15N 47 40 E
Badulla, Sri Lanka 40 R12 7 1N 81 7 E
Baena, Spain 19 D3 37 37N 4 20W
Baeza, Spain 19 D4 37 57N 3 25W
Bafatá, Guinea-Biss. 50 F2 12 8N 14 40W
Baffin B., Canada 4 B4 72 0N 64 0W
Baffin I., Canada 69 B12 68 0N 75 0W
Bafia, Cameroon 50 H7 4 40N 11 10 E
Bafing →, Mali 50 F2 13 49N 10 50W
Bafliyūn, Syria 44 B3 36 37N 36 59 E
Bafoulabé, Mali 50 F2 13 50N 10 55W
Bāfq, Iran 45 D7 31 40N 55 25 E
Bāft, Iran 45 D8 29 15N 56 38 E
Bafwasende, Zaïre 54 B2 1 3N 27 5 E
Bagamoyo, Tanzania 54 D4 6 28S 38 55 E
Bagamoyo □, Tanzania 54 D4 6 20S 38 30 E
Bagan Datoh, Malaysia 39 L3 3 59N 100 47 E
Bagan Serai, Malaysia 39 K3 5 1N 100 32 E
Baganga, Phil. 37 C7 7 34N 126 33 E
Bagani, Namibia 56 B3 18 7S 21 41 E
Bagansiapiapi, Indonesia 36 D2 2 12N 100 50 E
Bagasra, India 42 J4 21 30N 71 0 E
Bagdad, U.S.A. 85 L11 34 35N 115 53W
Bagdarin, Russia 27 D12 54 26N 113 36 E
Bagé, Brazil 95 C5 31 20S 54 15W
Bagenalstown = Muine Bheag, Ireland 13 D5 52 42N 6 58W
Baggs, U.S.A. 82 F10 41 2N 107 39W
Bagh, Pakistan 43 C5 33 59N 73 45 E
Baghdād, Iraq 44 C5 33 20N 44 30 E
Bagheria, Italy 20 E5 38 5N 13 30 E
Baghlān, Afghan. 40 A6 36 12N 69 0 E
Bagley, U.S.A. 80 B7 47 32N 95 24W
Bagotville, Canada 71 C5 48 22N 70 54W
Bagrationovsk, Russia 9 J19 54 23N 20 39 E
Baguio, Phil. 37 A6 16 26N 120 34 E
Bahadurgarh, India 42 E7 28 40N 76 57 E
Bahama, Canal Viejo de, W. Indies 88 B4 22 10N 77 30W
Bahamas ■, N. Amer. 89 B5 24 0N 75 0W
Baharampur, India 43 G13 24 2N 88 27 E
Bahau, Malaysia 39 L4 2 48N 102 26 E
Bahawalnagar, Pakistan 42 D5 30 0N 73 15 E
Bahawalpur, Pakistan 42 E4 29 24N 71 40 E
Baheri, India 43 E8 28 45N 79 34 E
Bahi, Tanzania 54 D4 5 58S 35 21 E
Bahi Swamp, Tanzania 54 D4 6 10S 35 0 E
Bahia = Salvador, Brazil 93 F11 13 0S 38 30W
Bahia □, Brazil 93 F10 12 0S 42 0W
Bahía, Is. de la, Honduras 88 C2 16 45N 86 15W

Bareilly

Bahía Blanca, Argentina 94 D3 38 35S 62 13W
Bahía de Caráquez, Ecuador 92 D2 0 40S 80 27W
Bahía Honda, Cuba 88 B3 22 54N 83 10W
Bahía Laura, Argentina 96 F3 48 10S 66 30W
Bahía Negra, Paraguay 92 H7 20 5S 58 5W
Bahmanzād, Iran 45 D6 31 15N 51 47 E
Bahr Aouk →, C.A.R. 52 C3 8 40N 19 0 E
Bahr el Ghazâl □, Sudan 48 F6 7 0N 28 0 E
Bahr Salamat →, Chad 51 G8 9 20N 18 0 E
Bahraich, India 43 F9 27 38N 81 37 E
Bahrain ■, Asia 45 E6 26 0N 50 35 E
Bahror, India 42 F7 27 51N 76 20 E
Bāhū Kalāt, Iran 45 E9 25 43N 61 25 E
Bai Bung, Mui, Vietnam 39 H5 8 38N 104 44 E
Bai Duc, Vietnam 38 C5 18 3N 105 49 E
Bai Thuong, Vietnam 38 C5 19 54N 105 23 E
Baia Mare, Romania 17 E12 47 40N 23 35 E
Baïbokoum, Chad 51 G8 7 46N 15 43 E
Baicheng, China 35 B12 45 38N 122 42 E
Baidoa, Somali Rep. 46 G3 3 8N 43 30 E
Baie Comeau, Canada 71 C6 49 12N 68 10W
Baie-St-Paul, Canada 71 C5 47 28N 70 32W
Baie Trinité, Canada 71 C6 49 25N 67 20W
Baie Verte, Canada 71 C8 49 55N 56 12W
Baihe, China 34 H6 32 50N 110 5 E
Ba'ījī, Iraq 44 C4 35 0N 43 30 E
Baikal, L. = Baykal, Oz., Russia 27 D11 53 0N 108 0 E
Baile Atha Cliath = Dublin, Ireland 13 C5 53 21N 6 15W
Băileşti, Romania 17 F12 44 1N 23 20 E
Bailundo, Angola 53 G3 12 10S 15 50 E
Bainbridge, Ga., U.S.A. 77 K3 30 55N 84 35W
Bainbridge, N.Y., U.S.A. 79 D9 42 18N 75 29W
Baing, Indonesia 37 F6 10 14S 120 34 E
Bainiu, China 34 H7 32 50N 112 15 E
Bainville, U.S.A. 80 A2 48 8N 104 13W
Bā'ir, Jordan 47 E5 30 45N 36 55 E
Baird, U.S.A. 81 J5 32 24N 99 24W
Baird Mts., U.S.A. 68 B3 67 0N 160 0W
Bairin Youqi, China 35 C10 43 30N 118 35 E
Bairin Zuoqi, China 35 C10 43 58N 119 15 E
Bairnsdale, Australia 63 F4 37 48S 147 36 E
Baisha, China 34 G7 34 20N 112 32 E
Baitadi, Nepal 43 E9 29 35N 80 25 E
Baiyin, China 34 F3 36 45N 104 14 E
Baiyu Shan, China 34 F4 37 15N 107 30 E
Baj Baj, India 43 H13 22 30N 88 5 E
Baja, Hungary 17 E10 46 12N 18 59 E
Baja, Pta., Mexico 86 B1 29 50N 116 0W
Baja California, Mexico 86 A1 31 10N 115 12W
Baja California □, Mexico 86 B2 30 0N 115 0W
Baja California Sur □, Mexico 86 B2 25 50N 111 50W
Bajamar, Canary Is. 22 F3 28 33N 16 20W
Bajana, India 42 H4 23 7N 71 49 E
Bājgīrān, Iran 45 B8 37 36N 58 24 E
Bajimba, Mt., Australia 63 D5 29 17S 152 6 E
Bajo Nuevo, Caribbean 88 C4 15 40N 78 50W
Bajool, Australia 62 C5 23 40S 150 35 E
Bakala, C.A.R. 51 G9 6 15N 20 20 E
Bakchar, Russia 26 D9 57 1N 82 5 E
Bakel, Senegal 50 F2 14 56N 12 20W
Baker, Calif., U.S.A. 85 K10 35 16N 116 4W
Baker, Mont., U.S.A. 80 B2 46 22N 104 17W
Baker, Oreg., U.S.A. 82 D5 44 47N 117 50W
Baker, L., Canada 68 B10 64 0N 96 0W
Baker I., Pac. Oc. 64 G10 0 10N 176 35W
Baker L., Australia 61 E4 26 54S 126 5 E
Baker Lake, Canada 68 B10 64 20N 96 3W
Baker Mt., U.S.A. 82 B3 48 50N 121 49W
Bakers Creek, Australia 62 C4 21 13S 149 7 E
Baker's Dozen Is., Canada 70 A4 56 45N 78 45W
Bakersfield, Calif., U.S.A. 85 K7 35 23N 119 1W
Bakersfield, Vt., U.S.A. 79 B12 44 45N 72 48W
Bākhtarān, Iran 44 C5 34 23N 47 0 E
Bākhtarān □, Iran 44 C5 34 0N 46 30 E
Bakı, Azerbaijan 25 F8 40 29N 49 56 E
Bakkafjörður, Iceland 8 C6 66 2N 14 48W
Bakony Forest = Bakony Hegyseg, Hungary 17 E9 47 10N 17 30 E
Bakony Hegyseg, Hungary 17 E9 47 10N 17 30 E
Bakouma, C.A.R. 51 G9 5 40N 22 56 E
Baku = Bakı, Azerbaijan 25 F8 40 29N 49 56 E
Bakutis Coast, Antarctica 5 D15 74 0S 120 0W
Baky = Bakı, Azerbaijan 25 F8 40 29N 49 56 E
Bala, Canada 78 A5 45 1N 79 37W
Bala, L., U.K. 10 E4 52 53N 3 37W
Balabac I., Phil. 36 C5 8 0N 117 0 E
Balabac Str., E. Indies 36 C5 7 53N 117 5 E
Balabagh, Afghan. 42 B4 34 25N 70 12 E
Ba'labakk, Lebanon 47 A5 34 0N 36 10 E
Balabalangan, Kepulauan, Indonesia 36 E5 2 20S 117 30 E
Balad, Iraq 44 C5 34 1N 44 9 E
Balad Rūz, Iraq 44 C5 33 42N 45 5 E
Bālādeh, Fārs, Iran 45 D6 29 17N 51 56 E
Bālādeh, Māzandaran, Iran 45 B6 36 12N 51 48 E
Balaghat, India 40 J12 21 49N 80 12 E
Balaghat Ra., India 40 K10 18 50N 76 30 E
Balaguer, Spain 19 B6 41 50N 0 50 E
Balaklava, Australia 63 E2 34 7S 138 22 E
Balaklava, Ukraine 25 F5 44 30N 33 30 E
Balakovo, Russia 24 D8 52 4N 47 55 E
Balancán, Mexico 87 D6 17 48N 91 32W
Balashov, Russia 24 D7 51 30N 43 10 E
Balasinor, India 42 H5 22 57N 73 23 E
Balasore = Baleshwar, India 41 J15 21 35N 87 3 E
Balaton, Hungary 17 E9 46 50N 17 40 E
Balbina, Reprêsa de, Brazil 92 D7 2 0S 59 30W
Balboa, Panama 88 E4 8 57N 79 34W
Balbriggan, Ireland 13 C5 53 37N 6 11W
Balcarce, Argentina 94 D4 38 0S 58 10W
Balcarres, Canada 73 C8 50 50N 103 35W
Balchik, Bulgaria 21 C13 43 28N 28 11 E
Balclutha, N.Z. 59 M2 46 15S 169 45 E
Bald Hd., Australia 61 G2 35 6S 118 1 E
Bald I., Australia 61 F2 34 57S 118 27 E
Bald Knob, U.S.A. 81 H9 35 19N 91 34W
Baldock L., Canada 73 B9 56 33N 97 57W
Baldwin, Fla., U.S.A. 77 K4 30 18N 81 59W
Baldwin, Mich., U.S.A. 76 D3 43 54N 85 51W
Baldwinsville, U.S.A. 79 C8 43 10N 76 20W
Baldy Peak, U.S.A. 83 K9 33 54N 109 34W
Baleares, Is., Spain 22 B10 39 30N 3 0 E
Balearic Is. = Baleares, Is., Spain 22 B10 39 30N 3 0 E
Baler, Phil. 37 A6 15 46N 121 34 E
Baleshwar, India 41 J15 21 35N 87 3 E
Balfate, Honduras 88 C2 15 48N 86 25W
Balfe's Creek, Australia 62 C4 20 12S 145 55 E
Bali, Cameroon 50 G7 5 54N 10 0 E
Bali, Greece 23 D6 35 25N 24 47 E
Bali, Indonesia 36 F5 8 20S 115 0 E
Bali □, Indonesia 36 F5 8 20S 115 0 E
Bali, Selat, Indonesia 37 H16 8 18S 114 25 E
Balikeşir, Turkey 21 E12 39 35N 27 58 E
Balikpapan, Indonesia 36 E5 1 10S 116 55 E
Balimbing, Phil. 37 C5 5 5N 119 58 E
Baling, Malaysia 39 K3 5 41N 100 55 E
Balipara, India 41 F18 26 50N 92 45 E
Baliza, Brazil 93 G8 16 0S 52 20W
Balkan Mts. = Stara Planina, Bulgaria 21 C10 43 15N 23 0 E
Balkhash = Balqash, Kazakstan 26 E8 46 50N 74 50 E
Balkhash, Ozero = Balqash Köl, Kazakstan 26 E8 46 0N 74 50 E
Balla, Bangla. 41 G17 24 10N 91 35 E
Ballachulish, U.K. 12 E3 56 41N 5 8W
Balladonia, Australia 61 F3 32 27S 123 51 E
Ballarat, Australia 63 F3 37 33S 143 50 E
Ballard, L., Australia 61 E3 29 20S 120 40 E
Ballater, U.K. 12 D5 57 3N 3 3W
Ballenas, Canal de, Mexico 86 B2 29 10N 113 45W
Balleny Is., Antarctica 5 C11 66 30S 163 0 E
Ballia, India 43 G11 25 46N 84 12 E
Ballidu, Australia 61 F2 30 35S 116 45 E
Ballina, Australia 63 D5 28 50S 153 31 E
Ballina, Mayo, Ireland 13 B2 54 7N 9 9W
Ballina, Tipp., Ireland 13 D3 52 49N 8 26W
Ballinasloe, Ireland 13 C3 53 20N 8 13W
Ballinger, U.S.A. 81 K5 31 45N 99 57W
Ballinrobe, Ireland 13 C2 53 38N 9 13W
Ballinskelligs B., Ireland 13 E1 51 48N 10 13W
Ballycastle, U.K. 13 A5 55 12N 6 15W
Ballymena, U.K. 13 B5 54 52N 6 17W
Ballymena □, U.K. 13 B5 54 53N 6 18W
Ballymoney, U.K. 13 A5 55 5N 6 31W
Ballymoney □, U.K. 13 A5 55 5N 6 23W
Ballyshannon, Ireland 13 B3 54 30N 8 11W
Balmaceda, Chile 96 F2 46 0S 71 50W
Balmoral, Australia 63 F3 37 15S 141 48 E
Balmoral, U.K. 12 D5 57 3N 3 13W
Balmorhea, U.S.A. 81 K3 30 59N 103 45W
Balonne →, Australia 63 D4 28 47S 147 56 E
Balqash, Kazakstan 26 E8 46 50N 74 50 E
Balqash Köl, Kazakstan 26 E8 46 0N 74 50 E
Balrampur, India 43 F10 27 30N 82 20 E
Balranald, Australia 63 E3 34 38S 143 33 E
Balsas, Mexico 87 D5 18 0N 99 40W
Balsas →, Mexico 86 D4 17 55N 102 10W
Balston Spa, U.S.A. 79 D11 43 0N 73 52W
Balta, Ukraine 17 D15 48 2N 29 45 E
Balta, U.S.A. 80 A4 48 10N 100 2W
Bălţi, Moldova 17 E14 47 48N 28 0 E
Baltic Sea, Europe 9 H18 57 0N 19 0 E
Baltimore, Ireland 13 E2 51 29N 9 22W
Baltimore, U.S.A. 76 F7 39 17N 76 37W
Baltit, Pakistan 43 A6 36 15N 74 40 E
Baltiysk, Russia 9 J18 54 41N 19 58 E
Baluchistan □, Pakistan 40 F4 27 30N 65 0 E
Balurghat, India 43 G13 25 15N 88 44 E
Balvi, Latvia 9 H22 57 8N 27 15 E
Balya, Turkey 21 E12 39 44N 27 35 E
Balygychan, Russia 27 C16 63 56N 154 12 E
Bam, Iran 45 D8 29 7N 58 14 E
Bama, Nigeria 51 F7 11 33N 13 41 E
Bamako, Mali 50 F3 12 34N 7 55W
Bamba, Mali 50 E4 17 5N 1 24W
Bambari, C.A.R. 51 G9 5 40N 20 35 E
Bambaroo, Australia 62 B4 18 50S 146 10 E
Bamberg, Germany 16 D6 49 54N 10 54 E
Bamberg, U.S.A. 77 J5 33 18N 81 2W
Bambili, Zaïre 54 B2 3 40N 26 0 E
Bamenda, Cameroon 50 G7 5 57N 10 11 E
Bamfield, Canada 72 D3 48 45N 125 10W
Bāmīān □, Afghan. 40 B5 35 0N 67 0 E
Bamiancheng, China 35 C13 43 15N 124 2 E
Bampūr, Iran 45 E9 27 15N 60 21 E
Ban Aranyaprathet, Thailand 38 F4 13 41N 102 30 E
Ban Ban, Laos 38 C4 19 31N 103 30 E
Ban Bang Hin, Thailand 39 H2 9 32N 98 35 E
Ban Chiang Klang, Thailand 38 C3 19 25N 100 55 E
Ban Chik, Laos 38 D4 17 15N 102 22 E
Ban Choho, Thailand 38 E4 15 2N 102 9 E
Ban Dan Lan Hoi, Thailand 38 D2 17 0N 99 35 E
Ban Don = Surat Thani, Thailand 39 H2 9 6N 99 20 E
Ban Don, Vietnam 38 F6 12 53N 107 48 E
Ban Don, Ao, Thailand 39 H2 9 20N 99 25 E
Ban Dong, Thailand 38 C3 19 30N 100 59 E
Ban Hong, Thailand 38 C2 18 18N 98 50 E
Ban Kaeng, Thailand 38 D3 17 29N 100 7 E
Ban Keun, Laos 38 C4 18 22N 102 35 E
Ban Khai, Thailand 38 F3 12 46N 101 18 E
Ban Kheun, Laos 38 B3 20 13N 101 7 E
Ban Khlong Kua, Thailand 39 J3 6 57N 100 8 E
Ban Khuan Mao, Thailand 39 J2 7 50N 99 37 E
Ban Khun Yuam, Thailand 38 C1 18 49N 97 57 E
Ban Ko Yai Chim, Thailand 39 G2 11 17N 99 26 E
Ban Kok, Thailand 38 D4 16 40N 103 40 E
Ban Laem, Thailand 38 F2 13 13N 99 59 E
Ban Lao Ngam, Laos 38 E6 15 28N 106 10 E
Ban Le Kathe, Thailand 38 E2 15 49N 98 53 E
Ban Mae Chedi, Thailand 38 C2 19 11N 99 31 E
Ban Mae Laeng, Thailand 38 B2 20 1N 99 17 E
Ban Mae Sariang, Thailand 38 C1 18 10N 97 56 E
Ban Mê Thuôt = Buon Me Thuot, Vietnam 38 F7 12 40N 108 3 E
Ban Mi, Thailand 38 E3 15 3N 100 32 E
Ban Muong Mo, Laos 38 C4 19 4N 103 58 E
Ban Na Mo, Laos 38 D5 17 7N 105 40 E
Ban Na San, Thailand 39 H2 8 53N 99 52 E
Ban Na Tong, Laos 38 B3 20 56N 101 47 E
Ban Nam Bac, Laos 38 B4 20 38N 102 20 E
Ban Nam Ma, Laos 38 A3 22 2N 101 37 E
Ban Ngang, Laos 38 E6 15 59N 106 11 E
Ban Nong Bok, Laos 38 D5 17 5N 104 48 E
Ban Nong Boua, Laos 38 E6 15 40N 106 33 E
Ban Nong Pling, Thailand 38 E3 15 40N 100 10 E
Ban Pak Chan, Thailand 39 G2 10 32N 98 51 E
Ban Phai, Thailand 38 D4 16 4N 102 44 E
Ban Pong, Thailand 38 F2 13 50N 99 55 E
Ban Ron Phibun, Thailand 39 H2 8 9N 99 51 E
Ban Sanam Chai, Thailand 39 J3 7 33N 100 25 E
Ban Sangkha, Thailand 38 E4 14 37N 103 52 E
Ban Tak, Thailand 38 D2 17 2N 99 4 E
Ban Tako, Thailand 38 E4 14 5N 102 40 E
Ban Tha Dua, Thailand 38 D2 17 59N 98 39 E
Ban Tha Li, Thailand 38 D3 17 37N 101 25 E
Ban Tha Nun, Thailand 39 H2 8 12N 98 18 E
Ban Thahine, Laos 38 E5 14 12N 105 33 E
Ban Xien Kok, Laos 38 B3 20 54N 100 39 E
Ban Yen Nhan, Vietnam 38 B6 20 57N 106 2 E
Banaba, Kiribati 64 H8 0 45S 169 50 E
Bañalbufar, Spain 22 B9 39 42N 2 31 E
Banalia, Zaïre 54 B2 1 32N 25 5 E
Banam, Cambodia 39 G5 11 20N 105 17 E
Banamba, Mali 50 F3 13 29N 7 22W
Banana, Australia 62 C5 24 28S 150 8 E
Bananal, I. do, Brazil 93 F8 11 30S 50 30W
Banaras = Varanasi, India 43 G10 25 22N 83 0 E
Banas →, Gujarat, India 42 H4 23 45N 71 25 E
Banas →, Mad. P., India 43 G9 24 15N 81 30 E
Banbān, Si. Arabia 44 E5 25 1N 46 35 E
Banbridge, U.K. 13 B5 54 22N 6 16W
Banbridge □, U.K. 13 B5 54 21N 6 16W
Banbury, U.K. 11 E6 52 4N 1 20W
Banchory, U.K. 12 D6 57 3N 2 29W
Bancroft, Canada 70 C4 45 3N 77 51W
Band Bonī, Iran 45 E8 25 30N 59 33 E
Band Qīr, Iran 45 D6 31 39N 48 53 E
Banda, India 43 G9 25 30N 80 26 E
Banda, Kepulauan, Indonesia 37 E7 4 37S 129 50 E
Banda Aceh, Indonesia 36 C1 5 35N 95 20 E
Banda Banda, Mt., Australia 63 E5 31 10S 152 28 E
Banda Elat, Indonesia 37 F8 5 40S 133 5 E
Banda Is. = Banda, Kepulauan, Indonesia 37 E7 4 37S 129 50 E
Banda Sea, Indonesia 37 F7 6 0S 130 0 E
Bandai-San, Japan 30 F10 37 36N 140 4 E
Bandān, Iran 45 D9 31 23N 60 44 E
Bandanaira, Indonesia 37 E7 4 32S 129 54 E
Bandanwara, India 42 F6 26 9N 74 38 E
Bandar = Machilipatnam, India 41 L12 16 12N 81 8 E
Bandār 'Abbās, Iran 45 E8 27 15N 56 15 E
Bandar-e Anzalī, Iran 45 B6 37 30N 49 30 E
Bandar-e Bushehr = Būshehr, Iran 45 D6 28 55N 50 55 E
Bandar-e Chārak, Iran 45 E7 26 45N 54 20 E
Bandar-e Deylam, Iran 45 D6 30 5N 50 10 E
Bandar-e Khomeynı, Iran 45 D6 30 30N 49 5 E
Bandar-e Lengeh, Iran 45 E7 26 35N 54 58 E
Bandar-e Maqām, Iran 45 E7 26 56N 53 29 E
Bandar-e Ma'shur, Iran 45 D6 30 35N 49 10 E
Bandar-e Nakhīlū, Iran 45 E7 26 58N 53 30 E
Bandar-e Rīg, Iran 45 D6 29 29N 50 38 E
Bandar-e Torkeman, Iran 45 B7 37 0N 54 10 E
Bandar Maharani = Muar, Malaysia 39 L4 2 3N 102 34 E
Bandar Penggaram = Batu Pahat, Malaysia 39 M4 1 50N 102 56 E
Bandar Seri Begawan, Brunei 36 C4 4 52N 115 0 E
Bandawe, Malawi 55 E3 11 58S 34 5 E
Bandeira, Pico da, Brazil 95 A7 20 26S 41 47W
Bandera, Argentina 94 B3 28 55S 62 20W
Bandera, U.S.A. 81 L5 29 44N 99 5W
Banderas, B. de, Mexico 86 C3 20 40N 105 30W
Bandiagara, Mali 50 F4 14 12N 3 29W
Bandırma, Turkey 21 D13 40 20N 28 0 E
Bandon, Ireland 13 E3 51 44N 8 44W
Bandon →, Ireland 13 E3 51 43N 8 37W
Bandula, Mozam. 55 F3 19 0S 33 7 E
Bandundu, Zaïre 52 E3 3 15S 17 22 E
Bandung, Indonesia 37 G12 6 54S 107 36 E
Bandya, Australia 61 E3 27 40S 122 5 E
Bāneh, Iran 44 C5 35 59N 45 53 E
Banes, Cuba 89 B4 21 0N 75 42W
Banff, Canada 72 C5 51 10N 115 34W
Banff, U.K. 12 D6 57 40N 2 33W
Banff Nat. Park, Canada 72 C5 51 30N 116 15W
Banfora, Burkina Faso 50 F4 10 40N 4 40W
Bang Fai →, Laos 38 D5 16 57N 104 45 E
Bang Hieng →, Laos 38 D5 16 10N 105 10 E
Bang Krathum, Thailand 38 D3 16 34N 100 18 E
Bang Lamung, Thailand 38 F3 13 3N 100 56 E
Bang Mun Nak, Thailand 38 D3 16 2N 100 23 E
Bang Pa In, Thailand 38 E3 14 14N 100 35 E
Bang Rakam, Thailand 38 D3 16 45N 100 7 E
Bang Saphan, Thailand 39 G2 11 14N 99 28 E
Bangala Dam, Zimbabwe 55 G3 21 7S 31 25 E
Bangalore, India 40 N10 12 59N 77 40 E
Bangaon, India 43 H13 23 0N 88 47 E
Bangassou, C.A.R. 52 D4 4 55N 23 7 E
Banggai, Kepulauan, Indonesia 37 E6 1 40S 123 30 E
Banggi, P., Malaysia 36 C5 7 17N 117 12 E
Banghāzī, Libya 51 B9 32 11N 20 3 E
Bangil, Indonesia 37 G15 7 36S 112 50 E
Bangka, P., Sulawesi, Indonesia 37 D7 1 50N 125 5 E
Bangka, P., Sumatera, Indonesia 36 E3 2 0S 105 50 E
Bangka, Selat, Indonesia 36 E3 2 30S 105 30 E
Bangkalan, Indonesia 37 G15 7 2S 112 46 E
Bangkinang, Indonesia 36 D2 0 18N 101 5 E
Bangko, Indonesia 36 E2 2 5S 102 9 E
Bangkok, Thailand 38 F3 13 45N 100 35 E
Bangladesh ■, Asia 41 H17 24 0N 90 0 E
Bangong Co, India 43 B8 35 50N 79 20 E
Bangor, Down, U.K. 13 B6 54 40N 5 40W
Bangor, Gwynedd, U.K. 10 D3 53 14N 4 8W
Bangor, Maine, U.S.A. 71 D6 44 48N 68 46W
Bangor, Pa., U.S.A. 79 F9 40 52N 75 13W
Bangued, Phil. 37 A6 17 40N 120 37 E
Bangui, C.A.R. 52 D3 4 23N 18 35 E
Banguru, Zaïre 54 B2 0 30N 27 10 E
Bangweulu, L., Zambia 55 E3 11 0S 30 0 E
Bangweulu Swamp, Zambia 55 E3 11 20S 30 15 E
Bani, Dom. Rep. 89 C5 18 16N 70 22W
Banī Sa'd, Iraq 44 C5 33 34N 44 32 E
Banī Walīd, Libya 51 B7 31 36N 13 53 E
Banihal Pass, India 43 C6 33 30N 75 12 E
Banīnah, Libya 51 B9 32 0N 20 12 E
Bāniyās, Syria 44 C3 35 10N 36 0 E
Banja Luka, Bos.-H. 20 B7 44 49N 17 11 E
Banjar, Indonesia 37 G13 7 24S 108 30 E
Banjarmasin, Indonesia 36 E4 3 20S 114 35 E
Banjarnegara, Indonesia 37 G13 7 24S 109 42 E
Banjul, Gambia 50 F1 13 28N 16 40W
Banka Banka, Australia 62 B1 18 50S 134 0 E
Banket, Zimbabwe 55 F3 17 27S 30 19 E
Bankipore, India 43 G11 25 35N 85 10 E
Banks I., B.C., Canada 72 C3 53 20N 130 0W
Banks I., N.W.T., Canada 68 A7 73 15N 121 30W
Banks Pen., N.Z. 59 K4 43 45S 173 15 E
Banks Str., Australia 62 G4 40 40S 148 10 E
Bankura, India 43 H12 23 11N 87 18 E
Bann →, Arm., U.K. 13 B5 54 30N 6 31W
Bann →, L'derry., U.K. 13 A5 55 8N 6 41W
Bannang Sata, Thailand 39 J3 6 16N 101 16 E
Banning, U.S.A. 85 M10 33 56N 116 53W
Banningville = Bandundu, Zaïre 52 E3 3 15S 17 22 E
Bannockburn, Canada 78 B7 44 39N 77 33W
Bannockburn, U.K. 12 E5 56 5N 3 55W
Bannockburn, Zimbabwe 55 G2 20 17S 29 48 E
Bannu, Pakistan 40 C7 33 0N 70 18 E
Banská Bystrica, Slovak Rep. 17 D10 48 46N 19 14 E
Banswara, India 42 H6 23 32N 74 24 E
Banten, Indonesia 37 G12 6 5S 106 8 E
Bantry, Ireland 13 E2 51 41N 9 27W
Bantry B., Ireland 13 E2 51 37N 9 44W
Bantul, Indonesia 37 G14 7 55S 110 19 E
Bantva, India 42 J4 21 29N 70 12 E
Banu, Afghan. 40 B6 35 35N 69 5 E
Banyak, Kepulauan, Indonesia 36 D1 2 10N 97 10 E
Banyo, Cameroon 50 G7 6 52N 11 45 E
Banyumas, Indonesia 37 G13 7 32S 109 18 E
Banyuwangi, Indonesia 37 H16 8 13S 114 21 E
Banzare Coast, Antarctica 5 C9 68 0S 125 0 E
Banzyville = Mobayi, Zaïre 52 D4 4 15N 21 8 E
Bao Ha, Vietnam 38 A5 22 11N 104 21 E
Bao Lac, Vietnam 38 A5 22 57N 105 40 E
Bao Loc, Vietnam 39 G6 11 32N 107 48 E
Baocheng, China 34 H4 33 12N 106 56 E
Baode, China 34 E6 39 1N 111 5 E
Baodi, China 35 E9 39 38N 117 20 E
Baoding, China 34 E8 38 50N 115 28 E
Baoji, China 34 G4 34 20N 107 5 E
Baoshan, China 32 D4 25 10N 99 5 E
Baotou, China 34 D6 40 32N 110 2 E
Baoying, China 35 H10 33 17N 119 20 E
Bap, India 42 F5 27 23N 72 18 E
Bapatla, India 41 M12 15 55N 80 30 E
Bāqerābād, Iran 45 C6 33 2N 51 58 E
Ba'qūbah, Iraq 44 C5 33 45N 44 50 E
Baquedano, Chile 94 A2 23 20S 69 52W
Bar, Montenegro, Yug. 21 C8 42 8N 19 8 E
Bar, Ukraine 17 D14 49 4N 27 40 E
Bar Bigha, India 43 G11 25 21N 85 47 E
Bar Harbor, U.S.A. 71 D6 44 23N 68 13W
Bar-le-Duc, France 18 B6 48 47N 5 10 E
Barabai, Indonesia 36 E5 2 32S 115 34 E
Barabinsk, Russia 26 D8 55 20N 78 20 E
Baraboo, U.S.A. 80 D10 43 28N 89 45W
Baracaldo, Spain 19 A4 43 18N 2 59W
Baracoa, Cuba 89 B5 20 20N 74 30W
Baradero, Argentina 94 C4 33 52S 59 29W
Baraga, U.S.A. 80 B10 46 47N 88 30W
Barahona, Dom. Rep. 89 C5 18 13N 71 7W
Barail Range, India 41 G18 25 15N 93 20 E
Barakhola, India 41 G18 25 0N 92 45 E
Barakot, India 43 J11 21 33N 84 59 E
Barakpur, India 43 H13 22 44N 88 30 E
Barakula, Australia 63 D5 26 30S 150 33 E
Baralaba, Australia 62 C4 24 13S 149 50 E
Baralzon L., Canada 73 B9 60 0N 98 3W
Baramula, India 43 B6 34 15N 74 20 E
Baran, India 42 G7 25 9N 76 40 E
Baranavichy, Belarus 17 B14 53 10N 26 0 E
Baranof I., U.S.A. 72 B1 57 0N 135 0W
Barão de Melgaço, Brazil 92 F6 11 50S 60 45W
Barapasi, Indonesia 37 E9 2 15S 137 5 E
Barasat, India 43 H13 22 46N 88 31 E
Barat Daya, Kepulauan, Indonesia 37 F7 7 30S 128 0 E
Barataria B., U.S.A. 81 L10 29 20N 89 55W
Baraut, India 42 E7 29 13N 77 7 E
Barbacena, Brazil 95 A7 21 15S 43 56W
Barbacoas, Colombia 92 C3 1 45N 78 0W
Barbados ■, W. Indies 89 D8 13 10N 59 30W
Barbastro, Spain 19 A6 42 2N 0 5 E
Barberton, S. Africa 57 D5 25 42S 31 2 E
Barberton, U.S.A. 78 E3 41 0N 81 39W
Barbourville, U.S.A. 77 G4 36 52N 83 53W
Barbuda, W. Indies 89 C7 17 30N 61 40W
Barcaldine, Australia 62 C4 23 43S 145 6 E
Barcellona Pozzo di Gotto, Italy 20 E6 38 9N 15 13 E
Barcelona, Spain 19 B7 41 21N 2 10 E
Barcelona, Venezuela 92 A6 10 10N 64 40W
Barcelos, Brazil 92 D6 1 0S 63 0W
Barcoo →, Australia 62 D3 25 30S 142 50 E
Bardai, Chad 51 D8 21 25N 17 0 E
Bardas Blancas, Argentina 94 D2 35 49S 69 45W
Barddhaman, India 43 H12 23 14N 87 39 E
Bardejov, Slovak Rep. 17 D11 49 18N 21 15 E
Bardera, Somali Rep. 46 G3 2 20N 42 27 E
Bardīyah, Libya 51 B9 31 45N 25 5 E
Bardsey I., U.K. 10 E3 52 45N 4 47W
Bardstown, U.S.A. 76 G3 37 49N 85 28W
Bareilly, India 43 E8 28 22N 79 27 E

Barents Sea

Bristol L.

Bolshoy Begichev, Ostrov, *Russia* **27 B12** 74 20N 112 30 E
Bolshoy Lyakhovskiy, Ostrov, *Russia* **27 B15** 73 35N 142 0 E
Bolshoy Tyuters, Ostrov, *Russia* **9 G22** 59 51N 27 13 E
Bolsward, *Neths.* **15 A5** 53 3N 5 32 E
Bolton, *Canada* **78 C5** 43 54N 79 45W
Bolton, *U.K.* **10 D5** 53 35N 2 26W
Bolu, *Turkey* **25 F5** 40 45N 31 35 E
Bolungavík, *Iceland* **8 C2** 66 9N 23 15W
Bolvadin, *Turkey* **25 G5** 38 45N 31 4 E
Bolzano, *Italy* **20 A4** 46 31N 11 22 E
Bom Despacho, *Brazil* **93 G9** 19 43S 45 15W
Bom Jesus da Lapa, *Brazil* **93 F10** 13 15S 43 25W
Boma, *Zaïre* **52 F2** 5 50S 13 4 E
Bomaderry, *Australia* **63 E5** 34 52S 150 37 E
Bombala, *Australia* **63 F4** 36 56S 149 15 E
Bombay, *India* **40 K8** 18 55N 72 50 E
Bomboma, *Zaïre* **52 D3** 2 25N 18 55 E
Bombombwa, *Zaïre* **54 B2** 1 40N 25 40 E
Bomili, *Zaïre* **54 B2** 1 45N 27 5 E
Bømlo, *Norway* **9 G11** 59 37N 5 13 E
Bomokandi →, *Zaïre* **54 B2** 3 39N 26 8 E
Bomongo, *Zaïre* **52 D3** 1 27N 18 21 E
Bomu →, *C.A.R.* **52 D4** 4 40N 22 30 E
Bon, C., *Tunisia* **51 A7** 37 1N 11 2 E
Bon Sar Pa, *Vietnam* **38 F6** 12 24N 107 35 E
Bonaire, *Neth. Ant.* **89 D6** 12 10N 68 15W
Bonang, *Australia* **63 F4** 37 11S 148 41 E
Bonanza, *Nic.* **88 D3** 13 54N 84 35W
Bonaparte Arch., *Australia* **60 B3** 14 0S 124 30 E
Bonaventure, *Canada* **71 C6** 48 5N 65 32W
Bonavista, *Canada* **71 C9** 48 40N 53 5W
Bonavista, C., *Canada* **71 C9** 48 42N 53 5W
Bondo, *Zaïre* **54 B1** 3 55N 23 53 E
Bondoukou, *Ivory C.* **50 G4** 8 2N 2 47W
Bondowoso, *Indonesia* **37 G15** 7 55S 113 49 E
Bone, Teluk, *Indonesia* **37 E6** 4 10S 120 50 E
Bonerate, *Indonesia* **37 F6** 7 25S 121 5 E
Bonerate, Kepulauan, *Indonesia* **37 F6** 6 30S 121 10 E
Bo'ness, *U.K.* **12 E5** 56 1N 3 37W
Bonete, Cerro, *Argentina* **94 B2** 27 55S 68 40W
Bong Son = Hoai Nhon, *Vietnam* **38 E7** 14 28N 109 1 E
Bongandanga, *Zaïre* **52 D4** 1 24N 21 3 E
Bongor, *Chad* **51 F8** 10 35N 15 20 E
Bonham, *U.S.A.* **81 J6** 33 35N 96 11W
Bonifacio, *France* **18 F8** 41 24N 9 10 E
Bonin Is. = Ogasawara Gunto, *Pac. Oc.* **28 G18** 27 0N 142 0 E
Bonn, *Germany* **16 C4** 50 46N 7 6 E
Bonne Terre, *U.S.A.* **81 G9** 37 55N 90 33W
Bonners Ferry, *U.S.A.* **82 B5** 48 42N 116 19W
Bonney, L., *Australia* **63 F3** 37 50S 140 20 E
Bonnie Downs, *Australia* **62 C3** 22 7S 143 50 E
Bonnie Rock, *Australia* **61 F2** 30 29S 118 22 E
Bonny, Bight of, *Africa* **52 D1** 3 30N 9 20 E
Bonnyville, *Canada* **73 C6** 54 20N 110 45W
Bonoi, *Indonesia* **37 E9** 1 45S 137 41 E
Bonsall, *U.S.A.* **85 M9** 33 16N 117 14W
Bontang, *Indonesia* **36 D5** 0 10N 117 30 E
Bonthain, *Indonesia* **37 F5** 5 34S 119 56 E
Bonthe, *S. Leone* **50 G2** 7 30N 12 33W
Bontoc, *Phil.* **37 A6** 17 7N 120 58 E
Bonython Ra., *Australia* **60 D4** 23 40S 128 45 E
Bookabie, *Australia* **61 F5** 31 50S 132 41 E
Booker, *U.S.A.* **81 G4** 36 27N 100 32W
Boolaboolka L., *Australia* **63 E3** 32 38S 143 10 E
Booligal, *Australia* **63 E3** 33 58S 144 53 E
Boom, *Belgium* **15 C4** 51 6N 4 20 E
Boonah, *Australia* **63 D5** 27 58S 152 41 E
Boone, *Iowa, U.S.A.* **80 D8** 42 4N 93 53W
Boone, *N.C., U.S.A.* **77 G5** 36 13N 81 41W
Booneville, *Ark., U.S.A.* **81 H8** 35 8N 93 55W
Booneville, *Miss., U.S.A.* **77 H1** 34 39N 88 34W
Boonville, *Calif., U.S.A.* **84 F3** 39 1N 123 22W
Boonville, *Ind., U.S.A.* **76 F2** 38 3N 87 16W
Boonville, *Mo., U.S.A.* **80 F8** 38 58N 92 44W
Boonville, *N.Y., U.S.A.* **79 C9** 43 29N 75 20W
Boorindal, *Australia* **63 E4** 30 22S 146 11 E
Boorowa, *Australia* **63 E4** 34 28S 148 44 E
Boothia, Gulf of, *Canada* **69 A11** 71 0N 90 0W
Boothia Pen., *Canada* **68 A10** 71 0N 94 0W
Bootle, *U.K.* **10 D4** 53 28N 3 1W
Booué, *Gabon* **52 E2** 0 5S 11 55 E
Boquete, *Panama* **88 E3** 8 46N 82 27W
Boquilla, Presa de la, *Mexico* **86 B3** 27 40N 105 30W
Boquillas del Carmen, *Mexico* **86 B4** 29 17N 102 53W
Bor, *Serbia, Yug.* **21 B10** 44 5N 22 7 E
Bôr, *Sudan* **51 G11** 6 10N 31 40 E
Bor Mashash, *Israel* **47 D3** 31 7N 34 50 E
Boradā →, *Syria* **47 B5** 33 33N 36 34 E
Borah Peak, *U.S.A.* **82 D7** 44 8N 113 47W
Borama, *Somali Rep.* **46 F3** 9 55N 43 7 E
Borås, *Sweden* **9 H15** 57 43N 12 56 E
Borāzjān, *Iran* **45 D6** 29 22N 51 10 E
Borba, *Brazil* **92 D7** 4 12S 59 34W
Borborema, Planalto da, *Brazil* **90 D7** 7 0S 37 0W
Bord Khūn-e Now, *Iran* **45 D6** 28 3N 51 28 E
Borda, C., *Australia* **63 F2** 35 45S 136 34 E
Bordeaux, *France* **18 D3** 44 50N 0 36W
Borden, *Australia* **61 F2** 34 3S 118 12 E
Borden, *Canada* **71 C7** 46 18N 63 47W
Borden I., *Canada* **4 B2** 78 30N 111 30W
Borders □, *U.K.* **12 F6** 55 35N 2 50W
Bordertown, *Australia* **63 F3** 36 19S 140 45 E
Borðeyri, *Iceland* **8 D3** 65 12N 21 6W
Bordj Fly Ste. Marie, *Algeria* **50 C4** 27 19N 2 32W
Bordj-in-Eker, *Algeria* **50 D6** 24 9N 5 3 E
Bordj Omar Driss, *Algeria* **50 C6** 28 10N 6 40 E
Bordj-Tarat, *Algeria* **50 C6** 25 55N 9 3 E
Borgå = Porvoo, *Finland* **9 F21** 60 24N 25 40 E
Borgarfjörður, *Iceland* **8 D7** 65 31N 13 49W
Borgarnes, *Iceland* **8 D3** 64 32N 21 55W
Børgefjellet, *Norway* **8 D15** 65 20N 13 45 E
Borger, *Neths.* **15 B6** 52 54N 6 44 E
Borger, *U.S.A.* **81 H4** 35 39N 101 24W
Borgholm, *Sweden* **9 H17** 56 52N 16 39 E
Borikhane, *Laos* **38 C4** 18 33N 103 43 E
Borisoglebsk, *Russia* **25 D7** 51 27N 42 5 E
Borisov = Barysaw, *Belarus* **17 A15** 54 17N 28 28 E
Borja, *Peru* **92 D3** 4 20S 77 40W
Borkou, *Chad* **51 E8** 18 15N 18 50 E
Borkum, *Germany* **16 B4** 53 34N 6 40 E
Borlänge, *Sweden* **9 F16** 60 29N 15 26 E
Borley, C., *Antarctica* **5 C5** 66 15S 52 30 E
Borneo, *E. Indies* **36 D5** 1 0N 115 0 E
Bornholm, *Denmark* **9 J16** 55 10N 15 0 E
Borobudur, *Indonesia* **37 G14** 7 36S 110 13 E
Borogontsy, *Russia* **27 C14** 62 42N 131 8 E
Boromo, *Burkina Faso* **50 F4** 11 45N 2 58W
Boron, *U.S.A.* **85 L9** 35 0N 117 39W
Borongan, *Phil.* **37 B7** 11 37N 125 26 E
Bororen, *Australia* **62 C5** 24 13S 151 33 E
Borovichi, *Russia* **24 C5** 58 25N 33 55 E
Borrego Springs, *U.S.A.* **85 M10** 33 15N 116 23W
Borroloola, *Australia* **62 B2** 16 4S 136 17 E
Borşa, *Romania* **17 E13** 47 41N 24 50 E
Borth, *U.K.* **11 E3** 52 29N 4 2W
Borūjerd, *Iran* **45 C6** 33 55N 48 50 E
Boryslav, *Ukraine* **17 D12** 49 18N 23 28 E
Borzya, *Russia* **27 D12** 50 24N 116 31 E
Bosa, *Italy* **20 D3** 40 18N 8 30 E
Bosanska Gradiška, *Bos.-H.* **20 B7** 45 10N 17 15 E
Bosaso, *Somali Rep.* **46 E4** 11 12N 49 18 E
Boscastle, *U.K.* **11 G3** 50 41N 4 42W
Boshan, *China* **35 F9** 36 28N 117 49 E
Boshof, *S. Africa* **56 D4** 28 31S 25 13 E
Boshrūyeh, *Iran* **45 C8** 33 50N 57 30 E
Bosna →, *Bos.-H.* **21 B8** 45 4N 18 29 E
Bosna i Hercegovina = Bosnia-Herzegovina ■, *Europe* **20 B7** 44 0N 17 0 E
Bosnia-Herzegovina ■, *Europe* **20 B7** 44 0N 17 0 E
Bosnik, *Indonesia* **37 E9** 1 5S 136 10 E
Bosobolo, *Zaïre* **52 D3** 4 15N 19 50 E
Bosporus = Karadeniz Boğazı, *Turkey* **21 D13** 41 10N 29 10 E
Bossangoa, *C.A.R.* **51 G8** 6 35N 17 30 E
Bossembélé, *C.A.R.* **51 G8** 5 25N 17 40 E
Bossier City, *U.S.A.* **81 J8** 32 31N 93 44W
Bosso, *Niger* **51 F7** 13 43N 13 19 E
Bostānābād, *Iran* **44 B5** 37 50N 46 50 E
Bosten Hu, *China* **32 B3** 41 55N 87 40 E
Boston, *U.K.* **10 E7** 52 59N 0 2W
Boston, *U.S.A.* **79 D13** 42 22N 71 4W
Boston Bar, *Canada* **72 D4** 49 52N 121 30W
Boswell, *Canada* **72 D5** 49 28N 116 45W
Boswell, *Okla., U.S.A.* **81 H7** 34 2N 95 52W
Boswell, *Pa., U.S.A.* **78 F5** 40 10N 79 2W
Botad, *India* **42 H4** 22 15N 71 40 E
Botany B., *Australia* **63 E5** 34 0S 151 14 E
Botene, *Laos* **38 D3** 17 35N 101 12 E
Bothaville, *S. Africa* **56 D4** 27 23S 26 34 E
Bothnia, G. of, *Europe* **8 E19** 63 0N 20 15 E
Bothwell, *Australia* **62 G4** 42 20S 147 1 E
Bothwell, *Canada* **78 D3** 42 38N 81 52W
Botletle →, *Botswana* **56 C3** 20 10S 23 15 E
Botoşani, *Romania* **17 E14** 47 42N 26 41 E
Botswana ■, *Africa* **56 C3** 22 0S 24 0 E
Bottineau, *U.S.A.* **80 A4** 48 50N 100 27W
Bottrop, *Germany* **15 C6** 51 31N 6 58 E
Botucatu, *Brazil* **95 A6** 22 55S 48 30W
Botwood, *Canada* **71 C8** 49 6N 55 23W
Bou Djébéha, *Mali* **50 E4** 18 25N 2 45W
Bou Izakarn, *Morocco* **50 C3** 29 12N 9 46W
Bouaké, *Ivory C.* **50 G3** 7 40N 5 2W
Bouar, *C.A.R.* **52 C3** 6 0N 15 40 E
Bouârfa, *Morocco* **50 B4** 32 32N 1 58W
Bouca, *C.A.R.* **51 G8** 6 45N 18 25 E
Boucaut B., *Australia* **62 A1** 12 0S 134 25 E
Bougainville C., *Australia* **60 B4** 13 57S 126 4 E
Bougainville Reef, *Australia* **62 B4** 15 30S 147 5 E
Bougie = Bejaia, *Algeria* **50 A6** 36 42N 5 2 E
Bougouni, *Mali* **50 F3** 11 30N 7 20W
Bouillon, *Belgium* **15 E5** 49 44N 5 3 E
Boulder, *Colo., U.S.A.* **80 E2** 40 1N 105 17W
Boulder, *Mont., U.S.A.* **82 C7** 46 14N 112 7W
Boulder City, *U.S.A.* **85 K12** 35 59N 114 50W
Boulder Creek, *U.S.A.* **84 H4** 37 7N 122 7W
Boulder Dam = Hoover Dam, *U.S.A.* **85 K12** 36 1N 114 44W
Boulia, *Australia* **62 C2** 22 52S 139 51 E
Boulogne-sur-Mer, *France* **18 A4** 50 42N 1 36 E
Boultoum, *Niger* **50 F7** 14 45N 10 25 E
Boun Neua, *Laos* **38 B3** 21 38N 101 54 E
Boun Tai, *Laos* **38 B3** 21 23N 101 58 E
Bouna, *Ivory C.* **50 G4** 9 10N 3 0W
Boundary Peak, *U.S.A.* **84 H8** 37 51N 118 21W
Boundiali, *Ivory C.* **50 G3** 9 30N 6 20W
Bountiful, *U.S.A.* **82 F8** 40 53N 111 53W
Bounty Is., *Pac. Oc.* **64 M9** 48 0S 178 30 E
Bourbonnais, *France* **18 C5** 46 28N 3 0 E
Bourem, *Mali* **50 E4** 17 0N 0 24W
Bourg-en-Bresse, *France* **18 C6** 46 13N 5 12 E
Bourg-St.-Maurice, *France* **18 D7** 45 35N 6 46 E
Bourges, *France* **18 C5** 47 9N 2 25 E
Bourget, *Canada* **79 A9** 45 26N 75 9W
Bourgogne, *France* **18 C6** 47 0N 4 50 E
Bourke, *Australia* **63 E4** 30 8S 145 55 E
Bournemouth, *U.K.* **11 G6** 50 43N 1 52W
Bouse, *U.S.A.* **85 M13** 33 56N 114 0W
Bousso, *Chad* **51 F8** 10 34N 16 52 E
Boutilimit, *Mauritania* **50 E2** 17 45N 14 40W
Bouvet I. = Bouvetøya, *Antarctica* **3 G10** 54 26S 3 24 E
Bouvetøya, *Antarctica* **3 G10** 54 26S 3 24 E
Bovigny, *Belgium* **15 D5** 50 12N 5 55 E
Bovill, *U.S.A.* **82 C5** 46 51N 116 24W
Bow Island, *Canada* **72 D6** 49 50N 111 23W
Bowbells, *U.S.A.* **80 A3** 48 48N 102 15W
Bowdle, *U.S.A.* **80 C5** 45 27N 99 39W
Bowelling, *Australia* **61 F2** 33 25S 116 30 E
Bowen, *Australia* **62 C4** 20 0S 148 16 E
Bowen Mts., *Australia* **63 F4** 37 0S 147 50 E
Bowie, *Ariz., U.S.A.* **83 K9** 32 19N 109 29W
Bowie, *Tex., U.S.A.* **81 J6** 33 34N 97 51W
Bowkān, *Iran* **44 B5** 36 31N 46 12 E
Bowland, Forest of, *U.K.* **10 D5** 54 0N 2 30W
Bowling Green, *Ky., U.S.A.* **76 G2** 36 59N 86 27W
Bowling Green, *Ohio, U.S.A.* **76 E4** 41 23N 83 39W
Bowling Green, C., *Australia* **62 B4** 19 19S 147 25 E
Bowman, *U.S.A.* **80 B3** 46 11N 103 24W
Bowman I., *Antarctica* **5 C8** 65 0S 104 0 E
Bowmans, *Australia* **63 E2** 34 10S 138 17 E
Bowmanville, *Canada* **70 D4** 43 55N 78 41W
Bowmore, *U.K.* **12 F2** 55 45N 6 17W
Bowral, *Australia* **63 E5** 34 26S 150 27 E
Bowraville, *Australia* **63 E5** 30 37S 152 52 E
Bowron →, *Canada* **72 C4** 54 3N 121 50W
Bowser L., *Canada* **72 B3** 56 30N 129 30W
Bowsman, *Canada* **73 C8** 52 14N 101 12W
Bowwood, *Zambia* **55 F2** 17 5S 26 20 E
Boxtel, *Neths.* **15 C5** 51 36N 5 20 E
Boyce, *U.S.A.* **81 K8** 31 23N 92 40W
Boyer →, *Canada* **72 B5** 58 27N 115 57W
Boyle, *Ireland* **13 C3** 53 59N 8 18W
Boyne →, *Ireland* **13 C5** 53 43N 6 15W
Boyne City, *U.S.A.* **76 C3** 45 13N 85 1W
Boynton Beach, *U.S.A.* **77 M5** 26 32N 80 4W
Boyoma, Chutes, *Zaïre* **54 B2** 0 35N 25 23 E
Boyup Brook, *Australia* **61 F2** 33 50S 116 23 E
Boz Dağları, *Turkey* **21 E13** 38 20N 28 0 E
Bozburun, *Turkey* **21 F13** 36 43N 28 8 E
Bozcaada, *Turkey* **21 E12** 39 49N 26 3 E
Bozdoğan, *Turkey* **21 F13** 37 40N 28 17 E
Bozeman, *U.S.A.* **82 D8** 45 41N 111 2W
Bozen = Bolzano, *Italy* **20 A4** 46 31N 11 22 E
Bozoum, *C.A.R.* **51 G8** 6 25N 16 35 E
Bra, *Italy* **20 B2** 44 42N 7 51 E
Brabant □, *Belgium* **15 D4** 50 46N 4 30 E
Brabant L., *Canada* **73 B8** 55 58N 103 43W
Brač, *Croatia* **20 C7** 43 20N 16 40 E
Bracadale, L., *U.K.* **12 D2** 57 20N 6 30W
Bracciano, L. di, *Italy* **20 C5** 42 7N 12 14 E
Bracebridge, *Canada* **70 C4** 45 2N 79 19W
Brach, *Libya* **51 C7** 27 31N 14 20 E
Bräcke, *Sweden* **9 E16** 62 45N 15 26 E
Brackettville, *U.S.A.* **81 L4** 29 19N 100 25W
Brad, *Romania* **17 E12** 46 10N 22 50 E
Bradenton, *U.S.A.* **77 M4** 27 30N 82 34W
Bradford, *Canada* **78 B5** 44 7N 79 34W
Bradford, *U.K.* **10 D6** 53 47N 1 45W
Bradford, *Pa., U.S.A.* **78 E6** 41 58N 78 38W
Bradford, *Vt., U.S.A.* **79 C12** 43 59N 72 9W
Bradley, *Ark., U.S.A.* **81 J8** 33 6N 93 39W
Bradley, *Calif., U.S.A.* **84 K6** 35 52N 120 48W
Bradley, *S. Dak., U.S.A.* **80 C6** 45 5N 97 39W
Bradley Institute, *Zimbabwe* **55 F3** 17 7S 31 25 E
Bradore Bay, *Canada* **71 B8** 51 27N 57 18W
Bradshaw, *Australia* **60 C5** 15 21S 130 16 E
Brady, *U.S.A.* **81 K5** 31 9N 99 20W
Braemar, *Australia* **63 E2** 33 12S 139 35 E
Braeside, *Canada* **79 A8** 45 28N 76 24W
Braga, *Portugal* **19 B1** 41 35N 8 25W
Bragado, *Argentina* **94 D3** 35 2S 60 27W
Bragança, *Brazil* **93 D9** 1 0S 47 2W
Bragança, *Portugal* **19 B2** 41 48N 6 50W
Bragança Paulista, *Brazil* **95 A6** 22 55S 46 32W
Brahmanbaria, *Bangla.* **41 H17** 23 58N 91 15 E
Brahmani →, *India* **41 J15** 20 39N 86 46 E
Brahmaputra →, *India* **43 G13** 23 58N 89 50 E
Braich-y-pwll, *U.K.* **10 E3** 52 47N 4 46W
Braidwood, *Australia* **63 F4** 35 27S 149 49 E
Brăila, *Romania* **17 F14** 45 19N 27 59 E
Brainerd, *U.S.A.* **80 B7** 46 22N 94 12W
Braintree, *U.K.* **11 F8** 51 53N 0 34 E
Braintree, *U.S.A.* **79 D14** 42 13N 71 0W
Brak →, *S. Africa* **56 D3** 29 35S 22 55 E
Brakwater, *Namibia* **56 C2** 22 28S 17 3 E
Bralorne, *Canada* **72 C4** 50 50N 122 50W
Brampton, *Canada* **70 D4** 43 45N 79 45W
Bramwell, *Australia* **62 A3** 12 8S 142 37 E
Branco →, *Brazil* **92 D6** 1 20S 61 50W
Brandenburg = Neubrandenburg, *Germany* **16 B7** 53 33N 13 15 E
Brandenburg, *Germany* **16 B7** 52 25N 12 33 E
Brandenburg □, *Germany* **16 B6** 52 50N 13 0 E
Brandfort, *S. Africa* **56 D4** 28 40S 26 30 E
Brandon, *Canada* **73 D9** 49 50N 99 57W
Brandon, *U.S.A.* **79 C11** 43 48N 73 4W
Brandon B., *Ireland* **13 D1** 52 17N 10 8W
Brandon Mt., *Ireland* **13 D1** 52 15N 10 15W
Brandsen, *Argentina* **94 D4** 35 10S 58 15W
Brandvlei, *S. Africa* **56 E3** 30 25S 20 30 E
Branford, *U.S.A.* **79 E12** 41 17N 72 49W
Braniewo, *Poland* **17 A10** 54 25N 19 50 E
Bransfield Str., *Antarctica* **5 C18** 63 0S 59 0W
Branson, *Colo., U.S.A.* **81 G3** 37 1N 103 53W
Branson, *Mo., U.S.A.* **81 G8** 36 39N 93 13W
Brantford, *Canada* **70 D3** 43 10N 80 15W
Branxholme, *Australia* **63 F3** 37 52S 141 49 E
Bras d'Or, L., *Canada* **71 C7** 45 50N 60 50W
Brasil, Planalto, *Brazil* **90 E6** 18 0S 46 30W
Brasiléia, *Brazil* **92 F5** 11 0S 68 45W
Brasília, *Brazil* **93 G9** 15 47S 47 55W
Braslaw, *Belarus* **9 J22** 55 38N 27 0 E
Braşov, *Romania* **17 F13** 45 38N 25 35 E
Brasschaat, *Belgium* **15 C4** 51 19N 4 27 E
Brassey, Banjaran, *Malaysia* **36 D5** 5 0N 117 15 E
Brassey Ra., *Australia* **61 E3** 25 8S 122 15 E
Brasstown Bald, *U.S.A.* **77 H4** 34 53N 83 49W
Brastad, *Sweden* **9 G14** 58 23N 11 30 E
Bratislava, *Slovak Rep.* **17 D9** 48 10N 17 7 E
Bratsk, *Russia* **27 D11** 56 10N 101 30 E
Brattleboro, *U.S.A.* **79 D12** 42 51N 72 34W
Braunau, *Austria* **16 D7** 48 15N 13 3 E
Braunschweig, *Germany* **16 B6** 52 15N 10 31 E
Braunton, *U.K.* **11 F3** 51 7N 4 10W
Brava, *Somali Rep.* **46 G3** 1 20N 44 8 E
Bravo del Norte →, *Mexico* **86 B5** 25 57N 97 9W
Bravo del Norte, R. → = Grande, Rio →, *U.S.A.* **81 N6** 25 58N 97 9W
Brawley, *U.S.A.* **85 N11** 32 59N 115 31W
Bray, *Ireland* **13 C5** 53 13N 6 7W
Bray, Mt., *Australia* **62 A1** 14 0S 134 30 E
Bray, Pays de, *France* **18 B4** 49 46N 1 26 E
Brazeau →, *Canada* **72 C5** 52 55N 115 14W
Brazil, *U.S.A.* **76 F2** 39 32N 87 8W
Brazil ■, *S. Amer.* **93 F9** 12 0S 50 0W
Brazilian Highlands = Brasil, Planalto, *Brazil* **90 E6** 18 0S 46 30W
Brazo Sur →, *S. Amer.* **94 B4** 25 21S 57 42W
Brazos →, *U.S.A.* **81 L7** 28 53N 95 23W
Brazzaville, *Congo* **52 E3** 4 9S 15 12 E
Brčko, *Bos.-H.* **21 B8** 44 54N 18 46 E
Breadalbane, *Australia* **62 C2** 23 50S 139 35 E
Breadalbane, *U.K.* **12 E4** 56 30N 4 15W
Breaden, L., *Australia* **61 E4** 25 51S 125 28 E
Breaksea Sd., *N.Z.* **59 L1** 45 35S 166 35 E
Bream B., *N.Z.* **59 F5** 35 56S 174 28 E
Bream Hd., *N.Z.* **59 F5** 35 51S 174 36 E
Breas, *Chile* **94 B1** 25 29S 70 24W
Brebes, *Indonesia* **37 G13** 6 52S 109 3 E
Brechin, *Canada* **78 B5** 44 32N 79 10W
Brechin, *U.K.* **12 E6** 56 44N 2 39W
Breckenridge, *Colo., U.S.A.* **82 G10** 39 29N 106 3W
Breckenridge, *Minn., U.S.A.* **80 B6** 46 16N 96 35W
Breckenridge, *Tex., U.S.A.* **81 J5** 32 45N 98 54W
Breckland, *U.K.* **11 E8** 52 30N 0 40 E
Brecon, *U.K.* **11 F4** 51 57N 3 23W
Brecon Beacons, *U.K.* **11 F4** 51 53N 3 26W
Breda, *Neths.* **15 C4** 51 35N 4 45 E
Bredasdorp, *S. Africa* **56 E3** 34 33S 20 2 E
Bredbo, *Australia* **63 F4** 35 58S 149 10 E
Bregenz, *Austria* **16 E5** 47 30N 9 45 E
Breiðafjörður, *Iceland* **8 D2** 65 15N 23 15W
Brejo, *Brazil* **93 D10** 3 41S 42 47W
Bremen, *Germany* **16 B5** 53 4N 8 47 E
Bremer I., *Australia* **62 A2** 12 5S 136 45 E
Bremerhaven, *Germany* **16 B5** 53 33N 8 36 E
Bremerton, *U.S.A.* **84 C4** 47 34N 122 38W
Brenham, *U.S.A.* **81 K6** 30 10N 96 24W
Brenner P., *Austria* **16 E6** 47 2N 11 30 E
Brent, *Canada* **70 C4** 46 2N 78 29W
Brent, *U.K.* **11 F7** 51 33N 0 16W
Brentwood, *U.K.* **11 F8** 51 37N 0 19 E
Brentwood, *U.S.A.* **79 F11** 40 47N 73 15W
Bréscia, *Italy* **20 B4** 45 33N 10 15 E
Breskens, *Neths.* **15 C3** 51 23N 3 33 E
Breslau = Wrocław, *Poland* **17 C9** 51 5N 17 5 E
Bressanone, *Italy* **20 A4** 46 43N 11 39 E
Bressay, *U.K.* **12 A7** 60 9N 1 6W
Brest, *Belarus* **17 B12** 52 10N 23 40 E
Brest, *France* **18 B1** 48 24N 4 31W
Brest-Litovsk = Brest, *Belarus* **17 B12** 52 10N 23 40 E
Bretagne, *France* **18 B2** 48 10N 3 0W
Breton, *Canada* **72 C6** 53 7N 114 28W
Breton Sd., *U.S.A.* **81 L10** 29 35N 89 15W
Brett, C., *N.Z.* **59 F5** 35 10S 174 20 E
Brevard, *U.S.A.* **77 H4** 35 14N 82 44W
Brewarrina, *Australia* **63 D4** 30 0S 146 51 E
Brewer, *U.S.A.* **71 D6** 44 48N 68 46W
Brewer, Mt., *U.S.A.* **84 J8** 36 44N 118 28W
Brewster, *N.Y., U.S.A.* **79 E11** 41 23N 73 37W
Brewster, *Wash., U.S.A.* **82 B4** 48 6N 119 47W
Brewster, Kap, *Greenland* **4 B6** 70 7N 22 0W
Brewton, *U.S.A.* **77 K2** 31 7N 87 4W
Breyten, *S. Africa* **57 D4** 26 16S 30 0 E
Brezhnev = Naberezhnyye Chelny, *Russia* **24 C9** 55 42N 52 19 E
Bria, *C.A.R.* **51 G9** 6 30N 21 58 E
Briançon, *France* **18 D7** 44 54N 6 39 E
Bribie I., *Australia* **63 D5** 27 0S 153 10 E
Bridgehampton, *U.S.A.* **79 F12** 40 56N 72 19W
Bridgend, *U.K.* **11 F4** 51 30N 3 34W
Bridgend □, *U.K.* **11 F4** 51 36N 3 36W
Bridgeport, *Calif., U.S.A.* **83 G4** 38 15N 119 14W
Bridgeport, *Conn., U.S.A.* **79 E11** 41 11N 73 12W
Bridgeport, *Nebr., U.S.A.* **80 E3** 41 40N 103 6W
Bridgeport, *Tex., U.S.A.* **81 J6** 33 13N 97 45W
Bridger, *U.S.A.* **82 D9** 45 18N 108 55W
Bridgeton, *U.S.A.* **76 F8** 39 26N 75 14W
Bridgetown, *Australia* **61 F2** 33 58S 116 7 E
Bridgetown, *Barbados* **89 D8** 13 5N 59 30W
Bridgetown, *Canada* **71 D6** 44 55N 65 18W
Bridgewater, *Canada* **71 D7** 44 25N 64 31W
Bridgewater, *Mass., U.S.A.* **79 E14** 41 59N 70 58W
Bridgewater, *S. Dak., U.S.A.* **80 D6** 43 33N 97 30W
Bridgewater, C., *Australia* **63 F3** 38 23S 141 23 E
Bridgnorth, *U.K.* **11 E5** 52 32N 2 25W
Bridgton, *U.S.A.* **79 B14** 44 3N 70 42W
Bridgwater, *U.K.* **11 F4** 51 8N 2 59W
Bridlington, *U.K.* **10 C7** 54 5N 0 12W
Bridport, *Australia* **62 G4** 40 59S 147 23 E
Bridport, *U.K.* **11 G5** 50 44N 2 45W
Brig, *Switz.* **16 E4** 46 18N 7 59 E
Brigg, *U.K.* **10 D7** 53 34N 0 28W
Briggsdale, *U.S.A.* **80 E2** 40 38N 104 20W
Brigham City, *U.S.A.* **82 F7** 41 31N 112 1W
Bright, *Australia* **63 F4** 36 42S 146 56 E
Brighton, *Australia* **63 F2** 35 5S 138 30 E
Brighton, *Canada* **70 D4** 44 2N 77 44W
Brighton, *U.K.* **11 G7** 50 49N 0 7W
Brighton, *U.S.A.* **80 F2** 39 59N 104 49W
Brilliant, *Canada* **72 D5** 49 19N 117 38W
Brilliant, *U.S.A.* **78 F4** 40 15N 80 39W
Brindisi, *Italy* **21 D7** 40 39N 17 55 E
Brinkley, *U.S.A.* **81 H9** 34 53N 91 12W
Brinkworth, *Australia* **63 E2** 33 42S 138 26 E
Brinnon, *U.S.A.* **84 C4** 47 41N 122 54W
Brion, I., *Canada* **71 C7** 47 46N 61 26W
Brisbane, *Australia* **63 D5** 27 25S 153 2 E
Brisbane →, *Australia* **63 D5** 27 24S 153 9 E
Bristol, *U.K.* **11 F5** 51 26N 2 35W
Bristol, *Conn., U.S.A.* **79 E12** 41 40N 72 57W
Bristol, *Pa., U.S.A.* **79 F10** 40 6N 74 51W
Bristol, *R.I., U.S.A.* **79 E13** 41 40N 71 16W
Bristol, *S. Dak., U.S.A.* **80 C6** 45 21N 97 45W
Bristol, *Tenn., U.S.A.* **77 G4** 36 36N 82 11W
Bristol □, *U.K.* **11 F5** 51 27N 2 36W
Bristol B., *U.S.A.* **68 C4** 58 0N 160 0W
Bristol Channel, *U.K.* **11 F3** 51 18N 4 30W
Bristol I., *Antarctica* **5 B1** 58 45S 28 0W
Bristol L., *U.S.A.* **83 J5** 34 23N 116 50W

Bristow

Bristow, U.S.A. 81 H6 35 50N 96 23W
British Columbia □, Canada 72 C3 55 0N 125 15W
British Isles, Europe 6 E5 54 0N 4 0W
Brits, S. Africa 57 D4 25 37S 27 48 E
Britstown, S. Africa 56 E3 30 37S 23 30 E
Britt, Canada 70 C3 45 46N 80 34W
Brittany = Bretagne, France 18 B2 48 10N 3 0W
Britton, U.S.A. 80 C6 45 48N 97 45W
Brive-la-Gaillarde, France 18 D4 45 10N 1 32 E
Brixen = Bressanone, Italy 20 A4 46 43N 11 39 E
Brixton, Australia 62 C3 23 32S 144 57 E
Brlik, Kazakstan 26 E8 43 40N 73 49 E
Brno, Czech. 17 D9 49 10N 16 35 E
Broad —►, U.S.A. 77 J5 34 1N 81 4W
Broad Arrow, Australia 61 F3 30 23S 121 15 E
Broad B., U.K. 12 C2 58 14N 6 18W
Broad Haven, Ireland 13 B2 54 20N 9 55W
Broad Law, U.K. 12 F5 55 30N 3 21W
Broad Sd., Australia 62 C4 22 0S 149 45 E
Broadhurst Ra., Australia 60 D3 22 30S 122 30 E
Broads, The, U.K. 10 E9 52 45N 1 30 E
Broadus, U.S.A. 80 C2 45 27N 105 25W
Broadview, Canada 73 C8 50 22N 102 35W
Brochet, Canada 73 B8 57 53N 101 40W
Brochet, L., Canada 73 B8 58 36N 101 35W
Brock, Canada 73 C7 51 26N 108 43W
Brocken, Germany 16 C6 51 47N 10 37 E
Brockport, U.S.A. 78 C7 43 13N 77 56W
Brockton, U.S.A. 79 D13 42 5N 71 1W
Brockville, Canada 70 D4 44 35N 75 41W
Brockway, Mont., U.S.A. 80 B2 47 18N 105 45W
Brockway, Pa., U.S.A. 78 E6 41 15N 78 47W
Brocton, U.S.A. 78 D5 42 23N 79 26W
Brodeur Pen., Canada 69 A11 72 30N 88 10W
Brodick, U.K. 12 F3 55 35N 5 9W
Brodnica, Poland 17 B10 53 15N 19 25 E
Brody, Ukraine 17 C13 50 5N 25 10 E
Brogan, U.S.A. 82 D5 44 15N 117 31W
Broken Arrow, U.S.A. 81 G7 36 3N 95 48W
Broken Bow, Nebr., U.S.A. 80 E5 41 24N 99 38W
Broken Bow, Okla., U.S.A. 81 H7 34 2N 94 44W
Broken Hill = Kabwe, Zambia 55 E2 14 30S 28 29 E
Broken Hill, Australia 63 E3 31 58S 141 29 E
Bromfield, U.K. 11 E5 52 24N 2 45W
Bromley, U.K. 11 F8 51 24N 0 2 E
Brønderslev, Denmark 9 H13 57 16N 9 57 E
Bronkhorstspruit, S. Africa 57 D4 25 46S 28 45 E
Brønnøysund, Norway 8 D15 65 28N 12 14 E
Bronte, U.S.A. 81 K4 31 53N 100 18W
Bronte Park, Australia 62 G4 42 8S 146 30 E
Brook Park, U.S.A. 78 E4 41 24N 80 51W
Brookfield, U.S.A. 80 F8 39 47N 93 4W
Brookhaven, U.S.A. 81 K9 31 35N 90 26W
Brookings, Oreg., U.S.A. 82 E1 42 3N 124 17W
Brookings, S. Dak., U.S.A. 80 C6 44 19N 96 48W
Brooklin, Canada 78 C6 43 55N 78 55W
Brooklyn Park, U.S.A. 80 C8 45 6N 93 23W
Brookmere, Canada 72 D4 49 52N 120 53W
Brooks, Canada 72 C6 50 35N 111 55W
Brooks B., Canada 72 C3 50 15N 127 55W
Brooks L., Canada 73 A7 61 55N 106 35W
Brooks Ra., U.S.A. 68 B5 68 40N 147 0W
Brooksville, U.S.A. 77 L4 28 33N 82 23W
Brookville, U.S.A. 76 F3 39 25N 85 1W
Brooloo, Australia 63 D5 26 30S 152 43 E
Broom, L., U.K. 12 D3 57 55N 5 15W
Broome, Australia 60 C3 18 0S 122 15 E
Broomehill, Australia 61 F2 33 51S 117 39 E
Brora, U.K. 12 C5 58 0N 3 52W
Brora —►, U.K. 12 C5 58 0N 3 51W
Brosna —►, Ireland 13 C4 53 14N 7 58W
Brothers, U.S.A. 82 E3 43 49N 120 36W
Brough, U.K. 10 C5 54 32N 2 18W
Broughton Island, Canada 69 B13 67 33N 63 0W
Broughty Ferry, U.K. 12 E6 56 29N 2 51W
Brouwershaven, Neths. 15 C3 51 45N 3 55 E
Browerville, U.S.A. 80 B7 46 5N 94 52W
Brown, Pt., Australia 63 E1 32 32S 133 50 E
Brown Willy, U.K. 11 G3 50 35N 4 37W
Brownfield, U.S.A. 81 J3 33 11N 102 17W
Browning, U.S.A. 82 B7 48 34N 113 1W
Brownlee, Canada 73 C7 50 43N 106 1W
Brownsville, Oreg., U.S.A. 82 D2 44 24N 122 59W
Brownsville, Tenn., U.S.A. 81 H10 35 36N 89 16W
Brownsville, Tex., U.S.A. 81 N6 25 54N 97 30W
Brownwood, U.S.A. 81 K5 31 43N 98 59W
Brownwood, L., U.S.A. 81 K5 31 51N 98 35W
Browse I., Australia 60 B3 14 7S 123 33 E
Bruas, Malaysia 39 K3 4 30N 100 47 E
Bruay-en-Artois, France 18 A5 50 29N 2 33 E
Bruce, Mt., Australia 60 D2 22 37S 118 8 E
Bruce Pen., Canada 78 A3 45 0N 81 30W
Bruce Rock, Australia 61 F2 31 52S 118 8 E
Bruck an der Leitha, Austria 17 D9 48 1N 16 47 E
Bruck an der Mur, Austria 16 E8 47 24N 15 16 E
Brue —►, U.K. 11 F5 51 13N 2 59W
Bruges = Brugge, Belgium 15 C3 51 13N 3 13 E
Brugge, Belgium 15 C3 51 13N 3 13 E
Brûlé, Canada 72 C5 53 15N 117 58W
Brumado, Brazil 93 F10 14 14S 41 40W
Brumunddal, Norway 9 F14 60 53N 10 56 E
Brunchilly, Australia 62 B1 18 50S 134 30 E
Brundidge, U.S.A. 77 K3 31 43N 85 49W
Bruneau, U.S.A. 82 E6 42 53N 115 48W
Bruneau —►, U.S.A. 82 E6 42 56N 115 57W
Brunei = Bandar Seri Begawan, Brunei 36 C4 4 52N 115 0 E
Brunei ■, Asia 36 D4 4 50N 115 0 E
Brunette Downs, Australia 62 B2 18 40S 135 55 E
Brunner, L., N.Z. 59 K3 42 37S 171 27 E
Bruno, Canada 73 C7 52 20N 105 30W
Brunswick = Braunschweig, Germany 16 B6 52 15N 10 31 E
Brunswick, Ga., U.S.A. 77 K5 31 10N 81 30W
Brunswick, Maine, U.S.A. 71 D6 43 55N 69 58W
Brunswick, Md., U.S.A. 76 F7 39 19N 77 38W
Brunswick, Mo., U.S.A. 80 F8 39 26N 93 8W
Brunswick, Ohio, U.S.A. 78 E3 41 14N 81 51W
Brunswick, Pen. de, Chile 96 G2 53 30S 71 30W
Brunswick B., Australia 60 C3 15 15S 124 50 E
Brunswick Junction, Australia 61 F2 33 15S 115 50 E
Bruny I., Australia 62 G4 43 20S 147 15 E
Brus Laguna, Honduras 88 C3 15 47N 84 35W
Brush, U.S.A. 80 E3 40 15N 103 37W
Brushton, U.S.A. 79 B10 44 50N 74 31W
Brusque, Brazil 95 B6 27 5S 49 0W
Brussel, Belgium 15 D4 50 51N 4 21 E
Brussels = Brussel, Belgium 15 D4 50 51N 4 21 E
Brussels, Canada 78 C3 43 44N 81 15W
Bruthen, Australia 63 F4 37 42S 147 50 E
Bruxelles = Brussel, Belgium 15 D4 50 51N 4 21 E
Bryan, Ohio, U.S.A. 76 E3 41 28N 84 33W
Bryan, Tex., U.S.A. 81 K6 30 40N 96 22W
Bryan, Mt., Australia 63 E2 33 30S 139 0 E
Bryansk, Russia 24 D5 53 13N 34 25 E
Bryant, U.S.A. 80 C6 44 35N 97 28W
Bryne, Norway 9 G11 58 44N 5 38 E
Bryson City, U.S.A. 77 H4 35 26N 83 27W
Bsharri, Lebanon 47 A5 34 15N 36 0 E
Bū Baqarah, U.A.E. 45 E8 25 35N 56 25 E
Bu Craa, W. Sahara 50 C2 26 45N 12 50W
Bū Ḥasā, U.A.E. 45 F7 23 30N 53 20 E
Bua Yai, Thailand 38 E4 15 33N 102 26 E
Buapinang, Indonesia 37 E6 4 40S 121 30 E
Buayan, Phil. 37 C7 6 3N 125 6 E
Bubanza, Burundi 54 C2 3 6S 29 23 E
Būbiyān, Kuwait 45 D6 29 45N 48 15 E
Bucaramanga, Colombia 92 B4 7 0N 73 0W
Buccaneer Arch., Australia 60 C3 16 7S 123 20 E
Buchach, Ukraine 17 D13 49 5N 25 25 E
Buchan, U.K. 12 D6 57 32N 2 21W
Buchan Ness, U.K. 12 D7 57 29N 1 46W
Buchanan, Canada 73 C8 51 40N 102 45W
Buchanan, Liberia 50 G2 5 57N 10 2W
Buchanan, L., Queens., Australia 62 C4 21 35S 145 52 E
Buchanan, L., W. Austral., Australia 61 E3 25 33S 123 2 E
Buchanan, L., U.S.A. 81 K5 30 45N 98 25W
Buchanan Cr. —►, Australia 62 B2 19 13S 136 33 E
Buchans, Canada 71 C8 48 50N 56 52W
Bucharest = Bucureşti, Romania 17 F14 44 27N 26 10 E
Buchon, Pt., U.S.A. 84 K6 35 15N 120 54W
Buckeye, U.S.A. 83 K7 33 22N 112 35W
Buckhannon, U.S.A. 76 F5 39 0N 80 8W
Buckhaven, U.K. 12 E5 56 11N 3 3W
Buckie, U.K. 12 D6 57 41N 2 58W
Buckingham, Canada 70 C4 45 37N 75 24W
Buckingham, U.K. 11 F7 51 59N 0 57W
Buckingham B., Australia 62 A2 12 10S 135 40 E
Buckinghamshire □, U.K. 11 F7 51 53N 0 55W
Buckle Hd., Australia 60 B4 14 26S 127 52 E
Buckleboo, Australia 63 E2 32 54S 136 12 E
Buckley, U.S.A. 82 C2 47 10N 122 2W
Buckley —►, Australia 62 C2 20 10S 138 49 E
Bucklin, U.S.A. 81 G5 37 33N 99 38W
Bucks L., U.S.A. 84 F5 39 54N 121 12W
Buctouche, Canada 71 C7 46 30N 64 45W
Bucureşti, Romania 17 F14 44 27N 26 10 E
Bucyrus, U.S.A. 76 E4 40 48N 82 59W
Budalin, Burma 41 H19 22 20N 95 10 E
Budapest, Hungary 17 E10 47 29N 19 5 E
Budaun, India 43 E8 28 5N 79 10 E
Budd Coast, Antarctica 5 C8 68 0S 112 0 E
Bude, U.K. 11 G3 50 49N 4 34W
Budennovsk, Russia 25 F7 44 50N 44 10 E
Budge Budge = Baj Baj, India 43 H13 22 30N 88 5 E
Budgewoi, Australia 63 E5 33 13S 151 34 E
Budjala, Zaïre 52 D3 2 50N 19 40 E
Buellton, U.S.A. 85 L6 34 37N 120 12W
Buena Park, U.S.A. 85 M9 33 52N 117 59W
Buena Vista, Colo., U.S.A. 83 G10 38 51N 106 8W
Buena Vista, Va., U.S.A. 76 G6 37 44N 79 21W
Buena Vista L., U.S.A. 85 K7 35 12N 119 18W
Buenaventura, Colombia 92 C3 3 53N 77 4W
Buenaventura, Mexico 86 B3 29 50N 107 30W
Buenos Aires, Argentina 94 C4 34 30S 58 20W
Buenos Aires, Costa Rica 88 E3 9 10N 83 20W
Buenos Aires □, Argentina 94 D4 36 30S 60 0W
Buenos Aires, L., Chile 96 F2 46 35S 72 30W
Buffalo, Mo., U.S.A. 81 G8 37 39N 93 6W
Buffalo, N.Y., U.S.A. 78 D6 42 53N 78 53W
Buffalo, Okla., U.S.A. 81 G5 36 50N 99 38W
Buffalo, S. Dak., U.S.A. 80 C3 45 35N 103 33W
Buffalo, Wyo., U.S.A. 82 D10 44 21N 106 42W
Buffalo —►, Canada 72 A5 60 5N 115 5W
Buffalo Head Hills, Canada 72 B5 57 25N 115 55W
Buffalo L., Canada 72 C6 52 27N 112 54W
Buffalo Narrows, Canada 73 B7 55 51N 108 29W
Buffels —►, S. Africa 56 D2 29 36S 17 3 E
Buford, U.S.A. 77 H4 34 10N 84 0W
Bug —► = Buh —►, Ukraine 25 E5 46 59N 31 58 E
Bug —►, Poland 17 B11 52 31N 21 5 E
Buga, Colombia 92 C3 4 0N 76 15W
Buganda, Uganda 54 C3 0 0 31 30 E
Buganga, Uganda 54 C3 0 3S 32 0 E
Bugel, Tanjung, Indonesia 36 F4 6 26S 111 3 E
Bugibba, Malta 23 D1 35 57N 14 25 E
Bugsuk, Phil. 36 C5 8 15N 117 15 E
Bugulma, Russia 24 D9 54 33N 52 48 E
Bugun Shara, Mongolia 32 B5 49 0N 104 0 E
Buguruslan, Russia 24 D9 53 39N 52 26 E
Buh —►, Ukraine 25 E5 46 59N 31 58 E
Buheirat-Murrat-el-Kubra, Egypt 51 B11 30 18N 32 26 E
Buhl, Idaho, U.S.A. 82 E6 42 36N 114 46W
Buhl, Minn., U.S.A. 80 B8 47 30N 92 46W
Buick, U.S.A. 81 G9 37 38N 91 2W
Builth Wells, U.K. 11 E4 52 9N 3 25W
Buir Nur, Mongolia 33 B6 47 50N 117 42 E
Bujumbura, Burundi 54 C2 3 16S 29 18 E
Bukachacha, Russia 27 D12 52 55N 116 50 E
Bukama, Zaïre 55 D2 9 10S 25 50 E
Bukavu, Zaïre 54 C2 2 20S 28 52 E
Bukene, Tanzania 54 C3 4 15S 32 48 E
Bukhara = Bukhoro, Uzbekistan 26 F7 39 48N 64 25 E
Bukhoro, Uzbekistan 26 F7 39 48N 64 25 E
Bukima, Tanzania 54 C3 1 50S 33 25 E
Bukit Mertajam, Malaysia 39 K3 5 22N 100 28 E
Bukittinggi, Indonesia 36 E2 0 20S 100 20 E
Bukoba, Tanzania 54 C3 1 20S 31 49 E
Bukoba □, Tanzania 54 C3 1 30S 32 0 E
Bukuya, Uganda 54 B3 0 40N 31 52 E
Bula, Indonesia 37 E8 3 6S 130 30 E
Bulahdelah, Australia 63 E5 32 23S 152 13 E
Bulan, Phil. 37 B6 12 40N 123 52 E
Bulandshahr, India 42 E7 28 28N 77 51 E
Bulawayo, Zimbabwe 55 G2 20 7S 28 32 E
Buldan, Turkey 21 E13 38 2N 28 50 E
Bulgaria ■, Europe 21 C11 42 35N 25 30 E
Bulgroo, Australia 63 D3 25 47S 143 58 E
Bulgunnia, Australia 63 E1 30 10S 134 53 E
Bulhar, Somali Rep. 46 E3 10 25N 44 30 E
Buli, Teluk, Indonesia 37 D7 1 5N 128 25 E
Buliluyan, C., Phil. 36 C5 8 20N 117 15 E
Bulkley —►, Canada 72 B3 55 15N 127 40W
Bull Shoals L., U.S.A. 81 G8 36 22N 92 35W
Bullara, Australia 60 D1 22 40S 114 3 E
Bullaring, Australia 61 F2 32 30S 117 45 E
Bulli, Australia 63 E5 34 15S 150 57 E
Bullock Creek, Australia 62 B3 17 43S 144 31 E
Bulloo —►, Australia 63 D3 28 43S 142 30 E
Bulloo Downs, Queens., Australia 63 D3 28 31S 142 57 E
Bulloo Downs, W. Austral., Australia 60 D2 24 0S 119 32 E
Bulloo L., Australia 63 D3 28 43S 142 25 E
Bulls, N.Z. 59 J5 40 10S 175 24 E
Bulnes, Chile 94 D1 36 42S 72 19W
Bulo Burti, Somali Rep. 46 G4 3 50N 45 33 E
Bulsar = Valsad, India 40 J8 20 40N 72 58 E
Bultfontein, S. Africa 56 D4 28 18S 26 10 E
Bulukumba, Indonesia 37 F6 5 33S 120 11 E
Bulun, Russia 27 B13 70 37N 127 30 E
Bulus, Russia 27 C13 63 10N 129 10 E
Bumba, Zaïre 52 D4 2 13N 22 30 E
Bumbiri I., Tanzania 54 C3 1 40S 31 55 E
Bumhpa Bum, Burma 41 F20 26 51N 97 14 E
Bumi —►, Zimbabwe 55 F2 17 0S 28 20 E
Buna, Kenya 54 B4 2 58N 39 30 E
Bunazi, Tanzania 54 C3 1 3S 31 23 E
Bunbah, Khalīj, Libya 51 B9 32 20N 23 15 E
Bunbury, Australia 61 F2 33 20S 115 35 E
Buncrana, Ireland 13 A4 55 8N 7 27W
Bundaberg, Australia 63 C5 24 54S 152 22 E
Bundey —►, Australia 62 C2 21 46S 135 37 E
Bundi, India 42 G6 25 30N 75 35 E
Bundooma, Australia 62 C1 24 54S 134 16 E
Bundoran, Ireland 13 B3 54 28N 8 16W
Bung Kan, Thailand 38 C4 18 23N 103 37 E
Bungatakada, Japan 31 H5 33 35N 131 25 E
Bungil Cr. —►, Australia 62 D4 27 5S 149 5 E
Bungo-Suidō, Japan 31 H6 33 0N 132 15 E
Bungoma, Kenya 54 B3 0 34N 34 34 E
Bungu, Tanzania 54 D4 7 35S 39 0 E
Bunia, Zaïre 54 B3 1 35N 30 20 E
Bunji, Pakistan 43 B6 35 45N 74 40 E
Bunkie, U.S.A. 81 K8 30 57N 92 11W
Bunnell, U.S.A. 77 L5 29 28N 81 16W
Buntok, Indonesia 36 E4 1 40S 114 58 E
Bunyu, Indonesia 36 D5 3 35N 117 50 E
Buol, Indonesia 37 D6 1 15N 121 32 E
Buon Brieng, Vietnam 38 F7 13 9N 108 12 E
Buon Me Thuot, Vietnam 38 F7 12 40N 108 3 E
Buong Long, Cambodia 38 F6 13 44N 106 59 E
Buorkhaya, Mys, Russia 27 B14 71 50N 132 40 E
Buqayq, Si. Arabia 45 E6 26 0N 49 45 E
Bur Acaba, Somali Rep. 46 G3 3 12N 44 20 E
Bûr Safâga, Egypt 51 C11 26 43N 33 57 E
Bûr Sa'îd, Egypt 51 B11 31 16N 32 18 E
Bûr Sûdân, Sudan 51 E12 19 32N 37 9 E
Bura, Kenya 54 C4 1 4S 39 58 E
Burao, Somali Rep. 46 F4 9 32N 45 32 E
Burāq, Syria 47 B5 33 11N 36 29 E
Buras, U.S.A. 81 L10 29 22N 89 32W
Buraydah, Si. Arabia 44 E5 26 20N 44 8 E
Burbank, U.S.A. 85 L8 34 11N 118 19W
Burcher, Australia 63 E4 33 30S 147 16 E
Burdekin —►, Australia 62 B4 19 38S 147 25 E
Burdett, Canada 72 D6 49 50N 111 32W
Burdur, Turkey 25 G5 37 45N 30 17 E
Burdwan = Barddhaman, India 43 H12 23 14N 87 39 E
Bure —►, U.K. 10 E9 52 38N 1 43 E
Bureya —►, Russia 27 E13 49 27N 129 30 E
Burford, Canada 78 C4 43 7N 80 27W
Burgas, Bulgaria 21 C12 42 33N 27 29 E
Burgeo, Canada 71 C8 47 37N 57 38W
Burgersdorp, S. Africa 56 E4 31 0S 26 20 E
Burges, Mt., Australia 61 F3 30 50S 121 5 E
Burgos, Spain 19 A4 42 21N 3 41W
Burgsvik, Sweden 9 H18 57 3N 18 19 E
Burgundy = Bourgogne, France 18 C6 47 0N 4 50 E
Burhaniye, Turkey 21 E12 39 30N 26 58 E
Burhanpur, India 40 J10 21 18N 76 14 E
Burias, Phil. 37 B6 12 55N 123 5 E
Burica, Pta., Costa Rica 88 E3 8 3N 82 51W
Burigi, L., Tanzania 54 C3 2 2S 31 22 E
Burin, Canada 71 C8 47 1N 55 14W
Buriram, Thailand 38 E4 15 0N 103 0 E
Burj Sāfitā, Syria 44 C3 34 48N 36 7 E
Burji, Ethiopia 51 G12 5 29N 37 51 E
Burkburnett, U.S.A. 81 H5 34 6N 98 34W
Burke, U.S.A. 82 C6 47 31N 115 49W
Burke —►, Australia 62 C2 23 12S 139 33 E
Burketown, Australia 62 B2 17 45S 139 33 E
Burkina Faso ■, Africa 50 F4 12 0N 1 0W
Burk's Falls, Canada 70 C4 45 37N 79 24W
Burley, U.S.A. 82 E7 42 32N 113 48W
Burlingame, U.S.A. 84 H4 37 35N 122 21W
Burlington, Canada 78 C5 43 18N 79 45W
Burlington, Colo., U.S.A. 80 F3 39 18N 102 16W
Burlington, Iowa, U.S.A. 80 E9 40 49N 91 14W
Burlington, Kans., U.S.A. 80 F7 38 12N 95 45W
Burlington, N.C., U.S.A. 77 G6 36 6N 79 26W
Burlington, N.J., U.S.A. 79 F10 40 4N 74 51W
Burlington, Vt., U.S.A. 79 B11 44 29N 73 12W
Burlington, Wash., U.S.A. 84 B4 48 28N 122 20W
Burlington, Wis., U.S.A. 76 D1 42 41N 88 17W
Burlyu-Tyube, Kazakstan 26 E8 46 30N 79 10 E
Burma ■, Asia 41 J20 21 0N 96 30 E
Burnaby I., Canada 72 C2 52 25N 131 19W
Burnet, U.S.A. 81 K5 30 45N 98 14W
Burney, U.S.A. 82 F3 40 53N 121 40W
Burngup, Australia 61 F2 33 2S 118 42 E
Burnham, U.S.A. 78 F7 40 38N 77 34W
Burnie, Australia 62 G4 41 4S 145 56 E
Burnley, U.K. 10 D5 53 47N 2 14W
Burns, Oreg., U.S.A. 82 E4 43 35N 119 3W
Burns, Wyo., U.S.A. 80 E2 41 12N 104 21W
Burns Lake, Canada 72 C3 54 20N 125 45W
Burnside —►, Canada 68 B9 66 51N 108 4W
Burnside, L., Australia 61 E3 25 22S 123 0 E
Burnsville, U.S.A. 80 C8 44 47N 93 17W
Burnt River, Canada 78 B6 44 41N 78 42W
Burntwood —►, Canada 73 B9 56 8N 96 34W
Burntwood L., Canada 73 B8 55 22N 100 26W
Burqān, Kuwait 44 D5 29 0N 47 57 E
Burra, Australia 63 E2 33 40S 138 55 E
Burramurra, Australia 62 C2 20 25S 137 15 E
Burren Junction, Australia 63 E4 30 7S 148 59 E
Burrendong Dam, Australia 63 E4 32 39S 149 6 E
Burrinjuck Res., Australia 63 F4 35 0S 148 36 E
Burro, Serranías del, Mexico 86 B4 29 0N 102 0W
Burruyacú, Argentina 94 B3 26 30S 64 40W
Burry Port, U.K. 11 F3 51 41N 4 15W
Bursa, Turkey 21 D13 40 15N 29 5 E
Burstall, Canada 73 C7 50 39N 109 54W
Burton L., Canada 70 B4 54 45N 78 20W
Burton upon Trent, U.K. 10 E6 52 48N 1 38W
Burtundy, Australia 63 E3 33 45S 142 15 E
Buru, Indonesia 37 E7 3 30S 126 30 E
Burûn, Râs, Egypt 47 D2 31 14N 33 7 E
Burundi ■, Africa 54 C3 3 15S 30 0 E
Bururi, Burundi 54 C2 3 57S 29 37 E
Burutu, Nigeria 50 G6 5 20N 5 29 E
Burwell, U.S.A. 80 E5 41 47N 99 8W
Bury, U.K. 10 D5 53 35N 2 17W
Bury St. Edmunds, U.K. 11 E8 52 15N 0 43 E
Buryatia □, Russia 27 D11 53 0N 110 0 E
Busango Swamp, Zambia 55 E2 14 15S 25 45 E
Buşayrah, Syria 44 C4 35 9N 40 26 E
Buşayyah, Iraq 44 D5 30 0N 46 10 E
Būshehr, Iran 45 D6 28 55N 50 55 E
Būshehr □, Iran 45 D6 28 20N 51 45 E
Bushell, Canada 73 B7 59 31N 108 45W
Bushenyi, Uganda 54 C3 0 35S 30 10 E
Bushire = Būshehr, Iran 45 D6 28 55N 50 55 E
Bushnell, Ill., U.S.A. 80 E9 40 33N 90 31W
Bushnell, Nebr., U.S.A. 80 E3 41 14N 103 54W
Busia □, Kenya 54 B3 0 25N 34 6 E
Businga, Zaïre 52 D4 3 16N 20 59 E
Busra ash Shām, Syria 47 C5 32 30N 36 25 E
Busselton, Australia 61 F2 33 42S 115 15 E
Bussum, Neths. 15 B5 52 16N 5 10 E
Busto Arsizio, Italy 20 B3 45 37N 8 51 E
Busu-Djanoa, Zaïre 52 D4 1 43N 21 23 E
Busuanga, Phil. 37 B5 12 10N 120 0 E
Buta, Zaïre 54 B1 2 50N 24 53 E
Butare, Rwanda 54 C2 2 31S 29 52 E
Butaritari, Kiribati 64 G9 3 30N 174 0 E
Bute, U.K. 12 F3 55 48N 5 2W
Bute Inlet, Canada 72 C4 50 40N 124 53W
Butemba, Uganda 54 B3 1 9N 31 37 E
Butembo, Zaïre 54 B2 0 9N 29 18 E
Butha Qi, China 33 B7 48 0N 122 32 E
Butiaba, Uganda 54 B3 1 50N 31 20 E
Butler, Mo., U.S.A. 80 F7 38 16N 94 20W
Butler, Pa., U.S.A. 78 F5 40 52N 79 54W
Buton, Indonesia 37 E6 5 0S 122 45 E
Butte, Mont., U.S.A. 82 C7 46 0N 112 32W
Butte, Nebr., U.S.A. 80 D5 42 58N 98 51W
Butte Creek —►, U.S.A. 84 F5 39 12N 121 56W
Butterworth = Gcuwa, S. Africa 57 E4 32 20S 28 11 E
Butterworth, Malaysia 39 K3 5 24N 100 23 E
Buttfield, Mt., Australia 61 D4 24 45S 128 9 E
Button B., Canada 73 B10 58 45N 94 23W
Buttonwillow, U.S.A. 85 K7 35 24N 119 28W
Butty Hd., Australia 61 F3 33 54S 121 39 E
Butuan, Phil. 37 C7 8 57N 125 33 E
Butung = Buton, Indonesia 37 E6 5 0S 122 45 E
Buturlinovka, Russia 25 D7 50 50N 40 35 E
Buxar, India 43 G10 25 34N 83 58 E
Buxtehude, Germany 16 B5 53 28N 9 39 E
Buxton, U.K. 10 D6 53 16N 1 54W
Buy, Russia 24 C7 58 28N 41 28 E
Büyük Menderes —►, Turkey 21 F12 37 28N 27 11 E
Büyükçekmece, Turkey 21 D13 41 2N 28 35 E
Buzău, Romania 17 F14 45 10N 26 50 E
Buzău —►, Romania 17 F14 45 26N 27 44 E
Buzen, Japan 31 H5 33 35N 131 5 E
Buzi —►, Mozam. 55 F3 19 50S 34 43 E
Buzuluk, Russia 24 D9 52 48N 52 12 E
Buzzards Bay, U.S.A. 79 E14 41 45N 70 37W
Bwana Mkubwe, Zaïre 55 E2 13 8S 28 38 E
Byarezina —►, Belarus 17 B16 52 33N 30 14 E
Bydgoszcz, Poland 17 B9 53 10N 18 0 E
Byelarus = Belarus ■, Europe 17 B14 53 30N 27 0 E
Byelorussia = Belarus ■, Europe 17 B14 53 30N 27 0 E
Byers, U.S.A. 80 F2 39 43N 104 14W
Byesville, U.S.A. 78 G3 39 58N 81 32W
Byhalia, U.S.A. 81 H10 34 52N 89 41W
Bykhaw, Belarus 17 B16 53 31N 30 14 E
Bykhov = Bykhaw, Belarus 17 B16 53 31N 30 14 E
Bylas, U.S.A. 83 K8 33 8N 110 7W
Bylot I., Canada 69 A12 73 13N 78 34W
Byrd, C., Antarctica 5 C17 69 38S 76 7W
Byro, Australia 61 E2 26 5S 116 11 E
Byrock, Australia 63 E4 30 40S 146 27 E
Byron Bay, Australia 63 D5 28 43S 153 37 E
Byrranga, Gory, Russia 27 B11 75 0N 100 0 E

Cape York Peninsula

Byrranga Mts. = Byrranga, Gory, Russia 27 B11 75 0N 100 0 E
Byske, Sweden 8 D19 64 57N 21 11 E
Byske älv →, Sweden 8 D19 64 57N 21 13 E
Bytom, Poland 17 C10 50 25N 18 54 E
Bytów, Poland 17 A9 54 10N 17 30 E
Byumba, Rwanda 54 C3 1 35S 30 4 E

C

Ca →, Vietnam 38 C5 18 45N 105 45 E
Ca Mau = Quan Long, Vietnam 39 H5 9 7N 105 8 E
Ca Mau, Mui = Bai Bung, Mui, Vietnam 39 H5 8 38N 104 44 E
Ca Na, Vietnam 39 G7 11 20N 108 54 E
Caacupé, Paraguay 94 B4 25 23S 57 5W
Caála, Angola 53 G3 12 46S 15 30 E
Caamano Sd., Canada 72 C3 52 55N 129 25W
Caazapá, Paraguay 94 B4 26 8S 56 19W
Caazapá □, Paraguay 95 B4 26 10S 56 0W
Caballeria, C. de, Spain 22 A11 40 5N 4 5 E
Cabanatuan, Phil. 37 A6 15 30N 120 58 E
Cabano, Canada 71 C6 47 40N 68 56W
Cabazon, U.S.A. 85 M10 33 55N 116 47W
Cabedelo, Brazil 93 E12 7 0S 34 50W
Cabildo, Chile 94 C1 32 30S 71 5W
Cabimas, Venezuela 92 A4 10 23N 71 25W
Cabinda, Angola 52 F2 5 33S 12 11 E
Cabinda □, Angola 52 F2 5 0S 12 30 E
Cabinet Mts., U.S.A. 82 C6 48 0N 115 30W
Cabo Blanco, Argentina 96 F3 47 15S 65 47W
Cabo Frio, Brazil 95 A7 22 51S 42 3W
Cabo Pantoja, Peru 92 D3 1 0S 75 10W
Cabonga, Réservoir, Canada 70 C4 47 20N 76 40W
Cabool, U.S.A. 81 G8 37 7N 92 6W
Caboolture, Australia 63 D5 27 5S 152 58 E
Cabora Bassa Dam = Cahora Bassa Dam, Mozam. 55 F3 15 20S 32 50 E
Caborca, Mexico 86 A2 30 40N 112 10W
Cabot, Mt., U.S.A. 79 B13 44 30N 71 25W
Cabot Str., Canada 71 C8 47 15N 59 40W
Cabra, Spain 19 D3 37 30N 4 28W
Cabrera, Spain 22 B9 39 8N 2 57 E
Cabri, Canada 73 C7 50 35N 108 25W
Cabriel →, Spain 19 C5 39 14N 1 3W
Čačak, Serbia, Yug. 21 C9 43 54N 20 20 E
Cáceres, Brazil 92 G7 16 5S 57 40W
Cáceres, Spain 19 C2 39 26N 6 23W
Cache Bay, Canada 70 C4 46 22N 80 0W
Cache Cr. →, U.S.A. 84 G5 38 42N 121 42W
Cachi, Argentina 94 B2 25 5S 66 10W
Cachimbo, Serra do, Brazil 93 E7 9 30S 55 30W
Cachoeira, Brazil 93 F11 12 30S 39 0W
Cachoeira de Itapemirim, Brazil 95 A7 20 51S 41 7W
Cachoeira do Sul, Brazil 95 C5 30 3S 52 53W
Cacólo, Angola 52 G3 10 9S 19 21 E
Caconda, Angola 53 G3 13 48S 15 8 E
Cacongo, Angola 52 F2 5 11S 12 5 E
Caddo, U.S.A. 81 H6 34 7N 96 16W
Cadell Cr. →, Australia 62 C3 22 35S 141 51 E
Cader Idris, U.K. 10 E4 52 42N 3 53W
Cadibarrawirracanna, L., Australia 63 D2 28 52S 135 27 E
Cadillac, Canada 70 C4 48 14N 78 23W
Cadillac, U.S.A. 76 C3 44 15N 85 24W
Cadiz, Phil. 37 B6 10 57N 123 15 E
Cádiz, Spain 19 D2 36 30N 6 20W
Cadiz, U.S.A. 78 F4 40 22N 81 0W
Cádiz, G. de, Spain 19 D2 36 40N 7 0W
Cadney Park, Australia 63 D1 27 55S 134 3 E
Cadomin, Canada 72 C5 53 2N 117 20W
Cadotte →, Canada 72 B5 56 43N 117 10W
Cadoux, Australia 61 F2 30 46S 117 7 E
Caen, France 18 B3 49 10N 0 22W
Caernarfon, U.K. 10 D3 53 8N 4 16W
Caernarfon B., U.K. 10 D3 53 4N 4 40W
Caernarvon = Caernarfon, U.K. 10 D3 53 8N 4 16W
Caerphilly, U.K. 11 F4 51 35N 3 13W
Caerphilly □, U.K. 11 F4 51 37N 3 12W
Caesarea, Israel 47 C3 32 30N 34 53 E
Caeté, Brazil 93 G10 19 55S 43 40W
Caetité, Brazil 93 F10 13 50S 42 32W
Cafayate, Argentina 94 B2 26 2S 66 0W
Cafu, Angola 56 B2 16 30S 15 8 E
Cagayan →, Phil. 37 A6 18 25N 121 42 E
Cagayan de Oro, Phil. 37 C6 8 30N 124 40 E
Cágliari, Italy 20 E3 39 13N 9 7 E
Cágliari, G. di, Italy 20 E3 39 8N 9 11 E
Caguas, Puerto Rico 89 C6 18 14N 66 2W
Caha Mts., Ireland 13 E2 51 45N 9 40W
Cahama, Angola 56 B1 16 17S 14 19 E
Caher, Ireland 13 D4 52 22N 7 56W
Caherciveen, Ireland 13 E1 51 56N 10 14W
Cahora Bassa Dam, Mozam. 55 F3 15 20S 32 50 E
Cahore Pt., Ireland 13 D5 52 33N 6 12W
Cahors, France 18 D4 44 27N 1 27 E
Cahuapanas, Peru 92 E3 5 15S 77 0W
Cahul, Moldova 17 F15 45 50N 28 15 E
Cai Bau, Dao, Vietnam 38 B6 21 10N 107 27 E
Cai Nuoc, Vietnam 39 H5 8 56N 105 1 E
Caia, Mozam. 55 F4 17 51S 35 24 E
Caianda, Angola 55 E1 11 2S 23 31 E
Caibarién, Cuba 88 B4 22 30N 79 30W
Caicara, Venezuela 92 B5 7 38N 66 10W
Caicó, Brazil 93 E11 6 20S 37 0W
Caicos Is., W. Indies 89 B5 21 40N 71 40W
Caicos Passage, W. Indies 89 B5 22 45N 72 45W
Caird Coast, Antarctica 5 D1 75 0S 25 0W
Cairn Gorm, U.K. 12 D5 57 7N 3 39W
Cairn Toul, U.K. 12 D5 57 3N 3 44W
Cairngorm Mts., U.K. 12 D5 57 6N 3 42W
Cairns, Australia 62 B4 16 57S 145 45 E
Cairo = El Qâhira, Egypt 51 B11 30 1N 31 14 E
Cairo, Ga., U.S.A. 77 K3 30 52N 84 13W
Cairo, Ill., U.S.A. 81 G10 37 0N 89 11W
Caithness, Ord of, U.K. 12 C5 58 8N 3 36W
Caiundo, Angola 53 H3 15 50S 17 28 E
Caiza, Bolivia 92 H5 20 2S 65 40W
Cajamarca, Peru 92 E3 7 5S 78 28W
Cajàzeiras, Brazil 93 E11 6 52S 38 30W
Cala d'Or, Spain 22 B10 39 23N 3 14 E
Cala Figuera, C., Spain 22 B9 39 27N 2 31 E
Cala Forcat, Spain 22 A10 40 0N 3 47 E
Cala Mayor, Spain 22 B9 39 33N 2 37 E
Cala Mezquida, Spain 22 B11 39 55N 4 16 E
Cala Millor, Spain 22 B10 39 35N 3 22 E
Cala Ratjada, Spain 22 B10 39 43N 3 27 E
Calabar, Nigeria 50 H6 4 57N 8 20 E
Calábria □, Italy 20 E7 39 0N 16 30 E
Calafate, Argentina 96 G2 50 19S 72 15W
Calahorra, Spain 19 A5 42 18N 1 59W
Calais, France 18 A4 50 57N 1 56 E
Calais, U.S.A. 71 C6 45 11N 67 17W
Calalaste, Cord. de, Argentina 94 B2 25 0S 67 0W
Calama, Brazil 92 E6 8 0S 62 50W
Calama, Chile 94 A2 22 30S 68 55W
Calamar, Bolívar, Colombia 92 A4 10 15N 74 55W
Calamar, Vaupés, Colombia 92 C4 1 58N 72 32W
Calamian Group, Phil. 37 B5 11 50N 119 55 E
Calamocha, Spain 19 B5 40 50N 1 17W
Calán Porter, Spain 22 B11 39 52N 4 8 E
Calang, Indonesia 36 D1 4 37N 95 37 E
Calapan, Phil. 37 B6 13 25N 121 7 E
Călăraşi, Romania 17 F14 44 12N 27 20 E
Calatayud, Spain 19 B5 41 20N 1 40W
Calauag, Phil. 37 B6 13 55N 122 15 E
Calavite, C., Phil. 37 B6 13 26N 120 20 E
Calbayog, Phil. 37 B6 12 4N 124 38 E
Calca, Peru 92 F4 13 22S 72 0W
Calcasieu L., U.S.A. 81 L8 29 55N 93 18W
Calcutta, India 43 H13 22 36N 88 24 E
Caldas da Rainha, Portugal 19 C1 39 24N 9 8W
Calder →, U.K. 10 D6 53 44N 1 22W
Caldera, Chile 94 B1 27 5S 70 55W
Caldwell, Idaho, U.S.A. 82 E5 43 40N 116 41W
Caldwell, Kans., U.S.A. 81 G6 37 2N 97 37W
Caldwell, Tex., U.S.A. 81 K6 30 32N 96 42W
Caledon, S. Africa 56 E2 34 14S 19 26 E
Caledon →, S. Africa 56 E4 30 31S 26 5 E
Caledon B., Australia 62 A2 12 45S 137 0 E
Caledonia, Canada 78 C5 43 7N 79 58W
Caledonia, U.S.A. 78 D7 42 58N 77 51W
Calemba, Angola 56 B2 16 0S 15 44 E
Calexico, U.S.A. 85 N11 32 40N 115 30W
Calf of Man, U.K. 10 C3 54 3N 4 48W
Calgary, Canada 72 C6 51 0N 114 10W
Calheta, Madeira 22 D2 32 44N 17 11W
Calhoun, U.S.A. 77 H3 34 30N 84 57W
Cali, Colombia 92 C3 3 25N 76 35W
Calicut, India 40 P9 11 15N 75 43 E
Caliente, U.S.A. 83 H6 37 37N 114 31W
California, Mo., U.S.A. 80 F8 38 38N 92 34W
California, Pa., U.S.A. 78 F5 40 4N 79 54W
California □, U.S.A. 83 H4 37 30N 119 30W
California, Baja, Mexico 86 A1 32 10N 115 12W
California, Baja, T.N. □ = Baja California □, Mexico 86 B2 30 0N 115 0W
California, Baja, T.S. □ = Baja California Sur □, Mexico 86 B2 25 50N 111 50W
California, G. de, Mexico 86 B2 27 0N 111 0W
California City, U.S.A. 85 K9 35 10N 117 55W
California Hot Springs, U.S.A. 85 K8 35 51N 118 41W
Calingasta, Argentina 94 C2 31 15S 69 30W
Calipatria, U.S.A. 85 M11 33 8N 115 31W
Calistoga, U.S.A. 84 G4 38 35N 122 35W
Calitzdorp, S. Africa 56 E3 33 33S 21 42 E
Callabonna, L., Australia 63 D3 29 40S 140 5 E
Callan, Ireland 13 D4 52 32N 7 24W
Callander, U.K. 12 E4 56 15N 4 13W
Callao, Peru 92 F3 12 0S 77 0W
Callaway, U.S.A. 80 E5 41 18N 99 56W
Calles, Mexico 87 C5 23 2N 98 42W
Callide, Australia 62 C5 24 18S 150 28 E
Calling Lake, Canada 72 B6 55 15N 113 12W
Calliope, Australia 62 C5 24 0S 151 16 E
Calola, Angola 56 B2 16 25S 17 48 E
Caloundra, Australia 63 D5 26 45S 153 10 E
Calpella, U.S.A. 84 F3 39 14N 123 12W
Calpine, U.S.A. 84 F6 39 40N 120 27W
Calstock, Canada 70 C3 49 47N 84 9W
Caltagirone, Italy 20 F6 37 14N 14 31 E
Caltanissetta, Italy 20 F6 37 29N 14 4 E
Calulo, Angola 52 G2 10 1S 14 56 E
Calumet, U.S.A. 76 B1 47 14N 88 27W
Calunda, Angola 53 G4 12 7S 23 36 E
Calvert, U.S.A. 81 K6 30 59N 96 40W
Calvert →, Australia 62 B2 16 17S 137 44 E
Calvert Hills, Australia 62 B2 17 15S 137 20 E
Calvert I., Canada 72 C3 51 30N 128 0W
Calvert Ra., Australia 60 D3 24 0S 122 30 E
Calvi, France 18 E8 42 34N 8 45 E
Calvià, Spain 19 C7 39 34N 2 31 E
Calvillo, Mexico 86 C4 21 51N 102 43W
Calvinia, S. Africa 56 E2 31 28S 19 45 E
Calwa, U.S.A. 84 J7 36 42N 119 46W
Cam →, U.K. 11 E8 52 21N 0 16 E
Cam Lam, Vietnam 39 G7 11 54N 109 10 E
Cam Pha, Vietnam 38 B6 21 7N 107 18 E
Cam Ranh, Vietnam 39 G7 11 54N 109 12 E
Cam Xuyen, Vietnam 38 C6 18 15N 106 0 E
Camabatela, Angola 52 F3 8 20S 15 26 E
Camacha, Madeira 22 D3 32 41N 16 49W
Camacho, Mexico 86 C4 24 25N 102 18W
Camacupa, Angola 53 G3 11 58S 17 22 E
Camagüey, Cuba 88 B4 21 20N 78 0W
Camaná, Peru 92 G4 16 30S 72 50W
Camanche Reservoir, U.S.A. 84 G6 38 14N 121 1W
Camaquã →, Brazil 95 C5 31 17S 51 47W
Câmara de Lobos, Madeira 22 D3 32 39N 16 59W
Camargo, Bolivia 92 H5 20 38S 65 15W
Camargue, France 18 E6 43 34N 4 34 E
Camarillo, U.S.A. 85 L7 34 13N 119 2W
Camarón, C., Honduras 88 C2 16 0N 85 5W
Camarones, Argentina 96 E3 44 50S 65 40W
Camas, U.S.A. 84 E4 45 35N 122 24W
Camas Valley, U.S.A. 82 E2 43 2N 123 40W
Cambará, Brazil 95 A5 23 2S 50 5W
Cambay = Khambhat, India 42 H5 22 23N 72 33 E
Cambay, G. of = Khambat, G. of, India 42 J5 20 45N 72 30 E
Cambodia ■, Asia 38 F5 12 15N 105 0 E
Camborne, U.K. 11 G2 50 12N 5 19W
Cambrai, France 18 A5 50 11N 3 14 E
Cambria, U.S.A. 83 J3 35 34N 121 5W
Cambrian Mts., U.K. 11 E4 52 3N 3 57W
Cambridge, Canada 70 D3 43 23N 80 15W
Cambridge, Jamaica 88 C4 18 18N 77 54W
Cambridge, N.Z. 59 G5 37 54S 175 29 E
Cambridge, U.K. 11 E8 52 12N 0 8 E
Cambridge, Idaho, U.S.A. 82 D5 44 34N 116 41W
Cambridge, Mass., U.S.A. 79 D13 42 22N 71 6W
Cambridge, Md., U.S.A. 76 F7 38 34N 76 5W
Cambridge, Minn., U.S.A. 80 C8 45 34N 93 13W
Cambridge, N.Y., U.S.A. 79 C11 43 2N 73 22W
Cambridge, Nebr., U.S.A. 80 E4 40 17N 100 10W
Cambridge, Ohio, U.S.A. 78 F3 40 2N 81 35W
Cambridge Bay, Canada 68 B9 69 10N 105 0W
Cambridge G., Australia 60 B4 14 55S 128 15 E
Cambridge Springs, U.S.A. 78 E4 41 48N 80 4W
Cambridgeshire □, U.K. 11 E8 52 25N 0 7W
Cambuci, Brazil 95 A7 21 35S 41 55W
Cambundi-Catembo, Angola 52 G3 10 10S 17 35 E
Camden, Ala., U.S.A. 77 K2 31 59N 87 17W
Camden, Ark., U.S.A. 81 J8 33 35N 92 50W
Camden, Maine, U.S.A. 71 D6 44 13N 69 4W
Camden, N.J., U.S.A. 79 G9 39 56N 75 7W
Camden, S.C., U.S.A. 77 H5 34 16N 80 36W
Camden Sd., Australia 60 C3 15 27S 124 25 E
Camdenton, U.S.A. 81 F8 38 1N 92 45W
Cameron, Ariz., U.S.A. 83 J8 35 53N 111 25W
Cameron, La., U.S.A. 81 L8 29 48N 93 20W
Cameron, Mo., U.S.A. 80 F7 39 44N 94 14W
Cameron, Tex., U.S.A. 81 K6 30 51N 96 59W
Cameron Falls, Canada 70 C2 49 8N 88 19W
Cameron Highlands, Malaysia 39 K3 4 27N 101 22 E
Cameron Hills, Canada 72 B5 59 48N 118 0W
Cameroon ■, Africa 51 G7 6 0N 12 30 E
Cameroun, Mt., Cameroon 50 H6 4 13N 9 10 E
Cametá, Brazil 93 D9 2 12S 49 30W
Caminha, Portugal 19 B1 41 50N 8 50W
Camino, U.S.A. 84 G6 38 44N 120 41W
Camira Creek, Australia 63 D5 29 15S 152 58 E
Camissombo, Angola 52 F4 8 7S 20 38 E
Cammal, U.S.A. 78 E7 41 24N 77 28W
Camocim, Brazil 93 D10 2 55S 40 50W
Camooweal, Australia 62 B2 19 56S 138 7 E
Camopi →, Fr. Guiana 93 C8 3 10N 52 20W
Camp Crook, U.S.A. 80 C3 45 33N 103 59W
Camp Nelson, U.S.A. 85 J8 36 8N 118 39W
Camp Wood, U.S.A. 81 L4 29 40N 100 1W
Campana, Argentina 94 C4 34 10S 58 55W
Campana, I., Chile 96 F1 48 20S 75 20W
Campanário, Madeira 22 D2 32 39N 17 2W
Campânia □, Italy 20 D6 41 0N 14 30 E
Campbell, S. Africa 56 D3 28 48S 23 44 E
Campbell, Calif., U.S.A. 84 H5 37 17N 121 57W
Campbell, Ohio, U.S.A. 78 E4 41 5N 80 37W
Campbell I., Pac. Oc. 64 N8 52 30S 169 0 E
Campbell L., Canada 73 A7 63 14N 106 55W
Campbell River, Canada 72 C3 50 5N 125 20W
Campbell Town, Australia 62 G4 41 52S 147 30 E
Campbellford, Canada 78 B7 44 18N 77 48W
Campbellpur, Pakistan 42 C5 33 46N 72 26 E
Campbellsville, U.S.A. 76 G3 37 21N 85 20W
Campbellton, Canada 71 C6 47 57N 66 43W
Campbelltown, Australia 63 E5 34 4S 150 49 E
Campbeltown, U.K. 12 F3 55 26N 5 36W
Campeche, Mexico 87 D6 19 50N 90 32W
Campeche □, Mexico 87 D6 19 50N 90 32W
Campeche, B. de, Mexico 87 D6 19 30N 93 0W
Camperdown, Australia 63 F3 38 14S 143 9 E
Camperville, Canada 73 C8 51 59N 100 9W
Campina Grande, Brazil 93 E11 7 20S 35 47W
Campinas, Brazil 95 A6 22 50S 47 0W
Campo, Cameroon 52 D1 2 22N 9 50 E
Campo Belo, Brazil 93 H9 20 52S 45 16W
Campo Formoso, Brazil 93 F10 10 30S 40 20W
Campo Grande, Brazil 93 H8 20 25S 54 40W
Campo Maíor, Brazil 93 D10 4 50S 42 12W
Campo Mourão, Brazil 95 A5 24 3S 52 22W
Campoalegre, Colombia 92 C3 2 41N 75 20W
Campobasso, Italy 20 D6 41 34N 14 39 E
Campos, Brazil 95 A7 21 50S 41 20W
Campos Belos, Brazil 93 F9 13 10S 47 3W
Campos del Puerto, Spain 22 B10 39 26N 3 1 E
Campos Novos, Brazil 95 B5 27 21S 51 50W
Camptonville, U.S.A. 84 F5 39 27N 121 3W
Campuya →, Peru 92 D4 1 40S 73 30W
Camrose, Canada 72 C6 53 0N 112 50W
Camsell Portage, Canada 73 B7 59 37N 109 15W
Çan, Turkey 21 D12 40 2N 27 3 E
Can Clavo, Spain 22 C7 38 57N 1 27 E
Can Creu, Spain 22 C7 38 58N 1 28 E
Can Gio, Vietnam 39 G6 10 25N 106 58 E
Can Tho, Vietnam 39 G5 10 2N 105 46 E
Canaan, U.S.A. 79 D11 42 2N 73 20W
Canada ■, N. Amer. 68 C10 60 0N 100 0W
Cañada de Gómez, Argentina 94 C3 32 40S 61 30W
Canadian, U.S.A. 81 H4 35 55N 100 23W
Canadian →, U.S.A. 81 H7 35 28N 95 3W
Canadian Shield, Canada 69 C10 53 0N 75 0W
Çanakkale, Turkey 21 D12 40 8N 26 24 E
Çanakkale Boğazı, Turkey 21 D12 40 17N 26 32 E
Canal Flats, Canada 72 C5 50 10N 115 48W
Canalejas, Argentina 94 D2 35 15S 66 34W
Canals, Argentina 94 C3 33 35S 62 53W
Canandaigua, U.S.A. 78 D7 42 54N 77 17W
Cananea, Mexico 86 A2 31 0N 110 20W
Canarias, Is., Atl. Oc. 22 F4 28 30N 16 0W
Canarreos, Arch. de los, Cuba 88 B3 21 35N 81 40W
Canary Is. = Canarias, Is., Atl. Oc. 22 F4 28 30N 16 0W
Canatlán, Mexico 86 C4 24 31N 104 47W
Canaveral, C., U.S.A. 77 L5 28 27N 80 32W
Canavieiras, Brazil 93 G11 15 39S 39 0W
Canbelego, Australia 63 E4 31 32S 146 18 E
Canberra, Australia 63 F4 35 15S 149 8 E
Canby, Calif., U.S.A. 82 F3 41 27N 120 52W
Canby, Minn., U.S.A. 80 C6 44 43N 96 16W
Canby, Oreg., U.S.A. 84 E4 45 16N 122 42W
Cancún, Mexico 87 C7 21 8N 86 44W
Candala, Somali Rep. 46 E4 11 30N 49 58 E
Candelaria, Argentina 95 B4 27 29S 55 44W
Candelaria, Canary Is. 22 F3 28 22N 16 22W
Candelo, Australia 63 F4 36 47S 149 43 E
Candia = Iraklion, Greece 23 D7 35 20N 25 12 E
Candle L., Canada 73 C7 53 50N 105 18W
Candlemas I., Antarctica 5 B1 57 3S 26 40W
Cando, U.S.A. 80 A5 48 32N 99 12W
Canea = Khaniá, Greece 23 D6 35 30N 24 4 E
Canelones, Uruguay 95 C4 34 32S 56 17W
Cañete, Chile 94 D1 37 50S 73 30W
Cañete, Peru 92 F3 13 8S 76 30W
Cangas de Narcea, Spain 19 A2 43 10N 6 32W
Canguaretama, Brazil 93 E11 6 20S 35 5W
Canguçu, Brazil 95 C5 31 22S 52 43W
Cangzhou, China 34 E9 38 19N 116 52 E
Canicattì, Italy 20 F5 37 21N 13 51 E
Canigou, Mt., France 18 E5 42 31N 2 27 E
Canim Lake, Canada 72 C4 51 47N 120 54W
Canindeyu □, Paraguay 95 A4 24 10S 55 0W
Canipaan, Phil. 36 C5 8 33N 117 15 E
Canisteo, U.S.A. 78 D7 42 16N 77 36W
Canisteo →, U.S.A. 78 D7 42 7N 77 8W
Cañitas, Mexico 86 C4 23 36N 102 43W
Çankırı, Turkey 25 F5 40 40N 33 37 E
Cankuzo, Burundi 54 C3 3 10S 30 31 E
Canmore, Canada 72 C5 51 7N 115 18W
Cann River, Australia 63 F4 37 35S 149 7 E
Canna, U.K. 12 D2 57 3N 6 33W
Cannanore, India 40 P9 11 53N 75 27 E
Cannes, France 18 E7 43 32N 7 1 E
Canning Town = Port Canning, India 43 H13 22 23N 88 40 E
Cannington, Canada 78 B5 44 20N 79 2W
Cannock, U.K. 10 E5 52 41N 2 1W
Cannon Ball →, U.S.A. 80 B4 46 20N 100 38W
Cannondale Mt., Australia 62 D4 25 13S 148 57 E
Canoas, Brazil 95 B5 29 56S 51 11W
Canoe L., Canada 73 B7 55 10N 108 15W
Canon City, U.S.A. 80 F2 38 27N 105 14W
Canora, Canada 73 C8 51 40N 102 30W
Canowindra, Australia 63 E4 33 35S 148 38 E
Canso, Canada 71 C7 45 20N 61 0W
Cantabria □, Spain 19 A4 43 10N 4 0W
Cantabrian Mts. = Cantábrica, Cordillera, Spain 19 A3 43 0N 5 10W
Cantábrica Cordillera, Spain 19 A3 43 0N 5 10W
Cantal, Plomb du, France 18 D5 45 3N 2 45 E
Canterbury, Australia 62 D3 25 23S 141 53 E
Canterbury, U.K. 11 F9 51 16N 1 6 E
Canterbury □, N.Z. 59 K3 43 45S 171 19 E
Canterbury Bight, N.Z. 59 L3 44 16S 171 55 E
Canterbury Plains, N.Z. 59 K3 43 55S 171 22 E
Cantil, U.S.A. 85 K9 35 18N 117 58W
Canton = Guangzhou, China 33 D6 23 5N 113 10 E
Canton, Ga., U.S.A. 77 H3 34 14N 84 29W
Canton, Ill., U.S.A. 80 E9 40 33N 90 2W
Canton, Miss., U.S.A. 81 J9 32 37N 90 2W
Canton, Mo., U.S.A. 80 E9 40 8N 91 32W
Canton, N.Y., U.S.A. 79 B9 44 36N 75 10W
Canton, Ohio, U.S.A. 78 F3 40 48N 81 23W
Canton, Okla., U.S.A. 81 G5 36 3N 98 35W
Canton, S. Dak., U.S.A. 80 D6 43 18N 96 35W
Canton L., U.S.A. 81 G5 36 6N 98 35W
Canudos, Brazil 92 E7 7 13S 58 5W
Canutama, Brazil 92 E6 6 30S 64 20W
Canutillo, U.S.A. 83 L10 31 55N 106 36W
Canyon, Tex., U.S.A. 81 H4 34 59N 101 55W
Canyon, Wyo., U.S.A. 82 D8 44 43N 110 36W
Canyonlands National Park, U.S.A. 83 G9 38 15N 110 0W
Canyonville, U.S.A. 82 E2 42 56N 123 17W
Cao Bang, Vietnam 38 A6 22 40N 106 15 E
Cao He →, China 35 D13 40 10N 124 32 E
Cao Lanh, Vietnam 39 G5 10 27N 105 38 E
Cao Xian, China 34 G8 34 50N 115 35 E
Cap-aux-Meules, Canada 71 C7 47 23N 61 52W
Cap-Chat, Canada 71 C6 49 6N 66 40W
Cap-de-la-Madeleine, Canada 70 C5 46 22N 72 31W
Cap-Haïtien, Haiti 89 C5 19 40N 72 20W
Cap St.-Jacques = Vung Tau, Vietnam 39 G6 10 21N 107 4 E
Capa, Vietnam 38 A4 22 21N 103 50 E
Capaia, Angola 52 F4 8 27S 20 13 E
Capanaparo →, Venezuela 92 B5 7 1N 67 7W
Cape →, Australia 62 C4 20 59S 146 51 E
Cape Barren I., Australia 62 G4 40 25S 148 15 E
Cape Breton Highlands Nat. Park, Canada 71 C7 46 50N 60 40W
Cape Breton I., Canada 71 C7 46 0N 60 30W
Cape Charles, U.S.A. 76 G8 37 16N 76 1W
Cape Coast, Ghana 50 G4 5 5N 1 15W
Cape Coral, U.S.A. 77 M5 26 33N 81 57W
Cape Dorset, Canada 69 B12 64 14N 76 32W
Cape Dyer, Canada 69 B13 66 30N 61 22W
Cape Fear →, U.S.A. 77 H6 33 53N 78 1W
Cape Girardeau, U.S.A. 81 G10 37 19N 89 32W
Cape Jervis, Australia 63 F2 35 40S 138 5 E
Cape May, U.S.A. 76 F8 38 56N 74 56W
Cape May Point, U.S.A. 75 C12 38 56N 74 58W
Cape Tormentine, Canada 71 C7 46 8N 63 47W
Cape Town, S. Africa 56 E2 33 55S 18 22 E
Cape Verde Is. ■, Atl. Oc. 49 E1 17 10N 25 20W
Cape Vincent, U.S.A. 79 B8 44 8N 76 20W
Cape York Peninsula, Australia 62 A3 12 0S 142 30 E

Chilko, L.

Chadan, *Russia* **27 D10** 51 17N 91 35 E
Chadileuvú →, *Argentina* **94 D2** 37 46S 66 0W
Chadiza, *Zambia* **55 E3** 14 45S 32 27 E
Chadron, *U.S.A.* **80 D3** 42 50N 103 0W
Chadyr-Lunga = Ceadâr-Lunga, *Moldova* **17 E15** 46 3N 28 51 E
Chae Hom, *Thailand* **38 C2** 18 43N 99 35 E
Chaem →, *Thailand* **38 C2** 18 11N 98 38 E
Chaeryŏng, *N. Korea* **35 E13** 38 24N 125 36 E
Chagai Hills, *Afghan.* **40 E3** 29 30N 63 0 E
Chagda, *Russia* **27 D14** 58 45N 130 38 E
Chagos Arch., *Ind. Oc.* **29 K11** 6 0S 72 0 E
Chāh Ākhvor, *Iran* **45 C8** 32 41N 59 40 E
Chāh Bahār, *Iran* **45 E9** 25 20N 60 40 E
Chāh-e-Malek, *Iran* **45 D8** 28 35N 59 7 E
Chāh Kavīr, *Iran* **45 D7** 31 45N 54 52 E
Chahar Burjak, *Afghan.* **40 D3** 30 15N 62 0 E
Chaibasa, *India* **41 H14** 22 42N 85 49 E
Chainat, *Thailand* **38 E3** 15 11N 100 8 E
Chaiya, *Thailand* **39 H2** 9 23N 99 14 E
Chaj Doab, *Pakistan* **42 C5** 32 15N 73 0 E
Chajari, *Argentina* **94 C4** 30 42S 58 0W
Chake Chake, *Tanzania* **54 D4** 5 15S 39 45 E
Chakhānsūr, *Afghan.* **40 D3** 31 10N 62 0 E
Chakonipau, L., *Canada* **71 A6** 56 18N 68 30W
Chakradharpur, *India* **43 H11** 22 45N 85 40 E
Chakwal, *Pakistan* **42 C5** 32 56N 72 53 E
Chala, *Peru* **92 G4** 15 48S 74 20W
Chalchihuites, *Mexico* **86 C4** 23 29N 103 53W
Chalcis = Khalkís, *Greece* **21 E10** 38 27N 23 42 E
Chaleur B., *Canada* **71 C6** 47 55N 65 30W
Chalfant, *U.S.A.* **84 H8** 37 32N 118 21W
Chalhuanca, *Peru* **92 F4** 14 15S 73 15W
Chalisgaon, *India* **40 J9** 20 30N 75 10 E
Chalky Inlet, *N.Z.* **59 M1** 46 3S 166 31 E
Challapata, *Bolivia* **92 G5** 18 53S 66 50W
Challis, *U.S.A.* **82 D6** 44 30N 114 14W
Chalna, *India* **43 H13** 22 36N 89 35 E
Chalon-sur-Saône, *France* **18 C6** 46 48N 4 50 E
Châlons-en-Champagne, *France* **18 B6** 48 58N 4 20 E
Chalyaphum, *Thailand* **38 E4** 15 48N 102 2 E
Cham, Cu Lao, *Vietnam* **38 E7** 15 57N 108 30 E
Chama, *U.S.A.* **83 H10** 36 54N 106 35W
Chaman, *Pakistan* **40 D5** 30 58N 66 25 E
Chamba, *India* **42 C7** 32 35N 76 10 E
Chamba, *Tanzania* **55 E4** 11 37S 37 0 E
Chambal →, *India* **43 F8** 26 29N 79 15 E
Chamberlain, *U.S.A.* **80 D5** 43 49N 99 20W
Chamberlain →, *Australia* **60 C4** 15 30S 127 54 E
Chambers, *U.S.A.* **83 J9** 35 11N 109 26W
Chambersburg, *U.S.A.* **76 F7** 39 56N 77 40W
Chambéry, *France* **18 D6** 45 34N 5 55 E
Chambly, *Canada* **79 A11** 45 27N 73 17W
Chambord, *Canada* **71 C5** 48 25N 72 6W
Chamchamal, *Iraq* **44 C5** 35 32N 44 50 E
Chamela, *Mexico* **86 D3** 19 32N 105 5W
Chamical, *Argentina* **94 C2** 30 22S 66 27W
Chamkar Luong, *Cambodia* **39 G4** 11 0N 103 45 E
Chamonix-Mont Blanc, *France* **18 D7** 45 55N 6 51 E
Champa, *India* **43 H10** 22 2N 82 43 E
Champagne, *Canada* **72 A1** 60 49N 136 30W
Champagne, *France* **18 B6** 48 40N 4 20 E
Champaign, *U.S.A.* **76 E1** 40 7N 88 15W
Champassak, *Laos* **38 E5** 14 53N 105 52 E
Champlain, *Canada* **76 B9** 46 27N 72 24W
Champlain, *U.S.A.* **79 B11** 44 59N 73 27W
Champlain, L., *U.S.A.* **79 B11** 44 40N 73 20W
Champotón, *Mexico* **87 D6** 19 20N 90 50W
Chana, *Thailand* **39 J3** 6 55N 100 44 E
Chañaral, *Chile* **94 B1** 26 23S 70 40W
Chanārān, *Iran* **45 B8** 36 39N 59 6 E
Chanasma, *India* **42 H5** 23 44N 72 5 E
Chandannagar, *India* **43 H13** 22 52N 88 24 E
Chandausi, *India* **43 E8** 28 27N 78 49 E
Chandeleur Is., *U.S.A.* **81 L10** 29 55N 88 57W
Chandeleur Sd., *U.S.A.* **81 L10** 29 55N 89 0W
Chandigarh, *India* **42 D7** 30 43N 76 47 E
Chandler, *Australia* **63 D1** 27 0S 133 19 E
Chandler, *Canada* **71 C7** 48 18N 64 46W
Chandler, *Ariz., U.S.A.* **83 K8** 33 18N 111 50W
Chandler, *Okla., U.S.A.* **81 H6** 35 42N 96 53W
Chandpur, *Bangla.* **41 H17** 23 8N 90 45 E
Chandpur, *India* **42 E8** 29 8N 78 19 E
Chandrapur, *India* **40 K11** 19 57N 79 25 E
Chānf, *Iran* **45 E9** 26 38N 60 29 E
Chang, *Pakistan* **42 F3** 26 59N 68 30 E
Chang, Ko, *Thailand* **39 F4** 12 0N 102 23 E
Ch'ang Chiang = Chang Jiang →, *China* **33 C7** 31 48N 121 10 E
Chang Jiang →, *China* **33 C7** 31 48N 121 10 E
Changa, *India* **43 C7** 33 53N 77 35 E
Changanacheri, *India* **40 Q10** 9 25N 76 31 E
Changane →, *Mozam.* **57 C5** 24 30S 33 30 E
Changbai, *China* **35 D15** 41 25N 128 5 E
Changbai Shan, *China* **35 C15** 42 20N 129 0 E
Changchiak'ou = Zhangjiakou, *China* **34 D8** 40 48N 114 55 E
Ch'angchou = Changzhou, *China* **33 C6** 31 47N 119 58 E
Changchun, *China* **35 C13** 43 57N 125 17 E
Changchunling, *China* **35 B13** 45 18N 125 27 E
Changde, *China* **33 D6** 29 4N 111 35 E
Changdo-ri, *N. Korea* **35 E14** 38 30N 127 40 E
Changhai = Shanghai, *China* **33 C7** 31 15N 121 26 E
Changhua, *Taiwan* **33 D7** 24 2N 120 30 E
Changhŭng, *S. Korea* **35 G14** 34 41N 126 52 E
Changhŭngni, *N. Korea* **35 D15** 40 24N 128 19 E
Changjiang, *China* **38 C7** 19 20N 108 55 E
Changjin, *N. Korea* **35 D14** 40 23N 127 15 E
Changjin-chŏsuji, *N. Korea* **35 D14** 40 30N 127 15 E
Changli, *China* **35 E10** 39 40N 119 13 E
Changling, *China* **35 B12** 44 20N 123 58 E
Changlun, *Malaysia* **39 J3** 6 25N 100 26 E
Changping, *China* **34 D9** 40 14N 116 12 E
Changsha, *China* **33 D6** 28 12N 113 0 E
Changwu, *China* **34 G4** 35 10N 107 45 E
Changyi, *China* **35 F10** 36 40N 119 30 E
Changyŏn, *N. Korea* **35 E13** 38 15N 125 6 E
Changyuan, *China* **34 G8** 35 15N 114 42 E
Changzhi, *China* **34 F7** 36 10N 113 6 E
Changzhou, *China* **33 C6** 31 47N 119 58 E
Chanhanga, *Angola* **56 B1** 16 0S 14 8 E
Channapatna, *India* **40 N10** 12 40N 77 15 E
Channel Is., *U.K.* **11 H5** 49 19N 2 24W
Channel Is., *U.S.A.* **85 M7** 33 40N 119 15W
Channel-Port aux Basques, *Canada* **71 C8** 47 30N 59 9W
Channing, *Mich., U.S.A.* **76 B1** 46 9N 88 5W
Channing, *Tex., U.S.A.* **81 H3** 35 41N 102 20W
Chantada, *Spain* **19 A2** 42 36N 7 46W
Chanthaburi, *Thailand* **38 F4** 12 38N 102 12 E
Chantrey Inlet, *Canada* **68 B10** 67 48N 96 20W
Chanute, *U.S.A.* **81 G7** 37 41N 95 27W
Chao Phraya →, *Thailand* **38 F3** 13 32N 100 36 E
Chao Phraya Lowlands, *Thailand* **38 E3** 15 30N 100 0 E
Chao'an, *China* **33 D6** 23 42N 116 32 E
Chaocheng, *China* **34 F8** 36 4N 115 37 E
Chaoyang, *China* **35 D11** 41 35N 120 22 E
Chapala, *Mozam.* **55 F4** 15 50S 37 35 E
Chapala, L. de, *Mexico* **86 C4** 20 10N 103 20W
Chapayev, *Kazakstan* **25 D9** 50 25N 51 10 E
Chapayevsk, *Russia* **24 D8** 53 0N 49 40 E
Chapecó, *Brazil* **95 B5** 27 14S 52 41W
Chapel Hill, *U.S.A.* **77 H6** 35 55N 79 4W
Chapleau, *Canada* **70 C3** 47 50N 83 24W
Chaplin, *Canada* **73 C7** 50 28N 106 40W
Chapra = Chhapra, *India* **43 G11** 25 48N 84 44 E
Châr, *Mauritania* **50 D2** 21 32N 12 45W
Chara, *Russia* **27 D12** 56 54N 118 20 E
Charadai, *Argentina* **94 B4** 27 35S 59 55W
Charagua, *Bolivia* **92 G6** 19 45S 63 10W
Charaña, *Bolivia* **92 G5** 17 30S 69 25W
Charata, *Argentina* **94 B3** 27 13S 61 14W
Charcas, *Mexico* **86 C4** 23 10N 101 20W
Charcoal L., *Canada* **73 B8** 58 49N 102 22W
Chard, *U.K.* **11 G5** 50 52N 2 58W
Chardara, *Kazakstan* **26 E7** 41 16N 67 59 E
Chardon, *U.S.A.* **78 E3** 41 35N 81 12W
Chardzhou = Chärjew, *Turkmenistan* **26 F7** 39 6N 63 34 E
Charente →, *France* **18 D3** 45 57N 1 5W
Chari →, *Chad* **51 F7** 12 58N 14 31 E
Chārīkār, *Afghan.* **40 B6** 35 0N 69 10 E
Chariton →, *U.S.A.* **80 F8** 39 19N 92 58W
Chärjew, *Turkmenistan* **26 F7** 39 6N 63 34 E
Charkhari, *India* **43 G8** 25 24N 79 45 E
Charkhi Dadri, *India* **42 E7** 28 37N 76 17 E
Charleroi, *Belgium* **15 D4** 50 24N 4 27 E
Charleroi, *U.S.A.* **78 F5** 40 9N 79 57W
Charles, C., *U.S.A.* **76 G8** 37 7N 75 58W
Charles City, *U.S.A.* **80 D8** 43 4N 92 41W
Charles L., *Canada* **73 B6** 59 50N 110 33W
Charles Town, *U.S.A.* **76 F7** 39 17N 77 52W
Charleston, *Ill., U.S.A.* **76 F1** 39 30N 88 10W
Charleston, *Miss., U.S.A.* **81 H9** 34 1N 90 4W
Charleston, *Mo., U.S.A.* **81 G10** 36 55N 89 21W
Charleston, *S.C., U.S.A.* **77 J6** 32 46N 79 56W
Charleston, *W. Va., U.S.A.* **76 F5** 38 21N 81 38W
Charleston Peak, *U.S.A.* **85 J11** 36 16N 115 42W
Charlestown, *S. Africa* **57 D4** 27 26S 29 53 E
Charlestown, *U.S.A.* **76 F3** 38 27N 85 40W
Charlesville, *Zaïre* **52 F4** 5 27S 20 59 E
Charleville = Rath Luirc, *Ireland* **13 D3** 52 21N 8 40W
Charleville, *Australia* **63 D4** 26 24S 146 15 E
Charleville-Mézières, *France* **18 B6** 49 44N 4 40 E
Charlevoix, *U.S.A.* **76 C3** 45 19N 85 16W
Charlotte, *Mich., U.S.A.* **76 D3** 42 34N 84 50W
Charlotte, *N.C., U.S.A.* **77 H5** 35 13N 80 51W
Charlotte Amalie, *Virgin Is.* **89 C7** 18 21N 64 56W
Charlotte Harbor, *U.S.A.* **77 M4** 26 50N 82 10W
Charlottesville, *U.S.A.* **76 F6** 38 2N 78 30W
Charlottetown, *Canada* **71 C7** 46 14N 63 8W
Charlton, *Australia* **63 F3** 36 16S 143 24 E
Charlton, *U.S.A.* **80 E8** 40 59N 93 20W
Charlton I., *Canada* **70 B4** 52 0N 79 20W
Charny, *Canada* **71 C5** 46 43N 71 15W
Charolles, *France* **18 C6** 46 27N 4 16 E
Charouine, *Algeria* **50 C4** 29 0N 0 15W
Charre, *Mozam.* **55 F4** 17 13S 35 10 E
Charsadda, *Pakistan* **42 B4** 34 7N 71 45 E
Charters Towers, *Australia* **62 C4** 20 5S 146 13 E
Chartres, *France* **18 B4** 48 29N 1 30 E
Chascomús, *Argentina* **94 D4** 35 30S 58 0W
Chasefu, *Zambia* **55 E3** 11 55S 33 8 E
Chasovnya-Uchurskaya, *Russia* **27 D14** 57 15N 132 50 E
Chât, *Iran* **45 B7** 37 59N 55 16 E
Châteaubriant, *France* **18 C3** 47 43N 1 23W
Châteaulin, *France* **18 B1** 48 11N 4 8W
Châteauroux, *France* **18 C4** 46 50N 1 40 E
Châtellerault, *France* **18 C4** 46 50N 0 30 E
Chatfield, *U.S.A.* **80 D9** 43 51N 92 11W
Chatham, *N.B., Canada* **71 C6** 47 2N 65 28W
Chatham, *Ont., Canada* **70 D3** 42 24N 82 11W
Chatham, *U.K.* **11 F8** 51 22N 0 32 E
Chatham, *La., U.S.A.* **81 J8** 32 18N 92 27W
Chatham, *N.Y., U.S.A.* **79 D11** 42 21N 73 36W
Chatham Is., *Pac. Oc.* **64 M10** 44 0S 176 40W
Chatham Str., *U.S.A.* **72 B2** 57 0N 134 40W
Chatmohar, *Bangla.* **43 G13** 24 15N 89 15 E
Chatra, *India* **43 G11** 24 12N 84 56 E
Chatrapur, *India* **41 K14** 19 22N 85 2 E
Chats, L. des, *Canada* **79 A8** 45 30N 76 20W
Chatsworth, *Canada* **78 B4** 44 27N 80 54W
Chatsworth, *Zimbabwe* **55 F3** 19 38S 31 13 E
Chattahoochee →, *U.S.A.* **77 K3** 30 54N 84 57W
Chattanooga, *U.S.A.* **77 H3** 35 3N 85 19W
Chaturat, *Thailand* **38 E3** 15 40N 101 51 E
Chau Doc, *Vietnam* **39 G5** 10 42N 105 7 E
Chauk, *Burma* **41 J19** 20 53N 94 49 E
Chaukan La, *Burma* **41 F20** 27 0N 97 15 E
Chaumont, *France* **18 B6** 48 7N 5 8 E
Chaumont, *U.S.A.* **79 B8** 44 4N 76 8W
Chautauqua L., *U.S.A.* **78 D5** 42 10N 79 24W
Chauvin, *Canada* **73 C6** 52 45N 110 10W
Chaves, *Brazil* **93 D9** 0 15S 49 55W
Chaves, *Portugal* **19 B2** 41 45N 7 32W
Chavuma, *Zambia* **53 G4** 13 4S 22 40 E
Chawang, *Thailand* **39 H2** 8 25N 99 30 E
Chaykovskiy, *Russia* **24 C9** 56 47N 54 9 E
Chazy, *U.S.A.* **79 B11** 44 53N 73 26W
Cheb, *Czech.* **16 C7** 50 9N 12 28 E
Cheboksary, *Russia* **24 C8** 56 8N 47 12 E
Cheboygan, *U.S.A.* **76 C3** 45 39N 84 29W
Chech, Erg, *Africa* **50 D4** 25 0N 2 15W
Chechenia □, *Russia* **25 F8** 43 30N 45 29 E
Checheno-Ingush Republic = Chechenia □, *Russia* **25 F8** 43 30N 45 29 E
Chechnya = Chechenia □, *Russia* **25 F8** 43 30N 45 29 E
Chechon, *S. Korea* **35 F15** 37 8N 128 12 E
Checleset B., *Canada* **72 C3** 50 5N 127 35W
Checotah, *U.S.A.* **81 H7** 35 28N 95 31W
Chedabucto B., *Canada* **71 C7** 45 25N 61 8W
Cheduba I., *Burma* **41 K18** 18 45N 93 40 E
Cheepie, *Australia* **63 D4** 26 33S 145 1 E
Chegdomyn, *Russia* **27 D14** 51 7N 133 1 E
Chegga, *Mauritania* **50 C3** 25 27N 5 40W
Chegutu, *Zimbabwe* **55 F3** 18 10S 30 14 E
Chehalis, *U.S.A.* **84 D4** 46 40N 122 58W
Cheju Do, *S. Korea* **35 H14** 33 29N 126 34 E
Chekiang = Zhejiang □, *China* **33 D7** 29 0N 120 0 E
Chela, Sa. da, *Angola* **56 B1** 16 20S 13 20 E
Chelan, *U.S.A.* **82 C4** 47 51N 120 1W
Chelan, L., *U.S.A.* **82 C3** 48 11N 120 30W
Cheleken, *Turkmenistan* **25 G9** 39 34N 53 16 E
Chelforó, *Argentina* **96 D3** 39 0S 66 33W
Chelkar = Shalqar, *Kazakstan* **26 E6** 47 48N 59 39 E
Chelkar Tengiz, Solonchak, *Kazakstan* **26 E7** 48 5N 63 7 E
Chełm, *Poland* **17 C12** 51 8N 23 30 E
Chełmno, *Poland* **17 B10** 53 20N 18 30 E
Chelmsford, *U.K.* **11 F8** 51 44N 0 29 E
Chelsea, *Okla., U.S.A.* **81 G7** 36 32N 95 26W
Chelsea, *Vt., U.S.A.* **79 C12** 43 59N 72 27W
Cheltenham, *U.K.* **11 F5** 51 54N 2 4W
Chelyabinsk, *Russia* **26 D7** 55 10N 61 24 E
Chelyuskin, C., *Russia* **28 B14** 77 30N 103 0 E
Chemainus, *Canada* **72 D4** 48 55N 123 42W
Chemnitz, *Germany* **16 C7** 50 51N 12 54 E
Chemult, *U.S.A.* **82 E3** 43 14N 121 47W
Chen, Gora, *Russia* **27 C15** 65 16N 141 50 E
Chenab →, *Pakistan* **42 D4** 30 23N 71 2 E
Chenango Forks, *U.S.A.* **79 D9** 42 15N 75 51W
Chencha, *Ethiopia* **51 G12** 6 15N 37 32 E
Cheney, *U.S.A.* **82 C5** 47 30N 117 35W
Cheng Xian, *China* **34 H3** 33 43N 105 42 E
Chengcheng, *China* **34 G5** 35 8N 109 56 E
Chengchou = Zhengzhou, *China* **34 G7** 34 45N 113 34 E
Chengde, *China* **35 D9** 40 59N 117 58 E
Chengdu, *China* **32 C5** 30 38N 104 2 E
Chenggu, *China* **34 H4** 33 10N 107 21 E
Chengjiang, *China* **32 D5** 24 39N 103 0 E
Ch'engtu = Chengdu, *China* **32 C5** 30 38N 104 2 E
Chengwu, *China* **34 G8** 34 58N 115 50 E
Chengyang, *China* **35 F11** 36 18N 120 21 E
Chenjiagang, *China* **35 G10** 34 23N 119 47 E
Chenkán, *Mexico* **87 D6** 19 8N 90 58W
Chennai = Madras, *India* **40 N12** 13 8N 80 19 E
Cheo Reo, *Vietnam* **38 F7** 13 25N 108 28 E
Cheom Ksan, *Cambodia* **38 E5** 14 13N 104 56 E
Chepén, *Peru* **92 E3** 7 15S 79 23W
Chepes, *Argentina* **94 C2** 31 20S 66 35W
Chepo, *Panama* **88 E4** 9 10N 79 6W
Cheptulil, Mt., *Kenya* **54 B4** 1 25N 35 35 E
Chequamegon B., *U.S.A.* **80 B9** 46 40N 90 30W
Cher →, *France* **18 C4** 47 21N 0 29 E
Cheraw, *U.S.A.* **77 H6** 34 42N 79 53W
Cherbourg, *France* **18 B3** 49 39N 1 40W
Cherchell, *Algeria* **50 A5** 36 35N 2 12 E
Cherdyn, *Russia* **24 B10** 60 24N 56 29 E
Cheremkhovo, *Russia* **27 D11** 53 8N 103 1 E
Cherepanovo, *Russia* **26 D9** 54 15N 83 30 E
Cherepovets, *Russia* **24 C6** 59 5N 37 55 E
Chergui, Chott ech, *Algeria* **50 B5** 34 21N 0 25 E
Cherikov = Cherykaw, *Belarus* **17 B16** 53 32N 31 20 E
Cherkasy, *Ukraine* **25 E5** 49 27N 32 4 E
Cherlak, *Russia* **26 D8** 54 15N 74 55 E
Chernaya, *Russia* **27 B9** 70 30N 89 10 E
Chernigov = Chernihiv, *Ukraine* **24 D5** 51 28N 31 20 E
Chernihiv, *Ukraine* **24 D5** 51 28N 31 20 E
Chernikovsk, *Russia* **24 D10** 54 48N 56 8 E
Chernivtsi, *Ukraine* **17 D13** 48 15N 25 52 E
Chernobyl = Chornobyl, *Ukraine* **17 C16** 51 20N 30 15 E
Chernogorsk, *Russia* **27 D10** 53 49N 91 18 E
Chernovtsy = Chernivtsi, *Ukraine* **17 D13** 48 15N 25 52 E
Chernyakhovsk, *Russia* **9 J19** 54 36N 21 48 E
Chernyshovskiy, *Russia* **27 C12** 63 0N 112 30 E
Cherokee, *Iowa, U.S.A.* **80 D7** 42 45N 95 33W
Cherokee, *Okla., U.S.A.* **81 G5** 36 45N 98 21W
Cherokees, Lake O' The, *U.S.A.* **81 G7** 36 28N 95 2W
Cherquenco, *Chile* **96 D2** 38 35S 72 0W
Cherrapunji, *India* **41 G17** 25 17N 91 47 E
Cherry Creek, *U.S.A.* **82 G6** 39 54N 114 53W
Cherry Valley, *U.S.A.* **85 M10** 33 59N 116 57W
Cherryvale, *U.S.A.* **81 G7** 37 16N 95 33W
Cherskiy, *Russia* **27 C17** 68 45N 161 18 E
Cherskogo Khrebet, *Russia* **27 C15** 65 0N 143 0 E
Cherven, *Belarus* **17 B15** 53 45N 28 28 E
Chervonohrad, *Ukraine* **17 C13** 50 25N 24 10 E
Cherwell →, *U.K.* **11 F6** 51 44N 1 14W
Cherykaw, *Belarus* **17 B16** 53 32N 31 20 E
Chesapeake, *U.S.A.* **76 G7** 36 50N 76 17W
Chesapeake B., *U.S.A.* **76 F7** 38 0N 76 10W
Cheshire □, *U.K.* **10 D5** 53 14N 2 30W
Cheshskaya Guba, *Russia* **24 A8** 67 20N 47 0 E
Cheslatta L., *Canada* **72 C3** 53 49N 125 20W
Chesley, *Canada* **78 B3** 44 17N 81 5W
Chester, *U.K.* **10 D5** 53 12N 2 53W
Chester, *Calif., U.S.A.* **82 F3** 40 19N 121 14W
Chester, *Ill., U.S.A.* **81 G10** 37 55N 89 49W
Chester, *Mont., U.S.A.* **82 B8** 48 31N 110 58W
Chester, *Pa., U.S.A.* **76 F8** 39 51N 75 22W
Chester, *S.C., U.S.A.* **77 H5** 34 43N 81 12W
Chesterfield, *U.K.* **10 D6** 53 15N 1 25W
Chesterfield, Is., *N. Cal.* **64 J7** 19 52S 158 15 E
Chesterfield Inlet, *Canada* **68 B10** 63 30N 90 45W
Chesterton Ra., *Australia* **63 D4** 25 30S 147 27 E
Chesterville, *Canada* **79 A9** 45 6N 75 14W
Chesuncook L., *U.S.A.* **71 C6** 46 0N 69 21W
Chéticamp, *Canada* **71 C7** 46 37N 60 59W
Chetumal, B. de, *Mexico* **87 D7** 18 40N 88 10W
Chetwynd, *Canada* **72 B4** 55 45N 121 36W
Cheviot, The, *U.K.* **10 B5** 55 29N 2 9W
Cheviot Hills, *U.K.* **10 B5** 55 20N 2 30W
Cheviot Ra., *Australia* **62 D3** 25 20S 143 45 E
Chew Bahir, *Ethiopia* **51 H12** 4 40N 36 50 E
Chewelah, *U.S.A.* **82 B5** 48 17N 117 43W
Cheyenne, *Okla., U.S.A.* **81 H5** 35 37N 99 40W
Cheyenne, *Wyo., U.S.A.* **80 E2** 41 8N 104 49W
Cheyenne →, *U.S.A.* **80 C4** 44 41N 101 18W
Cheyenne Wells, *U.S.A.* **80 F3** 38 49N 102 21W
Cheyne B., *Australia* **61 F2** 34 35S 118 50 E
Chhabra, *India* **42 G7** 24 40N 76 54 E
Chhapra, *India* **43 G11** 25 48N 84 44 E
Chhata, *India* **42 F7** 27 42N 77 30 E
Chhatarpur, *India* **43 G8** 24 55N 79 35 E
Chhep, *Cambodia* **38 F5** 13 45N 105 24 E
Chhindwara, *India* **43 H8** 22 2N 78 59 E
Chhlong, *Cambodia* **39 F5** 12 15N 105 58 E
Chhuk, *Cambodia* **39 G5** 10 46N 104 28 E
Chi →, *Thailand* **38 E5** 15 11N 104 43 E
Chiai, *Taiwan* **33 D7** 23 29N 120 25 E
Chiamis, *Indonesia* **37 G13** 7 20S 108 21 E
Chiamussu = Jiamusi, *China* **33 B8** 46 40N 130 26 E
Chiang Dao, *Thailand* **38 C2** 19 22N 98 58 E
Chiang Kham, *Thailand* **38 C3** 19 32N 100 18 E
Chiang Khan, *Thailand* **38 D3** 17 52N 101 36 E
Chiang Khong, *Thailand* **38 B3** 20 17N 100 24 E
Chiang Mai, *Thailand* **38 C2** 18 47N 98 59 E
Chiang Saen, *Thailand* **38 B3** 20 16N 100 5 E
Chiange, *Angola* **53 H2** 15 35S 13 40 E
Chiapa →, *Mexico* **87 D6** 16 42N 93 0W
Chiapa de Corzo, *Mexico* **87 D6** 16 42N 93 0W
Chiapas □, *Mexico* **87 D6** 17 0N 92 45W
Chiautla, *Mexico* **87 D5** 18 18N 98 34W
Chiávari, *Italy* **20 B3** 44 19N 9 19 E
Chiavenna, *Italy* **20 A3** 46 19N 9 24 E
Chiba, *Japan* **31 G10** 35 30N 140 7 E
Chibabava, *Mozam.* **57 C5** 20 17S 33 35 E
Chibatu, *Indonesia* **37 G12** 7 6S 107 59 E
Chibemba, *Cunene, Angola* **53 H2** 15 48S 14 8 E
Chibemba, *Huila, Angola* **56 B2** 16 20S 15 20 E
Chibia, *Angola* **53 H2** 15 10S 13 42 E
Chibougamau, *Canada* **70 C5** 49 56N 74 24W
Chibougamau L., *Canada* **70 C5** 49 50N 74 20W
Chibuk, *Nigeria* **51 F7** 10 52N 12 50 E
Chic-Chocs, Mts., *Canada* **71 C6** 48 55N 66 0W
Chicacole = Srikakulam, *India* **41 K13** 18 14N 83 58 E
Chicago, *U.S.A.* **76 E2** 41 53N 87 38W
Chicago Heights, *U.S.A.* **76 E2** 41 30N 87 38W
Chichagof I., *U.S.A.* **72 B1** 57 30N 135 30W
Chicheng, *China* **34 D8** 40 55N 115 55 E
Chichester, *U.K.* **11 G7** 50 50N 0 47W
Chichibu, *Japan* **31 F9** 36 5N 139 10 E
Ch'ich'ihaerh = Qiqihar, *China* **27 E13** 47 26N 124 0 E
Chickasha, *U.S.A.* **81 H5** 35 3N 97 58W
Chiclana de la Frontera, *Spain* **19 D2** 36 26N 6 9W
Chiclayo, *Peru* **92 E3** 6 42S 79 50W
Chico, *U.S.A.* **84 F5** 39 44N 121 50W
Chico →, *Chubut, Argentina* **96 E3** 44 0S 67 0W
Chico →, *Santa Cruz, Argentina* **96 G3** 50 0S 68 30W
Chicomo, *Mozam.* **57 C5** 24 31S 34 6 E
Chicontepec, *Mexico* **87 C5** 20 58N 98 10W
Chicopee, *U.S.A.* **79 D12** 42 9N 72 37W
Chicoutimi, *Canada* **71 C5** 48 28N 71 5W
Chicualacuala, *Mozam.* **57 C5** 22 6S 31 42 E
Chidambaram, *India* **40 P11** 11 20N 79 45 E
Chidenguele, *Mozam.* **57 C5** 24 55S 34 11 E
Chidley, C., *Canada* **69 B13** 60 23N 64 26W
Chiede, *Angola* **56 B2** 17 15S 16 22 E
Chiefs Pt., *Canada* **78 B3** 44 41N 81 18W
Chiem Hoa, *Vietnam* **38 A5** 22 12N 105 17 E
Chiemsee, *Germany* **16 E7** 47 53N 12 28 E
Chiengi, *Zambia* **55 D2** 8 45S 29 10 E
Chiengmai = Chiang Mai, *Thailand* **38 C2** 18 47N 98 59 E
Chiese →, *Italy* **20 B4** 45 8N 10 25 E
Chieti, *Italy* **20 C6** 42 21N 14 10 E
Chifeng, *China* **35 C10** 42 18N 118 58 E
Chignecto B., *Canada* **71 C7** 45 30N 64 40W
Chiguana, *Bolivia* **94 A2** 21 0S 67 58W
Chiha-ri, *N. Korea* **35 E14** 38 40N 126 30 E
Chihli, G. of = Bo Hai, *China* **35 E10** 39 0N 119 0 E
Chihli, G. of = Po Hai, *China* **28 F15** 38 30N 119 0 E
Chihuahua, *Mexico* **86 B3** 28 40N 106 3W
Chihuahua □, *Mexico* **86 B3** 28 40N 106 3W
Chiili, *Kazakstan* **26 E7** 44 20N 66 15 E
Chik Bollapur, *India* **40 N10** 13 25N 77 45 E
Chikmagalur, *India* **40 N9** 13 15N 75 45 E
Chikwawa, *Malawi* **55 F3** 16 2S 34 50 E
Chilac, *Mexico* **87 D5** 18 20N 97 24W
Chilako →, *Canada* **72 C4** 53 53N 122 57W
Chilam Chavki, *Pakistan* **43 B6** 35 5N 75 5 E
Chilanga, *Zambia* **55 F2** 15 33S 28 16 E
Chilapa, *Mexico* **87 D5** 17 40N 99 11W
Chilas, *Pakistan* **43 B6** 35 25N 74 5 E
Chilaw, *Sri Lanka* **40 R11** 7 30N 79 50 E
Chilcotin →, *Canada* **72 C4** 51 44N 122 23W
Childers, *Australia* **63 D5** 25 15S 152 17 E
Childress, *U.S.A.* **81 H4** 34 25N 100 13W
Chile ■, *S. Amer.* **96 D2** 35 0S 72 0W
Chile Rise, *Pac. Oc.* **65 L13** 38 0S 92 0W
Chilecito, *Argentina* **94 B2** 29 10S 67 30W
Chilete, *Peru* **92 E3** 7 10S 78 50W
Chililabombwe, *Zambia* **55 E2** 12 18S 27 43 E
Chilin = Jilin, *China* **35 C14** 43 44N 126 30 E
Chilka L., *India* **41 K14** 19 40N 85 25 E
Chilko →, *Canada* **72 C4** 52 0N 123 40W
Chilko, L., *Canada* **72 C4** 51 20N 124 10W

Corinth, G. of = Korinthiakós Kólpos, Greece 21 E10 38 16N 22 30 E
Corinto, Brazil 93 G10 18 20S 44 30W
Corinto, Nic. 88 D2 12 30N 87 10W
Cork, Ireland 13 E3 51 54N 8 29W
Cork □, Ireland 13 E3 51 57N 8 40W
Cork Harbour, Ireland 13 E3 51 47N 8 16W
Çorlu, Turkey 21 D12 41 11N 27 49 E
Cormack L., Canada 72 A4 60 56N 121 37W
Cormorant, Canada 73 C8 54 14N 100 35W
Cormorant L., Canada 73 C8 54 15N 100 50W
Corn Is. = Maiz, Is. del, Nic. 88 D3 12 15N 83 4W
Cornélio Procópio, Brazil 95 A5 23 7S 50 40W
Cornell, U.S.A. 80 C9 45 10N 91 9W
Corner Brook, Canada 71 C8 48 57N 57 58W
Corneşti, Moldova 17 E15 47 21N 28 1 E
Corning, Ark., U.S.A. 81 G9 36 25N 90 35W
Corning, Calif., U.S.A. 82 G2 39 56N 122 11W
Corning, Iowa, U.S.A. 80 E7 40 59N 94 44W
Corning, N.Y., U.S.A. 78 D7 42 9N 77 3W
Cornwall, Canada 70 C5 45 2N 74 44W
Cornwall □, U.K. 11 G3 50 26N 4 40W
Corny Pt., Australia 63 E2 34 55S 137 0 E
Coro, Venezuela 92 A5 11 25N 69 41W
Coroatá, Brazil 93 D10 4 8S 44 0W
Corocoro, Bolivia 92 G5 17 15S 68 28W
Coroico, Bolivia 92 G5 16 0S 67 50W
Coromandel, N.Z. 59 G5 36 45S 175 31 E
Coromandel Coast, India 40 N12 12 30N 81 0 E
Corona, Australia 63 E3 31 16S 141 24 E
Corona, Calif., U.S.A. 85 M9 33 53N 117 34W
Corona, N. Mex., U.S.A. 83 J11 34 15N 105 36W
Coronado, U.S.A. 85 N9 32 41N 117 11W
Coronado, B. de, Costa Rica 88 E3 9 0N 83 40W
Coronados, Is. los, U.S.A. 85 N9 32 25N 117 15W
Coronation, Canada 72 C6 52 5N 111 27W
Coronation Gulf, Canada 68 B8 68 25N 110 0W
Coronation I., Antarctica 5 C18 60 45S 46 0W
Coronation I., U.S.A. 72 B2 55 52N 134 20W
Coronation Is., Australia 60 B3 14 57S 124 55 E
Coronda, Argentina 94 C3 31 58S 60 56W
Coronel, Chile 94 D1 37 0S 73 10W
Coronel Bogado, Paraguay 94 B4 27 11S 56 18W
Coronel Dorrego, Argentina 94 D3 38 40S 61 10W
Coronel Oviedo, Paraguay 94 B4 25 24S 56 30W
Coronel Pringles, Argentina 94 D3 38 0S 61 30W
Coronel Suárez, Argentina 94 D3 37 30S 61 52W
Coronel Vidal, Argentina 94 D4 37 28S 57 45W
Corowa, Australia 63 F4 35 58S 146 21 E
Corozal, Belize 87 D7 18 23N 88 23W
Corpus, Argentina 95 B4 27 10S 55 30W
Corpus Christi, U.S.A. 81 M6 27 47N 97 24W
Corpus Christi, L., U.S.A. 81 L6 28 2N 97 52W
Corque, Bolivia 92 G5 18 20S 67 41W
Corralejo, Canary Is. 22 F6 28 43N 13 53W
Correntes, C. das, Mozam. 57 C6 24 6S 35 34 E
Corrib, L., Ireland 13 C2 53 27N 9 16W
Corrientes, Argentina 94 B4 27 30S 58 45W
Corrientes □, Argentina 94 B4 28 0S 57 0W
Corrientes →, Argentina 94 C4 30 42S 59 38W
Corrientes →, Peru 92 D4 3 43S 74 35W
Corrientes, C., Colombia 92 B3 5 30N 77 34W
Corrientes, C., Cuba 88 B3 21 43N 84 30W
Corrientes, C., Mexico 86 C3 20 25N 105 42W
Corrigan, U.S.A. 81 K7 31 0N 94 52W
Corrigin, Australia 61 F2 32 20S 117 53 E
Corry, U.S.A. 78 E5 41 55N 79 39W
Corse, France 18 F8 42 0N 9 0 E
Corse, C., France 18 E8 43 1N 9 25 E
Corsica = Corse, France 18 F8 42 0N 9 0 E
Corsicana, U.S.A. 81 J6 32 6N 96 28W
Corte, France 18 E8 42 19N 9 11 E
Cortez, U.S.A. 83 H9 37 21N 108 35W
Cortland, U.S.A. 79 D8 42 36N 76 11W
Çorum, Turkey 25 F5 40 30N 34 57 E
Corumbá, Brazil 92 G7 19 0S 57 30W
Corumbá de Goiás, Brazil 93 G9 16 0S 48 50W
Corunna = La Coruña, Spain 19 A1 43 20N 8 25W
Corvallis, U.S.A. 82 D2 44 34N 123 16W
Corvette, L. de la, Canada 70 B5 53 25N 74 3W
Corydon, U.S.A. 80 E8 40 46N 93 19W
Cosalá, Mexico 86 C3 24 28N 106 40W
Cosamaloapan, Mexico 87 D5 18 23N 95 50W
Cosenza, Italy 20 E7 39 18N 16 15 E
Coshocton, U.S.A. 78 F3 40 16N 81 51W
Cosmo Newberry, Australia 61 E3 28 0S 122 54 E
Coso Junction, U.S.A. 85 J9 36 3N 117 57W
Coso Pk., U.S.A. 85 J9 36 13N 117 44W
Cosquín, Argentina 94 C3 31 15S 64 30W
Costa Blanca, Spain 19 C5 38 25N 0 10W
Costa Brava, Spain 19 B7 41 30N 3 0 E
Costa del Sol, Spain 19 D3 36 30N 4 30W
Costa Dorada, Spain 19 B6 41 12N 1 15 E
Costa Mesa, U.S.A. 85 M9 33 38N 117 55W
Costa Rica ■, Cent. Amer. 88 D3 10 0N 84 0W
Costilla, U.S.A. 83 H11 36 59N 105 32W
Cosumnes →, U.S.A. 84 G5 38 16N 121 26W
Cotabato, Phil. 37 C6 7 14N 124 15 E
Cotagaita, Bolivia 94 A2 20 45S 65 40W
Côte d'Azur, France 18 E7 43 25N 7 10 E
Côte-d'Ivoire ■ = Ivory Coast ■, Africa 50 G3 7 30N 5 0W
Coteau des Prairies, U.S.A. 80 C6 45 20N 97 50W
Coteau du Missouri, U.S.A. 80 B4 47 0N 100 0W
Coteau Landing, Canada 79 A10 45 15N 74 13W
Cotentin, France 18 B3 49 15N 1 30W
Cotillo, Canary Is. 22 F5 28 41N 14 1W
Cotonou, Benin 50 G5 6 20N 2 25 E
Cotopaxi, Ecuador 92 D3 0 40S 78 30W
Cotswold Hills, U.K. 11 F5 51 42N 2 10W
Cottage Grove, U.S.A. 82 E2 43 48N 123 3W
Cottbus, Germany 16 C8 51 45N 14 20 E
Cottingham, U.K. 10 C5 53 47N 0 23W
Cottonwood, U.S.A. 83 J7 34 45N 112 1W
Cotulla, U.S.A. 81 L5 28 26N 99 14W
Coudersport, U.S.A. 78 E6 41 46N 78 1W
Couedic, C. du, Australia 63 F2 36 5S 136 40 E
Coulee City, U.S.A. 82 C4 47 37N 119 17W
Coulman I., Antarctica 5 D11 73 35S 170 0 E
Coulonge →, Canada 70 C4 45 52N 76 46W
Coulterville, U.S.A. 84 H6 37 43N 120 12W
Council, Alaska, U.S.A. 68 B3 64 55N 163 45W
Council, Idaho, U.S.A. 82 D5 44 44N 116 26W
Council Bluffs, U.S.A. 80 E7 41 16N 95 52W
Council Grove, U.S.A. 80 F6 38 40N 96 29W
Coupeville, U.S.A. 84 B4 48 13N 122 41W
Courantyne →, S. Amer. 92 B7 5 55N 57 5W
Courtenay, Canada 72 D3 49 45N 125 0W
Courtland, U.S.A. 84 G5 38 20N 121 34W
Courtrai = Kortrijk, Belgium 15 D3 50 50N 3 17 E
Courtright, Canada 78 D2 42 49N 82 28W
Coushatta, U.S.A. 81 J8 32 1N 93 21W
Coutts, Canada 72 D6 49 0N 111 57W
Coventry, U.K. 11 E6 52 25N 1 28W
Coventry L., Canada 73 A7 61 15N 106 15W
Covilhã, Portugal 19 B2 40 17N 7 31W
Covington, Ga., U.S.A. 77 J4 33 36N 83 51W
Covington, Ky., U.S.A. 76 F3 39 5N 84 31W
Covington, Okla., U.S.A. 81 G6 36 18N 97 35W
Covington, Tenn., U.S.A. 81 H10 35 34N 89 39W
Cowal, L., Australia 63 E4 33 40S 147 25 E
Cowan, Canada 73 C8 52 5N 100 45W
Cowan, L., Australia 61 F3 31 45S 121 45 E
Cowan L., Canada 73 C7 54 0N 107 15W
Cowangie, Australia 63 F3 35 12S 141 26 E
Cowansville, Canada 79 A12 45 14N 72 46W
Cowarie, Australia 63 D2 27 45S 138 15 E
Cowcowing Lakes, Australia 61 F2 30 55S 117 20 E
Cowdenbeath, U.K. 12 E5 56 7N 3 21W
Cowell, Australia 63 E2 33 39S 136 56 E
Cowes, U.K. 11 G6 50 45N 1 18W
Cowlitz →, U.S.A. 84 D4 46 6N 122 55W
Cowra, Australia 63 E4 33 49S 148 42 E
Coxilha Grande, Brazil 95 B5 28 18S 51 30W
Coxim, Brazil 93 G8 18 30S 54 55W
Cox's Bazar, Bangla. 41 J17 21 26N 91 59 E
Cox's Cove, Canada 71 C8 49 7N 58 5W
Coyame, Mexico 86 B3 29 28N 105 6W
Coyote Wells, U.S.A. 85 N11 32 44N 115 58W
Coyuca de Benítez, Mexico 87 D4 17 1N 100 8W
Coyuca de Catalan, Mexico 86 D4 18 18N 100 41W
Cozad, U.S.A. 80 E5 40 52N 99 59W
Cozumel, Mexico 87 C7 20 31N 86 55W
Cozumel, I. de, Mexico 87 C7 20 30N 86 40W
Craboon, Australia 63 E4 32 3S 149 30 E
Cracow = Kraków, Poland 17 C10 50 4N 19 57 E
Cracow, Australia 63 D5 25 17S 150 17 E
Cradock, S. Africa 56 E4 32 8S 25 36 E
Craig, Alaska, U.S.A. 72 B2 55 29N 133 9W
Craig, Colo., U.S.A. 82 F10 40 31N 107 33W
Craigavon, U.K. 13 B5 54 27N 6 23W
Craigmore, Zimbabwe 55 G3 20 28S 32 50 E
Crailsheim, Germany 16 D6 49 8N 10 5 E
Craiova, Romania 17 F12 44 21N 23 48 E
Cramsie, Australia 62 C3 23 20S 144 15 E
Cranberry Portage, Canada 73 C8 54 35N 101 23W
Cranbrook, Tas., Australia 62 G4 42 0S 148 5 E
Cranbrook, W. Austral., Australia 61 F2 34 18S 117 33 E
Cranbrook, Canada 72 D5 49 30N 115 46W
Crandon, U.S.A. 80 C10 45 34N 88 54W
Crane, Oreg., U.S.A. 82 E4 43 25N 118 35W
Crane, Tex., U.S.A. 81 K3 31 24N 102 21W
Cranston, U.S.A. 79 E13 41 47N 71 26W
Crater L., U.S.A. 82 E2 42 56N 122 6W
Crateús, Brazil 93 E10 5 10S 40 39W
Crato, Brazil 93 E11 7 10S 39 25W
Crawford, U.S.A. 80 D3 42 41N 103 25W
Crawfordsville, U.S.A. 76 E2 40 2N 86 54W
Crawley, U.K. 11 F7 51 7N 0 11W
Crazy Mts., U.S.A. 82 C8 46 12N 110 20W
Crean L., Canada 73 C7 54 5N 106 9W
Crediton, Canada 78 C3 43 17N 81 33W
Credo, Australia 61 F3 30 28S 120 45 E
Cree →, Canada 73 B7 58 57N 105 47W
Cree →, U.K. 12 G4 54 55N 4 25W
Cree L., Canada 73 B7 57 30N 106 30W
Creede, U.S.A. 83 H10 37 51N 106 56W
Creel, Mexico 86 B3 27 45N 107 38W
Creighton, U.S.A. 80 D6 42 28N 97 54W
Crema, Italy 20 B3 45 22N 9 41 E
Cremona, Italy 20 B4 45 7N 10 2 E
Cres, Croatia 16 F8 44 58N 14 25 E
Cresbard, U.S.A. 80 C5 45 10N 98 57W
Crescent, Okla., U.S.A. 81 H6 35 57N 97 36W
Crescent, Oreg., U.S.A. 82 E3 43 28N 121 42W
Crescent City, U.S.A. 82 F1 41 45N 124 12W
Crespo, Argentina 94 C3 32 2S 60 19W
Cressy, Australia 63 F3 38 2S 143 40 E
Crested Butte, U.S.A. 83 G10 38 52N 106 59W
Crestline, Calif., U.S.A. 85 L9 34 14N 117 18W
Crestline, Ohio, U.S.A. 78 F2 40 47N 82 44W
Creston, Canada 72 D5 49 10N 116 31W
Creston, Calif., U.S.A. 84 K6 35 32N 120 33W
Creston, Iowa, U.S.A. 80 E7 41 4N 94 22W
Creston, Wash., U.S.A. 82 C4 47 46N 118 31W
Crestview, Calif., U.S.A. 84 H8 37 46N 118 58W
Crestview, Fla., U.S.A. 77 K2 30 46N 86 34W
Crete = Kríti, Greece 23 D7 35 15N 25 0 E
Crete, U.S.A. 80 E6 40 38N 96 58W
Créteil, France 18 B5 48 47N 2 28 E
Creus, C. de, Spain 19 A7 42 20N 3 19 E
Creuse →, France 18 C4 47 0N 0 34 E
Crewe, U.K. 10 D5 53 6N 2 26W
Criciúma, Brazil 95 B6 28 40S 49 23W
Crieff, U.K. 12 E5 56 22N 3 50W
Crimean Pen. = Krymskyy Pivostriv, Ukraine 25 E5 45 0N 34 0 E
Crişul Alb →, Romania 17 E11 46 42N 21 17 E
Crişul Negru →, Romania 17 E11 46 42N 21 16 E
Crna Gora = Montenegro □, Yugoslavia 21 C8 42 40N 19 20 E
Crna Gora, Serbia, Yug. 21 C9 42 10N 21 30 E
Crna Reka →, Macedonia 21 D9 41 33N 21 59 E
Croagh Patrick, Ireland 13 C2 53 46N 9 40W
Croatia ■, Europe 16 F9 45 20N 16 0 E
Crocker, Banjaran, Malaysia 36 C5 5 40N 116 30 E
Crockett, U.S.A. 81 K7 31 19N 95 27W
Crocodile = Krokodil →, Mozam. 57 D5 25 14S 32 18 E
Crocodile Is., Australia 62 A1 12 3S 134 58 E
Croix, L. La, Canada 70 C1 48 20N 92 15W
Croker, C., Australia 60 B5 10 58S 132 35 E
Croker I., Australia 60 B5 11 12S 132 32 E
Cromarty, Canada 73 B10 58 3N 94 9W
Cromarty, U.K. 12 D4 57 40N 4 2W
Cromer, U.K. 10 E9 52 56N 1 17 E
Cromwell, N.Z. 59 L2 45 3S 169 14 E
Cronulla, Australia 63 E5 34 3S 151 8 E
Crooked →, Canada 72 C4 54 50N 122 54W
Crooked →, U.S.A. 82 D3 44 32N 121 16W
Crooked I., Bahamas 89 B5 22 50N 74 10W
Crooked Island Passage, Bahamas 89 B5 23 0N 74 30W
Crookston, Minn., U.S.A. 80 B6 47 47N 96 37W
Crookston, Nebr., U.S.A. 80 D4 42 56N 100 45W
Crooksville, U.S.A. 76 F4 39 46N 82 6W
Crookwell, Australia 63 E4 34 28S 149 24 E
Crosby, Minn., U.S.A. 80 B8 46 29N 93 58W
Crosby, N. Dak., U.S.A. 73 D8 48 55N 103 18W
Crosby, Pa., U.S.A. 78 E6 41 45N 78 23W
Crosbyton, U.S.A. 81 J4 33 40N 101 14W
Cross City, U.S.A. 77 L4 29 38N 83 7W
Cross Fell, U.K. 10 C5 54 43N 2 28W
Cross L., Canada 73 C9 54 45N 97 30W
Cross Plains, U.S.A. 81 J5 32 8N 99 11W
Cross Sound, U.S.A. 68 C6 58 0N 135 0W
Crossett, U.S.A. 81 J9 33 8N 91 58W
Crossfield, Canada 72 C6 51 25N 114 0W
Crosshaven, Ireland 13 E3 51 47N 8 17W
Croton-on-Hudson, U.S.A. 79 E11 41 12N 73 55W
Crotone, Italy 20 E7 39 5N 17 8 E
Crow →, Canada 72 B4 59 41N 124 20W
Crow Agency, U.S.A. 82 D10 45 36N 107 28W
Crow Hd., Ireland 13 E1 51 35N 10 9W
Crowell, U.S.A. 81 J5 33 59N 99 43W
Crowley, U.S.A. 81 K8 30 13N 92 22W
Crowley, L., U.S.A. 84 H8 37 35N 118 42W
Crown Point, U.S.A. 76 E2 41 25N 87 22W
Crows Landing, U.S.A. 84 H5 37 23N 121 6W
Crows Nest, Australia 63 D5 27 16S 152 4 E
Crowsnest Pass, Canada 72 D6 49 40N 114 40W
Croydon, Australia 62 B3 18 13S 142 14 E
Croydon, U.K. 11 F7 51 22N 0 5W
Crozet Is., Ind. Oc. 3 G12 46 27S 52 0 E
Cruz, C., Cuba 88 C4 19 50N 77 50W
Cruz Alta, Brazil 95 B5 28 45S 53 40W
Cruz del Eje, Argentina 94 C3 30 45S 64 50W
Cruzeiro, Brazil 95 A7 22 33S 45 0W
Cruzeiro do Oeste, Brazil 95 A5 23 46S 53 4W
Cruzeiro do Sul, Brazil 92 E4 7 35S 72 35W
Cry L., Canada 72 B3 58 45N 129 0W
Crystal Bay, U.S.A. 84 F7 39 15N 120 0W
Crystal Brook, Australia 63 E2 33 21S 138 12 E
Crystal City, Mo., U.S.A. 80 F9 38 13N 90 23W
Crystal City, Tex., U.S.A. 81 L5 28 41N 99 50W
Crystal Falls, U.S.A. 76 B1 46 5N 88 20W
Crystal River, U.S.A. 77 L4 28 54N 82 35W
Crystal Springs, U.S.A. 81 K9 31 59N 90 21W
Csongrád, Hungary 17 E11 46 43N 20 12 E
Cu Lao Hon, Vietnam 39 G7 10 54N 108 18 E
Cua Rao, Vietnam 38 C5 19 16N 104 27 E
Cuácua →, Mozam. 55 F4 17 54S 37 0 E
Cuamato, Angola 56 B2 17 2S 15 7 E
Cuamba, Mozam. 55 E4 14 45S 36 22 E
Cuando →, Angola 53 H4 17 30S 23 15 E
Cuando Cubango □, Angola 56 B3 16 25S 20 0 E
Cuangar, Angola 56 B2 17 36S 18 39 E
Cuanza →, Angola 48 G5 9 2S 13 30 E
Cuarto →, Argentina 94 C3 33 25S 63 2W
Cuatrociénegas, Mexico 86 B4 26 59N 102 5W
Cuauhtémoc, Mexico 86 B3 28 25N 106 52W
Cuba, N. Mex., U.S.A. 83 J10 36 1N 107 4W
Cuba, N.Y., U.S.A. 78 D6 42 13N 78 17W
Cuba ■, W. Indies 88 B4 22 0N 79 0W
Cuballing, Australia 61 F2 32 50S 117 10 E
Cubango →, Africa 56 B3 18 50S 22 25 E
Cuchi, Angola 53 G3 14 37S 16 58 E
Cuchumatanes, Sierra de los, Guatemala 88 C1 15 35N 91 25W
Cucurpe, Mexico 86 A2 30 20N 110 43W
Cúcuta, Colombia 92 B4 7 54N 72 31W
Cuddalore, India 40 P11 11 46N 79 45 E
Cuddapah, India 40 M11 14 30N 78 47 E
Cuddapan, L., Australia 62 D3 25 45S 141 26 E
Cudgewa, Australia 63 F4 36 10S 147 42 E
Cue, Australia 61 E2 27 25S 117 54 E
Cuenca, Ecuador 92 D3 2 50S 79 9W
Cuenca, Spain 19 B4 40 5N 2 10W
Cuenca, Serranía de, Spain 19 C5 39 55N 1 50W
Cuernavaca, Mexico 87 D5 18 55N 99 15W
Cuero, U.S.A. 81 L6 29 6N 97 17W
Cuervo, U.S.A. 81 H2 35 2N 104 25W
Cuevas del Almanzora, Spain 19 D5 37 18N 1 58W
Cuevo, Bolivia 92 H6 20 15S 63 30W
Cuiabá, Brazil 93 G7 15 30S 56 0W
Cuiabá →, Brazil 93 G7 17 5S 56 36W
Cuilco, Guatemala 88 C1 15 24N 91 58W
Cuillin Hills, U.K. 12 D2 57 13N 6 15W
Cuillin Sd., U.K. 12 D2 57 4N 6 20W
Cuima, Angola 53 G3 13 25S 15 45 E
Cuito →, Angola 56 B3 18 1S 20 48 E
Cuitzeo, L. de, Mexico 86 D4 19 55N 101 5W
Cukai, Malaysia 39 K4 4 13N 103 25 E
Culbertson, U.S.A. 80 A2 48 9N 104 31W
Culcairn, Australia 63 F4 35 41S 147 3 E
Culgoa →, Australia 63 D4 29 56S 146 20 E
Culiacán, Mexico 86 C3 24 50N 107 23W
Culiacán →, Mexico 86 C3 24 30N 107 42W
Culion, Phil. 37 B6 11 54N 120 1 E
Cullarin Ra., Australia 63 E4 34 30S 149 30 E
Cullen, U.K. 12 D6 57 42N 2 49W
Cullen Pt., Australia 62 A3 11 57S 141 54 E
Cullera, Spain 19 C5 39 9N 0 17W
Cullman, U.S.A. 77 H2 34 11N 86 51W
Culloden, U.K. 12 D4 57 30N 4 9W
Culpeper, U.S.A. 76 F7 38 30N 78 0W
Culuene →, Brazil 93 F8 12 56S 52 51W
Culver, Pt., Australia 61 F3 32 54S 124 43 E
Culverden, N.Z. 59 K4 42 47S 172 49 E
Cumaná, Venezuela 92 A6 10 30N 64 5W
Cumberland, Canada 72 D3 49 40N 125 0W
Cumberland, Md., U.S.A. 76 F6 39 39N 78 46W
Cumberland, Wis., U.S.A. 80 C8 45 32N 92 1W
Cumberland →, U.S.A. 77 G2 36 15N 87 0W
Cumberland I., U.S.A. 77 K5 30 50N 81 25W
Cumberland Is., Australia 62 C4 20 35S 149 10 E
Cumberland L., Canada 73 C8 54 3N 102 18W
Cumberland Pen., Canada 69 B13 67 0N 64 0W
Cumberland Plateau, U.S.A. 77 H3 36 0N 85 0W
Cumberland Sd., Canada 69 B13 65 30N 66 0W
Cumborah, Australia 63 D4 29 40S 147 45 E
Cumbria □, U.K. 10 C5 54 42N 2 52W
Cumbrian Mts., U.K. 10 C4 54 30N 3 0W
Cumbum, India 40 M11 15 40N 79 10 E
Cummings Mt., U.S.A. 85 K8 35 2N 118 34W
Cummins, Australia 63 E2 34 16S 135 43 E
Cumnock, Australia 63 E4 32 59S 148 46 E
Cumnock, U.K. 12 F4 55 28N 4 17W
Cumpas, Mexico 86 A3 30 0N 109 48W
Cumplida, Pta., Canary Is. 22 F2 28 50N 17 48W
Cuncumén, Chile 94 C1 31 53S 70 38W
Cundeelee, Australia 61 F3 30 43S 123 26 E
Cunderdin, Australia 61 F2 31 37S 117 12 E
Cunene →, Angola 56 B1 17 20S 11 50 E
Cúneo, Italy 20 B2 44 23N 7 32 E
Cunillera, I., Spain 22 C7 38 59N 1 13 E
Cunnamulla, Australia 63 D4 28 2S 145 38 E
Cupar, Canada 73 C8 50 57N 104 10W
Cupar, U.K. 12 E5 56 19N 3 1W
Cupica, G. de, Colombia 92 B3 6 25N 77 30W
Curaçao, Neth. Ant. 89 D6 12 10N 69 0W
Curanilahue, Chile 94 D1 37 29S 73 28W
Curaray →, Peru 92 D4 2 20S 74 5W
Curepto, Chile 94 D1 35 8S 72 1W
Curiapo, Venezuela 92 B6 8 33N 61 5W
Curicó, Chile 94 C1 34 55S 71 20W
Curicó □, Chile 94 C1 34 50S 71 15W
Curitiba, Brazil 95 B6 25 20S 49 10W
Currabubula, Australia 63 E5 31 16S 150 44 E
Currais Novos, Brazil 93 E11 6 13S 36 30W
Curralinho, Brazil 93 D9 1 45S 49 46W
Currant, U.S.A. 82 G6 38 51N 115 32W
Curraweena, Australia 63 E4 30 47S 145 54 E
Currawilla, Australia 62 D3 25 10S 141 20 E
Current →, U.S.A. 81 G9 36 15N 90 55W
Currie, Australia 62 F3 39 56S 143 53 E
Currie, U.S.A. 82 F6 40 16N 114 45W
Currituck Sd., U.S.A. 77 G8 36 20N 75 52W
Curtea de Argeş, Romania 17 F13 45 12N 24 42 E
Curtis, U.S.A. 80 E4 40 38N 100 31W
Curtis Group, Australia 62 F4 39 30S 146 37 E
Curtis I., Australia 62 C5 23 35S 151 10 E
Curuápanema →, Brazil 93 D7 2 25S 55 2W
Curuçá, Brazil 93 D9 0 43S 47 50W
Curuguaty, Paraguay 95 A4 24 31S 55 42W
Çürüksu Çayi →, Turkey 21 F13 37 27N 27 11 E
Curup, Indonesia 36 E2 4 26S 102 13 E
Cururupu, Brazil 93 D10 1 50S 44 50W
Curuzú Cuatiá, Argentina 94 B4 29 50S 58 5W
Cushing, U.S.A. 81 H6 35 59N 96 46W
Cushing, Mt., Canada 72 B3 57 35N 126 57W
Cusihuiriáchic, Mexico 86 B3 28 10N 106 50W
Custer, U.S.A. 80 D3 43 46N 103 36W
Cut Bank, U.S.A. 82 B7 48 38N 112 20W
Cuthbert, U.S.A. 77 K3 31 46N 84 48W
Cutler, U.S.A. 84 J7 36 31N 119 17W
Cuttaburra →, Australia 63 D3 29 43S 144 22 E
Cuttack, India 41 J14 20 25N 85 57 E
Cuvier, C., Australia 61 D1 23 14S 113 22 E
Cuvier I., N.Z. 59 G5 36 27S 175 50 E
Cuxhaven, Germany 16 B5 53 51N 8 41 E
Cuyahoga Falls, U.S.A. 78 E3 41 8N 81 29W
Cuyo, Phil. 37 B6 10 50N 121 5 E
Cuzco, Bolivia 92 H5 20 0S 66 50W
Cuzco, Peru 92 F4 13 32S 72 0W
Cwmbran, U.K. 11 F4 51 39N 3 2W
Cyangugu, Rwanda 54 C2 2 29S 28 54 E
Cyclades = Kikládhes, Greece 21 F11 37 20N 24 30 E
Cygnet, Australia 62 G4 43 8S 147 1 E
Cynthiana, U.S.A. 76 F3 38 23N 84 18W
Cypress Hills, Canada 73 D7 49 40N 109 30W
Cyprus ■, Asia 23 E12 35 0N 33 0 E
Cyrenaica, Libya 51 C9 27 0N 23 0 E
Cyrene = Shaḥḥāt, Libya 51 B9 32 48N 21 54 E
Czar, Canada 73 C6 52 27N 110 50W
Czech Rep. ■, Europe 16 D8 50 0N 15 0 E
Częstochowa, Poland 17 C10 50 49N 19 7 E

D

Da →, Vietnam 38 B5 21 15N 105 20 E
Da Hinggan Ling, China 33 B7 48 0N 121 0 E
Da Lat, Vietnam 39 G7 11 56N 108 25 E
Da Nang, Vietnam 38 D7 16 4N 108 13 E
Da Qaidam, China 32 C4 37 50N 95 15 E
Da Yunhe →, China 35 G11 34 25N 120 5 E
Da'an, China 35 B13 45 30N 124 7 E
Daba Shan, China 33 C5 32 0N 109 0 E
Dabakala, Ivory C. 50 G4 8 15N 4 20W
Dabhoi, India 42 H5 22 10N 73 20 E
Dabo, Indonesia 36 E2 0 30S 104 33 E
Dabola, Guinea 50 F2 10 50N 11 5W
Daboya, Ghana 50 G4 9 30N 1 20W
Dabung, Malaysia 39 K4 5 23N 102 1 E
Dacca = Dhaka, Bangla. 43 H14 23 43N 90 26 E
Dacca = Dhaka □, Bangla. 43 G14 24 25N 90 25 E
Dachau, Germany 16 D6 48 15N 11 26 E
Dadanawa, Guyana 92 C7 2 50N 59 30W
Dade City, U.S.A. 77 L4 28 22N 82 11W
Dadra and Nagar Haveli □, India 40 J8 20 5N 73 0 E

Dera Ghazi Khan

Dadri = Charkhi Dadri, India 42 E7 28 37N 76 17 E
Dadu, Pakistan 42 F2 26 45N 67 45 E
Daet, Phil. 37 B6 14 2N 122 55 E
Dagana, Senegal 50 E1 16 30N 15 35W
Dagestan □, Russia 25 F8 42 30N 47 0 E
Daggett, U.S.A. 85 L10 34 52N 116 52W
Daghestan Republic = Dagestan □, Russia 25 F8 42 30N 47 0 E
Dagö = Hiiumaa, Estonia 9 G20 58 50N 22 45 E
Dagu, China 35 E9 38 59N 117 40 E
Dagupan, Phil. 37 A6 16 3N 120 20 E
Dahlak Kebir, Eritrea 46 D3 15 50N 40 10 E
Dahlonega, U.S.A. 77 H4 34 32N 83 59W
Dahod, India 42 H6 22 50N 74 15 E
Dahomey = Benin ■, Africa 50 G5 10 0N 2 0 E
Dahra, Senegal 50 E1 15 22N 15 30W
Dai Hao, Vietnam 38 C6 18 1N 106 25 E
Dai-Sen, Japan 31 G6 35 22N 133 32 E
Dai Xian, China 34 E7 39 4N 112 58 E
Daicheng, China 34 E9 38 42N 116 38 E
Daingean, Ireland 13 C4 53 18N 7 17W
Daintree, Australia 62 B4 16 20S 145 20 E
Daiō-Misaki, Japan 31 G8 34 15N 136 45 E
Dairût, Egypt 51 C11 27 34N 30 43 E
Daisetsu-Zan, Japan 30 C11 43 30N 142 57 E
Dajarra, Australia 62 C2 21 42S 139 30 E
Dak Dam, Cambodia 38 F6 12 20N 107 21 E
Dak Nhe, Vietnam 38 E6 15 28N 107 48 E
Dak Pek, Vietnam 38 E6 15 4N 107 44 E
Dak Song, Vietnam 39 F6 12 19N 107 35 E
Dak Sui, Vietnam 38 E6 14 55N 107 43 E
Dakar, Senegal 50 F1 14 34N 17 29W
Dakhla, W. Sahara 50 D1 23 50N 15 53W
Dakhla, El Wâhât el-, Egypt 51 C10 25 30N 28 50 E
Dakhovskaya, Russia 25 F7 44 13N 40 13 E
Dakor, India 42 H5 22 45N 73 11 E
Dakota City, U.S.A. 80 D6 42 25N 96 25W
Đakovica, Serbia, Yug. 21 C9 42 22N 20 26 E
Dalachi, China 34 F3 36 48N 105 0 E
Dalai Nur, China 34 C9 43 20N 116 45 E
Dālakī, Iran 45 D6 29 26N 51 17 E
Dalälven, Sweden 9 F17 60 12N 16 43 E
Dalaman →, Turkey 21 F13 36 41N 28 43 E
Dalandzadgad, Mongolia 34 C3 43 27N 104 30 E
Dalarna, Sweden 9 F16 61 0N 14 0 E
Dālbandīn, Pakistan 40 E4 29 0N 64 23 E
Dalbeattie, U.K. 12 G5 54 56N 3 50W
Dalby, Australia 63 D5 27 10S 151 17 E
Dalgān, Iran 45 E8 27 31N 59 19 E
Dalhart, U.S.A. 81 G3 36 4N 102 31W
Dalhousie, Canada 71 C6 48 5N 66 26W
Dalhousie, India 42 C6 32 38N 75 58 E
Dali, Shaanxi, China 34 G5 34 48N 109 58 E
Dali, Yunnan, China 32 D5 25 40N 100 10 E
Dalian, China 35 E11 38 50N 121 40 E
Daliang Shan, China 32 D5 28 0N 102 45 E
Daling He →, China 35 D11 40 55N 121 40 E
Dāliyat el Karmel, Israel 47 C4 32 43N 35 2 E
Dalkeith, U.K. 12 F5 55 54N 3 4W
Dall I., U.S.A. 72 C2 54 59N 133 25W
Dallarnil, Australia 63 D5 25 19S 152 2 E
Dallas, Oreg., U.S.A. 82 D2 44 55N 123 19W
Dallas, Tex., U.S.A. 81 J6 32 47N 96 49W
Dalmacija, Croatia 20 C7 43 20N 17 0 E
Dalmatia = Dalmacija, Croatia 20 C7 43 20N 17 0 E
Dalmellington, U.K. 12 F4 55 19N 4 23W
Dalnegorsk, Russia 27 E14 44 32N 135 33 E
Dalnerechensk, Russia 27 E14 45 50N 133 40 E
Daloa, Ivory C. 50 G3 7 0N 6 30W
Dalsland, Sweden 9 G14 58 50N 12 15 E
Daltenganj, India 43 G11 24 0N 84 4 E
Dalton, Canada 70 C3 48 11N 84 1W
Dalton, Ga., U.S.A. 77 H3 34 46N 84 58W
Dalton, Mass., U.S.A. 79 D11 42 28N 73 11W
Dalton, Nebr., U.S.A. 80 E3 41 25N 102 58W
Dalton Iceberg Tongue, Antarctica 5 C9 66 15S 121 30 E
Dalvík, Iceland 8 D4 65 58N 18 32W
Daly →, Australia 60 B5 13 35S 130 19 E
Daly City, U.S.A. 84 H4 37 42N 122 28W
Daly L., Canada 73 B7 56 32N 105 39W
Daly Waters, Australia 62 B1 16 15S 133 24 E
Dam Doi, Vietnam 39 H5 8 50N 105 12 E
Dam Ha, Vietnam 38 B6 21 21N 107 36 E
Daman, India 40 J8 20 25N 72 57 E
Dāmaneh, Iran 45 C6 33 1N 50 29 E
Damanhûr, Egypt 51 B11 31 0N 30 30 E
Damanzhuang, China 34 E9 38 5N 116 35 E
Damar, Indonesia 37 F7 7 7S 128 40 E
Damaraland, Namibia 56 C2 21 0S 17 0 E
Damascus = Dimashq, Syria 47 B5 33 30N 36 18 E
Damāvand, Iran 45 C7 35 47N 52 0 E
Damāvand, Qolleh-ye, Iran 45 C7 35 56N 52 10 E
Damba, Angola 52 F3 6 44S 15 20 E
Dame Marie, Haiti 89 C5 18 36N 74 26W
Dāmghān, Iran 45 B7 36 10N 54 17 E
Damiel, Spain 19 C4 39 4N 3 37W
Damietta = Dumyât, Egypt 51 B11 31 24N 31 48 E
Daming, China 34 F8 36 15N 115 6 E
Damīr Qābū, Syria 44 B4 36 58N 41 51 E
Dammam = Ad Dammām, Si. Arabia 45 E6 26 20N 50 5 E
Damodar →, India 43 H12 23 17N 87 35 E
Damoh, India 43 H8 23 50N 79 28 E
Dampier, Australia 60 D2 20 41S 116 42 E
Dampier, Selat, Indonesia 37 E8 0 40S 131 0 E
Dampier Arch., Australia 60 D2 20 38S 116 32 E
Damrei, Chuor Phnum, Cambodia 39 G4 11 30N 103 0 E
Dana, Indonesia 37 F6 11 0S 122 52 E
Dana, L., Canada 70 B4 50 53N 77 20W
Dana, Mt., U.S.A. 84 H7 37 54N 119 12W
Danbury, U.S.A. 79 E11 41 24N 73 28W
Danby L., U.S.A. 83 J6 34 13N 115 5W
Dand, Afghan. 42 D1 31 28N 65 32 E
Dandaragan, Australia 61 F2 30 40S 115 40 E
Dandeldhura, Nepal 43 E9 29 20N 80 35 E
Dandeli, India 40 M9 15 5N 74 30 E
Dandenong, Australia 63 F4 38 0S 145 15 E
Dandong, China 35 D13 40 10N 124 20 E
Danfeng, China 34 H6 33 45N 110 25 E
Danforth, U.S.A. 71 C6 45 40N 67 52W
Danger Is. = Pukapuka, Cook Is. 65 J11 10 53S 165 49W
Danger Pt., S. Africa 56 E2 34 40S 19 17 E
Dangora, Nigeria 50 F6 11 30N 8 7 E
Dangrek, Phnom, Thailand 38 E5 14 15N 105 0 E
Dangriga, Belize 87 D7 17 0N 88 13W
Dangshan, China 34 G9 34 27N 116 22 E
Daniel, U.S.A. 82 E8 42 52N 110 4W
Daniel's Harbour, Canada 71 B8 50 13N 57 35W
Danielskuil, S. Africa 56 D3 28 11S 23 33 E
Danielson, U.S.A. 79 E13 41 48N 71 53W
Danilov, Russia 24 C7 58 16N 40 13 E
Daning, China 34 F6 36 28N 110 45 E
Danissa, Kenya 54 B5 3 15N 40 58 E
Dankhar Gompa, India 40 C11 32 10N 78 10 E
Danlí, Honduras 88 D2 14 4N 86 35W
Dannemora, U.S.A. 79 B11 44 43N 73 44W
Dannevirke, N.Z. 59 J6 40 12S 176 8 E
Dannhauser, S. Africa 57 D5 28 0S 30 3 E
Dansville, U.S.A. 78 D7 42 34N 77 42W
Dantan, India 43 J12 21 57N 87 20 E
Dante, Somali Rep. 46 E5 10 25N 51 16 E
Danube = Dunărea →, Europe 17 F15 45 20N 29 40 E
Danube →, Europe 17 F15 45 20N 29 40 E
Danvers, U.S.A. 79 D14 42 34N 70 56W
Danville, Ill., U.S.A. 76 E2 40 8N 87 37W
Danville, Ky., U.S.A. 76 G3 37 39N 84 46W
Danville, Va., U.S.A. 77 G6 36 36N 79 23W
Danzig = Gdańsk, Poland 17 A10 54 22N 18 40 E
Dao, Phil. 37 B6 10 30N 121 57 E
Daoud = Aïn Beïda, Algeria 50 A6 35 50N 7 29 E
Daqing Shan, China 34 D6 40 40N 111 0 E
Dar Banda, Africa 48 F6 8 0N 23 0 E
Dar el Beida = Casablanca, Morocco 50 B3 33 36N 7 36W
Dar es Salaam, Tanzania 54 D4 6 50S 39 12 E
Dar Mazār, Iran 45 D8 29 14N 57 20 E
Dar'ā, Syria 47 C5 32 36N 36 7 E
Dar'ā □, Syria 47 C5 32 55N 36 10 E
Dārāb, Iran 45 D7 28 50N 54 30 E
Daraj, Libya 50 B7 30 10N 10 28 E
Dārān, Iran 45 C6 32 59N 50 24 E
Dārayyā, Syria 47 B5 33 28N 36 15 E
Darband, Pakistan 42 B5 34 20N 72 50 E
Darband, Kūh-e, Iran 45 D8 31 34N 57 8 E
Darbhanga, India 43 F11 26 15N 85 55 E
Darby, U.S.A. 82 C6 46 1N 114 11W
Dardanelle, Ark., U.S.A. 81 H8 35 13N 93 9W
Dardanelle, Calif., U.S.A. 84 G7 38 20N 119 50W
Dardanelles = Çanakkale Boğazı, Turkey 21 D12 40 17N 26 32 E
Dārestān, Iran 45 D8 29 9N 58 42 E
Dârfûr, Sudan 51 F9 13 40N 24 0 E
Dargai, Pakistan 42 B4 34 25N 71 55 E
Dargan Ata, Uzbekistan 26 E7 40 29N 62 10 E
Dargaville, N.Z. 59 F4 35 57S 173 52 E
Darhan Muminggan Lianheqi, China 34 D6 41 40N 110 28 E
Darica, Turkey 21 D13 40 45N 29 23 E
Darién, G. del, Colombia 92 B3 9 0N 77 0W
Dariganga, Mongolia 34 B7 45 21N 113 45 E
Darjeeling = Darjiling, India 43 F13 27 3N 88 18 E
Darjiling, India 43 F13 27 3N 88 18 E
Dark Cove, Canada 71 C9 48 47N 54 13W
Darkan, Australia 61 F2 33 20S 116 43 E
Darkhazīneh, Iran 45 D6 31 54N 48 39 E
Darkot Pass, Pakistan 43 A5 36 45N 73 26 E
Darling →, Australia 63 E3 34 4S 141 54 E
Darling Downs, Australia 63 D5 27 30S 150 30 E
Darling Ra., Australia 61 F2 32 30S 116 0 E
Darlington, U.K. 10 C6 54 32N 1 33W
Darlington, S.C., U.S.A. 77 H6 34 18N 79 52W
Darlington, Wis., U.S.A. 80 D9 42 41N 90 7W
Darlington, L., S. Africa 56 E4 33 10S 25 9 E
Darlot, L., Australia 61 E3 27 48S 121 35 E
Darłowo, Poland 16 A9 54 25N 16 25 E
Darmstadt, Germany 16 D5 49 51N 8 39 E
Darnah, Libya 51 B9 32 45N 22 45 E
Darnall, S. Africa 57 D5 29 23S 31 18 E
Darnley, C., Antarctica 5 C6 68 0S 69 0 E
Darnley B., Canada 68 B7 69 30N 123 30W
Darr, Australia 62 C3 23 13S 144 7 E
Darr →, Australia 62 C3 23 39S 143 50 E
Darrington, U.S.A. 82 B3 48 15N 121 36W
Dart →, U.K. 11 G4 50 24N 3 39W
Dart, C., Antarctica 5 D14 73 6S 126 20W
Dartmoor, U.K. 11 G4 50 38N 3 57W
Dartmouth, Australia 62 C3 23 31S 144 44 E
Dartmouth, Canada 71 D7 44 40N 63 30W
Dartmouth, U.K. 11 G4 50 21N 3 36W
Dartmouth, L., Australia 63 D4 26 4S 145 18 E
Dartuch, C., Spain 22 B10 39 55N 3 49 E
Darvaza, Turkmenistan 26 E6 40 11N 58 24 E
Darvel, Teluk, Malaysia 37 D5 4 50N 118 20 E
Darwha, India 40 J10 20 15N 77 45 E
Darwin, Australia 60 B5 12 25S 130 51 E
Darwin, U.S.A. 85 J9 36 15N 117 35W
Darwin River, Australia 60 B5 12 50S 130 58 E
Daryoi Amu = Amudarya →, Uzbekistan 26 E6 43 58N 59 34 E
Dās, U.A.E. 45 E7 25 20N 53 30 E
Dashetai, China 34 D5 41 0N 109 5 E
Dashhowuz, Turkmenistan 26 E6 41 49N 59 58 E
Dasht, Iran 45 B8 37 17N 56 7 E
Dasht →, Pakistan 40 G2 25 10N 61 40 E
Dasht-e Mārgow, Afghan. 40 D3 30 40N 62 30 E
Dasht-i-Nawar, Afghan. 42 C3 33 52N 68 0 E
Daska, Pakistan 42 C6 32 20N 74 20 E
Datça, Turkey 21 F12 36 46N 27 40 E
Datia, India 43 G8 25 39N 78 27 E
Datong, China 34 D7 40 6N 113 18 E
Datu, Tanjung, Indonesia 36 D3 2 5N 109 39 E
Datu Piang, Phil. 37 C6 7 2N 124 30 E
Daugava →, Latvia 9 H21 57 4N 24 3 E
Daugavpils, Latvia 9 J22 55 53N 26 32 E
Daulpur, India 42 F7 26 45N 77 59 E
Dauphin, Canada 73 C8 51 9N 100 5W
Dauphin I., U.S.A. 77 K1 30 15N 88 11W
Dauphin L., Canada 73 C9 51 20N 99 45W
Dauphiné, France 18 D6 45 15N 5 25 E
Dausa, India 42 F7 26 52N 76 20 E
Davangere, India 40 M9 14 25N 75 55 E
Davao, Phil. 37 C7 7 0N 125 40 E
Davao, G. of, Phil. 37 C7 6 30N 125 48 E
Dāvar Panāh, Iran 45 E9 27 25N 62 15 E
Davenport, Calif., U.S.A. 84 H4 37 1N 122 12W
Davenport, Iowa, U.S.A. 80 E9 41 32N 90 35W
Davenport, Wash., U.S.A. 82 C4 47 39N 118 9W
Davenport Downs, Australia 62 C3 24 8S 141 7 E
Davenport Ra., Australia 62 C1 20 28S 134 0 E
David, Panama 88 E3 8 30N 82 30W
David City, U.S.A. 80 E6 41 15N 97 8W
David Gorodok = Davyd Haradok, Belarus 17 B14 52 4N 27 8 E
Davidson, Canada 73 C7 51 16N 105 59W
Davis, U.S.A. 84 G5 38 33N 121 44W
Davis Dam, U.S.A. 85 K12 35 11N 114 34W
Davis Inlet, Canada 71 A7 55 50N 60 59W
Davis Mts., U.S.A. 81 K2 30 50N 103 55W
Davis Sea, Antarctica 5 C7 66 0S 92 0 E
Davis Str., N. Amer. 69 B14 65 0N 58 0W
Davos, Switz. 16 E5 46 48N 9 49 E
Davy L., Canada 73 B7 58 53N 108 18W
Davyd Haradok, Belarus 17 B14 52 4N 27 8 E
Dawes Ra., Australia 62 C5 24 40S 150 40 E
Dawson, Canada 68 B6 64 10N 139 30W
Dawson, Ga., U.S.A. 77 K3 31 46N 84 27W
Dawson, N. Dak., U.S.A. 80 B5 46 52N 99 45W
Dawson, I., Chile 96 G2 53 50S 70 50W
Dawson Creek, Canada 72 B4 55 45N 120 15W
Dawson Inlet, Canada 73 A10 61 50N 93 25W
Dawson Ra., Australia 62 C4 24 30S 149 48 E
Dax, France 18 E3 43 44N 1 3W
Daxian, China 32 C5 31 15N 107 23 E
Daxindian, China 35 F11 37 30N 120 50 E
Daxinggou, China 35 C15 43 25N 129 40 E
Daxue Shan, China 32 C5 30 30N 101 30 E
Daylesford, Australia 63 F3 37 21S 144 9 E
Dayr az Zawr, Syria 44 C4 35 20N 40 5 E
Daysland, Canada 72 C6 52 50N 112 20W
Dayton, Nev., U.S.A. 84 F7 39 14N 119 36W
Dayton, Ohio, U.S.A. 76 F3 39 45N 84 12W
Dayton, Pa., U.S.A. 78 F5 40 53N 79 15W
Dayton, Tenn., U.S.A. 77 H3 35 30N 85 1W
Dayton, Wash., U.S.A. 82 C4 46 19N 117 59W
Daytona Beach, U.S.A. 77 L5 29 13N 81 1W
Dayville, U.S.A. 82 D4 44 28N 119 32W
De Aar, S. Africa 56 E3 30 39S 24 0 E
De Funiak Springs, U.S.A. 77 K2 30 43N 86 7W
De Grey, Australia 60 D2 20 12S 119 12 E
De Grey →, Australia 60 D2 20 12S 119 13 E
De Kalb, U.S.A. 80 E10 41 56N 88 46W
De Land, U.S.A. 77 L5 29 2N 81 18W
De Leon, U.S.A. 81 J5 32 7N 98 32W
De Pere, U.S.A. 76 C1 44 27N 88 4W
De Queen, U.S.A. 81 H7 34 2N 94 21W
De Quincy, U.S.A. 81 K8 30 27N 93 26W
De Ridder, U.S.A. 81 K8 30 51N 93 17W
De Smet, U.S.A. 80 C6 44 23N 97 33W
De Soto, U.S.A. 80 F9 38 8N 90 34W
De Tour Village, U.S.A. 76 C4 46 0N 83 56W
De Witt, U.S.A. 81 H9 34 18N 91 20W
Dead Sea, Asia 47 D4 31 30N 35 30 E
Deadwood, U.S.A. 80 C3 44 23N 103 44W
Deadwood L., Canada 72 B3 59 10N 128 30W
Deakin, Australia 61 F4 30 46S 128 58 E
Deal, U.K. 11 F9 51 13N 1 25 E
Deal I., Australia 62 F4 39 30S 147 20 E
Dealesville, S. Africa 56 D4 28 41S 25 44 E
Dean, Forest of, U.K. 11 F5 51 45N 2 33W
Deán Funes, Argentina 94 C3 30 20S 64 20W
Dearborn, U.S.A. 70 D3 42 19N 83 11W
Dease →, Canada 72 B3 59 56N 128 32W
Dease L., Canada 72 B2 58 40N 130 5W
Dease Lake, Canada 72 B2 58 25N 130 6W
Death Valley, U.S.A. 85 J10 36 15N 116 50W
Death Valley Junction, U.S.A. 85 J10 36 20N 116 25W
Death Valley National Monument, U.S.A. 85 J10 36 45N 117 15W
Deba Habe, Nigeria 50 F7 10 14N 11 20 E
Debar, Macedonia 21 D9 41 31N 20 30 E
Debden, Canada 73 C7 53 30N 106 50W
Dębica, Poland 17 C11 50 2N 21 25 E
Debolt, Canada 72 B5 55 12N 118 1W
Deborah East, L., Australia 61 F2 30 45S 119 0 E
Deborah West, L., Australia 61 F2 30 45S 118 50 E
Debre Markos, Ethiopia 51 F12 10 20N 37 40 E
Debre Tabor, Ethiopia 51 F12 11 50N 38 26 E
Debrecen, Hungary 17 E11 47 33N 21 42 E
Decatur, Ala., U.S.A. 77 H2 34 36N 86 59W
Decatur, Ga., U.S.A. 77 J3 33 47N 84 18W
Decatur, Ill., U.S.A. 80 F10 39 51N 88 57W
Decatur, Ind., U.S.A. 76 E3 40 50N 84 56W
Decatur, Tex., U.S.A. 81 J6 33 14N 97 35W
Deccan, India 40 M10 18 0N 79 0 E
Deception L., Canada 73 B8 56 33N 104 13W
Děčín, Czech. 16 C8 50 47N 14 12 E
Deckerville, U.S.A. 78 C2 43 32N 82 44W
Decorah, U.S.A. 80 D9 43 18N 91 48W
Dedéagach = Alexandroúpolis, Greece 21 D11 40 50N 25 54 E
Dedham, U.S.A. 79 D13 42 15N 71 10W
Dédougou, Burkina Faso 50 F4 12 30N 3 25W
Dedza, Malawi 55 E3 14 20S 34 20 E
Dee →, C. of Aberd., U.K. 12 D6 57 9N 2 5W
Dee →, Wales, U.K. 10 D4 53 22N 3 17W
Deep B., Canada 72 A5 61 15N 116 35W
Deep Well, Australia 62 C1 24 20S 134 0 E
Deepwater, Australia 63 D5 29 25S 151 51 E
Deer →, Canada 73 B10 58 23N 94 13W
Deer Lake, Nfld., Canada 71 C8 49 11N 57 27W
Deer Lake, Ont., Canada 73 C10 52 36N 94 20W
Deer Lodge, U.S.A. 82 C7 46 24N 112 44W
Deer Park, U.S.A. 82 C5 47 57N 117 28W
Deer River, U.S.A. 80 B8 47 20N 93 48W
Deeral, Australia 62 B4 17 14S 145 55 E
Deerdepoort, S. Africa 56 C4 24 37S 26 27 E
Deferiet, U.S.A. 79 B9 44 2N 75 41W
Defiance, U.S.A. 76 E3 41 17N 84 22W
Degeh Bur, Ethiopia 46 F3 8 11N 43 31 E
Deggendorf, Germany 16 D7 48 50N 12 57 E
Deh Bīd, Iran 45 D7 30 39N 53 11 E
Deh-e Shīr, Iran 45 D7 31 29N 53 45 E
Dehaj, Iran 45 D7 30 42N 54 53 E
Dehdez, Iran 45 D6 31 43N 50 17 E
Dehestān, Iran 45 D7 28 30N 55 35 E
Dehgolān, Iran 44 C5 35 17N 47 25 E
Dehi Titan, Afghan. 40 C3 33 45N 63 50 E
Dehibat, Tunisia 50 B7 32 0N 10 47 E
Dehlorān, Iran 44 C5 32 41N 47 16 E
Dehnow-e Kūhestān, Iran 45 E8 27 58N 58 32 E
Dehra Dun, India 42 D8 30 20N 78 4 E
Dehri, India 43 G11 24 50N 84 15 E
Dehui, China 35 B13 44 30N 125 40 E
Deinze, Belgium 15 D3 50 59N 3 32 E
Dej, Romania 17 E12 47 10N 23 52 E
Dekese, Zaïre 52 E4 3 24S 21 24 E
Del Mar, U.S.A. 85 N9 32 58N 117 16W
Del Norte, U.S.A. 83 H10 37 41N 106 21W
Del Rio, U.S.A. 81 L4 29 22N 100 54W
Delano, U.S.A. 85 K7 35 46N 119 15W
Delareyville, S. Africa 56 D4 26 41S 25 26 E
Delavan, U.S.A. 80 D10 42 38N 88 39W
Delaware, U.S.A. 76 E4 40 18N 83 4W
Delaware □, U.S.A. 76 F8 39 0N 75 20W
Delaware →, U.S.A. 76 F8 39 15N 75 20W
Delaware B., U.S.A. 75 C12 39 0N 75 10W
Delegate, Australia 63 F4 37 4S 148 56 E
Delft, Neths. 15 B4 52 1N 4 22 E
Delfzijl, Neths. 15 A6 53 20N 6 55 E
Delgado, C., Mozam. 55 E5 10 45S 40 40 E
Delgerhet, Mongolia 34 B6 45 50N 110 30 E
Delgo, Sudan 51 D11 20 6N 30 40 E
Delhi, Canada 78 D4 42 51N 80 30W
Delhi, India 42 E7 28 38N 77 17 E
Delhi, U.S.A. 79 D10 42 17N 74 55W
Delia, Canada 72 C6 51 38N 112 23W
Delice →, Turkey 25 G5 39 45N 34 15 E
Delicias, Mexico 86 B3 28 10N 105 30W
Delījān, Iran 45 C6 33 59N 50 40 E
Déline, Canada 68 B7 65 10N 123 30W
Dell City, U.S.A. 83 L11 31 56N 105 12W
Dell Rapids, U.S.A. 80 D6 43 50N 96 43W
Delmar, U.S.A. 79 D11 42 37N 73 47W
Delmenhorst, Germany 16 B5 53 3N 8 37 E
Delmiro Gouveia, Brazil 93 E11 9 24S 38 6W
Delong, Ostrova, Russia 27 B15 76 40N 149 20 E
Deloraine, Australia 62 G4 41 30S 146 40 E
Deloraine, Canada 73 D8 49 15N 100 29W
Delphi, U.S.A. 76 E2 40 36N 86 41W
Delphos, U.S.A. 76 E3 40 51N 84 21W
Delportshoop, S. Africa 56 D3 28 22S 24 20 E
Delray Beach, U.S.A. 77 M5 26 28N 80 4W
Delta, Colo., U.S.A. 83 G9 38 44N 108 4W
Delta, Utah, U.S.A. 82 G7 39 21N 112 35W
Delungra, Australia 63 D5 29 39S 150 51 E
Delvinë, Albania 21 E9 39 59N 20 4 E
Demanda, Sierra de la, Spain 19 A4 42 15N 3 0W
Demavand = Damāvand, Iran 45 C7 35 47N 52 0 E
Demba, Zaïre 52 F4 5 28S 22 15 E
Dembecha, Ethiopia 51 F12 10 32N 37 30 E
Dembia, Zaïre 54 B2 3 33N 25 48 E
Dembidolo, Ethiopia 51 G11 8 34N 34 50 E
Demer →, Belgium 15 D4 50 57N 4 42 E
Deming, N. Mex., U.S.A. 83 K10 32 16N 107 46W
Deming, Wash., U.S.A. 84 B4 48 50N 122 13W
Demini →, Brazil 92 D6 0 46S 62 56W
Demirci, Turkey 21 E13 39 2N 28 38 E
Demirköy, Turkey 21 D12 41 49N 27 45 E
Demopolis, U.S.A. 77 J2 32 31N 87 50W
Dempo, Indonesia 36 E2 4 2S 103 15 E
Den Burg, Neths. 15 A4 53 3N 4 47 E
Den Chai, Thailand 38 D3 17 59N 100 4 E
Den Haag = 's-Gravenhage, Neths. 15 B4 52 7N 4 17 E
Den Helder, Neths. 15 B4 52 57N 4 45 E
Den Oever, Neths. 15 B5 52 56N 5 2 E
Denain, France 15 D3 50 20N 3 22 E
Denair, U.S.A. 84 H6 37 32N 120 48W
Denau, Uzbekistan 26 F7 38 16N 67 54 E
Denbigh, U.K. 10 D4 53 12N 3 25W
Denbighshire □, U.K. 10 D4 53 8N 3 22W
Dendang, Indonesia 36 E3 3 7S 107 56 E
Dendermonde, Belgium 15 C4 51 2N 4 5 E
Dengfeng, China 34 G7 34 25N 113 2 E
Dengkou, China 34 D4 40 18N 106 55 E
Denham, Australia 61 E1 25 56S 113 31 E
Denham Ra., Australia 62 C4 21 55S 147 46 E
Denham Sd., Australia 61 E1 25 45S 113 15 E
Denia, Spain 19 C6 38 49N 0 8 E
Denial B., Australia 63 E1 32 14S 133 32 E
Deniliquin, Australia 63 F3 35 30S 144 58 E
Denison, Iowa, U.S.A. 80 D7 42 1N 95 21W
Denison, Tex., U.S.A. 81 J6 33 45N 96 33W
Denison Plains, Australia 60 C4 18 35S 128 0 E
Denizli, Turkey 25 G4 37 42N 29 2 E
Denman Glacier, Antarctica 5 C7 66 45S 99 25 E
Denmark, Australia 61 F2 34 59S 117 25 E
Denmark ■, Europe 9 J13 55 30N 9 0 E
Denmark Str., Atl. Oc. 4 C6 66 0N 30 0W
Dennison, U.S.A. 78 F3 40 24N 81 19W
Denpasar, Indonesia 36 F5 8 45S 115 14 E
Denton, Mont., U.S.A. 82 C9 47 19N 109 57W
Denton, Tex., U.S.A. 81 J6 33 13N 97 8W
D'Entrecasteaux, Pt., Australia 61 F2 34 50S 115 57 E
Denver, U.S.A. 80 F2 39 44N 104 59W
Denver City, U.S.A. 81 J3 32 58N 102 50W
Deoband, India 42 E7 29 42N 77 43 E
Deoghar, India 43 G12 24 30N 86 42 E
Deolali, India 40 K8 19 58N 73 50 E
Deoli = Devli, India 42 G6 25 50N 75 20 E
Deoria, India 43 F10 26 31N 83 48 E
Deosai Mts., Pakistan 43 B6 35 40N 75 0 E
Deping, China 35 F9 37 25N 116 58 E
Deposit, U.S.A. 79 D9 42 4N 75 25W
Depot Springs, Australia 61 E3 27 55S 120 3 E
Deputatskiy, Russia 27 C14 69 18N 139 54 E
Dera Ghazi Khan, Pakistan 42 D4 30 5N 70 43 E

E

Farsund

Enkhuizen, Neths. 15 B5 52 42N 5 17 E
Enna, Italy 20 F6 37 34N 14 16 E
Ennadai, Canada 73 A8 61 8N 100 53W
Ennadai L., Canada 73 A8 61 0N 101 0W
Ennedi, Chad 51 E9 17 15N 22 0 E
Enngonia, Australia 63 D4 29 21S 145 50 E
Ennis, Ireland 13 D3 52 51N 8 59W
Ennis, Mont., U.S.A. 82 D8 45 21N 111 44W
Ennis, Tex., U.S.A. 81 J6 32 20N 96 38W
Enniscorthy, Ireland 13 D5 52 30N 6 34W
Enniskillen, U.K. 13 B4 54 21N 7 39W
Ennistimon, Ireland 13 D2 52 57N 9 17W
Enns →, Austria 16 D8 48 14N 14 32 E
Enontekiö, Finland 8 B20 68 23N 23 37 E
Enriquillo, L., Dom. Rep. 89 C5 18 20N 72 5W
Enschede, Neths. 15 B6 52 13N 6 53 E
Ensenada, Argentina 94 C4 34 55S 57 55W
Ensenada, Mexico 86 A1 31 50N 116 50W
Ensiola, Pta., Spain 22 B9 39 7N 2 55 E
Entebbe, Uganda 54 B3 0 4N 32 28 E
Enterprise, Canada 72 A5 60 47N 115 45W
Enterprise, Oreg., U.S.A. 82 D5 45 25N 117 17W
Enterprise, Utah, U.S.A. 83 H7 37 34N 113 43W
Entre Ríos, Bolivia 94 A3 21 30S 64 25W
Entre Ríos □, Argentina 94 C4 30 30S 58 30W
Entroncamento, Portugal 19 C1 39 28N 8 28W
Enugu, Nigeria 50 G6 6 20N 7 30 E
Enugu Ezike, Nigeria 50 G6 7 0N 7 29 E
Enumclaw, U.S.A. 84 C5 47 12N 121 59W
Eólie, Is., Italy 20 E6 38 30N 14 57 E
Epe, Neths. 15 B5 52 21N 5 59 E
Épernay, France 18 B5 49 3N 3 56 E
Ephesus, Turkey 21 F12 37 55N 27 22 E
Ephraim, U.S.A. 82 G8 39 22N 111 35W
Ephrata, U.S.A. 82 C4 47 19N 119 33W
Épinal, France 18 B7 48 10N 6 27 E
Episkopi, Cyprus 23 E11 34 40N 32 54 E
Episkopí, Greece 23 D6 35 20N 24 20 E
Episkopi Bay, Cyprus 23 E11 34 35N 32 50 E
Epping, U.K. 11 F8 51 41N 0 7 E
Epukiro, Namibia 56 C2 21 40S 19 9 E
Equatorial Guinea ■, Africa 52 D1 2 0N 8 0 E
Er Rahad, Sudan 51 F11 12 45N 30 32 E
Er Rif, Morocco 50 A4 35 1N 4 1W
Er Roseires, Sudan 51 F11 11 55N 34 30 E
Erāwadī Myit = Irrawaddy →, Burma 41 M19 15 50N 95 6 E
Erbil = Arbīl, Iraq 44 B5 36 15N 44 5 E
Erciyaş Dağı, Turkey 25 G6 38 30N 35 30 E
Érd, Hungary 17 E10 47 22N 18 56 E
Erdao Jiang →, China 35 C14 43 0N 127 0 E
Erdek, Turkey 21 D12 40 23N 27 47 E
Erdene, Mongolia 34 B6 44 13N 111 10 E
Erebus, Mt., Antarctica 5 D11 77 35S 167 0 E
Erechim, Brazil 95 B5 27 35S 52 15W
Ereğli, Konya, Turkey 25 G5 37 31N 34 4 E
Ereğli, Zonguldak, Turkey 25 F5 41 15N 31 24 E
Erenhot, China 34 C7 43 48N 112 2 E
Eresma →, Spain 19 B3 41 26N 4 45W
Erewadi Myitwanya, Burma 41 M19 15 30N 95 0 E
Erfenisdam, S. Africa 56 D4 28 30S 26 50 E
Erfurt, Germany 16 C6 50 58N 11 2 E
Ergeni Vozvyshennost, Russia 25 E7 47 0N 44 0 E
Ērgli, Latvia 9 H21 56 54N 25 38 E
Eriboll, L., U.K. 12 C4 58 30N 4 42W
Érice, Italy 20 E5 38 2N 12 35 E
Erie, U.S.A. 78 D4 42 8N 80 5W
Erie, L., N. Amer. 78 D3 42 15N 81 0W
Erie Canal, U.S.A. 78 C6 43 5N 78 43W
Erieau, Canada 78 D3 42 16N 81 57W
Erigavo, Somali Rep. 46 E4 10 35N 47 20 E
Erikoúsa, Greece 23 A3 39 53N 19 34 E
Eriksdale, Canada 73 C9 50 52N 98 7W
Erímanthos, Greece 21 F9 37 57N 21 50 E
Erimo-misaki, Japan 30 D11 41 50N 143 15 E
Eritrea ■, Africa 51 F12 14 0N 38 30 E
Erlangen, Germany 16 D6 49 36N 11 0 E
Erldunda, Australia 62 D1 25 14S 133 12 E
Ermelo, Neths. 15 B5 52 18N 5 35 E
Ermelo, S. Africa 57 D4 26 31S 29 59 E
Ermones, Greece 23 A3 39 37N 19 46 E
Ermoúpolis = Síros, Greece 21 F11 37 28N 24 57 E
Ernakulam = Cochin, India 40 Q10 9 59N 76 22 E
Erne →, Ireland 13 B3 54 30N 8 16W
Erne, Lower L., U.K. 13 B4 54 28N 7 47W
Erne, Upper L., U.K. 13 B4 54 14N 7 32W
Ernest Giles Ra., Australia 61 E3 27 0S 123 45 E
Erode, India 40 P10 11 24N 77 45 E
Eromanga, Australia 63 D3 26 40S 143 11 E
Erongo, Namibia 56 C2 21 39S 15 58 E
Errabiddy, Australia 61 E2 25 25S 117 5 E
Erramala Hills, India 40 M11 15 30N 78 15 E
Errigal, Ireland 13 A3 55 2N 8 6W
Erris Hd., Ireland 13 B1 54 19N 10 0W
Erskine, U.S.A. 80 B7 47 40N 96 0W
Ertis → = Irtysh →, Russia 26 C7 61 4N 68 52 E
Erwin, U.S.A. 77 G4 36 9N 82 25W
Erzgebirge, Germany 16 C7 50 27N 12 55 E
Erzin, Russia 27 D10 50 15N 95 10 E
Erzincan, Turkey 25 G6 39 46N 39 30 E
Erzurum, Turkey 25 G7 39 57N 41 15 E
Es Caló, Spain 22 C8 38 40N 1 30 E
Es Caná, Spain 22 B8 39 2N 1 36 E
Es Sahrâ' Esh Sharqîya, Egypt 51 C11 27 30N 32 30 E
Es Sînâ', Egypt 51 C11 29 0N 34 0 E
Esambo, Zaïre 54 C1 3 48S 23 30 E
Esan-Misaki, Japan 30 D10 41 40N 141 10 E
Esashi, Hokkaidō, Japan 30 B11 44 56N 142 35 E
Esashi, Hokkaidō, Japan 30 D10 41 52N 140 7 E
Esbjerg, Denmark 9 J13 55 29N 8 29 E
Escalante, U.S.A. 83 H8 37 47N 111 36W
Escalante →, U.S.A. 83 H8 37 24N 110 57W
Escalón, Mexico 86 B4 26 46N 104 20W
Escambia →, U.S.A. 77 K2 30 32N 87 11W
Escanaba, U.S.A. 76 C2 45 45N 87 4W
Esch-sur-Alzette, Lux. 18 B6 49 32N 6 0 E
Escondido, U.S.A. 85 M9 33 7N 117 5W
Escuinapa, Mexico 86 C3 22 50N 105 50W
Escuintla, Guatemala 88 D1 14 20N 90 48W
Esenguly, Turkmenistan 26 F6 37 37N 53 59 E
Eşfahān, Iran 45 C6 32 39N 51 43 E
Esfideh, Iran 45 C8 33 39N 59 46 E
Esh Sham = Dimashq, Syria 47 B5 33 30N 36 18 E
Eshowe, S. Africa 57 D5 28 50S 31 30 E
Esil → = Ishim →, Russia 26 D8 57 45N 71 10 E
Esk →, Cumb., U.K. 12 G5 54 58N 3 2W
Esk →, N. Yorks., U.K. 10 C7 54 30N 0 37W
Eskifjörður, Iceland 8 D7 65 3N 13 55W
Eskilstuna, Sweden 9 G17 59 22N 16 32 E
Eskimo Pt., Canada 73 A10 61 10N 94 15W
Eskişehir, Turkey 25 G5 39 50N 30 35 E
Esla →, Spain 19 B2 41 29N 6 3W
Eslāmābād-e Gharb, Iran 44 C5 34 10N 46 30 E
Eşme, Turkey 21 E13 38 23N 28 58 E
Esmeraldas, Ecuador 92 C3 1 0N 79 40W
Espalmador, I., Spain 22 C7 38 47N 1 26 E
Espanola, Canada 70 C3 46 15N 81 46W
Espardell, I. del, Spain 22 C7 38 48N 1 29 E
Esparta, Costa Rica 88 E3 9 59N 84 40W
Esperance, Australia 61 F3 33 45S 121 55 E
Esperance B., Australia 61 F3 33 48S 121 55 E
Esperanza, Argentina 94 C3 31 29S 61 3W
Espichel, C., Portugal 19 C1 38 22N 9 16W
Espigão, Serra do, Brazil 95 B5 26 35S 50 30W
Espinal, Colombia 92 C4 4 9N 74 53W
Espinazo, Sierra del = Espinhaço, Serra do, Brazil 93 G10 17 30S 43 30W
Espinhaço, Serra do, Brazil 93 G10 17 30S 43 30W
Espinilho, Serra do, Brazil 95 B5 28 30S 55 0W
Espírito Santo □, Brazil 93 G10 20 0S 40 45W
Espíritu Santo, B. del, Mexico 87 D7 19 15N 87 0W
Espíritu Santo, I., Mexico 86 C2 24 30N 110 23W
Espita, Mexico 87 C7 21 1N 88 19W
Espoo, Finland 9 F21 60 12N 24 40 E
Espungabera, Mozam. 57 C5 20 29S 32 45 E
Esquel, Argentina 96 E2 42 55S 71 20W
Esquina, Argentina 94 B4 30 0S 59 30W
Essaouira, Morocco 50 B3 31 32N 9 42W
Essebie, Zaïre 54 B3 2 58N 30 40 E
Essen, Belgium 15 C4 51 28N 4 28 E
Essen, Germany 16 C4 51 28N 7 0 E
Essendon, Mt., Australia 61 E3 25 0S 120 29 E
Essequibo →, Guyana 92 B7 6 50N 58 30W
Essex, Canada 78 D2 42 10N 82 49W
Essex, Calif., U.S.A. 85 L11 34 44N 115 15W
Essex, N.Y., U.S.A. 79 B11 44 19N 73 21W
Essex □, U.K. 11 F8 51 54N 0 27 E
Esslingen, Germany 16 D5 48 44N 9 18 E
Estados, I. de Los, Argentina 96 G4 54 40S 64 30W
Eşṭahbānāt, Iran 45 D7 29 8N 54 4 E
Estallenchs, Spain 22 B9 39 39N 2 29 E
Estância, Brazil 93 F11 11 16S 37 26W
Estancia, U.S.A. 83 J10 34 46N 106 4W
Estārm, Iran 45 D8 28 21N 58 21 E
Estcourt, S. Africa 57 D4 29 0S 29 53 E
Estelí, Nic. 88 D2 13 9N 86 22W
Estelline, S. Dak., U.S.A. 80 C6 44 35N 96 54W
Estelline, Tex., U.S.A. 81 H4 34 33N 100 26W
Esterhazy, Canada 73 C8 50 37N 102 5W
Estevan, Canada 73 D8 49 10N 102 59W
Estevan Group, Canada 72 C3 53 3N 129 38W
Estherville, U.S.A. 80 D7 43 24N 94 50W
Eston, Canada 73 C7 51 8N 108 40W
Estonia ■, Europe 9 G21 58 30N 25 30 E
Estrêla, Serra da, Portugal 19 B2 40 10N 7 45W
Estremoz, Portugal 19 C2 38 51N 7 39W
Estrondo, Serra do, Brazil 93 E9 7 20S 48 0W
Esztergom, Hungary 17 E10 47 47N 18 44 E
Etadunna, Australia 63 D2 28 43S 138 38 E
Etah, India 43 F8 27 35N 78 40 E
Etamamu, Canada 71 B8 50 18N 59 59W
Étampes, France 18 B5 48 26N 2 10 E
Etanga, Namibia 56 B1 17 55S 13 0 E
Etawah, India 43 F8 26 48N 79 6 E
Etawah →, U.S.A. 77 H3 34 20N 84 15W
Etawney L., Canada 73 B9 57 50N 96 50W
Ethel, U.S.A. 84 D4 46 32N 122 46W
Ethel Creek, Australia 60 D3 22 55S 120 11 E
Ethelbert, Canada 73 C8 51 32N 100 25W
Ethiopia ■, Africa 46 F3 8 0N 40 0 E
Ethiopian Highlands, Ethiopia 28 J7 10 0N 37 0 E
Etive, L., U.K. 12 E3 56 29N 5 10W
Etna, Italy 20 F6 37 50N 14 55 E
Etoile, Zaïre 55 E2 11 33S 27 30 E
Etolin I., U.S.A. 72 B2 56 5N 132 20W
Etosha Pan, Namibia 56 B2 18 40S 16 30 E
Etowah, U.S.A. 77 H3 35 20N 84 32W
Ettrick Water →, U.K. 12 F6 55 31N 2 55W
Etuku, Zaïre 54 C2 3 42S 25 45 E
Etzatlán, Mexico 86 C4 20 48N 104 5W
Euboea = Évvoia, Greece 21 E11 38 30N 24 0 E
Eucla Motel, Australia 61 F4 31 41S 128 52 E
Euclid, U.S.A. 78 E3 41 34N 81 32W
Eucumbene, L., Australia 63 F4 36 2S 148 40 E
Eudora, U.S.A. 81 J9 33 7N 91 16W
Eufaula, Ala., U.S.A. 77 K3 31 54N 85 9W
Eufaula, Okla., U.S.A. 81 H7 35 17N 95 35W
Eufaula L., U.S.A. 81 H7 35 18N 95 21W
Eugene, U.S.A. 82 E2 44 5N 123 4W
Eugowra, Australia 63 E4 33 22S 148 24 E
Eulo, Australia 63 D4 28 10S 145 3 E
Eunice, La., U.S.A. 81 K8 30 30N 92 25W
Eunice, N. Mex., U.S.A. 81 J3 32 26N 103 10W
Eupen, Belgium 15 D6 50 37N 6 3 E
Euphrates = Furāt, Nahr al →, Asia 44 D5 31 0N 47 25 E
Eureka, Canada 4 B3 80 0N 85 56W
Eureka, Calif., U.S.A. 82 F1 40 47N 124 9W
Eureka, Kans., U.S.A. 81 G6 37 49N 96 17W
Eureka, Mont., U.S.A. 82 B6 48 53N 115 3W
Eureka, Nev., U.S.A. 82 G5 39 31N 115 58W
Eureka, S. Dak., U.S.A. 80 C5 45 46N 99 38W
Eureka, Utah, U.S.A. 82 G7 39 58N 112 7W
Eureka, Mt., Australia 61 E3 26 35S 121 35 E
Euroa, Australia 63 F4 36 44S 145 35 E
Europa, Î., Ind. Oc. 53 J8 22 20S 40 22 E
Europa, Picos de, Spain 19 A3 43 10N 4 49W
Europa, Pta. de, Gib. 19 D3 36 3N 5 21W
Europa Pt. = Europa, Pta. de, Gib. 19 D3 36 3N 5 21W
Europoort, Neths. 15 C4 51 57N 4 10 E
Eustis, U.S.A. 77 L5 28 51N 81 41W
Eutsuk L., Canada 72 C3 53 20N 126 45W
Eva Downs, Australia 62 B1 18 1S 134 52 E
Evale, Angola 56 B2 16 33S 15 44 E
Evans, U.S.A. 80 E2 40 23N 104 41W
Evans Head, Australia 63 D5 29 7S 153 27 E
Evans L., Canada 70 B4 50 50N 77 0W
Evans Mills, U.S.A. 79 B9 44 6N 75 48W
Evanston, Ill., U.S.A. 76 D2 42 3N 87 41W
Evanston, Wyo., U.S.A. 82 F8 41 16N 110 58W
Evansville, Ind., U.S.A. 76 F2 37 58N 87 35W
Evansville, Wis., U.S.A. 80 D10 42 47N 89 18W
Evaz, Iran 45 E7 27 46N 53 59 E
Eveleth, U.S.A. 80 B8 47 28N 92 32W
Evensk, Russia 27 C16 62 12N 159 30 E
Everard, L., Australia 63 E1 31 30S 135 0 E
Everard Park, Australia 61 E5 27 1S 132 43 E
Everard Ras., Australia 61 E5 27 5S 132 28 E
Everest, Mt., Nepal 43 E12 28 5N 86 58 E
Everett, Pa., U.S.A. 78 F6 40 1N 78 23W
Everett, Wash., U.S.A. 84 C4 47 59N 122 12W
Everglades, The, U.S.A. 77 N5 25 50N 81 0W
Everglades City, U.S.A. 77 N5 25 52N 81 23W
Everglades National Park, U.S.A. 77 N5 25 30N 81 0W
Evergreen, U.S.A. 77 K2 31 26N 86 57W
Everson, U.S.A. 82 B2 48 57N 122 22W
Evesham, U.K. 11 E6 52 6N 1 56W
Evinayong, Eq. Guin. 52 D2 1 26N 10 35 E
Evje, Norway 9 G12 58 36N 7 51 E
Évora, Portugal 19 C2 38 33N 7 57W
Evowghlī, Iran 44 B5 38 43N 45 13 E
Évreux, France 18 B4 49 3N 1 8 E
Évros →, Bulgaria 21 D12 41 40N 26 34 E
Evry, France 18 B5 48 38N 2 27 E
Évvoia, Greece 21 E11 38 30N 24 0 E
Ewe, L., U.K. 12 D3 57 49N 5 38W
Ewing, U.S.A. 80 D5 42 16N 98 21W
Ewo, Congo 52 E2 0 48S 14 45 E
Exaltación, Bolivia 92 F5 13 10S 65 20W
Excelsior Springs, U.S.A. 80 F7 39 20N 94 13W
Exe →, U.K. 11 G4 50 41N 3 29W
Exeter, Canada 78 C3 43 21N 81 29W
Exeter, U.K. 11 G4 50 43N 3 31W
Exeter, Calif., U.S.A. 83 H4 36 18N 119 9W
Exeter, N.H., U.S.A. 79 D14 42 59N 70 57W
Exeter, Nebr., U.S.A. 80 E6 40 39N 97 27W
Exmoor, U.K. 11 F4 51 12N 3 45W
Exmouth, Australia 60 D1 21 54S 114 10 E
Exmouth, U.K. 11 G4 50 37N 3 25W
Exmouth G., Australia 60 D1 22 15S 114 15 E
Expedition Ra., Australia 62 C4 24 30S 149 12 E
Extremadura □, Spain 19 C2 39 30N 6 5W
Exuma Sound, Bahamas 88 B4 24 30N 76 20W
Eyasi, L., Tanzania 54 C4 3 30S 35 0 E
Eyeberry L., Canada 73 A8 63 8N 104 43W
Eyemouth, U.K. 12 F6 55 52N 2 5W
Eyjafjörður, Iceland 8 C4 66 15N 18 30W
Eyre, Australia 61 F4 32 15S 126 18 E
Eyre (North), L., Australia 63 D2 28 30S 137 20 E
Eyre (South), L., Australia 63 D2 29 18S 137 25 E
Eyre Cr. →, Australia 63 D2 26 40S 139 0 E
Eyre Mts., N.Z. 59 L2 45 25S 168 25 E
Eyre Pen., Australia 63 E2 33 30S 136 17 E
Eysturoy, Færoe Is. 8 E9 62 13N 6 54W
Eyvānkī, Iran 45 C6 35 24N 51 56 E
Ezine, Turkey 21 E12 39 48N 26 20 E
Ezouza →, Cyprus 23 E11 34 44N 32 27 E

F

F.Y.R.O.M. = Macedonia ■, Europe 21 D9 41 53N 21 40 E
Fabens, U.S.A. 83 L10 31 30N 106 10W
Fabriano, Italy 20 C5 43 20N 12 54 E
Facatativá, Colombia 92 C4 4 49N 74 22W
Fachi, Niger 50 E7 18 6N 11 34 E
Fada, Chad 51 E9 17 13N 21 34 E
Fada-n-Gourma, Burkina Faso 50 F5 12 10N 0 30 E
Faddeyevskiy, Ostrov, Russia 27 B15 76 0N 144 0 E
Fadghāmī, Syria 44 C4 35 53N 40 52 E
Faenza, Italy 20 B4 44 17N 11 53 E
Færoe Is. = Føroyar, Atl. Oc. 8 F9 62 0N 7 0W
Făgăras, Romania 17 F13 45 48N 24 58 E
Fagersta, Sweden 9 F16 60 1N 15 46 E
Fagnano, L., Argentina 96 G3 54 30S 68 0W
Fahliān, Iran 45 D6 30 11N 51 28 E
Fahraj, Kermān, Iran 45 D8 29 0N 59 0 E
Fahraj, Yazd, Iran 45 D7 31 46N 54 36 E
Faial, Madeira 22 D3 32 47N 16 53W
Fair Hd., U.K. 13 A5 55 14N 6 9W
Fair Oaks, U.S.A. 84 G5 38 39N 121 16W
Fairbank, U.S.A. 83 L8 31 43N 110 11W
Fairbanks, U.S.A. 68 B5 64 51N 147 43W
Fairbury, U.S.A. 80 E6 40 8N 97 11W
Fairfax, U.S.A. 81 G6 36 34N 96 42W
Fairfield, Ala., U.S.A. 77 J2 33 29N 86 55W
Fairfield, Calif., U.S.A. 84 G4 38 15N 122 3W
Fairfield, Conn., U.S.A. 79 E11 41 9N 73 16W
Fairfield, Idaho, U.S.A. 82 E6 43 21N 114 44W
Fairfield, Ill., U.S.A. 76 F1 38 23N 88 22W
Fairfield, Iowa, U.S.A. 80 E9 40 56N 91 57W
Fairfield, Mont., U.S.A. 82 C8 47 37N 111 59W
Fairfield, Tex., U.S.A. 81 K7 31 44N 96 10W
Fairford, Canada 73 C9 51 37N 98 38W
Fairhope, U.S.A. 77 K2 30 31N 87 54W
Fairlie, N.Z. 59 L3 44 5S 170 49 E
Fairmead, U.S.A. 84 H6 37 5N 120 10W
Fairmont, Minn., U.S.A. 80 D7 43 39N 94 28W
Fairmont, W. Va., U.S.A. 76 F5 39 29N 80 9W
Fairmount, U.S.A. 85 L8 34 45N 118 26W
Fairplay, U.S.A. 83 G11 39 15N 106 2W
Fairport, U.S.A. 78 C7 43 6N 77 27W
Fairport Harbor, U.S.A. 78 E3 41 45N 81 17W
Fairview, Australia 62 B3 15 31S 144 17 E
Fairview, Canada 72 B5 56 5N 118 25W
Fairview, Mont., U.S.A. 80 B2 47 51N 104 3W
Fairview, Okla., U.S.A. 81 G5 36 16N 98 29W
Fairview, Utah, U.S.A. 82 G8 39 50N 111 0W
Fairweather, Mt., U.S.A. 68 C6 58 55N 137 32W
Faisalabad, Pakistan 42 D5 31 30N 73 5 E
Faith, U.S.A. 80 C3 45 2N 102 2W
Faizabad, India 43 F10 26 45N 82 10 E
Fajardo, Puerto Rico 89 C6 18 20N 65 39W
Fakfak, Indonesia 37 E8 3 0S 132 15 E
Faku, China 35 C12 42 32N 123 21 E
Falaise, France 18 B3 48 54N 0 12W
Falaise, Mui, Vietnam 38 C5 19 6N 105 45 E
Falam, Burma 41 H18 23 0N 93 45 E
Falcón, C., Spain 22 C7 38 50N 1 23 E
Falcon Dam, U.S.A. 81 M5 26 50N 99 20W
Falconara Marittima, Italy 20 C5 43 37N 13 24 E
Falcone, C., Italy 20 D3 40 58N 8 12 E
Falconer, U.S.A. 78 D5 42 7N 79 13W
Faleshty = Făleşti, Moldova 17 E14 47 32N 27 44 E
Făleşti, Moldova 17 E14 47 32N 27 44 E
Falfurrias, U.S.A. 81 M5 27 14N 98 9W
Falher, Canada 72 B5 55 44N 117 15W
Falirakí, Greece 23 C10 36 22N 28 12 E
Falkenberg, Sweden 9 H15 56 54N 12 30 E
Falkirk, U.K. 12 F5 56 0N 3 47W
Falkirk □, U.K. 12 F5 55 58N 3 49W
Falkland Is. □, Atl. Oc. 96 G5 51 30S 59 0W
Falkland Sd., Falk. Is. 96 G5 52 0S 60 0W
Falköping, Sweden 9 G15 58 12N 13 33 E
Fall River, U.S.A. 79 E13 41 43N 71 10W
Fall River Mills, U.S.A. 82 F3 41 3N 121 26W
Fallbrook, U.S.A. 83 K5 33 25N 117 12W
Fallbrook, Calif., U.S.A. 85 M9 33 23N 117 15W
Fallon, Mont., U.S.A. 80 B2 46 50N 105 8W
Fallon, Nev., U.S.A. 82 G4 39 28N 118 47W
Falls City, Nebr., U.S.A. 80 E7 40 3N 95 36W
Falls City, Oreg., U.S.A. 82 D2 44 52N 123 26W
Falls Creek, U.S.A. 78 E6 41 9N 78 48W
Falmouth, Jamaica 88 C4 18 30N 77 40W
Falmouth, U.K. 11 G2 50 9N 5 5W
Falmouth, U.S.A. 76 F3 38 41N 84 20W
False B., S. Africa 56 E2 34 15S 18 40 E
Falso, C., Honduras 88 C3 15 12N 83 21W
Falster, Denmark 9 J14 54 45N 11 55 E
Falsterbo, Sweden 9 J15 55 23N 12 50 E
Fălticeni, Romania 17 E14 47 21N 26 20 E
Falun, Sweden 9 F16 60 37N 15 37 E
Famagusta, Cyprus 23 D12 35 8N 33 55 E
Famagusta Bay, Cyprus 23 D13 35 15N 34 0 E
Famatina, Sierra de, Argentina 94 B2 27 30S 68 0W
Family L., Canada 73 C9 51 54N 95 27W
Famoso, U.S.A. 85 K7 35 37N 119 12W
Fan Xian, China 34 G8 35 55N 115 38 E
Fandriana, Madag. 57 C8 20 14S 47 21 E
Fang, Thailand 38 C2 19 55N 99 13 E
Fangcheng, China 34 H7 33 18N 112 59 E
Fangshan, China 34 E6 38 3N 111 25 E
Fangzi, China 35 F10 36 33N 119 10 E
Fanjiatun, China 35 C13 43 40N 125 15 E
Fannich, L., U.K. 12 D4 57 38N 4 59W
Fannūj, Iran 45 E8 26 35N 59 38 E
Fanny Bay, Canada 72 D4 49 37N 124 48W
Fanø, Denmark 9 J13 55 25N 8 25 E
Fano, Italy 20 C5 43 50N 13 1 E
Fanshaw, U.S.A. 72 B2 57 11N 133 30W
Fanshi, China 34 E7 39 12N 113 20 E
Fao = Al Fāw, Iraq 45 D6 30 0N 48 30 E
Faqirwali, Pakistan 42 E5 29 27N 73 0 E
Faradje, Zaïre 54 B2 3 50N 29 45 E
Farafangana, Madag. 57 C8 22 49S 47 50 E
Farāh, Afghan. 40 C3 32 20N 62 7 E
Farāh □, Afghan. 40 C3 32 25N 62 10 E
Farahalana, Madag. 57 A9 14 26S 50 10 E
Faranah, Guinea 50 F2 10 3N 10 45W
Farasān, Jazā'ir, Si. Arabia 46 D3 16 45N 41 55 E
Farasan Is. = Farasān, Jazā'ir, Si. Arabia 46 D3 16 45N 41 55 E
Faratsiho, Madag. 57 B8 19 24S 46 57 E
Fareham, U.K. 11 G6 50 51N 1 11W
Farewell, C., N.Z. 59 J4 40 29S 172 43 E
Farewell C. = Farvel, Kap, Greenland 4 D5 59 48N 43 55W
Farghona, Uzbekistan 26 E8 40 23N 71 19 E
Fargo, U.S.A. 80 B6 46 53N 96 48W
Fār'iah, W. al →, West Bank 47 C4 32 12N 35 27 E
Faribault, U.S.A. 80 C8 44 18N 93 16W
Faridkot, India 42 D6 30 44N 74 45 E
Faridpur, Bangla. 43 H13 23 15N 89 55 E
Farim, Guinea-Biss. 50 F1 12 27N 15 9W
Farīmān, Iran 45 C8 35 40N 59 49 E
Farina, Australia 63 E2 30 3S 138 15 E
Fariones, Pta., Canary Is. 22 E6 29 13N 13 28W
Farmerville, U.S.A. 81 J8 32 47N 92 24W
Farmington, Calif., U.S.A. 84 H6 37 55N 120 59W
Farmington, N.H., U.S.A. 79 C13 43 24N 71 4W
Farmington, N. Mex., U.S.A. 83 H9 36 44N 108 12W
Farmington, Utah, U.S.A. 82 F8 41 0N 111 12W
Farmington →, U.S.A. 79 E12 41 51N 72 38W
Farmville, U.S.A. 76 G6 37 18N 78 24W
Farnborough, U.K. 11 F7 51 16N 0 45W
Farne Is., U.K. 10 B6 55 38N 1 37W
Farnham, Canada 79 A12 45 17N 72 59W
Faro, Brazil 93 D7 2 10S 56 39W
Faro, Portugal 19 D2 37 2N 7 55W
Fårö, Sweden 9 H18 57 55N 19 5 E
Farquhar, C., Australia 61 D1 23 50S 113 36 E
Farrars Cr. →, Australia 62 D3 25 35S 140 43 E
Farrāshband, Iran 45 D7 28 57N 52 5 E
Farrell, U.S.A. 78 E4 41 13N 80 30W
Farrell Flat, Australia 63 E2 33 48S 138 48 E
Farrokhī, Iran 45 C8 33 50N 59 31 E
Farruch, C., Spain 22 B10 39 47N 3 21 E
Farrukhabad-cum-Fatehgarh, India 43 F8 27 30N 79 32 E
Fārs □, Iran 45 D7 29 30N 55 0 E
Fársala, Greece 21 E10 39 17N 22 23 E
Farsund, Norway 9 G12 58 5N 6 55 E

Garmāb

Greece

Gō-no-ura, Japan 31 H4 33 44N 129 40 E
Go Quao, Vietnam 39 H5 9 43N 105 17 E
Goa, India 40 M8 15 33N 73 59 E
Goa □, India 40 M8 15 33N 73 59 E
Goalen Hd., Australia 63 F5 36 33S 150 4 E
Goalpara, India 41 F17 26 10N 90 40 E
Goalundo Ghat, Bangla. 43 H13 23 50N 89 47 E
Goat Fell, U.K. 12 F3 55 38N 5 11W
Goba, Ethiopia 46 F2 7 1N 39 59 E
Goba, Mozam. 57 D5 26 15S 32 13 E
Gobabis, Namibia 56 C2 22 30S 19 0 E
Gobi, Asia 34 C5 44 0N 111 0 E
Gobō, Japan 31 H7 33 53N 135 10 E
Gochas, Namibia 56 C2 24 59S 18 55 E
Godavari →, India 41 L13 16 25N 82 18 E
Godavari Point, India 41 L13 17 0N 82 20 E
Godbout, Canada 71 C6 49 20N 67 38W
Godda, India 43 G12 24 50N 87 13 E
Goderich, Canada 70 D3 43 45N 81 41W
Godhavn, Greenland 4 C5 69 15N 53 38W
Godhra, India 42 H5 22 49N 73 40 E
Godoy Cruz, Argentina 94 C2 32 56S 68 52W
Gods →, Canada 73 B10 56 22N 92 51W
Gods L., Canada 73 C10 54 40N 94 15W
Godthåb, Greenland 69 B14 64 10N 51 35W
Godwin Austen = K2, Pakistan 43 B7 35 58N 76 32 E
Goeie Hoop, Kaap die = Good Hope, C. of, S. Africa 56 E2 34 24S 18 30 E
Goéland, L. au, Canada 70 C4 49 50N 76 48W
Goeree, Neths. 15 C3 51 50N 4 0 E
Goes, Neths. 15 C3 51 30N 3 55 E
Gogama, Canada 70 C3 47 35N 81 43W
Gogango, Australia 62 C5 23 40S 150 2 E
Gogebic, L., U.S.A. 80 B10 46 30N 89 35W
Gogra = Ghaghara →, India 43 G11 25 45N 84 40 E
Goiânia, Brazil 93 G9 16 43S 49 20W
Goiás, Brazil 93 G8 15 55S 50 10W
Goiás □, Brazil 93 F9 12 10S 48 0W
Goio-Ere, Brazil 95 A5 24 12S 53 1W
Gojō, Japan 31 G7 34 21N 135 42 E
Gojra, Pakistan 42 D5 31 10N 72 40 E
Gokarannath, India 43 F9 27 57N 80 39 E
Gökçeada, Turkey 21 D11 40 10N 25 50 E
Gokteik, Burma 41 H20 22 26N 97 0 E
Gokurt, Pakistan 42 E2 29 40N 67 26 E
Gola, India 43 E9 28 3N 80 32 E
Golakganj, India 43 F13 26 8N 89 52 E
Golan Heights = Hagolan, Syria 47 B4 33 0N 35 45 E
Golāshkerd, Iran 45 E8 27 59N 57 16 E
Golchikha, Russia 4 B12 71 45N 83 30 E
Golconda, U.S.A. 82 F5 40 58N 117 30W
Gold Beach, U.S.A. 82 E1 42 25N 124 25W
Gold Coast, Australia 63 D5 28 0S 153 25 E
Gold Coast, W. Afr. 48 F3 4 0N 1 40W
Gold Hill, U.S.A. 82 E2 42 26N 123 3W
Golden, Canada 72 C5 51 20N 116 59W
Golden, U.S.A. 80 F2 39 42N 105 15W
Golden B., N.Z. 59 J4 40 40S 172 50 E
Golden Gate, U.S.A. 82 H2 37 54N 122 30W
Golden Hinde, Canada 72 D3 49 40N 125 44W
Golden Lake, Canada 78 A7 45 34N 77 21W
Golden Prairie, Canada 73 C7 50 13N 109 37W
Golden Vale, Ireland 13 D3 52 33N 8 17W
Goldendale, U.S.A. 82 D3 45 49N 120 50W
Goldfield, U.S.A. 83 H5 37 42N 117 14W
Goldfields, Canada 73 B7 59 28N 108 29W
Goldsand L., Canada 73 B8 57 2N 101 8W
Goldsboro, U.S.A. 77 H7 35 23N 77 59W
Goldsmith, U.S.A. 81 K3 31 59N 102 37W
Goldsworthy, Australia 60 D2 20 21S 119 30 E
Goldthwaite, U.S.A. 81 K5 31 27N 98 34W
Golęniów, Poland 16 B8 53 35N 14 50 E
Golestānak, Iran 45 D7 30 36N 54 14 E
Goleta, U.S.A. 85 L7 34 27N 119 50W
Golfito, Costa Rica 88 E3 8 41N 83 5W
Golfo Aranci, Italy 20 D3 40 59N 9 38 E
Goliad, U.S.A. 81 L6 28 40N 97 23W
Golpāyegān, Iran 45 C6 33 27N 50 18 E
Golra, Pakistan 42 C5 33 37N 72 56 E
Golspie, U.K. 12 D5 57 58N 3 59W
Goma, Rwanda 54 C2 2 11S 29 18 E
Goma, Zaïre 54 C2 1 37S 29 10 E
Gomati →, India 43 G10 25 32N 83 11 E
Gombari, Zaïre 54 B2 2 45N 29 3 E
Gombe →, Tanzania 54 C3 4 38S 31 40 E
Gomel = Homyel, Belarus 17 B16 52 28N 31 0 E
Gomera, Canary Is. 22 F2 28 7N 17 14W
Gómez Palacio, Mexico 86 B4 25 40N 104 0W
Gomīshān, Iran 45 B7 37 4N 54 6 E
Gomogomo, Indonesia 37 F8 6 39S 134 43 E
Gomoh, India 41 H15 23 52N 86 10 E
Gompa = Ganta, Liberia 50 G3 7 15N 8 59W
Gonābād, Iran 45 C8 34 15N 58 45 E
Gonaïves, Haiti 89 C5 19 20N 72 42W
Gonâve, G. de la, Haiti 89 C5 19 29N 72 42W
Gonâve, I. de la, Haiti 89 C5 18 45N 73 0W
Gonbab-e Kāvūs, Iran 45 B7 37 20N 55 25 E
Gonda, India 43 F9 27 9N 81 58 E
Gondal, India 42 J4 21 58N 70 52 E
Gonder, Ethiopia 51 F12 12 39N 37 30 E
Gondia, India 40 J12 21 23N 80 10 E
Gondola, Mozam. 55 F3 19 10S 33 37 E
Gönen, Turkey 21 D12 40 6N 27 39 E
Gonghe, China 32 C5 36 18N 100 32 E
Gongolgon, Australia 63 E4 30 21S 146 54 E
Goniri, Nigeria 51 F7 11 30N 12 15 E
Gonzales, Calif., U.S.A. 83 H3 36 30N 121 26W
Gonzales, Tex., U.S.A. 81 L6 29 30N 97 27W
González Chaves, Argentina 94 D3 38 2S 60 5W
Good Hope, C. of, S. Africa 56 E2 34 24S 18 30 E
Gooderham, Canada 70 D4 44 54N 78 21W
Goodeve, Canada 73 C8 51 4N 103 10W
Gooding, U.S.A. 82 E6 42 56N 114 43W
Goodland, U.S.A. 80 F4 39 21N 101 43W
Goodnight, U.S.A. 81 H4 35 2N 101 11W
Goodooga, Australia 63 D4 29 3S 147 28 E
Goodsoil, Canada 73 C7 54 24N 109 13W
Goodsprings, U.S.A. 83 J6 35 50N 115 26W
Goole, U.K. 10 D7 53 42N 0 53W
Goolgowi, Australia 63 E4 33 58S 145 41 E
Goomalling, Australia 61 F2 31 15S 116 49 E
Goombalie, Australia 63 D4 29 59S 145 26 E
Goonda, Mozam. 55 F3 19 48S 33 57 E
Goondiwindi, Australia 63 D5 28 30S 150 21 E
Goongarrie, L., Australia 61 F3 30 3S 121 9 E
Goonyella, Australia 62 C4 21 47S 147 58 E
Goor, Neths. 15 B6 52 13N 6 33 E
Gooray, Australia 63 D5 28 25S 150 2 E
Goose →, Canada 71 B7 53 20N 60 35W
Goose L., U.S.A. 82 F3 41 56N 120 26W
Gop, India 40 H6 22 5N 69 50 E
Gopalganj, India 43 F11 26 28N 84 30 E
Göppingen, Germany 16 D5 48 42N 9 39 E
Gorakhpur, India 43 F10 26 47N 83 23 E
Goražde, Bos.-H. 21 C8 43 38N 18 58 E
Gorda, U.S.A. 84 K5 35 53N 121 26W
Gorda, Pta., Canary Is. 22 F2 28 45N 18 0W
Gorda, Pta., Nic. 88 D3 14 20N 83 10W
Gordan B., Australia 60 B5 11 35S 130 10 E
Gordon, U.S.A. 80 D3 42 48N 102 12W
Gordon →, Australia 62 G4 42 27S 145 30 E
Gordon Downs, Australia 60 C4 18 48S 128 33 E
Gordon L., Alta., Canada 73 B6 56 30N 110 25W
Gordon L., N.W.T., Canada 72 A6 63 5N 113 11W
Gordonvale, Australia 62 B4 17 5S 145 50 E
Gore, Australia 63 D5 28 17S 151 30 E
Goré, Chad 51 G8 7 59N 16 31 E
Gore, Ethiopia 51 G12 8 12N 35 32 E
Gore, N.Z. 59 M2 46 5S 168 58 E
Gore Bay, Canada 70 C3 45 57N 82 28W
Gorey, Ireland 13 D5 52 41N 6 18W
Gorg, Iran 45 D8 29 29N 59 43 E
Gorgān, Iran 45 B7 36 50N 54 29 E
Gorgona, I., Colombia 92 C3 3 0N 78 10W
Gorham, U.S.A. 79 B13 44 23N 71 10W
Gorinchem, Neths. 15 C4 51 50N 4 59 E
Gorízia, Italy 20 B5 45 56N 13 37 E
Gorki = Nizhniy Novgorod, Russia 24 C7 56 20N 44 0 E
Gorkiy = Nizhniy Novgorod, Russia 24 C7 56 20N 44 0 E
Gorkovskoye Vdkhr., Russia 24 C7 57 2N 43 4 E
Görlitz, Germany 16 C8 51 9N 14 58 E
Gorlovka = Horlivka, Ukraine 25 E6 48 19N 38 5 E
Gorman, Calif., U.S.A. 85 L8 34 47N 118 51W
Gorman, Tex., U.S.A. 81 J5 32 12N 98 41W
Gorna Dzhumayo = Blagoevgrad, Bulgaria 21 C10 42 2N 23 5 E
Gorna Oryakhovitsa, Bulgaria 21 C11 43 7N 25 40 E
Gorno-Altay □, Russia 26 D9 51 0N 86 0 E
Gorno-Altaysk, Russia 26 D9 51 50N 86 5 E
Gorno Slinkino = Gornopravdinsk, Russia 26 C8 60 5N 70 0 E
Gornopravdinsk, Russia 26 C8 60 5N 70 0 E
Gornyatski, Russia 24 A11 67 32N 64 3 E
Gornyi, Russia 30 B6 44 57N 133 59 E
Gorodenka = Horodenka, Ukraine 17 D13 48 41N 25 29 E
Gorodok = Horodok, Ukraine 17 D12 49 46N 23 32 E
Gorokhov = Horokhiv, Ukraine 17 C13 50 30N 24 45 E
Goromonzi, Zimbabwe 55 F3 17 52S 31 22 E
Gorongose →, Mozam. 57 C5 20 30S 34 40 E
Gorongoza, Mozam. 55 F3 18 44S 34 2 E
Gorongoza, Sa. da, Mozam. 55 F3 18 27S 34 2 E
Gorontalo, Indonesia 37 D6 0 35N 123 5 E
Gort, Ireland 13 C3 53 3N 8 49W
Gortis, Greece 23 D6 35 4N 24 58 E
Gorzów Wielkopolski, Poland 16 B8 52 43N 15 15 E
Gosford, Australia 63 E5 33 23S 151 18 E
Goshen, Calif., U.S.A. 84 J7 36 21N 119 25W
Goshen, Ind., U.S.A. 76 E3 41 35N 85 50W
Goshen, N.Y., U.S.A. 79 E10 41 24N 74 20W
Goshogawara, Japan 30 D10 40 48N 140 27 E
Goslar, Germany 16 C6 51 54N 10 25 E
Gospič, Croatia 16 F8 44 35N 15 23 E
Gosport, U.K. 11 G6 50 48N 1 9W
Gosse →, Australia 62 B1 19 32S 134 37 E
Göta älv →, Sweden 9 H14 57 42N 11 54 E
Göta kanal, Sweden 9 G16 58 30N 15 58 E
Götaland, Sweden 9 G15 57 30N 14 30 E
Göteborg, Sweden 9 H14 57 43N 11 59 E
Gotha, Germany 16 C6 50 56N 10 42 E
Gothenburg = Göteborg, Sweden 9 H14 57 43N 11 59 E
Gothenburg, U.S.A. 80 E4 40 56N 100 10W
Gotland, Sweden 9 H18 57 30N 18 33 E
Gotska Sandön, Sweden 9 G18 58 24N 19 15 E
Gōtsu, Japan 31 G6 35 0N 132 14 E
Göttingen, Germany 16 C5 51 31N 9 55 E
Gottwaldov = Zlin, Czech. 17 D9 49 14N 17 40 E
Goubangzi, China 35 D11 41 20N 121 52 E
Gouda, Neths. 15 B4 52 1N 4 42 E
Goúdhoura, Ákra, Greece 23 E8 34 59N 26 6 E
Gough I., Atl. Oc. 2 G9 40 10S 9 45W
Gouin, Rés., Canada 70 C5 48 35N 74 40W
Goulburn, Australia 63 E4 34 44S 149 44 E
Goulburn Is., Australia 62 A1 11 40S 133 20 E
Gounou-Gaya, Chad 51 G8 9 38N 15 31 E
Gouri, Chad 51 E8 19 36N 19 36 E
Gourits →, S. Africa 56 E3 34 21S 21 52 E
Gourma Rharous, Mali 50 E4 16 55N 1 50W
Goúrnais, Greece 23 D7 35 19N 25 16 E
Gourock Ra., Australia 63 F4 36 0S 149 25 E
Gouverneur, U.S.A. 79 B9 44 20N 75 28W
Gouviá, Greece 23 A3 39 39N 19 50 E
Govan, Canada 73 C8 51 20N 105 0W
Governador Valadares, Brazil 93 G10 18 15S 41 57W
Governor's Harbour, Bahamas 88 A4 25 10N 76 14W
Gowan Ra., Australia 62 C4 25 0S 145 0 E
Gowanda, U.S.A. 78 D6 42 28N 78 56W
Gowd-e Zirreh, Afghan. 40 E3 29 45N 62 0 E
Gower, U.K. 11 F3 51 35N 4 10W
Gowna, L., Ireland 13 C4 53 51N 7 34W
Goya, Argentina 94 B4 29 10S 59 10W
Goyder Lagoon, Australia 63 D2 27 3S 138 58 E
Goyllarisquisga, Peru 92 F3 10 31S 76 24W
Goz Beïda, Chad 51 F9 12 10N 21 20 E
Gozo, Malta 23 C1 36 3N 14 13 E
Graaff-Reinet, S. Africa 56 E3 32 13S 24 32 E
Gračac, Croatia 16 F8 44 18N 15 57 E
Grace, U.S.A. 82 E8 42 35N 111 44W
Graceville, U.S.A. 80 C6 45 34N 96 26W
Gracias a Dios, C., Honduras 88 C3 15 0N 83 10W
Graciosa, I., Canary Is. 22 E6 29 15N 13 32W
Grado, Spain 19 A2 43 23N 6 4W
Gradule, Australia 63 D4 28 32S 149 15 E
Grady, U.S.A. 81 H3 34 49N 103 19W
Grafton, Australia 63 D5 29 38S 152 58 E
Grafton, U.S.A. 80 A6 48 25N 97 25W
Graham, Canada 70 C1 49 20N 90 30W
Graham, N.C., U.S.A. 77 G6 36 5N 79 25W
Graham, Tex., U.S.A. 81 J5 33 6N 98 35W
Graham →, Canada 72 B4 56 31N 122 17W
Graham, Mt., U.S.A. 83 K9 32 42N 109 52W
Graham Bell, Os., Russia 26 A7 81 0N 62 0 E
Graham I., Canada 72 C2 53 40N 132 30W
Graham Land, Antarctica 5 C17 65 0S 64 0W
Grahamdale, Canada 73 C9 51 23N 98 30W
Grahamstown, S. Africa 56 E4 33 19S 26 31 E
Grain Coast, W. Afr. 48 F2 4 20N 10 0W
Grajaú, Brazil 93 E9 5 50S 46 4W
Grajaú →, Brazil 93 D10 3 41S 44 48W
Grampian Highlands = Grampian Mts., U.K. 12 E5 56 50N 4 0W
Grampian Mts., U.K. 12 E5 56 50N 4 0W
Gran Canaria, Canary Is. 22 F4 27 55N 15 35W
Gran Chaco, S. Amer. 94 B3 25 0S 61 0W
Gran Paradiso, Italy 20 B2 45 33N 7 17 E
Gran Sasso d'Italia, Italy 20 C5 42 27N 13 42 E
Granada, Nic. 88 D2 11 58N 86 0W
Granada, Spain 19 D4 37 10N 3 35W
Granada, U.S.A. 81 F3 38 4N 102 19W
Granadilla de Abona, Canary Is. 22 F3 28 7N 16 33W
Granard, Ireland 13 C4 53 47N 7 30W
Granbury, U.S.A. 81 J6 32 27N 97 47W
Granby, Canada 70 C5 45 25N 72 45W
Grand →, Mo., U.S.A. 80 F8 39 23N 93 7W
Grand →, S. Dak., U.S.A. 80 C4 45 40N 100 45W
Grand Bahama, Bahamas 88 A4 26 40N 78 30W
Grand Bank, Canada 71 C8 47 6N 55 48W
Grand Bassam, Ivory C. 50 G4 5 10N 3 49W
Grand-Bourg, Guadeloupe 89 C7 15 53N 61 19W
Grand Canal = Yun Ho →, China 35 E9 39 10N 117 10 E
Grand Canyon, U.S.A. 83 H7 36 3N 112 9W
Grand Canyon National Park, U.S.A. 83 H7 36 15N 112 30W
Grand Cayman, Cayman Is. 88 C3 19 20N 81 20W
Grand Coulee, U.S.A. 82 C4 47 57N 119 0W
Grand Coulee Dam, U.S.A. 82 C4 47 57N 118 59W
Grand Falls, Canada 71 C8 48 56N 55 40W
Grand Forks, Canada 72 D5 49 0N 118 30W
Grand Forks, U.S.A. 80 B6 47 55N 97 3W
Grand Haven, U.S.A. 76 D2 43 4N 86 13W
Grand I., U.S.A. 76 B2 46 31N 86 40W
Grand Island, U.S.A. 80 E5 40 55N 98 21W
Grand Isle, U.S.A. 81 L10 29 14N 90 0W
Grand Junction, U.S.A. 83 G9 39 4N 108 33W
Grand L., N.B., Canada 71 C6 45 57N 66 7W
Grand L., Nfld., Canada 71 C8 49 0N 57 30W
Grand L., Nfld., Canada 71 B7 53 40N 60 30W
Grand L., U.S.A. 81 L8 29 55N 92 47W
Grand Lac Victoria, Canada 70 C4 47 35N 77 35W
Grand Lahou, Ivory C. 50 G3 5 10N 5 5W
Grand Lake, U.S.A. 82 F11 40 15N 105 49W
Grand Manan I., Canada 71 D6 44 45N 66 52W
Grand Marais, Canada 80 B9 47 45N 90 25W
Grand Marais, U.S.A. 76 B3 46 40N 85 59W
Grand-Mère, Canada 70 C5 46 36N 72 40W
Grand Portage, U.S.A. 70 C2 47 58N 89 41W
Grand Prairie, U.S.A. 81 J6 32 47N 97 0W
Grand Rapids, Canada 73 C9 53 12N 99 19W
Grand Rapids, Mich., U.S.A. 76 D2 42 58N 85 40W
Grand Rapids, Minn., U.S.A. 80 B8 47 14N 93 31W
Grand St.-Bernard, Col du, Europe 16 F4 45 50N 7 10 E
Grand Teton, U.S.A. 82 E8 43 54N 111 50W
Grand Valley, U.S.A. 82 G9 39 27N 108 3W
Grand View, Canada 73 C8 51 10N 100 42W
Grande →, Jujuy, Argentina 94 A2 24 20S 65 2W
Grande →, Mendoza, Argentina 94 D2 36 52S 69 45W
Grande →, Bolivia 92 G6 15 51S 64 39W
Grande →, Bahia, Brazil 93 F10 11 30S 44 30W
Grande →, Minas Gerais, Brazil 93 H8 20 6S 51 4W
Grande, B., Argentina 96 G3 50 30S 68 20W
Grande, Rio →, U.S.A. 81 N6 25 58N 97 9W
Grande Baie, Canada 71 C5 48 19N 70 52W
Grande Baleine, R. de la →, Canada 70 A4 55 16N 77 47W
Grande Cache, Canada 72 C5 53 53N 119 8W
Grande de Santiago →, Mexico 86 C3 21 36N 105 26W
Grande-Entrée, Canada 71 C7 47 30N 61 40W
Grande Prairie, Canada 72 B5 55 10N 118 50W
Grande-Rivière, Canada 71 C7 48 26N 64 30W
Grande-Vallée, Canada 71 C6 49 14N 65 8W
Grandes-Bergeronnes, Canada 71 C6 48 16N 69 35W
Grandfalls, U.S.A. 81 K3 31 20N 102 51W
Grandoe Mines, Canada 72 B3 56 29N 129 54W
Grandview, U.S.A. 82 C4 46 15N 119 54W
Graneros, Chile 94 C1 34 5S 70 45W
Grangemouth, U.K. 12 E5 56 1N 3 42W
Granger, Wash., U.S.A. 82 C3 46 21N 120 11W
Granger, Wyo., U.S.A. 82 F9 41 35N 109 58W
Grangeville, U.S.A. 82 D5 45 56N 116 7W
Granite City, U.S.A. 80 F9 38 42N 90 9W
Granite Falls, U.S.A. 80 C7 44 49N 95 33W
Granite Mt., U.S.A. 85 M10 33 5N 116 28W
Granite Peak, Australia 61 E3 25 40S 121 20 E
Granite Peak, U.S.A. 82 D9 45 10N 109 48W
Granity, N.Z. 59 J3 41 39S 171 51 E
Granja, Brazil 93 D10 3 7S 40 50W
Granollers, Spain 19 B7 41 39N 2 18 E
Grant, U.S.A. 80 E4 40 53N 101 42W
Grant, Mt., U.S.A. 82 G4 38 34N 118 48W
Grant City, U.S.A. 80 E7 40 29N 94 25W
Grant I., Australia 60 B5 11 10S 132 52 E
Grant Range, U.S.A. 83 G6 38 30N 115 25W
Grantham, U.K. 10 E7 52 55N 0 38W
Grantown-on-Spey, U.K. 12 D5 57 20N 3 36W
Grants, U.S.A. 83 J10 35 9N 107 52W
Grants Pass, U.S.A. 82 E2 42 26N 123 19W
Grantsburg, U.S.A. 80 C8 45 47N 92 41W
Grantsville, U.S.A. 82 F7 40 36N 112 28W
Granville, France 18 B3 48 50N 1 35W
Granville, N. Dak., U.S.A. 80 A4 48 16N 100 47W
Granville, N.Y., U.S.A. 76 D9 43 24N 73 16W
Granville L., Canada 73 B8 56 18N 100 30W
Grapeland, U.S.A. 81 K7 31 30N 95 29W
Gras, L. de, Canada 68 B8 64 30N 110 30W
Graskop, S. Africa 57 C5 24 56S 30 49 E
Grass →, Canada 73 B9 56 3N 96 33W
Grass Range, U.S.A. 82 C9 47 0N 109 0W
Grass River Prov. Park, Canada 73 C8 54 40N 100 50W
Grass Valley, Calif., U.S.A. 84 F6 39 13N 121 4W
Grass Valley, Oreg., U.S.A. 82 D3 45 22N 120 47W
Grasse, France 18 E7 43 38N 6 56 E
Grassmere, Australia 63 E3 31 24S 142 38 E
Graulhet, France 18 E4 43 45N 1 59 E
Gravelbourg, Canada 73 D7 49 50N 106 35W
's-Gravenhage, Neths. 15 B4 52 7N 4 17 E
Gravenhurst, Canada 78 B5 44 52N 79 20W
Gravesend, Australia 63 D5 29 35S 150 20 E
Gravesend, U.K. 11 F8 51 26N 0 22 E
Gravois, Pointe-à-, Haiti 89 C5 18 15N 73 56W
Grayling, U.S.A. 76 C3 44 40N 84 43W
Grayling →, Canada 72 B3 59 21N 125 0W
Grays Harbor, U.S.A. 82 C1 46 59N 124 1W
Grays L., U.S.A. 82 E8 43 4N 111 26W
Grays River, U.S.A. 84 D3 46 21N 123 37W
Grayson, Canada 73 C8 50 45N 102 40W
Graz, Austria 16 E8 47 4N 15 27 E
Greasy L., Canada 72 A4 62 55N 122 12W
Great Abaco I., Bahamas 88 A4 26 25N 77 10W
Great Artesian Basin, Australia 62 C3 23 0S 144 0 E
Great Australian Bight, Australia 61 F5 33 30S 130 0 E
Great Bahama Bank, Bahamas 88 B4 23 15N 78 0W
Great Barrier I., N.Z. 59 G5 36 11S 175 25 E
Great Barrier Reef, Australia 62 B4 18 0S 146 50 E
Great Barrington, U.S.A. 79 D11 42 12N 73 22W
Great Basin, U.S.A. 82 G5 40 0N 117 0W
Great Bear →, Canada 68 B7 65 0N 124 0W
Great Bear L., Canada 68 B7 65 30N 120 0W
Great Belt = Store Bælt, Denmark 9 J14 55 20N 11 0 E
Great Bend, Kans., U.S.A. 80 F5 38 22N 98 46W
Great Bend, Pa., U.S.A. 79 E9 41 58N 75 45W
Great Blasket I., Ireland 13 D1 52 6N 10 32W
Great Britain, Europe 6 E5 54 0N 2 15W
Great Central, Canada 72 D3 49 20N 125 10W
Great Dividing Ra., Australia 62 C4 23 0S 146 0 E
Great Driffield = Driffield, U.K. 10 C7 54 0N 0 26W
Great Exuma I., Bahamas 88 B4 23 30N 75 50W
Great Falls, Canada 73 C9 50 27N 96 1W
Great Falls, U.S.A. 82 C8 47 30N 111 17W
Great Fish = Groot Vis →, S. Africa 56 E4 33 28S 27 5 E
Great Guana Cay, Bahamas 88 B4 24 0N 76 20W
Great Harbour Deep, Canada 71 B8 50 25N 56 32W
Great I., Canada 73 B9 58 53N 96 35W
Great Inagua I., Bahamas 89 B5 21 0N 73 20W
Great Indian Desert = Thar Desert, India 42 F4 28 0N 72 0 E
Great Karoo, S. Africa 56 E3 31 55S 21 0 E
Great Lake, Australia 62 G4 41 50S 146 40 E
Great Malvern, U.K. 11 E5 52 7N 2 18W
Great Ormes Head, U.K. 10 D4 53 20N 3 52W
Great Ouse →, U.K. 10 E8 52 48N 0 21 E
Great Palm I., Australia 62 B4 18 45S 146 40 E
Great Plains, N. Amer. 74 A6 47 0N 105 0W
Great Ruaha →, Tanzania 54 D4 7 56S 37 52 E
Great Saint Bernard P. = Grand St.-Bernard, Col du, Europe 16 F4 45 50N 7 10 E
Great Salt L., U.S.A. 82 F7 41 15N 112 40W
Great Salt Lake Desert, U.S.A. 82 F7 40 50N 113 30W
Great Salt Plains L., U.S.A. 81 G5 36 45N 98 8W
Great Sandy Desert, Australia 60 D3 21 0S 124 0 E
Great Sangi = Sangihe, P., Indonesia 37 D7 3 45N 125 30 E
Great Slave L., Canada 72 A5 61 23N 115 38W
Great Smoky Mts. Nat. Pk., U.S.A. 77 H4 35 40N 83 40W
Great Stour = Stour →, U.K. 11 F9 51 18N 1 22 E
Great Victoria Desert, Australia 61 E4 29 30S 126 30 E
Great Wall, China 34 E5 38 30N 109 30 E
Great Whernside, U.K. 10 C6 54 10N 1 58W
Great Yarmouth, U.K. 10 E9 52 37N 1 44 E
Greater Antilles, W. Indies 89 C5 17 40N 74 0W
Greater London □, U.K. 11 F7 51 31N 0 6W
Greater Manchester □, U.K. 10 D5 53 30N 2 15W
Greater Sunda Is., Indonesia 36 F4 7 0S 112 0 E
Greco, C., Cyprus 23 E13 34 57N 34 5 E
Gredos, Sierra de, Spain 19 B3 40 20N 5 0W
Greece, U.S.A. 78 C7 43 13N 77 41W
Greece ■, Europe 21 E9 40 0N 23 0 E

Heinze Is.

Hajipur, India 43 G11 25 45N 85 13 E
Hājjī Muḩsin, Iraq 44 C5 32 35N 45 29 E
Ḩājjīābād, Eşfahan, Iran 45 C7 33 41N 54 50 E
Ḩājjīābād, Hormozgān, Iran 45 D7 28 19N 55 55 E
Hajnówka, Poland 17 B12 52 47N 23 35 E
Hakansson, Mts., Zaïre 55 D2 8 40S 25 45 E
Hakken-Zan, Japan 31 G7 34 10N 135 54 E
Hakodate, Japan 30 D10 41 45N 140 44 E
Haku-San, Japan 31 F8 36 9N 136 46 E
Hakui, Japan 31 F8 36 53N 136 47 E
Hala, Pakistan 40 G6 25 43N 68 20 E
Ḩalab, Syria 44 B3 36 10N 37 15 E
Ḩalabjah, Iraq 44 C5 35 10N 45 58 E
Halaib, Sudan 51 D12 22 12N 36 30 E
Hālat 'Ammār, Si. Arabia 44 D3 29 10N 36 4 E
Halbā, Lebanon 47 A5 34 34N 36 6 E
Halberstadt, Germany 16 C6 51 54N 11 3 E
Halcombe, N.Z. 59 J5 40 8S 175 30 E
Halcon, Mt., Phil. 37 B6 13 0N 121 30 E
Halden, Norway 9 G14 59 9N 11 23 E
Haldia, India 41 H16 22 5N 88 3 E
Haldwani, India 43 E8 29 31N 79 30 E
Hale →, Australia 62 C2 24 56S 135 53 E
Haleakala Crater, U.S.A. 74 H16 20 43N 156 16W
Haleyville, U.S.A. 77 H2 34 14N 87 37W
Halfway →, Canada 72 B4 56 12N 121 32W
Haliburton, Canada 70 C4 45 3N 78 30W
Halifax, Australia 62 B4 18 32S 146 22 E
Halifax, Canada 71 D7 44 38N 63 35W
Halifax, U.K. 10 D6 53 43N 1 52W
Halifax B., Australia 62 B4 18 50S 147 0 E
Halifax I., Namibia 56 D2 26 38S 15 4 E
Halil →, Iran 45 E8 27 40N 58 30 E
Hall Beach, Canada 69 B11 68 46N 81 12W
Hall Pt., Australia 60 C3 15 40S 124 23 E
Halland, Sweden 9 H15 57 8N 12 47 E
Halle, Belgium 15 D4 50 44N 4 13 E
Halle, Germany 16 C6 51 30N 11 56 E
Hällefors, Sweden 9 G16 59 47N 14 31 E
Hallett, Australia 63 E2 33 25S 138 55 E
Hallettsville, U.S.A. 81 L6 29 27N 96 57W
Halliday, U.S.A. 80 B3 47 21N 102 20W
Halliday L., Canada 73 A7 61 21N 108 56W
Hallim, S. Korea 35 H14 33 24N 126 15 E
Hallingdalselva →, Norway 9 F13 60 40N 8 50 E
Hallock, U.S.A. 73 D9 48 47N 96 57W
Halls Creek, Australia 60 C4 18 16S 127 38 E
Hallsberg, Sweden 9 G16 59 5N 15 7 E
Hallstead, U.S.A. 79 E9 41 58N 75 45W
Halmahera, Indonesia 37 D7 0 40N 128 0 E
Halmstad, Sweden 9 H15 56 41N 12 52 E
Halq el Oued, Tunisia 51 A7 36 53N 10 18 E
Hälsingborg = Helsingborg, Sweden 9 H15 56 3N 12 42 E
Hälsingland, Sweden 9 F16 61 40N 16 5 E
Halstad, U.S.A. 80 B6 47 21N 96 50W
Halti, Finland 8 B19 69 17N 21 18 E
Halul, Qatar 45 E7 25 40N 52 40 E
Ḩalvān, Iran 45 C8 33 57N 56 15 E
Ham Tan, Vietnam 39 G6 10 40N 107 45 E
Ham Yen, Vietnam 38 A5 22 4N 105 3 E
Hamab, Namibia 56 D2 28 7S 19 16 E
Hamada, Japan 31 G6 34 56N 132 4 E
Hamadān, Iran 45 C6 34 52N 48 32 E
Hamadān □, Iran 45 C6 35 0N 49 0 E
Ḩamāh, Syria 44 C3 35 5N 36 40 E
Hamamatsu, Japan 31 G8 34 45N 137 45 E
Hamar, Norway 9 F14 60 48N 11 7 E
Hambantota, Sri Lanka 40 R12 6 10N 81 10 E
Hamber Prov. Park, Canada 72 C5 52 20N 118 0W
Hamburg, Germany 16 B5 53 33N 9 59 E
Hamburg, Ark., U.S.A. 81 J9 33 14N 91 48W
Hamburg, Iowa, U.S.A. 80 E7 40 36N 95 39W
Hamburg, N.Y., U.S.A. 78 D6 42 43N 78 50W
Hamburg, Pa., U.S.A. 79 F9 40 33N 75 59W
Ḩamḑ, W. al →, Si. Arabia 44 E3 24 55N 36 20 E
Hamden, U.S.A. 79 E12 41 23N 72 54W
Häme, Finland 9 F20 61 38N 25 10 E
Hämeenlinna, Finland 9 F21 61 0N 24 28 E
Hamelin Pool, Australia 61 E1 26 22S 114 20 E
Hameln, Germany 16 B5 52 6N 9 21 E
Hamerkaz □, Israel 47 C3 32 15N 34 55 E
Hamersley Ra., Australia 60 D2 22 0S 117 45 E
Hamhung, N. Korea 35 E14 39 54N 127 30 E
Hami, China 32 B4 42 55N 93 25 E
Hamilton, Australia 63 F3 37 45S 142 2 E
Hamilton, Canada 70 D4 43 15N 79 50W
Hamilton, N.Z. 59 G5 37 47S 175 19 E
Hamilton, U.K. 12 F4 55 46N 4 2W
Hamilton, Mo., U.S.A. 80 F8 39 45N 93 59W
Hamilton, Mont., U.S.A. 82 C6 46 15N 114 10W
Hamilton, N.Y., U.S.A. 79 D9 42 50N 75 33W
Hamilton, Ohio, U.S.A. 76 F3 39 24N 84 34W
Hamilton, Tex., U.S.A. 81 K5 31 42N 98 7W
Hamilton →, Australia 62 C2 23 30S 139 47 E
Hamilton City, U.S.A. 84 F4 39 45N 122 1W
Hamilton Hotel, Australia 62 C3 22 45S 140 40 E
Hamilton Inlet, Canada 71 B8 54 0N 57 30W
Hamina, Finland 9 F22 60 34N 27 12 E
Hamiota, Canada 73 C8 50 11N 100 38W
Hamlet, U.S.A. 77 H6 34 53N 79 42W
Hamley Bridge, Australia 63 E2 34 17S 138 35 E
Hamlin = Hameln, Germany 16 B5 52 6N 9 21 E
Hamlin, N.Y., U.S.A. 78 C7 43 17N 77 55W
Hamlin, Tex., U.S.A. 81 J4 32 53N 100 8W
Hamm, Germany 16 C4 51 40N 7 50 E
Hammerfest, Norway 8 A20 70 39N 23 41 E
Hammond, Ind., U.S.A. 76 E2 41 38N 87 30W
Hammond, La., U.S.A. 81 K9 30 30N 90 28W
Hammonton, U.S.A. 76 F8 39 39N 74 48W
Hampden, N.Z. 59 L3 45 18S 170 50 E
Hampshire □, U.K. 11 F6 51 7N 1 23W
Hampshire Downs, U.K. 11 F6 51 15N 1 10W
Hampton, Ark., U.S.A. 81 J8 33 32N 92 28W
Hampton, Iowa, U.S.A. 80 D8 42 45N 93 13W
Hampton, N.H., U.S.A. 79 D14 42 57N 70 50W
Hampton, S.C., U.S.A. 77 J5 32 52N 81 7W
Hampton, Va., U.S.A. 76 G7 37 2N 76 21W
Hampton Tableland, Australia 61 F4 32 0S 127 0 E
Hamrat esh Sheykh, Sudan 51 F10 14 38N 27 55 E
Hamyang, S. Korea 35 G14 35 32N 127 42 E
Han Pijesak, Bos.-H. 21 B8 44 5N 18 57 E
Hana, U.S.A. 74 H17 20 45N 155 59W
Hanak, Si. Arabia 44 E3 25 32N 37 0 E
Hanamaki, Japan 30 E10 39 23N 141 7 E
Hanang, Tanzania 54 C4 4 30S 35 25 E
Hanau, Germany 16 C5 50 7N 8 56 E
Hanbogd, Mongolia 34 C4 43 11N 107 10 E
Hancheng, China 34 G6 35 31N 110 25 E
Hancock, Mich., U.S.A. 80 B10 47 8N 88 35W
Hancock, Minn., U.S.A. 80 C7 45 30N 95 48W
Hancock, N.Y., U.S.A. 79 E9 41 57N 75 17W
Handa, Japan 31 G8 34 53N 136 55 E
Handa, Somali Rep. 46 E5 10 37N 51 2 E
Handan, China 34 F8 36 35N 114 28 E
Handeni, Tanzania 54 D4 5 25S 38 2 E
Handeni □, Tanzania 54 D4 5 30S 38 0 E
Handwara, India 43 B6 34 21N 74 20 E
Hanegev, Israel 47 E3 30 50N 35 0 E
Haney, Canada 72 D4 49 12N 122 40W
Hanford, U.S.A. 83 H4 36 20N 119 39W
Hang Chat, Thailand 38 C2 18 20N 99 21 E
Hang Dong, Thailand 38 C2 18 41N 98 55 E
Hangang →, S. Korea 35 F14 37 50N 126 30 E
Hangayn Nuruu, Mongolia 32 B4 47 30N 99 0 E
Hangchou = Hangzhou, China 33 C7 30 18N 120 11 E
Hanggin Houqi, China 34 D4 40 58N 107 4 E
Hanggin Qi, China 34 E5 39 52N 108 50 E
Hangu, China 35 E9 39 18N 117 53 E
Hangzhou, China 33 C7 30 18N 120 11 E
Hangzhou Wan, China 33 C7 30 15N 120 45 E
Hanhongor, Mongolia 34 C3 43 55N 104 28 E
Ḩanīdh, Si. Arabia 45 E6 26 35N 48 38 E
Ḩanīsh, Yemen 46 E3 13 45N 42 46 E
Hankinson, U.S.A. 80 B6 46 4N 96 54W
Hanko, Finland 9 G20 59 50N 22 57 E
Hanksville, U.S.A. 83 G8 38 22N 110 43W
Hanle, India 43 C8 32 42N 79 4 E
Hanmer Springs, N.Z. 59 K4 42 32S 172 50 E
Hann →, Australia 60 C4 17 26S 126 17 E
Hann, Mt., Australia 60 C4 15 45S 126 0 E
Hanna, Canada 72 C6 51 40N 111 54W
Hannaford, U.S.A. 80 B5 47 19N 98 11W
Hannah, U.S.A. 80 A5 48 58N 98 42W
Hannah B., Canada 70 B4 51 40N 80 0W
Hannibal, U.S.A. 80 F9 39 42N 91 22W
Hannover, Germany 16 B5 52 22N 9 46 E
Hanoi, Vietnam 32 D5 21 5N 105 55 E
Hanover = Hannover, Germany 16 B5 52 22N 9 46 E
Hanover, Canada 78 B3 44 9N 81 2W
Hanover, S. Africa 56 E3 31 4S 24 29 E
Hanover, N.H., U.S.A. 79 C12 43 42N 72 17W
Hanover, Ohio, U.S.A. 78 F2 40 4N 82 16W
Hanover, Pa., U.S.A. 76 F7 39 48N 76 59W
Hanover, I., Chile 96 G2 51 0S 74 50W
Hansi, India 42 E6 29 10N 75 57 E
Hanson, L., Australia 63 E2 31 0S 136 15 E
Hantsavichy, Belarus 17 B14 52 49N 26 30 E
Hanzhong, China 34 H4 33 10N 107 1 E
Hanzhuang, China 35 G9 34 33N 117 23 E
Haora, India 43 H13 22 37N 88 20 E
Haparanda, Sweden 8 D21 65 52N 24 8 E
Happy, U.S.A. 81 H4 34 45N 101 52W
Happy Camp, U.S.A. 82 F2 41 48N 123 23W
Happy Valley-Goose Bay, Canada 71 B7 53 15N 60 20W
Hapsu, N. Korea 35 D15 41 13N 128 51 E
Hapur, India 42 E7 28 45N 77 45 E
Ḩaql, Si. Arabia 47 F3 29 10N 34 58 E
Har, Indonesia 37 F8 5 16S 133 14 E
Har-Ayrag, Mongolia 34 B5 45 47N 109 16 E
Har Hu, China 32 C4 38 20N 97 38 E
Har Us Nuur, Mongolia 32 B4 48 0N 92 0 E
Har Yehuda, Israel 47 D3 31 35N 34 57 E
Ḩaraḑ, Si. Arabia 46 C4 24 22N 49 0 E
Haranomachi, Japan 30 F10 37 38N 140 58 E
Harardera, Somali Rep. 46 G4 4 33N 47 38 E
Harare, Zimbabwe 55 F3 17 43S 31 2 E
Harazé, Chad 51 F8 14 20N 19 12 E
Harbin, China 35 B14 45 48N 126 40 E
Harbor Beach, U.S.A. 76 D4 43 51N 82 39W
Harbor Springs, U.S.A. 76 C3 45 26N 85 0W
Harbour Breton, Canada 71 C8 47 29N 55 50W
Harbour Grace, Canada 71 C9 47 40N 53 22W
Harda, India 42 H7 22 27N 77 5 E
Hardangerfjorden, Norway 9 F12 60 5N 6 0 E
Hardangervidda, Norway 9 F12 60 7N 7 20 E
Hardap Dam, Namibia 56 C2 24 32S 17 50 E
Hardenberg, Neths. 15 B6 52 34N 6 37 E
Harderwijk, Neths. 15 B5 52 21N 5 38 E
Hardey →, Australia 60 D2 22 45S 116 8 E
Hardin, U.S.A. 82 D10 45 44N 107 37W
Harding, S. Africa 57 E4 30 35S 29 55 E
Harding Ra., Australia 60 C3 16 17S 124 55 E
Hardisty, Canada 72 C6 52 40N 111 18W
Hardman, U.S.A. 82 D4 45 10N 119 41W
Hardoi, India 43 F9 27 26N 80 6 E
Hardwar = Haridwar, India 42 E8 29 58N 78 9 E
Hardwick, U.S.A. 79 B12 44 30N 72 22W
Hardy, U.S.A. 81 G9 36 19N 91 29W
Hardy, Pen., Chile 96 H3 55 30S 68 20W
Hare B., Canada 71 B8 51 15N 55 45W
Hareid, Norway 9 E12 62 22N 6 1 E
Harer, Ethiopia 46 F3 9 20N 42 8 E
Hargeisa, Somali Rep. 46 F3 9 30N 44 2 E
Hari →, Indonesia 36 E2 1 16S 104 5 E
Haria, Canary Is. 22 E6 29 8N 13 32W
Haridwar, India 42 E8 29 58N 78 9 E
Haringhata →, Bangla. 41 J16 22 0N 89 58 E
Harīrūd →, Asia 40 A2 37 24N 60 38 E
Härjedalen, Sweden 9 E15 62 22N 13 5 E
Harlan, Iowa, U.S.A. 80 E7 41 39N 95 19W
Harlan, Ky., U.S.A. 77 G4 36 51N 83 19W
Harlech, U.K. 10 E3 52 52N 4 6W
Harlem, U.S.A. 82 B9 48 32N 108 47W
Harlingen, Neths. 15 A5 53 11N 5 25 E
Harlingen, U.S.A. 81 M6 26 12N 97 42W
Harlowton, U.S.A. 82 C9 46 26N 109 50W
Harney Basin, U.S.A. 82 E4 43 30N 119 0W
Harney L., U.S.A. 82 E4 43 14N 119 8W
Harney Peak, U.S.A. 80 D3 43 52N 103 32W
Härnösand, Sweden 9 E17 62 38N 17 55 E
Harp L., Canada 71 A7 55 5N 61 50W
Harrand, Pakistan 42 E4 29 28N 70 3 E
Harriman, U.S.A. 77 H3 35 56N 84 33W
Harrington Harbour, Canada 71 B8 50 31N 59 30W
Harris, U.K. 12 D2 57 50N 6 55W
Harris, Sd. of, U.K. 12 D1 57 44N 7 6W
Harris L., Australia 63 E2 31 10S 135 10 E
Harrisburg, Ill., U.S.A. 81 G10 37 44N 88 32W
Harrisburg, Nebr., U.S.A. 80 E3 41 33N 103 44W
Harrisburg, Oreg., U.S.A. 82 D2 44 16N 123 10W
Harrisburg, Pa., U.S.A. 78 F8 40 16N 76 53W
Harrismith, S. Africa 57 D4 28 15S 29 8 E
Harrison, Ark., U.S.A. 81 G8 36 14N 93 7W
Harrison, Idaho, U.S.A. 82 C5 47 27N 116 47W
Harrison, Nebr., U.S.A. 80 D3 42 41N 103 53W
Harrison, C., Canada 71 B8 54 55N 57 55W
Harrison Bay, U.S.A. 68 A4 70 40N 151 0W
Harrison L., Canada 72 D4 49 33N 121 50W
Harrisonburg, U.S.A. 76 F6 38 27N 78 52W
Harrisonville, U.S.A. 80 F7 38 39N 94 21W
Harriston, Canada 70 D3 43 57N 80 53W
Harrisville, U.S.A. 78 B1 44 39N 83 17W
Harrogate, U.K. 10 D6 54 0N 1 33W
Harrow, U.K. 11 F7 51 35N 0 21W
Harsīn, Iran 44 C5 34 18N 47 33 E
Harstad, Norway 8 B17 68 48N 16 30 E
Hart, U.S.A. 76 D2 43 42N 86 22W
Hart, L., Australia 63 E2 31 10S 136 25 E
Hartbees →, S. Africa 56 D3 28 45S 20 32 E
Hartford, Conn., U.S.A. 79 E12 41 46N 72 41W
Hartford, Ky., U.S.A. 76 G2 37 27N 86 55W
Hartford, S. Dak., U.S.A. 80 D6 43 38N 96 57W
Hartford, Wis., U.S.A. 80 D10 43 19N 88 22W
Hartford City, U.S.A. 76 E3 40 27N 85 22W
Hartland, Canada 71 C6 46 20N 67 32W
Hartland Pt., U.K. 11 F3 51 1N 4 32W
Hartlepool, U.K. 10 C6 54 42N 1 13W
Hartlepool □, U.K. 10 C6 54 42N 1 17W
Hartley Bay, Canada 72 C3 53 25N 129 15W
Hartmannberge, Namibia 56 B1 17 0S 13 0 E
Hartney, Canada 73 D8 49 30N 100 35W
Harts →, S. Africa 56 D3 28 24S 24 17 E
Hartselle, U.S.A. 77 H2 34 27N 86 56W
Hartshorne, U.S.A. 81 H7 34 51N 95 34W
Hartsville, U.S.A. 77 H5 34 23N 80 4W
Hartwell, U.S.A. 77 H4 34 21N 82 56W
Harunabad, Pakistan 42 E5 29 35N 73 8 E
Harvand, Iran 45 D7 28 25N 55 43 E
Harvey, Australia 61 F2 33 5S 115 54 E
Harvey, Ill., U.S.A. 76 E2 41 36N 87 50W
Harvey, N. Dak., U.S.A. 80 B5 47 47N 99 56W
Harwich, U.K. 11 F9 51 56N 1 17 E
Haryana □, India 42 E7 29 0N 76 10 E
Haryn →, Belarus 17 B14 52 7N 27 17 E
Harz, Germany 16 C6 51 38N 10 44 E
Hasan Kiādeh, Iran 45 B6 37 24N 49 58 E
Ḩasanābād, Iran 45 C7 32 8N 52 44 E
Hasanpur, India 42 E8 28 43N 78 17 E
Hashimoto, Japan 31 G7 34 19N 135 37 E
Hashtjerd, Iran 45 C6 35 52N 50 40 E
Haskell, Okla., U.S.A. 81 H7 35 50N 95 40W
Haskell, Tex., U.S.A. 81 J5 33 10N 99 44W
Hasselt, Belgium 15 D5 50 56N 5 21 E
Hassi Inifel, Algeria 50 C5 29 50N 3 41 E
Hassi Messaoud, Algeria 50 B6 31 51N 6 1 E
Hässleholm, Sweden 9 H15 56 10N 13 46 E
Hastings, N.Z. 59 H6 39 39S 176 52 E
Hastings, U.K. 11 G8 50 51N 0 35 E
Hastings, Mich., U.S.A. 76 D3 42 39N 85 17W
Hastings, Minn., U.S.A. 80 C8 44 44N 92 51W
Hastings, Nebr., U.S.A. 80 E5 40 35N 98 23W
Hastings Ra., Australia 63 E5 31 15S 152 14 E
Hat Yai, Thailand 39 J3 7 1N 100 27 E
Hatanbulag, Mongolia 34 C5 43 8N 109 5 E
Hatay = Antalya, Turkey 25 G5 36 52N 30 45 E
Hatch, U.S.A. 83 K10 32 40N 107 9W
Hatches Creek, Australia 62 C2 20 56S 135 12 E
Hatchet L., Canada 73 B8 58 36N 103 40W
Hateruma-Shima, Japan 31 M1 24 3N 123 47 E
Hatfield P.O., Australia 63 E3 33 54S 143 49 E
Hatgal, Mongolia 32 A5 50 26N 100 9 E
Hathras, India 42 F8 27 36N 78 6 E
Hatia, Bangla. 41 H17 22 30N 91 5 E
Hato Mayor, Dom. Rep. 89 C6 18 46N 69 15W
Hattah, Australia 63 E3 34 48S 142 17 E
Hatteras, C., U.S.A. 77 H8 35 14N 75 32W
Hattiesburg, U.S.A. 81 K10 31 20N 89 17W
Hatvan, Hungary 17 E10 47 40N 19 45 E
Hau Bon = Cheo Reo, Vietnam 38 F7 13 25N 108 28 E
Hau Duc, Vietnam 38 E7 15 20N 108 13 E
Haugesund, Norway 9 G11 59 23N 5 13 E
Haukipudas, Finland 8 D21 65 12N 25 20 E
Haultain →, Canada 73 B7 55 51N 106 46W
Hauraki G., N.Z. 59 G5 36 35S 175 5 E
Haut Atlas, Morocco 50 B3 32 30N 5 0W
Haut Zaïre □, Zaïre 54 B2 2 20N 26 0 E
Hauterive, Canada 71 C6 49 10N 68 16W
Hautes Fagnes = Hohe Venn, Belgium 15 D6 50 30N 6 5 E
Hauts Plateaux, Algeria 50 A5 35 0N 1 0 E
Havana = La Habana, Cuba 88 B3 23 8N 82 22W
Havana, U.S.A. 80 E9 40 18N 90 4W
Havant, U.K. 11 G7 50 51N 0 58W
Havasu, L., U.S.A. 85 L12 34 18N 114 28W
Havel →, Germany 16 B7 52 50N 12 3 E
Havelange, Belgium 15 D5 50 23N 5 15 E
Havelian, Pakistan 42 B5 34 2N 73 10 E
Havelock, N.B., Canada 71 C6 46 2N 65 24W
Havelock, Ont., Canada 70 D4 44 26N 77 53W
Havelock, N.Z. 59 J4 41 17S 173 48 E
Haverfordwest, U.K. 11 F3 51 48N 4 58W
Haverhill, U.S.A. 79 D13 42 47N 71 5W
Havering, U.K. 11 F8 51 34N 0 13 E
Haverstraw, U.S.A. 79 E11 41 12N 73 58W
Havířov, Czech Rep. 17 D10 49 46N 18 20 E
Havlíčkův Brod, Czech. 16 D8 49 36N 15 33 E
Havre, U.S.A. 82 B9 48 33N 109 41W
Havre-Aubert, Canada 71 C7 47 12N 61 56W
Havre-St.-Pierre, Canada 71 B7 50 18N 63 33W
Haw →, U.S.A. 77 H6 35 36N 79 3W
Hawaii □, U.S.A. 74 H16 19 30N 156 30W
Hawaii I., Pac. Oc. 74 J17 20 0N 155 0W
Hawaiian Is., Pac. Oc. 74 H17 20 30N 156 0W
Hawaiian Ridge, Pac. Oc. 65 E11 24 0N 165 0W
Hawarden, Canada 73 C7 51 25N 106 36W
Hawarden, U.S.A. 80 D6 43 0N 96 29W
Hawea, L., N.Z. 59 L2 44 28S 169 19 E
Hawera, N.Z. 59 H5 39 35S 174 19 E
Hawick, U.K. 12 F6 55 26N 2 47W
Hawk Junction, Canada 70 C3 48 5N 84 38W
Hawke B., N.Z. 59 H6 39 25S 177 20 E
Hawker, Australia 63 E2 31 59S 138 22 E
Hawkesbury, Canada 70 C5 45 37N 74 37W
Hawkesbury I., Canada 72 C3 53 37N 129 3W
Hawkesbury Pt., Australia 62 A1 11 55S 134 5 E
Hawkinsville, U.S.A. 77 J4 32 17N 83 28W
Hawkwood, Australia 63 D5 25 45S 150 50 E
Hawley, U.S.A. 80 B6 46 53N 96 19W
Hawrān, Syria 47 C5 32 45N 36 15 E
Hawsh Mūssá, Lebanon 47 B4 33 45N 35 55 E
Hawthorne, U.S.A. 82 G4 38 32N 118 38W
Haxtun, U.S.A. 80 E3 40 39N 102 38W
Hay, Australia 63 E3 34 30S 144 51 E
Hay →, Australia 62 C2 24 50S 138 0 E
Hay →, Canada 72 A5 60 50N 116 26W
Hay, C., Australia 60 B4 14 5S 129 29 E
Hay L., Canada 72 B5 58 50N 118 50W
Hay Lakes, Canada 72 C6 53 12N 113 2W
Hay-on-Wye, U.K. 11 E4 52 5N 3 8W
Hay River, Canada 72 A5 60 51N 115 44W
Hay Springs, U.S.A. 80 D3 42 41N 102 41W
Haya, Indonesia 37 E7 3 19S 129 37 E
Hayachine-San, Japan 30 E10 39 34N 141 29 E
Hayden, Ariz., U.S.A. 83 K8 33 0N 110 47W
Hayden, Colo., U.S.A. 82 F10 40 30N 107 16W
Haydon, Australia 62 B3 18 0S 141 30 E
Hayes, U.S.A. 80 C4 44 23N 101 1W
Hayes →, Canada 73 B10 57 3N 92 12W
Haynesville, U.S.A. 81 J8 32 58N 93 8W
Hayrabolu, Turkey 21 D12 41 12N 27 5 E
Hays, Canada 72 C6 50 6N 111 48W
Hays, U.S.A. 80 F5 38 53N 99 20W
Haysyn, Ukraine 17 D15 48 57N 29 25 E
Hayvoron, Ukraine 17 D15 48 22N 29 52 E
Hayward, Calif., U.S.A. 84 H4 37 40N 122 5W
Hayward, Wis., U.S.A. 80 B9 46 1N 91 29W
Haywards Heath, U.K. 11 F7 51 0N 0 5W
Hazafon □, Israel 47 C4 32 40N 35 20 E
Hazarām, Kūh-e, Iran 45 D8 29 30N 57 18 E
Hazard, U.S.A. 76 G4 37 15N 83 12W
Hazaribag, India 43 H11 23 58N 85 26 E
Hazaribag Road, India 43 G11 24 12N 85 57 E
Hazelton, Canada 72 B3 55 20N 127 42W
Hazelton, U.S.A. 80 B4 46 29N 100 17W
Hazen, N. Dak., U.S.A. 80 B4 47 18N 101 38W
Hazen, Nev., U.S.A. 82 G4 39 34N 119 3W
Hazlehurst, Ga., U.S.A. 77 K4 31 52N 82 36W
Hazlehurst, Miss., U.S.A. 81 K9 31 52N 90 24W
Hazleton, U.S.A. 79 F9 40 57N 75 59W
Hazlett, L., Australia 60 D4 21 30S 128 48 E
Hazor, Israel 47 B4 33 2N 35 32 E
Head of Bight, Australia 61 F5 31 30S 131 25 E
Headlands, Zimbabwe 55 F3 18 15S 32 2 E
Healdsburg, U.S.A. 84 G4 38 37N 122 52W
Healdton, U.S.A. 81 H6 34 14N 97 29W
Healesville, Australia 63 F4 37 35S 145 30 E
Heanor, U.K. 10 D6 53 1N 1 21W
Heard I., Ind. Oc. 3 G13 53 0S 74 0 E
Hearne, U.S.A. 81 K6 30 53N 96 36W
Hearne B., Canada 73 A9 60 10N 99 10W
Hearne L., Canada 72 A6 62 20N 113 10W
Hearst, Canada 70 C3 49 40N 83 41W
Heart →, U.S.A. 80 B4 46 46N 100 50W
Heart's Content, Canada 71 C9 47 54N 53 27W
Heath Pt., Canada 71 C7 49 8N 61 40W
Heath Steele, Canada 71 C6 47 17N 66 5W
Heavener, U.S.A. 81 H7 34 53N 94 36W
Hebbronville, U.S.A. 81 M5 27 18N 98 41W
Hebei □, China 34 E9 39 0N 116 0 E
Hebel, Australia 63 D4 28 58S 147 47 E
Heber, U.S.A. 85 N11 32 44N 115 32W
Heber Springs, U.S.A. 81 H9 35 30N 92 2W
Hebert, Canada 73 C7 50 30N 107 10W
Hebgen L., U.S.A. 82 D8 44 52N 111 20W
Hebi, China 34 G8 35 57N 114 7 E
Hebrides, U.K. 12 D1 57 30N 7 0W
Hebron = Al Khalīl, West Bank 47 D4 31 32N 35 6 E
Hebron, Canada 69 C13 58 5N 62 30W
Hebron, N. Dak., U.S.A. 80 B3 46 54N 102 3W
Hebron, Nebr., U.S.A. 80 E6 40 10N 97 35W
Hecate Str., Canada 72 C2 53 10N 130 30W
Hechi, China 32 D5 24 40N 108 2 E
Hechuan, China 32 C5 30 2N 106 12 E
Hecla, U.S.A. 80 C5 45 53N 98 9W
Hecla I., Canada 73 C9 51 10N 96 43W
Hede, Sweden 9 E15 62 23N 13 30 E
Hedemora, Sweden 9 F16 60 18N 15 58 E
Hedley, U.S.A. 81 H4 34 52N 100 39W
Heemstede, Neths. 15 B4 52 22N 4 37 E
Heerde, Neths. 15 B6 52 24N 6 2 E
Heerenveen, Neths. 15 B5 52 57N 5 55 E
Heerlen, Neths. 18 A6 50 55N 5 58 E
Hefa, Israel 47 C3 32 46N 35 0 E
Hefa □, Israel 47 C4 32 40N 35 0 E
Hefei, China 33 C6 31 52N 117 18 E
Hegang, China 33 B8 47 20N 130 19 E
Heichengzhen, China 34 F4 36 24N 106 3 E
Heidelberg, Germany 16 D5 49 24N 8 42 E
Heidelberg, S. Africa 56 E3 34 6S 20 59 E
Heilbron, S. Africa 57 D4 27 16S 27 59 E
Heilbronn, Germany 16 D5 49 9N 9 13 E
Heilongjiang □, China 35 B14 48 0N 126 0 E
Heilunkiang = Heilongjiang □, China 35 B14 48 0N 126 0 E
Heimaey, Iceland 8 E3 63 26N 20 17W
Heinola, Finland 9 F22 61 13N 26 2 E
Heinze Is., Burma 41 M20 14 25N 97 45 E

Ilek, Russia **26 D6** 51 32N 53 21 E
Ilek —►, Russia **24 D9** 51 30N 53 22 E
Ilford, Canada **73 B9** 56 4N 95 35W
Ilfracombe, Australia **62 C3** 23 30S 144 30 E
Ilfracombe, U.K. **11 F3** 51 12N 4 8W
Ilhéus, Brazil **93 F11** 14 49S 39 2W
Ili —►, Kazakstan **26 E7** 45 53N 77 10 E
Ilich, Kazakstan **26 E7** 40 50N 68 27 E
Iliff, U.S.A. **80 E3** 40 45N 103 4W
Iligan, Phil. **37 C6** 8 12N 124 13 E
Ilion, U.S.A. **79 D9** 43 1N 75 2W
Ilkeston, U.K. **10 E6** 52 58N 1 19W
Illampu = Ancohuma, Nevada, Bolivia **92 G5** 16 0S 68 50W
Illana B., Phil. **37 C6** 7 35N 123 45 E
Illapel, Chile **94 C1** 32 0S 71 10W
Iller —►, Germany **16 D6** 48 23N 9 58 E
Illetas, Spain **22 B9** 39 32N 2 35 E
Illimani, Bolivia **92 G5** 16 30S 67 50W
Illinois □, U.S.A. **75 C9** 40 15N 89 30W
Illinois —►, U.S.A. **75 C8** 38 58N 90 28W
Illium = Troy, Turkey **21 E12** 39 57N 26 12 E
Ilmajoki, Finland **9 E20** 62 44N 22 34 E
Ilmen, Ozero, Russia **24 C5** 58 15N 31 10 E
Ilo, Peru **92 G4** 17 40S 71 20W
Iloilo, Phil. **37 B6** 10 45N 122 33 E
Ilorin, Nigeria **50 G5** 8 30N 4 35 E
Ilwaco, U.S.A. **84 D2** 46 19N 124 3W
Ilwaki, Indonesia **37 F7** 7 55S 126 30 E
Imabari, Japan **31 G6** 34 4N 133 0 E
Imaloto —►, Madag. **57 C8** 23 27S 45 13 E
Imandra, Ozero, Russia **24 A5** 67 30N 33 0 E
Imari, Japan **31 H4** 33 15N 129 52 E
Imbler, U.S.A. **82 D5** 45 28N 117 58W
imeni 26 Bakinskikh Komissarov = Neftçala, Azerbaijan **25 G8** 39 19N 49 12 E
imeni 26 Bakinskikh Komissarov, Turkmenistan **25 G9** 39 22N 54 10 E
Imeni Poliny Osipenko, Russia **27 D14** 52 30N 136 29 E
Imeri, Serra, Brazil **92 C5** 0 50N 65 25W
Imerimandroso, Madag. **57 B8** 17 26S 48 35 E
Imi, Ethiopia **46 F3** 6 28N 42 10 E
Imlay, U.S.A. **82 F4** 40 40N 118 9W
Imlay City, U.S.A. **78 C1** 43 2N 83 5W
Immingham, U.K. **10 D7** 53 37N 0 13W
Immokalee, U.S.A. **77 M5** 26 25N 81 25W
Imola, Italy **20 B4** 44 20N 11 42 E
Imperatriz, Brazil **93 E9** 5 30S 47 29W
Impéria, Italy **20 C3** 43 53N 8 3 E
Imperial, Canada **73 C7** 51 21N 105 28W
Imperial, Calif., U.S.A. **85 N11** 32 51N 115 34W
Imperial, Nebr., U.S.A. **80 E4** 40 31N 101 39W
Imperial Beach, U.S.A. **85 N9** 32 35N 117 8W
Imperial Dam, U.S.A. **85 N12** 32 55N 114 25W
Imperial Reservoir, U.S.A. **85 N12** 32 53N 114 28W
Imperial Valley, U.S.A. **85 N11** 33 0N 115 30W
Imperieuse Reef, Australia **60 C2** 17 36S 118 50 E
Impfondo, Congo **52 D3** 1 40N 18 0 E
Imphal, India **41 G18** 24 48N 93 56 E
İmroz = Gökçeada, Turkey **21 D11** 40 10N 25 50 E
Imuruan B., Phil. **37 B5** 10 40N 119 10 E
In Belbel, Algeria **50 C5** 27 55N 1 12 E
In Salah, Algeria **50 C5** 27 10N 2 32 E
Ina, Japan **31 G8** 35 50N 137 55 E
Inangahua Junction, N.Z. **59 J3** 41 52S 171 59 E
Inanwatan, Indonesia **37 E8** 2 10S 132 14 E
Iñapari, Peru **92 F5** 11 0S 69 40W
Inari, Finland **8 B22** 68 54N 27 5 E
Inarijärvi, Finland **8 B22** 69 0N 28 0 E
Inawashiro-Ko, Japan **30 F10** 37 29N 140 6 E
Inca, Spain **22 B9** 39 43N 2 54 E
Incaguasi, Chile **94 B1** 29 12S 71 5W
İnce Burun, Turkey **25 F5** 42 7N 34 56 E
Inchon, S. Korea **35 F14** 37 27N 126 40 E
İncirliova, Turkey **21 F12** 37 50N 27 41 E
Incomáti —►, Mozam. **57 D5** 25 46S 32 43 E
Indalsälven —►, Sweden **9 E17** 62 36N 17 30 E
Indaw, Burma **41 G20** 24 15N 96 5 E
Independence, Calif., U.S.A. **83 H4** 36 48N 118 12W
Independence, Iowa, U.S.A. **80 D9** 42 28N 91 54W
Independence, Kans., U.S.A. **81 G7** 37 14N 95 42W
Independence, Mo., U.S.A. **80 F7** 39 6N 94 25W
Independence, Oreg., U.S.A. **82 D2** 44 51N 123 11W
Independence Fjord, Greenland **4 A6** 82 10N 29 0W
Independence Mts., U.S.A. **82 F5** 41 20N 116 0W
Index, U.S.A. **84 C5** 47 50N 121 33W
India ■, Asia **40 K11** 20 0N 78 0 E
Indian —►, U.S.A. **77 M5** 27 59N 80 34W
Indian Cabins, Canada **72 B5** 59 52N 117 40W
Indian Harbour, Canada **71 B8** 54 27N 57 13W
Indian Head, Canada **73 C8** 50 30N 103 41W
Indian Ocean **28 K11** 5 0S 75 0 E
Indian Springs, U.S.A. **85 J11** 36 35N 115 40W
Indiana, U.S.A. **78 F5** 40 37N 79 9W
Indiana □, U.S.A. **76 E3** 40 0N 86 0W
Indianapolis, U.S.A. **76 F2** 39 46N 86 9W
Indianola, Iowa, U.S.A. **80 E8** 41 22N 93 34W
Indianola, Miss., U.S.A. **81 J9** 33 27N 90 39W
Indiga, Russia **24 A8** 67 38N 49 9 E
Indigirka —►, Russia **27 B15** 70 48N 148 54 E
Indio, U.S.A. **85 M10** 33 43N 116 13W
Indonesia ■, Asia **36 F5** 5 0S 115 0 E
Indore, India **42 H6** 22 42N 75 53 E
Indramayu, Indonesia **37 G13** 6 20S 108 19 E
Indravati —►, India **41 K12** 19 20N 80 20 E
Indre —►, France **18 C4** 47 16N 0 11 E
Indus —►, Pakistan **42 G2** 24 20N 67 47 E
Indus, Mouth of the, Pakistan **42 H2** 24 0N 68 0 E
İnebolu, Turkey **25 F5** 41 55N 33 40 E
Infiernillo, Presa del, Mexico **86 D4** 18 9N 102 0W
Ingende, Zaïre **52 E3** 0 12S 18 57 E
Ingenio, Canary Is. **22 G4** 27 55N 15 26W
Ingenio Santa Ana, Argentina **94 B2** 27 25S 65 40W
Ingersoll, Canada **78 C4** 43 4N 80 55W
Ingham, Australia **62 B4** 18 43S 146 10 E
Ingleborough, U.K. **10 C5** 54 10N 2 22W
Inglewood, Queens., Australia **63 D5** 28 25S 151 2 E
Inglewood, Vic., Australia **63 F3** 36 29S 143 53 E
Inglewood, N.Z. **59 H5** 39 9S 174 14 E
Inglewood, U.S.A. **85 M8** 33 58N 118 21W
Ingólfshöfði, Iceland **8 E5** 63 48N 16 39W
Ingolstadt, Germany **16 D6** 48 46N 11 26 E
Ingomar, U.S.A. **82 C10** 46 35N 107 23W
Ingonish, Canada **71 C7** 46 42N 60 18W
Ingraj Bazar, India **43 G13** 24 58N 88 10 E
Ingrid Christensen Coast, Antarctica **5 C6** 69 30S 76 0 E
Ingulec = Inhulec, Ukraine **25 E5** 47 42N 33 14 E
Ingwavuma, S. Africa **57 D5** 27 9S 31 59 E
Inhaca, I., Mozam. **57 D5** 26 1S 32 57 E
Inhafenga, Mozam. **57 C5** 20 36S 33 53 E
Inhambane, Mozam. **57 C6** 23 54S 35 30 E
Inhambane □, Mozam. **57 C5** 22 30S 34 20 E
Inhaminga, Mozam. **55 F4** 18 26S 35 0 E
Inharrime, Mozam. **57 C6** 24 30S 35 0 E
Inharrime —►, Mozam. **57 C6** 24 30S 35 0 E
Inhulec, Ukraine **25 E5** 47 42N 33 14 E
Ining = Yining, China **26 E9** 43 58N 81 10 E
Inírida —►, Colombia **92 C5** 3 55N 67 52W
Inishbofin, Ireland **13 C1** 53 37N 10 13W
Inishmore, Ireland **13 C2** 53 8N 9 45W
Inishowen Pen., Ireland **13 A4** 55 14N 7 15W
Injune, Australia **63 D4** 25 53S 148 32 E
Inklin, Canada **72 B2** 58 56N 133 5W
Inklin —►, Canada **72 B2** 58 50N 133 10W
Inkom, U.S.A. **82 E7** 42 48N 112 15W
Inle L., Burma **41 J20** 20 30N 96 58 E
Inn —►, Austria **16 D7** 48 35N 13 28 E
Innamincka, Australia **63 D3** 27 44S 140 46 E
Inner Hebrides, U.K. **12 D2** 57 0N 6 30W
Inner Mongolia = Nei Monggol Zizhiqu □, China **34 C6** 42 0N 112 0 E
Inner Sound, U.K. **12 D3** 57 30N 5 55W
Innerkip, Canada **78 C4** 43 13N 80 42W
Innetalling I., Canada **70 A4** 56 0N 79 0W
Innisfail, Australia **62 B4** 17 33S 146 5 E
Innisfail, Canada **72 C6** 52 0N 113 57W
In'no-shima, Japan **31 G6** 34 19N 133 10 E
Innsbruck, Austria **16 E6** 47 16N 11 23 E
Inny —►, Ireland **13 C4** 53 30N 7 50W
Inongo, Zaïre **52 E3** 1 55S 18 30 E
Inoucdjouac = Inukjuak, Canada **69 C12** 58 25N 78 15W
Inowrocław, Poland **17 B10** 52 50N 18 12 E
Inpundong, N. Korea **35 D14** 41 25N 126 34 E
Inquisivi, Bolivia **92 G5** 16 50S 67 10W
Inscription, C., Australia **61 E1** 25 29S 112 59 E
Insein, Burma **41 L20** 16 50N 96 5 E
Inta, Russia **24 A11** 66 5N 60 8 E
Intendente Alvear, Argentina **94 D3** 35 12S 63 32W
Interior, U.S.A. **80 D4** 43 44N 101 59W
Interlaken, Switz. **16 E4** 46 41N 7 50 E
International Falls, U.S.A. **80 A8** 48 36N 93 25W
Intiyaco, Argentina **94 B3** 28 43S 60 5W
Inukjuak, Canada **69 C12** 58 25N 78 15W
Inútil, B., Chile **96 G2** 53 30S 70 15W
Inuvik, Canada **68 B6** 68 16N 133 40W
Inveraray, U.K. **12 E3** 56 14N 5 5W
Inverbervie, U.K. **12 E6** 56 51N 2 17W
Invercargill, N.Z. **59 M2** 46 24S 168 24 E
Inverclyde □, U.K. **12 F4** 55 55N 4 49W
Inverell, Australia **63 D5** 29 45S 151 8 E
Invergordon, U.K. **12 D4** 57 41N 4 10W
Invermere, Canada **72 C5** 50 30N 116 2W
Inverness, Canada **71 C7** 46 15N 61 19W
Inverness, U.K. **12 D4** 57 29N 4 13W
Inverness, U.S.A. **77 L4** 28 50N 82 20W
Inverurie, U.K. **12 D6** 57 17N 2 23W
Inverway, Australia **60 C4** 17 50S 129 38 E
Investigator Group, Australia **63 E1** 34 45S 134 20 E
Investigator Str., Australia **63 F2** 35 30S 137 0 E
Inya, Russia **26 D9** 50 28N 86 37 E
Inyanga, Zimbabwe **55 F3** 18 12S 32 40 E
Inyangani, Zimbabwe **55 F3** 18 5S 32 50 E
Inyantue, Zimbabwe **55 F2** 18 30S 26 40 E
Inyo Mts., U.S.A. **83 H5** 36 40N 118 0W
Inyokern, U.S.A. **85 K9** 35 39N 117 49W
Inza, Russia **24 D8** 53 55N 46 25 E
Iō-Jima, Japan **31 J5** 30 48N 130 18 E
Ioánnina, Greece **21 E9** 39 42N 20 47 E
Iola, U.S.A. **81 G7** 37 55N 95 24W
Iona, U.K. **12 E2** 56 20N 6 25W
Ione, Calif., U.S.A. **84 G6** 38 21N 120 56W
Ione, Wash., U.S.A. **82 B5** 48 45N 117 25W
Ionia, U.S.A. **76 D3** 42 59N 85 4W
Ionian Is. = Iónioi Nísoi, Greece **21 E9** 38 40N 20 0 E
Ionian Sea, Medit. S. **21 E7** 37 30N 17 30 E
Iónioi Nísoi, Greece **21 E9** 38 40N 20 0 E
Íos, Greece **21 F11** 36 41N 25 20 E
Iowa □, U.S.A. **80 D8** 42 18N 93 30W
Iowa City, U.S.A. **80 E9** 41 40N 91 32W
Iowa Falls, U.S.A. **80 D8** 42 31N 93 16W
Ipala, Tanzania **54 C3** 4 30S 32 52 E
Ipameri, Brazil **93 G9** 17 44S 48 9W
Ipatinga, Brazil **93 G10** 19 32S 42 30W
Ipiales, Colombia **92 C3** 0 50N 77 37W
Ipin = Yibin, China **32 D5** 28 45N 104 32 E
Ipixuna, Brazil **92 E4** 7 0S 71 40W
Ipoh, Malaysia **39 K3** 4 35N 101 5 E
Ippy, C.A.R. **51 G9** 6 5N 21 7 E
Ipsala, Turkey **21 D12** 40 55N 26 23 E
Ipswich, Australia **63 D5** 27 35S 152 40 E
Ipswich, U.K. **11 E9** 52 4N 1 10 E
Ipswich, Mass., U.S.A. **79 D14** 42 41N 70 50W
Ipswich, S. Dak., U.S.A. **80 C5** 45 27N 99 2W
Ipu, Brazil **93 D10** 4 23S 40 44W
Iqaluit, Canada **69 B13** 63 44N 68 31W
Iquique, Chile **92 H4** 20 19S 70 5W
Iquitos, Peru **92 D4** 3 45S 73 10W
Irabu-Jima, Japan **31 M2** 24 50N 125 10 E
Iracoubo, Fr. Guiana **93 B8** 5 30N 53 10W
Īrafshān, Iran **45 E9** 26 42N 61 56 E
Iráklion, Greece **23 D7** 35 20N 25 12 E
Iráklion □, Greece **23 D7** 35 10N 25 10 E
Irala, Paraguay **95 B5** 25 55S 54 35W
Iramba □, Tanzania **54 C3** 4 30S 34 30 E
Iran ■, Asia **45 C7** 33 0N 53 0 E
Iran, Gunung-Gunung, Malaysia **36 D4** 2 20N 114 50 E
Iran, Plateau of, Asia **28 F9** 32 0N 55 0 E
Iran Ra. = Iran, Gunung-Gunung, Malaysia **36 D4** 2 20N 114 50 E
Īrānshahr, Iran **45 E9** 27 15N 60 40 E
Irapuato, Mexico **86 C4** 20 40N 101 30W
Iraq ■, Asia **44 C5** 33 0N 44 0 E
Irati, Brazil **95 B5** 25 25S 50 38W
Irbid, Jordan **47 C4** 32 35N 35 48 E
Irbid □, Jordan **47 C5** 32 15N 36 35 E
Irebu, Zaïre **52 E3** 0 40S 17 46 E
Ireland ■, Europe **13 D4** 53 50N 7 52W
Ireland's Eye, Ireland **13 C5** 53 24N 6 4W
Iret, Russia **27 C16** 60 3N 154 20 E
Irhyangdong, N. Korea **35 D15** 41 15N 129 30 E
Iri, S. Korea **35 G14** 35 59N 127 0 E
Irian Jaya □, Indonesia **37 E9** 4 0S 137 0 E
Iringa, Tanzania **54 D4** 7 48S 35 43 E
Iringa □, Tanzania **54 D4** 7 48S 35 43 E
Iriomote-Jima, Japan **31 M1** 24 19N 123 48 E
Iriona, Honduras **88 C2** 15 57N 85 11W
Iriri —►, Brazil **93 D8** 3 52S 52 37W
Irish Republic ■, Europe **13 D4** 53 0N 8 0W
Irish Sea, U.K. **10 D3** 53 38N 4 48W
Irkineyeva, Russia **27 D10** 58 30N 96 49 E
Irkutsk, Russia **27 D11** 52 18N 104 20 E
Irma, Canada **73 C6** 52 55N 111 14W
Irō-Zaki, Japan **31 G9** 34 36N 138 51 E
Iron Baron, Australia **63 E2** 32 58S 137 11 E
Iron Gate = Portile de Fier, Europe **17 F12** 44 42N 22 30 E
Iron Knob, Australia **63 E2** 32 46S 137 8 E
Iron Mountain, U.S.A. **76 C1** 45 49N 88 4W
Iron Ra., Australia **62 A3** 12 46S 143 16 E
Iron River, U.S.A. **80 B10** 46 6N 88 39W
Ironbridge, U.K. **11 E5** 52 38N 2 30W
Irondequoit, U.S.A. **78 C7** 43 13N 77 35W
Ironstone Kopje, Botswana **56 D3** 25 17S 24 5 E
Ironton, Mo., U.S.A. **81 G9** 37 36N 90 38W
Ironton, Ohio, U.S.A. **76 F4** 38 32N 82 41W
Ironwood, U.S.A. **80 B9** 46 27N 90 9W
Iroquois Falls, Canada **70 C3** 48 46N 80 41W
Irpin, Ukraine **17 C16** 50 30N 30 15 E
Irrara Cr. —►, Australia **63 D4** 29 35S 145 31 E
Irrawaddy □, Burma **41 L19** 17 0N 95 0 E
Irrawaddy —►, Burma **41 M19** 15 50N 95 6 E
Irtysh —►, Russia **26 C7** 61 4N 68 52 E
Irumu, Zaïre **54 B2** 1 32N 29 53 E
Irún, Spain **19 A5** 43 20N 1 52W
Irunea = Pamplona, Spain **19 A5** 42 48N 1 38W
Irvine, Canada **73 D6** 49 57N 110 16W
Irvine, U.K. **12 F4** 55 37N 4 41W
Irvine, Calif., U.S.A. **85 M9** 33 41N 117 46W
Irvine, Ky., U.S.A. **76 G4** 37 42N 83 58W
Irvinestown, U.K. **13 B4** 54 28N 7 40W
Irving, U.S.A. **81 J6** 32 49N 96 56W
Irvona, U.S.A. **78 F6** 40 46N 78 33W
Irwin —►, Australia **61 E1** 29 15S 114 54 E
Irymple, Australia **63 E3** 34 14S 142 8 E
Isaac —►, Australia **62 C4** 22 55S 149 20 E
Isabel, U.S.A. **80 C4** 45 24N 101 26W
Isabela, I., Mexico **86 C3** 21 51N 105 55W
Isabella, Phil. **37 C6** 6 40N 122 10 E
Isabella, Cord., Nic. **88 D2** 13 30N 85 25W
Isabella Ra., Australia **60 D3** 21 0S 121 4 E
Ísafjarðardjúp, Iceland **8 C2** 66 10N 23 0W
Ísafjörður, Iceland **8 C2** 66 5N 23 9W
Isagarh, India **42 G7** 24 48N 77 51 E
Isahaya, Japan **31 H5** 32 52N 130 2 E
Isaka, Tanzania **54 C3** 3 56S 32 59 E
Isangi, Zaïre **52 D4** 0 52N 24 10 E
Isar —►, Germany **16 D7** 48 48N 12 57 E
Íschia, Italy **20 D5** 40 44N 13 57 E
Isdell —►, Australia **60 C3** 16 27S 124 51 E
Ise, Japan **31 G8** 34 25N 136 45 E
Ise-Wan, Japan **31 G8** 34 43N 136 43 E
Iseramagazi, Tanzania **54 C3** 4 37S 32 10 E
Isère —►, France **18 D6** 44 59N 4 51 E
Isérnia, Italy **20 D6** 41 36N 14 14 E
Ishigaki-Shima, Japan **31 M2** 24 20N 124 10 E
Ishikari-Gawa —►, Japan **30 C10** 43 15N 141 23 E
Ishikari-Sammyaku, Japan **30 C11** 43 30N 143 0 E
Ishikari-Wan, Japan **30 C10** 43 25N 141 1 E
Ishikawa □, Japan **31 F8** 36 30N 136 30 E
Ishim, Russia **26 D7** 56 10N 69 30 E
Ishim —►, Russia **26 D8** 57 45N 71 10 E
Ishinomaki, Japan **30 E10** 38 32N 141 20 E
Ishioka, Japan **31 F10** 36 11N 140 16 E
Ishkuman, Pakistan **43 A5** 36 30N 73 50 E
Ishpeming, U.S.A. **76 B2** 46 29N 87 40W
Isil Kul, Russia **26 D8** 54 55N 71 16 E
Isiolo, Kenya **54 B4** 0 24N 37 33 E
Isiolo □, Kenya **54 B4** 2 30N 37 30 E
Isiro, Zaïre **54 B2** 2 53N 27 40 E
Isisford, Australia **62 C3** 24 15S 144 21 E
İskenderun, Turkey **25 G6** 36 32N 36 10 E
İskenderun Körfezi, Turkey **25 G6** 36 40N 35 50 E
Iskŭr —►, Bulgaria **21 C11** 43 45N 24 25 E
Iskut —►, Canada **72 B2** 56 45N 131 49W
Isla —►, U.K. **12 E5** 56 32N 3 20W
Isla Vista, U.S.A. **85 L7** 34 25N 119 53W
Islamabad, Pakistan **42 C5** 33 40N 73 10 E
Islamkot, Pakistan **42 G4** 24 42N 70 13 E
Island —►, Canada **72 A4** 60 25N 121 12W
Island Falls, Canada **70 C3** 49 35N 81 20W
Island Falls, U.S.A. **71 C6** 46 1N 68 16W
Island L., Canada **73 C10** 53 47N 94 25W
Island Lagoon, Australia **63 E2** 31 30S 136 40 E
Island Pond, U.S.A. **79 B13** 44 49N 71 53W
Islands, B. of, Canada **71 C8** 49 11N 58 15W
Islay, U.K. **12 F2** 55 46N 6 10W
Isle —►, France **18 D3** 44 55N 0 15W
Isle aux Morts, Canada **71 C8** 47 35N 59 0W
Isle of Wight □, U.K. **11 G6** 50 41N 1 17W
Isle Royale, U.S.A. **80 A10** 48 0N 88 54W
Isleta, U.S.A. **83 J10** 34 55N 106 42W
Isleton, U.S.A. **84 G5** 38 10N 121 37W
Ismail = Izmayil, Ukraine **17 F15** 45 22N 28 46 E
Ismâ'ilîya, Egypt **51 B11** 30 37N 32 18 E
Ismay, U.S.A. **80 B2** 46 30N 104 48W
Isna, Egypt **51 C11** 25 17N 32 30 E
Isogstalo, India **43 B8** 34 15N 78 46 E
Isparta, Turkey **25 G5** 37 47N 30 30 E
Ispica, Italy **20 F6** 36 47N 14 55 E
Israel ■, Asia **47 D3** 32 0N 34 50 E
Issoire, France **18 D5** 45 32N 3 15 E
Issyk-Kul = Ysyk-Köl, Kyrgyzstan **28 E11** 42 26N 76 12 E
Issyk-Kul, Ozero = Ysyk-Köl, Ozero, Kyrgyzstan **26 E8** 42 25N 77 15 E
Istaihah, U.A.E. **45 F7** 23 19N 54 4 E
İstanbul, Turkey **21 D13** 41 0N 29 0 E
Istiaía, Greece **21 E10** 38 57N 23 9 E
Istokpoga, L., U.S.A. **77 M5** 27 23N 81 17W
Istra, Croatia **16 F7** 45 10N 14 0 E
Istranca Dağlan, Turkey **21 D12** 41 48N 27 36 E
Istres, France **18 E6** 43 31N 4 59 E
Istria = Istra, Croatia **16 F7** 45 10N 14 0 E
Itá, Paraguay **94 B4** 25 29S 57 21W
Itabaiana, Brazil **93 E11** 7 18S 35 19W
Itaberaba, Brazil **93 F10** 12 32S 40 18W
Itabira, Brazil **93 G10** 19 37S 43 13W
Itabirito, Brazil **95 A7** 20 15S 43 48W
Itabuna, Brazil **93 F11** 14 48S 39 16W
Itaipú, Represa de, Brazil **95 B5** 25 30S 54 30W
Itaituba, Brazil **93 D7** 4 10S 55 50W
Itajaí, Brazil **95 B6** 27 50S 48 39W
Itajubá, Brazil **95 A6** 22 24S 45 30W
Itaka, Tanzania **55 D3** 8 50S 32 49 E
Italy ■, Europe **20 C5** 42 0N 13 0 E
Itampolo, Madag. **57 C7** 24 41S 43 57 E
Itapecuru-Mirim, Brazil **93 D10** 3 24S 44 20W
Itaperuna, Brazil **95 A7** 21 10S 41 54W
Itapetininga, Brazil **95 A6** 23 36S 48 7W
Itapeva, Brazil **95 A6** 23 59S 48 59W
Itapicuru —►, Bahia, Brazil **93 F11** 11 47S 37 32W
Itapicuru —►, Maranhão, Brazil **93 D10** 2 52S 44 12W
Itapipoca, Brazil **93 D11** 3 30S 39 35W
Itapuá □, Paraguay **95 B4** 26 40S 55 40W
Itaquari, Brazil **95 A7** 20 20S 40 25W
Itaquatiara, Brazil **92 D7** 2 58S 58 30W
Itaquí, Brazil **94 B4** 29 8S 56 30W
Itararé, Brazil **95 A6** 24 6S 49 23W
Itarsi, India **42 H7** 22 36N 77 51 E
Itatí, Argentina **94 B4** 27 16S 58 15W
Itatuba, Brazil **92 E6** 5 46S 63 20W
Itchen —►, U.K. **11 G6** 50 55N 1 22W
Itezhi Tezhi, L., Zambia **55 F2** 15 30S 25 30 E
Ithaca = Itháki, Greece **21 E9** 38 25N 20 40 E
Ithaca, U.S.A. **79 D8** 42 27N 76 30W
Itháki, Greece **21 E9** 38 25N 20 40 E
Ito, Japan **31 G9** 34 58N 139 5 E
Itoigawa, Japan **31 F8** 37 2N 137 51 E
Itonamas —►, Bolivia **92 F6** 12 28S 64 24W
Ittoqqortoormiit = Scoresbysund, Greenland **4 B6** 70 20N 23 0W
Itu, Brazil **95 A6** 23 17S 47 15W
Ituaçu, Brazil **93 F10** 13 50S 41 18W
Ituiutaba, Brazil **93 G9** 19 0S 49 25W
Itumbiara, Brazil **93 G9** 18 20S 49 10W
Ituna, Canada **73 C8** 51 10N 103 24W
Itunge Port, Tanzania **55 D3** 9 40S 33 55 E
Iturbe, Argentina **94 A2** 23 0S 65 25W
Ituri —►, Zaïre **54 B2** 1 40N 27 1 E
Iturup, Ostrov, Russia **27 E15** 45 0N 148 0 E
Ituyuro —►, Argentina **94 A3** 22 40S 63 50W
Itzehoe, Germany **16 B5** 53 55N 9 31 E
Ivaí —►, Brazil **95 A5** 23 18S 53 42W
Ivalo, Finland **8 B22** 68 38N 27 35 E
Ivalojoki —►, Finland **8 B22** 68 40N 27 40 E
Ivanava, Belarus **17 B13** 52 7N 25 29 E
Ivanhoe, N.S.W., Australia **63 E3** 32 56S 144 20 E
Ivanhoe, W. Austral., Australia **60 C4** 15 41S 128 41 E
Ivanhoe, U.S.A. **84 J7** 36 23N 119 13W
Ivanhoe L., Canada **73 A7** 60 25N 106 30W
Ivano-Frankivsk, Ukraine **17 D13** 48 40N 24 40 E
Ivano-Frankovsk = Ivano-Frankivsk, Ukraine **17 D13** 48 40N 24 40 E
Ivanovo = Ivanava, Belarus **17 B13** 52 7N 25 29 E
Ivanovo, Russia **24 C7** 57 5N 41 0 E
Ivato, Madag. **57 C8** 20 37S 47 10 E
Ivatsevichy, Belarus **17 B13** 52 43N 25 21 E
Ivdel, Russia **24 B11** 60 42N 60 24 E
Ivinheima —►, Brazil **95 A5** 23 14S 53 42W
Ivohibe, Madag. **57 C8** 22 31S 46 57 E
Ivory Coast ■, Africa **50 G3** 7 30N 5 0W
Ivrea, Italy **20 B2** 45 28N 7 52 E
Ivujivik, Canada **69 B12** 62 24N 77 55W
Iwahig, Phil. **36 C5** 8 36N 117 32 E
Iwaizumi, Japan **30 E10** 39 50N 141 45 E
Iwaki, Japan **31 F10** 37 3N 140 55 E
Iwakuni, Japan **31 G6** 34 15N 132 8 E
Iwamizawa, Japan **30 C10** 43 12N 141 46 E
Iwanai, Japan **30 C10** 42 58N 140 30 E
Iwata, Japan **31 G8** 34 42N 137 51 E
Iwate □, Japan **30 E10** 39 30N 141 30 E
Iwate-San, Japan **30 E10** 39 51N 141 0 E
Iwo, Nigeria **50 G5** 7 39N 4 9 E
Ixiamas, Bolivia **92 F5** 13 50S 68 5W
Ixopo, S. Africa **57 E5** 30 11S 30 5 E
Ixtepec, Mexico **87 D5** 16 32N 95 10W
Ixtlán del Río, Mexico **86 C4** 21 5N 104 21W
Iyo, Japan **31 H6** 33 45N 132 45 E
Izabal, L. de, Guatemala **88 C2** 15 30N 89 10W
Izamal, Mexico **87 C7** 20 56N 89 1W
Izegem, Belgium **15 D3** 50 55N 3 12 E
Izena-Shima, Japan **31 L3** 26 56N 127 56 E
Izhevsk, Russia **24 C9** 56 51N 53 14 E
Izmayil, Ukraine **17 F15** 45 22N 28 46 E
İzmir, Turkey **21 E12** 38 25N 27 8 E
İzmit, Turkey **25 F4** 40 45N 29 50 E
İznik Gölü, Turkey **21 D13** 40 27N 29 30 E
Izra, Syria **47 C5** 32 51N 36 15 E
Izu-Shotō, Japan **31 G10** 34 30N 140 0 E
Izumi-sano, Japan **31 G7** 34 23N 135 18 E
Izumo, Japan **31 G6** 35 20N 132 46 E
Izyaslav, Ukraine **17 C14** 50 5N 26 50 E

Juan de Fuca Str.

J

Jabal Lubnān, *Lebanon* 47 B4 33 45N 35 40 E
Jabalpur, *India* 43 H8 23 9N 79 58 E
Jabbūl, *Syria* 44 B3 36 4N 37 30 E
Jablah, *Syria* 44 C3 35 20N 36 0 E
Jablanica, *Macedonia* 21 D9 41 15N 20 30 E
Jablonec, *Czech.* 16 C8 50 43N 15 10 E
Jaboatão, *Brazil* 93 E11 8 7S 35 1W
Jaboticabal, *Brazil* 95 A6 21 15S 48 17W
Jaburu, *Brazil* 92 E6 5 30S 64 0W
Jaca, *Spain* 19 A5 42 35N 0 33W
Jacareí, *Brazil* 95 A6 23 20S 46 0W
Jacarèzinho, *Brazil* 95 A6 23 5S 49 58W
Jackman, *U.S.A.* 71 C5 45 35N 70 17W
Jacksboro, *U.S.A.* 81 J5 33 14N 98 15W
Jackson, *Australia* 63 D4 26 39S 149 39 E
Jackson, *Ala., U.S.A.* 77 K2 31 31N 87 53W
Jackson, *Calif., U.S.A.* 84 G6 38 21N 120 46W
Jackson, *Ky., U.S.A.* 76 G4 37 33N 83 23W
Jackson, *Mich., U.S.A.* 76 D3 42 15N 84 24W
Jackson, *Minn., U.S.A.* 80 D7 43 37N 95 1W
Jackson, *Miss., U.S.A.* 81 J9 32 18N 90 12W
Jackson, *Mo., U.S.A.* 81 G10 37 23N 89 40W
Jackson, *Ohio, U.S.A.* 76 F4 39 3N 82 39W
Jackson, *Tenn., U.S.A.* 77 H1 35 37N 88 49W
Jackson, *Wyo., U.S.A.* 82 E8 43 29N 110 46W
Jackson B., *N.Z.* 59 K2 43 58S 168 42 E
Jackson L., *U.S.A.* 82 E8 43 52N 110 36W
Jacksons, *N.Z.* 59 K3 42 46S 171 32 E
Jacksonville, *Ala., U.S.A.* 77 J3 33 49N 85 46W
Jacksonville, *Calif., U.S.A.* 84 H6 37 52N 120 24W
Jacksonville, *Fla., U.S.A.* 77 K5 30 20N 81 39W
Jacksonville, *Ill., U.S.A.* 80 F9 39 44N 90 14W
Jacksonville, *N.C., U.S.A.* 77 H7 34 45N 77 26W
Jacksonville, *Oreg., U.S.A.* 82 E2 42 19N 122 57W
Jacksonville, *Tex., U.S.A.* 81 K7 31 58N 95 17W
Jacksonville Beach, *U.S.A.* 77 K5 30 17N 81 24W
Jacmel, *Haiti* 89 C5 18 14N 72 32W
Jacob Lake, *U.S.A.* 83 H7 36 43N 112 13W
Jacobabad, *Pakistan* 42 E3 28 20N 68 29 E
Jacobina, *Brazil* 93 F10 11 11S 40 30W
Jacques-Cartier, Mt., *Canada* 71 C6 48 57N 66 0W
Jacuí →, *Brazil* 95 C5 30 2S 51 15W
Jacumba, *U.S.A.* 85 N10 32 37N 116 11W
Jacundá →, *Brazil* 93 D8 1 57S 50 26W
Jadotville = Likasi, *Zaïre* 55 E2 10 55S 26 48 E
Jādū, *Libya* 51 B7 32 0N 12 0 E
Jaén, *Peru* 92 E3 5 25S 78 40W
Jaén, *Spain* 19 D4 37 44N 3 43W
Jaffa = Tel Aviv-Yafo, *Israel* 47 C3 32 4N 34 48 E
Jaffa, C., *Australia* 63 F2 36 58S 139 40 E
Jaffna, *Sri Lanka* 40 Q12 9 45N 80 2 E
Jagadhri, *India* 42 D7 30 10N 77 20 E
Jagadishpur, *India* 43 G11 25 30N 84 21 E
Jagdalpur, *India* 41 K12 19 3N 82 0 E
Jagersfontein, *S. Africa* 56 D4 29 44S 25 27 E
Jagraon, *India* 40 D9 30 50N 75 25 E
Jagtial, *India* 40 K11 18 50N 79 0 E
Jaguariaíva, *Brazil* 95 A6 24 10S 49 50W
Jaguaribe →, *Brazil* 93 D11 4 25S 37 45W
Jagüey Grande, *Cuba* 88 B3 22 35N 81 7W
Jahangirabad, *India* 42 E8 28 19N 78 4 E
Jahrom, *Iran* 45 D7 28 30N 53 31 E
Jailolo, *Indonesia* 37 D7 1 5N 127 30 E
Jailolo, Selat, *Indonesia* 37 D7 0 5N 129 5 E
Jaipur, *India* 42 F6 27 0N 75 50 E
Jājarm, *Iran* 45 B8 36 58N 56 27 E
Jakarta, *Indonesia* 37 G12 6 9S 106 49 E
Jakobstad = Pietarsaari, *Finland* 8 E20 63 40N 22 43 E
Jal, *U.S.A.* 81 J3 32 7N 103 12W
Jalalabad, *Afghan.* 42 B4 34 30N 70 29 E
Jalalabad, *India* 43 F8 27 41N 79 42 E
Jalalpur Jattan, *Pakistan* 42 C6 32 38N 74 11 E
Jalama, *U.S.A.* 85 L6 34 29N 120 29W
Jalapa, *Guatemala* 88 D2 14 39N 89 59W
Jalapa Enríquez, *Mexico* 87 D5 19 32N 96 55W
Jalasjärvi, *Finland* 9 E20 62 29N 22 47 E
Jalaun, *India* 43 F8 26 8N 79 25 E
Jaleswar, *Nepal* 43 F11 26 38N 85 48 E
Jalgaon, *Maharashtra, India* 40 J10 21 2N 76 31 E
Jalgaon, *Maharashtra, India* 40 J9 21 0N 75 42 E
Jalībah, *Iraq* 44 D5 30 35N 46 32 E
Jalisco □, *Mexico* 86 C4 20 0N 104 0W
Jalkot, *Pakistan* 43 B5 35 14N 73 24 E
Jalna, *India* 40 K9 19 48N 75 38 E
Jalón →, *Spain* 19 B5 41 47N 1 4W
Jalpa, *Mexico* 86 C4 21 38N 102 58W
Jalpaiguri, *India* 41 F16 26 32N 88 46 E
Jaluit I., *Pac. Oc.* 64 G8 6 0N 169 30 E
Jalūlā, *Iraq* 44 C5 34 16N 45 10 E
Jamaica ■, *W. Indies* 88 C4 18 10N 77 30W
Jamalpur, *Bangla.* 41 G16 24 52N 89 56 E
Jamalpur, *India* 43 G12 25 18N 86 28 E
Jamalpurganj, *India* 43 H13 23 2N 88 1 E
Jamanxim →, *Brazil* 93 D7 4 43S 56 18W
Jambe, *Indonesia* 37 E8 1 15S 132 10 E
Jambi, *Indonesia* 36 E2 1 38S 103 30 E
Jambi □, *Indonesia* 36 E2 1 30S 102 30 E
Jambusar, *India* 42 H5 22 3N 72 51 E
James →, *U.S.A.* 80 D6 42 52N 97 18W
James B., *Canada* 69 C11 51 30N 80 0W
James Ras., *Australia* 60 D5 24 10S 132 30 E
James Ross I., *Antarctica* 5 C18 63 58S 57 50W
Jamestown, *Australia* 63 E2 33 10S 138 32 E
Jamestown, *S. Africa* 56 E4 31 6S 26 45 E
Jamestown, *Ky., U.S.A.* 76 G3 36 59N 85 4W
Jamestown, *N. Dak., U.S.A.* 80 B5 46 54N 98 42W
Jamestown, *N.Y., U.S.A.* 78 D5 42 6N 79 14W
Jamestown, *Pa., U.S.A.* 78 E4 41 29N 80 27W
Jamestown, *Tenn., U.S.A.* 77 G3 36 26N 84 56W
Jamīlābād, *Iran* 45 C6 34 24N 48 28 E
Jamiltepec, *Mexico* 87 D5 16 17N 97 49W
Jamkhandi, *India* 40 L9 16 30N 75 15 E
Jammu, *India* 42 C6 32 43N 74 54 E
Jammu & Kashmir □, *India* 43 B7 34 25N 77 0 E
Jamnagar, *India* 42 H4 22 30N 70 6 E
Jampur, *Pakistan* 42 E4 29 39N 70 40 E
Jamrud, *Pakistan* 42 C4 33 59N 71 24 E
Jämsä, *Finland* 9 F21 61 53N 25 10 E
Jamshedpur, *India* 43 H12 22 44N 86 12 E
Jamtara, *India* 43 H12 23 59N 86 49 E
Jämtland, *Sweden* 8 E15 63 31N 14 0 E
Jan L., *Canada* 73 C8 54 56N 102 55W
Jan Mayen, *Arctic* 4 B7 71 0N 9 0W
Janakkala, *Finland* 9 F21 60 54N 24 36 E
Jand, *Pakistan* 42 C5 33 30N 72 6 E
Jandaq, *Iran* 45 C7 34 3N 54 22 E
Jandia, *Canary Is.* 22 F5 28 6N 14 21W
Jandia, Pta. de, *Canary Is.* 22 F5 28 3N 14 31W
Jandola, *Pakistan* 42 C4 32 20N 70 9 E
Jandowae, *Australia* 63 D5 26 45S 151 7 E
Janesville, *U.S.A.* 80 D10 42 41N 89 1W
Janīn, *West Bank* 47 C4 32 28N 35 18 E
Janos, *Mexico* 86 A3 30 45N 108 10W
Januária, *Brazil* 93 G10 15 25S 44 25W
Janubio, *Canary Is.* 22 F6 28 56N 13 50W
Jaora, *India* 42 H6 23 40N 75 10 E
Japan ■, *Asia* 31 G8 36 0N 136 0 E
Japan, Sea of, *Asia* 30 E7 40 0N 135 0 E
Japan Trench, *Pac. Oc.* 28 F18 32 0N 142 0 E
Japen = Yapen, *Indonesia* 37 E9 1 50S 136 0 E
Japurá →, *Brazil* 92 D5 3 8S 65 46W
Jaque, *Panama* 92 B3 7 27N 78 8W
Jarābulus, *Syria* 44 B3 36 49N 38 1 E
Jarama →, *Spain* 19 B4 40 24N 3 32W
Jaranwala, *Pakistan* 42 D5 31 15N 73 26 E
Jarash, *Jordan* 47 C4 32 17N 35 54 E
Jardim, *Brazil* 94 A4 21 28S 56 2W
Jardines de la Reina, Is., *Cuba* 88 B4 20 50N 78 50W
Jargalang, *China* 35 C12 43 5N 122 55 E
Jargalant = Hovd, *Mongolia* 32 B4 48 2N 91 37 E
Jarīr, W. al →, *Si. Arabia* 44 E4 25 38N 42 30 E
Jarosław, *Poland* 17 C12 50 2N 22 42 E
Jarrahdale, *Australia* 61 F2 32 24S 116 5 E
Jarres, Plaine des, *Laos* 38 C4 19 27N 103 10 E
Jarso, *Ethiopia* 51 G12 5 15N 37 30 E
Jartai, *China* 34 E3 39 45N 105 48 E
Jarud Qi, *China* 35 B11 44 28N 120 50 E
Järvenpää, *Finland* 9 F21 60 29N 25 5 E
Jarvis, *Canada* 78 D4 42 53N 80 6W
Jarvis I., *Pac. Oc.* 65 H12 0 15S 159 55W
Jarwa, *India* 43 F10 27 38N 82 30 E
Jāsimīyah, *Iraq* 44 C5 33 45N 44 41 E
Jasin, *Malaysia* 39 L4 2 20N 102 26 E
Jāsk, *Iran* 45 E8 25 38N 57 45 E
Jasło, *Poland* 17 D11 49 45N 21 30 E
Jasper, *Alta., Canada* 72 C5 52 55N 118 5W
Jasper, *Ont., Canada* 79 B9 44 52N 75 57W
Jasper, *Ala., U.S.A.* 77 J2 33 50N 87 17W
Jasper, *Fla., U.S.A.* 77 K4 30 31N 82 57W
Jasper, *Minn., U.S.A.* 80 D6 43 51N 96 24W
Jasper, *Tex., U.S.A.* 81 K8 30 56N 94 1W
Jasper Nat. Park, *Canada* 72 C5 52 50N 118 8W
Jászberény, *Hungary* 17 E10 47 30N 19 55 E
Jataí, *Brazil* 93 G8 17 58S 51 48W
Jati, *Pakistan* 42 G3 24 20N 68 19 E
Jatibarang, *Indonesia* 37 G13 6 28S 108 18 E
Jatinegara, *Indonesia* 37 G12 6 13S 106 52 E
Játiva, *Spain* 19 C5 39 0N 0 32W
Jaú, *Brazil* 95 A6 22 10S 48 30W
Jauja, *Peru* 92 F3 11 45S 75 15W
Jaunpur, *India* 43 G10 25 46N 82 44 E
Java = Jawa, *Indonesia* 37 G14 7 0S 110 0 E
Java Sea, *Indonesia* 36 E3 4 35S 107 15 E
Java Trench, *Ind. Oc.* 64 H2 9 0S 105 0 E
Javhlant = Ulyasutay, *Mongolia* 32 B4 47 56N 97 28 E
Jawa, *Indonesia* 37 G14 7 0S 110 0 E
Jay, *U.S.A.* 81 G7 36 25N 94 48W
Jaya, Puncak, *Indonesia* 37 E9 3 57S 137 17 E
Jayanti, *India* 41 F16 26 45N 89 40 E
Jayapura, *Indonesia* 37 E10 2 28S 140 38 E
Jayawijaya, Pegunungan, *Indonesia* 37 E9 5 0S 139 0 E
Jaynagar, *India* 41 F15 26 43N 86 9 E
Jayrūd, *Syria* 44 C3 33 49N 36 44 E
Jayton, *U.S.A.* 81 J4 33 15N 100 34W
Jazīreh-ye Shīf, *Iran* 45 D6 29 4N 50 54 E
Jazminal, *Mexico* 86 C4 24 56N 101 25W
Jazzīn, *Lebanon* 47 B4 33 31N 35 35 E
Jean, *U.S.A.* 85 K11 35 47N 115 20W
Jean Marie River, *Canada* 72 A4 61 32N 120 38W
Jean Rabel, *Haiti* 89 C5 19 50N 73 5W
Jeanerette, *U.S.A.* 81 L9 29 55N 91 40W
Jeanette, Ostrov, *Russia* 27 B16 76 43N 158 0 E
Jeannette, *U.S.A.* 78 F5 40 20N 79 36W
Jebba, *Nigeria* 50 G5 9 9N 4 48 E
Jebel, Bahr el →, *Sudan* 51 G11 9 30N 30 25 E
Jedburgh, *U.K.* 12 F6 55 29N 2 33W
Jedda = Jiddah, *Si. Arabia* 46 C2 21 29N 39 10 E
Jędrzejów, *Poland* 17 C11 50 35N 20 15 E
Jedway, *Canada* 72 C2 52 17N 131 14W
Jefferson, *Iowa, U.S.A.* 80 D7 42 1N 94 23W
Jefferson, *Ohio, U.S.A.* 78 E4 41 44N 80 46W
Jefferson, *Tex., U.S.A.* 81 J7 32 46N 94 21W
Jefferson, *Wis., U.S.A.* 80 D10 43 0N 88 48W
Jefferson, Mt., *Nev., U.S.A.* 82 G5 38 51N 117 0W
Jefferson, Mt., *Oreg., U.S.A.* 82 D3 44 41N 121 48W
Jefferson City, *Mo., U.S.A.* 80 F8 38 34N 92 10W
Jefferson City, *Tenn., U.S.A.* 77 G4 36 7N 83 30W
Jeffersonville, *U.S.A.* 76 F3 38 17N 85 44W
Jega, *Nigeria* 50 F5 12 15N 4 23 E
Jēkabpils, *Latvia* 9 H21 56 29N 25 57 E
Jelenia Góra, *Poland* 16 C8 50 50N 15 45 E
Jelgava, *Latvia* 9 H20 56 41N 23 49 E
Jellicoe, *Canada* 70 C2 49 40N 87 30W
Jemaja, *Indonesia* 36 D3 3 5N 105 45 E
Jemaluang, *Malaysia* 39 L4 2 16N 103 52 E
Jember, *Indonesia* 37 H15 8 11S 113 41 E
Jembongan, *Malaysia* 36 C5 6 45N 117 20 E
Jemeppe, *Belgium* 15 D5 50 37N 5 30 E
Jena, *Germany* 16 C6 50 54N 11 35 E
Jena, *U.S.A.* 81 K8 31 41N 92 8W
Jenkins, *U.S.A.* 76 G4 37 10N 82 38W
Jenner, *U.S.A.* 84 G3 38 27N 123 7W
Jennings, *U.S.A.* 81 K8 30 13N 92 40W
Jennings →, *Canada* 72 B2 59 38N 132 5W
Jeparit, *Australia* 63 F3 36 8S 142 1 E
Jequié, *Brazil* 93 F10 13 51S 40 5W
Jequitinhonha, *Brazil* 93 G10 16 30S 41 0W
Jequitinhonha →, *Brazil* 93 G11 15 51S 38 53W
Jerada, *Morocco* 50 B4 34 17N 2 10W
Jerantut, *Malaysia* 39 L4 3 56N 102 22 E
Jérémie, *Haiti* 89 C5 18 40N 74 10W
Jerez, Punta, *Mexico* 87 C5 22 58N 97 40W
Jerez de García Salinas, *Mexico* 86 C4 22 39N 103 0W
Jerez de la Frontera, *Spain* 19 D2 36 41N 6 7W
Jerez de los Caballeros, *Spain* 19 C2 38 20N 6 45W
Jericho = Arīḩā, *Syria* 44 C3 35 49N 36 35 E
Jericho = El Arīḩā, *West Bank* 47 D4 31 52N 35 27 E
Jericho, *Australia* 62 C4 23 38S 146 6 E
Jerilderie, *Australia* 63 F4 35 20S 145 41 E
Jermyn, *U.S.A.* 79 E9 41 31N 75 31W
Jerome, *U.S.A.* 83 J8 34 45N 112 7W
Jersey, *U.K.* 11 H5 49 11N 2 7W
Jersey City, *U.S.A.* 79 F10 40 44N 74 4W
Jersey Shore, *U.S.A.* 78 E7 41 12N 77 15W
Jerseyville, *U.S.A.* 80 F9 39 7N 90 20W
Jerusalem, *Israel* 47 D4 31 47N 35 10 E
Jervis B., *Australia* 63 F5 35 8S 150 46 E
Jesselton = Kota Kinabalu, *Malaysia* 36 C5 6 0N 116 4 E
Jessore, *Bangla.* 41 H16 23 10N 89 10 E
Jesup, *U.S.A.* 77 K5 31 36N 81 53W
Jesús Carranza, *Mexico* 87 D5 17 28N 95 1W
Jesús María, *Argentina* 94 C3 30 59S 64 5W
Jetmore, *U.S.A.* 81 F5 38 4N 99 54W
Jetpur, *India* 42 J4 21 45N 70 10 E
Jevnaker, *Norway* 9 F14 60 15N 10 26 E
Jewett, *Ohio, U.S.A.* 78 F3 40 22N 81 2W
Jewett, *Tex., U.S.A.* 81 K6 31 22N 96 9W
Jewett City, *U.S.A.* 79 E13 41 36N 72 0W
Jeyḩūnābād, *Iran* 45 C6 34 58N 48 59 E
Jeypore, *India* 41 K13 18 50N 82 38 E
Jhajjar, *India* 42 E7 28 37N 76 42 E
Jhal Jhao, *Pakistan* 40 F4 26 20N 65 35 E
Jhalawar, *India* 42 G7 24 40N 76 10 E
Jhang Maghiana, *Pakistan* 42 D5 31 15N 72 22 E
Jhansi, *India* 43 G8 25 30N 78 36 E
Jharia, *India* 43 H12 23 45N 86 26 E
Jharsuguda, *India* 41 J14 21 56N 84 5 E
Jhelum, *Pakistan* 42 C5 33 0N 73 45 E
Jhelum →, *Pakistan* 42 D5 31 20N 72 10 E
Jhunjhunu, *India* 42 E6 28 10N 75 30 E
Ji Xian, *Hebei, China* 34 F8 37 35N 115 30 E
Ji Xian, *Henan, China* 34 G8 35 22N 114 5 E
Ji Xian, *Shanxi, China* 34 F6 36 7N 110 40 E
Jia Xian, *Henan, China* 34 H7 33 59N 113 12 E
Jia Xian, *Shaanxi, China* 34 E6 38 12N 110 28 E
Jiamusi, *China* 33 B8 46 40N 130 26 E
Ji'an, *Jiangxi, China* 33 D6 27 6N 114 59 E
Ji'an, *Jilin, China* 35 D14 41 5N 126 10 E
Jianchang, *China* 35 D11 40 55N 120 35 E
Jianchangying, *China* 35 D10 40 10N 118 50 E
Jiangcheng, *China* 32 D5 22 36N 101 52 E
Jiangmen, *China* 33 D6 22 32N 113 0 E
Jiangsu □, *China* 35 H10 33 0N 120 0 E
Jiangxi □, *China* 33 D6 27 30N 116 0 E
Jiao Xian, *China* 35 F11 36 18N 120 1 E
Jiaohe, *Hebei, China* 34 E9 38 2N 116 20 E
Jiaohe, *Jilin, China* 35 C14 43 40N 127 22 E
Jiaozhou Wan, *China* 35 F11 36 5N 120 10 E
Jiaozuo, *China* 34 G7 35 16N 113 12 E
Jiawang, *China* 35 G9 34 28N 117 26 E
Jiaxiang, *China* 34 G9 35 25N 116 20 E
Jiaxing, *China* 33 C7 30 49N 120 45 E
Jiayi = Chiai, *Taiwan* 33 D7 23 29N 120 25 E
Jibuti = Djibouti ■, *Africa* 46 E3 12 0N 43 0 E
Jicarón, I., *Panama* 88 E3 7 10N 81 50W
Jiddah, *Si. Arabia* 46 C2 21 29N 39 10 E
Jido, *India* 41 E19 29 2N 94 58 E
Jieshou, *China* 34 H8 33 18N 115 22 E
Jiexiu, *China* 34 F6 37 2N 111 55 E
Jiggalong, *Australia* 60 D3 23 21S 120 47 E
Jihlava, *Czech.* 16 D8 49 28N 15 35 E
Jihlava →, *Czech.* 17 D9 48 55N 16 36 E
Jijel, *Algeria* 50 A6 36 52N 5 50 E
Jijiga, *Ethiopia* 46 F3 9 20N 42 50 E
Jilin, *China* 35 C14 43 44N 126 30 E
Jilin □, *China* 35 C13 44 0N 127 0 E
Jilong = Chilung, *Taiwan* 33 D7 25 3N 121 45 E
Jima, *Ethiopia* 51 G12 7 40N 36 47 E
Jiménez, *Mexico* 86 B4 27 10N 104 54W
Jimo, *China* 35 F11 36 23N 120 30 E
Jin Xian, *Hebei, China* 34 E8 38 2N 115 2 E
Jin Xian, *Liaoning, China* 35 E11 38 55N 121 42 E
Jinan, *China* 34 F9 36 38N 117 1 E
Jincheng, *China* 34 G7 35 29N 112 50 E
Jind, *India* 42 E7 29 19N 76 22 E
Jindabyne, *Australia* 63 F4 36 25S 148 35 E
Jindrichuv Hradeç, *Czech.* 16 D8 49 10N 15 2 E
Jing He →, *China* 34 G5 34 27N 109 4 E
Jingbian, *China* 34 F5 37 20N 108 30 E
Jingchuan, *China* 34 G4 35 20N 107 20 E
Jingdezhen, *China* 33 D6 29 20N 117 11 E
Jinggu, *China* 32 D5 23 35N 100 41 E
Jinghai, *China* 34 E9 38 55N 116 55 E
Jingle, *China* 34 E6 38 20N 111 55 E
Jingning, *China* 34 G3 35 30N 105 43 E
Jingpo Hu, *China* 35 C15 43 55N 128 55 E
Jingtai, *China* 34 F3 37 10N 104 6 E
Jingxing, *China* 34 E8 38 2N 114 8 E
Jingyang, *China* 34 G5 34 30N 108 50 E
Jingyu, *China* 35 C14 42 25N 126 45 E
Jingyuan, *China* 34 F3 36 30N 104 40 E
Jingziguan, *China* 34 H6 33 15N 111 0 E
Jinhua, *China* 33 D6 29 8N 119 38 E
Jining, *Nei Mongol Zizhiqu, China* 34 D7 41 5N 113 0 E
Jining, *Shandong, China* 34 G9 35 22N 116 34 E
Jinja, *Uganda* 54 B3 0 25N 33 12 E
Jinjang, *Malaysia* 39 L3 3 13N 101 39 E
Jinji, *China* 34 F4 37 58N 106 8 E
Jinnah Barrage, *Pakistan* 40 C7 32 58N 71 33 E
Jinotega, *Nic.* 88 D2 13 6N 85 59W
Jinotepe, *Nic.* 88 D2 11 50N 86 10W
Jinsha Jiang →, *China* 32 D5 28 50N 104 36 E
Jinxi, *China* 35 D11 40 52N 120 50 E
Jinxiang, *China* 34 G9 35 5N 116 22 E
Jinzhou, *China* 35 D11 41 5N 121 3 E
Jiparaná →, *Brazil* 92 E6 8 3S 62 52W
Jipijapa, *Ecuador* 92 D2 1 0S 80 40W
Jiquilpan, *Mexico* 86 D4 19 57N 102 42W
Jishan, *China* 34 G6 35 34N 110 58 E
Jisr ash Shughūr, *Syria* 44 C3 35 49N 36 18 E
Jitarning, *Australia* 61 F2 32 48S 117 57 E
Jitra, *Malaysia* 39 J3 6 16N 100 25 E
Jiu →, *Romania* 17 F12 43 47N 23 48 E
Jiudengkou, *China* 34 E4 39 56N 106 40 E
Jiujiang, *China* 33 D6 29 42N 115 58 E
Jiutai, *China* 35 E13 44 10N 125 50 E
Jiuxiangcheng, *China* 34 H8 33 12N 114 50 E
Jiuxincheng, *China* 34 E8 39 17N 115 59 E
Jixi, *China* 35 B16 45 20N 130 50 E
Jiyang, *China* 35 F9 37 0N 117 12 E
Jīzān, *Si. Arabia* 46 D3 17 0N 42 20 E
Jize, *China* 34 F8 36 54N 114 56 E
Jizō-Zaki, *Japan* 31 G6 35 34N 133 20 E
Jizzakh, *Uzbekistan* 26 E7 40 6N 67 50 E
Joaçaba, *Brazil* 95 B5 27 5S 51 31W
João Pessoa, *Brazil* 93 E12 7 10S 34 52W
Joaquín V González, *Argentina* 94 B3 25 10S 64 0W
Jodhpur, *India* 42 F5 26 23N 73 8 E
Joensuu, *Finland* 24 B4 62 37N 29 49 E
Jofane, *Mozam.* 57 C5 21 15S 34 18 E
Jõgeva, *Estonia* 9 G22 58 45N 26 24 E
Joggins, *Canada* 71 C7 45 42N 64 27W
Jogjakarta = Yogyakarta, *Indonesia* 37 G14 7 49S 110 22 E
Johannesburg, *S. Africa* 57 D4 26 10S 28 2 E
Johannesburg, *U.S.A.* 85 K9 35 22N 117 38W
John Day, *U.S.A.* 82 D4 44 25N 118 57W
John Day →, *U.S.A.* 82 D3 45 44N 120 39W
John H. Kerr Reservoir, *U.S.A.* 77 G6 36 36N 78 18W
John o' Groats, *U.K.* 12 C5 58 38N 3 4W
Johnnie, *U.S.A.* 85 J10 36 25N 116 5W
John's Ra., *Australia* 62 C1 21 55S 133 23 E
Johnson, *U.S.A.* 81 G4 37 34N 101 45W
Johnson City, *N.Y., U.S.A.* 79 D9 42 7N 75 58W
Johnson City, *Tenn., U.S.A.* 77 G4 36 19N 82 21W
Johnson City, *Tex., U.S.A.* 81 K5 30 17N 98 25W
Johnsonburg, *U.S.A.* 78 E6 41 29N 78 41W
Johnsondale, *U.S.A.* 85 K8 35 58N 118 32W
Johnson's Crossing, *Canada* 72 A2 60 29N 133 18W
Johnston, L., *Australia* 61 F3 32 25S 120 30 E
Johnston Falls = Mambilima Falls, *Zambia* 55 E2 10 31S 28 45 E
Johnston I., *Pac. Oc.* 65 F11 17 10N 169 8W
Johnstone Str., *Canada* 72 C3 50 28N 126 0W
Johnstown, *N.Y., U.S.A.* 79 C10 43 0N 74 22W
Johnstown, *Pa., U.S.A.* 78 F6 40 20N 78 55W
Johor Baharu, *Malaysia* 39 M4 1 28N 103 46 E
Jõhvi, *Estonia* 9 G22 59 22N 27 27 E
Joinvile, *Brazil* 95 B6 26 15S 48 55W
Joinville I., *Antarctica* 5 C18 65 0S 55 30W
Jojutla, *Mexico* 87 D5 18 37N 99 11W
Jokkmokk, *Sweden* 8 C18 66 35N 19 50 E
Jökulsá á Bru →, *Iceland* 8 D6 65 40N 14 16W
Jökulsá á Fjöllum →, *Iceland* 8 C5 66 10N 16 30W
Jolfā, *Āzarbājān-e Sharqī, Iran* 44 B5 38 57N 45 38 E
Jolfā, *Eşfahan, Iran* 45 C6 32 58N 51 37 E
Joliet, *U.S.A.* 76 E1 41 32N 88 5W
Joliette, *Canada* 70 C5 46 3N 73 24W
Jolo, *Phil.* 37 C6 6 0N 121 0 E
Jolon, *U.S.A.* 84 K5 35 58N 121 9W
Jombang, *Indonesia* 37 G15 7 33S 112 14 E
Jome, *Indonesia* 37 E7 1 16S 127 30 E
Jonava, *Lithuania* 9 J21 55 8N 24 12 E
Jones Sound, *Canada* 4 B3 76 0N 85 0W
Jonesboro, *Ark., U.S.A.* 81 H9 35 50N 90 42W
Jonesboro, *Ill., U.S.A.* 81 G10 37 27N 89 16W
Jonesboro, *La., U.S.A.* 81 J8 32 15N 92 43W
Jonesport, *U.S.A.* 71 D6 44 32N 67 37W
Joniškis, *Lithuania* 9 H20 56 13N 23 35 E
Jönköping, *Sweden* 9 H16 57 45N 14 10 E
Jonquière, *Canada* 71 C5 48 27N 71 14W
Joplin, *U.S.A.* 81 G7 37 6N 94 31W
Jordan, *U.S.A.* 82 C10 47 19N 106 55W
Jordan ■, *Asia* 47 E5 31 0N 36 0 E
Jordan →, *Asia* 47 D4 31 48N 35 32 E
Jordan Valley, *U.S.A.* 82 E5 42 59N 117 3W
Jorhat, *India* 41 F19 26 45N 94 12 E
Jörn, *Sweden* 8 D19 65 4N 20 1 E
Jorong, *Indonesia* 36 E4 3 58S 114 56 E
Jørpeland, *Norway* 9 G11 59 3N 6 1 E
Jorquera →, *Chile* 94 B2 28 3S 69 58W
Jos, *Nigeria* 50 G6 9 53N 8 51 E
José Batlle y Ordóñez, *Uruguay* 95 C4 33 20S 55 10W
Joseph, *U.S.A.* 82 D5 45 21N 117 14W
Joseph, L., *Nfld., Canada* 71 B6 52 45N 65 18W
Joseph, L., *Ont., Canada* 78 A5 45 10N 79 44W
Joseph Bonaparte G., *Australia* 60 B4 14 35S 128 50 E
Joseph City, *U.S.A.* 83 J8 34 57N 110 20W
Joshua Tree, *U.S.A.* 85 L10 34 8N 116 19W
Joshua Tree National Monument, *U.S.A.* 85 M10 33 55N 116 0W
Jostedalsbreen, *Norway* 9 F12 61 40N 6 59 E
Jotunheimen, *Norway* 9 F13 61 35N 8 25 E
Jourdanton, *U.S.A.* 81 L5 28 55N 98 33W
Joussard, *Canada* 72 B5 55 22N 115 50W
Jovellanos, *Cuba* 88 B3 22 40N 81 10W
Ju Xian, *China* 35 F10 36 35N 118 20 E
Juan Aldama, *Mexico* 86 C4 24 20N 103 23W
Juan Bautista Alberdi, *Argentina* 94 C3 34 26S 61 48W
Juan de Fuca Str., *Canada* 84 B2 48 15N 124 0W

Juan de Nova

Juan de Nova, *Ind. Oc.* .. **57 B7** 17 3S 43 45 E
Juan Fernández, Arch. de, *Pac. Oc.* **90 G2** 33 50S 80 0W
Juan José Castelli, *Argentina* **94 B3** 25 27S 60 57W
Juan L. Lacaze, *Uruguay* . **94 C4** 34 26S 57 25W
Juankoski, *Finland* ..... **8 E23** 63 3N 28 19 E
Juárez, *Argentina* **94 D4** 37 40S 59 43W
Juárez, *Mexico* **85 N11** 32 20N 115 57W
Juárez, Sierra de, *Mexico* **86 A1** 32 0N 116 0W
Juàzeiro, *Brazil* **93 E10** 9 30S 40 30W
Juàzeiro do Norte, *Brazil* **93 E11** 7 10S 39 18W
Jubayl, *Lebanon* ...... **47 A4** 34 5N 35 39 E
Jubbah, *Si. Arabia* ..... **44 D4** 28 2N 40 56 E
Jubbulpore = Jabalpur, *India* .... **43 H8** 23 9N 79 58 E
Jubilee L., *Australia* .... **61 E4** 29 0S 126 50 E
Juby, C., *Morocco* **50 C2** 28 0N 12 59W
Júcar ─►, *Spain* **19 C5** 39 5N 0 10W
Júcaro, *Cuba* **88 B4** 21 37N 78 51W
Juchitán, *Mexico* **87 D5** 16 27N 95 5W
Judaea = Har Yehuda, *Israel* .... **47 D3** 31 35N 34 57 E
Judith ─►, *U.S.A.* **82 C9** 47 44N 109 39W
Judith, Pt., *U.S.A.* **79 E13** 41 22N 71 29W
Judith Gap, *U.S.A.* **82 C9** 46 41N 109 45W
Jugoslavia = Yugoslavia ■, *Europe* . **21 B9** 44 0N 20 0 E
Juigalpa, *Nic.* **88 D2** 12 6N 85 26W
Juiz de Fora, *Brazil* **95 A7** 21 43S 43 19W
Jujuy □, *Argentina* **94 A2** 23 20S 65 40W
Julesburg, *U.S.A.* **80 E3** 40 59N 102 16W
Juli, *Peru* **92 G5** 16 10S 69 25W
Julia Cr. ─►, *Australia* .. **62 C3** 20 0S 141 11 E
Julia Creek, *Australia* ... **62 C3** 20 39S 141 44 E
Juliaca, *Peru* **92 G4** 15 25S 70 10W
Julian, *U.S.A.* **85 M10** 33 4N 116 38W
Julianehåb, *Greenland* .. **4 C5** 60 43N 46 0W
Julimes, *Mexico* **86 B3** 28 25N 105 27W
Jullundur, *India* .... **42 D6** 31 20N 75 40 E
Julu, *China* .... **34 F8** 37 15N 115 2 E
Jumbo, *Zimbabwe* ..... **55 F3** 17 30S 30 58 E
Jumbo Pk., *U.S.A.* **85 J12** 36 12N 114 11W
Jumentos Cays, *Bahamas* **89 B4** 23 0N 75 40W
Jumet, *Belgium* .... **15 D4** 50 27N 4 25 E
Jumilla, *Spain* **19 C5** 38 28N 1 19W
Jumla, *Nepal* .... **43 E10** 29 15N 82 13 E
Jumna = Yamuna ─►, *India* .... **43 G9** 25 30N 81 53 E
Junagadh, *India* .... **42 J4** 21 30N 70 30 E
Junction, *Tex., U.S.A.* ... **81 K5** 30 29N 99 46W
Junction, *Utah, U.S.A.* ... **83 G7** 38 14N 112 13W
Junction B., *Australia* ... **62 A1** 11 52S 133 55 E
Junction City, *Kans., U.S.A.* **80 F6** 39 2N 96 50W
Junction City, *Oreg., U.S.A.* **82 D2** 44 13N 123 12W
Junction Pt., *Australia* ... **62 A1** 11 45S 133 50 E
Jundah, *Australia* ...... **62 C3** 24 46S 143 2 E
Jundiaí, *Brazil* **95 A6** 24 30S 47 0W
Juneau, *U.S.A.* **68 C6** 58 18N 134 25W
Junee, *Australia* .... **63 E4** 34 53S 147 35 E
Jungfrau, *Switz.* .... **16 E4** 46 32N 7 58 E
Junggar Pendi, *China* ... **32 B3** 44 30N 86 0 E
Jungshahi, *Pakistan* .... **42 G2** 24 52N 67 44 E
Juniata ─►, *U.S.A.* **78 F7** 40 30N 77 40W
Junín, *Argentina* **94 C3** 34 33S 60 57W
Junín de los Andes, *Argentina* **96 D2** 39 45S 71 0W
Jūniyah, *Lebanon* ..... **47 B4** 33 59N 35 38 E
Juntura, *U.S.A.* **82 E4** 43 45N 118 5W
Jupiter ─►, *Canada* **71 C7** 49 29N 63 37W
Jur, Nahr el ─►, *Sudan* . **51 G10** 8 45N 29 15 E
Jura = Jura, Mts. du, *Europe* .... **18 C7** 46 40N 6 5 E
Jura = Schwäbische Alb, *Germany* .... **16 D5** 48 20N 9 30 E
Jura, *U.K.* **12 F3** 56 0N 5 50W
Jura, Mts. du, *Europe* ... **18 C7** 46 40N 6 5 E
Jura, Sd. of, *U.K.* **12 F3** 55 57N 5 45W
Jurado, *Colombia* **92 B3** 7 7N 77 46W
Jurbarkas, *Lithuania* .... **9 J20** 55 6N 22 47 E
Jūrmala, *Latvia* .... **9 H20** 56 58N 23 34 E
Juruá ─►, *Brazil* **92 D5** 2 37S 65 44W
Juruena ─►, *Brazil* **92 E7** 7 20S 58 3W
Juruti, *Brazil* **93 D7** 2 9S 56 4W
Justo Daract, *Argentina* . **94 C2** 33 52S 65 12W
Juticalpa, *Honduras* **88 D2** 14 40N 86 12W
Jutland = Jylland, *Denmark* .... **9 H13** 56 25N 9 30 E
Juventud, I. de la, *Cuba* . **88 B3** 21 40N 82 40W
Juwain, *Afghan.* .... **40 D2** 31 45N 61 30 E
Jūy Zar, *Iran* .... **44 C5** 33 50N 46 18 E
Juye, *China* .... **34 G9** 35 22N 116 5 E
Jylland, *Denmark* ...... **9 H13** 56 25N 9 30 E
Jyväskylä, *Finland* ..... **9 E21** 62 14N 25 50 E

K

K2, *Pakistan* .... **43 B7** 35 58N 76 32 E
Kaap Plateau, *S. Africa* .. **56 D3** 28 30S 24 0 E
Kaapkruis, *Namibia* ..... **56 C1** 21 55S 13 57 E
Kaapstad = Cape Town, *S. Africa* .... **56 E2** 33 55S 18 22 E
Kabaena, *Indonesia* .... **37 F6** 5 15S 122 0 E
Kabala, *S. Leone* **50 G2** 9 38N 11 37W
Kabale, *Uganda* .... **54 C3** 1 15S 30 0 E
Kabalo, *Zaïre* .... **54 D2** 6 0S 27 0 E
Kabambare, *Zaïre* ..... **54 C2** 4 41S 27 39 E
Kabango, *Zaïre* .... **55 D2** 8 35S 28 30 E
Kabanjahe, *Indonesia* ... **36 D1** 3 6N 98 30 E
Kabara, *Mali* **50 E4** 16 40N 2 50W
Kabardino-Balkar Republic = Kabardino Balkaria □, *Russia* .... **25 F7** 43 30N 43 30 E
Kabardino Balkaria □, *Russia* .... **25 F7** 43 30N 43 30 E
Kabare, *Indonesia* ..... **37 E8** 0 4S 130 58 E
Kabarega Falls, *Uganda* . **54 B3** 2 15N 31 30 E
Kabasalan, *Phil.* .... **37 C6** 7 47N 122 44 E
Kabba, *Nigeria* .... **50 G6** 7 50N 6 3 E
Kabin Buri, *Thailand* .... **38 F3** 13 57N 101 43 E
Kabinakagami L., *Canada* **70 C3** 48 54N 84 25W
Kabīr, Zab al ─►, *Iraq* ... **44 C4** 36 1N 43 24 E
Kabkabīyah, *Sudan* ..... **51 F9** 13 50N 24 0 E
Kabompo, *Zambia* ..... **55 E1** 13 36S 24 14 E
Kabompo ─►, *Zambia* .. **53 G4** 14 10S 23 11 E
Kabondo, *Zaïre* .... **55 D2** 8 58S 25 40 E
Kabongo, *Zaïre* .... **54 D2** 7 22S 25 33 E
Kabra, *Australia* .... **62 C5** 23 25S 150 25 E
Kabūd Gonbad, *Iran* .... **45 B8** 37 5N 59 45 E
Kābul, *Afghan.* .... **42 B3** 34 28N 69 11 E
Kābul □, *Afghan.* ...... **40 B6** 34 30N 69 0 E
Kabul ─►, *Pakistan* .... **42 C5** 33 55N 72 14 E
Kabunga, *Zaïre* .... **54 C2** 1 38S 28 3 E
Kaburuang, *Indonesia* ... **37 D7** 3 50N 126 30 E
Kabwe, *Zambia* .... **55 E2** 14 30S 28 29 E
Kachchh, Gulf of, *India* .. **42 H3** 22 50N 69 15 E
Kachchh, Rann of, *India* . **42 G4** 24 0N 70 0 E
Kachebera, *Zambia* ..... **55 E3** 13 50S 32 50 E
Kachin □, *Burma* .... **41 F20** 26 0N 97 30 E
Kachira, L., *Uganda* .... **54 C3** 0 40S 31 7 E
Kachiry, *Kazakstan* ..... **26 D8** 53 10N 75 50 E
Kachot, *Cambodia* ..... **39 G4** 11 30N 103 3 E
Kaçkar, *Turkey* .... **25 F7** 40 45N 41 10 E
Kadan Kyun, *Burma* .... **36 B1** 12 30N 98 20 E
Kadanai ─►, *Afghan.* ... **42 D1** 31 22N 65 45 E
Kadi, *India* .... **42 H5** 23 18N 72 23 E
Kadina, *Australia* ...... **63 E2** 33 55S 137 43 E
Kadiyevka = Stakhanov, *Ukraine* .... **25 E6** 48 35N 38 40 E
Kadoka, *U.S.A.* **80 D4** 43 50N 101 31W
Kadoma, *Zimbabwe* .... **55 F2** 18 20S 29 52 E
Kâdugli, *Sudan* .... **51 F10** 11 0N 29 45 E
Kaduna, *Nigeria* .... **50 F6** 10 30N 7 21 E
Kaédi, *Mauritania* **50 E2** 16 9N 13 28W
Kaelé, *Cameroon* ...... **51 F7** 10 7N 14 27 E
Kaeng Khoï, *Thailand* ... **38 E3** 14 35N 101 0 E
Kaesŏng, *N. Korea* ..... **35 F14** 37 58N 126 35 E
Kāf, *Si. Arabia* .... **44 D3** 31 25N 37 29 E
Kafakumba, *Zaïre* ...... **52 F4** 9 38S 23 46 E
Kafan = Kapan, *Armenia* **25 G8** 39 18N 46 27 E
Kafanchan, *Nigeria* .... **50 G6** 9 40N 8 20 E
Kaffrine, *Senegal* **50 F1** 14 8N 15 36W
Kafia Kingi, *Sudan* ..... **51 G9** 9 20N 24 25 E
Kafinda, *Zambia* .... **55 E3** 12 32S 30 20 E
Kafirévs, Ákra, *Greece* .. **21 E11** 38 9N 24 38 E
Kafue, *Zambia* .... **55 F2** 15 46S 28 9 E
Kafue ─►, *Zambia* ..... **53 H5** 15 30S 29 0 E
Kafue Flats, *Zambia* .... **55 F2** 15 40S 27 25 E
Kafue Nat. Park, *Zambia* . **55 F2** 15 0S 25 30 E
Kafulwe, *Zambia* .... **55 D2** 9 0S 29 1 E
Kaga, *Afghan.* .... **42 B4** 34 14N 70 10 E
Kaga Bandoro, *C.A.R.* ... **51 G8** 7 0N 19 10 E
Kagan, *Uzbekistan* ..... **26 F7** 39 43N 64 33 E
Kagawa □, *Japan* ...... **31 G6** 34 15N 134 0 E
Kagera □, *Tanzania* .... **54 C3** 2 0S 31 30 E
Kagera ─►, *Uganda* .... **54 C3** 0 57S 31 47 E
Kagoshima, *Japan* ..... **31 J5** 31 35N 130 33 E
Kagoshima □, *Japan* .... **31 J5** 31 30N 130 30 E
Kagul = Cahul, *Moldova* . **17 F15** 45 50N 28 15 E
Kahak, *Iran* .... **45 B6** 36 6N 49 46 E
Kahama, *Tanzania* ..... **54 C3** 4 8S 32 30 E
Kahama □, *Tanzania* .... **54 C3** 3 50S 32 0 E
Kahang, *Malaysia* ...... **39 L4** 2 12N 103 32 E
Kahayan ─►, *Indonesia* . **36 E4** 3 40S 114 0 E
Kahe, *Tanzania* .... **54 C4** 3 30S 37 25 E
Kahemba, *Zaïre* .... **52 F3** 7 18S 18 55 E
Kahniah ─►, *Canada* **72 B4** 58 15N 120 55W
Kahnūj, *Iran* .... **45 E8** 27 55N 57 40 E
Kahoka, *U.S.A.* **80 E9** 40 25N 91 44W
Kahoolawe, *U.S.A.* **74 H16** 20 33N 156 37W
Kahramanmaraş, *Turkey* . **25 G6** 37 37N 36 53 E
Kahuta, *Pakistan* ...... **42 C5** 33 35N 73 24 E
Kai, Kepulauan, *Indonesia* **37 F8** 5 55S 132 45 E
Kai Besar, *Indonesia* .... **37 F8** 5 35S 133 0 E
Kai Is. = Kai, Kepulauan, *Indonesia* .... **37 F8** 5 55S 132 45 E
Kai Kecil, *Indonesia* .... **37 F8** 5 45S 132 40 E
Kaiama, *Nigeria* .... **50 G5** 9 36N 4 1 E
Kaiapoi, *N.Z.* .... **59 K4** 43 24S 172 40 E
Kaieteur Falls, *Guyana* .. **92 B7** 5 1N 59 10W
Kaifeng, *China* .... **34 G8** 34 48N 114 21 E
Kaikohe, *N.Z.* .... **59 F4** 35 25S 173 49 E
Kaikoura, *N.Z.* .... **59 K4** 42 25S 173 43 E
Kaikoura Ra., *N.Z.* ..... **59 J4** 41 59S 173 41 E
Kailu, *China* .... **35 C11** 43 38N 121 18 E
Kailua Kona, *U.S.A.* **74 J17** 19 39N 155 59W
Kaimana, *Indonesia* .... **37 E8** 3 39S 133 45 E
Kaimanawa Mts., *N.Z.* ... **59 H5** 39 15S 175 56 E
Kaimganj, *India* .... **43 F8** 27 33N 79 24 E
Kaimur Hills, *India* ..... **43 G9** 24 30N 82 0 E
Kaingaroa Forest, *N.Z.* .. **59 H6** 38 24S 176 30 E
Kainji Res., *Nigeria* .... **50 F5** 10 1N 4 40 E
Kainuu, *Finland* .... **8 D23** 64 30N 29 7 E
Kaipara Harbour, *N.Z.* ... **59 G5** 36 25S 174 14 E
Kaipokok B., *Canada* **71 B8** 54 54N 59 47W
Kairana, *India* .... **42 E7** 29 24N 77 15 E
Kaironi, *Indonesia* ..... **37 E8** 0 47S 133 40 E
Kairouan, *Tunisia* ..... **50 A7** 35 45N 10 5 E
Kaiserslautern, *Germany* **16 D4** 49 26N 7 45 E
Kaitaia, *N.Z.* .... **59 F4** 35 8S 173 17 E
Kaitangata, *N.Z.* ...... **59 M2** 46 17S 169 51 E
Kaithal, *India* .... **42 E7** 29 48N 76 26 E
Kaitu ─►, *Pakistan* .... **42 C4** 33 10N 70 30 E
Kaiwi Channel, *U.S.A.* ... **74 H16** 21 15N 157 30W
Kaiyuan, *China* .... **35 C13** 42 28N 124 1 E
Kajaani, *Finland* .... **8 D22** 64 17N 27 46 E
Kajabbi, *Australia* ..... **62 B3** 20 0S 140 1 E
Kajana = Kajaani, *Finland* **8 D22** 64 17N 27 46 E
Kajang, *Malaysia* ...... **39 L3** 2 59N 101 48 E
Kajiado, *Kenya* .... **54 C4** 1 53S 36 48 E
Kajiado □, *Kenya* ...... **54 C4** 2 0S 36 30 E
Kajo Kaji, *Sudan* ...... **51 H11** 3 58N 31 40 E
Kaka, *Sudan* .... **51 F11** 10 38N 32 10 E
Kakabeka Falls, *Canada* . **70 C2** 48 24N 89 37W
Kakamas, *S. Africa* ..... **56 D3** 28 45S 20 33 E
Kakamega, *Kenya* ...... **54 B3** 0 20N 34 46 E
Kakamega □, *Kenya* .... **54 B3** 0 20N 34 46 E
Kakanui Mts., *N.Z.* ..... **59 L3** 45 10S 170 30 E
Kake, *Japan* .... **31 G6** 34 36N 132 19 E
Kakegawa, *Japan* ...... **31 G9** 34 45N 138 1 E
Kakeroma-Jima, *Japan* .. **31 K4** 28 8N 129 14 E
Kakhovka, *Ukraine* ..... **25 E5** 46 45N 33 30 E
Kakhovske Vdskh., *Ukraine* **25 E5** 47 5N 34 0 E
Kakinada, *India* .... **41 L13** 16 57N 82 11 E
Kakisa ─►, *Canada* **72 A5** 61 3N 118 10W
Kakisa L., *Canada* **72 A5** 60 56N 117 43W
Kakogawa, *Japan* ...... **31 G7** 34 46N 134 51 E
Kakwa ─►, *Canada* **72 C5** 54 37N 118 28W
Kāl Gūsheh, *Iran* ...... **45 D8** 30 59N 58 12 E
Kal Safīd, *Iran* .... **44 C5** 34 52N 47 23 E
Kalabagh, *Pakistan* .... **42 C4** 33 0N 71 28 E
Kalabahi, *Indonesia* .... **37 F6** 8 13S 124 31 E
Kalabo, *Zambia* .... **53 G4** 14 58S 22 40 E
Kalach, *Russia* .... **25 D7** 50 22N 41 0 E
Kaladan ─►, *Burma* .... **41 J18** 20 20N 93 5 E
Kaladar, *Canada* **78 B7** 44 37N 77 5W
Kalahari, *Africa* .... **56 C3** 24 0S 21 30 E
Kalahari Gemsbok Nat. Park, *S. Africa* ...... **56 D3** 25 30S 20 30 E
Kalajoki, *Finland* ...... **8 D20** 64 12N 24 10 E
Kālak, *Iran* .... **45 E8** 25 29N 59 22 E
Kalakamati, *Botswana* ... **57 C4** 20 40S 27 25 E
Kalakan, *Russia* .... **27 D12** 55 15N 116 45 E
Kalakh, *Syria* .... **44 C3** 34 55N 36 10 E
K'alak'unlun Shank'ou, *Pakistan* .... **43 B7** 35 33N 77 46 E
Kalam, *Pakistan* .... **43 B5** 35 34N 72 30 E
Kalama, *U.S.A.* **84 E4** 46 1N 122 51W
Kalama, *Zaïre* .... **54 C2** 2 52S 28 35 E
Kalámai, *Greece* .... **21 F10** 37 3N 22 10 E
Kalamata = Kalámai, *Greece* .... **21 F10** 37 3N 22 10 E
Kalamazoo, *U.S.A.* **76 D3** 42 17N 85 35W
Kalamazoo ─►, *U.S.A.* .. **76 D2** 42 40N 86 10W
Kalambo Falls, *Tanzania* . **55 D3** 8 37S 31 35 E
Kalannie, *Australia* ..... **61 F2** 30 22S 117 5 E
Kalāntarī, *Iran* .... **45 C7** 32 10N 54 8 E
Kalao, *Indonesia* ...... **37 F6** 7 21S 121 0 E
Kalaotoa, *Indonesia* .... **37 F6** 7 20S 121 50 E
Kalasin, *Thailand* ...... **38 D4** 16 26N 103 30 E
Kalat, *Pakistan* .... **40 E5** 29 8N 66 31 E
Kalāteh, *Iran* .... **45 B7** 36 33N 55 41 E
Kalāteh-ye-Ganj, *Iran* ... **45 E8** 27 31N 57 55 E
Kalbarri, *Australia* ..... **61 E1** 27 40S 114 10 E
Kalce, *Slovenia* .... **16 F8** 45 54N 14 13 E
Kale, *Turkey* .... **21 F13** 37 27N 28 49 E
Kalegauk Kyun, *Burma* .. **41 M20** 15 33N 97 35 E
Kalehe, *Zaïre* .... **54 C2** 2 6S 28 50 E
Kalema, *Tanzania* ...... **54 C3** 1 12S 31 55 E
Kalemie, *Zaïre* .... **54 D2** 5 55S 29 9 E
Kalewa, *Burma* .... **41 H19** 23 10N 94 15 E
Kalgan = Zhangjiakou, *China* .... **34 D8** 40 48N 114 55 E
Kalgoorlie-Boulder, *Australia* .... **61 F3** 30 40S 121 22 E
Kaliakra, Nos, *Bulgaria* .. **21 C13** 43 21N 28 30 E
Kalianda, *Indonesia* .... **36 F3** 5 50S 105 45 E
Kalibo, *Phil.* .... **37 B6** 11 43N 122 22 E
Kaliganj, *Bangla.* ...... **43 H13** 22 25N 89 8 E
Kalima, *Zaïre* .... **54 C2** 2 33S 26 32 E
Kalimantan, *Indonesia* ... **36 E4** 0 0 114 0 E
Kalimantan Barat □, *Indonesia* .... **36 E4** 0 0 110 30 E
Kalimantan Selatan □, *Indonesia* .... **36 E5** 2 30S 115 30 E
Kalimantan Tengah □, *Indonesia* .... **36 E4** 2 0S 113 30 E
Kalimantan Timur □, *Indonesia* .... **36 D5** 1 30N 116 30 E
Kálimnos, *Greece* ...... **21 F12** 37 0N 27 0 E
Kalimpong, *India* ...... **43 F13** 27 4N 88 35 E
Kalinin = Tver, *Russia* .. **24 C6** 56 55N 35 55 E
Kaliningrad, *Kaliningd., Russia* .... **9 J19** 54 42N 20 32 E
Kaliningrad, *Moskva, Russia* .... **24 C6** 55 58N 37 54 E
Kalinkavichy, *Belarus* ... **17 B15** 52 12N 29 20 E
Kalinkovichi = Kalinkavichy, *Belarus* ... **17 B15** 52 12N 29 20 E
Kaliro, *Uganda* .... **54 B3** 0 56N 33 30 E
Kalispell, *U.S.A.* **82 B6** 48 12N 114 19W
Kalisz, *Poland* .... **17 C10** 51 45N 18 8 E
Kaliua, *Tanzania* ...... **54 D3** 5 5S 31 48 E
Kalix, *Sweden* .... **8 D20** 65 53N 23 12 E
Kalix ─►, *Sweden* ..... **8 D20** 65 50N 23 11 E
Kalka, *India* .... **42 D7** 30 46N 76 57 E
Kalkaska, *U.S.A.* **76 C3** 44 44N 85 11W
Kalkfeld, *Namibia* ...... **56 C2** 20 57S 16 14 E
Kalkfontein, *Botswana* ... **56 C3** 22 4S 20 57 E
Kalkrand, *Namibia* ..... **56 C2** 24 1S 17 35 E
Kallavesi, *Finland* ...... **8 E22** 62 58N 27 30 E
Kallsjön, *Sweden* ...... **8 E15** 63 38N 13 0 E
Kalmar, *Sweden* .... **9 H17** 56 40N 16 20 E
Kalmyk Republic = Kalmykia □, *Russia* .... **25 E8** 46 5N 46 1 E
Kalmykia □, *Russia* .... **25 E8** 46 5N 46 1 E
Kalmykovo, *Kazakstan* ... **25 E9** 49 0N 51 47 E
Kalna, *India* .... **43 H13** 23 13N 88 25 E
Kalocsa, *Hungary* ..... **17 E10** 46 32N 19 0 E
Kalokhorio, *Cyprus* ..... **23 E12** 34 51N 33 2 E
Kaloko, *Zaïre* .... **54 D2** 6 47S 25 48 E
Kalol, *Gujarat, India* .... **42 H5** 22 37N 73 31 E
Kalol, *Gujarat, India* .... **42 H5** 23 15N 72 33 E
Kalomo, *Zambia* .... **55 F2** 17 0S 26 30 E
Kalpi, *India* .... **43 F8** 26 8N 79 47 E
Kalu, *Pakistan* .... **42 G2** 25 5N 67 39 E
Kaluga, *Russia* .... **24 D6** 54 35N 36 10 E
Kalulushi, *Zambia* ..... **55 E2** 12 50S 28 3 E
Kalundborg, *Denmark* ... **9 J14** 55 41N 11 5 E
Kalush, *Ukraine* .... **17 D13** 49 3N 24 23 E
Kalutara, *Sri Lanka* .... **40 R11** 6 35N 80 0 E
Kalya, *Russia* .... **24 B10** 60 15N 59 59 E
Kama, *Zaïre* .... **54 C2** 3 30S 27 5 E
Kama ─►, *Russia* ..... **24 C9** 55 45N 52 0 E
Kamachumu, *Tanzania* ... **54 C3** 1 37S 31 37 E
Kamaishi, *Japan* ...... **30 E10** 39 16N 141 53 E
Kamalia, *Pakistan* ..... **42 D5** 30 44N 72 42 E
Kamapanda, *Zambia* ... **55 E1** 12 5S 24 0 E
Kamaran, *Yemen* .... **46 D3** 15 21N 42 35 E
Kamativi, *Zimbabwe* .... **55 F2** 18 15S 27 27 E
Kambalda, *Australia* .... **61 F3** 31 10S 121 37 E
Kambar, *Pakistan* ...... **42 F3** 27 37N 68 1 E
Kambarka, *Russia* ..... **24 C9** 56 15N 54 11 E
Kambolé, *Zambia* ...... **55 D3** 8 47S 30 48 E
Kambos, *Cyprus* .... **23 D11** 35 2N 32 44 E
Kambove, *Zaïre* .... **55 E2** 10 51S 26 33 E
Kamchatka, P-ov., *Russia* **27 D16** 57 0N 160 0 E
Kamchatka Pen. = Kamchatka, P-ov., *Russia* .... **27 D16** 57 0N 160 0 E
Kamchiya ─►, *Bulgaria* . **21 C12** 43 4N 27 44 E
Kamen, *Russia* .... **26 D9** 53 50N 81 30 E
Kamen-Rybolov, *Russia* . **30 B6** 44 46N 132 2 E
Kamenjak, Rt., *Croatia* ... **16 F7** 44 47N 13 55 E
Kamenka, *Russia* ...... **24 A7** 65 58N 44 0 E
Kamenka Bugskaya = Kamyanka-Buzka, *Ukraine* .... **17 C13** 50 8N 24 16 E
Kamensk Uralskiy, *Russia* **26 D7** 56 25N 62 2 E
Kamenskoye, *Russia* .... **27 C17** 62 45N 165 30 E
Kameoka, *Japan* ...... **31 G7** 35 0N 135 35 E
Kamiah, *U.S.A.* **82 C5** 46 14N 116 2W
Kamieskroon, *S. Africa* .. **56 E2** 30 9S 17 56 E
Kamilukuak, L., *Canada* .. **73 A8** 62 22N 101 40W
Kamin-Kashyrskyy, *Ukraine* .... **17 C13** 51 39N 24 56 E
Kamina, *Zaïre* .... **55 D1** 8 45S 25 0 E
Kaminak L., *Canada* **73 A9** 62 10N 95 0W
Kaminoyama, *Japan* .... **30 E10** 38 9N 140 17 E
Kamiros, *Greece* .... **23 C9** 36 20N 27 56 E
Kamituga, *Zaïre* .... **54 C2** 3 2S 28 10 E
Kamloops, *Canada* **72 C4** 50 40N 120 20W
Kamo, *Japan* .... **30 F9** 37 39N 139 3 E
Kamoke, *Pakistan* ..... **42 C6** 32 4N 74 4 E
Kampala, *Uganda* ...... **54 B3** 0 20N 32 30 E
Kampar, *Malaysia* ..... **39 K3** 4 18N 101 9 E
Kampar ─►, *Indonesia* .. **36 D2** 0 30N 103 8 E
Kampen, *Neths.* .... **15 B5** 52 33N 5 53 E
Kamphaeng Phet, *Thailand* .... **38 D2** 16 28N 99 30 E
Kampolombo, L., *Zambia* **55 E2** 11 37S 29 42 E
Kampong To, *Thailand* .. **39 J3** 6 3N 101 13 E
Kampot, *Cambodia* ..... **39 G5** 10 36N 104 10 E
Kampuchea = Cambodia ■, *Asia* .... **38 F5** 12 15N 105 0 E
Kampung ─►, *Indonesia* **37 F9** 5 44S 138 24 E
Kampung Air Putih, *Malaysia* .... **39 K4** 4 15N 103 10 E
Kampung Jerangau, *Malaysia* .... **39 K4** 4 50N 103 10 E
Kampung Raja, *Malaysia* **39 K4** 5 45N 102 35 E
Kampungbaru = Tolitoli, *Indonesia* .... **37 D6** 1 5N 120 50 E
Kamrau, Teluk, *Indonesia* **37 E8** 3 30S 133 36 E
Kamsack, *Canada* **73 C8** 51 34N 101 54W
Kamskoye Vdkhr., *Russia* **24 C10** 58 41N 56 7 E
Kamuchawie L., *Canada* . **73 B8** 56 18N 101 59W
Kamui-Misaki, *Japan* ... **30 C10** 43 20N 140 21 E
Kamyanets-Podilskyy, *Ukraine* .... **17 D14** 48 45N 26 40 E
Kamyanka-Buzka, *Ukraine* **17 C13** 50 8N 24 16 E
Kāmyārān, *Iran* .... **44 C5** 34 47N 46 56 E
Kamyshin, *Russia* ..... **25 D8** 50 10N 45 24 E
Kanaaupscow, *Canada* .. **70 B4** 54 2N 76 30W
Kanab, *U.S.A.* **83 H7** 37 3N 112 32W
Kanab ─►, *U.S.A.* **83 H7** 36 24N 112 38W
Kanagi, *Japan* .... **30 D10** 40 54N 140 27 E
Kanairiktok ─►, *Canada* . **71 A7** 55 2N 60 18W
Kananga, *Zaïre* .... **52 F4** 5 55S 22 18 E
Kanarraville, *U.S.A.* **83 H7** 37 32N 113 11W
Kanash, *Russia* .... **24 C8** 55 30N 47 32 E
Kanaskat, *U.S.A.* **84 C5** 47 19N 121 54W
Kanastraíon, Ákra = Palioúrion, Ákra, *Greece* **21 E10** 39 57N 23 45 E
Kanawha ─►, *U.S.A.* ... **76 F4** 38 50N 82 9W
Kanazawa, *Japan* ...... **31 F8** 36 30N 136 38 E
Kanchanaburi, *Thailand* . **38 E2** 14 2N 99 31 E
Kanchenjunga, *Nepal* ... **43 F13** 27 50N 88 10 E
Kanchipuram, *India* .... **40 N11** 12 52N 79 45 E
Kanda Kanda, *Zaïre* .... **52 F4** 6 52S 23 48 E
Kandahar = Qandahār, *Afghan.* .... **40 D4** 31 32N 65 30 E
Kandalaksha, *Russia* ... **24 A5** 67 9N 32 30 E
Kandalakshkiy Zaliv, *Russia* .... **24 A5** 66 0N 35 0 E
Kandalu, *Afghan.* ...... **40 E3** 29 55N 63 20 E
Kandangan, *Indonesia* ... **36 E5** 2 50S 115 20 E
Kandanos, *Greece* ..... **23 D5** 35 19N 23 44 E
Kandhkot, *Pakistan* .... **42 E3** 28 16N 69 8 E
Kandhla, *India* .... **42 E7** 29 18N 77 19 E
Kandi, *Benin* .... **50 F5** 11 7N 2 55 E
Kandi, *India* .... **43 H13** 23 58N 88 5 E
Kandla, *India* .... **42 H4** 23 0N 70 10 E
Kandos, *Australia* ..... **63 E4** 32 45S 149 58 E
Kandy, *Sri Lanka* ...... **40 R12** 7 18N 80 43 E
Kane, *U.S.A.* **78 E6** 41 40N 78 49W
Kane Basin, *Greenland* .. **4 B4** 79 1N 70 0W
Kangān, *Fārs, Iran* ..... **45 E7** 27 50N 52 3 E
Kangān, *Hormozgān, Iran* **45 E8** 25 48N 57 28 E
Kangar, *Malaysia* ...... **39 J3** 6 27N 100 12 E
Kangaroo I., *Australia* .. **63 F2** 35 45S 137 0 E
Kangasala, *Finland* .... **9 F21** 61 28N 24 4 E
Kangāvar, *Iran* .... **45 C6** 34 40N 48 0 E
Kangdong, *N. Korea* .... **35 E14** 39 9N 126 5 E
Kangean, Kepulauan, *Indonesia* .... **36 F5** 6 55S 115 23 E
Kangean Is. = Kangean, Kepulauan, *Indonesia* . **36 F5** 6 55S 115 23 E
Kanggye, *N. Korea* ..... **35 D14** 41 0N 126 35 E
Kanggyŏng, *S. Korea* ... **35 F14** 36 10N 127 0 E
Kanghwa, *S. Korea* .... **35 F14** 37 45N 126 30 E
Kangiqsualujjuaq, *Canada* **69 C13** 58 30N 65 59W
Kangiqsujuaq, *Canada* .. **69 B12** 61 30N 72 0W
Kangirsuk, *Canada* **69 B13** 60 0N 70 0W
Kangnŭng, *S. Korea* .... **35 F15** 37 45N 128 54 E
Kango, *Gabon* .... **52 D2** 0 11N 10 5 E
Kangping, *China* ...... **35 C12** 42 43N 123 18 E
Kangto, *India* .... **41 F18** 27 50N 92 35 E
Kaniama, *Zaïre* .... **54 D1** 7 30S 24 12 E
Kaniapiskau ─►, *Canada* **71 A6** 56 40N 69 30W
Kaniapiskau L., *Canada* .. **71 B6** 54 10N 69 55W
Kanin, Poluostrov, *Russia* **24 A8** 68 0N 45 0 E
Kanin Nos, Mys, *Russia* . **24 A7** 68 39N 43 32 E
Kanin Pen. = Kanin, Poluostrov, *Russia* .... **24 A8** 68 0N 45 0 E
Kaniva, *Australia* ...... **63 F3** 36 22S 141 18 E
Kanjut Sar, *Pakistan* .... **43 A6** 36 7N 75 25 E
Kankaanpää, *Finland* ... **9 F20** 61 44N 22 50 E
Kankakee, *U.S.A.* **76 E2** 41 7N 87 52W
Kankakee ─►, *U.S.A.* ... **76 E1** 41 23N 88 15W
Kankan, *Guinea* **50 F3** 10 23N 9 15W

Korea, South

Kinston, *U.S.A.* 77 H7 35 16N 77 35W
Kintampo, *Ghana* 50 G4 8 5N 1 41W
Kintap, *Indonesia* 36 E5 3 51S 115 13 E
Kintore Ra., *Australia* 60 D4 23 15S 128 47 E
Kintyre, *U.K.* 12 F3 55 30N 5 35W
Kintyre, Mull of, *U.K.* 12 F3 55 17N 5 47W
Kinushseo ~>, *Canada* 70 A3 55 15N 83 45W
Kinuso, *Canada* 72 B5 55 20N 115 25W
Kinyangiri, *Tanzania* 54 C3 4 25S 34 37 E
Kinzua, *U.S.A.* 78 E6 41 52N 78 58W
Kinzua Dam, *U.S.A.* 78 E5 41 53N 79 0W
Kiosk, *Canada* 70 C4 46 6N 78 53W
Kiowa, *Kans., U.S.A.* 81 G5 37 1N 98 29W
Kiowa, *Okla., U.S.A.* 81 H7 34 43N 95 54W
Kipahigan L., *Canada* 73 B8 55 20N 101 55W
Kipanga, *Tanzania* 54 D4 6 15S 35 20 E
Kiparissía, *Greece* 21 F9 37 15N 21 40 E
Kiparissiakós Kólpos, *Greece* 21 F9 37 25N 21 25 E
Kipembawe, *Tanzania* 54 D3 7 38S 33 27 E
Kipengere Ra., *Tanzania* 55 D3 9 12S 34 15 E
Kipili, *Tanzania* 54 D3 7 28S 30 32 E
Kipini, *Kenya* 54 C5 2 30S 40 32 E
Kipling, *Canada* 73 C8 50 6N 102 38W
Kippure, *Ireland* 13 C5 53 11N 6 21W
Kipushi, *Zaïre* 55 E2 11 48S 27 12 E
Kiratpur, *India* 42 E8 29 32N 78 12 E
Kirensk, *Russia* 27 D11 57 50N 107 55 E
Kirgella Rocks, *Australia* 61 F3 30 5S 122 50 E
Kirghizia ■ = Kyrgyzstan ■, *Asia* 26 E8 42 0N 75 0 E
Kirghizstan = Kyrgyzstan ■, *Asia* 26 E8 42 0N 75 0 E
Kirgiziya Steppe, *Eurasia* 25 D10 50 0N 55 0 E
Kiri, *Zaïre* 52 E3 1 29S 19 0 E
Kiribati ■, *Pac. Oc.* 64 H10 5 0S 180 0 E
Kırıkkale, *Turkey* 25 G5 39 51N 33 32 E
Kirillov, *Russia* 24 C6 59 49N 38 24 E
Kirin = Jilin, *China* 35 C14 43 44N 126 30 E
Kirin = Jilin □, *China* 35 C13 44 0N 127 0 E
Kiritimati, *Kiribati* 65 G12 1 58N 157 27W
Kirkcaldy, *U.K.* 12 E5 56 7N 3 9W
Kirkcudbright, *U.K.* 12 G4 54 50N 4 2W
Kirkee, *India* 40 K8 18 34N 73 56 E
Kirkenes, *Norway* 8 B23 69 40N 30 5 E
Kirkintilloch, *U.K.* 12 F4 55 56N 4 8W
Kirkjubæjarklaustur, *Iceland* 8 E4 63 47N 18 4W
Kirkkonummi, *Finland* 9 F21 60 8N 24 26 E
Kirkland, *U.S.A.* 83 J7 34 25N 112 43W
Kirkland Lake, *Canada* 70 C3 48 9N 80 2W
Kırklareli, *Turkey* 21 D12 41 44N 27 15 E
Kirksville, *U.S.A.* 80 E8 40 12N 92 35W
Kirkūk, *Iraq* 44 C5 35 30N 44 21 E
Kirkwall, *U.K.* 12 C6 58 59N 2 58W
Kirkwood, *S. Africa* 56 E4 33 22S 25 15 E
Kirov, *Russia* 24 C8 58 35N 49 40 E
Kirovabad = Gäncä, *Azerbaijan* 25 F8 40 45N 46 20 E
Kirovakan = Vanadzor, *Armenia* 25 F7 40 48N 44 30 E
Kirovograd = Kirovohrad, *Ukraine* 25 E5 48 35N 32 20 E
Kirovohrad, *Ukraine* 25 E5 48 35N 32 20 E
Kirovsk = Babadayhan, *Turkmenistan* 26 F7 37 42N 60 23 E
Kirovsk, *Russia* 24 A5 67 32N 33 41 E
Kirovskiy, *Kamchatka, Russia* 27 D16 54 27N 155 42 E
Kirovskiy, *Primorsk, Russia* 30 B6 45 7N 133 30 E
Kirriemuir, *U.K.* 12 E6 56 41N 3 1W
Kirsanov, *Russia* 24 D7 52 35N 42 40 E
Kırşehir, *Turkey* 25 G5 39 14N 34 5 E
Kirthar Range, *Pakistan* 42 F2 27 0N 67 0 E
Kiruna, *Sweden* 8 C19 67 52N 20 15 E
Kirundu, *Zaïre* 54 C2 0 50S 25 35 E
Kirup, *Australia* 61 F2 33 40S 115 50 E
Kiryū, *Japan* 31 F9 36 24N 139 20 E
Kisaga, *Tanzania* 54 C3 4 30S 34 23 E
Kisalaya, *Nic.* 88 D3 14 40N 84 3W
Kisámou, Kólpos, *Greece* 23 D5 35 30N 23 38 E
Kisanga, *Zaïre* 54 B2 2 30N 26 35 E
Kisangani, *Zaïre* 54 B2 0 35N 25 15 E
Kisar, *Indonesia* 37 F7 8 5S 127 10 E
Kisaran, *Indonesia* 36 D1 3 0N 99 37 E
Kisarawe, *Tanzania* 54 D4 6 53S 39 0 E
Kisarawe □, *Tanzania* 54 D4 7 3S 39 0 E
Kisarazu, *Japan* 31 G9 35 23N 139 55 E
Kiselevsk, *Russia* 26 D9 54 5N 86 39 E
Kishanganga ~>, *Pakistan* 43 B5 34 18N 73 28 E
Kishanganj, *India* 43 F13 26 3N 88 14 E
Kishangarh, *India* 42 F4 27 50N 70 30 E
Kishinev = Chişinău, *Moldova* 17 E15 47 0N 28 50 E
Kishiwada, *Japan* 31 G7 34 28N 135 22 E
Kishtwar, *India* 43 C6 33 20N 75 48 E
Kisii, *Kenya* 54 C3 0 40S 34 45 E
Kisii □, *Kenya* 54 C3 0 40S 34 45 E
Kisiju, *Tanzania* 54 D4 7 23S 39 19 E
Kisizi, *Uganda* 54 C2 1 0S 29 58 E
Kiska I., *U.S.A.* 68 C1 51 59N 177 30 E
Kiskatinaw ~>, *Canada* 72 B4 56 8N 120 10W
Kiskittogisu L., *Canada* 73 C9 54 13N 98 20W
Kiskörös, *Hungary* 17 E10 46 37N 19 20 E
Kiskunfélegyháza, *Hungary* 17 E10 46 42N 19 53 E
Kiskunhalas, *Hungary* 17 E10 46 28N 19 37 E
Kislovodsk, *Russia* 25 F7 43 50N 42 45 E
Kismayu = Chisimaio, *Somali Rep.* 49 G8 0 22S 42 32 E
Kiso-Gawa ~>, *Japan* 31 G8 35 20N 136 45 E
Kiso-Sammyaku, *Japan* 31 G8 35 45N 137 45 E
Kisofukushima, *Japan* 31 G8 35 52N 137 43 E
Kisoro, *Uganda* 54 C2 1 17S 29 48 E
Kissidougou, *Guinea* 50 G2 9 5N 10 5W
Kissimmee, *U.S.A.* 77 L5 28 18N 81 24W
Kissimmee ~>, *U.S.A.* 77 M5 27 9N 80 52W
Kississing L., *Canada* 73 B8 55 10N 101 20W
Kissónerga, *Cyprus* 23 E11 34 49N 32 24 E
Kisumu, *Kenya* 54 C3 0 3S 34 45 E
Kiswani, *Tanzania* 54 C4 4 5S 37 57 E
Kiswere, *Tanzania* 55 D4 9 27S 39 30 E
Kit Carson, *U.S.A.* 80 F3 38 46N 102 48W
Kita, *Mali* 50 F3 13 5N 9 25W
Kitab, *Uzbekistan* 26 F7 39 7N 66 52 E
Kitaibaraki, *Japan* 31 F10 36 50N 140 45 E
Kitakami, *Japan* 30 E10 39 20N 141 10 E
Kitakami-Gawa ~>, *Japan* 30 E10 38 25N 141 19 E
Kitakami-Sammyaku, *Japan* 30 E10 39 30N 141 30 E
Kitakata, *Japan* 30 F9 37 39N 139 52 E
Kitakyūshū, *Japan* 31 H5 33 50N 130 50 E
Kitale, *Kenya* 54 B4 1 0N 35 0 E
Kitami, *Japan* 30 C11 43 48N 143 54 E
Kitami-Sammyaku, *Japan* 30 B11 44 22N 142 43 E
Kitangiri, L., *Tanzania* 54 C3 4 5S 34 20 E
Kitaya, *Tanzania* 55 E5 10 38S 40 8 E
Kitchener, *Australia* 61 F3 30 55S 124 8 E
Kitchener, *Canada* 70 D3 43 27N 80 29W
Kitega = Gitega, *Burundi* 54 C2 3 26S 29 56 E
Kitengo, *Zaïre* 54 D1 7 26S 24 8 E
Kiteto □, *Tanzania* 54 C4 5 0S 37 0 E
Kitgum, *Uganda* 54 B3 3 17N 32 52 E
Kíthira, *Greece* 21 F10 36 8N 23 0 E
Kíthnos, *Greece* 21 F11 37 26N 24 27 E
Kiti, *Cyprus* 23 E12 34 50N 33 34 E
Kiti, C., *Cyprus* 23 E12 34 48N 33 36 E
Kitikmeot □, *Canada* 68 A9 70 0N 110 0W
Kitimat, *Canada* 72 C3 54 3N 128 38W
Kitinen ~>, *Finland* 8 C22 67 14N 27 27 E
Kitsuki, *Japan* 31 H5 33 25N 131 37 E
Kittakittaooloo, L., *Australia* 63 D2 28 3S 138 14 E
Kittanning, *U.S.A.* 78 F5 40 49N 79 31W
Kittatinny Mts., *U.S.A.* 79 E10 41 0N 75 0W
Kittery, *U.S.A.* 77 D10 43 5N 70 45W
Kittilä, *Finland* 8 C21 67 40N 24 51 E
Kitui, *Kenya* 54 C4 1 17S 38 0 E
Kitui □, *Kenya* 54 C4 1 30S 38 25 E
Kitwe, *Zambia* 55 E2 12 54S 28 13 E
Kivarli, *India* 42 G5 24 33N 72 46 E
Kivertsi, *Ukraine* 17 C13 50 50N 25 28 E
Kividhes, *Cyprus* 23 E11 34 46N 32 51 E
Kivu □, *Zaïre* 54 C2 3 10S 27 0 E
Kivu, L., *Zaïre* 54 C2 1 48S 29 0 E
Kiyev = Kyyiv, *Ukraine* 17 C16 50 30N 30 28 E
Kiyevskoye Vdkhr. = Kyyivske Vdskh., *Ukraine* 17 C16 51 0N 30 25 E
Kizel, *Russia* 24 C10 59 3N 57 40 E
Kiziguru, *Rwanda* 54 C3 1 46S 30 23 E
Kızıl Irmak ~>, *Turkey* 25 F6 41 44N 35 58 E
Kizil Jilga, *India* 43 B8 35 26N 78 50 E
Kizimkazi, *Tanzania* 54 D4 6 28S 39 30 E
Kizlyar, *Russia* 25 F8 43 51N 46 40 E
Kizyl-Arvat = Gyzylarbat, *Turkmenistan* 26 F6 39 4N 56 23 E
Kjölur, *Iceland* 8 D4 64 50N 19 25W
Kladno, *Czech.* 16 C8 50 10N 14 7 E
Klaeng, *Thailand* 38 F3 12 47N 101 39 E
Klagenfurt, *Austria* 16 E8 46 38N 14 20 E
Klaipeda, *Lithuania* 9 J19 55 43N 21 10 E
Klaksvík, *Færoe Is.* 8 E9 62 14N 6 35W
Klamath ~>, *U.S.A.* 82 F1 41 33N 124 5W
Klamath Falls, *U.S.A.* 82 E3 42 13N 121 46W
Klamath Mts., *U.S.A.* 82 F2 41 20N 123 0W
Klappan ~>, *Canada* 72 B3 58 0N 129 43W
Klarälven ~>, *Sweden* 9 G15 59 23N 13 32 E
Klaten, *Indonesia* 37 G14 7 43S 110 36 E
Klatovy, *Czech.* 16 D7 49 23N 13 18 E
Klawer, *S. Africa* 56 E2 31 44S 18 36 E
Klawock, *U.S.A.* 72 B2 55 33N 133 6W
Kleena Kleene, *Canada* 72 C4 52 0N 124 59W
Klein, *U.S.A.* 82 C9 46 24N 108 33W
Klein-Karas, *Namibia* 56 D2 27 33S 18 7 E
Klerksdorp, *S. Africa* 56 D4 26 53S 26 38 E
Kletsk = Klyetsk, *Belarus* 17 B14 53 5N 26 45 E
Kletskiy, *Russia* 26 E5 49 16N 43 11 E
Klickitat, *U.S.A.* 82 D3 45 49N 121 9W
Klickitat ~>, *U.S.A.* 84 E5 45 42N 121 17W
Klidhes, *Cyprus* 23 D13 35 42N 34 36 E
Klin, *Russia* 26 D4 56 20N 36 48 E
Klinaklini ~>, *Canada* 72 C3 51 21N 125 40W
Klipdale, *S. Africa* 56 E2 34 19S 19 57 E
Klipplaat, *S. Africa* 56 E3 33 1S 24 22 E
Kłodzko, *Poland* 17 C9 50 28N 16 38 E
Klondike, *Canada* 68 B6 64 0N 139 26W
Klouto, *Togo* 50 G5 6 57N 0 44 E
Kluane L., *Canada* 68 B6 61 15N 138 40W
Kluczbork, *Poland* 17 C10 50 58N 18 12 E
Klyetsk, *Belarus* 17 B14 53 5N 26 45 E
Klyuchevskaya, Gora, *Russia* 27 D17 55 50N 160 30 E
Knaresborough, *U.K.* 10 C6 54 1N 1 28W
Knee L., *Man., Canada* 73 B10 55 3N 94 45W
Knee L., *Sask., Canada* 73 B7 55 51N 107 0W
Knight Inlet, *Canada* 72 C3 50 45N 125 40W
Knighton, *U.K.* 11 E4 52 21N 3 3W
Knights Ferry, *U.S.A.* 84 H6 37 50N 120 40W
Knights Landing, *U.S.A.* 84 G5 38 48N 121 43W
Knob, C., *Australia* 61 F2 34 32S 119 16 E
Knockmealdown Mts., *Ireland* 13 D4 52 14N 7 56W
Knokke, *Belgium* 15 C3 51 20N 3 17 E
Knossós, *Greece* 23 D7 35 16N 25 10 E
Knox, *U.S.A.* 76 E2 41 18N 86 37W
Knox, C., *Canada* 72 C2 54 11N 133 5W
Knox City, *U.S.A.* 81 J5 33 25N 99 49W
Knox Coast, *Antarctica* 5 C8 66 30S 108 0 E
Knoxville, *Iowa, U.S.A.* 80 E8 41 19N 93 6W
Knoxville, *Tenn., U.S.A.* 77 H4 35 58N 83 55W
Knysna, *S. Africa* 56 E3 34 2S 23 2 E
Ko Kha, *Thailand* 38 C2 18 11N 99 24 E
Ko Tao, *Thailand* 39 G2 10 6N 99 48 E
Koartac = Quaqtaq, *Canada* 69 B13 60 55N 69 40W
Koba, *Aru, Indonesia* 37 F8 6 37S 134 37 E
Koba, *Bangka, Indonesia* 36 E3 2 26S 106 14 E
Kobarid, *Slovenia* 16 E7 46 15N 13 30 E
Kobayashi, *Japan* 31 J5 31 56N 130 59 E
Kobdo = Hovd, *Mongolia* 32 B4 48 2N 91 37 E
Kōbe, *Japan* 31 G7 34 45N 135 10 E
København, *Denmark* 9 J15 55 41N 12 34 E
Kōbi-Sho, *Japan* 31 M1 25 56N 123 41 E
Koblenz, *Germany* 16 C4 50 21N 7 36 E
Kobroor, Kepulauan, *Indonesia* 37 F8 6 10S 134 30 E
Kobryn, *Belarus* 17 B13 52 15N 24 22 E
Kocaeli = İzmit, *Turkey* 25 F4 40 45N 29 50 E
Kočani, *Macedonia* 21 D10 41 55N 22 25 E
Koch Bihar, *India* 41 F16 26 22N 89 29 E
Kochang, *S. Korea* 35 G14 35 41N 127 55 E
Kochas, *India* 43 G10 25 15N 83 56 E
Kocheya, *Russia* 27 D13 52 32N 120 42 E
Kōchi, *Japan* 31 H6 33 30N 133 35 E
Kōchi □, *Japan* 31 H6 33 40N 133 30 E
Kochiu = Gejiu, *China* 32 D5 23 20N 103 10 E
Kodiak, *U.S.A.* 68 C4 57 47N 152 24W
Kodiak I., *U.S.A.* 68 C4 57 30N 152 45W
Kodinar, *India* 42 J4 20 46N 70 46 E
Koes, *Namibia* 56 D2 26 0S 19 15 E
Koffiefontein, *S. Africa* 56 D4 29 30S 25 0 E
Kofiau, *Indonesia* 37 E7 1 11S 129 50 E
Koforidua, *Ghana* 50 G4 6 3N 0 17W
Kōfu, *Japan* 31 G9 35 40N 138 30 E
Koga, *Japan* 31 F9 36 11N 139 43 E
Kogaluk ~>, *Canada* 71 A7 56 12N 61 44W
Kogan, *Australia* 63 D5 27 2S 150 40 E
Køge, *Denmark* 9 J15 55 27N 12 11 E
Koh-i-Bābā, *Afghan.* 40 B5 34 30N 67 0 E
Koh-i-Khurd, *Afghan.* 42 C1 33 30N 65 59 E
Kohat, *Pakistan* 42 C4 33 40N 71 29 E
Kohima, *India* 41 G19 25 35N 94 10 E
Kohkīlūyeh va Būyer Aḩmadi □, *Iran* 45 D6 31 30N 50 30 E
Kohler Ra., *Antarctica* 5 D15 77 0S 110 0W
Kohtla-Järve, *Estonia* 9 G22 59 20N 27 20 E
Koillismaa, *Finland* 8 D23 65 44N 28 36 E
Koin-dong, *N. Korea* 35 D14 40 28N 126 18 E
Kojō, *N. Korea* 35 E14 38 58N 127 58 E
Kojonup, *Australia* 61 F2 33 48S 117 10 E
Kojūr, *Iran* 45 B6 36 23N 51 43 E
Kokand = Qūqon, *Uzbekistan* 26 E8 40 30N 70 57 E
Kokanee Glacier Prov. Park, *Canada* 72 D5 49 47N 117 10W
Kokas, *Indonesia* 37 E8 2 42S 132 26 E
Kokchetav = Kökshetaū, *Kazakstan* 26 D7 53 20N 69 25 E
Kokemäenjoki ~>, *Finland* 9 F19 61 32N 21 44 E
Kokkola, *Finland* 8 E20 63 50N 23 8 E
Koko Kyunzu, *Burma* 41 M18 14 10N 93 25 E
Kokomo, *U.S.A.* 76 E2 40 29N 86 8W
Kokonau, *Indonesia* 37 E9 4 43S 136 26 E
Koksan, *N. Korea* 35 E14 38 46N 126 40 E
Kökshetaū, *Kazakstan* 26 D7 53 20N 69 25 E
Koksoak ~>, *Canada* 69 C13 58 30N 68 10W
Kokstad, *S. Africa* 57 E4 30 32S 29 29 E
Kokubu, *Japan* 31 J5 31 44N 130 46 E
Kokuora, *Russia* 27 B15 71 35N 144 50 E
Kola, *Indonesia* 37 F8 5 35S 134 30 E
Kola, *Russia* 24 A5 68 45N 33 8 E
Kola Pen. = Kolskiy Poluostrov, *Russia* 24 A6 67 30N 38 0 E
Kolahoi, *India* 43 B6 34 12N 75 22 E
Kolaka, *Indonesia* 37 E6 4 3S 121 46 E
Kolar, *India* 40 N11 13 12N 78 15 E
Kolar Gold Fields, *India* 40 N11 12 58N 78 16 E
Kolari, *Finland* 8 C20 67 20N 23 48 E
Kolayat, *India* 40 F8 27 50N 72 50 E
Kolchugino = Leninsk-Kuznetskiy, *Russia* 26 D9 54 44N 86 10 E
Kolda, *Senegal* 50 F2 12 55N 14 57W
Kolding, *Denmark* 9 J13 55 30N 9 29 E
Kole, *Zaïre* 52 E4 3 16S 22 42 E
Kolepom = Yos Sudarso, Pulau, *Indonesia* 37 F9 8 0S 138 30 E
Kolguyev, Ostrov, *Russia* 24 A8 69 20N 48 30 E
Kolhapur, *India* 40 L9 16 43N 74 15 E
Kolín, *Czech.* 16 C8 50 2N 15 9 E
Kolkas Rags, *Latvia* 9 H20 57 46N 22 37 E
Kolmanskop, *Namibia* 56 D2 26 45S 15 14 E
Köln, *Germany* 16 C4 50 56N 6 57 E
Koło, *Poland* 17 B10 52 14N 18 40 E
Kołobrzeg, *Poland* 16 A8 54 10N 15 35 E
Kolokani, *Mali* 50 F3 13 35N 7 45W
Kolomna, *Russia* 24 C6 55 8N 38 45 E
Kolomyya, *Ukraine* 17 D13 48 31N 25 2 E
Kolonodale, *Indonesia* 37 E6 2 3S 121 25 E
Kolosib, *India* 41 G18 24 15N 92 45 E
Kolpashevo, *Russia* 26 D9 58 20N 83 5 E
Kolpino, *Russia* 24 C5 59 44N 30 39 E
Kolskiy Poluostrov, *Russia* 24 A6 67 30N 38 0 E
Kolskiy Zaliv, *Russia* 24 A5 69 23N 34 0 E
Kolwezi, *Zaïre* 55 E2 10 40S 25 25 E
Kolyma ~>, *Russia* 27 C17 69 30N 161 0 E
Kolymskoye Nagorye, *Russia* 27 C16 63 0N 157 0 E
Komandorskiye Is. = Komandorskiye Ostrova, *Russia* 27 D17 55 0N 167 0 E
Komandorskiye Ostrova, *Russia* 27 D17 55 0N 167 0 E
Komárno, *Slovak Rep.* 17 E10 47 49N 18 5 E
Komatipoort, *S. Africa* 57 D5 25 25S 31 55 E
Komatou Yialou, *Cyprus* 23 D13 35 25N 34 8 E
Komatsu, *Japan* 31 F8 36 25N 136 30 E
Komatsujima, *Japan* 31 H7 34 0N 134 35 E
Komi □, *Russia* 24 B10 64 0N 55 0 E
Kommunarsk = Alchevsk, *Ukraine* 25 E6 48 30N 38 45 E
Kommunizma, Pik, *Tajikistan* 26 F8 39 0N 72 2 E
Komodo, *Indonesia* 37 F5 8 37S 119 20 E
Komono, *Congo* 52 E2 3 10S 13 20 E
Komoran, Pulau, *Indonesia* 37 F9 8 18S 138 45 E
Komoro, *Japan* 31 F9 36 19N 138 26 E
Komotini, *Greece* 21 D11 41 9N 25 26 E
Kompasberg, *S. Africa* 56 E3 31 45S 24 32 E
Kompong Bang, *Cambodia* 39 F5 12 24N 104 40 E
Kompong Cham, *Cambodia* 39 F5 12 0N 105 30 E
Kompong Chhnang, *Cambodia* 39 F5 12 20N 104 35 E
Kompong Chikreng, *Cambodia* 38 F5 13 5N 104 18 E
Kompong Kleang, *Cambodia* 38 F5 13 6N 104 8 E
Kompong Luong, *Cambodia* 39 G5 11 49N 104 48 E
Kompong Pranak, *Cambodia* 38 F5 13 35N 104 55 E
Kompong Som, *Cambodia* 39 G4 10 38N 103 30 E
Kompong Som, Chhung, *Cambodia* 39 G4 10 50N 103 32 E
Kompong Speu, *Cambodia* 39 G5 11 26N 104 32 E
Kompong Sralao, *Cambodia* 38 E5 14 5N 105 46 E
Kompong Thom, *Cambodia* 38 F5 12 35N 104 51 E
Kompong Trabeck, *Cambodia* 38 F5 13 6N 105 14 E
Kompong Trabeck, *Cambodia* 39 G5 11 9N 105 28 E
Kompong Trach, *Cambodia* 39 G5 11 25N 105 48 E
Kompong Tralach, *Cambodia* 39 G5 11 54N 104 47 E
Komrat = Comrat, *Moldova* 17 E15 46 18N 28 40 E
Komsberg, *S. Africa* 56 E3 32 40S 20 45 E
Komsomolets, Ostrov, *Russia* 27 A10 80 30N 95 0 E
Komsomolsk, *Russia* 27 D14 50 30N 137 0 E
Konarhá □, *Afghan.* 40 B7 35 30N 71 3 E
Konārī, *Iran* 45 D6 28 13N 51 36 E
Konawa, *U.S.A.* 81 H6 34 58N 96 45W
Konch, *India* 43 G8 26 0N 79 10 E
Kondakovo, *Russia* 27 C16 69 36N 152 0 E
Konde, *Tanzania* 54 C4 4 57S 39 45 E
Kondinin, *Australia* 61 F2 32 34S 118 8 E
Kondoa, *Tanzania* 54 C4 4 55S 35 50 E
Kondoa □, *Tanzania* 54 D4 5 0S 36 0 E
Kondókali, *Greece* 23 A3 39 38N 19 51 E
Kondopaga, *Russia* 24 B5 62 12N 34 17 E
Kondratyevo, *Russia* 27 D10 57 22N 98 15 E
Konduga, *Nigeria* 51 F7 11 35N 13 26 E
Köneürgench, *Turkmenistan* 26 E6 42 19N 59 10 E
Konevo, *Russia* 24 B6 62 8N 39 20 E
Kong, *Ivory C.* 50 G4 8 54N 4 36W
Kong ~>, *Cambodia* 38 F5 13 32N 105 58 E
Kong, Koh, *Cambodia* 39 G4 11 20N 103 0 E
Kong Christian IX.s Land, *Greenland* 4 C6 68 0N 36 0W
Kong Christian X.s Land, *Greenland* 4 E6 74 0N 29 0W
Kong Franz Joseph Fd., *Greenland* 4 E6 73 30N 24 30W
Kong Frederik IX.s Land, *Greenland* 4 C5 67 0N 52 0W
Kong Frederik VI.s Kyst, *Greenland* 4 C5 63 0N 43 0W
Kong Frederik VIII.s Land, *Greenland* 4 B6 78 30N 26 0W
Kong Oscar Fjord, *Greenland* 4 B6 72 20N 24 0W
Kongju, *S. Korea* 35 F14 36 30N 127 0 E
Konglu, *Burma* 41 F20 27 13N 97 57 E
Kongolo, *Kasai Or., Zaïre* 54 D1 5 26S 24 49 E
Kongolo, *Shaba, Zaïre* 54 D2 5 22S 27 0 E
Kongor, *Sudan* 51 G11 7 1N 31 27 E
Kongsberg, *Norway* 9 G13 59 39N 9 39 E
Kongsvinger, *Norway* 9 F15 60 12N 12 2 E
Kongwa, *Tanzania* 54 D4 6 11S 36 26 E
Koni, *Zaïre* 55 E2 10 40S 27 11 E
Koni, Mts., *Zaïre* 55 E2 10 36S 27 10 E
Königsberg = Kaliningrad, *Russia* 9 J19 54 42N 20 32 E
Konin, *Poland* 17 B10 52 12N 18 15 E
Konjic, *Bos.-H.* 21 C7 43 42N 17 58 E
Konkiep, *Namibia* 56 D2 26 49S 17 15 E
Konosha, *Russia* 24 B7 61 0N 40 5 E
Kōnosu, *Japan* 31 F9 36 3N 139 31 E
Konotop, *Ukraine* 25 D5 51 12N 33 7 E
Końskie, *Poland* 17 C11 51 15N 20 23 E
Konstanz, *Germany* 16 E5 47 40N 9 10 E
Kont, *Iran* 45 E9 26 55N 61 50 E
Kontagora, *Nigeria* 50 F6 10 23N 5 27 E
Kontum, *Vietnam* 38 E7 14 24N 108 0 E
Kontum, Plateau du, *Vietnam* 38 E7 14 30N 108 30 E
Konya, *Turkey* 25 G5 37 52N 32 35 E
Konza, *Kenya* 54 C4 1 45S 37 7 E
Kookynie, *Australia* 61 E3 29 17S 121 22 E
Kooline, *Australia* 60 D2 22 57S 116 20 E
Kooloonong, *Australia* 63 E3 34 48S 143 10 E
Koolyanobbing, *Australia* 61 F2 30 48S 119 36 E
Koondrook, *Australia* 63 F3 35 33S 144 8 E
Koonibba, *Australia* 63 E1 31 54S 133 25 E
Koorawatha, *Australia* 63 E4 34 2S 148 33 E
Koorda, *Australia* 61 F2 30 48S 117 35 E
Kooskia, *U.S.A.* 82 C6 46 9N 115 59W
Kootenai ~>, *Canada* 82 B5 49 15N 117 39W
Kootenay L., *Canada* 72 D5 49 45N 116 50W
Kootenay Nat. Park, *Canada* 72 C5 51 0N 116 0W
Kootjieskolk, *S. Africa* 56 E3 31 15S 20 21 E
Kopaonik, *Serbia, Yug.* 21 C9 43 10N 20 50 E
Kópavogur, *Iceland* 8 D3 64 6N 21 55W
Koper, *Slovenia* 16 F7 45 31N 13 44 E
Kopervik, *Norway* 9 G11 59 17N 5 17 E
Kopeysk, *Russia* 26 D7 55 7N 61 37 E
Kopi, *Australia* 63 E2 33 24S 135 40 E
Köping, *Sweden* 9 G17 59 31N 16 3 E
Koppies, *S. Africa* 57 D4 27 20S 27 30 E
Koprivnica, *Croatia* 20 A7 46 12N 16 45 E
Kopychyntsi, *Ukraine* 17 D13 49 7N 25 58 E
Korab, *Macedonia* 21 D9 41 44N 20 40 E
Korakiána, *Greece* 23 A3 39 42N 19 45 E
Korba, *India* 43 H10 22 20N 82 45 E
Korbu, G., *Malaysia* 39 K3 4 41N 101 18 E
Korça, *Albania* 21 D9 40 37N 20 50 E
Korce = Korça, *Albania* 21 D9 40 37N 20 50 E
Korčula, *Croatia* 20 C7 42 56N 16 57 E
Kord Kūy, *Iran* 45 B7 36 48N 54 7 E
Kord Sheykh, *Iran* 45 D7 28 31N 52 53 E
Kordestān □, *Iran* 44 C5 36 0N 47 0 E
Kordofân, *Sudan* 51 F10 13 0N 29 0 E
Korea, North ■, *Asia* 35 E14 40 0N 127 0 E
Korea, South ■, *Asia* 35 F15 36 0N 128 0 E

Lansdowne

Kwataboahegan →, *Canada* **70 B3** 51 9N 80 50W
Kwatisore, *Indonesia* **37 E8** 3 18S 134 50 E
KwaZulu Natal □, *S. Africa* **57 D5** 29 0S 30 0 E
Kweichow = Guizhou □, *China* **32 D5** 27 0N 107 0 E
Kwekwe, *Zimbabwe* **55 F2** 18 58S 29 48 E
Kwidzyn, *Poland* **17 B10** 53 44N 18 55 E
Kwimba □, *Tanzania* **54 C3** 3 0S 33 0 E
Kwinana New Town, *Australia* **61 F2** 32 15S 115 47 E
Kwoka, *Indonesia* **37 E8** 0 31S 132 27 E
Kyabé, *Chad* **51 G8** 9 30N 19 0 E
Kyabra Cr. →, *Australia* **63 D3** 25 36S 142 55 E
Kyabram, *Australia* **63 F4** 36 19S 145 4 E
Kyaikto, *Burma* **38 D1** 17 20N 97 3 E
Kyakhta, *Russia* **27 D11** 50 30N 106 25 E
Kyancutta, *Australia* **63 E2** 33 8S 135 33 E
Kyangin, *Burma* **41 K19** 18 20N 95 20 E
Kyaukpadaung, *Burma* **41 J19** 20 52N 95 8 E
Kyaukpyu, *Burma* **41 K18** 19 28N 93 30 E
Kyaukse, *Burma* **41 J20** 21 36N 96 10 E
Kyburz, *U.S.A.* **84 G6** 38 47N 120 18W
Kyenjojo, *Uganda* **54 B3** 0 40N 30 37 E
Kyle Dam, *Zimbabwe* **55 G3** 20 15S 31 0 E
Kyle of Lochalsh, *U.K.* **12 D3** 57 17N 5 44W
Kymijoki →, *Finland* **9 F22** 60 30N 26 55 E
Kyneton, *Australia* **63 F3** 37 10S 144 29 E
Kynuna, *Australia* **62 C3** 21 37S 141 55 E
Kyō-ga-Saki, *Japan* **31 G7** 35 45N 135 15 E
Kyoga, L., *Uganda* **54 B3** 1 35N 33 0 E
Kyogle, *Australia* **63 D5** 28 40S 153 0 E
Kyongju, *S. Korea* **35 G15** 35 51N 129 14 E
Kyongpyaw, *Burma* **41 L19** 17 12N 95 10 E
Kyŏngsŏng, *N. Korea* **35 D15** 41 35N 129 36 E
Kyōto, *Japan* **31 G7** 35 0N 135 45 E
Kyōto □, *Japan* **31 G7** 35 15N 135 45 E
Kyparissovouno, *Cyprus* **23 D12** 35 19N 33 10 E
Kyperounda, *Cyprus* **23 E11** 34 56N 32 58 E
Kyren, *Russia* **27 D11** 51 45N 101 45 E
Kyrenia, *Cyprus* **23 D12** 35 20N 33 20 E
Kyrgyzstan ■, *Asia* **26 E8** 42 0N 75 0 E
Kyrönjoki →, *Finland* **8 E19** 63 14N 21 45 E
Kyrtylakh, *Russia* **27 C13** 65 30N 123 40 E
Kystatyam, *Russia* **27 C13** 67 20N 123 10 E
Kythréa, *Cyprus* **23 D12** 35 15N 33 29 E
Kyulyunken, *Russia* **27 C14** 64 10N 137 5 E
Kyunhla, *Burma* **41 H19** 23 25N 95 15 E
Kyuquot, *Canada* **72 C3** 50 3N 127 25W
Kyūshū, *Japan* **31 H5** 33 0N 131 0 E
Kyūshū □, *Japan* **31 H5** 33 0N 131 0 E
Kyūshū-Sanchi, *Japan* **31 H5** 32 35N 131 17 E
Kyustendil, *Bulgaria* **21 C10** 42 16N 22 41 E
Kyusyur, *Russia* **27 B13** 70 19N 127 30 E
Kywong, *Australia* **63 E4** 34 58S 146 44 E
Kyyiv, *Ukraine* **17 C16** 50 30N 30 28 E
Kyyivske Vdskh., *Ukraine* **17 C16** 51 0N 30 25 E
Kyzyl, *Russia* **27 D10** 51 50N 94 30 E
Kyzyl Kum, *Uzbekistan* **26 E7** 42 30N 65 0 E
Kyzyl-Kyya, *Kyrgyzstan* **26 E8** 40 16N 72 8 E
Kzyl-Orda = Qyzylorda, *Kazakstan* **26 E7** 44 48N 65 28 E

L

La Albufera, *Spain* **19 C5** 39 20N 0 27W
La Alcarria, *Spain* **19 B4** 40 31N 2 45W
La Asunción, *Venezuela* **92 A6** 11 2N 63 53W
La Banda, *Argentina* **94 B3** 27 45S 64 10W
La Barca, *Mexico* **86 C4** 20 20N 102 40W
La Barge, *U.S.A.* **82 E8** 42 16N 110 12W
La Belle, *U.S.A.* **77 M5** 26 46N 81 26W
La Biche →, *Canada* **72 B4** 59 57N 123 50W
La Bomba, *Mexico* **86 A1** 31 53N 115 2W
La Calera, *Chile* **94 C1** 32 50S 71 10W
La Canal, *Spain* **22 C7** 38 51N 1 23 E
La Carlota, *Argentina* **94 C3** 33 30S 63 20W
La Ceiba, *Honduras* **88 C2** 15 40N 86 50W
La Chaux de Fonds, *Switz.* **16 E4** 47 7N 6 50 E
La Cocha, *Argentina* **94 B2** 27 50S 65 40W
La Concordia, *Mexico* **87 D6** 16 8N 92 38W
La Conner, *U.S.A.* **82 B2** 48 23N 122 30W
La Coruña, *Spain* **19 A1** 43 20N 8 25W
La Crete, *Canada* **72 B5** 58 11N 116 24W
La Crosse, *Kans., U.S.A.* **80 F5** 38 32N 99 18W
La Crosse, *Wis., U.S.A.* **80 D9** 43 48N 91 15W
La Cruz, *Costa Rica* **88 D2** 11 4N 85 39W
La Cruz, *Mexico* **86 C3** 23 55N 106 54W
La Dorada, *Colombia* **92 B4** 5 30N 74 40W
La Escondida, *Mexico* **86 C5** 24 6N 99 55W
La Esmeralda, *Paraguay* **94 A3** 22 16S 62 33W
La Esperanza, *Cuba* **88 B3** 22 46N 83 44W
La Esperanza, *Honduras* **88 D2** 14 15N 88 10W
La Estrada, *Spain* **19 A1** 42 43N 8 27W
La Fayette, *U.S.A.* **77 H3** 34 42N 85 17W
La Fé, *Cuba* **88 B3** 22 2N 84 15W
La Follette, *U.S.A.* **77 G3** 36 23N 84 7W
La Grande, *U.S.A.* **82 D4** 45 20N 118 5W
La Grange, *Calif., U.S.A.* **84 H6** 37 42N 120 27W
La Grange, *Ga., U.S.A.* **77 J3** 33 2N 85 2W
La Grange, *Ky., U.S.A.* **76 F3** 38 25N 85 23W
La Grange, *Tex., U.S.A.* **81 L6** 29 54N 96 52W
La Guaira, *Venezuela* **92 A5** 10 36N 66 56W
La Güera, *Mauritania* **50 D1** 20 51N 17 0W
La Habana, *Cuba* **88 B3** 23 8N 82 22W
La Harpe, *U.S.A.* **80 E9** 40 35N 90 58W
La Independencia, *Mexico* **87 D6** 16 31N 91 47W
La Isabela, *Dom. Rep.* **89 C5** 19 58N 71 2W
La Jara, *U.S.A.* **83 H11** 37 16N 105 58W
La Junta, *U.S.A.* **81 F3** 37 59N 103 33W
La Laguna, *Canary Is.* **22 F3** 28 28N 16 18W
La Libertad, *Guatemala* **88 C1** 16 47N 90 7W
La Libertad, *Mexico* **86 B2** 29 55N 112 41W
La Ligua, *Chile* **94 C1** 32 30S 71 16W
La Línea de la Concepción, *Spain* **19 D3** 36 15N 5 23W
La Loche, *Canada* **73 B7** 56 29N 109 26W
La Louvière, *Belgium* **15 D4** 50 27N 4 10 E
La Malbaie, *Canada* **71 C5** 47 40N 70 10W
La Mancha, *Spain* **19 C4** 39 10N 2 54W
La Mesa, *Calif., U.S.A.* **85 N9** 32 46N 117 3W
La Mesa, *N. Mex., U.S.A.* **83 K10** 32 7N 106 42W
La Misión, *Mexico* **86 A1** 32 5N 116 50W
La Moure, *U.S.A.* **80 B5** 46 21N 98 18W
La Negra, *Chile* **94 A1** 23 46S 70 18W
La Oliva, *Canary Is.* **22 F6** 28 36N 13 57W
La Orotava, *Canary Is.* **22 F3** 28 22N 16 31W
La Palma, *Canary Is.* **22 F2** 28 40N 17 50W
La Palma, *Panama* **88 E4** 8 15N 78 0W
La Palma del Condado, *Spain* **19 D2** 37 21N 6 38W
La Paloma, *Chile* **94 C1** 30 35S 71 0W
La Pampa □, *Argentina* **94 D2** 36 50S 66 0W
La Paragua, *Venezuela* **92 B6** 6 50N 63 20W
La Paz, *Entre Ríos, Argentina* **94 C4** 30 50S 59 45W
La Paz, *San Luis, Argentina* **94 C2** 33 30S 67 20W
La Paz, *Bolivia* **92 G5** 16 20S 68 10W
La Paz, *Honduras* **88 D2** 14 20N 87 47W
La Paz, *Mexico* **86 C2** 24 10N 110 20W
La Paz Centro, *Nic.* **88 D2** 12 20N 86 41W
La Pedrera, *Colombia* **92 D5** 1 18S 69 43W
La Perouse Str., *Asia* **30 B11** 45 40N 142 0 E
La Pesca, *Mexico* **87 C5** 23 46N 97 47W
La Piedad, *Mexico* **86 C4** 20 20N 102 1W
La Pine, *U.S.A.* **82 E3** 43 40N 121 30W
La Plant, *U.S.A.* **80 C4** 45 9N 100 39W
La Plata, *Argentina* **94 D4** 35 0S 57 55W
La Porte, *U.S.A.* **76 E2** 41 36N 86 43W
La Purísima, *Mexico* **86 B2** 26 10N 112 4W
La Push, *U.S.A.* **84 C2** 47 55N 124 38W
La Quiaca, *Argentina* **94 A2** 22 5S 65 35W
La Reine, *Canada* **70 C4** 48 50N 79 30W
La Restinga, *Canary Is.* **22 G2** 27 38N 17 59W
La Rioja, *Argentina* **94 B2** 29 20S 67 0W
La Rioja □, *Argentina* **94 B2** 29 30S 67 0W
La Rioja □, *Spain* **19 A4** 42 20N 2 20W
La Robla, *Spain* **19 A3** 42 50N 5 41W
La Roche-sur-Yon, *France* **18 C3** 46 40N 1 25W
La Rochelle, *France* **18 C3** 46 10N 1 9W
La Roda, *Spain* **19 C4** 39 13N 2 15W
La Romana, *Dom. Rep.* **89 C6** 18 27N 68 57W
La Ronge, *Canada* **73 B7** 55 5N 105 20W
La Rumorosa, *Mexico* **85 N10** 32 33N 116 4W
La Sabina, *Spain* **22 C7** 38 44N 1 25 E
La Salle, *U.S.A.* **80 E10** 41 20N 89 6W
La Santa, *Canary Is.* **22 E6** 29 5N 13 40W
La Sarre, *Canada* **70 C4** 48 45N 79 15W
La Scie, *Canada* **71 C8** 49 57N 55 36W
La Selva Beach, *U.S.A.* **84 J5** 36 56N 121 51W
La Serena, *Chile* **94 B1** 29 55S 71 10W
La Seyne-sur-Mer, *France* **18 E6** 43 7N 5 52 E
La Spézia, *Italy* **20 B3** 44 7N 9 50 E
La Tortuga, *Venezuela* **89 D6** 11 0N 65 22W
La Tuque, *Canada* **70 C5** 47 30N 72 50W
La Unión, *Chile* **96 E2** 40 10S 73 0W
La Unión, *El Salv.* **88 D2** 13 20N 87 50W
La Unión, *Mexico* **86 D4** 17 58N 101 49W
La Urbana, *Venezuela* **92 B5** 7 8N 66 56W
La Vega, *Dom. Rep.* **89 C5** 19 20N 70 30W
La Venta, *Mexico* **87 D6** 18 8N 94 3W
La Ventura, *Mexico* **86 C4** 24 38N 100 54W
Labe = Elbe →, *Europe* **16 B5** 53 50N 9 0 E
Labé, *Guinea* **50 F2** 11 24N 12 16W
Laberge, L., *Canada* **72 A1** 61 11N 135 12W
Labis, *Malaysia* **39 L4** 2 22N 103 2 E
Laboulaye, *Argentina* **94 C3** 34 10S 63 30W
Labrador, Coast of □, *Canada* **71 B7** 53 20N 61 0W
Labrador City, *Canada* **71 B6** 52 57N 66 55W
Lábrea, *Brazil* **92 E6** 7 15S 64 51W
Labuan, Pulau, *Malaysia* **36 C5** 5 21N 115 13 E
Labuha, *Indonesia* **37 E7** 0 30S 127 30 E
Labuhan, *Indonesia* **37 G11** 6 22S 105 50 E
Labuhanbajo, *Indonesia* **37 F6** 8 28S 120 1 E
Labuk, Telok, *Malaysia* **36 C5** 6 10N 117 50 E
Labyrinth, L., *Australia* **63 E2** 30 40S 135 11 E
Labytnangi, *Russia* **24 A12** 66 39N 66 21 E
Lac Allard, *Canada* **71 B7** 50 33N 63 24W
Lac Bouchette, *Canada* **71 C5** 48 16N 72 11W
Lac du Flambeau, *U.S.A.* **80 B10** 45 58N 89 53W
Lac Édouard, *Canada* **70 C5** 47 40N 72 16W
Lac La Biche, *Canada* **72 C6** 54 45N 111 58W
Lac la Martre = Wha Ti, *Canada* **68 B8** 63 8N 117 16W
Lac-Mégantic, *Canada* **71 C5** 45 35N 70 53W
Lac Seul, Res., *Canada* **70 B1** 50 25N 92 30W
Lac Thien, *Vietnam* **38 F7** 12 25N 108 11 E
Lacanau, *France* **18 D3** 44 58N 1 5W
Lacantúm →, *Mexico* **87 D6** 16 36N 90 40W
Laccadive Is. = Lakshadweep Is., *Ind. Oc.* **28 H11** 10 0N 72 30 E
Lacepede B., *Australia* **63 F2** 36 40S 139 40 E
Lacepede Is., *Australia* **60 C3** 16 55S 122 0 E
Lacerdónia, *Mozam.* **55 F4** 18 3S 35 35 E
Lacey, *U.S.A.* **84 C4** 47 7N 122 49W
Lachhmangarh, *India* **42 F6** 27 50N 75 4 E
Lachi, *Pakistan* **42 C4** 33 25N 71 20 E
Lachine, *Canada* **70 C5** 45 30N 73 40W
Lachlan →, *Australia* **63 E3** 34 22S 143 55 E
Lachute, *Canada* **70 C5** 45 39N 74 21W
Lackawanna, *U.S.A.* **78 D6** 42 50N 78 50W
Lacolle, *Canada* **79 A11** 45 5N 73 22W
Lacombe, *Canada* **72 C6** 52 30N 113 44W
Lacona, *U.S.A.* **79 C8** 43 39N 76 10W
Laconia, *U.S.A.* **79 C13** 43 32N 71 28W
Lacrosse, *U.S.A.* **82 C5** 46 51N 117 58W
Ladakh Ra., *India* **43 B8** 34 0N 78 0 E
Ladismith, *S. Africa* **56 E3** 33 28S 21 15 E
Lādīz, *Iran* **45 D9** 28 55N 61 15 E
Ladnun, *India* **42 F6** 27 38N 74 25 E
Ladoga, L. = Ladozhskoye Ozero, *Russia* **24 B5** 61 15N 30 30 E
Ladozhskoye Ozero, *Russia* **24 B5** 61 15N 30 30 E
Lady Grey, *S. Africa* **56 E4** 30 43S 27 13 E
Ladybrand, *S. Africa* **56 D4** 29 9S 27 29 E
Ladysmith, *Canada* **72 D4** 49 0N 123 49W
Ladysmith, *S. Africa* **57 D4** 28 32S 29 46 E
Ladysmith, *U.S.A.* **80 C9** 45 28N 91 12W
Lae, *Papua N. G.* **64 H6** 6 40S 147 2 E
Laem Ngop, *Thailand* **39 F4** 12 10N 102 26 E
Laem Pho, *Thailand* **39 J3** 6 55N 101 19 E
Læsø, *Denmark* **9 H14** 57 15N 10 53 E
Lafayette, *Colo., U.S.A.* **80 F2** 39 58N 105 12W
Lafayette, *Ind., U.S.A.* **76 E2** 40 25N 86 54W
Lafayette, *La., U.S.A.* **81 K9** 30 14N 92 1W
Lafayette, *Tenn., U.S.A.* **77 G3** 36 31N 86 2W
Laferte →, *Canada* **72 A5** 61 53N 117 44W
Lafia, *Nigeria* **50 G6** 8 30N 8 34 E
Lafleche, *Canada* **73 D7** 49 45N 106 40W
Lagan →, *U.K.* **13 B6** 54 36N 5 55W
Lagarfljót →, *Iceland* **8 D6** 65 40N 14 18W
Lågen →, *Oppland, Norway* **9 F14** 61 8N 10 25 E
Lågen →, *Vestfold, Norway* **9 G14** 59 3N 10 3 E
Laghouat, *Algeria* **50 B5** 33 50N 2 59 E
Lagonoy Gulf, *Phil.* **37 B6** 13 50N 123 50 E
Lagos, *Nigeria* **50 G5** 6 25N 3 27 E
Lagos, *Portugal* **19 D1** 37 5N 8 41W
Lagos de Moreno, *Mexico* **86 C4** 21 21N 101 55W
Lagrange, *Australia* **60 C3** 18 45S 121 43 E
Lagrange B., *Australia* **60 C3** 18 38S 121 42 E
Laguna, *Brazil* **95 B6** 28 30S 48 50W
Laguna, *U.S.A.* **83 J10** 35 2N 107 25W
Laguna Beach, *U.S.A.* **85 M9** 33 33N 117 47W
Laguna Limpia, *Argentina* **94 B4** 26 32S 59 45W
Laguna Madre, *U.S.A.* **87 B5** 27 0N 97 20W
Lagunas, *Chile* **94 A2** 21 0S 69 45W
Lagunas, *Peru* **92 E3** 5 10S 75 35W
Lahad Datu, *Malaysia* **37 C5** 5 0N 118 20 E
Lahan Sai, *Thailand* **38 E4** 14 25N 102 52 E
Lahanam, *Laos* **38 D5** 16 16N 105 16 E
Laharpur, *India* **43 F9** 27 43N 80 56 E
Lahat, *Indonesia* **36 E2** 3 45S 103 30 E
Lahewa, *Indonesia* **36 D1** 1 22N 97 12 E
Lāhījān, *Iran* **45 B6** 37 10N 50 6 E
Lahn →, *Germany* **16 C4** 50 19N 7 37 E
Laholm, *Sweden* **9 H15** 56 30N 13 2 E
Lahontan Reservoir, *U.S.A.* **82 G4** 39 28N 119 4W
Lahore, *Pakistan* **42 D6** 31 32N 74 22 E
Lahti, *Finland* **9 F21** 60 58N 25 40 E
Lahtis = Lahti, *Finland* **9 F21** 60 58N 25 40 E
Laï, *Chad* **51 G8** 9 25N 16 18 E
Lai Chau, *Vietnam* **38 A4** 22 5N 103 3 E
Laidley, *Australia* **63 D5** 27 39S 152 20 E
Laikipia □, *Kenya* **54 B4** 0 30N 36 30 E
Laingsburg, *S. Africa* **56 E3** 33 9S 20 52 E
Lainio älv →, *Sweden* **8 C20** 67 35N 22 40 E
Lairg, *U.K.* **12 C4** 58 2N 4 24W
Laishui, *China* **34 E8** 39 23N 115 45 E
Laiwu, *China* **35 F9** 36 15N 117 40 E
Laixi, *China* **35 F11** 36 50N 120 31 E
Laiyang, *China* **35 F11** 36 59N 120 45 E
Laiyuan, *China* **34 E8** 39 20N 114 40 E
Laizhou Wan, *China* **35 F10** 37 30N 119 30 E
Laja →, *Mexico* **86 C4** 20 55N 100 46W
Lajere, *Nigeria* **50 F7** 12 10N 11 25 E
Lajes, *Brazil* **95 B5** 27 48S 50 20W
Lak Sao, *Laos* **38 C5** 18 11N 104 59 E
Lakaband, *Pakistan* **42 D3** 31 2N 69 15 E
Lake Alpine, *U.S.A.* **84 G7** 38 29N 120 0W
Lake Andes, *U.S.A.* **80 D5** 43 9N 98 32W
Lake Anse, *U.S.A.* **76 B1** 46 42N 88 25W
Lake Arthur, *U.S.A.* **81 K8** 30 5N 92 41W
Lake Cargelligo, *Australia* **63 E4** 33 15S 146 22 E
Lake Charles, *U.S.A.* **81 K8** 30 14N 93 13W
Lake City, *Colo., U.S.A.* **83 G10** 38 2N 107 19W
Lake City, *Fla., U.S.A.* **77 K4** 30 11N 82 38W
Lake City, *Iowa, U.S.A.* **80 D7** 42 16N 94 44W
Lake City, *Mich., U.S.A.* **76 C3** 44 20N 85 13W
Lake City, *Minn., U.S.A.* **80 C8** 44 27N 92 16W
Lake City, *Pa., U.S.A.* **78 D4** 42 1N 80 21W
Lake City, *S.C., U.S.A.* **77 J6** 33 52N 79 45W
Lake George, *U.S.A.* **79 C11** 43 26N 73 43W
Lake Grace, *Australia* **61 F2** 33 7S 118 28 E
Lake Harbour = Kimmirut, *Canada* **69 B13** 62 50N 69 50W
Lake Havasu City, *U.S.A.* **85 L12** 34 27N 114 22W
Lake Hughes, *U.S.A.* **85 L8** 34 41N 118 26W
Lake Isabella, *U.S.A.* **85 K8** 35 38N 118 28W
Lake King, *Australia* **61 F2** 33 5S 119 45 E
Lake Lenore, *Canada* **73 C8** 52 24N 104 59W
Lake Louise, *Canada* **72 C5** 51 30N 116 10W
Lake Mead National Recreation Area, *U.S.A.* **85 K12** 36 15N 114 30W
Lake Mills, *U.S.A.* **80 D8** 43 25N 93 32W
Lake Nash, *Australia* **62 C2** 20 57S 138 0 E
Lake Providence, *U.S.A.* **81 J9** 32 48N 91 10W
Lake River, *Canada* **70 B3** 54 30N 82 31W
Lake Superior Prov. Park, *Canada* **70 C3** 47 45N 84 45W
Lake Village, *U.S.A.* **81 J9** 33 20N 91 17W
Lake Wales, *U.S.A.* **77 M5** 27 54N 81 35W
Lake Worth, *U.S.A.* **77 M5** 26 37N 80 3W
Lakefield, *Canada* **70 D4** 44 25N 78 16W
Lakeland, *Australia* **62 B3** 15 49S 144 57 E
Lakeland, *U.S.A.* **77 L5** 28 3N 81 57W
Lakemba, *Fiji* **59 D9** 18 13S 178 47W
Lakeport, *U.S.A.* **84 F4** 39 3N 122 55W
Lakes Entrance, *Australia* **63 F4** 37 50S 148 0 E
Lakeside, *Ariz., U.S.A.* **83 J9** 34 9N 109 58W
Lakeside, *Calif., U.S.A.* **85 N10** 32 52N 116 55W
Lakeside, *Nebr., U.S.A.* **80 D3** 42 3N 102 26W
Lakeview, *U.S.A.* **82 E3** 42 11N 120 21W
Lakewood, *Colo., U.S.A.* **80 F2** 39 44N 105 5W
Lakewood, *N.J., U.S.A.* **79 F10** 40 6N 74 13W
Lakewood, *Ohio, U.S.A.* **78 E3** 41 29N 81 48W
Lakewood Center, *U.S.A.* **84 C4** 47 11N 122 32W
Lakhaniá, *Greece* **23 D9** 35 58N 27 54 E
Lakhonpheng, *Laos* **38 E5** 15 54N 105 34 E
Lakhpat, *India* **42 H3** 23 48N 68 47 E
Lakin, *U.S.A.* **81 G4** 37 57N 101 15W
Lakitusaki →, *Canada* **70 B3** 54 21N 82 25W
Lákkoi, *Greece* **23 D5** 35 24N 23 57 E
Lakonikós Kólpos, *Greece* **21 F10** 36 40N 22 40 E
Lakor, *Indonesia* **37 F7** 8 15S 128 17 E
Lakota, *Ivory C.* **50 G3** 5 50N 5 30W
Lakota, *U.S.A.* **80 A5** 48 2N 98 21W
Laksefjorden, *Norway* **8 A22** 70 45N 26 50 E
Lakselv, *Norway* **8 A21** 70 2N 25 0 E
Lakshadweep Is., *Ind. Oc.* **28 H11** 10 0N 72 30 E
Lakshmikantapur, *India* **43 H13** 22 5N 88 20 E
Lala Ghat, *India* **41 G18** 24 30N 92 40 E
Lala Musa, *Pakistan* **42 C5** 32 40N 73 57 E
Lalago, *Tanzania* **54 C3** 3 28S 33 58 E
Lalapanzi, *Zimbabwe* **55 F3** 19 20S 30 15 E
Lalganj, *India* **43 G11** 25 52N 85 13 E
Lalibela, *Ethiopia* **51 F12** 12 2N 39 2 E
Lalin, *China* **35 B14** 45 12N 127 0 E
Lalín, *Spain* **19 A1** 42 40N 8 5W
Lalin He →, *China* **35 B13** 45 32N 125 40 E
Lalitapur = Patan, *Nepal* **41 F14** 27 40N 85 20 E
Lalitpur, *India* **43 G8** 24 42N 78 28 E
Lam, *Vietnam* **38 B6** 21 21N 106 31 E
Lam Pao Res., *Thailand* **38 D4** 16 50N 103 15 E
Lamaing, *Burma* **41 M20** 15 25N 97 53 E
Lamar, *Colo., U.S.A.* **80 F3** 38 5N 102 37W
Lamar, *Mo., U.S.A.* **81 G7** 37 30N 94 16W
Lamas, *Peru* **92 E3** 6 28S 76 31W
Lambaréné, *Gabon* **52 E2** 0 41S 10 12 E
Lambasa, *Fiji* **59 C8** 16 30S 179 10 E
Lambay I., *Ireland* **13 C5** 53 29N 6 1W
Lambert, *U.S.A.* **80 B2** 47 41N 104 37W
Lambert Glacier, *Antarctica* **5 D6** 71 0S 70 0 E
Lamberts Bay, *S. Africa* **56 E2** 32 5S 18 17 E
Lame, *Nigeria* **50 F6** 10 30N 9 20 E
Lame Deer, *U.S.A.* **82 D10** 45 37N 106 40W
Lamego, *Portugal* **19 B2** 41 5N 7 52W
Lamèque, *Canada* **71 C7** 47 45N 64 38W
Lameroo, *Australia* **63 F3** 35 19S 140 33 E
Lamesa, *U.S.A.* **81 J4** 32 44N 101 58W
Lamía, *Greece* **21 E10** 38 55N 22 26 E
Lammermuir Hills, *U.K.* **12 F6** 55 50N 2 40W
Lamon Bay, *Phil.* **37 B6** 14 30N 122 20 E
Lamont, *Canada* **72 C6** 53 46N 112 50W
Lamont, *U.S.A.* **85 K8** 35 15N 118 55W
Lampa, *Peru* **92 G4** 15 22S 70 22W
Lampang, *Thailand* **38 C2** 18 16N 99 32 E
Lampasas, *U.S.A.* **81 K5** 31 4N 98 11W
Lampazos de Naranjo, *Mexico* **86 B4** 27 2N 100 32W
Lampedusa, *Medit. S.* **20 G5** 35 36N 12 40 E
Lampeter, *U.K.* **11 E3** 52 7N 4 4W
Lampione, *Medit. S.* **20 G5** 35 33N 12 20 E
Lampman, *Canada* **73 D8** 49 25N 102 50W
Lamprey, *Canada* **73 B10** 58 33N 94 8W
Lampung □, *Indonesia* **36 F2** 5 30S 104 30 E
Lamu, *Kenya* **54 C5** 2 16S 40 55 E
Lamu □, *Kenya* **54 C5** 2 0S 40 45 E
Lamy, *U.S.A.* **83 J11** 35 29N 105 53W
Lan Xian, *China* **34 E6** 38 15N 111 35 E
Lanai I., *U.S.A.* **74 H16** 20 50N 156 55W
Lanak La, *India* **43 B8** 34 27N 79 32 E
Lanak'o Shank'ou = Lanak La, *India* **43 B8** 34 27N 79 32 E
Lanao, L., *Phil.* **37 C6** 7 52N 124 15 E
Lanark, *Canada* **79 A8** 45 1N 76 22W
Lanark, *U.K.* **12 F5** 55 40N 3 47W
Lancang Jiang →, *China* **32 D5** 21 40N 101 10 E
Lancashire □, *U.K.* **10 D5** 53 50N 2 48W
Lancaster, *Canada* **79 A10** 45 10N 74 30W
Lancaster, *U.K.* **10 C5** 54 3N 2 48W
Lancaster, *Calif., U.S.A.* **85 L8** 34 42N 118 8W
Lancaster, *Ky., U.S.A.* **76 G3** 37 37N 84 35W
Lancaster, *N.H., U.S.A.* **79 B13** 44 29N 71 34W
Lancaster, *N.Y., U.S.A.* **78 D6** 42 54N 78 40W
Lancaster, *Pa., U.S.A.* **79 F8** 40 2N 76 19W
Lancaster, *S.C., U.S.A.* **77 H5** 34 43N 80 46W
Lancaster, *Wis., U.S.A.* **80 D9** 42 51N 90 43W
Lancaster Sd., *Canada* **69 A11** 74 13N 84 0W
Lancer, *Canada* **73 C7** 50 48N 108 53W
Lanchow = Lanzhou, *China* **34 F2** 36 1N 103 52 E
Lanciano, *Italy* **20 C6** 42 14N 14 23 E
Lancun, *China* **35 F11** 36 25N 120 10 E
Landeck, *Austria* **16 E6** 47 9N 10 34 E
Landen, *Belgium* **15 D5** 50 45N 5 3 E
Lander, *U.S.A.* **82 E9** 42 50N 108 44W
Lander →, *Australia* **60 D5** 22 0S 132 0 E
Landes, *France* **18 D3** 44 0N 1 0W
Landi Kotal, *Pakistan* **42 B4** 34 7N 71 6 E
Landor, *Australia* **61 E2** 25 10S 116 54 E
Land's End, *U.K.* **11 G2** 50 4N 5 44W
Landsborough Cr. →, *Australia* **62 C3** 22 28S 144 35 E
Landshut, *Germany* **16 D7** 48 34N 12 8 E
Landskrona, *Sweden* **9 J15** 55 53N 12 50 E
Lanesboro, *U.S.A.* **79 E9** 41 57N 75 34W
Lanett, *U.S.A.* **77 J3** 32 52N 85 12W
Lang Bay, *Canada* **72 D4** 49 45N 124 21W
Lang Qua, *Vietnam* **38 A5** 22 16N 104 27 E
Lang Shan, *China* **34 D4** 41 0N 106 30 E
Lang Son, *Vietnam* **38 B6** 21 52N 106 42 E
Lang Suan, *Thailand* **39 H2** 9 57N 99 4 E
La'nga Co, *China* **41 D12** 30 45N 81 15 E
Langar, *Iran* **45 C9** 35 23N 60 25 E
Langara I., *Canada* **72 C2** 54 14N 133 1W
Langdon, *U.S.A.* **80 A5** 48 45N 98 22W
Langeberg, *S. Africa* **56 E3** 33 55S 21 0 E
Langeberge, *S. Africa* **56 D3** 28 15S 22 33 E
Langeland, *Denmark* **9 J14** 54 56N 10 48 E
Langenburg, *Canada* **73 C8** 50 51N 101 43W
Langholm, *U.K.* **12 F6** 55 9N 3 0W
Langjökull, *Iceland* **8 D3** 64 39N 20 12W
Langkawi, P., *Malaysia* **39 J2** 6 25N 99 45 E
Langklip, *S. Africa* **56 D3** 28 12S 20 20 E
Langkon, *Malaysia* **36 C5** 6 30N 116 40 E
Langlade, *St- P. & M.* **71 C8** 46 50N 56 20W
Langlois, *U.S.A.* **82 E1** 42 56N 124 27W
Langøya, *Norway* **8 B16** 68 45N 14 50 E
Langres, *France* **18 C6** 47 52N 5 20 E
Langres, Plateau de, *France* **18 C6** 47 45N 5 3 E
Langsa, *Indonesia* **36 D1** 4 30N 97 57 E
Langtry, *U.S.A.* **81 L4** 29 49N 101 34W
Langu, *Thailand* **39 J2** 6 53N 99 47 E
Languedoc, *France* **18 E5** 43 58N 3 55 E
Langxiangzhen, *China* **34 E9** 39 43N 116 8 E
Lanigan, *Canada* **73 C7** 51 51N 105 2W
Lankao, *China* **34 G8** 34 48N 114 50 E
Länkäran, *Azerbaijan* **25 G8** 38 48N 48 52 E
Lannion, *France* **18 B2** 48 46N 3 29W
L'Annonciation, *Canada* **70 C5** 46 25N 74 55W
Lansdale, *U.S.A.* **79 F9** 40 14N 75 17W
Lansdowne, *Australia* **63 E5** 31 48S 152 30 E
Lansdowne, *Canada* **79 B8** 44 24N 76 1W

Lansdowne House

Maluku

McGehee, U.S.A. 81 J9 33 38N 91 24W
McGill, U.S.A. 82 G6 39 23N 114 47W
Macgillycuddy's Reeks, Ireland 13 D2 51 58N 9 45W
MacGregor, Canada 73 D9 49 57N 98 48W
McGregor, U.S.A. 80 D9 43 1N 91 11W
McGregor →, Canada 72 B4 55 10N 122 0W
McGregor Ra., Australia 63 D3 27 0S 142 45 E
Mach, Pakistan 40 E5 29 50N 67 20 E
Māch Kowr, Iran 45 E9 25 48N 61 28 E
Machado = Jiparaná →, Brazil 92 E6 8 3S 62 52W
Machagai, Argentina 94 B3 26 56S 60 2W
Machakos, Kenya 54 C4 1 30S 37 15 E
Machakos □, Kenya 54 C4 1 30S 37 15 E
Machala, Ecuador 92 D3 3 20S 79 57W
Machanga, Mozam. 57 C6 20 59S 35 0 E
Machattie, L., Australia 62 C2 24 50S 139 48 E
Machava, Mozam. 57 D5 25 54S 32 28 E
Machece, Mozam. 55 F4 19 15S 35 32 E
Machevna, Russia 27 C18 61 20N 172 20 E
Machias, U.S.A. 71 D6 44 43N 67 28W
Machichi →, Canada 73 B10 57 3N 92 6W
Machico, Madeira 22 D3 32 43N 16 44W
Machilipatnam, India 41 L12 16 12N 81 8 E
Machiques, Venezuela 92 A4 10 4N 72 34W
Machupicchu, Peru 92 F4 13 8S 72 30W
Machynlleth, U.K. 11 E4 52 35N 3 50W
McIlwraith Ra., Australia 62 A3 13 50S 143 20 E
McIntosh, U.S.A. 80 C4 45 55N 101 21W
McIntosh L., Canada 73 B8 55 45N 105 0W
Macintosh Ra., Australia 61 E4 27 39S 125 32 E
Macintyre →, Australia 63 D5 28 37S 150 47 E
Mackay, Australia 62 C4 21 8S 149 11 E
Mackay, U.S.A. 82 E7 43 55N 113 37W
MacKay →, Canada 72 B6 57 10N 111 38W
Mackay, L., Australia 60 D4 22 30S 129 0 E
McKay Ra., Australia 60 D3 23 0S 122 30 E
McKeesport, U.S.A. 78 F5 40 21N 79 52W
McKenna, U.S.A. 84 D4 46 56N 122 33W
Mackenzie, Canada 72 B4 55 20N 123 5W
McKenzie, U.S.A. 77 G1 36 8N 88 31W
Mackenzie →, Australia 62 C4 23 38S 149 46 E
Mackenzie →, Canada 68 B6 69 10N 134 20W
McKenzie →, U.S.A. 82 D2 44 7N 123 6W
Mackenzie Bay, Canada 4 B1 69 0N 137 30W
Mackenzie City = Linden, Guyana 92 B7 6 0N 58 10W
Mackenzie Highway, Canada 72 B5 58 0N 117 15W
Mackenzie Mts., Canada 68 B6 64 0N 130 0W
Mackinaw City, U.S.A. 76 C3 45 47N 84 44W
McKinlay, Australia 62 C3 21 16S 141 18 E
McKinlay →, Australia 62 C3 20 50S 141 28 E
McKinley, Mt., U.S.A. 68 B4 63 4N 151 0W
McKinley Sea, Arctic 4 A7 82 0N 0 0 E
McKinney, U.S.A. 81 J6 33 12N 96 37W
Mackinnon Road, Kenya 54 C4 3 40S 39 1 E
Macksville, Australia 63 E5 30 40S 152 56 E
McLaughlin, U.S.A. 80 C4 45 49N 100 49W
Maclean, Australia 63 D5 29 26S 153 16 E
McLean, U.S.A. 81 H4 35 14N 100 36W
McLeansboro, U.S.A. 80 F10 38 6N 88 32W
Maclear, S. Africa 57 E4 31 2S 28 23 E
Macleay →, Australia 63 E5 30 56S 153 0 E
McLennan, Canada 72 B5 55 42N 116 50W
MacLeod, B., Canada 73 A7 62 53N 110 0W
McLeod, L., Australia 61 D1 24 9S 113 47 E
MacLeod Lake, Canada 72 C4 54 58N 123 0W
McLoughlin, Mt., U.S.A. 82 E2 42 27N 122 19W
McLure, Canada 72 C4 51 2N 120 13W
McMechen, U.S.A. 78 G4 39 57N 80 44W
McMillan, L., U.S.A. 81 J2 32 36N 104 21W
McMinnville, Oreg., U.S.A. 82 D2 45 13N 123 12W
McMinnville, Tenn., U.S.A. 77 H3 35 41N 85 46W
McMorran, Canada 73 C7 51 19N 108 42W
McMurdo Sd., Antarctica 5 D11 77 0S 170 0 E
McMurray = Fort McMurray, Canada 72 B6 56 44N 111 7W
McMurray, U.S.A. 84 B4 48 19N 122 14W
McNary, U.S.A. 83 J9 34 4N 109 51W
MacNutt, Canada 73 C8 51 5N 101 36W
Macodoene, Mozam. 57 C6 23 32S 35 5 E
Macomb, U.S.A. 80 E9 40 27N 90 40W
Mâcon, France 18 C6 46 19N 4 50 E
Macon, Ga., U.S.A. 77 J4 32 51N 83 38W
Macon, Miss., U.S.A. 77 J1 33 7N 88 34W
Macon, Mo., U.S.A. 80 F8 39 44N 92 28W
Macondo, Angola 53 G4 12 37S 23 46 E
Macossa, Mozam. 55 F3 17 55S 33 56 E
Macoun L., Canada 73 B8 56 32N 103 40W
Macovane, Mozam. 57 C6 21 30S 35 2 E
McPherson, U.S.A. 80 F6 38 22N 97 40W
McPherson Pk., U.S.A. 85 L7 34 53N 119 53W
McPherson Ra., Australia 63 D5 28 15S 153 15 E
Macquarie Harbour, Australia 62 G4 42 15S 145 23 E
Macquarie Is., Pac. Oc. 64 N7 54 36S 158 55 E
MacRobertson Land, Antarctica 5 D6 71 0S 64 0 E
Macroom, Ireland 13 E3 51 54N 8 57W
Macroy, Australia 60 D2 20 53S 118 2 E
MacTier, Canada 78 A5 45 9N 79 46W
Macubela, Mozam. 55 F4 16 53S 37 49 E
Macuiza, Mozam. 55 F3 18 7S 34 29 E
Macuse, Mozam. 55 F4 17 45S 37 10 E
Macuspana, Mexico 87 D6 17 46N 92 36W
Macusse, Angola 56 B3 17 48S 20 23 E
McVille, U.S.A. 80 B5 47 46N 98 11W
Madadeni, S. Africa 57 D5 27 43S 30 3 E
Madagali, Nigeria 51 F7 10 56N 13 33 E
Madagascar ■, Africa 57 C8 20 0S 47 0 E
Madā'in Sālih, Si. Arabia 44 E3 26 46N 37 57 E
Madama, Niger 51 D7 22 0N 13 40 E
Madame I., Canada 71 C7 45 30N 60 58W
Madaoua, Niger 50 F6 14 5N 6 27 E
Madaripur, Bangla. 41 H17 23 19N 90 15 E
Madauk, Burma 41 L20 17 56N 96 52 E
Madawaska, Canada 78 A7 45 30N 78 0W
Madawaska →, Canada 78 A8 45 27N 76 21W
Madaya, Burma 41 H20 22 12N 96 10 E
Maddalena, Italy 20 D3 41 15N 9 23 E
Madeira, Atl. Oc. 22 D3 32 50N 17 0W
Madeira →, Brazil 92 D7 3 22S 58 45W
Madeleine, Is. de la, Canada 71 C7 47 30N 61 40W
Madera, U.S.A. 83 H3 36 57N 120 3W
Madha, India 40 L9 18 0N 75 30 E
Madhubani, India 43 F12 26 21N 86 7 E
Madhya Pradesh □, India 42 J7 22 50N 78 0 E
Madikeri, India 40 N9 12 30N 75 45 E
Madill, U.S.A. 81 H6 34 6N 96 46W
Madimba, Zaïre 52 E3 4 58S 15 5 E
Ma'din, Syria 44 C3 35 45N 39 36 E
Madīnat ash Sha'b, Yemen 46 E3 12 50N 45 0 E
Madingou, Congo 52 E2 4 10S 13 33 E
Madirovalo, Madag. 57 B8 16 26S 46 32 E
Madison, Calif., U.S.A. 84 G5 38 41N 121 59W
Madison, Fla., U.S.A. 77 K4 30 28N 83 25W
Madison, Ind., U.S.A. 76 F3 38 44N 85 23W
Madison, Nebr., U.S.A. 80 E6 41 50N 97 27W
Madison, Ohio, U.S.A. 78 E3 41 46N 81 3W
Madison, S. Dak., U.S.A. 80 D6 44 0N 97 7W
Madison, Wis., U.S.A. 80 D10 43 4N 89 24W
Madison →, U.S.A. 82 D8 45 56N 111 31W
Madisonville, Ky., U.S.A. 76 G2 37 20N 87 30W
Madisonville, Tex., U.S.A. 81 K7 30 57N 95 55W
Madista, Botswana 56 C4 21 15S 25 6 E
Madiun, Indonesia 37 G14 7 38S 111 32 E
Madley, U.K. 11 E5 52 2N 2 51W
Madona, Latvia 9 H22 56 53N 26 5 E
Madras = Tamil Nadu □, India 40 P10 11 0N 77 0 E
Madras, India 40 N12 13 8N 80 19 E
Madras, U.S.A. 82 D3 44 38N 121 8W
Madre, L., Mexico 87 B5 25 0N 97 30W
Madre, Laguna, U.S.A. 81 M6 27 0N 97 30W
Madre, Sierra, Phil. 37 A6 17 0N 122 0 E
Madre de Dios →, Bolivia 92 F5 10 59S 66 8W
Madre de Dios, I., Chile 96 G1 50 20S 75 10W
Madre del Sur, Sierra, Mexico 87 D5 17 30N 100 0W
Madre Occidental, Sierra, Mexico 86 B3 27 0N 107 0W
Madre Oriental, Sierra, Mexico 86 C4 25 0N 100 0W
Madri, India 42 G5 24 16N 73 32 E
Madrid, Spain 19 B4 40 25N 3 45W
Madura, Selat, Indonesia 37 G15 7 30S 113 20 E
Madura Motel, Australia 61 F4 31 55S 127 0 E
Madurai, India 40 Q11 9 55N 78 10 E
Madurantakam, India 40 N11 12 30N 79 50 E
Mae Chan, Thailand 38 B2 20 9N 99 52 E
Mae Hong Son, Thailand 38 C2 19 16N 98 1 E
Mae Khlong →, Thailand 38 F3 13 24N 100 0 E
Mae Phrik, Thailand 38 D2 17 27N 99 7 E
Mae Ramat, Thailand 38 D2 16 58N 98 31 E
Mae Rim, Thailand 38 C2 18 54N 98 57 E
Mae Sot, Thailand 38 D2 16 43N 98 34 E
Mae Suai, Thailand 38 C2 19 39N 99 33 E
Mae Tha, Thailand 38 C2 18 28N 99 8 E
Maebashi, Japan 31 F9 36 24N 139 4 E
Maesteg, U.K. 11 F4 51 36N 3 40W
Maestra, Sierra, Cuba 88 B4 20 15N 77 0W
Maestrazgo, Mts. del, Spain 19 B5 40 30N 0 25W
Maevatanana, Madag. 57 B8 16 56S 46 49 E
Mafeking = Mafikeng, S. Africa 56 D4 25 50S 25 38 E
Mafeking, Canada 73 C8 52 40N 101 10W
Mafeteng, Lesotho 56 D4 29 51S 27 15 E
Maffra, Australia 63 F4 37 53S 146 58 E
Mafia I., Tanzania 54 D4 7 45S 39 50 E
Mafikeng, S. Africa 56 D4 25 50S 25 38 E
Mafra, Brazil 95 B6 26 10S 49 55W
Mafra, Portugal 19 C1 38 55N 9 20W
Mafungabusi Plateau, Zimbabwe 55 F2 18 30S 29 8 E
Magadan, Russia 27 D16 59 38N 150 50 E
Magadi, Kenya 54 C4 1 54S 36 19 E
Magadi, L., Kenya 54 C4 1 54S 36 19 E
Magaliesburg, S. Africa 57 D4 26 0S 27 32 E
Magallanes, Estrecho de, Chile 96 G2 52 30S 75 0W
Magangué, Colombia 92 B4 9 14N 74 45W
Magburaka, S. Leone 50 G2 8 47N 12 0W
Magdalen Is. = Madeleine, Is. de la, Canada 71 C7 47 30N 61 40W
Magdalena, Argentina 94 D4 35 5S 57 30W
Magdalena, Bolivia 92 F6 13 13S 63 57W
Magdalena, Malaysia 36 D5 4 25N 117 55 E
Magdalena, Mexico 86 A2 30 50N 112 0W
Magdalena, U.S.A. 83 J10 34 7N 107 15W
Magdalena →, Colombia 92 A4 11 6N 74 51W
Magdalena →, Mexico 86 A2 30 40N 112 25W
Magdalena, B., Mexico 86 C2 24 30N 112 10W
Magdalena, Llano de la, Mexico 86 C2 25 0N 111 30W
Magdeburg, Germany 16 B6 52 7N 11 38 E
Magdelaine Cays, Australia 62 B5 16 33S 150 18 E
Magee, U.S.A. 81 K10 31 52N 89 44W
Magee, I., U.K. 13 B6 54 48N 5 43W
Magelang, Indonesia 37 G14 7 29S 110 13 E
Magellan's Str. = Magallanes, Estrecho de, Chile 96 G2 52 30S 75 0W
Magenta, L., Australia 61 F2 33 30S 119 2 E
Magerøya, Norway 8 A21 71 3N 25 40 E
Maggiore, L., Italy 20 B3 45 57N 8 39 E
Magherafelt, U.K. 13 B5 54 45N 6 37W
Magistralnyy, Russia 27 D11 56 16N 107 36 E
Magnetic Pole (North) = North Magnetic Pole, Canada 4 B2 77 58N 102 8W
Magnetic Pole (South) = South Magnetic Pole, Antarctica 5 C9 64 8S 138 8 E
Magnitogorsk, Russia 24 D10 53 27N 59 4 E
Magnolia, Ark., U.S.A. 81 J8 33 16N 93 14W
Magnolia, Miss., U.S.A. 81 K9 31 9N 90 28W
Magog, Canada 71 C5 45 18N 72 9W
Magoro, Uganda 54 B3 1 45N 34 12 E
Magosa = Famagusta, Cyprus 23 D12 35 8N 33 55 E
Magouládhes, Greece 23 A3 39 45N 19 42 E
Magoye, Zambia 55 F2 16 1S 27 30 E
Magpie L., Canada 71 B7 51 0N 64 41W
Magrath, Canada 72 D6 49 25N 112 50W
Magu □, Tanzania 54 C3 2 31S 33 28 E
Maguarinho, C., Brazil 93 D9 0 15S 48 30W
Mağusa = Famagusta, Cyprus 23 D12 35 8N 33 55 E
Maguse L., Canada 73 A9 61 40N 95 10W
Maguse Pt., Canada 73 A10 61 20N 93 50W
Magwe, Burma 41 J19 20 10N 95 0 E
Maha Sarakham, Thailand 38 D4 16 12N 103 16 E
Mahābād, Iran 44 B5 36 50N 45 45 E
Mahabharat Lekh, Nepal 43 E9 28 30N 82 0 E
Mahabo, Madag. 57 C7 20 23S 44 40 E
Mahadeo Hills, India 42 H8 22 20N 78 30 E
Mahagi, Zaïre 54 B3 2 20N 31 0 E
Mahajamba →, Madag. 57 B8 15 33S 47 8 E
Mahajamba, Helodranon' i, Madag. 57 B8 15 24S 47 5 E
Mahajan, India 42 E5 28 48N 73 56 E
Mahajanga, Madag. 57 B8 15 40S 46 25 E
Mahajanga □, Madag. 57 B8 17 0S 47 0 E
Mahajilo →, Madag. 57 B8 19 42S 45 22 E
Mahakam →, Indonesia 36 E5 0 35S 117 17 E
Mahalapye, Botswana 56 C4 23 1S 26 51 E
Maḩallāt, Iran 45 C6 33 55N 50 30 E
Māhān, Iran 45 D8 30 5N 57 18 E
Mahanadi →, India 41 J15 20 20N 86 25 E
Mahanoro, Madag. 57 B8 19 54S 48 48 E
Mahanoy City, U.S.A. 79 F8 40 49N 76 9W
Maharashtra □, India 40 J9 20 30N 75 30 E
Mahari Mts., Tanzania 54 D2 6 20S 30 0 E
Mahasham, W. →, Egypt 47 E3 30 15N 34 10 E
Mahasolo, Madag. 57 B8 19 7S 46 22 E
Mahattat ash Shīdīyah, Jordan 47 F4 29 55N 35 55 E
Mahattat 'Unayzah, Jordan 47 E4 30 30N 35 47 E
Mahaxay, Laos 38 D5 17 22N 105 12 E
Mahbubnagar, India 40 L10 16 45N 77 59 E
Maḩḑah, Oman 45 E7 24 24N 55 59 E
Mahdia, Tunisia 51 A7 35 28N 11 0 E
Mahe, India 43 C8 33 10N 78 32 E
Mahenge, Tanzania 55 D4 8 45S 36 41 E
Maheno, N.Z. 59 L3 45 10S 170 50 E
Mahesana, India 42 H5 23 39N 72 26 E
Mahia Pen., N.Z. 59 H6 39 9S 177 55 E
Mahilyow, Belarus 17 B16 53 55N 30 18 E
Mahmud Kot, Pakistan 42 D4 30 16N 71 0 E
Mahnomen, U.S.A. 80 B7 47 19N 95 58W
Mahoba, India 43 G8 25 15N 79 55 E
Mahón, Spain 22 B11 39 53N 4 16 E
Mahone Bay, Canada 71 D7 44 30N 64 20W
Mai-Ndombe, L., Zaïre 52 E3 2 0S 18 20 E
Mai-Sai, Thailand 38 B2 20 20N 99 55 E
Maicurú →, Brazil 93 D8 2 14S 54 17W
Maidan Khula, Afghan. 42 C3 33 36N 69 50 E
Maidenhead, U.K. 11 F7 51 31N 0 42W
Maidstone, Canada 73 C7 53 5N 109 20W
Maidstone, U.K. 11 F8 51 16N 0 32 E
Maiduguri, Nigeria 51 F7 12 0N 13 20 E
Maijdi, Bangla. 41 H17 22 48N 91 10 E
Maikala Ra., India 41 J12 22 0N 81 0 E
Mailsi, Pakistan 42 E5 29 48N 72 15 E
Main →, Germany 16 C5 50 0N 8 18 E
Main →, U.K. 13 B5 54 48N 6 18W
Main Centre, Canada 73 C7 50 35N 107 21W
Maine, France 18 C3 47 55N 0 25W
Maine □, U.S.A. 71 C6 45 20N 69 0W
Maine →, Ireland 13 D2 52 9N 9 45W
Maingkwan, Burma 41 F20 26 15N 96 37 E
Mainit, L., Phil. 37 C7 9 31N 125 30 E
Mainland, Orkney, U.K. 12 C5 58 59N 3 8W
Mainland, Shet., U.K. 12 A7 60 15N 1 22W
Mainpuri, India 43 F8 27 18N 79 4 E
Maintirano, Madag. 57 B7 18 3S 44 1 E
Mainz, Germany 16 C5 50 1N 8 14 E
Maipú, Argentina 94 D4 36 52S 57 50W
Maiquetía, Venezuela 92 A5 10 36N 66 57W
Mairabari, India 41 F18 26 30N 92 22 E
Maisí, Cuba 89 B5 20 17N 74 9W
Maisi, Pta. de, Cuba 89 B5 20 10N 74 10W
Maitland, N.S.W., Australia 63 E5 32 33S 151 36 E
Maitland, S. Austral., Australia 63 E2 34 23S 137 40 E
Maitland →, Canada 78 C3 43 45N 81 43W
Maiz, Is. del, Nic. 88 D3 12 15N 83 4W
Maizuru, Japan 31 G7 35 25N 135 22 E
Majalengka, Indonesia 37 G13 6 50S 108 13 E
Majene, Indonesia 37 E5 3 38S 118 57 E
Maji, Ethiopia 51 G12 6 12N 35 30 E
Major, Canada 73 C7 51 52N 109 37W
Majorca = Mallorca, Spain 22 B10 39 30N 3 0 E
Maka, Senegal 50 F2 13 40N 14 10W
Makale, Indonesia 37 E5 3 6S 119 51 E
Makamba, Burundi 54 C2 4 8S 29 49 E
Makari, Cameroon 52 B2 12 35N 14 28 E
Makarikari = Makgadikgadi Salt Pans, Botswana 56 C4 20 40S 25 45 E
Makarovo, Russia 27 D11 57 40N 107 45 E
Makasar = Ujung Pandang, Indonesia 37 F5 5 10S 119 20 E
Makasar, Selat, Indonesia 37 E5 1 0S 118 20 E
Makasar, Str. of = Makasar, Selat, Indonesia 37 E5 1 0S 118 20 E
Makat, Kazakstan 25 E9 47 39N 53 19 E
Makedhonía □, Greece 21 D10 40 39N 22 0 E
Makedonija = Macedonia ■, Europe 21 D9 41 53N 21 40 E
Makena, U.S.A. 74 H16 20 39N 156 27W
Makeni, S. Leone 50 G2 8 55N 12 5W
Makeyevka = Makiyivka, Ukraine 25 E6 48 0N 38 0 E
Makgadikgadi Salt Pans, Botswana 56 C4 20 40S 25 45 E
Makhachkala, Russia 25 F8 43 0N 47 30 E
Makhmūr, Iraq 44 C4 35 46N 43 35 E
Makian, Indonesia 37 D7 0 20N 127 20 E
Makindu, Kenya 54 C4 2 18S 37 50 E
Makinsk, Kazakstan 26 D8 52 37N 70 26 E
Makiyivka, Ukraine 25 E6 48 0N 38 0 E
Makkah, Si. Arabia 46 C2 21 30N 39 54 E
Makkovik, Canada 71 A8 55 10N 59 10W
Makó, Hungary 17 E11 46 14N 20 33 E
Makokou, Gabon 52 D2 0 40N 12 50 E
Makongo, Zaïre 54 B2 3 25N 26 17 E
Makoro, Zaïre 54 B2 3 10N 29 59 E
Makoua, Congo 52 E3 0 5S 15 50 E
Makrai, India 40 H10 22 2N 77 0 E
Makran Coast Range, Pakistan 40 G4 25 40N 64 0 E
Makrana, India 42 F6 27 2N 74 46 E
Makriyialos, Greece 23 D7 35 2N 25 59 E
Maksimkin Yar, Russia 26 D9 58 42N 86 50 E
Mākū, Iran 44 B5 39 15N 44 31 E
Makumbi, Zaïre 52 F4 5 50S 20 43 E
Makunda, Botswana 56 C3 22 30S 20 7 E
Makurazaki, Japan 31 J5 31 15N 130 20 E
Makurdi, Nigeria 50 G6 7 43N 8 35 E
Makūyeh, Iran 45 D7 28 7N 53 9 E
Makwassie, S. Africa 56 D4 27 17S 26 0 E
Mal B., Ireland 13 D2 52 50N 9 30W
Mala, Pta., Panama 88 E3 7 28N 80 2W
Malabang, Phil. 37 C6 7 36N 124 3 E
Malabar Coast, India 40 P9 11 0N 75 0 E
Malabo = Rey Malabo, Eq. Guin. 50 H6 3 45N 8 50 E
Malacca, Str. of, Indonesia 39 L3 3 0N 101 0 E
Malad City, U.S.A. 82 E7 42 12N 112 15W
Maladzyechna, Belarus 17 A14 54 20N 26 50 E
Málaga, Spain 19 D3 36 43N 4 23W
Malaga, U.S.A. 81 J2 32 14N 104 4W
Malagarasi, Tanzania 54 D3 5 5S 30 50 E
Malagarasi →, Tanzania 54 D2 5 12S 29 47 E
Malaimbandy, Madag. 57 C8 20 20S 45 36 E
Malakâl, Sudan 51 G11 9 33N 31 40 E
Malakand, Pakistan 42 B4 34 40N 71 55 E
Malakoff, U.S.A. 81 J7 32 10N 96 1W
Malamyzh, Russia 27 E14 49 50N 136 50 E
Malang, Indonesia 37 G15 7 59S 112 45 E
Malangen, Norway 8 B18 69 24N 18 37 E
Malanje, Angola 52 F3 9 36S 16 17 E
Mälaren, Sweden 9 G17 59 30N 17 10 E
Malargüe, Argentina 94 D2 35 32S 69 30W
Malartic, Canada 70 C4 48 9N 78 9W
Malaryta, Belarus 17 C13 51 50N 24 3 E
Malatya, Turkey 25 G6 38 25N 38 20 E
Malawi ■, Africa 55 E3 11 55S 34 0 E
Malawi, L., Africa 55 E3 12 30S 34 30 E
Malay Pen., Asia 39 J3 7 25N 100 0 E
Malaybalay, Phil. 37 C7 8 5N 125 7 E
Malāyer, Iran 45 C6 34 19N 48 51 E
Malaysia ■, Asia 36 D4 5 0N 110 0 E
Malazgirt, Turkey 25 G7 39 10N 42 33 E
Malbon, Australia 62 C3 21 5S 140 17 E
Malbooma, Australia 63 E1 30 41S 134 11 E
Malbork, Poland 17 B10 54 3N 19 1 E
Malcolm, Australia 61 E3 28 51S 121 25 E
Malcolm, Pt., Australia 61 F3 33 48S 123 45 E
Maldegem, Belgium 15 C3 51 14N 3 26 E
Malden, Mass., U.S.A. 79 D13 42 26N 71 4W
Malden, Mo., U.S.A. 81 G10 36 34N 89 57W
Malden I., Kiribati 65 H12 4 3S 155 1W
Maldives ■, Ind. Oc. 29 J11 5 0N 73 0 E
Maldonado, Uruguay 95 C5 34 59S 55 0W
Maldonado, Punta, Mexico 87 D5 16 19N 98 35W
Malé Karpaty, Slovak Rep. 17 D9 48 30N 17 20 E
Maléa, Ákra, Greece 21 F10 36 28N 23 7 E
Malegaon, India 40 J9 20 30N 74 38 E
Malei, Mozam. 55 F4 17 12S 36 58 E
Malek Kandī, Iran 44 B5 37 9N 46 6 E
Malela, Zaïre 54 C2 4 22S 26 8 E
Malema, Mozam. 55 E4 14 57S 37 20 E
Máleme, Greece 23 D5 35 31N 23 49 E
Malerkotla, India 42 D6 30 32N 75 58 E
Máles, Greece 23 D7 35 6N 25 35 E
Malgomaj, Sweden 8 D17 64 40N 16 30 E
Malha, Sudan 51 E10 15 8N 25 10 E
Malheur →, U.S.A. 82 D5 44 4N 116 59W
Malheur L., U.S.A. 82 E4 43 20N 118 48W
Mali ■, Africa 50 E4 17 0N 3 0W
Mali →, Burma 41 G20 25 40N 97 40 E
Malibu, U.S.A. 85 L8 34 2N 118 41W
Malik, Indonesia 37 E6 0 39S 123 16 E
Malili, Indonesia 37 E6 2 42S 121 6 E
Malimba, Mts., Zaïre 54 D2 7 30S 29 30 E
Malin Hd., Ireland 13 A4 55 23N 7 23W
Malindi, Kenya 54 C5 3 12S 40 5 E
Malines = Mechelen, Belgium 15 C4 51 2N 4 29 E
Malino, Indonesia 37 D6 1 0N 121 0 E
Malinyi, Tanzania 55 D4 8 56S 36 0 E
Malita, Phil. 37 C7 6 19N 125 39 E
Malkara, Turkey 21 D12 40 53N 26 53 E
Mallacoota, Australia 63 F4 37 40S 149 40 E
Mallacoota Inlet, Australia 63 F4 37 34S 149 40 E
Mallaig, U.K. 12 E3 57 0N 5 50W
Mallawan, India 43 F9 27 4N 80 12 E
Mallawi, Egypt 51 C11 27 44N 30 44 E
Mállia, Greece 23 D7 35 17N 25 27 E
Mallión, Kólpos, Greece 23 D7 35 19N 25 27 E
Mallorca, Spain 22 B10 39 30N 3 0 E
Mallorytown, Canada 79 B9 44 29N 75 53W
Mallow, Ireland 13 D3 52 8N 8 39W
Malmberget, Sweden 8 C19 67 11N 20 40 E
Malmédy, Belgium 15 D6 50 25N 6 2 E
Malmesbury, S. Africa 56 E2 33 28S 18 41 E
Malmö, Sweden 9 J15 55 36N 12 59 E
Malolos, Phil. 37 B6 14 50N 120 49 E
Malombe L., Malawi 55 E4 14 40S 35 15 E
Malone, U.S.A. 79 B10 44 51N 74 18W
Måløy, Norway 9 F11 61 57N 5 6 E
Malozemelskaya Tundra, Russia 24 A9 67 0N 50 0 E
Malpaso, Canary Is. 22 G1 27 43N 18 3W
Malpelo, Colombia 92 C2 4 3N 81 35W
Malta, Idaho, U.S.A. 82 E7 42 18N 113 22W
Malta, Mont., U.S.A. 82 B10 48 21N 107 52W
Malta ■, Europe 23 D1 35 50N 14 30 E
Maltahöhe, Namibia 56 C2 24 55S 17 0 E
Malton, Canada 78 C5 43 42N 79 38W
Malton, U.K. 10 C7 54 8N 0 49W
Maluku, Indonesia 37 E7 1 0S 127 0 E
Maluku □, Indonesia 37 E7 3 0S 128 0 E

Maluku Sea

Maluku Sea = Molucca Sea, Indonesia **37 E6** 2 0S 124 0 E
Malvan, India **40 L8** 16 2N 73 30 E
Malvern, U.S.A. **81 H8** 34 22N 92 49W
Malvern Hills, U.K. **11 E5** 52 0N 2 19W
Malvinas, Is. = Falkland Is. □, Atl. Oc. **96 G5** 51 30S 59 0W
Malya, Tanzania **54 C3** 3 5S 33 38 E
Malyn, Ukraine **17 C15** 50 46N 29 3 E
Malyy Lyakhovskiy, Ostrov, Russia **27 B15** 74 7N 140 36 E
Malyy Nimnyr, Russia **27 D13** 57 50N 125 10 E
Mama, Russia **27 D12** 58 18N 112 54 E
Mamanguape, Brazil **93 E11** 6 50S 35 4W
Mamasa, Indonesia **37 E5** 2 55S 119 20 E
Mambasa, Zaïre **54 B2** 1 22N 29 3 E
Mamberamo →, Indonesia **37 E9** 2 0S 137 50 E
Mambilima Falls, Zambia **55 E2** 10 31S 28 45 E
Mambirima, Zaïre **55 E2** 11 25S 27 33 E
Mambo, Tanzania **54 C4** 4 52S 38 22 E
Mambrui, Kenya **54 C5** 3 5S 40 5 E
Mamburao, Phil. **37 B6** 13 13N 120 39 E
Mameigwess L., Canada **70 B2** 52 35N 87 50W
Mamfe, Cameroon **50 G6** 5 50N 9 15 E
Mammoth, U.S.A. **83 K8** 32 43N 110 39W
Mamoré →, Bolivia **92 F5** 10 23S 65 53W
Mamou, Guinea **50 F2** 10 15N 12 0W
Mamuju, Indonesia **37 E5** 2 41S 118 50 E
Man, Ivory C. **50 G3** 7 30N 7 40W
Man, I. of, U.K. **10 C3** 54 15N 4 30W
Man Na, Burma **41 H20** 23 27N 97 19 E
Mana, Fr. Guiana **93 B8** 5 45N 53 55W
Manaar, G. of = Mannar, G. of, Asia **40 Q11** 8 30N 79 0 E
Manacapuru, Brazil **92 D6** 3 16S 60 37W
Manacor, Spain **22 B10** 39 34N 3 13 E
Manado, Indonesia **37 D6** 1 29N 124 51 E
Managua, Nic. **88 D2** 12 6N 86 20W
Managua, L., Nic. **88 D2** 12 20N 86 30W
Manakara, Madag. **57 C8** 22 8S 48 1 E
Manama = Al Manāmah, Bahrain **45 E6** 26 10N 50 30 E
Manambao →, Madag. **57 B7** 17 35S 44 0 E
Manambato, Madag. **57 A8** 13 43S 49 7 E
Manambolo →, Madag. **57 B7** 19 18S 44 22 E
Manambolosy, Madag. **57 B8** 16 2S 49 40 E
Mananara, Madag. **57 B8** 16 10S 49 46 E
Mananara →, Madag. **57 C8** 23 21S 47 42 E
Mananjary, Madag. **57 C8** 21 13S 48 20 E
Manantenina, Madag. **57 C8** 24 17S 47 19 E
Manaos = Manaus, Brazil **92 D7** 3 0S 60 0W
Manapouri, N.Z. **59 L1** 45 34S 167 39 E
Manapouri, L., N.Z. **59 L1** 45 32S 167 32 E
Manas, China **32 B3** 44 17N 85 56 E
Manas →, India **41 F17** 26 12N 90 40 E
Manaslu, Nepal **43 E11** 28 33N 84 33 E
Manasquan, U.S.A. **79 F10** 40 8N 74 3W
Manassa, U.S.A. **83 H11** 37 11N 105 56W
Manaung, Burma **41 K18** 18 45N 93 40 E
Manaus, Brazil **92 D7** 3 0S 60 0W
Manawan L., Canada **73 B8** 55 24N 103 14W
Manay, Phil. **37 C7** 7 17N 126 33 E
Manbij, Syria **44 B3** 36 31N 37 57 E
Mancelona, U.S.A. **76 C3** 44 54N 85 4W
Manchester, U.K. **10 D5** 53 29N 2 12W
Manchester, Calif., U.S.A. **84 G3** 38 58N 123 41W
Manchester, Conn., U.S.A. **79 E12** 41 47N 72 31W
Manchester, Ga., U.S.A. **77 J3** 32 51N 84 37W
Manchester, Iowa, U.S.A. **80 D9** 42 29N 91 27W
Manchester, Ky., U.S.A. **76 G4** 37 9N 83 46W
Manchester, N.H., U.S.A. **79 D13** 42 59N 71 28W
Manchester, N.Y., U.S.A. **78 D7** 42 56N 77 16W
Manchester, Vt., U.S.A. **79 C11** 43 10N 73 5W
Manchester L., Canada **73 A7** 61 28N 107 29W
Manchuria = Dongbei, China **35 D13** 42 0N 125 0 E
Manchurian Plain, China **28 E16** 47 0N 124 0 E
Mand →, Iran **45 D7** 28 20N 52 30 E
Manda, Chunya, Tanzania **54 D3** 6 51S 32 29 E
Manda, Ludewe, Tanzania **55 E3** 10 30S 34 40 E
Mandabé, Madag. **57 C7** 21 0S 44 55 E
Mandaguari, Brazil **95 A5** 23 32S 51 42W
Mandah, Mongolia **34 B5** 44 27N 108 2 E
Mandal, Norway **9 G12** 58 2N 7 25 E
Mandalay, Burma **41 J20** 22 0N 96 4 E
Mandale = Mandalay, Burma **41 J20** 22 0N 96 4 E
Mandalgovi, Mongolia **34 B4** 45 45N 106 10 E
Mandalī, Iraq **44 C5** 33 43N 45 28 E
Mandan, U.S.A. **80 B4** 46 50N 100 54W
Mandar, Teluk, Indonesia **37 E5** 3 35S 119 15 E
Mandaue, Phil. **37 B6** 10 20N 123 56 E
Mandera, Kenya **54 B5** 3 55N 41 53 E
Mandera □, Kenya **54 B5** 3 30N 41 0 E
Mandi, India **42 D7** 31 39N 76 58 E
Mandimba, Mozam. **55 E4** 14 20S 35 40 E
Mandioli, Indonesia **37 E7** 0 40S 127 20 E
Mandla, India **43 H9** 22 39N 80 30 E
Mandoto, Madag. **57 B8** 19 34S 46 17 E
Mandra, Pakistan **42 C5** 33 23N 73 12 E
Mandrare →, Madag. **57 D8** 25 10S 46 30 E
Mandritsara, Madag. **57 B8** 15 50S 48 49 E
Mandsaur, India **42 G6** 24 3N 75 8 E
Mandurah, Australia **61 F2** 32 36S 115 48 E
Mandvi, India **42 H3** 22 51N 69 22 E
Mandya, India **40 N10** 12 30N 77 0 E
Mandzai, Pakistan **42 D2** 30 55N 67 6 E
Maneh, Iran **45 B8** 37 39N 57 7 E
Maneroo, Australia **62 C3** 23 22S 143 53 E
Maneroo Cr. →, Australia **62 C3** 23 21S 143 53 E
Manfalût, Egypt **51 C11** 27 20N 30 52 E
Manfred, Australia **63 E3** 33 19S 143 45 E
Manfredónia, Italy **20 D6** 41 38N 15 55 E
Mangalia, Romania **17 G15** 43 50N 28 35 E
Mangalore, India **40 N9** 12 55N 74 47 E
Mangaweka, N.Z. **59 H5** 39 48S 175 47 E
Manggar, Indonesia **36 E3** 2 50S 108 10 E
Manggawitu, Indonesia **37 E8** 4 8S 133 32 E
Mangkalihat, Tanjung, Indonesia **37 D5** 1 2N 118 59 E
Mangla Dam, Pakistan **43 C5** 33 9N 73 44 E
Manglaur, India **42 E7** 29 44N 77 49 E
Mangnai, China **32 C4** 37 52N 91 43 E
Mango, Togo **50 F5** 10 20N 0 30 E
Mangoche, Malawi **55 E4** 14 25S 35 16 E
Mangoky →, Madag. **57 C7** 21 29S 43 41 E
Mangole, Indonesia **37 E7** 1 50S 125 55 E
Mangombe, Zaïre **54 C2** 1 20S 26 48 E
Mangonui, N.Z. **59 F4** 35 1S 173 32 E
Mangueigne, Chad **51 F9** 10 30N 21 15 E
Mangueira, L. da, Brazil **95 C5** 33 0S 52 50W
Mangum, U.S.A. **81 H5** 34 53N 99 30W
Mangyshlak Poluostrov, Kazakstan **26 E6** 44 30N 52 30 E
Manhattan, U.S.A. **80 F6** 39 11N 96 35W
Manhiça, Mozam. **57 D5** 25 23S 32 49 E
Manhuaçu, Brazil **93 H10** 20 15S 42 2W
Mania →, Madag. **57 B8** 19 42S 45 22 E
Manica, Mozam. **57 B5** 18 58S 32 59 E
Manica e Sofala □, Mozam. **57 B5** 19 10S 33 45 E
Manicaland □, Zimbabwe **55 F3** 19 0S 32 30 E
Manicoré, Brazil **92 E6** 5 48S 61 16W
Manicouagan →, Canada **71 C6** 49 30N 68 30W
Manifah, Si. Arabia **45 E6** 27 44N 49 0 E
Manifold, Australia **62 C5** 22 41S 150 40 E
Manifold, C., Australia **62 C5** 22 41S 150 50 E
Manigotagan, Canada **73 C9** 51 6N 96 18W
Manihiki, Cook Is. **65 J11** 10 24S 161 1W
Manika, Plateau de la, Zaïre **55 E2** 10 0S 25 5 E
Manila, Phil. **37 B6** 14 40N 121 3 E
Manila, U.S.A. **82 F9** 40 59N 109 43W
Manila B., Phil. **37 B6** 14 40N 120 35 E
Manilla, Australia **63 E5** 30 45S 150 43 E
Maningrida, Australia **62 A1** 12 3S 134 13 E
Manipur □, India **41 G18** 25 0N 94 0 E
Manipur →, Burma **41 H19** 23 45N 94 20 E
Manisa, Turkey **21 E12** 38 38N 27 30 E
Manistee, U.S.A. **76 C2** 44 15N 86 19W
Manistee →, U.S.A. **76 C2** 44 15N 86 21W
Manistique, U.S.A. **76 C2** 45 57N 86 15W
Manito L., Canada **73 C7** 52 43N 109 43W
Manitoba □, Canada **73 B9** 55 30N 97 0W
Manitoba, L., Canada **73 C9** 51 0N 98 45W
Manitou, Canada **73 D9** 49 15N 98 32W
Manitou I., U.S.A. **70 C2** 47 25N 87 37W
Manitou Is., U.S.A. **76 C2** 45 8N 86 0W
Manitou L., Canada **71 B6** 50 55N 65 17W
Manitou Springs, U.S.A. **80 F2** 38 52N 104 55W
Manitoulin I., Canada **70 C3** 45 40N 82 30W
Manitowaning, Canada **70 C3** 45 46N 81 49W
Manitowoc, U.S.A. **76 C2** 44 5N 87 40W
Manizales, Colombia **92 B3** 5 5N 75 32W
Manja, Madag. **57 C7** 21 26S 44 20 E
Manjacaze, Mozam. **57 C5** 24 45S 34 0 E
Manjakandriana, Madag. **57 B8** 18 55S 47 47 E
Manjhand, Pakistan **42 G3** 25 50N 68 10 E
Manjil, Iran **45 B6** 36 46N 49 30 E
Manjimup, Australia **61 F2** 34 15S 116 6 E
Manjra →, India **40 K10** 18 49N 77 52 E
Mankato, Kans., U.S.A. **80 F5** 39 47N 98 13W
Mankato, Minn., U.S.A. **80 C8** 44 10N 94 0W
Mankayane, Swaziland **57 D5** 26 40S 31 4 E
Mankono, Ivory C. **50 G3** 8 1N 6 10W
Mankota, Canada **73 D7** 49 25N 107 5W
Manlay, Mongolia **34 B4** 44 9N 107 0 E
Manly, Australia **63 E5** 33 48S 151 17 E
Manmad, India **40 J9** 20 18N 74 28 E
Mann Ras., Australia **61 E5** 26 6S 130 5 E
Manna, Indonesia **36 E2** 4 25S 102 55 E
Mannahill, Australia **63 E3** 32 25S 140 0 E
Mannar, Sri Lanka **40 Q11** 9 1N 79 54 E
Mannar, G. of, Asia **40 Q11** 8 30N 79 0 E
Mannar I., Sri Lanka **40 Q11** 9 5N 79 45 E
Mannheim, Germany **16 D5** 49 29N 8 29 E
Manning, Canada **72 B5** 56 53N 117 39W
Manning, Oreg., U.S.A. **84 E3** 45 45N 123 13W
Manning, S.C., U.S.A. **77 J5** 33 42N 80 13W
Manning Prov. Park, Canada **72 D4** 49 5N 120 45W
Mannington, U.S.A. **76 F5** 39 32N 80 21W
Mannum, Australia **63 E2** 34 50S 139 20 E
Mano, S. Leone **50 G2** 8 3N 12 2W
Manokwari, Indonesia **37 E8** 0 54S 134 0 E
Manombo, Madag. **57 C7** 22 57S 43 28 E
Manono, Zaïre **54 D2** 7 15S 27 25 E
Manosque, France **18 E6** 43 49N 5 47 E
Manouane, L., Canada **71 B5** 50 45N 70 45W
Manpojin, N. Korea **35 D14** 41 6N 126 24 E
Manresa, Spain **19 B6** 41 48N 1 50 E
Mansa, Gujarat, India **42 H5** 23 27N 72 45 E
Mansa, Punjab, India **42 E6** 30 0N 75 27 E
Mansa, Zambia **55 E2** 11 13S 28 55 E
Mansehra, Pakistan **42 B5** 34 20N 73 15 E
Mansel I., Canada **69 B11** 62 0N 80 0W
Mansfield, Australia **63 F4** 37 4S 146 6 E
Mansfield, U.K. **10 D6** 53 9N 1 11W
Mansfield, La., U.S.A. **81 J8** 32 2N 93 43W
Mansfield, Mass., U.S.A. **79 D13** 42 2N 71 13W
Mansfield, Ohio, U.S.A. **78 F2** 40 45N 82 31W
Mansfield, Pa., U.S.A. **78 E7** 41 48N 77 5W
Mansfield, Wash., U.S.A. **82 C4** 47 49N 119 38W
Manson Creek, Canada **72 B4** 55 37N 124 32W
Manta, Ecuador **92 D2** 1 0S 80 40W
Mantalingajan, Mt., Phil. **36 C5** 8 55N 117 45 E
Mantare, Tanzania **54 C3** 2 42S 33 13 E
Manteca, U.S.A. **83 H3** 37 48N 121 13W
Manteo, U.S.A. **77 H8** 35 55N 75 40W
Mantes-la-Jolie, France **18 B4** 48 58N 1 41 E
Manthani, India **40 K11** 18 40N 79 35 E
Manti, U.S.A. **82 G8** 39 16N 111 38W
Mantiqueira, Serra da, Brazil **95 A7** 22 0S 44 0W
Manton, U.S.A. **76 C3** 44 25N 85 24W
Mántova, Italy **20 B4** 45 9N 10 48 E
Mänttä, Finland **9 E21** 62 0N 24 40 E
Mantua = Mántova, Italy **20 B4** 45 9N 10 48 E
Manu, Peru **92 F4** 12 10S 70 51W
Manua Is., Amer. Samoa **59 B14** 14 13S 169 35W
Manuae, Cook Is. **65 J12** 19 30S 159 0W
Manuel Alves →, Brazil **93 F9** 11 19S 48 28W
Manui, Indonesia **37 E6** 3 35S 123 5 E
Manville, U.S.A. **80 D2** 42 47N 104 37W
Many, U.S.A. **81 K8** 31 34N 93 29W
Manyara, L., Tanzania **54 C4** 3 40S 35 50 E
Manych-Gudilo, Ozero, Russia **25 E7** 46 24N 42 38 E
Manyonga →, Tanzania **54 C3** 4 10S 34 15 E
Manyoni, Tanzania **54 D3** 5 45S 34 55 E
Manyoni □, Tanzania **54 D3** 6 30S 34 30 E
Manzai, Pakistan **42 C4** 32 12N 70 15 E
Manzanares, Spain **19 C4** 39 2N 3 22W
Manzanillo, Cuba **88 B4** 20 20N 77 31W
Manzanillo, Mexico **86 D4** 19 0N 104 20W
Manzanillo, Pta., Panama **88 E4** 9 30N 79 40W
Manzano Mts., U.S.A. **83 J10** 34 40N 106 20W
Manzarīyeh, Iran **45 C6** 34 53N 50 50 E
Manzhouli, China **33 B6** 49 35N 117 25 E
Manzini, Swaziland **57 D5** 26 30S 31 25 E
Mao, Chad **51 F8** 14 4N 15 19 E
Maoke, Pegunungan, Indonesia **37 E9** 3 40S 137 30 E
Maolin, China **35 C12** 43 58N 123 30 E
Maoming, China **33 D6** 21 50N 110 54 E
Maoxing, China **35 B13** 45 28N 124 40 E
Mapam Yumco, China **32 C3** 30 45N 81 28 E
Mapastepec, Mexico **87 D6** 15 26N 92 54W
Mapia, Kepulauan, Indonesia **37 D8** 0 50N 134 20 E
Mapimí, Mexico **86 B4** 25 50N 103 50W
Mapimí, Bolsón de, Mexico **86 B4** 27 30N 104 15W
Mapinga, Tanzania **54 D4** 6 40S 39 12 E
Mapinhane, Mozam. **57 C6** 22 20S 35 0 E
Maple Creek, Canada **73 D7** 49 55N 109 29W
Maple Valley, U.S.A. **84 C4** 47 25N 122 3W
Mapleton, U.S.A. **82 D2** 44 2N 123 52W
Mapuera →, Brazil **92 D7** 1 5S 57 2W
Maputo, Mozam. **57 D5** 25 58S 32 32 E
Maputo, B. de, Mozam. **57 D5** 25 50S 32 45 E
Maqiaohe, China **35 B16** 44 40N 130 30 E
Maqnā, Si. Arabia **44 D2** 28 25N 34 50 E
Maquela do Zombo, Angola **52 F3** 6 0S 15 15 E
Maquinchao, Argentina **96 E3** 41 15S 68 50W
Maquoketa, U.S.A. **80 D9** 42 4N 90 40W
Mar, Serra do, Brazil **95 B6** 25 30S 49 0W
Mar Chiquita, L., Argentina **94 C3** 30 40S 62 50W
Mar del Plata, Argentina **94 D4** 38 0S 57 30W
Mar Menor, Spain **19 D5** 37 40N 0 45W
Mara, Tanzania **54 C3** 1 30S 34 32 E
Mara □, Tanzania **54 C3** 1 45S 34 20 E
Maraã, Brazil **92 D5** 1 52S 65 25W
Marabá, Brazil **93 E9** 5 20S 49 5W
Maracá, I. de, Brazil **93 C8** 2 10N 50 30W
Maracaibo, Venezuela **92 A4** 10 40N 71 37W
Maracaibo, L. de, Venezuela **92 B4** 9 40N 71 30W
Maracaju, Brazil **95 A4** 21 38S 55 9W
Maracay, Venezuela **92 A5** 10 15N 67 28W
Marādah, Libya **51 C8** 29 15N 19 15 E
Maradi, Niger **50 F6** 13 29N 7 20 E
Marāgheh, Iran **44 B5** 37 30N 46 12 E
Marāh, Si. Arabia **44 E5** 25 0N 45 35 E
Marajó, I. de, Brazil **93 D9** 1 0S 49 30W
Marākand, Iran **44 B5** 38 51N 45 16 E
Maralal, Kenya **54 B4** 1 0N 36 38 E
Maralinga, Australia **61 F5** 30 13S 131 32 E
Marama, Australia **63 F3** 35 10S 140 10 E
Marampa, S. Leone **50 G2** 8 45N 12 28W
Maran, Malaysia **39 L4** 3 35N 102 45 E
Marana, U.S.A. **83 K8** 32 27N 111 13W
Maranboy, Australia **60 B5** 14 40S 132 39 E
Marand, Iran **44 B5** 38 30N 45 45 E
Marang, Malaysia **39 K4** 5 12N 103 13 E
Maranguape, Brazil **93 D11** 3 55S 38 50W
Maranhão = São Luís, Brazil **93 D10** 2 39S 44 15W
Maranhão □, Brazil **93 E9** 5 0S 46 0W
Maranoa →, Australia **63 D4** 27 50S 148 37 E
Marañón →, Peru **92 D4** 4 30S 73 35W
Marão, Mozam. **57 C5** 24 18S 34 2 E
Maraş = Kahramanmaraş, Turkey **25 G6** 37 37N 36 53 E
Marathasa □, Cyprus **23 E11** 34 59N 32 51 E
Marathon, Australia **62 C3** 20 51S 143 32 E
Marathon, Canada **70 C2** 48 44N 86 23W
Marathon, N.Y., U.S.A. **79 D8** 42 27N 76 2W
Marathon, Tex., U.S.A. **81 K3** 30 12N 103 15W
Marathóvouno, Cyprus **23 D12** 35 13N 33 37 E
Maratua, Indonesia **37 D5** 2 10N 118 35 E
Maravatío, Mexico **86 D4** 19 51N 100 25W
Marāwih, U.A.E. **45 E7** 24 18N 53 18 E
Marbella, Spain **19 D3** 36 30N 4 57W
Marble Bar, Australia **60 D2** 21 9S 119 44 E
Marble Falls, U.S.A. **81 K5** 30 35N 98 16W
Marblehead, U.S.A. **79 D14** 42 30N 70 51W
Marburg, Germany **16 C5** 50 47N 8 46 E
March, U.K. **11 E8** 52 33N 0 5 E
Marche, France **18 C4** 46 5N 1 20 E
Marche-en-Famenne, Belgium **15 D5** 50 14N 5 19 E
Marchena, Spain **19 D3** 37 18N 5 23W
Marcos Juárez, Argentina **94 C3** 32 42S 62 5W
Marcus I. = Minami-Tori-Shima, Pac. Oc. **64 E7** 24 0N 153 45 E
Marcus Necker Ridge, Pac. Oc. **64 F9** 20 0N 175 0 E
Marcy, Mt., U.S.A. **79 B11** 44 7N 73 56W
Mardan, Pakistan **42 B5** 34 20N 72 0 E
Mardie, Australia **60 D2** 21 12S 115 59 E
Mardin, Turkey **25 G7** 37 20N 40 43 E
Maree, L., U.K. **12 D3** 57 40N 5 26W
Mareeba, Australia **62 B4** 16 59S 145 28 E
Marek = Stanke Dimitrov, Bulgaria **21 C10** 42 17N 23 9 E
Marek, Indonesia **37 E6** 4 41S 120 24 E
Marengo, U.S.A. **80 E8** 41 48N 92 4W
Marenyi, Kenya **54 C4** 4 22S 39 8 E
Marerano, Madag. **57 C7** 21 23S 44 52 E
Marfa, U.S.A. **81 K2** 30 19N 104 1W
Marfa Pt., Malta **23 D1** 35 59N 14 19 E
Margaret →, Australia **60 C4** 18 9S 125 41 E
Margaret Bay, Canada **72 C3** 51 20N 127 35W
Margaret L., Canada **72 B5** 58 56N 115 25W
Margaret River, Australia **60 C4** 18 38S 126 52 E
Margarita, I. de, Venezuela **92 A6** 11 0N 64 0W
Margaritovo, Russia **30 C7** 43 25N 134 45 E
Margate, S. Africa **57 E5** 30 50S 30 20 E
Margate, U.K. **11 F9** 51 23N 1 23 E
Margelan = Marghilon, Uzbekistan **26 E8** 40 27N 71 42 E
Marghilon, Uzbekistan **26 E8** 40 27N 71 42 E
Marguerite, Canada **72 C4** 52 30N 122 25W
Mari El □, Russia **24 C8** 56 30N 48 0 E
Mari Republic □ = Mari El □, Russia **24 C8** 56 30N 48 0 E
María Elena, Chile **94 A2** 22 18S 69 40W
María Grande, Argentina **94 C4** 31 45S 59 55W
Maria I., N. Terr., Australia **62 A2** 14 52S 135 45 E
Maria I., Tas., Australia **62 G4** 42 35S 148 0 E
Maria van Diemen, C., N.Z. **59 F4** 34 29S 172 40 E
Mariakani, Kenya **54 C4** 3 50S 39 27 E
Marian L., Canada **72 A5** 63 0N 116 15W
Mariana Trench, Pac. Oc. **28 H18** 13 0N 145 0 E
Marianao, Cuba **88 B3** 23 8N 82 24W
Marianna, Ark., U.S.A. **81 H9** 34 46N 90 46W
Marianna, Fla., U.S.A. **77 K3** 30 46N 85 14W
Marias →, U.S.A. **82 C8** 47 56N 110 30W
Mariato, Punta, Panama **88 E3** 7 12N 80 52W
Ma'rib, Yemen **46 D4** 15 25N 45 21 E
Maribor, Slovenia **16 E8** 46 36N 15 40 E
Marico →, Africa **56 C4** 23 35S 26 57 E
Maricopa, Ariz., U.S.A. **83 K7** 33 4N 112 3W
Maricopa, Calif., U.S.A. **85 K7** 35 4N 119 24W
Maricourt, Canada **69 C12** 56 34N 70 49W
Marīdī, Sudan **51 H10** 4 55N 29 25 E
Marie Byrd Land, Antarctica **5 D14** 79 30S 125 0W
Marie-Galante, Guadeloupe **89 C7** 15 56N 61 16W
Mariecourt = Kangiqsujuaq, Canada **69 B12** 61 30N 72 0W
Marienberg, Neths. **15 B6** 52 2N 6 35 E
Marienbourg, Belgium **15 D4** 50 6N 4 31 E
Mariental, Namibia **56 C2** 24 36S 18 0 E
Marienville, U.S.A. **78 E5** 41 28N 79 8W
Mariestad, Sweden **9 G15** 58 43N 13 50 E
Marietta, Ga., U.S.A. **77 J3** 33 57N 84 33W
Marietta, Ohio, U.S.A. **76 F5** 39 25N 81 27W
Marieville, Canada **79 A11** 45 26N 73 10W
Mariinsk, Russia **26 D9** 56 10N 87 20 E
Marijampolė, Lithuania **9 J20** 54 33N 23 19 E
Marília, Brazil **95 A5** 22 13S 50 0W
Marillana, Australia **60 D2** 22 37S 119 16 E
Marín, Spain **19 A1** 42 23N 8 42W
Marina, U.S.A. **84 J5** 36 41N 121 48W
Marina Plains, Australia **62 A3** 14 37S 143 57 E
Marinduque, Phil. **37 B6** 13 25N 122 0 E
Marine City, U.S.A. **76 D4** 42 43N 82 30W
Marinette, U.S.A. **76 C2** 45 6N 87 38W
Maringá, Brazil **95 A5** 23 26S 52 2W
Marion, Ala., U.S.A. **77 J2** 32 38N 87 19W
Marion, Ill., U.S.A. **81 G10** 37 44N 88 56W
Marion, Ind., U.S.A. **76 E3** 40 32N 85 40W
Marion, Iowa, U.S.A. **80 D9** 42 2N 91 36W
Marion, Kans., U.S.A. **80 F6** 38 21N 97 1W
Marion, Mich., U.S.A. **76 C3** 44 6N 85 9W
Marion, N.C., U.S.A. **77 H4** 35 41N 82 1W
Marion, Ohio, U.S.A. **76 E4** 40 35N 83 8W
Marion, S.C., U.S.A. **77 H6** 34 11N 79 24W
Marion, Va., U.S.A. **77 G5** 36 50N 81 31W
Marion, L., U.S.A. **77 J5** 33 28N 80 10W
Mariposa, U.S.A. **83 H4** 37 29N 119 58W
Mariscal Estigarribia, Paraguay **94 A3** 22 3S 60 40W
Maritime Alps = Maritimes, Alpes, Europe **16 F4** 44 10N 7 10 E
Maritimes, Alpes, Europe **16 F4** 44 10N 7 10 E
Maritsa = Évros →, Bulgaria **21 D12** 41 40N 26 34 E
Maritsa, Greece **23 C10** 36 22N 28 10 E
Mariupol, Ukraine **25 E6** 47 5N 37 31 E
Marīvān, Iran **44 C5** 35 30N 46 25 E
Markazī □, Iran **45 C6** 35 0N 49 30 E
Markdale, Canada **78 B4** 44 19N 80 39W
Marked Tree, U.S.A. **81 H9** 35 32N 90 25W
Marken, Neths. **15 B5** 52 26N 5 12 E
Market Drayton, U.K. **10 E5** 52 54N 2 29W
Market Harborough, U.K. **11 E7** 52 29N 0 55W
Markham, Canada **78 C5** 43 52N 79 16W
Markham, Mt., Antarctica **5 E11** 83 0S 164 0 E
Markham L., Canada **73 A8** 62 30N 102 35W
Markleeville, U.S.A. **84 G7** 38 42N 119 47W
Markovo, Russia **27 C17** 64 40N 169 40 E
Marks, Russia **24 D8** 51 45N 46 50 E
Marksville, U.S.A. **81 K8** 31 8N 92 4W
Marla, Australia **63 D1** 27 19S 133 33 E
Marlboro, U.S.A. **79 D13** 42 19N 71 33W
Marlborough, Australia **62 C4** 22 46S 149 52 E
Marlborough Downs, U.K. **11 F6** 51 27N 1 53W
Marlin, U.S.A. **81 K6** 31 18N 96 54W
Marlow, U.S.A. **81 H6** 34 39N 97 58W
Marmagao, India **40 M8** 15 25N 73 56 E
Marmara, Turkey **21 D12** 40 35N 27 38 E
Marmara, Sea of = Marmara Denizi, Turkey **21 D13** 40 45N 28 15 E
Marmara Denizi, Turkey **21 D13** 40 45N 28 15 E
Marmaris, Turkey **21 F13** 36 50N 28 14 E
Marmarth, U.S.A. **80 B3** 46 18N 103 54W
Marmion, Mt., Australia **61 E2** 29 16S 119 50 E
Marmion L., Canada **70 C1** 48 55N 91 20W
Marmolada, Mte., Italy **20 A4** 46 26N 11 51 E
Marmora, Canada **70 D4** 44 28N 77 41W
Marne →, France **18 B5** 48 48N 2 24 E
Maroala, Madag. **57 B8** 15 23S 47 59 E
Maroantsetra, Madag. **57 B8** 15 26S 49 44 E
Maromandia, Madag. **57 A8** 14 13S 48 5 E
Marondera, Zimbabwe **55 F3** 18 5S 31 42 E
Maroni →, Fr. Guiana **93 B8** 5 30N 54 0W
Maroochydore, Australia **63 D5** 26 29S 153 5 E
Maroona, Australia **63 F3** 37 27S 142 54 E
Marosakoa, Madag. **57 B8** 15 26S 46 38 E
Maroua, Cameroon **51 F7** 10 40N 14 20 E
Marovoay, Madag. **57 B8** 16 6S 46 39 E
Marquard, S. Africa **56 D4** 28 40S 27 28 E
Marquesas Is. = Marquises, Is., Pac. Oc. **65 H14** 9 30S 140 0W
Marquette, U.S.A. **76 B2** 46 33N 87 24W
Marquises, Is., Pac. Oc. **65 H14** 9 30S 140 0W

Mekhtar

Marracuene, Mozam. 57 D5 25 45S 32 35 E
Marrakech, Morocco 50 B3 31 9N 8 0W
Marrawah, Australia 62 G3 40 55S 144 42 E
Marree, Australia 63 D2 29 39S 138 1 E
Marrilla, Australia 60 D1 22 31S 114 25 E
Marrimane, Mozam. 57 C5 22 58S 33 34 E
Marromeu, Mozam. 57 B6 18 15S 36 25 E
Marrowie Cr. →, Australia 63 E4 33 23S 145 40 E
Marrubane, Mozam. 55 F4 18 0S 37 0 E
Marrupa, Mozam. 55 E4 13 8S 37 30 E
Marsá Matrûh, Egypt 51 B10 31 19N 27 9 E
Marsá Susah, Libya 51 B9 32 52N 21 59 E
Marsabit, Kenya 54 B4 2 18N 38 0 E
Marsabit □, Kenya 54 B4 2 45N 37 45 E
Marsala, Italy 20 F5 37 48N 12 26 E
Marsalforn, Malta 23 C1 36 4N 14 15 E
Marsden, Australia 63 E4 33 47S 147 32 E
Marseille, France 18 E6 43 18N 5 23 E
Marseilles = Marseille, France 18 E6 43 18N 5 23 E
Marsh I., U.S.A. 81 L9 29 34N 91 53W
Marsh L., U.S.A. 80 C6 45 5N 96 0W
Marshall, Liberia 50 G2 6 8N 10 22W
Marshall, Ark., U.S.A. 81 H8 35 55N 92 38W
Marshall, Mich., U.S.A. 76 D3 42 16N 84 58W
Marshall, Minn., U.S.A. 80 C7 44 25N 95 45W
Marshall, Mo., U.S.A. 80 F8 39 7N 93 12W
Marshall, Tex., U.S.A. 81 J7 32 33N 94 23W
Marshall →, Australia 62 C2 22 59S 136 59 E
Marshall Is. ■, Pac. Oc. 64 G9 9 0N 171 0 E
Marshalltown, U.S.A. 80 D8 42 3N 92 55W
Marshfield, Mo., U.S.A. 81 G8 37 15N 92 54W
Marshfield, Wis., U.S.A. 80 C9 44 40N 90 10W
Marshūn, Iran 45 B6 36 19N 49 23 E
Märsta, Sweden 9 G17 59 37N 17 52 E
Mart, U.S.A. 81 K6 31 33N 96 50W
Martaban, Burma 41 L20 16 30N 97 35 E
Martaban, G. of, Burma 41 L20 16 5N 96 30 E
Martapura, Kalimantan, Indonesia 36 E4 3 22S 114 47 E
Martapura, Sumatera, Indonesia 36 E2 4 19S 104 22 E
Marte, Nigeria 51 F7 12 23N 13 46 E
Martelange, Belgium 15 E5 49 49N 5 43 E
Martha's Vineyard, U.S.A. 79 E14 41 25N 70 38W
Martigny, Switz. 16 E4 46 6N 7 3 E
Martigues, France 18 E6 43 24N 5 4 E
Martin, Slovak Rep. 17 D10 49 6N 18 48 E
Martin, S. Dak., U.S.A. 80 D4 43 11N 101 44W
Martin, Tenn., U.S.A. 81 G10 36 21N 88 51W
Martin L., U.S.A. 77 J3 32 41N 85 55W
Martina Franca, Italy 20 D7 40 42N 17 20 E
Martinborough, N.Z. 59 J5 41 14S 175 29 E
Martinez, U.S.A. 84 G4 38 1N 122 8W
Martinique ■, W. Indies 89 D7 14 40N 61 0W
Martinique Passage, W. Indies 89 C7 15 15N 61 0W
Martinópolis, Brazil 95 A5 22 11S 51 12W
Martins Ferry, U.S.A. 78 F4 40 6N 80 44W
Martinsburg, Pa., U.S.A. 78 F6 40 19N 78 20W
Martinsburg, W. Va., U.S.A. 76 F7 39 27N 77 58W
Martinsville, Ind., U.S.A. 76 F2 39 26N 86 25W
Martinsville, Va., U.S.A. 77 G6 36 41N 79 52W
Marton, N.Z. 59 J5 40 4S 175 23 E
Martos, Spain 19 D4 37 44N 3 58W
Marudi, Malaysia 36 D4 4 11N 114 19 E
Ma'ruf, Afghan. 40 D5 31 30N 67 6 E
Marugame, Japan 31 G6 34 15N 133 40 E
Marulan, Australia 63 E5 34 43S 150 3 E
Marunga, Angola 56 B3 17 28S 20 2 E
Marungu, Mts., Zaïre 54 D2 7 30S 30 0 E
Marvast, Iran 45 D7 30 30N 54 15 E
Marwar, India 42 G5 25 43N 73 45 E
Mary, Turkmenistan 26 F7 37 40N 61 50 E
Mary Frances L., Canada 73 A7 63 19N 106 13W
Mary Kathleen, Australia 62 C2 20 44S 139 48 E
Maryborough = Port Laoise, Ireland 13 C4 53 2N 7 18W
Maryborough, Queens., Australia 63 D5 25 31S 152 37 E
Maryborough, Vic., Australia 63 F3 37 0S 143 44 E
Maryfield, Canada 73 D8 49 50N 101 35W
Maryland □, U.S.A. 76 F7 39 0N 76 30W
Maryland Junction, Zimbabwe 55 F3 17 45S 30 31 E
Maryport, U.K. 10 C4 54 44N 3 28W
Mary's Harbour, Canada 71 B8 52 18N 55 51W
Marystown, Canada 71 C8 47 10N 55 10W
Marysvale, U.S.A. 83 G7 38 27N 112 14W
Marysville, Canada 72 D5 49 35N 116 0W
Marysville, Calif., U.S.A. 84 F5 39 9N 121 35W
Marysville, Kans., U.S.A. 80 F6 39 51N 96 39W
Marysville, Mich., U.S.A. 78 D2 42 54N 82 29W
Marysville, Ohio, U.S.A. 76 E4 40 14N 83 22W
Marysville, Wash., U.S.A. 84 B4 48 3N 122 11W
Maryvale, Australia 63 D5 28 4S 152 12 E
Maryville, U.S.A. 77 H4 35 46N 83 58W
Marzūq, Libya 51 C7 25 53N 13 57 E
Masahunga, Tanzania 54 C3 2 6S 33 18 E
Masai, Malaysia 39 M4 1 29N 103 55 E
Masai Steppe, Tanzania 54 C4 4 30S 36 30 E
Masaka, Uganda 54 C3 0 21S 31 45 E
Masalembo, Kepulauan, Indonesia 36 F4 5 35S 114 30 E
Masalima, Kepulauan, Indonesia 36 F5 5 4S 117 5 E
Masamba, Indonesia 37 E6 2 30S 120 15 E
Masan, S. Korea 35 G15 35 11N 128 32 E
Masasi, Tanzania 55 E4 10 45S 38 52 E
Masasi □, Tanzania 55 E4 10 45S 38 50 E
Masaya, Nic. 88 D2 12 0N 86 7W
Masbate, Phil. 37 B6 12 21N 123 36 E
Mascara, Algeria 50 A5 35 26N 0 6 E
Mascota, Mexico 86 C4 20 30N 104 50W
Masela, Indonesia 37 F7 8 9S 129 51 E
Maseru, Lesotho 56 D4 29 18S 27 30 E
Mashaba, Zimbabwe 55 G3 20 2S 30 29 E
Mashābih, Si. Arabia 44 E3 25 35N 36 30 E
Masherbrum, Pakistan 43 B7 35 38N 76 18 E
Mashhad, Iran 45 B8 36 20N 59 35 E
Mashīz, Iran 45 D8 29 56N 56 37 E
Mashkel, Hamun-i-, Pakistan 40 E3 28 30N 63 0 E
Mashki Chāh, Pakistan 40 E3 29 5N 62 30 E
Mashonaland Central □, Zimbabwe 57 B5 17 30S 31 0 E
Mashonaland East □, Zimbabwe 57 B5 18 0S 32 0 E
Mashonaland West □, Zimbabwe 57 B4 17 30S 29 30 E
Masi Manimba, Zaïre 52 E3 4 40S 17 54 E
Masindi, Uganda 54 B3 1 40N 31 43 E
Masindi Port, Uganda 54 B3 1 43N 32 2 E
Masisea, Peru 92 E4 8 35S 74 22W
Masisi, Zaïre 54 C2 1 23S 28 49 E
Masjed Soleyman, Iran 45 D6 31 55N 49 18 E
Mask, L., Ireland 13 C2 53 36N 9 22W
Masoala, Tanjon' i, Madag. 57 B9 15 59S 50 13 E
Masoarivo, Madag. 57 B7 19 3S 44 19 E
Masohi, Indonesia 37 E7 3 20S 128 55 E
Masomeloka, Madag. 57 C8 20 17S 48 37 E
Mason, Nev., U.S.A. 84 G7 38 56N 119 8W
Mason, Tex., U.S.A. 81 K5 30 45N 99 14W
Mason City, U.S.A. 80 D8 43 9N 93 12W
Maspalomas, Canary Is. 22 G4 27 46N 15 35W
Maspalomas, Pta., Canary Is. 22 G4 27 43N 15 36W
Masqat, Oman 46 C6 23 37N 58 36 E
Massa, Italy 20 B4 44 1N 10 9 E
Massachusetts □, U.S.A. 79 D12 42 30N 72 0W
Massachusetts B., U.S.A. 79 D14 42 20N 70 50W
Massaguet, Chad 51 F8 12 28N 15 26 E
Massakory, Chad 51 F8 13 0N 15 49 E
Massanella, Spain 22 B9 39 48N 2 51 E
Massangena, Mozam. 57 C5 21 34S 33 0 E
Massawa = Mitsiwa, Eritrea 51 E12 15 35N 39 25 E
Massena, U.S.A. 79 B10 44 56N 74 54W
Massénya, Chad 51 F8 11 21N 16 9 E
Masset, Canada 72 C2 54 2N 132 10W
Massif Central, France 18 D5 44 55N 3 0 E
Massillon, U.S.A. 78 F3 40 48N 81 32W
Massinga, Mozam. 57 C6 23 15S 35 22 E
Masson, Canada 79 A9 45 32N 75 25W
Masson I., Antarctica 5 C7 66 10S 93 20 E
Mastanli = Momchilgrad, Bulgaria 21 D11 41 33N 25 23 E
Masterton, N.Z. 59 J5 40 56S 175 39 E
Mastuj, Pakistan 43 A5 36 20N 72 36 E
Mastung, Pakistan 40 E5 29 50N 66 56 E
Masty, Belarus 17 B13 53 27N 24 38 E
Masuda, Japan 31 G5 34 40N 131 51 E
Masvingo, Zimbabwe 55 G3 20 8S 30 49 E
Masvingo □, Zimbabwe 55 G3 21 0S 31 30 E
Maswa □, Tanzania 54 C3 3 30S 34 0 E
Maşyāf, Syria 44 C3 35 4N 36 20 E
Matabeleland North □, Zimbabwe 55 F2 19 0S 28 0 E
Matabeleland South □, Zimbabwe 55 G2 21 0S 29 0 E
Mataboor, Indonesia 37 E9 1 41S 138 3 E
Matachewan, Canada 70 C3 47 56N 80 39W
Matadi, Zaïre 52 F2 5 52S 13 31 E
Matagalpa, Nic. 88 D2 13 0N 85 58W
Matagami, Canada 70 C4 49 45N 77 34W
Matagami, L., Canada 70 C4 49 50N 77 40W
Matagorda, U.S.A. 81 L7 28 42N 95 58W
Matagorda B., U.S.A. 81 L6 28 40N 96 0W
Matagorda I., U.S.A. 81 L6 28 15N 96 30W
Matak, P., Indonesia 39 L6 3 18N 106 16 E
Matakana, Australia 63 E4 32 59S 145 54 E
Mátala, Greece 23 E6 34 59N 24 45 E
Matam, Senegal 50 E2 15 34N 13 17W
Matamoros, Campeche, Mexico 87 D6 18 50N 90 50W
Matamoros, Coahuila, Mexico 86 B4 25 33N 103 15W
Matamoros, Puebla, Mexico 87 D5 18 2N 98 17W
Matamoros, Tamaulipas, Mexico 87 B5 25 50N 97 30W
Ma'ṭan as Sarra, Libya 51 D9 21 45N 22 0 E
Matandu →, Tanzania 55 D3 8 45S 34 19 E
Matane, Canada 71 C6 48 50N 67 33W
Matanzas, Cuba 88 B3 23 0N 81 40W
Matapan, C. = Tainaron, Ákra, Greece 21 F10 36 22N 22 27 E
Matapédia, Canada 71 C6 48 0N 66 59W
Matara, Sri Lanka 40 S12 5 58N 80 30 E
Mataram, Indonesia 36 F5 8 41S 116 10 E
Matarani, Peru 92 G4 17 0S 72 10W
Mataranka, Australia 60 B5 14 55S 133 4 E
Matarma, Râs, Egypt 47 E1 30 27N 32 44 E
Mataró, Spain 19 B7 41 32N 2 29 E
Matatiele, S. Africa 57 E4 30 20S 28 49 E
Mataura, N.Z. 59 M2 46 11S 168 51 E
Matehuala, Mexico 86 C4 23 40N 100 40W
Mateke Hills, Zimbabwe 55 G3 21 48S 31 0 E
Matera, Italy 20 D7 40 40N 16 36 E
Matetsi, Zimbabwe 55 F2 18 12S 26 0 E
Matheson Island, Canada 73 C9 51 45N 96 56W
Mathis, U.S.A. 81 L6 28 6N 97 50W
Mathura, India 42 F7 27 30N 77 40 E
Mati, Phil. 37 C7 6 55N 126 15 E
Matías Romero, Mexico 87 D5 16 53N 95 2W
Matibane, Mozam. 55 E5 14 49S 40 45 E
Matima, Botswana 56 C3 20 15S 24 26 E
Matiri Ra., N.Z. 59 J4 41 38S 172 20 E
Matlock, U.K. 10 D6 53 9N 1 33W
Matmata, Tunisia 50 B6 33 37N 9 59 E
Mato Grosso □, Brazil 93 F8 14 0S 55 0W
Mato Grosso, Planalto do, Brazil 93 G8 15 0S 55 0W
Mato Grosso, Plateau of, Brazil 90 E5 15 0S 54 0W
Mato Grosso do Sul □, Brazil 93 G8 18 0S 55 0W
Matochkin Shar, Russia 26 B6 73 10N 56 40 E
Matopo Hills, Zimbabwe 55 G2 20 36S 28 20 E
Matopos, Zimbabwe 55 G2 20 20S 28 29 E
Matosinhos, Portugal 19 B1 41 11N 8 42W
Matsue, Japan 31 G6 35 25N 133 10 E
Matsumae, Japan 30 D10 41 26N 140 7 E
Matsumoto, Japan 31 F9 36 15N 138 0 E
Matsusaka, Japan 31 G8 34 34N 136 32 E
Matsuura, Japan 31 H4 33 20N 129 49 E
Matsuyama, Japan 31 H6 33 45N 132 45 E
Mattagami →, Canada 70 B3 50 43N 81 29W
Mattancheri, India 40 Q10 9 50N 76 15 E
Mattawa, Canada 70 C4 46 20N 78 45W
Mattawamkeag, U.S.A. 71 C6 45 32N 68 21W
Matterhorn, Switz. 16 F4 45 58N 7 39 E
Matthew Town, Bahamas 89 B5 20 57N 73 40W
Matthew's Ridge, Guyana 92 B6 7 37N 60 10W
Mattice, Canada 70 C3 49 40N 83 20W
Mattituck, U.S.A. 79 F12 40 59N 72 32W
Matuba, Mozam. 57 C5 24 28S 32 49 E
Matucana, Peru 92 F3 11 55S 76 25W
Matun, Afghan. 42 C3 33 22N 69 58 E
Maturín, Venezuela 92 B6 9 45N 63 11W
Mau, India 43 G10 25 56N 83 33 E
Mau Escarpment, Kenya 54 C4 0 40S 36 0 E
Mau Ranipur, India 43 G8 25 16N 79 8 E
Maubeuge, France 18 A6 50 17N 3 57 E
Maud, Pt., Australia 60 D1 23 6S 113 45 E
Maude, Australia 63 E3 34 29S 144 18 E
Maudin Sun, Burma 41 M19 16 0N 94 30 E
Maués, Brazil 92 D7 3 20S 57 45W
Mauganj, India 41 G12 24 50N 81 55 E
Maui, U.S.A. 74 H16 20 48N 156 20W
Maulamyaing = Moulmein, Burma 41 L20 16 30N 97 40 E
Maule □, Chile 94 D1 36 5S 72 30W
Maumee, U.S.A. 76 E4 41 34N 83 39W
Maumee →, U.S.A. 76 E4 41 42N 83 28W
Maumere, Indonesia 37 F6 8 38S 122 13 E
Maun, Botswana 56 B3 20 0S 23 26 E
Mauna Kea, U.S.A. 74 J17 19 50N 155 28W
Mauna Loa, U.S.A. 74 J17 19 30N 155 35W
Maungmagan Kyunzu, Burma 41 M20 14 0N 97 48 E
Maupin, U.S.A. 82 D3 45 11N 121 5W
Maurepas, L., U.S.A. 81 K9 30 15N 90 30W
Maurice, L., Australia 61 E5 29 30S 131 0 E
Mauritania ■, Africa 50 D3 20 50N 10 0W
Mauritius ■, Ind. Oc. 49 J9 20 0S 57 0 E
Mauston, U.S.A. 80 D9 43 48N 90 5W
Mavinga, Angola 53 H4 15 50S 20 21 E
Mavli, India 42 G5 24 45N 73 55 E
Mavuradonha Mts., Zimbabwe 55 F3 16 30S 31 30 E
Mawa, Zaïre 54 B2 2 45N 26 40 E
Mawana, India 42 E7 29 6N 77 58 E
Mawand, Pakistan 42 E3 29 33N 68 38 E
Mawk Mai, Burma 41 J20 20 14N 97 37 E
Mawlaik, Burma 41 H19 23 40N 94 26 E
Mawquq, Si. Arabia 44 E4 27 25N 41 8 E
Mawson Coast, Antarctica 5 C6 68 30S 63 0 E
Max, U.S.A. 80 B4 47 49N 101 18W
Maxcanú, Mexico 87 C6 20 40N 92 0W
Maxesibeni, S. Africa 57 E4 30 49S 29 23 E
Maxhamish L., Canada 72 B4 59 50N 123 17W
Maxixe, Mozam. 57 C6 23 54S 35 17 E
Maxville, Canada 79 A10 45 17N 74 51W
Maxwell, U.S.A. 84 F4 39 17N 122 11W
Maxwelton, Australia 62 C3 20 43S 142 41 E
May Downs, Australia 62 C4 22 38S 148 55 E
May Pen, Jamaica 88 C4 17 58N 77 15W
Maya →, Russia 27 D14 60 28N 134 28 E
Maya Mts., Belize 87 D7 16 30N 89 0W
Mayaguana, Bahamas 89 B5 22 30N 72 44W
Mayagüez, Puerto Rico 89 C6 18 12N 67 9W
Mayāmey, Iran 45 B7 36 24N 55 42 E
Mayari, Cuba 89 B4 20 40N 75 41W
Maybell, U.S.A. 82 F9 40 31N 108 5W
Maydān, Iraq 44 C5 34 55N 45 37 E
Maydena, Australia 62 G4 42 45S 146 30 E
Mayenne →, France 18 C3 47 30N 0 32W
Mayer, U.S.A. 83 J7 34 24N 112 14W
Mayerthorpe, Canada 72 C5 53 57N 115 8W
Mayfield, U.S.A. 77 G1 36 44N 88 38W
Mayhill, U.S.A. 83 K11 32 53N 105 29W
Maykop, Russia 25 F7 44 35N 40 10 E
Maymyo, Burma 38 A1 22 2N 96 28 E
Maynard, U.S.A. 84 C4 47 59N 122 55W
Maynard Hills, Australia 61 E2 28 28S 119 49 E
Mayne →, Australia 62 C3 23 40S 141 55 E
Maynooth, Ireland 13 C5 53 23N 6 34W
Mayo, Canada 68 B6 63 38N 135 57W
Mayo □, Ireland 13 C2 53 53N 9 3W
Mayo L., Canada 68 B6 63 45N 135 0W
Mayon Volcano, Phil. 37 B6 13 15N 123 41 E
Mayor I., N.Z. 59 G6 37 16S 176 17 E
Mayotte, I., Mayotte 49 H8 12 50S 45 10 E
Mayson L., Canada 73 B7 57 55N 107 10W
Maysville, U.S.A. 76 F4 38 39N 83 46W
Mayu, Indonesia 37 D7 1 30N 126 30 E
Mayville, N. Dak., U.S.A. 80 B6 47 30N 97 20W
Mayville, N.Y., U.S.A. 78 D5 42 15N 79 30W
Mayya, Russia 27 C14 61 44N 130 18 E
Mazabuka, Zambia 55 F2 15 52S 27 44 E
Mazagán = El Jadida, Morocco 50 B3 33 11N 8 17W
Mazagão, Brazil 93 D8 0 7S 51 16W
Mazán, Peru 92 D4 3 30S 73 0W
Māzandarān □, Iran 45 B7 36 30N 52 0 E
Mazapil, Mexico 86 C4 24 38N 101 34W
Mazara del Vallo, Italy 20 F5 37 39N 12 35 E
Mazarredo, Argentina 96 F3 47 10S 66 50W
Mazarrón, Spain 19 D5 37 38N 1 19W
Mazaruni →, Guyana 92 B7 6 25N 58 35W
Mazatán, Mexico 86 B2 29 0N 110 8W
Mazatenango, Guatemala 88 D1 14 35N 91 30W
Mazatlán, Mexico 86 C3 23 13N 106 25W
Mažeikiai, Lithuania 9 H20 56 20N 22 20 E
Māzhān, Iran 45 C8 32 30N 59 0 E
Mazīnān, Iran 45 B8 36 19N 56 56 E
Mazoe, Mozam. 55 F3 16 42S 33 7 E
Mazoe →, Mozam. 55 F3 16 20S 33 30 E
Mazowe, Zimbabwe 55 F3 17 28S 30 58 E
Mazurian Lakes = Mazurski, Pojezierze, Poland 17 B11 53 50N 21 0 E
Mazurski, Pojezierze, Poland 17 B11 53 50N 21 0 E
Mazyr, Belarus 17 B15 51 59N 29 15 E
Mbabane, Swaziland 57 D5 26 18S 31 6 E
Mbaïki, C.A.R. 52 D3 3 53N 18 1 E
Mbala, Zambia 55 D3 8 46S 31 24 E
Mbale, Uganda 54 B3 1 8N 34 12 E
Mbalmayo, Cameroon 52 D2 3 33N 11 33 E
Mbamba Bay, Tanzania 55 E3 11 13S 34 49 E
Mbandaka, Zaïre 52 D3 0 1N 18 18 E
Mbanza Congo, Angola 52 F2 6 18S 14 16 E
Mbanza Ngungu, Zaïre 52 F2 5 12S 14 53 E
Mbarara, Uganda 54 C3 0 35S 30 40 E
Mbashe →, S. Africa 57 E4 32 15S 28 54 E
Mbenkuru →, Tanzania 55 D4 9 25S 39 50 E
Mberengwa, Zimbabwe 55 G2 20 29S 29 57 E
Mberengwa, Mt., Zimbabwe 55 G2 20 37S 29 55 E
Mbesuma, Zambia 55 D3 10 0S 32 2 E
Mbeya, Tanzania 55 D3 8 54S 33 29 E
Mbeya □, Tanzania 54 D3 8 15S 33 30 E
Mbinga, Tanzania 55 E4 10 50S 35 0 E
Mbinga □, Tanzania 55 E3 10 50S 35 0 E
Mbini □, Eq. Guin. 52 D2 1 30N 10 0 E
Mbour, Senegal 50 F1 14 22N 16 54W
Mbout, Mauritania 50 E2 16 1N 12 38W
Mbozi □, Tanzania 55 D3 9 0S 32 50 E
Mbuji-Mayi, Zaïre 54 D1 6 9S 23 40 E
Mbulu, Tanzania 54 C4 3 45S 35 30 E
Mbulu □, Tanzania 54 C4 3 52S 35 33 E
Mburucuyá, Argentina 94 B4 28 1S 58 14W
Mchinja, Tanzania 55 D4 9 44S 39 45 E
Mchinji, Malawi 55 E3 13 47S 32 58 E
Mead, L., U.S.A. 85 J12 36 1N 114 44W
Meade, U.S.A. 81 G4 37 17N 100 20W
Meadow, Australia 61 E1 26 35S 114 40 E
Meadow Lake, Canada 73 C7 54 10N 108 26W
Meadow Lake Prov. Park, Canada 73 C7 54 27N 109 0W
Meadow Valley Wash →, U.S.A. 85 J12 36 40N 114 34W
Meadville, U.S.A. 78 E4 41 39N 80 9W
Meaford, Canada 70 D3 44 36N 80 35W
Mealy Mts., Canada 71 B8 53 10N 58 0W
Meander River, Canada 72 B5 59 2N 117 42W
Meares, C., U.S.A. 82 D2 45 37N 124 0W
Mearim →, Brazil 93 D10 3 4S 44 35W
Meath □, Ireland 13 C5 53 40N 6 57W
Meath Park, Canada 73 C7 53 27N 105 22W
Meaux, France 18 B5 48 58N 2 50 E
Mebechi-Gawa →, Japan 30 D10 40 31N 141 31 E
Mecanhelas, Mozam. 55 F4 15 12S 35 54 E
Mecca = Makkah, Si. Arabia 46 C2 21 30N 39 54 E
Mecca, U.S.A. 85 M10 33 34N 116 5W
Mechanicsburg, U.S.A. 78 F8 40 13N 77 1W
Mechanicville, U.S.A. 79 D11 42 54N 73 41W
Mechelen, Belgium 15 C4 51 2N 4 29 E
Mecheria, Algeria 50 B4 33 35N 0 18W
Mecklenburg, Germany 16 B6 53 33N 11 40 E
Mecklenburger Bucht, Germany 16 A6 54 20N 11 40 E
Meconta, Mozam. 55 E4 14 59S 39 50 E
Meda, Australia 60 C3 17 22S 123 59 E
Medan, Indonesia 36 D1 3 40N 98 38 E
Medanosa, Pta., Argentina 96 F3 48 8S 66 0W
Medéa, Algeria 50 A5 36 12N 2 50 E
Medellín, Colombia 92 B3 6 15N 75 35W
Medelpad, Sweden 9 E17 62 33N 16 30 E
Medemblik, Neths. 15 B5 52 46N 5 8 E
Mederdra, Mauritania 50 E1 17 0N 15 38W
Medford, Mass., U.S.A. 79 D13 42 25N 71 7W
Medford, Oreg., U.S.A. 82 E2 42 19N 122 52W
Medford, Wis., U.S.A. 80 C9 45 9N 90 20W
Medgidia, Romania 17 F15 44 15N 28 19 E
Media Agua, Argentina 94 C2 31 58S 68 25W
Media Luna, Argentina 94 C2 34 45S 66 44W
Mediaş, Romania 17 E13 46 9N 24 22 E
Medical Lake, U.S.A. 82 C5 47 34N 117 41W
Medicine Bow, U.S.A. 82 F10 41 54N 106 12W
Medicine Bow Pk., U.S.A. 82 F10 41 21N 106 19W
Medicine Bow Ra., U.S.A. 82 F10 41 10N 106 25W
Medicine Hat, Canada 73 D6 50 0N 110 45W
Medicine Lake, U.S.A. 80 A2 48 30N 104 30W
Medicine Lodge, U.S.A. 81 G5 37 17N 98 35W
Medina = Al Madīnah, Si. Arabia 46 C2 24 35N 39 52 E
Medina, N. Dak., U.S.A. 80 B5 46 54N 99 18W
Medina, N.Y., U.S.A. 78 C6 43 13N 78 23W
Medina, Ohio, U.S.A. 78 E3 41 8N 81 52W
Medina →, U.S.A. 81 L5 29 16N 98 29W
Medina del Campo, Spain 19 B3 41 18N 4 55W
Medina L., U.S.A. 81 L5 29 32N 98 56W
Medina-Sidonia, Spain 19 D3 36 28N 5 57W
Medinipur, India 43 H12 22 25N 87 21 E
Mediterranean Sea, Europe 6 H7 35 0N 15 0 E
Medley, Canada 73 C6 54 25N 110 16W
Médoc, France 18 D3 45 10N 0 50W
Medstead, Canada 73 C7 53 19N 108 5W
Medveditsa →, Russia 25 E7 49 35N 42 41 E
Medvezhi, Ostrava, Russia 27 B17 71 0N 161 0 E
Medvezhyegorsk, Russia 24 B5 63 0N 34 25 E
Medway →, U.K. 11 F8 51 27N 0 46 E
Meeberrie, Australia 61 E2 26 57S 115 51 E
Meekatharra, Australia 61 E2 26 32S 118 29 E
Meeker, U.S.A. 82 F10 40 2N 107 55W
Meerut, India 42 E7 29 1N 77 42 E
Meeteetse, U.S.A. 82 D9 44 9N 108 52W
Mega, Ethiopia 51 H12 3 57N 38 19 E
Mégara, Greece 21 F10 37 58N 23 22 E
Meghalaya □, India 41 G17 25 50N 91 0 E
Mégiscane, L., Canada 70 C4 48 35N 75 55W
Mehndawal, India 43 F10 26 58N 83 5 E
Mehr Jān, Iran 45 C7 33 50N 55 6 E
Mehrābād, Iran 44 B5 36 53N 47 55 E
Mehrān, Iran 44 C5 33 7N 46 10 E
Mehrīz, Iran 45 D7 31 35N 54 28 E
Mei Xian, Guangdong, China 33 D6 24 16N 116 6 E
Mei Xian, Shaanxi, China 34 G4 34 18N 107 55 E
Meiganga, Cameroon 52 C2 6 30N 14 25 E
Meiktila, Burma 41 J19 20 53N 95 54 E
Meissen, Germany 16 C7 51 9N 13 29 E
Mejillones, Chile 94 A1 23 10S 70 30W
Meka, Australia 61 E2 27 25S 116 48 E
Mékambo, Gabon 52 D2 1 2N 13 50 E
Mekdela, Ethiopia 51 F12 11 24N 39 10 E
Mekhtar, Pakistan 40 D6 30 30N 69 15 E

North Las Vegas

North Las Vegas, *U.S.A.* . 85 J11 36 12N 115 7W
North Lincolnshire □, *U.K.* 10 D7 53 36N 0 30W
North Little Rock, *U.S.A.* . 81 H8 34 45N 92 16W
North Loup →, *U.S.A.* . . 80 E5 41 17N 98 24W
North Magnetic Pole, *Canada* 4 B2 77 58N 102 8W
North Minch, *U.K.* 12 C3 58 5N 5 55W
North Nahanni →, *Canada* 72 A4 62 15N 123 20W
North Olmsted, *U.S.A.* . . 78 E3 41 25N 81 56W
North Ossetia □, *Russia* . 25 F7 43 30N 44 30 E
North Pagai, I. = Pagai Utara, *Indonesia* . . . . . . 36 E2 2 35S 100 0 E
North Palisade, *U.S.A.* . . . 83 H4 37 6N 118 31W
North Platte, *U.S.A.* 80 E4 41 8N 100 46W
North Platte →, *U.S.A.* . 80 E4 41 7N 100 42W
North Pole, *Arctic* . . . . . . 4 A 90 0N 0 0 E
North Portal, *Canada* 73 D8 49 0N 102 33W
North Powder, *U.S.A.* . . . 82 D5 45 2N 117 55W
North Pt., *Canada* 71 C7 47 5N 64 0W
North Rhine Westphalia □ = Nordrhein-Westfalen □, *Germany* 16 C4 51 45N 7 30 E
North Ronaldsay, *U.K.* . . . 12 B6 59 22N 2 26W
North Saskatchewan →, *Canada* 73 C7 53 15N 105 5W
North Sea, *Europe* . . . . . . 6 D6 56 0N 4 0 E
North Somerset □, *U.K.* . 11 F5 51 24N 2 45W
North Sporades = Voríai Sporádhes, *Greece* . . . . 21 E10 39 15N 23 30 E
North Sydney, *Canada* . . 71 C7 46 12N 60 15W
North Taranaki Bight, *N.Z.* 59 H5 38 50S 174 15 E
North Thompson →, *Canada* 72 C4 50 40N 120 20W
North Tonawanda, *U.S.A.* 78 C6 43 2N 78 53W
North Troy, *U.S.A.* 79 B12 45 0N 72 24W
North Truchas Pk., *U.S.A.* 83 J11 36 0N 105 30W
North Twin I., *Canada* . . . 70 B3 53 20N 80 0W
North Tyne →, *U.K.* 10 C5 55 0N 2 8W
North Uist, *U.K.* 12 D1 57 40N 7 15W
North Vancouver, *Canada* 72 D4 49 25N 123 3W
North Vernon, *U.S.A.* . . . 76 F3 39 0N 85 38W
North Wabasca L., *Canada* 72 B6 56 0N 113 55W
North Walsham, *U.K.* . . . 10 E9 52 50N 1 22 E
North-West □, *S. Africa* . 56 D4 27 0S 25 0 E
North West C., *Australia* . 60 D1 21 45S 114 9 E
North West Christmas I. Ridge, *Pac. Oc.* 65 G11 6 30N 165 0W
North West Frontier □, *Pakistan* . . . . 42 C4 34 0N 72 0 E
North West Highlands, *U.K.* 12 D3 57 33N 4 58W
North West Providence Channel, *W. Indies* 88 A4 26 0N 78 0W
North West River, *Canada* 71 B7 53 30N 60 10W
North West Territories □, *Canada* 68 B9 67 0N 110 0W
North Western □, *Zambia* 55 E2 13 30S 25 30 E
North York Moors, *U.K.* . 10 C7 54 23N 0 53W
North Yorkshire □, *U.K.* . 10 C6 54 15N 1 25W
Northallerton, *U.K.* 10 C6 54 20N 1 26W
Northam, *S. Africa* . . . . . 56 C4 24 56S 27 18 E
Northampton, *Australia* . 61 E1 28 27S 114 33 E
Northampton, *U.K.* 11 E7 52 15N 0 53W
Northampton, *Mass., U.S.A.* 79 D12 42 19N 72 38W
Northampton, *Pa., U.S.A.* 79 F9 40 41N 75 30W
Northampton Downs, *Australia* . . . . 62 C4 24 35S 145 48 E
Northamptonshire □, *U.K.* 11 E7 52 16N 0 55W
Northbridge, *U.S.A.* 79 D13 42 9N 71 39W
Northcliffe, *Australia* . . . . 61 F2 34 39S 116 7 E
Northern □, *Malawi* . . . . . 55 E3 11 0S 34 0 E
Northern □, *Uganda* . . . . . 54 B3 3 5N 32 30 E
Northern □, *Zambia* . . . . . 55 E3 10 30S 31 0 E
Northern Cape □, *S. Africa* 56 D3 30 0S 20 0 E
Northern Circars, *India* . . 41 L13 17 30N 82 30 E
Northern Indian L., *Canada* 73 B9 57 20N 97 20W
Northern Ireland □, *U.K.* . 13 B5 54 45N 7 0W
Northern Light, L., *Canada* 70 C1 48 15N 90 39W
Northern Marianas ■, *Pac. Oc.* . . . . 64 F6 17 0N 145 0 E
Northern Territory □, *Australia* . . . . 60 D5 20 0S 133 0 E
Northern Transvaal □, *S. Africa* . . . . 57 C4 24 0S 29 0 E
Northfield, *U.S.A.* 80 C8 44 27N 93 9W
Northland □, *N.Z.* . . . . . . 59 F4 35 30S 173 30 E
Northome, *U.S.A.* 80 B7 47 52N 94 17W
Northport, *Ala., U.S.A.* . . 77 J2 33 14N 87 35W
Northport, *Mich., U.S.A.* . 76 C3 45 8N 85 37W
Northport, *Wash., U.S.A.* 82 B5 48 55N 117 48W
Northumberland □, *U.K.* . 10 B5 55 12N 2 0W
Northumberland, C., *Australia* . . . . 63 F3 38 5S 140 40 E
Northumberland Is., *Australia* . . . . 62 C4 21 30S 149 50 E
Northumberland Str., *Canada* 71 C7 46 20N 64 0W
Northwich, *U.K.* 10 D5 53 15N 2 31W
Northwood, *Iowa, U.S.A.* 80 D8 43 27N 93 13W
Northwood, *N. Dak., U.S.A.* 80 B6 47 44N 97 34W
Norton, *U.S.A.* 80 F5 39 50N 99 53W
Norton, *Zimbabwe* . . . . . . 55 F3 17 52S 30 40 E
Norton Sd., *U.S.A.* 68 B3 63 50N 164 0W
Norwalk, *Calif., U.S.A.* . . . 85 M8 33 54N 118 5W
Norwalk, *Conn., U.S.A.* . . 79 E11 41 7N 73 22W
Norwalk, *Ohio, U.S.A.* . . . 78 E2 41 15N 82 37W
Norway, *U.S.A.* 76 C2 45 47N 87 55W
Norway ■, *Europe* . . . . . . 8 E14 63 0N 11 0 E
Norway House, *Canada* . . 73 C9 53 59N 97 50W
Norwegian Sea, *Atl. Oc.* . 4 C8 66 0N 1 0 E
Norwich, *Canada* 78 D4 42 59N 80 36W
Norwich, *U.K.* . . . . 10 E9 52 38N 1 18 E
Norwich, *Conn., U.S.A.* . . 79 E12 41 31N 72 5W
Norwich, *N.Y., U.S.A.* . . . 79 D9 42 32N 75 32W
Norwood, *Canada* 78 B7 44 23N 77 59W
Noshiro, *Japan* . . . . 30 D10 40 12N 140 0 E
Nosok, *Russia* . . . . 26 B9 70 10N 82 20 E
Noss Hd., *U.K.* 12 C5 58 28N 3 3W
Nossob →, *S. Africa* . . . 56 D3 26 55S 20 45 E
Nosy Bé, *Madag.* . . . . 53 G9 13 25S 48 15 E
Nosy Boraha, *Madag.* . . . . 57 B8 16 50S 49 55 E
Nosy Mitsio, *Madag.* . . . . . 53 G9 12 54S 48 36 E
Nosy Varika, *Madag.* . . . . 57 C8 20 35S 48 32 E
Noteć →, *Poland* . . . . . . 16 B8 52 44N 15 26 E
Notigi Dam, *Canada* 73 B9 56 40N 99 10W
Notikewin →, *Canada* . . 72 B5 57 2N 117 38W
Notodden, *Norway* . . . . . 9 G13 59 35N 9 17 E
Notre-Dame, *Canada* 71 C7 46 18N 64 46W
Notre Dame B., *Canada* . 71 C8 49 45N 55 30W
Notre Dame de Koartac = Quaqtaq, *Canada* 69 B13 60 55N 69 40W
Notre Dame d'Ivugivic = Ivujivik, *Canada* 69 B12 62 24N 77 55W
Nottaway →, *Canada* . . 70 B4 51 22N 78 55W
Nottingham, *U.K.* 10 E6 52 58N 1 10W
Nottinghamshire □, *U.K.* 10 D7 53 10N 1 3W
Nottoway →, *U.S.A.* . . . 76 G7 36 33N 76 55W
Notwane →, *Botswana* . 56 C4 23 35S 26 58 E
Nouâdhibou, *Mauritania* . 50 D1 20 54N 17 0W
Nouâdhibou, Ras, *Mauritania* 50 D1 20 50N 17 0W
Nouakchott, *Mauritania* . . 50 E1 18 9N 15 58W
Nouméa, *N. Cal.* . . . . 64 K8 22 17S 166 30 E
Noupoort, *S. Africa* . . . . . 56 E3 31 10S 24 57 E
Nouveau Comptoir = Wemindji, *Canada* 70 B4 53 0N 78 49W
Nouvelle-Calédonie = New Caledonia ■, *Pac. Oc.* . . . . 64 K8 21 0S 165 0 E
Nova Casa Nova, *Brazil* . . 93 E10 9 25S 41 5W
Nova Cruz, *Brazil* 93 E11 6 28S 35 25W
Nova Esperança, *Brazil* . . 95 A5 23 8S 52 24W
Nova Friburgo, *Brazil* . . . 95 A7 22 16S 42 30W
Nova Gaia = Cambundi-Catembo, *Angola* . . . . . 52 G3 10 10S 17 35 E
Nova Iguaçu, *Brazil* 95 A7 22 45S 43 28W
Nova Iorque, *Brazil* 93 E10 7 0S 44 5W
Nova Lima, *Brazil* 95 A7 19 59S 43 51W
Nova Lisboa = Huambo, *Angola* . . . . 53 G3 12 42S 15 54 E
Nova Lusitânia, *Mozam.* . 55 F3 19 50S 34 34 E
Nova Mambone, *Mozam.* . 57 C6 21 0S 35 3 E
Nova Scotia □, *Canada* . . 71 C7 45 10N 63 0W
Nova Sofala, *Mozam.* . . . . 57 C5 20 7S 34 42 E
Nova Venécia, *Brazil* 93 G10 18 45S 40 24W
Nova Zagora, *Bulgaria* . . . 21 C11 42 32N 25 59 E
Novara, *Italy* . . . . 20 B3 45 28N 8 38 E
Novato, *U.S.A.* 84 G4 38 6N 122 35W
Novaya Ladoga, *Russia* . . 24 B5 60 7N 32 16 E
Novaya Lyalya, *Russia* . . . 26 D7 59 4N 60 45 E
Novaya Sibir, Ostrov, *Russia* . . . . 27 B16 75 10N 150 0 E
Novaya Zemlya, *Russia* . . 26 B6 75 0N 56 0 E
Nové Zámky, *Slovak Rep.* 17 D10 48 2N 18 8 E
Novgorod, *Russia* . . . . . . 24 C5 58 30N 31 25 E
Novgorod-Severskiy = Novhorod-Siverskyy, *Ukraine* . . . . 24 D5 52 2N 33 10 E
Novhorod-Siverskyy, *Ukraine* . . . . 24 D5 52 2N 33 10 E
Novi Lígure, *Italy* . . . . 20 B3 44 46N 8 47 E
Novi Pazar, *Serbia, Yug.* . 21 C9 43 12N 20 28 E
Novi Sad, *Serbia, Yug.* . . 21 B8 45 18N 19 52 E
Nôvo Hamburgo, *Brazil* . . 95 B5 29 37S 51 7W
Novo Mesto, *Slovenia* . . . 16 F8 45 48N 15 10 E
Novo Remanso, *Brazil* . . . 93 E10 9 41S 42 4W
Novoataysk, *Russia* . . . . . 26 D9 53 30N 84 0 E
Novocherkassk, *Russia* . . 25 E7 47 27N 40 15 E
Novogrudok = Navahrudak, *Belarus* . . 17 B13 53 40N 25 50 E
Novohrad-Volynskyy, *Ukraine* . . . . 17 C14 50 34N 27 35 E
Novokachalinsk, *Russia* . . 30 B6 45 5N 132 0 E
Novokazalinsk = Zhangaqazaly, *Kazakstan* . . . . 26 E7 45 48N 62 6 E
Novokuybyshevsk, *Russia* 24 D8 53 7N 49 58 E
Novokuznetsk, *Russia* . . . 26 D9 53 45N 87 10 E
Novomoskovsk, *Russia* . . . 24 D6 54 5N 38 15 E
Novorossiysk, *Russia* . . . . 25 F6 44 43N 37 46 E
Novorybnoye, *Russia* . . . . 27 B11 72 50N 105 50 E
Novoselytsya, *Ukraine* . . . 17 D14 48 14N 26 15 E
Novoshakhtinsk, *Russia* . . 25 E6 47 46N 39 58 E
Novosibirsk, *Russia* . . . . . 26 D9 55 0N 83 5 E
Novosibirskiye Ostrova, *Russia* . . . . 27 B15 75 0N 142 0 E
Novotroitsk, *Russia* . . . . . 26 D6 51 10N 58 15 E
Novouzensk, *Russia* . . . . . 25 D8 50 32N 48 17 E
Novovolynsk, *Ukraine* . . . 17 C13 50 45N 24 4 E
Novska, *Croatia* . . . . 20 B7 45 19N 17 0 E
Novyy Port, *Russia* . . . . . 26 C8 67 40N 72 30 E
Now Shahr, *Iran* . . . . 45 B6 36 40N 51 30 E
Nowa Sól, *Poland* . . . . . . 16 C8 51 48N 15 44 E
Nowbarān, *Iran* . . . . 45 C6 35 8N 49 42 E
Nowghāb, *Iran* . . . . 45 C8 33 53N 59 4 E
Nowgong, *India* . . . . 41 F18 26 20N 92 50 E
Nowra, *Australia* . . . . 63 E5 34 53S 150 35 E
Nowshera, *Pakistan* . . . . . 40 B8 34 0N 72 0 E
Nowy Sącz, *Poland* . . . . . 17 D11 49 40N 20 41 E
Nowy Targ, *Poland* . . . . . 17 D11 49 29N 20 2 E
Nowy Tomyśl, *Poland* . . . 16 B9 52 19N 16 10 E
Noxen, *U.S.A.* 79 E8 41 25N 76 4W
Noxon, *U.S.A.* 82 C6 48 0N 115 43W
Noyes I., *U.S.A.* 72 B2 55 30N 133 40W
Noyon, *France* . . . . 18 B5 49 34N 2 59 E
Noyon, *Mongolia* . . . . 34 C2 43 2N 102 4 E
Nsanje, *Malawi* . . . . 55 F4 16 55S 35 12 E
Nsawam, *Ghana* 50 G4 5 50N 0 24W
Nsomba, *Zambia* . . . . 55 E2 10 45S 29 51 E
Nsukka, *Nigeria* . . . . 50 G6 6 51N 7 29 E
Nu Jiang →, *China* . . . . 32 D4 29 58N 97 25 E
Nu Shan, *China* . . . . 32 D4 26 0N 99 20 E
Nubia, *Africa* . . . . 48 D7 21 0N 32 0 E
Nubian Desert = Nûbîya, Es Sahrâ En, *Sudan* . . 51 D11 21 30N 33 30 E
Nûbîya, Es Sahrâ En, *Sudan* . . . . 51 D11 21 30N 33 30 E
Ñuble □, *Chile* 94 D1 37 0S 72 0W
Nuboai, *Indonesia* . . . . . . 37 E9 2 10S 136 30 E
Nubra →, *India* . . . . . . 43 B7 34 35N 77 35 E
Nueces →, *U.S.A.* 81 M6 27 51N 97 30W
Nueltin L., *Canada* 73 A9 60 30N 99 30W
Nueva Asunción □, *Paraguay* 94 A3 21 0S 61 0W
Nueva Gerona, *Cuba* 88 B3 21 53N 82 49W
Nueva Imperial, *Chile* . . . 96 D2 38 45S 72 58W
Nueva Palmira, *Uruguay* . 94 C4 33 52S 58 20W
Nueva Rosita, *Mexico* . . . 86 B4 28 0N 101 11W
Nueva San Salvador, *El Salv.* 88 D2 13 40N 89 18W
Nuéve de Julio, *Argentina* 94 D3 35 30S 61 0W
Nuevitas, *Cuba* 88 B4 21 30N 77 20W
Nuevo, G., *Argentina* 96 E4 43 0S 64 30W
Nuevo Guerrero, *Mexico* . 87 B5 26 34N 99 15W
Nuevo Laredo, *Mexico* . . 87 B5 27 30N 99 30W
Nuevo León □, *Mexico* . . 86 C4 25 0N 100 0W
Nugget Pt., *N.Z.* . . . . 59 M2 46 27S 169 50 E
Nuhaka, *N.Z.* . . . . 59 H6 39 3S 177 45 E
Nukey Bluff, *Australia* . . . 63 E2 32 26S 135 29 E
Nukheila, *Sudan* . . . . 51 E10 19 1N 26 21 E
Nuku'alofa, *Tonga* 59 E11 21 10S 174 0W
Nukus, *Uzbekistan* . . . . . . 26 E6 42 27N 59 41 E
Nulato, *U.S.A.* 68 B4 64 43N 158 6W
Nullagine →, *Australia* . . 60 D3 21 20S 120 20 E
Nullarbor, *Australia* . . . . . 61 F5 31 28S 130 55 E
Nullarbor Plain, *Australia* 61 F4 31 10S 129 0 E
Numalla, L., *Australia* . . . 63 D3 28 43S 144 20 E
Numan, *Nigeria* . . . . 51 G7 9 29N 12 3 E
Numata, *Japan* . . . . 31 F9 36 45N 139 4 E
Numazu, *Japan* . . . . 31 G9 35 7N 138 51 E
Numbulwar, *Australia* . . . . 62 A2 14 15S 135 45 E
Numfoor, *Indonesia* . . . . . 37 E8 1 0S 134 50 E
Numurkah, *Australia* . . . . 63 F4 36 5S 145 26 E
Nunaksaluk I., *Canada* . . . 71 A7 55 49N 60 20W
Nuneaton, *U.K.* 11 E6 52 32N 1 27W
Nungo, *Mozam.* . . . . 55 E4 13 23S 37 43 E
Nungwe, *Tanzania* . . . . . . 54 C3 2 48S 32 2 E
Nunivak I., *U.S.A.* 68 B3 60 10N 166 30W
Nunkun, *India* . . . . 43 C7 33 57N 76 2 E
Nunspeet, *Neths.* . . . . 15 B5 52 21N 5 45 E
Núoro, *Italy* . . . . 20 D3 40 20N 9 20 E
Nūrābād, *Iran* . . . . 45 E8 27 47N 57 12 E
Nuremberg = Nürnberg, *Germany* . . . . 16 D6 49 27N 11 3 E
Nuri, *Mexico* 86 B3 28 2N 109 22W
Nurina, *Australia* . . . . 61 F4 30 56S 126 33 E
Nuriootpa, *Australia* . . . . 63 E2 34 27S 139 0 E
Nurmes, *Finland* . . . . 8 E23 63 33N 29 10 E
Nürnberg, *Germany* . . . . 16 D6 49 27N 11 3 E
Nurran, L. = Terewah, L., *Australia* . . . . 63 D4 29 52S 147 35 E
Nurrari Lakes, *Australia* . 61 E5 29 1S 130 5 E
Nusa Barung, *Indonesia* . 37 H15 8 10S 113 30 E
Nusa Kambangan, *Indonesia* . . . . 37 G13 7 40S 108 10 E
Nusa Tenggara Barat □, *Indonesia* . . . . 36 F5 8 50S 117 30 E
Nusa Tenggara Timur □, *Indonesia* . . . . 37 F6 9 30S 122 0 E
Nusaybin, *Turkey* . . . . 25 G7 37 3N 41 10 E
Nushki, *Pakistan* . . . . 42 E2 29 35N 66 0 E
Nutak, *Canada* 69 C13 57 28N 61 59W
Nutwood Downs, *Australia* 62 B1 15 49S 134 10 E
Nuuk = Godthåb, *Greenland* 69 B14 64 10N 51 35W
Nuwakot, *Nepal* . . . . 43 E10 28 10N 83 55 E
Nuweveldberge, *S. Africa* 56 E3 32 10S 21 45 E
Nuyts, C., *Australia* . . . . . 61 F5 32 2S 132 21 E
Nuyts Arch., *Australia* . . . 63 E1 32 35S 133 20 E
Nxau-Nxau, *Botswana* . . . 56 B3 18 57S 21 4 E
Nyack, *U.S.A.* 79 E11 41 5N 73 55W
Nyah West, *Australia* . . . . 63 F3 35 16S 143 21 E
Nyahanga, *Tanzania* . . . . . 54 C3 2 20S 33 37 E
Nyahua, *Tanzania* . . . . . . 54 D3 5 25S 33 23 E
Nyahururu, *Kenya* . . . . . . 54 B4 0 2N 36 27 E
Nyainqentanglha Shan, *China* . . . . 32 D3 30 0N 90 0 E
Nyakanazi, *Tanzania* . . . . 54 C3 3 2S 31 10 E
Nyâlâ, *Sudan* . . . . 51 F9 12 2N 24 58 E
Nyamandhlovu, *Zimbabwe* . . . . 55 F2 19 55S 28 16 E
Nyambiti, *Tanzania* . . . . . 54 C3 2 48S 33 27 E
Nyamwaga, *Tanzania* . . . . 54 C3 1 27S 34 33 E
Nyandekwa, *Tanzania* . . . . 54 C3 3 57S 32 32 E
Nyandoma, *Russia* . . . . . . 24 B7 61 40N 40 12 E
Nyangana, *Namibia* . . . . . . 56 B3 18 0S 20 40 E
Nyanguge, *Tanzania* . . . . . 54 C3 2 30S 33 12 E
Nyanza, *Burundi* . . . . 54 C2 4 21S 29 36 E
Nyanza, *Rwanda* . . . . 54 C2 2 20S 29 42 E
Nyanza □, *Kenya* . . . . . . 54 C3 0 10S 34 15 E
Nyarling →, *Canada* 72 A6 60 41N 113 23W
Nyasa, L. = Malawi, L., *Africa* . . . . 55 E3 12 30S 34 30 E
Nyasvizh, *Belarus* . . . . . . 17 B14 53 14N 26 38 E
Nyazepetrovsk, *Russia* . . 24 C10 56 3N 59 36 E
Nyazura, *Zimbabwe* . . . . . 55 F3 18 40S 32 16 E
Nyazwidzi →, *Zimbabwe* 55 F3 20 0S 31 17 E
Nybro, *Sweden* . . . . 9 H16 56 44N 15 55 E
Nyda, *Russia* . . . . 26 C8 66 40N 72 58 E
Nyeri, *Kenya* . . . . 54 C4 0 23S 36 56 E
Nyíregyháza, *Hungary* . . . 17 E11 47 58N 21 47 E
Nykøbing, *Storstrøm, Denmark* . . . . 9 J14 54 56N 11 52 E
Nykøbing, *Vestsjælland, Denmark* . . . . 9 J14 55 55N 11 40 E
Nykøbing, *Viborg, Denmark* . . . . 9 H13 56 48N 8 51 E
Nyköping, *Sweden* . . . . . 9 G17 58 45N 17 0 E
Nylstroom, *S. Africa* . . . . 57 C4 24 42S 28 22 E
Nymagee, *Australia* . . . . . 63 E4 32 7S 146 20 E
Nynäshamn, *Sweden* . . . . 9 G17 58 54N 17 57 E
Nyngan, *Australia* . . . . . . 63 E4 31 30S 147 8 E
Nyoman = Neman →, *Lithuania* . . . . 9 J19 55 25N 21 10 E
Nysa, *Poland* . . . . 17 C9 50 30N 17 22 E
Nysa →, *Europe* . . . . 16 B8 52 4N 14 46 E
Nyssa, *U.S.A.* 82 E5 43 53N 117 0W
Nyunzu, *Zaïre* . . . . 54 D2 5 57S 27 58 E
Nyurbe, *Russia* . . . . 27 C12 63 17N 118 28 E
Nzega, *Tanzania* . . . . 54 C3 4 10S 33 12 E
Nzega □, *Tanzania* . . . . . 54 C3 4 10S 33 10 E
N'Zérékoré, *Guinea* 50 G3 7 49N 8 48W
Nzeto, *Angola* . . . . 52 F2 7 10S 12 52 E
Nzilo, Chutes de, *Zaïre* . . 55 E2 10 18S 25 27 E
Nzubuka, *Tanzania* . . . . . . 54 C3 4 45S 32 50 E

O

Ō-Shima, *Nagasaki, Japan* 31 G4 34 29N 129 33 E
Ō-Shima, *Shizuoka, Japan* 31 G9 34 44N 139 24 E
Oacoma, *U.S.A.* 80 D5 43 48N 99 24W
Oahe, L., *U.S.A.* 80 C4 44 27N 100 24W
Oahe Dam, *U.S.A.* 80 C4 44 27N 100 24W
Oahu, *U.S.A.* 74 H16 21 28N 157 58W
Oak Creek, *U.S.A.* 82 F10 40 16N 106 57W
Oak Harbor, *U.S.A.* 84 B4 48 18N 122 39W
Oak Hill, *U.S.A.* 76 G5 37 59N 81 9W
Oak Park, *U.S.A.* 76 E2 41 53N 87 47W
Oak Ridge, *U.S.A.* 77 G3 36 1N 84 16W
Oak View, *U.S.A.* 85 L7 34 24N 119 18W
Oakan-Dake, *Japan* . . . . . 30 C12 43 27N 144 10 E
Oakbank, *Australia* . . . . . 63 E3 33 4S 140 33 E
Oakdale, *Calif., U.S.A.* . . . 83 H3 37 46N 120 51W
Oakdale, *La., U.S.A.* 81 K8 30 49N 92 40W
Oakengates, *U.K.* 10 E5 52 41N 2 26W
Oakes, *U.S.A.* 80 B5 46 8N 98 6W
Oakesdale, *U.S.A.* 82 C5 47 8N 117 15W
Oakey, *Australia* . . . . 63 D5 27 25S 151 43 E
Oakham, *U.K.* 10 E7 52 40N 0 43W
Oakhurst, *U.S.A.* 84 H7 37 19N 119 40W
Oakland, *Calif., U.S.A.* . . . 83 H2 37 49N 122 16W
Oakland, *Oreg., U.S.A.* . . . 82 E2 43 25N 123 18W
Oakland City, *U.S.A.* 76 F2 38 20N 87 21W
Oakley, *Idaho, U.S.A.* 82 E7 42 15N 113 53W
Oakley, *Kans., U.S.A.* 80 F4 39 8N 100 51W
Oakover →, *Australia* . . 60 D3 21 0S 120 40 E
Oakridge, *U.S.A.* 82 E2 43 45N 122 28W
Oakville, *U.S.A.* 84 D3 46 51N 123 14W
Oamaru, *N.Z.* . . . . 59 L3 45 5S 170 59 E
Oasis, *Calif., U.S.A.* 85 M10 33 28N 116 6W
Oasis, *Nev., U.S.A.* 84 H9 37 29N 117 55W
Oates Land, *Antarctica* . . 5 C11 69 0S 160 0 E
Oatman, *U.S.A.* 85 K12 35 1N 114 19W
Oaxaca, *Mexico* 87 D5 17 2N 96 40W
Oaxaca □, *Mexico* 87 D5 17 0N 97 0W
Ob →, *Russia* . . . . 26 C7 66 45N 69 30 E
Oba, *Canada* 70 C3 49 4N 84 7W
Obama, *Japan* . . . . 31 G7 35 30N 135 45 E
Oban, *U.K.* 12 E3 56 25N 5 29W
Obbia, *Somali Rep.* . . . . . 46 F4 5 25N 48 30 E
Obed, *Canada* 72 C5 53 30N 117 10W
Obera, *Argentina* 95 B4 27 21S 55 2W
Oberhausen, *Germany* . . . 16 C4 51 28N 6 51 E
Oberlin, *Kans., U.S.A.* . . . 80 F4 39 49N 100 32W
Oberlin, *La., U.S.A.* 81 K8 30 37N 92 46W
Oberlin, *Ohio, U.S.A.* 78 E2 41 18N 82 13W
Oberon, *Australia* . . . . 63 E4 33 45S 149 52 E
Obi, Kepulauan, *Indonesia* 37 E7 1 23S 127 45 E
Obi Is. = Obi, Kepulauan, *Indonesia* . . . . 37 E7 1 23S 127 45 E
Óbidos, *Brazil* 93 D7 1 50S 55 30W
Obihiro, *Japan* . . . . 30 C11 42 56N 143 12 E
Obilatu, *Indonesia* . . . . . . 37 E7 1 25S 127 20 E
Obluchye, *Russia* . . . . 27 E14 49 1N 131 4 E
Obo, *C.A.R.* . . . . 54 A2 5 20N 26 32 E
Oboa, Mt., *Uganda* . . . . . 54 B3 1 45N 34 45 E
Oboyan, *Russia* . . . . 26 D4 51 15N 36 21 E
Obozerskaya = Obozerskiy, *Russia* . . . . 26 C5 63 34N 40 21 E
Obozerskiy, *Russia* . . . . . . 26 C5 63 34N 40 21 E
Observatory Inlet, *Canada* 72 B3 55 10N 129 54W
Obshchi Syrt, *Russia* . . . . 6 E16 52 0N 53 0 E
Obskaya Guba, *Russia* . . . 26 C8 69 0N 73 0 E
Obuasi, *Ghana* 50 G4 6 17N 1 40W
Ocala, *U.S.A.* 77 L4 29 11N 82 8W
Ocampo, *Mexico* 86 B3 28 9N 108 24W
Ocaña, *Spain* 19 C4 39 55N 3 30W
Ocanomowoc, *U.S.A.* 80 D10 43 7N 88 30W
Ocate, *U.S.A.* 81 G2 36 11N 105 3W
Occidental, Cordillera, *Colombia* 92 C3 5 0N 76 0W
Ocean City, *N.J., U.S.A.* . . 76 F8 39 17N 74 35W
Ocean City, *Wash., U.S.A.* 84 C2 47 4N 124 10W
Ocean I. = Banaba, *Kiribati* . . . . 64 H8 0 45S 169 50 E
Ocean Park, *U.S.A.* 84 D2 46 30N 124 3W
Oceano, *U.S.A.* 85 K6 35 6N 120 37W
Oceanport, *U.S.A.* 79 F10 40 19N 74 3W
Oceanside, *U.S.A.* 85 M9 33 12N 117 23W
Ochil Hills, *U.K.* 12 E5 56 14N 3 40W
Ochre River, *Canada* 73 C9 51 4N 99 47W
Ocilla, *U.S.A.* 77 K4 31 36N 83 15W
Ocmulgee →, *U.S.A.* . . . 77 K4 31 58N 82 33W
Ocnița, *Moldova* . . . . 17 D14 48 25N 27 30 E
Oconee →, *U.S.A.* 77 K4 31 58N 82 33W
Oconto, *U.S.A.* 76 C2 44 53N 87 52W
Oconto Falls, *U.S.A.* 76 C1 44 52N 88 9W
Ocosingo, *Mexico* 87 D6 17 10N 92 15W
Ocotal, *Nic.* 88 D2 13 41N 86 31W
Ocotlán, *Mexico* 86 C4 20 21N 102 42W
Octave, *U.S.A.* 83 J7 34 10N 112 43W
Ocumare del Tuy, *Venezuela* 92 A5 10 7N 66 46W
Ōda, *Japan* . . . . 31 G6 35 11N 132 30 E
Ódáðahraun, *Iceland* 8 D5 65 5N 17 0W
Odate, *Japan* . . . . 30 D10 40 16N 140 34 E
Odawara, *Japan* . . . . 31 G9 35 20N 139 6 E
Odda, *Norway* . . . . 9 F12 60 3N 6 35 E
Oddur, *Somali Rep.* . . . . . 46 G3 4 11N 43 52 E
Odei →, *Canada* 73 B9 56 6N 96 54W
Ödemiș, *Turkey* . . . . 21 E13 38 15N 28 0 E
Odendaalsrus, *S. Africa* . . 56 D4 27 48S 26 45 E
Odense, *Denmark* . . . . 9 J14 55 22N 10 23 E
Oder →, *Germany* . . . . . . 16 B8 53 33N 14 38 E
Odesa, *Ukraine* . . . . 25 E5 46 30N 30 45 E
Odessa = Odesa, *Ukraine* 25 E5 46 30N 30 45 E
Odessa, *Canada* 79 B8 44 17N 76 43W
Odessa, *Tex., U.S.A.* 81 K3 31 52N 102 23W
Odessa, *Wash., U.S.A.* . . . 82 C4 47 20N 118 41W
Odiakwe, *Botswana* . . . . . 56 C4 20 12S 25 17 E
Odienné, *Ivory C.* 50 G3 9 30N 7 34W
Odintsovo, *Russia* . . . . . . 24 C6 55 39N 37 15 E
O'Donnell, *U.S.A.* 81 J4 32 58N 101 50W
Odorheiu Secuiesc, *Romania* . . . . 17 E13 46 21N 25 21 E
Odra = Oder →, *Germany* . . . . 16 B8 53 33N 14 38 E

149

Oshnovīyeh

Oshnovīyeh, Iran 44 B5 37 2N 45 6 E
Oshogbo, Nigeria 50 G5 7 48N 4 37 E
Oshtorīnān, Iran 45 C6 34 1N 48 38 E
Oshwe, Zaïre 52 E3 3 25S 19 28 E
Osijek, Croatia 21 B8 45 34N 18 41 E
Osipenko = Berdyansk, Ukraine 25 E6 46 45N 36 50 E
Osipovichi = Asipovichy, Belarus 17 B15 53 19N 28 33 E
Osizweni, S. Africa 57 D5 27 49S 30 7 E
Oskaloosa, U.S.A. 80 E8 41 18N 92 39W
Oskarshamn, Sweden 9 H17 57 15N 16 27 E
Oskélanéo, Canada 70 C4 48 5N 75 15W
Öskemen, Kazakstan 26 E9 50 0N 82 36 E
Oslo, Norway 9 G14 59 55N 10 45 E
Oslob, Phil. 37 C6 9 31N 123 26 E
Oslofjorden, Norway 9 G14 59 20N 10 35 E
Osmanabad, India 40 K10 18 5N 76 10 E
Osmaniye, Turkey 25 G6 37 5N 36 10 E
Osnabrück, Germany 16 B5 52 17N 8 3 E
Osorio, Brazil 95 B5 29 53S 50 17W
Osorno, Chile 96 E2 40 25S 73 0W
Osoyoos, Canada 72 D5 49 0N 119 30W
Osøyri, Norway 9 F11 60 9N 5 30 E
Ospika →, Canada 72 B4 56 20N 124 0W
Osprey Reef, Australia 62 A4 13 52S 146 36 E
Oss, Neths. 15 C5 51 46N 5 32 E
Ossa, Mt., Australia 62 G4 41 52S 146 3 E
Óssa, Oros, Greece 21 E10 39 47N 22 42 E
Ossabaw I., U.S.A. 77 K5 31 50N 81 5W
Ossining, U.S.A. 79 E11 41 10N 73 55W
Ossipee, U.S.A. 79 C13 43 41N 71 7W
Ossokmanuan L., Canada 71 B7 53 25N 65 0W
Ossora, Russia 27 D17 59 20N 163 13 E
Ostend = Oostende, Belgium 15 C2 51 15N 2 54 E
Oster, Ukraine 17 C16 50 57N 30 53 E
Österdalälven, Sweden 9 F16 61 30N 13 45 E
Østerdalen, Norway 9 F14 61 40N 10 50 E
Östersund, Sweden 8 E16 63 10N 14 38 E
Ostfriesische Inseln, Germany 16 B4 53 42N 7 0 E
Ostrava, Czech. 17 D10 49 51N 18 18 E
Ostróda, Poland 17 B10 53 42N 19 58 E
Ostroh, Ukraine 17 C14 50 20N 26 30 E
Ostrołęka, Poland 17 B11 53 4N 21 32 E
Ostrów Mazowiecka, Poland 17 B11 52 50N 21 51 E
Ostrów Wielkopolski, Poland 17 C9 51 36N 17 44 E
Ostrowiec-Świętokrzyski, Poland 17 C11 50 55N 21 22 E
Ostuni, Italy 21 D7 40 44N 17 35 E
Ōsumi-Kaikyō, Japan 31 J5 30 55N 131 0 E
Ōsumi-Shotō, Japan 31 J5 30 30N 130 0 E
Osuna, Spain 19 D3 37 14N 5 8W
Oswego, U.S.A. 79 C8 43 27N 76 31W
Oswestry, U.K. 10 E4 52 52N 3 3W
Oświęcim, Poland 17 C10 50 2N 19 11 E
Otago □, N.Z. 59 L2 45 15S 170 0 E
Otago Harbour, N.Z. 59 L3 45 47S 170 42 E
Ōtake, Japan 31 G6 34 12N 132 13 E
Otaki, N.Z. 59 J5 40 45S 175 10 E
Otaru, Japan 30 C10 43 10N 141 0 E
Otaru-Wan = Ishikari-Wan, Japan 30 C10 43 25N 141 1 E
Otavalo, Ecuador 92 C3 0 13N 78 20W
Otavi, Namibia 56 B2 19 40S 17 24 E
Otchinjau, Angola 56 B1 16 30S 13 56 E
Othello, U.S.A. 82 C4 46 50N 119 10W
Otira Gorge, N.Z. 59 K3 42 53S 171 33 E
Otis, U.S.A. 80 E3 40 9N 102 58W
Otjiwarongo, Namibia 56 C2 20 30S 16 33 E
Otoineppu, Japan 30 B11 44 44N 142 16 E
Otorohanga, N.Z. 59 H5 38 12S 175 14 E
Otoskwin →, Canada 70 B2 52 13N 88 6W
Otosquen, Canada 73 C8 53 17N 102 1W
Otra →, Norway 9 G13 58 9N 8 1 E
Otranto, Italy 21 D8 40 9N 18 28 E
Otranto, C. d', Italy 21 D8 40 7N 18 30 E
Otranto, Str. of, Italy 21 D8 40 15N 18 40 E
Otse, S. Africa 56 D4 25 2S 25 45 E
Ōtsu, Japan 31 G7 35 0N 135 50 E
Ōtsuki, Japan 31 G9 35 36N 138 57 E
Ottawa = Outaouais →, Canada 70 C5 45 27N 74 8W
Ottawa, Canada 70 C4 45 27N 75 42W
Ottawa, Ill., U.S.A. 80 E10 41 21N 88 51W
Ottawa, Kans., U.S.A. 80 F7 38 37N 95 16W
Ottawa Is., Canada 69 C11 59 35N 80 10W
Otter L., Canada 73 B8 55 35N 104 39W
Otter Rapids, Ont., Canada 70 B3 50 11N 81 39W
Otter Rapids, Sask., Canada 73 B8 55 38N 104 44W
Otterville, Canada 78 D4 42 55N 80 36W
Otto Beit Bridge, Zimbabwe 55 F2 15 59S 28 56 E
Ottosdal, S. Africa 56 D4 26 46S 25 59 E
Ottumwa, U.S.A. 80 E8 41 1N 92 25W
Oturkpo, Nigeria 50 G6 7 16N 8 8 E
Otway, B., Chile 96 G2 53 30S 74 0W
Otway, C., Australia 63 F3 38 52S 143 30 E
Otwock, Poland 17 B11 52 5N 21 20 E
Ou →, Laos 38 B4 20 4N 102 13 E
Ou Neua, Laos 38 A3 22 18N 101 48 E
Ou-Sammyaku, Japan 30 E10 39 20N 140 35 E
Ouachita →, U.S.A. 81 K9 31 38N 91 49W
Ouachita, L., U.S.A. 81 H8 34 34N 93 12W
Ouachita Mts., U.S.A. 81 H7 34 40N 94 25W
Ouadâne, Mauritania 50 D2 20 50N 11 40W
Ouadda, C.A.R. 51 G9 8 15N 22 20 E
Ouagadougou, Burkina Faso 50 F4 12 25N 1 30W
Ouahran = Oran, Algeria 50 A4 35 45N 0 39W
Ouallene, Algeria 50 D5 24 41N 1 11 E
Ouanda Djallé, C.A.R. 51 G9 8 55N 22 53 E
Ouango, C.A.R. 52 D4 4 19N 22 30 E
Ouargla, Algeria 50 B6 31 59N 5 16 E
Ouarzazate, Morocco 50 B3 30 55N 6 50W
Oubangi →, Zaïre 52 E3 0 30S 17 50 E
Ouddorp, Neths. 15 C3 51 50N 3 57 E
Oude Rijn →, Neths. 15 B4 52 12N 4 24 E
Oudenaarde, Belgium 15 D3 50 50N 3 37 E
Oudtshoorn, S. Africa 56 E3 33 35S 22 14 E
Ouessant, I. d', France 18 B1 48 28N 5 6W
Ouesso, Congo 52 D3 1 37N 16 5 E
Ouest, Pte., Canada 71 C7 49 52N 64 40W
Ouezzane, Morocco 50 B3 34 51N 5 35W
Ouidah, Benin 50 G5 6 25N 2 0 E
Oujda, Morocco 50 B4 34 41N 1 55W
Oujeft, Mauritania 50 D2 20 2N 13 0W
Oulainen, Finland 8 D21 64 17N 24 47 E
Ouled Djellal, Algeria 50 B6 34 28N 5 2 E
Oulu, Finland 8 D21 65 1N 25 29 E
Oulujärvi, Finland 8 D22 64 25N 27 15 E
Oulujoki →, Finland 8 D21 65 1N 25 30 E
Oum Chalouba, Chad 51 E9 15 48N 20 46 E
Ounasjoki →, Finland 8 C21 66 31N 25 40 E
Ounguati, Namibia 56 C2 22 0S 15 46 E
Ounianga-Kébir, Chad 51 E9 19 4N 20 29 E
Ounianga Sérir, Chad 51 E9 18 54N 20 51 E
Our →, Lux. 15 E6 49 55N 6 5 E
Ouray, U.S.A. 83 G10 38 1N 107 40W
Ourense = Orense, Spain 19 A2 42 19N 7 55W
Ouricuri, Brazil 93 E10 7 53S 40 5W
Ourinhos, Brazil 95 A6 23 0S 49 54W
Ouro Fino, Brazil 95 A6 22 16S 46 25W
Ouro Prêto, Brazil 95 A7 20 20S 43 30W
Ourthe →, Belgium 15 D5 50 29N 5 35 E
Ouse, Australia 62 G4 42 38S 146 42 E
Ouse →, E. Susx., U.K. 11 G8 50 47N 0 4 E
Ouse →, N. Yorks., U.K. 10 C8 53 44N 0 55W
Outaouais →, Canada 70 C5 45 27N 74 8W
Outardes →, Canada 71 C6 49 24N 69 30W
Outer Hebrides, U.K. 12 D1 57 30N 7 40W
Outer I., Canada 71 B8 51 10N 58 35W
Outjo, Namibia 56 C2 20 5S 16 7 E
Outlook, Canada 73 C7 51 30N 107 0W
Outlook, U.S.A. 80 A2 48 53N 104 47W
Outokumpu, Finland 8 E23 62 43N 29 1 E
Ouyen, Australia 63 F3 35 1S 142 22 E
Ovalau, Fiji 59 C8 17 40S 178 48 E
Ovalle, Chile 94 C1 30 33S 71 18W
Ovamboland, Namibia 56 B2 18 30S 16 0 E
Overflakkee, Neths. 15 C4 51 44N 4 10 E
Overijssel □, Neths. 15 B6 52 25N 6 35 E
Overland Park, U.S.A. 80 F7 38 55N 94 50W
Overpelt, Belgium 15 C5 51 12N 5 20 E
Overton, U.S.A. 85 J12 36 33N 114 27W
Övertorneå, Sweden 8 C20 66 23N 23 38 E
Ovid, U.S.A. 80 E3 40 58N 102 23W
Oviedo, Spain 19 A3 43 25N 5 50W
Oviši, Latvia 9 H19 57 33N 21 44 E
Övör Hangay □, Mongolia 34 B2 45 0N 102 30 E
Øvre Årdal, Norway 9 F12 61 19N 7 48 E
Ovruch, Ukraine 17 C15 51 25N 28 45 E
Owaka, N.Z. 59 M2 46 27S 169 40 E
Owambo = Ovamboland, Namibia 56 B2 18 30S 16 0 E
Owase, Japan 31 G8 34 7N 136 12 E
Owatonna, U.S.A. 80 C8 44 5N 93 14W
Owbeh, Afghan. 40 B3 34 28N 63 10 E
Owego, U.S.A. 79 D8 42 6N 76 16W
Owen Falls Dam, Uganda 54 B3 0 30N 33 5 E
Owen Sound, Canada 70 D3 44 35N 80 55W
Owendo, Gabon 52 D1 0 17N 9 30 E
Owens →, U.S.A. 84 J9 36 32N 117 59W
Owens L., U.S.A. 85 J9 36 26N 117 57W
Owensboro, U.S.A. 76 G2 37 46N 87 7W
Owensville, U.S.A. 80 F9 38 21N 91 30W
Owl →, Canada 73 B10 57 51N 92 44W
Owo, Nigeria 50 G6 7 10N 5 39 E
Owosso, U.S.A. 76 D3 43 0N 84 10W
Owyhee, U.S.A. 82 F5 41 57N 116 6W
Owyhee →, U.S.A. 82 E5 43 49N 117 2W
Owyhee, L., U.S.A. 82 E5 43 38N 117 14W
Öxarfjörður, Iceland 8 C5 66 15N 16 45W
Oxelösund, Sweden 9 G17 58 43N 17 15 E
Oxford, N.Z. 59 K4 43 18S 172 11 E
Oxford, U.K. 11 F6 51 46N 1 15W
Oxford, Miss., U.S.A. 81 H10 34 22N 89 31W
Oxford, N.C., U.S.A. 77 G6 36 19N 78 35W
Oxford, Ohio, U.S.A. 76 F3 39 31N 84 45W
Oxford L., Canada 73 C9 54 51N 95 37W
Oxfordshire □, U.K. 11 F6 51 48N 1 16W
Oxley, Australia 63 E3 34 11S 144 6 E
Oxnard, U.S.A. 85 L7 34 12N 119 11W
Oxus = Amudarya →, Uzbekistan 26 E6 43 58N 59 34 E
Oya, Malaysia 36 D4 2 55N 111 55 E
Oyama, Japan 31 F9 36 18N 139 48 E
Oyem, Gabon 52 D2 1 34N 11 31 E
Oyen, Canada 73 C6 51 22N 110 28W
Oykel →, U.K. 12 D4 57 56N 4 26W
Oymyakon, Russia 27 C15 63 25N 142 44 E
Oyo, Nigeria 50 G5 7 46N 3 56 E
Oyster Bay, U.S.A. 79 F11 40 52N 73 32W
Ōyūbari, Japan 30 C11 43 1N 142 5 E
Ozamiz, Phil. 37 C6 8 15N 123 50 E
Ozark, Ala., U.S.A. 77 K3 31 28N 85 39W
Ozark, Ark., U.S.A. 81 H8 35 29N 93 50W
Ozark, Mo., U.S.A. 81 G8 37 1N 93 12W
Ozark Plateau, U.S.A. 81 G9 37 20N 91 40W
Ozarks, L. of the, U.S.A. 80 F8 38 12N 92 38W
Ózd, Hungary 17 D11 48 14N 20 15 E
Ozette L., U.S.A. 84 B2 48 6N 124 38W
Ozona, U.S.A. 81 K4 30 43N 101 12W
Ozuluama, Mexico 87 C5 21 40N 97 50W

P

Pa-an, Burma 41 L20 16 51N 97 40 E
Pa Mong Dam, Thailand 38 D4 18 0N 102 22 E
Paamiut = Frederikshåb, Greenland 4 C5 62 0N 49 43W
Paarl, S. Africa 56 E2 33 45S 18 56 E
Paauilo, U.S.A. 74 H17 20 2N 155 22W
Pab Hills, Pakistan 42 F2 26 30N 66 45 E
Pabianice, Poland 17 C10 51 40N 19 20 E
Pabna, Bangla. 41 G16 24 1N 89 18 E
Pabo, Uganda 54 B3 3 1N 32 10 E
Pacaja →, Brazil 93 D8 1 56S 50 50W
Pacaraima, Sierra, Venezuela 92 C6 4 0N 62 30W
Pacasmayo, Peru 92 E3 7 20S 79 35W
Pachhar, India 42 G7 24 40N 77 42 E
Pachpadra, India 40 G8 25 58N 72 10 E
Pachuca, Mexico 87 C5 20 10N 98 40W
Pacific, Canada 72 C3 54 48N 128 28W
Pacific-Antarctic Ridge, Pac. Oc. 65 M16 43 0S 115 0W
Pacific Grove, U.S.A. 83 H3 36 38N 121 56W
Pacific Ocean, Pac. Oc. 65 G14 10 0N 140 0W
Pacifica, U.S.A. 84 H4 37 36N 122 30W
Pacitan, Indonesia 37 H14 8 12S 111 7 E
Packwood, U.S.A. 84 D5 46 36N 121 40W
Padaido, Kepulauan, Indonesia 37 E9 1 5S 138 0 E
Padang, Indonesia 36 E2 1 0S 100 20 E
Padangpanjang, Indonesia 36 E2 0 40S 100 20 E
Padangsidempuan, Indonesia 36 D1 1 30N 99 15 E
Paddockwood, Canada 73 C7 53 30N 105 30W
Paderborn, Germany 16 C5 51 42N 8 45 E
Padloping Island, Canada 69 B13 67 0N 62 50W
Pádova, Italy 20 B4 45 25N 11 53 E
Padra, India 42 H5 22 15N 73 7 E
Padrauna, India 43 F10 26 54N 83 59 E
Padre I., U.S.A. 81 M6 27 10N 97 25W
Padstow, U.K. 11 G3 50 33N 4 58W
Padua = Pádova, Italy 20 B4 45 25N 11 53 E
Paducah, Ky., U.S.A. 76 G1 37 5N 88 37W
Paducah, Tex., U.S.A. 81 H4 34 1N 100 18W
Paengnyong-do, S. Korea 35 F13 37 57N 124 40 E
Paeroa, N.Z. 59 G5 37 23S 175 41 E
Pafúri, Mozam. 57 C5 22 28S 31 17 E
Pag, Croatia 16 F8 44 25N 15 3 E
Pagadian, Phil. 37 C6 7 55N 123 30 E
Pagai Selatan, P., Indonesia 36 E2 3 0S 100 15 E
Pagai Utara, Indonesia 36 E2 2 35S 100 0 E
Pagalu = Annobón, Atl. Oc. 49 G4 1 25S 5 36 E
Pagastikós Kólpos, Greece 21 E10 39 15N 23 0 E
Pagatan, Indonesia 36 E5 3 33S 115 59 E
Page, Ariz., U.S.A. 83 H8 36 57N 111 27W
Page, N. Dak., U.S.A. 80 B6 47 10N 97 34W
Pago Pago, Amer. Samoa 59 B13 14 16S 170 43W
Pagosa Springs, U.S.A. 83 H10 37 16N 107 1W
Pagwa River, Canada 70 B2 50 2N 85 14W
Pahala, U.S.A. 74 J17 19 12N 155 29W
Pahang →, Malaysia 39 L4 3 30N 103 9 E
Pahiatua, N.Z. 59 J5 40 27S 175 50 E
Pahokee, U.S.A. 77 M5 26 50N 80 40W
Pahrump, U.S.A. 85 J11 36 12N 115 59W
Pahute Mesa, U.S.A. 84 H10 37 20N 116 45W
Pai, Thailand 38 C2 19 19N 98 27 E
Paia, U.S.A. 74 H16 20 54N 156 22W
Paicines, U.S.A. 84 J5 36 44N 121 17W
Paide, Estonia 9 G21 58 57N 25 31 E
Paignton, U.K. 11 G4 50 26N 3 35W
Päijänne, Finland 9 F21 61 30N 25 30 E
Painan, Indonesia 36 E2 1 21S 100 34 E
Painesville, U.S.A. 78 E3 41 43N 81 15W
Paint Hills = Wemindji, Canada 70 B4 53 0N 78 49W
Paint L., Canada 73 B9 55 28N 97 57W
Paint Rock, U.S.A. 81 K5 31 31N 99 55W
Painted Desert, U.S.A. 83 J8 36 0N 111 0W
Paintsville, U.S.A. 76 G4 37 49N 82 48W
País Vasco □, Spain 19 A4 42 50N 2 45W
Paisley, Canada 78 B3 44 18N 81 16W
Paisley, U.K. 12 F4 55 50N 4 25W
Paisley, U.S.A. 82 E3 42 42N 120 32W
Paita, Peru 92 E2 5 11S 81 9W
Pajares, Puerto de, Spain 19 A3 42 58N 5 46W
Pak Lay, Laos 38 C3 18 15N 101 27 E
Pak Phanang, Thailand 39 H3 8 21N 100 12 E
Pak Sane, Laos 38 C4 18 22N 103 39 E
Pak Song, Laos 38 E6 15 11N 106 14 E
Pak Suong, Laos 38 C4 19 58N 102 15 E
Pakaraima Mts., Guyana 92 B6 6 0N 60 0W
Pákhnes, Greece 23 D6 35 16N 24 4 E
Pakistan ■, Asia 42 E3 30 0N 70 0 E
Pakkading, Laos 38 C4 18 19N 103 59 E
Pakokku, Burma 41 J19 21 20N 95 0 E
Pakpattan, Pakistan 42 D5 30 25N 73 27 E
Pakse, Laos 38 E5 15 5N 105 52 E
Paktīā □, Afghan. 40 C6 33 0N 69 15 E
Pakwach, Uganda 54 B3 2 28N 31 27 E
Pala, Chad 51 G8 9 25N 15 5 E
Pala, U.S.A. 85 M9 33 22N 117 5W
Pala, Zaïre 54 D2 6 45S 29 30 E
Palabek, Uganda 54 B3 3 22N 32 33 E
Palacios, U.S.A. 81 L6 28 42N 96 13W
Palagruža, Croatia 20 C7 42 24N 16 15 E
Palaiókastron, Greece 23 D8 35 12N 26 15 E
Palaiokhóra, Greece 23 D5 35 16N 23 39 E
Palam, India 40 K10 19 0N 77 0 E
Palampur, India 42 C7 32 10N 76 30 E
Palana, Australia 62 F4 39 45S 147 55 E
Palana, Russia 27 D16 59 10N 159 59 E
Palanan, Phil. 37 A6 17 8N 122 29 E
Palanan Pt., Phil. 37 A6 17 17N 122 30 E
Palandri, Pakistan 43 C5 33 42N 73 40 E
Palanga, Lithuania 9 J19 55 58N 21 3 E
Palangkaraya, Indonesia 36 E4 2 16S 113 56 E
Palani Hills, India 40 P10 10 14N 77 33 E
Palanpur, India 42 G5 24 10N 72 25 E
Palanro, Indonesia 37 E5 3 21S 119 23 E
Palapye, Botswana 56 C4 22 30S 27 7 E
Palas, Pakistan 43 B5 35 4N 73 14 E
Palatka, Russia 27 C16 60 6N 150 54 E
Palatka, U.S.A. 77 L5 29 39N 81 38W
Palau ■, Pac. Oc. 28 J17 7 30N 134 30 E
Palawan, Phil. 36 C5 9 30N 118 30 E
Palayankottai, India 40 Q10 8 45N 77 45 E
Paldiski, Estonia 9 G21 59 23N 24 9 E
Paleleh, Indonesia 37 D6 1 10N 121 50 E
Palembang, Indonesia 36 E2 3 0S 104 50 E
Palencia, Spain 19 A3 42 1N 4 34W
Paleokastrítsa, Greece 23 A3 39 40N 19 41 E
Paleometokho, Cyprus 23 D12 35 7N 33 11 E
Palermo, Italy 20 E5 38 7N 13 22 E
Palermo, U.S.A. 82 G3 39 26N 121 33W
Palestine, Asia 47 D4 32 0N 35 0 E
Palestine, U.S.A. 81 K7 31 46N 95 38W
Paletwa, Burma 41 J18 21 10N 92 50 E
Palghat, India 40 P10 10 46N 76 42 E
Palgrave, Mt., Australia 60 D2 23 22S 115 58 E
Pali, India 42 G5 25 50N 73 20 E
Palioúrion, Ákra, Greece 21 E10 39 57N 23 45 E
Palisade, U.S.A. 80 E4 40 21N 101 7W
Palitana, India 42 J4 21 32N 71 49 E
Palizada, Mexico 87 D6 18 18N 92 8W
Palk Bay, Asia 40 Q11 9 30N 79 15 E
Palk Strait, Asia 40 Q11 10 0N 79 45 E
Palkānah, Iraq 44 C5 35 49N 44 26 E
Palla Road = Dinokwe, Botswana 56 C4 23 29S 26 37 E
Pallanza = Verbánia, Italy 20 B3 45 56N 8 33 E
Pallisa, Uganda 54 B3 1 12N 33 43 E
Pallu, India 42 E6 28 59N 74 14 E
Palm Bay, U.S.A. 77 L5 28 2N 80 35W
Palm Beach, U.S.A. 77 M6 26 43N 80 2W
Palm Desert, U.S.A. 85 M10 33 43N 116 22W
Palm Is., Australia 62 B4 18 40S 146 35 E
Palm Springs, U.S.A. 85 M10 33 50N 116 33W
Palma, Mozam. 55 E5 10 46S 40 29 E
Palma →, Brazil 93 F9 12 33S 47 52W
Palma, B. de, Spain 22 B9 39 30N 2 39 E
Palma de Mallorca, Spain 22 B9 39 35N 2 39 E
Palma Soriano, Cuba 88 B4 20 15N 76 0W
Palmares, Brazil 93 E11 8 41S 35 28W
Palmas, Brazil 95 B5 26 29S 52 0W
Palmas, C., Liberia 50 H3 4 27N 7 46W
Pálmas, G. di, Italy 20 E3 39 0N 8 30 E
Palmdale, U.S.A. 85 L8 34 35N 118 7W
Palmeira dos Índios, Brazil 93 E11 9 25S 36 37W
Palmeirinhas, Pta. das, Angola 52 F2 9 2S 12 57 E
Palmer, U.S.A. 68 B5 61 36N 149 7W
Palmer →, Australia 62 B3 16 0S 142 26 E
Palmer Arch., Antarctica 5 C17 64 15S 65 0W
Palmer Lake, U.S.A. 80 F2 39 7N 104 55W
Palmer Land, Antarctica 5 D18 73 0S 63 0W
Palmerston, Canada 78 C4 43 50N 80 51W
Palmerston, N.Z. 59 L3 45 29S 170 43 E
Palmerston North, N.Z. 59 J5 40 21S 175 39 E
Palmerton, U.S.A. 79 F9 40 48N 75 37W
Palmetto, U.S.A. 77 M4 27 31N 82 34W
Palmi, Italy 20 E6 38 21N 15 51 E
Palmira, Argentina 94 C2 32 59S 68 34W
Palmira, Colombia 92 C3 3 32N 76 16W
Palmyra = Tudmur, Syria 44 C3 34 36N 38 15 E
Palmyra, Mo., U.S.A. 80 F9 39 48N 91 32W
Palmyra, N.Y., U.S.A. 78 C7 43 5N 77 18W
Palmyra Is., Pac. Oc. 65 G11 5 52N 162 5W
Palo Alto, U.S.A. 83 H2 37 27N 122 10W
Palo Verde, U.S.A. 85 M12 33 26N 114 44W
Palopo, Indonesia 37 E6 3 0S 120 16 E
Palos, C. de, Spain 19 D5 37 38N 0 40W
Palos Verdes, U.S.A. 85 M8 33 48N 118 23W
Palos Verdes, Pt., U.S.A. 85 M8 33 43N 118 26W
Palouse, U.S.A. 82 C5 46 55N 117 4W
Palparara, Australia 62 C3 24 47S 141 28 E
Palu, Indonesia 37 E5 1 0S 119 52 E
Palu, Turkey 25 G7 38 45N 40 0 E
Paluan, Phil. 37 B6 13 26N 120 29 E
Palwal, India 42 E7 28 8N 77 19 E
Pama, Burkina Faso 50 F5 11 19N 0 44 E
Pamanukan, Indonesia 37 G12 6 16S 107 49 E
Pamekasan, Indonesia 37 G15 7 10S 113 28 E
Pamiers, France 18 E4 43 7N 1 39 E
Pamirs, Tajikistan 26 F8 37 40N 73 0 E
Pamlico →, U.S.A. 77 H7 35 20N 76 28W
Pamlico Sd., U.S.A. 77 H8 35 20N 76 0W
Pampa, U.S.A. 81 H4 35 32N 100 58W
Pampa de las Salinas, Argentina 94 C2 32 1S 66 58W
Pampanua, Indonesia 37 E6 4 16S 120 8 E
Pampas, Argentina 94 D3 35 0S 63 0W
Pampas, Peru 92 F4 12 20S 74 50W
Pamplona, Colombia 92 B4 7 23N 72 39W
Pamplona, Spain 19 A5 42 48N 1 38W
Pampoenpoort, S. Africa 56 E3 31 3S 22 40 E
Pana, U.S.A. 80 F10 39 23N 89 5W
Panaca, U.S.A. 83 H6 37 47N 114 23W
Panaitan, Indonesia 37 G11 6 36S 105 12 E
Panaji, India 40 M8 15 25N 73 50 E
Panamá, Panama 88 E4 9 0N 79 25W
Panama ■, Cent. Amer. 88 E4 8 48N 79 55W
Panamá, G. de, Panama 88 E4 8 4N 79 20W
Panama Canal, Panama 88 E4 9 10N 79 37W
Panama City, U.S.A. 77 K3 30 10N 85 40W
Panamint Range, U.S.A. 85 J9 36 20N 117 20W
Panamint Springs, U.S.A. 85 J9 36 20N 117 28W
Panão, Peru 92 E3 9 55S 75 55W
Panare, Thailand 39 J3 6 51N 101 30 E
Panarukan, Indonesia 37 G15 7 42S 113 56 E
Panay, Phil. 37 B6 11 10N 122 30 E
Panay, G., Phil. 37 B6 11 0N 122 30 E
Pancake Range, U.S.A. 83 G6 38 30N 115 50W
Pančevo, Serbia, Yug. 21 B9 44 52N 20 41 E
Pandan, Phil. 37 B6 11 45N 122 10 E
Pandegelang, Indonesia 37 G12 6 25N 106 5 E
Pandharpur, India 40 L9 17 41N 75 20 E
Pando, Uruguay 95 C4 34 44S 56 0W
Pando, L. = Hope, L., Australia 63 D2 28 24S 139 18 E
Pandokrátor, Greece 23 A3 39 45N 19 50 E
Pandora, Costa Rica 88 E3 9 43N 83 3W
Panevėžys, Lithuania 9 J21 55 42N 24 25 E
Panfilov, Kazakstan 26 E8 44 10N 80 0 E
Pang-Long, Burma 41 H21 23 11N 98 45 E
Pang-Yang, Burma 41 H21 22 7N 98 48 E
Panga, Zaïre 54 B2 1 52N 26 18 E
Pangalanes, Canal des, Madag. 57 C8 22 48S 47 50 E
Pangani, Tanzania 54 D4 5 25S 38 58 E
Pangani □, Tanzania 54 D4 5 25S 39 0 E
Pangani →, Tanzania 54 D4 5 26S 38 58 E
Pangfou = Bengbu, China 35 H9 32 58N 117 20 E
Pangil, Zaïre 54 C2 3 10S 26 35 E
Pangkah, Tanjung, Indonesia 37 G15 6 51S 112 33 E
Pangkajene, Indonesia 37 E5 4 46S 119 34 E
Pangkalanbrandan, Indonesia 36 D1 4 1N 98 20 E
Pangkalanbuun, Indonesia 36 E4 2 41S 111 37 E

153

Potrerillos

Ravenna

Ravenna, *Italy* **20 B5** 44 25N 12 12 E
Ravenna, *Nebr., U.S.A.* **80 E5** 41 1N 98 55W
Ravenna, *Ohio, U.S.A.* **78 E3** 41 9N 81 15W
Ravensburg, *Germany* **16 E5** 47 46N 9 36 E
Ravenshoe, *Australia* **62 B4** 17 37S 145 29 E
Ravensthorpe, *Australia* **61 F3** 33 35S 120 2 E
Ravenswood, *Australia* **62 C4** 20 6S 146 54 E
Ravenswood, *U.S.A.* **76 F5** 38 57N 81 46W
Ravi →, *Pakistan* **42 D4** 30 35N 71 49 E
Rawalpindi, *Pakistan* **42 C5** 33 38N 73 8 E
Rawāndūz, *Iraq* **44 B5** 36 40N 44 30 E
Rawang, *Malaysia* **39 L3** 3 20N 101 35 E
Rawdon, *Canada* **70 C5** 46 3N 73 40W
Rawene, *N.Z.* **59 F4** 35 25S 173 32 E
Rawlinna, *Australia* **61 F4** 30 58S 125 28 E
Rawlins, *U.S.A.* **82 F10** 41 47N 107 14W
Rawlinson Ra., *Australia* **61 D4** 24 40S 128 30 E
Rawson, *Argentina* **96 E3** 43 15S 65 5W
Ray, *U.S.A.* **80 A3** 48 21N 103 10W
Ray, C., *Canada* **71 C8** 47 33N 59 15W
Rayadurg, *India* **40 M10** 14 40N 76 50 E
Rayagada, *India* **41 K13** 19 15N 83 20 E
Raychikhinsk, *Russia* **27 E13** 49 46N 129 25 E
Rāyen, *Iran* **45 D8** 29 34N 57 26 E
Raymond, *Canada* **72 D6** 49 30N 112 35W
Raymond, *Calif., U.S.A.* **84 H7** 37 13N 119 54W
Raymond, *Wash., U.S.A.* **84 D3** 46 41N 123 44W
Raymondville, *U.S.A.* **81 M6** 26 29N 97 47W
Raymore, *Canada* **73 C8** 51 25N 104 31W
Rayne, *U.S.A.* **81 K8** 30 14N 92 16W
Rayón, *Mexico* **86 B2** 29 43N 110 35W
Rayong, *Thailand* **38 F3** 12 40N 101 20 E
Rayville, *U.S.A.* **81 J9** 32 29N 91 46W
Raz, Pte. du, *France* **18 C1** 48 2N 4 47W
Razan, *Iran* **45 C6** 35 23N 49 2 E
Razdel'naya = Rozdilna, *Ukraine* **17 E16** 46 50N 30 2 E
Razdolnoye, *Russia* **30 C5** 43 30N 131 52 E
Razeh, *Iran* **45 C6** 32 47N 48 9 E
Razelm, Lacul, *Romania* **17 F15** 44 50N 29 0 E
Razgrad, *Bulgaria* **21 C12** 43 33N 26 34 E
Razmak, *Pakistan* **42 C3** 32 45N 69 50 E
Ré, I. de, *France* **18 C3** 46 12N 1 30W
Reading, *U.K.* **11 F7** 51 27N 0 58W
Reading, *U.S.A.* **79 F9** 40 20N 75 56W
Realicó, *Argentina* **94 D3** 35 0S 64 15W
Reata, *Mexico* **86 B4** 26 8N 101 5W
Rebecca, L., *Australia* **61 F3** 30 0S 122 15 E
Rebi, *Indonesia* **37 F8** 6 23S 134 7 E
Rebiana, *Libya* **51 D9** 24 12N 22 10 E
Rebun-Tō, *Japan* **30 B10** 45 23N 141 2 E
Recherche, Arch. of the, *Australia* **61 F3** 34 15S 122 50 E
Rechytsa, *Belarus* **17 B16** 52 21N 30 24 E
Recife, *Brazil* **93 E12** 8 0S 35 0W
Recklinghausen, *Germany* **15 C7** 51 37N 7 12 E
Reconquista, *Argentina* **94 B4** 29 10S 59 45W
Recreo, *Argentina* **94 B2** 29 25S 65 10W
Red →, *La., U.S.A.* **81 K9** 31 1N 91 45W
Red →, *N. Dak., U.S.A.* **80 A6** 49 0N 97 15W
Red Bank, *U.S.A.* **79 F10** 40 21N 74 5W
Red Bay, *Canada* **71 B8** 51 44N 56 25W
Red Bluff, *U.S.A.* **82 F2** 40 11N 122 15W
Red Bluff L., *U.S.A.* **81 K3** 31 54N 103 55W
Red Cliffs, *Australia* **63 E3** 34 19S 142 11 E
Red Cloud, *U.S.A.* **80 E5** 40 5N 98 32W
Red Deer, *Canada* **72 C6** 52 20N 113 50W
Red Deer →, *Alta., Canada* **73 C6** 50 58N 110 0W
Red Deer →, *Man., Canada* **73 C8** 52 53N 101 1W
Red Deer L., *Canada* **73 C8** 52 55N 101 20W
Red Indian L., *Canada* **71 C8** 48 35N 57 0W
Red Lake, *Canada* **73 C10** 51 3N 93 49W
Red Lake Falls, *U.S.A.* **80 B6** 47 53N 96 16W
Red Lodge, *U.S.A.* **82 D9** 45 11N 109 15W
Red Mountain, *U.S.A.* **85 K9** 35 37N 117 38W
Red Oak, *U.S.A.* **80 E7** 41 1N 95 14W
Red Rock, *Canada* **70 C2** 48 55N 88 15W
Red Rock, L., *U.S.A.* **80 E8** 41 22N 92 59W
Red Rocks Pt., *Australia* **61 F4** 32 13S 127 32 E
Red Sea, *Asia* **46 C2** 25 0N 36 0 E
Red Slate Mt., *U.S.A.* **84 H8** 37 31N 118 52W
Red Sucker L., *Canada* **73 C10** 54 9N 93 40W
Red Tower Pass = Turnu Roşu, P., *Romania* **17 F13** 45 33N 24 17 E
Red Wing, *U.S.A.* **80 C8** 44 34N 92 31W
Redbridge, *U.K.* **11 F8** 51 35N 0 7 E
Redcar, *U.K.* **10 C6** 54 37N 1 4W
Redcar & Cleveland □, *U.K.* **10 C6** 54 29N 1 0W
Redcliff, *Canada* **73 C6** 50 10N 110 50W
Redcliffe, *Australia* **63 D5** 27 12S 153 0 E
Redcliffe, Mt., *Australia* **61 E3** 28 30S 121 30 E
Reddersburg, *S. Africa* **56 D4** 29 41S 26 10 E
Redding, *U.S.A.* **82 F2** 40 35N 122 24W
Redditch, *U.K.* **11 E6** 52 18N 1 55W
Redfield, *U.S.A.* **80 C5** 44 53N 98 31W
Redknife →, *Canada* **72 A5** 61 14N 119 22W
Redlands, *U.S.A.* **85 M9** 34 4N 117 11W
Redmond, *Australia* **61 F2** 34 55S 117 40 E
Redmond, *Oreg., U.S.A.* **82 D3** 44 17N 121 11W
Redmond, *Wash., U.S.A.* **84 C4** 47 41N 122 7W
Redon, *France* **18 C2** 47 40N 2 6W
Redonda, *Antigua* **89 C7** 16 58N 62 19W
Redondela, *Spain* **19 A1** 42 15N 8 38W
Redondo Beach, *U.S.A.* **85 M8** 33 50N 118 23W
Redrock Pt., *Canada* **72 A5** 62 11N 115 2W
Redruth, *U.K.* **11 G2** 50 14N 5 14W
Redvers, *Canada* **73 D8** 49 35N 101 40W
Redwater, *Canada* **72 C6** 53 55N 113 6W
Redwood, *U.S.A.* **79 B9** 44 18N 75 48W
Redwood City, *U.S.A.* **83 H2** 37 30N 122 15W
Redwood Falls, *U.S.A.* **80 C7** 44 32N 95 7W
Ree, L., *Ireland* **13 C4** 53 35N 8 0W
Reed, L., *Canada* **73 C8** 54 38N 100 30W
Reed City, *U.S.A.* **76 D3** 43 53N 85 31W
Reeder, *U.S.A.* **80 B3** 46 7N 102 57W
Reedley, *U.S.A.* **83 H4** 36 36N 119 27W
Reedsburg, *U.S.A.* **80 D9** 43 32N 90 0W
Reedsport, *U.S.A.* **82 E1** 43 42N 124 6W
Reefton, *N.Z.* **59 K3** 42 6S 171 51 E
Refugio, *U.S.A.* **81 L6** 28 18N 97 17W
Regensburg, *Germany* **16 D7** 49 1N 12 6 E
Réggio di Calábria, *Italy* **20 E6** 38 6N 15 39 E
Réggio nell'Emília, *Italy* **20 B4** 44 43N 10 36 E
Reghin, *Romania* **17 E13** 46 46N 24 42 E
Regina, *Canada* **73 C8** 50 27N 104 35W
Registro, *Brazil* **95 A6** 24 29S 47 49W
Rehar →, *India* **43 H10** 23 55N 82 40 E
Rehoboth, *Namibia* **56 C2** 23 15S 17 4 E
Rehovot, *Israel* **47 D3** 31 54N 34 48 E
Rei-Bouba, *Cameroon* **51 G7** 8 40N 14 15 E
Reichenbach, *Germany* **16 C7** 50 37N 12 17 E
Reid, *Australia* **61 F4** 30 49S 128 26 E
Reid River, *Australia* **62 B4** 19 40S 146 48 E
Reidsville, *U.S.A.* **77 G6** 36 21N 79 40W
Reigate, *U.K.* **11 F7** 51 14N 0 12W
Reims, *France* **18 B6** 49 15N 4 1 E
Reina Adelaida, Arch., *Chile* **96 G2** 52 20S 74 0W
Reinbeck, *U.S.A.* **80 D8** 42 19N 92 36W
Reindeer →, *Canada* **73 B8** 55 36N 103 11W
Reindeer I., *Canada* **73 C9** 52 30N 98 0W
Reindeer L., *Canada* **73 B8** 57 15N 102 15W
Reinga, C., *N.Z.* **59 F4** 34 25S 172 43 E
Reinosa, *Spain* **19 A3** 43 2N 4 15W
Reitz, *S. Africa* **57 D4** 27 48S 28 29 E
Reivilo, *S. Africa* **56 D3** 27 36S 24 8 E
Rekinniki, *Russia* **27 C17** 60 51N 163 40 E
Reliance, *Canada* **73 A7** 63 0N 109 20W
Remarkable, Mt., *Australia* **63 E2** 32 48S 138 10 E
Rembang, *Indonesia* **37 G14** 6 42S 111 21 E
Remedios, *Panama* **88 E3** 8 15N 81 50W
Remeshk, *Iran* **45 E8** 26 55N 58 50 E
Remich, *Lux.* **15 E6** 49 32N 6 22 E
Ren Xian, *China* **34 F8** 37 8N 114 40 E
Rendsburg, *Germany* **16 A5** 54 17N 9 39 E
Rene, *Russia* **27 C19** 66 2N 179 25W
Renfrew, *Canada* **70 C4** 45 30N 76 40W
Renfrew, *U.K.* **12 F4** 55 52N 4 24W
Renfrewshire □, *U.K.* **12 F4** 55 49N 4 38W
Rengat, *Indonesia* **36 E2** 0 30S 102 45 E
Rengo, *Chile* **94 C1** 34 24S 70 50W
Reni, *Ukraine* **17 F15** 45 28N 28 15 E
Renk, *Sudan* **51 F11** 11 50N 32 50 E
Renkum, *Neths.* **15 C5** 51 58N 5 43 E
Renmark, *Australia* **63 E3** 34 11S 140 43 E
Rennell Sd., *Canada* **72 C2** 53 23N 132 35W
Renner Springs T.O., *Australia* **62 B1** 18 20S 133 47 E
Rennes, *France* **18 B3** 48 7N 1 41W
Reno, *U.S.A.* **84 F7** 39 31N 119 48W
Reno →, *Italy* **20 B5** 44 38N 12 16 E
Renovo, *U.S.A.* **78 E7** 41 20N 77 45W
Renqiu, *China* **34 E9** 38 43N 116 5 E
Rensselaer, *Ind., U.S.A.* **76 E2** 40 57N 87 9W
Rensselaer, *N.Y., U.S.A.* **79 D11** 42 38N 73 45W
Rentería, *Spain* **19 A5** 43 19N 1 54W
Renton, *U.S.A.* **84 C4** 47 29N 122 12W
Reotipur, *India* **43 G10** 25 33N 83 45 E
Republic, *Mich., U.S.A.* **76 B2** 46 25N 87 59W
Republic, *Wash., U.S.A.* **82 B4** 48 39N 118 44W
Republican →, *U.S.A.* **80 F6** 39 4N 96 48W
Republican City, *U.S.A.* **80 E5** 40 6N 99 13W
Repulse Bay, *Canada* **69 B11** 66 30N 86 30W
Requena, *Peru* **92 E4** 5 5S 73 52W
Requena, *Spain* **19 C5** 39 30N 1 4W
Resadiye = Datça, *Turkey* **21 F12** 36 46N 27 40 E
Reserve, *Canada* **73 C8** 52 28N 102 39W
Reserve, *U.S.A.* **83 K9** 33 43N 108 45W
Resht = Rasht, *Iran* **45 B6** 37 20N 49 40 E
Resistencia, *Argentina* **94 B4** 27 30S 59 0W
Reşiţa, *Romania* **17 F11** 45 18N 21 53 E
Resolution I., *Canada* **69 B13** 61 30N 65 0W
Resolution I., *N.Z.* **59 L1** 45 40S 166 40 E
Ressano Garcia, *Mozam.* **57 D5** 25 25S 32 0 E
Reston, *Canada* **73 D8** 49 33N 101 6W
Retalhuleu, *Guatemala* **88 D1** 14 33N 91 46W
Retenue, L. de, *Zaïre* **55 E2** 11 0S 27 0 E
Retford, *U.K.* **10 D7** 53 19N 0 56W
Réthimnon, *Greece* **23 D6** 35 18N 24 30 E
Réthimnon □, *Greece* **23 D6** 35 23N 24 28 E
Réunion ■, *Ind. Oc.* **49 J9** 21 0S 56 0 E
Reus, *Spain* **19 B6** 41 10N 1 5 E
Reutlingen, *Germany* **16 D5** 48 29N 9 12 E
Reval = Tallinn, *Estonia* **9 G21** 59 22N 24 48 E
Revda, *Russia* **24 C10** 56 48N 59 57 E
Revelganj, *India* **43 G11** 25 50N 84 40 E
Revelstoke, *Canada* **72 C5** 51 0N 118 10W
Revilla Gigedo, Is., *Pac. Oc.* **66 H8** 18 40N 112 0W
Revillagigedo I., *U.S.A.* **72 B2** 55 50N 131 20W
Revuè →, *Mozam.* **55 F3** 19 50S 34 0 E
Rewa, *India* **43 G9** 24 33N 81 25 E
Rewari, *India* **42 E7** 28 15N 76 40 E
Rexburg, *U.S.A.* **82 E8** 43 49N 111 47W
Rey, *Iran* **45 C6** 35 35N 51 25 E
Rey Malabo, *Eq. Guin.* **50 H6** 3 45N 8 50 E
Reyðarfjörður, *Iceland* **8 D6** 65 2N 14 13W
Reyes, Pt., *U.S.A.* **84 H3** 38 0N 123 0W
Reykjahlið, *Iceland* **8 D5** 65 40N 16 55W
Reykjanes, *Iceland* **8 E2** 63 48N 22 40W
Reykjavík, *Iceland* **8 D3** 64 10N 21 57W
Reynolds, *Canada* **73 D9** 49 40N 95 55W
Reynolds Ra., *Australia* **60 D5** 22 30S 133 0 E
Reynoldsville, *U.S.A.* **78 E6** 41 5N 78 58W
Reynosa, *Mexico* **87 B5** 26 5N 98 18W
Rēzekne, *Latvia* **9 H22** 56 30N 27 17 E
Rezvān, *Iran* **45 E8** 27 34N 56 6 E
Rhayader, *U.K.* **11 E4** 52 18N 3 29W
Rheden, *Neths.* **15 B6** 52 3N 6 3 E
Rhein, *Canada* **73 C8** 51 25N 102 15W
Rhein →, *Europe* **15 C6** 51 52N 6 2 E
Rhein-Main-Donau-Kanal, *Germany* **16 D6** 49 15N 11 15 E
Rheine, *Germany* **16 B4** 52 17N 7 26 E
Rheinland-Pfalz □, *Germany* **16 C4** 50 0N 7 0 E
Rhin = Rhein →, *Europe* **15 C6** 51 52N 6 2 E
Rhine = Rhein →, *Europe* **15 C6** 51 52N 6 2 E
Rhineland-Palatinate □ = Rheinland-Pfalz □, *Germany* **16 C4** 50 0N 7 0 E
Rhinelander, *U.S.A.* **80 C10** 45 38N 89 25W
Rhino Camp, *Uganda* **54 B3** 3 0N 31 22 E
Rhode Island □, *U.S.A.* **79 E13** 41 40N 71 30W
Rhodes = Ródhos, *Greece* **23 C10** 36 15N 28 10 E
Rhodesia = Zimbabwe ■, *Africa* **55 F2** 19 0S 30 0 E
Rhodope Mts. = Rhodopi Planina, *Bulgaria* **21 D11** 41 40N 24 20 E
Rhodopi Planina, *Bulgaria* **21 D11** 41 40N 24 20 E
Rhön = Hohe Rhön, *Germany* **16 C5** 50 24N 9 58 E
Rhondda, *U.K.* **11 F4** 51 39N 3 31W
Rhondda Cynon Taff □, *U.K.* **11 F4** 51 42N 3 27W
Rhône →, *France* **18 E6** 43 28N 4 42 E
Rhum, *U.K.* **12 E2** 57 0N 6 20W
Rhyl, *U.K.* **10 D4** 53 20N 3 29W
Rhymney, *U.K.* **11 F4** 51 46N 3 17W
Riachão, *Brazil* **93 E9** 7 20S 46 37W
Riasi, *India* **43 C6** 33 10N 74 50 E
Riau □, *Indonesia* **36 D2** 0 0 102 35 E
Riau, Kepulauan, *Indonesia* **36 D2** 0 30N 104 20 E
Riau Arch. = Riau, Kepulauan, *Indonesia* **36 D2** 0 30N 104 20 E
Ribadeo, *Spain* **19 A2** 43 35N 7 5W
Ribble →, *U.K.* **10 C5** 53 52N 2 25W
Ribe, *Denmark* **9 J13** 55 19N 8 44 E
Ribeira Brava, *Madeira* **22 D2** 32 41N 17 4W
Ribeirão Prêto, *Brazil* **95 A6** 21 10S 47 50W
Riberalta, *Bolivia* **92 F5** 11 0S 66 0W
Rîbniţa, *Moldova* **17 E15** 47 45N 29 0 E
Riccarton, *N.Z.* **59 K4** 43 32S 172 37 E
Rice, *U.S.A.* **85 L12** 34 5N 114 51W
Rice L., *Canada* **78 B6** 44 12N 78 10W
Rice Lake, *U.S.A.* **80 C9** 45 30N 91 44W
Rich Hill, *U.S.A.* **81 F7** 38 6N 94 22W
Richards Bay, *S. Africa* **57 D5** 28 48S 32 6 E
Richards L., *Canada* **73 B7** 59 10N 107 10W
Richardson →, *Canada* **73 B6** 58 25N 111 14W
Richardson Springs, *U.S.A.* **84 F5** 39 51N 121 46W
Richardton, *U.S.A.* **80 B3** 46 53N 102 19W
Riche, C., *Australia* **61 F2** 34 36S 118 47 E
Richey, *U.S.A.* **80 B2** 47 39N 105 4W
Richfield, *Idaho, U.S.A.* **82 E6** 43 3N 114 9W
Richfield, *Utah, U.S.A.* **83 G8** 38 46N 112 5W
Richford, *U.S.A.* **79 B12** 45 0N 72 40W
Richibucto, *Canada* **71 C7** 46 42N 64 54W
Richland, *Ga., U.S.A.* **77 J3** 32 5N 84 40W
Richland, *Oreg., U.S.A.* **82 D5** 44 46N 117 10W
Richland, *Wash., U.S.A.* **82 C4** 46 17N 119 18W
Richland Center, *U.S.A.* **80 D9** 43 21N 90 23W
Richlands, *U.S.A.* **76 G5** 37 6N 81 48W
Richmond, *N.S.W., Australia* **63 E5** 33 35S 150 42 E
Richmond, *Queens., Australia* **62 C3** 20 43S 143 8 E
Richmond, *N.Z.* **59 J4** 41 20S 173 12 E
Richmond, *U.K.* **10 C6** 54 25N 1 43W
Richmond, *Calif., U.S.A.* **84 H4** 37 56N 122 21W
Richmond, *Ind., U.S.A.* **76 F3** 39 50N 84 53W
Richmond, *Ky., U.S.A.* **76 G3** 37 45N 84 18W
Richmond, *Mich., U.S.A.* **78 D2** 42 49N 82 45W
Richmond, *Mo., U.S.A.* **80 F8** 39 17N 93 58W
Richmond, *Tex., U.S.A.* **81 L7** 29 35N 95 46W
Richmond, *Utah, U.S.A.* **82 F8** 41 56N 111 48W
Richmond, *Va., U.S.A.* **76 G7** 37 33N 77 27W
Richmond Ra., *Australia* **63 D5** 29 0S 152 45 E
Richmond-upon-Thames, *U.K.* **11 F7** 51 27N 0 17W
Richton, *U.S.A.* **77 K1** 31 16N 88 56W
Richwood, *U.S.A.* **76 F5** 38 14N 80 32W
Ridder = Leninogorsk, *Kazakstan* **26 D9** 50 20N 83 30 E
Ridgecrest, *U.S.A.* **85 K9** 35 38N 117 40W
Ridgedale, *Canada* **73 C8** 53 0N 104 10W
Ridgefield, *U.S.A.* **84 E4** 45 49N 122 45W
Ridgeland, *U.S.A.* **77 J5** 32 29N 80 59W
Ridgelands, *Australia* **62 C5** 23 16S 150 17 E
Ridgetown, *Canada* **70 D3** 42 26N 81 52W
Ridgewood, *U.S.A.* **79 F10** 40 59N 74 7W
Ridgway, *U.S.A.* **78 E6** 41 25N 78 44W
Riding Mountain Nat. Park, *Canada* **73 C8** 50 50N 100 0W
Ridley, Mt., *Australia* **61 F3** 33 12S 122 7 E
Ried, *Austria* **16 D7** 48 14N 13 30 E
Riesa, *Germany* **16 C7** 51 17N 13 17 E
Riet →, *S. Africa* **56 D3** 29 0S 23 54 E
Rieti, *Italy* **20 C5** 42 24N 12 51 E
Riffe L., *U.S.A.* **84 D4** 46 32N 122 26W
Rifle, *U.S.A.* **82 G10** 39 32N 107 47W
Rift Valley □, *Kenya* **54 B4** 0 20N 36 0 E
Rig Rig, *Chad* **51 F7** 14 13N 14 25 E
Rīga, *Latvia* **9 H21** 56 53N 24 8 E
Riga, G. of, *Latvia* **9 H20** 57 40N 23 45 E
Rīgān, *Iran* **45 D8** 28 37N 58 58 E
Rīgas Jūras Līcis = Riga, G. of, *Latvia* **9 H20** 57 40N 23 45 E
Rigaud, *Canada* **79 A10** 45 29N 74 18W
Rigby, *U.S.A.* **82 E8** 43 40N 111 55W
Rīgestān □, *Afghan.* **40 D4** 30 15N 65 0 E
Riggins, *U.S.A.* **82 D5** 45 25N 116 19W
Rigolet, *Canada* **71 B8** 54 10N 58 23W
Riihimäki, *Finland* **9 F21** 60 45N 24 48 E
Riiser-Larsen-halvøya, *Antarctica* **5 C4** 68 0S 35 0 E
Rijeka, *Croatia* **16 F8** 45 20N 14 21 E
Rijn →, *Neths.* **15 B4** 52 12N 4 21 E
Rijssen, *Neths.* **15 B6** 52 19N 6 31 E
Rijswijk, *Neths.* **15 B4** 52 4N 4 22 E
Rikuzentakada, *Japan* **30 E10** 39 0N 141 40 E
Riley, *U.S.A.* **82 E4** 43 32N 119 28W
Rimah, Wadi ar →, *Si. Arabia* **44 E4** 26 5N 41 30 E
Rimbey, *Canada* **72 C6** 52 35N 114 15W
Rimini, *Italy* **20 B5** 44 3N 12 33 E
Rîmnicu Sărat, *Romania* **17 F14** 45 26N 27 3 E
Rîmnicu Vîlcea, *Romania* **17 F13** 45 9N 24 21 E
Rimouski, *Canada* **71 C6** 48 27N 68 30W
Rimrock, *U.S.A.* **84 D5** 46 38N 121 10W
Rinca, *Indonesia* **37 F5** 8 45S 119 35 E
Rincón de Romos, *Mexico* **86 C4** 22 14N 102 18W
Rinconada, *Argentina* **94 A2** 22 26S 66 10W
Ringkøbing, *Denmark* **9 H13** 56 5N 8 15 E
Ringling, *U.S.A.* **82 C8** 46 16N 110 49W
Ringvassøy, *Norway* **8 B18** 69 56N 19 15 E
Rinjani, *Indonesia* **36 F5** 8 24S 116 28 E
Rio Branco, *Brazil* **92 E5** 9 58S 67 49W
Río Branco, *Uruguay* **95 C5** 32 40S 53 40W
Rio Brilhante, *Brazil* **95 A5** 21 48S 54 33W
Rio Claro, *Brazil* **95 A6** 22 19S 47 35W
Rio Claro, *Trin. & Tob.* **89 D7** 10 20N 61 25W
Río Colorado, *Argentina* **96 D4** 39 0S 64 0W
Río Cuarto, *Argentina* **94 C3** 33 10S 64 25W
Rio das Pedras, *Mozam.* **57 C6** 23 8S 35 28 E
Rio de Janeiro, *Brazil* **95 A7** 23 0S 43 12W
Rio de Janeiro □, *Brazil* **95 A7** 22 50S 43 0W
Rio do Sul, *Brazil* **95 B6** 27 13S 49 37W
Río Gallegos, *Argentina* **96 G3** 51 35S 69 15W
Río Grande, *Argentina* **96 G3** 53 50S 67 45W
Rio Grande, *Brazil* **95 C5** 32 0S 52 20W
Río Grande, *Mexico* **86 C4** 23 50N 103 2W
Río Grande, *Nic.* **88 D3** 12 54N 83 33W
Rio Grande →, *U.S.A.* **81 N6** 25 57N 97 9W
Rio Grande City, *U.S.A.* **81 M5** 26 23N 98 49W
Río Grande del Norte →, *N. Amer.* **75 E7** 26 0N 97 0W
Rio Grande do Norte □, *Brazil* **93 E11** 5 40S 36 0W
Rio Grande do Sul □, *Brazil* **95 C5** 30 0S 53 0W
Río Hato, *Panama* **88 E3** 8 22N 80 10W
Rio Lagartos, *Mexico* **87 C7** 21 36N 88 10W
Rio Largo, *Brazil* **93 E11** 9 28S 35 50W
Río Mulatos, *Bolivia* **92 G5** 19 40S 66 50W
Río Muni = Mbini □, *Eq. Guin.* **52 D2** 1 30N 10 0 E
Rio Negro, *Brazil* **95 B6** 26 0S 49 55W
Rio Pardo, *Brazil* **95 C5** 30 0S 52 30W
Río Segundo, *Argentina* **94 C3** 31 40S 63 59W
Río Tercero, *Argentina* **94 C3** 32 15S 64 8W
Rio Verde, *Brazil* **93 G8** 17 50S 51 0W
Río Verde, *Mexico* **87 C5** 21 56N 99 59W
Rio Vista, *U.S.A.* **84 G5** 38 10N 121 42W
Ríobamba, *Ecuador* **92 D3** 1 50S 78 45W
Ríohacha, *Colombia* **92 A4** 11 33N 72 55W
Ríosucio, *Caldas, Colombia* **92 B3** 5 30N 75 40W
Ríosucio, *Choco, Colombia* **92 B3** 7 27N 77 7W
Riou L., *Canada* **73 B7** 59 7N 106 25W
Ripley, *Canada* **78 B3** 44 4N 81 35W
Ripley, *Calif., U.S.A.* **85 M12** 33 32N 114 39W
Ripley, *N.Y., U.S.A.* **78 D5** 42 16N 79 43W
Ripley, *Tenn., U.S.A.* **81 H10** 35 45N 89 32W
Ripon, *U.K.* **10 C6** 54 9N 1 31W
Ripon, *Calif., U.S.A.* **84 H5** 37 44N 121 7W
Ripon, *Wis., U.S.A.* **76 D1** 43 51N 88 50W
Risalpur, *Pakistan* **42 B4** 34 3N 71 59 E
Rishā', W. ar →, *Si. Arabia* **44 E5** 25 33N 44 5 E
Rishiri-Tō, *Japan* **30 B10** 45 11N 141 15 E
Rishon le Ziyyon, *Israel* **47 D3** 31 58N 34 48 E
Rison, *U.S.A.* **81 J8** 33 58N 92 11W
Risør, *Norway* **9 G13** 58 43N 9 13 E
Rittman, *U.S.A.* **78 F3** 40 58N 81 47W
Ritzville, *U.S.A.* **82 C4** 47 8N 118 23W
Riva del Garda, *Italy* **20 B4** 45 53N 10 50 E
Rivadavia, *Buenos Aires, Argentina* **94 D3** 35 29S 62 59W
Rivadavia, *Mendoza, Argentina* **94 C2** 33 13S 68 30W
Rivadavia, *Salta, Argentina* **94 A3** 24 5S 62 54W
Rivadavia, *Chile* **94 B1** 29 57S 70 35W
Rivas, *Nic.* **88 D2** 11 30N 85 50W
Rivera, *Uruguay* **95 C4** 31 0S 55 50W
Riverdale, *U.S.A.* **84 J7** 36 26N 119 52W
Riverhead, *U.S.A.* **79 F12** 40 55N 72 40W
Riverhurst, *Canada* **73 C7** 50 55N 106 50W
Riverina, *Australia* **61 E3** 29 45S 120 40 E
Rivers, *Canada* **73 C8** 50 2N 100 14W
Rivers, L. of the, *Canada* **73 D7** 49 49N 105 44W
Rivers Inlet, *Canada* **72 C3** 51 42N 127 15W
Riversdale, *S. Africa* **56 E3** 34 7S 21 15 E
Riverside, *Calif., U.S.A.* **85 M9** 33 59N 117 22W
Riverside, *Wyo., U.S.A.* **82 F10** 41 13N 106 47W
Riversleigh, *Australia* **62 B2** 19 5S 138 40 E
Riverton, *Australia* **63 E2** 34 10S 138 46 E
Riverton, *Canada* **73 C9** 51 1N 97 0W
Riverton, *N.Z.* **59 M1** 46 21S 168 0 E
Riverton, *U.S.A.* **82 E9** 43 2N 108 23W
Riverton Heights, *U.S.A.* **84 C4** 47 28N 122 17W
Riviera di Levante, *Italy* **20 B3** 44 15N 9 30 E
Riviera di Ponente, *Italy* **20 B3** 44 10N 8 20 E
Rivière-à-Pierre, *Canada* **71 C5** 46 59N 72 11W
Rivière-au-Renard, *Canada* **71 C7** 48 59N 64 23W
Rivière-du-Loup, *Canada* **71 C6** 47 50N 69 30W
Rivière-Pentecôte, *Canada* **71 C6** 49 57N 67 1W
Rivière-Pilote, *Martinique* **89 D7** 14 26N 60 53W
Rivne, *Ukraine* **17 C14** 50 40N 26 10 E
Rívoli, *Italy* **20 B2** 45 3N 7 31 E
Rivoli B., *Australia* **63 F3** 37 32S 140 3 E
Riyadh = Ar Riyāḍ, *Si. Arabia* **46 C4** 24 41N 46 42 E
Rize, *Turkey* **25 F7** 41 0N 40 30 E
Rizhao, *China* **35 G10** 35 25N 119 30 E
Rizokarpaso, *Cyprus* **23 D13** 35 36N 34 23 E
Rizzuto, C., *Italy* **20 E7** 38 53N 17 5 E
Rjukan, *Norway* **9 G13** 59 54N 8 33 E
Road Town, *Virgin Is.* **89 C7** 18 27N 64 37W
Roag, L., *U.K.* **12 C2** 58 12N 6 51W
Roanne, *France* **18 C6** 46 3N 4 4 E
Roanoke, *Ala., U.S.A.* **77 J3** 33 9N 85 22W
Roanoke, *Va., U.S.A.* **76 G6** 37 16N 79 56W
Roanoke →, *U.S.A.* **77 H7** 35 57N 76 42W
Roanoke I., *U.S.A.* **77 H8** 35 55N 75 40W
Roanoke Rapids, *U.S.A.* **77 G7** 36 28N 77 40W
Roatán, *Honduras* **88 C2** 16 18N 86 35W
Robbins I., *Australia* **62 G4** 40 42S 145 0 E
Robe →, *Australia* **60 D2** 21 42S 116 15 E
Robe →, *Ireland* **13 C2** 53 38N 9 10W
Robert Lee, *U.S.A.* **81 K4** 31 54N 100 29W
Roberts, *U.S.A.* **82 E7** 43 43N 112 8W
Robertsganj, *India* **43 G10** 24 44N 83 4 E
Robertson, *S. Africa* **56 E2** 33 46S 19 50 E
Robertson I., *Antarctica* **5 C18** 65 15S 59 30W

Sanderson, U.S.A. 81 K3 30 9N 102 24W
Sandfly L., Canada 73 B7 55 43N 106 6W
Sandgate, Australia 63 D5 27 18S 153 3 E
Sandia, Peru 92 F5 14 10S 69 30W
Sandnes, Norway 9 G11 58 50N 5 45 E
Sandness, U.K. 12 A7 60 18N 1 40W
Sandnessjøen, Norway 8 C15 66 2N 12 38 E
Sandoa, Zaïre 52 F4 9 41S 23 0 E
Sandomierz, Poland 17 C11 50 40N 21 43 E
Sandover →, Australia 62 C2 21 43S 136 32 E
Sandoway, Burma 41 K19 18 20N 94 30 E
Sandoy, Færoe Is. 8 F9 61 52N 6 46W
Sandpoint, U.S.A. 82 B5 48 17N 116 33W
Sandringham, U.K. 10 E8 52 51N 0 31 E
Sandspit, Canada 72 C2 53 14N 131 49W
Sandstone, Australia 61 E2 27 59S 119 16 E
Sandusky, Mich., U.S.A. 78 C2 43 25N 82 50W
Sandusky, Ohio, U.S.A. 78 E2 41 27N 82 42W
Sandviken, Sweden 9 F17 60 38N 16 46 E
Sandwich, C., Australia 62 B4 18 14S 146 18 E
Sandwich B., Canada 71 B8 53 40N 57 15W
Sandwich B., Namibia 56 C1 23 25S 14 20 E
Sandwip Chan., Bangla. 41 H17 22 35N 91 35 E
Sandy, Nev., U.S.A. 85 K11 35 49N 115 36W
Sandy, Oreg., U.S.A. 84 E4 45 24N 122 16W
Sandy, Utah, U.S.A. 82 F8 40 35N 111 50W
Sandy Bight, Australia 61 F3 33 50S 123 20 E
Sandy C., Queens., Australia 62 C5 24 42S 153 15 E
Sandy C., Tas., Australia 62 G3 41 25S 144 45 E
Sandy Cay, Bahamas 89 B4 23 13N 75 18W
Sandy Cr. →, U.S.A. 82 F9 41 51N 109 47W
Sandy L., Canada 70 B1 53 2N 93 0W
Sandy Lake, Canada 70 B1 53 0N 93 15W
Sandy Narrows, Canada 73 B8 55 5N 103 4W
Sanford, Fla., U.S.A. 77 L5 28 48N 81 16W
Sanford, Maine, U.S.A. 79 C14 43 27N 70 47W
Sanford, N.C., U.S.A. 77 H6 35 29N 79 10W
Sanford →, Australia 61 E2 27 22S 115 53 E
Sanford, Mt., U.S.A. 68 B5 62 13N 144 8W
Sang-i-Masha, Afghan. 42 C2 33 8N 67 27 E
Sanga, Mozam. 55 E4 12 22S 35 21 E
Sanga →, Congo 52 E3 1 5S 17 0 E
Sanga-Tolon, Russia 27 C15 61 50N 149 40 E
Sangamner, India 40 K9 19 37N 74 15 E
Sangar, Afghan. 42 C1 32 56N 65 30 E
Sangar, Russia 27 C13 64 2N 127 31 E
Sangar Sarai, Afghan. 42 B4 34 27N 70 35 E
Sangasangadalam, Indonesia 36 E5 0 36S 117 13 E
Sange, Zaïre 54 D2 6 58S 28 21 E
Sangeang, Indonesia 37 F5 8 12S 119 6 E
Sanger, U.S.A. 83 H4 36 42N 119 33W
Sangerhausen, Germany 16 C6 51 28N 11 18 E
Sanggan He →, China 34 E9 38 12N 117 15 E
Sanggau, Indonesia 36 D4 0 5N 110 30 E
Sangihe, Kepulauan, Indonesia 37 D7 3 0N 126 0 E
Sangihe, P., Indonesia 37 D7 3 45N 125 30 E
Sangju, S. Korea 35 F15 36 25N 128 10 E
Sangkapura, Indonesia 36 F4 5 52S 112 40 E
Sangkhla, Thailand 38 E2 14 57N 98 28 E
Sangli, India 40 L9 16 55N 74 33 E
Sangmélina, Cameroon 52 D2 2 57N 12 1 E
Sangre de Cristo Mts., U.S.A. 81 G2 37 0N 105 0W
Sangudo, Canada 72 C6 53 50N 114 54W
Sanje, Uganda 54 C3 0 49S 31 30 E
Sanjo, Japan 30 F9 37 37N 138 57 E
Sankt Gallen, Switz. 16 E5 47 26N 9 22 E
Sankt Moritz, Switz. 16 E5 46 30N 9 50 E
Sankt-Peterburg, Russia 24 C5 59 55N 30 20 E
Sankt Pölten, Austria 16 D8 48 12N 15 38 E
Sankuru →, Zaïre 52 E4 4 17S 20 25 E
Sanliurfa, Turkey 25 G6 37 12N 38 50 E
Sanlúcar de Barrameda, Spain 19 D2 36 46N 6 21W
Sanmenxia, China 34 G6 34 47N 111 12 E
Sanming, China 33 D6 26 15N 117 40 E
Sannaspos, S. Africa 56 D4 29 6S 26 34 E
Sannicandro Gargánico, Italy 20 D6 41 50N 15 34 E
Sannieshof, S. Africa 56 D4 26 30S 25 47 E
Sannin, J., Lebanon 47 B4 33 57N 35 52 E
Sanok, Poland 17 D12 49 35N 22 10 E
Sanquhar, U.K. 12 F5 55 22N 3 54W
Santa Ana, Bolivia 92 F5 13 50S 65 40W
Santa Ana, Ecuador 92 D2 1 16S 80 20W
Santa Ana, El Salv. 88 D2 14 0N 89 31W
Santa Ana, Mexico 86 A2 30 31N 111 8W
Santa Ana, U.S.A. 85 M9 33 46N 117 52W
Santa Barbara, Honduras 88 D2 14 53N 88 14W
Santa Bárbara, Mexico 86 B3 26 48N 105 50W
Santa Barbara, U.S.A. 85 L7 34 25N 119 42W
Santa Barbara Channel, U.S.A. 85 L7 34 15N 120 0W
Santa Barbara I., U.S.A. 85 M7 33 29N 119 2W
Santa Catalina, Mexico 86 B2 25 40N 110 50W
Santa Catalina, Gulf of, U.S.A. 85 N9 33 10N 117 50W
Santa Catalina I., U.S.A. 85 M8 33 23N 118 25W
Santa Catarina □, Brazil 95 B6 27 25S 48 30W
Santa Catarina, I. de, Brazil 95 B6 27 30S 48 40W
Santa Cecília, Brazil 95 B5 26 56S 50 18W
Santa Clara, Cuba 88 B4 22 20N 80 0W
Santa Clara, Calif., U.S.A. 83 H3 37 21N 121 57W
Santa Clara, Utah, U.S.A. 83 H7 37 8N 113 39W
Santa Clara de Olimar, Uruguay 95 C5 32 50S 54 54W
Santa Clotilde, Peru 92 D4 2 33S 73 45W
Santa Coloma de Gramanet, Spain 19 B7 41 27N 2 13 E
Santa Cruz, Argentina 96 G3 50 0S 68 32W
Santa Cruz, Bolivia 92 G6 17 43S 63 10W
Santa Cruz, Chile 94 C1 34 38S 71 27W
Santa Cruz, Costa Rica 88 D2 10 15N 85 35W
Santa Cruz, Madeira 22 D3 32 42N 16 46W
Santa Cruz, Phil. 37 B6 14 20N 121 24 E
Santa Cruz, U.S.A. 83 H2 36 58N 122 1W
Santa Cruz →, Argentina 96 G3 50 10S 68 20W
Santa Cruz de la Palma, Canary Is. 22 F2 28 41N 17 46W
Santa Cruz de Tenerife, Canary Is. 22 F3 28 28N 16 15W
Santa Cruz del Norte, Cuba 88 B3 23 9N 81 55W
Santa Cruz del Sur, Cuba 88 B4 20 44N 78 0W
Santa Cruz do Rio Pardo, Brazil 95 A6 22 54S 49 37W
Santa Cruz do Sul, Brazil 95 B5 29 42S 52 25W
Santa Cruz I., Solomon Is. 64 J8 10 30S 166 0 E
Santa Cruz I., U.S.A. 85 M7 34 1N 119 43W
Santa Domingo, Cay, Bahamas 88 B4 21 25N 75 15W
Santa Elena, Argentina 94 C4 30 58S 59 47W
Santa Elena, Ecuador 92 D2 2 16S 80 52W
Santa Elena, C., Costa Rica 88 D2 10 54N 85 56W
Santa Eugenia, Pta., Mexico 86 B1 27 50N 115 5W
Santa Eulalia, Spain 22 C8 38 59N 1 32 E
Santa Fe, Argentina 94 C3 31 35S 60 41W
Santa Fe, U.S.A. 83 J11 35 41N 105 57W
Santa Fé □, Argentina 94 C3 31 50S 60 55W
Santa Filomena, Brazil 93 E9 9 6S 45 50W
Santa Galdana, Spain 22 B10 39 56N 3 58 E
Santa Gertrudis, Spain 22 B7 39 0N 1 26 E
Santa Inés, Spain 22 B7 39 3N 1 21 E
Santa Inés, I., Chile 96 G2 54 0S 73 0W
Santa Isabel = Rey Malabo, Eq. Guin. 50 H6 3 45N 8 50 E
Santa Isabel, Argentina 94 D2 36 10S 66 54W
Santa Isabel, Brazil 93 F8 11 45S 51 30W
Santa Lucía, Corrientes, Argentina 94 B4 28 58S 59 5W
Santa Lucía, San Juan, Argentina 94 C2 31 30S 68 30W
Santa Lucía, Uruguay 94 C4 34 27S 56 24W
Santa Lucia Range, U.S.A. 83 J3 36 0N 121 20W
Santa Magdalena, I., Mexico 86 C2 24 40N 112 15W
Santa Margarita, Argentina 94 D3 38 28S 61 35W
Santa Margarita, Mexico 86 C2 24 30N 111 50W
Santa Margarita, Spain 22 B10 39 42N 3 6 E
Santa Margarita, U.S.A. 84 K6 35 23N 120 37W
Santa Margarita →, U.S.A. 85 M9 33 13N 117 23W
Santa María, Argentina 94 B2 26 40S 66 0W
Santa Maria, Brazil 95 B5 29 40S 53 48W
Santa María, Spain 22 B9 39 38N 2 47 E
Santa Maria, U.S.A. 85 L6 34 57N 120 26W
Santa María →, Mexico 86 A3 31 0N 107 14W
Santa María, B. de, Mexico 86 B3 25 10N 108 40W
Santa Maria da Vitória, Brazil 93 F10 13 24S 44 12W
Santa Maria di Leuca, C., Italy 21 E8 39 47N 18 22 E
Santa Marta, Colombia 92 A4 11 15N 74 13W
Santa Marta, Sierra Nevada de, Colombia 92 A4 10 55N 73 50W
Santa Marta Grande, C., Brazil 95 B6 28 43S 48 50W
Santa Maura = Levkás, Greece 21 E9 38 40N 20 43 E
Santa Monica, U.S.A. 85 M8 34 1N 118 29W
Santa Ponsa, Spain 22 B9 39 30N 2 28 E
Santa Rita, U.S.A. 83 K10 32 48N 108 4W
Santa Rosa, La Pampa, Argentina 94 D3 36 40S 64 17W
Santa Rosa, San Luis, Argentina 94 C2 32 21S 65 10W
Santa Rosa, Bolivia 92 F5 10 36S 67 20W
Santa Rosa, Brazil 95 B5 27 52S 54 29W
Santa Rosa, Calif., U.S.A. 84 G4 38 26N 122 43W
Santa Rosa, N. Mex., U.S.A. 81 H2 34 57N 104 41W
Santa Rosa de Copán, Honduras 88 D2 14 47N 88 46W
Santa Rosa de Río Primero, Argentina 94 C3 31 8S 63 20W
Santa Rosa I., Calif., U.S.A. 85 M6 33 58N 120 6W
Santa Rosa I., Fla., U.S.A. 77 K2 30 20N 86 50W
Santa Rosa Range, U.S.A. 82 F5 41 45N 117 40W
Santa Rosalía, Mexico 86 B2 27 20N 112 20W
Santa Sylvina, Argentina 94 B3 27 50S 61 10W
Santa Tecla = Nueva San Salvador, El Salv. 88 D2 13 40N 89 18W
Santa Teresa, Argentina 94 C3 33 25S 60 47W
Santa Teresa, Mexico 87 B5 25 17N 97 51W
Santa Vitória do Palmar, Brazil 95 C5 33 32S 53 25W
Santa Ynez →, U.S.A. 85 L6 35 41N 120 36W
Santa Ynez Mts., U.S.A. 85 L6 34 30N 120 0W
Santa Ysabel, U.S.A. 85 M10 33 7N 116 40W
Santai, China 32 C5 31 5N 104 58 E
Santana, Madeira 22 D3 32 48N 16 52W
Santana, Coxilha de, Brazil 95 C4 30 50S 55 35W
Santana do Livramento, Brazil 95 C4 30 55S 55 30W
Santanayi, Spain 22 B10 39 20N 3 5 E
Santander, Spain 19 A4 43 27N 3 51W
Santander Jiménez, Mexico 87 C5 24 11N 98 29W
Sant'Antíoco, Italy 20 E3 39 4N 8 27 E
Santaquin, U.S.A. 82 G8 39 59N 111 47W
Santarém, Brazil 93 D8 2 25S 54 42W
Santarém, Portugal 19 C1 39 12N 8 42W
Santaren Channel, W. Indies 88 B4 24 0N 79 30W
Santee, U.S.A. 85 N10 32 50N 116 58W
Santiago, Brazil 95 B5 29 11S 54 52W
Santiago, Chile 94 C1 33 24S 70 40W
Santiago, Panama 88 E3 8 0N 81 0W
Santiago □, Chile 94 C1 33 30S 70 50W
Santiago →, Mexico 66 G9 25 11N 105 26W
Santiago →, Peru 92 D3 4 27S 77 38W
Santiago de Compostela, Spain 19 A1 42 52N 8 37W
Santiago de Cuba, Cuba 88 C4 20 0N 75 49W
Santiago de los Cabelleros, Dom. Rep. 89 C5 19 30N 70 40W
Santiago del Estero, Argentina 94 B3 27 50S 64 15W
Santiago del Estero □, Argentina 94 B3 27 40S 63 15W
Santiago del Teide, Canary Is. 22 F3 28 17N 16 48W
Santiago Ixcuintla, Mexico 86 C3 21 50N 105 11W
Santiago Papasquiaro, Mexico 86 B3 25 0N 105 20W
Santiaguillo, L. de, Mexico 86 C4 24 50N 104 50W
Santo Amaro, Brazil 93 F11 12 30S 38 43W
Santo Anastácio, Brazil 95 A5 21 58S 51 39W
Santo André, Brazil 95 A6 23 39S 46 29W
Santo Ângelo, Brazil 95 B5 28 15S 54 15W
Santo Antonio, Brazil 93 G7 15 50S 56 0W
Santo Corazón, Bolivia 92 G7 18 0S 58 45W
Santo Domingo, Dom. Rep. 89 C6 18 30N 69 59W
Santo Domingo, Baja Calif., Mexico 86 A1 30 43N 116 2W
Santo Domingo, Baja Calif. S., Mexico 86 B2 25 32N 112 2W
Santo Domingo, Nic. 88 D3 12 14N 84 59W
Santo Tomás, Mexico 86 A1 31 33N 116 24W
Santo Tomás, Peru 92 F4 14 26S 72 8W
Santo Tomé, Argentina 95 B4 28 40S 56 5W
Santo Tomé de Guayana = Ciudad Guayana, Venezuela 92 B6 8 0N 62 30W
Santoña, Spain 19 A4 43 29N 3 27W
Santoríni = Thíra, Greece 21 F11 36 23N 25 27 E
Santos, Brazil 95 A6 24 0S 46 20W
Santos Dumont, Brazil 95 A7 22 55S 43 10W
Sanyuan, China 34 G5 34 35N 108 58 E
Sanza Pombo, Angola 52 F3 7 18S 15 56 E
São Anastácio, Brazil 95 A5 22 0S 51 40W
São Bernardo de Campo, Brazil 95 A6 23 45S 46 34W
São Borja, Brazil 95 B4 28 39S 56 0W
São Carlos, Brazil 95 A6 22 0S 47 50W
São Cristóvão, Brazil 93 F11 11 1S 37 15W
São Domingos, Brazil 93 F9 13 25S 46 19W
São Francisco, Brazil 93 G10 16 0S 44 50W
São Francisco →, Brazil 93 F11 10 30S 36 24W
São Francisco do Sul, Brazil 95 B6 26 15S 48 36W
São Gabriel, Brazil 95 C5 30 20S 54 20W
São Gonçalo, Brazil 95 A7 22 48S 43 5W
Sao Hill, Tanzania 55 D4 8 20S 35 12 E
São João da Boa Vista, Brazil 95 A6 22 0S 46 52W
São João da Madeira, Portugal 19 B1 40 54N 8 30W
São João del Rei, Brazil 95 A7 21 8S 44 15W
São João do Araguaia, Brazil 93 E9 5 23S 48 46W
São João do Piauí, Brazil 93 E10 8 21S 42 15W
São Jorge, Pta. de, Madeira 22 D3 32 50N 16 53W
São José do Rio Prêto, Brazil 95 A6 20 50S 49 20W
São José dos Campos, Brazil 95 A6 23 7S 45 52W
São Leopoldo, Brazil 95 B5 29 50S 51 10W
São Lourenço, Brazil 95 A6 22 7S 45 3W
São Lourenço →, Brazil 93 G7 17 53S 57 27W
São Lourenço, Pta. de, Madeira 22 D3 32 44N 16 39W
São Luís, Brazil 93 D10 2 39S 44 15W
São Luís Gonzaga, Brazil 95 B5 28 25S 55 0W
São Marcos →, Brazil 93 G9 18 15S 47 37W
São Marcos, B. de, Brazil 93 D10 2 0S 44 0W
São Mateus, Brazil 93 G11 18 44S 39 50W
São Paulo, Brazil 95 A6 23 32S 46 37W
São Paulo □, Brazil 95 A6 22 0S 49 0W
São Paulo, I., Atl. Oc. 2 D8 0 50N 31 40W
São Roque, Madeira 22 D3 32 46N 16 48W
São Roque, C. de, Brazil 93 E11 5 30S 35 16W
São Sebastião, I. de, Brazil 95 A6 23 50S 45 18W
São Sebastião do Paraíso, Brazil 95 A6 20 54S 46 59W
São Tomé, Atl. Oc. 48 F4 0 10N 6 39 E
São Tomé, C. de, Brazil 95 A7 22 0S 40 59W
São Tomé & Principe ■, Africa 49 F4 0 12N 6 39 E
São Vicente, Brazil 95 A6 23 57S 46 23W
São Vicente, Madeira 22 D2 32 48N 17 3W
São Vicente, C. de, Portugal 19 D1 37 0N 9 0W
Saona, I., Dom. Rep. 89 C6 18 10N 68 40W
Saône →, France 18 D6 45 44N 4 50 E
Saonek, Indonesia 37 E8 0 22S 130 55 E
Saparua, Indonesia 37 E7 3 33S 128 40 E
Sapele, Nigeria 50 G6 5 50N 5 40 E
Sapelo I., U.S.A. 77 K5 31 25N 81 12W
Saposoa, Peru 92 E3 6 55S 76 45W
Sappho, U.S.A. 84 B2 48 4N 124 16W
Sapporo, Japan 30 C10 43 0N 141 21 E
Sapudi, Indonesia 37 G16 7 6S 114 20 E
Sapulpa, U.S.A. 81 G7 35 59N 96 5W
Saqqez, Iran 44 B5 36 15N 46 20 E
Sar Dasht, Iran 45 C6 32 32N 48 52 E
Sar Gachīneh, Iran 45 D6 30 31N 51 31 E
Sar Planina, Macedonia 21 C9 42 10N 21 0 E
Sara Buri, Thailand 38 E3 14 30N 100 55 E
Sarāb, Iran 44 B5 37 55N 47 40 E
Sarabadi, Iraq 44 C5 33 1N 44 48 E
Sarada →, India 41 F12 27 21N 81 23 E
Saragossa = Zaragoza, Spain 19 B5 41 39N 0 53W
Saraguro, Ecuador 92 D3 3 35S 79 16W
Sarajevo, Bos.-H. 21 C8 43 52N 18 26 E
Saran, G., Indonesia 36 E4 0 30S 111 25 E
Saranac Lake, U.S.A. 79 B10 44 20N 74 8W
Saranda, Tanzania 54 D3 5 45S 34 59 E
Sarandi del Yi, Uruguay 95 C4 33 18S 55 38W
Sarandi Grande, Uruguay 94 C4 33 44S 56 20W
Sarangani B., Phil. 37 C7 6 0N 125 13 E
Sarangani Is., Phil. 37 C7 5 25N 125 25 E
Sarangarh, India 41 J13 21 30N 83 5 E
Saransk, Russia 24 D8 54 10N 45 10 E
Sarapul, Russia 24 C9 56 28N 53 48 E
Sarasota, U.S.A. 77 M4 27 20N 82 32W
Saratoga, Calif., U.S.A. 84 H4 37 16N 122 2W
Saratoga, Wyo., U.S.A. 82 F10 41 27N 106 49W
Saratoga Springs, U.S.A. 79 C11 43 5N 73 47W
Saratov, Russia 24 D8 51 30N 46 2 E
Saravane, Laos 38 E6 15 43N 106 25 E
Sarawak □, Malaysia 36 D4 2 0N 113 0 E
Saray, Turkey 21 D12 41 26N 27 55 E
Sarayköy, Turkey 21 F13 37 55N 28 54 E
Sarbāz, Iran 45 E9 26 38N 61 19 E
Sarbīsheh, Iran 45 C8 32 30N 59 40 E
Sarda → = Sarada →, India 41 F12 27 21N 81 23 E
Sardalas, Libya 50 C7 25 50N 10 34 E
Sardarshahr, India 42 E6 28 30N 74 29 E
Sardegna □, Italy 20 D3 40 0N 9 0 E
Sardhana, India 42 E7 29 9N 77 39 E
Sardina, Pta., Canary Is. 22 F4 28 9N 15 44W
Sardinia = Sardegna □, Italy 20 D3 40 0N 9 0 E
Sardis, Turkey 21 E12 38 28N 28 2 E
Sārdūīyeh = Dar Mazār, Iran 45 D8 29 14N 57 20 E
Sargent, U.S.A. 80 E5 41 39N 99 22W
Sargodha, Pakistan 42 C5 32 10N 72 40 E
Sarh, Chad 51 G8 9 5N 18 23 E
Sārī, Iran 45 B7 36 30N 53 4 E
Sarıgöl, Turkey 21 E13 38 14N 28 41 E
Sarikei, Malaysia 36 D4 2 8N 111 30 E
Sarina, Australia 62 C4 21 22S 149 13 E
Sarita, U.S.A. 81 M6 27 13N 97 47W
Sariwŏn, N. Korea 35 E13 38 31N 125 46 E
Sark, U.K. 11 H5 49 25N 2 22W
Şarköy, Turkey 21 D12 40 36N 27 6 E
Sarlat-la-Canéda, France 18 D4 44 54N 1 13 E
Sarles, U.S.A. 80 A5 48 58N 99 0W
Sarmi, Indonesia 37 E9 1 49S 138 44 E
Sarmiento, Argentina 96 F3 45 35S 69 5W
Särna, Sweden 9 F15 61 41N 13 8 E
Sarnia, Canada 70 D3 42 58N 82 23W
Sarny, Ukraine 24 D4 51 17N 26 40 E
Sarolangun, Indonesia 36 E2 2 19S 102 42 E
Saronikós Kólpos, Greece 21 F10 37 45N 23 45 E
Saros Körfezi, Turkey 21 D12 40 30N 26 15 E
Sarpsborg, Norway 9 G14 59 16N 11 7 E
Sarre = Saar →, Europe 16 D4 49 41N 6 32 E
Sarreguemines, France 18 B7 49 5N 7 4 E
Sarro, Mali 50 F3 13 40N 5 15W
Sarthe →, France 18 C3 47 33N 0 31W
Sartynya, Russia 26 C7 63 22N 63 11 E
Sarvestān, Iran 45 D7 29 20N 53 10 E
Sary-Tash, Kyrgyzstan 26 F8 39 44N 73 15 E
Saryshagan, Kazakstan 26 E8 46 12N 73 38 E
Sasabeneh, Ethiopia 46 F3 7 59N 44 43 E
Sasaram, India 43 G11 24 57N 84 5 E
Sasebo, Japan 31 H4 33 10N 129 43 E
Saser, India 43 B7 34 50N 77 50 E
Saskatchewan □, Canada 73 C7 54 40N 106 0W
Saskatchewan →, Canada 73 C8 53 37N 100 40W
Saskatoon, Canada 73 C7 52 10N 106 38W
Saskylakh, Russia 27 B12 71 55N 114 1 E
Sasolburg, S. Africa 57 D4 26 46S 27 49 E
Sasovo, Russia 24 D7 54 25N 41 55 E
Sassandra, Ivory C. 50 H3 4 55N 6 8W
Sassandra →, Ivory C. 50 H3 4 58N 6 5W
Sássari, Italy 20 D3 40 43N 8 34 E
Sassnitz, Germany 16 A7 54 29N 13 39 E
Sassuolo, Italy 20 B4 44 33N 10 47 E
Sasumua Dam, Kenya 54 C4 0 45S 36 40 E
Sasyk, Ozero, Ukraine 17 F15 45 45N 29 20 E
Sata-Misaki, Japan 31 J5 31 0N 130 40 E
Satadougou, Mali 50 F2 12 25N 11 25W
Satakunta, Finland 9 F20 61 45N 23 0 E
Satanta, U.S.A. 81 G4 37 26N 100 59W
Satara, India 40 L8 17 44N 73 58 E
Satilla →, U.S.A. 77 K5 30 59N 81 29W
Satka, Russia 24 C10 55 3N 59 1 E
Satmala Hills, India 40 J9 20 15N 74 40 E
Satna, India 43 G9 24 35N 80 50 E
Sátoraljaújhely, Hungary 17 D11 48 25N 21 41 E
Satpura Ra., India 42 J7 21 25N 76 10 E
Satsuna-Shotō, Japan 31 K5 30 0N 130 0 E
Sattahip, Thailand 38 F3 12 41N 100 54 E
Satu Mare, Romania 17 E12 47 46N 22 55 E
Satui, Indonesia 36 E5 3 50S 115 27 E
Satun, Thailand 39 J3 6 43N 100 2 E
Saturnina →, Brazil 92 F7 12 15S 58 10W
Sauce, Argentina 94 C4 30 5S 58 46W
Sauceda, Mexico 86 B4 25 55N 101 18W
Saucillo, Mexico 86 B3 28 1N 105 17W
Sauda, Norway 9 G12 59 40N 6 20 E
Sauðarkrókur, Iceland 8 D4 65 45N 19 40W
Saudi Arabia ■, Asia 46 B3 26 0N 44 0 E
Sauer →, Germany 15 E6 49 44N 6 31 E
Sauerland, Germany 16 C4 51 12N 7 59 E
Saugeen →, Canada 78 B3 44 30N 81 22W
Saugerties, U.S.A. 79 D11 42 5N 73 57W
Sauk Centre, U.S.A. 80 C7 45 44N 94 57W
Sauk Rapids, U.S.A. 80 C7 45 35N 94 10W
Sault Ste. Marie, Canada 70 C3 46 30N 84 20W
Sault Ste. Marie, U.S.A. 76 B3 46 30N 84 21W
Saumlaki, Indonesia 37 F8 7 55S 131 20 E
Saumur, France 18 C3 47 15N 0 5W
Saunders C., N.Z. 59 L3 45 53S 170 45 E
Saunders I., Antarctica 5 B1 57 48S 26 28W
Saunders Point, Australia 61 E4 27 52S 125 38 E
Sauri, Nigeria 50 F6 11 42N 6 44 E
Saurimo, Angola 52 F4 9 40S 20 12 E
Sausalito, U.S.A. 84 H4 37 51N 122 29W
Savá, Honduras 88 C2 15 32N 86 15W
Sava →, Serbia, Yug. 21 B9 44 50N 20 26 E
Savage, U.S.A. 80 B2 47 27N 104 21W
Savage I. = Niue, Cook Is. 65 J11 19 2S 169 54W
Savai'i, W. Samoa 59 A12 13 28S 172 24W
Savalou, Benin 50 G5 7 57N 1 58 E
Savane, Mozam. 55 F4 19 37S 35 8 E
Savanna, U.S.A. 80 D9 42 5N 90 8W
Savanna la Mar, Jamaica 88 C4 18 10N 78 10W
Savannah, Ga., U.S.A. 77 J5 32 5N 81 6W
Savannah, Mo., U.S.A. 80 F7 39 56N 94 50W
Savannah, Tenn., U.S.A. 77 H1 35 14N 88 15W
Savannah →, U.S.A. 77 J5 32 2N 80 53W
Savannakhet, Laos 38 D5 16 30N 104 49 E
Savant L., Canada 70 B1 50 16N 90 44W
Savant Lake, Canada 70 B1 50 14N 90 40W

Shāndak

Shāndak, Iran 45 D9 28 28N 60 27 E
Shandon, U.S.A. 84 K6 35 39N 120 23W
Shandong □, China 35 F10 36 0N 118 0 E
Shandong Bandao, China 35 F11 37 0N 121 0 E
Shang Xian, China 34 H5 33 50N 109 58 E
Shangalowe, Zaïre 55 E2 10 50S 26 30 E
Shangani →, Zimbabwe 55 F2 18 41S 27 10 E
Shangbancheng, China 35 D10 40 50N 118 1 E
Shangdu, China 34 D7 41 30N 113 30 E
Shanghai, China 33 C7 31 15N 121 26 E
Shanghe, China 35 F9 37 20N 117 10 E
Shangnan, China 34 H6 33 32N 110 50 E
Shangqiu, China 34 G8 34 26N 115 36 E
Shangrao, China 33 D6 28 25N 117 59 E
Shangshui, China 34 H8 33 42N 114 35 E
Shangzhi, China 35 B14 45 22N 127 56 E
Shanhetun, China 35 B14 44 33N 127 15 E
Shaniko, U.S.A. 82 D3 45 0N 120 45W
Shannon, N.Z. 59 J5 40 33S 175 25 E
Shannon →, Ireland 13 D2 52 35N 9 30W
Shansi = Shanxi □, China 34 F7 37 0N 112 0 E
Shantar, Ostrov Bolshoy, Russia 27 D14 55 9N 137 40 E
Shantipur, India 43 H13 23 17N 88 25 E
Shantou, China 33 D6 23 18N 116 40 E
Shantung = Shandong □, China 35 F10 36 0N 118 0 E
Shanxi □, China 34 F7 37 0N 112 0 E
Shanyang, China 34 H5 33 31N 109 55 E
Shanyin, China 34 E7 39 25N 112 56 E
Shaoguan, China 33 D6 24 48N 113 35 E
Shaoxing, China 33 C7 30 0N 120 35 E
Shaoyang, China 33 D6 27 14N 111 25 E
Shapinsay, U.K. 12 B6 59 3N 2 51W
Shaqra', Si. Arabia 44 E5 25 15N 45 16 E
Shaqrā', Yemen 46 E4 13 22N 45 44 E
Sharbot Lake, Canada 79 B8 44 46N 76 41W
Shari, Japan 30 C12 43 55N 144 40 E
Sharjah = Ash Shāriqah, U.A.E. 45 E7 25 23N 55 26 E
Shark B., Australia 61 E1 25 30S 113 32 E
Sharon, Mass., U.S.A. 79 D13 42 7N 71 11W
Sharon, Pa., U.S.A. 78 E4 41 14N 80 31W
Sharon Springs, U.S.A. 80 F4 38 54N 101 45W
Sharp Pt., Australia 62 A3 10 58S 142 43 E
Sharpe L., Canada 73 C10 54 24N 93 40W
Sharpsville, U.S.A. 78 E4 41 15N 80 29W
Sharya, Russia 24 C8 58 22N 45 20 E
Shashi, Botswana 57 C4 21 15S 27 27 E
Shashi, China 33 C6 30 25N 112 14 E
Shashi →, Africa 55 G2 21 14S 29 20 E
Shasta, Mt., U.S.A. 82 F2 41 25N 122 12W
Shasta L., U.S.A. 82 F2 40 43N 122 25W
Shatt al'Arab →, Iraq 45 D6 29 57N 48 34 E
Shattuck, U.S.A. 81 G5 36 16N 99 53W
Shaunavon, Canada 73 D7 49 35N 108 25W
Shaver L., U.S.A. 84 H7 37 9N 119 18W
Shaw →, Australia 60 D2 20 21S 119 17 E
Shaw I., Australia 62 C4 20 30S 149 2 E
Shawanaga, Canada 78 A4 45 31N 80 17W
Shawano, U.S.A. 76 C1 44 47N 88 36W
Shawinigan, Canada 70 C5 46 35N 72 50W
Shawnee, U.S.A. 81 H6 35 20N 96 55W
Shaybārā, Si. Arabia 44 E3 25 26N 36 47 E
Shaykh Sa'īd, Iraq 44 C5 32 34N 46 17 E
Shcherbakov = Rybinsk, Russia 24 C6 58 5N 38 50 E
Shchuchinsk, Kazakstan 26 D8 52 56N 70 12 E
She Xian, China 34 F7 36 30N 113 40 E
Shebele = Scebeli, Wabi →, Somali Rep. 46 G3 2 0N 44 0 E
Sheboygan, U.S.A. 76 D2 43 46N 87 45W
Shediac, Canada 71 C7 46 14N 64 32W
Sheelin, L., Ireland 13 C4 53 48N 7 20W
Sheep Haven, Ireland 13 A4 55 11N 7 52W
Sheerness, U.K. 11 F8 51 26N 0 47 E
Sheet Harbour, Canada 71 D7 44 56N 62 31W
Sheffield, U.K. 10 D6 53 23N 1 28W
Sheffield, Ala., U.S.A. 77 H2 34 46N 87 41W
Sheffield, Mass., U.S.A. 79 D11 42 5N 73 21W
Sheffield, Pa., U.S.A. 78 E5 41 42N 79 3W
Sheffield, Tex., U.S.A. 81 K4 30 41N 101 49W
Sheho, Canada 73 C8 51 35N 103 13W
Sheikhpura, India 43 G11 25 9N 85 53 E
Shekhupura, Pakistan 42 D5 31 42N 73 58 E
Shelburne, N.S., Canada 71 D6 43 47N 65 20W
Shelburne, Ont., Canada 70 D3 44 4N 80 15W
Shelburne, U.S.A. 79 B11 44 23N 73 14W
Shelburne B., Australia 62 A3 11 50S 142 50 E
Shelburne Falls, U.S.A. 79 D12 42 36N 72 45W
Shelby, Mich., U.S.A. 76 D2 43 37N 86 22W
Shelby, Mont., U.S.A. 82 B8 48 30N 111 51W
Shelby, N.C., U.S.A. 77 H5 35 17N 81 32W
Shelby, Ohio, U.S.A. 78 F2 40 53N 82 40W
Shelbyville, Ill., U.S.A. 80 F10 39 24N 88 48W
Shelbyville, Ind., U.S.A. 76 F3 39 31N 85 47W
Shelbyville, Tenn., U.S.A. 77 H2 35 29N 86 28W
Sheldon, U.S.A. 80 D7 43 11N 95 51W
Sheldrake, Canada 71 B7 50 20N 64 51W
Shelikhova, Zaliv, Russia 27 D16 59 30N 157 0 E
Shell Lake, Canada 73 C7 53 19N 107 2W
Shell Lakes, Australia 61 E4 29 20S 127 30 E
Shellbrook, Canada 73 C7 53 13N 106 24W
Shellharbour, Australia 63 E5 34 31S 150 51 E
Shelling Rocks, Ireland 13 E1 51 45N 10 35W
Shelton, Conn., U.S.A. 79 E11 41 19N 73 5W
Shelton, Wash., U.S.A. 84 C3 47 13N 123 6W
Shen Xian, China 34 F8 36 15N 115 40 E
Shenandoah, Iowa, U.S.A. 80 E7 40 46N 95 22W
Shenandoah, Pa., U.S.A. 79 F8 40 49N 76 12W
Shenandoah, Va., U.S.A. 76 F6 38 29N 78 37W
Shenandoah →, U.S.A. 76 F7 39 19N 77 44W
Shenchi, China 34 E7 39 8N 112 10 E
Shendam, Nigeria 50 G6 8 49N 9 30 E
Shendī, Sudan 51 E11 16 46N 33 22 E
Shengfang, China 34 E9 39 3N 116 42 E
Shenjingzi, China 35 B13 44 40N 124 30 E
Shenmu, China 34 E6 38 50N 110 29 E
Shenqiu, China 34 H8 33 25N 115 5 E
Shenqiucheng, China 34 H8 33 24N 115 2 E
Shensi = Shaanxi □, China 34 G5 35 0N 109 0 E
Shenyang, China 35 D12 41 48N 123 27 E
Sheopur Kalan, India 40 G10 25 40N 76 40 E
Shepetivka, Ukraine 17 C14 50 10N 27 10 E
Shepetovka = Shepetivka, Ukraine 17 C14 50 10N 27 10 E
Shepparton, Australia 63 F4 36 23S 145 26 E
Sheqi, China 34 H7 33 12N 112 57 E
Sher Qila, Pakistan 43 A6 36 7N 74 2 E
Sherborne, U.K. 11 G5 50 57N 2 31W
Sherbro I., S. Leone 50 G2 7 30N 12 40W
Sherbrooke, Canada 71 C5 45 28N 71 57W
Sheridan, Ark., U.S.A. 81 H8 34 19N 92 24W
Sheridan, Wyo., U.S.A. 82 D10 44 48N 106 58W
Sherkot, India 43 E8 29 22N 78 35 E
Sherman, U.S.A. 81 J6 33 40N 96 35W
Sherridon, Canada 73 B8 55 8N 101 5W
Sherwood, N. Dak., U.S.A. 80 A4 48 57N 101 38W
Sherwood, Tex., U.S.A. 81 K4 31 18N 100 45W
Sherwood Forest, U.K. 10 D6 53 6N 1 7W
Sheslay, Canada 72 B2 58 17N 131 52W
Sheslay →, Canada 72 B2 58 48N 132 5W
Shethanei L., Canada 73 B9 58 48N 97 50W
Shetland □, U.K. 12 A7 60 30N 1 30W
Shetland Is., U.K. 12 A7 60 30N 1 30W
Sheyenne, U.S.A. 80 B5 47 50N 99 7W
Sheyenne →, U.S.A. 80 B6 47 2N 96 50W
Shibām, Yemen 46 D4 16 0N 48 36 E
Shibata, Japan 30 F9 37 57N 139 20 E
Shibecha, Japan 30 C12 43 17N 144 36 E
Shibetsu, Japan 30 B11 44 10N 142 23 E
Shibogama L., Canada 70 B2 53 35N 88 15W
Shibushi, Japan 31 J5 31 25N 131 8 E
Shickshock Mts. = Chic-Chocs, Mts., Canada 71 C6 48 55N 66 0W
Shidao, China 35 F12 36 50N 122 25 E
Shido, Japan 31 G7 34 19N 134 10 E
Shiel, L., U.K. 12 E3 56 48N 5 34W
Shield, C., Australia 62 A2 13 20S 136 20 E
Shiga □, Japan 31 G8 35 20N 136 0 E
Shigaib, Sudan 51 E9 15 5N 23 35 E
Shiguaigou, China 34 D6 40 52N 110 15 E
Shihchiachuangi = Shijiazhuang, China 34 E8 38 2N 114 28 E
Shijiazhuang, China 34 E8 38 2N 114 28 E
Shikarpur, India 42 E8 28 17N 78 7 E
Shikarpur, Pakistan 42 F3 27 57N 68 39 E
Shikoku □, Japan 31 H6 33 30N 133 30 E
Shikoku-Sanchi, Japan 31 H6 33 30N 133 30 E
Shilabo, Ethiopia 46 F3 6 22N 44 32 E
Shiliguri, India 41 F16 26 45N 88 25 E
Shilka, Russia 27 D12 52 0N 115 55 E
Shilka →, Russia 27 D13 53 20N 121 26 E
Shillelagh, Ireland 13 D5 52 45N 6 32W
Shillong, India 41 G17 25 35N 91 53 E
Shilo, West Bank 47 C4 32 4N 35 18 E
Shilou, China 34 F6 37 0N 110 48 E
Shimabara, Japan 31 H5 32 48N 130 20 E
Shimada, Japan 31 G9 34 49N 138 10 E
Shimane □, Japan 31 G6 35 0N 132 30 E
Shimanovsk, Russia 27 D13 52 15N 127 30 E
Shimizu, Japan 31 G9 35 0N 138 30 E
Shimodate, Japan 31 F9 36 20N 139 55 E
Shimoga, India 40 N9 13 57N 75 32 E
Shimoni, Kenya 54 C4 4 38S 39 20 E
Shimonoseki, Japan 31 H5 33 58N 130 55 E
Shimpuru Rapids, Angola 56 B2 17 45S 19 55 E
Shin, L., U.K. 12 C4 58 5N 4 30W
Shin-Tone →, Japan 31 G10 35 44N 140 51 E
Shinano →, Japan 31 F9 36 50N 138 30 E
Shīndand, Afghan. 40 C3 33 12N 62 8 E
Shingleton, U.S.A. 70 C2 46 21N 86 28W
Shingū, Japan 31 H7 33 40N 135 55 E
Shinjō, Japan 30 E10 38 46N 140 18 E
Shinshār, Syria 47 A5 34 36N 36 43 E
Shinyanga, Tanzania 54 C3 3 45S 33 27 E
Shinyanga □, Tanzania 54 C3 3 50S 34 0 E
Shiogama, Japan 30 E10 38 19N 141 1 E
Shiojiri, Japan 31 F8 36 6N 137 58 E
Ship I., U.S.A. 81 K10 30 13N 88 55W
Shipehenski Prokhod, Bulgaria 21 C11 42 45N 25 15 E
Shiping, China 32 D5 23 45N 102 23 E
Shipki La, India 40 D11 31 45N 78 40 E
Shippegan, Canada 71 C7 47 45N 64 45W
Shippensburg, U.S.A. 78 F7 40 3N 77 31W
Shiprock, U.S.A. 83 H9 36 47N 108 41W
Shiqma, N. →, Israel 47 D3 31 37N 34 30 E
Shiquan, China 34 H5 33 5N 108 15 E
Shīr Kūh, Iran 45 D7 31 39N 54 3 E
Shiragami-Misaki, Japan 30 D10 41 24N 140 12 E
Shirakawa, Fukushima, Japan 31 F10 37 7N 140 13 E
Shirakawa, Gifu, Japan 31 F8 36 17N 136 56 E
Shirane-San, Gumma, Japan 31 F9 36 48N 139 22 E
Shirane-San, Yamanashi, Japan 31 G9 35 42N 138 9 E
Shiraoi, Japan 30 C10 42 33N 141 21 E
Shīrāz, Iran 45 D7 29 42N 52 30 E
Shire →, Africa 55 F4 17 42S 35 19 E
Shiretoko-Misaki, Japan 30 B12 44 21N 145 20 E
Shirinab →, Pakistan 42 D2 30 15N 66 28 E
Shiriya-Zaki, Japan 30 D10 41 25N 141 30 E
Shiroishi, Japan 30 E10 38 0N 140 37 E
Shīrvān, Iran 45 B8 37 30N 57 50 E
Shirwa, L. = Chilwa, L., Malawi 55 F4 15 15S 35 40 E
Shivpuri, India 42 G7 25 26N 77 42 E
Shixian, China 35 C15 43 5N 129 50 E
Shizuishan, China 34 E4 39 15N 106 50 E
Shizuoka, Japan 31 G9 34 57N 138 24 E
Shizuoka □, Japan 31 G9 35 15N 138 40 E
Shklov = Shklow, Belarus 17 A16 54 16N 30 15 E
Shklow, Belarus 17 A16 54 16N 30 15 E
Shkoder = Shkodra, Albania 21 C8 42 4N 19 32 E
Shkodra, Albania 21 C8 42 4N 19 32 E
Shkumbini →, Albania 21 D8 41 2N 19 31 E
Shmidta, O., Russia 27 A10 81 0N 91 0 E
Shō-Gawa →, Japan 31 F8 36 47N 137 4 E
Shoal Lake, Canada 73 C8 50 30N 100 35W
Shōdo-Shima, Japan 31 G7 34 30N 134 15 E
Shoeburyness, U.K. 11 F8 51 32N 0 49 E
Sholapur = Solapur, India 40 L9 17 43N 75 56 E
Shologontsy, Russia 27 C12 66 13N 114 0 E
Shōmrōn, West Bank 47 C4 32 15N 35 13 E
Shoshone, Calif., U.S.A. 85 K10 35 58N 116 16W
Shoshone, Idaho, U.S.A. 82 E6 42 56N 114 25W
Shoshone L., U.S.A. 82 D8 44 22N 110 43W
Shoshone Mts., U.S.A. 82 G5 39 20N 117 25W
Shoshong, Botswana 56 C4 22 56S 26 31 E
Shoshoni, U.S.A. 82 E9 43 14N 108 7W
Shouguang, China 35 F10 37 52N 118 45 E
Shouyang, China 34 F7 37 54N 113 8 E
Show Low, U.S.A. 83 J9 34 15N 110 2W
Shreveport, U.S.A. 81 J8 32 31N 93 45W
Shrewsbury, U.K. 10 E5 52 43N 2 45W
Shrirampur, India 43 H13 22 44N 88 21 E
Shropshire □, U.K. 11 E5 52 36N 2 45W
Shu, Kazakstan 26 E8 43 36N 73 42 E
Shu →, Kazakstan 28 E10 45 0N 67 44 E
Shuangcheng, China 35 B14 45 20N 126 15 E
Shuanggou, China 35 G9 34 2N 117 30 E
Shuangliao, China 35 C12 43 29N 123 30 E
Shuangshanzi, China 35 D10 40 20N 119 8 E
Shuangyang, China 35 C13 43 28N 125 40 E
Shuangyashan, China 33 B8 46 28N 131 5 E
Shuguri Falls, Tanzania 55 D4 8 33S 37 22 E
Shuiye, China 34 F8 36 7N 114 8 E
Shujalpur, India 42 H7 23 18N 76 46 E
Shukpa Kunzang, India 43 B8 34 22N 78 22 E
Shulan, China 35 B14 44 28N 127 0 E
Shule, China 32 C2 39 25N 76 3 E
Shumagin Is., U.S.A. 68 C4 55 7N 159 45W
Shumikha, Russia 26 D7 55 10N 63 15 E
Shungnak, U.S.A. 68 B4 66 52N 157 9W
Shuo Xian, China 34 E7 39 20N 112 33 E
Shūr →, Iran 45 D7 28 30N 55 0 E
Shūr Āb, Iran 45 C6 34 23N 51 11 E
Shūr Gaz, Iran 45 D8 29 10N 59 20 E
Shūrāb, Iran 45 C8 33 43N 56 29 E
Shūrjestān, Iran 45 D7 31 24N 52 25 E
Shurugwi, Zimbabwe 55 F3 19 40S 30 0 E
Shūsf, Iran 45 D9 31 50N 60 5 E
Shūshtar, Iran 45 D6 32 0N 48 50 E
Shuswap L., Canada 72 C5 50 55N 119 3W
Shuyang, China 35 G10 34 10N 118 42 E
Shūzū, Iran 45 D7 29 52N 54 30 E
Shwebo, Burma 41 H19 22 30N 95 45 E
Shwegu, Burma 41 G20 24 15N 96 26 E
Shweli →, Burma 41 H20 23 45N 96 45 E
Shymkent, Kazakstan 26 E7 42 18N 69 36 E
Shyok, India 43 B8 34 15N 78 12 E
Shyok →, Pakistan 43 B6 35 13N 75 53 E
Si Chon, Thailand 39 H2 9 0N 99 54 E
Si Kiang = Xi Jiang →, China 33 D6 22 5N 113 20 E
Si-ngan = Xi'an, China 34 G5 34 15N 109 0 E
Si Prachan, Thailand 38 E3 14 37N 100 9 E
Si Racha, Thailand 38 F3 13 10N 100 48 E
Si Xian, China 35 H9 33 30N 117 50 E
Siahan Range, Pakistan 40 F4 27 30N 64 40 E
Siaksriindrapura, Indonesia 36 D2 0 51N 102 0 E
Sialkot, Pakistan 42 C6 32 32N 74 30 E
Siam = Thailand ■, Asia 38 E4 16 0N 102 0 E
Siantan, P., Indonesia 39 L6 3 10N 106 15 E
Siāreh, Iran 45 D9 28 5N 60 14 E
Siargao, Phil. 37 C7 9 52N 126 3 E
Siari, Pakistan 43 B7 34 55N 76 40 E
Siasi, Phil. 37 C6 5 34N 120 50 E
Siau, Indonesia 37 D7 2 50N 125 25 E
Šiauliai, Lithuania 9 J20 55 56N 23 15 E
Siaya □, Kenya 54 B3 0 0 34 20 E
Sibay, Russia 24 D10 52 42N 58 39 E
Sibayi, L., S. Africa 57 D5 27 20S 32 45 E
Šibenik, Croatia 20 C6 43 48N 15 54 E
Siberia, Russia 4 D13 60 0N 100 0 E
Siberut, Indonesia 36 E1 1 30S 99 0 E
Sibi, Pakistan 42 E2 29 30N 67 54 E
Sibil, Indonesia 37 E10 4 59S 140 35 E
Sibiti, Congo 52 E2 3 38S 13 19 E
Sibiu, Romania 17 F13 45 45N 24 9 E
Sibley, Iowa, U.S.A. 80 D7 43 24N 95 45W
Sibley, La., U.S.A. 81 J8 32 33N 93 18W
Sibolga, Indonesia 36 D1 1 42N 98 45 E
Sibsagar, India 41 F19 27 0N 94 36 E
Sibu, Malaysia 36 D4 2 18N 111 49 E
Sibuco, Phil. 37 C6 7 20N 122 10 E
Sibuguey B., Phil. 37 C6 7 50N 122 45 E
Sibut, C.A.R. 51 G8 5 46N 19 10 E
Sibutu, Phil. 37 D5 4 45N 119 30 E
Sibutu Passage, E. Indies 37 D5 4 50N 120 0 E
Sibuyan, Phil. 37 B6 12 25N 122 40 E
Sibuyan Sea, Phil. 37 B6 12 30N 122 20 E
Sicamous, Canada 72 C5 50 49N 119 0W
Sichuan □, China 32 C5 31 0N 104 0 E
Sicilia, Italy 20 F6 37 30N 14 30 E
Sicily = Sicilia, Italy 20 F6 37 30N 14 30 E
Sicuani, Peru 92 F4 14 21S 71 10W
Sidári, Greece 23 A3 39 47N 19 41 E
Siddhapur, India 42 H5 23 56N 72 25 E
Siddipet, India 40 K11 18 5N 78 51 E
Sidéradougou, Burkina Faso 50 F4 10 42N 4 12W
Sídheros, Ákra, Greece 23 D8 35 19N 26 19 E
Sîdi Barrâni, Egypt 51 B10 31 38N 25 58 E
Sidi-bel-Abbès, Algeria 50 A4 35 13N 0 39W
Sidlaw Hills, U.K. 12 E5 56 32N 3 2W
Sidley, Mt., Antarctica 5 D14 77 2S 126 2W
Sidmouth, U.K. 11 G4 50 40N 3 15W
Sidmouth, C., Australia 62 A3 13 25S 143 36 E
Sidney, Canada 72 D4 48 39N 123 24W
Sidney, Mont., U.S.A. 80 B2 47 43N 104 9W
Sidney, N.Y., U.S.A. 79 D9 42 19N 75 24W
Sidney, Nebr., U.S.A. 80 E3 41 8N 102 59W
Sidney, Ohio, U.S.A. 76 E3 40 17N 84 9W
Sidoarjo, Indonesia 37 G15 7 27S 112 43 E
Sidon = Saydā, Lebanon 47 B4 33 35N 35 25 E
Sidra, G. of = Surt, Khalīj, Libya 51 B8 31 40N 18 30 E
Sidra, G. of, Libya 48 C5 31 40N 18 30 E
Siedlce, Poland 17 B12 52 10N 22 20 E
Sieg →, Germany 16 C4 50 46N 7 6 E
Siegen, Germany 16 C5 50 51N 8 0 E
Siem Pang, Cambodia 38 E6 14 7N 106 23 E
Siem Reap, Cambodia 38 F4 13 20N 103 52 E
Siena, Italy 20 C4 43 19N 11 21 E
Sieradz, Poland 17 C10 51 37N 18 41 E
Sierra Blanca, U.S.A. 83 L11 31 11N 105 22W
Sierra Blanca Peak, U.S.A. 83 K11 33 23N 105 49W
Sierra City, U.S.A. 84 F6 39 34N 120 38W
Sierra Colorada, Argentina 96 E3 40 35S 67 50W
Sierra Gorda, Chile 94 A2 22 50S 69 15W
Sierra Leone ■, W. Afr. 50 G2 9 0N 12 0W
Sierra Madre, Mexico 87 D6 16 0N 93 0W
Sierra Mojada, Mexico 86 B4 27 19N 103 42W
Sierraville, U.S.A. 84 F6 39 36N 120 22W
Sífnos, Greece 21 F11 37 0N 24 45 E
Sifton, Canada 73 C8 51 21N 100 8W
Sifton Pass, Canada 72 B3 57 52N 126 15W
Sighetu-Marmatiei, Romania 17 E12 47 57N 23 52 E
Sighişoara, Romania 17 E13 46 12N 24 50 E
Sigli, Indonesia 36 C1 5 25N 96 0 E
Siglufjörður, Iceland 8 C4 66 12N 18 55W
Signal, U.S.A. 85 L13 34 30N 113 38W
Signal Pk., U.S.A. 85 M12 33 20N 114 2W
Sigsig, Ecuador 92 D3 3 0S 78 50W
Sigtuna, Sweden 9 G17 59 36N 17 44 E
Sigüenza, Spain 19 B4 41 3N 2 40W
Siguiri, Guinea 50 F3 11 31N 9 10W
Sigulda, Latvia 9 H21 57 10N 24 55 E
Sigurd, U.S.A. 83 G8 38 50N 111 58W
Sihanoukville = Kompong Som, Cambodia 39 G4 10 38N 103 30 E
Siikajoki →, Finland 8 D21 64 50N 24 43 E
Siilinjärvi, Finland 8 E22 63 4N 27 39 E
Sijarira Ra., Zimbabwe 55 F2 17 36S 27 45 E
Sikao, Thailand 39 J2 7 34N 99 21 E
Sikar, India 42 F6 27 33N 75 10 E
Sikasso, Mali 50 F3 11 18N 5 35W
Sikeston, U.S.A. 81 G10 36 53N 89 35W
Sikhote Alin, Khrebet, Russia 27 E14 45 0N 136 0 E
Sikhote Alin Ra. = Sikhote Alin, Khrebet, Russia 27 E14 45 0N 136 0 E
Síkinos, Greece 21 F11 36 40N 25 8 E
Sikkani Chief →, Canada 72 B4 57 47N 122 15W
Sikkim □, India 41 F16 27 50N 88 30 E
Sikotu-Ko, Japan 30 C10 42 45N 141 25 E
Sil →, Spain 19 A2 42 27N 7 43W
Silacayoapan, Mexico 87 D5 17 30N 98 9W
Silchar, India 41 G18 24 49N 92 48 E
Silcox, Canada 73 B10 57 12N 94 10W
Siler City, U.S.A. 77 H6 35 44N 79 28W
Silesia = Śląsk, Poland 16 C9 51 0N 16 30 E
Silgarhi Doti, Nepal 43 E9 29 15N 81 0 E
Silghat, India 41 F18 26 35N 93 0 E
Silifke, Turkey 25 G5 36 22N 33 58 E
Siliguri = Shiliguri, India 41 F16 26 45N 88 25 E
Siling Co, China 32 C3 31 50N 89 20 E
Silistra, Bulgaria 21 B12 44 6N 27 19 E
Silivri, Turkey 21 D13 41 4N 28 14 E
Siljan, Sweden 9 F16 60 55N 14 45 E
Silkeborg, Denmark 9 H13 56 10N 9 32 E
Sillajhuay, Cordillera, Chile 92 G5 19 46S 68 40W
Sillamäe, Estonia 9 G22 59 24N 27 45 E
Siloam Springs, U.S.A. 81 G7 36 11N 94 32W
Silsbee, U.S.A. 81 K7 30 21N 94 11W
Šilute, Lithuania 9 J19 55 21N 21 33 E
Silva Porto = Kuito, Angola 53 G3 12 22S 16 55 E
Silver City, N. Mex., U.S.A. 83 K9 32 46N 108 17W
Silver City, Nev., U.S.A. 82 G4 39 15N 119 48W
Silver Cr. →, U.S.A. 82 E4 43 16N 119 13W
Silver Creek, U.S.A. 78 D5 42 33N 79 10W
Silver L., Calif., U.S.A. 84 G6 38 39N 120 6W
Silver L., Calif., U.S.A. 85 K10 35 21N 116 7W
Silver Lake, U.S.A. 82 E3 43 8N 121 3W
Silver Streams, S. Africa 56 D3 28 20S 23 33 E
Silverton, Colo., U.S.A. 83 H10 37 49N 107 40W
Silverton, Tex., U.S.A. 81 H4 34 28N 101 19W
Silvies →, U.S.A. 82 E4 43 34N 119 2W
Simanggang, Malaysia 36 D4 1 15N 111 32 E
Simard, L., Canada 70 C4 47 40N 78 40W
Simav, Turkey 21 E13 39 4N 28 58 E
Simba, Tanzania 54 C4 2 10S 37 36 E
Simbirsk, Russia 24 D8 54 20N 48 25 E
Simbo, Tanzania 54 C2 4 51S 29 41 E
Simcoe, Canada 70 D3 42 50N 80 20W
Simcoe, L., Canada 70 D4 44 25N 79 20W
Simenga, Russia 27 C11 62 42N 108 25 E
Simeria, Romania 17 F12 45 51N 23 1 E
Simeulue, Indonesia 36 D1 2 45N 95 45 E
Simferopol, Ukraine 25 F5 44 55N 34 3 E
Sími, Greece 21 F12 36 35N 27 50 E
Simi Valley, U.S.A. 85 L8 34 16N 118 47W
Simikot, Nepal 43 E9 30 0N 81 50 E
Simla, India 42 D7 31 2N 77 9 E
Simmie, Canada 73 D7 49 56N 108 6W
Simmler, U.S.A. 85 K7 35 21N 119 59W
Simojoki →, Finland 8 D21 65 35N 25 1 E
Simojovel, Mexico 87 D6 17 12N 92 38W
Simonette →, Canada 72 B5 55 9N 118 15W
Simonstown, S. Africa 56 E2 34 14S 18 26 E
Simplon P., Switz. 16 E5 46 15N 8 3 E
Simpson Desert, Australia 62 D2 25 0S 137 0 E
Simpungdong, N. Korea 35 D15 40 56N 129 29 E
Simrishamn, Sweden 9 J16 55 33N 14 22 E
Simunjan, Malaysia 36 D4 1 25N 110 45 E
Simushir, Ostrov, Russia 27 E16 46 50N 152 30 E
Sinabang, Indonesia 36 D1 2 30N 96 24 E
Sinadogo, Somali Rep. 46 F4 5 50N 47 0 E
Sinai = Es Sînâ', Egypt 51 C11 29 0N 34 0 E
Sinai, Mt. = Mûsa, G., Egypt 51 C11 28 33N 33 59 E
Sinai Peninsula, Egypt 47 F2 29 30N 34 0 E
Sinaloa □, Mexico 86 C3 25 0N 107 30W
Sinaloa de Levya, Mexico 86 B3 25 50N 108 20W
Sinarádhes, Greece 23 A3 39 34N 19 51 E
Sīnāwan, Libya 50 B7 31 0N 10 37 E
Sincelejo, Colombia 92 B3 9 18N 75 24W
Sinchang, N. Korea 35 D15 40 7N 128 28 E
Sinchang-ni, N. Korea 35 E14 39 24N 126 8 E
Sinclair, U.S.A. 82 F10 41 47N 107 7W
Sinclair Mills, Canada 72 C4 54 5N 121 40W
Sincorá, Serra do, Brazil 93 F10 13 30S 41 0W
Sind, Pakistan 42 G3 26 0N 68 30 E

163

Songpan

Songpan, *China* **32 C5** 32 40N 103 30 E
Songwe, *Zaïre* **54 C2** 3 20S 26 16 E
Songwe →, *Africa* **55 D3** 9 44S 33 58 E
Sonid Youqi, *China* **34 C7** 42 45N 112 48 E
Sonipat, *India* **42 E7** 29 0N 77 5 E
Sonmiani, *Pakistan* **42 G2** 25 25N 66 40 E
Sono →, *Brazil* **93 E9** 9 58S 48 11W
Sonora, *Calif., U.S.A.* **83 H3** 37 59N 120 23W
Sonora, *Tex., U.S.A.* **81 K4** 30 34N 100 39W
Sonora □, *Mexico* **86 B2** 29 0N 111 0W
Sonora →, *Mexico* **86 B2** 28 50N 111 33W
Sonora Desert, *U.S.A.* **85 L12** 33 40N 114 15W
Sonoyta, *Mexico* **86 A2** 31 51N 112 50W
Sŏnsan, *S. Korea* **35 F15** 36 14N 128 17 E
Sonsonate, *El Salv.* **88 D2** 13 43N 89 44W
Soochow = Suzhou, *China* **33 C7** 31 19N 120 38 E
Sop Hao, *Laos* **38 B5** 20 33N 104 27 E
Sop Prap, *Thailand* **38 D2** 17 53N 99 20 E
Sopi, *Indonesia* **37 D7** 2 34N 128 28 E
Sopot, *Poland* **17 A10** 54 27N 18 31 E
Sopron, *Hungary* **17 E9** 47 45N 16 32 E
Sop's Arm, *Canada* **71 C8** 49 46N 56 56W
Sopur, *India* **43 B6** 34 18N 74 27 E
Sør-Rondane, *Antarctica* **5 D4** 72 0S 25 0 E
Sorah, *Pakistan* **42 F3** 27 13N 68 56 E
Sorata, *Bolivia* **92 G5** 15 50S 68 40W
Sorel, *Canada* **70 C5** 46 0N 73 10W
Soreq, N. →, *Israel* **47 D3** 31 57N 34 43 E
Sorgono, *Italy* **20 D3** 40 1N 9 6 E
Soria, *Spain* **19 B4** 41 43N 2 32W
Soriano, *Uruguay* **94 C4** 33 24S 58 19W
Sorkh, Kuh-e, *Iran* **45 C8** 35 40N 58 30 E
Soroca, *Moldova* **17 D15** 48 8N 28 12 E
Sorocaba, *Brazil* **95 A6** 23 31S 47 27W
Sorochinsk, *Russia* **24 D9** 52 26N 53 10 E
Soroki = Soroca, *Moldova* **17 D15** 48 8N 28 12 E
Soron, *India* **43 F8** 27 55N 78 45 E
Sorong, *Indonesia* **37 E8** 0 55S 131 15 E
Soroní, *Greece* **23 C10** 36 21N 28 1 E
Soroti, *Uganda* **54 B3** 1 43N 33 35 E
Sørøya, *Norway* **8 A20** 70 40N 22 30 E
Sørøysundet, *Norway* **8 A20** 70 25N 23 0 E
Sorrento, *Australia* **63 F3** 38 22S 144 47 E
Sorsele, *Sweden* **8 D17** 65 31N 17 30 E
Sorsogon, *Phil.* **37 B6** 13 0N 124 0 E
Sortavala, *Russia* **24 B5** 61 42N 30 41 E
Sortland, *Norway* **8 B16** 68 42N 15 25 E
Sŏsan, *S. Korea* **35 F14** 36 47N 126 27 E
Soscumica, L., *Canada* **70 B4** 50 15N 77 27W
Sosnogorsk, *Russia* **24 B9** 63 37N 53 51 E
Sosnovka, *Russia* **27 D11** 54 9N 109 35 E
Sosnowiec, *Poland* **17 C10** 50 20N 19 10 E
Sŏsura, *N. Korea* **35 C16** 42 16N 130 36 E
Sosva, *Russia* **24 C11** 59 10N 61 50 E
Sotkamo, *Finland* **8 D23** 64 8N 28 23 E
Soto la Marina →, *Mexico* **87 C5** 23 40N 97 40W
Sotuta, *Mexico* **87 C7** 20 29N 89 43W
Souanké, *Congo* **52 D2** 2 10N 14 3 E
Soúdha, *Greece* **23 D6** 35 29N 24 4 E
Soúdhas, Kólpos, *Greece* **23 D6** 35 25N 24 10 E
Soukhouma, *Laos* **38 E5** 14 38N 105 48 E
Sŏul, *S. Korea* **35 F14** 37 31N 126 58 E
Sound, The, *U.K.* **11 G3** 50 20N 4 10W
Sources, Mt. aux, *Lesotho* **57 D4** 28 45S 28 50 E
Soure, *Brazil* **93 D9** 0 35S 48 30W
Souris, *Man., Canada* **73 D8** 49 40N 100 20W
Souris, *P.E.I., Canada* **71 C7** 46 21N 62 15W
Souris →, *Canada* **80 A5** 49 40N 99 34W
Sousa, *Brazil* **93 E11** 6 45S 38 10W
Sousel, *Brazil* **93 D8** 2 38S 52 29W
Sousse, *Tunisia* **51 A7** 35 50N 10 38 E
South Africa ■, *Africa* **56 E3** 32 0S 23 0 E
South Atlantic Ocean **90 H7** 20 0S 10 0W
South Aulatsivik I., *Canada* **71 A7** 56 45N 61 30W
South Australia □, *Australia* **63 E2** 32 0S 139 0 E
South Ayrshire □, *U.K.* **12 F4** 55 18N 4 41W
South Baldy, *U.S.A.* **83 J10** 33 59N 107 11W
South Bend, *Ind., U.S.A.* **76 E2** 41 41N 86 15W
South Bend, *Wash., U.S.A.* **84 D3** 46 40N 123 48W
South Boston, *U.S.A.* **77 G6** 36 42N 78 54W
South Branch, *Canada* **71 C8** 47 55N 59 2W
South Brook, *Canada* **71 C8** 49 26N 56 5W
South Carolina □, *U.S.A.* **77 J5** 34 0N 81 0W
South Charleston, *U.S.A.* **76 F5** 38 22N 81 44W
South China Sea, *Asia* **36 C4** 10 0N 113 0 E
South Dakota □, *U.S.A.* **80 C5** 44 15N 100 0W
South Downs, *U.K.* **11 G7** 50 52N 0 25W
South East C., *Australia* **62 G4** 43 40S 146 50 E
South East Is., *Australia* **61 F3** 34 17S 123 30 E
South Esk →, *U.K.* **12 E5** 56 43N 2 31W
South Foreland, *U.K.* **11 F9** 51 8N 1 24 E
South Fork →, *U.S.A.* **82 C7** 47 54N 113 15W
South Fork, American →, *U.S.A.* **84 G5** 38 45N 121 5W
South Fork, Feather →, *U.S.A.* **84 F5** 39 17N 121 36W
South Georgia, *Antarctica* **5 B1** 54 30S 37 0W
South Gloucestershire □, *U.K.* **11 F5** 51 32N 2 28W
South Haven, *U.S.A.* **76 D2** 42 24N 86 16W
South Henik, L., *Canada* **73 A9** 61 30N 97 30W
South Honshu Ridge, *Pac. Oc.* **64 E6** 23 0N 143 0 E
South Horr, *Kenya* **54 B4** 2 12N 36 56 E
South I., *Kenya* **54 B4** 2 35N 36 35 E
South I., *N.Z.* **59 L3** 44 0S 170 0 E
South Invercargill, *N.Z.* **59 M2** 46 26S 168 23 E
South Knife →, *Canada* **73 B10** 58 55N 94 37W
South Korea ■, *Asia* **35 F15** 36 0N 128 0 E
South Lake Tahoe, *U.S.A.* **84 G6** 38 57N 119 59W
South Lanarkshire □, *U.K.* **12 F5** 55 37N 3 53W
South Loup →, *U.S.A.* **80 E5** 41 4N 98 39W
South Magnetic Pole, *Antarctica* **5 C9** 64 8S 138 8 E
South Milwaukee, *U.S.A.* **76 D2** 42 55N 87 52W
South Molton, *U.K.* **11 F4** 51 1N 3 51W
South Nahanni →, *Canada* **72 A4** 61 3N 123 21W
South Natuna Is. = Natuna Selatan, Kepulauan, *Indonesia* **39 L7** 2 45N 109 0 E
South Negril Pt., *Jamaica* **88 C4** 18 14N 78 30W
South Orkney Is., *Antarctica* **5 C18** 63 0S 45 0W
South Pagai, I. = Pagai Selatan, P., *Indonesia* **36 E2** 3 0S 100 15 E
South Pass, *U.S.A.* **82 E9** 42 20N 108 58W
South Pittsburg, *U.S.A.* **77 H3** 35 1N 85 42W
South Platte →, *U.S.A.* **80 E4** 41 7N 100 42W
South Pole, *Antarctica* **5 E** 90 0S 0 0 E
South Porcupine, *Canada* **70 C3** 48 30N 81 12W
South River, *Canada* **70 C4** 45 52N 79 23W
South River, *U.S.A.* **79 F10** 40 27N 74 23W
South Ronaldsay, *U.K.* **12 C6** 58 48N 2 58W
South Sandwich Is., *Antarctica* **5 B1** 57 0S 27 0W
South Saskatchewan →, *Canada* **73 C7** 53 15N 105 5W
South Seal →, *Canada* **73 B9** 58 48N 98 8W
South Shetland Is., *Antarctica* **5 C18** 62 0S 59 0W
South Shields, *U.K.* **10 C6** 55 0N 1 25W
South Sioux City, *U.S.A.* **80 D6** 42 28N 96 24W
South Taranaki Bight, *N.Z.* **59 H5** 39 40S 174 5 E
South Thompson →, *Canada* **72 C4** 50 40N 120 20W
South Twin I., *Canada* **70 B4** 53 7N 79 52W
South Tyne →, *U.K.* **10 C5** 54 59N 2 8W
South Uist, *U.K.* **12 D1** 57 20N 7 15W
South West Africa = Namibia ■, *Africa* **56 C2** 22 0S 18 9 E
South West C., *Australia* **62 G4** 43 34S 146 3 E
South Yorkshire □, *U.K.* **10 D6** 53 27N 1 36W
Southampton, *Canada* **70 D3** 44 30N 81 25W
Southampton, *U.K.* **11 G6** 50 54N 1 23W
Southampton, *U.S.A.* **79 F12** 40 53N 72 23W
Southampton I., *Canada* **69 B11** 64 30N 84 0W
Southbridge, *N.Z.* **59 K4** 43 48S 172 16 E
Southbridge, *U.S.A.* **79 D12** 42 5N 72 2W
Southend, *Canada* **73 B8** 56 19N 103 22W
Southend-on-Sea, *U.K.* **11 F8** 51 32N 0 44 E
Southern □, *Malawi* **55 F4** 15 0S 35 0 E
Southern □, *Uganda* **54 C3** 0 15S 31 30 E
Southern □, *Zambia* **55 F2** 16 20S 26 20 E
Southern Alps, *N.Z.* **59 K3** 43 41S 170 11 E
Southern Cross, *Australia* **61 F2** 31 12S 119 15 E
Southern Hills, *Australia* **61 F3** 32 15S 122 40 E
Southern Indian L., *Canada* **73 B9** 57 10N 98 30W
Southern Ocean, *Antarctica* **5 C6** 62 0S 60 0 E
Southern Pines, *U.S.A.* **77 H6** 35 11N 79 24W
Southern Uplands, *U.K.* **12 F5** 55 28N 3 52W
Southington, *U.S.A.* **79 E12** 41 36N 72 53W
Southold, *U.S.A.* **79 E12** 41 4N 72 26W
Southport, *Australia* **63 D5** 27 58S 153 25 E
Southport, *U.K.* **10 D4** 53 39N 3 0W
Southport, *U.S.A.* **77 J6** 33 55N 78 1W
Southwest C., *N.Z.* **59 M1** 47 17S 167 28 E
Southwold, *U.K.* **11 E9** 52 20N 1 41 E
Soutpansberg, *S. Africa* **57 C4** 23 0S 29 30 E
Sovetsk, *Kaliningd., Russia* **9 J19** 55 6N 21 50 E
Sovetsk, *Kirov, Russia* **24 C8** 57 38N 48 53 E
Sovetskaya Gavan, *Russia* **27 E15** 48 50N 140 5 E
Soweto, *S. Africa* **57 D4** 26 14S 27 54 E
Sōya-Kaikyō = La Perouse Str., *Asia* **30 B11** 45 40N 142 0 E
Sōya-Misaki, *Japan* **30 B10** 45 30N 141 55 E
Soyo, *Angola* **52 F2** 6 13S 12 20 E
Sozh →, *Belarus* **17 B16** 51 57N 30 48 E
Spa, *Belgium* **15 D5** 50 29N 5 53 E
Spain ■, *Europe* **19 B4** 39 0N 4 0W
Spalding, *Australia* **63 E2** 33 30S 138 37 E
Spalding, *U.K.* **10 E7** 52 48N 0 9W
Spalding, *U.S.A.* **80 E5** 41 42N 98 22W
Spangler, *U.S.A.* **78 F6** 40 39N 78 48W
Spaniard's Bay, *Canada* **71 C9** 47 38N 53 20W
Spanish, *Canada* **70 C3** 46 12N 82 20W
Spanish Fork, *U.S.A.* **82 F8** 40 7N 111 39W
Spanish Town, *Jamaica* **88 C4** 18 0N 76 57W
Sparks, *U.S.A.* **84 F7** 39 32N 119 45W
Sparta = Spárti, *Greece* **21 F10** 37 5N 22 25 E
Sparta, *Ga., U.S.A.* **77 J4** 33 17N 82 58W
Sparta, *Wis., U.S.A.* **80 D9** 43 56N 90 49W
Spartanburg, *U.S.A.* **77 H4** 34 56N 81 57W
Spartansburg, *U.S.A.* **78 E5** 41 49N 79 41W
Spárti, *Greece* **21 F10** 37 5N 22 25 E
Spartivento, C., *Calabria, Italy* **20 F7** 37 55N 16 4 E
Spartivento, C., *Sard., Italy* **20 E3** 38 53N 8 50 E
Spassk Dalniy, *Russia* **27 E14** 44 40N 132 48 E
Spátha, Ákra, *Greece* **23 D5** 35 42N 23 43 E
Spatsizi →, *Canada* **72 B3** 57 42N 128 7W
Spearfish, *U.S.A.* **80 C3** 44 30N 103 52W
Spearman, *U.S.A.* **81 G4** 36 12N 101 12W
Speers, *Canada* **73 C7** 52 43N 107 34W
Speightstown, *Barbados* **89 D8** 13 15N 59 39W
Speke Gulf, *Tanzania* **54 C3** 2 20S 32 50 E
Spencer, *Idaho, U.S.A.* **82 D7** 44 22N 112 11W
Spencer, *Iowa, U.S.A.* **80 D7** 43 9N 95 9W
Spencer, *N.Y., U.S.A.* **79 D8** 42 13N 76 30W
Spencer, *Nebr., U.S.A.* **80 D5** 42 53N 98 42W
Spencer, *W. Va., U.S.A.* **76 F5** 38 48N 81 21W
Spencer, C., *Australia* **63 F2** 35 20S 136 53 E
Spencer B., *Namibia* **56 D1** 25 30S 14 47 E
Spencer G., *Australia* **63 E2** 34 0S 137 20 E
Spencerville, *Canada* **79 B9** 44 51N 75 33W
Spences Bridge, *Canada* **72 C4** 50 25N 121 20W
Spenser Mts., *N.Z.* **59 K4** 42 15S 172 45 E
Sperrin Mts., *U.K.* **13 B5** 54 50N 7 0W
Spey →, *U.K.* **12 D5** 57 40N 3 6W
Speyer, *Germany* **16 D5** 49 29N 8 25 E
Spíli, *Greece* **23 D6** 35 13N 24 31 E
Spin Baldak = Qala-i-Jadid, *Afghan.* **42 D2** 31 1N 66 25 E
Spinalónga, *Greece* **23 D7** 35 18N 25 44 E
Spirit Lake, *Idaho, U.S.A.* **82 C5** 47 58N 116 52W
Spirit Lake, *Wash., U.S.A.* **84 D4** 46 15N 122 9W
Spirit River, *Canada* **72 B5** 55 45N 118 50W
Spiritwood, *Canada* **73 C7** 53 24N 107 33W
Spithead, *U.K.* **11 G6** 50 45N 1 10W
Spitzbergen = Svalbard, *Arctic* **4 B8** 78 0N 17 0 E
Spjelkavik, *Norway* **9 E12** 62 28N 6 22 E
Split, *Croatia* **20 C7** 43 31N 16 26 E
Split L., *Canada* **73 B9** 56 8N 96 15W
Spofford, *U.S.A.* **81 L4** 29 10N 100 25W
Spokane, *U.S.A.* **82 C5** 47 40N 117 24W
Spoleto, *Italy* **20 C5** 42 44N 12 44 E
Spooner, *U.S.A.* **80 C9** 45 50N 91 53W
Sporyy Navolok, Mys, *Russia* **26 B7** 75 50N 68 40 E
Spragge, *Canada* **70 C3** 46 15N 82 40W
Sprague, *U.S.A.* **82 C5** 47 18N 117 59W
Sprague River, *U.S.A.* **82 E3** 42 27N 121 30W
Spratly Is., *S. China Sea* **36 C4** 8 20N 112 0 E
Spray, *U.S.A.* **82 D4** 44 50N 119 48W
Spree →, *Germany* **16 B7** 52 32N 13 13 E
Sprengisandur, *Iceland* **8 D5** 64 52N 18 7W
Spring City, *U.S.A.* **82 G8** 39 29N 111 30W
Spring Garden, *U.S.A.* **84 F6** 39 52N 120 47W
Spring Mts., *U.S.A.* **83 H6** 36 0N 115 45W
Spring Valley, *Calif., U.S.A.* **85 N10** 32 45N 117 5W
Spring Valley, *Minn., U.S.A.* **80 D8** 43 41N 92 23W
Springbok, *S. Africa* **56 D2** 29 42S 17 54 E
Springdale, *Canada* **71 C8** 49 30N 56 6W
Springdale, *Ark., U.S.A.* **81 G7** 36 11N 94 8W
Springdale, *Wash., U.S.A.* **82 B5** 48 4N 117 45W
Springer, *U.S.A.* **81 G2** 36 22N 104 36W
Springerville, *U.S.A.* **83 J9** 34 8N 109 17W
Springfield, *Canada* **78 D4** 42 50N 80 56W
Springfield, *N.Z.* **59 K3** 43 19S 171 56 E
Springfield, *Colo., U.S.A.* **81 G3** 37 24N 102 37W
Springfield, *Ill., U.S.A.* **80 F10** 39 48N 89 39W
Springfield, *Mass., U.S.A.* **79 D12** 42 6N 72 35W
Springfield, *Mo., U.S.A.* **81 G8** 37 13N 93 17W
Springfield, *Ohio, U.S.A.* **76 F4** 39 55N 83 49W
Springfield, *Oreg., U.S.A.* **82 D2** 44 3N 123 1W
Springfield, *Tenn., U.S.A.* **77 G2** 36 31N 86 53W
Springfield, *Vt., U.S.A.* **79 C12** 43 18N 72 29W
Springfontein, *S. Africa* **56 E4** 30 15S 25 40 E
Springhill, *Canada* **71 C7** 45 40N 64 4W
Springhouse, *Canada* **72 C4** 51 56N 122 7W
Springhurst, *Australia* **63 F4** 36 10S 146 31 E
Springs, *S. Africa* **57 D4** 26 13S 28 25 E
Springsure, *Australia* **62 C4** 24 8S 148 6 E
Springvale, *Queens., Australia* **62 C3** 23 33S 140 42 E
Springvale, *W. Austral., Australia* **60 C4** 17 48S 127 41 E
Springvale, *U.S.A.* **79 C14** 43 28N 70 48W
Springville, *Calif., U.S.A.* **84 J8** 36 8N 118 49W
Springville, *N.Y., U.S.A.* **78 D6** 42 31N 78 40W
Springville, *Utah, U.S.A.* **82 F8** 40 10N 111 37W
Springwater, *Canada* **73 C7** 51 58N 108 23W
Spruce-Creek, *U.S.A.* **78 F6** 40 36N 78 9W
Spur, *U.S.A.* **81 J4** 33 28N 100 52W
Spurn Hd., *U.K.* **10 D8** 53 35N 0 8 E
Spuzzum, *Canada* **72 D4** 49 37N 121 23W
Squam L., *U.S.A.* **79 C13** 43 45N 71 32W
Squamish, *Canada* **72 D4** 49 45N 123 10W
Square Islands, *Canada* **71 B8** 52 47N 55 47W
Squires, Mt., *Australia* **61 E4** 26 14S 127 28 E
Sragen, *Indonesia* **37 G14** 7 26S 111 2 E
Srbija = Serbia □, *Yugoslavia* **21 C9** 43 30N 21 0 E
Sre Khtum, *Cambodia* **39 F6** 12 10N 106 52 E
Sre Umbell, *Cambodia* **39 G4** 11 8N 103 46 E
Srebrnica, *Bos.-H.* **21 B8** 44 10N 19 18 E
Sredinny Ra. = Sredinnyy Khrebet, *Russia* **27 D16** 57 0N 160 0 E
Sredinnyy Khrebet, *Russia* **27 D16** 57 0N 160 0 E
Sredne Tambovskoye, *Russia* **27 D14** 50 55N 137 45 E
Srednekolymsk, *Russia* **27 C16** 67 27N 153 40 E
Srednevilyuysk, *Russia* **27 C13** 63 50N 123 5 E
Śrem, *Poland* **17 B9** 52 6N 17 2 E
Sremska Mitrovica, *Serbia, Yug.* **21 B8** 44 59N 19 33 E
Srepok →, *Cambodia* **38 F6** 13 33N 106 16 E
Sretensk, *Russia* **27 D12** 52 10N 117 40 E
Sri Lanka ■, *Asia* **40 R12** 7 30N 80 50 E
Srikakulam, *India* **41 K13** 18 14N 83 58 E
Srinagar, *India* **43 B6** 34 5N 74 50 E
Staaten →, *Australia* **62 B3** 16 24S 141 17 E
Stade, *Germany* **16 B5** 53 35N 9 29 E
Stadskanaal, *Neths.* **15 A6** 53 4N 6 55 E
Staffa, *U.K.* **12 E2** 56 27N 6 21W
Stafford, *U.K.* **10 E5** 52 49N 2 7W
Stafford, *U.S.A.* **81 G5** 37 58N 98 36W
Stafford Springs, *U.S.A.* **79 E12** 41 57N 72 18W
Staffordshire □, *U.K.* **10 E5** 52 53N 2 10W
Staines, *U.K.* **11 F7** 51 26N 0 29W
Stakhanov, *Ukraine* **25 E6** 48 35N 38 40 E
Stalingrad = Volgograd, *Russia* **25 E7** 48 40N 44 25 E
Staliniri = Tskhinvali, *Georgia* **25 F7** 42 14N 44 1 E
Stalino = Donetsk, *Ukraine* **25 E6** 48 0N 37 45 E
Stalinogorsk = Novomoskovsk, *Russia* **24 D6** 54 5N 38 15 E
Stalis, *Greece* **23 D7** 35 17N 25 25 E
Stalowa Wola, *Poland* **17 C12** 50 34N 22 3 E
Stalybridge, *U.K.* **10 D5** 53 28N 2 3W
Stamford, *Australia* **62 C3** 21 15S 143 46 E
Stamford, *U.K.* **11 E7** 52 39N 0 29W
Stamford, *Conn., U.S.A.* **79 E11** 41 3N 73 32W
Stamford, *Tex., U.S.A.* **81 J5** 32 57N 99 48W
Stamps, *U.S.A.* **81 J8** 33 22N 93 30W
Stanberry, *U.S.A.* **80 E7** 40 13N 94 35W
Standerton, *S. Africa* **57 D4** 26 55S 29 7 E
Standish, *U.S.A.* **76 D4** 43 59N 83 57W
Stanford, *U.S.A.* **82 C8** 47 9N 110 13W
Stanger, *S. Africa* **57 D5** 29 27S 31 14 E
Stanislaus →, *U.S.A.* **84 H5** 37 40N 121 14W
Stanislav = Ivano-Frankivsk, *Ukraine* **17 D13** 48 40N 24 40 E
Stanke Dimitrov, *Bulgaria* **21 C10** 42 17N 23 9 E
Stanley, *Australia* **62 G4** 40 46S 145 19 E
Stanley, *N.B., Canada* **71 C6** 46 20N 66 44W
Stanley, *Sask., Canada* **73 B8** 55 24N 104 22W
Stanley, *Falk. Is.* **96 G5** 51 40S 59 51W
Stanley, *Idaho, U.S.A.* **82 D6** 44 13N 114 56W
Stanley, *N. Dak., U.S.A.* **80 A3** 48 19N 102 23W
Stanley, *N.Y., U.S.A.* **78 D7** 42 48N 77 6W
Stanley, *Wis., U.S.A.* **80 C9** 44 58N 90 56W
Stanovoy Khrebet, *Russia* **27 D13** 55 0N 130 0 E
Stanovoy Ra. = Stanovoy Khrebet, *Russia* **27 D13** 55 0N 130 0 E
Stansmore Ra., *Australia* **60 D4** 21 23S 128 33 E
Stanthorpe, *Australia* **63 D5** 28 36S 151 59 E
Stanton, *U.S.A.* **81 J4** 32 8N 101 48W
Stanwood, *U.S.A.* **84 B4** 48 15N 122 23W
Staples, *U.S.A.* **80 B7** 46 21N 94 48W
Stapleton, *U.S.A.* **80 E4** 41 29N 100 31W
Star City, *Canada* **73 C8** 52 50N 104 20W
Stara Planina, *Bulgaria* **21 C10** 43 15N 23 0 E
Stara Zagora, *Bulgaria* **21 C11** 42 26N 25 39 E
Starachowice, *Poland* **17 C11** 51 3N 21 2 E
Staraya Russa, *Russia* **24 C5** 57 58N 31 23 E
Starbuck I., *Kiribati* **65 H12** 5 37S 155 55W
Stargard Szczeciński, *Poland* **16 B8** 53 20N 15 0 E
Staritsa, *Russia* **24 C5** 56 33N 34 55 E
Starke, *U.S.A.* **77 K4** 29 57N 82 7W
Starkville, *Colo., U.S.A.* **81 G2** 37 8N 104 30W
Starkville, *Miss., U.S.A.* **77 J1** 33 28N 88 49W
Starogard Gdański, *Poland* **17 B10** 53 59N 18 30 E
Starokonstantinov = Starokonstyantyniv, *Ukraine* **17 D14** 49 48N 27 10 E
Starokonstyantyniv, *Ukraine* **17 D14** 49 48N 27 10 E
Start Pt., *U.K.* **11 G4** 50 13N 3 39W
Staryy Chartoriysk, *Ukraine* **17 C13** 51 15N 25 54 E
Staryy Kheydzhan, *Russia* **27 C15** 60 0N 144 50 E
Staryy Oskol, *Russia* **24 D6** 51 19N 37 55 E
State College, *U.S.A.* **78 F7** 40 48N 77 52W
Stateline, *U.S.A.* **84 G7** 38 57N 119 56W
Staten, I. = Estados, I. de Los, *Argentina* **96 G4** 54 40S 64 30W
Staten, I., *Argentina* **90 J4** 54 40S 64 0W
Staten I., *U.S.A.* **79 F10** 40 35N 74 9W
Statesboro, *U.S.A.* **77 J5** 32 27N 81 47W
Statesville, *U.S.A.* **77 H5** 35 47N 80 53W
Stauffer, *U.S.A.* **85 L7** 34 45N 119 3W
Staunton, *Ill., U.S.A.* **80 F10** 39 1N 89 47W
Staunton, *Va., U.S.A.* **76 F6** 38 9N 79 4W
Stavanger, *Norway* **9 G11** 58 57N 5 40 E
Staveley, *N.Z.* **59 K3** 43 40S 171 32 E
Stavelot, *Belgium* **15 D5** 50 23N 5 55 E
Staveren, *Neths.* **15 B5** 52 53N 5 22 E
Stavern, *Norway* **9 G14** 59 0N 10 1 E
Stavropol, *Russia* **25 E7** 45 5N 42 0 E
Stavros, *Cyprus* **23 D11** 35 1N 32 38 E
Stavrós, *Greece* **23 D6** 35 12N 24 45 E
Stavros, Ákra, *Greece* **23 D6** 35 26N 24 58 E
Stawell, *Australia* **63 F3** 37 5S 142 47 E
Stawell →, *Australia* **62 C3** 20 20S 142 55 E
Stayner, *Canada* **78 B4** 44 25N 80 5W
Steamboat Springs, *U.S.A.* **82 F10** 40 29N 106 50W
Steele, *U.S.A.* **80 B5** 46 51N 99 55W
Steelton, *U.S.A.* **78 F8** 40 14N 76 50W
Steelville, *U.S.A.* **81 G9** 37 58N 91 22W
Steen River, *Canada* **72 B5** 59 40N 117 12W
Steenkool = Bintuni, *Indonesia* **37 E8** 2 7S 133 32 E
Steenwijk, *Neths.* **15 B6** 52 47N 6 7 E
Steep Pt., *Australia* **61 E1** 26 8S 113 8 E
Steep Rock, *Canada* **73 C9** 51 30N 98 48W
Stefanie L. = Chew Bahir, *Ethiopia* **51 H12** 4 40N 36 50 E
Stefansson Bay, *Antarctica* **5 C5** 67 20S 59 8 E
Steiermark □, *Austria* **16 E8** 47 26N 15 0 E
Steilacoom, *U.S.A.* **84 C4** 47 10N 122 36W
Steinbach, *Canada* **73 D9** 49 32N 96 40W
Steinfort, *Lux.* **15 E5** 49 39N 5 55 E
Steinkjer, *Norway* **8 D14** 64 1N 11 31 E
Steinkopf, *S. Africa* **56 D2** 29 18S 17 43 E
Stellarton, *Canada* **71 C7** 45 32N 62 30W
Stellenbosch, *S. Africa* **56 E2** 33 58S 18 50 E
Stendal, *Germany* **16 B6** 52 36N 11 53 E
Steornabhaigh = Stornoway, *U.K.* **12 C2** 58 13N 6 23W
Stepanakert = Xankändi, *Azerbaijan* **25 G8** 39 52N 46 49 E
Stephen, *U.S.A.* **80 A6** 48 27N 96 53W
Stephens Creek, *Australia* **63 E3** 31 50S 141 30 E
Stephens I., *Canada* **72 C2** 54 10N 130 45W
Stephenville, *Canada* **71 C8** 48 31N 58 35W
Stephenville, *U.S.A.* **81 J5** 32 13N 98 12W
Stepnoi = Elista, *Russia* **25 E7** 46 16N 44 14 E
Stepnyak, *Kazakstan* **26 D8** 52 50N 70 50 E
Steppe, *Asia* **28 D9** 50 0N 50 0 E
Sterkstroom, *S. Africa* **56 E4** 31 32S 26 32 E
Sterling, *Colo., U.S.A.* **80 E3** 40 37N 103 13W
Sterling, *Ill., U.S.A.* **80 E10** 41 48N 89 42W
Sterling, *Kans., U.S.A.* **80 F5** 38 13N 98 12W
Sterling City, *U.S.A.* **81 K4** 31 51N 101 0W
Sterling Run, *U.S.A.* **78 E6** 41 25N 78 12W
Sterlitamak, *Russia* **24 D10** 53 40N 56 0 E
Stérnes, *Greece* **23 D6** 35 30N 24 9 E
Stettin = Szczecin, *Poland* **16 B8** 53 27N 14 27 E
Stettiner Haff, *Germany* **16 B8** 53 47N 14 15 E
Stettler, *Canada* **72 C6** 52 19N 112 40W
Steubenville, *U.S.A.* **78 F4** 40 22N 80 37W
Stevens Point, *U.S.A.* **80 C10** 44 31N 89 34W
Stevenson, *U.S.A.* **84 E5** 45 42N 121 53W
Stevenson L., *Canada* **73 C9** 53 55N 96 0W
Stewart, *B.C., Canada* **72 B3** 55 56N 129 57W
Stewart, *N.W.T., Canada* **68 B6** 63 19N 139 26W
Stewart, *U.S.A.* **84 F7** 39 5N 119 46W
Stewart, C., *Australia* **62 A1** 11 57S 134 56 E
Stewart, I., *Chile* **96 G2** 54 50S 71 15W
Stewart I., *N.Z.* **59 M1** 46 58S 167 54 E
Stewarts Point, *U.S.A.* **84 G3** 38 39N 123 24W
Stewiacke, *Canada* **71 C7** 45 9N 63 22W
Steynsburg, *S. Africa* **56 E4** 31 15S 25 49 E
Steyr, *Austria* **16 D8** 48 3N 14 25 E
Steytlerville, *S. Africa* **56 E3** 33 17S 24 19 E
Stigler, *U.S.A.* **81 H7** 35 15N 95 8W
Stikine →, *Canada* **72 B2** 56 40N 132 30W
Stilfontein, *S. Africa* **56 D4** 26 51S 26 50 E
Stillwater, *N.Z.* **59 K3** 42 27S 171 20 E
Stillwater, *Minn., U.S.A.* **80 C8** 45 3N 92 49W
Stillwater, *N.Y., U.S.A.* **79 D11** 42 55N 73 41W

Sweetwater

Stillwater, *Okla., U.S.A.* . . **81 G6** 36 7N 97 4W
Stillwater Range, *U.S.A.* . **82 G4** 39 50N 118 5W
Stilwell, *U.S.A.* **81 H7** 35 49N 94 38W
Štip, *Macedonia* . . . . **21 D10** 41 42N 22 10 E
Stirling, *Australia* . . . . . . **62 B3** 17 12S 141 35 E
Stirling, *Canada* **72 D6** 49 30N 112 30W
Stirling, *U.K.* **12 E5** 56 8N 3 57W
Stirling □, *U.K.* **12 E4** 56 12N 4 18W
Stirling Ra., *Australia* . . . **61 F2** 34 23S 118 0 E
Stittsville, *Canada* **79 A9** 45 15N 75 55W
Stjernøya, *Norway* . . . . . . **8 A20** 70 20N 22 40 E
Stjørdalshalsen, *Norway* . **8 E14** 63 29N 10 51 E
Stockerau, *Austria* . . . . . . **16 D9** 48 24N 16 12 E
Stockett, *U.S.A.* **82 C8** 47 21N 111 10W
Stockholm, *Sweden* . . . . . **9 G18** 59 20N 18 3 E
Stockport, *U.K.* **10 D5** 53 25N 2 9W
Stockton, *Calif., U.S.A.* . . **83 H3** 37 58N 121 17W
Stockton, *Kans., U.S.A.* . . **80 F5** 39 26N 99 16W
Stockton, *Mo., U.S.A.* . . . **81 G8** 37 42N 93 48W
Stockton-on-Tees, *U.K.* . . **10 C6** 54 35N 1 19W
Stockton-on-Tees □, *U.K.* **10 C6** 54 35N 1 19W
Stoke on Trent, *U.K.* **10 D5** 53 1N 2 11W
Stokes Bay, *Canada* **70 C3** 45 0N 81 28W
Stokes Pt., *Australia* . . . . **62 G3** 40 10S 143 56 E
Stokes Ra., *Australia* . . . . **60 C5** 15 50S 130 50 E
Stokksnes, *Iceland* **8 D6** 64 14N 14 58W
Stokmarknes, *Norway* . . . **8 B16** 68 34N 14 54 E
Stolac, *Bos.-H.* . . . . **21 C7** 43 5N 17 59 E
Stolbovaya, *Russia* . . . . . **27 C16** 64 50N 153 50 E
Stolbovoy, Ostrov, *Russia* **27 D17** 74 44N 135 14 E
Stolbtsy = Stowbtsy, *Belarus* . . . . **17 B14** 53 30N 26 43 E
Stolin, *Belarus* . . . . **17 C14** 51 53N 26 50 E
Stomion, *Greece* . . . . **23 D5** 35 21N 23 32 E
Stonehaven, *U.K.* **12 E6** 56 59N 2 12W
Stonehenge, *Australia* . . . **62 C3** 24 22S 143 17 E
Stonewall, *Canada* **73 C9** 50 10N 97 19W
Stony L., *Man., Canada* . . **73 B9** 58 51N 98 40W
Stony L., *Ont., Canada* . . **78 B6** 44 30N 78 5W
Stony Rapids, *Canada* . . . **73 B7** 59 16N 105 50W
Stony Tunguska = Podkamennaya Tunguska →, *Russia* . **27 C10** 61 50N 90 13 E
Stonyford, *U.S.A.* **84 F4** 39 23N 122 33W
Stora Lulevatten, *Sweden* **8 C18** 67 10N 19 30 E
Storavan, *Sweden* . . . . . . **8 D18** 65 45N 18 10 E
Stord, *Norway* . . . . **9 G11** 59 52N 5 23 E
Store Bælt, *Denmark* . . . . **9 J14** 55 20N 11 0 E
Store Creek, *Australia* . . . **63 E4** 32 54S 149 6 E
Storm B., *Australia* . . . . . **62 G4** 43 10S 147 30 E
Storm Lake, *U.S.A.* **80 D7** 42 39N 95 13W
Stormberge, *S. Africa* . . . **56 E4** 31 16S 26 17 E
Stormsrivier, *S. Africa* . . . **56 E3** 33 59S 23 52 E
Stornoway, *U.K.* **12 C2** 58 13N 6 23W
Storozhinets = Storozhynets, *Ukraine* . **17 D13** 48 14N 25 45 E
Storozhynets, *Ukraine* . . . **17 D13** 48 14N 25 45 E
Storsjön, *Sweden* . . . . . . **8 E16** 63 9N 14 30 E
Storuman, *Sweden* . . . . . **8 D17** 65 5N 17 10 E
Storuman, sjö, *Sweden* . . **8 D17** 65 13N 16 50 E
Stoughton, *Canada* **73 D8** 49 40N 103 0W
Stour →, *Dorset, U.K.* . . . **11 G5** 50 43N 1 47W
Stour →, *Here. & Worcs., U.K.* **11 E5** 52 21N 2 17W
Stour →, *Kent, U.K.* . . . . **11 F9** 51 18N 1 22 E
Stour →, *Suffolk, U.K.* . . **11 F9** 51 57N 1 4 E
Stourbridge, *U.K.* **11 E5** 52 28N 2 8W
Stout, L., *Canada* **73 C10** 52 0N 94 40W
Stove Pipe Wells Village, *U.S.A.* **85 J9** 36 35N 117 11W
Stowbtsy, *Belarus* . . . . . . **17 B14** 53 30N 26 43 E
Stowmarket, *U.K.* . . . . **11 E9** 52 12N 1 0 E
Strabane, *U.K.* **13 B4** 54 50N 7 27W
Strabane □, *U.K.* **13 B4** 54 45N 7 25W
Strahan, *Australia* . . . . . . **62 G4** 42 9S 145 20 E
Stralsund, *Germany* . . . . . **16 A7** 54 18N 13 4 E
Strand, *S. Africa* . . . . **56 E2** 34 9S 18 48 E
Stranda, *Møre og Romsdal, Norway* . . . . **9 E12** 62 19N 6 58 E
Stranda, *Nord-Trøndelag, Norway* . . . . **8 E14** 63 33N 10 14 E
Strangford L., *U.K.* **13 B6** 54 30N 5 37W
Strangsville, *U.S.A.* **78 E3** 41 19N 81 50W
Stranraer, *U.K.* **12 G3** 54 54N 5 1W
Strasbourg, *Canada* **73 C8** 51 4N 104 55W
Strasbourg, *France* . . . . . **18 B7** 48 35N 7 42 E
Strasburg, *U.S.A.* **80 B4** 46 8N 100 10W
Stratford, *Canada* **70 D3** 43 23N 81 0W
Stratford, *N.Z.* . . . . **59 H5** 39 20S 174 19 E
Stratford, *Calif., U.S.A.* . . **83 H4** 36 11N 119 49W
Stratford, *Conn., U.S.A.* . **79 E11** 41 12N 73 8W
Stratford, *Tex., U.S.A.* . . . **81 G3** 36 20N 102 4W
Stratford-upon-Avon, *U.K.* **11 E6** 52 12N 1 42W
Strath Spey, *U.K.* **12 D5** 57 9N 3 49W
Strathalbyn, *Australia* . . . **63 F2** 35 13S 138 53 E
Strathcona Prov. Park, *Canada* **72 D3** 49 38N 125 40W
Strathmore, *Australia* . . . **62 B3** 17 50S 142 35 E
Strathmore, *Canada* **72 C6** 51 5N 113 18W
Strathmore, *U.K.* **12 E5** 56 37N 3 7W
Strathmore, *U.S.A.* **84 J7** 36 9N 119 4W
Strathnaver, *Canada* **72 C4** 53 20N 122 33W
Strathpeffer, *U.K.* **12 D4** 57 35N 4 32W
Strathroy, *Canada* **70 D3** 42 58N 81 38W
Strathy Pt., *U.K.* **12 C4** 58 36N 4 1W
Stratton, *U.S.A.* **80 F3** 39 19N 102 36W
Straubing, *Germany* . . . . . **16 D7** 48 52N 12 34 E
Straumnes, *Iceland* **8 C2** 66 26N 23 8W
Strawberry Reservoir, *U.S.A.* **82 F8** 40 8N 111 9W
Strawn, *U.S.A.* **81 J5** 32 33N 98 30W
Streaky B., *Australia* . . . . **63 E1** 32 48S 134 13 E
Streaky Bay, *Australia* . . . **63 E1** 32 51S 134 18 E
Streator, *U.S.A.* **80 E10** 41 8N 88 50W
Streeter, *U.S.A.* **80 B5** 46 39N 99 21W
Streetsville, *Canada* **78 C5** 43 35N 79 42W
Strelka, *Russia* . . . . **27 D10** 58 5N 93 3 E
Streng →, *Cambodia* . . . **38 F4** 13 12N 103 37 E
Streymoy, *Færoe Is.* **8 E9** 62 8N 7 5W
Strezhevoy, *Russia* . . . . . . **26 C8** 60 42N 77 34 E
Strimón →, *Greece* . . . . . **21 D10** 40 46N 23 51 E
Strimonikós Kólpos, *Greece* . . . . **21 D11** 40 33N 24 0 E
Strómboli, *Italy* . . . . **20 E6** 38 47N 15 13 E
Stromeferry, *U.K.* **12 D3** 57 21N 5 33W
Stromness, *U.K.* **12 C5** 58 58N 3 17W
Stromsburg, *U.S.A.* **80 E6** 41 7N 97 36W
Strömstad, *Sweden* . . . . . **9 G14** 58 56N 11 10 E
Strömsund, *Sweden* . . . . . **8 E16** 63 51N 15 33 E
Stronsay, *U.K.* **12 B6** 59 7N 2 35W
Stroud, *U.K.* **11 F5** 51 45N 2 13W
Stroud Road, *Australia* . . **63 E5** 32 18S 151 57 E
Stroudsburg, *U.S.A.* **79 F9** 40 59N 75 12W
Stroumbi, *Cyprus* . . . . **23 E11** 34 53N 32 29 E
Struer, *Denmark* . . . . **9 H13** 56 30N 8 35 E
Strumica, *Macedonia* . . . . **21 D10** 41 28N 22 41 E
Struthers, *Canada* **70 C2** 48 41N 85 51W
Struthers, *U.S.A.* **78 E4** 41 4N 80 39W
Stryker, *U.S.A.* **82 B6** 48 41N 114 46W
Stryy, *Ukraine* . . . . **17 D12** 49 16N 23 48 E
Strzelecki Cr. →, *Australia* . . . . **63 D2** 29 37S 139 59 E
Stuart, *Fla., U.S.A.* **77 M5** 27 12N 80 15W
Stuart, *Nebr., U.S.A.* **80 D5** 42 36N 99 8W
Stuart →, *Canada* **72 C4** 54 0N 123 35W
Stuart Bluff Ra., *Australia* **60 D5** 22 50S 131 52 E
Stuart L., *Canada* **72 C4** 54 30N 124 30W
Stuart Ra., *Australia* . . . . **63 D1** 29 10S 134 56 E
Stull, L., *Canada* **70 B1** 54 24N 92 34W
Stung Treng, *Cambodia* . . **38 F5** 13 31N 105 58 E
Stupart →, *Canada* **73 B10** 56 0N 93 25W
Sturgeon B., *Canada* **73 C9** 52 0N 97 50W
Sturgeon Bay, *U.S.A.* **76 C2** 44 50N 87 23W
Sturgeon Falls, *Canada* . . **70 C4** 46 25N 79 57W
Sturgeon L., *Alta., Canada* **72 B5** 55 6N 117 32W
Sturgeon L., *Ont., Canada* **70 B1** 50 0N 90 45W
Sturgeon L., *Ont., Canada* **78 B6** 44 28N 78 43W
Sturgis, *Mich., U.S.A.* **76 E3** 41 48N 85 25W
Sturgis, *S. Dak., U.S.A.* . . **80 C3** 44 25N 103 31W
Sturt Cr. →, *Australia* . . . **60 C4** 19 8S 127 50 E
Sturt Creek, *Australia* . . . **60 C4** 19 12S 128 8 E
Stutterheim, *S. Africa* . . . **56 E4** 32 33S 27 28 E
Stuttgart, *Germany* . . . . . **16 D5** 48 48N 9 11 E
Stuttgart, *U.S.A.* **81 H9** 34 30N 91 33W
Stuyvesant, *U.S.A.* **79 D11** 42 23N 73 45W
Stykkishólmur, *Iceland* . . **8 D2** 65 2N 22 40W
Styria = Steiermark □, *Austria* . . . . **16 E8** 47 26N 15 0 E
Su Xian, *China* . . . . **34 H9** 33 41N 116 59 E
Suakin, *Sudan* . . . . **51 E12** 19 8N 37 20 E
Suan, *N. Korea* . . . . **35 E14** 38 42N 126 22 E
Suaqui, *Mexico* **86 B3** 29 12N 109 41W
Subang, *Indonesia* . . . . . . **37 G12** 6 34S 107 45 E
Subansiri →, *India* . . . . . . **41 F18** 26 48N 93 50 E
Subayhah, *Si. Arabia* . . . . **44 D3** 30 2N 38 50 E
Subi, *Indonesia* . . . . **39 L7** 2 58N 108 50 E
Subotica, *Serbia, Yug.* . . . **21 A8** 46 6N 19 39 E
Success, *Canada* **73 C7** 50 28N 108 6W
Suceava, *Romania* . . . . . . **17 E14** 47 38N 26 16 E
Suchan, *Russia* . . . . **30 C6** 43 8N 133 9 E
Suchitoto, *El Salv.* **88 D2** 13 56N 89 0W
Suchou = Suzhou, *China* . **33 C7** 31 19N 120 38 E
Süchow = Xuzhou, *China* . **35 G9** 34 18N 117 10 E
Suck →, *Ireland* **13 C3** 53 17N 8 3W
Sucre, *Bolivia* **92 G5** 19 0S 65 15W
Sud, Pte., *Canada* **71 C7** 49 3N 62 14W
Sud-Ouest, Pte. du, *Canada* **71 C7** 49 23N 63 36W
Sudan, *U.S.A.* **81 H3** 34 4N 102 32W
Sudan ■, *Africa* . . . . **51 E11** 15 0N 30 0 E
Sudbury, *Canada* **70 C3** 46 30N 81 0W
Sudbury, *U.K.* . . . . **11 E8** 52 2N 0 45 E
Sûdd, *Sudan* . . . . **51 G11** 8 20N 30 0 E
Sudeten Mts. = Sudety, *Europe* . . . . **17 C9** 50 20N 16 45 E
Sudety, *Europe* . . . . **17 C9** 50 20N 16 45 E
Suðuroy, *Færoe Is.* **8 F9** 61 32N 6 50W
Sudi, *Tanzania* . . . . **55 E4** 10 11S 39 57 E
Sudirman, Pegunungan, *Indonesia* . . . . **37 E9** 4 30S 137 0 E
Sueca, *Spain* **19 C5** 39 12N 0 21W
Suez = El Suweis, *Egypt* . **51 C11** 29 58N 32 31 E
Suez, G. of = Suweis, Khalîg el, *Egypt* . . . . . . **51 C11** 28 40N 33 0 E
Suffield, *Canada* **73 C6** 50 12N 111 10W
Suffolk, *U.S.A.* **76 G7** 36 44N 76 35W
Suffolk □, *U.K.* . . . . **11 E9** 52 16N 1 0 E
Sugar City, *U.S.A.* **80 F3** 38 14N 103 40W
Sugluk = Salluit, *Canada* **69 B12** 62 14N 75 38W
Suhār, *Oman* . . . . **45 E8** 24 20N 56 40 E
Sühbaatar □, *Mongolia* . . **34 B8** 45 30N 114 0 E
Suhl, *Germany* . . . . **16 C6** 50 36N 10 42 E
Sui Xian, *China* . . . . **34 G8** 34 25N 115 2 E
Suide, *China* . . . . **34 F6** 37 30N 110 12 E
Suifenhe, *China* . . . . **35 B16** 44 25N 131 10 E
Suihua, *China* . . . . **33 B7** 46 32N 126 55 E
Suining, *China* . . . . **35 H9** 33 56N 117 58 E
Suiping, *China* . . . . **34 H7** 33 10N 113 59 E
Suir →, *Ireland* **13 D4** 52 16N 7 9W
Suiyang, *China* . . . . **35 B16** 44 30N 130 56 E
Suizhong, *China* . . . . **35 D11** 40 21N 120 20 E
Sujangarh, *India* . . . . **42 F6** 27 42N 74 31 E
Sukabumi, *Indonesia* . . . . **37 G12** 6 56S 106 50 E
Sukadana, *Kalimantan, Indonesia* . . . . **36 E3** 1 10S 110 0 E
Sukadana, *Sumatera, Indonesia* . . . . **36 F3** 5 5S 105 33 E
Sukagawa, *Japan* . . . . **31 F10** 37 17N 140 23 E
Sukaraja, *Indonesia* . . . . . **36 E4** 2 28S 110 25 E
Sukarnapura = Jayapura, *Indonesia* . . . . **37 E10** 2 28S 140 38 E
Sukchŏn, *N. Korea* . . . . . . **35 E13** 39 22N 125 35 E
Sukhona →, *Russia* . . . . . **24 C6** 61 15N 46 39 E
Sukhothai, *Thailand* . . . . . **38 D2** 17 1N 99 49 E
Sukhumi = Sokhumi, *Georgia* . . . . **25 F7** 43 0N 41 0 E
Sukkur, *Pakistan* . . . . **42 F3** 27 42N 68 54 E
Sukkur Barrage, *Pakistan* **42 F3** 27 40N 68 50 E
Sukumo, *Japan* . . . . **31 H6** 32 56N 132 44 E
Sukunka →, *Canada* **72 B4** 55 45N 121 15W
Sula, Kepulauan, *Indonesia* . . . . **37 E7** 1 45S 125 0 E
Sulaco →, *Honduras* **88 C2** 15 2N 87 44W
Sulaiman Range, *Pakistan* **42 D3** 30 30N 69 50 E
Sūlār, *Iran* . . . . **45 D6** 31 53N 51 54 E
Sulawesi □, *Indonesia* . . . **37 E6** 2 0S 120 0 E
Sulawesi Sea = Celebes Sea, *Indonesia* . . . . **37 D6** 3 0N 123 0 E
Sulima, *S. Leone* **50 G2** 6 58N 11 32W
Sulina, *Romania* . . . . **17 F15** 45 10N 29 40 E
Sulitjelma, *Norway* . . . . . **8 C17** 67 9N 16 3 E
Sullana, *Peru* **92 D2** 4 52S 80 39W
Sullivan, *Ill., U.S.A.* **80 F10** 39 36N 88 37W
Sullivan, *Ind., U.S.A.* **76 F2** 39 6N 87 24W
Sullivan, *Mo., U.S.A.* **80 F9** 38 13N 91 10W
Sullivan Bay, *Canada* . . . **72 C3** 50 55N 126 50W
Sulphur, *La., U.S.A.* **81 K8** 30 14N 93 23W
Sulphur, *Okla., U.S.A.* . . . **81 H6** 34 31N 96 58W
Sulphur Pt., *Canada* **72 A6** 60 56N 114 48W
Sulphur Springs, *U.S.A.* . **81 J7** 33 8N 95 36W
Sulphur Springs Draw →, *U.S.A.* **81 J4** 32 12N 101 36W
Sultan, *Canada* **70 C3** 47 36N 82 47W
Sultan, *U.S.A.* **84 C5** 47 52N 121 49W
Sultanpur, *India* . . . . **43 F10** 26 18N 82 4 E
Sultsa, *Russia* . . . . **24 B8** 63 27N 46 2 E
Sulu Arch., *Phil.* . . . . **37 C6** 6 0N 121 0 E
Sulu Sea, *E. Indies* . . . . . . **37 C6** 8 0N 120 0 E
Suluq, *Libya* . . . . **51 B9** 31 44N 20 14 E
Sulzberger Ice Shelf, *Antarctica* . . . . **5 D10** 78 0S 150 0 E
Sumalata, *Indonesia* . . . . **37 D6** 1 0N 122 31 E
Sumampa, *Argentina* **94 B3** 29 25S 63 29W
Sumatera □, *Indonesia* . . **36 D2** 0 40N 100 20 E
Sumatra = Sumatera □, *Indonesia* . . . . **36 D2** 0 40N 100 20 E
Sumatra, *U.S.A.* **82 C10** 46 37N 107 33W
Sumba, *Indonesia* . . . . . . **37 F5** 9 45S 119 35 E
Sumba, Selat, *Indonesia* . **37 F5** 9 0S 118 40 E
Sumbawa, *Indonesia* . . . . **36 F5** 8 26S 117 30 E
Sumbawa Besar, *Indonesia* . . . . **36 F5** 8 30S 117 26 E
Sumbawanga □, *Tanzania* **54 D3** 8 0S 31 30 E
Sumbe, *Angola* . . . . **52 G2** 11 10S 13 48 E
Sumburgh Hd., *U.K.* **12 B7** 59 52N 1 17W
Sumdo, *India* . . . . **43 B8** 35 6N 78 41 E
Sumedang, *Indonesia* . . . . **37 G12** 6 52S 107 55 E
Šumen, *Bulgaria* . . . . **21 C12** 43 18N 26 55 E
Sumenep, *Indonesia* . . . . **37 G15** 7 1S 113 52 E
Sumgait = Sumqayıt, *Azerbaijan* . . . . **25 F8** 40 34N 49 38 E
Summer L., *U.S.A.* **82 E3** 42 50N 120 45W
Summerland, *Canada* **72 D5** 49 32N 119 41W
Summerside, *Canada* **71 C7** 46 24N 63 47W
Summerville, *Ga., U.S.A.* . **77 H3** 34 29N 85 21W
Summerville, *S.C., U.S.A.* **77 J5** 33 1N 80 11W
Summit Lake, *Canada* . . . **72 C4** 54 20N 122 40W
Summit Peak, *U.S.A.* **83 H10** 37 21N 106 42W
Sumner, *Iowa, U.S.A.* **80 D8** 42 51N 92 6W
Sumner, *Wash., U.S.A.* . . **84 C4** 47 12N 122 14W
Sumoto, *Japan* . . . . **31 G7** 34 21N 134 54 E
Šumperk, *Czech.* . . . . **17 D9** 49 59N 17 0 E
Sumqayıt, *Azerbaijan* . . . . **25 F8** 40 34N 49 38 E
Sumter, *U.S.A.* **77 J5** 33 55N 80 21W
Sumy, *Ukraine* . . . . **25 D5** 50 57N 34 50 E
Sun City, *Ariz., U.S.A.* . . . **83 K7** 33 36N 112 17W
Sun City, *Calif., U.S.A.* . . **85 M9** 33 42N 117 11W
Sunagawa, *Japan* . . . . **30 C10** 43 29N 141 55 E
Sunan, *N. Korea* . . . . **35 E13** 39 15N 125 40 E
Sunart, L., *U.K.* **12 E3** 56 42N 5 43W
Sunburst, *U.S.A.* **82 B8** 48 53N 111 55W
Sunbury, *Australia* . . . . . . **63 F3** 37 35S 144 44 E
Sunbury, *U.S.A.* **79 F8** 40 52N 76 48W
Sunchales, *Argentina* . . . **94 C3** 30 58S 61 35W
Suncho Corral, *Argentina* **94 B3** 27 55S 63 27W
Sunchon, *S. Korea* . . . . . **35 G14** 34 52N 127 31 E
Suncook, *U.S.A.* **79 C13** 43 8N 71 27W
Sunda, Selat, *Indonesia* . . **36 F3** 6 20S 105 30 E
Sunda Is., *Indonesia* . . . . **28 K14** 5 0S 105 0 E
Sunda Str. = Sunda, Selat, *Indonesia* . . . . . . **36 F3** 6 20S 105 30 E
Sundance, *U.S.A.* **80 C2** 44 24N 104 23W
Sundarbans, The, *Asia* . . **41 J16** 22 0N 89 0 E
Sundargarh, *India* . . . . . . **41 H14** 22 4N 84 5 E
Sundays = Sondags →, *S. Africa* . . . . **56 E4** 33 44S 25 51 E
Sunderland, *Canada* **78 B5** 44 16N 79 4W
Sunderland, *U.K.* **10 C6** 54 55N 1 23W
Sundre, *Canada* **72 C6** 51 49N 114 38W
Sundridge, *Canada* **70 C4** 45 45N 79 25W
Sundsvall, *Sweden* . . . . . . **9 E17** 62 23N 17 17 E
Sung Hei, *Vietnam* . . . . . . **39 G6** 10 20N 106 2 E
Sungai Kolok, *Thailand* . . **39 J3** 6 2N 101 58 E
Sungai Lembing, *Malaysia* **39 L4** 3 55N 103 3 E
Sungai Patani, *Malaysia* . . **39 K3** 5 37N 100 30 E
Sungaigerong, *Indonesia* . **36 E2** 2 59S 104 52 E
Sungailiat, *Indonesia* . . . . **36 E3** 1 51S 106 8 E
Sungaipakning, *Indonesia* **36 D2** 1 19N 102 0 E
Sungaipenuh, *Indonesia* . . **36 E2** 2 1S 101 20 E
Sungaitiram, *Indonesia* . . . **36 E5** 0 45S 117 8 E
Sungari = Songhua Jiang →, *China* . . . . . **33 B8** 47 45N 132 30 E
Sungguminasa, *Indonesia* **37 F5** 5 17S 119 30 E
Sunghua Chiang = Songhua Jiang →, *China* . . . . **33 B8** 47 45N 132 30 E
Sunndalsøra, *Norway* . . . **9 E13** 62 40N 8 33 E
Sunnyside, *Utah, U.S.A.* . . **82 G8** 39 34N 110 23W
Sunnyside, *Wash., U.S.A.* . **82 C3** 46 20N 120 0W
Sunnyvale, *U.S.A.* **83 H2** 37 23N 122 2W
Sunray, *U.S.A.* **81 G4** 36 1N 101 49W
Suntar, *Russia* . . . . **27 C12** 62 15N 117 30 E
Suomenselkä, *Finland* . . . **8 E21** 62 52N 24 0 E
Suomussalmi, *Finland* . . . **8 D23** 64 54N 29 10 E
Suoyarvi, *Russia* . . . . **24 B5** 62 3N 32 20 E
Supai, *U.S.A.* **83 H7** 36 15N 112 41W
Supaul, *India* . . . . **43 F12** 26 10N 86 40 E
Superior, *Ariz., U.S.A.* . . . **83 K8** 33 18N 111 6W
Superior, *Mont., U.S.A.* . . **82 C6** 47 12N 114 53W
Superior, *Nebr., U.S.A.* . . **80 E5** 40 1N 98 4W
Superior, *Wis., U.S.A.* . . . **80 B8** 46 44N 92 6W
Superior, L., *U.S.A.* **70 C2** 47 0N 87 0W
Suphan Buri, *Thailand* . . . **38 E3** 14 14N 100 10 E
Supiori, *Indonesia* . . . . . . **37 E9** 1 0S 136 0 E
Supung Sk., *China* . . . . . . **35 D13** 40 35N 124 50 E
Sūq Suwayq, *Si. Arabia* . . **44 E3** 24 23N 38 27 E
Suqian, *China* . . . . **35 H10** 33 54N 118 8 E
Sūr, *Lebanon* . . . . **47 B4** 33 19N 35 16 E
Sur, Pt., *U.S.A.* **83 H3** 36 18N 121 54W
Sura →, *Russia* . . . . **24 C8** 56 6N 46 0 E
Surab, *Pakistan* . . . . **42 E2** 28 25N 66 15 E
Surabaja = Surabaya, *Indonesia* . . . . **37 G15** 7 17S 112 45 E
Surabaya, *Indonesia* . . . . **37 G15** 7 17S 112 45 E
Surakarta, *Indonesia* . . . . **37 G14** 7 35S 110 48 E
Surat, *Australia* . . . . **63 D4** 27 10S 149 6 E
Surat, *India* . . . . **40 J8** 21 12N 72 55 E
Surat Thani, *Thailand* . . . **39 H2** 9 6N 99 20 E
Suratgarh, *India* . . . . **42 E5** 29 18N 73 55 E
Sûre = Sauer →, *Germany* . . . . **15 E6** 49 44N 6 31 E
Surendranagar, *India* . . . . **42 H4** 22 45N 71 40 E
Surf, *U.S.A.* **85 L6** 34 41N 120 36W
Surgut, *Russia* . . . . **26 C8** 61 14N 73 20 E
Suriapet, *India* . . . . **40 L11** 17 10N 79 40 E
Surigao, *Phil.* . . . . **37 C7** 9 47N 125 29 E
Surin, *Thailand* . . . . **38 E4** 14 50N 103 34 E
Surin Nua, Ko, *Thailand* . . **39 H1** 9 30N 97 55 E
Surinam ■, *S. Amer.* **93 C7** 4 0N 56 0W
Suriname ■ = Surinam ■, *S. Amer.* **93 C7** 4 0N 56 0W
Suriname →, *Surinam* . . **93 B7** 5 50N 55 15W
Sūrmaq, *Iran* . . . . **45 D7** 31 3N 52 48 E
Surprise L., *Canada* **72 B2** 59 40N 133 15W
Surrey □, *U.K.* **11 F7** 51 15N 0 31W
Surt, *Libya* . . . . **51 B8** 31 11N 16 39 E
Surt, Khalīj, *Libya* . . . . . . **51 B8** 31 40N 18 30 E
Surtsey, *Iceland* **8 E3** 63 20N 20 30W
Suruga-Wan, *Japan* . . . . . **31 G9** 34 45N 138 30 E
Susaki, *Japan* . . . . **31 H6** 33 22N 133 17 E
Sūsangerd, *Iran* . . . . **45 D6** 31 35N 48 6 E
Susanino, *Russia* . . . . **27 D15** 52 50N 140 14 E
Susanville, *U.S.A.* **82 F3** 40 25N 120 39W
Susquehanna →, *U.S.A.* . **79 G8** 39 33N 76 5W
Susquehanna Depot, *U.S.A.* **79 E9** 41 57N 75 36W
Susques, *Argentina* **94 A2** 23 35S 66 25W
Sussex, *Canada* **71 C6** 45 45N 65 37W
Sussex, *U.S.A.* **79 E10** 41 13N 74 37W
Sussex, E. □, *U.K.* . . . . . . **11 G8** 51 0N 0 20 E
Sussex, W. □, *U.K.* **11 G7** 51 0N 0 30W
Sustut →, *Canada* **72 B3** 56 20N 127 30W
Susuman, *Russia* . . . . **27 C15** 62 47N 148 10 E
Susunu, *Indonesia* . . . . . . **37 E8** 3 20S 133 25 E
Susurluk, *Turkey* . . . . **21 E13** 39 54N 28 8 E
Sutherland, *S. Africa* . . . . **56 E3** 32 24S 20 40 E
Sutherland, *U.S.A.* **80 E4** 41 10N 101 8W
Sutherland Falls, *N.Z.* . . . **59 L1** 44 48S 167 46 E
Sutherlin, *U.S.A.* **82 E2** 43 23N 123 19W
Sutlej →, *Pakistan* . . . . . . **42 E4** 29 23N 71 3 E
Sutter, *U.S.A.* **84 F5** 39 10N 121 45W
Sutter Creek, *U.S.A.* **84 G6** 38 24N 120 48W
Sutton, *Canada* **79 A12** 45 6N 72 37W
Sutton, *U.S.A.* **80 E6** 40 36N 97 52W
Sutton →, *Canada* **70 A3** 55 15N 83 45W
Sutton in Ashfield, *U.K.* . . **10 D6** 53 8N 1 16W
Suttor →, *Australia* . . . . . **62 C4** 21 36S 147 2 E
Suttsu, *Japan* . . . . **30 C10** 42 48N 140 14 E
Suva, *Fiji* . . . . **59 D8** 18 6S 178 30 E
Suva Planina, *Serbia, Yug.* **21 C10** 43 10N 22 5 E
Suvorov Is. = Suwarrow Is., *Cook Is.* **65 J11** 15 0S 163 0W
Suwałki, *Poland* . . . . **17 A12** 54 8N 22 59 E
Suwannaphum, *Thailand* . . **38 E4** 15 33N 103 47 E
Suwannee →, *U.S.A.* **77 L4** 29 17N 83 10W
Suwanose-Jima, *Japan* . . . **31 K4** 29 38N 129 43 E
Suwarrow Is., *Cook Is.* . . . **65 J11** 15 0S 163 0W
Suwayq aş Şuqban, *Iraq* . . **44 D5** 31 32N 46 7 E
Suweis, Khalîg el, *Egypt* . **51 C11** 28 40N 33 0 E
Suwŏn, *S. Korea* . . . . **35 F14** 37 17N 127 1 E
Suzdal, *Russia* . . . . **24 C7** 56 29N 40 26 E
Suzhou, *China* . . . . **33 C7** 31 19N 120 38 E
Suzu, *Japan* . . . . **31 F8** 37 25N 137 17 E
Suzu-Misaki, *Japan* . . . . . . **31 F8** 37 31N 137 21 E
Suzuka, *Japan* . . . . **31 G8** 34 55N 136 36 E
Svalbard, *Arctic* . . . . **4 B8** 78 0N 17 0 E
Svappavaara, *Sweden* . . . . **8 C19** 67 40N 21 3 E
Svartisen, *Norway* . . . . **8 C15** 66 40N 13 50 E
Svay Chek, *Cambodia* . . . . **38 F4** 13 48N 102 58 E
Svay Rieng, *Cambodia* . . . **39 G5** 11 5N 105 48 E
Svealand □, *Sweden* . . . . . **9 G16** 59 55N 15 0 E
Sveg, *Sweden* . . . . **9 E16** 62 2N 14 21 E
Svendborg, *Denmark* . . . . **9 J14** 55 4N 10 35 E
Sverdlovsk = Yekaterinburg, *Russia* . **24 C11** 56 50N 60 30 E
Sverdrup Is., *Canada* **4 B3** 79 0N 97 0W
Svetlaya, *Russia* . . . . **30 A9** 46 33N 138 18 E
Svetlogorsk = Svyetlahorsk, *Belarus* . **17 B15** 52 38N 29 46 E
Svetozarevo, *Serbia, Yug.* **21 C9** 44 5N 21 15 E
Svir →, *Russia* . . . . **24 B5** 60 30N 32 48 E
Svishtov, *Bulgaria* . . . . **21 C11** 43 36N 25 23 E
Svislach, *Belarus* . . . . **17 B13** 53 3N 24 2 E
Svobodnyy, *Russia* . . . . **27 D13** 51 20N 128 0 E
Svolvær, *Norway* . . . . **8 B16** 68 15N 14 34 E
Svyetlahorsk, *Belarus* . . . . **17 B15** 52 38N 29 46 E
Swabian Alps = Schwäbische Alb, *Germany* . . . . **16 D5** 48 20N 9 30 E
Swainsboro, *U.S.A.* **77 J4** 32 36N 82 20W
Swakopmund, *Namibia* . . . **56 C1** 22 37S 14 30 E
Swale →, *U.K.* **10 C6** 54 5N 1 20W
Swan Hill, *Australia* . . . . . . **63 F3** 35 20S 143 33 E
Swan Hills, *Canada* **72 C5** 54 42N 115 24W
Swan Is., *W. Indies* **88 C3** 17 22N 83 57W
Swan L., *Canada* **73 C8** 52 30N 100 40W
Swan River, *Canada* **73 C8** 52 10N 101 16W
Swanage, *U.K.* **11 G6** 50 36N 1 58W
Swansea, *Australia* . . . . . . **63 E5** 33 3S 151 35 E
Swansea, *U.K.* **11 F4** 51 37N 3 57W
Swansea □, *U.K.* **11 F3** 51 38N 4 3W
Swar →, *Pakistan* . . . . **43 B5** 34 40N 72 5 E
Swartberge, *S. Africa* . . . . **56 E3** 33 20S 22 0 E
Swartmodder, *S. Africa* . . . **56 D3** 28 1S 20 32 E
Swartruggens, *S. Africa* . . **56 D4** 25 39S 26 42 E
Swastika, *Canada* **70 C3** 48 7N 80 6W
Swatow = Shantou, *China* **33 D6** 23 18N 116 40 E
Swaziland ■, *Africa* . . . . . . **57 D5** 26 30S 31 30 E
Sweden ■, *Europe* . . . . **9 G16** 57 0N 15 0 E
Sweet Home, *U.S.A.* **82 D2** 44 24N 122 44W
Sweetwater, *Nev., U.S.A.* . **84 G7** 38 27N 119 9W
Sweetwater, *Tex., U.S.A.* . **81 J4** 32 28N 100 25W

Sweetwater

Theun

Tarragona, *Spain* . . . . **19 B6** 41 5N 1 17 E
Tarrasa, *Spain* . . . . **19 B7** 41 34N 2 1 E
Tarrytown, *U.S.A.* **79 E11** 41 4N 73 52W
Tarshiha = Me'ona, *Israel* **47 B4** 33 1N 35 15 E
Tarso Emissi, *Chad* . . . . . **51 D8** 21 27N 18 36 E
Tarsus, *Turkey* . . . . **25 G5** 36 58N 34 55 E
Tartagal, *Argentina* **94 A3** 22 30S 63 50W
Tartu, *Estonia* . . . . **9 G22** 58 20N 26 44 E
Ṭarṭūs, *Syria* . . . . **44 C2** 34 55N 35 55 E
Tarumizu, *Japan* . . . . **31 J5** 31 29N 130 42 E
Tarutao, Ko, *Thailand* . . . **39 J2** 6 33N 99 40 E
Tarutung, *Indonesia* . . . . **36 D1** 2 0N 98 54 E
Tasāwah, *Libya* . . . . **51 C7** 26 0N 13 30 E
Taschereau, *Canada* **70 C4** 48 40N 78 40W
Taseko —►, *Canada* **72 C4** 52 8N 123 45W
Tash-Kömür, *Kyrgyzstan* . **26 E8** 41 40N 72 10 E
Tash-Kumyr = Tash-Kömür, *Kyrgyzstan* . . . . **26 E8** 41 40N 72 10 E
Tashauz = Dashhowuz, *Turkmenistan* . . . . **26 E6** 41 49N 59 58 E
Tashi Chho Dzong = Thimphu, *Bhutan* . . . . . **41 F16** 27 31N 89 45 E
Tashkent = Toshkent, *Uzbekistan* . . . . **26 E7** 41 20N 69 10 E
Tashtagol, *Russia* . . . . **26 D9** 52 47N 87 53 E
Tasikmalaya, *Indonesia* . . **37 G13** 7 18S 108 12 E
Tåsjön, *Sweden* . . . . **8 D16** 64 15N 15 40 E
Taskan, *Russia* . . . . **27 C16** 62 59N 150 20 E
Tasman B., *N.Z.* . . . . **59 J4** 40 59S 173 25 E
Tasman Mts., *N.Z.* . . . . . . **59 J4** 41 3S 172 25 E
Tasman Pen., *Australia* . . **62 G4** 43 10S 148 0 E
Tasman Sea, *Pac. Oc.* . . . . **64 L8** 36 0S 160 0 E
Tasmania □, *Australia* . . . **62 G4** 42 0S 146 30 E
Tassili n-Ajjer, *Algeria* . . . **48 D4** 25 47N 8 1 E
Tasu Sd., *Canada* **72 C2** 52 47N 132 2W
Tatabánya, *Hungary* . . . . . **17 E10** 47 32N 18 25 E
Tatar Republic □ = Tatarstan □, *Russia* . . . **24 C9** 55 30N 51 30 E
Tatarbunary, *Ukraine* . . . . **17 F15** 45 50N 29 39 E
Tatarsk, *Russia* . . . . **26 D8** 55 14N 76 0 E
Tatarstan □, *Russia* . . . . . **24 C9** 55 30N 51 30 E
Tateyama, *Japan* . . . . **31 G9** 35 0N 139 50 E
Tathlina L., *Canada* **72 A5** 60 33N 117 39W
Tathra, *Australia* . . . . **63 F4** 36 44S 149 59 E
Tatinnai L., *Canada* **73 A9** 60 55N 97 40W
Tatnam, C., *Canada* **73 B10** 57 16N 91 0W
Tatra = Tatry, *Slovak Rep.* **17 D11** 49 20N 20 0 E
Tatry, *Slovak Rep.* . . . . . . **17 D11** 49 20N 20 0 E
Tatsuno, *Japan* . . . . **31 G7** 34 52N 134 33 E
Tatta, *Pakistan* . . . . **42 G2** 24 42N 67 55 E
Tatuí, *Brazil* **95 A6** 23 25S 47 53W
Tatum, *U.S.A.* **81 J3** 33 16N 103 19W
Tat'ung = Datong, *China* **34 D7** 40 6N 113 18 E
Tatvan, *Turkey* . . . . **25 G7** 38 31N 42 15 E
Taubaté, *Brazil* **95 A6** 23 0S 45 36W
Tauern, *Austria* . . . . **16 E7** 47 15N 12 40 E
Taumarunui, *N.Z.* . . . . **59 H5** 38 53S 175 15 E
Taumaturgo, *Brazil* **92 E4** 8 54S 72 51W
Taung, *S. Africa* . . . . **56 D3** 27 33S 24 47 E
Taungdwingyi, *Burma* . . . **41 J19** 20 1N 95 40 E
Taunggyi, *Burma* . . . . **41 J20** 20 50N 97 0 E
Taungup, *Burma* . . . . **41 K19** 18 51N 94 14 E
Taungup Pass, *Burma* . . . . **41 K19** 18 40N 94 45 E
Taungup Taunggya, *Burma* . . . . **41 K18** 18 20N 93 40 E
Taunsa Barrage, *Pakistan* **42 D4** 30 42N 70 50 E
Taunton, *U.K.* **11 F4** 51 1N 3 5W
Taunton, *U.S.A.* **79 E13** 41 54N 71 6W
Taunus, *Germany* . . . . **16 C5** 50 13N 8 34 E
Taupo, *N.Z.* . . . . **59 H6** 38 41S 176 7 E
Taupo, L., *N.Z.* . . . . **59 H5** 38 46S 175 55 E
Taurage, *Lithuania* . . . . . . **9 J20** 55 14N 22 16 E
Tauranga, *N.Z.* . . . . **59 G6** 37 42S 176 11 E
Tauranga Harb., *N.Z.* . . . . **59 G6** 37 30S 176 5 E
Taurianova, *Italy* . . . . **20 E7** 38 21N 16 1 E
Taurus Mts. = Toros Dağlan, *Turkey* . . . . **25 G5** 37 0N 32 30 E
Tavda, *Russia* . . . . **26 D7** 58 7N 65 8 E
Tavda —►, *Russia* . . . . . . **26 D7** 57 47N 67 18 E
Taveta, *Tanzania* . . . . **54 C4** 3 23S 37 37 E
Taveuni, *Fiji* **59 C9** 16 51S 179 58W
Tavira, *Portugal* **19 D2** 37 8N 7 40W
Tavistock, *Canada* **78 C4** 43 19N 80 50W
Tavistock, *U.K.* **11 G3** 50 33N 4 9W
Tavoy, *Burma* . . . . **38 E2** 14 2N 98 12 E
Taw —►, *U.K.* **11 F3** 51 4N 4 4W
Tawas City, *U.S.A.* **76 C4** 44 16N 83 31W
Tawau, *Malaysia* . . . . **36 D5** 4 20N 117 55 E
Tawitawi, *Phil.* . . . . **37 B6** 5 10N 120 0 E
Taxila, *Pakistan* . . . . **42 C5** 33 42N 72 52 E
Tay —►, *U.K.* **12 E5** 56 37N 3 38W
Tay, Firth of, *U.K.* **12 E5** 56 25N 3 8W
Tay, L., *Australia* . . . . **61 F3** 32 55S 120 48 E
Tay, L., *U.K.* **12 E4** 56 32N 4 8W
Tay Ninh, *Vietnam* . . . . . . **39 G6** 11 20N 106 5 E
Tayabamba, *Peru* **92 E3** 8 15S 77 16W
Taylakova, *Russia* . . . . . . **26 D8** 59 13N 74 0 E
Taylakovy = Taylakova, *Russia* . . . . **26 D8** 59 13N 74 0 E
Taylor, *Canada* **72 B4** 56 13N 120 40W
Taylor, *Nebr., U.S.A.* **80 E5** 41 46N 99 23W
Taylor, *Pa., U.S.A.* **79 E9** 41 23N 75 43W
Taylor, *Tex., U.S.A.* **81 K6** 30 34N 97 25W
Taylor, Mt., *U.S.A.* **83 J10** 35 14N 107 37W
Taylorville, *U.S.A.* **80 F10** 39 33N 89 18W
Taymā, *Si. Arabia* . . . . . . **44 E3** 27 35N 38 45 E
Taymyr, Oz., *Russia* . . . . . **27 B11** 74 20N 102 0 E
Taymyr, Poluostrov, *Russia* . . . . **27 B11** 75 0N 100 0 E
Tayport, *U.K.* **12 E6** 56 27N 2 52W
Tayshet, *Russia* . . . . **27 D10** 55 58N 98 1 E
Taytay, *Phil.* . . . . **37 B5** 10 45N 119 30 E
Taz —►, *Russia* . . . . **26 C8** 67 32N 78 40 E
Taza, *Morocco* **50 B4** 34 16N 4 6W
Tāzah Khurmātū, *Iraq* . . . **44 C5** 35 18N 44 20 E
Tazawa-Ko, *Japan* . . . . . . **30 E10** 39 43N 140 40 E
Tazin L., *Canada* **73 B7** 59 44N 108 42W
Tazovskiy, *Russia* . . . . **26 C8** 67 30N 78 44 E
Tbilisi, *Georgia* . . . . **25 F7** 41 43N 44 50 E
Tchad = Chad ■, *Africa* . **51 E8** 15 0N 17 15 E
Tchad, L., *Chad* . . . . **51 F7** 13 30N 14 30 E
Tch'eng-tou = Chengdu, *China* . . . . **32 C5** 30 38N 104 2 E
Tchentlo L., *Canada* **72 B4** 55 15N 125 0W
Tchibanga, *Gabon* . . . . . . **52 E2** 2 45S 11 0 E
Tch'ong-k'ing = Chongqing, *China* . . . . **32 D5** 29 35N 106 25 E
Tczew, *Poland* . . . . **17 A10** 54 8N 18 50 E
Te Anau, L., *N.Z.* . . . . **59 L1** 45 15S 167 45 E
Te Aroha, *N.Z.* . . . . **59 G5** 37 32S 175 44 E
Te Awamutu, *N.Z.* . . . . . . **59 H5** 38 1S 175 20 E
Te Kuiti, *N.Z.* . . . . **59 H5** 38 20S 175 11 E
Te Puke, *N.Z.* . . . . **59 G6** 37 46S 176 22 E
Te Waewae B., *N.Z.* . . . . . **59 M1** 46 13S 167 33 E
Tea Tree, *Australia* . . . . . **62 C1** 22 5S 133 22 E
Teague, *U.S.A.* **81 K6** 31 38N 96 17W
Teapa, *Mexico* **87 D6** 18 35N 92 56W
Tebakang, *Malaysia* . . . . . **36 D4** 1 6N 110 30 E
Tébessa, *Algeria* . . . . **50 A6** 35 22N 8 8 E
Tebicuary —►, *Paraguay* **94 B4** 26 36S 58 16W
Tebingtinggi, *Indonesia* . . **36 D1** 3 20N 99 9 E
Tecate, *Mexico* **85 N10** 32 34N 116 38W
Tecomán, *Mexico* **86 D4** 18 55N 103 53W
Tecopa, *U.S.A.* **85 K10** 35 51N 116 13W
Tecoripa, *Mexico* **86 B3** 28 37N 109 57W
Tecuala, *Mexico* **86 C3** 22 23N 105 27W
Tecuci, *Romania* . . . . **17 F14** 45 51N 27 27 E
Tecumseh, *U.S.A.* **76 D4** 42 0N 83 57W
Tedzhen = Tejen, *Turkmenistan* . . . . **26 F7** 37 23N 60 31 E
Tees —►, *U.K.* **10 C6** 54 37N 1 10W
Teesside, *U.K.* **10 C6** 54 36N 1 15W
Teeswater, *Canada* **78 C3** 43 59N 81 17W
Tefé, *Brazil* **92 D6** 3 25S 64 50W
Tegal, *Indonesia* . . . . **37 G13** 6 52S 109 8 E
Tegelen, *Neths.* . . . . **15 C6** 51 20N 6 9 E
Teghra, *India* . . . . **43 G11** 25 30N 85 34 E
Tegid, L. = Bala, L., *U.K.* . **10 E4** 52 53N 3 37W
Tegina, *Nigeria* . . . . **50 F6** 10 5N 6 11 E
Tegucigalpa, *Honduras* . . **88 D2** 14 5N 87 14W
Tehachapi, *U.S.A.* **85 K8** 35 8N 118 27W
Tehachapi Mts., *U.S.A.* . . **85 L8** 35 0N 118 30W
Tehrān, *Iran* . . . . **45 C6** 35 44N 51 30 E
Tehuacán, *Mexico* **87 D5** 18 30N 97 30W
Tehuantepec, *Mexico* . . . **87 D5** 16 21N 95 13W
Tehuantepec, G. de, *Mexico* **87 D5** 15 50N 95 12W
Tehuantepec, Istmo de, *Mexico* **87 D6** 17 0N 94 30W
Teide, *Canary Is.* **22 F3** 28 15N 16 38W
Teifi —►, *U.K.* **11 E3** 52 5N 4 41W
Teign —►, *U.K.* **11 G4** 50 32N 3 32W
Teignmouth, *U.K.* **11 G4** 50 33N 3 31W
Tejen, *Turkmenistan* . . . . **26 F7** 37 23N 60 31 E
Tejo —►, *Europe* **19 C1** 38 40N 9 24W
Tejon Pass, *U.S.A.* **85 L8** 34 49N 118 53W
Tekamah, *U.S.A.* **80 E6** 41 47N 96 13W
Tekapo, L., *N.Z.* . . . . **59 K3** 43 53S 170 33 E
Tekax, *Mexico* **87 C7** 20 11N 89 18W
Tekeli, *Kazakstan* . . . . **26 E8** 44 50N 79 0 E
Tekirdağ, *Turkey* . . . . **21 D12** 40 58N 27 30 E
Tekkali, *India* . . . . **41 K14** 18 37N 84 15 E
Tekoa, *U.S.A.* **82 C5** 47 14N 117 4W
Tel Aviv-Yafo, *Israel* . . . . . **47 C3** 32 4N 34 48 E
Tel Lakhish, *Israel* . . . . . . **47 D3** 31 34N 34 51 E
Tel Megiddo, *Israel* . . . . . **47 C4** 32 35N 35 11 E
Tela, *Honduras* **88 C2** 15 40N 87 28W
Telanaipura = Jambi, *Indonesia* . . . . **36 E2** 1 38S 103 30 E
Telavi, *Georgia* . . . . **25 F8** 42 0N 45 30 E
Telde, *Canary Is.* **22 G4** 27 59N 15 25W
Telegraph Creek, *Canada* **72 B2** 58 0N 131 10W
Telekhany = Tsyelyakhany, *Belarus* . **17 B13** 52 30N 25 46 E
Telemark, *Norway* . . . . . . **9 G12** 59 15N 7 40 E
Telén, *Argentina* **94 D2** 36 15S 65 31W
Teleng, *Iran* . . . . **45 E9** 25 47N 61 3 E
Teles Pires —►, *Brazil* . . . **92 E7** 7 21S 58 3W
Telescope Pk., *U.S.A.* . . . **85 J9** 36 10N 117 5W
Telford, *U.K.* **10 E5** 52 40N 2 27W
Télimélé, *Guinea* **50 F2** 10 54N 13 2W
Telkwa, *Canada* **72 C3** 54 41N 127 5W
Tell City, *U.S.A.* **76 G2** 37 57N 86 46W
Tellicherry, *India* . . . . **40 P9** 11 45N 75 30 E
Telluride, *U.S.A.* **83 H10** 37 56N 107 49W
Teloloapán, *Mexico* **87 D5** 18 21N 99 51W
Telpos Iz, *Russia* . . . . **24 B10** 63 16N 59 13 E
Telsen, *Argentina* **96 E3** 42 30S 66 50W
Telšiai, *Lithuania* . . . . **9 H20** 55 59N 22 14 E
Teluk Anson, *Malaysia* . . . **39 K3** 4 3N 101 0 E
Teluk Betung = Tanjungkarang Telukbetung, *Indonesia* **36 F3** 5 20S 105 10 E
Teluk Intan = Teluk Anson, *Malaysia* . . . . . **39 K3** 4 3N 101 0 E
Telukbutun, *Indonesia* . . . **39 K7** 4 13N 108 12 E
Telukdalem, *Indonesia* . . . **36 D1** 0 33N 97 50 E
Tema, *Ghana* . . . . **50 G5** 5 41N 0 0 E
Temanggung, *Indonesia* . **37 G14** 7 18S 110 10 E
Temapache, *Mexico* **87 C5** 21 4N 97 38W
Temax, *Mexico* **87 C7** 21 10N 88 50W
Temba, *S. Africa* . . . . **57 D4** 25 20S 28 17 E
Tembe, *Zaïre* . . . . **54 C2** 0 16S 28 14 E
Temblor Range, *U.S.A.* . . **85 K7** 35 20N 119 50W
Teme —►, *U.K.* **11 E5** 52 11N 2 13W
Temecula, *U.S.A.* **85 M9** 33 30N 117 9W
Temerloh, *Malaysia* . . . . . **39 L4** 3 27N 102 25 E
Temir, *Kazakstan* . . . . **26 E6** 49 1N 57 14 E
Temirtau, *Kazakstan* . . . . **26 D8** 50 5N 72 56 E
Temirtau, *Russia* . . . . **26 D9** 53 10N 87 30 E
Témiscaming, *Canada* . . . **70 C4** 46 44N 79 5W
Temma, *Australia* . . . . **62 G3** 41 12S 144 48 E
Temora, *Australia* . . . . . . **63 E4** 34 30S 147 30 E
Temosachic, *Mexico* **86 B3** 28 58N 107 50W
Tempe, *U.S.A.* **83 K8** 33 25N 111 56W
Tempe Downs, *Australia* . **60 D5** 24 22S 132 24 E
Tempiute, *U.S.A.* **84 H11** 37 39N 115 38W
Temple, *U.S.A.* **81 K6** 31 6N 97 21W
Temple B., *Australia* . . . . **62 A3** 12 15S 143 3 E
Templemore, *Ireland* **13 D4** 52 47N 7 51W
Templeton, *U.S.A.* **84 K6** 35 33N 120 42W
Templeton —►, *Australia* **62 C2** 21 0S 138 40 E
Tempoal, *Mexico* **87 C5** 21 31N 98 23W
Temuco, *Chile* **96 D2** 38 45S 72 40W
Temuka, *N.Z.* . . . . **59 L3** 44 14S 171 17 E
Tenabo, *Mexico* **87 C6** 20 2N 90 12W
Tenaha, *U.S.A.* **81 K7** 31 57N 94 15W
Tenali, *India* . . . . **40 L12** 16 15N 80 35 E
Tenancingo, *Mexico* **87 D5** 19 0N 99 33W
Tenango, *Mexico* **87 D5** 19 7N 99 33W
Tenasserim, *Burma* . . . . . **39 F2** 12 6N 99 3 E
Tenasserim □, *Burma* . . . **38 F2** 14 0N 98 30 E
Tenby, *U.K.* **11 F3** 51 40N 4 42W
Tenda, Col di, *France* . . . **20 B2** 44 7N 7 36 E
Tendaho, *Ethiopia* . . . . . . **46 E3** 11 48N 40 54 E
Tenerife, *Canary Is.* **22 F3** 28 15N 16 35W
Tenerife, Pico, *Canary Is.* **22 G1** 27 43N 18 1W
Teng Xian, *China* . . . . **35 G9** 35 5N 117 10 E
Tengah □, *Indonesia* . . . . **37 E6** 2 0S 122 0 E
Tengah Kepulauan, *Indonesia* . . . . **36 F5** 7 5S 118 15 E
Tengchong, *China* . . . . **32 D4** 25 0N 98 28 E
Tengchowfu = Penglai, *China* . . . . **35 F11** 37 48N 120 42 E
Tenggara □, *Indonesia* . . **37 E6** 3 0S 122 0 E
Tenggarong, *Indonesia* . . **36 E5** 0 24S 116 58 E
Tenggol, P., *Malaysia* . . . **39 K4** 4 48N 103 41 E
Tengiz, Ozero, *Kazakstan* **26 D7** 50 30N 69 0 E
Tenino, *U.S.A.* **84 D4** 46 51N 122 51W
Tenkasi, *India* . . . . **40 Q10** 8 55N 77 20 E
Tenke, *Shaba, Zaïre* . . . . . **55 E2** 11 22S 26 40 E
Tenke, *Shaba, Zaïre* . . . . . **55 E2** 10 32S 26 7 E
Tenkodogo, *Burkina Faso* **50 F4** 11 54N 0 19W
Tennant Creek, *Australia* . **62 B1** 19 30S 134 15 E
Tennessee □, *U.S.A.* **77 H2** 36 0N 86 30W
Tennessee —►, *U.S.A.* . . . **76 G1** 37 4N 88 34W
Tennille, *U.S.A.* **77 J4** 32 56N 82 48W
Teno, Pta. de, *Canary Is.* . **22 F3** 28 21N 16 55W
Tenom, *Malaysia* . . . . **36 C5** 5 4N 115 57 E
Tenosique, *Mexico* **87 D6** 17 30N 91 24W
Tenryū-Gawa —►, *Japan* **31 G8** 35 39N 137 48 E
Tent L., *Canada* **73 A7** 62 25N 107 54W
Tenterfield, *Australia* . . . . **63 D5** 29 0S 152 0 E
Teófilo Otoni, *Brazil* **93 G10** 17 50S 41 30W
Teotihuacán, *Mexico* **87 D5** 19 44N 98 50W
Tepa, *Indonesia* . . . . **37 F7** 7 52S 129 31 E
Tepalcatepec —►, *Mexico* **86 D4** 18 35N 101 59W
Tepehuanes, *Mexico* **86 B3** 25 21N 105 44W
Tepetongo, *Mexico* **86 C4** 22 28N 103 9W
Tepic, *Mexico* **86 C4** 21 30N 104 54W
Teplice, *Czech.* . . . . **16 C7** 50 40N 13 48 E
Tepoca, C., *Mexico* **86 A2** 30 20N 112 25W
Tequila, *Mexico* **86 C4** 20 54N 103 47W
Ter —►, *Spain* . . . . **19 A7** 42 2N 3 12 E
Ter Apel, *Neths.* . . . . **15 B7** 52 53N 7 5 E
Téra, *Niger* . . . . **50 F5** 14 0N 0 45 E
Teraina, *Kiribati* **65 G11** 4 43N 160 25W
Téramo, *Italy* . . . . **20 C5** 42 39N 13 42 E
Terang, *Australia* . . . . **63 F3** 38 15S 142 55 E
Tercero —►, *Argentina* . . **94 C3** 32 58S 61 47W
Terebovlya, *Ukraine* . . . . **17 D13** 49 18N 25 44 E
Terek —►, *Russia* . . . . **25 F8** 44 0N 47 30 E
Teresina, *Brazil* **93 E10** 5 9S 42 45W
Terewah, L., *Australia* . . . **63 D4** 29 52S 147 35 E
Terhazza, *Mali* **50 D3** 23 38N 5 22W
Teridgerie Cr. —►, *Australia* . . . . **63 E4** 30 25S 148 50 E
Termez = Termiz, *Uzbekistan* . . . . **26 F7** 37 15N 67 15 E
Términi Imerese, *Italy* . . . **20 F5** 37 59N 13 42 E
Términos, L. de, *Mexico* . **87 D6** 18 35N 91 30W
Termiz, *Uzbekistan* . . . . . **26 F7** 37 15N 67 15 E
Térmoli, *Italy* . . . . **20 C6** 42 0N 15 0 E
Ternate, *Indonesia* . . . . . . **37 D7** 0 45N 127 25 E
Terneuzen, *Neths.* . . . . . . **15 C3** 51 20N 3 50 E
Terney, *Russia* . . . . **27 E14** 45 3N 136 37 E
Terni, *Italy* . . . . **20 C5** 42 34N 12 37 E
Ternopil, *Ukraine* . . . . **17 D13** 49 30N 25 40 E
Ternopol = Ternopil, *Ukraine* . . . . **17 D13** 49 30N 25 40 E
Terowie, *N.S.W., Australia* **63 E4** 32 27S 147 52 E
Terowie, *S. Austral., Australia* . . . . **63 E2** 33 8S 138 55 E
Terra Bella, *U.S.A.* **85 K7** 35 58N 119 3W
Terrace, *Canada* **72 C3** 54 30N 128 35W
Terrace Bay, *Canada* **70 C2** 48 47N 87 5W
Terracina, *Italy* . . . . **20 D5** 41 17N 13 15 E
Terralba, *Italy* . . . . **20 E3** 39 43N 8 39 E
Terranova = Ólbia, *Italy* . **20 D3** 40 55N 9 31 E
Terrassa = Tarrasa, *Spain* **19 B7** 41 34N 2 1 E
Terre Haute, *U.S.A.* **76 F2** 39 28N 87 25W
Terrebonne B., *U.S.A.* . . . **81 L9** 29 5N 90 35W
Terrell, *U.S.A.* **81 J6** 32 44N 96 17W
Terrenceville, *Canada* . . . **71 C9** 47 40N 54 44W
Terrick Terrick, *Australia* . **62 C4** 24 44S 145 5 E
Terry, *U.S.A.* **80 B2** 46 47N 105 19W
Terschelling, *Neths.* . . . . . **15 A5** 53 25N 5 20 E
Teruel, *Spain* **19 B5** 40 22N 1 8W
Tervola, *Finland* . . . . **8 C21** 66 6N 24 49 E
Teryaweyna L., *Australia* . **63 E3** 32 18S 143 22 E
Teshio, *Japan* . . . . **30 B10** 44 53N 141 44 E
Teshio-Gawa —►, *Japan* . **30 B10** 44 53N 141 45 E
Tesiyn Gol —►, *Mongolia* **32 A4** 50 40N 93 20 E
Teslin, *Canada* **72 A2** 60 10N 132 43W
Teslin —►, *Canada* **72 A2** 61 34N 134 35W
Teslin L., *Canada* **72 A2** 60 15N 132 57W
Tessalit, *Mali* . . . . **50 D5** 20 12N 1 0 E
Tessaoua, *Niger* . . . . **50 F6** 13 47N 7 56 E
Test —►, *U.K.* **11 F6** 50 56N 1 29W
Tetachuck L., *Canada* **72 C3** 53 18N 125 55W
Tetas, Pta., *Chile* **94 A1** 23 31S 70 38W
Tete, *Mozam.* . . . . **55 F3** 16 13S 33 33 E
Tete □, *Mozam.* . . . . **55 F3** 15 15S 32 40 E
Teterev —►, *Ukraine* . . . . **17 C16** 51 1N 30 5 E
Teteven, *Bulgaria* . . . . **21 C11** 42 58N 24 17 E
Tethul —►, *Canada* **72 A6** 60 35N 112 12W
Tetiyev, *Ukraine* . . . . **17 D15** 49 22N 29 38 E
Teton —►, *U.S.A.* **82 C8** 47 56N 110 31W
Tétouan, *Morocco* **50 A3** 35 35N 5 21W
Tetovo, *Macedonia* . . . . . **21 C9** 42 1N 21 2 E
Tetyukhe Pristan, *Russia* . **30 B7** 44 22N 135 48 E
Teuco —►, *Argentina* **94 B3** 25 35S 60 11W
Teulon, *Canada* **73 C9** 50 23N 97 16W
Teun, *Indonesia* . . . . **37 F7** 6 59S 129 8 E
Teutoburger Wald, *Germany* . . . . **16 B5** 52 5N 8 22 E
Tévere —►, *Italy* . . . . **20 D5** 41 44N 12 14 E
Teverya, *Israel* . . . . **47 C4** 32 47N 35 32 E
Teviot —►, *U.K.* **12 F6** 55 29N 2 38W
Tewantin, *Australia* . . . . . **63 D5** 26 27S 153 3 E
Tewkesbury, *U.K.* **11 F5** 51 59N 2 9W
Texada I., *Canada* **72 D4** 49 40N 124 25W
Texarkana, *Ark., U.S.A.* . . **81 J8** 33 26N 94 2W
Texarkana, *Tex., U.S.A.* . . **81 J7** 33 26N 94 3W
Texas, *Australia* . . . . **63 D5** 28 49S 151 9 E
Texas □, *U.S.A.* **81 K5** 31 40N 98 30W
Texas City, *U.S.A.* **81 L7** 29 24N 94 54W
Texel, *Neths.* . . . . **15 A4** 53 5N 4 50 E
Texhoma, *U.S.A.* **81 G4** 36 30N 101 47W
Texline, *U.S.A.* **81 G3** 36 23N 103 2W
Texoma, L., *U.S.A.* **81 J6** 33 50N 96 34W
Tezin, *Afghan.* . . . . **42 B3** 34 24N 69 30 E
Teziutlán, *Mexico* **87 D5** 19 50N 97 22W
Tezpur, *India* . . . . **41 F18** 26 40N 92 45 E
Tezzeron L., *Canada* **72 C4** 54 43N 124 30W
Tha-anne —►, *Canada* . . **73 A10** 60 31N 94 37W
Tha Deua, *Laos* . . . . **38 D4** 17 57N 102 53 E
Tha Deua, *Laos* . . . . **38 C3** 19 26N 101 50 E
Tha Pla, *Thailand* . . . . **38 D3** 17 48N 100 32 E
Tha Rua, *Thailand* . . . . . . **38 E3** 14 34N 100 44 E
Tha Sala, *Thailand* . . . . . . **39 H2** 8 40N 99 56 E
Tha Song Yang, *Thailand* **38 D1** 17 34N 97 55 E
Thaba Putsoa, *Lesotho* . . **57 D4** 29 45S 28 0 E
Thabana Ntlenyana, *Lesotho* . . . . **57 D4** 29 30S 29 16 E
Thabazimbi, *S. Africa* . . . **57 C4** 24 40S 27 21 E
Thai Binh, *Vietnam* . . . . . **38 B6** 20 35N 106 1 E
Thai Hoa, *Vietnam* . . . . . . **38 C5** 19 20N 105 20 E
Thai Muang, *Thailand* . . . **39 H2** 8 24N 98 16 E
Thai Nguyen, *Vietnam* . . . **38 B5** 21 35N 105 55 E
Thailand ■, *Asia* . . . . **38 E4** 16 0N 102 0 E
Thailand, G. of, *Asia* . . . . **39 G3** 11 30N 101 0 E
Thakhek, *Laos* . . . . **38 D5** 17 25N 104 45 E
Thal, *Pakistan* . . . . **42 C4** 33 28N 70 33 E
Thal Desert, *Pakistan* . . . **42 D4** 31 10N 71 30 E
Thala La, *Burma* . . . . **41 E20** 28 25N 97 23 E
Thalabarivat, *Cambodia* . . **38 F5** 13 33N 105 57 E
Thallon, *Australia* . . . . **63 D4** 28 39S 148 49 E
Thame —►, *U.K.* **11 F6** 51 39N 1 9W
Thames, *N.Z.* . . . . **59 G5** 37 7S 175 34 E
Thames —►, *Canada* **70 D3** 42 20N 82 25W
Thames —►, *U.K.* . . . . **11 F8** 51 29N 0 34 E
Thames —►, *U.S.A.* **79 E12** 41 18N 72 5W
Thamesdown □, *U.K.* **11 F6** 51 33N 1 47W
Thamesford, *Canada* **78 C3** 43 4N 81 0W
Thamesville, *Canada* **78 D3** 42 33N 81 59W
Than Uyen, *Vietnam* . . . . **38 B4** 22 0N 103 54 E
Thane, *India* . . . . **40 K8** 19 12N 72 59 E
Thanesar, *India* . . . . **42 D7** 30 1N 76 52 E
Thanet, I. of, *U.K.* . . . . . . **11 F9** 51 21N 1 20 E
Thangoo, *Australia* . . . . . . **60 C3** 18 10S 122 22 E
Thangool, *Australia* . . . . . **62 C5** 24 38S 150 42 E
Thanh Hoa, *Vietnam* . . . . . **38 C5** 19 48N 105 46 E
Thanh Hung, *Vietnam* . . . . **39 H5** 9 55N 105 43 E
Thanh Pho Ho Chi Minh = Phanh Bho Ho Chi Minh, *Vietnam* . . . . **39 G6** 10 58N 106 40 E
Thanh Thuy, *Vietnam* . . . **38 A5** 22 55N 104 51 E
Thanjavur, *India* . . . . **40 P11** 10 48N 79 12 E
Thap Sakae, *Thailand* . . . **39 G2** 11 30N 99 37 E
Thap Than, *Thailand* . . . . **38 E2** 15 27N 99 54 E
Thar Desert, *India* . . . . . . **42 F4** 28 0N 72 0 E
Tharad, *India* . . . . **42 G4** 24 30N 71 44 E
Thargomindah, *Australia* **63 D3** 27 58S 143 46 E
Tharrawaddy, *Burma* . . . . **41 L19** 17 38N 95 48 E
Tharthār, Mileh, *Iraq* . . . . **44 C4** 34 0N 43 15 E
Tharthār, W. ath —►, *Iraq* **44 C4** 33 59N 43 12 E
Thásos, *Greece* . . . . **21 D11** 40 40N 24 40 E
That Khe, *Vietnam* . . . . . . **38 A6** 22 16N 106 28 E
Thatcher, *Ariz., U.S.A.* . . . **83 K9** 32 51N 109 46W
Thatcher, *Colo., U.S.A.* . . . **81 G2** 37 33N 104 7W
Thaton, *Burma* . . . . **41 L20** 16 55N 97 22 E
Thaungdut, *Burma* . . . . . . **41 G19** 24 30N 94 40 E
Thayer, *U.S.A.* **81 G9** 36 31N 91 33W
Thayetmyo, *Burma* . . . . . . **41 K19** 19 20N 95 10 E
Thazi, *Burma* . . . . **41 J20** 21 0N 96 5 E
The Alberga —►, *Australia* **63 D2** 27 6S 135 33 E
The Bight, *Bahamas* **89 B4** 24 19N 75 24W
The Coorong, *Australia* . . . **63 F2** 35 50S 139 20 E
The Dalles, *U.S.A.* **82 D3** 45 36N 121 10W
The English Company's Is., *Australia* . . . . **62 A2** 11 50S 136 32 E
The Frome —►, *Australia* . **63 D2** 29 8S 137 54 E
The Grampians, *Australia* **63 F3** 37 0S 142 20 E
The Great Divide = Great Dividing Ra., *Australia* . **62 C4** 23 0S 146 0 E
The Hague = 's-Gravenhage, *Neths.* . . . **15 B4** 52 7N 4 17 E
The Hamilton —►, *Australia* . . . . **63 D2** 26 40S 135 19 E
The Macumba —►, *Australia* . . . . **63 D2** 27 52S 137 12 E
The Neales —►, *Australia* **63 D2** 28 8S 136 47 E
The Officer —►, *Australia* **61 E5** 27 46S 132 30 E
The Pas, *Canada* **73 C8** 53 45N 101 15W
The Range, *Zimbabwe* . . . **55 F3** 19 2S 31 2 E
The Rock, *Australia* . . . . . . **63 F4** 35 15S 147 2 E
The Salt L., *Australia* . . . . **63 E3** 30 6S 142 8 E
The Stevenson —►, *Australia* . . . . **63 D2** 27 6S 135 33 E
The Warburton —►, *Australia* . . . . **63 D2** 28 4S 137 28 E
Thebes = Thívai, *Greece* . **21 E10** 38 19N 23 19 E
Thedford, *Canada* **78 C3** 43 9N 81 51W
Thedford, *U.S.A.* **80 E4** 41 59N 100 35W
Theebine, *Australia* . . . . . **63 D5** 25 57S 152 34 E
Thekulthili L., *Canada* . . . **73 A7** 61 3N 110 0W
Thelon —►, *Canada* **73 A8** 62 35N 104 3W
Theodore, *Australia* . . . . . **62 C5** 24 55S 150 3 E
Thepha, *Thailand* . . . . **39 J3** 6 52N 100 58 E
Theresa, *U.S.A.* **79 B9** 44 13N 75 48W
Thermaïkós Kólpos, *Greece* . . . . **21 D10** 40 15N 22 45 E
Thermopolis, *U.S.A.* **82 E9** 43 39N 108 13W
Thermopylae P., *Greece* . . **21 E10** 38 48N 22 35 E
Thessalon, *Canada* **70 C3** 46 20N 83 30W
Thessaloniki, *Greece* . . . . **21 D10** 40 38N 22 58 E
Thessaloniki, Gulf of = Thermaïkós Kólpos, *Greece* . . . . **21 D10** 40 15N 22 45 E
Thetford, *U.K.* . . . . **11 E8** 52 25N 0 45 E
Thetford Mines, *Canada* . **71 C5** 46 8N 71 18W
Theun —►, *Laos* . . . . **38 C5** 18 19N 104 0 E

Turabah

W

Westend

Westend, *U.S.A.* **85 K9** 35 42N 117 24W
Westerland, *Germany* **9 J13** 54 54N 8 17 E
Western □, *Kenya* **54 B3** 0 30N 34 30 E
Western □, *Uganda* **54 B3** 1 45N 31 30 E
Western □, *Zambia* **55 F1** 15 15S 24 30 E
Western Australia □, *Australia* **61 E2** 25 0S 118 0 E
Western Cape □, *S. Africa* **56 E3** 34 0S 20 0 E
Western Dvina = Daugava —►, *Latvia* **9 H21** 57 4N 24 3 E
Western Ghats, *India* **40 N9** 14 0N 75 0 E
Western Isles □, *U.K.* **12 D1** 57 30N 7 10W
Western Sahara ■, *Africa* **50 D2** 25 0N 13 0W
Western Samoa ■, *Pac. Oc.* **59 A13** 14 0S 172 0W
Westernport, *U.S.A.* **76 F6** 39 29N 79 3W
Westerschelde —►, *Neths.* **15 C3** 51 25N 3 25 E
Westerwald, *Germany* **16 C4** 50 38N 7 56 E
Westfield, *Mass., U.S.A.* **79 D12** 42 7N 72 45W
Westfield, *N.Y., U.S.A.* **78 D5** 42 20N 79 35W
Westfield, *Pa., U.S.A.* **78 E7** 41 55N 77 32W
Westhope, *U.S.A.* **80 A4** 48 55N 101 1W
Westland Bight, *N.Z.* **59 K3** 42 55S 170 5 E
Westlock, *Canada* **72 C6** 54 9N 113 55W
Westmeath □, *Ireland* **13 C4** 53 33N 7 34W
Westminster, *U.S.A.* **76 F7** 39 34N 76 59W
Westmorland, *U.S.A.* **83 K6** 33 2N 115 37W
Weston, *Malaysia* **36 C5** 5 10N 115 35 E
Weston, *Oreg., U.S.A.* **82 D4** 45 49N 118 26W
Weston, *W. Va., U.S.A.* **76 F5** 39 2N 80 28W
Weston I., *Canada* **70 B4** 52 33N 79 36W
Weston-super-Mare, *U.K.* **11 F5** 51 21N 2 58W
Westport, *Canada* **79 B8** 44 40N 76 25W
Westport, *Ireland* **13 C2** 53 48N 9 31W
Westport, *N.Z.* **59 J3** 41 46S 171 37 E
Westport, *Oreg., U.S.A.* **84 D3** 46 8N 123 23W
Westport, *Wash., U.S.A.* **82 C1** 46 53N 124 6W
Westray, *Canada* **73 C8** 53 36N 101 24W
Westray, *U.K.* **12 B6** 59 18N 3 0W
Westree, *Canada* **70 C3** 47 26N 81 34W
Westville, *Calif., U.S.A.* **84 F6** 39 8N 120 42W
Westville, *Ill., U.S.A.* **76 E2** 40 2N 87 38W
Westville, *Okla., U.S.A.* **81 G7** 35 58N 94 40W
Westwood, *U.S.A.* **82 F3** 40 18N 121 0W
Wetar, *Indonesia* **37 F7** 7 30S 126 30 E
Wetaskiwin, *Canada* **72 C6** 52 55N 113 24W
Wethersfield, *U.S.A.* **79 E12** 41 42N 72 40W
Wetteren, *Belgium* **15 D3** 51 0N 3 52 E
Wetzlar, *Germany* **16 C5** 50 32N 8 31 E
Wewoka, *U.S.A.* **81 H6** 35 9N 96 30W
Wexford, *Ireland* **13 D5** 52 20N 6 28W
Wexford □, *Ireland* **13 D5** 52 20N 6 25W
Wexford Harbour, *Ireland* **13 D5** 52 20N 6 25W
Weyburn, *Canada* **73 D8** 49 40N 103 50W
Weyburn L., *Canada* **72 A5** 63 0N 117 59W
Weymouth, *Canada* **71 D6** 44 30N 66 1W
Weymouth, *U.K.* **11 G5** 50 37N 2 28W
Weymouth, *U.S.A.* **79 D14** 42 13N 70 58W
Weymouth, C., *Australia* **62 A3** 12 37S 143 27 E
Wha Ti, *Canada* **68 B8** 63 8N 117 16W
Whakatane, *N.Z.* **59 G6** 37 57S 177 1 E
Whale —►, *Canada* **71 A6** 58 15N 67 40W
Whale Cove, *Canada* **73 A10** 62 11N 92 36W
Whales, B. of, *Antarctica* **5 D12** 78 0S 165 0W
Whalsay, *U.K.* **12 A7** 60 22N 0 59W
Whangamomona, *N.Z.* **59 H5** 39 8S 174 44 E
Whangarei, *N.Z.* **59 F5** 35 43S 174 21 E
Whangarei Harb., *N.Z.* **59 F5** 35 45S 174 28 E
Wharfe —►, *U.K.* **10 D6** 53 51N 1 9W
Wharfedale, *U.K.* **10 C5** 54 6N 2 1W
Wharton, *N.J., U.S.A.* **79 F10** 40 54N 74 35W
Wharton, *Pa., U.S.A.* **78 E6** 41 31N 78 1W
Wharton, *Tex., U.S.A.* **81 L6** 29 19N 96 6W
Wheatland, *Calif., U.S.A.* **84 F5** 39 1N 121 25W
Wheatland, *Wyo., U.S.A.* **80 D2** 42 3N 104 58W
Wheatley, *Canada* **78 D2** 42 6N 82 27W
Wheaton, *U.S.A.* **80 C6** 45 48N 96 30W
Wheelbarrow Pk., *U.S.A.* **84 H10** 37 26N 116 5W
Wheeler, *Oreg., U.S.A.* **82 D2** 45 41N 123 53W
Wheeler, *Tex., U.S.A.* **81 H4** 35 27N 100 16W
Wheeler —►, *Canada* **73 B7** 57 25N 105 30W
Wheeler Pk., *N. Mex., U.S.A.* **83 H11** 36 34N 105 25W
Wheeler Pk., *Nev., U.S.A.* **83 G6** 38 57N 114 15W
Wheeler Ridge, *U.S.A.* **85 L8** 35 0N 118 57W
Wheeling, *U.S.A.* **78 F4** 40 4N 80 43W
Whernside, *U.K.* **10 C5** 54 14N 2 24W
Whidbey I., *U.S.A.* **72 D4** 48 12N 122 17W
Whiskey Gap, *Canada* **72 D6** 49 0N 113 3W
Whiskey Jack L., *Canada* **73 B8** 58 23N 101 55W
Whistleduck Cr. —►, *Australia* **62 C2** 20 15S 135 18 E
Whitby, *Canada* **78 C6** 43 52N 78 56W
Whitby, *U.K.* **10 C7** 54 29N 0 37W
White —►, *Ark., U.S.A.* **81 J9** 33 57N 91 5W
White —►, *Ind., U.S.A.* **76 F2** 38 25N 87 45W
White —►, *S. Dak., U.S.A.* **80 D5** 43 42N 99 27W
White —►, *Utah, U.S.A.* **82 F9** 40 4N 109 41W
White —►, *Wash., U.S.A.* **84 C4** 47 12N 122 15W
White, L., *Australia* **60 D4** 21 9S 128 56 E
White B., *Canada* **71 B8** 50 0N 56 35W
White Bear Res., *Canada* **71 C8** 48 10N 57 5W
White Bird, *U.S.A.* **82 D5** 45 46N 116 18W
White Butte, *U.S.A.* **80 B3** 46 23N 103 18W
White City, *U.S.A.* **80 F6** 38 48N 96 44W
White Cliffs, *Australia* **63 E3** 30 50S 143 10 E
White Deer, *U.S.A.* **81 H4** 35 26N 101 10W
White Hall, *U.S.A.* **80 F9** 39 26N 90 24W
White Haven, *U.S.A.* **79 E9** 41 4N 75 47W
White Horse, Vale of, *U.K.* **11 F6** 51 37N 1 30W
White I., *N.Z.* **59 G6** 37 30S 177 13 E
White L., *Canada* **79 A8** 45 18N 76 31W
White L., *U.S.A.* **81 L8** 29 44N 92 30W
White Mts., *Calif., U.S.A.* **83 H4** 37 30N 118 15W
White Mts., *N.H., U.S.A.* **75 B12** 44 15N 71 15W
White Nile = Nîl el Abyad —►, *Sudan* **51 E11** 15 38N 32 31 E
White Otter L., *Canada* **70 C1** 49 5N 91 55W
White Pass, *Canada* **72 B1** 59 40N 135 3W
White Pass, *U.S.A.* **84 D5** 46 38N 121 24W
White Plains, *U.S.A.* **79 E11** 41 2N 73 46W
White River, *Canada* **70 C2** 48 35N 85 20W
White River, *S. Africa* **57 D5** 25 20S 31 0 E
White River, *U.S.A.* **80 D4** 43 34N 100 45W
White Russia = Belarus ■, *Europe* **17 B14** 53 30N 27 0 E
White Sea = Beloye More, *Russia* **24 A6** 66 30N 38 0 E
White Sulphur Springs, *Mont., U.S.A.* **82 C8** 46 33N 110 54W
White Sulphur Springs, *W. Va., U.S.A.* **76 G5** 37 48N 80 18W
White Swan, *U.S.A.* **84 D6** 46 23N 120 44W
Whitecliffs, *N.Z.* **59 K3** 43 26S 171 55 E
Whitecourt, *Canada* **72 C5** 54 10N 115 45W
Whiteface, *U.S.A.* **81 J3** 33 36N 102 37W
Whitefield, *U.S.A.* **79 B13** 44 23N 71 37W
Whitefish, *U.S.A.* **82 B6** 48 25N 114 20W
Whitefish L., *Canada* **73 A7** 62 41N 106 48W
Whitefish Point, *U.S.A.* **76 B3** 46 45N 84 59W
Whitegull, L., *Canada* **71 A7** 55 27N 64 17W
Whitehall, *Mich., U.S.A.* **76 D2** 43 24N 86 21W
Whitehall, *Mont., U.S.A.* **82 D7** 45 52N 112 6W
Whitehall, *N.Y., U.S.A.* **79 C11** 43 33N 73 24W
Whitehall, *Wis., U.S.A.* **80 C9** 44 22N 91 19W
Whitehaven, *U.K.* **10 C4** 54 33N 3 35W
Whitehorse, *Canada* **72 A1** 60 43N 135 3W
Whitemark, *Australia* **62 G4** 40 7S 148 3 E
Whitemouth, *Canada* **73 D9** 49 57N 95 58W
Whitesboro, *N.Y., U.S.A.* **79 C9** 43 7N 75 18W
Whitesboro, *Tex., U.S.A.* **81 J6** 33 39N 96 54W
Whiteshell Prov. Park, *Canada* **73 C9** 50 0N 95 40W
Whitetail, *U.S.A.* **80 A2** 48 54N 105 10W
Whiteville, *U.S.A.* **77 H6** 34 20N 78 42W
Whitewater, *U.S.A.* **76 D1** 42 50N 88 44W
Whitewater Baldy, *U.S.A.* **83 K9** 33 20N 108 39W
Whitewater L., *Canada* **70 B2** 50 50N 89 10W
Whitewood, *Australia* **62 C3** 21 28S 143 30 E
Whitewood, *Canada* **73 C8** 50 20N 102 20W
Whitfield, *Australia* **63 F4** 36 42S 146 24 E
Whithorn, *U.K.* **12 G4** 54 44N 4 26W
Whitianga, *N.Z.* **59 G5** 36 47S 175 41 E
Whitman, *U.S.A.* **79 D14** 42 5N 70 56W
Whitmire, *U.S.A.* **77 H5** 34 30N 81 37W
Whitney, *Canada* **78 A6** 45 31N 78 14W
Whitney, Mt., *U.S.A.* **83 H4** 36 35N 118 18W
Whitney Point, *U.S.A.* **79 D9** 42 20N 75 58W
Whitstable, *U.K.* **11 F9** 51 21N 1 3 E
Whitsunday I., *Australia* **62 C4** 20 15S 149 4 E
Whittier, *U.S.A.* **85 M8** 33 58N 118 3W
Whittlesea, *Australia* **63 F4** 37 27S 145 9 E
Whitwell, *U.S.A.* **77 H3** 35 12N 85 31W
Wholdaia L., *Canada* **73 A8** 60 43N 104 20W
Whyalla, *Australia* **63 E2** 33 2S 137 30 E
Whyjonta, *Australia* **63 D3** 29 41S 142 28 E
Wiarton, *Canada* **78 B3** 44 40N 81 10W
Wibaux, *U.S.A.* **80 B2** 46 59N 104 11W
Wichian Buri, *Thailand* **38 E3** 15 39N 101 7 E
Wichita, *U.S.A.* **81 G6** 37 42N 97 20W
Wichita Falls, *U.S.A.* **81 J5** 33 54N 98 30W
Wick, *U.K.* **12 C5** 58 26N 3 5W
Wickenburg, *U.S.A.* **83 K7** 33 58N 112 44W
Wickepin, *Australia* **61 F2** 32 50S 117 30 E
Wickham, C., *Australia* **62 F3** 39 35S 143 57 E
Wickliffe, *U.S.A.* **78 E3** 41 36N 81 28W
Wicklow, *Ireland* **13 D5** 52 59N 6 3W
Wicklow □, *Ireland* **13 D5** 52 57N 6 25W
Wicklow Hd., *Ireland* **13 D5** 52 58N 6 0W
Widgiemooltha, *Australia* **61 F3** 31 30S 121 34 E
Widnes, *U.K.* **10 D5** 53 23N 2 45W
Wieluń, *Poland* **17 C10** 51 15N 18 34 E
Wien, *Austria* **16 D9** 48 12N 16 22 E
Wiener Neustadt, *Austria* **16 E9** 47 49N 16 16 E
Wierden, *Neths.* **15 B6** 52 22N 6 35 E
Wiesbaden, *Germany* **16 C5** 50 4N 8 14 E
Wigan, *U.K.* **10 D5** 53 33N 2 38W
Wiggins, *Colo., U.S.A.* **80 E2** 40 14N 104 4W
Wiggins, *Miss., U.S.A.* **81 K10** 30 51N 89 8W
Wight, I. of □, *U.K.* **11 G6** 50 40N 1 20W
Wigtown, *U.K.* **12 G4** 54 53N 4 27W
Wigtown B., *U.K.* **12 G4** 54 46N 4 15W
Wilber, *U.S.A.* **80 E6** 40 29N 96 58W
Wilberforce, *Canada* **78 A6** 45 2N 78 13W
Wilberforce, C., *Australia* **62 A2** 11 54S 136 35 E
Wilburton, *U.S.A.* **81 H7** 34 55N 95 19W
Wilcannia, *Australia* **63 E3** 31 30S 143 26 E
Wilcox, *U.S.A.* **78 E6** 41 35N 78 41W
Wildrose, *Calif., U.S.A.* **85 J9** 36 14N 117 11W
Wildrose, *N. Dak., U.S.A.* **80 A3** 48 38N 103 11W
Wildspitze, *Austria* **16 E6** 46 53N 10 53 E
Wildwood, *U.S.A.* **76 F8** 38 59N 74 50W
Wilge —►, *S. Africa* **57 D4** 27 3S 28 20 E
Wilhelm II Coast, *Antarctica* **5 C7** 68 0S 90 0 E
Wilhelmshaven, *Germany* **16 B5** 53 31N 8 7 E
Wilhelmstal, *Namibia* **56 C2** 21 58S 16 21 E
Wilkes-Barre, *U.S.A.* **79 E9** 41 15N 75 53W
Wilkesboro, *U.S.A.* **77 G5** 36 9N 81 10W
Wilkie, *Canada* **73 C7** 52 27N 108 42W
Wilkinsburg, *U.S.A.* **78 F5** 40 26N 79 53W
Wilkinson Lakes, *Australia* **61 E5** 29 40S 132 39 E
Willamina, *U.S.A.* **82 D2** 45 5N 123 29W
Willandra Billabong Creek —►, *Australia* **63 E4** 33 22S 145 52 E
Willapa B., *U.S.A.* **82 C2** 46 40N 124 0W
Willapa Hills, *U.S.A.* **84 D3** 46 35N 123 25W
Willard, *N. Mex., U.S.A.* **83 J10** 34 36N 106 2W
Willard, *Utah, U.S.A.* **82 F7** 41 25N 112 2W
Willcox, *U.S.A.* **83 K9** 32 15N 109 50W
Willemstad, *Neth. Ant.* **89 D6** 12 5N 69 0W
Willeroo, *Australia* **60 C5** 15 14S 131 37 E
William —►, *Canada* **73 B7** 59 8N 109 19W
William Creek, *Australia* **63 D2** 28 58S 136 22 E
Williambury, *Australia* **61 D2** 23 45S 115 12 E
Williams, *Australia* **61 F2** 33 2S 116 52 E
Williams, *Ariz., U.S.A.* **83 J7** 35 15N 112 11W
Williams, *Calif., U.S.A.* **84 F4** 39 9N 122 9W
Williams Lake, *Canada* **72 C4** 52 10N 122 10W
Williamsburg, *Ky., U.S.A.* **77 G3** 36 44N 84 10W
Williamsburg, *Pa., U.S.A.* **78 F6** 40 28N 78 12W
Williamsburg, *Va., U.S.A.* **76 G7** 37 17N 76 44W
Williamson, *N.Y., U.S.A.* **78 C7** 43 14N 77 11W
Williamson, *W. Va., U.S.A.* **76 G4** 37 41N 82 17W
Williamsport, *U.S.A.* **78 E7** 41 15N 77 0W
Williamston, *U.S.A.* **77 H7** 35 51N 77 4W
Williamstown, *Australia* **63 F3** 37 51S 144 52 E
Williamstown, *Mass., U.S.A.* **79 D11** 42 41N 73 12W
Williamstown, *N.Y., U.S.A.* **79 C9** 43 26N 75 53W
Williamsville, *U.S.A.* **81 G9** 36 58N 90 33W
Willimantic, *U.S.A.* **79 E12** 41 43N 72 13W
Willis Group, *Australia* **62 B5** 16 18S 150 0 E
Williston, *S. Africa* **56 E3** 31 20S 20 53 E
Williston, *Fla., U.S.A.* **77 L4** 29 23N 82 27W
Williston, *N. Dak., U.S.A.* **80 A3** 48 9N 103 37W
Williston L., *Canada* **72 B4** 56 0N 124 0W
Willits, *U.S.A.* **82 G2** 39 25N 123 21W
Willmar, *U.S.A.* **80 C7** 45 7N 95 3W
Willoughby, *U.S.A.* **78 E3** 41 39N 81 24W
Willow Bunch, *Canada* **73 D7** 49 20N 105 35W
Willow L., *Canada* **72 A5** 62 10N 119 8W
Willow Lake, *U.S.A.* **80 C6** 44 38N 97 38W
Willow Springs, *U.S.A.* **81 G8** 37 0N 91 58W
Willow Wall, The, *China* **35 C12** 42 10N 122 0 E
Willowlake —►, *Canada* **72 A4** 62 42N 123 8W
Willowmore, *S. Africa* **56 E3** 33 15S 23 30 E
Willows, *Australia* **62 C4** 23 39S 147 25 E
Willows, *U.S.A.* **84 F4** 39 31N 122 12W
Willowvale = Gatyana, *S. Africa* **57 E4** 32 16S 28 31 E
Wills, L., *Australia* **60 D4** 21 25S 128 51 E
Wills Cr. —►, *Australia* **62 C3** 22 43S 140 2 E
Wills Point, *U.S.A.* **81 J7** 32 43N 96 1W
Willunga, *Australia* **63 F2** 35 15S 138 30 E
Wilmette, *U.S.A.* **76 D2** 42 5N 87 42W
Wilmington, *Australia* **63 E2** 32 39S 138 7 E
Wilmington, *Del., U.S.A.* **76 F8** 39 45N 75 33W
Wilmington, *Ill., U.S.A.* **76 E1** 41 18N 88 9W
Wilmington, *N.C., U.S.A.* **77 H7** 34 14N 77 55W
Wilmington, *Ohio, U.S.A.* **76 F4** 39 27N 83 50W
Wilpena Cr. —►, *Australia* **63 E2** 31 25S 139 29 E
Wilsall, *U.S.A.* **82 D8** 45 59N 110 38W
Wilson, *U.S.A.* **77 H7** 35 44N 77 55W
Wilson —►, *Queens., Australia* **63 D3** 27 38S 141 24 E
Wilson —►, *W. Austral., Australia* **60 C4** 16 48S 128 16 E
Wilson Bluff, *Australia* **61 F4** 31 41S 129 0 E
Wilsons Promontory, *Australia* **63 F4** 38 55S 146 25 E
Wilton, *U.K.* **11 F6** 51 5N 1 51W
Wilton, *U.S.A.* **80 B4** 47 10N 100 47W
Wilton —►, *Australia* **62 A1** 14 45S 134 33 E
Wiltshire □, *U.K.* **11 F6** 51 18N 1 53W
Wiltz, *Lux.* **15 E5** 49 57N 5 55 E
Wiluna, *Australia* **61 E3** 26 36S 120 14 E
Wimmera —►, *Australia* **63 F3** 36 8S 141 56 E
Winam G., *Kenya* **54 C3** 0 20S 34 15 E
Winburg, *S. Africa* **56 D4** 28 30S 27 2 E
Winchendon, *U.S.A.* **79 D12** 42 41N 72 3W
Winchester, *U.K.* **11 F6** 51 4N 1 18W
Winchester, *Conn., U.S.A.* **79 E11** 41 53N 73 9W
Winchester, *Idaho, U.S.A.* **82 C5** 46 14N 116 38W
Winchester, *Ind., U.S.A.* **76 E3** 40 10N 84 59W
Winchester, *Ky., U.S.A.* **76 G3** 38 0N 84 11W
Winchester, *N.H., U.S.A.* **79 D12** 42 46N 72 23W
Winchester, *Nev., U.S.A.* **85 J11** 36 6N 115 10W
Winchester, *Tenn., U.S.A.* **77 H2** 35 11N 86 7W
Winchester, *Va., U.S.A.* **76 F6** 39 11N 78 10W
Wind —►, *U.S.A.* **82 E9** 43 12N 108 12W
Wind River Range, *U.S.A.* **82 E9** 43 0N 109 30W
Windau = Ventspils, *Latvia* **9 H19** 57 25N 21 32 E
Windber, *U.S.A.* **78 F6** 40 14N 78 50W
Windermere, L., *U.K.* **10 C5** 54 22N 2 56W
Windfall, *Canada* **72 C5** 54 12N 116 13W
Windflower L., *Canada* **72 A5** 62 52N 118 30W
Windhoek, *Namibia* **56 C2** 22 35S 17 4 E
Windom, *U.S.A.* **80 D7** 43 52N 95 7W
Windorah, *Australia* **62 D3** 25 24S 142 36 E
Window Rock, *U.S.A.* **83 J9** 35 41N 109 3W
Windrush —►, *U.K.* **11 F6** 51 43N 1 24W
Windsor, *Australia* **63 E5** 33 37S 150 50 E
Windsor, *N.S., Canada* **71 D7** 44 59N 64 5W
Windsor, *Nfld., Canada* **71 C8** 48 57N 55 40W
Windsor, *Ont., Canada* **70 D3** 42 18N 83 0W
Windsor, *U.K.* **11 F7** 51 29N 0 36W
Windsor, *Colo., U.S.A.* **80 E2** 40 29N 104 54W
Windsor, *Conn., U.S.A.* **79 E12** 41 50N 72 39W
Windsor, *Mo., U.S.A.* **80 F8** 38 32N 93 31W
Windsor, *N.Y., U.S.A.* **79 D9** 42 5N 75 37W
Windsor, *Vt., U.S.A.* **79 C12** 43 29N 72 24W
Windsorton, *S. Africa* **56 D3** 28 16S 24 44 E
Windward Is., *W. Indies* **89 D7** 13 0N 61 0W
Windward Passage = Vientos, Paso de los, *Caribbean* **89 C5** 20 0N 74 0W
Windy L., *Canada* **73 A8** 60 20N 100 2W
Winefred L., *Canada* **73 B6** 55 30N 110 30W
Winfield, *U.S.A.* **81 G6** 37 15N 96 59W
Wingate Mts., *Australia* **60 B5** 14 25S 130 40 E
Wingen, *Australia* **63 E5** 31 54S 150 54 E
Wingham, *Australia* **63 E5** 31 48S 152 22 E
Wingham, *Canada* **70 D3** 43 55N 81 20W
Winifred, *U.S.A.* **82 C9** 47 34N 109 23W
Winisk, *Canada* **70 A2** 55 20N 85 15W
Winisk —►, *Canada* **70 A2** 55 17N 85 5W
Winisk L., *Canada* **70 B2** 52 55N 87 22W
Wink, *U.S.A.* **81 K3** 31 45N 103 9W
Winkler, *Canada* **73 D9** 49 10N 97 56W
Winlock, *U.S.A.* **84 D4** 46 30N 122 56W
Winneba, *Ghana* **50 G4** 5 25N 0 36W
Winnebago, *U.S.A.* **80 D7** 43 46N 94 10W
Winnebago, L., *U.S.A.* **76 D1** 44 0N 88 26W
Winnecke Cr. —►, *Australia* **60 C5** 18 35S 131 34 E
Winnemucca, *U.S.A.* **82 F5** 40 58N 117 44W
Winnemucca L., *U.S.A.* **82 F4** 40 7N 119 21W
Winner, *U.S.A.* **80 D5** 43 22N 99 52W
Winnett, *U.S.A.* **82 C9** 47 0N 108 21W
Winnfield, *U.S.A.* **81 K8** 31 56N 92 38W
Winnibigoshish, L., *U.S.A.* **80 B7** 47 27N 94 13W
Winning, *Australia* **60 D1** 23 9S 114 30 E
Winnipeg, *Canada* **73 D9** 49 54N 97 9W
Winnipeg —►, *Canada* **73 C9** 50 38N 96 19W
Winnipeg, L., *Canada* **73 C9** 52 0N 97 0W
Winnipeg Beach, *Canada* **73 C9** 50 30N 96 58W
Winnipegosis, *Canada* **73 C9** 51 39N 99 55W
Winnipegosis L., *Canada* **73 C9** 52 30N 100 0W
Winnipesaukee, L., *U.S.A.* **79 C13** 43 38N 71 21W
Winnsboro, *La., U.S.A.* **81 J9** 32 10N 91 43W
Winnsboro, *S.C., U.S.A.* **77 H5** 34 23N 81 5W
Winnsboro, *Tex., U.S.A.* **81 J7** 32 58N 95 17W
Winokapau, L., *Canada* **71 B7** 53 15N 62 50W
Winona, *Minn., U.S.A.* **80 C9** 44 3N 91 39W
Winona, *Miss., U.S.A.* **81 J10** 33 29N 89 44W
Winooski, *U.S.A.* **79 B11** 44 29N 73 11W
Winschoten, *Neths.* **15 A7** 53 9N 7 3 E
Winslow, *Ariz., U.S.A.* **83 J8** 35 2N 110 42W
Winslow, *Wash., U.S.A.* **84 C4** 47 38N 122 31W
Winsted, *U.S.A.* **79 E11** 41 55N 73 4W
Winston-Salem, *U.S.A.* **77 G5** 36 6N 80 15W
Winter Garden, *U.S.A.* **77 L5** 28 34N 81 35W
Winter Haven, *U.S.A.* **77 M5** 28 1N 81 44W
Winter Park, *U.S.A.* **77 L5** 28 36N 81 20W
Winterhaven, *U.S.A.* **85 N12** 32 47N 114 39W
Winters, *Calif., U.S.A.* **84 G5** 38 32N 121 58W
Winters, *Tex., U.S.A.* **81 K5** 31 58N 99 58W
Winterset, *U.S.A.* **80 E7** 41 20N 94 1W
Wintersville, *U.S.A.* **78 F4** 40 23N 80 42W
Winterswijk, *Neths.* **15 C6** 51 58N 6 43 E
Winterthur, *Switz.* **16 E5** 47 30N 8 44 E
Winthrop, *Minn., U.S.A.* **80 C7** 44 32N 94 22W
Winthrop, *Wash., U.S.A.* **82 B3** 48 28N 120 10W
Winton, *Australia* **62 C3** 22 24S 143 3 E
Winton, *N.Z.* **59 M2** 46 8S 168 20 E
Winton, *U.S.A.* **77 G7** 36 24N 76 56W
Wirral, *U.K.* **10 D4** 53 25N 3 0W
Wirrulla, *Australia* **63 E1** 32 24S 134 31 E
Wisbech, *U.K.* **10 E8** 52 41N 0 9 E
Wisconsin □, *U.S.A.* **80 C10** 44 45N 89 30W
Wisconsin —►, *U.S.A.* **80 D9** 43 0N 91 15W
Wisconsin Dells, *U.S.A.* **80 D10** 43 38N 89 46W
Wisconsin Rapids, *U.S.A.* **80 C10** 44 23N 89 49W
Wisdom, *U.S.A.* **82 D7** 45 37N 113 27W
Wishaw, *U.K.* **12 F5** 55 46N 3 54W
Wishek, *U.S.A.* **80 B5** 46 16N 99 33W
Wisła —►, *Poland* **17 A10** 54 22N 18 55 E
Wismar, *Germany* **16 B6** 53 54N 11 29 E
Wisner, *U.S.A.* **80 E6** 41 59N 96 55W
Witbank, *S. Africa* **57 D4** 25 51S 29 14 E
Witdraai, *S. Africa* **56 D3** 26 58S 20 48 E
Witham —►, *U.K.* **10 D7** 52 59N 0 2W
Withernsea, *U.K.* **10 D8** 53 44N 0 1 E
Witney, *U.K.* **11 F6** 51 48N 1 28W
Witnossob —►, *Namibia* **56 D3** 26 55S 20 37 E
Witten, *Germany* **15 C7** 51 26N 7 20 E
Wittenberg, *Germany* **16 C7** 51 53N 12 39 E
Wittenberge, *Germany* **16 B6** 53 0N 11 45 E
Wittenoom, *Australia* **60 D2** 22 15S 118 20 E
Wkra —►, *Poland* **17 B11** 52 27N 20 44 E
Wlingi, *Indonesia* **37 H15** 8 5S 112 25 E
Włocławek, *Poland* **17 B10** 52 40N 19 3 E
Włodawa, *Poland* **17 C12** 51 33N 23 31 E
Woburn, *U.S.A.* **79 D13** 42 29N 71 9W
Wodian, *China* **34 H7** 32 50N 112 35 E
Wodonga, *Australia* **63 F4** 36 5S 146 50 E
Wokam, *Indonesia* **37 F8** 5 45S 134 28 E
Wolf —►, *Canada* **72 A2** 60 17N 132 33W
Wolf Creek, *U.S.A.* **82 C7** 47 0N 112 4W
Wolf L., *Canada* **72 A2** 60 24N 131 40W
Wolf Point, *U.S.A.* **80 A2** 48 5N 105 39W
Wolfe I., *Canada* **70 D4** 44 7N 76 20W
Wolfsberg, *Austria* **16 E8** 46 50N 14 52 E
Wolfsburg, *Germany* **16 B6** 52 25N 10 48 E
Wolin, *Poland* **16 B8** 53 50N 14 37 E
Wollaston, Is., *Chile* **96 H3** 55 40S 67 30W
Wollaston L., *Canada* **73 B8** 58 7N 103 10W
Wollaston Pen., *Canada* **68 B8** 69 30N 115 0W
Wollogorang, *Australia* **62 B2** 17 13S 137 57 E
Wollongong, *Australia* **63 E5** 34 25S 150 54 E
Wolmaransstad, *S. Africa* **56 D4** 27 12S 25 59 E
Wolseley, *Australia* **63 F3** 36 23S 140 54 E
Wolseley, *Canada* **73 C8** 50 25N 103 15W
Wolseley, *S. Africa* **56 E2** 33 26S 19 7 E
Wolstenholme, C., *Canada* **66 C12** 62 35N 77 30W
Wolvega, *Neths.* **15 B6** 52 52N 6 0 E
Wolverhampton, *U.K.* **11 E5** 52 35N 2 7W
Wonarah, *Australia* **62 B2** 19 55S 136 20 E
Wondai, *Australia* **63 D5** 26 20S 151 49 E
Wongalarroo L., *Australia* **63 E3** 31 32S 144 0 E
Wongan Hills, *Australia* **61 F2** 30 51S 116 37 E
Wongawol, *Australia* **61 E3** 26 5S 121 55 E
Wŏnju, *S. Korea* **35 F14** 37 22N 127 58 E
Wonosari, *Indonesia* **37 G14** 7 58S 110 36 E
Wŏnsan, *N. Korea* **35 E14** 39 11N 127 27 E
Wonthaggi, *Australia* **63 F4** 38 37S 145 37 E
Woocalla, *Australia* **63 E2** 31 42S 137 12 E
Wood Buffalo Nat. Park, *Canada* **72 B6** 59 0N 113 41W
Wood Is., *Australia* **60 C3** 16 24S 123 19 E
Wood L., *Canada* **73 B8** 55 17N 103 17W
Wood Lake, *U.S.A.* **80 D4** 42 38N 100 14W
Woodah I., *Australia* **62 A2** 13 27S 136 10 E
Woodanilling, *Australia* **61 F2** 33 31S 117 24 E
Woodbridge, *Canada* **78 C5** 43 47N 79 36W
Woodburn, *Australia* **63 D5** 29 6S 153 23 E
Woodenbong, *Australia* **63 D5** 28 24S 152 39 E
Woodend, *Australia* **63 F3** 37 20S 144 33 E
Woodfords, *U.S.A.* **84 G7** 38 47N 119 50W
Woodgreen, *Australia* **62 C1** 22 26S 134 12 E
Woodlake, *U.S.A.* **84 J7** 36 25N 119 6W
Woodland, *U.S.A.* **84 G5** 38 41N 121 46W
Woodlands, *Australia* **60 D2** 24 46S 118 8 E
Woodpecker, *Canada* **72 C4** 53 30N 122 40W
Woodridge, *Canada* **73 D9** 49 20N 96 9W
Woodroffe, Mt., *Australia* **61 E5** 26 20S 131 45 E
Woodruff, *Ariz., U.S.A.* **83 J8** 34 51N 110 1W
Woodruff, *Utah, U.S.A.* **82 F8** 41 31N 111 10W
Woods, L., *Australia* **62 B1** 17 50S 133 30 E
Woods, L., *Canada* **71 B6** 54 30N 65 13W
Woods, L. of the, *Canada* **73 D10** 49 15N 94 45W
Woodstock, *Queens., Australia* **62 B4** 19 35S 146 50 E
Woodstock, *W. Austral., Australia* **60 D2** 21 41S 118 57 E
Woodstock, *N.B., Canada* **71 C6** 46 11N 67 37W
Woodstock, *Ont., Canada* **70 D3** 43 10N 80 45W
Woodstock, *U.K.* **11 F6** 51 51N 1 20W
Woodstock, *Ill., U.S.A.* **80 D10** 42 19N 88 27W
Woodstock, *Vt., U.S.A.* **79 C12** 43 37N 72 31W
Woodsville, *U.S.A.* **79 B13** 44 9N 72 2W
Woodville, *N.Z.* **59 J5** 40 20S 175 53 E

Woodville, *U.S.A.* **81 K7** 30 47N 94 25W
Woodward, *U.S.A.* **81 G5** 36 26N 99 24W
Woody, *U.S.A.* **85 K8** 35 42N 118 50W
Woolamai, C., *Australia* . **63 F4** 38 30S 145 23 E
Woolgoolga, *Australia* ... **63 E5** 30 6S 153 11 E
Woombye, *Australia* .... **63 D5** 26 40S 152 55 E
Woomera, *Australia* ..... **63 E2** 31 5S 136 50 E
Woonsocket, *R.I., U.S.A.* . **79 D13** 42 0N 71 31W
Woonsocket, *S. Dak., U.S.A.* **80 C5** 44 3N 98 17W
Wooramel, *Australia* .... **61 E1** 25 45S 114 17 E
Wooramel →, *Australia* **61 E1** 25 47S 114 10 E
Wooroloo, *Australia* .... **61 F2** 31 48S 116 18 E
Wooster, *U.S.A.* **78 F3** 40 48N 81 56W
Worcester, *S. Africa* .... **56 E2** 33 39S 19 27 E
Worcester, *U.K.* **11 E5** 52 11N 2 12W
Worcester, *Mass., U.S.A.* **79 D13** 42 16N 71 48W
Worcester, *N.Y., U.S.A.* .. **79 D10** 42 36N 74 45W
Workington, *U.K.* **10 C4** 54 39N 3 33W
Worksop, *U.K.* **10 D6** 53 18N 1 7W
Workum, *Neths.* .... **15 B5** 52 59N 5 26 E
Worland, *U.S.A.* **82 D10** 44 1N 107 57W
Worms, *Germany* .... **16 D5** 49 37N 8 21 E
Wortham, *U.S.A.* **81 K6** 31 47N 96 28W
Worthing, *U.K.* **11 G7** 50 49N 0 21W
Worthington, *U.S.A.* **80 D7** 43 37N 95 36W
Wosi, *Indonesia* .... **37 E7** 0 15S 128 0 E
Wou-han = Wuhan, *China* **33 C6** 30 31N 114 18 E
Wour, *Chad* .... **51 D8** 21 14N 16 0 E
Wousi = Wuxi, *China* ... **33 C7** 31 33N 120 18 E
Wowoni, *Indonesia* ..... **37 E6** 4 5S 123 5 E
Woy Woy, *Australia* .... **63 E5** 33 30S 151 19 E
Wrangel I. = Vrangelya, Ostrov, *Russia* .... **27 B19** 71 0N 180 0 E
Wrangell, *U.S.A.* **68 C6** 56 28N 132 23W
Wrangell I., *U.S.A.* **72 B2** 56 16N 132 12W
Wrangell Mts., *U.S.A.* ... **68 B5** 61 30N 142 0W
Wrath, C., *U.K.* **12 C3** 58 38N 5 1W
Wray, *U.S.A.* **80 E3** 40 5N 102 13W
Wrekin, The, *U.K.* **10 E5** 52 41N 2 32W
Wrens, *U.S.A.* **77 J4** 33 12N 82 23W
Wrexham, *U.K.* **10 D4** 53 3N 3 0W
Wrexham □, *U.K.* **10 D5** 53 1N 2 58W
Wright, *Canada* **72 C4** 51 52N 121 40W
Wright, *Phil.* .... **37 B7** 11 42N 125 2 E
Wrightson Mt., *U.S.A.* ... **83 L8** 31 42N 110 51W
Wrightwood, *U.S.A.* **85 L9** 34 21N 117 38W
Wrigley, *Canada* **68 B7** 63 16N 123 37W
Wrocław, *Poland* .... **17 C9** 51 5N 17 5 E
Września, *Poland* ...... **17 B9** 52 21N 17 36 E
Wu Jiang →, *China* .... **32 D5** 29 40N 107 20 E
Wu'an, *China* .... **34 F8** 36 40N 114 15 E
Wubin, *Australia* .... **61 F2** 30 6S 116 37 E
Wubu, *China* .... **34 F6** 37 28N 110 42 E
Wuchang, *China* .... **35 B14** 44 55N 127 5 E
Wucheng, *China* .... **34 F9** 37 12N 116 20 E
Wuchuan, *China* .... **34 D6** 41 5N 111 28 E
Wudi, *China* .... **35 F9** 37 40N 117 35 E
Wuding He →, *China* ... **34 F6** 37 2N 110 23 E
Wudu, *China* .... **34 H3** 33 22N 104 54 E
Wuhan, *China* .... **33 C6** 30 31N 114 18 E
Wuhe, *China* .... **35 H9** 33 10N 117 50 E
Wuhsi = Wuxi, *China* ... **33 C7** 31 33N 120 18 E
Wuhu, *China* .... **33 C6** 31 22N 118 21 E
Wukari, *Nigeria* .... **50 G6** 7 51N 9 42 E
Wulajie, *China* .... **35 B14** 44 6N 126 33 E
Wulanbulang, *China* .... **34 D6** 41 5N 110 55 E
Wulian, *China* .... **35 G10** 35 40N 119 12 E
Wuliaru, *Indonesia* ..... **37 F8** 7 27S 131 0 E
Wuluk'omushih Ling, *China* .... **32 C3** 36 25N 87 25 E
Wulumuchi = Ürümqi, *China* .... **26 E9** 43 45N 87 45 E
Wum, *Cameroon* .... **50 G7** 6 24N 10 2 E
Wunnummin L., *Canada* . **70 B2** 52 55N 89 10W
Wuntho, *Burma* .... **41 H19** 23 55N 95 45 E
Wuppertal, *Germany* .... **16 C4** 51 16N 7 12 E
Wuppertal, *S. Africa* .... **56 E2** 32 13S 19 12 E
Wuqing, *China* .... **35 E9** 39 23N 117 4 E
Wurung, *Australia* ...... **62 B3** 19 13S 140 38 E
Würzburg, *Germany* .... **16 D5** 49 46N 9 55 E
Wushan, *China* .... **34 G3** 34 43N 104 53 E
Wusuli Jiang = Ussuri →, *Asia* ...... **30 A7** 48 27N 135 0 E
Wutai, *China* .... **34 E7** 38 40N 113 12 E
Wuting = Huimin, *China* . **35 F9** 37 27N 117 28 E
Wutonghaolai, *China* ... **35 C11** 42 50N 120 5 E
Wutongqiao, *China* ..... **32 D5** 29 22N 103 50 E
Wuwei, *China* .... **32 C5** 37 57N 102 34 E
Wuxi, *China* .... **33 C7** 31 33N 120 18 E
Wuxiang, *China* .... **34 F7** 36 49N 112 50 E
Wuxing, *China* .... **33 C7** 30 51N 120 8 E
Wuyang, *China* .... **34 H7** 33 25N 113 35 E
Wuyi, *China* .... **34 F8** 37 46N 115 56 E
Wuyi Shan, *China* ...... **33 D6** 27 0N 117 0 E
Wuyuan, *China* .... **34 D5** 41 2N 108 20 E
Wuzhai, *China* .... **34 E6** 38 54N 111 48 E
Wuzhi Shan, *China* ..... **38 C7** 18 45N 109 45 E
Wuzhong, *China* .... **34 E4** 38 2N 106 12 E
Wuzhou, *China* .... **33 D6** 23 30N 111 18 E
Wyaaba Cr. →, *Australia* **62 B3** 16 27S 141 35 E
Wyalkatchem, *Australia* . **61 F2** 31 8S 117 22 E
Wyalusing, *U.S.A.* **79 E8** 41 40N 76 16W
Wyandotte, *U.S.A.* **76 D4** 42 12N 83 9W
Wyandra, *Australia* ..... **63 D4** 27 12S 145 56 E
Wyangala Res., *Australia* **63 E4** 33 54S 149 0 E
Wyara, L., *Australia* .... **63 D3** 28 42S 144 14 E
Wycheproof, *Australia* .. **63 F3** 36 5S 143 17 E
Wye →, *U.K.* **11 F5** 51 38N 2 40W
Wyemandoo, *Australia* .. **61 E2** 28 28S 118 29 E
Wymondham, *U.K.* **11 E7** 52 45N 0 43W
Wymore, *U.S.A.* **80 E6** 40 7N 96 40W
Wynbring, *Australia* .... **63 E1** 30 33S 133 32 E
Wyndham, *Australia* .... **60 C4** 15 33S 128 3 E
Wyndham, *N.Z.* .... **59 M2** 46 20S 168 51 E
Wyndmere, *U.S.A.* **80 B6** 46 16N 97 8W
Wynne, *U.S.A.* **81 H9** 35 14N 90 47W
Wynnum, *Australia* ..... **63 D5** 27 27S 153 9 E
Wynyard, *Australia* ..... **62 G4** 41 5S 145 44 E
Wynyard, *Canada* **73 C8** 51 45N 104 10W
Wyola, L., *Australia* .... **61 E5** 29 8S 130 17 E
Wyoming □, *U.S.A.* **82 E10** 43 0N 107 30W
Wyong, *Australia* ...... **63 E5** 33 14S 151 24 E
Wytheville, *U.S.A.* **76 G5** 36 57N 81 5W

X

Xai-Xai, *Mozam.* .... **57 D5** 25 6S 33 31 E
Xainza, *China* .... **32 C3** 30 58N 88 35 E
Xangongo, *Angola* ...... **56 B2** 16 45S 15 5 E
Xankändi, *Azerbaijan* ... **25 G8** 39 52N 46 49 E
Xánthi, *Greece* .... **21 D11** 41 10N 24 58 E
Xapuri, *Brazil* **92 F5** 10 35S 68 35W
Xar Moron He →, *China* **35 C11** 43 25N 120 35 E
Xau, L., *Botswana* ...... **56 C3** 21 15S 24 44 E
Xavantina, *Brazil* **95 A5** 21 15S 52 48W
Xenia, *U.S.A.* **76 F4** 39 41N 83 56W
Xeropotamos →, *Cyprus* **23 E11** 34 42N 32 33 E
Xhora, *S. Africa* .... **57 E4** 31 55S 28 38 E
Xhumo, *Botswana* ...... **56 C3** 21 7S 24 35 E
Xi Jiang →, *China* ..... **33 D6** 22 5N 113 20 E
Xi Xian, *China* .... **34 F6** 36 41N 110 58 E
Xia Xian, *China* .... **34 G6** 35 8N 111 12 E
Xiachengzi, *China* ...... **35 B16** 44 40N 130 18 E
Xiaguan, *China* .... **32 D5** 25 32N 100 16 E
Xiajin, *China* .... **34 F8** 36 56N 116 0 E
Xiamen, *China* .... **33 D6** 24 25N 118 4 E
Xi'an, *China* .... **34 G5** 34 15N 109 0 E
Xian Xian, *China* .... **34 E9** 38 12N 116 6 E
Xiang Jiang →, *China* .. **33 D6** 28 55N 112 50 E
Xiangcheng, *Henan, China* **34 H8** 33 29N 114 52 E
Xiangcheng, *Henan, China* **34 H7** 33 50N 113 27 E
Xiangfan, *China* .... **33 C6** 32 2N 112 8 E
Xianghuang Qi, *China* ... **34 C7** 42 2N 113 50 E
Xiangning, *China* .... **34 G6** 35 58N 110 50 E
Xiangquan, *China* ...... **34 F7** 36 30N 113 1 E
Xiangshui, *China* .... **35 G10** 34 12N 119 33 E
Xiangtan, *China* .... **33 D6** 27 51N 112 54 E
Xianyang, *China* .... **34 G5** 34 20N 108 40 E
Xiao Hinggan Ling, *China* **33 B7** 49 0N 127 0 E
Xiao Xian, *China* .... **34 G9** 34 15N 116 55 E
Xiaoyi, *China* .... **34 F6** 37 8N 111 48 E
Xiawa, *China* .... **35 C11** 42 35N 120 38 E
Xiayi, *China* .... **34 G9** 34 15N 116 10 E
Xichang, *China* .... **32 D5** 27 51N 102 19 E
Xichuan, *China* .... **34 H6** 33 0N 111 30 E
Xieng Khouang, *Laos* ... **38 C4** 19 17N 103 25 E
Xifei He →, *China* ..... **34 H9** 32 45N 116 40 E
Xifeng, *China* .... **35 C13** 42 42N 124 45 E
Xifengzhen, *China* ...... **34 G4** 35 40N 107 40 E
Xigazê, *China* .... **32 D3** 29 5N 88 45 E
Xihe, *China* .... **34 G3** 34 2N 105 20 E
Xihua, *China* .... **34 H8** 33 45N 114 30 E
Xiliao He →, *China* .... **35 C12** 43 32N 123 35 E
Xin Xian, *China* .... **34 E7** 38 22N 112 46 E
Xinavane, *Mozam.* ...... **57 D5** 25 2S 32 47 E
Xinbin, *China* .... **35 D13** 41 40N 125 2 E
Xing Xian, *China* .... **34 E6** 38 27N 111 7 E
Xing'an, *China* .... **33 D6** 25 38N 110 40 E
Xingcheng, *China* ...... **35 D11** 40 40N 120 45 E
Xinghe, *China* .... **34 D7** 40 55N 113 55 E
Xinghua, *China* .... **35 H10** 32 58N 119 48 E
Xinglong, *China* .... **35 D9** 40 25N 117 30 E
Xingping, *China* .... **34 G5** 34 20N 108 28 E
Xingtai, *China* .... **34 F8** 37 3N 114 32 E
Xingu →, *Brazil* **93 D8** 1 30S 51 53W
Xingyang, *China* .... **34 G7** 34 45N 112 52 E
Xinhe, *China* .... **34 F8** 37 30N 115 15 E
Xining, *China* .... **32 C5** 36 34N 101 40 E
Xinjiang, *China* .... **34 G6** 35 34N 111 11 E
Xinjiang Uygur Zizhiqu □, *China* .... **32 B3** 42 0N 86 0 E
Xinjin, *China* .... **35 E11** 39 25N 121 58 E
Xinkai He →, *China* .... **35 C12** 43 32N 123 35 E
Xinle, *China* .... **34 E8** 38 25N 114 40 E
Xinlitun, *China* .... **35 D12** 42 0N 122 8 E
Xinmin, *China* .... **35 D12** 41 59N 122 50 E
Xintai, *China* .... **35 G9** 35 55N 117 45 E
Xinxiang, *China* .... **34 G7** 35 18N 113 50 E
Xinzhan, *China* .... **35 C14** 43 50N 127 18 E
Xinzheng, *China* .... **34 G7** 34 20N 113 45 E
Xiong Xian, *China* ..... **34 E9** 38 59N 116 8 E
Xiongyuecheng, *China* .. **35 D12** 40 12N 122 5 E
Xiping, *Henan, China* ... **34 H8** 33 22N 114 5 E
Xiping, *Henan, China* ... **34 H6** 33 25N 111 8 E
Xique-Xique, *Brazil* **93 F10** 10 50S 42 40W
Xisha Qundao = Paracel Is., *S. China Sea* ...... **36 A4** 15 50N 112 0 E
Xiuyan, *China* .... **35 D12** 40 18N 123 11 E
Xixabangma Feng, *China* **41 E14** 28 20N 85 40 E
Xixia, *China* .... **34 H6** 33 25N 111 29 E
Xixiang, *China* .... **34 H4** 33 0N 107 44 E
Xiyang, *China* .... **34 F7** 37 38N 113 38 E
Xizang □, *China* .... **32 C3** 32 0N 88 0 E
Xlendi, *Malta* .... **23 C1** 36 1N 14 12 E
Xuan Loc, *Vietnam* ..... **39 G6** 10 56N 107 14 E
Xuanhua, *China* .... **34 D8** 40 40N 115 2 E
Xuchang, *China* .... **34 G7** 34 2N 113 48 E
Xun Xian, *China* .... **34 G8** 35 42N 114 33 E
Xunyang, *China* .... **34 H5** 32 48N 109 22 E
Xunyi, *China* .... **34 G5** 35 8N 108 20 E
Xushui, *China* .... **34 E8** 39 2N 115 40 E
Xuyen Moc, *Vietnam* ... **39 G6** 10 34N 107 25 E
Xuzhou, *China* .... **35 G9** 34 18N 117 10 E
Xylophagou, *Cyprus* .... **23 E12** 34 54N 33 51 E

Y

Ya Xian, *China* .... **38 C7** 18 14N 109 29 E
Yaamba, *Australia* ...... **62 C5** 23 8S 150 22 E
Yaapeet, *Australia* ..... **63 F3** 35 45S 142 3 E
Yabelo, *Ethiopia* .... **51 H12** 4 50N 38 8 E
Yablonovy Ra. = Yablonovyy Khrebet, *Russia* .... **27 D12** 53 0N 114 0 E
Yablonovyy Khrebet, *Russia* .... **27 D12** 53 0N 114 0 E
Yabrai Shan, *China* ..... **34 E2** 39 40N 103 0 E
Yabrūd, *Syria* .... **47 B5** 33 58N 36 39 E
Yacheng, *China* .... **33 E5** 18 22N 109 6 E
Yacuiba, *Bolivia* **94 A3** 22 0S 63 43W
Yadgir, *India* .... **40 L10** 16 45N 77 5 E
Yadkin →, *U.S.A.* **77 H5** 35 29N 80 9W
Yagodnoye, *Russia* ..... **27 C15** 62 33N 149 40 E
Yagoua, *Cameroon* ..... **52 B3** 10 20N 15 13 E
Yaha, *Thailand* .... **39 J3** 6 29N 101 8 E
Yahila, *Zaïre* .... **54 B1** 0 13N 24 28 E
Yahk, *Canada* **72 D5** 49 6N 116 10W
Yahuma, *Zaïre* .... **52 D4** 1 0N 23 10 E
Yaita, *Japan* .... **31 F9** 36 48N 139 56 E
Yaiza, *Canary Is.* **22 F6** 28 57N 13 46W
Yakima, *U.S.A.* **82 C3** 46 36N 120 31W
Yakima →, *U.S.A.* **82 C3** 47 0N 120 30W
Yakovlevka, *Russia* .... **30 B6** 44 26N 133 28 E
Yaku-Shima, *Japan* .... **31 J5** 30 20N 130 30 E
Yakutat, *U.S.A.* **68 C6** 59 33N 139 44W
Yakutia = Sakha □, *Russia* **27 C13** 62 0N 130 0 E
Yakutsk, *Russia* .... **27 C13** 62 5N 129 50 E
Yala, *Thailand* .... **39 J3** 6 33N 101 18 E
Yalbalgo, *Australia* .... **61 E1** 25 10S 114 45 E
Yalboroo, *Australia* .... **62 C4** 20 50S 148 40 E
Yale, *U.S.A.* **78 C2** 43 8N 82 48W
Yalgoo, *Australia* ...... **61 E2** 28 16S 116 39 E
Yalinga, *C.A.R.* .... **51 G9** 6 33N 23 10 E
Yalkubul, Punta, *Mexico* . **87 C7** 21 32N 88 37W
Yalleroi, *Australia* ..... **62 C4** 24 3S 145 42 E
Yalobusha →, *U.S.A.* .. **81 J9** 33 33N 90 10W
Yalong Jiang →, *China* . **32 D5** 26 40N 101 55 E
Yalova, *Turkey* .... **21 D13** 40 41N 29 15 E
Yalta, *Ukraine* .... **25 F5** 44 30N 34 10 E
Yalu Jiang →, *China* ... **35 E13** 40 0N 124 22 E
Yalutorovsk, *Russia* .... **26 D7** 56 41N 66 12 E
Yam Ha Melaḥ = Dead Sea, *Asia* .... **47 D4** 31 30N 35 30 E
Yam Kinneret, *Israel* ... **47 C4** 32 45N 35 35 E
Yamada, *Japan* .... **31 H5** 33 33N 130 49 E
Yamagata, *Japan* ...... **30 E10** 38 15N 140 15 E
Yamagata □, *Japan* .... **30 E10** 38 30N 140 0 E
Yamaguchi, *Japan* ..... **31 G5** 34 10N 131 32 E
Yamaguchi □, *Japan* ... **31 G5** 34 20N 131 40 E
Yamal, Poluostrov, *Russia* **26 B8** 71 0N 70 0 E
Yamal Pen. = Yamal, Poluostrov, *Russia* .... **26 B8** 71 0N 70 0 E
Yamanashi □, *Japan* ... **31 G9** 35 40N 138 40 E
Yamantau, Gora, *Russia* . **24 D10** 54 15N 58 6 E
Yamba, *N.S.W., Australia* **63 D5** 29 26S 153 23 E
Yamba, *S. Austral., Australia* .... **63 E3** 34 10S 140 52 E
Yambah, *Australia* ..... **62 C1** 23 10S 133 50 E
Yambarran Ra., *Australia* **60 C5** 15 10S 130 25 E
Yâmbiô, *Sudan* .... **51 H10** 4 35N 28 16 E
Yambol, *Bulgaria* ...... **21 C12** 42 30N 26 36 E
Yamdena, *Indonesia* .... **37 F8** 7 45S 131 20 E
Yame, *Japan* .... **31 H5** 33 13N 130 35 E
Yamethin, *Burma* ...... **41 J20** 20 29N 96 18 E
Yamma-Yamma, L., *Australia* .... **63 D3** 26 16S 141 20 E
Yamoussoukro, *Ivory C.* . **50 G3** 6 49N 5 17W
Yampa →, *U.S.A.* **82 F9** 40 32N 108 59W
Yampi Sd., *Australia* .... **60 C3** 16 8S 123 38 E
Yampil, *Moldova* .... **17 D15** 48 15N 28 15 E
Yampol = Yampil, *Moldova* .... **17 D15** 48 15N 28 15 E
Yamuna →, *India* ...... **43 G9** 25 30N 81 53 E
Yamzho Yumco, *China* .. **32 D4** 28 48N 90 35 E
Yana →, *Russia* .... **27 B14** 71 30N 136 0 E
Yanac, *Australia* ...... **63 F3** 36 8S 141 25 E
Yanagawa, *Japan* ...... **31 H5** 33 10N 130 24 E
Yanai, *Japan* .... **31 H6** 33 58N 132 7 E
Yan'an, *China* .... **34 F5** 36 35N 109 26 E
Yanaul, *Russia* .... **24 C10** 56 25N 55 0 E
Yanbu 'al Baḥr, *Si. Arabia* **44 F3** 24 0N 38 5 E
Yancannia, *Australia* ... **63 E3** 30 12S 142 35 E
Yanchang, *China* ...... **34 F6** 36 43N 110 1 E
Yancheng, *Henan, China* . **34 H7** 33 35N 114 0 E
Yancheng, *Jiangsu, China* **35 H11** 33 23N 120 8 E
Yanchi, *China* .... **34 F4** 37 48N 107 20 E
Yanchuan, *China* ...... **34 F6** 36 51N 110 10 E
Yanco Cr. →, *Australia* . **63 F4** 35 14S 145 35 E
Yandal, *Australia* ...... **61 E3** 27 35S 121 10 E
Yandanooka, *Australia* .. **61 E2** 29 18S 115 29 E
Yandaran, *Australia* .... **62 C5** 24 43S 152 6 E
Yandoon, *Burma* ...... **41 L19** 17 0N 95 40 E
Yang Xian, *China* ...... **34 H4** 33 15N 107 30 E
Yangambi, *Zaïre* .... **54 B1** 0 47N 24 20 E
Yangcheng, *China* ..... **34 G7** 35 28N 112 22 E
Yangch'ü = Taiyuan, *China* .... **34 F7** 37 52N 112 33 E
Yanggao, *China* .... **34 D7** 40 21N 113 55 E
Yanggu, *China* .... **34 F8** 36 8N 115 43 E
Yangliuqing, *China* .... **35 E9** 39 2N 117 5 E
Yangon = Rangoon, *Burma* .... **41 L20** 16 45N 96 20 E
Yangpingguan, *China* ... **34 H4** 32 58N 106 5 E
Yangquan, *China* ...... **34 F7** 37 58N 113 31 E
Yangtze Kiang = Chang Jiang →, *China* ..... **33 C7** 31 48N 121 10 E
Yangyang, *S. Korea* .... **35 E15** 38 4N 128 38 E
Yangyuan, *China* ...... **34 D8** 40 1N 114 10 E
Yangzhou, *China* ...... **33 C6** 32 21N 119 26 E
Yanji, *China* .... **35 C15** 42 59N 129 30 E
Yankton, *U.S.A.* **80 D6** 42 53N 97 23W
Yanna, *Australia* ...... **63 D4** 26 58S 146 0 E
Yanonge, *Zaïre* .... **54 B1** 0 35N 24 38 E
Yanqi, *China* .... **32 B3** 42 5N 86 35 E
Yanqing, *China* .... **34 D8** 40 30N 115 58 E
Yanshan, *China* .... **35 E9** 38 4N 117 22 E
Yanshou, *China* .... **35 B15** 45 28N 128 22 E
Yantabulla, *Australia* ... **63 D4** 29 21S 145 0 E
Yantai, *China* .... **35 F11** 37 34N 121 22 E
Yanykurgan, *Kazakstan* . **26 E7** 43 50N 68 48 E
Yanzhou, *China* .... **34 G9** 35 35N 116 49 E
Yao, *Chad* .... **51 F8** 12 56N 17 33 E
Yao Xian, *China* .... **34 G5** 34 55N 108 59 E
Yao Yai, Ko, *Thailand* .. **39 J2** 8 0N 98 35 E
Yaoundé, *Cameroon* .... **50 H7** 3 50N 11 35 E
Yaowan, *China* .... **35 G10** 34 15N 118 3 E
Yap I., *Pac. Oc.* .... **64 G5** 9 30N 138 10 E
Yapen, *Indonesia* ...... **37 E9** 1 50S 136 0 E
Yapen, Selat, *Indonesia* . **37 E9** 1 20S 136 10 E
Yappar →, *Australia* ... **62 B3** 18 22S 141 16 E
Yaqui →, *Mexico* **86 B2** 27 37N 110 39W
Yar-Sale, *Russia* .... **26 C8** 66 50N 70 50 E
Yaraka, *Australia* ...... **62 C3** 24 53S 144 3 E
Yaransk, *Russia* .... **24 C8** 57 22N 47 49 E
Yardea P.O., *Australia* .. **63 E2** 32 23S 135 32 E
Yare →, *U.K.* .... **11 E9** 52 35N 1 38 E
Yaremcha, *Ukraine* .... **17 D13** 48 27N 24 33 E
Yarensk, *Russia* .... **24 B8** 62 11N 49 15 E
Yarí →, *Colombia* **92 D4** 0 20S 72 20W
Yarkand = Shache, *China* **32 C2** 38 20N 77 10 E
Yarker, *Canada* **79 B8** 44 23N 76 46W
Yarkhun →, *Pakistan* ... **43 A5** 36 17N 72 30 E
Yarmouth, *Canada* **71 D6** 43 50N 66 7W
Yarmūk →, *Syria* ...... **47 C4** 32 42N 35 40 E
Yaroslavl, *Russia* ...... **24 C6** 57 35N 39 55 E
Yarqa, W. →, *Egypt* .... **47 F2** 30 0N 33 49 E
Yarra Yarra Lakes, *Australia* .... **61 E2** 29 40S 115 45 E
Yarraden, *Australia* .... **62 A3** 14 17S 143 15 E
Yarraloola, *Australia* ... **60 D2** 21 33S 115 52 E
Yarram, *Australia* ...... **63 F4** 38 29S 146 39 E
Yarraman, *Australia* .... **63 D5** 26 50S 152 0 E
Yarranvale, *Australia* ... **63 D4** 26 50S 145 20 E
Yarras, *Australia* ...... **63 E5** 31 25S 152 20 E
Yarrowmere, *Australia* .. **62 C4** 21 27S 145 53 E
Yartsevo, *Russia* ...... **27 C10** 60 20N 90 0 E
Yasawa Group, *Fiji* .... **59 C7** 17 0S 177 23 E
Yaselda, *Belarus* ...... **17 B14** 52 7N 26 28 E
Yasin, *Pakistan* .... **43 A5** 36 24N 73 23 E
Yasinski, L., *Canada* **70 B4** 53 16N 77 35W
Yasinya, *Ukraine* ...... **17 D13** 48 16N 24 21 E
Yasothon, *Thailand* .... **38 E5** 15 50N 104 10 E
Yass, *Australia* .... **63 E4** 34 49S 148 54 E
Yatağan, *Turkey* .... **21 F13** 37 20N 28 10 E
Yates Center, *U.S.A.* ... **81 G7** 37 53N 95 44W
Yathkyed L., *Canada* ... **73 A9** 62 40N 98 0W
Yatsushiro, *Japan* ..... **31 H5** 32 30N 130 40 E
Yatta Plateau, *Kenya* ... **54 C4** 2 0S 38 0 E
Yauyos, *Peru* **92 F3** 12 19S 75 50W
Yavari →, *Peru* **92 D4** 4 21S 70 2W
Yavatmal, *India* .... **40 J11** 20 20N 78 15 E
Yavne, *Israel* .... **47 D3** 31 52N 34 45 E
Yavoriv, *Ukraine* ...... **17 D12** 49 55N 23 20 E
Yavorov = Yavoriv, *Ukraine* .... **17 D12** 49 55N 23 20 E
Yawatahama, *Japan* .... **31 H6** 33 27N 132 24 E
Yayama-Rettō, *Japan* ... **31 M1** 24 30N 123 40 E
Yazd, *Iran* .... **45 D7** 31 55N 54 27 E
Yazd □, *Iran* .... **45 D7** 32 0N 55 0 E
Yazoo →, *U.S.A.* **81 J9** 32 22N 90 54W
Yazoo City, *U.S.A.* **81 J9** 32 51N 90 25W
Yding Skovhøj, *Denmark* **9 J13** 55 59N 9 46 E
Ye Xian, *Henan, China* .. **34 H7** 33 35N 113 25 E
Ye Xian, *Shandong, China* **35 F10** 37 8N 119 57 E
Yealering, *Australia* .... **61 F2** 32 36S 117 36 E
Yebyu, *Burma* .... **41 M21** 14 15N 98 13 E
Yechŏn, *S. Korea* ..... **35 F15** 36 39N 128 27 E
Yecla, *Spain* **19 C5** 38 35N 1 5W
Yécora, *Mexico* **86 B3** 28 20N 108 58W
Yedintsy = Edinița, *Moldova* .... **17 D14** 48 9N 27 18 E
Yeeda, *Australia* ...... **60 C3** 17 31S 123 38 E
Yeelanna, *Australia* .... **63 E2** 34 9S 135 45 E
Yegros, *Paraguay* **94 B4** 26 20S 56 25W
Yehuda, Midbar, *Israel* .. **47 D4** 31 35N 35 15 E
Yei, *Sudan* .... **51 H11** 4 9N 30 40 E
Yekaterinburg, *Russia* .. **24 C11** 56 50N 60 30 E
Yekaterinodar = Krasnodar, *Russia* .... **25 E6** 45 5N 39 0 E
Yelanskoye, *Russia* .... **27 C13** 61 25N 128 0 E
Yelarbon, *Australia* .... **63 D5** 28 33S 150 38 E
Yelets, *Russia* .... **24 D6** 52 40N 38 30 E
Yelizavetgrad = Kirovohrad, *Ukraine* ... **25 E5** 48 35N 32 20 E
Yell, *U.K.* **12 A7** 60 35N 1 5W
Yell Sd., *U.K.* **12 A7** 60 33N 1 15W
Yellow Sea, *China* ..... **35 G12** 35 0N 123 0 E
Yellowhead Pass, *Canada* **72 C5** 52 53N 118 25W
Yellowknife, *Canada* **72 A6** 62 27N 114 29W
Yellowknife →, *Canada* . **72 A6** 62 31N 114 19W
Yellowstone →, *U.S.A.* . **80 B3** 47 59N 103 59W
Yellowstone L., *U.S.A.* .. **82 D8** 44 27N 110 22W
Yellowstone National Park, *U.S.A.* **82 D8** 44 40N 110 30W
Yellowtail Res., *U.S.A.* .. **82 D9** 45 6N 108 8W
Yelsk, *Belarus* .... **17 C15** 51 50N 29 10 E
Yelvertoft, *Australia* .... **62 C2** 20 13S 138 45 E
Yemen ■, *Asia* .... **46 E3** 15 0N 44 0 E
Yen Bai, *Vietnam* ...... **38 B5** 21 42N 104 52 E
Yenangyaung, *Burma* ... **41 J19** 20 30N 95 0 E
Yenbo = Yanbu 'al Baḥr, *Si. Arabia* .... **44 F3** 24 0N 38 5 E
Yenda, *Australia* ...... **63 E4** 34 13S 146 14 E
Yenice, *Turkey* .... **21 E12** 39 55N 27 17 E
Yenisey →, *Russia* .... **26 B9** 71 50N 82 40 E
Yeniseysk, *Russia* ..... **27 D10** 58 27N 92 13 E
Yeniseyskiy Zaliv, *Russia* **26 B9** 72 20N 81 0 E
Yennádhi, *Greece* ..... **23 C9** 36 2N 27 56 E
Yenyuka, *Russia* ...... **27 D13** 57 57N 121 15 E
Yeo, L., *Australia* ..... **61 E3** 28 0S 124 30 E
Yeola, *India* .... **40 J9** 20 2N 74 30 E
Yeoryioúpolis, *Greece* .. **23 D6** 35 20N 24 15 E
Yeovil, *U.K.* **11 G5** 50 57N 2 38W
Yeppoon, *Australia* .... **62 C5** 23 5S 150 47 E
Yerbent, *Turkmenistan* .. **26 F6** 39 30N 58 50 E
Yerbogachen, *Russia* ... **27 C11** 61 16N 108 0 E
Yerevan, *Armenia* ..... **25 F7** 40 10N 44 31 E
Yerilla, *Australia* ...... **61 E3** 29 24S 121 47 E
Yermak, *Kazakstan* .... **26 D8** 52 2N 76 55 E
Yermakovo, *Russia* .... **27 D13** 52 25N 126 20 E
Yermo, *U.S.A.* **85 L10** 34 54N 116 50W
Yerofey Pavlovich, *Russia* **27 D13** 54 0N 122 0 E
Yerólakkos, *Cyprus* .... **23 D12** 35 11N 33 15 E
Yeropol, *Russia* .... **27 C17** 65 15N 168 40 E
Yeropótamos →, *Greece* **23 D6** 35 3N 24 50 E
Yeroskipos, *Cyprus* .... **23 E11** 34 46N 32 28 E
Yershov, *Russia* ...... **25 D8** 51 23N 48 27 E
Yerushalayim = Jerusalem, *Israel* ..... **47 D4** 31 47N 35 10 E
Yes Tor, *U.K.* **11 G4** 50 41N 4 0W
Yesan, *S. Korea* ...... **35 F14** 36 41N 126 51 E
Yeso, *U.S.A.* **81 H2** 34 26N 104 37W
Yessey, *Russia* .... **27 C11** 68 29N 102 10 E
Yeu, I. d', *France* **18 C2** 46 42N 2 20W
Yevpatoriya, *Ukraine* ... **25 E5** 45 15N 33 20 E
Yeysk, *Russia* .... **25 E6** 46 40N 38 12 E
Yezd = Yazd, *Iran* ..... **45 D7** 31 55N 54 27 E
Yhati, *Paraguay* **94 B4** 25 0S 56 35W
Yhú, *Paraguay* **95 B4** 25 0S 56 0W
Yi →, *Uruguay* **94 C4** 33 7S 57 8W

WORLD: REGIONS IN THE NEWS

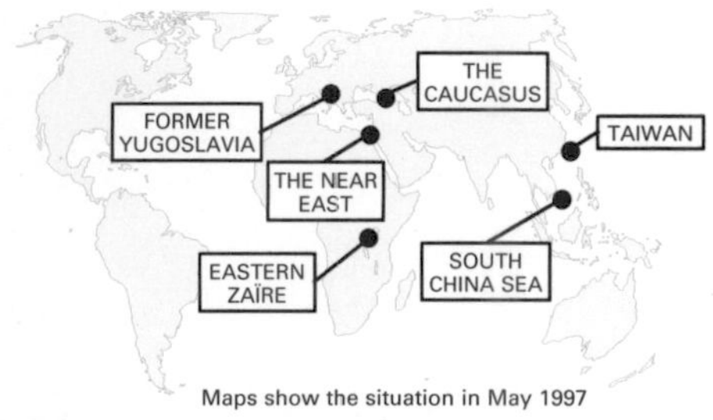

FORMER YUGOSLAVIA

THE CAUCASUS

THE NEAR EAST

TAIWAN

EASTERN ZAÏRE

SOUTH CHINA SEA

Maps show the situation in May 1997

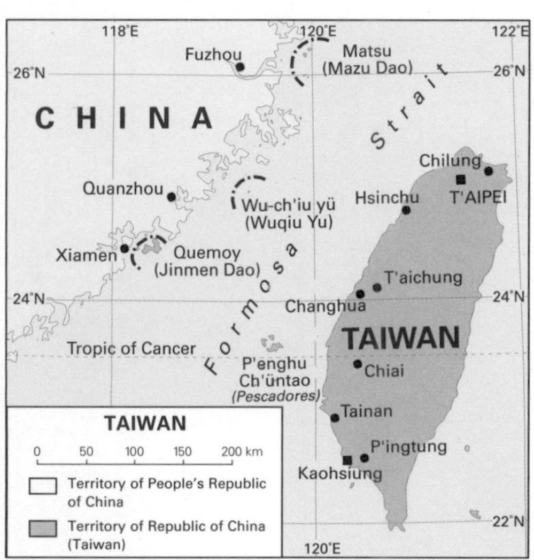

CHINA

Fuzhou
Matsu (Mazu Dao)
26°N
118°E
120°E
122°E
26°N

Quanzhou
Wu-ch'iu yü (Wuqiu Yu)
Chilung
Hsinchu
T'AIPEI

Xiamen
Quemoy (Jinmen Dao)
T'aichung

Changhua
24°N
24°N

Tropic of Cancer
TAIWAN
Chiai

P'enghu Ch'üntao (Pescadores)
Tainan
P'ingtung

Kaohsiung
22°N
120°E

TAIWAN

0   50   100   150   200 km

☐ Territory of People's Republic of China
☐ Territory of Republic of China (Taiwan)

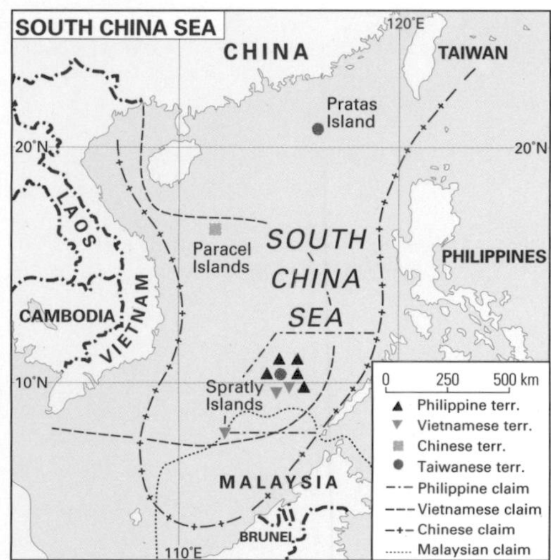

SOUTH CHINA SEA

CHINA
120°E
TAIWAN

Pratas Island
20°N
20°N

LAOS

VIETNAM

SOUTH CHINA SEA

Paracel Islands

PHILIPPINES

CAMBODIA

10°N

Spratly Islands
▲ Philippine terr.
▼ Vietnamese terr.
■ Chinese terr.
● Taiwanese terr.

MALAYSIA

BRUNEI

110°E

0   250   500 km

–·–· Philippine claim
– – – Vietnamese claim
–+–+ Chinese claim
········ Malaysian claim

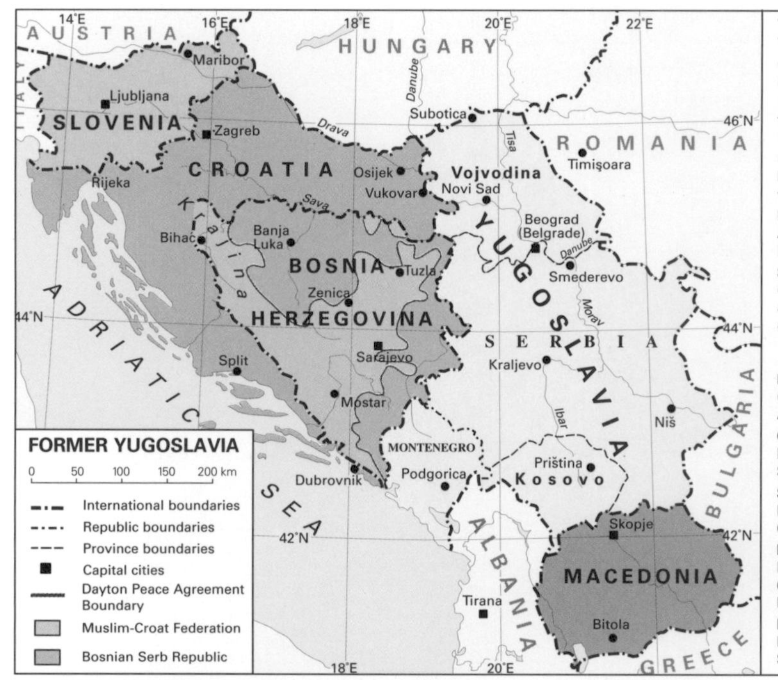

AUSTRIA
14°E
16°E
HUNGARY
18°E
20°E
22°E

Maribor

SLOVENIA
Ljubljana
Zagreb
Drava
46°N
ROMANIA

CROATIA
Osijek
Vojvodina
Timişoara

Rijeka
Vukovar
Novi Sad

Bihać
Banja Luka
Beograd (Belgrade)
Smederevo

BOSNIA
Zenica
Tuzla

44°N
HERZEGOVINA
Sarajevo
SERBIA
44°N

Split
Kraljevo

BULGARIA

Mostar

MONTENEGRO
Niš

Dubrovnik
Podgorica
Priština
Kosovo

42°N
Skopje
42°N

ALBANIA
MACEDONIA

Tirana
Bitola

18°E
20°E
GREECE

FORMER YUGOSLAVIA

0   50   100   150   200 km

–·–· International boundaries
– – – Republic boundaries
– – – Province boundaries
■ Capital cities
▬▬ Dayton Peace Agreement Boundary
☐ Muslim-Croat Federation
☐ Bosnian Serb Republic

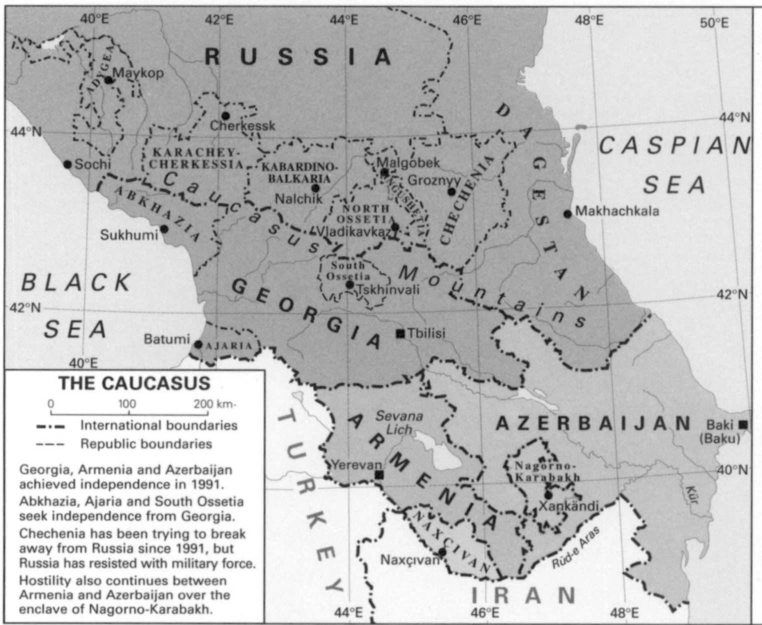

40°E
42°E
44°E
46°E
48°E
50°E

Maykop
RUSSIA
CASPIAN SEA

Cherkessk
44°N

Sochi
KARACHEY-CHERKESSIA
KABARDINO-BALKARIA
Malgobek
Groznyy

Nalchik
NORTH OSSETIA
CHECHENIA
DAGESTAN

ABKHAZIA
Vladikavkaz
Makhachkala

Sukhumi
Caucasus
South Ossetia
Mountains

BLACK SEA
42°N
GEORGIA
Tskhinvali
42°N

Batumi
AJARIA

Tbilisi

AZERBAIJAN
Baki (Baku)

40°E
Sevana Lich

Yerevan
ARMENIA
Nagorno-Karabakh
40°N

TURKEY
Xankändi

NAXÇIVAN
Rüd-e Aras

Naxçivan
IRAN

44°E
46°E
48°E

THE CAUCASUS

0   100   200 km

–·–· International boundaries
– – – Republic boundaries

Georgia, Armenia and Azerbaijan achieved independence in 1991. Abkhazia, Ajaria and South Ossetia seek independence from Georgia. Chechenia has been trying to break away from Russia since 1991, but Russia has resisted with military force. Hostility also continues between Armenia and Azerbaijan over the enclave of Nagorno-Karabakh.

THE BREAK-UP OF YUGOSLAVIA
The former country of Yugoslavia comprised six republics. In 1991 Slovenia and Croatia declared independence. Bosnia-Herzegovina followed in 1992 and Macedonia in 1993. Yugoslavia now comprises the remaining two republics, Serbia and Montenegro.

YUGOSLAVIA
Population: 10,881,000 (Serb 62.6%, Albanian 16.5%, Montenegrin 5%, Hungarian 3.3%, Muslim 3.2%)

Serbia Population: 6,060,000 (Serb 87.7%, excluding the former autonomous provinces of Kosovo and Vojvodina)
Kosovo Population: 1,989,050
Vojvodina Population: 2,131,900

Montenegro Population: 700,050 (Montenegrin 61.9%, Muslim 14.6%, Albanian 7%)

CROATIA
Population: 4,900,000 (Croat 78.1%, Serb 12.2%)

SLOVENIA
Population: 2,000,000 (Slovene 88%, Croat 3%, Serb 2%)

MACEDONIA (F. Y. R. O. M.)
Population: 2,173,000 (Macedonian 64%, Albanian 21.7%, Turkish 5%, Romanian 3%, Serb 2%)

BOSNIA-HERZEGOVINA
Population: 4,400,000 (Muslim 49%, Serb 31.2%, Croat 17.2%)

COUNTRIES AND REPUBLICS OF THE CAUCASUS REGION

RUSSIAN REPUBLICS IN THE NEWS
North Ossetia (Alania) Population: 695,000 (Ossetian 53%, Russian 29%, Chechen 5.2%, Armenian 1.9%)
Chechenia Population: 1,308,000 (Chechen and Ingush 70.7%, Russian 23.1%, Armenian 1.2%)
Ingushetia (Split from Chechenia in June 1993) Population: 250,000

GEORGIA
Population: 5,448,000 (Georgian 70.1%, Armenian 8.1%, Russian 6.3%, Azerbaijani 5.7%, Ossetian 3%, Greek 2%, Abkhazian 2%)
Abkhazia Population: 537,500 (Georgian 45.7%, Abkhazian 17.8%, Armenian 14.6%, Russian 14.3%)
Ajaria Population: 382,000 (Georgian 82.8%, Russian 7.7%, Armenian 4%)

ARMENIA
Population: 3,603,000 (Armenian 93%, Azerbaijani 3%)
Nagorno-Karabakh Population: 192,400 (Armenian 76.9%, Azerbaijani 21.5%)

AZERBAIJAN
Population: 7,559,000 (Azerbaijani 83%, Russian 6%, Armenian 6%, Lezgin 2%)
Naxçivan Population: 300,400

ISRAEL
Population: 5,696,000 (inc. East Jerusalem and Jewish settlers in the areas under Israeli administration. (Jewish 82%, Arab Muslim 13.8%, Arab Christian 2.5%, Druze 1.7%)

West Bank
Population: 1,122,900 (Palestinian Arabs 97% [of whom Arab Muslim 85%, Jewish 7%, Christian 8%])

Gaza Strip
Population: 748,400 (Arab Muslim 98%)

JORDAN
Population: 5,547,000 (Arab 99% [of whom about 50% are Palestinian Arab])

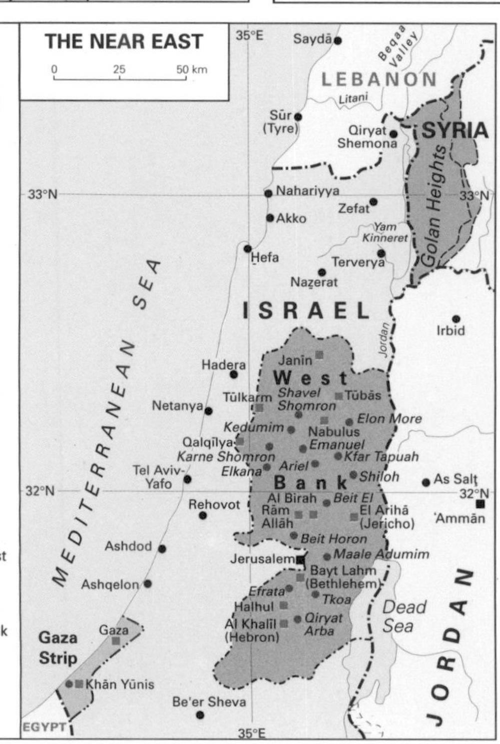

THE NEAR EAST

0   25   50 km

35°E
Saydā
Bekaa Valley

LEBANON

Litani

Sür (Tyre)
Qiryat Shemona
SYRIA

Nahariyya
Zefat
Golan Heights
33°N

Akko
Yam Kinneret

Hefa
Terverya

Nazerat

MEDITERRANEAN SEA

ISRAEL
Irbid

Hadera
Janin
Jordan

Netanya
Tülkarm
Shavei Shomron
Tübäs

Kedumim
Elon More

Qalqilya
Nabulus
Emanuel
Kfar Tapuah
As Salt
32°N

Tel Aviv-Yafo
Karne Shomron
Ariel
Shiloh

Elkana
West Bank

Rehovot
Al Birah
Rām Allāh
Beit El
El Arihã (Jericho)
'Ammān

Ashdod
Beit Horon
Maale Adumim

Jerusalem
Bayt Lahm (Bethlehem)

Ashqelon
Efrata
Tkoa
Halhul

Al Khalīl (Hebron)
Qiryat Arba

Gaza
Dead Sea

Gaza Strip
JORDAN

Khân Yūnis

Be'er Sheva

EGYPT
35°E

–·–· 1949 Armistice Line
– – – 1974 Cease-fire Lines
● Efrata — Main Jewish settlements in the West Bank and Gaza Strip
■ Halhul — Main Palestinian Arab towns in the West Bank and Gaza Strip
■ 'Amman — Capital cities

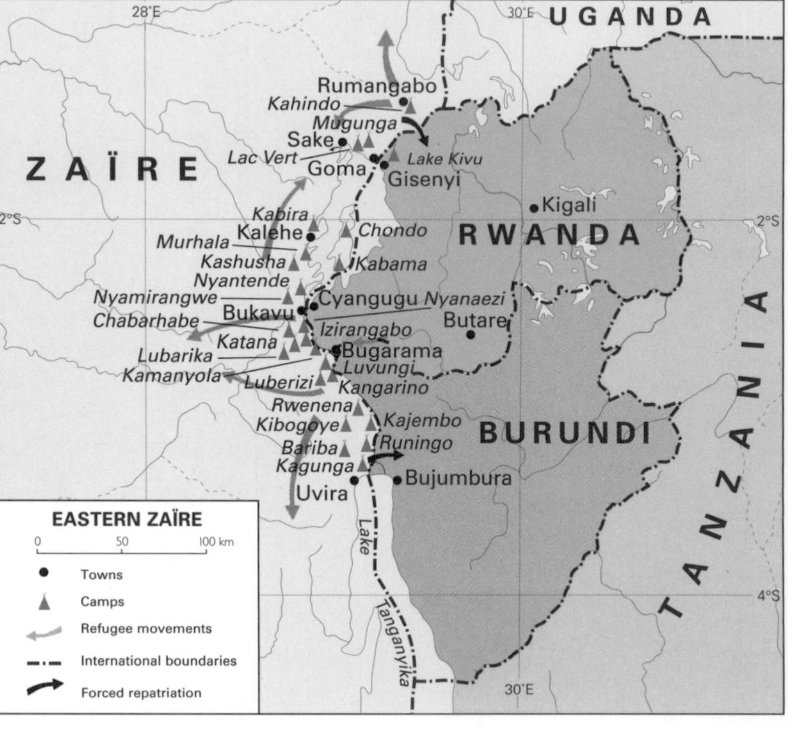

28°E
UGANDA
30°E

Rumangabo
Kahindo
Mugunga

Sake
Lac Vert
Goma
Lake Kivu
Gisenyi

ZAÏRE
Kigali
2°S

Kabira
Murhala
Kalehe
Chondo
RWANDA

Kashusha
Kabama

Nyamirangwe
Nyantende
Cyangugu
Nyanaezi

Chabarhabe
Bukavu
Izirangabo
Butare

Lubarika
Katana
Bugarama
Luvungi

Kamanyola
Luberizi
Kangarino

Rwenena
Kajembo

Kibogoye
Runingo
BURUNDI

Bariba
Kagunga

Uvira
Bujumbura

Lake Tanganyika

TANZANIA

4°S
30°E

EASTERN ZAÏRE

0   50   100 km

● Towns
▲ Camps
→ Refugee movements
–·–· International boundaries
➤ Forced repatriation

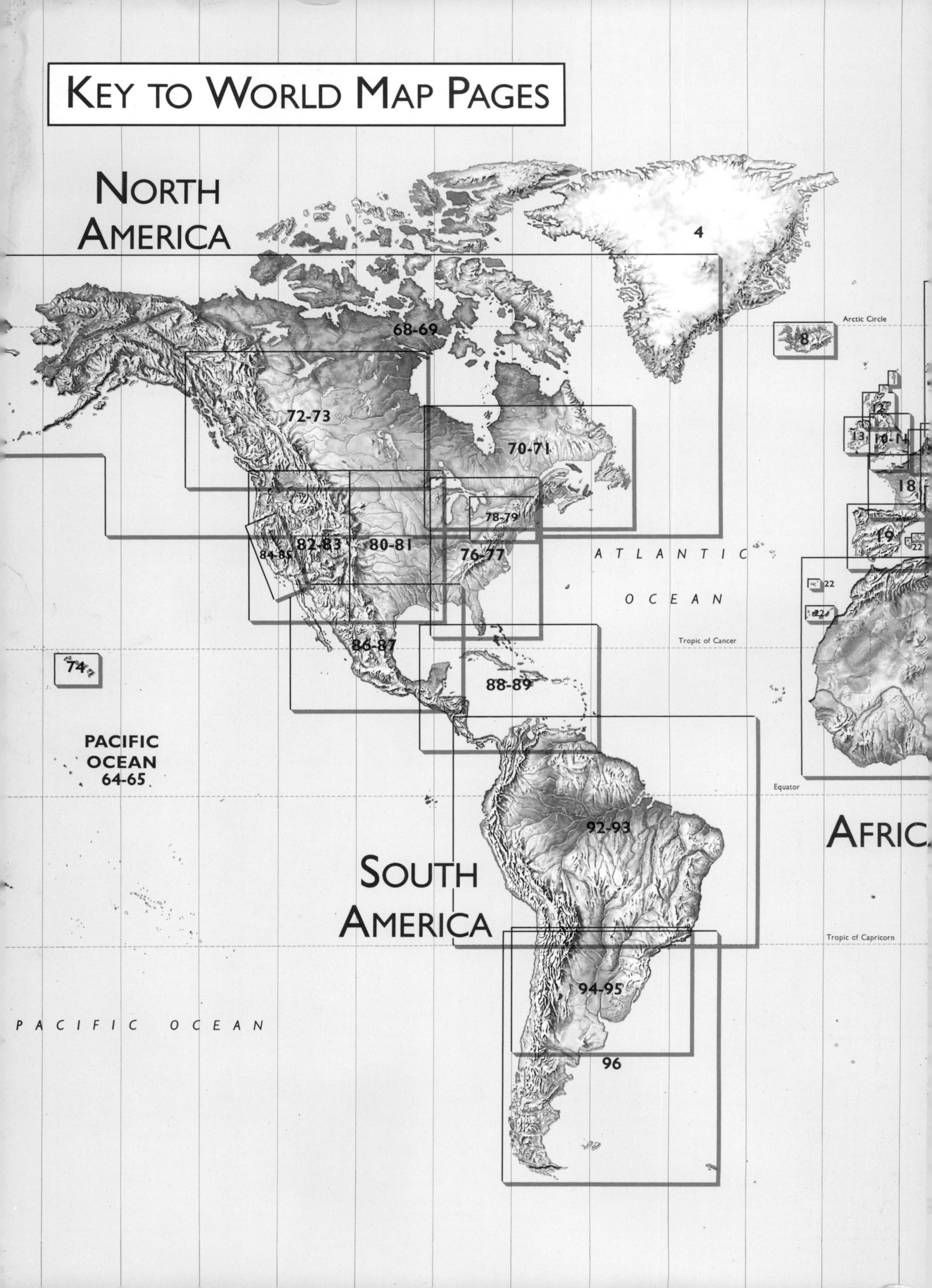

KEY TO WORLD MAP PAGES

NORTH AMERICA

4

Arctic Circle

8

68-69

72-73

70-71

78-79

12

13

10 11

18

82-83

80-81

19

84-85

76-77

A T L A N T I C

22

O C E A N

22

74

86-87

Tropic of Cancer

22

88-89

**PACIFIC
OCEAN
64-65**

92-93

AFRICA

Equator

SOUTH AMERICA

Tropic of Capricorn

P A C I F I C   O C E A N

94-95

96